CLARKSON & HILL'S CONFLICT OF LAWS

CLARKSON & HILL'S CONFLICT OF LAWS

Fifth Edition

JONATHAN HILL LLB, LLM, PhD
Professor of Law, University of Bristol

MÁIRE NÍ SHÚILLEABHÁIN BCL, LLM, PhD
Assistant Professor in Law, University College Dublin

UNIVERSITY PRESS

Great Clarendon Street, Oxford, OX2 6DP,
United Kingdom

Oxford University Press is a department of the University of Oxford.
It furthers the University's objective of excellence in research, scholarship,
and education by publishing worldwide. Oxford is a registered trade mark of
Oxford University Press in the UK and in certain other countries

© Oxford University Press 2016

The moral rights of the authors have been asserted

Second edition 2002
Third edition 2006
Fourth edition 2011

Impression: 3

All rights reserved. No part of this publication may be reproduced, stored in
a retrieval system, or transmitted, in any form or by any means, without the
prior permission in writing of Oxford University Press, or as expressly permitted
by law, by licence or under terms agreed with the appropriate reprographics
rights organization. Enquiries concerning reproduction outside the scope of the
above should be sent to the Rights Department, Oxford University Press, at the
address above

You must not circulate this work in any other form
and you must impose this same condition on any acquirer

Public sector information reproduced under Open Government Licence v3.0
(http://www.nationalarchives.gov.uk/doc/open-government-licence/open-government-licence.htm)

Published in the United States of America by Oxford University Press
198 Madison Avenue, New York, NY 10016, United States of America

British Library Cataloguing in Publication Data
Data available

Library of Congress Control Number: 2016943273

ISBN 978-0-19-873229-7

Printed and bound by CPI Group (UK) Ltd,
Croydon, CR0 4YY

Links to third party websites are provided by Oxford in good faith and
for information only. Oxford disclaims any responsibility for the materials
contained in any third party website referenced in this work.

Contents

Preface	vii
CMV Clarkson	ix
New to this Edition	xi
Table of Legislation	xiii
Table of International Conventions	xix
Table of Secondary Legislation	xxi
Table of Cases	xxix

1 Introduction — 1
  I Nature of the subject — 1
  II The conflicts process — 7

2 Civil jurisdiction — 57
  I Introduction — 57
  II Bases of jurisdiction in personam — 68
  III Declining jurisdiction and staying proceedings — 116
  IV Provisional measures — 150
  V Restraining foreign proceedings: anti-suit injunctions — 157

3 Foreign judgments — 167
  I Introduction — 167
  II Recognition and enforcement at common law — 170
  III Statutory regimes based on the common law — 192
  IV Recognition and enforcement under the Brussels I Recast — 194
  V United Kingdom judgments — 209

4 Contractual obligations — 211
  I Introduction — 211
  II Rome I Regulation: general considerations — 213
  III Determining the applicable law — 216
  IV The limits of the applicable law — 239
  V Specific contracts: articles 5 to 8 — 247
  VI Particular aspects of the contract — 254

5 Non-contractual obligations — 267
  I Choice of law in tort: introduction — 267
  II The Rome II Regulation: introduction — 269
  III The Rome II Regulation: tortious obligations — 273
  IV The Rome II Regulation: other non-contractual obligations — 289
  V The Rome II Regulation: general provisions — 295
  VI Non-contractual obligations excluded from the Rome II Regulation — 302
  VII The interaction of non-contractual obligations and contractual obligations — 309

6 Domicile, nationality, and habitual residence — 315
　I　Introduction — 315
　II　Domicile: introduction — 317
　III　Species of domicile — 320
　IV　Nationality — 339
　V　Habitual residence — 340

7 Marriage — 353
　I　Introduction — 353
　II　Formal validity — 358
　III　Essential validity — 364
　IV　Renvoi — 383
　V　Public policy — 386
　VI　Same-sex marriages and civil partnerships — 387
　VII　Polygamous marriages — 394

8 Matrimonial causes — 408
　I　Jurisdiction of the English court — 408
　II　Choice of law — 428
　III　Recognition of foreign judgments — 431
　IV　Financial provision — 461

9 Property — 471
　I　Movables and immovables — 471
　II　Transfers inter vivos — 473
　III　Matrimonial property — 485
　IV　Succession — 496

Index — 511

Preface

This is the fifth edition of a book that originally grew out of Tony Jaffey's *Introduction to the Conflict of Laws* (Butterworths, 1988); it is the first by the new editorial team of Hill and Ní Shúilleabháin. Previous editions have drawn attention to the increasing Europeanisation of the English conflict of laws in recent decades. Since the fourth edition, that evolutionary process has continued (albeit at a more modest pace); significant developments addressed in this edition include the revision of the Brussels I Regulation ('the Brussels I Recast') and the planned revision of the Brussels II *bis* Regulation. In terms of the topics discussed in this book, the common law which once dominated the field is now restricted to less than half of civil jurisdiction and judgments (Chapters 2 and 3), domicile (Chapter 6), marriage (Chapter 7), and choice of law rules relating to property (Chapter 9); the remainder derives from EU legislation.

As regards its structure and coverage, this edition closely follows the fourth edition. Of course, developments both in terms of legislation and case law have necessitated the substantial re-writing of most chapters. The aim of this edition (like that of previous editions) remains to provide a clear and full account of those topics in private international law which are covered in typical undergraduate (and many postgraduate) modules.

For the sake of simplicity, throughout the text we have used 'he', 'his', and 'him' to signify 'he or she', 'his or her', and 'him or her'. We have also used 'England' and 'English law' to signify 'England and Wales' and 'the law of England and Wales'.

We are grateful to Tony Jaffey for having provided us with the opportunity to use his work as a point of departure for the development of this book. We are also grateful to the various editors at Oxford University Press with whom we have worked for the care and diligence they have shown throughout the production process.

As far as possible, this edition has been written with reference to the law as on 1 January 2016, though it has been possible to incorporate some later material.

Jonathan Hill
Máire Ní Shúilleabháin
March 2016

CMV Clarkson

This is the first edition of this book since Chris Clarkson's retirement. This preface is, therefore, an appropriate place for me to pay tribute to Chris' contribution to this work—and more generally.

I first met Chris in 1991 when he joined the Faculty of Law, University of Bristol. Almost immediately, we were thrown together—in the sense that we were jointly allocated the teaching of the Conflict of Laws. Although Chris is almost certainly better known by the legal community at large as a criminal lawyer of distinction, his contribution to the teaching of the Conflict of Laws was no less significant. He was a famously charismatic lecturer (by his own admission, a bit of a showman), idolised by his students. Teaching the Conflict of Laws with Chris was always a lot of fun.

Chris remained in Bristol for only four years—until he was lured away to the University of Leicester. Fortunately for me, shortly after moving to Leicester, Chris was approached by Tony Jaffey to see whether he would be interested in working on a new edition of *Introduction to the Conflict of Laws* (1988). Chris was keen to take on the project—but not on his own. That is where I came in, how our working relationship developed in a new direction, and how our friendship was firmly cemented; I will always look back on our collaboration over the first four editions of this book with pleasure and, putting false modesty to one side, some measure of satisfaction. Chris was kind enough to suggest in the preface to the fourth edition that he was leaving the book 'in good hands' (p viii). I hope this edition does not cause him to revise that opinion.

Jonathan Hill
March 2016

New to this Edition

1. The chapters on civil jurisdiction and foreign judgments have been substantially re-written to take account of the changes brought about by the entry into force of the Brussels I Recast.
2. Chapters dealing with choice of law in contractual and non-contractual obligations have been revised to address the expanding body of jurisprudence generated by the Rome Regulations.
3. Chapters on connecting factors and marriage have been substantially revised to take account of significant new case law on habitual residence and the formal validity of marriage.
4. Chapters on marriage and matrimonial causes have been revised in light of the Marriage (Same Sex Couples) Act 2013.
5. Proposed reform of Brussels II *bis* is discussed in the chapter on matrimonial causes.

Table of Legislation

Table of Statutes

Administration of Estates Act 1925 . . . 1.83
Administration of Justice Act 1920 . . . 3.6,
    3.80–3.83, 3.84
    s 9(2)(a) . . . 3.81
    s 9(2)(b) . . . 3.81
    s 9(2)(c) . . . 3.81
    s 9(2)(d)–(f) . . . 3.82
    s 9(4) . . . 2.255
    s 9(5) . . . 3.83
Adoption and Children Act 2002
    s 67(1) . . . 6.17, 6.30
    s 67(2) . . . 6.18
Arbitration Act 1975 . . . 2.250
Arbitration Act 1996 . . . 2.249, 2.250
    s 5 . . . 2.250
    s 5(2)(c) . . . 2.250
    s 5(4) . . . 2.250
    s 5(6) . . . 2.250
    s 9 . . . 2.250, 2.254, 2.255
    s 9(1) . . . 2.251
    s 9(3) . . . 2.253
    s 81(1)(a) . . . 2.252

Bills of Exchange Act 1882 . . . 4.8

Child Abduction and Custody Act 1985 . . . 6.77
    Sch 1, art 4 . . . 6.71
Civil Evidence Act 1972
    s 4(1) . . . 1.139
    s 4(2) . . . 1.140
Civil Jurisdiction and Judgments Act
    1982 . . . 3.127
    s 3(3) . . . 2.11
    s 16 . . . 2.21
    s 18 . . . 3.127
    s 19 . . . 3.127
    s 25 . . . 2.173, 2.285, 2.286, 2.287, 2.288, 2.289
    s 25(1) . . . 2.286
    s 25(2) . . . 2.289
    s 25(3) . . . 2.286
    s 30 . . . 2.260
    s 32 . . . 3.75, 3.77, 3.82, 3.86, 3.93, 3.128
    s 32(1)(b) . . . 3.75
    s 32(1)(c) . . . 3.75
    s 32(2) . . . 3.75
    s 32(3) . . . 3.76
    s 32(4) . . . 3.128

s 33(1)(a) . . . 3.19
s 33(1)(b) . . . 3.19
s 33(1)(c) . . . 3.20
s 34 . . . 3.45, 3.46, 3.54, 3.56
Sch 4 . . . 2.21–2.23, 2.269
Sch 4, r 1 . . . 2.22, 2.62
Sch 4, r 3(a) . . . 2.76
Sch 4, r 11(a) . . . 2.41
Sch 4, r 16 . . . 2.284
Sch 6 . . . 3.6, 3.127
Sch 6, para 10(b) . . . 3.128
Sch 7 . . . 3.6, 3.127
Sch 7, para 9(b) . . . 3.128
Civil Liability (Contribution) Act 1978 . . . 2.160
Civil Partnership Act 2004 . . . 1.110, 1.130, 7.11,
    7.76, 7.77, 7.92, 7.104, 7.105, 7.107, 7.110,
    7.122, 7.123, 8.62, 8.148, 9.45
    s 3 . . . 7.34, 7.119
    s 3(1)(c) . . . 7.65
    s 4 . . . 7.119
    s 8 . . . 7.119
    s 11(b) . . . 7.119
    s 32 . . . 7.19
    s 33 . . . 7.19
    s 49(b) . . . 7.19
    s 49(c) . . . 7.19
    s 50 . . . 7.116
    s 50(1)(a) . . . 7.71
    s 50(1)(c) . . . 7.76
    s 54(8)(a) . . . 7.116
    s 54(8)(b) . . . 7.116
    s 54(8)(c) . . . 7.116
    s 54(10) . . . 7.116
    s 210 . . . 7.32, 7.108
    s 210(2) . . . 7.109
    s 211 . . . 7.33, 7.108
    s 212(1)(a) . . . 7.112
    s 212(1A) . . . 7.122
    s 212(1)(b)(i) . . . 7.111, 7.123
    s 212(1)(b)(ii) . . . 7.111
    s 212(2) . . . 1.110, 7.113, 7.114
    s 212(3) . . . 7.92
    s 213 . . . 7.112
    s 214 . . . 7.112
    s 215(1) . . . 1.110, 7.92, 7.110
    s 215(1)(a) . . . 7.114
    s 215(1)(b) . . . 7.113
    s 216 . . . 7.116
    s 216(1) . . . 7.111, 7.123

s 217 ... 7.114
s 218 ... 7.117
ss 219–221 ... 8.54
s 221(1)(c) ... 8.55
ss 233–238 ... 8.148
s 238 ... 7.87
Sch 1, Pt 1 ... 7.114
Sch 20 ... 7.112
Civil Procedure Act 1997 ... 2.290
Clandestine Marriages Act 1753 ... 7.27
Common Law Procedure Act 1854 ... 3.36
Companies Act 2006 ... 2.143, 2.144, 2.145
   Pt 34 ... 2.144
   s 1044 ... 2.144
   s 1046 ... 2.144
   s 1139(2)(a) ... 2.144
   s 1139(2)(b) ... 2.144
Companies Act 2008 ... 2.252
Consumer Rights Act 2015 ... 4.124
   Pt 2 ... 4.124, 4.125
   s 62(1) ... 4.124
   s 74(1) ... 4.124
Contracts (Applicable Law) Act 1990 ... 4.6
   s 2(2) ... 4.99, 4.176
Criminal Justice Act 1988 ... 3.70

Defamation Act 2013
   s 9 ... 2.157
Domicile and Matrimonial Proceedings Act 1973 ... 6.26, 6.27, 6.29, 6.31, 6.32, 6.34, 7.120, 8.1, 8.3, 8.21, 8.35, 8.42, 8.44, 9.50, 9.59, 9.89
   s 1(1) ... 6.34
   s 1(2) ... 6.34
   s 3(1) ... 6.27, 6.31
   s 4(2) ... 6.18, 6.29
   s 4(2)(a) ... 6.29
   s 4(2)(b) ... 6.29
   s 4(3) ... 6.29
   s 4(4) ... 6.28
   s 5 ... 8.21
   s 5(2) ... 8.3, 8.5
   s 5(2)(b) ... 6.71, 8.20, 8.32, 8.180
   s 5(3) ... 8.3, 8.5
   s 5(6) ... 8.36, 8.54
   s 5(6A) ... 8.39
   s 5(6)(b) ... 8.47
   s 16(1) ... 8.98
   Sch 1 ... 8.54
   Sch 1, para 3(2) ... 8.36
   Sch 1, para 4(2) ... 8.40
   Sch 1, para 8 ... 8.36
   Sch 1, para 9 ... 8.30, 8.32
   Sch 1, para 9(1) ... 8.38, 8.40
   Sch 1, para 9(2) ... 8.36, 8.41
   Sch A1 ... 7.120, 8.54
   Sch A1, para 2(1)(c) ... 7.120, 8.55

Family Law Act 1986 ... 1.165, 3.73, 6.78, 7.98, 8.62, 8.66, 8.67, 8.81, 8.83, 8.84, 8.87, 8.91, 8.98, 8.99, 8.101, 8.102, 8.103, 8.106, 8.108, 8.117, 8.118, 8.122, 8.137, 8.143, 8.148, 8.150, 8.155, 8.158, 8.159, 8.160, 8.161, 8.164
   s 44 ... 8.62, 8.84, 8.115
   s 44(1) ... 8.98
   s 44(2) ... 8.84
   s 46 ... 8.84, 8.115
   ss 46–52 ... 8.62
   s 46(1) ... 6.14, 8.85, 8.111
   s 46(1)(a) ... 3.73, 8.91, 8.117, 8.164
   s 46(1)(b)(i) ... 6.71, 6.78
   s 46(1)(b)(iii) ... 6.65
   s 46(2) ... 8.109, 8.110, 8.111, 8.112, 8.119
   s 46(2)(a) ... 3.73, 8.91, 8.164
   s 46(3)(a) ... 8.117
   s 46(3)(b) ... 8.119
   s 46(5) ... 1.105, 6.14, 8.85, 8.110
   s 48(1) ... 8.94
   s 48(3) ... 8.94
   s 49(1) ... 8.90, 8.93
   s 49(2) ... 8.90
   s 49(3) ... 8.90, 8.93
   s 50 ... 7.87, 7.89, 7.98
   s 51(1) ... 8.84, 8.123, 8.157
   s 51(2) ... 8.84, 8.123
   s 51(3) ... 8.137
   s 51(3)(a) ... 1.161, 1.165, 8.131, 8.160
   s 51(3)(a)(i) ... 8.125, 8.129, 8.143
   s 51(3)(a)(ii) ... 8.128, 8.143
   s 51(3)(b) ... 8.147
   s 51(3)(c) ... 1.157, 8.132, 8.161
   s 51(4) ... 8.147
   s 54(1) ... 8.102
   ss 55–57 ... 6.71
   s 57(3)(b) ... 6.78
   s 56 ... 9.113
Family Law Act 1996
   Pt IV ... 7.158
   s 63(5) ... 7.158
Family Law Reform Act 1987
   s 22 ... 9.113
Family Law (Scotland) Act 2006
   s 22 ... 6.32
Fatal Accidents Acts ... 3.46
Finance Act 1996
   s 200 ... 6.53
Forced Marriage (Civil Protection) Act 2007 ... 7.103
Foreign Judgments (Reciprocal Enforcement) Act 1933 ... 3.6, 3.80, 3.84–3.86
   s 1(2)(a) ... 3.85
   s 1(2)(b) ... 3.85
   s 4(1)(a)(ii) ... 3.85
   s 4(1)(a)(iii) ... 3.86
   s 4(1)(a)(iv) ... 3.86

s 4(1)(a)(v) ... 3.86
s 4(1)(b) ... 3.86
s 4(2)(a) ... 3.85
s 4(2)(a)(iv) ... 3.85
s 4(2)(a)(v) ... 3.85
s 6 ... 3.85
Foreign Limitation Periods Act 1984 ... 1.96, 5.119
  s 1 ... 1.90
  s 1(1) ... 1.96
  s 2(1) ... 1.96
  s 2(2) ... 1.96
  s 3 ... 3.48
Foreign Marriage Act 1892 ... 7.32

Gender Recognition Act 2004 ... 7.116

Hire-Purchase and Small Debt (Scotland) Act 1932 ... 4.107
Human Fertilisation and Embryology Act 2008
  s 42 ... 6.18
  s 48(6) ... 6.18
  s 54(1) ... 6.17, 6.30
  s 54(4)(b) ... 6.12
Human Rights Act 1998 ... 2.4

Immigration Act 1971
  s 5(4) ... 7.160
Immigration Act 1988
  s 2(2) ... 7.160
Immigration Act 2014
  Sch 4(2), para 22 ... 7.119
Inheritance (Provision for Family and Dependants) Act 1975 ... 7.155, 9.45, 9.69, 9.70, 9.83
  s 1(1) ... 9.83
  s 1(1A) ... 7.157
  s 1(2) ... 7.157
  s 25(4) ... 7.157
Inheritance Tax Act 1984
  s 267 ... 6.6, 6.12

Landlord and Tenant Act 1985 ... 4.93
  s 11(1)(a) ... 4.93
  s 12 ... 4.93
Late Payment of Commercial Debts (Interest) Act 1998
  s 12 ... 4.104
Law of Property Act 1925
  s 184 ... 1.79
Law of Property (Miscellaneous Provisions) Act 1989
  s 2 ... 4.151
Law Reform (Miscellaneous Provisions) Act 1949
  s 1 ... 8.1
Law Reform (Personal Injuries) Act 1948
  s 1(3) ... 5.129, 5.134, 5.136

Law Reform (Succession) Act 1995
  s 2(3) ... 7.157

Maintenance Agreements Act 1957
  s 1 ... 9.64
Maintenance Orders Act 1950
  Pt II ... 8.189
Maintenance Orders (Facilities for Enforcement) Act 1920 ... 8.182, 8.187, 8.190
Maintenance Orders (Reciprocal Enforcement) Act 1972 ... 8.182, 8.187, 8.190
  Pt I ... 8.190
  Pt II ... 8.182
Marine Insurance Act 1906
  s 34(3) ... 4.93
  s 39(1) ... 4.93
  Sch ... 4.33
Marriage Act 1949 ... 7.134
  s 1(4)–(8) ... 7.62
  s 2 ... 7.65, 7.69
  s 24 ... 7.19
  s 25 ... 7.19
  s 44(3) ... 7.13
  s 48 ... 7.19
  s 49 ... 7.19
  s 75 ... 7.19
  s 75(2)(a) ... 7.134
Marriage (Enabling) Act 1960 ... 7.62
  s 1 ... 7.62
  s 1(3) ... 7.57, 7.62, 7.63
Marriage (Prohibited Degrees of Relationship) Act 1986
  s 1(7) ... 7.62
Marriage (Registrar General's Licence) Act 1970
  s 16 ... 7.19
Marriage (Same Sex Couples) Act 2013 ... 7.11, 7.32, 7.33, 7.120, 7.121
  s 1 ... 7.120
  s 9 ... 7.121
  s 10 ... 7.122
  s 10(1) ... 7.122
  s 11(1) ... 7.120
  Sch 3, Pt 1, para 1 ... 8.148
  Sch 4, Pt 4 ... 7.120
  Sch 4, Pt 4, para 6(4) ... 8.54
  Sch 4, Pt 4 para 8 ... 8.54
  Sch 6 ... 7.32
  Sch 6, para 1(2)(a) ... 7.32
  Sch 6, para 1(2)(b) ... 7.32
  Sch 6, para 1(2)(c) ... 7.32
  Sch 6, para 1(2)(d) ... 7.32
  Sch 6, para 8(2) ... 7.33
  Explanatory Notes ... 7.120
Married Women's Property Act 1882 ... 7.158
Matrimonial Causes Act 1937
  s 13 ... 8.1
Matrimonial Causes Act 1973 ... 9.66, 9.71

s 1 ... 7.152
s 1(2)(a) ... 7.151
s 1(2)(c) ... 7.152
s 11 ... 7.145
s 11(b) ... 7.146
s 11(d) ... 7.128, 7.136, 7.137, 7.138, 7.140, 7.144, 7.145, 7.146
s 12(1)(a) ... 7.77
s 12(1)(b) ... 7.77
s 12(1)(c) ... 7.71
s 12(1)(e) ... 7.76
s 12(1)(f) ... 7.76
s 12(2) ... 7.77
s 13(3) ... 7.76
s 14 ... 7.145
s 14(1) ... 7.140, 7.145
s 25 ... 9.73
s 25(1) ... 9.64, 9.65, 9.66, 9.67
s 34 ... 9.64
s 35 ... 9.64
s 46(1)(a) ... 8.1
s 46(1)(b) ... 8.1
s 47 ... 7.125
s 47(4) ... 7.152
Matrimonial and Family Proceedings Act 1984 ... 8.46
  Pt III ... 1.175, 8.108, 8.136, 8.140, 8.183, 8.184, 8.185, 8.186
  s 12 ... 8.64, 8.183
  s 13(1) ... 8.185
  s 15 ... 8.184
  s 16(1) ... 8.185
  s 16(2)(a)–(c) ... 8.185
  s 16(2)(d) ... 8.185
  s 16(2)(e) ... 8.185
  s 16(2)(g) ... 8.185
  s 16(2)(h) ... 8.185
  s 16(2)(i) ... 8.185
Matrimonial Proceedings (Polygamous Marriages) Act 1972 ... 7.125, 7.148, 7.152

Patents Act 1977
  s 30(1) ... 9.5
Perjury Act 1911
  s 3 ... 7.19
Private International Law (Miscellaneous Provisions) Act 1995 ... 5.30, 5.91, 5.104, 5.122, 5.123, 5.124, 5.125, 5.137, 7.128, 7.138, 7.139, 7.140, 7.141
  Pt III ... 5.5, 5.31, 5.104, 5.122, 5.123–5.127
  s 5(1) ... 7.138, 7.140
  s 5(2) ... 7.139, 7.140
  s 6(1) ... 7.141
  s 6(2) ... 7.141
  s 6(3)–(5) ... 7.141
  s 6(6) ... 7.141
  s 9(1) ... 5.123

s 9(3) ... 5.104
s 9(5) ... 5.124
s 11 ... 5.124, 5.126
s 11(1) ... 5.125
s 11(2)(a) ... 5.125
s 11(2)(b) ... 5.125
s 11(2)(c) ... 5.125
s 12 ... 5.126, 5.127
s 13 ... 5.104
Sch, para 2(2) ... 7.128
Sch, para 2(3)(b) ... 7.152
Protection of Trading Interests Act 1980 ... 3.78, 3.79
  s 5 ... 3.79, 3.82, 3.86
  s 6 ... 3.79

Recognition of Divorces and Legal Separations Act 1971 ... 8.66, 8.87, 8.88, 8.98, 8.100, 8.103, 8.104, 8.150
  s 2 ... 8.103
  s 2(b) ... 8.91
  s 3 ... 8.117
  s 3(1)(a) ... 6.71
  s 6 ... 8.100
Recognition of Trusts Act 1987
  s 1(1) ... 5.10

Sale of Goods Act 1979 ... 4.102
  s 25(1) ... 9.22
Senior Courts Act 1981 ... 2.31, 2.32, 2.34
  ss 20–24 ... 2.31
  s 20(2)(e) ... 2.31
  s 20(2)(g) ... 2.31
  s 20(2)(h) ... 2.31
  s 21(2) ... 2.31
  s 21(3) ... 2.31
  s 21(4) ... 2.31
  s 21(5) ... 2.6
  s 37 ... 2.298
  s 37(1) ... 2.290
Sexual Offences Act 2003
  s 9 ... 7.67
  s 64 ... 7.64
Sexual Offences (Conspiracy and Incitement) Act 1996 ... 7.69
Social Security Contributions and Benefits Act 1992
  s 121(1)(b) ... 7.159
  s 147(5) ... 7.159
Statute of Frauds 1677 ... 4.151
  s 4 ... 1.95

Unfair Contract Terms Act 1977 ... 4.104–4.105, 4.125
  s 2(1) ... 4.105
  s 26 ... 4.104
  s 27(1) ... 4.104
  s 27(2) ... 4.105

Wills Act 1963 . . . 9.81, 9.94, 9.101, 9.109
   s 1 . . . 6.65, 6.78, 9.81
   s 2(1)(a) . . . 9.81
   s 2(1)(b) . . . 9.94
   s 2(1)(c) . . . 9.87
   s 3 . . . 1.90
   s 4 . . . 9.85
   s 6(1) . . . 9.109
   s 6(3) . . . 9.81

Australia

Family Law Act 1975
   s 39(3) . . . 6.12

Trade Practices Act 1974
   s 81(1A) . . . 3.79

France

Civil Code . . . 4.36
   art 14 . . . 2.183, 3.97
   art 171 . . . 7.8
   art 476 . . . 4.164
   art 481 . . . 4.164
   art 1123 . . . 4.164
   art 1124 . . . 4.164

Germany

Civil Code . . . 1.80, 1.81, 1.83

Malta

Marriage Act 1975
   s 18 . . . 1.82

Pakistan

Muslim Family Laws Ordinance 1961 . . . 8.103, 8.104, 8.115, 8.143

United States of America

Carriage of Goods by Sea Act 1936 . . . 4.37

Table of International Conventions

Accession Conventions . . . 2.11

Brussels Convention on Jurisdiction and
the Enforcement of Judgments in Civil
and Commercial Matters 1968 (Brussels I
Convention) . . . 1.13, 1.14, 1.15, 2.7, 2.8, 2.9,
2.11, 2.13, 2.90, 2.195, 2.205, 2.211, 2.244,
2.273, 2.314, 2.315, 3.69, 3.84, 3.115, 4.6, 8.26
art 2 . . . 8.29
art 5(1) . . . 4.135, 5.18
art 21 . . . 8.178
art 27(2) . . . 3.118
Brussels Convention on Jurisdiction and the
Recognition and Enforcement of Judgments
in Matrimonial Matters 1998 (Brussels II
Convention) . . . 1.14, 6.91, 8.4, 8.9, 8.67
art 2(2) . . . 8.13

Convention on Jurisdiction and the Enforcement
of Judgments in Civil and Commercial Matters
1968 *see* Brussels Convention on Jurisdiction
and the Enforcement of Judgments in Civil
and Commercial Matters 1968 (Brussels I
Convention)
Convention on Jurisdiction and the Recognition
and Enforcement of Judgments in Matrimonial
Matters 1998 *see* Brussels Convention
on Jurisdiction and the Recognition and
Enforcement of Judgments in Matrimonial
Matters 1998 (Brussels II Convention)
Convention on the Contract for the International
Carriage of Goods by Road 1956 . . . 2.33, 2.35
Convention on the Law Applicable to Trusts and
on their Recognition
art 8 . . . 5.10

European Convention on Human Rights 1950
(ECHR) . . . 2.4, 3.70, 3.110, 7.123, 8.77, 9.50
art 6 . . . 1.167, 2.4, 2.254, 3.70, 3.110, 3.122
art 6(1) . . . 2.4, 3.70
art 12 . . . 7.17
art 14 . . . 9.50
Protocol 1, art 1 . . . 9.50

Hague Choice of Court Convention
2005 . . . 2.47, 2.164, 2.244–2.248, 2.274,
2.278, 3.15
art 1(1) . . . 2.245
art 1(2) . . . 2.245
art 5 . . . 2.164, 2.246
art 6 . . . 2.247, 2.274

art 6(c) . . . 2.248
art 8 . . . 3.15
art 9 . . . 3.15
Hague Convention on the Civil Aspects of
International Child Abduction 1980 . . . 6.77,
6.80, 6.90, 6.96
Hague Convention on the Conflict of Laws
Relating to the Form of Testamentary
Dispositions 1961 . . . 9.81
Hague Convention on the International Recovery
of Child Support and other Forms of Family
Maintenance . . . 8.184, 8.187
Hague Convention on the Recognition of
Divorces and Legal Separations 1970 . . . 8.89
Hague Protocol of 23 November 2007 on
the Law Applicable to Maintenance
Obligations . . . 1.107,
8.187, 8.191

International Convention for the Unification of
Certain Rules Concerning Civil Jurisdiction in
Matters of Collision 1952 . . . 2.31, 2.33
International Convention for the Unification
of Certain Rules Relating to the Arrest of
Seagoing Ships 1952 . . . 2.31, 2.33, 2.34

Lugano Convention on Jurisdiction and the
Enforcement of Judgments in Civil and
Commercial Matters 1988 . . . 2.9, 3.6, 3.84,
8.174
Lugano Convention on Jurisdiction and the
Enforcement of Judgments in Civil and
Commercial Matters Revised 2007 . . . 2.9, 3.6,
3.84, 8.174
Title III . . . 3.6

New York Convention on the Recognition and
Enforcement of Foreign Arbitral Awards
1958 . . . 2.244, 2.249, 2.319, 3.88, 3.95, 3.96,
3.109, 4.8
art II . . . 2.249

Paris Convention on Third Party Liability in the
Field of Nuclear Energy 1960 . . . 5.11

Rome Convention on the Law Applicable to
Contractual Obligations 1980 . . . 1.13, 1.14,
2.138, 4.6, 4.9, 4.12, 4.50, 4.58, 4.61, 4.64, 4.66,
4.68, 4.72, 4.74, 4.78, 4.85, 4.107, 4.111, 4.170,
4.176, 4.177, 5.6
art 3(1) . . . 4.15

art 4 . . . 4.50, 4.61, 4.63, 4.66–4.69
art 4(2)–(4) . . . 4.61
art 4(4) . . . 4.116
art 4(5) . . . 4.61, 4.64
art 7(1) . . . 4.99

Treaty of Amsterdam 1997 . . . 1.15, 1.17, 5.6
art 61 . . . 1.15
art 65 . . . 1.15
Treaty on the Functioning of the European Union (TFEU) . . . 1.15, 1.17
Part 1, Title IV . . . 2.81
art 57 . . . 2.81
art 67 . . . 1.15
art 81 . . . 1.15
art 101 . . . 2.252, 5.55
art 102 . . . 2.252, 5.55
art 267 . . . 2.10, 2.21, 3.92, 4.11, 4.108
Treaty of Rome
art 220 . . . 1.13

UN Convention on Consent to Marriage, Minimum Age for Marriage and Registration of Marriages 1962 . . . 7.25

Vienna Convention on Civil Liability for Nuclear Damage 1963 . . . 5.11

Table of Secondary Legislation

United Kingdom

Civil Jurisdiction and Judgments Act
  1982 (Interim Relief) Order 1997 (SI
  1997/302) . . . 2.286
Civil Jurisdiction and Judgments (Maintenance)
  Regulations 2011 (SI 2011/1484) . . . 8.184
Civil Jurisdiction and Judgments Order 2001 (SI
  2001/3929)
  Sch 1, para 9(2) . . . 2.27
  Sch 1, para 9(3) . . . 2.27
  Sch 1, para 9(5) . . . 2.27
  Sch 1, para 9(6) . . . 2.27
Civil Partnership (Armed Forces) Order 2005 (SI
  2005/3188) . . . 7.108
Civil Partnership (Jurisdiction and Recognition
  of Judgments) Regulations 2005 (SI
  2005/3334) . . . 8.54, 8.148
Civil Partnership (Registration Abroad
  and Certificates) Order 2005 (SI
  2005/2761) . . . 7.108
Civil Partnership (Supplementary Provisions
  relating to the Recognition of Overseas
  Dissolutions, Annulments or Legal
  Separations) (England and Wales and
  Northern Ireland) Regulations 2005 (SI
  2005/3104)
  reg 3 . . . 8.148
Civil Procedure Rules 1998 (CPR)
  (SI 3132/1998) . . . 2.126, 2.150, 2.164,
  2.170, 2.287
  r 6.9 . . . 2.142, 2.143, 2.145
  r 6.9(2) . . . 2.142, 2.145
  r 6.11 . . . 2.149
  r 6.33 . . . 2.19, 2.65
  r 6.36 . . . 2.24, 2.25, 2.141, 2.149, 2.150, 2.151,
    2.159, 2.170, 2.176, 2.177, 2.183, 2.213,
    2.217, 2.240, 2.241, 2.247, 2.287, 3.13, 3.37,
    3.38
  r 6.37(1)(b) . . . 2.152
  r 6.37(3) . . . 2.151
  r 6.40(3)(c) . . . 2.151
  PD 6B, para 3.1 . . . 2.24, 2.65, 2.141, 2.150,
    2.153, 2.159, 2.175, 2.176
  PD 6B, para 3.1(1) . . . 2.176
  PD 6B, para 3.1(5) . . . 2.287
  PD 6B, para 3.1(6)(a) . . . 2.161
  PD 6B, para 3.1(6)(b) . . . 2.162
  PD 6B, para 3.1(6)(c) . . . 2.163. 2.298, 4.32
  PD 6B, para 3.1(6)(d) . . . 2.149, 2.164
  PD 6B, para 3.1(9) . . . 3.38
  PD 6B, para 3.1(10) . . . 2.176
  PD 6B, para 3.1(11) . . . 2.176
  PD 6B, para 3.1(12) . . . 2.176
  PD 6B, para 3.1(12A) . . . 2.176
  PD 6B, para 3.1(17) . . . 2.176
  PD 6B, para 3.1(20) . . . 2.176
  r 7.2(1) . . . 2.184
  r 7.2(2) . . . 2.184
  Pt 20 . . . 2.174
  Pt 24 . . . 2.254
Commercial Agents (Council Directive)
  Regulations 1993 (SI 1993/3053) . . . 4.108
Consular Marriages and Marriages under
  Foreign Law (No 2) Order 2014 (SI 2014/3265)
  art 4(4)(a) . . . 7.32

European Communities (Jurisdiction and
  Judgments in Matrimonial and Parental
  Responsibility Matters) Regulations 2005
  (SI 2005/265)
  reg 3 . . . 8.5
  reg 3(5) . . . 8.39
European Communities (Matrimonial
  Jurisdiction and Judgments) Regulations 2001
  (SI 2001/310) . . . 8.30
  reg 3 . . . 8.5

Family Procedure (Civil Partnership:
  Staying of Proceedings) Rules 2010 (SI
  2010/2986) . . . 8.54
Human Fertilisation and Embryology (Parental
  Orders) Regulations 2010 (SI 2010/985)
  sch 1 . . . 6.18

Income Support (General) Regulations 1987
  (SI 1987/1967)
  reg 2(1) . . . 7.159

Law Applicable to Contractual Obligations
  (England and Wales and Northern Ireland)
  Regulations 2009 (SI 2009/3064) . . . 4.10
Law Applicable to Contractual Obligations
  (Scotland) Regulations 2009 (SSI
  2009/410) . . . 4.10
Law Applicable to Non-Contractual Obligations
  (England and Wales and Northern Ireland)
  Regulations 2008 (SI 2008/2986) . . . 5.17

Law Applicable to Non-Contractual Obligations (Scotland) Regulations 2008 (SSI 2008/404) ... 5.17

Marriage Act 1949 (Remedial) Order 2007 (SI 2007/438) ... 7.62
Marriage of Same Sex Couples (Conversion of Civil Partnership) Regulations 2014 (SI 2014/3181) ... 7.121
Marriage (Same Sex Couples) (Jurisdiction and Recognition of Judgments) Regulations 2014 (SI 2014/543) ... 8.54, 8.62, 8.148

Overseas Companies Regulations 2009 (SI 2009/1801) ... 2.143
  reg 7(1) ... 2.144
Overseas Marriage (Armed Forces) Order 2014 (SI 2014/1108) ... 7.33

Protection of Trading Interests (Australian Trade Practices) Order 1988 (SI 1988/569) ... 3.79

Unfair Terms in Consumer Contracts Regulations 1999 (SI 1999/2083) ... 4.124

European Union

Decisions

Council Decision No 2001/470/EC ... 1.144
Commission Decision No 2009/26/EC ... 4.9
Commission Decision No 2009/451/EC ... 8.187
Council Decision No 2009/568/EC ... 1.144
  art 1(2) ... 1.144
  art 3(1)(c) ... 1.144

Directives

Directive No 73/239/EEC
  art 5(d) ... 4.127
Directive No 86/653/EEC (Commercial Agents Directive) ... 4.101, 4.108
Directive No 88/357/EEC
  art 2(d) ... 4.127
Directive No 93/13/EEC ... 4.124
Directive No 96/71/EC ... 4.139
Directive No 2000/31/EC (E-Commerce Directive) ... 5.29
  art 3 ... 5.29
Directive No 2002/83/EC
  art 1(1)(g) ... 4.127

Regulations

Brussels I Regulation *see* EC Regulation No 44/2001 (Brussels I Regulation)
Brussels II Regulation *see* EC Regulation No 1347/2000 (Brussels II Regulation)
Brussels II *bis* Regulation *see* EC Regulation No 2201/2003 (Brussels II *bis* Regulation)

Community Trade Mark Regulation
  art 93(5) ... 2.104

Evidence Regulation *see* EC Regulation No 1206/2001 (Evidence Regulation)

Insolvency Regulation *see* EC Regulation No 1346/2000 (Old Insolvency Regulation)

Maintenance Regulation *see* EC Regulation No 4/2009 (Maintenance Regulation)

Rome I Regulation *see* EC Regulation 593/2008 (Rome I Regulation)
Rome II Regulation *see* EC Regulation 864/2007 (Rome II Regulation)
Rome III *see* EU Regulation 1259/2010 (Rome III)

Service Regulation *see* EC Regulation No 1393/2007 (Service Regulation)

EC Regulation No 1346/2000 (Old Insolvency Regulation) ... 1.15, 2.15
EC Regulation No 1347/2000 (Brussels II Regulation) ... 6.72, 6.91, 8.4, 8.29, 8.30, 8.42, 8.45
  recital (12) ... 8.13
EC Regulation No 44/2001 (Brussels I Regulation) ... 1.15, 2.9, 2.11, 2.13, 2.16, 2.54, 2.85, 2.195, 2.196, 2.205, 2.211, 2.265, 2.268, 2.269, 2.273, 2.275, 2.295, 2.312, 2.314, 2.316, 2.318, 2.319, 2.321, 3.6, 3.84, 3.87, 3.90, 3.94, 3.100, 4.12, 5.8, 5.84, 8.26, 8.32, 8.166, 8.167, 8.169, 8.170
  recital (19) ... 2.11
  art 2 ... 8.32
  art 5(2) ... 8.166, 8.167
  art 5(3) ... 5.28
  art 7(1) ... 4.7
EC Regulation No 1206/2001 (Evidence Regulation) ... 1.15
EC Regulation No 2201/2003 (Brussels II *bis* Regulation) ... 1.15, 1.157, 6.71, 6.72, 6.75, 6.76, 6.78, 6.87, 6.90, 6.91, 6.92, 6.93, 6.94, 6.95, 6.96, 6.97, 6.99, 8.4, 8.5, 8.7, 8.13, 8.15, 8.21, 8.22, 8.23, 8.29, 8.30, 8.32, 8.33, 8.34, 8.39, 8.48, 8.50, 8.53, 8.54, 8.59, 8.62, 8.67, 8.68–8.82, 8.99, 8.113, 8.148, 8.150, 8.155, 8.158, 8.160, 8.161, 8.166, 8.180
  recital (8) ... 8.166
  recital (21) ... 8.70, 8.75
  Ch II ... 8.6

Ch III ... 8.70
art 1(1) ... 8.68
art 1(3)(e) ... 8.166
art 3 ... 6.95, 8.6–8.13, 8.14, 8.15, 8.16, 8.20,
    8.22, 8.29, 8.30, 8.32, 8.38, 8.48, 8.50, 8.52,
    8.53, 8.54, 8.180
art 3(1) ... 8.6
art 3(1)(b) ... 8.13
art 3(2) ... 8.13
art 4 ... 8.13, 8.14, 8.15, 8.16
art 5 ... 8.13, 8.14, 8.15, 8.16
art 6 ... 8.5, 8.13, 8.15, 8.16, 8.50, 8.52
art 7 ... 8.50, 8.52, 8.70
art 7(1) ... 8.15, 8.16, 8.17
art 7(2) ... 8.18, 8.19
art 8(1) ... 6.97
art 15(3)(c) ... 6.65
art 16 ... 8.26
art 16(1)(a) ... 8.26
art 16(1)(b) ... 8.26
art 18(1) ... 8.24
art 19 ... 8.25–8.26, 8.27, 8.32, 8.39, 8.54
art 19(1) ... 8.6, 8.25
art 19(2) ... 8.26
art 21 ... 8.71
art 21(2) ... 8.72
art 21(3) ... 8.73
art 21(4) ... 8.74
art 22 ... 8.75, 8.148
art 22(a) ... 8.76, 8.77, 8.161
art 22(b) ... 8.78, 8.131, 8.160
art 22(c) ... 8.79, 8.157
art 22(d) ... 8.80, 8.157
art 24 ... 8.70, 8.76
art 25 ... 8.70, 8.76, 8.161
art 26 ... 8.70, 8.76
art 65 ... 8.51
EC Regulation No 805/2004 (European
    Enforcement Order Regulation) ... 2.134,
    3.103
EC Regulation No 1896/2006 (European Order
    for Payment Procedure Regulation) ... 3.103
EC Regulation No 861/2007 (European Small
    Claims Procedure Regulation) ... 3.103
EC Regulation No 864/2007 (Rome II
    Regulation) ... 1.15, 1.17, 1.18, 1.91, 1.94,
    1.97, 1.99, 1.107, 1.157, 4.6, 4.12, 4.62, 4.177,
    5.6, 5.7, 5.8, 5.9, 5.10, 5.11, 5.12, 5.13, 5.15,
    5.16, 5.17, 5.1, 5.19, 5.20, 5.22, 5.23, 5.24, 5.31,
    5.41, 5.44, 5.45, 5.46, 5.50, 5.60, 5.63, 5.67,
    5.68, 5.73, 5.75, 5.83, 5.86–5.103, 5.104–5.121,
    5.122, 5.123, 5.124, 5.130, 5.135, 6.72
recital (1) ... 5.13
recital (6) ... 5.23
recital (7) ... 5.8, 5.28
recital (9) ... 5.8
recital (10) ... 4.8
recital (11) ... 5.8, 5.12, 5.21

recital (14) ... 5.23
recital (16) ... 5.25
recital (17) ... 5.25
recital (18) ... 5.34
recital (19) ... 5.45
recital (20) ... 5.46, 5.47
recital (23) ... 5.55
recital (24) ... 5.57
recital (25) ... 5.58
recital (26) ... 5.58, 5.64
recital (27) ... 5.65
recital (28) ... 5.65
recital (30) ... 5.83
recital (31) ... 5.86
recital (32) ... 5.91, 5.98
recital (33) ... 5.92
recital (34) ... 5.43
recital (39) ... 5.6
recital (40) ... 5.6
art 1(1) ... 1.91, 5.8
art 1(1)(g) ... 5.104
art 1(2) ... 5.9
art 1(2)(a) ... 5.10
art 1(2)(b) ... 5.10
art 1(2)(c) ... 5.10
art 1(2)(d) ... 5.10
art 1(2)(e) ... 5.10
art 1(2)(f) ... 5.11
art 1(2)(g) ... 5.11, 5.123
art 1(3) ... 1.94, 5.9, 5.91
art 2 ... 5.12
art 2(2) ... 5.15
art 2(3) ... 5.15
art 3 ... 5.13
art 3(1) ... 5.87
art 4 ... 5.20, 5.21, 5.22, 5.23–5.44, 5.45, 5.46,
    5.52, 5.54, 5.57, 5.61, 5.64, 5.65, 5.79, 5.135
art 4(1) ... 1.91, 5.15, 5.25–5.29, 5.30, 5.33,
    5.34, 5.35, 5.36, 5.41, 5.58, 5.125, 5.135
art 4(2) ... 5.15, 5.30, 5.31, 5.32, 5.33, 5.34,
    5.35, 5.36, 5.52, 5.65, 5.95, 6.94
art 4(3) ... 5.19, 5.27, 5.34–5.42, 5.89, 5.131,
    5.135, 5.136, 5.137
art 5 ... 5.46–5.52
arts 5–9 ... 5.21, 5.45–5.66
art 5(1) ... 5.15, 5.52, 5.95
art 5(1)(a) ... 5.48, 5.49, 5.52
art 5(1)(b) ... 5.48, 5.49
art 5(1)(c) ... 5.48
art 5(1), proviso ... 5.48
art 5(2) ... 5.19, 5.52, 5.89
art 6 ... 5.53–5.56, 5.90
art 6(1) ... 5.54
art 6(2) ... 5.54
art 6(3) ... 5.55
art 7 ... 5.57–5.63
art 8 ... 5.64, 5.90
art 8(2) ... 5.64

art 8(3) . . . 5.64
art 9 . . . 5.65–5.66
art 10 . . . 5.22, 5.69–5.79, 5.84
art 10(1) . . . 4.177, 5.19, 5.71, 5.72, 5.75, 5.76, 5.78
art 10(1)–(3) . . . 5.79
art 10(2) . . . 5.78, 5.95
art 10(3) . . . 5.78, 5.79
art 10(4) . . . 5.79, 5.89
art 11 . . . 5.80–5.82, 5.84
art 11(1) . . . 5.19, 5.80, 5.81, 5.82
art 11(2) . . . 5.82, 5.95
art 11(3) . . . 5.82
art 11(4) . . . 5.81, 5.82, 5.89
art 12 . . . 4.8, 5.83–5.85
art 12(1) . . . 5.84
art 12(1)(e) . . . 5.71
art 12(2)(a) . . . 5.85
art 12(2)(b) . . . 5.85, 5.95
art 12(2)(c) . . . 5.85, 5.89
art 13 . . . 5.64
art 14 . . . 5.19, 5.41, 5.56, 5.64, 5.86–5.90
art 14(1) . . . 5.87
art 14(1)(b) . . . 5.89
art 14(2) . . . 5.90
art 14(3) . . . 5.90
art 15 . . . 5.91
art 15(c) . . . 1.99, 5.72, 5.92, 5.94, 5.121
art 15(d) . . . 5.94
art 15(h) . . . 1.97, 5.119
art 16 . . . 5.97, 5.136
art 17 . . . 5.43–5.44, 5.61, 5.62, 5.63
art 18 . . . 5.103
art 22(1) . . . 1.94
art 23 . . . 5.30, 5.95
art 23(1) . . . 5.96
art 23(2) . . . 5.96
art 24 . . . 1.107, 5.16
art 25(2) . . . 5.17
art 26 . . . 1.17, 5.97
art 30(2) . . . 5.11
art 31 . . . 5.6
art 32 . . . 5.6
EC Regulation No 1393/2007 (Service Regulation) . . . 1.15
EC Regulation No 593/2008 (Rome I Regulation) . . . 1.15, 1.17, 1.91, 1.94, 1.97, 1.100, 1.107, 1.157, 4.6–4.13, 4.14, 4.22, 4.25, 4.45, 4.49, 4.50, 4.57, 4.58, 4.66, 4.67, 4.68, 4.71, 4.73, 4.74, 4.78, 4.82, 4.83, 4.89, 4.90, 4.95, 4.101, 4.109, 4.113, 4.114, 4.124, 4.142, 4.143, 4.149, 4.151, 4.166, 4.169, 4.177, 4.179, 4.181, 5.8, 5.17, 5.18, 5.19, 5.22, 5.71, 5.87, 5.90, 5.121, 5.130, 5.131, 5.132, 5.135, 5.136, 5.137, 6.72, 9.28, 9.31, 9.32, 9.33, 9.42, 9.68
recital (7) . . . 4.12
recital (11) . . . 4.15
recital (12) . . . 4.25
recital (13) . . . 4.16
recital (14) . . . 4.16
recital (17) . . . 4.52
recital (19) . . . 4.57
recital (20) . . . 4.61, 4.73
recital (21) . . . 4.78
recital (22) . . . 4.116
recital (24) . . . 4.123
recital (32) . . . 4.123
recital (34) . . . 4.139
recital (36) . . . 4.135
recital (38) . . . 9.35
recital (45) . . . 4.9
recital (46) . . . 4.9
art 1(1) . . . 1.90, 4.7
art 1(2)–(3) . . . 4.8
art 1(2)(a) . . . 4.161
art 1(2)(b) . . . 9.31
art 1(2)(c) . . . 9.31, 9.68
art 1(2)(j) . . . 9.33
art 1(3) . . . 1.94, 4.179
art 2 . . . 4.9
art 3 . . . 4.14, 4.15, 4.16, 4.17, 4.22, 4.32, 4.33, 4.42, 4.49, 4.51, 4.86, 4.92, 4.97, 4.123, 4.127, 4.128, 4.152, 5.90, 9.32
arts 3–8 . . . 4.140
art 3(1) . . . 4.15, 4.22, 4.41, 4.45, 4.101, 5.87
art 3(2) . . . 4.47, 4.49
art 3(3) . . . 4.90, 4.92, 4.93, 4.94, 4.95, 4.96, 4.97, 4.101, 4.102, 5.90
art 3(4) . . . 4.90, 4.92, 5.90
art 3(5) . . . 4.145, 4.147
art 4 . . . 1.35, 4.14, 4.22, 4.46, 4.49, 4.50, 4.56, 4.60, 4.61, 4.62, 4.63, 4.67, 4.68, 4.70, 4.75, 4.89, 4.97, 4.101, 4.102, 4.117, 4.123, 4.127, 4.128, 4.134, 4.148, 4.152, 9.32
art 4(1) . . . 4.51–4.55, 4.56, 4.59, 4.60, 4.61, 4.62, 4.68, 4.75, 4.76, 4.77, 4.82
art 4(1)(a) . . . 4.51, 4.52, 4.53, 4.60, 4.73, 4.83, 4.86, 4.143
art 4(1)(b) . . . 4.51, 4.52, 4.53, 4.58
art 4(1)(c) . . . 4.51, 4.54
art 4(1)(d) . . . 4.51, 4.55
art 4(1)(e) . . . 4.51, 4.52, 4.55
art 4(1)(f) . . . 4.51, 4.52, 4.55
art 4(1)(g) . . . 4.51, 4.54
art 4(1)(h) . . . 4.51
art 4(2) . . . 4.56–4.59, 4.60, 4.61, 4.62, 4.68, 4.75, 4.76, 4.77, 4.82, 4.85
art 4(3) . . . 4.60–4.76, 4.119, 4.137
art 4(4) . . . 4.59, 4.77–4.81
art 5 . . . 4.51, 4.115–4.121, 4.123
arts 5–8 . . . 4.14, 4.114
art 5(1) . . . 4.116, 4.117, 4.118, 4.119
art 5(2) . . . 4.105, 4.120, 4.121, 4.131
art 5(3) . . . 4.119

TABLE OF SECONDARY LEGISLATION

art 6 . . . 4.51, 4.122–4.125, 4.133, 4.153
art 6(1) . . . 4.122, 4.123
art 6(2) . . . 4.90, 4.122
art 6(3) . . . 4.123
art 6(4) . . . 4.105, 4.123
art 7 . . . 4.8, 4.51, 4.123, 4.126–4.132
art 7(1) . . . 4.127
art 7(2) . . . 4.127
art 7(3) . . . 4.130
art 7(3)(a) . . . 4.129, 4.130
art 7(3)(b) . . . 4.129, 4.130
art 7(3)(c) . . . 4.129
art 7(3)(d) . . . 4.129
art 7(3)(e) . . . 4.129, 4.130
art 7(4) . . . 4.132
art 7(5) . . . 4.129
art 7(6) . . . 4.127
art 8 . . . 4.51, 4.133–4.139
art 8(1) . . . 4.90, 4.138, 5.136
art 8(2) . . . 4.135, 5.136
art 8(3) . . . 4.136
art 8(4) . . . 4.137
art 9 . . . 4.97, 4.102, 4.105, 4.124, 4.125
art 9(1) . . . 4.90, 4.97
art 9(2) . . . 1.160, 4.101, 4.105, 4.107, 4.109, 4.113, 4.124, 4.125, 5.97, 5.136
art 9(3) . . . 1.42, 4.98, 4.99, 4.100, 4.170, 4.173, 4.174, 4.175
art 10 . . . 4.141, 4.147, 9.32
art 10(1) . . . 4.142
art 10(2) . . . 4.148, 4.149
art 11 . . . 4.151, 4.153, 9.32
art 11(1) . . . 1.95, 4.152
art 11(2) . . . 4.152
art 11(3) . . . 4.153
art 11(4) . . . 4.153
art 11(5) . . . 4.153
art 12 . . . 9.32
art 12(1) . . . 4.169
art 12(1)(a) . . . 4.165
art 12(1)(b) . . . 4.166
art 12(1)(c) . . . 1.100, 4.167, 4.180, 4.181, 5.121
art 12(1)(d) . . . 1.97, 4.168, 4.175, 5.119
art 12(1)(e) . . . 4.176, 4.177, 5.71, 5.76
art 12(1)(j) . . . 9.33
art 12(2) . . . 4.166, 5.62
art 13 . . . 4.8, 4.155, 4.161–4.164, 9.32, 9.33
art 14 . . . 9.28
art 14(1) . . . 9.32, 9.35, 9.41
art 14(2) . . . 9.30, 9.41
art 15 . . . 1.107
art 18(1) . . . 1.94
art 19 . . . 4.52, 4.56, 4.82–4.86, 4.117, 4.150, 5.95
art 19(1) . . . 4.86
art 19(2) . . . 4.84, 4.85
art 19(3) . . . 4.82
art 20 . . . 4.13, 5.16
art 21 . . . 1.17, 1.157, 4.109, 4.113
art 22(2) . . . 4.10
art 28 . . . 4.6
EC Regulation No 4/2009 (Maintenance Regulation) . . . 1.15 1.107, 8.166, 8.167, 8.168, 8.169, 8.172, 8.179, 8.180, 8.181, 8.184, 8.187, 8.191, 9.73
recital (15) . . . 8.167
recital (16) . . . 8.175, 8.176
recital (19) . . . 8.170
recital (44) . . . 8.167
Ch VII . . . 8.191
art 2(3) . . . 8.170, 8.176
art 2(1)(10) . . . 8.172
art 3 . . . 6.72, 8.167, 8.170, 8.172
art 3(c) . . . 8.180
art 4 . . . 8.170
art 4(1) . . . 8.170
art 4(2) . . . 8.170
art 4(3) . . . 8.170
art 5 . . . 8.171
art 6 . . . 6.65, 8.170, 8.174
art 7 . . . 8.175, 8.176
art 8(1) . . . 8.184, 8.185
art 8(2)(a) . . . 8.184
art 8(2)(b) . . . 8.184
art 8(2)(c) . . . 8.184
art 8(2)(d) . . . 8.184
art 10 . . . 8.167
art 12 . . . 8.177, 8.178
art 13 . . . 8.177
art 15 . . . 8.187
art 17 . . . 8.191
art 26 . . . 8.191
art 68(1) . . . 8.167
art 69 . . . 8.182
EU Regulation No 1259/2010 (Rome III) . . . 1.15, 6.72, 8.50, 8.53, 8.59–8.60
recital (6) . . . 8.60
recital (14) . . . 8.60
art 5(1) . . . 8.60
art 8 . . . 8.60
EU Regulation No 650/2012 (Succession Regulation) . . . 1.15, 1.17, 1.109, 1.125, 1.130, 6.72, 9.116–9.121
recital (23) . . . 9.119
recital (57) . . . 1.119, 1.120
art 1(2)(k)–(l) . . . 9.119
art 4 . . . 9.118
art 20 . . . 9.118
art 21(1) . . . 9.118
art 21(2) . . . 9.118
art 22(1) . . . 9.118
art 30 . . . 9.119
art 34 . . . 1.109, 1.119, 1.120

art 34(1) . . . 9.118
art 83(1) . . . 9.118
EU Regulation No 1215/2012 (Brussels I Recast) . . . 1.15, 1.18, 1.105, 1.157, 1.162, 2.7, 2.8–2.20, 2.21, 2.22, 2.23, 2.26, 2.27, 2.28, 2.33, 2.34, 2.35, 2.36, 2.37, 2.46, 2.47, 2.59, 2.66, 2.84, 2.129, 2.132, 2.140, 2.142, 2.143, 2.164, 2.172, 2.175, 2.177, 2.179, 2.180, 2.181, 2.182, 2.197, 2.198, 2.205, 2.212, 2.232, 2.241, 2.245, 2.256, 2.265, 2.269, 2.272, 2.273, 2.274, 2.276, 2.278, 2.279, 2.280, 2.284, 2.313–2.321, 3.5, 3.6, 3.9, 3.73, 3.88, 3.89–3.98, 3.101, 3.102, 3.108, 4.6, 4.8, 5.19, 6.7, 8.4, 8.26, 8.69, 8.71, 8.72, 8.73, 8.79, 8.179
recital (12) . . . 3.95, 3.96
recital (22) . . . 2.197
recital (24) . . . 2.211
recital (26) . . . 3.88
recital (34) . . . 2.11
Chap I . . . 2.9, 2.13
Chap II . . . 2.9, 2.13, 2.21, 2.34, 2.37, 2.46, 2.55, 2.58, 2.63, 2.65, 2.114, 2.119, 2.126, 2.129, 2.139, 2.143, 2.265, 2.272, 2.280, 2.317, 3.92, 3.97, 3.104, 3.123
Chap II, Section 3, insurance . . . 2.129, 2.131, 2.133, 2.197
Chap II, Sections 3–5 . . . 2.130
Chap II, Section 4, consumer contracts . . . 2.129, 2.134, 2.197
Chap II, Section 5, employment contracts . . . 2.119, 2.129, 2.138, 2.197
Chap III . . . 2.9, 2.194, 3.6, 3.88, 3.90, 3.91, 3.92, 3.93, 3.96, 3.97, 3.98, 3.99, 3.101, 3.102, 3.103, 3.113, 3.126
Chap IV . . . 3.90
art 1 . . . 2.14, 2.16, 2.19, 2.37, 2.140, 2.176, 2.182, 2.235, 2.256, 2.285, 2.286, 2.317, 3.6, 3.92, 3.93, 3.94, 3.123, 4.7
art 1(2) . . . 2.15
art 1(2)(a) . . . 8.179
art 1(2)(d) . . . 2.318, 3.89
art 1(2)(e) . . . 8.166
art 2(a) . . . 3.89, 3.90, 3.101
art 4 . . . 2.17, 2.22, 2.55, 2.62, 2.64, 2.65, 2.78, 2.114, 2.127, 2.180, 2.207, 2.209, 2.268, 2.271, 2.272, 5.14, 8.32
art 5 . . . 2.19, 8.17
art 5(2) . . . 3.97
art 6 . . . 2.20, 2.38, 2.59, 2.129, 2.317, 3.97, 3.104, 8.17
art 7 . . . 1.91, 2.63, 2.64, 2.65, 2.66, 2.69, 2.78, 2.150, 2.207, 2.209, 2.268, 5.19
art 7(1) . . . 2.13, 2.22, 2.64, 2.66, 2.67, 2.68, 2.69, 2.71, 2.72, 2.74, 2.75, 2.76, 2.77, 2.80, 2.87, 2.90, 2.115, 2.126, 2.180, 5.18, 5.19, 5.130

art 7(1)(a) . . . 2.70, 2.76, 2.77, 2.79, 2.80, 2.81, 2.93
art 7(1)(b) . . . 2.76, 2.81, 2.84, 2.86, 2.87, 2.89, 2.90, 2.91, 2.92, 2.93, 4.52
art 7(1)(c) . . . 2.93
art 7(2) . . . 2.22, 2.64, 2.65, 2.66, 2.67, 2.68, 2.69, 2.71, 2.94, 2.95, 2.96, 2.97, 2.99, 2.100, 2.101, 2.102, 2.106, 2.108, 2.168, 2.169, 5.18, 5.19, 5.28, 5.130
art 7(3) . . . 2.64
art 7(4) . . . 2.64
art 7(5) . . . 2.64, 2.109, 2.110, 2.111, 2.112, 2.113, 2.129
art 7(6) . . . 2.64
art 7(7) . . . 2.64
art 8 . . . 2.63, 2.64, 2.65, 2.114, 2.150, 2.175, 2.207, 2.209, 3.123
art 8(1) . . . 2.115, 2.116, 2.117, 2.118, 2.119, 2.120, 2.121, 2.122, 2.123
art 8(2) . . . 2.124, 2.125, 2.126, 2.174
art 8(3) . . . 2.127, 2.128
art 8(4) . . . 2.114
art 9 . . . 2.63, 2.207, 2.209
art 10 . . . 2.129
arts 10–16 . . . 2.131, 3.106
art 11(1) . . . 2.131
art 11(2) . . . 2.131
art 12 . . . 2.131
art 13(1) . . . 2.131
art 13(2) . . . 2.131
art 14(1) . . . 2.131
art 15 . . . 2.132
art 16 . . . 2.132
art 17 . . . 2.44, 2.136, 4.123
arts 17–19 . . . 2.134, 3.106
art 17(1) . . . 2.129, 2.134
art 17(1)(c) . . . 2.134
art 17(2) . . . 2.135
art 17(3) . . . 2.134
art 18 . . . 2.38
art 18(1) . . . 2.38, 2.58, 2.59, 2.135
art 18(2) . . . 2.135
art 19 . . . 2.136
art 20 . . . 2.129
arts 20–23 . . . 2.138, 3.106
art 20(2) . . . 2.138
art 21 . . . 2.38
art 21(1)(b)(i) . . . 2.138
art 21(1)(b)(ii) . . . 2.138
art 21(2) . . . 2.38, 2.58, 2.59, 2.138
art 22 . . . 2.138
art 23 . . . 2.139, 2.311
art 24 . . . 2.21, 2.38, 2.39, 2.40, 2.57, 2.59, 2.61, 2.181, 2.194, 2.272, 2.276, 2.277, 2.280, 2.284, 3.106
art 24(1) . . . 2.20, 2.23, 2.40, 2.41, 2.42, 2.43, 2.44, 2.45, 2.256

art 25 . . . 2.23, 2.38, 2.46, 2.47, 2.49, 2.50, 2.51, 2.52, 2.55, 2.56, 2.57, 2.59, 2.79, 2.114, 2.149, 2.164, 2.197, 2.239, 2.268, 2.272, 2.276, 2.277, 2.278, 2.279, 2.280
art 25(1) . . . 2.47, 2.48, 2.50, 2.51, 2.54, 2.55, 2.56
art 25(1)(b) . . . 2.53
art 25(1)(c) . . . 2.51, 2.53
art 25(2) . . . 2.51
art 25(4) . . . 2.57
art 25(5) . . . 2.48
art 26 . . . 2.46, 2.57, 2.59, 2.60, 2.61, 2.129
art 26(1) . . . 8.171
art 27 . . . 2.40
art 28 . . . 3.120
art 28(1) . . . 2.19
art 28(2) . . . 2.19
art 29 . . . 2.181, 2.182, 2.183, 2.184, 2.185–2.186, 2.188, 2.189, 2.191, 2.192, 2.194, 2.197, 2.199, 2.206, 2.207, 2.211, 2.222, 2.265, 2.269, 2.272, 2.273, 2.313, 8.25
arts 29–33 . . . 2.38
arts 29–34 . . . 3.123
art 30 . . . 2.181, 2.182, 2.183, 2.184, 2.185, 2.190, 2.191, 2.199, 2.200, 2.202, 2.203, 2.204, 2.206, 2.211, 2.265, 2.269, 2.272, 2.273, 2.313, 8.25
art 30(1) . . . 2.201
art 30(2) . . . 2.201
art 30(3) . . . 2.199
art 31(1) . . . 2.181
art 31(2) . . . 2.197, 2.198, 3.107
art 31(3) . . . 2.197
art 31(4) . . . 2.197
art 32(1)(a) . . . 2.184
art 32(1)(b) . . . 2.184
art 32(4) . . . 3.93
art 33 . . . 2.206, 2.207, 2.211, 2.265, 2.271, 2.273, 2.280, 3.123, 8.33, 8.34, 8.52
art 33(1) . . . 2.207, 2.208
art 33(3) . . . 2.208, 2.211
art 34 . . . 2.206, 2.209, 2.211, 2.265, 2.271, 2.273, 2.280, 3.123, 8.33, 8.34, 8.52
art 34(1) . . . 2.209
art 34(2) . . . 2.210
art 35 . . . 2.188, 2.284, 2.285, 2.298, 3.90
art 35(1)(b) . . . 3.122
art 36 . . . 3.99
art 36(1) . . . 3.98
art 37(1) . . . 3.98
art 38 . . . 3.103
art 39 . . . 3.73, 3.101, 3.102
arts 39–51 . . . 3.102
art 42 . . . 3.102
art 43 . . . 3.102
art 45 . . . 3.98, 3.102, 3.103, 3.111
art 45(1)(a) . . . 3.108, 8.77
art 45(1)(b) . . . 3.114, 3.115, 3.116, 3.117, 3.118, 3.119, 3.120, 3.121, 3.122, 8.78
art 45(1)(c) . . . 3.123, 3.124, 8.79
art 45(1)(d) . . . 2.280, 3.123, 3.125, 3.126, 8.82
art 45(1)(e) . . . 3.106
art 45(1)(e)(ii) . . . 2.194
art 45(2) . . . 3.106
art 45(3) . . . 3.104
art 46 . . . 3.102
art 49 . . . 3.102
art 50 . . . 3.102
art 51 . . . 3.103
art 52 . . . 3.103, 3.111
art 53 . . . 3.98, 3.102
art 54 . . . 3.88
art 55 . . . 3.101
art 62(1) . . . 2.27
art 62(2) . . . 1.104, 2.28
art 63 . . . 2.30
art 63(1) . . . 2.29
art 63(2) . . . 2.29
art 73 . . . 2.33, 2.35
art 73(2) . . . 3.95, 3.96, 3.110
Annex 1 . . . 3.98
EU Regulation No 606/2013 on mutual recognition of protection measures in civil matters . . . 1.15
EU Regulation No 655/2014 (European Account Preservation Order Regulation) . . . 1.15, 2.281
EU Regulation No 848/2015 (New Insolvency Regulation) . . . 1.15, 2.15
EU Regulation No 2421/2015 . . . 3.103

Table of Cases

Alphabetical Listing

7E Communications Ltd v Vertex
   Antennentechnik GmbH (2007) . . . 2.52

A (Abduction: Habitual Residence), Re
   (1996) . . . 6.89
A (Abduction: Habitual Residence), Re
   (2007) . . . 6.84
A (Children), Re (2014) . . . 6.65, 6.78, 6.79, 6.90,
   6.96, 6.99
A (Foreign Surrogacy: South Africa), Re
   (2015) . . . 6.13
A and B (Parental Order: Domicile), Re
   (2014) . . . 6.13, 6.53
A v A (Child Abduction) (1993) . . . 6.84
A v B (2007) . . . 2.254
A v B: C–184/14 (2015) . . . 8.173
A v B: C-489/14 (2016) . . . 8.26
A v L (2010) . . . 8.94, 8.105, 8.108, 8.129, 8.133
A v T (Ancilliary Relief: Cultural Factors)
   (2004) . . . 8.187
A-G for Alberta v Cook (1926) . . . 6.33
A-G of Ceylon v Reid (1965) . . . 7.149, 7.150
A-G of New Zealand v Ortiz (1984) . . . 1.149,
   1.153
A-G (UK) v Heinemann Publishers Australia Pty
   Ltd (No 2) (1988) . . . 1.154
A-G for the United Kingdom v Wellington
   Newspapers Ltd (1988) . . . 1.154
A-G of Zambia v Meer Care & Desai
   (2006) . . . 2.175
A Local Authority v X (2014) . . . 7.66
AA v BB (2015) . . . 8.177
AB v JJB (EU Maintenance Regulation:
   Modification Application Procedure)
   (2015) . . . 8.191
Abbassi v Abbassi (2006) . . . 8.91
ABCI v Banque Franco-Tunisienne
   (2003) . . . 2.169
Abela v Baadarani (2013) . . . 2.150
Abidin Daver, The (1984) . . . 1.164, 2.32, 2.214,
   2.216, 2.221, 2.236, 2.238
Abouloff v Oppenheimer & Co (1882) . . . 3.68
Accentuate Ltd v Asigra Inc (2010) . . . 4.108
Activis UK Ltd v Eli Lily and Co (2015) . . . 5.9

Adams v Cape Industries plc (1990) . . . 1.161,
   1.165, 3.8, 3.15, 3.16, 3.18, 3.23, 3.24, 3.25,
   3.27, 3.28, 3.31, 3.38, 3.64, 3.66, 3.85
Adams v Clutterbuck (1883) . . . 2.263, 9.8
Adams v National Bank of Greece and Athens SA
   (1961) . . . 1.75
Addison v Brown (1954) . . . 1.163
Aeolian, The (2001) . . . 4.47
AES Ust-Kamenogorsk Hydropower Plant LLP
   v Ust-Kamenogorsk Hydropower Plant JSC
   (2013) . . . 2.298
African Fertilizers and Chemicals Nig Ltd v BD
   Shipsnavo GmbH & Co Reederei KG
   (2011) . . . 2.319, 3.124
Agbaje v Agbaje (2009) . . . 8.186
Agbaje v Agbaje (2010) . . . 8.185, 8.186
Agnew v Lansförsäkringsbølagens AB
   (2001) . . . 2.73, 2.75
AH v PH (Scandinavian Marriage Settlement)
   (2014) . . . 9.71
Ahmed v Mustafa (2015) . . . 8.49
AIG Europe SA v QBE International Insurance
   Ltd (2001) . . . 2.52
AIG Europe (UK) Ltd v The Ethniki
   (2000) . . . 2.77
Air Foyle Ltd v Center Capital Ltd
   (2003) . . . 9.16
Airbus Industrie GIE v Patel (1999) . . . 2.301,
   2.305
Akande v Balfour Beatty Construction Ltd
   (1998) . . . 3.17
Aksionairnoye Obschestvo AM Luther v James
   Sagor & Co (1921) . . . 9.43
Al-Bassam v Al-Bassam (2004) . . . 9.82
Al Habtoor v Fotheringham (2001) . . . 6.88
Al-Saedy v Musawi (Presumption of Marriage)
   (2011) . . . 7.23
Albaforth, The (1984) . . . 2.157, 3.38
Alberta Inc v Katanga Mining Ltd
   (2009) . . . 2.30
Albon v Naza Motor Trading Sdn Bhd
   (2007) . . . 2.160, 2.250
Albon v Naza Motor Trading Sdn Bhd (No 4)
   (2008) . . . 2.298, 2.301
Alfa Laval Tumba AB v Separator Spares
   International Ltd (2013) . . . 2.138
Alfonso-Brown v Milwood (2006) . . . 7.4, 7.72

Alfred Dunhill Ltd v Diffusion Internationale de Maroquinerie de Prestige SARL (2001) . . . 2.102
Ali v Ali (1968) . . . 7.147
Allen v Depuy International Ltd (2015) . . . 5.6
Alliance Bank JSC v Aquanta Corporation (2013) . . . 2.160
Alltrans Inc v Interdom Holdings Ltd (1991) . . . 2.287
Altertext Inc v Advanced Data Communications Ltd (1985) . . . 2.290
Altimo Holdings & Investments Ltd v Kyrgyz Mobil Tel Ltd (2012). . . . 2.154, 2.158, 2.234, 2.235
Aluminium Industrie Vaassen BV v Romalpa Aluminium Ltd (1976) . . . 1.138
A-M v A-M (2001) . . . 7.4, 7.134
Amalgamated Metal Trading Ltd v Baron (2012) . . . 2.151
American Motorists Insurance Co v Cellstar Corporation (2003) . . . 4.39
Amin Rasheed Shipping Corpn v Kuwait Insurance Co (1984) . . . 2.157, 2.215, 2.237, 4.3, 4.13, 4.33
AMT Futures Ltd v Marzillier, Dr Meier & Dr Gunter Rechtsanwaltsgesellschaft mbH (2015) . . . 2.100
Anderson v Eric Anderson Radio and TV Pty Ltd (1966) . . . 5.110
Andrew Weir Shipping Ltd v Wartsila UK Ltd (2004) . . . 2.123
Angelic Grace, The (1995) . . . 2.307, 2.318, 2.319
Annesley, Re (1926) . . . 1.104, 1.109, 1.115, 1.120, 1.129, 6.14, 9.82, 9.108
Anton Durbeck GmbH v Den Norske Bank ASA (2003) . . . 2.111
Anton Durbeck GmbH v Den Norske Bank ASA (2006) . . . 5.127
Apostolides v Orams: C–420/07 (2009) . . . 3.89, 3.101, 3.108, 3.122
Apostolides v Orams (2010) . . . 3.109
Apple Corps Ltd v Apple Computer Inc (2004) . . . 2.161, 4.59
Apt v Apt (1948) . . . 1.70, 1.90, 7.13
Arab Bank Ltd v Barclays Bank (1953) . . . 5.75
Arab Business Consortium International Finance and Investment Co v Banque Franco-Tunisienne (1997) . . . 2.168
Arab Monetary Fund v Hashim (1996) . . . 5.93
Arab Monetary Fund v Hashim (No 9) (1994) . . . 5.74
Ark Therapeutics plc v True North Capital Ltd (2006) . . . 2.218, 4.57
Armar Shipping Co Ltd v Caisse Algérienne d'Assurance et de Réassurance (1981) . . . 4.48
Armitage v A-G (1906) . . . 8.65
Armstrong v Armstrong (2003) . . . 6.85

A/S D/S Svendborg v Wansa (1997) . . . 2.309
Asaad v Kurter (2014) . . . 7.5, 7.10, 7.17, 7.23
Ashton Investments Ltd v OJSC Russian Aluminium (2007) . . . 2.176
Ashurst v Pollard (2001) . . . 2.43
Askew, Re (1930) . . . 1.109, 1.129
Askin v Absa Bank Ltd (1999) . . . 2.235
ASML Netherlands BV v Semiconductor Industry Services GmbH (SEMIS): C–283/05 (2006) . . . 3.115, 3.121
Atlantic Star, The (1973) . . . 2.213
Atlantic Star, The (1974) . . . 2.32, 2.214, 2.216
Attock Cement Co Ltd v Romanian Bank for Foreign Trade (1989) . . . 4.35
Attorney General . . . see A-G
AV Pound & Co Ltd v MW Hardy & Co Inc (1956) . . . 4.172
Avotins v Latvia App No 17502/07 (2016) . . . 3.122

B (Abduction) (No 2), Re (1993) . . . 6.88
B (Child Abduction: Habitual Residence), Re (1994) . . . 6.88
B v B (Divorce: Northern Cyprus) (2000) . . . 8.126, 8.133
B v S (Financial Remedy: Marital Property Regime) (2012) . . . 9.71
B v UK (2006) . . . 7.62
Babanaft International Co SA v Bassatne (1990) . . . 2.290, 2.293
Babcock v Jackson (1963) . . . 1.47, 1.56, 5.32
Baghlaf Al Zafer Factory Co BR for Industry Ltd v Pakistan National Shipping Co (1998) . . . 2.232, 2.242
Baghlaf Al Zafer Factory Co BR for Industry Ltd v Pakistan National Shipping Co (No 2) (2000) . . . 2.178
Baindail v Baindail (1946) . . . 7.153, 7.154, 9.112
Baker v Ian McCall International Ltd (2000) . . . 3.59
Baltic Flame, The (2001) . . . 2.173
Baltic Shipping v Translink Shipping Ltd (1995) . . . 2.297
Bamgbose v Daniel (1955) . . . 7.154
Banco Atlantico SA v British Bank of the Middle East (1990) . . . 2.233
Banco Nacional de Commercio Exterior Snc v Empresa de Telecomunicaciones de Cuba SA (2007) . . . 2.295
Banco Nacionel de Cuba, Re (2001) . . . 2.176
Bank of Africa Ltd v Cohen (1909) . . . 9.7, 9.13
Bank of Baroda v Vysya Bank (1994) . . . 4.58, 4.68, 4.74, 4.85
Bank of China v NBM LLC (2002) . . . 2.297
Bank of Dubai Ltd v Abbas (1997) . . . 2.27
Bank of New York Mellon v GV Films (2010) . . . 2.55

Bank of Tokyo-Mitsubishi v Baskan Gida Sanayi Ve Pazarlama (2004) . . . 2.188
Bank St Petersburg OJSC v Arkhangelsky (2014) . . . 1.96, 2.298
Bank voor Handel en Scheepvaart NV v Slatford (1953) . . . 1.156, 9.43
Bankes, Re (1902) . . . 9.68
Banque Cantonale de Genève v Polevent Ltd (2016) . . . 5.78
Barclays Bank plc v Ente Nazionale di Prevedenza (2015) . . . 2.187, 2.203
Barings plc v Coopers & Lybrand (1997) . . . 2.175
Barnett's Trusts, Re (1902) . . . 1.78
Barrie's Estate, Re (1949) . . . 9.97, 9.104
Barros Mattos Junior v MacDaniels (2005) . . . 5.78
Barry v Bradshaw (2000) . . . 2.77
Barton v Golden Sun Holidays Ltd (in liquidation) (2007) . . . 2.124
Base Metal Trading Ltd v Shamurin (2005) . . . 5.77, 5.131
BAT Industries plc v Windward Prospects Ltd (2014) 2.223
Bata v Bata (1948) . . . 5.106
Bater v Bater (1906) . . . 8.133
BDMS Ltd v Rafael Advanced Defence Systems (2015) . . . 2.255
Beaudoin v Trudel (1937) . . . 9.69
Beaumont, Re (1893) . . . 6.28
Beijing Jianlong Heavy Industry Group v Golden Ocean Group Ltd (2013) . . . 4.172
Bell v Kennedy (1868) . . . 6.37
Belletti v Morici (2009) . . . 2.173, 2.289, 2.294
Benaim & Co v Debono (1924) . . . 2.161
Benincasa v Dentalkit Srl: C-269/95 (1997) . . . 2.48, 2.134
Berchtold, Re (1923) . . . 9.2, 9.3
Berezovsky v Michaels (2000) . . . 2.157, 3.38
Berkovits v Grinberg (1995) . . . 8.117, 8.118
Berliner Verkehrsbetriebe (BVG) v JP Morgan NA: C-144/10 (2011) . . . 2.39, 2.40
Bernhard v Harrah's Club (1976) . . . 1.52
Berthiaume v Dastous (1930) . . . 7.22
Besix v Wasserreinigungsbau Alfred Kretzschmar GmbH & Co KG: C-256/00 (2002) . . . 2.80
Bethell, Re (1888) . . . 7.135
Bhatia Shipping and Agencies PVT Ltd v Aclobex Metals Ltd (2005) . . . 4.48
Bheekhun v Williams (1999) . . . 6.47
Bianco v Bennett (2015) . . . 5.25
Bilta (UK) Ltd v Nazir (2010) . . . 2.253
Bischoffsheim, Re (1948) . . . 6.18
Black v Yates (1992) . . . 3.46

Black-Clawson International Ltd v Papierwerke Waldhof-Aschaffenburg AG (1975) . . . 3.48, 3.85
Blanckaert and Willems PVBA v Trost: 139/80 (1981) . . . 2.110
Bloch v Bloch (2003) . . . 8.49
Blohn v Desser (1962) . . . 3.15
Blue Sky One Ltd v Mahan Air (2010) . . . 1.108, 1.141, 9.24
Blue Tropic Ltd v Chkhartishvili (2014) . . . 2.268
Bodley Head Ltd v Flegon (1972) . . . 4.157
Bohez v Wiertz: C-4/14 (2015) . . . 3.101
Boissevain v Weil (1950) . . . 4.107
Bols Distilleries BV (trading as Bols Royal Distilleries) v Superior Yacht Services Ltd (2007) . . . 2.51
Bonacina, Re (1912) . . . 1.90, 4.7, 5.20
Bonhams 1793 Ltd v Lawson (2015) . . . 9.16
Bonython v Commonwealth of Australia (1951) . . . 4.3
Booth v Phillips (2004) . . . 2.169
Boreh v Republic of Djibouti (2015) . . . 2.292
Boss Group Ltd v Boss France SA (1996) . . . 2.72, 2.95
Bouygues Offshore SA v Caspian Shipping Co (Nos 1, 3, 4 and 5) (1998) . . . 2.240, 2.309
Bowling v Cox (1926) . . . 2.170
Boys v Chaplin (1971) . . . 1.99, 1.162, 5.4, 5.32, 5.91, 5.107, 5.108, 5.109, 5.112, 5.113, 5.114, 5.115, 5.120, 5.121
BP Exploration Co (Libya) Ltd v Hunt (1976) . . . 2.161
BP plc v Aon Ltd (2006) . . . 2.241
Bremer v Freeman (1857) . . . 1.126
Brenner and Noller v Dean Witter Reynolds Inc: C-318/93 (1994) . . . 2.135
Breuning v Breuning (2002) . . . 6.34, 6.89, 8.29
Brinkibon Ltd v Stahag Stahl und Stahlwarenhandelsgesellschaft mbH (1983) . . . 2.161
Bristow Helicopters Ltd v Sikorsky Aircraft Corporation (2004) . . . 5.125
British Airways Board v Laker Airways Ltd (1985) . . . 2.299
British American Tobacco Switzerland SA v Exel Europe Ltd (2015) . . . 2.35
British Arab Commercial Bank v Bank of Communications (2011) . . . 4.74
British South Africa Co v Companhia de Moçambique (1893) . . . 2.257, 2.260, 2.263, 2.264
Brodin v A/R Seljan (1973) . . . 5.134, 5.135, 5.136, 5.137
Brogsitter v Fabrication de Montres Normandes EURL: C-548/12 (2014) . . . 1.91, 2.66, 2.71
Brokaw v Seatrain UK Ltd (1971) . . . 1.151

Broken Hill Proprietary Co Ltd v Xenakis (1982) . . . 4.35
Brook v Brook (1861) . . . 7.60, 7.78
Brown v Brown (1981) . . . 6.21
Brown v Innovatorone plc (2011). . . . 2.118, 2.121
Brownlie v Four Seasons Holdings Inc (2016) . . . 2.161, 2.169, 5.26
Brunsden v Humphrey (1884) . . . 3.57
Buchanan v Rucker (1808) . . . 3.12
Buehler v Chronos Richardson Ltd (1998) . . . 3.40
Burns v Burns (2008) . . . 7.6, 7.10
Buswell v IRC (1974) . . . 6.50, 6.53
Butler v Butler (1997) . . . 8.44

C (a minor) v Hackney London Borough Council (1996) . . . 3.59
C (Abduction: Habitual Residence), Re (2004) . . . 6.88
C v C (2001) . . . 8.45
C v C (Divorce: Jurisdiction) (2005) . . . 8.26
C v M: C–376/14 (2014) . . . 6.99
C v S (Divorce: Jurisdiction) (2011) . . . 6.94, 6.95, 8.26
Cadre SA v Astra Asigurari SA (2006) . . . 2.301
Calyon v Wytwornia Sprzetu Komunikacynego PZL Swidnik SA (2009) . . . 2.53
Cameron v Cameron (1996) . . . 6.89
Cammell v Sewell (1860) . . . 9.16, 9.18, 9.19
Campbell Connelly & Co Ltd v Noble (1963) . . . 9.31, 9.38
Canada Trust Co v Stolzenberg (No 2) (1998) . . . 2.154
Canada Trust Co v Stolzenberg (No 2) (2002) . . . 2.37, 2.62
Canadian Pacific Rly Co v Parent (1917) . . . 5.134
Canyon Offshore Ltd v GDF Suez E&P Nederland BV (2015) . . . 2.80
Capital Trust Investments Ltd v Radio Design TJ AB (2002) . . . 2.253
Car Trim GmbH v KeySafety Systems Srl: C–381/08 (2010) . . . 2.82, 2.85, 2.86
Carl Zeiss Stiftung v Rayner & Keeler Ltd (No 2) (1967) . . . 3.54, 3.58, 3.59
Carlson v Rio Tinto plc (1999) . . . 2.232
Carrick v Hancock (1895) . . . 3.24
Cartel Damage Claims (CDC) Hydrogen Peroxide SA v Akzo Nobel NV: C–352/13 (2015) . . . 2.48, 2.100, 2.105, 2.118
Cartier Parfums-Lunettes SAS v Ziegler France SA: C–1/13 (2014) . . . 2.185
Carvalho v Hull, Blyth (Angola) Ltd (1979) . . . 2.243, 2.248
Carvill America Inc v Camperdown UK Ltd (2005) . . . 2.152, 2.154, 2.173

Casdagli v Casdagli (1919) . . . 6.53
Casey v Casey (1949) . . . 7.78
Casio Computer Co Ltd v Sayo (2001) . . . 2.95
Castanho v Brown & Root (UK) Ltd (1981) . . . 2.300
Castrique v Imrie (1870) . . . 3.5
Catalyst Investment Group Ltd v Lewinsohn (2010) . . . 2.271, 2.274, 2.276
Caterpillar Financial Services Corp v SNC Passion (2004) . . . 4.95
Catlin Syndicate Ltd v Adams Land & Cattle Co (2006) . . . 4.29
CC v DD (2014) . . . 6.13
CC v NC (2015) . . . 6.95
CEF Holdings Ltd v Mundey (2011) . . . 2.138
Centro Internationale Handelsbank AG v Morgan Grenfell Trade Finance Ltd (1997) . . . 2.202
Century Credit Corp v Richard (1962) . . . 9.22
Česká podnikatelská pojišťovna as, Vienna Insurance Group v Bilas: C–111/09 (2010) . . . 2.129
Ceska Sporitelna AS v Feichter: C–419/11 (2013) . . . 2.81, 2.134
Ceskoslovenska Obchodni Banka AS v Nomura International plc (2003) . . . 2.231
CFEM Façades SA v Bovis Construction Ltd (1992) . . . 3.90
CGU International Insurance plc v Szabo (2002) . . . 2.225
Chadha & Oiscom Technologies Inc v Dow Jones & Co Inc (1999) . . . 2.157
Chai v Peng (2015) . . . 6.87
Chai v Peng (Estoppel: Foreign Judgment) (No 1) (2015) . . . 8.41
Chai v Peng (Jurisdiction: Forum Conveniens) (No 2) (2015) . . . 8.45
Chandler v Chandler (2011) . . . 6.14
Channel Tunnel Group Ltd v Balfour Beatty Construction Ltd (1993) . . . 2.254
Chaparral, The (1968) . . . 2.240
Charron v Montreal Trust Co (1958) . . . 4.157
Chase Manhattan Bank NA v Israel-British Bank (London) Ltd (1981) . . . 5.78
Chase v Ram Technical Services Ltd (2000) . . . 2.221
Chaudhary v Chaudhary (1985) . . . 1.167, 8.100, 8.103, 8.104, 8.106, 8.108, 8.112, 8.146
Chaudhry v Chaudhry (1976) . . . 7.158
Cheang Thye Phin v Tan Ah Loy (1920) . . . 7.155
Chellaram v Chellaram (No 2) (2002) . . . 2.142
Cheni v Cheni (1965) . . . 7.62, 7.64, 7.67, 7.100, 7.102, 7.147
Cherney v Deripaska (2007) . . . 2.27
Cherney v Deripaska (No 2) (2010) . . . 2.227
Chetti v Chetti (1909) . . . 7.102
Chief Adjudication Officer v Bath (2000) . . . 7.19

Chiwell v Carlyon (1897) . . . 9.61
Choo Eng Choon v Neo Chan Neo (Six Widows' Case) (1908) . . . 7.155
Choudhary v Bhattar (2010) . . . 2.39, 2.275
Church of Scientology of California v Metropolitan Police Commissioner (1976) . . . 5.108
Cinnamon European Structured Credit Master Fund v Banco Commercial Portugues SA (2010) . . . 2.48
Citi-March Ltd v Neptune Orient Lines Ltd (1996) . . . 2.242
Citibank NA v Rafidian Bank (2003) . . . 3.110
City & Country Properties Ltd v Kamali (2007) . . . 2.142
City of Westminster v C (2009) . . . 7.21
Clarke v Fennoscandia Ltd (1998) . . . 3.128
Claxton Engineering Services Ltd v TXM Olaj-es Gazkutato Kft (No 2) (2011) . . . 2.298
Cleveland Museum of Art v Capricorn Art International SA (1990) . . . 2.222
Cohn, Re (1945) . . . 1.79, 1.83, 1.89
Coin Controls Ltd v Suzo International (UK) Ltd (1999) . . . 2.264
Coleman v Shang (1961) . . . 7.155
Collens, Re (1986) . . . 9.105
Collier v Rivaz (1841) . . . 1.126
Color Drack GmbH v Lexx International Vertriebs GmbH: C-386/05 (2007) . . . 2.87
Colt Industries Inc v Sarlie (No 2) (1966) . . . 3.40
Comet Group plc v Unika Computer SA (2004) . . . 3.90
Commercial Marine & Piling Ltd v Pierse Contracting Ltd (2009) . . . 4.74
Compagnie Tunisienne de Navigation SA v Compagnie d'Armement Maritime SA (1971) . . . 4.3, 4.19, 4.26, 4.31, 4.32
Compania Sud Americana de Vapores SA v Hin-Pro International Logistics Ltd (2015) . . . 2.307
Conductive Inkjet Technology Ltd v Uni-Pixel Displays Inc (2014) . . . 2.161
Connelly v RTZ Corp plc (1998) . . . 2.232
Continental Bank NA v Aeakos Compania Naviera SA (1994) . . . 2.56, 2.195, 2.307, 2.314
Cook Industries Inc v Galliher (1979) . . . 2.290
Cook v Plummer (2008) . . . 8.31
Cook v Virgin Media Ltd (2016) . . . 2.269
Cooley v Ramsay (2008) . . . 2.169
Cooper v Cooper (1888) . . . 4.156
Cooper Tire & Rubber Co Europe Ltd v Dow Deutschland Inc (2010) . . . 2.203
Coreck Maritime GmbH v Handelsveem BV: C-387/98 (2000) . . . 2.50, 2.274
Corman-Collins SA v La Maison du Whisky SA: C-9/12 (2014) . . . 2.19, 2.81

Coty Germany GmbH v First Note Perfumes NV: C-360/12 (2014) . . . 2.104
Coupland v Arabian Gulf Oil Co (1983) . . . 1.99, 5.108, 5.131, 5.133
Coursier v Fortis Bank: C-267/97 (1999) . . . 3.101
Courtney, Re (1840) . . . 2.261
Cox v Ergo Versicherung (2014) . . . 1.99, 5.91, 5.121
Coys of Kensington Automobiles Ltd v Pugliese (2011). . . . 2.52
Craignish, Re (1892) . . . 6.53
Cramer v Cramer (1987) . . . 6.47, 6.49
Crédit Agricole Indosuez v Unicof Ltd (2004) . . . 2.223
Crédit Suisse Fides Trust SA v Cuoghi (1998) . . . 2.289, 2.293, 2.294
Crédit Suisse Financial Products v Société Générale d'Entreprises (1997) . . . 2.52
Cronos Containers NV v Palatin (2003) . . . 2.95
Cunnington, Re (1924) . . . 9.86
Curati v Perdoni (2013) . . . 9.86
Custom Made Commercial Ltd v Stawa Metallbau GmbH: C-288/92 (1994) . . . 2.77
Cutliffe's Will Trusts, Re (1940) . . . 9.2
Cyganik v Agulian (2005) . . . 6.56
Cyganik v Agulian (2006) . . . 6.20, 6.21

D v D (1994) . . . 8.91, 8.127, 8.143
Dadourian Group International Inc v Simms (2006) . . . 2.297
Dadourian Group International Inc v Simms (No 2) (2007) . . . 2.297
Dallah Real Estate and Tourism Co v Ministry of Religious Affairs of the Government of Pakistan (2010) . . . 1.106
D'Almeida Araujo (J) Lda v Sir Frederick Becker & Co Ltd (1953) . . . 1.99
Dal Al Arkar Real Estate Development Co v Refai (2015) . . . 2.39
Daniel v Foster (1989) . . . 2.22
Danmarks Rederiforening v Lo Landsorganisation I Sverige: C-18/02 (2004) . . . 2.95
Dansommer A/S v Götz: C-8/98 (2000) . . . 2.44
Danvaern Production A/S v Schuhfabriken Otterbeck GmbH & Co: C-341/93 (1995) . . . 2.128
De Cavel v De Cavel (No 1): 143/78 (1979) . . . 3.101, 8.179
De Dampierre v De Dampierre (1988) . . . 8.42, 8.43, 8.44
De Nicols, Re (1900) . . . 9.61, 9.62
De Nicols v Curlier (1900) . . . 9.55, 9.56, 9.59, 9.61
De Reneville v De Reneville (1948) . . . 1.90, 7.10, 7.78

de Wolf v Harry Cox BV: 42/76 (1976) ... 3.102
Debaecker v Bouwman: 49/84 (1985) ... 3.118
Debt Collection London Ltd v SK Slavia Praha-Fotbal AS (2011) ... 2.184
Definitely Maybe (Touring) Ltd v Marek Lieberberg Konzertagentur GmbH (2001) ... 4.69, 4.71
Deichland, The (1990) ... 2.34
Dellar v Zivy (2007) ... 6.53, 9.82, 9.86
Denilauler v SNC Couchet Frères: 125/79 (1980) ... 3.89
Derby & Co Ltd v Weldon (1990) ... 2.292
Derby & Co Ltd v Weldon (Nos 3 and 4) (1990) ... 2.297
Derby & Co Ltd v Weldon (No 6) (1990) ... 2.292, 2.293
Deschamps v Miller (1908) ... 1.168, 2.259, 2.262
Desert Sun Loan Corp v Hill (1996) ... 3.17, 3.20, 3.40, 3.47, 3.51, 3.59
Deutsche Bank AG v Asia Pacific Broadband Wireless Communications Inc (2008) ... 2.48
Deutsche Bank AG v Highland Crusader Offshore Partners LP (2010) ... 2.300, 2.310
Deutsche Bank AG v Sebastian Holdings Inc (2010) ... 2.275
Deutsche Bank AG v Sebastian Holdings Inc (No 2) (2011) ... 2.48
Deutsche Bank AG London Branch v Petromena ASA (2015) ... 2.48
DHL GBS (UK) Ltd v Fallimento Finmatica SPA (2009) ... 3.94
Diageo Brands BV v Simiramida-04 EOOD: C-681/13 (2015) ... 3.108
Dimskal Shipping Co SA v International Transport Workers' Federation (1992) ... 5.75
Distillers Co (Biochemicals) Ltd v Thompson (1971) ... 5.106
Divall v Divall (2014) ... 6.36, 6.53, 6.62
Dolphin Maritime & Aviation Services Ltd v Sveriges Angfartygs Assurans Forening (2009) ... 2.100, 5.28
Domicrest Ltd v Swiss Bank Corp (1999) ... 2.102
Donaldson v Donaldson (1949) ... 6.55
Donkers v Storm Aviation Ltd (2015) ... 5.127
Donohue v Armco Inc (2002) ... 2.307, 2.309
Dornoch Ltd v Westminster International BV (2009) ... 1.108
Doucet v Geoghegan (1878) ... 6.44
Downing v Al Tameer Establishment (2002) ... 2.255
Drammeh v Drammeh (1970) ... 7.150
Drevon v Drevon (1864) ... 6.50
Drouot Assurances SA v Consolidated Metallurgical Industries (CMI Industrial Sites): C-351/96 (1998) ... 2.191
Duarte v Black & Decker Corporation (2008) ... 4.111, 4.138

Duder v Amsterdamsch Trustees Kantoor (1902) ... 2.290
Duhur-Johnson v Duhur-Johnson (Attorney General Intervening) (2005) ... 8.127, 8.139
Duijnstee v Goderbauer: 288/82 (1983) ... 2.39
Dukali v Lamrani (Attorney General Intervening) (2012) ... 7.21, 8.183
Duke of Marlborough v A-G (1945) ... 9.68
Duke of Wellington, Re (1947) ... 1.129, 1.141
Duke of Wellington, Re (1948) ... 2.263
Dulles' Settlement (No 2), Re (1951) ... 2.148
Dumez France SA v Hessische Landesbank: C-220/88 (1990) ... 2.100
Dunlop Pneumatic Tyre Co Ltd v Actien-Gesellschaft für Motor und Motorfahrzeugbau Vorm Cudell & Co (1902) ... 2.145
Dynamite Act v Rio Tinto Co Ltd (1918) ... 1.172, 4.111

E v E (2007) ... 6.88
E v E (2015) ... 8.26
EA v AP (2014) ... 8.173
Earl Caithness, Re (1891) ... 9.97
Earl Nelson v Lord Bridport (1846) ... 9.7
East West Corp v DKBS 1912 (2002) ... 4.166
eco cosmetics GmbH & Co KG v Dupuy: C-119/13 & C-120/13 (2015) ... 3.103
Ecom Agroindustrial Corp Ltd v Mosharaf Composite Textile Mill Ltd (2013) ... 2.307
Electrosteel Europe SA v Edil Centro SpA: C-87/10 (2011). ... 2.84
ED & F Man (Sugar) Ltd v Haryanto (No 2) (1991) ... 3.72
eDate Advertising GmbH v X; Martinez v MGN Ltd: C-509/09 & C-161/10 (2012). ... 2.107, 5.29
Edmunds v Simmonds (2001) ... 5.31, 5.127
EF Hutton & Co (London) Ltd v Mofarrij (1989) ... 2.153
Effer SpA v Kantner: 38/81 (1982) ... 2.72
Egerton's Will Trusts, Re (1956) ... 9.51, 9.52, 9.53
Egon Oldendorff v Libera Corp (1995) ... 4.32, 4.150
EI du Pont de Nemours & Co v Agnew (1987) ... 2.222, 2.225
El Ajou v Dollar Land Holdings plc (1993) ... 5.78
El Amria, The (1981) ... 2.216, 2.242
El Fadl v El Fadl (2000) ... 8.105, 8.143, 8.145
El Majdoub v CarsOnTheWeb Deutschland GmbH: C-322/14 (2015) ... 2.51
Elefanten Schuh GmbH v Jacqmain: 150/80 (1981) ... 2.51, 2.57, 2.60, 2.204, 8.171
Eleftheria, The (1970) ... 2.242, 2.278
Elektrim SA v Vivendi Holdings 1 Corporation (2009) ... 2.298

Elektrim SA v Vivendi Universal SA (No 2) (2007) ... 2.298
Ella v Ella (2007) ... 8.29, 8.45
Emanuel v Symon (1908) ... 3.13, 3.14, 3.21, 3.22, 3.24
Emeraldian Limited Partnership v Wellmix Shipping Ltd (2010). ... 4.111
Emin v Yeldag (2002) ... 8.133
Emrek v Sabranovic: C-218/12 (2014) ... 2.134
Engler v Janus Versand GmbH: C-27/02 (2005) ... 2.134
English v Donnelly (1958) ... 4.107
Ennstone Building Products Ltd v Stanger Ltd (2002) ... 4.68, 4.69
Entores Ltd v Miles Far East Corp (1955) ... 2.161
Epsilon Rosa, The (2002) ... 4.150
Equitas Ltd v Allstate Insurance Co (2009) ... 2.239, 2.268
Equitas Ltd v Wave City Shipping Co Ltd (2005) ... 2.95
'ERGO Insurance' SE v 'If P&C Insurance' AS: C-359/14 & C-475/14 (2016) ... 4.7, 5.12, 5.91
Erich Gasser GmbH v Misat Srl: C-116/02 (2003) ... 2.195, 2.196, 2.197, 2.198, 2.320, 8.178
Eroglu v Eroglu (1994) ... 8.133, 8.134
Erste Group Bank AG v JSC 'VMZ Red October' (2015) ... 2.169
Estasis Salotti di Colzani Aimo v RÜWA Polstereimaschinen GmbH: 24/76 (1976) ... 2.52
Et Plus SA v Welter (2006) ... 2.252
ETI Euro Telecom International NV v Republic of Bolivia (2009) ... 2.286
Ets A de Bloos SPRL v Société en commandite par actions Bouyer: 14/76 (1976) ... 2.77, 2.110, 2.112
Euro-Diam Ltd v Bathurst (1987) ... 4.174
Evans Marshall & Co Ltd v Bertola SA (1973) ... 2.242
Ex p Rucker (1834) ... 9.4
Excalibur Ventures LLC v Keystone Inc (2011) ... 2.298

F Berghoefer GmbH & Co KG v ASA SA: 221/84 (1985) ... 2.52
F (Child Abduction), Re (1992) ... 6.84
F v F (Divorce: Jurisdiction) (2009) ... 6.53, 8.20
Fahnenbrock v Greek Republic: C-226/13, C-245/13, C-247/13 & C-578/13 (2106) ... 2.14
Falco Privatstiftung v Weller-Lindhorst: C-533/07 (2009) ... 2.18, 2.81, 2.90
Faraday Reinsurance Co Ltd v Howden North America Inc (2012) ... 2.222
Fatima, Re (1986) ... 8.104, 8.117

FBTO Schadeverzekeringen NV v Odenbreit: C-463/06 (2007) ... 2.131
Fergusson's Will, Re (1902) ... 9.85
Fern Computer Consultancy Ltd v Intergraph Cadworx & Analysis Solutions Inc (2014) ... 4.101, 4.108
Ferrexpo AG v Gilson Investments Ltd (2012) ... 2.276
Feyerick v Hubbard (1902) ... 3.15, 3.63
Fibrosa Spolka Akcyjna v Fairbairn Lawson Combe Barbour Ltd (1943) ... 5.75
Fidelitas Shipping Co Ltd v V/O Exportchleb (1966) ... 3.58
Fiona Trust & Holding Corporation v Privalov (2007) ... 2.48, 2.251
Firma Hengst Import BV v Campese: C-474/93 (1995) ... 3.117
Fitzgerald, Re (1904) ... 9.68
FKI Engineering Ltd v Stribog Ltd (2011) ... 2.199
FlyLAL-Lithuanian Airlines SAS v Starptautiska Lidosta Riga VAS: C-302/13 (2015) ... 2.14, 2.39, 3.88, 3.108, 3.110
Flynn, Re (1968) ... 6.8, 6.61
Folien Fischer v Ritrama SpA: C-133/11 (2013) ... 2.11, 2.72, 2.95
Fonderie Officine Meccaniche Tacconi SpA v Heinrich Wagner Sinto Maschinenfabrik GmbH: C-334/00 (2002) ... 2.73, 2.95, 5.84
Football Dataco Ltd v Sportradar (2011) ... 2.186
Fordyce v Bridges (1848) ... 9.84
Foster v Driscoll (1929) ... 1.172, 4.172
Fourie v Le Roux (2007) ... 2.287
FR Lürssen Werft GmbH & Co KG v Halle (2010) ... 2.225
FR Lürssen Werft GmbH & Co KG v Halle (2011) ... 4.35
Frahuil SA v Assitalia SpA: C-265/02 (2004) ... 2.14
Frankel's Estate v The Master (1950) ... 7.41, 7.44
Freeport plc v Arnoldsson: C-98/06 (2007) ... 2.117, 2.123
Freights Queen, The (1977) ... 4.35
Freistaat Bayern v Blijdenstein: C-433/01 (2004) ... 2.14
Freke v Lord Carbery (1873) ... 9.3, 9.95
Fuld's Estate (No 3), Re (1968) ... 6.16, 6.43, 6.46, 6.47, 6.49, 6.52, 6.54, 6.63, 9.79, 9.109
Fulham Football Club (1987) Ltd v Richards (2012) ... 2.252
Furse, Re (1980) ... 6.44, 6.53

G, Re (1966) ... 6.32
G and M, Re (2014) ... 6.13
G v de Visser: C-292/10 (2013) ... 2.19, 2.58, 2.140, 3.103

G v G (2016) ... 8.179
Gabriel v Schlank & Schick GmbH: C-96/00 (2000) ... 2.134
Gaillard v Chekili: C-518/99 (2001) ... 2.43
Galaxias Steamship Co Ltd v Panagos Christofis (1948) ... 5.128
Galeries Segoura SPRL v Bonakdarian: 25/76 (1976) ... 2.52
Galloway v Goldstein (2012) ... 7.4
Gambazzi v Daimler Chrysler Canada Inc: C-394/07 (2009) ... 2.289, 3.90, 3.110
Gan Insurance Co Ltd v Tai Ping Insurance Co Ltd (1999) ... 2.225, 4.33
Gantner Electronic GmbH v Basch Expoitatie Maatschappij BV: C-111/01 (2003) ... 2.187
Gard Marine and Energy Ltd v Glacier Reinsurance AG (2011) ... 4.33, 4.74
Gate Gourmet Luxembourg IV Sarl v Morby (2015) ... 6.52
Gemeente Steenbergen v Baten: C-271/00 (2002) ... 2.14, 2.15
General Star International Indemnity Ltd v Stirling Cooke Brown Reinsurance Brokers Ltd (2003) ... 2.299
Gesellschaft für Antriebstechnik mbH & Co KG v Lamellen und Kupplungsbau Beteiligungs KG: C-4/03 (2006) ... 2.39
GIE Groupe Concorde v Master of the Vessel Suhadiwarno Panjan: C-440/97 (1999) ... 2.79
Glaxosmithkline v Rouard: C-462/06 (2008) ... 2.119, 2.129
Glencore International AG v Metro Trading International Inc (2001) ... 1.108, 5.125, 9.16, 9.24
Global 5000 Ltd v Wadhawan (2012) ... 2.152, 2.160
Global Multimedia International Ltd v Ara Media Services (2007) ... 2.148, 2.175
Godard v Gray (1870) ... 3.61
Goldbet Sportwetten GmbH v Sperindeo: C-144/12 (2014) ... 3.103
Golden Acres Ltd v Queensland Estates Pty Ltd (1969) ... 4.3
Golden Endurance, The (2015) ... 2.225, 2.298, 2.302
Golden Ocean Group Ltd v Salgaocar Mining Industries Pvt Ltd (2012) ... 2.225, 4.35
Golubovich v Golubovich (2010) ... 1.157, 1.165, 1.170, 8.136, 8.138, 8.140
Gomez v Gomez-Moche Vives (2008) ... 2.265, 2.268
Gomez v Gomez-Moche Vives (2009) ... 2.64, 2.265
Good Challenger, The (2004) ... 3.58
Goshawk Dedicated Ltd v Life Receivables Ireland Ltd (2008) ... 2.271

Goshawk Dedicated Ltd v Life Receivables Ireland Ltd (2009) ... 2.271
Gotha City v Sotheby's (No 2) (1998) ... 9.16
Gothaer Allgemeine Versicherung AG v Samskip GmbH: C-456/11 (2013) ... 3.88, 3.89, 3.99, 3.100
Gourdain v Nadler: 133/78 (1979) ... 2.15
Government of India v Taylor (1955) ... 1.146, 1.151
Government of the United States v Montgomery (No 2) (2004) ... 3.70
Grant v McAuliffe (1953) ... 1.90
Gray v Formosa (1963) ... 1.82, 1.165, 1.170, 6.34, 7.102, 8.162, 8.163
Greene Wood & McLean LLP v Templeton Insurance Ltd (2009) ... 2.160
Grell v Levy (1864) ... 1.171
Groupement d'intérêt économique (GIE) Réunion Européenne v Zurich España: C-77/04 (2005) ... 2.125, 2.131
Gruber v Bay Wa AG: C-464/01 (2005) ... 2.134
Grupo Torras SA v Al-Sabah (No 5) (2001) ... 5.22
Gubisch Maschinenfabrik KG v Palumbo: 144/86 (1987) ... 2.186, 2.188, 2.189
Guerrero v Moterrico Metals plc (2009) ... 2.288

H (Abduction: Habitual Residence: Consent), Re (2000) ... 6.86
H v H (2015) ... 8.65
H v H (Talaq Divorce) (2008) ... 8.108, 8.143
H v H (Validity of Japanese Divorce) (2007) ... 8.105, 8.108, 8.111, 8.138, 8.139
H v S (Recognition of Overseas Divorce) (2012) ... 8.105
Hacker v Euro-Relais GmbH: C-280/90 (1992) ... 2.44
Hadadi v Hadadi: C-168/08 (2009) ... 6.95, 8.6, 8.13
Haeger & Schmidt GmbH v Mutuelles du Mans assurances IARD: C-305/13 (2015) ... 4.60, 4.116
Hagen, The (1908) ... 2.153
Haji-Ioannou (Deceased), Re (2009) ... 1.116, 1.129, 6.42, 9.108
Halki Shipping Corp v Sopex Oils Ltd (1998) ... 2.254
Halley, The (1868) ... 5.107, 5.109, 5.115
Halpern v Halpern (Nos 1 and 2) (2008) ... 4.16
Hamed v Stevens (2013) ... 2.261
Hamlin v Hamlin (1986) ... 2.262
Hamlyn & Co v Talisker Distillery (1894) ... 4.26
Handelskwekerij GJ Bier BV v Mines de Potasse d'Alsace SA: 21/76 (1976) ... 2.97, 2.98, 2.106, 5.28, 5.57, 5.58
Haque v Haque (1962) ... 9.112

Har-Shefi v Har-Shefi (No 2) (1953) . . . 8.98
Harding v Wealands (2005) . . . 5.121
Harding v Wealands (2007) . . . 1.99, 5.91, 5.121, 5.127
Harley v Smith (2010) . . . 1.96, 5.101
Harris v Quine (1869) . . . 3.48
Harrison v Harrison (1953) . . . 6.31, 6.32
Harrods (Buenos Aires) Ltd, Re (1992) . . . 2.266
Harvie v Farnie (1881) . . . 8.65
Hashmi v Hashmi (1972) . . . 6.18
Hassett v South Eastern Health Board: C-372/07 (2008) . . . 2.39
Haugesund Kommune v Depfa ACS Bank (2012) . . . 4.154
Haumschild v Continental Casualty Co (1959) . . . 1.90
Hayward, Re (1997) . . . 2.41
Hazell v Hammersmith and Fulham London Borough Council (1992) . . . 2.75
Heidberg, The (1994) . . . 3.94
Hejduk v EnergieAgentur.NRW GmbH: C-441/13 (2015) . . . 2.99, 2.103
Hellmann's Will, Re (1866) . . . 9.80
Hemain v Hemain (1988) . . . 8.49
Henderson v Henderson (1843) . . . 3.112
Henderson v Henderson (1967) . . . 6.16, 6.17, 6.20
Henderson v Jaouen (2002) . . . 2.101
Hendrikman v Magenta Druck & Verlag GmbH: C-78/95 (1996) . . . 3.108, 3.114
Henwood v Barlow Clowes International Ltd (2008) . . . 6.20, 6.21, 6.22, 6.23, 6.39, 6.49, 6.62
Herceg Novi v Ming Galaxy (1998) . . . 2.232
Hesperides Hotels Ltd v Muftizade (1979) . . . 2.260
Hewitson v Hewitson (1995) . . . 8.186
Hi Hotel HCF SARL v Spoering: C-387/12 (2014) . . . 2.104, 2.106
Hillside (New Media) Ltd v Baasland (2010) . . . 4.58, 5.28
Hincks v Gallardo (2013) . . . 7.123
Hobohm v Benedikt Kampik Ltd & Co KG: C-297/14 (2016) . . . 2.134
Hoffmann v Krieg: 145/86 (1988) . . . 3.88, 3.108, 3.124
Holliday v Musa (2010) . . . 6.41, 6.53
Holmes v Holmes (1989) . . . 8.186
Holterman Ferho Exploitatie BV v Spies von Bullesheim: C-47/14 (2015) . . . 2.138
Homawoo v GMF Assurance SA: C-412/10 (2011) . . . 5.6
Homestake Gold of Australia Ltd v Peninsula Gold Pty Ltd (1996) . . . 4.157
Hooshmand v Ghasmezadegan (2000) . . . 7.27, 7.29
Hoskins v Matthews (1856) . . . 6.55

Hotel Alpenhof GesmbH v Heller (2010) . . . 2.134
Hough v P & O Containers Ltd (1999) . . . 2.114
House of Spring Gardens Ltd v Waite (1991) . . . 3.69
Hoyles, Re (1911) . . . 1.90, 9.4
Hudson v Leigh (Status of Non-Marriage) (2009) . . . 7.4, 7.5, 7.8
Hulse v Chambers (2001) . . . 5.125
Huntington v Attrill (1893) . . . 1.146, 1.147
Hussain v Hussain (1983) . . . 7.136, 7.137, 7.138, 7.147
Hyde v Hyde (1866) . . . 7.125, 7.136
Hypotecni banka as v Lindner: C-327/10 (2011) . . . 2.14, 2.18, 2.19, 2.135, 2.140

Ikimi v Ikimi (2002) . . . 6.73, 6.80, 6.85, 6.86, 6.93, 8.21
Ilsinger v Dreschers: C-180/06 (2009) . . . 2.134
Import Export Metro Ltd v Compania Sud Americana de Vapores SA (2003) . . . 2.241
Industrie Tessili Italiana Como v Dunlop AG: 12/76 (1976) . . . 2.79
Indyka v Indyka (1969) . . . 7.46, 8.65, 8.86
Inglis v Robertson (1898) . . . 9.17
Ingmar GB Ltd v Eaton Leonard Technologies Inc: C-381/98 (2000) . . . 4.108
Ingosstrakh Insurance Co Ltd v Latvian Shipping Company (2000) . . . 2.241
Insured Financial Structures Ltd v Elektrocieplownia Tychy SA (2003) . . . 2.55
Integral Petroleum SA v SCU-Finanz AG (2015) . . . 4.8, 4.154, 4.156
Intercontainer Interfrigo SC (ICF) v Balkenende Oosthuizen BV: C-133/08 (2009) . . . 4.66, 4.67, 4.68, 4.116
Interdesco SA v Nullifire Ltd (1992) . . . 1.161, 3.112
International Credit and Investment Company (Overseas) Ltd v Shaikh Kamal Adham (1999) . . . 2.232
International Transport Workers' Federation v Viking Line ABP (2005) . . . 2.62
Internationale Nederlanden Aviation Lease BV v Civil Aviation Authority (1997) . . . 2.185
Iran Continental Shelf Oil Co v IRI International Corp (2002) . . . 4.17, 4.85
Iran Continental Shelf Oil Co v IRI International Corp (2004) . . . 4.9, 4.69
Iraqi Civilian Litigation, Re (2016) . . . 5.119
IRC v Bullock (1976) . . . 6.20, 6.45, 6.46, 6.47, 6.52, 6.53, 6.63, 6.64, 6.67, 6.70
IRC v Duchess of Portland (1982) . . . 6.34, 6.38, 6.58
Irini A (No 2), The (1999) . . . 3.40
Irish Shipping Ltd v Commercial Union Assurance Co plc (1991) . . . 2.233

Irvin v Irvin (2001) . . . 6.42, 6.53
Isaac Penhas v Tan Soo Eng (1953) . . . 7.27, 7.132
ISC Technologies Ltd v Guerin (1992) . . . 2.171
Islamic Republic of Iran v Barakat Galleries Ltd (2009) . . . 9.43
Islamic Republic of Iran v Berend (2007) . . . 1.108, 9.24
Ismail v Choudhry (2016) . . . 7.17
Ispahani v Bank Melli Iran (1998) . . . 4.172
Israel Discount Bank of New York v Hadjipateras (1984) . . . 3.20, 3.71
Italian Leather SpA v WECO Polstermöbel GmbH & Co: C-80/90 (2002) . . . 3.90, 3.103, 3.124
Ivan Zagubanski, The (2002) . . . 3.94
Ivleva (formerly Yates) v Yates (2014) . . . 8.141

J (Abduction: Custody Rights), Re (1990) . . . 6.74, 6.79, 6.88
J (Jurisdiction), Re (2007) . . . 6.53
Jabbour v Custodian of Israeli Absentee's Property (1954) . . . 9.27
Jacobs v Motor Insurers' Bureau (2010) . . . 1.99, 5.91
Jacobs v Motor Insurers' Bureau (2011) . . . 1.108, 5.91
Jacobson v Frachon (1927) . . . 3.63
Jakob Handte & Co GmbH v Traitements Mécano-chimiques des Surfaces SA: C-26/91 (1992) . . . 2.67, 2.71, 5.18
James Miller & Partners Ltd v Whitworth Street Estates (Manchester) Ltd (1970) . . . 4.3, 4.33
James, Re (1908) . . . 6.55
Jarrett v Barclays Bank plc (1999) . . . 2.44
JB (Child Abduction) (Rights of Custody: Spain), Re (2004) . . . 1.129, 1.130
Jefferson v O'Connor (2014) . . . 8.24
Jet Holdings Inc v Patel (1990) . . . 3.67, 3.68
Jeyaretnam v Mahmood (1992) . . . 2.236
JKN v JCN (2011) . . . 8.32, 8.33, 8.34, 8.40
Jogia (a bankrupt), Re (1988) . . . 2.170, 5.78
John Pfeiffer Pty Ltd v Rogerson (2000) . . . 1.92, 5.121
Johnson, Re (1903) . . . 9.112
Johnson v Coventry Churchill International Ltd (1992) . . . 5.115
Joint Stock Co Aeroflot–Russian Airlines v Berezovsky (2013) . . . 2.37
Joint Stock Co 'Aeroflot–Russian Airlines v Berezovsky' (2014) . . . 3.40
Joint Stock Company VTB Bank v Skurikhin (2013) . . . 2.289
Jones v Assurances Generales de France (AGF) SA (2010) . . . 2.131
Jones v Trollope Colls Cementation Overseas Ltd (1990) . . . 5.101

Jordan v Jordan (2001) . . . 8.186
Jordan Grand Prix Ltd v Baltic Insurance Group (1999) . . . 2.129, 2.131
Joyce v Joyce (1979) . . . 1.170, 8.129, 8.130, 8.140
JP Morgan v Primacom (2005) . . . 2.196, 2.203
JSC BTA Bank v Ablyazov (2013) . . . 2.39
JSC BTA Bank v Granton Trade Ltd (2011) . . . 2.223
JV, Re (2014) . . . 6.53

K, Re: A Local Authority v N and Others (2007) . . . 7.67
K v A (2015) . . . 7.23
Kainz v Pantherwerke AG: C-45/13 (2015) . . . 2.102
Kalfelis v Bankhaus Schröder, Münchmeyer, Hengst & Co: 189/87 (1988) . . . 1.91, 2.64, 2.66, 2.67, 2.68, 2.121
Kapetan Georgis, The (1988) . . . 2.223
Kapur v Kapur (1984) . . . 6.86, 6.88, 8.58
Karafarin Bank v Mansoury-dara (2009) . . . 2.232, 2.275, 3.45
Kaufman v Gerson (1904) . . . 1.167, 4.110
Kazakhstan Kagazy plc v Arip (2014) . . . 2.288, 2.292
Keefe v Mapfre Mutualidad Cia De Seguros Y Reaseguros SA (2016) . . . 2.131
Kellman v Kellman (2000) . . . 1.157, 8.92, 8.93, 8.132
Kelly v Selwyn (1905) . . . 9.42
Kenburn Waste Management Ltd v Bergman (2002) . . . 4.72
Kendall v Kendall (1977) . . . 1.167, 8.133
Kensington International Ltd v Republic of Congo (2008) . . . 2.293
Kenward v Kenward (1951) . . . 7.75
King v Lewis (2003) . . . 2.157, 2.168
Kinnear v Falconfilms NV (1996) . . . 2.124
Kitechnology BV v Unicor GmbH RahnPlastmaschinen (1994) . . . 2.48, 2.167
KL (A Child), Re (2014) . . . 6.78, 6.99
Klein v Rhodos Management Ltd: C-73/04 (2005) . . . 2.39, 2.44
Kleinwort Benson Ltd v City of Glasgow District Council: C-346/93 (1995) . . . 2.21
Kleinwort Benson Ltd v Glasgow City Council (1996) . . . 2.69
Kleinwort Benson Ltd v Glasgow City Council (1999) . . . 2.69, 2.74, 2.75
Kleinwort Sons & Co v Ungarische Baumwolle Industrie Akt (1939) . . . 4.169
Klomps v Michel: 166/80 (1981) . . . 3.116, 3.117
Kochanski v Kochanska (1958) . . . 7.31
Koelzsch v Grand Duchy of Luxembourg: C-29/10 (2012) . . . 2.138, 4.135
Kolassa v Barclays Bank plc: C-375/13 (2015) . . . 2.11, 2.37, 2.100, 2.134

Kolden Holdings Ltd v Rodette Commerce Ltd (2008) . . . 2.191
Kolmar Group AG v Visen Industries Ltd (2010) . . . 2.52
Komninos S, The (1990) . . . 4.28
Komninos S, The (1991) . . . 4.3, 4.27, 4.29
Komu v Komu: C–605/14 (2016) . . . 2.42
Konamaneni v Rolls-Royce Industrial Power (India) Ltd (2002) . . . 2.231
Kongress Agentur Hagen GmbH v Zeehaghe BV: C–365/88 (1990) . . . 2.13, 2.126
Konkola Copper Mines plc v Coromin Ltd (2005) . . . 2.275, 2.277
Konkola Copper Mines plc v Coromin Ltd (No 2) (2002) . . . 2.241
Korea National Insurance Corporation v Allianz Global Corporate & Specialty AG (2009) . . . 3.67
Krejci Lager & Umschlagbetriebs GMBH v Olbrich Transport und Logistik GMBH: C–469/12 (2014). . . . 2.65, 2.81
Krell v Henderson (1960) . . . 1.56
Krenge v Krenge (1999) . . . 8.45, 8.46
Kribi, The (2001) . . . 2.4
Kroch v Rossell et Cie (1937) . . . 2.157
Krombach v Bamberski: C–7/98 (2000) . . . 3.104, 3.108, 3.110
Kronhofer v Maier: C–168/02 (2004) . . . 2.100
Kuwait Airways Corp v Iraqi Airways Co (Nos 4 and 5) (2002) . . . 1.155, 1.162, 1.163, 1.167, 1.170, 5.102, 9.43
Kuwait Oil Tanker SAK v Al Bader (2000) . . . 5.7
Kwok Chi Leung Karl v Estate Duty Comrs (1988) . . . 9.27

L-K v K (No 2) (2007) . . . 6.75, 6.93, 6.94
Laemthong International Lines Co Ltd v Artis (2005) . . . 2.288
Lafarge Plasterboard Ltd v Fritz Peters & Co KG (2000) . . . 2.53
Lamagni v Lamagni (1995) . . . 8.186
Land Berlin v Sapir: C–645/11 (2013) . . . 2.14
Land Oberösterreich v ČEZ as: C–343/04 (2006) . . . 2.43
Landhurst Leasing plc v Marcq (1998) . . . 3.89
Langley's Settlement Trusts, Re (1961) . . . 1.148
Lashley v Hog (1804) . . . 9.58
Late Emperor Napoleon Bonaparte, Re (1853) . . . 6.54
Law Debenture Trust Corporation plc v Elektrim Finance BV (2005) . . . 2.250
Lawlor v Sandvik Mining and Construction Mobile Crushers and Screens Ltd (2012) . . . 4.72
Lawlor v Sandvik Mining and Construction Mobile Crushers and Screens Ltd (2013) . . . 4.22

Lawrence v Lawrence (1985) . . . 7.46, 7.47, 7.50, 7.52, 7.80, 7.82, 7.86, 7.87, 7.88, 7.89
Lazar v Allianz SpA: C–350/14 (2016) . . . 5.26
LC (Children), Re (2014) . . . 6.78, 6.99
Le Feuvre v Sullivan (1855) . . . 9.42
Le Mesurier v Le Mesurier (1895) . . . 8.1
Leathertex Divisione Sintetici SpA v Bodotex BVBA: C–420/97 (1999) . . . 2.78
Lechouritou v Dimosio tis Omospondiakis Dimokratias tis Germanias: C–292/05 (2007) . . . 2.14, 5.8
Lee v Abdy (1886) . . . 9.39
Lee v Lau (1967) . . . 1.90, 7.127
Lehman Brothers Bankhaus AG I. Ins v CMA CGM (2013) . . . 2.202
Leman-Klammers v Klammers (2008) . . . 8.26
Lemenda Trading Co Ltd v African Middle East Petroleum Co Ltd (1988) . . . 1.169
Lepre v Lepre (1965) . . . 1.165, 7.10, 7.102, 8.162
Leroux v Brown (1852) . . . 1.95, 1.96, 4.151
Letang v Cooper (1965) . . . 3.55
Lewal's Settlement Trusts, Re (1918) . . . 9.79
Lewis v Eliades (2004) . . . 3.79
Liao Eng Kiat v Burswood Nominees Ltd (2005) . . . 3.70
Liaw v Lee (Non-Recognition of Divorce) (2016) . . . 8.77, 8.131, 8.141
Libyan Arab Foreign Bank v Bankers Trust Co (1989) . . . 4.174
Lieber v Göbel: C–292/93 (1994) . . . 2.43
Limit (No 3) Ltd v PDV Insurance Co (2005) . . . 2.225
Linuzs v Latmar Holdings Corp (2013) . . . 2.62, 2.118
Lipkin Gorman v Karpnale Ltd (1991) . . . 5.68
Littauer Glove Corp v FW Millington (1928) . . . 3.27
LK v K (No 3) (2007) . . . 8.26
Lloyd Evans, Re (1947) . . . 6.60
Lloyd v Lloyd (1962) . . . 6.12
Lloyd's Register of Shipping v Société Campenon Bernard: C–439/93 (1995) . . . 2.111, 2.113
Lodge v Lodge (1963) . . . 7.16
Lombard North Central plc v GATX Corp (2012) . . . 2.251
London Helicopters Ltd v Heliportugal LDA-INAC (2006) . . . 2.100, 2.102
Lord Advocate v Jaffrey (1921) . . . 6.33
L'Oreal SA v Bellure NV (2008) . . . 5.53
Louis Dreyfus Commodities Kenya Ltd v Bolster Shipping Co Ltd (2010) . . . 2.307
LS (Mut'a or sighé) Iran (2007) . . . 7.7
Lubbe v Cape plc (2000) . . . 2.4, 2.217, 2.232, 2.266
Lucasfilm Ltd v Ainsworth (2012) . . . 2.62, 2.264, 3.27
Luckwell v Limata (2014) . . . 9.66

Lucky Lady, The (2013) . . . 2.225
Lukandwa v Birungi (2012) . . . 7.23
Lupofresh Ltd v Sapporo Breweries Ltd (2014) . . . 4.141

M v M (Abduction: England and Scotland) (1997) . . . 6.82
M v M (Divorce: Domicile) (2011) . . . 6.50, 8.45
M v W (Application After New Zealand Financial Agreement) (2015) . . . 8.172
MA v JA (2013) . . . 7.5
MA v SK; S Investments v MA (Financial Relief After Saudi Divorce) (2016) . . . 8.186
Macartney, Re (1921) . . . 1.167, 3.71
McCabe v McCabe (1994) . . . 7.25
McFeetridge v Stewarts and Lloyds Ltd (1913) . . . 4.160
McGraw-Hill v Deutsche Apotheker- und Arztebank EG (2014) . . . 2.111
Machado v Fontes (1897) . . . 5.109
Maciej Rataj, The (1991) . . . 2.202
Mackender v Feldia AG (1967) . . . 2.241
McKenzie, Re (1951) . . . 6.17
Mackinnon v Iberia Shipping Co (1954) . . . 5.109
Maclean v Cristall (1849) . . . 7.28
MacLeod v MacLeod (2010) . . . 9.65
Macmillan Inc v Bishopsgate Investment Trust plc (No 3) (1995) . . . 1.121
Macmillan Inc v Bishopsgate Investment Trust plc (No 3) (1996) . . . 1.68, 1.90, 1.108, 5.73, 9.5, 9.16, 9.37, 9.38
MacShannon v Rockware Glass Ltd (1978) . . . 2.214
Madoff Securities International Ltd v Raven (2012) . . . 2.116
Maersk Olie and Gas A/S v Firma M de Haan and M de Boer: C–39/02 (2004) . . . 2.187, 2.188, 3.89, 3.114
Magdalena Fernández v Commission: T–90/92 (1993). . . . 6.72
Mahamdia v People's Democratic Republic of Algeria: C–154/11 (2012) . . . 2.138
Maharanee of Baroda v Wildenstein (1972) . . . 1.3, 1.4, 1.23, 1.35, 1.38, 1.61, 1.64, 1.174, 2.142, 3.24
Maher v Groupama Grand Est (2009) . . . 1.99, 5.91
Maher v Groupama Grand Est (2010) . . . 2.131, 5.121
Mahme Trust Reg v Lloyds TSB Bank plc (2004) . . . 2.265
Mahonia Ltd v JP Morgan Chase Bank (2003) . . . 4.174

Mainschiffahrts-Genossenschaft eG (MSG) v Les Gravières Rhénanes Sarl: C–106/95 (1997) . . . 2.51, 2.79
Maldonado's Estate, Re (1954) . . . 1.77, 1.78, 1.83, 1.89
Male v Roberts (1790) . . . 4.156
Maletic v lastminute.com GmbH: C–478/12 (2014) . . . 2.14
Mamdani v Mamdani (1984) . . . 8.130
Maple Leaf Macro Volatility Master Fund v Rouvroy (2009) . . . 2.48
Maples v Melamud (1988) . . . 6.61, 8.117
Marc Rich & Co AG v Società Italiana Impianti (No 2) (1992) . . . 3.19, 3.75
Marc Rich & Co AG v Società Italiana Impianti, The Atlantic Emperor: C–190/89 (1991) . . . 2.15, 2.16, 3.94
Marconi Communications International Ltd v PT Pan Indonesia Bank Ltd (2005) . . . 4.74
Marconi Communications International Ltd v PT Pan Indonesia Bank Ltd (2007) . . . 4.72
Maria Hertogh, Re (1951) . . . 7.70
Mariannina, The (1983) . . . 4.48
Marinari v Lloyds Bank plc: C–364/93 (1995) . . . 2.100, 5.28
Marinos v Marinos (2007) . . . 6.75, 6.92, 6.93, 6.94, 6.95, 8.11
Mark v Mark (2006) . . . 6.6, 6.13, 6.40, 6.49, 6.74, 6.87
Maronier v Larmer (2003) . . . 3.110
Marshall v Motor Insurers' Bureau (2015) . . . 5.30, 5.35, 5.36
Martin, Re (1900) . . . 1.90, 6.56, 9.49, 9.89
Martinez v MGN Ltd (2012) . . . 2.107
Martrade Shipping & Transport GmbH v United Enterprises Corpn (2015) . . . 4.104, 4.116
Marubeni Hong Kong and South China Ltd v Mongolian Government (2002) . . . 4.22, 4.32
Masri v Consolidated Contractors International (UK) Ltd (2006) . . . 2.116
Masri v Consolidated Contractors International (UK) Ltd (No 2) (2009) . . . 2.39, 2.273, 2.282, 2.291, 2.295, 2.297
Masri v Consolidated Contractors International (UK) Ltd (No 3) (2009) . . . 2.298, 2.301
Masters v Leaver (2000) . . . 3.65
Maudslay, Re (1900) . . . 9.42
Mauritius Commercial Bank Ltd v Hestia Holdings Ltd (2013) . . . 2.56, 4.47
May v May and Lehmann (1943) . . . 6.55
Mazur Media Ltd v Mazur Media GmbH (2004) . . . 2.71
MBM Fabri-Clad Ltd v Eisen-und Huttenwerke Thale AG (2000) . . . 2.77
MC Pearl, The (1997) . . . 2.242
MD Gemini, The (2012). . . . 2.308, 2.310
Meeth v Glacetal: 23/78 (1978) . . . 2.55

M'Elroy v M'Allister (1949) . . . 5.109, 5.111
Melzer v MF Global UK Ltd: C–228/11 (2013) . . . 2.104
Merchant International Co Ltd v Natsionalna Aktsionerna Kompaniia Naftogaz Ukrainy (2012) . . . 3.70
Mercredi v Chaffe: C–497/10 (2010) . . . 4.86, 6.98
Meridien BIAO Bank GmbH v Bank of New York (1997) . . . 4.167
Merker v Merker (1963) . . . 3.74, 7.31, 8.152, 8.164
Merrill Lynch Capital Services Inc v Municipality of Piraeus (1997) . . . 4.154
Messier-Dowty Ltd v Sabena SA (2000) . . . 2.218
Messina v Smith (1971) . . . 8.88
Metall und Rohstoff AG v Donaldson Lufkin & Jenrette Inc (1990) . . . 2.168, 5.105, 5.106
Mette v Mette (1859) . . . 7.62
Meyer, Re (1971) . . . 8.135
MH v MH (2015) . . . 8.26
Micallef's Estate, Re (1977) . . . 9.97
Middle Eastern Oil LLC v National Bank of Abu Dhabi (2009) . . . 5.137
Middleton v Middleton (1967) . . . 1.165, 8.133
Midgulf International Ltd v Groupe Chimique Tunisien (2010) . . . 2.317
Midland Bank plc v Laker Airways Ltd (1986) . . . 2.305
Mietz v Intership Yachting Sneek BV: C–99/96 (1999) . . . 2.134, 2.284
Miles Platt Ltd v Townroe Ltd (2003) . . . 2.188
Miliangos v George Frank (Textiles) Ltd (1976) . . . 4.182
Miller, Re (1914) . . . 9.95, 9.96
Minalmet GmbH v Brandeis Ltd: C–123/91 (1992) . . . 3.117
Ministry of Defence and Support of the Armed Forces for Iran v Faz Aviation Ltd (2007) . . . 2.62
Missouri Steamship Co, Re (1889) . . . 4.40
Mitchell, Re (1954) . . . 1.83
Mittal v Mittal (2014) . . . 8.33, 8.34, 8.40
MO v RO (2013) . . . 7.25
Mobil Cerro Negro Ltd v Petroleos de Venezuela SA (2008) . . . 2.294
Mohamed v Knott (1969) . . . 7.45, 7.67, 7.68, 7.125
Mölnlycke Health Care AB v BSN Medical Ltd (2010) . . . 2.191
Molton Street Capital LLP v Shooters Hill Capital Partners LLP (2015) . . . 4.68
Moore v Moore (2006) . . . 6.92
Moore v Moore (2007) . . . 8.179, 8.186
Mora Shipping Inc v Axa Corporate Solutions Assurance SA (2005) . . . 2.80
Morgan v Cilento (2004) . . . 6.61

Morin v Bonhams & Brooks Ltd (2004) . . . 5.86, 5.137
Morley v Reiter Engineering GmbH (2012) . . . 2.37
Morris v Davies (2011) . . . 6.53
Motorola Credit Corp v Uzan (No 2) (2004) . . . 2.289, 2.296
Moynihan v Moynihan (Nos 1 and 2) (1997) . . . 6.55
MRA v NRK (2011) . . . 7.21
MS v PS (2016) . . . 8.191
Muhlleitner v Yusufi: C–190/11 (2012) . . . 2.134
Multinational Gas and Petrochemical Co v Multinational Gas and Petrochemical Services Inc (1983) . . . 2.175
Munro v Munro (2008) . . . 6.52, 6.75, 6.94, 8.12
Murthy v Sivajothi (1999) . . . 3.18
Musawi v RE International (UK) Ltd (2008) . . . 4.16
Musurus's Estate, Re (1936) . . . 1.78

N (Jurisdiction), Re (2007) . . . 8.13
N v D (Customary Marriage) (2015) . . . 7.20, 7.25
N v N (Stay of Maintenance Proceedings) (2014) . . . 8.177
Nabb Brothers Ltd v Lloyds Bank International (Guernsey) Ltd (2005) . . . 2.170
Nabi v Heaton (1981) . . . 7.149
Nabi v Heaton (1983) . . . 7.158
National Bank of Greece and Athens SA v Metliss (1958) . . . 1.75
National Mortgage and Agency Co of New Zealand Ltd v Gosselin (1922) . . . 2.162
NB Three Shipping Ltd v Harebell Shipping Ltd (2005) . . . 2.250
Neilson v Overseas Projects Corporation of Victoria Ltd (2005) . . . 1.116, 1.129, 1.130, 5.124
Nessa v Chief Adjudication Officer (1999) . . . 6.74, 6.79, 6.83, 6.84
Netherlands State v Rüffer: 814/79 (1980) . . . 2.14
Neumeier v Kuehner (1972) . . . 1.57
New Hampshire Insurance Co v Phillips Electronics North America Corp (1998) . . . 2.218
New Hampshire Insurance Co v Strabag Bau AG (1992) . . . 2.133
New York Life Insurance Co v Public Trustee (1924) . . . 9.27
Newmarch v Newmarch (1978) . . . 8.129, 8.138, 8.139
Newsat Holdings Ltd v Zani (2006) . . . 2.169
Niche Products Ltd v Macdermid Offshore Solutions LLC (2014). . . . 2.222
Nile Rhapsody, The (1994) . . . 2.241

Ninemia Maritime Corp v Trave Schiffahrtsgesellschaft mbH und Co KG (1983) . . . 2.288
Nipponkoa Insurance Co (Europe) Ltd v Inter-Zuid Transport BV: C–452/12 (2014) . . . 2.35
Njegos, The (1936) . . . 4.35
Noble Assurance Co v Gerling-Konzern General Insurance Co (2007) . . . 2.301
Nomihold Securities Inc v Mobile Telesystems Finance SA (2012) . . . 2.293
Nomura International plc v Banca Monte Dei Paschi Di Siena SpA (2014) . . . 2.203
Nordglimt, The (1988) . . . 2.34, 2.192
Norris v Chambres (1861) . . . 2.259
Norton v Florence Land and Public Works Co (1877) . . . 9.7
Nouvion v Freeman (1889) . . . 3.40
Novus Aviation Ltd v Onur Air Tasimacilik AS (2009) . . . 2.225
NP v KRP (Recognition of Foreign Divorce) (2014) . . . 8.106, 8.139
Nurnberger Allgemeine Versicherungs AG v Portbridge Transport BV: C–148/03 (2004) . . . 2.33
Nygh & Kasey (2010) . . . 7.27

Oceanconnect UK Ltd v Angara Maritime Ltd (2010) . . . 2.301
Ochsenbein v Papelier (1873) . . . 3.67
O'Donoghue v United Kingdom (2011) . . . 7.17
ÖFAB v Koot: C–147/12 (2015) . . . 2.71, 2.95, 2.97, 2.102, 5.18
Official Solicitor v Yemoh (2011) . . . 7.155
Offshore Rental Co Inc v Continental Oil Co (1978) . . . 1.53
Ogden v Ogden (1908) . . . 1.71–1.77, 1.84, 1.86, 1.88, 1.89, 7.15, 7.16, 7.17, 7.57
Oinoussin Pride, The (1991) . . . 2.223
O'Keefe, Re (1940) . . . 1.109, 1.129, 9.108
Olafisoye v Olafisoye (Jurisdiction) (2011) . . . 6.94, 6.95
Olafisoye v Olafisoye (No 2) (Recognition) (2011) . . . 8.141
Olympic Galaxy, The (2006) . . . 2.222
Omega King, The (2011) . . . 2.157
Onobrauche v Onobrauche (1978) . . . 7.147, 7.151, 7.152
Ophthalmic Innovations International (UK) Ltd v Ophthalmic Innovations International Inc (2005) . . . 4.57
Oppenheimer v Cattermole (1976) . . . 1.167
Oppenheimer v Louis Rosenthal & Co AG (1937) . . . 2.235
OT Africa Line Ltd v Magic Sportswear Corp (2005) . . . 2.240
OT Africa Line Ltd v Magic Sportswear Corp (2006) . . . 2.240, 2.307, 2.317

Otobo v Otobo (2003) . . . 8.44, 8.45
OTP Bank Nyilvánosan Müködö Részvénytársaság v Hochtief Solution AG: C–519/12 (2015) . . . 2.71, 5.18
Overseas Union Insurance Ltd v New Hampshire Insurance Co: C–351/89 (1991) . . . 2.183, 2.193
Owens Bank Ltd v Bracco (1992) . . . 1.161, 3.68
Owens Bank Ltd v Bracco (No 2): C–129/92 (1994) . . . 2.39, 2.182, 2.203
Owens Bank Ltd v Etoile Commerciale SA (1995) . . . 3.69
Owners of the cargo lately laden on board the ship 'Tatry' v Owners of the ship 'Maciej Rataj': C–406/92 (1994) . . . 2.35, 2.187, 2.189, 2.190, 2.192, 2.200
Owusu v Jackson: C–281/02 (2005) . . . 2.14, 2.175, 2.267, 2.268, 2.270, 2.271, 2.273, 2.274, 2.275, 2.276, 2.277, 2.278, 2.280, 8.29, 8.30, 8.31, 8.32, 8.34

P v M: C–507/14 (2015) . . . 8.26
Pacific International Sports Clubs Ltd v Soccer Marketing International Ltd (2010) . . . 2.220
Pacific Maritime (Asia) Ltd v Holystone Overseas Ltd (2008) . . . 2.288
Padolecchia v Padolecchia (1968) . . . 7.85
Paine, Re (1940) . . . 7.58, 7.62
Painer v Standard Verlags GmbH: C–145/10 (2012). . . . 2.117, 2.122
Pakistan v Zardari (2006) . . . 2.176
Pammer v Reederei Karl Schluter GmbH & Co KG; Hotel Alpenhof GesmbH v Heller: C–585/08 & C–144/09 (2010) . . . 2.134
Papadopoulos v Papadopoulos (1930) . . . 8.164
Parfitt v Thompson (1844) . . . 4.93
Parkasho v Singh (1968) . . . 1.140, 7.147
Parouth, The (1982) . . . 4.30
Partenreederei ms Tilly Russ v NV Haven & Vervoerbedrijf Nova: 71/83 (1984) . . . 2.52, 2.53
Patel v Patel (2000) . . . 2.253
Pattni v Ali (2007) . . . 3.5, 3.17
Pazpena de Vire v Pazpena de Vire (2001) . . . 7.23, 7.25
Peer International Corp v Termidor Music Publishers Ltd (2004) . . . 1.156, 9.38, 9.43
Peh Teck Quee v Bayerische Landesbank Girozentrale (2001) . . . 4.3
Pemberton v Hughes (1899) . . . 1.165, 3.64
Pendy Plastic Products BV v Pluspunkt Handelsgesellschaft mbH: 228/81 (1982) . . . 3.120
Peng v Chai (2015) . . . 8.41, 8.44
Penn v Lord Baltimore (1750) . . . 2.261
Perdoni v Curati (2011) . . . 6.21, 6.44, 6.46, 6.49, 6.52, 6.53

Perrini v Perrini (1979) . . . 7.86
Petroleo Brasiliero SA v Mellitus Shipping Inc (2001) . . . 2.175
Petter v EMC Europe Ltd (2016) . . . 2.312
Philipson-Stow v IRC (1961) . . . 9.96, 9.103
Phillips v Eyre (1870) . . . 1.160, 5.105, 5.107, 5.109
Phoenix Marine Inc v China Ocean Shipping Co (1999) . . . 1.140
Pinckney v KDG Mediatech AG: C–170/12 (2014) . . . 2.99
Pioneer Container, The (1994) . . . 2.241, 2.242
Pittalis v Sherefettin (1986) . . . 2.250
P-J (Children)(Abduction: Consent), Re (2010) . . . 6.96
Plummer v IRC (1988) . . . 6.39, 6.58
Po, The (1991) . . . 2.34
Pocket Kings Ltd v Safenames Ltd (2010) . . . 3.42
Polly Peck International plc (in administration) (No 4), Re (1998) . . . 2.260
Polly Peck International plc v Nadir (1992) . . . 2.171, 2.293
Polskie Ratownictwo Okretowe v Rallo Vito & C SNC (2010) . . . 2.52
Ponticelli v Ponticelli (1958) . . . 7.78
Poon v Tan (1973) . . . 7.152
Potinger v Wightman (1817) . . . 6.28
Powell Duffryn plc v Petereit: C–214/89 (1992) . . . 2.49
Power Curber International Ltd v National Bank of Kuwait SAK (1981) . . . 9.27
Préservatrice foncière TIARD SA v Netherlands: C–266/01 (2003) . . . 2.14
Preston v Preston (1963) . . . 7.27, 7.31
Prestrioka, The (2003) . . . 2.220, 2.230
Princess Olga Paley v Weisz (1929) . . . 9.43
Prinsengracht, The (1993) . . . 2.34
Proceedings brought by A, Re: C–523/07 (2009) . . . 4.86, 6.75, 6.97
Proceedings brought by Schneider: C–386/12(2014) . . . 2.43
Proceedings concerning Gazprom OAO: C–536/13 (2015) . . . 2.15, 3.88, 3.89
Protector Alarms Ltd v Maxim Alarms Ltd (1978) . . . 2.290
Pruller-Frey v Brodnig: C–240/14 (2015) . . . 5.103
Pugh v Pugh (1951) . . . 7.68, 7.69
Pugliese v Finmeccanica SpA: C–437/00 (2003) . . . 2.138
Puttick v A-G (1980) . . . 6.40, 6.55

QRS1 ApS v Frandsen (1999) . . . 1.151
Quazi v Quazi (1980) . . . 1.130, 8.103, 8.104, 8.106
Quoraishi v Quoraishi (1985) . . . 7.152

Qureshi v Qureshi (1972) . . . 6.53, 6.61, 7.134, 8.98

R v Bham (1966) . . . 7.134
R v Brentwood Superintendent Registrar of Marriages, ex p Arias (1968) . . . 1.110, 1.116, 1.163, 7.56, 7.85, 7.91, 7.93, 7.94, 7.98
R v Department of Health, ex p Misra (1996) . . . 7.159
R v International Trustee for Protection of Bondholders Akt (1937) . . . 4.37
R v M (2011) . . . 7.20
R v Millis (1844) . . . 7.27
R v R (Divorce: Hemain Injunction) (2005) . . . 8.29, 8.49
R v R (Divorce: Jurisdiction: Domicile) (2006) . . . 6.20
R v R (Divorce: Stay of Proceedings) (1994) . . . 8.40, 8.46
R v Registrar General of Births, Deaths and Marriages, ex p Minhas (1977) . . . 8.120
R v Sagoo (1975) . . . 7.153
R v Sarwan Singh (1962) . . . 7.153
R (Arogundade) v Secretary of State for Business, Innovation and Skills (2013) . . . 6.87
R (Baiai) v Secretary of State for the Home Dept (2008) . . . 7.17
R (Cornwall Council) v Secretary of State for Health (2016) . . . 6.74
R Griggs Group Ltd v Evans (2005) . . . 2.262
Radhakrishna Hospitality Service Private Ltd v EIH Ltd (1999) . . . 2.231
Radmacher v Granatino (2011) . . . 9.46, 9.63, 9.65, 9.66, 9.67, 9.71
Radwan v Radwan (No 2) (1973) . . . 7.54, 7.143, 7.144, 7.145, 7.146, 7.147
Raiffeisen Zentralbank Österreich AG v Five Star General Trading LLC (2001) . . . 1.87, 1.89, 9.35, 9.40, 9.41
Ralli Bros v Compania Naviera Sota y Aznar (1920) . . . 4.172
Ramsay v Liverpool Royal Infirmary (1930) . . . 6.13, 6.20, 6.37, 6.43
Rapisarda v Colladon (2015) . . . 8.76
Raulin v Fischer (1911) . . . 3.42
Ray v Sekhri (2014) . . . 6.21, 6.62
Razelos v Razelos (No 2) (1970) . . . 2.262
Realchemie Nederland BV v Bayer Cropscience AG: C–406/09 (2012) . . . 3.90, 3.101
Red Sea Insurance Co Ltd v Bouygues SA (1995) . . . 5.115, 5.116
Reeve v Plummer (2015) . . . 3.115, 3.116, 3.122
Refco Inc v Eastern Trading Co (1999) . . . 2.288, 2.289
Refcomp SPA v AXA Corporate Solutions Assurance SA: C–543/10 (2013) . . . 2.47

Regazzoni v KC Sethia (1944) Ltd (1956)... 1.151
Regazzoni v KC Sethia (1944) Ltd (1958)... 1.172, 4.111
Régie Nationale des Usines Renault SA v Maxicar SpA: C-38/98 (2000)... 3.108, 3.109
Régie Nationale des Usines Renault SA v Zhang (2002).... 5.121
Rehder v Air Baltic Corporation: C-204/08 (2009)... 2.89
Reich v Purcell (1967)... 1.50, 1.59
Reichert v Dresdner Bank: C-115/88 (1990)... 2.42, 2.43
Reichert v Dresdner Bank (No 2): C-261/90 (1992)... 2.39, 2.95, 2.284
Rein v Stein (1892)... 2.93
Reisch Montage AG v Kiesel Baumaschinen Handels GmbH: C-103/05 (2006)... 2.117, 2.118
Relfo Ltd (in liquidation) v Varsani (2011)... 2.142
Republic of Haiti v Duvalier (1990)... 2.188, 2.285, 2.293, 2.295
Republic of India v India Steamship Co Ltd (1993)... 2.192, 3.46, 3.56
Republic of India v India Steamship Co (No 2) (1998)... 2.6, 2.192, 3.45, 3.54
Republic of Kazakhstan v Istil (No 2) (2008)... 2.298
Republica de Guatemala v Nunez (1927)... 9.39
Réunion Européenne SA v Splietoff's Bevachtingskantoor BV: C-51/97 (1998)... 2.68, 2.101, 2.120, 2.123, 2.204
Revenue and Customs Commissioners v Sunico APS: C-49/12 (2013)... 2.14
Richard West & Partners (Inverness) Ltd v Dick (1969)... 2.262
Risk v Risk (1951)... 7.135
Robert v Robert (1947)... 7.78
Robey & Co v Snaefell Mining Co Ltd (1887)... 2.93
Roche Nederland BV v Primus: C-539/03 (2006)... 2.121, 2.122
Roerig v Valiant Trawlers Ltd (2002)... 5.123, 5.125
Rome v Punjab National Bank (No 2) (1989)... 2.144
Roneleigh Ltd v MII Exports Inc (1989)... 2.231
Rosengarten v Downes (2002)... 8.55
Rösler v Rottwinkel: 241/83 (1985)... 2.44, 2.45
Ross, Re (1930)... 1.109, 1.120, 1.125, 1.129, 2.263, 9.82, 9.102, 9.107, 9.108
Rosseel NV v Oriental Commercial Shipping (UK) Ltd (1990)... 2.293, 2.294
Rothnie, The (1996)... 2.241
Rousillon v Rousillon (1880)... 1.171, 4.111

Royal & Sun Alliance Insurance plc v Rolls-Royce plc (2010)... 2.275
Royal Bank of Canada v Coöperative Centrale Raiffeisen-Boerenleenbank BA (2004)... 2.310
Royal Bank of Scotland plc v Fal Oil Co Ltd (2013)... 2.296
Royal Bank of Scotland plc v Highland Financial Partners LP (2012)... 2.308
Royal Boskalis Westminster NV v Mountain (1999)... 1.142, 4.110, 4.174
Royal Exchange Assurance Corp v Sjoforsakrings Aktiebolaget Vega (1902)... 4.40
RS (Forced Marriage Protection Order), Re (2015)... 7.103
Rubin v Eurofinance SA (2013)... 3.13, 3.24
Ruding v Smith (1821)... 7.29
Russ v Russ (1964)... 8.98
Rutten v Cross Medical Ltd: C-383/95 (1997)... 2.138, 4.135
Ryanair Ltd v Esso Italiana Srl (2015)... 2.251

S (A Minor) (Custody: Habitual Residence), Re (1998)... 6.84
S (Habitual Residence), Re (2010)... 6.84
S (Hospital Patient: Foreign Curator), Re (1996)... 6.60
S v A Bank (1997)... 4.172
S v S (Brussels II Revised: Art 19(1) and (3): Reference to CJEU) (2015)... 8.26
S v S (Divorce: Staying Proceedings) (1997)... 8.45, 8.46
S v S (Hemain Injunction) (2010)... 8.49
SA Consortium General Textiles v Sun and Sand Agencies Ltd (1978)... 3.17, 3.42, 3.70, 3.74, 5.98
Sabah Shipyard (Pakistan) Ltd v Islamic Republic of Pakistan (2003)... 2.310
Sabbagh v Sabbagh (1985)... 8.127, 8.130
St Paul Dairy Industries NV v Unibel Exser BVBA: C-104/03 (2005)... 2.284
St Pierre v South American Stores (Gath and Chaves) Ltd (1936)... 2.213
Saldhana v Beals (2003)... 3.37
Salvesen (or von Lorang) v Austrian Property Administrator (1927)... 8.153
Salzgitter Mannesmann Handel GmbH v SC Laminorul SA: C-157/12 (2014)... 3.125
Samcrete Egypt Engineers and Contractors SAE v Land Rover Exports Ltd (2002)... 4.17, 4.68, 4.74
Samengo-Turner v Marsh & McLennan (Services) Ltd (2007)... 2.311, 2.312
Sanders v van der Putte: 73/77 (1977)... 2.44
SAR Schotte GmbH v Parfums Rothschild SARL: 218/86 (1987)... 2.110

Sarrio SA v Kuwait Investment Authority
   (1997) . . . 2.269
Sarrio SA v Kuwait Investment Authority
   (1999) . . . 2.200
Saward v Saward (2013) . . . 6.92
Seven Licensing Co Sarl v FFG Platinum SA
   (2012) . . . 2.199
Saxby v Fulton (1909) . . . 1.171
Sayers v International Drilling Co NV
   (1971) . . . 1.90, 5.129, 5.132, 5.133, 5.136
Scarpetta v Lowenfeld (1911) . . . 3.63
Schapira v Ahronson (1998) . . . 2.157
Schibsby v Westenholz (1870) . . . 3.9
Schiffahrtsgesellschaft Detlev von Appen
   GmbH v Voest Alpine Intertrading GmbH
   (1997) . . . 2.298
Schlecker v Boedeker: C-64/12 (2014) . . . 4.137
Schnapper, Re (1928) . . . 9.80
Schwebel v Ungar (1963) . . . 7.88, 7.89
Scott v A-G (1886) . . . 1.167, 7.102
Scottish & Newcastle International Ltd v Othon
   Ghalanos Ltd (2008) . . . 2.86
SCT Industri AB (in liquidation) v Alpenblume
   AB: C-111/08 (2009) . . . 2.15
Scullard, Re (1957) . . . 6.33
Sea Assets v PT Garuda Indonesia
   (2000) . . . 2.145
Seaconsar Far East Ltd v Bank Markazi Jomhouri
   Islami Iran (1994) . . . 2.151, 2.152
Seaward Quest, The (2007) . . . 2.102
Securities and Investment Board v Lloyd-Wright
   (1993) . . . 2.292
Sehota, Re (1978) . . . 7.155
Sekhri v Ray (2014) . . . 6.21, 6.44, 6.49, 6.52,
   6.53
Selot's Trusts, Re (1902) . . . 1.148
Sennar (No 2), The (1985) . . . 3.49, 3.51, 3.100
Services Europe Atlantique Sud (SEAS)
   v Stockholms Rederiaktiebolag Svea
   (1979) . . . 4.182
SET Select Energy GmbH v F&M Bunkering Ltd
   (2014) . . . 2.188
Sfeir & Co v National Insurance Co of New
   Zealand (1964) . . . 3.15, 3.82
SH v NB (Marriage: Consent) (2010) . . . 7.71,
   7.73, 7.75
Shah v Barnet London Borough Council
   (1983) . . . 6.73, 6.74, 6.80, 6.81, 6.88, 6.89
Shamil Bank of Bahrain EC v Beximco
   Pharmaceuticals Ltd (2004) . . . 4.16
Sharab v Al-Saud (2009) . . . 2.161, 2.232
Sharif v Sharif (1980) . . . 8.104
Shearson Lehman Hutton v
   TVB Treuhandgesellschaft für
   Vermögensverwaltung und Beteiligungen
   mbH: C-89/91 (1993) . . . 2.134, 2.137
Shenavai v Kreischer: 266/85 (1987) . . . 2.77

Sherdley v Nordea Life and Pension SA
   (2013) . . . 2.131, 2.132
Shevill v Presse Alliance SA: C-68/93
   (1995) . . . 2.96, 2.106, 2.107
Shevill v Presse Alliance SA (1996) . . . 2.96
Showlag v Mansour (1995) . . . 3.72
Siber Energy Ltd v Tchigirinski (2012) . . . 2.117
Simon Engineering plc v Butte Mining plc (No 2)
   (1996) . . . 2.302
Simonin v Mallac (1860) . . . 1.88, 1.89, 7.17
Simpson v Intralinks (2012) . . . 2.139
Sinha Peerage Claim (1946) . . . 7.147, 7.154
Sirdar Gurdyal Singh v Rajah of Faridkote
   (1894) . . . 3.13
Siskina (Owners of cargo lately laden on board) v
   Distos Compania Naviera SA (1979) . . . 2.153,
   2.286
Skier Star, The (2008) . . . 2.308
Skype Technologies SA v Joltid Ltd
   (2011) . . . 2.271, 2.309
Slutsker v Haron Investments Ltd
   (2012) . . . 9.62
Slutsker v Haron Investments Ltd
   (2014) . . . 9.50, 9.52
Smith, Re (1916) . . . 2.262, 9.12
Smith v McInerney (1994) . . . 9.64
Smyth v Behbehani (1999) . . . 2.223
Snookes v Jani-King (GB) Ltd (2006) . . . 2.47
Société d'Informatique Service Réalisation
   Organisation v Ampersand Software BV
   (1994) . . . 3.112
Société d'Informatique Service Réalisation
   Organisation v Ampersand Software BV:
   C-432/93 (1995) . . . 3.112
Société Eram Shipping Co Ltd v Hong Kong and
   Shanghai Banking Corp Ltd (2004) . . . 1.75
Société Financière Industrielle du Peloux v Axa
   Belgium: C-112/03 (2005) . . . 2.132
Société Générale de Paris v Dreyfus Bros
   (1885) . . . 2.213
Société Nationale Industrielle Aérospatiale v Lee
   Kui Jak (1987) . . . 2.301, 2.303, 2.305
Société Nouvelle des Papeteries de l'Aa SA v BV
   Machinefabrike BOA (1992) . . . 4.64
Sohio Supply Co v Gatoil (USA) Inc
   (1989) . . . 2.307
Solo Kleinmotoren GmbH v Boch: C-414/92
   (1994) . . . 3.90, 3.108
Solovyev v Solovyeva (2015) . . . 8.84
Solvay SA v Honeywell Fluorine Products Europe
   BV: C-616/10, (2012) . . . 2.117, 2.121, 2.284
Somafer SA v Saar-Ferngas AG: 33/78
   (1978) . . . 2.12, 2.110, 2.111
Sonatrach Petroleum Corp v Ferrell International
   Ltd (2002) . . . 4.18, 4.48
Sonntag v Waidmann: C-172/91 (1993) . . . 2.14,
   3.114

Sony Computer Entertainment Ltd v RH Freight Services Ltd (2007) . . . 2.191
Sottomayor v De Barros (1877) . . . 7.57, 7.62
Sottomayor v De Barros (No 2) (1879) . . . 1.160, 7.15, 7.16, 7.57, 7.58, 7.63, 7.70, 8.159
Source Ltd v TUV Rheinland Holding AG (1998) . . . 2.71
South Carolina Insurance Co v Assurantie Maatschappij De Zeven Provincien NV (1987) . . . 2.300
SOVAG-Schwarzmeer und Ostsee Versicherungs-Aktiengesellschaft v If Vahinkovakuutusyhtio Oy: C-521/14 (2016) . . . 2.124
Sowa v Sowa (1961) . . . 7.125
Speed Investments Ltd v Formula One Holdings Ltd (2005) . . . 2.194
Spiliada Maritime Corp v Cansulex Ltd (1987) . . . 2.4, 2.151, 2.155, 2.214, 2.215, 2.224, 2.225, 2.226, 2.230, 2.231, 2.238, 8.44, 8.46, 8.47
Spliethoff's Bevrachtingskantoor BV v Bank of China Ltd (2015) . . . 3.19, 3.75
SPRL Arcado v SA Haviland: 9/87 (1988) . . . 1.91, 2.66
SSL International plc v TTK LIG Ltd (2012) . . . 2.143
Stafford Allen & Sons Ltd v Pacific Steam Navigation Co (1956) . . . 4.37
Standard Bank London Ltd v Apostolakis (2000) . . . 2.134
Standard Bank plc v EFAD Real Estate Company WLL (2014) . . . 2.152
Star Reefers Pool Inc v JFC Group Co Ltd (2012) . . . 2.301, 2.304
Starkowski v A-G (1954) . . . 7.20
Starlight International Inc v Bruce (2002) . . . 3.17
Starlight Shipping Co v Allianz Marine & Aviation Versicherungs AG (2014) . . . 2.184, 2.187, 2.203, 2.251, 2.307
Starlight Shipping Co v Allianz Marine & Aviation Versicherungs AG (No 2) (2014) . . . 2.307
State of Norway's Application (Nos 1 and 2), Re (1990) . . . 1.146, 1.153
Steamship Mutual Underwriting Association (Bermuda) Ltd v Sulpicio Lines Inc (2008) . . . 2.298
Steel v Steel (1888) . . . 6.53
Steinfeld and Keidan v Secretary of State for Education (2016) . . . 7.123
Stevens v Head (1993) . . . 5.121
Stichting Shell Pensioenfonds v Krys (2015) . . . 2.308
Stolt Sydness, The (1997) . . . 4.38
Stonebridge Underwriting Ltd v Ontario Municipal Insurance Exchange (2010) . . . 2.222, 4.33
Stretford v Football Association Ltd (2007) . . . 2.254
Studd v Cook (1883) . . . 9.96
Sulaiman v Juffali (2002) . . . 8.120
Sulamerica Cia Nacional de Seguros SA v Enesa Engelharia SA (2013) . . . 2.255, 4.8
Sundelind Lopez v Lopez Lizazo: C-68/07 (2007) . . . 8.8, 8.16
Swaddling v Adjudication Officer: C-90/97 (1999) . . . 4.86, 6.72, 6.92
SwissMarine Services SA v Gupta Coal India Private Ltd (2015) . . . 2.307
Syal v Heyward (1948) . . . 3.68
Szalatnay-Stacho v Fink (1947) . . . 5.105
Szechter v Szechter (1971) . . . 1.142, 6.49, 7.73–7.75
Szyrocka v SiGer Technologie GmbH: C-215/11 (2012) . . . 3.103

T v P (Jurisdiction: Lugano Convention and Forum Conveniens) (2013) . . . 8.46
T v T (1995) . . . 8.47
T v T (Hemain Injunction) (2014) . . . 8.49
T&N Ltd v Royal & Sun Alliance plc (2002) . . . 2.254
Taczanowska v Taczanowski (1957) . . . 1.110, 1.116, 1.126, 7.30, 7.31, 7.90, 7.93, 7.96
Talbot v Berkshire County Council (1994) . . . 3.57
Tan v Choy (2015) . . . 6.92, 6.93, 8.11
Tasarruf Mevduarti Sigorta Fonu v Demirel (2007) . . . 2.176
Taurus Petroleum v State Oil Marketing Co of the Ministry of Oil, Iraq (2016) . . . 9.27
Tavoulareas v Tsavliris (No 2) (2007) . . . 3.119
Teekay Tankers Ltd v STX Offshore & Shipping Co (2015) . . . 2.144, 2.225
Teletalk Mobil Engineers v Jyske Bank (1998) . . . 1.151
Texaco Melbourne, The (1994) . . . 4.182
Thoday v Thoday (1964) . . . 3.55
Thomas Cook Belgium NV v Thurner Hotel GmbH: C-245/14 (2016) . . . 3.103
Through Transport Mutual Insurance Association (Eurasia) Ltd v New India Assurance Co Ltd (2005) . . . 2.318
Tiernan v Magen Insurance Co Ltd (2000) . . . 2.233
Toepfer International GmbH v Molino Boschi SRL (1996) . . . 2.308
Tolten, The (1946) . . . 2.261
Tomkinson v First Pennsylvania Banking and Trust Co (1961) . . . 4.182
Tonicstar Ltd v American Home Assurance Co (2005) . . . 2.301

Torok v Torok (1973) . . . 8.89
Toyota Tsucho Sugar Trading Ltd v Prolat Srl (2015) . . . 4.142
Tracomin SA v Sudan Oil Seeds (1983) . . . 3.77
Tracomin v Sudan Oil Seeds Co Ltd (No 2) (1983) . . . 2.307
Trade Agency Ltd v Seramico Investments Ltd: C-619/10 (2012) . . . 3.110, 3.120
Trademark Licensing Co Ltd v Leofelis SA (2010) . . . 2.183
Trafigura Beheer BV v Kookmin Bank Co (2006) . . . 5.137
Trafigura Beheer BV v Kookmin Bank Co (No 2) (2007) . . . 2.301
Trasporti Castelletti Spedizione Internazionali SpA v Hugo Trumpy SpA: C-159/97 (1999) . . . 2.50, 2.51, 2.53
Travers v Holley (1953) . . . 8.65
Traversa v Freddi (2011) . . . 8.179
Trendex Trading Corp v Crédit Suisse (1982) . . . 1.171
Trident Turboprop (Dublin) Ltd v First Flight Couriers Ltd (2010) . . . 4.104
Trussler v Trussler (2003) . . . 8.26
TSN Kunststoffrecycling GmbH v Jurgens (2002) . . . 3.116
Turner v Grovit: C-159/02 (2004) . . . 2.315, 2.316, 8.48
Turner v Grovit (1999) . . . 2.315
Turner v Grovit (2000) . . . 2.315
Turner v Grovit (2002) . . . 2.301, 2.305, 2.315, 2.316

UBS AG v HSH Nordbank AG (2009) . . . 2.48, 2.239, 2.268
UBS Ltd v Regione Calabria (2012) . . . 2.200
Udny v Udny (1869) . . . 6.17, 6.23, 6.28, 6.43, 6.54
Underwriting Members of Lloyd's Syndicate 980 v Sinco SA (2009) . . . 2.188
Unibank A/S v Christensen: C-260/97 (1999) . . . 3.90
Union Discount Co Ltd v Union Discount Cal Ltd (2002) . . . 2.307
Union International Insurance Co Ltd v Jubilee Insurance Co Ltd (1991) . . . 2.162
Union Transport plc v Continental Lines SA (1992) . . . 2.77
United Antwerp Maritime Agencies NV v Navigation Maritime Bulgare: C-184/12 (2014) . . . 4.101
United Film Distribution Ltd v Chhabria (2001) . . . 2.173
United States Securities and Exchange Commission v Manterfield (2010) . . . 2.292, 9.43

United States v Inkley (1989) . . . 1.147, 1.153, 3.42
United States of America v Abacha (2015) . . . 2.289
Universal General Insurance Co (USIG) v Group Josi Reinsurance Co SA: C-412/98 (2000) . . . 2.36, 2.131
Urquhart v Butterfield (1887) . . . 6.35
USF Ltd v Aqua Technology Hanson NV/SA (2001) . . . 2.72

V, Re (1996) . . . 6.80
V v B (Abduction) (1991) . . . 6.84
V v V (Divorce: Jurisdiction) (2011) . . . 6.93, 8.11
Vadala v Lawes (1890) . . . 3.68
van den Boogaard v Laumen: C-220/95 (1997) . . . 8.179
Van Uden Maritime BV v Firma Deco-Line: C-391/95 (1998) . . . 2.15, 2.282, 2.284, 2.294, 2.295, 2.296, 3.94
Vanquelin v Bouard (1863) . . . 3.40, 3.74
Vapenik v Thurner: C-508/12 (2014) . . . 2.134
Varna (No 2), The (1994) . . . 2.221
Verein für Konsumenteninformation v Henkel: C-167/00 (2002) . . . 2.94
Vervaeke v Smith (1981) . . . 1.90, 1.130, 7.57
Vervaeke v Smith (1983) . . . 1.171, 3.72, 7.46, 7.47, 7.54, 7.72, 7.73, 7.80, 8.158, 8.163
Vidal-Hall v Google Inc (2015) . . . 2.167
Ville de Bauge v China (2015) . . . 8.26
Vishva Abha, The (1990) . . . 2.232
Vishva Ajay, The (1989) . . . 2.231
Vita Food Products Inc v Unus Shipping Co Ltd (1939) . . . 4.3
Vitol SA v Capri Marine Ltd (2011) . . . 2.307
Vogel v R & A Kohnstamm Ltd (1973) . . . 3.15, 3.29
Voogsgeerd v Navimer SA: C-384/10 (2012) . . . 2.138, 4.134, 4.135, 4.136
Vorarlberger Gebietskrankenkasse v WGV-Schwäbische Allgemeine Versicherungs AG: C-347/08 (2010) . . . 2.131
VTB Capital plc v Nutritek International Corpn (2013) . . . 2.156, 2.157, 2.225, 3.38

W, Re (2013) . . . 6.13
W v W (1993) . . . 9.50
W v W (1997) . . . 8.47
Wadi Sudr, The (2010) . . . 3.94, 3.109
Wahda Bank v Arab Bank (1996) . . . 4.35
Wahl v A-G (1932) . . . 6.50, 6.52
Wall v Mutuelle de Poitiers Assurances (2014) . . . 5.9, 5.91
Wallach, Re (1950) . . . 6.33
Wasa International Insurance Co v Lexington Insurance Co (2010) . . . 4.33

Watkins v North American Land and Timber Co Ltd (1904) . . . 2.142
Watson v First Choice Holidays and Flights Ltd (2001) . . . 2.123
Way v Way (1950) . . . 7.75, 7.78
WD Fairway (No 3), The (2009) . . . 9.16
Wealands v CLC Contractors Ltd (1999) . . . 2.254
Webb v Webb: C-294/92 (1994) . . . 2.43
Weber v Universal Ogden Services Ltd: C-37/00 (2002) . . . 2.138
Weber v Weber: C-438/12 (2015) . . . 2.42, 2.194
Weissfisch v Julius (2006) . . . 2.298
Welch v Tennent (1891) . . . 9.60, 9.61
Wencel v Zakład Ubezpieczeń Społecznych w Białymstoku: C-589/10 (2013) . . . 6.95
Wermuth v Wermuth (No 1) (2003) . . . 2.284
West Tankers Inc v Allianz SpA (formerly RAS Riunione Adriatica di Sicurta SpA) (2007) . . . 2.318, 2.319, 2.320
West Tankers Inc v Allianz SpA (formerly RAS Riunione Adriatica di Sicurta SpA): C-185/07 (2009) . . . 2.15, 2.16, 2.319, 2.321, 3.94, 3.95
Western Bulk Shipowning III A/S v Carbofer Maritime Trading ApS (2012) . . . 2.288
Western Regent, The (2005) . . . 2.301
Westminster City Council v C (2009) . . . 1.167, 7.21, 7.47, 7.52, 7.57, 7.71, 7.73, 7.100, 7.103
Wicken v Wicken (1999) . . . 8.147
Wight v Eckhardt Marine GmbH (2004) . . . 1.75
Wilkinson v Kitzinger (No 2) (2007) . . . 7.53, 7.122
Williams & Humbert Ltd v W & H Trade Marks (Jersey) Ltd (1986) . . . 1.167, 9.43
Williams and Glyn's Bank plc v Astro Dinamico Cia Naviera SA (1984) . . . 2.148
Williams v Colonial Bank (1888) . . . 9.5
Winans v A-G (1904) . . . 6.16, 6.20
Winkworth v Christie, Manson and Woods Ltd (1980) . . . 9.19, 9.20, 9.21, 9.23
Winnetka Trading Corp v Julius Baer International Ltd (2009) . . . 2.275
Winrow v Hemphill (2015) . . . 5.30, 5.36, 5.39, 5.91, 5.96, 6.94
Winter, The (2000) . . . 2.188
Wintersteiger AG v Products 4U Sondermaschinenbau GmbH: C-523/10 (2012) . . . 2.97, 2.99, 2.103
Witted v Galbraith (1893) . . . 2.172
WMS Gaming Inc v B Plus Giocolegale Ltd (2012) . . . 2.191
Wolfenden v Wolfenden (1946) . . . 7.27, 7.28
Wood v Wood (1957) . . . 6.53
Wood Floor Solutions Andreas Domberger GmbH v Silva Trade SA: C-19/09 (2010) . . . 2.88
Worms v De Valdor (1880) . . . 1.148

WPP Holdings Italy Srl v Benatti (2006) . . . 2.138
WPP Holdings Italy Srl v Benatti (2007) . . . 2.95
Wright v Deccan Chargers Sporting Ventures Ltd (2011) . . . 2.225

X City Council v MB (2006) . . . 7.35
XCC v AA (2012) . . . 7.103
Xin Yang, The (1996) . . . 2.269
Xing Su Hai, The (1995) . . . 2.118

Y, Re (1985) . . . 6.29
Yordanova v Iordanov (2013) . . . 8.77
Youell v La Réunion Aérienne (2009) . . . 2.16
Young v Anglo American South Africa Ltd (2014) . . . 2.29
Yukos Capital Sarl v OJSC Rosneft Oil Co (No 2) (2014) . . . 3.58, 9.43
Z (Abduction), Re (2009) . . . 6.88, 6.89
Z v Z (Divorce: Jurisdiction) (2010) . . . 6.75, 6.93, 6.94, 8.9
Z and B v C (Parental Order: Domicile) (2012) . . . 6.46, 6.53
Z and Z, Re (2013) . . . 6.78, 6.86
Z v Z (No 2) (Financial Remedy: Marriage Contract) (2012) . . . 9.71
Zaal v Zaal (1982) . . . 8.104
Zambia Steel and Building Supplies Ltd v James Clark & Eaton Ltd (1986) . . . 2.250
Zanelli v Zanelli (1948) . . . 8.56
Zelger v Salinitri: 56/79 (1980) . . . 2.79
Zivlin v Baal Taxa (1998) . . . 2.225
Zivnostenska Banka National Corp v Frankman (1950) . . . 4.169
Zuid-Chemie BV v Philippo's Mineralenfabriek NV/SA: C-189/08 (2009) . . . 2.99

Numerical Listing of ECJ Cases

(These cases are also included in the preceding Alphabetical Listing)

12/76: Industrie Tessili Italiana Como v Dunlop AG (1976) . . . 2.79
14/76: Ets A de Bloos SPRL v Société en commandite par actions Bouyer (1976) . . . 2.77, 2.110, 2.112
21/76: Handelskwekerij GJ Bier BV v Mines de Potasse d'Alsace SA (1976) . . . 2.97, 2.98, 2.106, 5.28, 5.57, 5.58
24/76: Estasis Salotti di Colzani Aimo v RÜWA Polstereimaschinen GmbH (1976) . . . 2.52
25/76: Galeries Segoura SPRL v Bonakdarian (1976) . . . 2.52
42/76: de Wolf v Harry Cox BV (1976) . . . 3.102
73/77: Sanders v van der Putte (1977) . . . 2.44
23/78: Meeth v Glacetal (1978) . . . 2.55

33/78: Somafer SA v Saar-Ferngas AG (1978) ... 2.12, 2.110, 2.111
143/78: De Cavel v De Cavel (No 1) (1979) ... 3.101, 8.179
56/79: Zelger v Salinitri (1980) ... 2.79
125/79: Denilauler v SNC Couchet Frères (1980) ... 3.89
133/78: Gourdain v Nadler (1979) ... 2.15
814/79: Netherlands State v Rüffer (1980) ... 2.14
139/80: Blanckaert and Willems PVBA v Trost (1981) ... 2.110
150/80: Elefanten Schuh GmbH v Jacqmain (1981) ... 2.51, 2.57, 2.60, 2.204, 8.171
166/80: Klomps v Michel (1981) ... 3.116, 3.117
38/81: Effer SpA v Kantner (1982) ... 2.72
228/81: Pendy Plastic Products BV v Pluspunkt Handelsgesellschaft mbH (1982) ... 3.120
288/82: Duijnstee v Goderbauer (1983) ... 2.39
71/83: Partenreederei ms Tilly Russ v NV Haven & Vervoerbedrijf Nova (1984) ... 2.52, 2.53
241/83: Rösler v Rottwinkel (1985) ... 2.44, 2.45
49/84: Debaecker v Bouwman (1985) ... 3.118
221/84: F Berghoefer GmbH & Co KG v ASA SA (1985) ... 2.52
266/85: Shenavai v Kreischer (1987) ... 2.77
144/86: Gubisch Maschinenfabrik KG v Palumbo (1987) ... 2.186, 2.188, 2.189
145/86: Hoffmann v Krieg (1988) ... 3.88, 3.108, 3.124
218/86: SAR Schotte GmbH v Parfums Rothschild SARL (1987) ... 2.110
9/87: SPRL Arcado v SA Haviland (1988) ... 1.91, 2.66
189/87: Kalfelis v Bankhaus Schröder, Münchmeyer, Hengst & Co (1988) ... 1.91, 2.64, 2.66, 2.67, 2.68, 2.121
C-115/88: Reichert v Dresdner Bank (1990) ... 2.42, 2.43
C-220/88: Dumez France SA v Hessische Landesbank (1990) ... 2.100
C-365/88: Kongress Agentur Hagen GmbH v Zeehaghe BV (1990) ... 2.13, 2.126
C-190/89: Marc Rich & Co AG v Società Italiana Impianti, The Atlantic Emperor (1991) ... 2.15, 2.16, 3.94
C-214/89: Powell Duffryn plc v Petereit (1992) ... 2.49
C-351/89: Overseas Union Insurance Ltd v New Hampshire Insurance Co (1991) ... 2.183, 2.193
C-80/90: Italian Leather SpA v WECO Polstermöbel GmbH & Co (2002) ... 3.90, 3.103, 3.124
C-261/90: Reichert v Dresdner Bank (No 2) (1992) ... 2.39, 2.95, 2.284

C-280/90: Hacker v Euro-Relais GmbH (1992) ... 2.44
C-26/91: Jakob Handte & Co GmbH v Traitements Mécano-chimiques des Surfaces SA (1992) ... 2.67, 2.71, 5.18
C-89/91: Shearson Lehman Hutton v TVB Treuhandgesellschaft für Vermögensverwaltung und Beteiligungen mbH (1993) ... 2.134, 2.137
C-123/91: Minalmet GmbH v Brandeis Ltd (1992) ... 3.117
C-172/91: Sonntag v Waidmann (1993) ... 2.14, 3.114
T-90/92: Magdalena Fernández v Commission (1993). ... 6.72
C-129/92: Owens Bank Ltd v Bracco (No 2) (1994) ... 2.39, 2.182, 2.203
C-288/92: Custom Made Commercial Ltd v Stawa Metallbau GmbH (1994) ... 2.77
C-294/92: Webb v Webb (1994) ... 2.43
C-406/92: Owners of the cargo lately laden on board the ship 'Tatry' v Owners of the ship 'Maciej Rataj' (1994) ... 2.35, 2.187, 2.189, 2.190, 2.192, 2.200
C-414/92: Solo Kleinmotoren GmbH v Boch (1994) ... 3.90, 3.108
C-68/93: Shevill v Presse Alliance SA (1995) ... 2.96, 2.106, 2.107
C-292/93: Lieber v Göbel (1994) ... 2.43
C-318/93: Brenner and Noller v Dean Witter Reynolds Inc (1994) ... 2.135
C-341/93: Danvaern Production A/S v Schuhfabriken Otterbeck GmbH & Co (1995) ... 2.128
C-346/93: Kleinwort Benson Ltd v City of Glasgow District Council (1995) ... 2.21
C-364/93: Marinari v Lloyds Bank plc (1995) ... 2.100, 5.28
C-432/93: Société d'Informatique Service Réalisation Organisation v Ampersand Software BV (1995) ... 3.112
C-439/93: Lloyd's Register of Shipping v Société Campenon Bernard (1995) ... 2.111, 2.113
C-474/93: Firma Hengst Import BV v Campese (1995) ... 3.117
C-78/95: Hendrikman v Magenta Druck & Verlag GmbH (1996) ... 3.108, 3.114
C-106/95: Mainschiffahrts-Genossenschaft eG (MSG) v Les Gravières Rhénanes Sarl (1997) ... 2.51, 2.79
C-220/95: van den Boogaard v Laumen (1997) ... 8.179
C-269/95: Benincasa v Dentalkit Srl (1997) ... 2.48, 2.134
C-383/95: Rutten v Cross Medical Ltd (1997) ... 2.138, 4.135

C-391/95: Van Uden Maritime BV v Firma
Deco-Line (1998) . . . 2.15, 2.282, 2.284, 2.294,
2.295, 2.296, 3.94
C-99/96: Mietz v Intership Yachting Sneek BV
(1999) . . . 2.134, 2.284
C-351/96: Drouot Assurances SA v Consolidated
Metallurgical Industries (CMI Industrial Sites)
(1998) . . . 2.191
C-51/97: Réunion Européenne SA v Splietoff's
Bevachtingskantoor BV (1998) . . . 2.68, 2.101,
2.120, 2.123, 2.204
C-90/97: Swaddling v Adjudication Officer
(1999) . . . 4.86, 6.72, 6.92
C-159/97: Trasporti Castelletti Spedizione
Internazionali SpA v Hugo Trumpy SpA
(1999) . . . 2.50, 2.51, 2.53
C-260/97: Unibank A/S v Christensen
(1999) . . . 3.90
C-267/97: Coursier v Fortis Bank
(1999) . . . 3.101
C-420/97: Leathertex Divisione Sintetici SpA v
Bodotex BVBA (1999) . . . 2.78
C-440/97: GIE Groupe Concorde v Master of the
Vessel Suhadiwarno Panjan (1999) . . . 2.79
C-7/98: Krombach v Bamberski
(2000) . . . 3.104, 3.108, 3.110
C-8/98: Dansommer A/S v Götz (2000) . . . 2.44
C-38/98: Régie Nationale des Usines Renault SA
v Maxicar SpA (2000) . . . 3.108, 3.109
C-381/98: Ingmar GB Ltd v Eaton Leonard
Technologies Inc (2000) . . . 4.108
C-387/98: Coreck Maritime GmbH v
Handelsveem BV (2000) . . . 2.50, 2.274
C-412/98: Universal General Insurance Co
(USIG) v Group Josi Reinsurance Co SA
(2000) . . . 2.36, 2.131
C-518/99: Gaillard v Chekili (2001) . . . 2.43
C-37/00: Weber v Universal Ogden Services Ltd
(2002) . . . 2.138
C-96/00: Gabriel v Schlank & Schick GmbH
(2000) . . . 2.134
C-167/00: Verein für Konsumenteninformation
v Henkel (2002) . . . 2.94
C-256/00: Besix v Wasserreinigungsbau Alfred
Kretzschmar GmbH & Co KG (2002) . . . 2.80
C-271/00: Gemeente Steenbergen v Baten
(2002) . . . 2.14, 2.15
C-334/00: Fonderie Officine Mecchaniche
Tacconi SpA v Heinrich Wagner Sinto
Maschinenfabrik GmbH (2002) . . . 2.73, 2.95,
5.84
C-437/00: Pugliese v Finmeccanica SpA
(2003) . . . 2.138
C-111/01: Gantner Electronic GmbH v Basch
Expoitatie Maatschappij BV (2003) . . . 2.187
C-266/01: Préservatrice foncière TIARD SA
(2003) . . . 2.14

C-433/01: Freistaat Bayern v Blijdenstein
(2004) . . . 2.14
C-464/01: Gruber v Bay Wa AG (2005) . . . 2.134
C-18/02: Danmarks Rederiforening v Lo
Landsorganisation I Sverige (2004) . . . 2.95
C-27/02: Engler v Janus Versand GmbH
(2005) . . . 2.134
C-39/02: Maersk Olie and Gas A/S v Firma M de
Haan and M de Boer (2004) . . . 2.187, 2.188,
3.89, 3.114
C-116/02: Erich Gasser GmbH v Misat Srl
(2003) . . . 2.195, 2.196, 2.197, 2.198, 2.320,
8.178
C-159/02: Turner v Grovit (2004) . . . 2.315,
2.316, 8.48
C-168/02: Kronhofer v Maier (2004) . . . 2.100
C-265/02: Frahuil SA v Assitalia SpA
(2004) . . . 2.14
C-281/02: Owusu v Jackson (2005) . . . 2.14,
2.175, 2.267, 2.268, 2.270, 2.271, 2.273, 2.274,
2.275, 2.276, 2.277, 2.278, 2.280, 8.29, 8.30,
8.31, 8.32, 8.34
C-4/03: Gesellschaft für Antriebstechnik mbH
& Co KG v Lamellen und Kupplungsbau
Beteiligungs KG (2006) . . . 2.39
C-104/03: St Paul Dairy Industries NV v Unibel
Exser BVBA (2005) . . . 2.284
C-112/03: Société financière industrielle du
Peloux v Axa Belgium (2005) . . . 2.132
C-148/03: Nurnberger Allgemeine Versicherungs
AG v Portbridge Transport BV (2004) . . . 2.33
C-539/03: Roche Nederland BV v Primus
(2006) . . . 2.121, 2.122
C-73/04: Klein v Rhodos Management Ltd
(2005) . . . 2.39, 2.44
C-77/04: Groupement d'intérêt économique
(GIE) Réunion Européenne v Zurich España
(2005) . . . 2.125, 2.131
C-343/04: Land Oberösterreich v ČEZ as
(2006) . . . 2.43
C-103/05: Reisch Montage AG v Kiesel
Baumaschinen Handels GmbH
(2006) . . . 2.117, 2.118
C-283/05: ASML Netherlands BV v
Semiconductor Industry Services GmbH
(SEMIS) (2006) . . . 3.115, 3.121
C-292/05: Lechouritou v Dimosio tis
Omospondiakis Dimokratias tis Germanias
(2007) . . . 2.14, 5.8
C-386/05: Color Drack GmbH v Lexx
International Vertriebs GmbH (2007) . . . 2.87,
2.88
C-98/06: Freeport plc v Arnoldsson
(2007) . . . 2.117, 2.123
C-180/06: Ilsinger v Dreschers (2009) . . . 2.134
C-462/06: Glaxosmithkline v Rouard
(2008) . . . 2.119, 2.129

C-463/06: FBTO Schadeverzekeringen NV v
   Odenbreit (2007) . . . 2.131
C-68/07: Sundelind Lopez v Lopez Lizazo
   (2007) . . . 8.8, 8.16
C-185/07: West Tankers Inc v Allianz SpA
   (formerly RAS Riunione Adriatica di Sicurta
   SpA) (2009) . . . 2.15, 2.16, 2.319, 2.321,
   3.94, 3.95
C-372/07: Hassett v South Eastern Health Board
   (2008) . . . 2.39
C-394/07: Gambazzi v Daimler Chrysler Canada
   Inc (2009) . . . 2.289, 3.90, 3.110
C-420/07: Apostolides v Orams (2009) . . . 3.89,
   3.101, 3.108, 3.122
C-523/07: Proceedings Brought by A, Re
   (2009) . . . 4.86, 6.75, 6.97
C-533/07: Falco Privatstiftung v Weller-
   Lindhorst (2009) . . . 2.18, 2.81, 2.90
C-111/08: SCT Industri AB (in liquidation) v
   Alpenblume AB (2009) . . . 2.15
C-133/08: Intercontainer Interfrigo SC (ICF) v
   Balkenende Oosthuizen BV (2009) . . . 4.66,
   4.67, 4.68, 4.116
C-168/08: Hadadi v Hadadi (2009) . . . 6.95, 8.6,
   8.13
C-189/08: Zuid-Chemie BV v Philippo's
   Mineralenfabriek NV/SA (2009) . . . 2.99
C-204/08: Rehder v Air Baltic Corporation
   (2009) . . . 2.89
C-347/08: Vorarlberger Gebietskrankenkasse v
   WGV-Schwäbische Allgemeine Versicherungs
   AG (2010) . . . 2.131
C-381/08: Car Trim GmbH v KeySafety Systems
   Srl (2010) . . . 2.82, 2.85, 2.86
C-585/08 & C-144/09: Pammer v Reederei Karl
   Schluter GmbH & Co KG; Hotel Alpenhof
   GesmbH v Heller (2010) . . . 2.134
C-19/09: Wood Floor Solutions Andreas
   Domberger GmbH v Silva Trade SA
   (2010) . . . 2.88
C-111/09: Česká podnikatelská pojišťovna
   as, Vienna Insurance Group v Bilas
   (2010) . . . 2.129
C-406/09: Realchemie Nederland BV v Bayer
   Cropscience AG (2012) . . . 3.90, 3.101
C-509/09 & C-161/10: eDate Advertising GmbH
   v X; Martinez v MGN Ltd (2012) . . . 2.107,
   5.29
C-29/10: Koelzsch v Grand Duchy of
   Luxembourg (2012) . . . 2.138, 4.135
C-144/10: Berliner Verkehrsbetriebe (BVG) v JP
   Morgan NA (2011) . . . 2.39, 2.40
C-145/10: Painer v Standard Verlags GmbH
   (2012). . . . 2.117, 2.122
C-292/10: G v de Visser (2013) . . . 2.19, 2.58,
   2.140, 3.103

C-327/10: Hypotecni banka as v Lindner
   (2011) . . . 2.14, 2.18, 2.19, 2.135, 2.140
C-384/10: Voogsgeerd v Navimer SA
   (2012) . . . 2.138, 4.134, 4.135, 4.136
C-412/10: Homawoo v GMF Assurances SA
   (2011) . . . 5.6
C-497/10: Mercredi v Chaffe (2010) . . . 4.86,
   6.98
C-523/10: Wintersteiger AG v Products 4U
   Sondermaschinenbau GmbH (2012) . . . 2.97,
   2.99, 2.103
C-543/10: Refcomp SPA v AXA Corporate
   Solutions Assurance SA (2013) . . . 2.47
C-589/10: Wencel v Zaklad Ubezpieczeń
   Spolecznych w Bialymstoku (2013) . . . 6.95
C-616/10: Solvay SA v Honeywell Fluorine
   Products Europe BV (2012) . . . 2.117, 2.121,
   2.284
C-619/10: Trade Agency Ltd v Seramico
   Investments Ltd (2012) . . . 3.110, 3.120
C-133/11: Folien Fischer v Ritrama SpA
   (2013) . . . 2.11, 2.72, 2.95
C-154/11: Mahamdia v People's Democratic
   Republic of Algeria (2012) . . . 2.138
C-190/11: Muhlleitner v Yusufi (2012) . . . 2.134
C-215/11: Szyrocka v SiGer Technologie GmbH
   (2012) . . . 3.103
C-228/11: Melzer v MF Global UK Ltd
   (2013) . . . 2.104
C-419/11: Ceska Sporitelna AS v Feichter
   (2013) . . . 2.81, 2.134
C-456/11: Gothaer Allgemeine Versicherung AG
   v Samskip GmbH (2013) . . . 3.88, 3.89, 3.99,
   3.100
C-645/11: Land Berlin v Sapir (2013) . . . 2.14
C-9/12: Corman-Collins SA v La Maison du
   Whisky SA (2014) . . . 2.19, 2.81
C-49/12: Revenue and Customs Commissioners
   v Sunico APS (2013). . . . 2.14
C-64/12: Schlecker v Boedeker (2014) . . . 4.137
C-144/12: Goldbet Sportwetten GmbH v
   Sperindeo (2014) . . . 3.103
C-147/12: ÖFAB v Koot (2015) . . . 2.71, 2.95,
   2.97, 2.102, 5.18
C-157/12: Salzgitter Mannesmann Handel
   GmbH v SC Laminorul SA (2014) . . . 3.125
C-170/12: Pinckney v KDG Mediatech AG
   (2014) . . . 2.99
C-184/12: United Antwerp Maritime Agencies
   NV v Navigation Maritime Bulgare
   (2014) . . . 4.101
C-218/12: Emrek v Sabranovic (2014) . . . 2.134
C-360/12: Coty Germany GmbH v First Note
   Perfumes NV (2014) . . . 2.104
C-386/12: Proceedings brought by Schneider
   (2014) . . . 2.43

C-387/12: Hi Hotel HCF SARL v Spoering (2014) . . . 2.104, 2.106
C-438/12: Weber v Weber (2015) . . . 2.42, 2.194
C-452/12: Nipponkoa Insurance Co (Europe) Ltd v Inter-Zuid Transport BV (2014) . . . 2.35
C-469/12: Krejci Lager & Umschlagbetriebs GMBH v Olbrich Transport und Logistik GMBH (2014). . . . 2.65, 2.81
C-478/12: Maletic v lastminute.com GmbH (2014) . . . 2.14
C-508/12: Vapenik v Thurner (2014) . . . 2.134
C-519/12: OTP Bank Nyilvánosan Müködö Részvénytársaság v Hochtief Solution AG (2015) . . . 2.71, 5.18
C-548/12: Brogsitter v Fabrication de Montres Normandes EURL (2014) . . . 1.91, 2.66, 2.71
C-1/13: Cartier Parfums-Lunettes SAS v Ziegler France SA (2014) . . . 2.185
C-45/13: Kainz v Pantherwerke AG (2015) . . . 2.102
C-119/13 & C-120/13: eco cosmetics GmbH & Co KG v Dupuy (2015) . . . 3.103
C-226/13, C-245/13, C-247/13 & C-578/13: Fahnenbrock v Greek Republic (2016) . . . 2.14
C-302/13: FlyLAL-Lithuanian Airlines SAS v Starptautiska Lidosta Riga VAS (2015) . . . 2.14, 2.39, 3.88, 3.108, 3.110
C-305/13: Haeger & Schmidt GmbH v Mutuelles du Mans assurances IARD (2015) . . . 4.60, 4.116

C-352/13: Cartel Damage Claims (CDC) Hydrogen Peroxide SA v Akzo Nobel NV (2015) . . . 2.48, 2.100, 2.105, 2.118
C-375/13: Kolassa v Barclays Bank plc (2015) . . . 2.11, 2.37, 2.100, 2.134
C-441/13: Hejduk v EnergieAgentur.NRW GmbH (2015) . . . 2.99, 2.103
C-536/13: Proceedings concerning Gazprom OAO (2015) . . . 2.15, 3.88, 3.89
C-681/13: Diageo Brands BV v Simiramida-04 EOOD (2015) . . . 3.108
C-4/14 Bohez v Wiertz (2015) . . . 3.101
C-47/14: Holterman Ferho Exploitatie BV v Spies von Bullesheim (2015) . . . 2.138
C-184/14: A v B (2015) . . . 8.173
C-240/14: Pruller-Frey v Brodnig (2015) . . . 5.103
C-245/14: Thomas Cook Belgium NV v Thurner Hotel GmbH (2016) . . . 3.103
C-297/14: Hobohm v Benedikt Kampik Ltd & Co KG (2016) . . . 2.134
C-322/14: El Majdoub v CarsOnTheWeb Deutschland GmbH (2015) . . . 2.51
C-350/14: Lazar v Allianz SpA (2016) . . . 5.26
C-359/14 & C-475/14: 'ERGO Insurance' SE v 'If P&C Insurance' AS (2016) . . . 4.7, 5.12, 5.91
C-376/14: C v M (2014) . . . 6.99
C-489/14: A v B (2016) . . . 8.26
C-507/14: P v M (2015) . . . 8.26
C-521/14: SOVAG-Schwarzmeer und Ostsee Versicherungs-Aktiengesellschaft v If Vahinkovakuutusyhtio Oy (2016) . . . 2.124
C-605/14: Komu v Komu (2016) . . . 2.42

1

Introduction

I Nature of the subject

1.1 The part of the law of England and Wales[1] called the conflict of laws or private international law deals with cases before the English court which have connections with foreign countries. The foreign elements in the case may be events which have taken place in foreign countries, or they may be the foreign domicile, residence, or place of business of the parties. For example, a case may involve a contract between an English resident and a French company, made by correspondence, and to be performed partly in England and partly in France or in a third country. Alternatively, the English court may be hearing a tort case in which an English defendant's conduct in New York caused injury to a Mexican visitor there. Another example is a situation in which the English court has to decide on the validity of a marriage celebrated in France between an English woman and an Egyptian man. In short, any case involving a foreign element raises potential conflict of laws issues.

A Overview

1.2 This requisite foreign element can arise in one of three ways, or, to put it differently, the conflict of laws is concerned with the following three questions: (i) jurisdiction, (ii) choice of law, and (iii) the recognition and enforcement of foreign judgments.

1. Jurisdiction

1.3 The first point which may have to be decided in a case having foreign elements is whether the English court has power to deal with the case at all. This raises the issue of when foreigners or persons having little or no link with England should be able to sue or be sued in the English courts. For example, in *Maharanee of Baroda v Wildenstein*[2] the plaintiff, a French resident, purchased a painting from the defendant, an international art dealer also resident in France. The painting was allegedly by Boucher. When the plaintiff discovered that the painting was probably not by Boucher at all, she commenced an action for rescission of the contract of sale by serving a writ on the defendant while he was on a brief visit to England. In many ways, the most appropriate jurisdiction for this litigation

---

[1] Throughout the remainder of this book 'England' is used to signify 'England and Wales' and 'English law' to signify 'the law of England and Wales'.
[2] [1972] 2 QB 283.

was France: the contract was made in France between two French residents and was governed by French law. However, the plaintiff wanted to sue in England because there might have been problems in having her expert evidence admitted in French proceedings and there would have been severe delays in having the action heard in France. The problem for the conflict of laws is whether the English court should assume jurisdiction to hear such a case that involves only the most tenuous of connections with England.

2. Choice of law

1.4 If the English court does assume jurisdiction, the next question is whether in deciding the case it will apply the rules of English law or those of a foreign country with which the case has connections. For instance, when the English court decided it had jurisdiction in *Maharanee of Baroda*[3] (as it did, under the law as it then stood), it then had to decide whether the legal issue (misrepresentation leading to rescission) was to be governed by English law (the law of the forum, known commonly as the lex fori) or by French law.

1.5 While the novice to this area of law might assume that English courts can apply only English law, the reality is that in appropriate cases the English court can apply a foreign law to resolve the legal issue. The rules that determine which law the court applies in a case involving foreign elements are called choice of law rules. Their characteristic form is shown by the following examples: the formal validity of a marriage is governed by the law of the country in which the marriage was celebrated; the material validity of a contract is governed by the law expressly or impliedly chosen by the parties; questions of title to immovable property are governed by the law of the country in which the property is situated.

3. Recognition and enforcement of foreign judgments

1.6 The question here concerns when the judgments of foreign courts are given effect in England. Suppose a claimant, having obtained a judgment against an English defendant in a New York court for damages for breach of contract, wishes to have the judgment satisfied out of the defendant's assets in England. Will the New York judgment be enforced, or will the claimant have to bring fresh proceedings in the English court to establish the claim? Alternatively, the question may be the recognition of a foreign divorce. A husband and wife living in England are Muslims; the husband pays a visit to a Muslim country of which he is a citizen where he divorces his wife under the Islamic law prevailing there by declaring three times that he divorces her. Is the divorce effective in England? Answering these questions is the third and final task of the conflict of laws.

B Terminology

1.7 This subject has two alternative titles: the conflict of laws and private international law. The reason for the first of these is obvious. It is concerned with cases in which the parties or other relevant issues are connected with more than one country. Different

---

[3] Ibid.

countries have different laws and there can be a 'conflict' in the sense that more than one country might have jurisdiction and more than one law could be applied. Conflict of laws rules are designed to eliminate these conflicts by indicating which court should have jurisdiction and which of the 'conflicting' laws should be applied. So far as the second title is concerned, the subject is 'international' because the facts of the case or the parties to it are connected with a country or countries other than England. It is 'private' as opposed to 'public' international law because it is not concerned with the relations of states with each other, but with the disputes of persons[4] arising out of their marriages, contracts, wills, torts, and other private law matters. It is not international in the sense of being a body of law shared by all countries.[5]

1.8 The English conflict of laws (or private international law) is just as much a part of English law as is the law of contract or the law of tort, but at a different level of classification. For present purposes, English law can be divided into two parts: English conflict of laws and English domestic law.[6] As was seen above, the conflict of laws can be subdivided into rules relating to jurisdiction, choice of law, and the recognition of foreign judgments. English domestic law can be subdivided into contract, tort, family law, property law, and so on. Domestic law, then, consists of the substantive rules defining and regulating people's rights and duties, the application of which directly determines the outcome of legal disputes. If a case before the English court has no foreign elements, the court simply applies the appropriate rules of English domestic law. But, if the case does have foreign elements, the court must turn to the English conflict of laws. The first question will be whether the court has jurisdiction. If not, the claimant must find a foreign court which has jurisdiction under its law. If the English court does have jurisdiction, however, then the English choice of law rules come into play. They will direct the court whether to apply English domestic law or the domestic law of one or more foreign countries in deciding the case.

1.9 English law, therefore, includes English conflict of laws as well as English domestic law. Similarly, French law includes French conflict of laws as well as French domestic law. Very often, however, the expression 'English law' is used to mean English domestic law only, excluding English conflict of laws. When it is said that a particular issue is governed by 'French law', that normally means French domestic law only, excluding the French conflict of laws, although occasionally, as shall be seen, the reference is to French conflict of laws.

C Meaning of 'country'

1.10 For the purposes of the conflict of laws, a 'country' is any territorial unit having its own separate system of law, whether or not it constitutes an independent state politically. So, in the conflicts context, England, Scotland, and Northern Ireland are

---

[4] Which may, of course, include legal persons, such as companies, and governments and other public authorities.
[5] But see Mills, 'The Private History of International Law' (2006) 55 ICLQ 1.
[6] Synonyms for 'domestic law' include 'internal law', 'municipal law', and 'local law'.

separate countries because they have separate legal systems. The United Kingdom cannot be the relevant country for the purposes of those branches of private law for which there is no such thing as the law of the United Kingdom. Similarly, each of the states of the United States, each Canadian province, and each Australian state is treated as a separate country for most conflict of laws purposes. One needs to know, for instance, whether a tort caused harm in Ontario, not whether it caused harm in Canada. Of course, it does not follow that a country, for conflicts purposes, cannot coincide with a sovereign independent state for the purposes of public international law. Indeed, usually they do coincide, for most states have a uniform legal system throughout their territory.

1.11 In the United States and other federal countries, the convenient expression 'law district' is often used to denote a country in the conflict of laws sense.

D The changing nature of the subject: the influence of the EU

1.12 Writing in 1935, Cheshire famously stated that the conflict of laws 'has been only lightly touched by the paralysing hand of the Parliamentary draftsman'.[7] No such assertion could plausibly be made in the twenty-first century. The modern conflict of laws in England is dominated by legislation, much of which either is derived from international conventions to which the United Kingdom is a party or takes the form of EU Regulations. Indeed, by far the most profound changes to English private international law in the last half-century have resulted from the activities of the European Union (formerly the European Community).

1.13 The seed from which the modern law has grown was article 220 of the Treaty of Rome under which the Member States of the EEC (as it then was) undertook to 'enter into negotiations with each other with a view to securing . . . the simplification of formalities governing the reciprocal recognition and enforcement of judgments of courts or tribunals'. In due course, negotiations led to the adoption by the original six EEC Member States of the Brussels Convention of 1968.[8] Subject to some important exceptions, the Convention created a uniform scheme for the allocation of jurisdiction and the recognition and enforcement of judgments in civil and commercial matters. It did not, however, address choice of law issues, a deficiency which was addressed by negotiations which, in 1980, ultimately resulted in the Rome Convention on the law applicable to contractual obligations. The original idea had been to create a convention which, to complement the Brussels Convention, covered choice of law in both contractual and non-contractual obligations, thereby creating an integrated European framework for the main conflict of laws questions which arise in commercial cases. However, as the Member States were unable to reach agreement on non-contractual obligations, the Rome Convention was limited to choice of law in contract and the aim which inspired

---

[7] See the preface to *Private International Law* (1935).
[8] As the European Community expanded in the 1970s, 1980s, and 1990s, the new Member States acceded to the Brussels Convention by means of a series of accession conventions.

the Rome Convention was not finally realised until towards the end of the first decade of the twenty-first century.

1.14 The undoubted success of the Brussels and Rome Conventions encouraged the institutions of the European Community to press on with further harmonisation measures in the field of private international law. In the 1990s work started on matters which were excluded from the Brussels and Rome Conventions—most significantly, insolvency (which had been excluded from the Brussels Convention's jurisdiction and judgments regime), the cross-border service of documents, and aspects of family law. This work led to three conventions: the Insolvency Convention (which covered jurisdiction, choice of law, and the recognition and enforcement of judgments), the Brussels II Convention (which addressed jurisdiction and judgments relating to matrimonial causes and certain parental responsibility matters), and the Service Convention.

1.15 However, these conventions never became part of the law of the Member States in this form. On the entry into force of the Treaty of Amsterdam in 1999, the European Community acquired legislative competence in relation to judicial co-operation in civil matters[9] and it was decided that the existing instruments—not only the conventions which were already in force (such as the Brussels Convention) but also those which had been agreed, but not yet brought into effect (such as the Insolvency Convention)—should be re-cast as Regulations. In the early years of the twenty-first century a series of Regulations were adopted translating (with amendments) the various conventions into mainstream European law. Furthermore, the new legislative competence conferred by the Treaty of Amsterdam and confirmed by the Treaty on the Functioning of the European Union of 2008 was used (and has continued to be used) to extend the reach of EU private international law—in both the commercial and family law areas. In the commercial field, legislation provides a unified European framework of conflict of laws rules in the following areas: jurisdiction and judgments in civil and commercial matters (the Brussels I Recast[10] replacing the Brussels I Regulation[11]); choice of law for contractual obligations (the Rome I Regulation[12]); choice of law for non-contractual obligations (the Rome II Regulation[13]); cross-border service of documents in civil and commercial matters (the Service Regulation[14]); the taking of evidence abroad in civil and commercial matters (the Evidence Regulation[15]); jurisdiction, choice of law, and judgments in insolvency (the Insolvency Regulation[16]). In the family law

[9] Arts 61 and 65. These provisions were replaced by TFEU, arts 67 and 81.
[10] Regulation (EU) No 1215/2012, OJ 2012 L351/1.
[11] Regulation (EC) No 44/2001, OJ 2001 L12/1.
[12] Regulation (EC) No 593/2008, OJ 2008 L177/6.
[13] Regulation (EC) No 864/2007, OJ 2007 L199/40.
[14] Regulation (EC) No 1393/2007, OJ 2007 L324/79.
[15] Regulation (EC) No 1206/2001, OJ 2001 L174/1.
[16] Regulation (EU) No 848/2015, OJ 2015 L141/19, which will replace the original Regulation (Regulation (EC) No 1346/2000, OJ 2001 L160/1) from June 2017. In addition to the Regulations listed above, the European Union has also adopted a Regulation establishing a European Account Preservation Order allowing for the cross-border freezing of bank accounts: Regulation (EU) No 655/2014, OJ 2014 L189/59 (the United Kingdom has, however, opted out).

field, European legislation covers: jurisdiction and judgments in proceedings relating to matrimonial causes and matters of parental responsibility (the Brussels II *bis* Regulation[17]) and jurisdiction, choice of law and judgments in relation to maintenance obligations (the Maintenance Regulation[18]). An EU Regulation on jurisdiction, choice of law, and judgments in succession matters has also been adopted (the Succession Regulation[19]) but the United Kingdom is not participating in this Regulation. There has been enhanced co-operation between 16 Member States (not including the United Kingdom) in the area of the law applicable to divorce and legal separation (Rome III)[20] and there is a proposal for further enhanced co-operation on jurisdiction, choice of law, and judgments in matrimonial property matters.[21]

1.16 The effect of all this legislative activity at the European level has been to transform the English conflict of laws. To anyone familiar with the English conflict of laws as it was in 1985, the current state of the law is completely unrecognisable; the majority of the issues considered in this book are, at least in part, regulated by the regimes created by European legislation. As indicated above, however, these European regimes are neither completely uniform nor comprehensive. Lack of uniformity results from two factors.

1.17 First, many of the European instruments make concessions to the sensitivities of the Member States; for example, although the Rome Regulations lay down choice of law rules for identifying the law applicable to contractual and non-contractual obligations, both Regulations provide that a Member State court may refuse to apply a provision of the governing law if its application would be manifestly contrary to the forum's public policy.[22] As public policy varies from one country to another, the outcome of a particular dispute may depend on whether the dispute is resolved by the courts of Member State X rather than by those of Member State Y, even though both Member States are bound to apply the same choice of law rules. Secondly, some of the Member States negotiated a position whereby they can choose whether or not to opt in to the judicial co-operation measures under the Treaty of Amsterdam (since replaced by provisions of the Treaty on the Functioning of the European Union). For example, Denmark is not bound by the Rome Regulations and the United Kingdom has not opted into the Succession Regulation.

1.18 Lack of comprehensiveness results from the fact that certain matters are excluded from specific Regulations (for example, the Rome II Regulation on choice of law relating to

---

[17] Regulation (EC) No 2201/2003, OJ 2003 L338/1.
[18] Regulation (EC) No 4/2009, OJ 2009 L7/1. The European Union has also adopted a Regulation on mutual recognition of protection measures in civil matters (providing cross-border protection to victims of domestic violence): Regulation (EU) No 606/2013, OJ 2013 L181/4.
[19] Regulation (EU) No 650/2012, OJ 2012 L201/07.
[20] Regulation (EU) No 1259/2010, OJ 2010 L343/10. Originally 14 Member States participated in Rome III and Lithuania and Greece opted in subsequently: see OJ 2012 L323/18; OJ 2014 L23/41. For some of the background to this Regulation, see *Proposal for a Council Regulation implementing enhanced cooperation in the area of the law applicable to divorce and legal separation* COM (2010) 105 final.
[21] COM (2016) 108 final.
[22] Rome I Regulation, art 21; Rome II Regulation, art 26.

non-contractual obligations does not apply to, inter alia, defamation; subject to limited exceptions, the Brussels I Recast does not determine the court's jurisdiction if the defendant is not domiciled in a Member State). This means that, even in areas where the European legislation applies, the traditional English conflict of laws rules have a residual role; they continue to apply in relation to those matters which are not regulated by the European rules. For example, whereas the Brussels I Recast covers the recognition and enforcement of Member State judgments in civil and commercial matters, the traditional English common law rules (and statutory schemes based on the common law) continue to determine whether a commercial judgment granted by the courts of a country which is not a Member State is entitled to recognition and enforcement in England. This type of structure—with the European rules and the residual, traditional rules operating in parallel, each with their separate spheres of operation—will be seen in many of the following chapters.

II The conflicts process

1.19 Tracing the various stages of proceedings which raise conflict of laws issues involves examining the problems of jurisdiction and choice of law. A few words concerning the recognition and enforcement of foreign judgments are also appropriate at this stage.

A Jurisdiction

1.20 The first issue for resolution in any conflicts case is whether the English court has jurisdiction. There is an argument that the English courts should be open to anyone. It is good for commerce, lucrative for English lawyers, and the standards of British justice are respected internationally, especially in commercial fields. This argument is particularly forceful when the parties to an international contract have agreed in their contract that the English courts should have jurisdiction. On the other hand, there is a formidable case for saying that proceedings should be heard only in *appropriate* courts, that is, courts having some genuine connection with the parties and/or the cause of action. Defendants and witnesses should not have to undergo the expense and inconvenience of having to travel around the world to participate in legal proceedings. Opening one's courts to the whole world encourages 'forum shopping' (the process of shopping around the world's courts until one finds a court where one is likely to obtain the most successful outcome) which is not conducive to settled international business. Further, if judgment is obtained in an inappropriate forum, the defendant may well not have any assets in that jurisdiction against which the judgment can be enforced and it may be necessary to commence further proceedings elsewhere to enforce the judgment. One of the objects of a modern and coherent system of private international law ought to be the avoidance of such a multiplicity of proceedings.

1.21 Accordingly, it is argued that before an English court assumes jurisdiction in a case involving foreign elements, there needs to be a careful investigation of all the relevant considerations, such as the interests of the parties and whether, having regard to the events and the evidence, the English court is an appropriate forum to decide the dispute.

1.22 It is, of course, important to bear in mind here that different degrees of connection (and thus different jurisdictional rules) might be required for different areas of law. For example, in an action for breach of contract the connection with England need not be particularly strong and it could suffice that the contract should have been performed in England or that the contract is governed by English law. On the other hand, in a divorce or annulment case a stronger connection with England may be desirable because such actions are more likely to involve protective policies which vary from one legal culture to another. Accordingly, there is a good argument for saying that only those belonging here in the sense of being, at least, resident here, should be permitted to obtain a divorce or annulment from the English courts.

1.23 The central problem is one of ascertaining whether the parties and/or the cause of action have a sufficiently close connection with England to justify the English court assuming jurisdiction. As shall be seen, the issue of choice of law involves similar considerations. Choice of law rules are structured to lead to the application of a law which has a close connection with either the parties or the cause of action. At first, this would seem to indicate that, if a court is sufficiently closely connected to the parties or the cause of action to justify the assumption of jurisdiction, its law would be a closely connected law, meaning that choice of law rules could be dispensed with and courts could apply their own law (the lex fori). Such a solution would be simpler, cheaper, and more certain than courts trying to apply foreign laws. Indeed, there is something to be said for this approach. Under present jurisdictional rules an English court today would not have jurisdiction in a case such as *Maharanee of Baroda*,[23] meaning that it would not have to concern itself with French law. Equally, continuing with the contract example, by assuming jurisdiction only in cases where the English forum is an appropriate and closely connected court, there is a good chance that English law will be the applicable law.

1.24 Accordingly, there can be little doubt that, in some senses, it is the jurisdictional rules that are of most importance today. In the majority of cases, once the jurisdiction question is resolved, that puts an end to the contentious issues; the forum can apply its own law and there might be little or no dispute as to the outcome. Indeed, once jurisdictional issues are resolved and the venue for the parties' dispute is determined, most cases—at least in the commercial sphere—are settled.[24]

1.25 It must be stressed, however, that there is no perfect symmetry between jurisdictional and choice of law rules. While both are structured to identify a country or law of close connection, the policy considerations underlying each are rather different. In particular, there are many contexts in which the jurisdictional rules are designed to ensure

---

[23] *Maharanee of Baroda v Wildenstein* [1972] 2 QB 283.
[24] See Fentiman, *International Commercial Litigation* (2nd edn, 2015) para 7.09.

that England is *an* appropriate forum (for example, in terms of practical convenience and location of evidence); there might be others equally appropriate. Indeed, as shall be seen, there might be another country that is more appropriate but nevertheless the English court will proceed to hear the case if justice will not be done in the foreign court.[25] Choice of law rules, on the other hand, are designed to be more exclusive in the sense of leading to only one applicable law, generally the *most* appropriate law, and considerations of practical convenience are less important.

1.26 As will be seen, there are different views as to whether the allocation of jurisdiction should be based on fixed rules (which prioritise certainty and predictability)—or whether jurisdictional rules should be more open-textured and fact-sensitive, allowing for a more tailored identification of the most appropriate forum (but often at a cost in terms of encouraging the parties to devote resources to 'satellite' litigation on the question of venue). The common law has favoured a more nuanced assessment of jurisdiction, while EU Regulations tend to adopt a more rigid and structured approach.

1.27 Finally, it should be noted that while the jurisdictional hurdle always has to be overcome in every conflicts case, in practice it is frequently not a live issue because the parties have agreed to the English court having jurisdiction. In particular in the context of international commercial litigation in the High Court, it is not uncommon for the parties to have agreed to English jurisdiction.[26]

B Choice of law

1.28 Once it has been determined that it possesses jurisdiction, the court is in a position to apply the relevant choice of law rule that leads to the applicable law (lex causae). As noted above, this applicable law may be English law or a foreign law.

1. Rationale of choice of law rules

1.29 At this point an obvious question presents itself. *Why* should an English court apply foreign law? If the parties have chosen litigation in England, surely it is not unreasonable that English law be applied. Further, if the English court decides not to apply English law, *which* foreign law will it apply?

1.30 There are several reasons for applying foreign law rather than English law. The following explanation of these reasons will reveal not just *why* foreign law is applied but also help indicate *which* foreign law is applicable.

(A) *Achieving justice between the parties*

1.31 One of the most important factors underlying choice of law rules is the desire to achieve justice between the parties (sometimes called 'conflicts justice'). This notion is manifested in two ways.

---

[25] See paras 2.227–2.236.
[26] A majority of disputes initiated in the Commercial Court concern at least one party which is not English: Fentiman, *International Commercial Litigation* (2nd edn, 2015) para 1.15.

(i) Giving effect to the parties' intentions

1.32 One of the principles which underlie the whole of private law is the principle of party autonomy. Such autonomy is not unfettered; it may be limited by policy considerations (such as the public interest in a system of free competition). Nevertheless, party autonomy is a reasonable starting-point in the conflict of laws, just as it is in other areas of private law.[27]

1.33 The desire to give effect to the common intention of the parties, unless there is good reason to the contrary, supports the rule that parties should be free to choose the law applicable to a contract[28] or, in certain situations, the law applicable to a tort.[29] There may, of course, be problems when deciding how far the chosen law should prevail over the mandatory rules of another country's law, designed to protect its public interest.[30]

1.34 Related to the principle of party autonomy is the principle (sometimes referred to as the favor validatis) that when parties freely enter legal transactions or create legal relationships such transactions and relationships should generally be effective.[31] It is recognised, for example, that choice of law rules should normally seek to uphold the validity of marriages.[32] Of course, systems of law contain rules which are designed to render certain transactions and relationships invalid and these rules cannot simply be ignored. However, such rules should not be applied—thereby invalidating a particular transaction or relationship—unless, in the light of the territorial connections of the facts and the parties, there is a sufficient ground for doing so.

(ii) Giving effect to the parties' legitimate expectations

1.35 The principle that effect should be given to the legitimate expectations of the parties is not unconnected to the principle of party autonomy. Where, for example, parties make a choice of law, the expressed will of the parties is a clear indication of their expectations. However, the principle of giving effect to reasonable expectations goes further than simply respecting the parties' express intentions. Some simple examples will illustrate the point that always applying English law, instead of a foreign law, could lead to a highly inappropriate outcome that would defeat the reasonable expectations of the parties. In *Maharanee of Baroda v Wildenstein*[33] two French residents entered into a contract in France. In these circumstances, it is appropriate that, in the absence of a choice of the governing law by the parties, French law should be applied by the English court; it is the law which the parties would reasonably have expected to apply and the law of the country by reference to which they can be deemed to have contracted. It is the law with which they can be presumed to have been familiar or, at any rate, if they had sought legal advice at the time of contracting, it would have been advice on French

---

[27] See Nygh, *Autonomy in International Contracts* (1999); Harris, 'Contractual Freedom in the Conflict of Laws' (2000) 20 OJLS 247; Carruthers, 'Party Autonomy in the Legal Regulation of Adult Relationships: What Place for Party Choice in Private International Law?' (2012) 61 ICLQ 881.
[28] See paras 4.16–4.20.   [29] See paras 5.86–5.90.   [30] See paras 4.87–4.113.
[31] See Ehrenzweig, 'Contracts in the Conflict of Laws' (1959) 59 Col LR 973, 988.
[32] See paras 7.40, 7.53.   [33] [1972] 2 QB 283.

law. The English choice of law rule in contractual situations where the parties have not chosen the applicable law is that the contract is governed by the law of the country with which it is (or is deemed to be) most closely connected[34]—which in this case would have been French law.

1.36 Another illustration can be taken from the field of family law. Consider the example of an English couple who are working in California for a year and decide to get married there by way of a ceremony in a hot air balloon—a form of marriage permitted under Californian law. They complete all of the paperwork required by the Californian authorities and comply with all of the local formalities—although these are different from those required for marriage in England. If the validity of such a marriage were to be tested some years later in the English courts it would be highly unjust to apply English law, which insists on a different set of formalities for a marriage. The parties got married in the only way they could in California—by relying on Californian law and formalities. Their reasonable expectations would be frustrated by the application of anything other than Californian law. Accordingly, the rule is that the formalities of a marriage are governed by the lex loci celebrationis (the law of the place where the marriage ceremony was conducted). One further example will suffice. Suppose a British person emigrates to Spain and lives there for 50 years before dying without having made a will. Which law should govern the question of intestate succession if that issue should arise in English proceedings? The obvious answer is the law of the country in which the deceased was domiciled—in the sense of having a settled home and living permanently—at the time of death. This is the law which the deceased might reasonably have expected to be the applicable law. Either such a person can be presumed to be familiar with this law, or, if seeking legal advice as to whether to make a will or not, it would have been advice on Spanish law that would have been sought. The application of English law—the law of the forum—in this case would result in the inappropriate and unjust result that the deceased's property would devolve according to the laws of a country with which the deceased was no longer connected. Accordingly, a clear choice of law rule has developed to meet such cases: intestate succession to movables is governed by the law of the deceased's domicile at the date of death.

1.37 It must not be thought that the most appropriate foreign law is necessarily the one that the parties would have *wanted* to apply. If an Englishman goes temporarily to Saudi Arabia and there marries two women in polygamous form, he might want and hope that the law of Saudi Arabia would apply and that these marriages would be regarded as valid. However, such a person should reasonably *expect* that English law would be applicable to such an important matter (which is concerned with the essential validity of a marriage, rather than simply its formal validity). This is not on a par with matters of formality—such as getting married in a hot air balloon. In this case, if the man is domiciled in England, his reasonable expectations would have to be that English law would apply to the marriage. He should recognise that on fundamental matters such as

---

[34] Rome I Regulation, art 4.

capacity to contract a polygamous marriage, the policy interests of England, a country committed to monogamy, will be held to prevail over the particular interests of the parties in question. Accordingly, a choice of law rule has been developed to reflect this: capacity to marry is governed by the law of domicile.[35]

1.38 These examples demonstrate the prevailing approach adopted by English law to the issue of choice of law: in the absence of party choice, the parties can be deemed reasonably to expect their relationships and transactions to be governed by the law with which those relationships and transactions are most closely connected. In the *Maharanee of Baroda* case, France was the country with which the contract was most closely connected; the formal validity of the Californian marriage was most closely connected with California; the person dying in Spain was most closely connected with Spain.

1.39 This is sometimes referred to as the 'proper law' approach: finding the law with which a particular transaction or legal relationship is most closely connected. Most connecting factors[36] within choice of law rules are aimed at locating this proper law. For example, in disputes involving immovable property, the choice of law rule is that the law of the country where the property is situated (the lex situs) is the applicable law. The rules on domicile seek to pinpoint the country to which a person 'belongs'. Tort liability is generally governed by the law of the place where the tort is committed (lex loci delicti) or where the damage is sustained (lex loci damni). However, when these basic choice of law rules do not lead to the application of the most closely connected law, they can give way to that latter law. For example, where a tort is more closely connected with a country other than where the tort was committed (for example, if both parties were from another country), the law of this other country can be applied, as a 'proper law exception'.

1.40 In other areas of law the basic choice of law rule has explicitly been the proper law. Under the English common law conflict of laws rules relating to contractual obligations, the basic rule was that the proper law, the law of closest connection, applied in cases where the parties had not chosen an applicable law. As a result of EU developments, this rule has been largely replaced by more focused choice of law rules (for example, that contracts for the sale of goods are governed by the law of the country where the seller has his habitual residence) but there is express provision that where the contract is manifestly more closely connected with another country, the law of that other country shall apply.[37]

(B) Protecting or advancing the public interest

1.41 Some legal rules have as their purpose (or one of their main purposes) the protection or advancement of the public interest. For example, some rules which invalidate marriages are designed to protect the public interest of the forum. An illustration of this is the rule of English law that a valid polygamous marriage cannot be contracted in England; one of the main purposes of this rule is to protect and buttress the institution of monogamous marriage. It is inevitable that the conflicts rules of a country will give

---

[35] This is considered in Chapter 7.   [36] See paras 1.102–1.105.   [37] See paras 4.60–4.74.

full scope to its own rules which are considered vital for the protection of the public interest. Each country has 'interests asserted either directly on its own behalf, such as the protection of its currency or security, or on behalf of those members of the community who need protection, such as consumers and employees'.[38] Accordingly, even though the parties are domiciled in a country where polygamy is lawful and even though they intend to return to that country after their marriage in England, any purported polygamous marriage in England is not valid.

1.42 Even when the country which has a public interest is not the forum, the English court may still seek to advance the public interest of a foreign country, despite the foreign country's interest taking priority over principles of conflicts justice which are designed to achieve a just solution between litigants. For example, article 9(3) of the Rome I Regulation provides that effect may be given to the overriding mandatory provisions of the law of the country where the contract is to be performed if such performance would be unlawful in that country. This provision allows for the public interests of foreign countries (as expressed in overriding mandatory rules) to be given priority over principles of conflicts justice (notably, the principle that the parties' intentions and reasonable expectations should be respected). The effect of article 9(3) is not that the interest of a foreign country necessarily takes precedence over the intentions (or expectations) of the parties in all cases; it all depends on the circumstances. Where, for example, a contract is invalid according to a rule of country X which is intended to protect the public interest, it would not necessarily be right to apply the rule to a contract—even though it falls within the policy of the rule—if the party who would suffer loss from the invalidation of the contract did not belong to country X and the contract's connections with country X were not such that it could reasonably have been anticipated that the contract might be affected by its law.

1.43 Recognising the importance of taking account of the public interest—and the purpose or policy of legal rules—has led, primarily in the United States, to an approach to choice of law called 'interest analysis'.[39] This approach has been particularly influential there in multi-state tort cases but can be applied to most choice of law rules.

(i) Interest analysis

(a) Deducing the applicability of a legal rule from its policy

1.44 Interest analysis involves trying to glean from the legal rule itself the extent to which it is applicable in a particular case having foreign elements by construing it according to its purpose or policy. The basic method is to start with an examination of the policies underlying the laws which might conceivably apply to the particular facts of the case. In a tort case, for example, the competing laws may include the lex fori, the lex loci delicti, and the laws of the countries with which the parties are closely connected.

---

[38] Nygh, 'The Reasonable Expectations of the Parties as a Guide to the Choice of Law in Contract and in Tort' (1995) 251 Hag Rec 269, 376.
[39] Most influential has been the writing on 'governmental interest analysis' by Brainerd Currie, *Selected Essays in the Conflict of Laws* (1963).

1.45 If, on investigating the policy of a rule, it is found that, having regard to the foreign elements, the facts of the case do not fall within the scope of that policy, there is no point in applying that rule. The rule should be applied only in cases for which it was designed. If the case does fall within the policy of the rule—and to apply the rule will advance the policy—there is a reason to apply it. Depending on whether or not the policy of the rule of a particular country calls for its application to the facts of the case, it is said that the country has (or does not have) an interest in its rule being applied. The premise of this approach is that a country has an interest that the policies underlying its legal rules should be advanced. According to this analysis, France has an interest in the application of French consumer protection rules to a dispute arising out of a contract involving a French consumer.

1.46 The application of this method may lead to the conclusion that, on the facts of the particular case, only one country has an interest in its rule being applied. In this situation, which is known as a 'false conflict', interest analysis requires the application of the law of that country. Where, for example, a married couple from country X are involved in a road accident in country Y, it is not unreasonable to conclude that only country X has an interest in the question whether the wife can sue her husband for injuries caused by his negligence.

1.47 This interest analysis approach is well illustrated by the New York case of *Babcock v Jackson*.[40] P and D were both residents of the state of New York. While they were on a brief trip to Ontario in D's car, P was injured as a result of D's negligent driving. P sued D in New York. Under the law of Ontario, D was not liable because of Ontario's 'guest statute', under which a driver was not liable for injury caused negligently to a gratuitous passenger; D was, however, liable under the law of New York, which had no such statute.

1.48 The New York Court of Appeals rejected the traditional view that liability in tort is necessarily governed by the lex loci delicti. It held instead that the issue whether the driver was liable to his gratuitous passenger should be decided by the law of the country which, in relation to that issue, had the most significant relationship with the events and the parties. Which country that was depended on the purposes and the relevant rules of the laws of Ontario and New York. The purposes of the Ontario statute included the prevention of fraudulent claims by passengers, in collusion with drivers, against insurance companies and the protection of motorists from an unfair liability to passengers to whom they had given a free lift. But, the Ontario statute was concerned to protect insurance companies and motorists from Ontario, not those from New York (as the driver and his insurer were in this case). As Fuld J, who gave the leading judgment, said:

> Whether New York defendants are imposed upon or their insurers defrauded by a New York plaintiff is scarcely a valid legislative concern of Ontario simply because the accident occurred there, any more so than if the accident had happened in some other jurisdiction.[41]

---

[40] 12 NY 2d 473 (1963). The decision was also reported in England: [1963] 2 Lloyd's Rep 286.
[41] [1963] 2 Lloyd's Rep 286 at 290.

1.49 The case did, however, fall within the policy of the New York rule, the purpose of which was to ensure that even gratuitous passengers were fully compensated. In the circumstances of the case there was every reason for applying New York law. So, P succeeded, notwithstanding the fact that D was not liable according to the lex loci delicti. However, the court stressed that, had the issue been a different one, the law of Ontario might have had the most significant relationship. If, for example, the issue had been the manner in which D had been driving, the law of Ontario would have been the applicable law.

1.50 A similar approach was adopted in the Californian case of *Reich v Purcell*,[42] where the plaintiff's wife was killed in Missouri as a result of the negligent driving of the defendant. The plaintiff and his wife came from Ohio; the defendant was Californian. The plaintiff sued for damages in California. A Missouri statute limited the damages in a wrongful death action to $25,000, but under the laws of Ohio and California the plaintiff was entitled to his full loss of $55,000. The court held that Missouri had no interest in the application of its statute, for the concern of Missouri law was to avoid imposing excessive financial burdens on Missouri defendants. Ohio, however, had an interest in the application of its law, whose policy afforded full compensation for injured parties, because the plaintiff resided in Ohio. California, the policy of whose law was the same as Ohio's, had no interest in the application of its law, for the injured party was not a Californian. Accordingly, the law of Ohio was applied. Interest analysis thus revealed that there was a false conflict: only one law (that of Ohio) had an interest in the application of its rule and the outcome of the case.

1.51 However, it is also possible that the particular facts of the case fall within the scope of the policy of two or more of the competing laws, an example of a 'true conflict'. For example, a 'marriage of convenience' contracted by a woman domiciled in Belgium, under whose law the marriage is void, and a man domiciled in England, under whose law the marriage is valid, gives rise to a true conflict. In this type of case, some basis has to be found for choosing between the competing laws. Which country's policy is to be preferred?

1.52 Currie's view was that if one of the countries having an interest is the forum—and the apparent conflict cannot be eliminated by a moderate and restrained interpretation of the competing laws—the law of the forum must be applied. This approach does not solve the problem when the forum is 'disinterested' and the conflict is between the laws of two other countries (though in many cases where the forum is disinterested one would expect the case to have an insufficiently strong connection with the forum to justify the exercise of jurisdiction). An alternative view is that the strengths of the conflicting interests should be weighed.[43] According to the 'comparative impairment' approach[44] the court should seek to determine which state's interest would be more impaired if its policy were subordinated to the policy of the other state.[45]

---

[42] 432 P 2d 727 (1967).
[43] See, eg, Von Mehren and Trautman, *The Law of Multistate Problems: Cases and Materials on Conflict of Laws* (1965) pp 76–7, 341–2, 376–8.
[44] Baxter, 'Choice of Law and the Federal System' (1963) 16 Stan LR 1.
[45] *Bernhard v Harrah's Club* 546 P 2d 719 (1976).

1.53 This comparative impairment approach can be illustrated by the Californian case of *Offshore Rental Co Inc v Continental Oil Co*,[46] in which a 'key' employee of a Californian company was injured in Louisiana by the negligence of the Louisiana defendant. Under Californian law, an employer had a cause of action against a person who negligently injured his key employee. Under the law of Louisiana, the employer had no such cause of action. The court held that the policy of the Californian rule was to protect Californian employers from loss arising from such injury and that the opposite Louisiana rule was to protect negligent tortfeasors acting within Louisiana's borders from the financial hardships which would be caused by the imposition of legal liability in such a case. So, both California and Louisiana had an interest in the application of its rule. The court decided in favour of the application of the law of Louisiana on the basis of the comparative impairment theory.

1.54 The most valuable feature of governmental interest analysis as a method is that it avoids the pointless application of a legal rule when the purpose of the rule would not be served by applying it. Suppose a rule of country X makes void a provision in a contract under which an employee agrees with his employer not to compete with his employer after the end of the employment. If the only purpose of that rule is to promote competition in country X there would seem little point in applying the rule to a restraint of trade provision which is to operate in country Y, not country X. If, by the law of country Y, the provision is valid it would be sensible to apply the rule of country Y. A choice of law rule which led to the application of the law of country X, simply because that law was the law applicable to the contract, would seem defective.

(b) The limits of interest analysis

1.55 Taken to its logical conclusion, interest analysis leads to the view that choice of law rules are unnecessary. The methodology of interest analysis is premised on the notion that the sphere of application of any rule of law can be determined by reference to its policy. Interest analysis postulates that a conflict of laws can be resolved by a consideration of the strength of the competing policies. As far as English (or EU) law is concerned, it has never been seriously suggested that choice of law rules can be dispensed with. Nevertheless, there seems little doubt that the content of choice of law rules is, to a certain extent, determined by the policy considerations which are articulated by interest analysis theorists. Traditional choice of law rules are not abstractly plucked out of the air; they are shaped by various influences and concerns. The idea that a particular transaction, relationship, or event should be governed by the law of the country with which it is most closely connected is explicable, at least in part, by the fact that the country of closest connection is the country which is likely, from the point of view of policy, to have the greatest interest.

1.56 While many would concede that interest analysis can make a positive contribution towards an understanding of important issues in choice of law, few would seek to

---

[46] 583 P 2d 721 (1978).

maintain that the theory is not subject to limits. A central problem is that the policy of a rule does not always give clear guidance as to its applicability in a case having foreign connections. The apparent simplicity of cases such as *Babcock v Jackson* hides the fact that there may be the greatest difficulty in deciding what the policy or purpose of a given rule is. Consider the converse of *Babcock v Jackson*: the driver and his gratuitous passenger (both from Ontario) are involved in an accident in New York. The passenger sues in New York. Ontario would have an interest in its guest statute being applied. Would New York have an interest in its rule, that the gratuitous passenger is entitled to compensation, being applied? If the purpose of the rule is regarded as being only to secure compensation for the victim of an accident, it could be argued that New York has no concern whether or not an Ontario passenger is compensated by an Ontario driver. But perhaps it is also a purpose of the New York rule of liability to deter negligent driving. Then, of course, New York will have an interest in its rule being applied to an accident in New York, wherever the parties come from. Then both countries have an interest. On such facts the New York court in *Krell v Henderson*[47] applied New York law.

1.57 The opposite situation is where neither country is found to have an interest: the case comes within the purpose of neither country's rule. That would be the position if a New York driver gave a gratuitous lift to an Ontario passenger in Ontario—as long as it is assumed that the purposes of the Ontario statute are to protect drivers and insurers and of the New York rule, to secure compensation for injured passengers and to promote safe driving in New York. In such a case, the New York court in *Neumeier v Kuehner*[48] applied Ontario law as the lex loci delicti.

1.58 While the results achieved in the leading cases discussed above are not difficult to defend, the process of reasoning is more questionable. It might be suggested that the whole approach to the rules in question is fallacious. The basis of the court's analysis seems in the end to be little more than that each rule under consideration is more favourable to one party than is the corresponding rule of another country. To maintain that the concern of a law which limits damages to $25,000 is to protect defendants from excessive financial burdens is only plausible if the comparison is with laws which do not limit damages. In comparison with laws allowing even less than $25,000 to be recovered, it would make little sense to say that the concern of the Missouri law was to protect defendants. Of course, a country which previously allowed full recovery of damages may pass a statute which limits damages to a certain amount. In such a case the purpose of the legislation may well be to protect defendants from excessive financial burdens. However, it is quite another matter to say that the purpose of the resulting law, as amended, is to protect defendants. The true position is that the purpose of the new law, like that of the previous law, is to provide a just solution between the parties. It is simply that the perception of what is just in such a case has changed, the balance having been tilted more towards the defendant.

---

[47] 270 NYS 2d 552 (1960).   [48] 286 NE 2d 454 (1972).

1.59 The effect of the interest analysis approach in cases such as *Reich v Purcell* seems to be that a country has an interest in its law being applied when it favours a party belonging to that country, but not when it is against him (or when the law favours a party who belongs to another country).

1.60 Quite apart from the difficulties of discerning the purposes and policies of rules of law, the odd conclusion that the facts of a case may fall within the purpose of neither country's rule suggests the possibility that this whole way of looking at things may be misconceived. Many rules of private law are not primarily designed to protect the public interest, whether by deterring harmful conduct or encouraging useful conduct or otherwise. Their function is to decide disputes between people, arising out of their relationships with each other or the effects of the conduct of one or another. Their purpose is to do justice between people, in the sense of producing a fair and reasonable solution to the dispute. But a rule's purpose in doing justice between parties to a dispute can tell us nothing about its applicability in a case having foreign elements. It makes little sense to ask whether a country has (or does not have) an interest in the application of its rule when the policy of the rule is to do justice between the parties. The only answer would be that the rule is intended to be applied to disputes in that country's courts, unless its choice of law rules direct that another country's standards of justice should be applied. The problem is simply that different countries have different concepts of what is the just solution in a particular case. The traditional function of choice of law rules is to indicate to the court in what circumstances, in view of the foreign connections, it should prefer the standards of justice of another country to its own.

(C) Achieving uniformity of decision

1.61 Another reason for applying foreign laws or, at least, for not always applying the law of the forum is that this can lead to uniformity of decision irrespective of where the litigation is actually brought. In a case with international connections, the courts of two or more countries may each have jurisdiction under their own law. If these courts each applied their domestic law to decide the case, the outcome of the case might depend purely on where the case was brought. The claimant would have the advantage of being able to choose to sue in the court whose law would be most favourable (a simple example of forum shopping), which is arguably unfair to the defendant. In matrimonial cases, if the courts of different countries each applied their own laws, parties might be regarded as married to each other in some countries, but single in others (a situation known as a 'limping marriage'), hardly an ideal state of affairs. On the other hand, if courts in different countries were to apply conflict rules with some of them applying foreign laws, these problems could be overcome. If, in a factual situation like the one that arose in *Maharanee of Baroda*, both French and English courts would apply French law, one reason for forum shopping would be removed.

1.62 It must be emphasised that the willingness of courts to apply foreign laws does not guarantee uniformity of decision because each country has its own choice of law rules, whose content may differ. Thus the English choice of law rule might direct the English court to apply the law of France in a case in which the French choice of law rule would require the French court to apply English law. Attempts have been made to harmonise the choice of law rules (and the jurisdictional and recognition rules) of different countries by means of international conventions (particularly those concluded under the auspices of the Hague Conference on Private International Law) and regional conventions and legislation (particularly within the European Union). While the former have had only limited success, as has already been seen, European legislation has achieved a high degree of uniformity at a regional level. Also, a doctrine known as renvoi is sometimes used, in a rather haphazard way, to achieve uniformity, as shall be seen.

1.63 It should be noted that the fact that different countries have different choice of law rules is only one reason why litigation may be brought in a seemingly inappropriate forum. Even when both countries adopt the same choice of law rule, there might still be procedural advantages for the claimant to bring proceedings in one country rather than another which means that forum shopping will still continue. For example, in *Maharanee of Baroda* it was questions surrounding the admissibility of evidence and possible delay in France that prompted the plaintiff to sue in England.

2. How can foreign law be applied?

1.64 Having accepted that justice might best be served by the application of a foreign law, another question nevertheless presents itself. How can an English judge apply foreign law? Is it not an abdication of sovereignty for an English judge sitting in an English court to apply, say, Mexican law? This question is easily answered. While one constantly refers to judges 'applying' foreign law, this is not technically correct. The truth is that the only law the judge applies is the English conflict of laws rule, which is clearly as much a part of English law as any other English rule. That English rule might refer the matter to a foreign law. The judge, however, being untrained in foreign laws, cannot 'apply' that foreign law, but rather relies on an expert who gives evidence on that foreign law as a matter of *fact* and the judge then applies that foreign fact solution to decide the case. In a sense, this is no different from what happens in every domestic case. In an English murder prosecution, the relevant law that is applied is that the defendant must have acted with intent to kill or cause grievous bodily harm. Whether the defendant actually possessed such an intention is a matter of fact which needs to be established by evidence. That finding of fact resolves the case. So too, in the conflict of laws. In *Maharanee of Baroda v Wildenstein*[49] the English conflicts rule at that time was that matters of contract should be governed by the law of closest connection, which would have been French law. That rule is the law applied in the case. To reach an outcome, however, the facts need to be applied to the law. The French solution to the problem is part of the relevant facts. Evidence must be given as to what that French fact solution would be and the case can then be decided.

---

[49] [1972] 2 QB 283.

3. Mechanics of the process

1.65 Having established the rationale of, and justification for, choice of law rules that can lead to the application of either English or a foreign law, it is now necessary to explain the mechanics of this process. This raises several important and sometimes complex issues.

(A) Classification

(i) Introduction

1.66 The conflict of laws is highly compartmentalised. For example, there are different choice of law rules for movables and immovables. If a British person living in Mexico were to die intestate, the rule for determining how the deceased's property should devolve is as follows: intestate succession to movables is governed by the law of the deceased's domicile at the date of death (lex domicilii ultimi). The court has to ascertain where the deceased was domiciled at the relevant time and then, using expert evidence, has to ascertain what the relevant intestate succession rules of that country are so that it can dispose of the case according to those rules. If, however, this same intestate person were to leave an estate consisting of land, the appropriate rule would be: intestate succession to immovable property is governed by the law of the place where the land is situated (lex situs). This compartmentalisation is also evident in relation to the validity of marriage. To determine the validity of a marriage there are two rules to be applied: formal validity of marriage (details relating to the marriage ceremony such as the number of witnesses and how the ceremony needs to be performed) is governed by the law of the place where the marriage took place (lex loci celebrationis) and essential validity of marriage (the important matters relating to the parties themselves such as the age at which they can marry) is normally governed by the law of the parties' domicile at the date of the marriage. To take a final example: if a dispute relates to whether a will is revoked by a subsequent marriage, one has to determine whether this is an issue relating to matrimonial property or succession. If it is the former, the applicable law is the law of the matrimonial domicile. If it is the latter, the relevant choice of law rule refers to the law of the deceased's domicile (for movables).

1.67 As a result of there being different choice of law rules for such closely related questions, the first step in the choice of law process is to categorise the factual situation or the relevant foreign rule into a precise legal category. This process of allocating the relevant facts or relevant legal rules into a legal category is known as classification or characterisation.

1.68 Classification has been the subject of a great deal of academic discussion.[50] Various kinds of classification problem can arise, and, indeed, a major point of academic disagreement in a particular case may be over what it is that has to be characterised: the

---

[50] See Dicey, Morris and Collins, *The Conflict of Laws* (15th edn, 2012) pp 38–55; Cheshire, North and Fawcett, *Private International Law* (14th edn, 2008) pp 41–50; Falconbridge, *Selected Essays on the Conflict of Laws* (2nd edn, 1954); Robertson, *Characterization in the Conflict of Laws* (1940); Harris, 'Does Choice of Law Make Any Sense?' (2004) 57 CLP 305.

facts, the cause of action, the legal issue, rules of domestic law, or rules of foreign law.[51] The main problem that arises at this stage, however, is one of determining by which law the process of classification is to be effected. Should this question be resolved by the lex fori or by the potentially applicable foreign law?

(ii) Approaches to classification

1.69 Although various theories have been advanced by writers, the courts have used differing approaches without expressly espousing any particular theory.

(a) The lex fori

1.70 Traditionally, the answer is that it is for the lex fori, English law, to classify facts or legal rules into a legal category. Two examples will illustrate this approach. In *Apt v Apt*,[52] an English domiciled woman accepted a marriage proposal from an Argentinian domiciliary. Unable to attend her marriage ceremony, she executed a power of attorney authorising a friend to stand in for her at the ceremony which was duly celebrated by proxy in Argentina. In assessing the validity of this marriage, the English court had to classify the issue as being one relating to essentials or one relating to formalities. If, on the one hand, it had decided that the issue of proxy marriages affected essentials, the marriage would have been held void: the essential validity of a marriage is governed by the law of domicile; the woman was domiciled in England and by English law proxy marriages are not valid. On the other hand, if this were a matter relating to formal validity, the lex loci celebrationis, Argentinian law, could be applied, under which the marriage was valid. The English court, without any reference to the Argentinian classification of the issue, decided that under English law this was a matter of formal validity and, therefore, the marriage was valid.

1.71 The second example is the case of *Ogden v Ogden*,[53] which concerned a French domiciliary who married in England without obtaining his parents' consent. Under French law the fact that he had not obtained this consent rendered the marriage voidable, but under English law he was old enough that such consent was not required. This divergence presented a problem of classification. If the requirement of parental consent was classified as relating to capacity to marry, any rules of the law of the husband's domicile which are rules of capacity must be applied. If, however, this was classified as a matter relating to formal validity, any rules of the law of the country in which the marriage was celebrated which are rules of formal validity are to be applied. So, was the French rule one of capacity, in which case it would be applicable? Or was it a rule of formality, in which case it would not be applicable? The English court classified it as a rule of formal validity, which meant that it was not to be applied, for the marriage had been celebrated in England. Accordingly, the marriage was held to be valid.

---

[51] See, eg, *Macmillan Inc v Bishopsgate Investment Trust plc (No 3)* [1996] 1 WLR 387, where there are references to classifying the 'issue', 'the question in this action', 'the relevant rule of law', and a 'judicial concept or category'. See, further, Forsyth, 'Characterisation Revisited: An Essay in the Theory and Practice of the English Conflict of Laws' (1998) 114 LQR 141.
[52] [1948] P 83.   [53] [1908] P 46.

1.72 This case demonstrates the illusory nature of the dispute whether it is facts or legal rules that are being classified. One approach is to assert that the facts of this case had to be classified into one of the two legal categories as relating to either capacity or formal validity. Having categorised the facts as raising the legal issue of formal validity, the court was able to apply the appropriate choice of law rule. The parties married in England by which law the husband did not need parental consent and, accordingly, the marriage was declared valid. The other approach is that the only live issue in this case concerned the French rule that a man of the husband's age needed parental consent without which the marriage was voidable. The court had to classify this French rule as relating to capacity (in which case it would have been applicable) or to formalities (in which case it was not applicable). The court adopted the latter approach and the marriage was valid. It made no difference which approach was adopted. In essence, the English court was having to classify the legal issue and whether the relevant rule (relating to parental consent) fell within that legal categorisation. It makes no difference whether the categorisation of the issue preceded the determination of whether the French rule came within that category, or whether it was the classification of the French rule that determined the category. The outcome, and the process by which that outcome was achieved, is the same. It is the failure to grasp this simple point that has generated much of the confusion surrounding the classification problem.

1.73 According to the lex fori approach, English domestic rules should be classified in the same way as they are in domestic law, and foreign domestic rules should be classified in the same way as the equivalent English domestic rules. In English domestic law the rule that a minor requires parental consent for marriage is classified as a rule of formality, and in *Ogden v Ogden* the court assumed that the equivalent French rule should be classified in the same way. The main advantage of this approach, apart from simplicity and predictability, is that it enables the English court to maintain control over its own conflicts rules; otherwise, it 'would no longer be master in its own home'.[54] To apply any other law presupposes that it is an applicable law (that is what the words 'lex causae' signify). It is impossible to be referred to a foreign lex causae other than by means of a choice of law rule and choice of law rules can only be attached to legal categories. It follows that this initial categorisation can only be effected by the lex fori because at that stage one does not know what the lex causae is. However, this rationale does not stand up to close analysis. In *Ogden v Ogden* there were only two possible applicable laws, English law and French law, and the reason that French law was a possibly applicable law was because of the English conflict of laws rule that capacity is governed by the law of domicile. If, for example, the French domiciliary had been a German national and habitually resident in Italy, the laws of Germany and Italy would not have been potentially applicable laws because there is no English choice of law rule that any aspect of validity of marriage is governed by the law of nationality or habitual residence. In short, the issue could have been classified by French law without the English court 'losing control' over its conflicts rules.

---

[54] Dicey, Morris and Collins, *The Conflict of Laws* (15th edn, 2012) p 42.

1.74 There are two main disadvantages of the lex fori approach. First, purporting to apply a foreign law, but ignoring its classifications, can result in applying a distorted law that is effectively the law of 'nowhere'. Imagine if the laws of England and France in *Ogden v Ogden* had been reversed so that lack of parental consent was regarded as a matter of capacity by English law and a matter of formal validity by French law. Classification by the lex fori would result in the French rule being construed as relating to capacity and hence applicable, thereby invalidating the marriage, despite the fact that by French law itself its rule would not have been applicable on the facts. It is argued that it is pointless purporting to apply a foreign law, unless it is applied in toto, including its classification rules. This argument, however, is premised on the assumption that application of a foreign law actually means applying the law as it would be applied by the foreign court. This, however, is rarely the case. Whenever the doctrine of renvoi[55] is not applied there is a risk that the law being applied is not the same as would actually be applied by the foreign court and, as shall be examined shortly, there are good reasons for rejecting the doctrine of renvoi.

1.75 The second claimed disadvantage of the lex fori approach is that the similarity between the foreign rule and the English rule may be superficial and misleading, for the nature, purpose, and effects of the foreign rule may be quite different from those of the English rule. That was so in *Ogden v Ogden* for, under English law, if a party marries without parental consent, the marriage is nevertheless valid, while by French law the marriage was voidable. This difference might well require different classification for conflicts purposes. Further, the English court will often be called upon to classify legal rules, issues, or institutions that have no analogy in English law. For example, English law has no obvious counterpart to the continental regimes of community of property, to the adoption of adults, to opposite-sex registered partnership, to polygamy, to legally binding agreements not supported by consideration, and so on. The short answer to this last point is that one of the main functions of the conflict of laws is to deal legally with just such situations that do not exist in English law; foreign legal concepts cannot be disregarded just because they are unknown to English law. Accordingly, following the lex fori approach, the English court simply identifies the nearest English analogue to the foreign provision. For example, cases involving polygamous marriages of foreign domiciliaries are classified as matters of marriage. Such classifications are effected, not by following the nomenclature adopted by the foreign law, but by examining the incidents of the status or legal relationship to ascertain its nearest English counterpart.[56]

(b) The lex causae

1.76 The alternative theory is that classification should be according to the lex causae, which means that a legal rule should be classified according to the law of which it is a part.

---

[55] Under the doctrine of renvoi, the lex causae is interpreted as meaning the whole of the applicable law, including its conflict of laws rules. See paras 1.106–1.130.

[56] See, eg, *National Bank of Greece and Athens SA v Metliss* [1958] AC 509; *Adams v National Bank of Greece and Athens SA* [1961] AC 255; *Wight v Eckhardt Marine GmbH* [2004] 1 AC 147; *Société Eram Shipping Co Ltd v Hong Kong and Shanghai Banking Corp Ltd* [2004] 1 AC 260. These cases are discussed fully in Dicey, Morris and Collins, *The Conflict of Laws* (15th edn, 2012) pp 47–9.

The English court should classify a French rule as it is classified in French law, not in the way the equivalent English rule is classified by English law. If the English court has to decide the validity of the marriage of a person who at the time of the marriage was domiciled in France, then the English court must apply all rules which French law regards as rules of capacity. The court did not do this in *Ogden v Ogden*,[57] where the rule about parental consent was classified by French law as one of capacity.

1.77 A case in which the English court did follow the lex causae approach is *Re Maldonado's Estate*.[58] The deceased died intestate, domiciled in Spain, leaving movable property in England. She left no next-of-kin. In these circumstances, by English law, the Crown was entitled to the property as bona vacantia, while by Spanish law the Spanish state was entitled to it. Many countries have the rule that if a person dies intestate leaving no relatives entitled to succeed to his estate, then the property goes to the state. But, the rule is classified differently in different systems. In some systems it is regarded as a rule of succession, the state succeeding to the property as intestate heir in the same way as an individual. In other systems, the rule that the property goes to the state is regarded not as a rule of succession but as one of property law, under which the state is entitled to seize ownerless property. Such a right of the state to take ownerless property is called the ius regale.

1.78 There were two choice of law rules to be considered in *Re Maldonado*. One was that intestate succession to movables is governed by the law of the country in which the deceased was domiciled at her death. The other was that the acquisition of title to movable property otherwise than by succession (including the right to seize ownerless property) is governed by the law of the country where the property is situated. If the Spanish rule under which the state was entitled to the property were classified as a rule of succession, then it would be applicable because the deceased died domiciled in Spain. If, however, it were classified as a rule of property law, then it would not be applied, for the property was in England, not Spain. In that situation the Crown would take the estate. The evidence showed that by Spanish law the state's right to the estate was regarded as a right of succession. The court held that as the succession was governed by Spanish law, all rules which, according to Spanish law, were rules of succession should be applied by the English court. In other words, it followed the lex causae approach. The consequence was that the Spanish state took the estate. In other cases[59] where, according to the foreign law which governed the succession, the state's right to the property was a ius regale, not a right of succession, the English estates of intestates who died without next-of-kin were awarded to the Crown.

1.79 Another case where classification was effected according to the lex causae was *Re Cohn*.[60] In this case a mother and daughter were both killed in an air-raid in London in 1941. By the mother's will the daughter succeeded to the mother's estate if the daughter survived the mother. It could not, however, be ascertained whether either had survived

---

[57] [1908] P 46.   [58] [1954] P 223.
[59] *Re Barnett's Trusts* [1902] 1 Ch 847; *Re Musurus's Estate* [1936] 2 All ER 1666.   [60] [1945] Ch 5.

the other, both having been killed in the same explosion. As the mother had been domiciled in Germany at the time of her death, the succession to her estate was governed by German law. Under English law, as provided by section 184 of the Law of Property Act 1925, under such circumstances 'such deaths shall . . . be presumed to have occurred in order of seniority, and accordingly the younger shall be deemed to have survived the elder'. According to German law, however, there was a provision that, if it could not be proved which had died first, it was presumed that they died simultaneously. Which presumption was applicable?

1.80 The court first examined the English provision and rejected the view that the presumption was a rule of procedure, in which case it would have had to apply, following the general rule that all questions of procedure are governed by the lex fori. It was not part of the law of evidence of the lex fori which assisted in the resolution of the factual question of who died first; rather it was a substantive rule of succession, in effect laying down who should be entitled to succeed to a deceased person's estate when it was unknown whether or not some other person had survived her. The court then examined the German presumption to ascertain whether it was a rule of evidence (in which case it would not have been applicable) or a rule of succession (which would be applicable). This classification was effected according to the lex causae. Construing the provision according to its location in the German Civil Code, it was concluded that it was a rule of succession which could be applied. Accordingly, the daughter did not take under the will.

1.81 This case highlights one of the problems with this approach to classification. If the German rule had been found to be a rule of evidence (as it could easily have been as the English court went no further than examining where the provision appeared in the German Civil Code), it could not have been applied. As the English rule was also not applicable, the result would have been an impasse with neither law applicable. Similarly, there would have been a problem had the court decided that the English presumption was procedural, but the German one was substantive. In this situation both laws would have been potentially applicable, although in such cases there can be little doubt that the English procedural rule would have trumped the foreign substantive provision.

1.82 It is clear that, in addition to the above problems, classification according to the lex causae does not necessarily produce a satisfactory result. Suppose that, before 1975,[61] a Roman Catholic man domiciled in Malta married a woman domiciled in Scotland in a register office in England. By Maltese law the marriage was void because the husband, being a Roman Catholic, could validly marry only in a Catholic church. If the Maltese rule were classified as a rule of formalities, the Maltese invalidity would be immaterial, because the marriage was celebrated in England, not Malta. Maltese law, however, classified its rule as one of essential validity rather than form. If the English court classified the rule in that way the marriage would be void, because Maltese law would be

---

[61] Maltese law on this point was altered by the Marriage Act 1975, s 18.

applicable under the relevant English choice of law rule. However, the English court would consider the marriage valid,[62] and rightly so. The English conflicts rule that formalities of marriage are governed by the lex loci celebrationis is surely designed precisely to deal with such questions as whether a marriage must be celebrated in a church. If the English court were to accept the Maltese classification of its rule as one of essential validity, it would be contradicting the policy of its own conflicts rule.

1.83 It is by no means clear that the lex causae approach was the correct one in *Re Maldonado*. Is it sensible that in such cases the question whether the Crown or the foreign state takes the property should depend on how the foreign law chooses to label its rule? The facts of the situation and the issue to be decided are the same whatever the foreign classification, so the same choice of law rule should apply, however the foreign law chooses to classify its rule.[63] Why should the outcome in *Re Cohn* have depended on the location of the presumption in the German Civil Code?

(c) The better view[64]

1.84 The reason why the court has to classify issues is to decide within which choice of law rule they fall. The problem then is for the court to ascertain the scope of its own choice of law rule. Like all rules, choice of law rules are expressed in general terms, so their meaning may have to be elucidated to decide the particular case. In a case like *Ogden v Ogden*,[65] the problem really is to decide what sorts of domestic rules come within the meaning of 'capacity' for the purposes of the choice of law rule that capacity to marry is governed by the law of the domicile, and what sorts of domestic rules come within the meaning of 'formalities' for the purposes of the choice of law rule that formal validity is governed by the lex loci celebrationis.

1.85 There is nothing peculiar to the conflict of laws in this need to determine the scope of a rule of law and to interpret it to see whether it extends to a doubtful case. The same has to be done with rules of contract, tort, or any other area of law in hard cases. The main difference is that the subject-matter of domestic rules of contract or tort is fact; the question is whether the particular facts fall within the rule in question. The subject-matter of choice of law rules is not facts but rules of domestic law; the question is whether the domestic rule in question falls within the scope of the choice of law rule.

1.86 How is the court to determine the scope of its choice of law rules in novel cases in order to decide within which of them the domestic rule in question comes? As when determining the scope of any other rule, it should seek out the reason or policy behind the possibly relevant choice of law rules and, on that basis, decide which is the appropriate

---

[62] *Gray v Formosa* [1963] P 259.
[63] The better approach would be to classify all the domestic rules as ones of property. It has been held that the Crown's right to take the estate under the Administration of Estates Act 1925 is a right of succession: *Re Mitchell* [1954] Ch 525; but it must also be a ius regale for conflicts purposes, otherwise no state might be entitled to the property.
[64] This approach is similar to that of Lipstein, 'Conflict of Laws 1921–1971: The Way Ahead' [1972B] CLJ 67, 77–83.
[65] [1908] P 46.

one for the instant case. For example, suppose that the reason for the choice of law rule for capacity to marry is that the laws of the countries to which the parties belong are the appropriate ones to decide whether the marriage relationship in question is permissible (because those are the countries whose laws are most fitted to determine whether an intending spouse has sufficient judgement or maturity), while the reason for the choice of law rule for formal validity is that if the marriage relationship is permissible, the law most appropriate to determine how it should be celebrated is the law of the country where it is celebrated. Should it not follow that the French rule in *Ogden v Ogden* requiring parental consent for a valid marriage should have been treated as a rule of capacity?

1.87 It might be found in a particular case that the domestic rule in question does not fit comfortably within the reason or policy behind any existing choice of law rule. In such a case a new choice of law rule will have to be formulated, on the basis of the more general principles underlying choice of law. The various legal categories recognised by the law are 'man-made, not natural. They have no inherent value, beyond their purpose in assisting to select the most appropriate law.'[66] For example, it may be that the most suitable solution to the problem of determining which law decides whether a will is revoked by marriage is the creation of a separate conflicts category for this issue.[67]

1.88 In determining the scope of substantive rules of domestic law to see whether the facts of the particular case fall within them, it is of course first necessary that the facts should have been correctly ascertained if the right result is to be reached. Similarly, when determining the scope of choice of law rules to see whether particular domestic rules fall within their rationale or policy, it is necessary that the true nature and effect of those domestic rules be ascertained. For example, if the French rule about parental consent in *Ogden v Ogden* should have been classified as one of capacity, it does not follow that the different French rule about such consent which was at issue in *Simonin v Mallac*[68] is also a rule of capacity. In the latter case, the relevant rule provided that the marriage was ultimately permissible without consent if consent had been formally requested and refused three times.[69] Such a rule can reasonably be regarded as being concerned with the manner of celebrating a permissible marriage relationship. In ascertaining the true nature and effects of the domestic rules, English or foreign, their classification within the laws to which they belong will be helpful. However, such classification cannot be conclusive, because after the nature and effect of the domestic rules have been determined, the question still remains whether they fall within the meaning of the English choice of law rule.

(iii) English law

1.89 The English courts have generally not bothered themselves with the difficult issues raised in the preceding sections and, with notable exceptions such as *Re Maldonado*[70] and

---

[66] Mance LJ in *Raiffeisen Zentralbank Österreich AG v Five Star General Trading LLC* [2001] QB 825 at 840.
[67] See para 9.89.   [68] (1860) 2 Sw & Tr 67.   [69] See para 7.17.   [70] [1954] P 223.

Re Cohn,[71] have tended to classify all issues according to the lex fori. Recent dicta, however, have started emphasising that 'the conflict of laws does not depend (like a game or even an election) upon the application of rigid rules, but upon a search for appropriate principles to meet particular situations'[72] and that while classification is to be effected by the lex fori this process must be undertaken in a 'broad internationalist spirit'.[73]

1.90 Numerous examples of such classifications will be encountered in this book: the requirement of parental consent[74] and laws permitting proxy marriages[75] have been classified as relating to formal validity of marriage; whether parties can lawfully contract marriages of convenience[76] and the effect of impotence and wilful refusal to consummate a marriage[77] have been held to be matters affecting the essential validity of a marriage; marriages where a man is permitted one primary wife and several secondary wives or concubines (who have some, but lesser, legal rights) have been classified as polygamous marriages;[78] whether a will is revoked by marriage has been classed as a matter of matrimonial property;[79] agreements not supported by consideration that are contractually binding by the law governing the agreement have been classified as contracts;[80] a contractual defence to a claim in tort has been classified as a matter of contract;[81] whether a bona fide purchase of shares provides a defence to a claim for restitution is a matter of property in shares;[82] whether one spouse is liable to another in tort has been held in the United States to be a matter of status and not tort;[83] whether a cause of action survives against the estate of a deceased tortfeasor has been treated in the United States as a matter relating to the administration of an estate and not as a matter of tort.[84] The problem of classification has also been addressed occasionally by statute. Section 3 of the Wills Act 1963 provides that any requirements of a foreign law that certain types of testators must observe special formalities and that some types of witnesses must possess certain qualifications are to be treated as formal requirements. Whether a claim is barred by lapse of time is classified by section 1 of the Foreign Limitation Periods Act 1984 as substantive, rather than procedural.

1.91 A few notable exceptions to the lex fori rule exist in English law. First, it is well established that whether property is movable or immovable is to be determined by the lex situs.[85] Secondly, as a consequence of the increasing Europeanisation of the conflict of laws, many concepts are being given an autonomous interpretation.[86] For example,

---

[71] [1945] Ch 5.
[72] Mance LJ in *Raiffeisen Zentralbank Österreich AG v Five Star General Trading LLC* [2001] QB 825 at 841.
[73] Ibid, 840.   [74] *Ogden v Ogden* [1908] P 46; *Simonin v Mallac* (1860) 2 Sw & Tr 67.
[75] *Apt v Apt* [1948] P 83.   [76] *Vervaeke v Smith* [1981] Fam 77.
[77] *De Reneville v De Reneville* [1948] P 100.   [78] *Lee v Lau* [1967] P 14.
[79] *Re Martin* [1900] P 211.
[80] *Re Bonacina* [1912] 2 Ch 394. This would still be the case under the Rome I Regulation, art 1(1). See Chapter 4.
[81] The majority view in *Sayers v International Drilling Co NV* [1971] 1 WLR 1176.
[82] *Macmillan Inc v Bishopsgate Investment Trust plc (No 3)* [1996] 1 WLR 387.
[83] *Haumschild v Continental Casualty Co* 7 Wis 2d 130, 95 NW 2d 814 (1959).
[84] *Grant v McAuliffe* 41 Cal 2d 859 (1953).   [85] *Re Hoyles* [1911] 1 Ch 179.
[86] See, generally, Illmer, 'Neutrality Matters—Some Thoughts about the Rome Regulations and the So-called Dichotomy of Substance and Procedure in European Private International Law' (2009) 28 CJQ 237.

whether a matter relates to contract or tort for the purposes of article 7 of the Brussels I Recast is to be determined by European law as opposed to domestic English law.[87] For the purposes of the Rome I Regulation it would appear that the term 'contractual obligations', used to define the scope of the Regulation, should also be given an autonomous European meaning.[88] It follows that an issue could be construed as contractual by European law and thus within the ambit of the Rome I Regulation, despite the fact that, under domestic English law, it might be construed as tortious. Similarly, under the Rome II Regulation the concepts of 'non-contractual obligations'[89] and 'non-contractual obligations arising out of a tort/delict'[90] must be given an autonomous interpretation. This means that some issues could be classified as tortious even though they do not constitute a tort under domestic English law. However, these European classifications of concepts and issues are not true exceptions to the lex fori rule in that European law is part of English law. Further exceptions relating to the classification of matters as substantive and procedural exist; these are examined in the following section.

(iv) Substance and procedure

1.92 As a general rule, matters of substance are governed by the applicable law while matters of procedure are governed by the lex fori, English law. Issues of substance are those relating to the 'existence, extent or enforceability of the rights or duties of the parties'.[91] Issues of procedure are those concerned with the method of trial, such as rules of evidence, where it would not be practicable for the English court to use foreign procedures to try a dispute simply because, for example, a contract was governed by French law.

1.93 However, in certain contexts the distinction between substance and procedure is far from clear-cut[92] and English courts, either because of considerations of convenience or through a desire to avoid the application of a foreign law in a particular situation, used to take an expansive view of what constitutes procedure with the result that doubtful cases were classified as procedural. However, as the following examples show, English law, particularly where it has been influenced by European developments, is now adopting a more balanced approach through a broader interpretation of what constitutes a substantive matter.[93]

(a) Evidence

1.94 The traditional position was that all matters of evidence (for example, admissibility of evidence, requirements of written evidence, burdens of proof, presumptions, etc)

---

[87] Case 9/87 *SPRL Arcado v SA Haviland* [1988] ECR 1539; Case 189/87 *Kalfelis v Bankhaus Schröder, Münchmeyer, Hengst & Co* [1988] ECR 5565; Case C–548/12 *Brogsitter v Fabrication de Montres Normandes EURL* [2014] ILPr 20.
[88] See para 4.7.   [89] Art 1(1).   [90] Art 4(1).
[91] *John Pfeiffer Pty Ltd v Rogerson* (2000) 203 CLR 503 at 543 (High Court, Australia).
[92] See generally Garnett, *Substance and Procedure in Private International Law* (2012).
[93] Carruthers, 'Substance and Procedure in the Conflict of Laws: A Continuing Debate in Relation to Damages' (2004) 53 ICLQ 691.

were regarded as procedural matters to be governed by the lex fori. While this still remains the general rule, in several important respects this position has been eroded by European developments. For example, while both the Rome I Regulation (dealing with contractual obligations) and the Rome II Regulation (dealing with non-contractual obligations) provide that matters of evidence and procedure are excluded from their scope,[94] with regard to the burden of proof and presumptions both Regulations provide that these matters are governed by the applicable law.[95]

1.95 With regard to the requirement of written evidence, section 4 of the Statute of Frauds (1677) provided that actions could not be brought on certain contracts in the absence of a written agreement or other document signed by the party being sued. This statute applies now only to contracts of guarantee. In *Leroux v Brown*[96] it was held that the provisions of this statute are procedural and, therefore, applicable to contracts governed by a foreign law. This decision would now be decided differently as article 11(1) of the Rome I Regulation provides that a contract is formally valid if it complies with, inter alia, the law governing the contract or the law of the country where it was concluded.

(b) Statutes of limitation

1.96 A similar approach to that in *Leroux v Brown*[97] used to be taken by the courts to statutes of limitation—that is, laws laying down periods within which claims of various kinds can be brought. At common law, the law as to limitation is generally regarded as procedural. The common law approach was, however, replaced by the Foreign Limitation Periods Act 1984, which provides that where any matter is governed by the law of a foreign country, then that country's law on limitation shall apply irrespective of whether it classifies the rule as substantive or procedural,[98] except where application of the foreign law would conflict with public policy.[99] A rule will conflict with public policy, inter alia, to the extent that its application would cause undue hardship to a party.[100]

1.97 European developments have further eroded the original common law position. With regard to contractual obligations, the Rome I Regulation provides that the applicable law governs 'the various ways of extinguishing obligations, and prescription and limitation of actions'.[101] With regard to non-contractual obligations, the Rome II Regulation provides that the applicable law shall govern 'the manner in which an obligation may be extinguished and the rules of prescription and limitation, including rules relating to the commencement, interruption and suspension of a period of prescription or limitation'.[102]

---

[94] Art 1(3) of both Regulations. This does not necessarily mean that such matters must be governed by the lex fori; their exclusion from the scope of the Regulations means that national laws can decide whether to apply the lex fori or the lex causae: Illmer, 'Neutrality Matters—Some Thoughts about the Rome Regulations and the So-called Dichotomy of Substance and Procedure in European Private International Law' (2009) 28 CJQ 237, 242.
[95] Rome I Regulation, art 18(1); Rome II Regulation, art 22(1). [96] (1852) 12 CB 801.
[97] Ibid. [98] S 1(1). [99] S 2(1).
[100] S 2(2). See *Harley v Smith* [2010] CP Rep 33; *Bank St Petersburg v Arkhangelsky* [2014] 1 WLR 4360.
[101] Art 12(1)(d). [102] Art 15(h).

(c) Remedies and damages

1.98 The traditional view is that, in relation to both contracts and torts, the nature of the remedy is a question of procedure so that, for example, it is for English law to determine whether specific performance or an injunction can be granted or only damages awarded. Given the modern trend to limit 'procedure' to matters which govern and regulate the mode and conduct of the proceedings, the traditional view may require reconsideration. For example, it has been argued that whether a remedy of specific performance should be granted is not an issue that affects the mode of conduct of court proceedings; rather, whether such a remedy is available is part of the substance of the claim and so should be characterised as substantive.[103]

1.99 As regards damages, questions of substance—such as remoteness of damage[104] and the kind of loss for which damages are recoverable (for example, non-pecuniary as well as pecuniary)[105]—are governed by the lex causae.[106] For example in *Boys v Chaplin*[107] a majority of the House of Lords concluded that whether a particular head of damage (pain and suffering) could be claimed was a substantive matter to be determined by the lex causae. On the other hand, questions relating to the measure or quantification of damages are classified as procedural and are governed by the lex fori, English law.[108] In *Boys v Chaplin* the question of how much money should be awarded for pain and suffering was determined by English principles of quantification. This rule was reaffirmed by the House of Lords in *Harding v Wealands*.[109] While this approach still applies to the tort of defamation,[110] for all other non-contractual obligations the Rome II Regulation provides that the applicable law governs 'the existence, the nature and the assessment of damage or the remedy claimed'.[111]

1.100 With regard to contract, the Rome I Regulation provides that the consequences of breach 'including the assessment of damages in so far as it is governed by rules of law' is a substantive matter governed by the applicable law provided it is 'within the limits of the powers conferred on the court by its procedural law'.[112] The precise effect of this provision is, as yet, untested. Nevertheless, as many issues of quantification (such as whether the claimant is entitled to the loss value of damaged property or the cost of repairing it) are mainly determined by the operation of legal rules,[113] it seems likely that a fairly broad range of matters that were traditionally classified as procedural should now be classified as substantive.

---

[103] Panagopoulos, 'Substance and Procedure in Private International Law' (2005) 1 Journal of Private International Law 69, 87.
[104] *D'Almeida Araujo (J) Lda v Sir Frederick Becker & Co Ltd* [1953] 2 QB 329.
[105] *Boys v Chaplin* [1971] AC 356.   [106] See also *Cox v Ergo Versicherung* [2014] AC 1379.
[107] [1971] AC 356.   [108] *Coupland v Arabian Gulf Petroleum Co* [1983] 1 WLR 1136.
[109] [2007] 2 AC 1. In the Court of Appeal it had been held that a rule which places a cap on damages is a substantive rule and that procedural matters should be limited to the modes or rules used to govern and regulate the conduct of the court's proceedings ([2005] 1 WLR 1539). This approach was disapproved by the House of Lords.
[110] See paras 5.119–5.121.
[111] Art 15(c). See *Maher v Groupama Grand Est* [2009] 1 WLR 1752; *Jacobs v Motor Insurers' Bureau* [2010] 1 All ER (Comm) 1128.
[112] Art 12(1)(c).   [113] See para 4.181.

1.101 This approach of limiting the matters to be classified as procedural is to be welcomed. The main rationale of subjecting issues of procedure to the rules of the lex fori is that of convenience. Such a rationale collapses in cases where the English court is dealing with, for example, heads of damages that do not exist in the forum. In such cases applying foreign rules of assessment may actually be more convenient.[114] Further, the more matters are classified as substantive and not procedural, the less is the risk of applying a distorted law. The function of choice of law rules is to identify an appropriate law which, as far as possible, should be applied as a coherent whole. Matters should only be classified as procedural if the English court is 'genuinely procedurally incompetent' to apply the foreign law.[115]

(B) Connecting factors

1.102 The characteristic form of choice of law rules is to identify the governing law by means of a connecting factor, consisting of a link between an event, a thing, a transaction, or a person, on the one hand, and a country, on the other. For example, in the rule that the essential validity of marriage is governed by the law of domicile, domicile is the connecting factor; it provides the connection or link with a country. Connecting factors may be quite precise—for example, title to land is governed by the law of the country in which the land is situated; the formal validity of a marriage is governed by the law of the country in which the marriage was celebrated. Some connecting factors are, however, rather vague; for example, at common law, in the absence of choice by the parties, the validity of a contract is governed by the law of the country with which the contract has its closest connection.

1.103 The rules of jurisdiction and recognition of foreign judgments also make use of connecting factors in determining the circumstances in which the English court should exercise jurisdiction or recognise a foreign judgment. For example, an English court has jurisdiction to grant a divorce if, inter alia, both spouses are habitually resident or domiciled in England[116] and many foreign divorces can be recognised, inter alia, if either party was domiciled or habitually resident in the foreign country at the date of the commencement of the divorce proceedings.[117]

1.104 A potential problem is that some common connecting factors, such as domicile, can be interpreted differently in different countries. For example, the concept of domicile is widely used in the United States but has there acquired a rather different meaning from that adopted under English law. If one were trying to decide whether a person had acquired a domicile in Texas, should one adopt the English or the Texan meaning of 'domicile'? Or, to put the matter more technically, by which law should the connecting factor, domicile, be classified? Again, the answer is for most purposes clear. Any

---

[114] Carruthers, 'Substance and Procedure in the Conflict of Laws: A Continuing Debate in Relation to Damages' (2004) 53 ICLQ 691, 709.
[115] Harris, 'Does Choice of Law Make any Sense?' (2004) 57 CLP 305, 311.   [116] See paras 8.7–8.13.
[117] Different rules apply to the recognition of divorces granted by the courts of most Member States of the European Union. See Chapter 8.

such classification must be made by English law, the lex fori. For example, when it is necessary to decide whether a person is domiciled in Texas, it is the English interpretation of domicile[118] that is employed. This is because no foreign law becomes potentially applicable until there has been a reference to it by an English choice of law rule with an English connecting factor. For instance, there might be a dispute as to whether a person is domiciled in Texas or California. Clearly, neither of these laws could be permitted to determine the outcome as they might both, under their respective laws, conclude that the person was domiciled there. The whole point of choice of law rules is to lead to the application of the appropriate law as determined by English law.

1.105 There are, however, a few exceptions to this well-established rule. For example, a foreign divorce, separation, or annulment (obtained in a non-Member State) can be recognised if either party was domiciled in the foreign country according to that country's conception of domicile in family matters.[119] Another exception is that in order to determine whether a person is domiciled in another Member State for the purposes of the Brussels I Recast, the English court must apply the law of that state.[120]

(C) Renvoi

(i) Introduction

1.106 Once the factual issue has been classified, a choice of law rule containing a connecting factor can be attached which will lead to the lex causae. This law might be, and indeed often is, English law. In such cases the role of the conflict of laws is complete and the matter can simply be decided according to domestic English law. However, when the lex causae is a foreign law, a further problem arises. Does this mean that the foreign domestic rules are applicable or should the foreign law in its entirety, including its choice of law rules, be applied? If the latter approach is adopted, the process is known as renvoi.[121] Take a simple example of intestate succession to movables (the factual issue) which is governed by the law of the deceased's domicile at the date of death (the choice of law rule) and suppose that the deceased was a British national who died domiciled in Mexico. The choice of law rule leads to the application of Mexican law. Does this mean the domestic (non-conflict) Mexican law of intestate succession which will determine how the property should devolve, or does it mean Mexican law in its entirety, including the Mexican conflicts rule? If it is the latter, one might find (as is common in civil law systems) that the Mexican conflicts rule would refer the question of intestate succession, not to the law of domicile, but to the law of nationality. In other words, under Mexican law this might be a conflicts case that would result in the application of British law. Assuming this is taken to mean English law,[122] does this mean the English domestic rules on intestate succession, or does it mean the whole of English

---

[118] *Re Annesley* [1926] Ch 692.   [119] Family Law Act 1986, s 46(5).   [120] Art 62(2).

[121] In some cases, for example determining the existence of an arbitration agreement in an international context, the domestic law of a country might involve the application of transnational law or rules. This is not renvoi, which involves applying another system of law: Lord Collins in *Dallah Real Estate and Tourism Co v Ministry of Religious Affairs of the Government of Pakistan* [2010] 3 WLR 1472 at [124], [125].

[122] See para 1.129.

law, including English conflicts rules? If it means the latter, it has already been seen that the English choice of law rules would refer to Mexican law. In short, if this approach were adopted one would have an impasse with the case being continually referred back and forth between English and Mexican law. This process of taking account of foreign conflicts rules which refer the case back to its starting-point is called remission. Where the foreign law's conflicts rules would refer the case to the law of a third country, the process is called transmission.

(ii) Application of renvoi in English law

1.107 It must be stressed at the outset that the doctrine of renvoi is not used in the vast majority of cases. It can only possibly be utilised if one party to the litigation expressly pleads it. Because of the cost and difficulty involved in proving foreign countries' choice of law rules and their rules on renvoi, this is seldom done. Furthermore, in most of the important commercial areas of the conflict of laws that now dominate the subject, the use of renvoi is expressly outlawed. For example, the doctrine of renvoi is excluded in the field of contract by the Rome I Regulation[123] and in cases involving non-contractual obligations by the Rome II Regulation.[124]

1.108 In areas where renvoi has not been expressly excluded, there is a 'presumption' that the doctrine is not applicable and there needs to be a 'strong reason' for it to be applied.[125] There are two approaches that could be adopted to determining whether the presumption should be rebutted. First, this could be done on a case-by-case, fact-specific basis under which the applicability of renvoi would depend on an evaluation of the policy of the English choice of law rule and the relevant foreign law: 'one should not answer the question in advance in such a manner as may, inadvertently, preclude application of the policy adopted by the foreign law'.[126] However, because such an approach could lead to uncertainty and 'a Tennysonian wilderness of single instances',[127] most English cases adopt the second approach that renvoi should apply only to certain 'classes of case'.[128] Following this latter approach, renvoi is generally regarded as not applicable in most commercial areas of law.[129] Equally, it does not apply to cases involving title to movable property.[130]

---

[123] Art 15.
[124] Art 24. Renvoi is also excluded by the Hague Protocol of 23 November 2007 on the Law Applicable to Maintenance Obligations which applies in tandem with the EU Maintenance Regulation but which has not been ratified by the United Kingdom. See para 8.187.
[125] *Jacobs v Motor Insurers Bureau* [2011] 1 WLR 2609 at [27].
[126] *Dornoch Ltd v Westminster International BV* [2009] 2 Lloyds Rep 191 at [89].
[127] Beatson J in *Blue Sky One Ltd v Mahan Air* [2010] EWHC 631 (Comm) at [172].   [128] Ibid, [173].
[129] For example, in matters relating to insurance, mortgages, negotiable instruments, partnerships, and dissolution of foreign companies (Cheshire, North and Fawcett, *Private International Law* (14th edn, 2008) p 71) and matters concerning title to shares in a company (*Macmillan Inc v Bishopsgate Investment Trust plc (No 3)* [1996] 1 WLR 387 at 399).
[130] Although there is some support for the application of renvoi in such cases (*Glencore International AG v Metro Trading International Inc* [2001] 1 Lloyd's Rep 284 at 297), more recent cases have rejected its application in this field: *Islamic Republic of Iran v Berend* [2007] 2 All ER (Comm) 132; *Blue Sky One Ltd v Mahan Air* [2010] EWHC 631 (Comm) at [172].

1.109 On the other hand, the doctrine has been applied in certain non-commercial classes of case. In particular, it has been applied to questions of intestate succession[131] and the essential validity of wills.[132] The EU Succession Regulation (in which the United Kingdom is not participating) also permits some use of renvoi: '[t]he application of the law of any third State specified by this Regulation shall mean the application of the rules of law in force in that State, including its rules of private international law in so far as those rules make a *renvoi* (a) to the law of a Member State; or (b) to the law of another third State which would apply its own law'.[133] It has also been applied to legitimation by subsequent marriage at common law.[134] It is generally accepted that renvoi should apply to cases involving title to immovable property.[135]

1.110 With regard to marriage, there is one case[136] in which renvoi was applied to capacity to marry after a foreign divorce. In addition, there is some authority[137] that if a marriage is not formally valid by the domestic law of the country in which it was celebrated, it will suffice if it is valid under the conflicts rules of that country. Most significantly, the doctrine received statutory endorsement (for the first time) in the field of civil partnerships. Under the Civil Partnership Act 2004 the parties must have capacity to enter into the relationship by the relevant law and must comply with the formalities of the relevant law.[138] The 'relevant law' is defined as the law of the country where the relationship is registered 'including its rules of private international law'.[139]

(iii) Approaches to renvoi

1.111 There are several approaches that can be adopted when there is a difference between the English and the relevant country's choice of law rules. The English court can either 'reject renvoi' and simply apply the domestic rules of the foreign country or it can take account of the foreign country's conflicts rules. If the latter course is adopted, this can be done in one of two ways: either by applying 'partial' or 'single' renvoi, on the one hand, or by applying 'total' or 'double' renvoi (also known as the 'foreign court theory'), on the other.

(a) Rejection of renvoi

1.112 If the doctrine of renvoi is rejected, when an English conflicts rule refers a matter to a foreign law, this is taken to mean the domestic, non-conflicts rules of that country. For example, if a person dies intestate domiciled in Mexico, the English conflicts rule requires that the distribution of the person's movable property should be governed by Mexican law as the law of domicile at the date of death. If renvoi is rejected, this means that the domestic rules of Mexican intestacy law are applied (for example, that the estate should be divided in set proportions between the surviving spouse and the children of the marriage). The fact that a Mexican court might regard this as a conflict of laws case and refer the matter to another law is disregarded.

---

[131] *Re O'Keefe* [1940] Ch 124.   [132] *Re Annesley* [1926] Ch 692; *Re Ross* [1930] 1 Ch 377.
[133] Art 34.   [134] *Re Askew* [1930] 2 Ch 259.   [135] *Re Ross* [1930] 1 Ch 377.
[136] *R v Brentwood Superintendent Registrar of Marriages, ex p Arias* [1968] 2 QB 956.
[137] *Taczanowska v Taczanowski* [1957] P 301.   [138] S 215(1).   [139] S 212(2).

(b) Partial renvoi

1.113 Under partial or single renvoi, the English court takes account of the conflicts rules of the country indicated by the English choice of law rule and applies the domestic law of the country referred to by that foreign choice of law rule. For example, suppose the English court has to decide who is entitled to movable property left in England by an intestate who died domiciled in Mexico, but who was a citizen of the United Kingdom. According to the English choice of law rule, the succession is governed by the law of the deceased's domicile, Mexican law. By Mexican choice of law rules, let it be supposed, intestate succession is governed by the law of the deceased's nationality at the date of his death, which is (let it be assumed again for the moment) English law. If, in these circumstances, the English court were to 'accept the remission' back to English law and apply English domestic law, without any further consideration of what the Mexican court would do in such a case, it would be following the doctrine of partial renvoi. This doctrine is used in some civil law countries.

(c) Total renvoi

1.114 Under total renvoi, also known as double renvoi or the foreign court theory of renvoi, the English court deals with the case in the same way as it would be dealt with by the court of the foreign country referred to by the English choice of law rule. The English judge has to 'don the mantle' of the foreign judge and try to decide the case exactly as the foreign judge would decide it. This means applying not only the foreign country's choice of law rule, but also its doctrine of renvoi and thus applying whatever domestic law the foreign court would apply. In the above example, where a citizen of the United Kingdom died domiciled in Mexico, the English choice of law rule refers to Mexican law. The English court, under total renvoi, applies not only the Mexican choice of law rule that the succession is governed by the law of nationality, English law, but also the Mexican rule relating to renvoi. So, if Mexican law adopts the doctrine of partial renvoi (or 'accepts the renvoi')—that is, if the Mexican court would take its choice of law rule to refer to English conflict of laws rules, and would accordingly apply Mexican domestic law—the English court would do likewise. If, however, Mexico rejects the doctrine of renvoi, so that its court would take its choice of law rule to refer to English domestic law, the English court would apply English domestic law.[140]

1.115 The operation of total renvoi is well illustrated by the case of *Re Annesley*,[141] where the testatrix, a British subject, died domiciled in France. The English court had to decide who was entitled to movable property she left in England. Her will was valid by English domestic law, but invalid by French domestic law to the extent that she had failed to leave two-thirds of her property to her children. Under the English choice of law rule, the essential validity of the will was governed by French law as the law of her domicile at her death. Russell J took this to mean that he must decide the case as a French court would decide it. By French choice of law rules, the succession was governed by English

---

[140] For a consideration of the problems that would result if Mexican law were to adopt total renvoi, see para 1.129.
[141] [1926] Ch 692.

law. But would a French court simply apply English domestic law (that is, reject renvoi), or would it 'accept the renvoi' (that is, use partial renvoi) and thus apply French domestic law? The experts on French law disagreed on this question, but it was held that the better view was that the French court would accept the renvoi. Accordingly, French domestic law was applied.

1.116 To the extent that renvoi is adopted in the English conflict of laws it seems to take the form of total, rather than partial, renvoi.[142] It is true that, in some cases where renvoi has been used, there has been no mention of the foreign country's rules of renvoi, but that can be explained in one case[143] on the basis that the foreign choice of law rule referred to the law of a second foreign country (transmission), as opposed to pointing back to England (remission), and the conflicts rule of the second foreign country was the same as that of the first. In such a case, a choice between total and partial renvoi does not arise. Of other cases[144] it could be argued that, in the absence of evidence that a foreign country uses renvoi, it is to be assumed that it does not (in which case the result is the same whether the English court uses total or partial renvoi).

(iv) Advantages of renvoi

1.117 There are several alleged advantages to the application of renvoi. First, it is claimed that it is self-defeating to purport to apply a foreign law unless one applies the solution that would actually be applied by the courts of the foreign country. If a British person dies intestate domiciled in Mexico leaving a movable estate in England, a court would be applying the law of 'nowhere' if it were to apply Mexican domestic law and ignore the fact that a Mexican court would (let it be assumed) not itself apply Mexican law, but would treat the case as a conflicts case and apply English law. According to this argument, the doctrine of partial renvoi is as objectionable as rejecting renvoi because under partial renvoi one is simply assuming (without investigation) that the foreign court would reject renvoi and apply the domestic law of the country to which its conflicts rules refer.

1.118 This so-called justification of renvoi is, however, problematic and depends upon the assumption that application of a foreign law means applying the solution that a foreign court would actually apply.[145] It is naïve to assert that an English court ever 'really' applies foreign law. The reality is that English rules on classification, the non-applicability of foreign procedural rules and the doctrine of public policy all ensure that often foreign law is not applied in its totality as it would be applied by the foreign court.

1.119 Secondly, it is claimed that, in some situations, renvoi will protect the reasonable expectations of the parties.[146] For example, if the parties to a contract stipulate that the

---

[142] *Re Haji-Ioannou (Deceased)* [2009] ILPr 56 at [57]. This approach was approved by a majority of the High Court of Australia in *Neilson v Overseas Projects Corporation of Victoria Ltd* (2005) 223 CLR 331. See Dickinson, 'Renvoi: the Comeback Kid?' (2006) 122 LQR 183.
[143] *R v Brentwood Superintendent Registrar of Marriages, ex p Arias* [1968] 2 QB 956.
[144] Eg, *Taczanowska v Taczanowski* [1957] P 301.
[145] Harris, 'Does Choice of Law make any Sense?' (2004) 57 CLP 305.
[146] Anton, *Private International Law* (1967) p 58.

Turkish courts should have jurisdiction, it is clear they must have wanted a Turkish court to hear the issue and arguable that they expected that that court would apply Turkish law including its rules of the conflict of laws.[147] Such a jurisdiction clause will often be regarded as an implied choice of law.[148] Accordingly, if an English court were exercising jurisdiction in such a case, arguably the application of Turkish law should include Turkish conflicts rules. However, a better solution to this problem is achieved through jurisdiction rules. If there is a jurisdiction clause in favour of Turkey, English courts should normally stay any proceedings here in favour of the Turkish courts.[149] If, however, the English court does assume jurisdiction in such a situation, this will normally be because both parties to the litigation have submitted to the jurisdiction of the English courts. Such a submission must be deemed to include an acceptance of English choice of law rules which do not include renvoi in cases of contract. Where the parties to a contract make an express choice of the law to govern the contract it would be highly artificial to deem them to expect that law to include its conflict of laws rules.[150] The reality is that such parties 'almost certainly envisage that the domestic law'[151] of that country will be applied. Accordingly, applying renvoi in such cases would amount to defeating the principle of party autonomy underlying this particular choice of law rule.

1.120 Thirdly, it is often stated that the principal reason for resorting to total renvoi is to achieve uniformity in terms of the resolution of the case,[152] irrespective of the country in whose court the claim is brought.[153] If the English court decides the case in exactly the same way as the court of a foreign country would decide it, by using the foreign country's conflicts rules, including its rules of renvoi, then uniformity with that country results. And if that country is the one with which, apart from England, the case and the parties are most closely connected, then a good deal has been achieved. Thus, in *Re Annesley*[154] and *Re Ross*,[155] the deceased's property in England and abroad was distributed according to the same domestic law.

1.121 However, with the English courts adopting their own view of classification and perhaps resorting to the doctrine of public policy, uniformity of decision is, in reality, unattainable: 'this cannot be achieved by judicial mental gymnastics but only by international conventions'.[156]

1.122 Further, choice of law rules are designed to select the domestic law which is appropriate (whether in terms of public or private interests). Their main purpose cannot be

---

[147] Briggs, 'In Praise and Defence of Renvoi' (1998) 47 ICLQ 877, 881.
[148] See paras 4.21–4.32.   [149] See Chapter 2.
[150] See recital (57) to Regulation (EU) No 650/2012 (the EU Succession Regulation): while the Regulation (at art 34) allows for renvoi to be used in certain cases, it is 'excluded in situations where the deceased had made a choice of law in favour of the law of a third State'.
[151] Harris, 'Does Choice of Law make any Sense?' (2004) 57 CLP 305, 345.
[152] See recital (57) to Regulation (EU) No 650/2012 (the EU Succession Regulation): the Regulation (at art 34) allows for renvoi in certain cases to 'ensure international consistency'.
[153] Jaffey, *Introduction to the Conflict of Laws* (1988) pp 262–3; Hughes, 'The Insolubility of Renvoi and its Consequences' (2010) 6 Journal of Private International Law 195.
[154] [1926] Ch 692.   [155] [1930] 1 Ch 377.
[156] *Macmillan Inc v Bishopsgate Investment Trust plc (No 3)* [1995] 1 WLR 978 at 1008.

to achieve uniformity by choosing the conflicts rules of some other country to select the appropriate domestic law. If that were the function of the choice of law rules of all countries, then, of course, no domestic law could be found to apply to the case at all. Furthermore, a vicious circle would result if the country to which the English choice of law rule referred also used total renvoi. The doctrine can only work if the other country either does not accept the doctrine of renvoi at all, or uses partial renvoi.

1.123 The quest for uniformity of outcome presupposes that there be uniformity between the 'right' countries. However, renvoi could achieve uniformity between the 'wrong' countries. For example, using renvoi in the field of marriage could bring about uniformity of status between countries to which the person concerned no longer belongs, perhaps even removing a uniformity with countries with which he is now connected. This would occur in a marriage case where the domicile or nationality of the parties has changed since the marriage. If uniformity were the overriding objective in a marriage case, the proper course would be to apply the conflicts rules of the countries with which the parties are connected by domicile and nationality at the time of the English proceedings, whenever those rules are all in agreement. Such an approach would require a substantial revision of choice of law rules, and their rationale, as presently understood.

1.124 Fourthly, it is argued that renvoi can operate as a deterrent to forum shopping. There would be little point in forum shopping in England if the English courts were to apply the more appropriate foreign law as it would be applied by the foreign court.[157] There are two responses to this argument: (i) while some people forum shop to obtain a better result on the substance of the law,[158] others are seeking procedural or other advantages associated with the operation of the legal system in the chosen country; (ii) the most obvious mechanism to prevent forum shopping is through the development of jurisdictional rules preventing forum shopping.[159]

1.125 Fifthly, there is an argument for total renvoi in cases concerning title to immovable property situated abroad. The choice of law rule that title to immovable property is governed by the lex situs is based not merely on the view that the domestic law of the situs is normally the appropriate law to govern the matter, but also on the fact that the property is under the control of the authorities of the situs, without whose concurrence an English judgment on questions of title can be of no effect. It is for this reason that the English courts do not normally exercise jurisdiction in such a case.[160] In the exceptional cases where they do exercise jurisdiction, for example, when the court is administering an estate which, in addition to the foreign immovable, includes property in England,[161] the possibility of the decision being nugatory in the foreign country is reduced if the

---

[157] Briggs, 'In Praise and Defence of Renvoi' (1998) 47 ICLQ 877, 881.
[158] Harris, 'Does Choice of Law make any Sense?' (2004) 57 CLP 305, 352.
[159] Cf Harris, 'Does Choice of Law Make any Sense?' (2004) 57 CLP 305, where it is argued that both jurisdictional and choice of law rules should unite to combat forum shopping.
[160] See paras 2.256–2.263.
[161] As in *Re Ross* [1930] 1 Ch 377.

case is decided according to the domestic law that the court of the situs would apply. While there is some force to this argument, it is possible to overstate the importance of applying the lex situs as the foreign court would apply it on the ground that the property is ultimately subject to the control of the authorities of that country. This argument presupposes that foreign courts would never recognise English judgments that did not apply the foreign law in exactly the same way as the foreign court would have done. Such a premise is clearly misconceived. Indeed, the lex situs rule for intestate succession to immovables had already been abandoned in most civil law countries[162] and the EU Succession Regulation does not use the lex situs rule for immovables.[163] If the lex situs rule itself is being abandoned, at least for some purposes, it is difficult to take too seriously the claims of total renvoi in those fields where the lex situs rule still prevails.

1.126 Finally, and possibly most significantly, the doctrine of renvoi can be utilised as a convenient expedient to avoid the application of a foreign law that would lead to an undesirable result. Indeed, it was such thinking that was behind the introduction of renvoi in English law in *Collier v Rivaz*.[164] In this case the court was concerned with the formal validity of a will and six codicils made by a British person domiciled in Belgium. Under the strict conflicts rule then in existence, formal validity of wills was governed exclusively by the law of the testator's domicile at the date of death. The will and two of the codicils complied with domestic Belgian law and, accordingly, were held to be formally valid. The remaining four codicils were not formally valid by Belgian domestic law, but, desirous of upholding their validity, Sir Herbert Jenner applied the Belgian conflicts rule which referred the matter to English law[165] under which they were valid. Little can be said in support of this approach[166] where the court had its cake and ate it by applying renvoi to certain testamentary instruments and rejecting renvoi in respect of others so as to ensure that all were ultimately valid. Nevertheless, it demonstrates how the doctrine can be used as a means of enabling courts to reach what they perceive to be a just result. Another similar example can be seen in the approach adopted in *Taczanowska v Taczanowski*.[167] The parties in this case, two Polish domiciliaries and nationals, married in Italy at the end of the Second World War without complying with the Italian formalities of marriage. The English choice of law rule referred to the lex loci celebrationis. On discovering that the marriage was formally invalid under Italian domestic law, Karminski J attempted to uphold the validity of the marriage by having recourse to the doctrine of renvoi and applying the Italian conflicts rule that formal validity of a marriage is governed by the law of the parties' nationality.[168] This approach was, however, in vain as it transpired that the marriage was also formally invalid by Polish law. Determined to achieve his objective, Karminski J fell back on the fiction that the parties had contracted a valid English common law marriage.[169] It was clear

---

[162] Dicey, Morris and Collins, *The Conflict of Laws* (15th edn, 2012) p 1417.
[163] See paras 9.116–9.121.   [164] (1841) 2 Curt 855.
[165] According to Belgian law the testator was domiciled in England. This decision was before nationality became a widely accepted connecting factor in civil law countries.
[166] *Collier v Rivaz* was disapproved in *Bremer v Freeman* (1857) 10 Moo PCC 306.
[167] [1957] P 301.   [168] See paras 7.30, 7.90.   [169] See para 7.30.

that the court was determined to uphold the validity of this marriage and the doctrine of renvoi was seen as one possible means of enabling the 'just' result to be achieved.

(v) Disadvantages of renvoi

1.127 None of the arguments in favour of renvoi is capable of withstanding close analysis. Additionally, strong arguments can be advanced against application of the doctrine.

1.128 Renvoi involves the English court applying the conflicts rules of a foreign country in preference to its own rules. An English choice of law rule, for instance that succession to movable property is governed by the law of the deceased's domicile, is designed to select the domestic law that is regarded by the English conflict of laws as appropriate for the cases covered by the rule. English law regards the law of a person's domicile—as opposed to the law of nationality—as best identifying the system of law to which that person belongs. Application of the doctrine of renvoi will often amount to nothing less than the substitution of nationality for domicile as the appropriate connecting factor. The rule that intestate succession to movables is governed by the law of domicile was developed on the assumption that application of the law of a person's 'home' would best accord with the reasonable expectations of the deceased. He might have refrained from making a will because he was content that his property should devolve in accordance with the local rules governing intestate succession. Application of the domestic law of some other country would defeat the reasonable expectations of the deceased and amounts to a negation of the policy underlying the English conflicts rule.

1.129 There are also practical difficulties involved in the application of renvoi. One arises when the conflicts rule of the foreign country refers to the law of a person's nationality, and the person concerned is a national of the United Kingdom or the United States or some other state consisting of more than one law district.[170] In some cases there may be clear evidence of how the foreign law would resolve this problem[171] but in other cases the foreign law may be deficient or uncertain in its rules prescribing which is the domestic law to be applied in such a case.[172] In such cases there has been an alarming tendency by the English courts to assume, or to allow the foreign expert to assume,[173] that either the national law of a British person is the law of his domicile of origin[174] or that it must mean English law.[175] Either assumption is patent nonsense and results in the application of a law that might not have been indicated by either the English or the foreign conflicts rule. Also, difficulties have been experienced in deciding what the foreign country's rules of renvoi are (as, of course, has to be done under total renvoi), especially when the question is unsettled in the foreign country itself.[176] The result is unpredictability of outcome and, at times, the application of an absurd and unrealistic

---

[170] On the problem of reference to countries which comprise more than one law district, see Christandl, 'Multi-unit States in European Union Private International Law' (2013) 9 Journal of Private International Law 219.
[171] *Re Haji-Ioannou (Deceased)* [2009] ILPr 46 at [29].   [172] See, eg, *Re O'Keefe* [1940] Ch 124.
[173] *Re JB (Child Abduction) (Rights of Custody: Spain)* [2004] 1 FLR 796 at 797.   [174] Ibid.
[175] *Re Ross* [1930] 1 Ch 377; *Re Askew* [1930] 2 Ch 259.
[176] *Re Annesley* [1926] Ch 692; *Re Duke of Wellington* [1947] Ch 506.

law. For example, in *Re O'Keefe*[177] the result was that the intestate succession to the movable estate of an Italian domiciliary was governed by the law of the Republic of Ireland, a country which the deceased had only once briefly visited and which had only come into political existence while she was living in Italy. Finally, the doctrine of total renvoi can apply only if the foreign country either rejects renvoi or applies partial renvoi. If the foreign country also applies total renvoi, the English court would have to attempt to resolve the case as the foreign court would do, only to discover that the foreign court would try to decide the case as the English court would do. The result would be stalemate—although, of course, it would be possible to apply a secondary rule[178] to break the deadlock. For example, it was suggested in the Australian High Court decision of *Neilson v Overseas Projects Corporation of Victoria Ltd*[179] that, in such a case, the domestic law of the forum should be applied. Nevertheless, it is difficult to justify a doctrine whose existence is premised on the assumption that no other country in the world adopts it.[180]

1.130 In view of the above objections, it is hoped that the doctrine of renvoi is fast approaching its sell-by date. However, the Law Commission[181] has not chosen to condemn the doctrine and the English judiciary has seen fit to continue to make reference to the doctrine[182] even when it has not been pleaded.[183] Moreover, the Civil Partnership Act 2004 expressly endorses renvoi in relation to civil partnerships and its use has been sanctioned at a European level in the Succession Regulation. In Australia the doctrine has been approved in the field of tort.[184] On the other hand, more recent English decisions have demonstrated hostility to the doctrine even in areas where it was thought to be potentially applicable.[185] It is to be hoped that this trend continues.

(D) The incidental question

(i) Introduction

1.131 When English choice of law rules refer to a foreign law, an incidental question may arise which could be resolved by a different English conflicts rule or by the foreign law. For example, English conflicts rules could refer a matter of succession to Mexican law and under Mexican law the property could devolve to the legitimate children of the deceased. The main issue is one of succession. Whether the children are legitimate is an incidental question. How is this incidental question to be answered? English law

---

[177] [1940] Ch 124.
[178] Hughes, 'The Insolubility of Renvoi and Its Consequences' (2010) 6 Journal of Private International Law 195.
[179] (2005) 223 CLR 331.
[180] Lorenzen, 'The Qualification, Classification, or Characterization Problem in the Conflict of Laws' (1941) 50 Yale LJ 743, 753.
[181] See, eg, Law Com Working Paper No 89, *Private International Law: Choice of Law Rules in Marriage* (1985) para 3.39; Law Com No 165, *Private International Law: Choice of Law Rules in Marriage* (1987) paras 2.5, 2.6.
[182] See, eg, Lord Scarman in *Quazi v Quazi* [1980] AC 744 at 824; *Re JB (Child Abduction) (Rights of Custody: Spain)* [2004] 1 FLR 796.
[183] *Vervaeke v Smith* [1981] 1 All ER 55 at 87 (CA).
[184] *Neilson v Overseas Projects Corporation of Victoria Ltd* (2005) 223 CLR 331.
[185] See above n 130.

has choice of law rules relating to legitimacy, but so too does Mexican law. If they both agree on the issue, there is no problem. However, if they disagree, the question is whether the law governing the main issue should also govern the incidental question (the lex causae approach), or whether the English conflicts rules should themselves govern the incidental question (the lex fori approach).

1.132 Another example is where, under the foreign law applicable in a tort case, an exemption clause in a contract is a good defence so long as the contract is valid. The validity of the contract is then an incidental question. The law governing the contract could be determined either by the choice of law rules of the law governing the tort (the lex causae approach), or by English choice of law rules (the lex fori approach).

(ii) Relationship to renvoi

1.133 The problems and arguments concerning the incidental question are similar to those raised and canvassed in relation to renvoi. On the one hand, adopting the lex causae approach can be seen as similar to applying the doctrine of renvoi; one is striving to achieve the same solution as the foreign court. It can be argued, as with renvoi, that it is pointless referring to Mexican law which, in the above example, would allow the property to devolve only to legitimate children if we ignore the Mexican rules on who are actually legitimate children. If English conflicts rules are allowed to determine who is legitimate, this might allow persons to succeed to property even though they would not be so entitled under Mexican law. On the other hand, adopting the lex fori approach can be likened to rejecting renvoi; one is not seeking an illusory uniformity of result but, rather, giving full effect to the English choice of law rules. English conflicts rules on succession allow Mexican law to make the basic determination as to what class of persons are to succeed. English law has conflicts rules on legitimacy and these should not be displaced by the Mexican rules which could employ a connecting factor such as nationality which has been rejected by English law.

1.134 It is important to stress, however, that the parallel between renvoi and the lex causae approach to the incidental question is not exact. First, it need not be the choice of law rules of the foreign country that govern the incidental question. It could be the domestic law of the foreign country. Secondly, if it were the conflicts rules of the foreign country that governed the incidental question, the English authorities to date have not treated such rules in the same manner as when applying renvoi. In particular, there has been no attempt to apply total renvoi and deal with the incidental question in whatever way the foreign court would do. Similarly, the analogy between rejection of renvoi and the lex fori solution to the incidental question is imprecise. The argument for the rejection of renvoi is that it allows full scope to be given to the English conflicts rule, bearing in mind that that rule is shaped by policy considerations which are designed to lead to the domestic law of the foreign country. When the problem of the incidental question presents itself, one could give full effect to the English choice of law rule governing the main issue (by rejecting renvoi) even though one allowed the lex causae to govern the incidental question. The real issue is whether the English conflicts rule governing the incidental question should be displaced in such a manner.

(iii) The solution

1.135 The view widely accepted today is that there is no general rule applicable to all types of case.[186] Instead, there needs to be an examination and weighing of the relative strengths of the policies underlying each English conflicts rule[187] and a consideration of the practical consequences of each approach in the particular case.[188] Such a solution, however, leads inevitably to uncertainty and lack of predictability and raises the problem of how the relative policies of conflicts rules are to be established and then measured against each other. Accordingly, it is suggested that a better way forward would be acceptance of a general guiding principle applicable in most situations—but one that would give way to a different approach where policy or justice clearly demands such a result. Following this, it is submitted that the lex fori approach should normally be applied, but that in clear cases this could be displaced by the lex causae approach.

1.136 For example, using the earlier example, suppose that in a succession governed by Mexican law the issue arises as to whether a woman was the wife of the deceased. The parties could be validly married under English law and have lived for years in England. It would be extremely unfortunate if the Mexican rules on the validity of this marriage were allowed to prevail with the result that the 'wife' (by English law) were excluded from the succession. However, there can be situations where the lex fori approach should give way to the lex causae approach. For example, if there is no spouse or legitimate child under English conflicts rules, but there is such a person under Mexican law, policy dictates that they be allowed to succeed.

1.137 These arguments are elaborated later in this book in the two areas of law where this issue has most commonly arisen, namely capacity to marry after a preceding divorce or annulment,[189] and succession.[190]

(E) Proof of foreign law

1.138 Before an English court will apply foreign law, it is necessary not only for the relevant choice of law rule to indicate that an issue in the case is to be decided by a foreign law, but also for a litigant to plead and prove that law. Otherwise the court will simply apply English law. It will not apply a foreign law of its own motion. For example, in *Aluminium Industrie Vaassen BV v Romalpa Aluminium Ltd*[191] a contract contained a provision that it was to be governed by Dutch law but, as neither party chose to plead Dutch law before the English courts, the case was simply decided according to English law.

1.139 As seen earlier, the only *law* that is applied is the relevant conflicts rule. If that rule indicates that a foreign law is applicable, that foreign law must be proved as a matter of *fact*. Because foreign laws are regarded as mere facts of which judges have no

---

[186] Gottlieb, 'The Incidental Question Revisited—Theory and Practice in the Conflict of Laws' (1977) 26 ICLQ 734; Dicey, Morris and Collins, *The Conflict of Laws* (15th edn, 2012) p 56.
[187] Harris, 'Does Choice of Law Make any Sense?' (2004) 57 CLP 305.
[188] Dicey, Morris and Collins, *The Conflict of Laws* (15th edn, 2012) p 56.
[189] See paras 7.80–7.89.   [190] See paras 9.110–9.115.   [191] [1976] 1 WLR 676.

judicial knowledge, they have to be proved in court by the party alleging that they are applicable. This means that the normal rules of civil evidence for proof of facts are applicable. The foreign law has to be proved by the testimony of experts, who give evidence in the case in the same way as other expert witnesses. This expert must be someone who is qualified on account of 'knowledge or experience' of the foreign law.[192] Although it is possible to obtain evidence from non-legal specialists such as bankers, in most cases it is lawyers, whether practising or not, who provide the expert testimony.

1.140 Because foreign law is proved as a matter of fact, and not law, it used to be clear that any finding as to foreign law could not operate as a precedent. Even if the identical point arose the next day in a different case, the foreign law would need to be proved afresh. In order to avoid the expense and inconvenience involved in such cases, section 4(2) of the Civil Evidence Act 1972 provides that any such decision on foreign law, if reported or recorded in citable form, is admissible as evidence in any later case as establishing the relevant foreign law unless the contrary is proved. This effectively raises a presumption that the earlier decision is correct. While the presumption may be rebutted, the desirability of consistency renders the previous decision 'a weighty piece of evidence in itself'.[193] The rule in section 4(2) of the 1972 Act, coupled with the fact that appellate courts are far more willing to disturb these particular findings of fact by the trial judge, underlines the statement in *Parkasho v Singh* that, while foreign law must be proved as a question of fact, it is nevertheless 'a question of fact of a peculiar kind'.[194]

1.141 If there is a conflict in the evidence of the experts, then the English court will have to decide, on the basis of that evidence and the statutes, cases and other materials cited by the experts, what the foreign law correctly is, and it may even have to do so on a point which is not yet settled in the foreign country itself.[195]

1.142 As mentioned above, the onus is on the person alleging that the foreign law is applicable to prove that foreign law. In the absence of such proof, the court will apply English law. It is often stated that this is because there is a presumption that the foreign law is the same as English law.[196] An alternative and more modern analysis is that English law is always the applicable law unless and until the relevant foreign law is proved.[197] For instance, in *Szechter v Szechter*[198] the choice of law rules on validity of marriage indicated that Polish law was the applicable law. However, at the critical moment the expert witness had to go into hospital for an operation and was thus not available for

---

[192] Civil Evidence Act 1972, s 4(1).
[193] *Phoenix Marine Inc v China Ocean Shipping Co* [1999] CLC 478 at 481. [194] [1968] P 233 at 250.
[195] *Re Duke of Wellington* [1947] Ch 506 at 515; *Blue Sky One Ltd v Mahan Air* [2010] EWHC 631 (Comm) at [88].
[196] See, eg, *Royal Boskalis Westminster NV v Mountain* [1999] QB 674 at 725.
[197] Fentiman, 'Foreign Law in English Courts' (1992) 108 LQR 142 describes the old presumption as 'a cumbersome and inaccurate fiction' (at 148) in that it suggests that courts will go through the unrealistic process of ascertaining the applicable law and then just apply English law. See, generally, Fentiman, *Foreign Law in English Courts* (1998) pp 143–53, 183–6.
[198] [1971] P 286.

oral examination. In such circumstances, the court felt obliged to apply English law. Failing to prove foreign law has the same effect as choosing not to plead foreign law and in such cases the only law before the court is English law.

1.143 It ought to be noted that these rules apply only to the proof of foreign law. Thus, the Supreme Court does not need to have Scots law or the law of Northern Ireland proved to it, even when hearing an English appeal. Similarly, EU law does not have to be proved in the UK courts; it is not foreign law.

1.144 In 2002 a European Judicial Network (EJN) in civil and commercial matters was established, inter alia, to assist judges in Member States of the European Union in resolving difficulties in the interpretation or application of the laws of other Member States. In 2009 a revised Decision was agreed by the European Parliament and the European Council under which the courts of one Member State may apply to the Network for information on the content of the law of another Member State.[199] Such information is not binding on the requesting court.[200] It is anticipated that this provision, which is permissive (a court 'may' apply), is more likely to be utilised in those Member States with an inquisitorial system of civil procedure. In the English adversarial system, it would not be appropriate for the court to rely on the EJN; foreign law has to be pleaded and proved by the litigants and the court is not normally entitled to undertake its own research into the law of another country.

(F) Exclusion of foreign law

1.145 Despite its choice of law rules leading to a foreign law, an English court will not apply the following foreign laws: (a) foreign penal laws; (b) foreign revenue laws; (c) other public laws; and (d) laws contrary to public policy.

(i) Penal laws

1.146 In certain circumstances effect may be given to foreign penal laws as part of the lex causae governing a legal transaction. For example, an English court will not enforce a contract that is illegal by the law governing the contract. However, the English court will not *enforce*, whether directly or indirectly, a foreign penal law[201] as this would amount to recognising 'an assertion of sovereign authority by one state within the territory of another'.[202] In *Re State of Norway's Application (Nos 1 and 2)*[203] it was indicated that the English court has no jurisdiction to assist such an assertion of authority; in effect the English court is declining jurisdiction in such cases.

1.147 Whether a foreign law is penal is, consistent with the general principle, to be determined by English law, the lex fori.[204] A penal law means a law under which a fine

---

[199] Decision No 2009/568/EC of the European Parliament and of the Council of 18 June 2009 amending Council Decision No 2001/470/EC establishing a European Judicial Network in civil and commercial matters: OJ 2009 L168/35, art 1(2).
[200] Art 3(1)(c). [201] *Huntington v Attrill* [1893] AC 150.
[202] *Government of India v Taylor* [1955] AC 491 at 511.
[203] [1990] 1 AC 723. [204] *United States v Inkley* [1989] QB 255 at 265.

or other pecuniary penalty is recoverable, or property forfeited, for a crime or other breach of public law, at the instance of the state or someone representing the public.[205] The court will also not enforce a foreign judgment in respect of such a penalty. In *United States v Inkley*[206] an action was brought by the US government for the enforcement in England of a Florida judgment. The defendant had been released on bail in Florida, having given an appearance bond, and then absconded. Although the Florida judgment was a civil one, the Court of Appeal refused to enforce it on the basis that the purpose of the judgment was to enforce the criminal law of Florida.[207] Three criteria were laid down to determine whether a foreign law or judgment was penal and/or public: the party in whose favour the right was created; the purpose of the foreign law; and the general context of the case. In the *Inkley* case, despite the 'civil clothing',[208] all these considerations pointed to the Florida judgment being one aimed at enforcing the criminal law.

1.148 The English courts have, at times, adopted an unfortunately wide interpretation of what constitutes a penal matter. In a series of cases, it was decided that a foreign status which subjected a person to certain incapacities was to be regarded as penal—with the consequence that no effect was to be given to any of the incapacities. *Worms v De Valdor*[209] and *Re Selot's Trusts*[210] both concerned persons declared prodigals in France. An order of prodigality involves the appointment of a curator who is empowered to control the spending, and in certain respects manage the affairs, of a spendthrift. The prodigal is, therefore, to an extent disqualified from managing his own affairs. These disqualifications were regarded as being penal in nature. Similarly, in *Re Langley's Settlement Trusts*[211] it was held that an order declaring a person suffering from multiple sclerosis to be incompetent to manage certain of his affairs and appointing his wife to do so on his behalf was penal. These cases have been roundly condemned[212] on the basis that the foreign orders were designed to protect the person concerned rather than punish him. These cases represent unfortunate instances of the English court adopting a somewhat chauvinistic response that, if a status is unknown to English law, there must be something objectionable about it. It is to be hoped that these decisions will not be followed.

1.149 A wide view of what constitutes a penal matter may lead to a refusal to give effect to a foreign state's expropriation of property, even though the property was situated in that state at the relevant time, if it was not actually taken into the state's possession before removal from the state's territory. In *A-G of New Zealand v Ortiz*[213] a New Zealand statute provided that historic articles exported from New Zealand without the permission of the government should be forfeited to the Crown. When a historic article was

---

[205] *Huntington v Attrill* [1893] AC 150 at 155–8.   [206] [1989] QB 255.
[207] It was indicated, in the alternative, that this was a 'public law' which was similarly not enforceable (Ibid, 264).
[208] [1989] QB 255 a Ibid, 266.   [209] (1880) 49 LJ Ch 261.   [210] [1902] 1 Ch 488.
[211] [1961] 1 WLR 41; affd [1962] Ch 541.
[212] Eg, Cheshire, North and Fawcett, *Private International Law* (14th edn, 2008) pp 147–9.
[213] [1984] AC 1.

exported contrary to the statute, the New Zealand government, relying on the statute, sought to recover it in English proceedings. It was held that on its true construction, the effect of the statute was that an article was only forfeited when seized, so that in the present case no title to the article had ever passed to the New Zealand government on which an action could be founded for its recovery. However, it was held obiter in the Court of Appeal[214] that, even if the effect of the Act had been to transfer title to the New Zealand state before the article left New Zealand, the action in the English court must fail. The forfeiture under the statute was a penalty to the state for the contravention of a public law, and the action was, therefore, one to enforce a foreign penal law.

(ii) Revenue laws

1.150 The position with regard to revenue laws is similar to that affecting penal laws. Such laws can be recognised as valid rules of the law of the country in question, to be applied if that law is the lex causae under the ordinary English conflicts rules. So, if a contract is governed by the law of X and is invalid by that law because it contravenes a revenue law of X, it will be held invalid by the English court (unless to apply the foreign law would be contrary to public policy).

1.151 However, as with penal laws, it is a well-established principle that the English court will not enforce a foreign revenue law.[215] The reason why the English courts will not enforce foreign revenue laws is simply that they 'do not sit to collect taxes for another country'.[216] Accordingly, the public authorities of a foreign country cannot recover in the English court any sort of tax or duty payable under its laws. Nor will a foreign revenue law be enforced indirectly, for example by allowing the foreign government to recover property in England over which it claims a lien in respect of the owner's liability to unpaid tax (unless the property had actually previously been taken into possession by the foreign government in its own territory).[217] For example, in *QRS1 ApS v Frandsen*[218] it was held that a claim by the liquidator of Danish companies against the controlling shareholder of the companies was an unenforceable revenue claim because the only creditors were the Danish revenue authorities. Where, however, there are other creditors, in addition to the revenue authorities of a country, this principle will not apply.[219] Again, it is for English law, as the lex fori, to determine whether an issue relates to 'revenue law'.[220]

(iii) Public laws

1.152 As with penal and revenue laws, enforcement of a foreign country's public laws would amount to an assertion of sovereign authority over another state. As a result, English

---

[214] By Ackner and O'Connor LJJ; for Lord Denning's approach, see p 50. This aspect was not considered by the House of Lords.
[215] *Government of India v Taylor* [1955] AC 491.
[216] *Regazzoni v KC Sethia (1944) Ltd* [1956] 2 QB 490 at 515.
[217] *Brokaw v Seatrain UK Ltd* [1971] 2 QB 476.   [218] [1999] 1 WLR 2169.
[219] Smart, 'The Rule against Foreign Revenue Laws' (2000) 116 LQR 360 discussing the unreported case of *Teletalk Mobil Engineers v Jyske Bank* (1998).
[220] For a full list of such matters, see Dicey, Morris and Collins, *The Conflict of Laws* (15th edn, 2012) p 114.

courts have no power to entertain proceedings for the enforcement of a public law of a foreign state. The scope of this doctrine is, however, somewhat uncertain.

1.153 In *A-G of New Zealand v Ortiz*[221] Lord Denning, rather than classifying the New Zealand statute as penal, stated obiter that the New Zealand government's claim would fail as its statute was a public law. In *Re State of Norway's Application (Nos 1 and 2)*[222] the House of Lords accepted that there is a category of 'other public laws' which might not be revenue or penal laws but which, for similar reasons, were not enforceable in England.[223]

1.154 In the Australian case of *A-G (UK) v Heinemann Publishers Australia Pty Ltd (No 2)*[224] the High Court dismissed an action brought by the United Kingdom to restrain publication of the book *Spycatcher*, written by a former member of the British security services, on the ground that the claim arose out of acts of the British government seeking to exercise powers relating to the protection of national security. It was accepted that the court should not enforce foreign public laws.[225]

(iv) Public policy

(a) Introduction

1.155 A foreign rule which would normally be applicable, or a foreign judgment or decree which would normally be enforced or recognised, will not be given effect if to do so would be contrary to English public policy. Such a law or judgment is disregarded: 'It is as though it did not exist.'[226] The doctrine of public policy is most likely to be encountered in relation to the essential validity of marriages,[227] the validity and enforcement of contracts,[228] the recognition of foreign matrimonial decrees,[229] and the recognition and enforcement of other foreign judgments[230]—although it is relatively rare for the doctrine to be applied in this and other commercial spheres of law.

1.156 Two general points need to be made by way of introduction. First, the doctrine can only be used as a shield (to deny the application of an otherwise applicable foreign law) and not as a sword (to invoke the application of an otherwise inapplicable law). In *Peer International Corp v Termidor Musical Publishers Ltd*[231] it was held that public policy could not be elevated to a 'positive connecting factor' or to a 'positive force'. In this case a Cuban statute was enacted which affected copyright in England. The argument that this statute could, on public policy grounds, displace the well-established lex situs rule was rejected.[232]

---

[221] [1984] AC 1.   [222] [1990] 1 AC 723.
[223] See also *United States of America v Inkley* [1989] QB 255.   [224] (1988) 165 CLR 30.
[225] A different approach was adopted in New Zealand in relation to the same book in *A-G for the United Kingdom v Wellington Newspapers Ltd* [1988] 1 NZLR 129 where it was indicated obiter that the duty of confidentiality between the author and the British government could be enforced.
[226] *Kuwait Airways Corpn v Iraqi Airways Co (Nos 4 and 5)* [2002] 2 AC 883 at 991 (CA).
[227] See paras 7.100–7.103.   [228] See paras 4.109–4.113.   [229] See paras 8.76–8.77, 8.132–8.136.
[230] See paras 3.70–3.71, 3.108–3.113.   [231] [2004] Ch 212.
[232] See also *Bank voor Handel v Slatford* [1953] 1 QB 248. In the *Peer* case these views were obiter as the Cuban statute was found to be confiscatory.

1.157 Secondly, the doctrine of public policy, its ambit and extent, and the manner in which it is to be applied, has been entirely the creation of the common law. However, as the conflict of laws has been increasingly regulated by statute, the doctrine of public policy has been enshrined in such legislation and in EU Regulations.[233] These legislative norms, however, do not define the concept, whose meaning and role must be ascertained from the common law.[234] Commonly, such statutes and Regulations stipulate that the doctrine can be invoked only where a foreign law or judgment is 'manifestly' contrary to public policy.[235] It has been held that the inclusion of the word 'manifestly' means that this is 'a very high hurdle to clear'[236] and that the doctrine can be invoked only in 'truly exceptional' cases.[237]

(b) Limited scope of doctrine

1.158 The doctrine of public policy is used relatively sparingly in the English conflict of laws, especially in comparison with the laws of some foreign countries such as France and Germany.[238] There are several reasons for this.

1.159 First, many English choice of law rules have a 'forum-oriented bias'[239] with the result that English law is the applicable law and consequently there is no scope for the application of public policy. For example, the English choice of law rule in matters relating to divorce, judicial separation, and maintenance is that the lex fori applies. Any issue classified as procedural is automatically subject to English law and the English courts have, at least until recently, adopted a rather broad view as to what constitutes a matter of procedure.

1.160 Secondly, and in a similar vein, many choice of law rules are structured in such a manner as to give English law ultimate 'control' and prevent the unfettered application of foreign law. In tort, under the common law rules, which still apply to defamation claims, no liability can be imposed unless the claim is actionable under English law.[240] In essential validity of marriage, the rule in *Sottomayor v De Barros (No 2)*[241] ensures the displacement of the normal dual domicile doctrine in favour of English law when the parties marry in England and one of them is an English domiciliary. Further, the use of English overriding mandatory rules ensures that an otherwise applicable foreign law is not applied.[242]

1.161 Thirdly, there are many conflicts rules which, while framed in different terms, are either performing the same function as a doctrine of public policy or, alternatively, can

---

[233] Eg, in the Brussels I Recast, the Brussels II *bis* Regulation, the Rome I Regulation, and the Rome II Regulation. On the use of public policy in the EU instruments, see Kramberger Škerl, 'European Public Policy (With an Emphasis on *Exequatur* Proceedings)' (2011) 7 Journal of Private International Law 461.
[234] Although, as seen in Chapter 3, the Court of Justice will review the limits on recourse to domestic conceptions of public policy where EU legislation is concerned.
[235] Eg, Family Law Act 1986, s 51(3)(c); Rome I Regulation, art 21.
[236] *Kellman v Kellman* [2000] 1 FLR 785 at 798.
[237] *Golubovich v Golubovich* [2010] 3 WLR 1607 at [78].
[238] Dicey, Morris and Collins, *The Conflict of Laws* (15th edn, 2012) p 100.
[239] Carter, 'The Role of Public Policy in English Conflict of Laws' (1993) 42 ICLQ 1, 3.
[240] *Phillips v Eyre* (1870) LR 6 QB 1.   [241] (1879) 5 PD 94.
[242] Rome I Regulation, art 9(2).

be regarded as crystallisations of public policy. For example, the common law rule that a foreign judgment will not be recognised if the defendant was given insufficient notice of the foreign proceedings or was not given a reasonable opportunity to take part in those proceedings[243] is a rule requiring that foreign proceedings complied with the requirements of natural justice. Were such a rule not in existence, resort to the residual doctrine of public policy would be necessary. Similarly, the rule that a foreign commercial judgment obtained by fraud will not be recognised or enforced[244] can be regarded as a crystallisation of public policy. Under the Brussels I Recast, which does not expressly deal with the problem of judgments procured by fraud, the extent to which such judgments may be denied recognition or enforcement depends upon the application of the doctrine of public policy.[245]

1.162 Fourthly, there is recognition by the English judiciary that public policy is an 'unruly horse'[246] and that 'care must be taken to ensure that this animal is not allowed to wreak havoc in international pastures'.[247] Public policy should only be invoked 'exceptionally and with the greatest circumspection'.[248] It has been said that '[t]he golden rule is that care must be taken not to expand its application beyond the true limits of the principle. These limits demand that, where there is any room for doubt, judicial restraint must be exercised.'[249]

1.163 Many foreign laws are different and even strange to English eyes; if the doctrine of public policy were to be used to deny application to all such laws, the result would be a complete emasculation of the conflicts process; as has been stated, 'those who live in legal glass houses, however well constructed, should perhaps not be over-astute to throw stones at the laws of other countries'.[250] Accordingly, a distinction is drawn between domestic public policy and international public policy. Transactions which offend purely local (English) interests are not necessarily to be regarded as contrary to public policy when set on an international stage and having no direct impact upon, or posing no direct threat to, English institutions.[251] In *Addison v Brown*,[252] a maintenance agreement ousting the jurisdiction of the Californian court was recognised despite the fact that a similar agreement to oust the jurisdiction of the English court would have been void. Similarly, while no polygamous marriage can be contracted in England (as this would threaten the monogamous institution of marriage) and no talak divorce can take place in England (as this would offend local public policy by enabling

---

[243] Family Law Act 1986, s 51(3)(a); the same rule applies to recognition of commercial judgments under the traditional rules: *Adams v Cape Industries plc* [1990] Ch 433.
[244] *Owens Bank Ltd v Bracco* [1992] 2 AC 443.
[245] *Interdesco SA v Nullifire Ltd* [1992] 1 Lloyd's Rep 180.
[246] Lord Hodson in *Boys v Chaplin* [1971] AC 356 at 378.
[247] Carter, 'The Role of Public Policy in English Private International Law' (1993) 42 ICLQ 1, 3.
[248] Lord Nicholls in *Kuwait Airways Corpn v Iraqi Airways Co (Nos 4 and 5)* [2002] 2 AC 883 at 1078.
[249] Lord Hope at 1109.
[250] Sachs J in *R v Brentwood Superintendent of Marriages, ex p Arias* [1968] 3 WLR 531 at 537.
[251] 'Local values ought not lightly to be elevated into public policy on the transnational level': Lord Steyn in *Kuwait Airways Corpn v Iraqi Airways Co (Nos 4 and 5)* [2002] 2 AC 883 at 1101.
[252] [1954] 1 WLR 779.

the parties to circumvent the protections afforded by the English courts), polygamous marriages entered into abroad and foreign talaks, khulas, and gets are potentially entitled to recognition.[253]

1.164 Finally, but not unrelated to the previous point, it has been argued[254] that the growing acceptance by the English judiciary of international comity has led to a corresponding decline in the use of public policy to exclude the normally applicable foreign law. Increasingly, 'judicial chauvinism has been replaced by judicial comity'[255] with the result that using public policy is regarded as 'being discourteous to the foreign state whose law is excluded. It is like throwing stones at your neighbour's house'.[256]

1.165 Perhaps conscious of such considerations English judges have, at times, chosen to 'speak with forked tongues' and, while avoiding all reference to public policy as such, have refused to apply a foreign law or recognise a foreign judgment on the ground that it offends English notions of 'substantial justice'.[257] This discretion was mainly used in the field of recognition of foreign divorces and nullity decrees.[258] For example, in *Gray v Formosa*[259] a Maltese nullity decree, granted on the ground that the parties had not married in a Roman Catholic church, was refused recognition as offending English notions of substantial justice. This discretion to refuse recognition, in relation to such matrimonial decrees, has been abolished by the Family Law Act 1986,[260] which provides that recognition of the decree can be refused only if recognition would be 'manifestly contrary to public policy'. It is unfortunate that in relation to commercial judgments the Court of Appeal revived the doctrine of 'substantial justice' in *Adams v Cape Industries plc*.[261] In this case it was decided that a process whereby the amount of the plaintiffs' damages was averaged—with the plaintiffs being placed by their lawyers in four bands according to the seriousness of their injuries—rather than assessed following a judicial investigation into the injuries sustained by each plaintiff, offended English notions of substantial justice. No explanation of the relationship between public policy and substantial justice was provided. Given the fact that over the past century the ambit of public policy has been rigorously circumscribed, and that a new discretionary power based on substantial justice could be broad and unlimited, it is to be hoped that the difference between public policy and substantial justice is simply one of nomenclature.

---

[253] See paras 7.124–7.160, 8.97–8.121.
[254] Enonchong, 'Public Policy in the Conflict of Laws: A Chinese Wall Around Little England?' (1996) 45 ICLQ 633. Enonchong does not assert that comity is the basis of the conflict of laws, but rather that considerations of comity have led the English judiciary to become more internationalist in its approach.
[255] Lord Diplock in *The Abidin Daver* [1984] AC 398 at 411–12.
[256] Enonchong, 'Public Policy in the Conflict of Laws: A Chinese Wall Around Little England?' (1996) 45 ICLQ 633, 653.
[257] *Pemberton v Hughes* [1899] 1 Ch 781 at 790.
[258] See, eg, *Middleton v Middleton* [1967] P 62 at 69–70; *Lepre v Lepre* [1965] P 52.
[259] [1963] P 259.   [260] S 51(3)(a). See *Golubovich v Golubovich* [2010] 3 WLR 1607 at [45]–[47].
[261] [1990] Ch 433. See paras 3.63–3.66.

(c) Scope of doctrine

1.166 There seem to be two classes of case (which sometimes overlap) in which public policy may be invoked by the court. In the one class, the foreign rule is not applied, or the foreign judgment not recognised or enforced, because to do so in the circumstances of the case would offend fundamental English ideas of morality, decency, human liberty, or justice. In the other class of case, public policy is invoked because the case falls within the scope of an English rule whose purpose is to protect the public interest.

Contrary to English concepts of morality, decency, human liberty, or justice

1.167 A foreign law will not be applied and a foreign contract, status, transaction, or judgment will not be recognised or enforced if it is regarded as repugnant to fundamental English concepts of morality, decency, human liberty, or justice. Examples include the refusal to enforce rules prohibiting marriages between people of different races;[262] the refusal to recognise as valid marriages involving seriously mentally impaired persons;[263] the refusal to enforce a rule prohibiting the guilty party to a divorce from remarrying before the innocent party does so;[264] the refusal to enforce a rule upholding a contractual promise by a wife to repay money stolen by her husband as the price for a criminal prosecution not being brought against the latter;[265] the refusal to recognise or enforce judgments obtained by fraud[266] or duress;[267] the refusal to recognise a foreign maintenance agreement entitling a child to receive maintenance after minority;[268] and the refusal to recognise an extra-judicial divorce when the marriage had substantial connections with England and recognition would mean that the wife would have been deprived of the financial relief to which she would be entitled under English law.[269] Public policy is very seldom invoked to deny recognition to foreign commercial judgments; however, a foreign judgment could be denied recognition or enforcement if the foreign judgment did not respect the defendant's right to a fair trial under article 6 of the European Convention on Human Rights.[270] In the sphere of government expropriation of property, effect will not be given to 'foreign confiscatory laws which, by reason of their being discriminatory on grounds of race, religion, or the like, constitute so grave an infringement of human rights that they ought not to be recognised as laws at all'[271] (for example, Nazi laws providing for the confiscation of the property of Jews[272]). Similarly, foreign confiscatory orders that are in gross breach of clearly established principles of international law are regarded as contrary to English public policy.[273]

---

[262] See para 7.102.   [263] *Westminster City Council v C* [2009] Fam 11.
[264] *Scott v A-G* (1886) 11 PD 128.   [265] *Kaufman v Gerson* [1904] 1 KB 591.
[266] *Kendall v Kendall* [1977] Fam 208.   [267] *Kaufman v Gerson* [1904] 1 KB 591.
[268] *Re Macartney* [1921] 1 Ch 522.   [269] *Chaudhary v Chaudhary* [1985] Fam 19.
[270] See para 3.70. On public policy and human rights, see Thoma, 'The ECHR and the *Ordre Public* Exception in Private International Law' [2011] Nederlands Internationaal Privaatrecht 13; Oster, 'Public Policy and Human Rights' (2015) 11 Journal of Private International Law 542.
[271] *Williams & Humbert Ltd v W & H Trade Marks (Jersey) Ltd* [1986] AC 368 at 379.
[272] *Oppenheimer v Cattermole* [1976] AC 249 at 278, 282.
[273] *Kuwait Airways Corpn v Iraqi Airways Co (Nos 4 and 5)* [2002] 2 AC 883. In this case Iraqi decrees authorising the confiscation of Kuwaiti planes in breach of principles of public international law were held to be contrary to English public policy.

1.168 Cases of a similar kind, not usually described in terms of public policy, are those in which the English court refuses to enforce an obligation relating to foreign land arising from 'a fiduciary relationship or fraud, or other conduct which, in the view of the Court of Equity in this country, would be unconscionable'.[274] In such cases, overriding effect is given to English rules relating to fraud, the abuse of fiduciary relationships and other unconscionable conduct. In effect, public policy dictates the application of English rules even if the lex situs would normally be the governing law.

1.169 In all the above cases the doctrine of public policy can generally be invoked even if no English interests are affected. For example, the contract for the sale of a slave would today be regarded as so offensive that no English court would enforce it even if all connections in the case were with a foreign country. However, there are two possible qualifications to this proposition. First, transactions could be regarded as broadly immoral, but not so repugnant as to justify the application of public policy. In effect, they are regarded as 'quasi-immoral'. In such cases public policy will only be applied if the transaction is also regarded as immoral by another directly affected country. For example, in *Lemenda Trading Co Ltd v African Middle East Petroleum Co Ltd*[275] a contract (governed by English law) that the claimant would use influence with the minister in charge of oil companies in Qatar to procure renewal of a supply contract was described by Phillips J as 'contrary to ... general principles of morality'[276] but it was 'questionable whether the moral principles involved [were] so weighty'[277] as to justify a refusal to enforce the agreement unless the agreement was also contrary to public policy and unenforceable under the law of Qatar.

1.170 Secondly, even in seemingly obvious cases, it does not necessarily follow that public policy would be invoked irrespective of the context in which the issue arose. Public policy is not a 'hard edged concept'.[278] Take the example of the laws that existed in South Africa during the apartheid era prohibiting marriages between persons of different races. Suppose two South African domiciliaries of different races married in South Africa and then, the marriage having later broken down, they relied on the nullity of the marriage under South African law and remarried. It would be surprising if the English court, when called upon to assess the validity of either party's second marriage, were to use public policy to uphold the validity of the first marriage with the result that the second marriage would be void. It has been suggested that in such cases there could be an 'intermediate type of foreign law which, although intrinsically repugnant, cannot always be treated as unacceptably so'.[279] Justice in the particular case can override principled objections to a foreign law. A similar approach (albeit in reverse, justifying the invocation of public policy) can be discerned in cases concerning the recognition of foreign divorces where the doctrine of public policy tends to be used only where justice in the particular case so demands.[280] Most of the family law cases where public

---

[274] *Deschamps v Miller* [1908] 1 Ch 856 at 863.   [275] [1988] QB 448.   [276] Ibid, 461.   [277] Ibid.
[278] Brooke LJ in *Kuwait Airways Corpn v Iraqi Airways Co (Nos 4 and 5)* [2002] 2 AC 883 at 972.
[279] Carter, 'The Role of Public Policy in English Conflict of Laws' (1993) 42 ICLQ 1, 4.
[280] See, eg, *Joyce v Joyce* [1979] Fam 93; *Golubovich v Golubovich* [2010] 3 WLR 1607 at [81].

policy in the guise of substantial justice has been used are also explicable on a similar basis. For example, in *Gray v Formosa*,[281] where the Maltese nullity decree granted on the ground that the parties had not married in a Roman Catholic church was denied recognition, the court was strongly influenced by the injustice that would be caused to the wife were the decree to be recognised and the fact that such recognition would have entailed the conclusion that a marriage contracted in an English register office was void.

English interests threatened

1.171 The second class of case includes the application to contracts governed by a foreign law of English domestic rules which invalidate contractual provisions in order to protect the English public interest, for example a rule invalidating a clause in restraint of trade.[282] If the contract in question will tend to damage the English public interest in the way in which the rule is designed to prevent, it will be held invalid even though it is valid by its foreign applicable law. The English interest is only the protection of free trade in England and, therefore, it is only contracts restraining free trade in England that will be held contrary to public policy. Similarly, in *Trendex Trading Corpn v Crédit Suisse*[283] a champertous assignment of an English cause of action was regarded as void. A champertous contract relating to litigation in a country where champerty is lawful would be regarded as valid.[284] In *Saxby v Fulton*[285] a contract for the loan of money to be used for gambling in Monte Carlo was enforced; were the gambling to have taken place in England, the contract would have been unenforceable. Another instance falling in this class is the refusal of the House of Lords in *Vervaeke v Smith*[286] to recognise a Belgian decree annulling a marriage on the ground that the parties never intended to cohabit because, inter alia, the English rule that such a marriage is valid is one of public policy and the marriage in question had substantial connections with England. Had all the connections of the parties been with Belgium in this case, a different result would have been reached.

1.172 Included in this category of situations are those where a transaction threatens the national interests of the United Kingdom and its good relations with other states. Examples include the rule which prohibits trading with the enemy[287] and the refusal either to enforce a contract to import liquor contrary to a friendly country's prohibition laws[288] or to export prohibited commodities.[289]

C Recognition and enforcement of foreign judgments

1.173 The problem here is one of laying down criteria as to when foreign judgments should be recognised. Clearly, one could adopt a view that all foreign judgments should be recognised provided they were granted by the courts of an internationally recognised country. This approach is being adopted increasingly within the European Union; most

---

[281] [1963] P 259.   [282] *Rousillon v Rousillon* (1880) 14 Ch D 351.
[283] [1982] AC 679. See also *Grell v Levy* (1864) 16 CBNS 73.
[284] Dicey, Morris and Collins, *The Conflict of Laws* (15th edn, 2012) p 102.   [285] [1909] 2 KB 208.
[286] [1983] 1 AC 145.
[287] *Dynamite Act v Rio Tinto Co Ltd* [1918] AC 260.   [288] *Foster v Driscoll* [1929] 1 KB 470.
[289] *Regazzoni v KC Sethia (1944) Ltd* [1958] AC 301.

commercial and matrimonial judgments granted by the courts of a Member State are entitled to automatic recognition in England with only limited exceptions. However, this takes place within a context of agreed and harmonised restrictions on jurisdiction; as the courts of certain countries exercise extraordinarily wide jurisdiction, such an approach would be inappropriate on a worldwide basis. Once one moves away from the proposition that all judgments should be recognised to the more limited version whereby only some are recognised, one needs carefully to circumscribe the circumstances in which judgments will be recognised. Generally, as with matters of jurisdiction and choice of law, the issue is one of appropriateness and degree of connection.

1.174 Is the criterion of appropriateness for recognition the same as that required for the exercise of jurisdiction? The answer to this depends on the area of law involved. In the commercial sphere, there is a strong case for demanding that the foreign court have the same degree of connection with the parties and/or the cause of action as would be required for the exercise of jurisdiction in England. If an English court today would not regard itself as an appropriate forum in *Maharanee of Baroda v Wildenstein*,[290] there would be little justification in recognising a Mexican judgment if the only connection with Mexico was that Mr Wildenstein had been temporarily present there when the proceedings were commenced. In the commercial sphere the recognition rules should be premised largely on the same basis as the jurisdictional rules, namely that defendants should not have to trouble themselves with defending claims in inappropriate fora. The policy considerations dictating when a court should exercise jurisdiction apply with equal force to the recognition and enforcement of foreign judgments. A degree of symmetry between jurisdictional and recognition rules is part of the scheme of protection to which defendants are entitled.

1.175 On the other hand, in some areas of law it could be justifiable to have a more flexible criterion of appropriateness for recognition than for jurisdictional purposes. With divorce jurisdiction, for example, the English court has to decide whether to become involved with the parties' marriage at all. This decision could have a profound effect; it would result in a change of status for the parties; matters affecting property distribution, financial relief, and arrangements for children would often need determination. Forum shopping is likely to be encouraged if courts are ready to assume jurisdiction too readily in a case with foreign elements. Accordingly, a fairly close connection between the parties and England will often be required before jurisdiction is exercised. With recognition of foreign divorces, on the other hand, the forum shopping, if any, has already taken place. A foreign court of competent jurisdiction (according to its rules) has heard the case and adjudicated upon it. The parties may have relied on the foreign divorce and remarried. Particularly, now that the English court is empowered to grant financial relief when recognising foreign divorces,[291] there is usually little to be gained by a denial of recognition. Accordingly, it could be justifiable to have more flexible criteria for the recognition of foreign divorces than for the exercise of divorce jurisdiction.

[290] [1972] 2 QB 283.   [291] Matrimonial and Family Proceedings Act 1984, Pt III.

2

Civil jurisdiction

I Introduction

A General considerations

2.1 This chapter addresses the English court's jurisdiction other than in family law matters (which is dealt with in Chapter 8) and excluding a few other kinds of proceedings.[1]

2.2 Broadly speaking, questions of jurisdiction may be looked at from two angles—one positive, the other negative. Looked at positively, there are various reasons why the English court may be a suitable forum to decide a dispute that has foreign elements. One is that the parties have agreed or submitted to its jurisdiction. If both parties are content for litigation to proceed in England there can be little objection to the assumption of jurisdiction by the English court. A second ground is a connection between the defendant and England; it will seldom be an injustice to a person to have to defend a case in his own country. Thirdly, the English court may be appropriate because there is a connection between the substance of the claim and England. While it may cause a foreign defendant expense and inconvenience to defend proceedings in England, it may nevertheless be reasonable for the English court to deal with the case if relevant events occurred in England. For example, if the defendant is alleged to have committed a tort against an English claimant while on a visit to England, both fairness to the claimant and the ready availability of witnesses and other evidence make the English court an appropriate forum.

2.3 These positive considerations are only one half of the equation. Situations arise in which, although England is prima facie a suitable forum, there are good grounds for the courts of another country to try the case. There are various reasons why a foreign court may be a more appropriate forum, notwithstanding the fact that there is a sufficient connection with England to justify the assumption of jurisdiction by the English court. For example, it may be more convenient for the claim against the defendant to be joined to related proceedings already pending in a foreign forum when the claimant seeks to invoke the English court's jurisdiction. A jurisdictional inquiry involves not only an investigation of the potential bases on which the English court may assume jurisdiction, but also a consideration of countervailing factors which may point towards

---

[1] Such as administration of estates and bankruptcy.

the English court staying the proceedings or declining jurisdiction in favour of the courts of another country.

2.4 It has been suggested that certain aspects of English law relating to the assumption of jurisdiction may have to be reconsidered in light of the Human Rights Act 1998, which implements the European Convention on Human Rights (ECHR). In *Lubbe v Cape plc*[2] it was argued that, if the English proceedings were stayed, the claimants would be deprived of their right to a fair trial under article 6 of the ECHR. As the House of Lords refused to grant a stay under normal principles,[3] the argument did not have to be directly addressed. Nevertheless, Lord Bingham did not think that 'article 6 supports any conclusion which is not already reached on application of [the usual] principles'.[4] Although, in particular circumstances, the ECHR may become relevant, its role is unlikely to be other than marginal. Article 6 of the ECHR protects the right to a 'fair and public hearing before an independent and impartial tribunal established by law', but it says nothing about where that right has to be capable of being exercised.[5] Only in exceptional circumstances will jurisdiction rules designed to determine where litigation is to take place (rather than whether or not it can take place at all) run the risk of falling foul of the Human Rights Act 1998.[6]

2.5 In the context of the current discussion there are two types of claim which may be commenced in England: claims in personam and Admiralty claims in rem. A claim in personam is one in which the claimant seeks a judgment requiring the defendant to pay money, deliver property or do, or refrain from doing, some other act. A claimant who wishes to commence proceedings in personam must be able to serve a claim form on the defendant—either in England or abroad. In certain circumstances a claimant is able to serve process on the defendant as of right; in others the claimant requires the permission of the court. Typical proceedings in personam include claims for an injunction or damages in tort and claims for damages or specific performance for breach of contract.

2.6 Admiralty proceedings in rem are directed against property, usually a ship.[7] Although it is not uncommon for the ship to be referred to as the defendant in a claim in rem, the reality is that the claim is brought against the owner of the ship.[8] A typical case is where the claimant has a claim against a ship-owner in respect of his ship—for example, where the claimant's cargo has been damaged as a result of the negligent navigation of the vessel. Proceedings in rem are commenced by process being affixed to any suitable part of the superstructure of the ship. The claimant will normally

---

[2] [2000] 1 WLR 1545.
[3] As laid down in *Spiliada Maritime Corpn v Cansulex Ltd* [1987] AC 460. See paras 2.215–2.238.
[4] [2000] 1 WLR 1545 at 1561. [5] See Atkins J in *The Kribi* [2001] 1 Lloyd's Rep 76 at 87.
[6] See, generally, Fawcett, 'The Impact of Article 6(1) of the ECHR on Private International Law' (2007) 56 ICLQ 1.
[7] A claim in rem may also be directed at cargo or freight and, in certain circumstances, against aircraft: Senior Courts Act 1981, s 21(5).
[8] *Republic of India v India Steamship Co (No 2)* [1998] AC 878. See Teare, 'The Admiralty Action In Rem and the House of Lords' [1998] LMCLQ 33.

also seek to arrest the ship so that it can be sold to meet any judgment granted to the claimant. However, the owner will often avoid the arrest of the vessel (or obtain the vessel's release after its arrest) by giving security for the claim. In that case the proceedings assume a hybrid character; the claim continues in rem (notionally) against the ship and also in personam against the ship-owner who has submitted to the English court's jurisdiction by giving security. Where a claim is brought solely in rem the claimant is confined to the proceeds of sale of the ship for the satisfaction of his judgment, but the claimant is not so limited in a case which is brought both in rem and in personam.

B The structure of English law on jurisdiction in personam

2.7 There are three main regimes governing the in personam jurisdiction of the English court. The first, which has a European origin, is the Brussels I Recast (which is derived from the Brussels Convention on Jurisdiction and the Enforcement of Judgments in Civil and Commercial Matters). The second regime is a modified version of the European jurisdiction rules, which in certain circumstances allocates jurisdiction within the United Kingdom. Thirdly, there are the so-called traditional rules which apply in cases not regulated by the European rules and/or the modified version which allocate jurisdiction within the United Kingdom.[9] A brief introductory description of these regimes will be given before aspects of the law are analysed in more detail.

1. The Brussels I Recast

(A) Development

2.8 In the 1960s the original six Member States of the EEC[10] negotiated a convention to provide for uniform rules on jurisdiction in civil and commercial matters and for the reciprocal recognition and enforcement of judgments in such matters. These negotiations led to the signing of the Brussels Convention in 1968. As the EC expanded in the latter part of the twentieth century the new Member States acceded to the Brussels Convention.[11]

2.9 The next step in the development of the Brussels regime was the replacement of the Brussels Convention by the so-called Brussels I Regulation,[12] which came into force in 2002 (hereafter 'the 2002 Regulation'). The territorial scope of the 2002 Regulation

---

[9] In the 1990s the Hague Conference on Private International Law commenced work which, it was hoped, would lead to a worldwide jurisdiction and judgments convention (based, to some extent, on the European model). The final version of this convention, which was agreed in June 2005, was much less ambitious; it focuses only on the enforcement of jurisdiction agreements and the recognition and enforcement of judgments in cases where the court of origin assumed jurisdiction on the basis of the parties' agreement. The Convention came into force between the Member States of the European Union (except Denmark), on the one hand, and Mexico, on the other, on 1 October 2015.

[10] Belgium, Germany, France, Italy, Luxembourg, and the Netherlands.

[11] In 1978, Denmark, Ireland, and the United Kingdom; in 1982, Greece; in 1989, Spain and Portugal; in 1996, Austria, Finland, and Sweden.

[12] Regulation (EC) No 44/2001, OJ 2001 L12/1.

expanded as new Member States acceded to the EU.[13] The 2002 Regulation made provision for the European Commission to report on the functioning of the Regulation and, if appropriate, to make proposals for its amendment. This process of revision was initiated by the Commission in 2009[14] and a proposal for a revised Regulation was published towards the end of 2010.[15] The revised version—known as the Brussels I Recast[16] (also referred to as 'the Recast')—was enacted in 2012 and came into force in January 2015.[17] The first three Chapters of the Recast define its scope (Chapter I), set out detailed rules on jurisdiction (Chapter II), and make provision for the reciprocal recognition and enforcement of judgments (Chapter III).[18]

(B) Interpretation

2.10 Questions of interpretation under the Brussels I Recast may be referred to the Court of Justice in accordance with the terms of article 267 of the Treaty on the Functioning of the European Union (TFEU). Under article 267 TFEU, a court against which there is no judicial remedy under national law 'shall' make a reference if a ruling on a point of European law is necessary to enable the court to make its decision;[19] any other court or tribunal 'may' make such a reference.

2.11 In the context of the Brussels Convention, it was provided that, when ascertaining the meaning of provisions of the Convention the court may consider the official reports which accompanied the Convention and the various subsequent Accession Conventions,[20] of which the most important are the Jenard Report[21] and the Schlosser Report.[22] In view of the importance of continuity between the Brussels Convention, the 2002 Regulation and the Recast,[23] these reports remain relevant when the provisions

---

[13] In 2004, the Czech Republic, Cyprus, Estonia, Hungary, Latvia, Lithuania, Malta, Poland, Slovakia, and Slovenia; in 2007, Bulgaria and Romania; in 2013, Croatia.

[14] See *Report from the Commission . . . on the application of Council Regulation (EC) No 44/2001 on jurisdiction and the recognition and enforcement of judgments in civil and commercial matters*, COM (2009) 174 final; *Green Paper on the Review of Council Regulation (EC) No 44/2001 on Jurisdiction and the Recognition and Enforcement of Judgments in Civil and Commercial Matters* (hereafter '*Brussels I Recast Green Paper*'), COM (2009) 175 final.

[15] European Commission, *Proposal for a Regulation of the European Parliament and of the Council on jurisdiction and the recognition and enforcement of judgments in civil and commercial matters* (hereafter '*Brussels I Recast Proposal*'), COM (2010) 748 final.

[16] Regulation (EU) No 1215/2012, OJ 2012 L351/1. See Dickinson and Lein, *The Brussels I Regulation Recast* (2015); Mankowski and Magnus (eds), *Brussels Ibis Regulation* (2015); Nielsen, 'The New Brussels I Regulation' (2013) 50 CML Rev 503.

[17] Although Denmark did not participate in the adoption of the Brussels I Recast, the provisions of the Recast apply to relations between Denmark and the other EU Member States by virtue of a separate agreement: see OJ 2013 L79/4. The Lugano Convention regulates the relationship between, on the one hand, the EU Member States and, on the other, Iceland, Norway, and Switzerland. The current version of the Lugano Convention, dating from 2007, follows closely the text of the 2002 Regulation.

[18] There are a number of substantive differences between the Recast and the Lugano Convention. This chapter considers Chapters I and II of the Recast.

[19] In the context of English civil proceedings, the Supreme Court is, for nearly all practical purposes, the only court against whose decisions there is no judicial remedy.

[20] Civil Jurisdiction and Judgments Act 1982, s 3(3).   [21] OJ 1979 C59/1.   [22] OJ 1979 C59/71.

[23] 2002 Regulation, recital (19); Brussels I Recast, recital (34). See, eg, Case C-133/11 *Folien Fischer v Ritama SpA* [2013] QB 523; Case C-375/13 *Kolassa v Barclays Bank plc* [2015] ILPr 14.

of the Recast derived from the earlier instruments are under consideration, as does the extensive case law of the Court of Justice. The Court of Justice may also take account of the relevant travaux préparatoires, in particular the European Commission's proposals which preceded the adoption of the 2002 Regulation and the Recast.[24]

2.12 The Court of Justice has adopted a teleological style of interpretation; the Recast must be interpreted having regard to both its principles and objectives.[25] Because each of the different language versions is equally authoritative an ambiguity in the English text may be resolved by reference to other language versions.

2.13 The Court of Justice has been required to consider on numerous occasions whether a specific concept should be given an autonomous interpretation or a national one. This is a question of policy which has to be resolved by reference to the objectives of the instrument in question. Because the Brussels I Recast (like the Convention and the 2002 Regulation before it) aims to produce uniformity in the allocation of jurisdiction, the Court of Justice tends to impose an autonomous interpretation in relation to the terms used in Chapter I, which defines the material scope of the Recast, and the conceptual categories which determine the scope of the specific jurisdiction provisions in Chapter II. For example, whether a particular dispute concerns 'matters relating to a contract' for the purposes of article 7(1) has to be decided by reference to a supranational conception of 'contract' rather than a purely national one.[26] It is not, however, the aim of the Brussels I Recast to harmonise the systems of civil procedure of the Member States.[27] Accordingly, matters which relate to procedural consequences or the detailed operation of legal concepts are normally to be interpreted by reference to the relevant national law.

(C) Outline

2.14 Within its material scope, the Brussels I Recast determines the international jurisdiction of the courts of Member States (such as where an English claimant sues an English defendant in respect of a tort committed in Jamaica[28] or where a German national of unknown domicile is sued in the Czech Republic for payment of arrears on a mortgage loan[29]). The material scope of the Recast, which is defined by article 1, encompasses civil and commercial matters, but does not extend to revenue, customs, or administrative matters. In broad terms, the phrase 'civil and commercial matters' covers 'legal actions for compensation for disturbance of ownership and property rights, contractual performance and damages'.[30] Problems surrounding the scope of civil and commercial matters are likely to arise most frequently in cases where one of the parties to the

---

[24] *Brussels I Proposal*, COM (1999) 348 final; *Brussels I Recast Proposal*, COM (2010) 748 final.
[25] Case 33/78 *Somafer SA v Saar-Ferngas AG* [1978] ECR 2183.   [26] See para 2.71.
[27] Case 365/88 *Kongress Agentur Hagen GmbH v Zeehaghe BV* [1990] ECR I–1845.
[28] Case C–281/02 *Owusu v Jackson* [2005] ECR I–1383. See also Case C–478/12 *Maletic v lastminute.com GmbH* [2014] QB 424 (in which the claimant and the second defendant were domiciled in Austria).
[29] Case C–327/10 *Hypotecni banka as v Lindner* [2011] ECR I–11543.
[30] Joined Cases C–226/13, C–245/13, C–247/13 & C–578/13 *Fahnenbrock v Greek Republic* [2016] ILPr 4 at para 59.

litigation is a public authority. Proceedings fall outside the ambit of article 1 where the dispute involves a public authority acting in the exercise of its public authority powers.[31] However, a case involving a public authority is within the scope of the Recast if the relationship between the parties is governed by private law.[32] The Recast covers, for example, a claim by a public authority for recovery of overpaid compensation for the loss of real property from victims of persecution under the Nazi regime,[33] an action whereby a public authority claims damages for loss caused by a tortious conspiracy to commit VAT fraud,[34] and a claim for legal redress for damage resulting from the infringement of EU competition law.[35]

2.15 It is also provided that various matters are excluded from the Recast's scope.[36] Matters relating to the status or legal capacity of natural persons, rights in property arising out of a matrimonial relationship, and wills or succession are excluded. In addition, the Recast does not apply to bankruptcy, proceedings relating to the winding up of insolvent companies or other legal persons, judicial arrangements, compositions and analogous proceedings,[37] social security,[38] or arbitration. Of these exceptions the one which has posed most difficulty is the one relating to arbitration.[39]

2.16 When a question arises whether or not proceedings fall within the Recast's scope, reference must be made solely to the subject-matter of the dispute; if, by virtue of its subject-matter a dispute concerns one of the exceptions to article 1, the existence of a preliminary issue which is within the scope of article 1 does not bring the proceedings under the Recast.[40] By the same token, a civil or commercial claim (such as a claim for breach of contract) falls within the scope of the Recast, notwithstanding the fact that the court must, as a preliminary issue, determine whether or not the parties in dispute are bound by an arbitration clause, a question which is outside the scope of the

---

[31] Case 814/79 *Netherlands State v Rüffer* [1980] ECR 3807; Case C-172/91 *Sonntag v Waidmann* [1993] ECR I-1963; Case C-292/05 *Lechouritou v Dimosio tis Omospondiakis Dimokratias tis Germanias* [2007] ECR I-1519.

[32] Case C-271/00 *Gemeente Steenbergen v Baten* [2002] ECR I-10489; Case C-266/01 *Préservatrice foncière TIARD SA v Netherlands* [2003] ECR I-4867; Case C-433/01 *Freistaat Bayern v Blijdenstein* [2004] ECR I-981; Case C-265/02 *Frahuil SA v Assitalia SpA* [2004] ECR I-1543.

[33] Case C-645/11 *Land Berlin v Sapir* [2013] ILPr 29.

[34] Case C-49/12 *Revenue and Customs Commissioners v Sunico APS* [2013] ILPr 43, noted by Collins, (2014) 130 LQR 353.

[35] Case C-302/13 *FlyLAL-Lithuanian Airlines SAS v Starptautiska Lidosta Riga VAS* [2015] ILPr 2.

[36] Art 1(2).

[37] Case 133/78 *Gourdain v Nadler* [1979] ECR 733; Case C-111/08 *SCT Industri AB (in liquidation) v Alpenblume AB* [2009] ECR I-5655. As between EU Member States private international law aspects of insolvency proceedings are dealt with by Regulation (EC) No 848/2015, OJ 2015 L141/19 (replacing Regulation (EC) No 1346/2000, OJ 2000 L160/1).

[38] Case C-271/00 *Gemeente Steenbergen v Baten* [2002] ECR I-10489.

[39] Case C-190/89 *Marc Rich & Co AG v Società Italiana Impianti* [1991] ECR I-3855; Case C-391/95 *Van Uden Maritime BV v Firma Deco-Line* [1998] ECR I-7091; Case C-185/07 *West Tankers Inc v Allianz SpA* [2009] 1 AC 1138; Case C-536/13 *Proceedings concerning Gazprom OAO* [2015] 1 WLR 4937. For an evaluation of these cases, see Hartley, 'The Brussels I Regulation and Arbitration' (2014) 63 ICLQ 63. See the discussion at paras 2.318–2.321 and 3.93–3.96.

[40] Case C-190/89 *Marc Rich & Co AG v Società Italiana Impianti* [1991] ECR I-3855, para 26.

Recast. In *West Tankers Inc v Allianz SpA*[41] the question concerning the scope of the 2002 Regulation arose in a case in which the claimant applied for an injunction to restrain the defendant from pursuing Italian proceedings which were allegedly brought in breach of an arbitration agreement by which the parties were bound. The claimant argued that, as the purpose of the injunction was to enforce the arbitration agreement, the application fell outside the 2002 Regulation's scope. On a reference from the House of Lords, the Court of Justice decided that, notwithstanding the arbitration agreement, the Italian proceedings (which involved a claim in tort) concerned civil and commercial matters within the scope of the 2002 Regulation;[42] furthermore, an anti-suit injunction whose purpose was to obstruct the Italian proceedings was held to be incompatible with the Regulation.[43] Although the Recast does not alter the text of article 1 in this regard, it does introduce a new recital in response to the *West Tankers* decision. The significance of this recital, which relates to the recognition and enforcement of judgments, rather than the allocation of jurisdiction, is considered in the next chapter.[44]

2.17 As regards the allocation of jurisdiction under the Recast, the defendant's domicile[45] is 'the point on which the jurisdiction rules hinge'.[46] A defendant who is domiciled in a Member State may normally be sued in the courts of that state.[47] However, the Recast specifies circumstances in which a person domiciled in one Member State may be sued in other Member States. For example, where a person domiciled in England commits a tort in France the claimant has a choice whether to bring proceedings in England or in France; where an English company and a German company agree to refer a dispute to the jurisdiction of the German courts the German company may sue the English company in Germany.

2.18 In terms of basic philosophy, the Brussels I Recast favours certainty over flexibility. One of the central objectives of the Recast is to enable a claimant to identify easily the court (or courts) in which he may sue and the defendant reasonably to foresee before which court (or courts) he may be sued.[48] This approach is in marked contrast to the English traditional rules, whose operation is, to a large extent, based on judicial discretion.

2.19 Where proceedings are covered by article 1 of the Recast, the English court cannot assume jurisdiction over a defendant domiciled in another Member State on the basis of the traditional rules; a person domiciled in a Member State may be sued in the courts of another Member State only in accordance with the terms of the Recast.[49] Where proceedings are commenced in England against a person domiciled in another

---

[41] Case C–185/07 [2009] 1 AC 1138.
[42] See also *Youell v La Réunion Aérienne* [2009] 1 Lloyd's Rep 586.   [43] See paras 2.318–2.321.
[44] See paras 3.95–3.96.
[45] For the purposes of the Brussels I Recast 'domicile' has a special meaning and is different from the common law concept considered in Chapter 6. See paras 2.27–2.30.
[46] Jenard-Möller Report, OJ 1990 C189/65.   [47] Art 4.
[48] See, eg, Case C–533/07 *Falco Privatstiftung v Weller-Lindhorst* [2009] ECR I–3327, para 22; Case C–327/10 *Hypotecni banka as v Lindner* [2011] ECR I–11543, para 44.
[49] Art 5; Case 9/12 *Corman-Collins SA v La Maison du Whisky SA* [2014] QB 431. Where the English court has jurisdiction under the Brussels I Recast, the claim form may be served on the defendant out of the jurisdiction without the permission of the court: CPR r 6.33.

Member State and the defendant does not enter an appearance, if the Recast does not confer jurisdiction on the English court, the court must decline jurisdiction of its own motion.[50]

2.20 If the defendant is not domiciled in a Member State the general rule is that the court may apply its traditional rules on jurisdiction.[51] However, there are certain bases of jurisdiction under the Recast which apply regardless of domicile. For example, the effect of article 24(1) is that a dispute relating to the ownership of immovable property in Italy is within the exclusive jurisdiction of the Italian courts, whether the defendant is domiciled in Italy, another Member State or a third state (that is, a non-Member State). It is a mistake to think that the Recast does not apply to parties who are not domiciled in a Member State. The Brussels I Recast also includes provisions that are designed to reduce the incidence of conflicting judgments by preventing situations where the courts of two or more Member States may assume jurisdiction in relation to the same or related issues. According to these rules, where parallel proceedings involving the same parties and the same cause of action are brought in more than one Member State (lis pendens) the general rule is that any court other than the court 'first seised' must stay the proceedings or decline jurisdiction; where related proceedings are brought in different Member States, a court other than the court 'first seised' may, in the exercise of its discretion, stay the proceedings or, if certain conditions are fulfilled, decline jurisdiction.

2. Schedule 4 to the Civil Jurisdiction and Judgments Act 1982

2.21 Schedule 4, which is modelled on Chapter II of the Recast, applies when the defendant is domiciled in the United Kingdom (or article 24 of the Recast allocates exclusive jurisdiction to the courts of the United Kingdom) and the proceedings are within the material scope of the Recast.[52] However, the Court of Justice has no jurisdiction under article 267 TFEU to rule on the interpretation of schedule 4, even in relation to those of its provisions which are identical to the equivalent provisions of the Recast.[53] Schedule 4 operates in two main ways.

2.22 First, it supplements the Recast in those cases where its rules allocate jurisdiction to the United Kingdom but without specifying any particular part of the United Kingdom.[54] For example, the effect of article 4 of the Recast is simply that a person domiciled in the United Kingdom may be sued in the United Kingdom. Rule 1 of schedule 4 identifies the particular part (or parts[55]) of the United Kingdom in which proceedings may be

---

[50] Art 28(1). Under art 28(2), the court should normally stay the proceedings if the defendant has not been able to receive the document instituting the proceedings in sufficient time to enable him to arrange for his defence. But, see Case C-327/10 *Hypotecni banka as v Lindner* [2011] ECR I-11543; Case C-292/10 *G v de Visser* [2013] QB 168.
[51] Art 6.   [52] Civil Jurisdiction and Judgments Act 1982, s 16.
[53] Case C-346/93 *Kleinwort Benson Ltd v City of Glasgow District Council* [1995] ECR I-615.
[54] Where the Brussels I Recast allocates jurisdiction to a 'place' rather than to a Member State (eg, where art 7(1) or (2) applies) sch 4 to the Civil Jurisdiction and Judgments Act 1982 does not have to be invoked.
[55] *Daniel v Foster* 1989 SLT (Sh Ct) 90.

brought by providing that a person domiciled in a part of the United Kingdom may be sued in that part.

2.23 Secondly, schedule 4 allocates jurisdiction in cases which are internal to the United Kingdom but which have connections with more than one part of it.[56] The effect, so far as the English court is concerned, is that Scotland and Northern Ireland are (subject to modifications) treated as if they were Member States. If the defendant is domiciled in another part of the United Kingdom the English court will have jurisdiction only if it would have had jurisdiction had the defendant been domiciled in another Member State. The effect of schedule 4 is that, as regards disputes that fall within the material scope of the Recast, the English court cannot assume jurisdiction on the basis of the traditional rules if the defendant is domiciled in another part of the United Kingdom.

3. The traditional rules

2.24 At common law the basis of the English court's jurisdiction in claims in personam is that the defendant is amenable to the court's jurisdiction—in the sense that the claim form commencing the proceedings can be served on him (whether in England or abroad). If the defendant is present in England, process can be served on him in England. If the defendant is not present in England at the commencement of the proceedings, but he has submitted to being sued in England, the English court has jurisdiction. If the defendant cannot be served with process in England, and does not submit to the jurisdiction, then the court may have the power under CPR rule 6.36 to assume jurisdiction by giving permission for process to be served on the defendant out of the jurisdiction.[57] This power arises where, notwithstanding the fact that the defendant is foreign, there is a connection between the events or subject-matter of the dispute and England.

2.25 An important feature of the traditional rules is that the outer limits of the court's jurisdiction are fixed by the court's discretion. Where a defendant is served with process in England as of right (because he is physically in England at the time of service) the court may nevertheless grant a stay of the English proceedings at the request of the defendant on the basis that there is a more appropriate forum abroad (forum non conveniens). Similarly, in exercising its powers to give permission for service of process out of the jurisdiction under CPR rule 6.36 the court has discretion and will permit service only if it is shown that England is the appropriate forum (forum conveniens).

2.26 When the traditional rules are compared with the Brussels I Recast the obvious difference in approach is that under the Recast the assumption of jurisdiction is, for the most part, mandatory whereas under the traditional rules the scope of the court's jurisdiction is largely determined by the exercise of discretion on the basis of an assessment of whether the English court is the appropriate forum.

---

[56] Unless jurisdiction is allocated by the Brussels I Recast. See the discussion of art 24(1) at paras 2.39–2.45 and art 25 at paras 2.46–2.57.

[57] The jurisdictional bases ('gateways') which enable the court to permit service out of the jurisdiction under CPR r 6.36 are listed in CPR PD 6B para 3.1.

4. The meaning of 'domicile'

2.27 Under the Brussels I Recast the English court's jurisdiction may depend on whether the defendant is domiciled in England, in another part of the United Kingdom, in another Member State, or in a third state (that is, a non-Member State). It is provided that, as regards individuals, the law of each Member State determines whether a person is domiciled in that state.[58] For the purposes of the Recast, 'domicile' is given a special meaning, which is different from its meaning at common law and closer to the continental usage of this term: an individual is domiciled in the United Kingdom if he is resident in the United Kingdom and the nature and circumstances of his residence indicate that he has a substantial connection with the United Kingdom, which will be presumed to be so (unless the contrary is proved) if he has been resident in the United Kingdom for the last three months or more.[59] A person will be regarded as resident in a particular part of the United Kingdom if that place is his settled or usual place of abode.[60] Mere ownership of a house in England by the defendant does not amount to domicile if the defendant's use of the house is infrequent, intermittent, and fleeting.[61]

2.28 If an individual is not domiciled in the forum state according to its law, then a court of that state must decide whether he is domiciled in another Member State by applying the law of the latter state.[62] If, for example, an English court wishes to determine whether someone is domiciled in France (for the purposes of the Recast) it must apply French law.

2.29 As regards the domicile of companies and other legal persons, article 63(1) of the Recast lays down a uniform rule: a company or other legal person (or association of natural or legal persons) is domiciled at the place where it has its statutory seat or its central administration or its principal place of business.[63] A company's central administration is not determined by where board meetings and AGMs are held, but is located where the company (through its organs) takes the decisions that are essential for the company's operations—in other words, the place where the company conducts its entrepreneurial management.[64] The principal place of business is where the company's main economic activity takes place. In practice, the principal place of business of a company and its central administration will often be in the same country.

2.30 As article 63 refers to the relevant connecting factors as alternatives, it is possible for a company to have more than one domicile (where, for example, its central

---

[58] Art 62(1).
[59] Civil Jurisdiction and Judgments Order 2001, SI 2001/3929, sch 1, para 9(2), (6). To determine whether an individual is domiciled in England, the same test applies (mutatis mutandis): sch 1, para 9(3), (6). An individual is also to be regarded as domiciled in England if he is domiciled in the United Kingdom and resident in England and the nature and circumstances of his residence do not indicate that he has a substantial connection with any particular part of the United Kingdom: sch 1, para 9(5).
[60] *Bank of Dubai Ltd v Abbas* [1997] ILPr 308.
[61] *Cherney v Deripaska* [2007] 2 All ER (Comm) 785.   [62] Art 62(2).
[63] In the United Kingdom (and Ireland) the statutory seat means the registered office, or if there is no such office, the place of incorporation or, if there is no such place, the place under the law of which the formation took place: art 63(2).
[64] *Young v Anglo American South Africa Ltd* [2014] 2 CLC 143.

administration is in Italy, but its principal place of business is in Spain).[65] It is also possible for an individual to be regarded as domiciled in more than one Member State (where, for example, an individual is domiciled in England under English law and domiciled in Germany under German law).

C The structure of English law on jurisdiction in rem

2.31 The situations in which the claimant may invoke the court's Admiralty jurisdiction in rem are set out in provisions of the Senior Courts Act 1981.[66] Although these provisions are based on international conventions,[67] the terms of the 1981 Act are, in certain respects, broader than the conventions from which the domestic legislation is derived. The Act provides, for example, that the English court may assume jurisdiction in a case involving 'any claim for damage done by a ship'[68] or 'any claim for loss of or damage to goods carried in a ship'[69] or 'any claim arising out of any agreement relating to the carriage of goods in a ship or to the use or hire of a ship'.[70] As a general rule, where a claim falls within the scope of the court's Admiralty jurisdiction, proceedings in rem may be brought against the ship or property in connection with which the claim arises.[71] It is also provided that in certain circumstances a claim in rem can be brought against a sister ship of the ship in connection with which the claim arises.[72]

2.32 The Admiralty jurisdiction of the English court in rem is strictly territorial. Although there is no requirement that the claim or the parties should have any connection with England, the claimant may invoke the jurisdiction of the English court only if, first, the claim falls within one of the bases of jurisdiction outlined in the 1981 Act and, secondly, the ship in question can be served with the claim form in English territorial waters. However, just as with a claim in personam where jurisdiction is based on the defendant's presence in England, the court has discretion to grant a stay of proceedings on the ground of forum non conveniens. Indeed, several of the cases in which the forum-non-conveniens doctrine was developed were commenced as Admiralty actions in rem.[73]

2.33 The Brussels I Recast does not formally draw a distinction between cases involving claims in personam and cases involving Admiralty claims in rem. Although the impact of the Recast is limited by article 71 which preserves the effect of special conventions in the field of jurisdiction and the recognition and enforcement of judgments,[74] there are two important ways in which the Recast has a role to play with regard to claims in rem.

2.34 First, where the claim falls within the material scope of the Brussels I Recast and the person who is interested in contesting the claim in rem is domiciled in a Member

---

[65] See the discussion in *Alberta Inc v Katanga Mining Ltd* [2009] ILPr 14.   [66] Ss 20–24.
[67] There are two important conventions which date from 1952: the International Convention for the Unification of Certain Rules relating to the Arrest of Seagoing Ships and the International Convention for the Unification of Certain Rules concerning Civil Jurisdiction in Matters of Collision.
[68] S 20(2)(e).   [69] S 20(2)(g).   [70] S 20(2)(h).   [71] S 21(2) and (3).   [72] S 21(4).
[73] Eg, *The Atlantic Star* [1974] AC 436; *The Abidin Daver* [1984] AC 398.
[74] Such as the 1952 Arrest and Collision Conventions. See Case C-148/03 *Nürnberger Allgemeine Versicherungs AG v Portbridge Transport BV* [2004] ECR I-10327 (a case concerning the Convention on the Contract for the International Carriage of Goods by Road 1956).

State, the English court has jurisdiction only if the assumption of jurisdiction under the Senior Courts Act 1981 is consistent either with the special conventions preserved by article 71 or with the provisions of Chapter II of the Recast.[75] Where, for example, cargo-owners bring English proceedings in rem in respect of a vessel chartered by a German defendant, but refrain from arresting the vessel because the defendant puts up security for the claim, the English court does not have jurisdiction.[76] This is because, in such circumstances, the assumption of jurisdiction under the Senior Courts Act 1981 is authorised neither by the Recast (because the defendant is domiciled in Germany rather than in England) nor by the Arrest Convention (because the application of the Arrest Convention depends on the ship having been arrested). The fact that the court would have had jurisdiction under the Senior Courts Act 1981 if the defendant had not been domiciled in a Member State is irrelevant.

2.35 Secondly, because the special conventions preserved by article 71 do not address questions relating to parallel or related proceedings, the provisions of the Recast fill the gap. Where parallel or related proceedings are commenced in two or more Member States, the provisions of the Recast concerning lis pendens and related actions are relevant whether the proceedings are in personam or in rem.[77]

II Bases of jurisdiction in personam

2.36 When considering the bases on which the court may assume jurisdiction in personam it is important to distinguish those cases that are governed by the Brussels I Recast from those which fall under the traditional rules. Whether the case is determined by the Recast or the traditional rules, the territorial connections of the claimant—in terms of nationality, domicile, or residence—are generally irrelevant when deciding whether or not the claim is covered by the particular jurisdictional basis invoked by the claimant.[78]

A Bases of jurisdiction under the Brussels I Recast

2.37 Although the domicile of the defendant is the point on which the jurisdiction rules in Chapter II hinge, it is appropriate in cases falling within the material scope of the Recast—as determined by article 1—to start by considering those bases of jurisdiction

---

[75] See *The Po* [1991] 2 Lloyd's Rep 206; *The Nordglimt* [1988] QB 183; *The Deichland* [1990] 1 QB 361; *The Prinsengracht* [1993] 1 Lloyd's Rep 41.

[76] *The Deichland* [1990] 1 QB 361.

[77] Case C-406/92 *Owners of the cargo lately laden on board the ship 'Tatry' v Owners of the ship 'Maciej Rataj'* [1994] ECR I-5439. See also Case C-452/12 *Nipponkoa Insurance Co (Europe) Ltd v Inter-Zuid Transport BV* [2014] ILPr 10; *British American Tobacco Switzerland SA v Exel Europe Ltd* [2015] 3 WLR 1173 (both cases concerning carriage of goods under the Convention on the Contract for the International Carriage of Goods by Road).

[78] Other than in relation to a few specific provisions, the Brussels I Recast applies whether or not the claimant is domiciled in a Member State: Case C-412/98 *Universal General Insurance Co (USIG) v Group Josi Reinsurance Co SA* [2000] ECR I-5925.

which apply in relation to all defendants, regardless of their domicile. If the jurisdiction of the English court under the Recast is contested (for example, on the basis that England was not the place of performance of the contractual obligation in question or, in a tort case, the place where the harmful event occurred), the claimant must establish 'a good arguable case' that the conditions of the article invoked are satisfied.[79] The court is not required, however, to conduct a comprehensive taking of evidence at the stage of determining jurisdiction.[80]

1. General bases of jurisdiction which do not depend on the defendant being domiciled in a Member State

2.38 Article 6 provides that, except in cases where article 18(1), article 21(2), article 24, or article 25 is effective to confer jurisdiction on the courts of a Member State, if the defendant is not domiciled in a Member State, jurisdiction is to be determined by the traditional rules.[81]

(A) Exclusive jurisdiction

2.39 Article 24 allocates exclusive jurisdiction, regardless of the defendant's domicile,[82] in circumstances where the courts of a particular Member State are thought to be uniquely appropriate to adjudicate upon the subject-matter of the dispute. The five paragraphs of article 24 concern 'proceedings'[83] of various types: (1) certain proceedings relating to immovable property; (2) certain proceedings concerning the formation and dissolution of companies and partnerships and the validity of decisions of their organs;[84] (3) certain proceedings concerning entries in public registers; (4) certain proceedings concerning intellectual property rights;[85] and (5) proceedings concerning the enforcement of judgments.[86]

---

[79] *Canada Trust Co v Stolzenberg (No 2)* [2002] 1 AC 1. For an example of the application of the test, see *Morley v Reiter Engineering GmbH* [2012] ILPr 6. The requirement of a good arguable case is not satisfied if the arguments for and against are equal: *Joint Stock Co Aeroflot—Russian Airlines v Berezovsky* [2013] 2 CLC 206.

[80] Case C–375/13 *Kolassa v Barclays Bank plc* [2015] ILPr 14, para 64.

[81] Arts 18 and 21, which deal with consumer and employment contracts respectively, are considered at paras 2.134–2.139. It is also established that arts 29–33 apply regardless of domicile; these provisions are discussed at paras 2.180–2.211.

[82] In *Choudhary v Bhattar* [2010] 2 All ER 1031 the Court of Appeal held that, despite its explicit wording, the exclusive jurisdiction rule (now art 24 of the Recast) does not apply where the defendant is domiciled in a non-Member State if the conflict of jurisdiction is between a Member State and a non-Member State. However, this decision was wrongly decided as it is inconsistent with the case law of the Court of Justice (see, eg, Case C–73/04 *Klein v Rhodos Management Ltd* [2005] ECR I–8667, para 14). It seems clear that *Choudhary*'s case was decided per incuriam and should not be followed: *Dal Al Arkar Real Estate Development Co v Refai* [2015] 1 WLR 135.

[83] Applications for provisional measures are not 'proceedings' for the purposes of art 24: *JSC BTA Bank v Ablyazov* [2013] ILPr 53.

[84] See Case C–372/07 *Hassett v South Eastern Health Board* [2008] ECR I–7403; Case C–144/10 *Berliner Verkehrsbetriebe (BVG) v JP Morgan NA* [2011] 1 WLR 2087; Case C–302/13 *FlyLAL-Lithuanian Airlines SAS v Starptautiska Lidosta Riga VAS* [2015] ILPr 2.

[85] See Case 288/82 *Duijnstee v Goderbauer* [1983] ECR 3663; Case C–4/03 *Gesellschaft für Antriebstechnik mbH & Co KG v Lamellen und Kupplungsbau Beteiligungs KG* [2006] ECR I–6509.

[86] See Case C–261/90 *Reichert v Dresdner Bank (No 2)* [1992] ECR I–2149; Case C–129/92 *Owens Bank Ltd v Bracco* [1994] ECR I–117; *Masri v Consolidated Contractors International (UK) Ltd (No 2)* [2009] QB 450.

2.40 The jurisdiction rules in article 24 are mandatory and exclusive; they may not be departed from either by an agreement purporting to confer jurisdiction on the courts of another Member State or by submission to another forum. Their application is, however, dependent on the proceedings being principally concerned with matters covered by the jurisdiction rule in question.[87] If the claimant seeks to invoke the jurisdiction of the English court in a matter which, by virtue of the provisions of article 24, falls within the exclusive jurisdiction of the courts of another Member State, the English court must of its own motion decline jurisdiction.[88] As only the first of the five bases of exclusive jurisdiction has been repeatedly referred to the Court of Justice, the discussion which follows is limited to article 24(1).[89]

2.41 The general rule contained in article 24(1) provides that the courts of the Member State in which immovable property is situated have exclusive jurisdiction in proceedings which have as their object rights in rem in, or tenancies of, such property. If the immovable property is in England, the English court has jurisdiction irrespective of where the defendant is domiciled.[90] If, however, the property is situated in another Member State (or in another part of the United Kingdom), the English court may not assume jurisdiction, even if the defendant is domiciled in England.[91]

(i) Rights in rem in immovable property

2.42 Article 24(1) encompasses claims which seek to determine the extent, content, ownership, or possession of immovable property or the existence of other rights in rem therein and to provide the holders of those rights with the protection of the powers which attach to their interest.[92] For example, if land is occupied by squatters, a claim by the paper owner to evict the squatters and recover possession falls within the scope of article 24(1). Similarly, an application for a declaration that a right of pre-emption relating to land in Germany had not been validly exercised is within the exclusive jurisdiction of the German courts;[93] an action for the termination of a tenancy in common of immovable property by way of sale is within the scope of article 24(1).[94]

2.43 Conversely, there is a large body of case law indicating many types of legal proceedings which fall outside the scope of article 24(1). For example, an action which seeks to prevent a nuisance affecting land belonging to the claimant does not fall under article 24(1); although the basis of such an action is the interference with a right in rem in immovable property, the nature of the right is of only marginal significance.[95] Neither

---

[87] Case C-144/10 *Berliner Verkehrsbetriebe (BVG) v JP Morgan NA* [2011] 1 WLR 2087.
[88] Art 27.
[89] For consideration of the other paragraphs of what is now art 24, see Dicey, Morris and Collins, *The Conflict of Laws* (15th edn, 2012) pp 518–26.
[90] Art 24(1) of the Recast allocates jurisdiction to the courts of the United Kingdom; r 11(a) of sch 4 to the Civil Jurisdiction and Judgments Act 1982 gives exclusive jurisdiction to the English court.
[91] See, eg, *Re Hayward* [1997] Ch 45.
[92] Case 115/88 *Reichert v Dresdner Bank* [1990] ECR I-27, para 11.
[93] Case C-438/12 *Weber v Weber* [2015] Ch 140.
[94] Case C-605/14 *Komu v Komu*, [2016] 4 WLR 26.
[95] Case C-343/04 *Land Oberösterreich v ČEZ as* [2006] ECR I-4557, para 34.

a claim based on a contract for the transfer of ownership of immovable property[96] nor a claim for rescission of a contract for the sale of land and consequential damages[97] is covered by article 24(1). Where a defendant occupies immovable property for nine years under a transfer from the claimant which is subsequently declared by the courts to be void, a claim to recover compensation for use of the property during the nine-year period is not within the exclusive jurisdiction of the courts of the Member State in which the property is situated.[98] In addition, article 24(1) does not apply to a claim by a creditor to have a disposition of immovable property declared ineffective as against him on the ground that it was made in fraud of his rights by the debtor.[99] By the same token, an application by a person placed under guardianship for authorisation to dispose of his immovable property is linked to legal capacity and does not involve rights in rem in immovable property for the purposes of article 24(1).[100] English proceedings for a declaration that the defendant holds an apartment in the south of France on trust for the claimant and for an order that the defendant should execute such documents as are required to vest legal ownership in the claimant are outside the scope of article 24(1); as the claimant is not claiming that he already enjoys rights in relation to the property which are enforceable against the whole world, but is seeking only to assert rights as against the defendant, his claim is a claim in personam rather than a claim in rem within the meaning of article 24(1).[101] The application of this reasoning leads to the conclusion that the English court has jurisdiction to make an order for the sale of a villa situated in Portugal in a case where, following the bankruptcy of one of the owners, that person's trustee in bankruptcy applies for such an order.[102]

(ii) Tenancies of immovable property

2.44 In *Rösler v Rottwinkel*[103] the Court of Justice ruled that proceedings which have as their object a tenancy of immovable property (even a short holiday lease) include disputes as to the existence or interpretation of the lease and claims by the landlord for recovery of the premises, for rent and other charges, or for compensation for damage caused by the tenant, whether or not the proceedings are based on a right in rem.[104] However, article 24(1) does not apply to a dispute arising from an agreement by which one party is to take over from the other a business carried on in immovable property which the latter leases from a third party.[105] Article 24(1) does not apply to disputes which are only indirectly related to the use of the property let, such as a claim for the loss of holiday enjoyment and travel expenses[106] or disputes relating to holiday contracts

---

[96] Schlosser Report, OJ 1979 C59/122, para 172.
[97] Case C–518/99 *Gaillard v Chekili* [2001] ECR I–2771.
[98] Case C–292/93 *Lieber v Göbel* [1994] ECR I–2535.
[99] Case C–115/88 *Reichert v Dresdner Bank* [1990] ECR I–27.
[100] Case C–386/12 *Proceedings brought by Schneider* [2014] 2 WLR 1048.
[101] Case C–294/92 *Webb v Webb* [1994] ECR I–1717, para 15. For a criticism of this decision, see Briggs (1994) 14 YBEL 557.
[102] *Ashurst v Pollard* [2001] Ch 595.   [103] Case 241/83 [1985] ECR 99.
[104] See also Case C–8/98 *Dansommer A/S v Götz* [2000] ECR I–393.
[105] Case 73/77 *Sanders v van der Putte* [1977] ECR 2383.
[106] Case 241/83 *Rösler v Rottwinkel* [1985] ECR 99.

which include not only accommodation, but also other services, such as information and advice, the reservation of transport, reception on arrival, and insurance against cancellation.[107] Proceedings relating to disputes arising from financing arrangements concerning leases covered by article 24(1) fall outside the scope of the exclusive jurisdiction provisions.[108] Article 24(1) does not normally apply to claims arising out of timeshare contracts (at least, where the arrangement takes the form of a club membership contract under which the 'tenant's' entitlement may relate to different premises each year[109]); such agreements should be regarded as consumer contracts within the scope of article 17.[110]

2.45 The practical significance of *Rösler v Rottwinkel* with regard to short leases is limited by the fact that article 24(1) also provides that, in certain circumstances, the claimant may bring proceedings in the court of the Member State in which the defendant is domiciled. Where proceedings involve a tenancy for temporary private use for a maximum period of six consecutive months, the courts of the Member State in which the defendant is domiciled have jurisdiction, provided that the tenant is a natural person and that the landlord and the tenant are both domiciled in the same Member State. The forum designated by this rule relating to short leases is an alternative to the courts of the Member State in which the property is situated. If a cottage in England is let by its French owner to a French tenant for a period of three months, a dispute arising out of the tenancy may be litigated either in England or in France.

(B) Prorogation of jurisdiction: jurisdiction agreements

(i) Introduction

2.46 As a general rule, a person may confer jurisdiction on a court by consent. A party may consent by a formal agreement concluded within the context of a wider contractual relationship (such as a jurisdiction clause in a printed contract) or by submitting to the jurisdiction of a court after the commencement of proceedings by the claimant. The Brussels I Recast refers to both of these situations as examples of 'prorogation of jurisdiction'; by the parties' agreement or submission the jurisdiction of the courts of a Member State is thereby extended. Article 25 is concerned with the effects of jurisdiction agreements in favour of the courts of a Member State;[111] article 26, which enables a defendant to confer jurisdiction on the courts of a Member State by submission, is considered in a later section of this chapter.[112]

2.47 Under article 25(1), if the parties, regardless of their domicile, have agreed that a court or the courts of a particular Member State shall have jurisdiction over disputes relating

---

[107] Case C-280/90 *Hacker v Euro-Relais GmbH* [1992] ECR I-1111.
[108] *Jarrett v Barclays Bank plc* [1999] QB 1.
[109] Case C-73/04 *Klein v Rhodos Management Ltd* [2005] ECR I-8667.
[110] See European Commission, *Brussels I Proposal*, COM (1999) 348 final, p 16.
[111] Chapter II also includes specific rules relating to jurisdiction agreements in insurance contracts, consumer contracts, and individual contracts of employment. See paras 2.129–2.139.
[112] See paras 2.59–2.61.

to a particular legal relationship, then such court or courts will have jurisdiction,[113] provided that the agreement satisfies certain formal requirements.[114] The paradigm case covered by article 25 is where a dispute relates to a contract which contains a jurisdiction clause referring disputes to the courts of a particular country or place.[115] The application of article 25 does not depend on the situation having an international element; article 25 is effective to confer exclusive jurisdiction on the contractual forum in a case where parties domiciled in England enter a contract which includes a clause requiring any legal proceedings to be brought in London.[116]

2.48 The courts tend to construe jurisdiction clauses broadly, so as to cover all disputes between the contracting parties.[117] In a case where a contract contains a standard jurisdiction clause which refers disputes arising in connection with the agreement to specific courts, if the facts give rise to parallel claims in contract and tort, both claims fall within the scope of the clause.[118] An appropriately drafted jurisdiction clause may, for example, extend to tortious damages for breach of competition law.[119] Article 25(5) gives effect to the doctrine of separability, providing that the validity of a jurisdiction clause cannot be contested solely on the ground that the contract of which it forms a part is not valid. Accordingly, a dispute relating to the validity of a contract (which includes a jurisdiction clause) does not fall outside the scope of the jurisdiction clause, unless the basis on which the validity of the contract is challenged also calls into question the very existence of the jurisdiction clause itself (as opposed to the validity of the contract as a whole). The courts of a Member State which have been designated in a jurisdiction clause validly concluded under article 25(1) also have jurisdiction where the proceedings are for a declaration that the contract containing the jurisdiction clause is

---

[113] Where goods are sold from A to B and then from B to C, C cannot, in proceedings against A, rely upon a jurisdiction clause in the contract between A and B unless it is established that C actually consented to that clause under the conditions laid down in art 25: Case C-543/10 *Refcomp SPA v AXA Corporate Solutions Assurance SA* [2013] ILPr 17.

[114] The Hague Choice of Court Convention (see paras 2.244–2.248), which came into force between the Member States of the European Union and Mexico on 1 October 2015, overrides the provisions of the Recast in cases where one or more of the parties reside in Mexico, which is a Contracting State to the Convention but which is not bound by the Recast. If and when the Convention is in force in the United States, a jurisdiction agreement between an English company and a New York company will not be governed by art 25 of the Recast.

[115] See Ratkovic and Zgrabljic Rotar, 'Choice-of-court Agreements under the Brussels I Regulation (Recast)' (2013) 9 Journal of Private International Law 245.

[116] *Snookes v Jani-King (GB) Ltd* [2006] ILPr 19.

[117] The approach adopted in *Fiona Trust & Holding Corporation v Privalov* [2007] 4 All ER 951, a case concerning an arbitration clause, has been held to apply to jurisdiction clauses. See, eg, *Deutsche Bank AG v Asia Pacific Broadband Wireless Communications Inc* [2008] 2 Lloyd's Rep 619; *UBS AG v HSH Nordbank AG* [2009] 2 Lloyd's Rep 272; *Cinnamon European Structured Credit Master Fund v Banco Commercial Portugues SA* [2010] ILPr 11; *Deutsche Bank AG v Sebastian Holdings Inc (No 2)* [2011] 2 All ER (Comm) 245. However, in a case where parties to a contract (the first relationship) which includes a jurisdiction clause subsequently enter into a second legal relationship, a dispute arising from that second relationship is likely not to fall within the scope of the jurisdiction clause: *Deutsche Bank AG London Branch v Petromena ASA* [2015] 1 WLR 4225.

[118] *Kitechnology BV v Unicor GmbH Plastmaschinen* [1994] ILPr 568. See also *Maple Leaf Macro Volatility Master Fund v Rouvroy* [2009] 1 Lloyd's Rep 475 at [197]–[199].

[119] Case C-352/13 *Cartel Damage Claims (CDC) Hydrogen Peroxide SA v Akzo Nobel NV* [2015] QB 906.

void.¹²⁰ It is only if the jurisdiction clause itself comes under specific attack (for example, on the basis of duress, forgery, or non est factum) that a question arises as to the clause's effectiveness.¹²¹

2.49 The concept of 'an agreement conferring jurisdiction' is an independent one which is to be understood by reference to European law, rather than the law of the forum or the law governing the contract. Although a jurisdiction agreement normally takes the form of a provision in a contract, a clause conferring jurisdiction which appears in a company's articles of association is to be regarded as an agreement for the purposes of article 25.¹²²

2.50 There is no requirement that there should be any objective connection between the relationship in dispute and the contractual forum.¹²³ Article 25(1) applies even if neither the claimant nor the defendant is domiciled in a Member State; it has no application, however, to cases where the parties have chosen the courts of a non-Member State.¹²⁴ It is not necessary for the parties' agreement to identify directly the contractual forum; a jurisdiction clause in a bill of lading which indirectly identifies the contractual forum (by referring disputes to the court for the carrier's principal place of business) falls within article 25.¹²⁵

(ii) Formal requirements

2.51 Article 25(1) applies only if the jurisdiction agreement satisfies one of a range of alternative formal requirements.¹²⁶ To be effective a jurisdiction agreement must be (a) in writing or evidenced in writing;¹²⁷ or (b) in a form which accords with practices which the parties have established between themselves; or (c) in international trade or commerce in a form which accords with a usage of which the parties are or ought to have been aware and which in such trade or commerce is widely known to, and regularly observed by, parties to contracts of the type involved in the particular trade or commerce concerned. A party seeking to rely on a jurisdiction agreement must have a 'good arguable case' (that is to say, he must have a much better argument than the other party) that article 25(1)'s formal requirements are met.¹²⁸ Although the purpose of these requirements is to ensure that there is consensus between the parties, in cases covered by article 25(1)(c) consensus is presumed.¹²⁹

---

[120] Case C-269/95 *Benincasa v Dentalkit Srl* [1997] ECR I-3767.
[121] *Deutsche Bank AG v Asia Pacific Broadband Wireless Communications Inc* [2008] 2 Lloyd's Rep 619.
[122] Case C-214/89 *Powell Duffryn plc v Petereit* [1992] ECR I-1745.
[123] Case C-159/97 *Trasporti Castelletti Spedizione Internazionali SpA v Hugo Trumpy SpA* [1999] ECR I-1597, para 50.
[124] Case C-387/98 *Coreck Maritime GmbH v Handelsveem BV* [2000] ECR I-9337.   [125] Ibid.
[126] National courts cannot impose additional requirements, over and above those contained in art 25(1) itself: Case 150/80 *Elefanten Schuh v Jacqmain* [1981] ECR 1671; Case C-159/97 *Trasporti Castelletti Spedizione Internazionali SpA v Hugo Trumpy SpA* [1999] ECR I-1597.
[127] Any communication by electronic means which provides a durable record of the agreement is treated as 'writing': art 25(2). A so-called 'click-wrap' agreement is 'in writing' for the purposes of art 25: Case C-322/14 *El Majdoub v CarsOnTheWeb Deutschland GmbH* [2015] 1 WLR 3986.
[128] *Bols Distilleries BV (trading as Bols Royal Distilleries) v Superior Yacht Services Ltd* [2007] 1 WLR 12.
[129] Case C-106/95 *Mainschiffahrts-Genossenschaft eG (MSG) v Les Gravières Rhénanes Sarl* [1997] ECR I-911.

2.52 As a general rule, a jurisdiction agreement is 'in writing' only if it is contained in a document that is signed by both parties.[130] Furthermore, where a clause conferring jurisdiction is included in general conditions printed on the back of the contract, the agreement is 'in writing' if the contract signed by both parties contains an express reference to the general conditions.[131] Similarly, where A offers in writing to sell goods on A's standard terms (which contain a jurisdiction clause) and B accepts A's offer in writing, the formal requirements of article 25 are satisfied,[132] whether or not B reads or understands A's standard terms.[133] Where, having reached an oral agreement on jurisdiction, one of the parties sends written confirmation of that agreement to the other and the latter raises no objection, the agreement is to be regarded as 'evidenced in writing'.[134] Where, however, X and Y conclude a contract orally without expressly agreeing on jurisdiction, if X subsequently confirms the contract by sending to Y printed terms and conditions containing a jurisdiction clause, that clause is not 'in writing or evidenced in writing' unless Y accepts the terms and conditions in writing.[135]

2.53 An agreement which is not 'in writing or evidenced in writing' may, nevertheless, be effective under paragraph (b) or (c) of article 25(1). Where, for example, the parties orally conclude a contract for the carriage of goods, which is subsequently confirmed in writing when the carrier issues a bill of lading (which includes a jurisdiction clause), the requirements of article 25(1)(b) are satisfied, notwithstanding the absence of express written agreement by the shipper, if the carrier and the shipper have a continuing business relationship which is governed as a whole by the carrier's general conditions which contain the jurisdiction clause.[136] Even in the absence of a continuing trading relationship, such a jurisdiction clause may be effective if it conforms to trade usages. However, for the purposes of article 25(1)(c) it is not sufficient that, in international trade or commerce, a jurisdiction agreement is in a form which accords with practices in such trade or commerce of which the parties are or ought to have been aware; the usage must also be widely known in international trade or commerce and regularly observed by parties to contracts of the type involved in the particular trade or commerce concerned.[137]

---

[130] Case 71/83 *Partenreederei ms Tilly Russ v NV Haven & Vervoerbedrijf Nova* [1984] ECR 2417, para 16.
[131] Case 24/76 *Estasis Salotti di Colzani Aimo v RÜWA Polstereimaschinen GmbH* [1976] ECR 1831.
[132] *7E Communications Ltd v Vertex Antennentechnik GmbH* [2007] 1 WLR 2175. See also *Crédit Suisse Financial Products v Société Générale d'Entreprises* [1997] ILPr 165; *AIG Europe SA v QBE International Insurance Ltd* [2001] 2 Lloyd's Rep 268.
[133] *Coys of Kensington Automobiles Ltd v Pugliese* [2011] 2 All ER (Comm) 664.
[134] Case C-221/84 *F Berghoefer GmbH & Co KG v ASA SA* [1985] ECR 2699. See also *Polskie Ratownictwo Okretowe v Rallo Vito & C SNC* [2010] 1 Lloyd's Rep 384; *Kolmar Group AG v Visen Industries Ltd* [2010] ILPr 23.
[135] Case C-25/76 *Galeries Segoura SPRL v Bonakdarian* [1976] ECR 1851.
[136] Case 71/83 *Partenreederei ms Tilly Russ v NV Haven & Vervoerbedrijf Nova* [1984] ECR 2417. See also *Calyon v Wytwornia Sprzetu Komunikacynego PZL Swidnik SA* [2009] 2 All ER (Comm) 603. Cf *Lafarge Plasterboard Ltd v Fritz Peters & Co KG* [2000] 2 Lloyd's Rep 689.
[137] See Case C-159/97 *Trasporti Castelletti Spedizione Internazionali SpA v Hugo Trumpy SpA* [1999] ECR I-1597.

(iii) Material validity

2.54 Article 25(1) requires that the parties 'have agreed' to confer jurisdiction on particular courts; in the absence of such an agreement, the conditions of article 25(1) are not satisfied. Although article 25(1) itself determines whether an alleged agreement is formally valid, which law governs the agreement's material validity (for example, whether the defendant's consent is vitiated by mistake or duress)?[138] Under the 2002 Regulation, it was unclear whether the material validity of a jurisdiction clause should be governed by an autonomous European standard or by the law of a country (whether the law of the forum in which legal proceedings were brought, the law governing the contract as a whole or the law of the chosen forum). Article 25(1) of the Recast does not seek to lay down a uniform standard; instead, it provides a clear choice-of-law rule: questions of material validity are governed by the law of the chosen forum.[139]

(iv) Exclusive or non-exclusive?

2.55 Article 25(1) provides that the jurisdiction which is derived from the parties' agreement 'shall be exclusive unless the parties have agreed otherwise'. In a simple case where contracting parties agree on French jurisdiction, the claimant cannot bring proceedings in England even if, in the absence of the agreement, the English court would have been competent on the basis of the defendant's domicile in England. However, where the parties have concluded a non-exclusive jurisdiction agreement the claimant has the option of relying either on the agreement or on other provisions of Chapter II. So, where two parties domiciled in Germany conclude a non-exclusive jurisdiction agreement in favour of the English courts, either party may sue the other in England (on the basis of article 25) or in Germany (on the basis of article 4). Similarly, parties may, by their agreement, confer jurisdiction on the courts of more than one Member State; they may, for example, agree that if A sues B the German courts are to have jurisdiction, but that if B sues A the French courts are to have jurisdiction.[140] Whether a jurisdiction agreement is exclusive or non-exclusive depends on the words used and is a question of construction,[141] which ought to be answered by reference to the law of the chosen forum.

2.56 Whether a one-sided or unilateral jurisdiction clause (known in France as a *clause potestative*) is valid under article 25 of the Recast has divided opinion.[142] In *Soc Banque*

---

[138] Some suggest that material validity does not include questions of consent: see, eg, Brand, 'The Evolving Private International Law/Private Law Overlap in the European Union' in Mankowski and Wurmest, *Festschrift für Ulrich Magnus* (2014) pp 371–83. However, the better view is that art 25(1) of the Recast deals with questions of *material* consent: see Camilleri, 'Article 23: Formal Validity, Material Validity or Both?' (2011) 7 Journal of Private International Law 297.

[139] See Herranz Ballesteros, 'The Regime of Party Autonomy in the Brussels I Recast: The Solutions Adopted for Agreements on Jurisdiction' (2014) 10 Journal of Private International Law 291.

[140] Case 23/78 *Meeth v Glacetal* [1978] ECR 2133.

[141] See *Insured Financial Structures Ltd v Elektrocieplownia Tychy SA* [2003] QB 1260; *Bank of New York Mellon v GV Films* [2010] 1 Lloyd's Rep 365.

[142] See the discussion by Keyes and Marshall, 'Jurisdictional Agreements: Exclusive, Optional and Asymmetrical' (2015) 11 Journal of Private International Law 345.

privée Edmond de Rothschild Europe v X,[143] for example, the French courts declared a one-sided jurisdiction clause to be null and void.[144] From an English perspective, this decision is hard to accept. As article 25(1) seeks to give effect to both exclusive and non-exclusive clauses, it is not obvious why a clause which is exclusive for one of the parties, but non-exclusive for the other should not be upheld. There is no doubt that, as far as English practice is concerned, such one-sided jurisdiction clauses are regarded as valid and are routinely enforced according to their terms.[145]

(v) The relationship between article 25 and other provisions

2.57 Article 25 yields both to articles 24 and 26. So, if the dispute between the parties involves rights in rem relating to immovable property situated in France, the French courts have mandatory and exclusive jurisdiction, notwithstanding a jurisdiction agreement between the parties in favour of the courts of another Member State.[146] Similarly, in a case where the parties have agreed on the jurisdiction of the Italian courts, if the claimant issues proceedings in England and the defendant acknowledges service of process, the English court has jurisdiction; the defendant's submission— which is in effect a waiver of the jurisdiction clause—supersedes the earlier contractual agreement.[147]

2. General bases of jurisdiction with regard to defendants domiciled in a Member State

2.58 If jurisdiction is not allocated by the above provisions, which apply both to defendants who are domiciled in a Member State and to defendants who are not so domiciled, the domicile of the defendant is normally of crucial importance. If the defendant is domiciled in a Member State the court may assume jurisdiction only by virtue of the provisions of Chapter II;[148] if the defendant is not domiciled in a Member State, subject to article 18(1) and article 21(2),[149] the traditional rules are applicable.

(A) Prorogation of jurisdiction: submission

2.59 Although the Recast does not expressly provide that article 26 applies only to defendants who are domiciled in a Member State, this conclusion follows from article 6 which

---

[143] Noted by Briggs, 'One-Sided Jurisdiction Clauses: French Folly and Russian Menace' [2013] LMCLQ 137; Fentiman, 'Unilateral Jurisdiction Clauses in Europe' [2013] CLJ 24.

[144] The jurisdiction clause in a contract between the bank and one of its clients provided that 'disputes between Bank and Client shall be subject to the exclusive jurisdiction of the courts of Luxembourg, though Bank reserves the right to bring proceedings before the courts of the Client's domicile, or before any other court which would have jurisdiction apart from this agreement'.

[145] See, eg, *Continental Bank NA v Aeakos Compania Naviera SA* [1994] 1 WLR 588 and, more recently, *Mauritius Commercial Bank Ltd v Hestia Holdings Ltd* [2013] 2 All ER (Comm) 898 (which post-dated the decision of the French courts in the *Soc Banque privée Edmond de Rothschild Europe* case).

[146] Art 25(4).   [147] Case 150/80 *Elefanten Schuh GmbH v Jacqmain* [1981] ECR 1671.

[148] If the whereabouts of the defendant, who is a citizen of a Member State, is unknown, the claimant can, nevertheless, rely on the jurisdictional bases in Chapter II, unless there is firm evidence that the defendant is domiciled outside the European Union: Case C-292/10 *G v de Visser* [2013] QB 168.

[149] See paras 2.134–2.139.

states that, if the defendant is not domiciled in a Member State, the jurisdiction of the courts of each Member State is, subject to articles 18(1), 21(2), 24, and 25, to be determined by that state's traditional rules. As far as English law is concerned, it makes little difference whether article 26 or the equivalent traditional rules apply as it is well established under the traditional rules that a defendant may confer jurisdiction on the English court by submission.[150]

2.60 Article 26 provides that the court of a Member State has jurisdiction if the defendant enters an appearance in that court, unless the appearance was entered to contest the court's jurisdiction. By virtue of article 26 the court has jurisdiction if the defendant empowers a solicitor in England to accept service on his behalf and the solicitor does so. However, a defendant who appears, not to defend the claim on the merits but merely to contend that the court has no jurisdiction, does not submit to the court's jurisdiction. If, at the same time as contesting the court's jurisdiction, the defendant raises in the alternative a defence on the merits, jurisdiction is not conferred by article 26.[151]

2.61 Article 26 cannot override the exclusive jurisdiction provisions of article 24. If the English court has jurisdiction in relation to a dispute concerning immovable property situated in England the defendant cannot confer jurisdiction on the French courts by submitting to proceedings commenced by the claimant in France. However, a submission by appearance in England is effective to confer jurisdiction on the English court even if the parties had agreed, prior to the dispute, that the courts of another Member State were to have jurisdiction.[152]

(B) *Defendant domiciled in England*

2.62 Under article 4 a person domiciled in a Member State may be sued in the courts of that state. Where a defendant is domiciled in England article 4 of the Recast provides that the claimant may bring proceedings in the courts of the United Kingdom. The Civil Jurisdiction and Judgments Act 1982, through rule 1 of schedule 4, allocates jurisdiction to England—the part of the United Kingdom in which the defendant is domiciled. The relevant time at which the defendant's domicile must be established is when the claim form is issued, rather than when it is served.[153] This ground of jurisdiction is applicable even if neither the claimant nor the dispute has a connection with England (or with any Member State).[154] In *Lucasfilm Ltd v Ainsworth*,[155] for example, the Supreme Court held that a claim for breach of US copyright could be brought in England against a defendant domiciled in England.

---

[150] See paras 2.148–2.149.
[151] Case 150/80 *Elefanten Schuh GmbH v Jacqmain* [1981] ECR 1671.   [152] Ibid.
[153] *Canada Trust Co v Stolzenberg (No 2)* [2002] 1 AC 1; *Ministry of Defence and Support of the Armed Forces for Iran v Faz Aviation Ltd* [2007] ILPr 42; *Linuzs v Latmar Holdings Corp* [2013] ILPr 19.
[154] See, eg, *International Transport Workers' Federation v Viking Line ABP* [2005] 2 CLC 720. Whether the English court may stay the proceedings in such circumstances on the basis of forum non conveniens is discussed at paras 2.265–2.268.
[155] [2012] 1 AC 208.

(C) 'Special jurisdiction': alternatives to the domicile rule

2.63 The basic rule that a defendant shall be sued in the Member State in which he is domiciled must be considered in conjunction with the 'special jurisdiction' provisions of Chapter II—notably, articles 7 and 8[156]—according to which a person domiciled in a Member State may be sued in an alternative Member State.

2.64 Jurisdiction under article 7 is premised on the existence of a close connection between the claim and the forum (unlike article 4 which is based on the defendant's connections with the forum). Article 7 contains seven paragraphs of which the most important are paragraph (1), which concerns 'matters relating to a contract', and paragraph (2), which allocates jurisdiction in 'matters relating to tort'. Paragraph (5) is concerned with disputes 'arising out of the operations of a branch, agency or other establishment'.[157] Article 8, which deals with cases involving multiple claims and defendants, is based on the simple idea that it is often convenient for related proceedings to be heard by the same court. The bases of jurisdiction in articles 7 and 8 are derogations from the general principle contained in article 4 and the Court of Justice has indicated that these derogations should be interpreted strictly.[158]

2.65 In inspiration, articles 7 and 8 are similar to the traditional grounds of jurisdiction listed in CPR PD 6B para 3.1. Their operation is, however, very different. In cases where the claimant relies on any of the jurisdiction rules contained in Chapter II, process can be served on the defendant without the court's permission;[159] the claimant does not have to demonstrate that the forum in which the proceedings are brought is the most appropriate one. Where, for example, D, domiciled in France, negligently injures C in England, C may bring proceedings in France on the basis of article 4 or, relying on article 7(2), sue D in England (where the harmful event occurred). The choice is entirely for C;[160] there is no mechanism whereby D can require C to opt for one jurisdiction rather than another.

(i) Matters relating to a contract and to tort: introduction

2.66 Article 7 draws a distinction between 'matters relating to a contract' (article 7(1)) and 'matters relating to tort' (article 7(2)). For the purposes of article 7, 'contract' and 'tort' are autonomous concepts which must be interpreted by reference principally to the system and objectives of the Brussels I Recast, rather than in accordance with the law

---

[156] Art 9, the third article which confers 'special jurisdiction', concerns claims relating to the limitation of liability for the use or operation of a ship.

[157] The other paragraphs of art 7 deal with the following matters: (3) 'a civil claim for damages or restitution which is based on an act giving rise to criminal proceedings'; (4) 'a civil claim for the recovery of a cultural object'; (6) certain proceedings relating to trusts; (7) 'a dispute concerning the payment of remuneration claimed in respect of the salvage of a cargo or freight'. For the interpretation of art 7(6), see *Gomez v Gomez-Moche Vives* [2009] Ch 245.

[158] Case 189/87 *Kalfelis v Bankhaus Schröder, Münchmeyer, Hengst & Co* [1988] ECR 5565.

[159] CPR r 6.33.

[160] Case C-469/12 *Krejci Lager & Umschlagbetriebs GMBH v Olbrich Transport und Logistik GMBH* [2014] ILPr 8.

of the forum.[161] This means that a situation which according to English law would not be regarded as contractual may have to be classified as such for jurisdictional purposes.

2.67 Paragraphs (1) and (2) are mutually exclusive.[162] If the proceedings concern 'matters relating to a contract' the claimant cannot, relying on English law, invoke the English court's jurisdiction under article 7(2) by framing the claim in tort rather than in contract. Equally, if the proceedings concern 'matters relating to tort' the French courts may not assume jurisdiction under article 7(1) on the basis that the claim is contractual according to French law.[163] Where a claimant has a claim against a defendant part of which is based in tort and another part of which is based in contract, a court which has jurisdiction under article 7(2) over the claim in so far as it is based in tort does not have jurisdiction over that claim in so far as it is not so based.[164]

2.68 Whether paragraphs (1) and (2) necessarily encompass claims which are restitutionary, rather than contractual or tortious, is uncertain. In *Kalfelis v Bankhaus Schröder, Münchmeyer, Hengst & Co* the Court of Justice stated that article 7(2) must be regarded as covering 'all actions which seek to establish the liability of a defendant and which are not related to a "contract" within the meaning of article [7](1)'.[165] Although this statement appears to endorse the view that paragraphs (1) and (2), taken together, cover all situations in which the claimant seeks to establish the civil liability of the defendant, the judgment as a whole seems to accept the possibility of a situation in which an obligation is excluded from the scope of paragraph (2) (because it is not tortious) and is not within paragraph (1) (because it is not contractual either).

2.69 The House of Lords' decision in *Kleinwort Benson Ltd v Glasgow City Council*[166] indicates that a claim for restitution of money paid under a purported contract (which is void) falls neither within article 7(1) nor within article 7(2). In policy terms, there is no compelling reason why claims based on unjust enrichment should fit somewhere within article 7: 'If a claim cannot be brought within article [7], it can always be pursued in the courts of the defendant's domicile.'[167]

(ii) Jurisdiction in matters relating to a contract

2.70 Article 7(1)(a) provides that in matters relating to a contract a person who is domiciled in a Member State may be sued in another Member State if that is the place of

---

[161] Case 9/87 *SPRL Arcado v SA Haviland* [1988] ECR 1539; Case 189/87 *Kalfelis v Bankhaus Schröder, Münchmeyer, Hengst & Co* [1988] ECR 5565; Case C-548/12 *Brogsitter v Fabrication de Montres Normandes EURL* [2014] QB 753.
[162] Case 189/87 *Kalfelis v Bankhaus Schröder, Münchmeyer, Hengst & Co* [1988] ECR 5565. For discussion of the implications of this decision, see Zogg, 'Accumulation of Contractual and Tortious Causes of Action under the Judgments Regulation' (2013) 9 Journal of Private International Law 39.
[163] Case C-26/91 *Jakob Handte & Co GmbH v Traitements Mécano-chimiques des Surfaces SA* [1992] ECR I-3967.
[164] Case 189/87 *Kalfelis v Bankhaus Schröder, Münchmeyer, Hengst & Co* [1988] ECR 5565.
[165] [1988] ECR 5565, para 17. See also Case C-51/97 *Réunion Européenne SA v Splietoff's Bevachtingskantoor BV* [1998] ECR I-6511, para 22.
[166] [1999] 1 AC 153.
[167] Millett LJ in *Kleinwort Benson Ltd v Glasgow City Council* [1996] QB 678 at 698.

performance of the obligation in question.¹⁶⁸ This general principle is fleshed out by subparagraph (b), which indicates how the place of performance is to be determined in certain types of cases.

(a) Matters relating to a contract

2.71 The Court of Justice has ruled that article 7(1) 'is not to be understood as covering a situation in which there is no obligation freely assumed by one party towards another';¹⁶⁹ the application of article 7(1) depends on 'the establishment of a legal obligation freely consented to by one person towards another and on which the claimant's action is based'.¹⁷⁰ So, where a manufacturer sells defective goods to a wholesaler, who sells them to a retailer, the retailer's claim against the manufacturer is to be classified, for jurisdictional purposes, as tortious, even if the claim is regarded as contractual under the law of the forum. Conversely, a claim which is classified as tortious under the law of the forum is within the scope of article 7(1), rather than 7(2), if there is a contractual relationship between the parties and the conduct complained of, although tortious under the law of the forum, might be considered a breach of the terms of the contract.¹⁷¹ Where, under English law, the defendant's conduct constitutes both a breach of contract and a tort (such as negligence¹⁷² or conversion¹⁷³) article 7(1) allocates jurisdiction over the tortious claim to the court for the place of performance of the defendant's contractual obligation and the claimant cannot rely on article 7(2).

2.72 Article 7(1) is not rendered inapplicable merely by the fact that the defendant denies the existence of the contract on which the claim is based.¹⁷⁴ In *Boss Group Ltd v Boss France SA*¹⁷⁵ it was held that article 7(1) is applicable even in a case where the claimant seeks a declaration that a contract alleged by the defendant does not exist. The Court of Appeal relied on the inconsistency of the defendant contending both that the claimant was in breach of contract and that article 7(1) was inapplicable because there was no contract between the parties. Although the correctness of the decision was doubted, the Court of Appeal's analysis is consistent with the Court of Justice's later decision in *Folien Fischer v Ritrama SpA*,¹⁷⁶ a case involving jurisdiction in matters relating to tort.

2.73 In *Agnew v Lansförsäkringsbølagens AB*¹⁷⁷ the plaintiff sought to avoid a contract of reinsurance on the ground that the defendant had failed to comply with the duty to make

---

¹⁶⁸ For consideration of the rules that apply to matters relating to insurance, consumer contracts, and individual contracts of employment, see paras 2.129–2.139.
¹⁶⁹ Case C–26/91 *Jakob Handte & Co GmbH v Traitements Mécano-chimiques des Surfaces SA* [1992] ECR I–3967, para 15 (discussed by Hartley (1993) 18 ELRev 506).
¹⁷⁰ Case C–147/12 *ÖFAB v Koot* [2015] QB 20, para 33. See also Case C–519/12 *OTP Bank Nyilvánosan Müködö Részvénytársaság v Hochtief Solution AG* [2015] ILPr 30.
¹⁷¹ Case C–548/12 *Brogsitter v Fabrication de Montres Normandes EURL* [2014] QB 753; Dickinson, [2014] LMCLQ 466.
¹⁷² *Source Ltd v TUV Rheinland Holding AG* [1998] QB 54.
¹⁷³ *Mazur Media Ltd v Mazur Media GmbH* [2004] 1 WLR 2966.
¹⁷⁴ Case 38/81 *Effer SpA v Kantner* [1982] ECR 825.
¹⁷⁵ [1996] 4 All ER 970. See also *USF Ltd v Aqua Technology Hanson NV/SA* [2001] 1 All ER (Comm) 856.
¹⁷⁶ Case C–133/11 [2013] QB 253.   ¹⁷⁷ [2001] 1 AC 223.

fair presentation of the risk. The House of Lords held that the proceedings involved 'matters relating to a contract', notwithstanding the fact that, as a matter of English law, the defendant's obligation arose extra-contractually. Conversely, in the *Tacconi*[178] case, the Court of Justice ruled that a claim based on breach of a pre-contractual obligation to conduct contractual negotiations in good faith is a matter 'relating to tort' rather than a matter 'relating to a contract'. However, the cases are distinguishable: whereas in *Agnew v Lansförsäkringsbølagens AB* there was a concluded contract between the parties, in the *Tacconi* case there was never any contractual relationship.

2.74 The extent to which article 7(1) extends to restitutionary obligations is contentious. Although in *Kleinwort Benson Ltd v Glasgow City Council*[179] the House of Lords accepted the proposition that normally restitutionary claims fall outside the scope of article 7(1), Lord Goff suggested that certain types of proceedings, which would be regarded as restitutionary in nature according to English law (such as a claim to recover, on the ground of failure of consideration, money paid under a valid contract), might come within article 7(1).[180]

2.75 There is a degree of tension between the decisions in the *Agnew* and *Kleinwort Benson* cases. Whereas in *Kleinwort Benson* one of the reasons for holding that restitutionary claims normally fall outside article 7(1) was that, in such cases, there is no contractual obligation (breached by the defendant) which can serve as the basis of the claim, in the *Agnew* case it was held that a pre-contractual obligation imposed by the general law may qualify as the 'obligation in question' for the purposes of article 7(1). The solution to this tension may be to confine the decision in the *Kleinwort Benson* case to situations in which the invalidity of the contract is not in dispute.[181]

(b) The place of performance of the obligation in question: article 7(1)(a)

2.76 As regards the place of performance of the obligation in question, the current version of article 7(1) distinguishes two different types of situation.[182] A large number of contractual disputes arise out of contracts for the sale of goods and contracts for the provision of services; jurisdiction in these cases falls to be determined primarily by article 7(1)(b). As regards contracts not falling within these categories, article 7(1)(a) applies; under this provision jurisdiction turns on, first, designation of the obligation in question and, secondly, identification of the place of performance of that obligation.[183]

---

[178] Case C-334/00 *Fonderie Officine Mecchaniche Tacconi SpA v Heinrich Wagner Sinto Maschinenfabrik GmbH* [2002] ECR I-7357.

[179] [1999] 1 AC 153.

[180] At 171.

[181] Somewhat exceptionally, prior to the commencement of the *Kleinwort Benson* litigation, it had already been established, in related proceedings raising identical issues, that the contract in question was void ab initio (because it was ultra vires the local authority): *Hazell v Hammersmith and Fulham London Borough Council* [1992] 2 AC 1.

[182] In addition, there are specific provisions that apply to insurance contracts, consumer contracts, and employment contracts: see paras 2.129–2.139.

[183] In relation to intra-United Kingdom cases, r 3(a) of sch 4 to the Civil Jurisdiction and Judgments Act 1982 contains no counterpart to art 7(1)(b).

2.77 For the purposes of article 7(1)(a), the relevant obligation is, as a general rule, the obligation (allegedly breached by the defendant) on which the claim is based.[184] So, where A contracts with B to exchange a ton of potatoes for a ton of carrots, if A sues for B's failure to deliver the carrots, the obligation in question is B's obligation to deliver, even if B's non-performance is a response to the fact that the potatoes delivered by A are not of satisfactory quality. In the context of a contract under which A hires a car from B, if B sues A for the unpaid hire, the obligation in question is A's obligation to pay the hire charge. Where the claim is based on more than one obligation the court should be guided by the maxim 'accessorium sequitur principale'; jurisdiction under article 7(1)(a) should be determined by the principal obligation.[185] Where, for example, the claimant wishes to sue the defendant on the basis not only of the latter's failure to perform the principal obligation in England but also of a failure to perform an accessory obligation abroad, article 7(1)(a) allocates jurisdiction to the English court with regard to the entire claim. For example, in *Union Transport plc v Continental Lines SA*[186] the plaintiff brought proceedings in England against a Belgian company for failure, under the terms of a tbn[187] charter-party agreement, to nominate and provide a vessel to carry a cargo of telegraph poles from Florida to Bangladesh. Although Florida was the place of performance of the obligation to provide the vessel, the House of Lords held that the English court had jurisdiction over the entire claim under article 7(1) on the basis that the principal obligation was the obligation to nominate a vessel and that nomination should have been made in England.[188]

2.78 Where the defendant is in breach of two independent obligations of equal significance—rather than a principal obligation to which another is accessory—jurisdiction with regard to each obligation must be determined by the general rule.[189] In the *Leathertex* case,[190] the Belgian court thought that the defendant's obligation to give a reasonable period of notice on termination of a commercial agency agreement (in Belgium) was of the same significance as the obligation to pay commission under the agency contract (in Italy). This means that, where two independent obligations are to be performed in two different Member States, there is a danger that there will be a fragmentation of related proceedings. It must be remembered, however, that special jurisdiction under article 7 is an alternative to the general jurisdiction which is conferred by article 4; the claimant has the option of relying on article 4 and litigating the entire claim in the courts of the Member State in which the defendant is domiciled.

2.79 If the parties agree in their contract on the place of performance of the obligation on which the claim is based, article 7(1)(a) normally allocates jurisdiction to the courts for

---

[184] Case 14/76 *Ets A de Bloos SPRL v Société en commandite par actions Bouyer* [1976] ECR 1497. This ruling has been confirmed in subsequent cases such as Case C-288/92 *Custom Made Commercial Ltd v Stawa Metallbau GmbH* [1994] ECR I-2913.
[185] Case 266/85 *Shenavai v Kreischer* [1987] ECR 239.   [186] [1992] 1 WLR 15.
[187] To be nominated.
[188] See also *AIG Europe (UK) Ltd v The Ethniki* [2000] 2 All ER 566; *Barry v Bradshaw* [2000] CLC 455; *MBM Fabri-Clad Ltd v Eisen-und Huttenwerke Thale AG* [2000] ILPr 505.
[189] Case C-420/97 *Leathertex Divisione Sintetici SpA v Bodotex BVBA* [1999] ECR I-6747.
[190] Ibid.

that place.¹⁹¹ If, however, the agreed place of performance is fictitious (or abstract)—in the sense that it has no actual connection with the subject-matter of the contract—and is designed solely to establish jurisdiction (rather than to determine the real place of performance), the agreement is not effective to confer jurisdiction on the courts for that place unless it satisfies the requirements as to form laid down in article 25.¹⁹² In the absence of such agreement, the court whose jurisdiction is invoked must fix the place of performance by applying the law which, according to its own choice of law rules, governs the contract.¹⁹³ So, if the claimant seeks to proceed in England under article 7(1)(a), the court must decide, by reference to English choice of law rules, which law is applicable to the contract and determine the place of performance of the obligation in question in accordance with that law.

2.80 Article 7(1)(a) refers to the *place* of performance. Accordingly, jurisdiction in matters relating to a contract cannot be allocated by article 7(1) in a case where a place of performance cannot be identified. In *Besix v Wasserreinigungsbau Alfred Kretzschmar GmbH & Co KG*¹⁹⁴ the question was whether the place of performance of the defendants' contractual obligation to 'act exclusively and not to commit themselves to other partners' was Belgium (where one of the contracting parties was domiciled). The Court of Justice ruled that article 7(1) is not applicable where 'the place of performance cannot be determined because it consists in an undertaking not to do something which is not subject to any geographical limit and is, therefore, characterised by a multiplicity of places for its performance'.¹⁹⁵ The extent to which the *Besix* ruling is applicable in the situation where a positive obligation may be performed in more than one identifiable place (such as where the defendant is entitled to make payment under a contract in any one of a number of different countries) is yet to be definitively determined.¹⁹⁶

(c) The place of performance of the obligation in question: article 7(1)(b)

2.81 The potential scope of the general principle in article 7(1)(a) is significantly curtailed by article 7(1)(b), which expressly identifies the place of performance in relation to contracts for the sale of goods and contracts for the provision of services. As for the meaning of the concepts employed in article 7(1)(b), the Court of Justice has given some guidance. In *Falco Privatstiftung v Weller-Lindhorst*¹⁹⁷ it was held that a contract whereby the owner of an intellectual property right grants, in return for payment, a licence for use of the right in question is not a contract for the provision of services. It is not necessary that 'services' in article 7(1)(b) should be interpreted as broadly as it is

---

¹⁹¹ Case 56/79 *Zelger v Salinitri* [1980] ECR 89.
¹⁹² Case C-106/95 *Mainschiffahrts-Genossenschaft eG (MSG) v Les Gravières Rhénanes Sarl* [1997] ECR I-911.
¹⁹³ Case 12/76 *Industrie Tessili Italiana Como v Dunlop AG* [1976] ECR 1473; Case C-440/97 *GIE Groupe Concorde v Master of the Vessel Suhadiwarno Panjan* [1999] ECR I-6307.
¹⁹⁴ Case C-256/00 [2002] ECR I-1699.   ¹⁹⁵ Ibid, para 55.
¹⁹⁶ Compare *Mora Shipping Inc v Axa Corporate Solutions Assurance SA* [2005] 2 Lloyd's Rep 769 and *Canyon Offshore Ltd v GDF Suez E&P Nederland BV* [2015] ILPr 8.
¹⁹⁷ Case C-533/07 [2009] ECR I-3327.

in the context of article 57 TFEU;[198] in order for an agreement to constitute a contract for the provision of services for the purposes of article 7(1)(b) of the Recast, normally the party who is remunerated must carry out a particular activity in return for the payment.[199]

2.82 The distinction between the sale of goods and the provision of services was considered by the Court of Justice in *Car Trim GmbH v KeySafety Systems Srl*,[200] which involved contracts for the manufacture and delivery of car parts. The terms of the contract obliged the seller to manufacture components to the customer's specifications and the question arose whether the contract should be characterised as a contract for the sale of goods or a contract for the provision of services. The Court of Justice concluded that the fact that the customer laid down detailed requirements for the manufactured products was not relevant; the contracts in question did not involve the seller in working raw materials provided by the customer (which might be regarded as the provision of a service), but were fundamentally contracts for the sale of the goods manufactured by the seller, for whose quality the seller was legally responsible.

2.83 With regard to contracts for the sale of goods and the provision of services, the Recast adopts the 'characteristic obligation' theory; jurisdiction is determined by reference to the place of performance of the obligation which determines the nature of the contract, namely the seller's obligation to deliver the goods (in a contract for the sale of goods) and the obligation to perform the services (in a contract for the provision of services). So, where the proceedings relate to a contract for the sale of goods, the place of performance of the obligation in question is, unless otherwise agreed, the place in a Member State where, under the contract, the goods were delivered or should have been delivered. Where the proceedings relate to a contract for the provision of services, the place of performance is, unless otherwise agreed, the place in a Member State where the services were or should have been provided.

2.84 It will not normally be too difficult to determine the place where contractual services are to be performed. However, contracts of sale potentially pose more difficulty. Is the place of delivery to be determined by reference to the terms of the contract as interpreted by the applicable law or should the place of delivery be understood as referring to the factual destination of the goods? The wording of the Recast makes it clear that, if the parties have agreed the place of delivery, article 7(1)(b) allocates jurisdiction to the courts for that place. In *Electrosteel Europe SA v Edil Centro SpA* the Court of Justice ruled that use of the phrase 'under the contract' means that the court must take into account

---

[198] Art 57 defines 'services' for the purposes of the free movement of persons, services, and capital under Title IV of Part 1 of the TFEU.
[199] Case C–469/12 *Krejci Lager & Umschlagbetriebs GMBH v Olbrich Transport und Logistik GMBH* [2014] ILPr 8 (contract for storage is a contract for the provision of services); Case 9/12 *Corman-Collins SA v La Maison du Whisky SA* [2014] QB 431 (a distribution contract is a contract for the provision of services); Case C–419/11 *Ceska Sporitelna AS v Feichter* [2013] ILPr 22 (a contract of *aval*, a type of guarantee, is not a contract for the provision of services).
[200] Case C–381/08 [2010] ECR I–1255.

all the relevant clauses of the contract, including clauses generally recognised and applied in international commercial usage (such as Incoterms), in so far as they enable the place of delivery to be clearly identified.[201] In *Electrosteel*, a contract for the sale of goods between an Italian seller and a French buyer included the term: 'delivered free ex our business premises'. The seller argued that the Italian courts had jurisdiction on the basis that this contractual provision was equivalent to the 'ex works' Incoterm and that, consequently, Italy was the place of delivery 'under the contract'. The Court of Justice held that it was for the Italian court to determine whether or not the contractual term relied on by the seller amounted to an agreement to the effect that the seller's place of business was the agreed place of delivery.

2.85 What is the position, however, if the parties' contract fails to designate the place of delivery? The European Commission's proposal which formed the background to the 2002 Regulation suggests that the place of delivery was intended to be based on a purely factual criterion.[202] In the *Car Trim* case, the Court of Justice ruled that where the contract does not explicitly provide an answer, the place of delivery is the place where the physical transfer of the goods took place as a result of which the purchaser obtained, or should have obtained, actual power of disposal over those goods *at the final destination* of the sales transaction.[203]

2.86 In view of this ruling, the correctness of the earlier decision of the House of Lords in *Scottish & Newcastle International Ltd v Othon Ghalanos Ltd*[204] may be doubted. The seller contracted to sell goods which were to be shipped from Liverpool to Limassol (Cyprus). The buyer argued that since Limassol was entered as the 'Place of delivery' on the invoices, the English court did not have jurisdiction under article 7(1)(b). However, the seller had no legal interest in the goods once shipment had taken place as, under English law, which was the law governing the contract, property and risk passed to the buyers upon delivery of the goods to the carrier in Liverpool. The House of Lords held that the English court had jurisdiction as the place of delivery was Liverpool, where the seller had transferred the goods to the carrier. As, in this case, the contract did not expressly identify Liverpool as the place of delivery and Limassol was the *final destination* of the sales transaction, the ruling in the *Car Trim* case suggests that the English court should not have assumed jurisdiction in this situation.[205]

2.87 Article 7(1)(b) does not expressly indicate the solution if, under the contract, goods are to be delivered to (or services provided in) more than one place.[206] This question was considered by the Court of Justice in *Color Drack GmbH v Lexx International Vertriebs*

---

[201] Case C-87/10 [2011] ILPr 28, para 22.
[202] Case C-381/08 *Car Trim* [2010] ECR I-1255, para 52 (referring to European Commission, COM (1999) 348 final, p 14).
[203] Ibid, para 62. The result of the *Car Trim* ruling is that the place of delivery for the purposes of art 7(1)(b) may be different from the place of delivery under the substantive law governing the contract.
[204] [2008] 2 All ER 768. See Hare and Hinks [2008] LMCLQ 353.
[205] See, however, Briggs (2008) 79 BYIL 508.
[206] See Grusic, 'Jurisdiction in Complex Contracts under the Brussels I Regulation' (2011) 7 Journal of Private International Law 321.

GmbH,[207] a case in which the seller had undertaken to deliver goods to a number of retailers in different parts of Austria. The Court held that article 7(1) should be interpreted as allocating jurisdiction to a single place of performance; where the defendant undertook to deliver goods in several places in the same Member State, the court with jurisdiction was the court for the 'place of the principal delivery, which must be determined on the basis of economic criteria'.[208] If there is no principal place of delivery, the claimant can choose to bring proceedings in any of the places of delivery.[209]

2.88 Although, in the *Color Drack* case, the Court of Justice stated that it was not seeking to address the problems posed by the situation where different obligations under a contract are performed in different countries, the approach taken in *Color Drack* was followed in the context of a contract for services in which the defendant had undertaken to perform services in more than one Member State. In *Wood Floor Solutions Andreas Domberger GmbH v Silva Trade SA*[210] the dispute arose out of a contract of commercial agency under the terms of which the agent undertook to provide services in more than one Member State. The Court of Justice held that the court which has jurisdiction to hear and determine all the claims arising from the contract is the court in whose jurisdiction the place of the main provision of services is situated; in a contract of commercial agency, that place, if not determined by the terms of the contract, is the place where, in practice, the contract is mainly performed (provided that the provision of services in that place is not contrary to the parties' intentions as it appears from the provisions of the contract) or, where that place cannot be established, the place where the agent is domiciled.

2.89 The same basic analysis was employed in *Rehder v Air Baltic Corporation*,[211] which involved a claim for compensation following the cancellation by the defendant, a Latvian airline, of a flight from Germany to Lithuania. The Court of Justice held that, where there are several places at which services are provided, the court with jurisdiction is the court for the place where the main provision of services is carried out. The Court decided that, in a contract for air transport, the main provision of services occurs at both the place of departure and the place of arrival of the aircraft; as neither place can be identified as the 'principal' place of performance (on the basis of economic criteria), article 7(1)(b) allows the claimant to bring proceedings at either place.[212] Alternatively, the claimant may, relying on article 4, sue the airline in the Member State in which the airline is domiciled.

(d) Article 7(1) and close connection

2.90 The purpose of article 7(1) is to allocate jurisdiction by reference to a connecting factor which identifies a place which has a close connection with the dispute.[213] Where, for

---

[207] Case C-386/05 [2007] ECR I-3699. Harris (2007) 123 LQR 522. [208] Case C-386/05 [2007] ECR I-3699, para 40.
[209] Ibid, paras 42-43. [210] Case C-19/09 [2010] 1 WLR 1900.
[211] Case C-204/08 [2009] ECR I-6073. [212] Ibid, paras 42-44.
[213] Jenard Report, OJ 1979 C59/22. This rationale has been frequently repeated in the Court of Justice's case law. See, eg, Case C-533/07 *Falco Privatstiftung v Weller-Lindhorst* [2009] ECR I-3327, para 24.

example, an Irish company agrees to provide services in England for a Belgian client, in the event of the client's failure to pay for the services (for example, because the standard of the service is unsatisfactory) the English court may assume jurisdiction in relation to the Irish company's claim for payment. In these circumstances, it is the claimant's obligation to provide the services (not the defendant's obligation to pay for them) which localises the contract and determines jurisdiction for the purposes of article 7(1)(b). To this extent, the Recast is an improvement upon the equivalent provision of the Brussels Convention[214] (as interpreted by the Court of Justice) which adopted the 'specific obligation' theory—according to which jurisdiction in contractual matters is determined by reference to the specific obligation (of the defendant) on which the claim is based. In proceedings relating to a dispute arising out of a contract for the sale of goods, the place of performance of the seller's obligation to deliver the goods is more likely to be the factual centre of gravity of the dispute than the specific obligation on which the claim is based. Where, for example, defective goods are delivered to D in Germany and D refuses to pay for them, the dispute underlying C's claim for recovery of the price will normally have a closer connection with the place of delivery than the place of payment. However, it should not be assumed that the Recast will always allocate jurisdiction in contractual matters to a closely connected forum—for three reasons.

2.91 First, article 7(1)(b) applies not only to cases of defective performance (in which the place of performance will often have a close connection with the subject-matter of the dispute) but also to cases of non-performance (in which it is less certain that the intended place of performance will have a close factual connection with the dispute).

2.92 Secondly, as regards contracts for the sale of goods, the place designated by article 7(1)(b) is where, *under the contract*, the goods were (or should have been) delivered; it by no means follows that the contractual place of delivery is the place where the goods are actually delivered.

2.93 Thirdly, article 7(1)(b) applies only to contracts for the sale of goods and contracts for the provision of services and only where the place of delivery (or the place of the provision of services) is in a Member State. If article 7(1)(b) does not apply, article 7(1)(a) applies.[215] Consider, for example, a case in which C, an English seller, contracts with D, a German buyer, to deliver goods to premises in New York. If D fails to pay for the goods, can C sue D in England? As article 7(1)(b) does not apply (because the agreed place of delivery is not in a Member State), C should be able to rely on article 7(1)(a). Under article 7(1)(a) the obligation in question is D's obligation to pay and, if the contract is governed by English law (which is very likely[216]), the place of performance is England (as under English law the debtor must, as a general rule, seek out the creditor at his place of business and pay him there[217]).

---

[214] For criticism of the Convention on this point, see Hill, 'Jurisdiction in Matters Relating to a Contract under the Brussels Convention' (1995) 44 ICLQ 591; Kennett, 'Place of Performance and Predictability' (1995) 15 YBEL 193.
[215] Art 7(1)(c).   [216] See para 4.51.
[217] *Robey & Co v Snaefell Mining Co Ltd* (1887) 20 QBD 152; *Rein v Stein* [1892] 1 QB 753.

(iii) Jurisdiction in matters relating to tort

2.94 Article 7(2) provides that in matters relating to tort a person who is domiciled in a Member State may be sued in another Member State in the courts for the place where the harmful event occurred or may occur. This rule is based on the premise that the courts for the place where the harmful event occurs is usually the most appropriate in terms of proximity and the ease of taking evidence.[218] So, where C is injured in England in a road accident caused by the negligent driving of D, who is domiciled in Spain, article 7(2) enables C to sue D in England.

2.95 As a general rule, proceedings fall within the scope of article 7(2) if the claim is based on wrongful conduct committed (or threatened) by the defendant and the act caused (or would cause) harm to the claimant.[219] For example, article 7(2) covers: a dispute concerning the lawfulness of industrial action which allegedly caused loss to the claimant;[220] in a situation where there is no contract between the parties, a claim based on the pre-contractual liability of the defendant for having failed to conduct negotiations in good faith;[221] the situation where a creditor of a limited company seeks to establish the liability of a director and a shareholder of that company for the company's debts;[222] in the context of a case involving breach of trust, a constructive trust claim based upon dishonest assistance.[223] The Court of Justice, rejecting the opinion of the Advocate General, ruled that article 7(2) also applies to proceedings for a negative declaration (that is, that the claimant is not liable to the defendant in tort); although the parties' usual roles are reversed, the courts for the place of the harmful event (alleged by the defendant, rather than the claimant) have jurisdiction over the claimant's application for declaratory relief.[224]

2.96 Which law determines whether or not a particular event is to be regarded as 'harmful' for the purposes of article 7(2)? In *Shevill v Presse Alliance SA*[225] the defendant argued that the plaintiff could not invoke the jurisdiction of the English court in a libel case because the plaintiff, who had sought to rely solely on the presumption of harm, had failed to establish that a harmful event had occurred. The House of Lords rejected this argument. On the basis of the Court of Justice's opinion that 'the criteria for assessing whether the event in question is harmful . . . are . . . governed by . . . the substantive

---

[218] Case C-167/00 *Verein für Konsumenteninformation v Henkel* [2002] ECR I-8111, para 46.
[219] See Advocate General Gulmann in Case C-261/90 *Reichert v Dresdner Bank (No 2)* [1992] ECR I-2149 at 2169.
[220] Case C-18/02 *Danmarks Rederiforening v Lo Landsorganisation I Sverige* [2004] ECR I-1417.
[221] Case C-334/00 *Fonderie Officine Meccaniche Tacconi SpA v Heinrich Wagner Sinto Maschinenfabrik GmbH* [2002] ECR I-7357.
[222] Case C-147/12 *ÖFAB v Koot* [2015] QB 20, para 42.
[223] *Casio Computer Co Ltd v Sayo* [2001] ILPr 43; *Cronos Containers NV v Palatin* [2003] ILPr 16. See also *WPP Holdings Italy Srl v Benatti* [2007] 1 WLR 2316 (claim for breach of fiduciary duty involves matters relating to tort).
[224] Case C-133/11 *Folien Fischer v Ritrama SpA* [2013] QB 253. See also the English case law which foreshadowed the Court of Justice's decision: *Equitas Ltd v Wave City Shipping Co Ltd* [2005] 2 All ER (Comm) 301 (following *Boss Group Ltd v Boss France SA* [1996] 4 All ER 970).
[225] [1996] AC 959.

law determined by the national conflict of laws rules of the court seised',[226] it was held that it was purely a question of English law whether the publication was a harmful event. So, where English law presumes that the publication of a defamatory statement is harmful, that is sufficient for the application of article 7(2).

(a) Multiple locality cases

2.97 In cases where all the elements constituting a tort occur in the same place, article 7(2) is simple to apply. The position is potentially more difficult if the defendant's wrongful act is committed in one place and the claimant is injured in another. In *Bier v Mines de Potasse d'Alsace*[227] it was alleged that D, a French company, had discharged harmful chemicals into the Rhine in France as a result of which C, a nursery gardener in the Netherlands, who used polluted water from the Rhine, suffered damage to his property. Could C sue D in the Netherlands? The Court of Justice ruled that a harmful event occurs either at the place where the damage occurs or at the place of the event giving rise to it.[228] Article 7(2) gives the claimant the option of suing at either place.[229]

2.98 At first glance, the interpretation favoured by the Court of Justice seems to allow the claimant an excessively wide choice. However, as the Court of Justice pointed out in its judgment in the *Bier* case, 'the place of the event giving rise to the damage no less than the place where damage occurred can, depending on the case, constitute a significant connecting factor from the point of view of jurisdiction'.[230] Furthermore, in many cases involving a transnational tort, the place of the event giving rise to the damage is likely to coincide with the defendant's domicile.

(b) The place where the damage occurs

2.99 The place where the damage occurs is the place where the harm is inflicted. So, where the claimant alleges infringement by the defendant of a registered trademark, the damage occurs in the Member State where the trademark is registered.[231] Where the defendant makes a contaminated product in Belgium and sells it to the claimant for use in the manufacture of fertiliser in the Netherlands, the claimant may rely on article 7(2) to sue the defendant in the Netherlands.[232]

2.100 Under article 7(2), the place where the damage occurs does not refer to the place where the injury (in particular, financial loss) is suffered;[233] article 7(2) does not confer

---

[226] Case C–68/93 *Shevill v Presse Alliance SA* [1995] ECR I–415, para 41.
[227] Case 21/76 *Handelskwekerij GJ Bier BV v Mines de Potasse d'Alsace SA* [1976] ECR 1735.
[228] See also Case 523/10 *Wintersteiger AG v Products 4U Sondermaschinenbau GmbH* [2012] ILPr 23.
[229] The determination of the court (or courts) with jurisdiction under art 7(2) is not affected by the claim in question having been transferred by the party initially injured to the claimant: Case C–147/12 *ÖFAB v Koot* [2015] QB 20, para 59.
[230] Case 21/76 *Handelskwekerij GJ Bier BV v Mines de Potasse d'Alsace SA* [1976] ECR 1735, para 15.
[231] Case C–523/10 *Wintersteiger AG v Products 4U Sondermaschinenbau GmbH* [2012] ILPr 23. See also, in the context of breach of copyright claims, Case C–170/12 *Pinckney v KDG Mediatech AG* [2014] ILPr 7; Case C–441/13 *Hejduk v EnergieAgentur.NRW GmbH*, [2015] Bus LR 560.
[232] Case C–189/08 *Zuid-Chemie BV v Philippo's Mineralenfabriek NV/SA* [2009] ECR I–6917.
[233] See Lehmann, 'Where Does Economic Loss Occur?' (2011) 7 Journal of Private International Law 527.

jurisdiction on the courts for the place where the claimant feels the adverse consequences of an event that has already caused actual damage elsewhere.[234] The crucial factor is where the event giving rise to the damage produced its 'initial', 'direct', 'immediate', or 'physical' harmful effect.[235] On the one hand, where a claimant suffers damage as a result of anti-competitive behaviour by the defendant (or defendants), the place of the damage is where the claimant's registered office is located.[236] On the other, where a French company suffers loss when its German subsidiaries become insolvent as a result of the negligent advice of a German bank, Germany is both the place where the event giving rise to the damage occurs and the place where the damage occurs, even though it is in France that the claimant suffers injury.[237] Similarly, where an Italian claimant suffers financial loss in Italy consequential upon initial damage arising from the defendant's refusal to return promissory notes which the claimant has deposited in England, article 7(2) does not confer jurisdiction on the Italian courts; England is the place where the damage occurs, notwithstanding the fact that Italy is the place where the loss is suffered.[238] Where the harm suffered takes the form of the claimant failing to receive a payment to which he was entitled, the harm occurs at the place where the payment should have been made.[239]

2.101 The distinction between the place where the damage occurs and the place where the loss is suffered may be relevant not only in situations involving pure economic loss. For example, in a case where the claimant is injured in a road accident in France, the English courts do not have jurisdiction under article 7(2) even if the claimant can establish that he suffered an aggravation of his injuries in England and even if the worsening of his condition constitutes a fresh cause of action under French law; in these circumstances, the deterioration which occurs in England is a consequence of the original harmful event in France, rather than a new harmful event occurring in England.[240] Similarly, where goods are transported in sealed containers, if the owner of the goods brings a claim in tort against the carrier of the goods, the place where the harmful event occurred for the purposes of article 7(2) is the place where the carrier was to deliver the goods, rather than the place where the owner actually discovers that the goods are damaged.[241] In this type of case it is normally impossible to determine exactly where the goods were damaged; if, however, the place where the damage was discovered were treated as the relevant place for the purposes of article 7(2), it would

---

[234] Case C-168/02 *Kronhofer v Maier* [2004] ECR I-6009, para 21; Case C-375/13 *Kolassa v Barclays Bank plc* [2015] ILPr 14, para 48.
[235] See Simon J's summary of the Court of Justice's jurisprudence in *London Helicopters Ltd v Heliportugal LDA-INAC* [2006] 1 All ER (Comm) 595 at [20]. See also *AMT Futures Ltd v Marzillier, Dr Meier & Dr Gunter Rechtsanwaltsgesellschaft mbH* [2015] QB 699.
[236] Case 352/13 *Cartel Damage Claims (CDC) Hydrogen Peroxide SA v Akzo Nobel NV* [2015] QB 906.
[237] Case 220/88 *Dumez France SA v Hessische Landesbank* [1990] ECR 49.
[238] Case C-364/93 *Marinari v Lloyds Bank plc* [1995] ECR I-2719. See also Case C-168/02 *Kronhofer v Maier* [2004] ECR I-6009.
[239] *Dolphin Maritime & Aviation Services Ltd v Sveriges Angfartygs Assurans Forening* [2009] 2 Lloyd's Rep 123.
[240] *Henderson v Jaouen* [2002] 1 WLR 2971.
[241] Case C-51/97 *Réunion Européenne SA v Splietoff's Bevachtingskantoor BV* [1998] ECR I-6511.

mean that, in any case where the ultimate place of delivery is the claimant's place of business, the claimant would be able to bring proceedings in his home forum.

(c) The place of the event giving rise to the damage

2.102 In most situations, the localisation of the event giving rise to the damage presents few problems. Not all cases, however, are totally straightforward. For example, in a case involving a fraudulent or negligent misrepresentation contained in (say) a letter posted in France to a recipient in England, is the place of the event giving rise to the damage in France (where the misstatement originates) or in England (where the misstatement is received)? According to the English courts, in this type of case, the event giving rise to the damage occurs in France.[242] In a product liability case in which the defendant, having manufactured a machine in Germany, puts it on the market in England with no warning as to its defects and the claimant is injured by the machine in Ireland, the place of manufacture (Germany) is the place of the event giving rise to the damage for the purposes of article 7(2).[243] In a case where a creditor of a company sues members of the company for losses caused by the defendants' failure to monitor the company's financial situation effectively, the place of the event giving rise to the damage will normally be where the company's seat is located.[244]

2.103 Where it is alleged that a tort has been committed online, the place of the event giving rise to the damage is not the location of the server through which the allegedly tortious material was made available; using the location of a server as a connecting factor would not satisfy the Recast's requirement that the designation of the court (or courts) with jurisdiction should be foreseeable. In the online context, the event giving rise to the damage takes place where the person responsible for the uploading or activation of the material in question is established.[245]

2.104 Problems may also arise in tort cases where there is more than one perpetrator of the alleged tort. Where C claims that it suffered harm as a result of the actions of X (who acted in Germany) and D (who acted in England) and seeks to establish jurisdiction on the basis of the location of the event giving rise to the damage, C cannot sue D in Germany even if, under German law, the law of the forum, the acts of X can be attributed to D.[246] It would be contrary to the basic scheme of the Recast if it were possible to sue D in a forum with which he had no connection and in which he had not acted.

---

[242] *Domicrest Ltd v Swiss Bank Corpn* [1999] QB 548; *Alfred Dunhill Ltd v Diffusion Internationale de Maroquinerie de Prestige SARL* [2001] CLC 949; *London Helicopters Ltd v Heliportugal LDA-INAC* [2006] 1 All ER (Comm) 595; *The Seaward Quest* [2007] 2 Lloyd's Rep 308. In this type of case, the place of the damage will normally be where the communication is received and relied upon by the claimant.

[243] Case C-45/13 *Kainz v Pantherwerke AG* [2015] QB 34. Of course, on such facts, Ireland would be the place where the damage occurs.

[244] Case C-147/12 *ÖFAB v Koot* [2015] QB 20, para 54.

[245] Case C-523/10 *Wintersteiger AG v Products 4U Sondermaschinenbau GmbH* [2012] ILPr 23; Case C-441/13 *Hejduk v EnergieAgentur.NRW GmbH*, [2015] Bus LR 560.

[246] Case C-228/11 *Melzer v MF Global UK Ltd* [2013] QB 1112. See also Case C-360/12 *Coty Germany GmbH v First Note Perfumes NV* [2014] Bus LR (in the context of jurisdiction over trade mark infringement under art 93(5) of the Community Trade Mark Regulation).

In such a case, however, the claimant may be able to sue D in Germany on the basis that Germany was the place where the damage occurred.²⁴⁷

2.105 Similar problems arise in a case where a number of defendants cause damage to a range of claimants by means of anti-competitive behaviour (in the form of a single and continuous infringement) carried out in a number of Member States, at different times and in different places. In such a case, the place of the event giving rise to the damage is either the place in which the cartel was definitively concluded or the place in which one agreement in particular was concluded which is identifiable as the sole cause of the loss allegedly suffered by the claimant.²⁴⁸

(d) Article 7(2) and the infringement of personality rights

2.106 The application of the ruling in *Bier v Mines de Potasse d'Alsace* to the case of a libel by a newspaper article distributed in several Member States gives the claimant a wide choice of jurisdictions in which to sue.²⁴⁹ In *Shevill v Presse Alliance SA*²⁵⁰ the Court of Justice ruled that a claimant who alleges international libel by the print media may bring proceedings in the place where the publisher is established because that is the place of the event giving rise to the damage; if successful, the claimant will recover damages for all the loss he has suffered. Alternatively, the claimant may sue the defendant in any of the places where the publication is distributed, because that is where the damage occurs. However, in such a case, the claimant may recover damages only for the loss of reputation suffered in the particular Member State in which the proceedings are brought.²⁵¹ Suppose a publishing company which is domiciled in Belgium produces a newspaper which is distributed in France and England. A person who is defamed by the publication may sue the publisher in England for the damage to his reputation in England and may sue the publisher in France for the damage to his reputation in France. The potential disadvantage of having different courts ruling on various aspects of the same dispute can be avoided if the claimant litigates his entire claim in Belgium, the place where the publisher is established.

2.107 The *Shevill* ruling, formulated in the context of libel by print media, was adapted in *eDate Advertising GmbH v X*²⁵² a case where the claim was based on infringement of personality rights by means of content placed online. The Court of Justice held that the claimant can sue for all the damage either in the Member State where the publisher of the content is established (as in *Shevill*), or in the Member State in which the centre of the *claimant's* interests is based (normally, the Member State in which the claimant

---

²⁴⁷ Case C–387/12 *Hi Hotel HCF SARL v Spoering* [2014] 1 WLR 1912.
²⁴⁸ Case 352/13 *Cartel Damage Claims (CDC) Hydrogen Peroxide SA v Akzo Nobel NV* [2015] QB 906.
²⁴⁹ For a discussion of the human rights implications of 'libel tourism', see Fawcett, Ní Shúilleabháin and Shah, *Human Rights and Private International Law* (2016) ch 10.
²⁵⁰ Case C–68/93 [1995] ECR I–415.
²⁵¹ The same rule applies where it is alleged that the defendant infringed the claimant's copyright and that the infringement caused loss in more than one Member State: Case C–387/12 *Hi Hotel HCF SARL v Spoering* [2014] 1 WLR 1912.
²⁵² Joined cases C–509/09 & C–161/10 *eDate Advertising GmbH v X; Martinez v MGN Ltd* [2012] QB 654. See Gillies (2012) 61 ICLQ 1007; Nagy (2012) 8 Journal of Private International Law 251.

is habitually resident). The Court of Justice considered that the courts of the Member State in which the centre of the claimant's interests is based are the ones best placed to assess the impact which material placed online is likely to have on the claimant.[253] The claimant may also sue in any other Member State in which the content is accessible, but only in respect of the damage caused in that Member State.

(e) Threatened wrongs

2.108 Article 7(2) applies to cases of threatened wrongs as well as committed wrongs, thereby providing a clear ground of jurisdiction for preventive measures. Where, for example, a claimant seeks an injunction to prevent the publication of defamatory material, article 7(2) confers jurisdiction on the court for the place where the harm would occur if the publication were not prevented.

(iv) Branch, agency, or other establishment

2.109 Under article 7(5) a defendant domiciled in a Member State may, as regards a dispute arising out of the operations of a branch, agency, or other establishment, be sued in another Member State in the courts for the place in which the branch, agency, or other establishment is situated. So, a natural or legal person domiciled in France can be sued in England if it has a branch in England, provided that the dispute arises out of the branch's operations.

2.110 The words 'agency or other establishment' add little to 'branch', which normally displays the following characteristics: it is subject to the direction and control of the parent body; it has a place of business which has the appearance of permanency; it is able to transact business with third parties.[254] These characteristics seem not, however, to be of universal application. The Court of Justice has ruled that, for the purposes of article 7(5), a parent company may be regarded as a branch of one of its subsidiary companies (even though the two companies are legally independent of each other) if it appears to third parties that the parent is acting on behalf of the subsidiary.[255]

2.111 The concept of 'operations' comprises three categories of activity: (i) actions relating to contractual and non-contractual obligations concerning the management of the branch itself, (ii) actions relating to undertakings which have been entered into by the branch in the name of the parent, and (iii) actions concerning non-contractual obligations arising from the activities of the branch on behalf of the parent.[256] There is no requirement that undertakings in the second category should be performed in the Member State where the branch is situated[257] or that non-contractual obligations

---

[253] [2012] QB 654, para 48.
[254] Case 14/76 *Ets A de Bloos SPRL v Société en commandite par actions Bouyer* [1976] ECR 1497; Case 33/78 *Somafer SA v Saar-Ferngas AG* [1978] ECR 2183; Case 139/80 *Blanckaert and Willems PVBA v Trost* [1981] ECR 819.
[255] Case 218/86 *SAR Schotte GmbH v Parfums Rothschild SARL* [1987] ECR 4905.
[256] Case 33/78 *Somafer SA v Saar-Ferngas AG* [1978] ECR 2183.
[257] Case C-439/93 *Lloyd's Register of Shipping v Société Campenon Bernard* [1995] ECR I-961.

in the third category should have produced harmful effects in that Member State.[258] Article 7(5) is satisfied as long as the nexus between the branch and the dispute is such that it is natural to describe the dispute as one which arose out of the branch's activities.[259] Such a connection may exist where a Dutch defendant's English branch is responsible for the production of the marketing material on which the claimant's claim for negligent misstatement is founded.[260]

2.112 The purpose of article 7(5) is to enable a third party who comes into contact with the parent through the activities of a branch or agent to sue the parent at the place where the branch or agent is established. There is no reason why, in a dispute between the parent and an agent, the agent should be able to rely on article 7(5) to sue the parent in the place where the agency is situated.[261]

2.113 The rationale of article 7(5) is the presumed existence of a close connection between the dispute and the country in which the branch is located. However, if its conditions are satisfied, article 7(5) is effective to confer jurisdiction on the courts for the place where the branch is situated, whether or not the dispute is connected in a meaningful way with that place. Where, for example, an English company undertakes (through its French branch) to perform services in Spain (through its Spanish branch) the French courts have jurisdiction under article 7(5) in relation to the claim for damages based on the defendant's defective performance of the services in Spain.[262]

(v) Multiple parties and claims

2.114 Where a dispute involves more than two parties it is often just and convenient for all the claims and the defences to them to be decided at the same time by the same court. Article 8 seeks to mitigate the effects of those provisions of Chapter II which tend towards the fragmentation of various disputes arising out of a single set of facts. Nevertheless, article 8 cannot be used to undermine the effectiveness of exclusive jurisdiction agreements under article 25; in a case where the court has jurisdiction over D1 (under article 4) and prima facie jurisdiction over D2 (under article 8), jurisdiction over D2 cannot be exercised if that would conflict with a jurisdiction agreement (either between the claimant and D2 or between D1 and D2).[263] There are three paragraphs of article 8 to be considered.[264]

(a) Multiple defendants

2.115 Article 8(1) deals with the situation where the claimant wishes to sue two (or more) defendants—for example, because they are each liable to him or they are liable in the

---

[258] *Anton Durbeck GmbH v Den Norske Bank ASA* [2003] QB 1160.   [259] Ibid.
[260] *McGraw-Hill v Deutsche Apotheker- und Arztebank EG* [2014] 2 Lloyd's Rep 523.
[261] See the opinion of Advocate General Reishl in Case 14/76 *Ets A de Bloos SPRL v Société en commandite par actions Bouyer* [1976] ECR 1497 at 1519.
[262] Case C-439/93 *Lloyd's Register of Shipping v Société Campenon Bernard* [1995] ECR I-961.
[263] *Hough v P & O Containers Ltd* [1999] QB 834.
[264] Art 8(4) allows a mortgagee of immovable property to combine, in the Member State in which the property is situated, an action concerning the personal liability of the owner with an action for the enforced sale of the property.

alternative. Under article 8(1) each of a number of defendants domiciled in different Member States may be sued in the courts for the place where any one of them is domiciled. Where, for example, there are two joint debtors—one domiciled in England (D1), the other domiciled in France (D2)—the claimant may sue both in either country. However, article 8(1) cannot be invoked if none of the defendants is domiciled in the Member State in which proceedings are brought. Where, for example, C sues D1, who is domiciled in France, in England on the basis of article 7(1), C cannot rely on article 8(1) in order to join D2, who is domiciled in Germany, to those proceedings.

2.116 Where article 8(1) is engaged, there is no requirement that the claims against D1 and D2 should be pursued in the same proceedings; article 8(1) is wide enough to encompass defendants and claims in more than one action.[265] However, the same person must be the claimant in proceedings brought against D1 and D2.[266]

2.117 The Court of Justice's judgment in *Reisch Montage AG v Kiesel Baumaschinen Handels GmbH*[267] indicates that article 8(1) cannot be relied on where claims are brought under article 8(1) for the sole purpose of removing D2 from the jurisdiction of the courts of the Member State in which that defendant is domiciled. Although the text of article 8(1) does not support this view and the contrary position appears to have been taken in *Freeport plc v Arnoldsson*,[268] subsequent decisions of the Court of Justice confirm that article 8(1) does not allow an applicant to make a claim against a number of defendants with the sole object of ousting the jurisdiction of the courts of the Member State where one of those defendants is domiciled.[269] Accordingly, an attempt to join a co-defendant on the basis of article 8(1) may be refused if there is clear evidence of collusion or abuse.[270]

2.118 It has been established that, where D1 is domiciled in England and D2 is domiciled in another Member State, it is generally necessary for a claimant to satisfy the court that there is a serious issue to be tried against both D1 and D2.[271] However, once proceedings have been properly initiated against D2, article 8(1) does not cease to be applicable by virtue of the claimant obtaining a default judgment against D1.[272] Somewhat surprisingly, in the *Reisch Montage* case,[273] the Court of Justice decided that, where the claimant brought proceedings in Germany against D1 (domiciled in Germany) and D2 (domiciled in Austria), the German court had jurisdiction over the claim against D2 on the basis of article 8(1), notwithstanding the fact that, when D2 was joined to the proceedings, the action against D1 had become inadmissible. A similar issue arose in the *Cartel Damage Claims* case.[274] The Court of Justice held that, in a situation

---

[265] *Masri v Consolidated Contractors International (UK) Ltd* [2006] 1 WLR 830.
[266] *Madoff Securities International Ltd v Raven* [2012] 2 All ER (Comm) 634.
[267] Case C-103/05 [2006] ECR I-6827, para 32.   [268] Case C-98/06 [2007] ECR I-8319, para 54.
[269] Case C-145/10 *Painer v Standard Verlags GmbH* [2012] ECDR 6, para 78; Case C-616/10 *Solvay SA v Honeywell Fluorine Products Europe BV*, para 22.
[270] *Siber Energy Ltd v Tchigirinski* [2012] 2 All ER (Comm) 1285.
[271] *Brown v Innovatorone plc* [2011] ILPr 9. Compare *The Xing Su Hai* [1995] 2 Lloyd's Rep 15.
[272] *Linuzs v Latmar Holdings Corp* [2012] ILPr 19.   [273] Case C-103/05 [2006] ECR I-6827.
[274] Case 352/13 *Cartel Damage Claims (CDC) Hydrogen Peroxide SA v Akzo Nobel NV* [2015] QB 906.

involving a number of defendants which had participated in different places and at different times in a single and continuous infringement of EU competition law, if C brings proceedings in Germany against D1 (domiciled in Germany) and a number of other defendants (domiciled in other Member States), article 8(1) continues to confer jurisdiction on the German courts as regards the claims against the other defendants, even if the claim against D1 is withdrawn. This rule does not apply, however, if there is firm evidence to support the allegation that C and D1 had colluded in creating a situation in which the conditions of article 8(1) were artificially fulfilled or their fulfilment was artificially prolonged.

2.119 The Court of Justice has held that article 8(1) cannot be invoked by an employee who finds himself in dispute with two (allegedly joint) employers. In *Glaxosmithkline v Rouard*[275] C, who was employed first by D1 (a French company) and then by D2 (a UK company in the same group), claimed that he had been wrongfully dismissed. C started proceedings in France against D1 (on the basis of D1's domicile in France) and sought to join D2 to those proceedings. The Court, which disagreed with the Advocate General, adopted a literal reading of the relevant provisions and ruled that the jurisdiction rules in Section 5 dealing with employment contracts cannot be amended or supplemented by other jurisdiction rules laid down in Chapter II unless special reference to them is made in Section 5 itself.[276] Given that there is no reference to article 8(1) in Section 5,[277] article 8(1) does not apply in disputes relating to individual contracts of employment.

2.120 Because article 8(1) applies only to defendants domiciled in Member States, if proceedings are brought in England against D1 (who is domiciled in a Member State), article 8(1) does not confer jurisdiction on the English courts as regards D2 (who is not domiciled in a Member State). Equally, if proceedings are brought in England against D1 (who is not domiciled in a Member State), article 8(1) does not confer jurisdiction on the English courts as regards D2 (who is domiciled in a Member State).[278]

2.121 Article 8(1) provides that jurisdiction can be assumed over co-defendants who are domiciled in other Member States only if the claims are so closely connected that it is expedient to hear and determine them together to avoid the risk of irreconcilable judgments resulting from separate proceedings.[279] In order for this condition to be satisfied, it must be shown that there is in fact a realistic possibility of there being separate proceedings.[280] In *Roche Nederland BV v Primus*[281] the claimant alleged that a number of companies based in different Member States, but part of the same corporate group, had infringed the claimant's European patent. The claimant brought proceedings against the Dutch company in the Netherlands and sought to join the other defendants

---

[275] Case C-462/06 [2008] ECR I-3965.   [276] Case C-462/06 [2008] ECR I-3965, para 19.
[277] See paras 2.138–2.139.
[278] Case C-51/97 *Réunion Européenne SA v Splietoff's Bevachtingskantoor BV* [1998] ECR I-6511, para 46.
[279] The text of art 8(1) of the Brussels I Recast effectively incorporates the ruling in Case 189/87 *Kalfelis v Bankhaus Schröder, Münchmeyer, Hengst & Co* [1988] ECR 5565.
[280] *Brown v Innovatorone plc* [2011] ILPr 9.   [281] Case C-539/03 [2006] ECR I-6535.

on the basis of article 8(1). The Court of Justice held that the co-defendants could not be joined in this case as, in order for there to be irreconcilable judgments, 'it is not sufficient that there be a divergence in the outcome of the dispute, but that divergence must also arise in the context of the same situation of law and fact'.[282] There was no risk of irreconcilable judgments in the *Roche Nederland* case as, under the European patent system, each patent derived from a European patent application took effect as an independent, national patent governed by national law. So, as regards each alleged infringement, although the factual situation was the same, the legal situation was not.

2.122 However, the *Roche Nederland* case appears to have been qualified by the ruling in *Painer v Standard Verlags GmbH*,[283] although the Court of Justice has not explained the relationship between the two cases. In the *Painer* case, the claimant alleged copyright infringement by a number of German and Austrian defendants and sought to bring proceedings against all the defendants in Austria, notwithstanding the fact that the liability of the Austrian defendants was governed by Austrian law and that of the German defendants by German law. The Court of Justice ruled that article 8(1) is not inapplicable solely because actions against several defendants for substantially identical copyright infringements are brought on national legal grounds which vary from country to country; it was for the Austrian court to determine whether there was a risk of irreconcilable judgments if the claimant had to proceed against the Austrian and German defendants separately. Presumably, such a risk could have been thought to arise if, in terms of substance, the laws of Austria and Germany were identical on the relevant issues.

2.123 On the basis of the Court of Justice's controversial judgment in *Réunion Européenne SA v Splietoff's Bevachtingskantoor BV*,[284] it appeared that article 8(1) could not be invoked in a case involving two claims directed against different defendants and based in one instance on contractual liability and in the other on liability in tort.[285] However, in *Freeport plc v Arnoldsson*[286] the Court of Justice took the opportunity to resolve the misunderstandings to which the *Réunion Européenne* case had given rise. C brought proceedings in Sweden against D1, a Swedish company, and D2, an English company which was D1's parent company, for payment that was allegedly due under a contract between C and D2. D2 sought to rely on the *Réunion Européenne* case to contest the Swedish court's jurisdiction over it on the basis that the requirements of article 8(1) were not satisfied: whereas the claim against D1 was non-contractual in nature, the claim against D2 was for breach of contract. The Court of Justice had no hesitation in ruling that the Swedish court had jurisdiction over both claims in this type of situation; where an action is brought before the court for the place where one of the defendants is domiciled, article 8(1) applies notwithstanding the fact that the claims brought

---

[282] Ibid, para 26. See also Case C-616/10 *Solvay SA v Honeywell Fluorine Products Europe BV*, unreported.
[283] Case C-145/10 [2012] ECDR 6.   [284] Case C-51/97 [1998] ECR I-6511, para 50.
[285] It is now clear that, as some had suggested, the Court of Justice did not mean what it appeared to have said: *Watson v First Choice Holidays and Flights Ltd* [2001] 2 Lloyd's Rep 339; *Andrew Weir Shipping Ltd v Wartsila UK Ltd* [2004] 2 Lloyd's Rep 377.
[286] Case C-98/06 [2007] ECR I-8319.

against different defendants have different legal bases. According to the Court of Justice, as the *Réunion Européenne* case had involved a situation in which proceedings had been brought in a Member State in which none of the defendants was domiciled, the judgment had no bearing on the proper interpretation of article 8(1) (regardless of what national courts and commentators had thought). The effect of the *Freeport* decision is that where, for example, C is injured in a coach accident while on holiday in Spain, C's contractual claim against D1, the English tour operator, and his tortious claim against D2, the Spanish coach operator, are sufficiently closely connected for the purposes of article 8(1) to enable the English court to assume jurisdiction over C's claim against D2.

(b) Third-party proceedings

2.124 The main purpose of article 8(2) is to deal with the case where it is a defendant, rather than the claimant, who wishes to join a further party to the proceedings. For example, a case may arise in which C sues D1 and D1 wishes to join D2 as a party to the proceedings so that if D1 is held liable he can shift liability (either in whole or in part) to D2.[287] However, article 8(2) also covers situations in which a third party joins proceedings in order to protect his own interests—for example, by bringing against the defendant in the original proceedings a claim that is closely linked to the original proceedings.[288]

2.125 Article 8(2) provides that a person domiciled in a Member State may be joined as third party in the court of another Member State which is seised of the original proceedings. For example, where a German manufacturer sells defective goods to a Belgian wholesaler who sells them to an English retailer, if the English retailer sues the Belgian wholesaler in Belgium, the Belgian wholesaler can use article 8(2) to join the German manufacturer to the Belgian proceedings. A restriction imposed on article 8(2) is that it cannot be invoked if the proceedings were brought solely with the object of removing the third party from the jurisdiction of the court which would otherwise be competent; it is for the national court to determine whether such an abuse of process has occurred.[289]

2.126 Although the text of article 8(2) is potentially ambiguous, it should be possible for jurisdiction to be assumed under article 8(2) only in cases where jurisdiction against the first defendant is derived from the provisions of Chapter II. Where, for example, C invokes the jurisdiction of the English court against D1, a New York defendant, under the Civil Procedure Rules, D1 should not be able to use article 8(2) to join D2, domiciled in Germany, as a third party. There is, however, no requirement under article 8(2) that the original proceedings should be brought in the Member State in which the first

---

[287] See, eg, *Kinnear v Falconfilms NV* [1996] 1 WLR 920. Compare *Barton v Golden Sun Holidays Ltd (in liquidation)* [2007] ILPr 57 (in which jurisdiction was refused in a case where there was no risk of irreconcilable judgments).

[288] Case C-521/14 *SOVAG-Schwarzmeer und Ostsee Versicherungs-Aktiengesellschaft v If Vahinkovakuutusyhtiö Oy* [2016] ILPr 12.

[289] See Case C-77/04 *Groupement d'intérêt économique (GIE) Réunion européenne v Zurich España* [2005] ECR I-4509.

defendant is domiciled. Where, for example, C relies on article 7(1) to bring proceedings in the Netherlands against D1, a German company, D1 can invoke article 8(2) to join D2, another German company, as a third party.[290]

(c) Counterclaims

2.127 Article 8(3) provides that a person domiciled in a Member State may be sued on a counterclaim in the court in which the original claim is pending as long as the counterclaim arises from the same contract or facts on which the original claim was based. So, if C (domiciled in Italy) relies on article 4 to sue D in England, the English court has jurisdiction over D's counterclaim against C.

2.128 The Court of Justice has ruled that article 8(3) applies only to claims by defendants which may lead to the pronouncement of a separate judgment.[291] It does not, however, deal with the situation where the defendant pleads, as a defence, the existence of a claim which he allegedly has against the claimant and which would have the effect of wholly or partially excluding the claim, but which would not lead to a separate judgment; the defences which may be raised and the conditions under which they can be raised are determined by the law of the forum in which the claimant is proceeding.[292] Where, for example, C sues D for the recovery of a sum of money and D raises set-off as a defence, article 8(3) has no application; the defence is an integral part of the proceedings initiated by C and does not involve C being 'sued' within the meaning of article 8(3).

3. Jurisdiction in matters relating to insurance, consumer contracts, and employment contracts

2.129 Chapter II contains detailed provisions dealing with jurisdiction in matters relating to insurance (Section 3), consumer contracts (Section 4), and employment contracts (Section 5). These detailed provisions create self-contained and exclusive codes in relation to the matters within their scope; it is not possible for litigants to fall back on the other provisions of the Brussels I Recast (unless expressly authorised by the relevant provisions).[293] However, there appears to be an exception in cases where the defendant submits to a court which would not otherwise have jurisdiction under the specific provisions of Chapter II. The Court of Justice has held that a court to which jurisdiction is not allocated by the provisions of Section 3 is nevertheless competent under article 26 (submission) if the defendant enters an appearance and does not contest the court's jurisdiction.[294]

---

[290] Case 365/88 *Kongress Agentur Hagen GmbH v Zeehaghe BV* [1990] ECR I-1845.
[291] Case C-341/93 *Danvaern Production A/S v Schuhfabriken Otterbeck GmbH & Co* [1995] ECR I-2053.
[292] Ibid, paras 12-14.
[293] Case C-462/06 *Glaxosmithkline v Rouard* [2008] ECR I-3965. See also *Jordan Grand Prix Ltd v Baltic Insurance Group* [1999] 2 AC 127. Note that the rules dealing with insurance, consumer contracts, and employment contracts are 'without prejudice' to art 7(5) and art 6: arts 10, 17(1), 20.
[294] Case C-111/09 *Česká podnikatelská pojišťovna as, Vienna Insurance Group v Bilas* [2010] ECR I-4545. There is no reason to suppose that the position in relation to consumer contracts (Section 4) or employment contracts (Section 5) is different.

2.130 There are two important aspects of these special rules in Sections 3 to 5. First, the primary aim of the rules is to protect the party who from the socio-economic point of view is weaker—that is, the policyholder, the consumer, or the employee. As a general rule the weaker party is able to ensure that any litigation will take place in his home forum. Secondly, a jurisdiction clause in an insurance contract, a consumer contract, or an employment contract may be enforced against the weaker party only in limited circumstances.

(A) Matters relating to insurance

2.131 Under Section 3, which comprises articles 10–16, in a matter relating to insurance,[295] an insurer domiciled in a Member State may be sued not only in the courts of the Member State in which he is domiciled, but also in the Member State in which the weaker party (that is, as the case may be, the policyholder, the assured, or a beneficiary) is domiciled.[296] Moreover, an insurer, who is not domiciled in any Member State but has a branch or agency in a Member State, is, in relation to disputes arising out of the operations of the branch or agency, deemed to be domiciled in that state.[297] In respect of liability insurance or insurance of immovable property, the insurer may be sued in the courts for the place where the harmful event occurred.[298] With regard to liability insurance, an insurer (whether or not domiciled in a Member State[299]) may be joined to proceedings brought by the injured party against the insured.[300] As a general rule, the insurer may bring proceedings only in the Member State in which the defendant is domiciled.[301]

2.132 The effectiveness of a jurisdiction agreement in an insurance contract is determined by articles 15 and 16.[302] Such an agreement will be enforced in only five alternative situations: (1) it was entered into after the dispute arose; (2) the agreement allows the weaker

---

[295] The insurance provisions do not apply either to proceedings between insurers (Case C-77/04 *Groupement d'intérêt économique (GIE) Réunion européenne v Zurich España* [2005] ECR I-4509) or to proceedings relating to contracts of reinsurance (Case C-412/98 *Universal General Insurance Co (USIG) v Group Josi Reinsurance Co SA* [2000] ECR I-5925). However, claims brought by policyholders against reinsurers should fall within these provisions: European Commission, *Brussels I Proposal*, COM (1999) 348 final, p 15.

[296] Art 11(1). For the purposes of this provision, it is the domicile of the weaker party when the proceedings are commenced, rather than when the contract of insurance was concluded, that is relevant: *Sherdley v Nordea Life and Pension SA* [2013] ILPr 26. Where a direct action by an injured person against an insurer is permitted, the scope of art 11(1) is broadened by art 13(2), which allows an injured party who is not the policyholder, the insured or the beneficiary of the insurance contract to sue the insurer in the Member State in which the injured party is domiciled: Case C-463/06 *FBTO Schadeverzekeringen NV v Odenbreit* [2007] ECR I-11321; *Jones v Assurances Generales de France (AGF) SA* [2010] ILPr 4 (English victim of road accident in France entitled to sue French insurer of allegedly negligent (Irish) driver in England). See also *Maher v Groupama Grand Est* [2010] 1 WLR 1564; *Keefe v Mapfre Mutualidad Cia De Seguros Y Reaseguros SA* [2016] 1 WLR 905. Art 13(2) does not permit a social security institution, acting as statutory assignee of the rights of a person directly injured in a road accident, to bring proceedings against the insurer in the country in which the social security institution is domiciled: Case C-347/08 *Vorarlberger Gebietskrankenkasse v WGV-Schwäbische Allgemeine Versicherungs AG* [2010] ILPr 2.

[297] Art 11(2).   [298] Art 12.
[299] *Jordan Grand Prix Ltd v Baltic Insurance Group* [1999] 2 AC 127.
[300] Art 13(1).   [301] Art 14(1).   [302] See *Sherdley v Nordea Life and Pension SA* [2013] ILPr 26.

party a wider choice than that permitted by the other provisions of the Recast; (3) the agreement confers jurisdiction on the courts of the Member State in which both the policyholder and the insurer are domiciled;[303] (4) the policyholder is not domiciled in a Member State (unless the insurance is compulsory or relates to immovable property situated in a Member State); (5) the agreement forms part of a contract of insurance dealing with major risks as defined by article 16 (such as a contract of marine insurance).

2.133 Although the rules relating to insurance were designed for the protection of the small policyholder against the more powerful insurer, the application of Section 3 does not depend on it being shown that the policyholder is weak and in need of protection.[304]

(B) Consumer contracts

2.134 Section 4, which comprises articles 17–19, sets out provisions for the protection of consumers.[305] To fall within the scope of the consumer contract provisions, the dispute must arise out of a concluded contract[306] and one of the parties must have entered the contract for a purpose outside his trade or profession.[307] In addition, the contract must be one of the following: (a) a contract for the sale of goods on instalment credit terms;[308] or (b) a contract for a loan repayable by instalments, or for any other form of credit, made to finance the sale of goods; or (c) any other contract[309] concluded with a person who pursues commercial or professional activities in the Member State of the consumer's domicile or, by any means, directs such activities to that Member State and the contract falls within the scope of such activities.[310] According to the European Commission, the purpose of subparagraph (c) is to ensure that consumer contracts concluded via an interactive website accessible in the state of the consumer's domicile

---

[303] But, a jurisdiction clause cannot be enforced against a beneficiary who is not domiciled in the same Member State as the policyholder and the insurer unless the beneficiary has expressly subscribed to the clause: Case C-112/03 *Société financière industrielle du Peloux v Axa Belgium* [2005] ECR I-3707.

[304] *New Hampshire Insurance Co v Strabag Bau AG* [1992] 1 Lloyd's Rep 361.

[305] See Hill, *Cross-Border Consumer Contracts* (2008) chs 3 and 4.

[306] Case C-96/00 *Gabriel v Schlank & Schick GmbH* [2000] ECR I-6367; Case C-27/02 *Engler v Janus Versand GmbH* [2005] ECR I-481; Case C-180/06 *Ilsinger v Dreschers* [2009] ECR I-3961; Case C-375/13 *Kolassa v Barclays Bank plc* [2015] ILPr 14.

[307] Case C-464/01 *Gruber v Bay Wa AG* [2005] ECR I-439. See also *Standard Bank London Ltd v Apostolakis* [2000] ILPr 766. A person who enters a contract with a view to pursuing a trade or profession, not at the present time but in the future, is not a consumer: Case C-269/95 *Benincasa v Dentalkit Srl* [1997] ECR I-3767. Where a managing director or majority shareholder guarantees the debts of the company in question, the contract of guarantee is not a consumer contract: Case C-419/11 *Ceska Sporitelna AS v Feichter* [2013] ILPr 22.

[308] See Case C-89/91 *Shearson Lehman Hutton v TVB Treuhandgesellschaft für Vermögensverwaltung und Beteiligungen mbH* [1993] ECR I-139; Case C-99/96 *Mietz v Intership Yachting Sneek BV* [1999] ECR I-2277.

[309] Including contracts which, for an inclusive price, provide for a combination of travel and accommodation (package holidays) (see Cases C-585/08 & C-144/09 *Pammer v Reederei Karl Schlüter GmbH & Co KG; Hotel Alpenhof GesmbH v Heller* [2010] ECR I-12527) but excluding other contracts of transport: art 17(3).

[310] Art 17(1). There is no further requirement that the contract be concluded at a distance, rather than face-to-face: Case C-190/11 *Mühlleitner v Yusufi* [2012] ILPr 46. Some of the factors relevant for determining whether activities are directed to a particular Member State are considered in Case C-218/12 *Emrek v Sabranovic* [2014] ILPr 49. See also Case C-297/14 *Hobohm v Benedikt Kampik Ltd & Co KG* [2016] 2 WLR 940.

are covered by the special provisions.³¹¹ If a contract is concluded between two parties neither of whom was engaged in commercial or professional activities, neither party is a 'consumer' and the case falls outside the scope of Section 4.³¹²

2.135 If the supplier is domiciled in a Member State (or is deemed to be so domiciled by virtue of having a branch in a Member State³¹³), the consumer may sue the supplier in the courts for the place in which the supplier is domiciled (or deemed to be domiciled); alternatively, the consumer may sue the supplier in the courts of the Member State in which the consumer is domiciled, regardless of the supplier's domicile.³¹⁴ However, the consumer may be sued only in the Member State in which he is domiciled.³¹⁵

2.136 These rules are subject to the provisions which regulate jurisdiction agreements in consumer contracts. A jurisdiction agreement is effective in only three alternative situations: (1) it was concluded after the dispute arose; or (2) the agreement gives the consumer a wider choice of jurisdictions in which to sue than that permitted by the other provisions of the Regulation; or (3) the agreement is in favour of the courts of the Member State in which both the consumer and the supplier are domiciled.³¹⁶

2.137 These provisions are relevant only to the extent that a consumer is personally the claimant or defendant in proceedings; if A, a consumer, contracts with B and then assigns his rights under the contract to C, who is not a consumer, C is not able to rely on the consumer contract provisions even though A would have been able to do so.³¹⁷

(C) Employment contracts

2.138 Section 5, comprising articles 20–23, applies to claims in matters relating to³¹⁸ individual contracts of employment³¹⁹ and sets out provisions for the protection of employees.³²⁰

---

³¹¹ European Commission, *Brussels I Proposal*, COM (1999) 348 final, p 16. For consideration of the application of art 17(1)(c) in the context of e-commerce, see Cases C-585/08 & C-144/09 *Pammer v Reederei Karl Schlüter GmbH & Co KG; Hotel Alpenhof GesmbH v Heller* [2010] ECR I-12527.

³¹² Case C-508/12 *Vapenik v Thurner* [2014] 1 WLR 2486 (a case involving the European Enforcement Orders Regulation).

³¹³ Art 17(2).

³¹⁴ Art 18(1). See Case C-318/93 *Brenner and Noller v Dean Witter Reynolds Inc* [1994] ECR I-4275. Under art 18(1) of the Brussels I Recast an English consumer may sue a Scottish supplier in England, notwithstanding the fact that both parties are domiciled in the same Member State: European Commission, *Brussels I Proposal*, COM (1999) 348 final, p 17.

³¹⁵ Art 18(2). Or, in certain circumstances, the Member State in which the consumer was last domiciled: Case C-327/10 *Hypotecni banka as v Lindner* [2011] ECR I-11543.

³¹⁶ Art 19.

³¹⁷ Case C-89/91 *Shearson Lehman Hutton v TVB Treuhandgesellschaft für Vermögensverwaltung und Beteiligungen mbH* [1993] ECR I-139, para 23.

³¹⁸ To fall within the scope of Section 5, proceedings do not have to be 'under' the contract of employment; the 'relating to' test is broader and may cover claims pleaded in tort (or on some other legal basis): *Alfa Laval Tumba AB v Separator Spares International Ltd* [2013] 1 WLR 1110; *CEF Holdings Ltd v Mundey* [2012] FSR 35.

³¹⁹ For consideration of the characteristics of an employment contract, see Case C-47/14 *Holterman Ferho Exploitatie BV v Spies von Büllesheim* [2015] ILPr 44. As for the distinction between a contract of employment and a consultancy agreement, see *WPP Holdings Italy Srl v Benatti* [2006] 2 Lloyd's Rep 610 (Field J); [2007] 1 WLR 2316 (CA).

³²⁰ For the argument that Section 5 fails to meet the objective of employee protection, see Grusic, 'Jurisdiction in Employment Matters under Brussels I: A Reassessment' (2012) 61 ICLQ 91.

If the employer is domiciled in a Member State (or is deemed to be so domiciled by virtue of having a branch, agency, or other establishment[321] in a Member State), the employee may sue the employer in the Member State in which the employer is domiciled or deemed to be domiciled. Alternatively, the employee may sue the employer in the courts for the place where the employee habitually carries out his work[322] (or for the last place where he did so);[323] an employee who does not habitually carry out his work in any one country can sue the employer in the courts for the place where the business which engaged the employee is (or was) situated.[324] An employer not domiciled in a Member State may be sued in the courts for the place (in a Member State) where the employee habitually carries out his work or where he last did so.[325] The employee may be sued only in the Member State in which the employee is domiciled.[326]

2.139 These provisions may be departed from only where the parties have concluded a jurisdiction agreement which was entered into after the dispute arose[327] or where the jurisdiction agreement allows the employee to bring proceedings in courts other than those designated by the other employment contract provisions in Chapter II.[328]

B Bases of jurisdiction under the traditional rules

2.140 An important difference between the jurisdiction of the English court under the traditional rules and under the Brussels I Recast is that the assumption of the former jurisdiction is discretionary, depending on whether the English court is the appropriate forum, whereas the latter is, in the main, mandatory, the court not normally being free to decline jurisdiction. The traditional rules apply not only in cases which are not within the scope of article 1 of the Recast but also in situations falling within the scope of article 1 where the defendant is not domiciled in a Member State and jurisdiction is not allocated by any of the rules which apply regardless of domicile.[329] Accordingly, the

---

[321] An embassy may be an 'establishment' for the purposes of art 20(2): Case C-154/11 *Mahamdia v People's Democratic Republic of Algeria* [2012] ILPr 41.

[322] See Case C-383/95 *Rutten v Cross Medical Ltd* [1997] ECR I-57; Case C-37/00 *Weber v Universal Ogden Services Ltd* [2002] ECR I-2013; Case C-437/00 *Pugliese v Finmeccanica SpA* [2003] ECR I-3573. See also Case C-29/10 *Koelzsch v Grand Duchy of Luxembourg* [2012] QB 210 (a case decided under the related provision of the Rome Convention).

[323] Art 21(1)(b)(i).

[324] Art 21(1)(b)(ii). See Case C-384/10 *Voogsgeerd v Navimer SA* [2012] ILPr 16 (a case decided under the Rome Convention).

[325] Art 21(2).   [326] Art 22.

[327] See *Simpson v Intralinks* [2012] ILPr 34 (in which the English court had jurisdiction, notwithstanding a German jurisdiction clause in the contract of employment).

[328] Art 23. For the purposes of this provision, the 'other' courts may be the courts of a non-Member State: Case C-154/11 *Mahamdia v People's Democratic Republic of Algeria* [2012] ILPr 41.

[329] As regards a citizen of a Member State whose whereabouts is unknown, jurisdiction cannot be invoked under the traditional rules unless the court seised has firm evidence that the defendant is in fact domiciled outside the European Union: Case C-327/10 *Hypotecni banka as v Lindner* [2011] ECR I-11543, para 42; Case C-292/10 *G v de Visser* [2013] QB 168, para 40.

traditional rules apply both to cases involving arbitration (because the subject-matter of the dispute is outside the Recast's scope) and to a simple claim for breach of contract brought against, say, a Japanese corporation.

2.141 Under the traditional rules the English court has jurisdiction in three situations: (i) if the defendant is present in England when the claim form is served (though the court may stay the proceedings on the ground that another court is a more appropriate forum); (ii) if the defendant submits to the court's jurisdiction; (iii) if the claim falls within one of the grounds of jurisdiction ('gateways') set out in para 3.1 of Practice Direction 6B of the Civil Procedure Rules (hereafter 'CPR PD 6B') and the court, having decided that England is the appropriate forum, gives permission under CPR rule 6.36 for service of the claim form out of the jurisdiction.

1. Presence

(A) Individuals

2.142 If a natural person is not domiciled in a Member State (and jurisdiction is not determined by the provisions of the Brussels I Recast which apply regardless of domicile) the English court has jurisdiction if the claim form is served on the defendant in England.[330] Jurisdiction on the basis of presence is potentially very wide; it allows the claimant to bring proceedings in England merely because the defendant happens to be temporarily present in England when process is served.[331] In *Maharanee of Baroda v Wildenstein*,[332] for example, process was served on the defendant, who was resident abroad, while he was briefly visiting England in order to attend the Ascot races. If, however, the claimant fraudulently induces the defendant to come to England—with the aim of serving a claim form on him in England—the claim may be struck out as an abuse of process.[333]

(B) Companies

2.143 As regards matters within the Brussels I Recast's scope, a company which is domiciled in England may be sued in England and a company which is domiciled in another Member State may be sued in England only if the English court has jurisdiction under Chapter II of the Recast. A company which is not domiciled in a Member State, but which has a place of business in England, may be sued in England in accordance with either the provisions of the Companies Act 2006 (and the regulations made under it[334]) or CPR rule 6.9. Service of process on a senior officer of a foreign company which

---

[330] As regards permissible methods of service, see CPR r 6.9.
[331] If the defendant cannot be served personally, he may be served at his 'usual or last known residence' in England: CPR, r 6.9(2): see *Relfo Ltd (in liquidation) v Varsani* [2011] 1 WLR 1402. Controversially, the Court of Appeal allowed C to invoke the court's jurisdiction by serving the claim form on D by post at D's English address, even though D was out of the country at the relevant time: *City & Country Properties Ltd v Kamali* [2007] 1 WLR 1219. This decision is contrary to principle and the earlier decision of Lawrence Collins J in *Chellaram v Chellaram (No 2)* [2002] 3 All ER 17 (which the Court of Appeal in the *Kamali* case regarded as wrong) is to be preferred.
[332] [1972] 2 QB 283. [333] *Watkins v North American Land and Timber Co Ltd* (1904) 20 TLR 534.
[334] Overseas Companies Regulations 2009, SI 2009/1801.

does not have a place of business in England does not establish the jurisdiction of the English court under the traditional rules.[335]

(i) Companies Act 2006

2.144 Part 34 of the Companies Act 2006 lays down various requirements relating to 'overseas companies', which are defined as companies 'incorporated outside the United Kingdom'.[336] An overseas company which 'opens a UK establishment' is required to register certain information with the Registrar of Companies, including the establishment's address and the 'name and service address of every person resident in the United Kingdom authorised to accept service of documents on behalf of the company'.[337] Under section 1139(2)(a) of the 2006 Act, a document may be served on an overseas company by leaving it at, or sending it by post to, the registered address of any person resident in the United Kingdom who is authorised to accept service of documents on the company's behalf. Where an overseas company is registered under the 2006 Act, service may be effected by complying with this rule even if the company has ceased to have a place of business in England when the proceedings are commenced.[338] If there is no person authorised to accept service or, for some other reason, service cannot be effected, the overseas company can be served by leaving the claim form at, or sending it by post to, any place of business of the company in the United Kingdom.[339] There is no requirement under the Companies Act 2006 that the claim should have a connection with the conduct of the company's business in England.[340]

(ii) CPR rule 6.9

2.145 The rules under the Companies Act 2006 are supplemented by CPR rule 6.9, as a consequence of which the court's jurisdiction is effectively extended to almost any case in which a foreign company has a business presence in England.[341] As regards a company which is not incorporated or registered in England, CPR rule 6.9(2) allows process to be served at any place of business of the company within the jurisdiction. Not only is this rule in addition to the rules in the companies legislation which prescribe methods of service but also there is no requirement that the dispute should have any connection with the defendant's activities in England.[342] On the basis of CPR rule 6.9, where a foreign company occupies a stand for a few days at a trade exhibition in England, the English court has jurisdiction over the company if the claimant serves a claim form on the stand during the exhibition.[343]

---

[335] *SSL International plc v TTK LIG Ltd* [2012] 1 WLR 1842.   [336] Companies Act 2006, s 1044.
[337] Companies Act 2006, s 1046; Overseas Companies Regs 2009, reg 7(1).
[338] *Rome v Punjab National Bank (No 2)* [1989] 1 WLR 1211.
[339] Companies Act 2006, s 1139(2)(b).
[340] *Teekay Tankers Ltd v STX Offshore & Shipping Co* [2015] 2 All ER (Comm) 263.
[341] For criticism, see Enonchong, 'Service of Process in England on Overseas Companies and Article 5(5) of the Brussels Convention' (1999) 48 ICLQ 921; Rogerson, 'English Courts' Jurisdiction over Companies: How Important is Service of the Claim Form in England?' (2000) 3 CFILR 272.
[342] *Sea Assets v PT Garuda Indonesia* [2000] 4 All ER 371.
[343] As in *Dunlop Pneumatic Tyre Co Ltd v Actien-Gesellschaft für Motor und Motorfahrzeugbau Vorm Cudell & Co* [1902] 1 KB 342.

(C) Forum non conveniens

2.146 Where jurisdiction is based merely on the defendant's presence within the jurisdiction, it is quite possible that the dispute will have only a limited connection with England. In such circumstances it may seem unreasonable for a foreign defendant to have English proceedings forced upon him. In cases involving both natural and legal persons the court has discretion, under the doctrine of forum non conveniens, to stay proceedings. Normally, a stay will be granted if the defendant is able to show that there is another forum with which the parties' dispute is more closely connected; however, a stay will be refused if the claimant can satisfy the court that substantial justice will not be done in the more closely connected forum.

2.147 The doctrine of forum non conveniens is potentially misleading in two respects. First, the basis of the doctrine is appropriateness rather than simply convenience. In the context of applications for a stay of proceedings litigational convenience is only one of the factors which the court takes into account. Secondly, to obtain a stay of proceedings the defendant has to satisfy the court that there is another forum which is more appropriate than England, rather than to show that England is an inappropriate forum. It is theoretically possible for English proceedings to be stayed, notwithstanding the fact that England is *an* appropriate forum, because another forum is *more* appropriate.[344]

2. Submission

2.148 Under the traditional rules, the defendant's submission is sufficient to confer jurisdiction on the English court. Whereas any step taken voluntarily by the defendant to defend the claim on the merits amounts to submission,[345] a defendant who appears to contest the court's jurisdiction does not thereby submit.[346] Any jurisdictional challenge must be made prior to submission. A defendant who has submitted to the court cannot subsequently change his mind and obtain a stay of English proceedings on the basis of forum non conveniens, even if the case has little connection with England and a much stronger connection with another country.

2.149 It is not uncommon for foreign defendants to instruct solicitors in England to accept service on their behalf. Where a defendant agrees to submit to English jurisdiction and the agreement stipulates a method whereby process can be served in England, if the claimant complies with the terms of the agreement (for example, by sending the claim form to the defendant's English solicitors), the defendant will be regarded as having submitted.[347] A contract which contains a jurisdiction clause but does not specify the method whereby process can be served in England is not to be regarded as a submission to the English court. In such a case, however, either the court has jurisdiction under the Brussels I Recast[348] or jurisdiction may be exercised on a discretionary basis.[349]

---

[344] The doctrine of forum non conveniens is considered further at paras 2.215–2.238.
[345] See, eg, *Global Multimedia International Ltd v Ara Media Services* [2007] 1 All ER (Comm) 1160.
[346] *Re Dulles' Settlement (No 2)* [1951] Ch 842; *Williams and Glyn's Bank plc v Astro Dinamico Cia Naviera SA* [1984] 1 WLR 438.
[347] CPR r 6.11.   [348] Art 25. See paras 2.46–2.57.
[349] See CPR r 6.36, PD 6B para 3.1(6)(d). See para 2.164.

3. Service out of the jurisdiction with the permission of the court

(A) Introduction

2.150 As regards a defendant who is not domiciled in a Member State, the English court may assume 'long-arm' jurisdiction under the Civil Procedure Rules.[350] CPR rule 6.36 (which enables process to be served out of the jurisdiction in cases covered by CPR PD 6B para 3.1) is based on the idea that there are certain situations in which it is appropriate for proceedings to be conducted in England notwithstanding the fact that jurisdiction cannot be based on the defendant's presence in England or on his submission. Such situations arise most commonly in cases where there is a connection between the claim (rather than the defendant) and England. In functional terms, the bases of jurisdiction in CPR PD 6B para 3.1 are similar to articles 7 and 8 of the Brussels I Recast.

2.151 Jurisdiction under CPR rule 6.36, which is discretionary, enables the court to give the claimant permission to serve process on the defendant out of the jurisdiction.[351] The court will not give permission unless satisfied that England is 'the proper place in which to bring the claim'.[352] In *Seaconsar Far East Ltd v Bank Markazi Jomhouri Islami Iran*[353] the House of Lords confirmed that there are three issues to be considered, the third of which is derived from *Spiliada Maritime Corpn v Cansulex Ltd*.[354] Unless the claimant satisfies the court on all three issues permission will not be given.

(i) A serious issue to be tried

2.152 As regards the merits, the claimant must show that there is a serious issue to be tried.[355] The hurdle established by this requirement is 'not a high one'; it involves no more than the claimant having a real (as opposed to fanciful) prospect of success.[356] There is a 'serious issue' if there is a substantial question of fact or law which the claimant bona fide desires to have tried.[357] Where, however, the facts alleged by the claimant, if proved, would not provide a sufficient foundation for the claim, this requirement is not satisfied.[358]

(ii) A claim within the scope of CPR PD 6B para 3.1

2.153 The claimant must show that his claim falls within one of the 'gateways' listed in CPR PD 6B para 3.1. If this second issue turns on the proper interpretation of one of the gateways the court must be satisfied that the interpretation favoured by the claimant is

---

[350] Although jurisdiction based on service out has traditionally been characterised as 'exorbitant', in *Abela v Baadarani* [2013] 1 WLR 2043 the Supreme Court regarded this characterisation as no longer realistic given that litigation between residents of different states is a routine incident of commercial life: see Lord Sumption JSC at [53]. For differing views of Lord Sumption's short judgment, see Briggs [2013] LMCLQ 415; Dickinson (2014) 130 LQR 197; Collins (2014) 130 LQR 555.

[351] Service of process cannot be effected by a method which is not permitted under the law of the place of service: CPR r 6.40(3)(c). See *Amalgamated Metal Trading Ltd v Baron* [2012] 1 CLC 920.

[352] CPR r 6.37(3).   [353] [1994] 1 AC 438.   [354] [1987] AC 460.

[355] This condition overlaps with the requirement under CPR r 6.37(1)(b) that the claim must have 'a reasonable prospect of success': *Carvill America Incorporated v Camperdown UK Ltd* [2005] 2 Lloyd's Rep 457.

[356] See *Carvill America Incorporated v Camperdown UK Ltd* [2005] 2 Lloyd's Rep 457; *Standard Bank plc v EFAD Real Estate Company WLL* [2014] 3 All ER (Comm) 208.

[357] *Seaconsar Far East Ltd v Bank Jomhouri Islami Iran* [1994] 1 AC 438 at 452.

[358] See *Global 5000 Ltd v Wadhawan* [2012] 1 Lloyd's Rep 239.

the correct one.³⁵⁹ If there is ambiguity in the construction of the rules, such ambiguity should be resolved in the defendant's favour.³⁶⁰

2.154 Where the second issue turns on a disputed question of fact, the claimant is required to show merely a 'good arguable case' that his claim falls within the gateway in question. The claimant will be able to show a 'good arguable case' that the jurisdictional ground is satisfied if he has a strong argument, albeit one falling short of a balance of probabilities.³⁶¹ Nevertheless, the court will normally require the claimant to have 'a much better argument on the material available'.³⁶² Where, for example, the claimant seeks permission to serve out under gateway (6)(c)—on the basis that the claim relates to a contract governed by English law—the claimant must have a good arguable case not only that there was a contract between the claimant and the defendant but also that the contract in question was governed by English law; it is not enough for the claimant to show that, had there been a contract, English law would have been its applicable law.³⁶³

(iii) Forum conveniens

2.155 The court must also be satisfied that England is the forum conveniens—that is, the forum in which the case can most suitably be tried in the interests of the parties and for the ends of justice.³⁶⁴ The factors which are relevant for the question whether England is the forum conveniens are the same as those which the court must consider when deciding whether to stay proceedings on the ground of forum non conveniens in a case which is brought against a defendant who is present in England when process is served.

2.156 The determination of the appropriate forum requires the court to answer one overall question: has it been clearly and distinctly shown that England is the appropriate forum?³⁶⁵ In addressing this question the court is required to consider not only the various factors which connect the parties' dispute with England, on the one hand, and with other countries, on the other, but also whether or not substantial justice would be done in a closely connected foreign forum.

2.157 The issue is not simply one of practical convenience, but one of appropriateness, having regard to all the circumstances. So, the court must consider the nature of the dispute, the legal and practical issues involved, such questions as local knowledge, availability of witnesses and their evidence and expense.³⁶⁶ Regard should also be had to the jurisdictional gateway invoked by the claimant. In some cases the gateway is such that

---

³⁵⁹ *EF Hutton & Co (London) Ltd v Mofarrij* [1989] 1 WLR 488.
³⁶⁰ *The Hagen* [1908] P 189; *Siskina (Owners of cargo lately laden on board) v Distos Compania Naviera SA* [1979] AC 210.
³⁶¹ *Carvill America Incorporated v Camperdown UK Ltd* [2005] 2 Lloyd's Rep 457.
³⁶² Waller LJ in *Canada Trust Co v Stolzenberg (No 2)* [1998] 1 WLR 547 at 555; Lord Collins in *Altimo Holdings & Investments Ltd v Kyrgyz Mobil Tel Ltd* [2012] 1 WLR 1804 at [71].
³⁶³ See Rogerson, 'Problems of the Applicable Law of the Contract in the English Common Law Jurisdiction Rules: The Good Arguable Case' (2013) 9 Journal of Private International Law 387.
³⁶⁴ *Spiliada Maritime Corpn v Cansulex Ltd* [1987] AC 460.
³⁶⁵ *VTB Capital plc v Nutritek International Corpn* [2013] 2 AC 337.
³⁶⁶ Lord Wilberforce in *Amin Rasheed Shipping Corpn v Kuwait Insurance Co* [1984] AC 50 at 72.

permission will normally be granted. For example, the English court will normally be regarded as the appropriate forum in a claim in tort if the tort was committed in England and, as a result, the claim is governed by English law.[367] However, there is no rule to this effect. In *VTB Capital plc v Nutritek International Corpn*,[368] a case in which the claimant, an English subsidiary of a Russian bank, sought damages in deceit and conspiracy against Russian defendants in respect of torts allegedly committed in England, the Supreme Court dismissed the appeal against the lower courts' refusal to give permission to serve out of the jurisdiction. In other cases, the gateway relied on will carry less weight in relation to the appropriateness of the English forum. If England is the centre of gravity of the dispute, permission will be granted; if the factual and legal connecting factors do not suggest that England is the appropriate forum, permission should normally be refused.

2.158 Even if England is not the most closely connected forum, the court may give permission for service out of the jurisdiction if the claimant would not obtain justice in the natural forum. The appropriate test is whether 'there is a real risk that justice will not be obtained in the foreign court by reason of incompetence or lack of independence or corruption'[369] and there is no principle to the effect that the English court may not rule on such questions. Nevertheless the mere fact that the claimant will be deprived of a legitimate personal or juridical advantage if the English court does not assume jurisdiction is not decisive and the English court should be extremely cautious before deciding that there is a risk of injustice abroad.

(B) The jurisdictional gateways

2.159 CPR PD 6B para 3.1 contains more than a dozen gateways listing the various circumstances in which the court may grant permission to serve a claim form out of the jurisdiction under CPR rule 6.36. Only the most important and commonly relied on gateways are considered here in any detail.

(i) Contract

2.160 Gateway (6) sets out four types of case in which the English court may assume jurisdiction where 'a claim is made in respect of a contract'. The essence of gateway (6) is that

---

[367] *The Albaforth* [1984] 2 Lloyd's Rep 91; *Schapira v Ahronson* [1998] ILPr 587; *Berezovsky v Michaels* [2000] 1 WLR 1004; *King v Lewis* [2003] ILPr 16; *The Omega King* [2011] 2 Lloyd's Rep 206. If, in a libel case, the claimant is unable to satisfy the court that he has a sufficient reputation to protect in England, permission to serve out may be refused: *Kroch v Rossell et Cie* [1937] 1 All ER 725; *Chadha & Osicom Technologies Inc v Dow Jones & Co Inc* [1999] ILPr 829. See Morse, 'Rights Relating to Personality, Freedom of the Press and Private International Law: Some Common Law Comments' (2005) 58 CLP 133. The problems of so-called 'libel tourism' (see Hartley (2010) 59 ICLQ 25) was one of the factors behind s 9 of the Defamation Act 2013, which provides that, where an action in defamation is brought against a defendant who is not domiciled in an EU Member State, the English court does not have jurisdiction 'unless the court is satisfied that, of all the places in which the statement complained of has been published, England and Wales is clearly the most appropriate place in which to bring an action in respect of the statement'. Whether this adds anything of substance to the *Spiliada* test may be questioned: see Bennett, 'The Defamation Act 2013' (2012/13) 14 Yb PIL 173.
[368] [2013] 2 AC 337; Hare [2013] CLJ 280.
[369] Lord Collins in *Altimo Holdings & Investments Ltd v Kyrgyz Mobil Tel Ltd* [2012] 1 WLR 1804 at [95].

the claimant is suing in order to assert a contractual right or a right which arose as a result of the non-performance of a contract. The claim does not have to be a claim under a contract as long as it is closely connected with a contract.[370] Nor does the claimant have to be a party to the contract in respect of which the claim is made; for example, a claim for a contribution under the Civil Liability (Contribution) Act 1978 which has a connection with a contract is a claim in respect of that contract for the purposes of gateway (6) even if it is not a claim brought under a contract.[371] However, the defendant must be a party to the contract in question.[372] Where C's claim is under contract A, which has no connection with England, permission for service out of the jurisdiction cannot be based on the fact that contract A is connected to contract B, which does have an appropriate link with England.[373]

(a) Contract made in England

2.161 Permission may be granted if the contract was made within the jurisdiction.[374] Where the parties' acts in making the contract take place in different countries, the contract is regarded as made in the country where the last act occurred which was necessary for the conclusion of the contract—that is, the country in which the acceptance takes effect. A problem may arise because the laws of different countries have different rules on this matter. For example, in a contract concluded by correspondence the moment at which the acceptance is effective (whether, for example, on dispatch by the offeree or on receipt by the offeror) differs in different laws. For the purposes of gateway (6)(a), the rules of the English law of contract are applicable for determining the place where the contract was concluded, whether or not the contract is governed by English law.[375] So, in a postal case, the contract is made in the country where the acceptance is posted,[376] whereas if virtually instantaneous means of communication are used, such as telephone, the contract is made in the country where the acceptance is received.[377] Strict analysis in terms of offer and acceptance is not always appropriate; where, for example, two parties from different countries conclude a contract after a long period of negotiation, it may be more realistic to say that the contract is made in both countries.[378] Where a contract is made partly in England and partly abroad, gateway (6)(a) is satisfied if the contract which is the subject-matter of the proceedings was 'substantially made' within the jurisdiction.[379] A contract concluded in England, but amended abroad, is made within the jurisdiction for the purposes of gateway (6)(a).[380]

---

[370] *Albon v Naza Motor Trading Sdn Bhd* [2007] 1 WLR 2489 (which involved a claim for restitution).
[371] *Greene Wood & McLean LLP v Templeton Insurance Ltd* [2009] 1 WLR 2013.
[372] '[A] claim is not . . . properly described as "made in respect of a contract" where the contract in question is not one to which the defendant is party': Tomlinson LJ in *Alliance Bank JSC v Aquanta Corporation* [2013] 1 All ER (Comm) 819 at [71].
[373] *Global 5000 Ltd v Wadhawan* [2012] 1 Lloyd's Rep 239.   [374] CPR PD 6B para 3.1(6)(a).
[375] *Entores Ltd v Miles Far East Corpn* [1955] 2 QB 327.   [376] *Benaim & Co v Debono* [1924] AC 514.
[377] *Entores Ltd v Miles Far East Corpn* [1955] 2 QB 327; *Brinkibon Ltd v Stahag Stahl und Stahlwarenhandelsgesellschaft mbH* [1983] 2 AC 34; *Brownlie v Four Seasons Holdings Inc* [2016] 1 WLR 1814.
[378] *Apple Corps Ltd v Apple Computer Inc* [2004] 2 CLC 720; *Conductive Inkjet Technology Ltd v Uni-Pixel Displays Inc* [2014] 1 All ER (Comm) 654.
[379] Kerr J in *BP Exploration Co (Libya) Ltd v Hunt* [1976] 1 WLR 788 at 798.
[380] *Sharab v Al-Saud* [2009] 2 Lloyd's Rep 160.

(b) Contract made through an agent in England

2.162 Jurisdiction may be assumed if the contract was made by or through an agent trading or residing within the jurisdiction.[381] This gateway is not confined to the case where the English agent concludes the contract on behalf of a foreign principal (when, in any event, the contract is likely to be made within the jurisdiction) but also includes the case where the agent in England solicits an order from an English customer and sends it on to the principal abroad, who concludes the contract by accepting the order.[382] This gateway is limited to cases where the contract is concluded through the defendant's agent; the fact that the claimant concludes the contract through an agent in England is irrelevant.[383]

(c) Contract governed by English law

2.163 The claimant may seek to invoke the court's jurisdiction where a claim relates to a contract which is governed by English law.[384] Whether a contract is governed by English law has to be determined in accordance with English choice of law rules.[385]

(d) English jurisdiction clause

2.164 Jurisdiction may be exercised where the contract contains a term to the effect that the court shall have jurisdiction to determine any claim in respect of the contract.[386] This provision is largely superseded by article 25 of the Brussels I Recast. In most cases involving an English jurisdiction clause, article 25 allocates exclusive (and mandatory) jurisdiction to the English court.[387] However, article 25 does not apply if the subject-matter of the dispute falls outside the material scope of the Recast. Furthermore, a jurisdiction clause in favour of the English courts is governed by article 5 of the Hague Choice of Court Convention (rather than by article 25 of the Recast) if one of the parties is resident in a third state which is a Contracting State to the Convention, even if the other party is domiciled in an EU Member State. In the absence of any amendment to the CPR, if service out of the jurisdiction is required in a case where the English court's jurisdiction is derived from article 5 of the Convention, the claimant may obtain permission under gateway (6)(d).

(e) Negative declarations

2.165 Gateway (8) covers cases involving a claim for a declaration that no contract exists where, if the contract were found to exist, it would fall within one of the heads of jurisdiction set out in gateway (6).

(ii) Breach of contract in England

2.166 By virtue of gateway (7) the English court may assume jurisdiction over an absent defendant where the claim is made in respect of a breach of contract committed within

---

[381] CPR PD 6B para 3.1(6)(b).
[382] *National Mortgage and Agency Co of New Zealand Ltd v Gosselin* (1922) 38 TLR 832.
[383] *Union International Insurance Co Ltd v Jubilee Insurance Co Ltd* [1991] 1 WLR 415.
[384] CPR PD 6B para 3.1(6)(c).   [385] See Chapter 4.   [386] CPR PD 6B para 3.1(6)(d).
[387] See paras 2.46–2.57.

the jurisdiction. A breach is committed within the jurisdiction if the obligation not performed was, according to the terms of the contract or under the law applicable to it, required to be performed in England or if defective performance occurred in England. If the breach relied upon took the form of repudiation, that must have occurred in England.

(iii) Tort

2.167 Gateway (9) allows for permission to serve out to be granted in cases involving a claim in tort if (a) damage has been or will be sustained within the jurisdiction; or (b) the damage which has been or will be sustained results from an act committed, or likely to be committed, within the jurisdiction. To determine whether a claim is made in tort for the purposes of this rule, the court applies exclusively English law. It has been held, for example, that gateway (9) extends to a claim for misuse of private information (which is a tort),[388] although it does not cover a claim for breach of confidence (which is not).[389]

2.168 The form of words used in gateway (9)—which expressly adopts the approach of article 7(2) of the Brussels I Recast as interpreted by the Court of Justice—is designed to avoid the theoretical difficulties associated with trying to determine the place where a tort is committed in a case where the defendant commits the wrongful act in one country and the claimant suffers loss or damage in another. Gateway (9) allows the English court to assume jurisdiction if either some 'significant damage' was sustained in England or the damage resulted from 'substantial and efficacious acts' committed by the defendant in England (whether or not other substantial and efficacious acts were committed elsewhere).[390] Where the claimant alleges that he has been defamed by an internet posting, the wrongful act takes place in England if the material is downloaded in England; however, if permission to serve out is given in such a case, the claimant can be compensated only in respect of injury to his reputation suffered in England.[391]

2.169 Since gateway (9) mirrors article 7(2) of the Brussels I Recast, the same problems of interpretation arise, particularly in cases involving economic loss.[392] Not surprisingly, there are cases in which the English courts rely on the Court of Justice's jurisprudence under Brussels I when considering the operation of gateway (9).[393] Nevertheless, there are English authorities (albeit at first instance) in which the court has given permission for service out on the basis of a much broader view of the place where damage was sustained than that suggested by the Court of Justice's case law under Brussels I. For example, in *Booth v Phillips*[394] permission for service out was granted where, following the

---

[388] *Vidal-Hall v Google Inc* [2015] 3 WLR 409.
[389] *Kitechnology BV v Unicor GmbH Plastmaschinen* [1994] ILPr 568.
[390] Slade LJ in *Metall und Rohstoff AG v Donaldson Lufkin & Jenrette Inc* [1990] 1 QB 391 at 437. See also *Arab Business Consortium International Finance and Investment Co v Banque Franco-Tunisienne* [1997] 1 Lloyd's Rep 531.
[391] *King v Lewis* [2004] ILPr 31. [392] See paras 2.94–2.108.
[393] See, eg, *ABCI v Banque Franco-Tunisienne* [2003] 2 Lloyd's Rep 146; *Newsat Holdings Ltd v Zani* [2006] 1 Lloyd's Rep 707.
[394] [2004] 2 Lloyd's Rep 457.

death of her husband abroad, an English widow invoked the court's jurisdiction on the basis that her loss of financial dependency was damage sustained in England. Similarly, in *Cooley v Ramsey*[395] the victim of a traffic accident which occurred in Australia obtained permission to serve out of the jurisdiction on the basis that the economic loss he suffered following the Australian accident occurred in England. In neither of these factual scenarios would England be the place where the harmful event occurred for the purposes of article 7(2) of the Recast. In *Erste Group Bank AG v JSC 'VMZ Red October'*[396] the Court of Appeal expressed serious reservations as to the correctness of these cases, both of which can legitimately be regarded as having been wrongly decided.[397]

(iv) Restitution

2.170 Gateway (16) covers the case where, as regards a claim for restitution, the defendant's alleged liability arises out of acts committed within the jurisdiction. Whether this gateway extends to a claim based on an equitable proprietary interest is debatable.[398] There was no counterpart to gateway (16) under the procedural rules which were replaced by the CPR, and there is some uncertainty over the relationship between gateway (16) (restitution) and gateway (6) (contract). It is reasonable to suppose that, given that the implied contract theory of restitution is rejected by modern commentators,[399] claims for restitution should not normally be regarded as falling within the scope of gateway (6).[400] However, there is no reason to suppose that a claim for restitution which is founded on the rescission or discharge of a contract does not fall within gateway (6) as well as gateway (16).

2.171 Gateway (15) is primarily designed to enable proceedings to be brought in fraud cases against a foreign company which has not participated directly in the fraud, but which has been used by the persons who control it as a receptacle for the proceeds of the fraud. Under gateway (15) the court may assume jurisdiction in a case where the claim is made for a remedy against the defendant as constructive trustee (or as trustee of a resulting trust) and the claim arises out of acts committed or events occurring within the jurisdiction or relates to assets within the jurisdiction. A claimant is able to bring his claim within the scope of gateway (15) by showing that some of the relevant acts of the defendant were committed in England; the fact that the factual matrix also has connections with other countries does not automatically take the case outside gateway (15).[401] For example, it is not essential that the defendant acquired the knowledge upon which a claim to enforce an alleged constructive trust is based within the jurisdiction.[402]

---

[395] [2008] ILPr 27.   [396] [2015] EWCA Civ 379.
[397] See also *Brownlie v Four Seasons Holdings Inc* [2016] 1 WLR 1814.
[398] See *Nabb Brothers Ltd v Lloyds Bank International (Guernsey) Ltd* [2005] ILPr 37.
[399] See Briggs, 'Jurisdiction under Traditional Rules' in Rose (ed), *Restitution in the Conflict of Laws* (1995) p 49ff.
[400] *Bowling v Cox* [1926] AC 751 and *Re Jogia* [1988] 1 WLR 484, both of which rely on the now discredited implied contract theory, are of questionable authority in the context of CPR r 6.36.
[401] *ISC Technologies Ltd v Guerin* [1992] 2 Lloyd's Rep 430.
[402] *Polly Peck International plc v Nadir* (1992) *The Independent*, 2 September.

(v) Multiple defendants

2.172 In the context of gateway (3), where a claim is brought against a person on whom a claim form has been or will be served (D1), permission may be granted to serve process on a person out of the jurisdiction (D2) if (a) there is between the claimant (C) and D1 a real issue which it is reasonable for the court to try; and (b) D2 is a necessary or proper party to C's claim against D1. The first of these requirements ensures that the court will not give permission where it appears that the claim against D1 is not brought bona fide, but merely as a pretext to bring D2 before the English court.[403] For the purpose of gateway (3), jurisdiction over D1 may be based either on the Brussels I Recast (if D1 is domiciled in a Member State) or the traditional rules (if D1 is not domiciled in a Member State).

2.173 If D1 is served in England or abroad, the court may grant permission for process to be served on D2 abroad, even though the case would not come under any other rule. Where claims against a number of defendants arise out of the same series of transactions and involve common questions of fact, each defendant is to be regarded as a necessary or proper party for the purposes of gateway (3).[404]

2.174 Gateway (4) allows permission for service out to be given in relation to a Part 20 claim (third-party proceedings) where the third party is a necessary or proper party to the claim. Gateway (4) is the equivalent, under the traditional rules, of article 8(2) of the Brussels I Recast.[405]

2.175 Gateways (3) and (4) are different from the other important bases of jurisdiction contained in CPR PD 6B para 3.1 because they are not founded on a connection between the claim and the forum. For this reason, the courts should exercise 'caution' or 'special care' in cases falling within the scope of these provisions.[406] Gateways (3) and (4)—like article 8 of the Brussels I Recast—are based on the practical consideration that it is more convenient and economical for a dispute involving multiple parties to be litigated in a single forum rather than to be fragmented between a number of different courts.[407] It follows that where some of the defendants against whom the claimant is bringing proceedings are domiciled in a Member State and are amenable to the English court's jurisdiction under the Brussels I Recast, there will be a tendency for the court to regard England as the forum conveniens with regard to those defendants who are domiciled in third states; because, in this type of case, the court cannot stay proceedings against

---

[403] *Witted v Galbraith* [1893] 1 QB 577 (a case decided under a former rule which required the proceedings to have been 'properly brought' against D1).
[404] *United Film Distribution Ltd v Chhabria* [2001] 2 All ER (Comm) 865. See also *The Baltic Flame* [2001] 2 Lloyd's Rep 203; *Carvill America Inc v Camperdown UK Ltd* [2005] 2 Lloyd's Rep 457. Gateway (3) does not apply if the substantive proceedings are abroad and the only basis for the court's jurisdiction over D1 is Civil Jurisdiction and Judgments Act 1982, s 25 (which allows the courts, in certain cases, to grant provisional measures): *Belletti v Morici* [2009] ILPr 57.
[405] See paras 2.124–2.126.
[406] *Multinational Gas and Petrochemical Co v Multinational Gas and Petrochemical Services Inc* [1983] Ch 258; *Petroleo Brasiliero SA v Mellitus Shipping Inc* [2001] 1 All ER (Comm) 993.
[407] See *Barings plc v Coopers & Lybrand* [1997] ILPr 12.

a defendant who is domiciled in a Member State (other than for reasons provided by the Brussels I Recast itself),[408] proceedings are bound to take place in England and the only way of producing a situation in which all the issues (involving all the defendants) can be resolved in one set of proceedings is to allow liberal use of the power to serve out on the basis of gateways (3) and (4).[409]

(vi) Other bases of jurisdiction

2.176 The numerous other bases of jurisdiction listed in CPR PD 6B para 3.1 (in relation to which the English court may assume jurisdiction over an absent defendant by giving permission to serve out under CPR rule 6.36) include: claims brought against a defendant domiciled in England,[410] claims to enforce foreign judgments and arbitral awards,[411] claims relating to property located within the jurisdiction,[412] claims in respect of a trust which is governed by English law[413] or which provides that the English courts have jurisdiction,[414] claims in respect of UK taxes,[415] and claims under various statutes.[416]

III Declining jurisdiction and staying proceedings

2.177 The fact that there exists a basis on which the English court may assume jurisdiction (whether under the Brussels I Recast or under the traditional rules) does not necessarily mean that the litigation will proceed in England. There may be countervailing factors which mean that the English court should decline jurisdiction or grant a stay of the proceedings. Under the traditional rules the English court may grant a stay on the basis of forum non conveniens; this involves consideration of the same factors as those which determine whether the court will allow service of a claim form out of the jurisdiction under CPR rule 6.36 on the basis of forum conveniens. The Brussels I Recast contains provisions dealing with parallel and related proceedings which are designed to reduce the possibility of the courts of two or more countries rendering irreconcilable judgments.

2.178 Whereas declining jurisdiction is a definitive step which brings the proceedings to a close, a stay merely places the proceedings on hold. In practice, it normally makes

---

[408] Case C-281/02 *Owusu v Jackson* [2005] ECR I-1383. See paras 2.265–2.280.
[409] See the discussion in *Attorney General of Zambia v Meer Care & Desai* [2006] 1 CLC 436; *Global Multimedia International Ltd v Ara Media Services* [2007] 1 All ER (Comm) 1160.
[410] CPR PD 6B para 3.1(1). This paragraph applies only in cases which fall outside the scope of art 1 of the Brussels I Recast (such as where proceedings relate to arbitration).
[411] CPR PD 6B para 3.1(10). The presence of assets within the jurisdiction is not a pre-condition for the assumption of jurisdiction under this subparagraph: *Tasarruf Mevduarti Sigorta Fonu v Demirel* [2007] 1 WLR 2508.
[412] CPR PD 6B para 3.1(11) See *Re Banco Nacional de Cuba* [2001] 1 WLR 2039; *Pakistan v Zardari* [2006] 2 CLC 667. It has been held that confidential information contained in digital form on a server in England constitutes 'property located within the jurisdiction': *Ashton Investments Ltd v OJSC Russian Aluminium* [2007] 1 Lloyd's Rep 311.
[413] CPR PD 6B para 3.1(12). [414] CPR PD 6B para 3.1(12A).
[415] CPR PD 6B para 3.1(17). [416] CPR PD 6B para 3.1(20).

little difference whether the court stays proceedings or declines jurisdiction; while the stay is maintained the proceedings cannot continue. There are, however, situations in which the court may be justified in lifting a stay. Where, for example, English proceedings are stayed on the basis that there is another more appropriate forum abroad, if it subsequently transpires that the claim cannot be brought in the foreign forum the court may lift the stay to enable the claimant to pursue his claim in England.[417]

2.179 When considering whether or not the court should stay proceedings or decline jurisdiction it is important, once again, to draw a distinction between cases which fall within the relevant provisions of the Brussels I Recast and situations which are governed by the common law.

A The effect of parallel or related proceedings in another Member State

1. Introduction

2.180 Cases may arise under the Brussels I Recast where the courts of more than one Member State have jurisdiction. For example, in a dispute arising out of a contract, proceedings may be brought either in the Member State in which the defendant is domiciled (under article 4) or in the court for the place of performance of the obligation in question (under article 7(1)). Similarly, as a defendant may be domiciled in more than one Member State, more than one court may have general jurisdiction under article 4.

2.181 The primary objective of the Brussels I Recast is to facilitate the free flow of judgments between the Member States. If the courts of different Member States may issue conflicting judgments on the same or related questions the free flow of judgments is impeded. Accordingly, the Recast contains provisions which are designed to reduce the possibility of such conflicts. The Brussels I Recast draws a distinction between two types of situation. First, there are cases within article 29 concerning parallel proceedings or lis pendens—where the same parties are involved in litigation on the same issues in two or more Member States.[418] Secondly, article 30 deals with situations where related proceedings are being pursued in two or more Member States. The general approach of the Recast is to give precedence to the court 'first seised'. Before the discussion turns to specific aspects of articles 29 and 30, a number of general points which are applicable to both provisions should be addressed.

2.182 It is important to remember that the material scope of the Brussels I Recast is restricted to civil and commercial matters. If parallel or related proceedings are brought in two Member States articles 29 and 30 are engaged only if both sets of proceedings fall within the scope of article 1. Furthermore, articles 29 and 30 do not apply to proceedings, or

---

[417] See *Baghlaf Al Zafer Factory Co BR for Industry Ltd v Pakistan National Shipping Co (No 2)* [2000] 1 Lloyd's Rep 1.
[418] Art 31(1) of the Brussels I Recast provides that where proceedings fall within the exclusive jurisdiction of the courts of more than one Member State (for example, where the courts of two Member States have exclusive jurisdiction under the different parts of art 24) any court other than the court first seised is required to decline jurisdiction.

issues arising in proceedings, concerning the recognition and enforcement of judgments given in civil and commercial matters in non-Member States.[419] So, if a claimant starts proceedings to enforce a New York judgment in Italy and in England, articles 29 and 30 have no application even though the same issues (such as whether the judgment was procured by fraud) may be raised by the defendant in both sets of proceedings.

2.183 Articles 29 and 30 apply regardless of the domicile of the parties and regardless of the basis of jurisdiction on which the proceedings are founded.[420] So, article 29 is relevant in a case where A, a Brazilian company, brings proceedings in England against B, a French national domiciled in Senegal (relying on CPR rule 6.36), and B brings proceedings against A in France (relying on article 14 of the French Civil Code). For the purposes of article 29 it is irrelevant that neither party is domiciled in a Member State and that, as regards each set of proceedings, the claimant seeks to invoke the court's jurisdiction under traditional rules.

2.184 Central to the operation of articles 29 and 30 is the idea of the court 'first seised'. The Recast lays down a uniform rule for determining the moment at which a court is deemed to be seised of proceedings.[421] A court is generally seised when the document instituting the proceedings is lodged with the court; however, the court will not be regarded as having been seised at this time if the claimant subsequently fails to take the steps he was required to take to have service effected on the defendant.[422] Furthermore, if under the procedural law of the court in question, the document has to be served before being lodged with the court, the court is regarded as having been seised at the time when the document is received by the authority responsible for service—though the court will not be regarded as having been seised at this time if the claimant subsequently fails to take any necessary steps to have the document lodged with the court.[423]

2. Parallel proceedings

(A) The framework of article 29

2.185 Article 29 deals with the situation where proceedings involving the same cause of action and between the same parties are brought in the courts of different Member States. It is provided that any court other than the court first seised shall stay its proceedings until such time as the jurisdiction of the court first seised is established; if the

---

[419] Case C-129/92 *Owens Bank Ltd v Bracco (No 2)* [1994] ECR I-117.
[420] Case C-351/89 *Overseas Union Insurance Ltd v New Hampshire Insurance Co* [1991] ECR I-3317. See *Trademark Licensing Co Ltd v Leofelis SA* [2010] ILPr 16.
[421] In a case where, during the course of proceedings, claims are amended or new claims are introduced, the important moment for the purposes of arts 29 and 30 is when the court was seised of the proceedings as a whole (rather than when a particular claim was initiated): *Starlight Shipping Co v Allianz Marine & Aviation Versicherungs AG* [2014] 1 All ER 590.
[422] Art 32(1)(a). In the context of English proceedings, this means that the court is seised when the court issues a claim form at the request of the claimant: CPR r 7.2(1). A claim form is issued on the date entered on the form by the court: CPR r 7.2(2). For the operation of art 32(1), see *Debt Collection London Ltd v SK Slavia Praha-Fotbal AS* [2011] 1 WLR 866 (in which the claimant in Czech proceedings failed to pay the court fee required under Czech law for service of process on the English defendant).
[423] Art 32(1)(b).

jurisdiction of the court first seised is established,[424] any other court is required to decline jurisdiction. In the situation where A sues B in France and B challenges the jurisdiction of the French court and starts proceedings against A in England, the English court must stay the proceedings. If B's challenge to the French court's jurisdiction is successful, there is no obstacle to the continuation of the English proceedings and the stay will be lifted. If, however, B's challenge to the jurisdiction of the French court is rejected, the English court must decline jurisdiction.[425]

2.186 Although the English language version of article 29 refers only to 'the same cause of action . . . between the same parties', other language versions indicate that article 29 involves three elements: the same subject-matter (or object), the same cause of action and the same parties.[426] Relying on the jurisprudence of the Court of Justice, the English courts regard the terms 'cause' and 'object' to have wide meanings.[427]

(B) The same cause of action and the same subject-matter (or object)

2.187 The subject-matter (or object) of an action is 'the end the action has in view'.[428] Parallel proceedings have the same object where, for example, the question whether a contract is binding lies at the heart of the two sets of proceedings or where the issue of liability is central to both sets of proceedings. To determine whether two claims pending before the courts of two Member States have the same subject-matter, the court should take into account only the claims of the two claimants, to the exclusion of the defence submissions raised by the defendants.[429] The mere fact that two claims raise some common issues does not mean that the same 'cause' and 'object' are involved.[430]

2.188 Parallel proceedings involve the same cause of action where they are both based on the same contractual relationship or where the same facts and the same rule of law are relied on as the basis of each claim.[431] So, a contractual claim cannot involve the same cause of action as a tortious claim even if both claims arise out of the same overall factual situation.[432] Similarly, article 29 is not engaged by claims arising out of different

---

[424] The jurisdiction of the court first seised is 'established' if that court has not declined jurisdiction of its own motion and none of the defendants has contested the court's jurisdiction prior to submission of their first defence on the merits: Case C-1/13 *Cartier Parfums-Lunettes SAS v Ziegler France SA* [2014] ILPr 25, para 45.

[425] However, if proceedings in the court first seised are properly discontinued, arts 29 and 30 do not prevent proceedings on the same or related matters being brought in other Member States: *Internationale Nederlanden Aviation Lease BV v Civil Aviation Authority* [1997] 1 Lloyd's Rep 80.

[426] Case 144/86 *Gubisch Maschinenfabrik KG v Palumbo* [1987] ECR 4861.

[427] See Jacob LJ in *Football Dataco Ltd v Sportradar* [2011] 1 WLR 3049 at [34].

[428] Case C-406/92 *Owners of the cargo lately laden on board the ship 'Tatry' v Owners of the ship 'Maciej Rataj'* [1994] ECR I-5439, para 41.

[429] Case C-111/01 *Gantner Electronic GmbH v Basch Expoitatie Maatschappij BV* [2003] ECR I-4207, para 26; Case C-39/02 *Maersk Olie & Gas A/S v Firma M de Haan en W de Boer* [2004] ECR I-9657, para 36.

[430] *Starlight Shipping Co v Allianz Marine & Aviation Versicherungs AG* [2014] 1 All ER 590; *Barclays Bank plc v Ente Nazionale di Prevedenza* [2015] 2 Lloyd's Rep 527.

[431] Case 144/86 *Gubisch Maschinenfabrik KG v Palumbo* [1987] ECR 4861; Case C-39/02 *Maersk Olie & Gas A/S v Firma M de Haan en W de Boer* [2004] ECR I-9657.

[432] See, eg, *Bank of Tokyo-Mitsubishi v Baskan Gida Sanayi Ve Pazarlama* [2004] 2 Lloyd's Rep 395; *Underwriting Members of Lloyd's Syndicate 980 v Sinco SA* [2009] 1 All ER (Comm) 272.

contractual relationships.[433] An application for provisional measures in one Member State (under article 35) does not involve the same cause of action as substantive proceedings in another Member State.[434]

2.189 In *Gubisch Maschinenfabrik KG v Palumbo*[435] a German 'seller' started proceedings in Germany against an Italian 'buyer' to enforce the terms of a disputed contract and the 'buyer' subsequently started proceedings in Italy with a view to obtaining a declaration that the alleged contract was not binding on him. The Court of Justice ruled that the conditions of article 29 were satisfied and that the Italian court was required to decline jurisdiction. Had the Italian proceedings been commenced first, however, the German court would have had to decline jurisdiction. Article 29 lays down a strict 'first come, first served' rule; it makes no difference whether the proceedings in the court first seised involve a positive claim by A to establish the liability of B or a claim for a declaration of non-liability by B against A.[436]

(C) The same parties

2.190 In a situation involving only two parties the requirement that parallel proceedings should involve the same parties is simple enough to apply. The position is potentially more difficult where more than two parties are involved. What is the position, for example, where as a result of disputes arising out of a joint venture agreement between four parties (A, B, C, and D), A sues B and C in France and then B sues D and A in England? In *The Tatry*[437] the Court of Justice ruled that the obligation of the court second seised to decline jurisdiction applies only to the extent to which the parties to the proceedings pending before it are also parties to the proceedings before the court first seised; it does not prevent the proceedings from continuing between the other parties. So, in the above example, provided the parallel proceedings involve the same cause of action and the same object, the English court is required to decline jurisdiction as regards A, but not D. This approach obviously involves the danger that proceedings involving the same issues will be fragmented between the courts of different Member States. However, this danger can be averted, to some extent, by the application of article 30.

2.191 Article 29 raises difficult questions in multi-party cases where the interests of different parties overlap. For example, does article 29 apply in a case where, following a road accident involving cars driven by A and B, A sues B for negligence in France and C (B's insurer) sues A in England? If the interests of B (the insured) and C (the insurer) are identical, the two sets of proceedings are to be regarded as involving the same parties; if, however, the interests of B and C are not entirely congruent, the same parties are not involved in both sets of proceedings and article 29 does not apply (though, in

---

[433] *SET Select Energy GmbH v F&M Bunkering Ltd* [2014] 1 Lloyd's Rep 652.
[434] *Republic of Haiti v Duvalier* [1990] 1 QB 202; *The Winter* [2000] 2 Lloyd's Rep 298; *Miles Platt Ltd v Townroe Ltd* [2003] 1 All ER (Comm) 561.
[435] Case 144/86 [1987] ECR 4861.
[436] Case C-406/92 *Owners of the cargo lately laden on board the ship 'Tatry' v Owners of the ship 'Maciej Rataj'* [1994] ECR I-5439.
[437] Case C-406/92 [1994] ECR I-5439.

all probability, article 30 does).[438] In any particular situation it may be difficult to determine whether or not the interests of the parties are congruent. It seems clear, however, that where a judgment rendered against B would have the force of res judicata as against C, B and C are to be regarded as one and the same party for the purposes of article 29.[439] By contrast, two separate subsidiaries of the same parent company are not 'the same party' for the purposes of article 29.[440]

2.192 Questions surrounding the applicability of article 29 may also arise in cases involving proceedings in rem. If A starts Dutch proceedings in rem in relation to a ship owned by B and B starts proceedings in personam in England against A, are the two sets of proceedings between the same parties or not? It used to be thought that, since proceedings in rem are (notionally) brought against specific property (usually a ship) rather than a person, article 29 could not apply.[441] However, this view has been rejected and the older cases overruled; for the purposes of article 29, the person who has an interest in defending proceedings in rem (typically, the ship-owner) is a party to those proceedings.[442] So, if the claimant starts proceedings in rem in relation to a vessel in Belgium and then starts proceedings in personam in England against the ship-owner, the two sets of proceedings involve the same parties for the purposes of article 29.

(D) The relationship between the court first seised and the court second seised

2.193 As a general rule, it is not permissible for the court second seised to review the basis on which the court first seised assumed jurisdiction. As the Court of Justice stressed in *Overseas Union Insurance Ltd v New Hampshire Insurance Co*,[443] in no case is the court second seised in a better position than the court first seised to determine whether the latter has jurisdiction: either the jurisdiction of the court first seised is determined directly by the Brussels I Recast (which is common to both Member States) or jurisdiction is derived, by virtue of article 6, from the traditional rules of the state of the court first seised (in which case that court is clearly better placed to rule on the question of its own jurisdiction).

2.194 However, article 29 does not apply in cases where the court second seised has exclusive jurisdiction under article 24.[444] If the court first seised assumes jurisdiction contrary to the terms of article 24, the judgment of that court is not entitled to recognition and enforcement under Chapter III.[445] If proceedings are commenced

---

[438] See Case C-351/96 *Drouot Assurances SA v Consolidated Metallurgical Industries (CMI Industrial Sites)* [1998] ECR I-3075. See also *Sony Computer Entertainment Ltd v RH Freight Services Ltd* [2007] 2 Lloyd's Rep 463.
[439] *Kolden Holdings Ltd v Rodette Commerce Ltd* [2008] 1 Lloyd's Rep 435 (where X Ltd makes a valid legal assignment of its cause of action to Y Ltd, the two companies are 'the same party'). Compare *Mölnlycke Health Care AB v BSN Medical Ltd* [2010] ILPr 9.
[440] *WMS Gaming Inc v B Plus Giocolegale Ltd* [2012] ILPr 5. [441] *The Nordglimt* [1988] QB 183.
[442] Case C-406/92 *Owners of the cargo lately laden on board the ship 'Tatry' v Owners of the ship 'Maciej Rataj'* [1994] ECR I-5439; *Republic of India v India Steamship Co (No 2)* [1998] AC 878.
[443] Case C-351/89 [1991] ECR I-3317.
[444] Case C-438/12 *Weber v Weber* [2015] Ch 140, effectively confirming the earlier decision of the Court of Appeal in *Speed Investments Ltd v Formula One Holdings Ltd* [2005] 1 WLR 1936.
[445] Art 45(1)(e)(ii).

in another Member State in a matter which, by virtue of article 24, falls within the exclusive jurisdiction of the English court, it makes no sense to apply article 29 to prevent one of the parties from starting proceedings in England on the same issue.

2.195 Under the Convention and the 2002 Regulation there was controversy over whether jurisdiction derived from the parties' agreement took precedence over the provisions relating to parallel and related proceedings. In *Continental Bank NA v Aeakos Compania Naviera SA*[446] the Court of Appeal decided that, where proceedings are started in Greece (first) and England (second), the English court did not have to stay its proceedings if the dispute fell within the scope of an English jurisdiction clause between the parties. The Court of Justice, however, took the opposite view in *Erich Gasser GmbH v Misat Srl*,[447] a case involving a dispute between an Italian company (B) and an Austrian company (A), which arose from a contract containing an Austrian jurisdiction clause. B brought an action in Italy, a non-contractual forum, before A started proceedings on the same cause of action against B in Austria, the contractual forum. The Court of Justice decided that the Austrian court, being the court second seised, was bound to stay its proceedings: the court second seised was not entitled to decide whether or not the court first seised was justified in assuming jurisdiction and there was no exception to this principle in cases where there was (allegedly) a jurisdiction agreement referring the dispute in question to the court second seised. Under the *Gasser* ruling, it was for the court first seised (the non-contractual forum) to rule on the effect of a jurisdiction agreement in favour of the court second seised (the contractual forum).

2.196 Although the Court of Justice's view was supported by the text and structure of the 2002 Regulation, in policy terms the ruling was fundamentally unsatisfactory as its effect was to encourage delaying tactics by litigants. In a case involving a jurisdiction agreement, one of the parties, by bringing a torpedo action in a non-contractual forum, could paralyse proceedings in the contractual forum.[448] To make matters worse, the Court of Justice had ruled in *Gasser* that, even if the delay in the non-contractual forum was excessively long (as was very likely to be the case in relation to court proceedings in Italy), the court second seised could not pre-empt the decision of the court first seised on the jurisdictional issue.[449]

2.197 Not surprisingly, during the process that culminated in the enactment of the Recast, there was almost universal support for an amendment whose purpose was 'to enhance the effectiveness of exclusive choice-of-court agreements and to avoid abusive litigation tactics'.[450] The solution adopted by the Recast is to create an exception to the 'first come, first served' rule in article 29 and to give priority, in a case like *Gasser*, to the

---

[446] [1994] 1 WLR 588. [447] Case C-116/02 [2003] ECR I-14693.
[448] See, eg, *JP Morgan v Primacom* [2005] 2 All ER (Comm) 764.
[449] Case C-116/02 *Erich Gasser GmbH v Misat Srl* [2003] ECR I-14693, para 68.
[450] Brussels I Recast, recital (22). See also European Commission, *Brussels I Recast Green Paper*, COM (2009) 175 final, pp 5–6; European Commission, *Brussels I Recast Proposal*, COM (2010) 748 final, para 3.

contractual forum.⁴⁵¹ Article 31(2) provides that where, by virtue of article 25, the parties have conferred exclusive jurisdiction on a court of a Member State, any court of another Member State shall stay its proceedings. This obligation to stay arises only when the contractual forum is seised. So, in a case like *Gasser*, the Italian court would have to grant a stay only if proceedings are brought by A in Austria. If the contractual forum declines jurisdiction (for example, on the basis that the jurisdiction clause does not satisfy the requirements of article 25), the non-contractual forum may lift the stay. If, however, the jurisdiction of the contractual forum is established, the non-contractual forum must decline jurisdiction in favour of the contractual forum.⁴⁵²

2.198 The solution adopted by the Recast, by giving priority to the contractual forum (regardless of whether it was first or second seised), goes a long way to solving the problems revealed by the *Gasser* case. It should be noted, however, that article 31(2) also has the potential for causing delay. Simply by asserting the existence of a jurisdiction clause (whether it is legally effective or not), a litigant is able to obstruct the commencement of litigation in a forum with jurisdiction under the Recast and can require the other party, before initiating proceedings in his preferred forum, to obtain a judgment from the (alleged) contractual forum to the effect that the jurisdiction agreement is invalid or ineffective.

3. Related actions

2.199 Article 30 is designed to deal with situations not falling within the strict confines of article 29. Where related actions are pending in the courts of two Member States the court second seised has discretion to stay the proceedings (or in certain circumstances decline jurisdiction). Even when the two actions arise out of the same factual situation, if there is no risk of irreconcilable decisions, there is no basis for a stay under article 30.⁴⁵³ For the purposes of article 30, actions are deemed to be related where they are so closely connected that it is expedient to hear and determine them together to avoid the risk of irreconcilable judgments resulting from separate proceedings.⁴⁵⁴ Whether proceedings are related for the purposes of article 30 depends on the circumstances as they exist at the date of the application for a stay, rather than when the proceedings before the court second seised were commenced.⁴⁵⁵

2.200 Under article 30 the concept of related actions is a broad one; two actions may be related—on the basis that there is a risk of irreconcilable judgments—even if it would be perfectly possible for the judgments resulting from the two actions to be separately

---

⁴⁵¹ See Hartley, 'Choice-of-court Agreements and the New Brussels I Regulation' (2013) 129 LQR 309. For consideration of the question whether art 31(2) of the Recast applies in a case where proceedings in the non-contractual forum are related (but not identical) to the proceedings brought in the contractual forum, see Kenny and Hennigan, 'Choice-of-Court Agreements, the Italian Torpedo, and the Recast of the Brussels I Regulation' (2015) 64 ICLQ 197.
⁴⁵² Art 31(3). Art 31(2) and (3) do not apply to matters referred to in Sections 3 (insurance), 4 (consumer contracts), and 5 (employment contracts): art 31(4).
⁴⁵³ See Mummery LJ in *FKI Engineering Ltd v Stribog Ltd* [2011] 1 WLR 3264 at [44]. See also *Seven Licensing Co Sarl v FFG Platinum SA* [2012] ILPr 7.
⁴⁵⁴ Art 30(3).   ⁴⁵⁵ *FKI Engineering Ltd v Stribog Ltd* [2011] 1 WLR 3264.

enforced. The concept of related actions covers the case where there is a risk that the courts of two Member States may reach contradictory conclusions on questions of fact. For example, proceedings (in one Member State) brought by an owner of cargo which has been damaged while being carried by the defendant's ship are related to proceedings (in another Member State) brought by the ship-owner to obtain exoneration from or limitation of liability for damage to a similar cargo owned by others.[456] Whether actions pending in different courts are related should not turn on a sophisticated and difficult exercise of legal analysis; rather, there should be a broad common-sense approach to whether the actions in question are related.[457] Where, for example, two actions in different Member States involve overlapping issues, there can be little doubt that article 30 is engaged.[458] The court second seised should rely on article 30 whenever it considers that the reasoning of the court first seised may concern issues likely to be relevant in the proceedings before the court second seised.[459]

2.201 Where there are related actions in the courts of two Member States, the court second seised may stay its proceedings.[460] Furthermore, on the application of one of the parties, the court second seised may decline jurisdiction if both actions are pending at first instance and, under the law of the court first seised, the two actions can be consolidated.[461]

2.202 Article 30 does not indicate how the courts should exercise their discretion. The traditional understanding is that where article 30 applies the first duty of the court is to stay its proceedings.[462] Accordingly, in principle, when the court second seised is considering whether or not to stay proceedings under article 30, the degree of risk of irreconcilable judgments should be the major factor. The court second seised may be justified in refusing to stay its proceedings or to decline jurisdiction where, for example, the risk of irreconcilable judgments is very small[463] or the risk is dependent on a range of contingent matters.[464] If, however, the degree of connection between the English and foreign proceedings is such that resolution of the issues in the English proceedings would be easier after conclusion of the foreign proceedings, the English proceedings should be stayed pending the final outcome of the foreign proceedings.[465]

2.203 The risk of irreconcilable judgments is not the only relevant factor. The appropriateness of the competing fora is something that may be taken into account; the court second seised is entitled to have regard not only to the stage reached in each set of

---

[456] Case C–406/92 *Owners of the cargo lately laden on board the ship 'Tatry' v Owners of the ship 'Maciej Rataj'* [1994] ECR I–5439.
[457] Lord Saville in *Sarrio SA v Kuwait Investment Authority* [1999] 1 AC 32 at 40–1.
[458] See, eg, *UBS Ltd v Regione Calabria* [2012] ILPr 22.
[459] See Advocate General Tesauro in C–406/92 *Owners of the cargo lately laden on board the ship 'Tatry' v Owners of the ship 'Maciej Rataj'* [1994] ECR I–5439, para 28.
[460] Art 30(1).   [461] Art 30(2).
[462] Jenard Report, OJ 1979 C59/41.
[463] *The Maciej Rataj* [1991] 2 Lloyd's Rep 458 (revsd on other grounds [1992] 2 Lloyd's Rep 552).
[464] *Centro Internationale Handelsbank AG v Morgan Grenfell Trade Finance Ltd* [1997] CLC 870.
[465] *Lehman Brothers Bankhaus AG I. Ins v CMA CGM* [2013] 2 All ER (Comm) 557.

proceedings, but also to the proximity of the courts to the subject-matter of the case[466] and the length of time before judgment is likely to be rendered in the related foreign proceedings.[467] Where the court second seised has jurisdiction by virtue of the parties' agreement, that court may exercise its discretion against granting a stay under article 30 (thereby upholding the agreement).[468]

2.204 Article 30 does not expand the jurisdiction of the court first seised; it is a negative rule, which enables a court other than the court first seised to stay proceedings in a situation in which it has prima facie jurisdiction.[469] Consider a case where A sues B in France and then C sues A in England. If the English court grants a stay under article 30 on the basis that the English proceedings are related to the earlier French proceedings, the fact that the English court has granted a stay does not thereby confer jurisdiction on the French court in relation to C's claim against A.

B The effect of parallel or related proceedings in a non-Member State

2.205 Neither the Brussels Convention nor the 2002 Regulation made any attempt to address problems posed by parallel or related proceedings brought in a third state, rather than a Member State. This gap in the framework of Brussels I was a cause of both uncertainty and criticism. The Brussels I Recast contains provisions which go some way towards filling this gap. The amendments introduced by the Recast are, however, seriously flawed and leave almost as many questions unanswered as the 2002 Regulation which it replaced.

2.206 In the context of parallel and related proceedings in a third state, article 33 (lis pendens) and article 34 (related proceedings) are, in very broad terms, the provisions equivalent to articles 29 and 30 of the Recast. There are, however, very considerable differences between the operation of articles 29 and 30, on the one hand, and articles 33 and 34, on the other.

2.207 Article 33, unlike article 29, does not normally *require* parallel proceedings to be stayed or dismissed. Article 33 applies if the Member State court's jurisdiction is based on article 4 (domicile) or articles 7, 8, or 9 (special jurisdiction) and the Member State proceedings involve the same cause of action and are between the same parties as proceedings already commenced in a non-Member State. The Member State court may stay its proceedings under article 33(1) if: (a) it is expected that the third state court will give a judgment capable of recognition and enforcement in that Member State; and (b) the court of the Member State is satisfied that a stay is necessary for the proper administration of justice.

---

[466] See Advocate General Lenz in Case C-129/92 *Owens Bank v Bracco (No 2)* [1994] ECR I-117, para 76.
[467] *Cooper Tire & Rubber Co Europe Ltd v Dow Deutschland Inc* [2010] 2 CLC 104.
[468] *JP Morgan v Primacom* [2005] 2 All ER (Comm) 764; *Starlight Shipping Co v Allianz Marine & Aviation Versicherungs AG* [2014] 1 All ER 590; *Nomura International plc v Banca Monte Dei Paschi Di Siena SpA* [2014] 1 WLR 1584; *Barclays Bank plc v Ente Nazionale di Prevedenza* [2015] 2 Lloyd's Rep 527.
[469] Case 150/80 *Elefanten Schuh GmbH v Jacqmain* [1981] ECR 1671; Case C-51/97 *Réunion Européenne SA v Splietoff's Bevachtingskantoor BV* [1998] ECR I-6511.

2.208 Having granted a stay under article 33(1), the court may lift the stay if: (a) the non-Member State proceedings are themselves stayed or discontinued; (b) it appears that the non-Member State proceedings are unlikely to be concluded within a reasonable time; or (c) the continuation of the Member State proceedings is required for the proper administration of justice. However, if, when proceedings are commenced in the courts of a Member State, the parallel proceedings in a third state have already led to a judgment which is capable of recognition and enforcement in that Member State, the Member State court must dismiss its proceedings.[470]

2.209 Article 34 establishes the same basic regime for cases involving related proceedings in a third state. Article 34 is engaged if the Member State court's jurisdiction is based on one of articles 4, 7, 8, or 9 and the Member State proceedings are related to an action in a non-Member State. The Member State court may stay its proceedings on the basis of article 34(1) if: (a) it is expedient to hear and determine the related actions together to avoid the risk of irreconcilable judgments resulting from separate proceedings; (b) it is expected that the non-Member State court will give a judgment capable of recognition and enforcement in that Member State; and (c) the court of the Member State is satisfied that a stay is necessary for the proper administration of justice.

2.210 A stay may be lifted under article 34(2) if: (a) there is no longer a risk of irreconcilable judgments; (b) the non-Member State proceedings are stayed or discontinued; (c) the non-Member State proceedings are unlikely to lead to a judgment within a reasonable time frame; and (d) the continuation of the Member State proceedings is required for the proper administration of justice. In addition, the Member State court may dismiss its proceedings if the third state proceedings have resulted in a judgment which is capable of recognition and enforcement in that Member State.[471]

2.211 There are various features of articles 33 and 34 which should be emphasised. First, like articles 29 and 30, they give precedence to the court first seised. The possibility of proceedings being stayed on the basis of parallel or related proceedings in a third state depends on there being proceedings already pending before the courts of a third state when the Member State court is seised. Secondly, articles 33 and 34 follow article 30 in the sense that they confer discretion on the Member State court (except in the case envisaged by article 33(3)—where parallel proceedings in a third state have already led to an enforceable judgment). Thirdly, the operation of articles 33 and 34 is not easy to predict as both provisions employ a number of open-textured phrases—such as 'the proper administration of justice', 'unlikely to be concluded within a reasonable time'. Recital (24), however, draws attention to a number of factors which may be taken into account in the context of articles 33 and 34: connections between the facts of the case and the parties and the non-Member State concerned; the stage reached by the foreign proceedings; when the foreign court is likely to render a judgment; whether the foreign court has exclusive jurisdiction. Fourthly, the contours of articles 33 and 34 depend on each Member State's conflicts rules on the recognition and enforcement of foreign

[470] Art 33(3).   [471] Art 34(2).

(third state) judgments. The possibility of proceedings brought before a Member State court being stayed under articles 33 and 34 arises only if parallel or related proceedings in a non-Member state are likely to lead to a judgment which is enforceable under the national law of that Member State. The lack of legal uniformity as regards the enforcement of third state judgments means that the practical significance of articles 33 and 34 may differ markedly from one Member State to another. Finally, it seems that articles 33 and 34 of the Recast do not attempt to provide a solution to certain key problems which were identified as arising under the Brussels Convention and the 2002 Regulation. Consider, for example, the case where a New York company (A) and an English company (B) enter a contract which includes an exclusive jurisdiction clause in favour of the New York courts. If A sues B in England and, then, B sues A (on the same cause of action) in New York, there is nothing in articles 33 and 34 to allow the English court to stay the proceedings commenced by A, notwithstanding the fact that New York is the contractual forum.[472] The issues thrown up by this example are considered in a later section.[473]

C Staying proceedings on the basis of the doctrine of forum non conveniens

1. The development of the doctrine

2.212 An important difference between the jurisdiction of the English court under the traditional rules and that under the Brussels I Recast is that the assumption of the former jurisdiction is discretionary, while the latter is largely mandatory.

2.213 Where the claimant invokes the jurisdiction of the English court on the basis of the defendant's presence in England, or the claimant is seeking permission under CPR rule 6.36 for process to be served abroad, the court has discretion whether or not to assume jurisdiction. Originally, the approaches in the two classes of case were very different. For much of the twentieth century the court would not stay proceedings brought against a defendant who was present in England unless the bringing of the proceedings was vexatious or oppressive, which usually required proof of an intention by the claimant to harass the defendant.[474] Short of that, the claim would be tried in England even if the parties were foreigners and the facts of the dispute had no connection with England. If the claimant believed he would enjoy some advantage by suing in England, he was free to do so, as long as process could be served on the defendant in England. The traditional attitude of the English courts—which necessarily encouraged forum shopping—was summed up by Lord Denning's observation that 'if the forum is England, it is a good place to shop in, both for the quality of the goods and the speed of service'.[475] By contrast, in cases brought under CPR rule 6.36 (and its predecessors), it

---

[472] If, however, the New York proceedings had been commenced first, art 33 would be engaged.
[473] See paras 2.270–2.280.
[474] *St Pierre v South American Stores (Gath and Chaves) Ltd* [1936] 1 KB 382.
[475] *The Atlantic Star* [1973] QB 364 at 382.

has been established since the nineteenth century that permission to serve out requires the claimant to show that England is the appropriate forum.[476]

2.214 As a result of a series of cases decided in the 1970s and 1980s,[477] the differences between these two categories of case were largely reduced, though not entirely eliminated. The House of Lords moved from the position that a stay would be granted only if the English proceedings were vexatious or oppressive to the modern position that a stay should be granted if there is an available forum which is more appropriate than the English court. The culmination of this development is the speech of Lord Goff in *Spiliada Maritime Corpn v Cansulex Ltd*,[478] which forms the cornerstone of the modern law.

2. General principles

(A) The fundamental question

2.215 Although in *Amin Rasheed Shipping Corpn v Kuwait Insurance Co*[479] Lord Wilberforce expressed the view that the principles which had been formulated in relation to the staying of proceedings were of little assistance in service-out cases, the *Spiliada* case[480] establishes that the same fundamental principles apply where the defendant seeks a stay of proceedings which have been started as of right in England (forum non conveniens) and where the claimant seeks permission to serve a claim form on the defendant out of the jurisdiction (forum conveniens). The fundamental principle is to identify the court in which the case can be most suitably tried for the interests of the parties and the ends of justice.

2.216 The question which the court is required to consider runs a real risk of drawing the court into a consideration of the merits and demerits of foreign systems for the administration of justice. In the past, English judges were criticised for displaying 'judicial chauvinism', a feature of 'the good old days, the passing of which many may regret, when the inhabitants of this island felt an innate superiority over those unfortunate enough to belong to other races'.[481] More recently, however, a number of senior judges have gone out of their way to deprecate such chauvinism and to indicate that it has been replaced by 'judicial comity'.[482] When applying the test of appropriateness the English court should not pronounce upon the advantages and disadvantages of the system of administering justice in foreign countries as compared with the system of administering justice in England. To make such invidious comparisons 'is not consistent with the mutual respect which the courts of friendly states, each of which has a well developed system for the administration of justice, owe, or should owe to each other'.[483]

---

[476] *Société Générale de Paris v Dreyfus Bros* (1885) 29 Ch D 239.
[477] *The Atlantic Star* [1974] AC 436; *MacShannon v Rockware Glass Ltd* [1978] AC 795; *The Abidin Daver* [1984] AC 398.
[478] [1987] AC 460. For a policy-based evaluation of the law, see Fawcett, 'Trial in England or Abroad: The Underlying Policy Considerations' (1989) 9 OJLS 205.
[479] [1984] AC 50 at 72.   [480] *Spiliada Maritime Corpn v Cansulex Ltd* [1987] AC 460.
[481] Lord Reid in *The Atlantic Star* [1974] AC 436 at 453.
[482] See, in particular, the speech of Lord Diplock in *The Abidin Daver* [1984] AC 398 at 411.
[483] Brandon LJ in *The El Amria* [1981] 2 Lloyd's Rep 119 at 126.

(B) The determination of the appropriate forum

2.217 A stay will be granted on the ground of forum non conveniens if the defendant satisfies the court that there is another available forum, having competent jurisdiction,[484] which is clearly or distinctly a more appropriate forum than the English court. In cases where the court's jurisdiction under CPR rule 6.36 is invoked the burden is on the claimant to establish that England is the most appropriate forum. If there is no foreign forum which is available to the claimant as an alternative forum for resolution of the dispute the court will refuse to grant a stay (or will give permission to serve out). Assuming, however, that there is another available forum, in the context of an application for a stay of English proceedings, the court applies a two-stage test to determine whether the English court or the alternative forum is more appropriate.

(i) The first stage

2.218 At the first stage, the judge must consider which forum—the English court or a foreign one—is more closely connected with the dispute. The court must have regard to connecting factors which point towards one forum or the other as that with which the dispute has its most real and substantial connection. Relevant factors include the law governing the substance of the dispute and the places where the parties reside or carry on business as well as factors which affect convenience and expense (such as the availability of witnesses). Where the claim in England is for a negative declaration (rather than for positive relief such as damages), this fact alone does not affect the relative appropriateness of the English court and the alternative forum—as long as the negative declaration is sought for a valid reason and the grant of such a declaration would serve a useful purpose.[485] In a case where proceedings are brought in England on the basis of the defendant's presence within the jurisdiction, if the court concludes at this stage that there is no other forum which is more closely connected with the dispute than England, it will refuse a stay.

2.219 There is no finite list of connecting factors which the court must consider at the first stage; much depends on the circumstances of each particular case. A factor which is of special significance in one case may be regarded as largely irrelevant in another. In principle, at the first stage, the court is seeking to identify the centre of gravity of the dispute so that inconvenience and expense can be reduced. The decided cases suggest that the court will have regard to six factors.

(a) Territorial connections

2.220 The court will always consider the territorial connections of the parties and the location of the evidence. If both the parties are resident in a foreign country and all the evidence is abroad, England is obviously not the most closely connected forum.[486]

---

[484] In relation to the question whether or not a foreign forum is 'available', the basis on which the foreign court may assume jurisdiction is irrelevant: *Lubbe v Cape plc* [2000] 1 WLR 1545.

[485] *New Hampshire Insurance Co v Phillips Electronics North America Corpn* [1998] CLC 1062; *Messier-Dowty Ltd v Sabena SA* [2000] 1 WLR 2040; *Ark Therapeutics plc v True North Capital Ltd* [2006] 1 All ER (Comm) 138.

[486] See, eg, *The Prestrioka* [2003] 2 Lloyd's Rep 327; *Pacific International Sports Clubs Ltd v Soccer Marketing International Ltd* [2010] EWCA Civ 753.

(b) Lis alibi pendens

2.221 Where proceedings between the same parties arising out of the same dispute are also pending in a foreign court (lis alibi pendens) the English court will often be a less appropriate forum than it would have been in the absence of the foreign proceedings. The additional inconvenience and expense which results from allowing two sets of proceedings to be pursued concurrently in two different countries—where the same facts are in issue and the testimony of the same witnesses required—adds weight to the argument that the foreign court is the appropriate forum. The court must also bear in mind the danger that parallel proceedings in two countries may lead to conflicting judgments.[487] In *The Abidin Daver*,[488] for example, A (Turkish ship-owners) had started proceedings in Turkey, claiming compensation from B (Cuban ship-owners) for damage arising from a collision between their ships in Turkish waters. B then started proceedings in England claiming damages from A in respect of the collision. The House of Lords took the view that the English proceedings should be stayed.

2.222 Unlike article 29 of the Brussels I Recast, the traditional rules do not endorse a simple 'first come, first served' approach;[489] the existence of parallel or related proceedings abroad is only one factor—which has to be weighed against the other connecting factors.[490] Where proceedings in the foreign court have been started only a few days before the commencement of English proceedings, the existence of lis alibi pendens is of little or no significance. Where, however, the foreign proceedings are well-advanced and judgment is imminent the argument that the foreign court is the more appropriate forum is a very strong one.[491]

(c) Multiple parties

2.223 Where the factual matrix from which the dispute arises involves a multiplicity of parties the court will have regard to the desirability of ensuring that, as far as possible, all the disputes between the parties are resolved in one set of proceedings in a single forum. For example, in a case where A sues B in England and has a related claim against C, the English court may regard itself as being the appropriate forum for A's claim against C, even though England is not the centre of gravity of the dispute, if England provides a forum in which the related claims against B and C can be determined together.[492] Conversely, if a foreign court has jurisdiction to determine all the claims in multi-party proceedings—and the English court does not—this is an argument in favour of the foreign court being regarded as the appropriate forum.[493]

---

[487] *The Varna (No 2)* [1994] 2 Lloyd's Rep 41; *Chase v Ram Technical Services Ltd* [2000] 2 Lloyd's Rep 418.
[488] [1984] AC 398.   [489] *EI du Pont de Nemours & Co v Agnew* [1987] 2 Lloyd's Rep 585.
[490] *The Olympic Galaxy* [2006] 2 Lloyd's Rep 27; *Stonebridge Underwriting Ltd v Ontario Municipal Insurance Exchange* [2010] 2 CLC 349; *Faraday Reinsurance Co Ltd v Howden North America Inc* [2012] 2 CLC 956; *Niche Products Ltd v Macdermid Offshore Solutions LLC* [2014] FSR 21.
[491] *Cleveland Museum of Art v Capricorn Art International SA* [1990] 2 Lloyd's Rep 166.
[492] See, eg, *The Kapetan Georgis* [1988] 1 Lloyd's Rep 352; *Smyth v Behbehani* [1999] ILPr 584; *Crédit Agricole Indosuez v Unicof Ltd* [2004] 1 Lloyd's Rep 196; *JSC BTA Bank v Granton Trade Ltd* [2011] 2 All ER (Comm) 542; *BAT Industries plc v Windward Prospects Ltd* [2014] 2 All ER (Comm) 757.
[493] *The Oinoussin Pride* [1991] 1 Lloyd's Rep 126.

(d) The 'Cambridgeshire' factor

2.224 The balance of convenience may be tilted in favour of one forum rather than another because of the existence of other proceedings in that forum involving different parties but raising the same factual and legal issues. This is known as the *Cambridgeshire* factor. In the *Spiliada* case,[494] the dispute arose out of a contract made between the plaintiff ship-owners and the defendants, who carried on business in British Columbia. The contract was governed by English law. The plaintiffs claimed that damage had been caused to the ship by the defendants having loaded a cargo of sulphur when it was wet. A similar cargo had been loaded at the same time on another ship, the *Cambridgeshire*. When the plaintiffs sought to invoke the jurisdiction of the English court, the owners of the *Cambridgeshire* had already commenced proceedings against the defendants in England. These proceedings involved a similar claim and the same solicitors and insurers. The House of Lords held that the judge was justified in holding that England was the appropriate forum.

(e) The applicable law

2.225 Although the first stage of the *Spiliada* doctrine is usually dominated by a consideration of factual connections, the court will also have regard to the applicable law. While it is perfectly possible for the English court to apply a foreign law and for a foreign court to apply English law, where the dispute centres on legal rather than factual questions 'it is generally preferable, other things being equal, that a case should be tried in the country whose law applies'.[495] Although English judges are better placed than others to rule on questions of English law, the weight to be attached to the applicable law depends on the circumstances of the case.[496] If the dispute is essentially one of fact, the applicable law is of relatively little significance.[497] However, it is preferable for difficult questions of English law to be determined by the English courts which are experienced in dealing with such matters.[498] Similarly, if an issue of English public policy arises in the context of a dispute concerning a contract governed by English law that issue should be decided by the English court. Not only would proceedings in a foreign forum involve the extra expense and inconvenience of expert evidence from English lawyers, but also a question of English public policy is not 'capable of fair resolution in any foreign court, however distinguished and well instructed'.[499]

---

[494] [1987] AC 460.

[495] Lord Mance JSC in *VTB Capital plc v Nutritek International Corpn* [2013] 2 AC 337 at [46]. See also *Gan Insurance Co Ltd v Tai Ping Insurance Co Ltd* [1999] CLC 1270; *Zivlin v Baal Taxa* [1998] ILPr 106; *CGU International Insurance plc v Szabo* [2002] 1 All ER (Comm) 83; *Wright v Deccan Chargers Sporting Ventures Ltd* [2011] ILPr 37; *The Golden Endurance* [2015] 1 Lloyd's Rep 266; *Teekay Tankers Ltd v STX Offshore & Shipping Co* [2015] 2 All ER (Comm) 263.

[496] See, eg, *Novus Aviation Ltd v Onur Air Tasimacilik AS* [2009] 1 Lloyd's Rep 576; *The Lucky Lady* [2013] 2 Lloyd's Rep 104.

[497] See *Limit (No 3) Ltd v PDV Insurance Co* [2005] 2 All ER (Comm) 347.

[498] *FR Lürssen Werft GmbH & Co KG v Halle* [2010] 2 Lloyd's Rep 20; *Golden Ocean Group Ltd v Salgaocar Mining Industries Pvt Ltd* [2011] 1 CLC 125. Although both these cases went on appeal, the forum conveniens determination was not challenged.

[499] Bingham LJ in *EI du Pont de Nemours & Co v Agnew* [1987] 2 Lloyd's Rep 585 at 594.

(f) Documentary evidence

2.226 If documentary evidence is an important element in the equation, the language of the documents is relevant. If the question is whether England or Mexico is the appropriate forum, the fact that the dispute centres on documents which are drawn up in Spanish is an argument in favour of the Mexican court; if the relevant documents were in English, this would be a factor pointing towards England as the appropriate forum.[500]

(ii) The second stage

2.227 The second stage has to be considered only if, having regard to the relevant connecting factors at the first stage, the court thinks that the dispute is more closely connected with a foreign court. Where proceedings are brought in England as of right (because the defendant was present in England when the claim form was served), if the court would incline towards granting a stay on the basis that a foreign court is the forum with which the dispute is most closely connected, the claimant may seek to resist a stay at the second stage on the basis that substantial justice will not be done in the foreign forum. Notwithstanding the fact that England is not the centre of gravity of the dispute, the court will not grant a stay if it is satisfied that justice requires that the claimant should not be required to litigate abroad.[501]

2.228 At the second stage the burden is on the claimant to satisfy the court that there is a real risk that justice will not be obtained in the foreign forum. The court will consider all the circumstances of the case, including circumstances which go beyond those taken into account at the first stage. To succeed at the second stage it is not enough for the claimant to show that he has a legitimate personal or juridical advantage in proceedings in England. The fact that the claimant will be deprived of such an advantage if the dispute is not determined in England is not a sufficient reason for the court to assume jurisdiction, provided that the court is satisfied that substantial justice will be done in the available foreign forum.

2.229 Perhaps the most difficult issue at the second stage is to determine the dividing line between, on the one hand, a factor which is merely an advantage to the claimant and, on the other, a factor which is so important that, if denied to the claimant, there will be a denial of justice. A number of factors have been discussed by the courts.

(a) Time bars

2.230 If the claim is time-barred in the alternative forum, the court may decide that England is the most appropriate forum, notwithstanding the fact that the dispute is more closely connected with another forum. In a case where the claim is time-barred in the foreign court, but proceedings would not be time-barred in England, if the claimant did not act unreasonably in failing to commence proceedings abroad within the relevant limitation period, it would not normally be just for the English court to

---

[500] See Lord Goff in *Spiliada Maritime Corpn v Cansulex Ltd* [1987] AC 460 at 483.
[501] See, eg, *Cherney v Deripaska (No 2)* [2010] 3 All ER (Comm) 456.

stay the proceedings, unless the defendant agrees to waive the time-bar in the foreign court.[502]

(b) Procedural advantages: delays, damages, and costs

2.231 Although Lord Goff made it clear in the *Spiliada* case[503] that, as a general rule, an advantage to the claimant of proceeding in England, rather than abroad, should not be regarded as decisive, there are several reported instances where the court has decided that the fact that a particular advantage to the claimant is not available in the more closely connected forum means that justice would not be done if the English proceedings are stayed. For example, in *The Vishva Ajay*,[504] which involved a dispute arising out of a collision between two ships in Indian waters, the court refused to stay the proceedings on the basis that delay in India was likely to be at least six years and that a successful litigant in India would not be awarded costs on a realistic basis. By contrast, in *Radhakrishna Hospitality Service Private Ltd v EIH Ltd*,[505] another case in which India was the country with which the parties' dispute was most closely connected, less weight was given to the possibility that Indian proceedings would be significantly slower than English proceedings and a stay was granted.[506] In *Roneleigh Ltd v MII Exports Inc*,[507] a case in which New Jersey was plainly the more closely connected forum, the Court of Appeal upheld the judge's decision to allow service out of the jurisdiction. The basis of the decision was that, because the law of New Jersey does not allow a successful claimant to recover costs, substantial justice would not be done in the foreign forum.

2.232 As a general rule, the fact that the claimant, if successful, would recover higher damages in English proceedings than in proceedings abroad is not enough to justify the conclusion that proceedings should continue in England.[508] Nevertheless, there are cases in which it has been held that, where the difference between the damages which could be recovered in England and abroad is very considerable, it would amount to an injustice if the claimant were required to pursue his claim abroad.[509] The court may regard the fact that the claimant cannot afford to litigate abroad to be decisive. Where the claimant's financial predicament means that there is no possibility of the claim being litigated in the most closely connected forum, but litigation can be pursued in England (for example, because of the availability of legal aid or a conditional fee agreement between the claimant and his English solicitors) the court may decide that, in the interests of justice, English proceedings should not be stayed.[510] Similarly, in a case

---

[502] See Lord Goff in *Spiliada Maritime Corpn v Cansulex Ltd* [1987] AC 460 at 483. See also *The Prestrioka* [2003] 2 Lloyd's Rep 327.
[503] *Spiliada Maritime Corpn v Cansulex Ltd* [1987] AC 460.
[504] [1989] 2 Lloyd's Rep 558.   [505] [1999] 2 Lloyd's Rep 249.
[506] See also *Konamaneni v Rolls-Royce Industrial Power (India) Ltd* [2002] 1 All ER 979; *Ceskoslovenska Obchodni Banka AS v Nomura International plc* [2003] ILPr 20.
[507] [1989] 1 WLR 619.
[508] *Herceg Novi v Ming Galaxy* [1998] 4 All ER 238.
[509] *The Vishva Abha* [1990] 2 Lloyd's Rep 312 (damages limited to £367,500 under South African law; potential liability of £1.5 million under English law); *Baghlaf Al Zafer Factory Co BR for Industry Ltd v Pakistan National Shipping Co* [1998] 2 Lloyd's Rep 229.
[510] *Connelly v RTZ Corpn plc* [1998] AC 854. See also *Carlson v Rio Tinto plc* [1999] CLC 551.

where the claim is being brought by a large number of claimants and the alternative forum does not have either experience of, or adequate facilities for, dealing with such proceedings, the court may refuse to grant a stay on the basis that the English court (which does have the necessary experience and facilities) provides the most appropriate forum.[511] Finally, it has been held that, where a foreign judgment is more difficult to enforce internationally than an English judgment (which is enforceable in other Member States under the Brussels I Recast), it may be unjust to deprive the claimant of the advantage of proceeding in England.[512]

(c) Divergent choice of law rules

2.233 The court may conclude that justice will not be done abroad in circumstances where it is shown that the foreign court, applying its own choice of law principles, will reach a conclusion which is opposed to that which would be reached by the English court through the application of English conflicts rules.[513] For example, in a case where the rival jurisdictions are England and the United Arab Emirates, if the courts of the United Arab Emirates would apply the local law, under which the claimant is bound to fail, but the English court would—on the basis of English choice of law principles—apply Spanish law, according to which the claimant has an arguable claim, the English court is likely to assume jurisdiction, even though the United Arab Emirates is the more closely connected forum.[514] The approach in this type of case is based on the courts' view that it is not conducive to justice to require the claimant, who has—in the eyes of English private international law—an arguable claim, to litigate in a forum where his claim would inevitably be rejected. This approach is, however, hardly consistent with judicial comity.[515]

(d) Procedural fairness

2.234 If the defendant will not receive a fair hearing in the alternative forum—whether for political or ideological reasons, incompetence, lack of independence or corruption—this is a significant factor which is likely to tilt the balance in favour of England as the appropriate forum. The claimant does not, however, have to prove that he will not obtain justice abroad; a real risk of injustice is enough.[516]

2.235 In *Oppenheimer v Louis Rosenthal & Co AG*[517] leave was sought in 1937 for process to be served in Germany. Although in other circumstances the German court might well have been the more appropriate forum, leave was granted because the plaintiff, being a Jew, would probably not have received a fair trial in the German court and, indeed,

---

[511] *Lubbe v Cape plc* [2000] 1 WLR 1545.
[512] *International Credit and Investment Company (Overseas) Ltd v Shaikh Kamal Adham* [1999] ILPr 302; *Sharab v Al-Saud* [2009] 2 Lloyd's Rep 160; *Karafarin Bank v Mansoury-dara* [2009] 2 Lloyd's Rep 289.
[513] *Irish Shipping Ltd v Commercial Union Assurance Co plc* [1991] 2 QB 206; *Tiernan v Magen Insurance Co Ltd* [2000] ILPr 517.
[514] *Banco Atlantico SA v British Bank of the Middle East* [1990] 2 Lloyd's Rep 504.
[515] See Carter (1989) 60 BYIL 482 at 484–5.
[516] *Altimo Holdings & Investments Ltd v Kyrgyz Mobil Tel Ltd* [2012] 1 WLR 1804.
[517] [1937] 1 All ER 23.

might have been put in a concentration camp if he visited Germany. Similarly, a foreign court with which the dispute was closely connected was held not to be the appropriate forum in a case where substantial evidence of procedural failings (such as breach of principles of natural justice) and irrational conclusions created a risk of injustice.[518] However, it is not unjust to refuse a stay in a case where the principal reason for the claimant wanting not to litigate in a more closely connected foreign forum is to avoid being exposed to criminal charges in that country.[519]

2.236 It should not be thought that the court will simply accept an allegation by the claimant that he will not be given a fair trial abroad. A litigant's unsubstantiated fears as to the quality of justice in the alternative forum are not relevant[520] and a claimant who wishes to resist a stay on the basis that even-handed justice may not be done abroad 'must assert this candidly and support his allegations with positive and cogent evidence'.[521]

(iii) Weighing the factors

2.237 At the first stage, where the connecting factors point in different directions, the court has to weigh them against each other to decide where the balance of convenience lies. In *Amin Rasheed Shipping Corpn v Kuwait Insurance Co*,[522] for example, the plaintiff, a Liberian company resident in Dubai, had entered a contract of marine insurance with the defendant, a Kuwaiti insurance company. When a dispute arose between the parties the plaintiff wished to bring proceedings in England. The House of Lords, although holding that the parties had impliedly chosen English law as the applicable law, held that the judge had been right to conclude that England was not the appropriate forum. The factual issues 'could be determined as well in Kuwait as in England, possibly better, and with no clear overall balance of convenience'.[523] Although any legal questions were to be decided by English law, there was no reason to suppose that a Kuwaiti judge would have any difficulty in applying the relevant rules.

2.238 The problems of weighing the relevant factors are considerably greater at the second stage in cases where the court has to balance the fact that England is not the country with which the parties' dispute is most closely connected against the claimant's assertion that justice will not be done abroad. The range of factors which the court is entitled to consider is very wide and the authorities do not give any guidance on how these factors are to be weighed in any particular case. Inevitably, the test of appropriateness is rather open-textured and its application is unpredictable.[524] The *Spiliada* doctrine is open to the criticism that it unduly favours the English forum by giving the claimant two bites at the cherry. If England is the most closely connected forum, the English court will refuse to grant a stay (or will give permission to serve out); if England is not

---

[518] *Altimo Holdings & Investments Ltd v Kyrgyz Mobil Tel Ltd* [2012] 1 WLR 1804.
[519] *Askin v Absa Bank Ltd* [1999] ILPr 471.   [520] *Jeyaretnam v Mahmood* (1992) The Times, 21 May.
[521] Lord Diplock in *The Abidin Daver* [1984] AC 398 at 411.
[522] [1984] AC 50.   [523] Lord Wilberforce at 66.
[524] See Hill, 'Jurisdiction in Civil and Commercial Matters: Is There a Third Way?' (2001) 54 CLP 439. See also Arzandeh, 'Should the *Spiliada* Test Be Revised?' (2014) 10 Journal of Private International Law 89 (arguing that the second stage should be reformulated).

the most closely connected forum, the court may still decide that the claim should be litigated in England on the basis that justice will not be done in the foreign forum. As has been seen, the fact that the claimant has a significant advantage in suing in England rather than abroad may be regarded as of such importance that the court concludes that there would be a denial of justice if the case were not heard in England. However, the court will invariably assume jurisdiction in cases where England is the most closely connected forum as there is no scope for the defendant to challenge the jurisdiction of the English court on the basis that substantial justice will not be done in England. If a claimant can resist a stay of proceedings on the basis that damages abroad are derisory, why is a defendant not able to obtain a stay on the basis that English damages are much lower than those which would be awarded by the alternative forum? As the *Spiliada* doctrine is asymmetrical in this way, the boast that 'judicial chauvinism has been replaced by judicial comity'[525] should not be accepted too uncritically.

3. The effect of a dispute-resolution clause

(A) Cases involving a jurisdiction clause in favour of the English courts

2.239 In most cases where the parties choose English jurisdiction, article 25 of the Brussels I Recast applies and the English court's jurisdiction is mandatory.[526] In those cases where article 25 does not confer mandatory jurisdiction (for example, in situations falling outside the scope of article 1 of the Recast), whether the court is entitled to assume jurisdiction is determined by the traditional rules.

2.240 If the traditional rules apply, the court has discretion whether or not to assume jurisdiction. A defendant who, having agreed to English jurisdiction, is served with a claim form in England, may apply for a stay of proceedings (as long as he has not submitted to the English court's jurisdiction). However, it would require 'some exceptional justification'[527] for the English court to accede to the defendant's application and there is no reported case in which a stay has been granted in this situation.[528] If the defendant cannot be served with process in England, the court will—in the absence of strong reasons to the contrary—hold the parties to their bargain and give permission for service out of the jurisdiction under CPR rule 6.36.[529]

(B) Cases involving a jurisdiction clause in favour of the courts of a non-Member State

2.241 The English court will normally not permit proceedings to be conducted in England in breach of the terms of an agreement conferring exclusive jurisdiction on the courts of a third state. If, notwithstanding such an agreement, the English court's jurisdiction is

---

[525] Lord Diplock in *The Abidin Daver* [1984] AC 398 at 411.
[526] *Equitas Ltd v Allstate Insurance Co* [2009] 1 All ER (Comm) 1137; *UBS AG v HSH Nordbank AG* [2009] 2 Lloyd's Rep 272.
[527] Langley J in *OT Africa Line Ltd v Magic Sportswear Corp* [2005] 1 Lloyd's Rep 252 at 258; affd [2006] 1 All ER (Comm) 32.
[528] There is, however, a reported case where English proceedings were stayed on the plaintiff's application, notwithstanding an English jurisdiction agreement: *Bouygues Offshore SA v Caspian Shipping Co (Nos. 1, 3, 4 and 5)* [1998] 2 Lloyd's Rep 461.
[529] *The Chaparral* [1968] 2 Lloyd's Rep 158.

invoked under the traditional rules[530] (for example, because the defendant is not domiciled in a Member State), proceedings will normally be stayed (if service is effected in England)[531] or permission to serve out of the jurisdiction will normally be refused (if the claimant seeks to rely on CPR rule 6.36).[532] Although a non-exclusive jurisdiction clause may create a strong prima facie case that the contractual forum is the appropriate one,[533] such a clause is not conclusive.[534]

2.242 Notwithstanding the foreign jurisdiction clause, the court may, in the exercise of its discretion, assume jurisdiction if 'strong cause' is shown by the claimant.[535] The court may, for example, decide to assume jurisdiction if there are related proceedings already being conducted in England and there will be significant advantages—in terms of convenience and expense—if the claimant is permitted to sue the defendant in England.[536] The mere fact that the claimant has failed to bring proceedings in the contractual forum within the limitation period is not a sufficient cause for allowing proceedings to be brought in England.[537] However, if the limitation period has expired in the contractual forum and it was not unreasonable for the claimant not to have started proceedings within the limitation period, a stay of proceedings may be refused (unless the defendant undertakes to waive the time bar in the contractual forum).[538]

2.243 If the claimant can establish that he will not receive a fair trial in the contractual forum—for example for political or racial reasons—the English court may allow the claimant to sue in England in breach of the terms of the jurisdiction agreement. For example, in *Carvalho v Hull, Blyth (Angola) Ltd*[539] the plaintiff, who had fled Angola shortly after the start of the civil war, was able to sue the defendant in England even though the parties' contract (which had been concluded before the civil war) referred disputes to the Angolan courts. The court refused to grant a stay of the English proceedings not only because the post-revolution Angolan court was completely different from the court contemplated by the parties at the time of the contract[540] but also because there was a question whether the plaintiff would be treated fairly by the Angolan courts in view of the fact that he 'was the sort of person who would be anathema to the [new] government in Angola'.[541]

---

[530] For discussion of the position where the parties have agreed to the jurisdiction of a non-Member State and the English court's jurisdiction is based on the Brussels I Recast, see paras 2.270–2.280.
[531] *The Nile Rhapsody* [1994] 1 Lloyd's Rep 382; *The Pioneer Container* [1994] 2 AC 324.
[532] *Mackender v Feldia AG* [1967] 2 QB 590; *Ingosstrakh Insurance Co Ltd v Latvian Shipping Company* [2000] ILPr 164; *Konkola Copper Mines plc v Coromin Ltd (No 2)* [2002] 2 All ER (Comm) 400.
[533] *The Rothnie* [1996] 2 Lloyd's Rep 206; *Import Export Metro Ltd v Compania Sud Americana de Vapores SA* [2003] 1 Lloyd's Rep 405.
[534] *BP plc v Aon Ltd* [2006] 1 Lloyd's Rep 549.
[535] *The Eleftheria* [1970] P 94; *Evans Marshall & Co Ltd v Bertola SA* [1973] 1 WLR 349. See Peel, 'Exclusive Jurisdiction Agreements: Purity and Pragmatism in the Conflict of Laws' [1998] LMCLQ 182.
[536] *The El Amria* [1981] 2 Lloyd's Rep 119; *Citi-March Ltd v Neptune Orient Lines Ltd* [1996] 1 WLR 1367. See also *The MC Pearl* [1997] 1 Lloyd's Rep 566.
[537] *The Pioneer Container* [1994] 2 AC 324.
[538] *Baghlaf Al Zafer Factory Co BR for Industry Ltd v Pakistan National Shipping Co* [1998] 2 Lloyd's Rep 229.
[539] [1979] 1 WLR 1228.
[540] Before the civil war, Angolan courts applied Portuguese law and there was a right to appeal to the Supreme Court in Lisbon.
[541] Geoffrey Lane LJ at 1241.

(C) The Hague Choice of Court Convention

2.244 In the 1990s the Hague Conference on Private International Law started work on what, it was hoped, would result in a worldwide convention along the lines of the Brussels Convention. In fact, the result of negotiations was the Hague Choice of Court Convention which, in basic structure, looks much more like the New York Convention of 1958 (which makes provision for the enforcement of arbitration agreements and for the recognition and enforcement of arbitral awards) than the Brussels Convention (which is a comprehensive jurisdiction and judgments convention). The Choice of Court Convention, which was signed in 2005 and entered into force between Mexico and the Member States of the European Union (except Denmark) on 1 October 2015,[542] seeks to promote both the enforcement of jurisdiction agreements and the recognition and enforcement of judgments in cases where the court of origin assumed jurisdiction on the basis of a choice of court clause.

2.245 The Hague Convention, which applies to 'exclusive choice of court agreements concluded in civil or commercial matters',[543] determines the jurisdictional impact of exclusive jurisdiction agreements in favour of the courts of a Contracting State. If a choice of court agreement designates an EU Member State as the contractual forum, the Convention applies in cases where one of the parties is resident in a Contracting State to the Convention which is not an EU Member State. So, if one of the parties is resident in Mexico, a choice of court agreement in favour of the English courts falls within the scope of the Hague Convention, rather than the Brussels I Recast.

2.246 The basic jurisdiction rules in article 5 of the Convention are that the contractual forum 'shall have jurisdiction to decide a dispute to which the agreement applies, unless the agreement is null and void under the law of that State' and that the contractual forum 'shall not decline to exercise jurisdiction on the ground that the dispute should be decided in a court of another State'. Article 5 of the Convention does not bring about a significant change to the circumstances in which the English court assumes jurisdiction. Notwithstanding the fact that, under the traditional rules that applied before the entry into force of the Convention, the English court had a discretion in cases involving jurisdiction clauses, there appears to be no reported case in which the English court has failed to assume jurisdiction in a situation where the parties concluded an exclusive jurisdiction agreement in favour of the English courts.

2.247 What is the situation where the contractual forum is a Contracting State to the Convention which is not an EU Member State? If proceedings are brought in England (for example, on the basis of the defendant's presence in England or under CPR rule 6.36), the court is normally required by article 6 to 'suspend or dismiss proceedings to which an exclusive choice of court agreement applies'. However, article 6 of the

---

[542] The Convention has also been signed by the United States and Singapore.
[543] Art 1(1). Various matters are excluded, such as family law issues, consumer contracts, and employments contracts: art 1(2).

Convention provides that a choice of court agreement (or an alleged agreement) in favour of the courts of a Contracting State is not a bar to the assumption of jurisdiction by the courts of another Contracting State in five situations:

(a) the agreement is null and void under the law of the State of the chosen court;

(b) a party lacked the capacity to conclude the agreement under the law of the State of the court seised;

(c) giving effect to the agreement would lead to a manifest injustice or would be manifestly contrary to the public policy of the State of the court seised;

(d) for exceptional reasons beyond the control of the parties, the agreement cannot reasonably be performed; or

(e) the chosen court has decided not to hear the case.

2.248 Although a case like *Carvalho v Hull, Blyth (Angola) Ltd*[544] would most probably be decided in the same way under the Convention (on the basis of article 6(c)), the English court will, as a general rule, be unable to assume jurisdiction in cases where the contractual forum is a Contracting State to the Convention.

(D) Cases involving an arbitration clause

2.249 What position should the courts adopt in a situation where one party to an arbitration agreement starts legal proceedings in breach of the terms of that agreement? The issues raised by this type of situation are similar to those surrounding jurisdiction agreements. However, in this situation, the discretionary doctrines of English private international law are not relevant as the situation is governed by the provisions of the Arbitration Act 1996 which implement article II of the New York Convention of 1958. One of the purposes of the New York Convention was to ensure that arbitration agreements are respected and enforced. Where legal proceedings are brought in breach of an arbitration agreement, article II of the Convention obliges the courts of Contracting States to refer the parties to arbitration.

2.250 The English courts are required to grant a stay of proceedings only if a number of conditions are satisfied. First, the defendant must establish that there is an arbitration agreement between the parties,[545] which must be 'in writing'.[546] The expression 'in writing' is given a broad definition; the Act extends to agreements which are evidenced in writing[547] and to cases where the parties agree otherwise than in writing to terms which are in writing.[548] So, where a printed clause is orally or tacitly accepted (so that it becomes a term of the contract) it satisfies the formal requirements of the English

---

[544] [1979] 1 WLR 1228.

[545] For the purposes of s 9 of the Arbitration Act 1996, an agreement that one party, but not the other, may insist on arbitration is an arbitration agreement: *Pittalis v Sherefettin* [1986] QB 868; *NB Three Shipping Ltd v Harebell Shipping Ltd* [2005] 1 Lloyd's Rep 509; *Law Debenture Trust Corporation plc v Elektrim Finance BV* [2005] 2 Lloyd's Rep 755. If the court is not satisfied that an alleged arbitration agreement was ever concluded, a stay under the 1996 Act will be refused: *Albon v Naza Motor Trading Sdn Bhd* [2007] 2 All ER 719. In such a case, the court may, however, grant a discretionary stay under its inherent jurisdiction.

[546] S 5.   [547] S 5(2)(c).   [548] S 5(4).

legislation.[549] It is also provided that an agreement is 'in writing' if it is recorded by any means.[550]

2.251 Secondly, the legal proceedings in question must be 'in respect of a matter which under the agreement is to be referred to arbitration'.[551] To have the right to a stay the defendant needs to satisfy the court that the dispute falls within the arbitrator's jurisdiction. The court may have to decide, for example, whether the arbitration agreement is broad enough to cover a claim in tort brought by one party to the agreement against another or whether the dispute between parties can be said to be 'in relation to' the agreement between the parties. Such questions must be determined by reference to the proper law of the arbitration agreement. Under English law, the court will assume that the parties are likely to have intended any dispute arising out of the relationship between them to be decided by the same tribunal.[552] Accordingly, the tendency is to construe arbitration agreements broadly, rather than narrowly.[553]

2.252 Thirdly, the subject-matter of the dispute must be capable of settlement by arbitration.[554] Although the majority of commercial disputes are arbitrable,[555] there are limits. Because of the consensual nature of arbitration, an arbitrator cannot determine certain types of dispute which have implications not only for the parties. For example, an arbitrator cannot make an award in rem in a shipping dispute or make a binding award winding up a company.

2.253 Fourthly, the defendant in legal proceedings must apply for a stay after acknowledging the legal proceedings against him, but before submitting to the court's jurisdiction by taking a step in those proceedings to answer the substantive claim.[556] A party who applies for a stay but, subsequently or simultaneously, invokes or accepts the court's jurisdiction conditionally on the application for a stay failing, has not taken a step in the proceedings.[557]

2.254 If these conditions are satisfied, the defendant is, in principle, entitled to a stay and it is irrelevant that there would be potential advantages if the parties' dispute were considered by the court (for example, in a case where the dispute involves three parties, only two of whom are bound by the arbitration agreement).[558] By the same token, the

---

[549] See *Zambia Steel and Building Supplies Ltd v James Clark & Eaton Ltd* [1986] 2 Lloyd's Rep 225 (a case decided under the Arbitration Act 1975).
[550] S 5(6). [551] S 9(1).
[552] *Fiona Trust & Holding Corporation v Privalov* [2007] 4 All ER 951.
[553] *Lombard North Central plc v GATX Corp* [2012] 1 CLC 884; *Starlight Shipping Co v Allianz Marine & Aviation Versicherungs AG* [2014] 1 All ER 590. But, compare *Ryanair Ltd v Esso Italiana Srl* [2015] 1 All ER (Comm) 152.
[554] S 81(1)(a).
[555] For example, claims for breach of competition law under arts 101 and 102 TFEU are arbitrable: *Et Plus SA v Welter* [2006] 1 Lloyd's Rep 251; as regards claims under the Companies Act 2008, see *Fulham Football Club (1987) Ltd v Richards* [2012] Ch 333.
[556] S 9(3). See *Patel v Patel* [2000] QB 551; *Bilta (UK) Ltd v Nazir* [2010] 2 Lloyd's Rep 29.
[557] *Capital Trust Investments Ltd v Radio Design TJ AB* [2002] 2 All ER 159.
[558] *Wealands v CLC Contractors Ltd* [1999] 2 Lloyd's Rep 739.

court cannot refuse to grant a stay on the basis that the defendant has no prospect of successfully defending the claim and it would be quicker and cheaper if the court made a summary judgment under the procedure provided by Part 24 of the CPR.[559] If there is a dispute between the parties—that is to say, where the claimant advances a claim which the defendant does not admit—the grant of a stay is mandatory.[560] Attempts by litigants to persuade the court that the grant of a mandatory stay under section 9 of the Arbitration Act 1996 is inconsistent with the right to a fair trial under article 6 of the European Convention on Human Rights have not met with success.[561]

2.255 However, the defendant's prima facie right to a stay may be defeated. First, a stay will be refused if the claimant satisfies the court (on the balance of probabilities) that the arbitration agreement is 'null and void, inoperative or incapable of being performed'.[562] Whether or not the agreement is valid should also be referred to its proper law.[563] If D denies the existence of an arbitration agreement and C unequivocally accepts D's repudiation by commencing litigation, the arbitration agreement ceases to be operative and D cannot seek to revive the arbitration agreement and obtain a stay of proceedings under section 9 of the Arbitration Act 1996.[564] Conversely, an arbitration agreement does not become inoperative by virtue of an ICC arbitration being suspended because one of the parties refuses to bear its share of the advance costs of the arbitration.[565]

4. Cases involving immovable property or intellectual property rights not regulated by the Brussels I Recast

2.256 In a situation which falls within the scope of the Recast, article 24(1) provides that proceedings relating to rights in rem in, or tenancies of, immovable property are within the exclusive jurisdiction of the courts of the Member State in which the property is situated. However, the Brussels I Recast does not determine jurisdiction either if the subject-matter of the dispute is outside the scope of article 1 (for example, because it involves rights in property arising out of a matrimonial relationship) or if the immovable property in question is not situated in a Member State and the defendant is not domiciled in a Member State. These situations are governed by the traditional rules.

2.257 At common law, under the rule in *British South Africa Co v Companhia de Moçambique*,[566] the English court will not adjudicate on questions relating to the title to, or the right to the possession of, immovable property[567] out of the jurisdiction. Accordingly, in a case involving title to land in Brazil, the English court will not assume

---

[559] *Halki Shipping Corpn v Sopex Oils Ltd* [1998] 1 WLR 726.
[560] See Swinton Thomas LJ at 761. Even if the case is not one in which a stay is mandatory under the 1996 Act, the court may grant a stay under its inherent jurisdiction: *Channel Tunnel Group Ltd v Balfour Beatty Construction Ltd* [1993] AC 334; *T&N Ltd v Royal & Sun Alliance plc* [2002] CLC 1342; *A v B* [2007] 1 Lloyd's Rep 237.
[561] See, eg, *Stretford v Football Association Ltd* [2007] 2 Lloyd's Rep 31.   [562] S 9(4).
[563] See *Sulamérica Cia Nacional de Seguros SA v Enesa Engelharia SA* [2013] 1 WLR 102.
[564] *Downing v Al Tameer Establishment* [2002] 2 All ER (Comm) 545.
[565] *BDMS Ltd v Rafael Advanced Defence Systems* [2015] 1 All ER (Comm) 627.
[566] [1893] AC 602.
[567] For the distinction between movable and immovable property, see paras 9.1–9.5.

jurisdiction even if the claimant can serve the Brazilian defendant with the claim form in England or can invoke some other basis of jurisdiction recognised by the traditional rules.

2.258 Although the origin of the common law rule may have lain in procedural requirements, the justification for it today is, first, that, as immovable property is under the control of the authorities of the country where it is situated, whose law may refuse to recognise an English judgment relating to the property, such an exercise of jurisdiction would quite possibly be ineffective and, secondly, that the courts of the situs are the ones best able to apply their own often technical and complex rules about title to land.

2.259 In *Norris v Chambres*[568] the plaintiff had contracted to buy foreign land and paid a deposit to the vendor. The vendor repudiated the contract and sold the land to the defendant. The plaintiff brought proceedings against the defendant in England claiming that he was entitled to a lien over the land in respect of the deposit he had paid. The court held that it had no jurisdiction to decide whether the plaintiff had such a right over foreign land. The same approach is illustrated by *Deschamps v Miller*.[569] The plaintiff's father had acquired lands in India and subsequently transferred them to the defendant. The plaintiff claimed that his mother had been entitled, by virtue of the proprietary consequences of her marriage, to a half-share in the property and that, on his mother's death, he was entitled to succeed to this half-share. The court held that it lacked jurisdiction to decide the question.

2.260 Until late in the twentieth century the law was that the English court would not assume jurisdiction in respect of a tort affecting foreign land.[570] Section 30 of the Civil Jurisdiction and Judgments Act 1982 provides that the court is not deprived of jurisdiction in such a case 'unless the proceedings are principally concerned with a question of the title to, or the right to possession of' the property.[571]

2.261 While the court will not assume jurisdiction on a question as to the title to, or a right to possession of, a foreign immovable, it does not follow that it must not deal with any case having a connection with such property. For example, the court may exercise jurisdiction in rem against a ship to enforce a claim for damage done to foreign land.[572] More importantly, if the court has jurisdiction in contractual proceedings, that jurisdiction will not be ousted because the contract relates to foreign land. Moreover, the court will enforce an obligation arising from such a contract, or from a trust or some other source, not merely by an award of damages or other monetary relief, but even by ordering a party to transfer or create a right in foreign land.[573] In such a case, the court is not adjudicating on the present title to the land, on which

---

[568] (1861) 29 Beav 246; affd 3 De GF & J 583.   [569] [1908] 1 Ch 856.
[570] *British South Africa Co v Companhia de Moçambique* [1893] AC 602; *Hesperides Hotels Ltd v Muftizade* [1979] AC 508.
[571] See, eg, *Re Polly Peck International plc (in administration) (No 4)* [1998] 2 BCLC 185.
[572] *The Tolten* [1946] P 135.   [573] See *Hamed v Stevens* [2013] ILPr 37.

its decision may be ineffective; its order to transfer or create a title can be enforced in personam[574]—by committing the defendant for contempt if he does not comply with the order. However, the court will not order a party to do in relation to foreign land something which the law of the foreign country would not permit or enable him to do.[575]

2.262 A court may make a decree of specific performance in relation to the sale of foreign land[576] and may order a party to execute a mortgage over foreign land in fulfilment of a contractual promise to do so.[577] The court may also enforce an obligation to transfer or create a right in foreign land arising from 'a fiduciary relationship or fraud, or other conduct which, in the view of the Court of Equity in this country, would be unconscionable'.[578] Such orders cannot actually affect the title of foreign land; if, however, the defendant is amenable to the jurisdiction of the English court, such orders can be enforced in personam.[579]

2.263 The situations just considered are not exceptions to the rule that the English court will not adjudicate on the title to or right to possession of foreign immovables, but rather, fall outside its scope. There are, however, a number of true exceptions. First, where the court has jurisdiction over a deceased's estate which includes property in England the court will also determine entitlement to immovable property situated outside England which is part of that estate.[580] The basis of this jurisdiction, which is far from obvious, has not been satisfactorily explained by the courts, but the jurisdiction seems to be established. It should be noted that, because such proceedings fall outside the scope of the Brussels I Recast (which does not apply to wills and succession), this jurisdiction applies equally to immovable property in Member States and third states. Secondly, 'in the exercise of the undoubted jurisdiction of the courts it may become necessary incidentally to investigate and determine the title to foreign lands'.[581] It is not clear what cases would fall within this category.[582]

2.264 As regards foreign intellectual property (IP) rights, it has long been accepted that the *Moçambique* rule applies to registered interests (such as patents and registered trademarks) in the same way as foreign land; such interests are treated (by analogy) as territorial in nature.[583] Whether the same approach should be taken to unregistered IP rights has been the subject of controversy. In *Lucasfilm Ltd v Ainsworth*[584] the Supreme

---

[574] *Penn v Lord Baltimore* (1750) 1 Ves Sen 444. See the discussion by Wass, 'The Court's *in Personam* Jurisdiction in Cases Involving Foreign Land' (2014) 63 ICLQ 103.
[575] *Re Courtney* (1840) Mont & Ch 239.
[576] *Richard West & Partners (Inverness) Ltd v Dick* [1969] 2 Ch 424.
[577] *Re Smith* [1916] 2 Ch 206.   [578] *Deschamps v Miller* [1908] 1 Ch 856 at 863.
[579] See *Razelos v Razelos (No 2)* [1970] 1 WLR 392; *Hamlin v Hamlin* [1986] Fam 11. See also the obiter discussion in *R Griggs Group Ltd v Evans* [2005] Ch 153.
[580] *Re Ross* [1930] 1 Ch 377; *Re Duke of Wellington* [1948] Ch 118.
[581] *British South Africa Co v Companhia de Moçambique* [1893] AC 602.
[582] An example might be *Adams v Clutterbuck* (1883) 10 QBD 403 (which concerned a document executed in England conveying shooting rights over moorland in Scotland).
[583] See *Coin Controls Ltd v Suzo International (UK) Ltd* [1999] Ch 33.
[584] [2012] 1 AC 208.

Court undertook an exhaustive review of the scope of the non-justiciability rule derived from the *Moçambique* case[585] and concluded that, if the court has in personam jurisdiction over the defendant, claims relating to unregistered foreign IP rights can be pursued in England.

5. If jurisdiction is derived from the Brussels I Recast, is there any residual discretion in cases involving connections with non-Member States?

(A) Background and general principles

2.265 Apart from the specific provisions of the Brussels I Recast which set out the circumstances in which proceedings must (or may) be stayed,[586] the court has no general discretion under the Recast to stay proceedings. For example, where an English defendant is sued in England in relation to a road accident which occurred in France, the court cannot stay the proceedings on the basis that France is a more appropriate forum; this type of case is governed solely by the Brussels I Recast.[587] One of the most hotly debated questions under the 2002 Regulation was whether the English court may, in cases where its jurisdiction is derived from Chapter II, stay proceedings or decline jurisdiction in favour of the courts of a third state—whether in reliance on the doctrine of forum non conveniens or on some other basis.

2.266 According to the doctrine propounded by the Court of Appeal in *Re Harrods (Buenos Aires) Ltd*,[588] in a case where jurisdiction is based on the defendant's domicile in England the English court may grant a stay if the defendant satisfies the court that a non-Member State is a more appropriate forum. However, such were the question-marks over whether the *Harrods* case had been correctly decided,[589] it was widely recognised that, sooner or later, the issue would have to be referred to the Court of Justice.[590]

2.267 In *Owusu v Jackson*[591] C, who was domiciled in England, suffered personal injuries when diving into the sea at a private beach in Jamaica. C had been staying in a villa let to him by D1, also domiciled in England. C started English proceedings against D1 (for breach of an implied contractual term that the beach was reasonably safe) and several Jamaican companies, including the owner of the beach (for failing to warn swimmers of potential dangers). The Court of Appeal sought an answer from the Court of Justice to the question whether the English court was permitted to

---

[585] [1893] AC 602.
[586] As regards arts 29, 30, 33, and 34 of the Brussels I Recast, see paras 2.180–2.211.
[587] See, eg, *Mahme Trust Reg v Lloyds TSB Bank plc* [2004] 2 Lloyd's Rep 637; *Gomez v Gomez-Moche Vives* [2008] 3 WLR 309, affd (without consideration of the forum non conveniens point) [2009] Ch 245.
[588] [1992] Ch 72.
[589] See Lord Bingham in *Lubbe v Cape plc* [2000] 1 WLR 1545 at 1562.
[590] *Re Harrods (Buenos Aires) Ltd* was appealed to the House of Lords, which referred a number of questions to the Court of Justice (Case C–314/92), but before the reference was heard the dispute was settled.
[591] Case C–281/02 [2005] ECR I–1383. See Briggs, 'Forum Non Conveniens and Ideal Europeans' [2005] LMCLQ 378; Hare, 'Forum non conveniens in Europe: Game Over or Time for "Reflexion"?' [2006] JBL 157; Harris, 'Stays of Proceedings and the Brussels Convention' (2005) 54 ICLQ 933; Peel, 'Forum Non Conveniens and European Ideals' [2005] LMCLQ 363.

stay the proceedings against D1 on the ground that Jamaica was a more appropriate forum.[592]

2.268 The Court of Justice had no hesitation in concluding that, where a national court has jurisdiction on the basis of the defendant's domicile, it is precluded from declining that jurisdiction on the ground that a third state would be a more appropriate forum for the trial—even if there are no connecting factors linking the situation to any other Member State. In reaching this conclusion, the Court of Justice emphasised various points: (i) the domicile rule (article 4 of the Recast) is mandatory in nature; (ii) principles of legal certainty and predictability would be undermined if a national court were permitted to stay proceedings on a discretionary basis; (iii) as the doctrine of forum non conveniens is found in the laws of only some of the Member States, it would adversely affect the uniform application of Brussels I if those states were allowed to apply the doctrine in cases where jurisdiction is derived from article 4. Although the ruling in *Owusu v Jackson* refers only to cases where the national court's jurisdiction is based on the defendant's domicile,[593] the logic of the decision applies equally to situations involving other bases of jurisdiction under the Brussels I Recast (such as article 7[594] or article 25[595]).

(B) Cases where the grant of a stay is not inconsistent with the Brussels I Regulation

2.269 In a case which is internal to the United Kingdom and is governed entirely by schedule 4 to the Civil Jurisdiction and Judgments Act 1982, the Recast does not inhibit the discretion of the English court to stay proceedings in favour of the courts of Scotland or Northern Ireland.[596] In addition, where the English court is authorised by article 6 of the Brussels I Recast to assume jurisdiction under the traditional rules, a stay may be granted on the basis of forum non conveniens whether the alternative forum is a third state or another Member State.[597] Where, for example, process in relation to a dispute arising out of a road traffic accident in Germany is served on a New York resident during a fleeting visit to England, the English court should be able to stay the English proceedings on the ground that Germany is a more appropriate forum. If parallel or related proceedings have already been commenced in another Member State the English court must apply articles 29 and 30 before considering whether to grant a stay under its inherent jurisdiction.

(C) Outstanding questions

2.270 In *Owusu v Jackson* the Court of Appeal not only referred the question whether, in that case, the English court was precluded from granting a stay in favour of the Jamaican

---

[592] [2002] ILPr 45.
[593] For application of the *Owusu* ruling, see *Blue Tropic Ltd v Chkhartishvili* [2014] ILPr 33.
[594] *Gomez v Gomez-Moche Vives* [2008] 3 WLR 309.
[595] *Equitas Ltd v Allstate Insurance Co* [2009] 1 All ER (Comm) 1137; *UBS AG v HSH Nordbank AG* [2009] 2 Lloyd's Rep 272.
[596] *Cook v Virgin Media Ltd* [2016] ILPr 6.
[597] *The Xin Yang* [1996] 2 Lloyd's Rep 217; *Sarrio SA v Kuwait Investment Authority* [1997] 1 Lloyd's Rep 113.

courts on the basis of forum non conveniens, but also asked what the position would be in a case where the parties had agreed to the jurisdiction of the courts of a third state or where the dispute related to immovable property situated in a non-Member State or where parallel or related proceedings had been started in a third state before the commencement of proceedings in England. Although some consideration of this second question could have resolved several difficult issues, the Court of Justice declined to provide an answer on the basis that, in the *Owusu* case itself, this question was entirely hypothetical.

2.271 One potential approach to the second question is to take the Court of Justice at its word and to extrapolate the decision in *Owusu* to the three types of case to which the Court of Appeal referred in its second question. In its ruling in *Owusu* the Court of Justice stated that what is now article 4 of the Recast 'is mandatory in nature and . . . according to its terms, there can be no derogation from the principle it lays down except in the cases expressly provided for'.[598] If this statement is to be understood literally, the answer to the Court of Appeal's second question is that, if a national court has jurisdiction under article 4, proceedings may be stayed or jurisdiction declined only on the basis of articles 33 and 34 of the Recast. This position was adopted by the Irish High Court[599] and the same approach was taken in England by Barling J in *Catalyst Investment Group Ltd v Lewinsohn*.[600]

2.272 In policy terms, however, this absolutist view of article 4 has little to recommend it. Within the framework of the Brussels I Recast, article 4 is subordinate to other provisions in Chapter II. The provisions which take priority over article 4 reflect important policy choices of general application—such as (i) the allocation of exclusive jurisdiction in cases where the subject-matter of the dispute is very closely connected with a particular place (article 24), (ii) the enforcement of jurisdiction agreements (article 25) and (iii) the avoidance of parallel and related proceedings (articles 29 and 30).

2.273 Although the Brussels I Recast, unlike the Convention and the 2002 Regulation, includes provisions addressing parallel proceedings and related actions in third states (articles 33 and 34), these provisions—which, like articles 29 and 30, give priority to the court first seised—do not offer a convincing solution to the problems posed by jurisdiction agreements in favour of the courts of third states or by cases where the dispute is so closely connected with a third state that the courts of that state should be regarded as having exclusive jurisdiction. If, for example, the English court has to decline jurisdiction over proceedings brought against a defendant domiciled in England when the dispute falls within the scope of a jurisdiction clause in favour of the courts of another Member State, there is every reason to think that the court should also decline jurisdiction in a case where the parties' agreement refers the dispute to the courts of a

---

[598] Case C-281/02 [2005] ECR I-1383, para 37.
[599] *Goshawk Dedicated Ltd v Life Receivables Ireland Ltd* [2008] ILPr 50. The issue was subsequently referred to the Court of Justice by the Irish Supreme Court [2009] ILPr 26, but the case was resolved before the reference was heard.
[600] [2010] Ch 218. See also the observations in *Skype Technologies SA v Joltid Ltd* [2011] ILPr 8.

non-Member State. Whether the English court was first seised or second seised should not be the most significant factor. The same argument can be made with regard to disputes relating to immovable property. Furthermore, if a Member State court is not able to stay proceedings in such cases, there is a serious danger that practical problems will be generated by the fact that the same issues will be litigated both in a third state and a Member State. As Lawrence Collins LJ stated in *Masri v Consolidated Contractors International (UK) Ltd (No 2)*,[601] it would be odd if the English courts were not able to grant a stay of proceedings in the types of situation identified by the Court of Appeal in its second question in *Owusu*. All the practical arguments point towards a national court being able to decline jurisdiction in a situation involving connections with a non-Member State if the circumstances are such that jurisdiction would have been declined (or the proceedings stayed) had the connection in question been with a Member State.

2.274 Within the authorities, there are indications that the approach adopted in cases such as *Catalyst Investment Group Ltd v Lewinsohn* does not command universal support. The case law of the Court of Justice does not unequivocally support the absolutist approach; in *Owusu v Jackson* itself, both the Advocate General and the Court were at pains to make clear that they were not purporting to provide an answer to the Court of Appeal's second question. Accordingly, it would be somewhat perverse to regard the *Owusu* doctrine as providing the definitive answer to the whole range of problems which may arise where a dispute has connections with both a Member State and a third state. For example, before the *Owusu* case was decided, the Court of Justice seems to have accepted the idea that a Member State court may give effect to a jurisdiction clause in favour of the courts of a third state; in *Coreck Maritime GmbH v Handelsveem BV*[602] the Court of Justice stated that the validity of a jurisdiction clause in favour of the courts of a non-Member State is governed by its applicable law (as determined by the forum's choice of law rules). This part of the judgment appears implicitly to accept that, in a case where a Member State court decides that a jurisdiction clause in favour of a third state is valid, the court is entitled to give effect to the jurisdiction clause under its national law (for example, by staying its proceedings or declining jurisdiction), even if its jurisdiction is derived from the Brussels I Recast.[603]

2.275 There are also several English authorities which have rejected the notion that the *Owusu* doctrine applies in the types of cases identified by the Court of Appeal's second question in the *Owusu* case.[604] For example, in *Winnetka Trading Corp v Julius Baer*

---

[601] [2009] QB 450 at [125].
[602] Case C-387/98 [2000] ECR I-9337, para 19.
[603] If an agreement confers jurisdiction on the courts of a third state which is a party to the Hague Choice of Court Convention, the courts of Member States are (normally) required by art 6 of the Convention to suspend or dismiss proceedings brought in breach of the agreement. See paras 2.244–2.248.
[604] There is also a line of cases in which the court has side-stepped having to decide the issue: *Karafarin Bank v Mansoury-dara* [2009] 2 Lloyd's Rep 289; *Choudhary v Bhattar* [2010] 2 All ER 1031; *Deutsche Bank AG v Sebastian Holdings Inc* [2010] 1 All ER (Comm) 808; *Royal & Sun Alliance Insurance plc v Rolls-Royce plc* [2010] 2 CLC 84.

International Ltd[605] it was held that the English court may stay its proceedings in a case where the dispute falls within the scope of a jurisdiction clause in favour of the courts of a non-Member State, notwithstanding the fact that the court's jurisdiction is derived from Brussels I.[606]

2.276 If such a power to grant a stay or to decline jurisdiction exists, what is its legal basis? The most plausible answer to this question is that the relevant provisions of the Recast (in particular, articles 24 and 25) should be given so-called 'reflexive effect'.[607] In *Ferrexpo AG v Gilson Investments Ltd*[608] Andrew Smith J, having referred to the analysis in the fourth edition of this work, explicitly rejected the approach adopted in the *Catalyst* case and held that the provision which is now article 24 of the Recast should be applied reflexively in cases with an appropriate connection with a third state. But, exactly how the doctrine of 'reflexive effect' (if it exists) should operate is contentious. Theories of 'reflexive effect' may take one of a number of forms.

2.277 First, according to the most flexible approach, national courts should retain discretion under national law in cases which, in broad terms, involve the types of issues that are addressed by article 24 of the Recast and jurisdiction clauses in favour of the courts of a non-Member State. This approach, which appeals to some English courts,[609] does not depend on it being shown that, if the relevant connection were with a Member State rather than a non-Member State, the conditions of article 24 or 25 (as the case may be) would have been satisfied. However, the considerable hostility shown by the Court of Justice in *Owusu* to the operation of discretionary principles in the field of civil jurisdiction suggests that a version of the 'reflexive effect' theory which preserves the traditional English approach to the staying of proceedings is not the correct solution.[610]

2.278 Secondly, the doctrine of 'reflexive effect' may enable a Member State court to rely on domestic doctrines in cases where, had there been an equivalent connection with a Member State, the court would have been obliged by the Recast to decline jurisdiction. According to this approach, in a case where the parties, one of whom is domiciled in England, enter a contract which includes a New York jurisdiction clause, if the English party is sued in England, the court may rely on the *Eleftheria* test and, in the exercise of its discretion, stay its proceedings (or decide not to do so)—even though the court would have been obliged by article 25 to decline jurisdiction if the contractual forum

---

[605] [2009] 2 All ER (Comm) 735.
[606] See also *Konkola Copper Mines plc v Coromin Ltd* [2005] 2 All ER (Comm) 637 (in which the same view was expressed obiter).
[607] This possibility is alluded to (but neither approved nor rejected) by Advocate General Léger in Case C–281/02 *Owusu v Jackson* [2005] ECR I–1383, para 70.
[608] [2012] 1 Lloyd's Rep 528; De Verneuil Smith, Lasser and Rymkiewicz, 'Reflections on *Owusu*: The Radical Decision in *Ferrexpo*' (2012) 8 Journal of Private International Law 389; Goodwin (2013) 129 LQR 317.
[609] See, eg, *Konkola Copper Mines v Coromin Ltd* [2005] 2 All ER (Comm) 637.
[610] For a conflicting view, see Briggs, 'Forum Non Conveniens and Ideal Europeans' [2005] LMCLQ 378; Peel, 'Forum Non Conveniens and European Ideals' [2005] LMCLQ 363. See also Droz, *Compétence Judiciaire et Effets des Jugements dans le Marché Commun* (1972) pp 108–10.

had been a Member State.⁶¹¹ In terms of certainty and predictability, the advantage of this version of the 'reflexive effect' theory is that the circumstances in which a national court may stay proceedings or decline jurisdiction in favour of the courts of a third state are determined with precision (albeit indirectly) by the terms of the Recast itself. However, from the Court of Justice's perspective, the problem with the second version is that it runs the risk of introducing the kind of discretion and lack of uniformity which was considered to be so objectionable in the *Owusu* case. Accordingly, there must be considerable doubt as to whether the Court of Justice is likely to endorse it.

2.279 Thirdly, the strictest version of the 'reflexive effect' theory involves applying provisions of the Recast by analogy as though non-Member States were Member States. According to this approach, a national court has no discretion over whether its proceedings are to be stayed or its jurisdiction declined. Under this strict version of the 'reflexive effect' theory, where English proceedings concerning title to immovable property situated in New York are brought against a defendant domiciled in England, the court must decline jurisdiction if it would have declined jurisdiction had the immovable property been situated in a Member State; the English court must also decline jurisdiction in a case involving a jurisdiction clause in favour of the courts of a non-Member State—as long as the requirements of article 25 would have been satisfied had a Member State been the contractual forum. While this approach is not without its problems, one of its advantages is that it avoids the uncertainty and lack of uniformity which is implicit in allowing the application of doctrines of national law (such as forum non conveniens).

(D) Conclusion

2.280 There is no easy solution to the issues discussed in the preceding paragraphs. Part of the problem is that the provisions of the Recast which seek to regulate the jurisdictional relationship between the courts of Member States and those of third states (articles 33 and 34) adopt a 'first come, first served' approach without distinguishing run-of-the-mill cases from situations which involve either jurisdiction agreements or connecting factors which justify exclusive jurisdiction. Because articles 33 and 34 of the Recast so obviously fail to address the full range of issues surrounding cases involving connections with third states, the doctrine of 'reflexive effect' continues to offer an intellectually attractive solution to the problems generated by the largely inward-looking nature of the provisions of Chapter II.⁶¹² Given that, in *Owusu v Jackson*, the Court of Justice definitively rejected the discretionary approach previously favoured by the English courts, the only practical way of achieving a suitable jurisdictional balance between Member States and non-Member States is to give 'reflexive effect' (in some way) to articles 24 and 25 in cases involving connections with third states. Whether the Court of Justice will decide to adopt one of the possible versions of the 'reflexive effect' theory remains a matter for speculation.

---

⁶¹¹ If and when the United States becomes bound by the Hague Choice of Court Convention, this scenario will be regulated by the Convention. See paras 2.244–2.248. On the *Eleftheria* test, see para 2.242.

⁶¹² By contrast, art 45(1)(d) of the Recast expressly deals with the problem posed by conflicting judgments given by the courts of Member States and third states. See paras 3.123–3.126.

IV Provisional measures

A Introduction

2.281 One of the significant developments in the latter part of the twentieth century was the evolution of certain types of provisional measures designed to maintain the status quo pending the outcome of the dispute between the parties.[613] For example, the English court may grant a freezing injunction (commonly referred to as a Mareva injunction),[614] the purpose of which is to prevent the defendant from moving his assets or dissipating them, so that if the claim is successful there will be assets available to satisfy the judgment. By such orders the courts aim to frustrate the efforts of defendants who seek to make themselves immune from the court's final judgment.

2.282 Where the main proceedings are being conducted in England, plainly the English court has jurisdiction to grant such provisional measures as may be appropriate in the context of those proceedings.[615] More problematic, however, are cases where the main proceedings are being conducted in another country: may the English court grant provisional measures in support of those proceedings? Even more contentious is whether the English court may make orders requiring the defendant to do something or refrain from doing something not in England but in another country.

B Jurisdiction to grant provisional measures in support of foreign proceedings

2.283 Common sense would suggest that if proceedings are pending in one country and the defendant's assets are situated in another, the claimant ought to be able to obtain protective or interim relief by way of attachment in the country where the assets are to be found.[616] After a lengthy period of uncertainty and development, English law finally achieved this position in the 1990s.

1. Proceedings in another Member State (or another part of the United Kingdom)

2.284 Article 35 of the Brussels I Recast provides that application may be made to the courts of a Member State for such provisional, including protective, measures as may be available under the law of that state, even if the courts of another Member State have jurisdiction

---

[613] Collins, 'Provisional and Protective Measures in International Litigation' in *Essays in International Litigation and the Conflict of Laws* (1994) pp 1–188.
[614] Regulation (EU) No 655/2014, 2014 OJ L189/59, established a European Account Preservation Order (which shares several of the characteristics of an English freezing injunction); the United Kingdom, however, did not take part in the adoption of the Regulation and is not bound by it or subject to its application.
[615] Case C-391/95 *Van Uden Maritime BV v Firma Deco-Line* [1998] ECR I-7091; *Masri v Consolidated Contractors International (UK) Ltd (No 2)* [2009] QB 450.
[616] See Collins, 'The Siskina Again: An Opportunity Missed' (1996) 112 LQR 8.

as to the substance of the matter.[617] Although this provision should apply only in relation to matters within the material scope of the Brussels I Recast, the Court of Justice has held that article 35 applies where a claimant seeks provisional measures in support of arbitration proceedings (rather than court proceedings in another Member State) as long as the rights which the claimant is seeking to safeguard are civil or commercial in nature.[618] Article 35 covers measures which are intended to preserve a factual or legal situation in one Member State so as to safeguard rights which are the subject-matter of litigation in a court of another Member State which has jurisdiction as to the substance of the matter.[619] Accordingly, a measure ordering the hearing of a witness so that the applicant can determine whether a potential claim is well founded and decide whether or not to commence proceedings is not a provisional measure for the purposes of article 35.[620] A measure is not within the scope of article 35 if its provisional character is not guaranteed; a court order requiring the defendant to make an unconditional interim payment falls outside article 35 unless the defendant can obtain repayment if the claimant is unsuccessful.[621] Freezing injunctions are provisional measures for the purposes of article 35.

2.285 Article 35 does not in itself confer jurisdiction on an English court to grant a freezing injunction in support of foreign proceedings. It is, however, provided by section 25 of the Civil Jurisdiction and Judgments Act 1982 that the court may grant interim relief in cases where the subject-matter of the litigation falls within the scope of article 1 of the Brussels I Recast and the proceedings have been commenced or are to be commenced in a Member State other than the United Kingdom (or in another part of the United Kingdom), whether or not the defendant is otherwise amenable to the jurisdiction of the court. Where proceedings have been commenced in France, the claimant may apply to the English court for an injunction freezing the defendant's assets, even though the court does not have jurisdiction over the substantive claim.[622] The power to grant interim relief in support of proceedings in another Member State exists whether or not the defendant is domiciled in a Member State.

2. Proceedings in a third state and proceedings outside the scope of article 1 of the Brussels I Recast

2.286 At common law, the English court does not have jurisdiction to order provisional measures in support of foreign proceedings.[623] Towards the end of the twentieth

---

[617] Sch 4 to the Civil Jurisdiction and Judgments Act 1982 (r 16) lays down the same rule for cases where the courts of another part of the United Kingdom have jurisdiction as to the substantive proceedings. Art 35 is not precluded in a case where the other Member State court has exclusive jurisdiction under art 24: Case C–616/10 *Solvay SA v Honeywell Fluorine Products Europe BV*, unreported.

[618] Case C–391/95 *Van Uden Maritime BV v Firma Deco-Line* [1998] ECR I–7091. But, see the doubts expressed by Petrochilos, 'Arbitration and Interim Measures: In the Twilight of the Brussels Convention' [2000] LMCLQ 99.

[619] Case C–261/90 *Reichert v Dresdner Bank AG (No 2)* [1992] ECR I–2149, para 34.

[620] Case C–104/03 *St Paul Dairy Industries NV v Unibel Exser BVBA* [2005] ECR I–3481.

[621] Case C–391/95 *Van Uden Maritime BV v Firma Deco-Line* [1998] ECR I–7091; Case C–99/96 *Mietz v Intership Yachting Sneek BV* [1999] ECR I–2277. See also *Wermuth v Wermuth* [2003] 1 WLR 942.

[622] See *Republic of Haiti v Duvalier* [1990] 1 QB 202.

[623] *Siskina (Owners of cargo lately laden on board) v Distos Compania Naviera SA* [1979] AC 210.

century the position at common law came under considerable criticism and, in due course, section 25 of the Civil Jurisdiction and Judgments Act 1982 was extended not only to cases falling outside the scope of article 1 but also to cases covered by article 1 involving proceedings in a non-Member State.[624] However, the foreign proceedings must be court proceedings on the substance of the dispute between the parties; under section 25 of the 1982 Act, the English court may not grant provisional measures in support of an arbitration or in relation to proceedings ancillary to an arbitration which are pending in another country.[625]

3. Procedural issues

2.287 Where a claim is made for an interim remedy under section 25 of the 1982 Act, the Civil Procedure Rules make provision for the claim form to be served out of the jurisdiction with the permission of the court.[626] There is no requirement that the foreign proceedings in respect of which the interim remedy is sought should be international in nature; where a French claimant sues a French defendant in France, the English court is not prevented from giving permission to serve out.[627] Furthermore, the English court may grant a freezing injunction to support foreign proceedings even before the foreign proceedings have been commenced; it is sufficient that such proceedings are intended.[628]

4. Discretion

2.288 In the context of an application for interim relief under section 25 of the 1982 Act, the first issue is whether the conditions for the grant of the relief would have been satisfied if the main proceedings had been pending in England. A freezing injunction will not be granted unless the claimant can establish not only that he has a good arguable case on the merits[629] but also that refusal of the order would involve a real risk that a judgment in favour of the claimant would remain unsatisfied.[630] A claimant might reasonably anticipate that, if the application succeeds, the injunction will cover the highest amount in respect of which he has a good arguable case (including a sum for interest and costs).[631] The claimant must normally provide a cross-undertaking in damages to indemnify the defendant for losses in the event of the substantive claim failing or to compensate any third party who suffers injury by reason of the injunction. If, had the main proceedings been commenced in England, the court would not have granted provisional relief, the power conferred by section 25 will not be exercised.

---

[624] The power to extend s 25(1) was provided by s 25(3) of the 1982 Act, which was exercised by the introduction of the Civil Jurisdiction and Judgments Act 1982 (Interim Relief) Order 1997, SI 1997/302.
[625] *ETI Euro Telecom International NV v Republic of Bolivia* [2009] 1 WLR 665.
[626] CPR r 6.36, PD 6B para 3.1(5).   [627] *Alltrans Inc v Interdom Holdings Ltd* [1991] 4 All ER 458.
[628] *Fourie v Le Roux* [2007] 1 WLR 320.
[629] For the meaning of 'good arguable case' in this context, see *Kazakhstan Kagazy plc v Arip* [2014] 1 CLC 451. For an example of the judge being 'just about satisfied' by the strength of the claimants' case, see Gloster J in *Guerrero v Moterrico Metals plc* [2009] EWHC 2475 (QB) at [26].
[630] *Ninemia Maritime Corpn v Trave Schiffahrtsgesellschaft mbH und Co KG* [1983] 1 WLR 1412; *Refco Inc v Eastern Trading Co* [1999] 1 Lloyd's Rep 159; *Laemthong International Lines Co Ltd v Artis* [2005] 1 Lloyd's Rep 100. If there is no risk of dissipation, an injunction should not be granted: see, eg, *Western Bulk Shipowning III A/S v Carbofer Maritime Trading ApS* [2012] 1 CLC 954.
[631] See *Pacific Maritime (Asia) Ltd v Holystone Overseas Ltd* [2008] 1 Lloyd's Rep 371.

2.289 If, however, the necessary conditions are satisfied the court has to consider whether the fact that the court does not have jurisdiction other than under section 25 makes it inexpedient to grant the interim relief.[632] A significant factor in the inexpediency question is the connection (or lack of it) with England.[633] Equally important is the impact of any order granted by the English court on the foreign proceedings. It would, for example, be inexpedient for jurisdiction under section 25 to be exercised if the grant of interim relief would obstruct or hamper the management of the case by the foreign court seised of the substantive proceedings.[634] Relief will also be refused if an injunction would not support or otherwise assist the substantive proceedings being conducted abroad[635] or if there would be no sanction available against the defendant in the event of his non-compliance with the English order.[636] Where the substantive proceedings are taking place in England, such sanction may take the form of barring a defendant who refuses to comply with the court's order from defending the claim on the merits.[637] Where, however, the application is for a freezing order in support of foreign proceedings, the court normally has no effective sanction for disobedience if the defendant is neither resident in England nor has any assets in England.[638]

C Extraterritorial orders

2.290 As a matter of principle there is no reason why provisional measures granted by the court should be limited to acts performed in England or to assets located in England. If a defendant who is amenable to the court's jurisdiction commits an act in breach of the terms of an injunction, the act amounts to a contempt regardless of whether the act was committed in England or abroad. The court has the power under section 37(1) of the Senior Courts Act 1981 to appoint a receiver over assets which are abroad,[639] to make a search order (frequently referred to as an Anton Piller order) in respect of foreign premises,[640] and to grant a freezing injunction in relation to the defendant's assets, regardless of their location.[641]

---

[632] Civil Jurisdiction and Judgments Act 1983, s 25(2).
[633] *Joint Stock Company VTB Bank v Skurikhin* [2013] 2 All ER (Comm) 418.
[634] *Crédit Suisse Fides Trust SA v Cuoghi* [1998] QB 818; *Refco Inc v Eastern Trading Co* [1999] 1 Lloyd's Rep 159.
[635] *United States of America v Abacha* [2015] 1 WLR 1917.
[636] *Motorola Credit Corpn v Uzan (No 2)* [2004] 1 WLR 113.
[637] In this type of case, a question arises whether an English judgment on the merits may be refused recognition and enforcement in other countries on the ground of public policy. See Case C-394/07 *Gambazzi v Daimler Chrysler Canada Inc* [2009] ECR I-2563, discussed at para 3.110.
[638] *Belletti v Morici* [2009] ILPr 57; *Mobil Cerro Negro Ltd v Petroleos de Venezuela SA* [2008] 1 Lloyd's Rep 684.
[639] *Duder v Amsterdamsch Trustees Kantoor* [1902] 2 Ch 132.
[640] Although the court's powers under Civil Procedure Act 1997 are limited to premises in England, the court's inherent jurisdiction is wider: *Cook Industries Inc v Galliher* [1979] Ch 439. See also *Protector Alarms Ltd v Maxim Alarms Ltd* [1978] FSR 442; *Altertext Inc v Advanced Data Communications Ltd* [1985] 1 WLR 457.
[641] The power to grant a freezing injunction in relation to foreign assets was first recognised in *Babanaft International Co SA v Bassatne* [1990] Ch 13.

2.291 The fact that the court has the power to grant provisional measures which seek to restrain the defendant from performing certain acts abroad does not mean that such a power should be liberally exercised. The mere fact that an order is in personam and is directed towards someone who is subject to the court's personal jurisdiction does not exclude the possibility that the making of the order would be contrary to public international law and outside the court's subject-matter jurisdiction.[642] To avoid exceeding the jurisdictional limits imposed by public international law, the court must, when faced with an application for an extraterritorial order, consider (a) the defendant's connection with England, (b) whether the proposed order is exorbitant in terms of jurisdiction, and (c) whether the order has impermissible effects on foreign parties.[643] As a matter of public international law, state A is not permitted to trespass upon the authority of state B, by attempting to seize assets situated within the jurisdiction of state B or compelling the citizens of state B to do acts within the territory of state B.[644]

2.292 The propriety of granting extraterritorial provisional measures has been considered most frequently by the courts in the context of applications for a 'worldwide' freezing injunction. Although it is firmly established that the English court's jurisdiction to grant a freezing injunction against a person depends not on the court's territorial jurisdiction over assets located in England but on the court's unlimited jurisdiction in personam against any person who is properly made a party to English proceedings,[645] an extraterritorial Mareva injunction will be granted only in exceptional circumstances.[646] So that the balance is not tilted too much in the claimant's favour, where a claimant makes an application without notice (as is usual), the claimant is normally required to (i) give an undertaking in damages in the event of the claim being unsuccessful;[647] and (ii) make proper disclosure of all matters relevant to the exercise of the court's discretion to grant a worldwide injunction. Failure to make proper disclosure will normally lead to the injunction being discharged[648] (unless the non-disclosure is minor[649]).

2.293 The court will consider the grant of extraterritorial relief only if the defendant has insufficient English assets to satisfy the claim. In an appropriate case the court may even order the transfer of foreign assets from one foreign country (where the final judgment will not be entitled to recognition) to another (where a judgment in the claimant's favour will be recognised).[650] As a matter of discretion, an extraterritorial

---

[642] See Lawrence Collins LJ in *Masri v Consolidated Contractors International (UK) Ltd (No 2)* [2009] QB 450 at [35].
[643] Ibid at [59]. [644] Ibid at [47].
[645] See Dillon LJ in *Derby & Co Ltd v Weldon (No 6)* [1990] 1 WLR 1139 at 1149.
[646] See, eg, May LJ in *Derby & Co Ltd v Weldon* [1990] Ch 48 at 55.
[647] See, however, cases in which this requirement was waived in favour of a public body acting in the performance of a public duty: *Securities and Investment Board v Lloyd-Wright* [1993] 4 All ER 210; *United States Securities and Exchange Commission v Manterfield* [2010] 1 WLR 172.
[648] See, eg, *Boreh v Republic of Djibouti* [2015] 3 All ER 577.
[649] *Kazakhstan Kagazy plc v Arip* [2014] 1 CLC 451.
[650] *Derby & Co Ltd v Weldon (No 6)* [1990] 1 WLR 1139.

freezing injunction is more likely to be made after judgment than before[651] and the court will also be more inclined to grant Mareva relief in cases where the claim is proprietary rather than personal.[652] Although it has been said that the court should not normally grant an extraterritorial freezing injunction in cases where the claimant is seeking to enforce a foreign judgment in England,[653] the correctness of this view has been doubted.[654] Although freezing injunctions permit the defendant to carry on his business in the ordinary way and to meet his debts or other obligations as they come due,[655] the court may, in exceptional circumstances, order a defendant not to perform contracts to which he has already become bound and not to trade with a particular partner in the future.[656]

2.294 In *Van Uden Maritime BV v Firma Deco-Line*,[657] the Court of Justice ruled that the granting of provisional measures in support of substantive proceedings in another Member State is conditional on the existence of 'a real connecting link' between the subject-matter of the measures sought and the territorial jurisdiction of the court before which those measures are sought.[658] As a general rule, unless England is the forum for the substantive dispute between the parties, the court should confine itself to assets within the jurisdiction.[659] In a suitable case, however, the court may grant a worldwide freezing injunction in support of proceedings abroad. Such an order will not normally be granted unless the defendant has a sufficiently strong connection with England; worldwide orders are most likely in a case where the defendant is amenable to the in personam jurisdiction of the English court (such as where the defendant is domiciled in England).[660] If the defendant neither is domiciled in England, nor owns substantial assets in England, the grant of an extraterritorial order is not normally appropriate.[661] Indeed, in a case where the defendant is not domiciled in England, whether the court may, in support of proceedings in another Member State, grant an extraterritorial freezing injunction in relation to foreign assets is contentious.

2.295 Somewhat exceptionally, extraterritorial relief was granted in *Republic of Haiti v Duvalier*,[662] a case in which the defendants neither were domiciled in England nor had assets in England. The Republic started proceedings in France against the defendants, who comprised Baby Doc Duvalier and various members of his family, who, prior to their flight from Haiti, had allegedly embezzled significant sums of money belonging

---

[651] *Babanaft International Co SA v Bassatne* [1990] Ch 13.
[652] *Republic of Haiti v Duvalier* [1990] 1 QB 202.
[653] *Rosseel NV v Oriental Commercial Shipping (UK) Ltd* [1990] 1 WLR 1387.
[654] *Crédit Suisse Fides Trust SA v Cuoghi* [1998] QB 818.
[655] See, eg, *Polly Peck International plc v Nadir* [1992] 2 Lloyd's Rep 238; *Nomihold Securities Inc v Mobile Telesystems Finance SA* [2012] 1 All ER (Comm) 223.
[656] *Kensington International Ltd v Republic of Congo* [2008] 1 Lloyd's Rep 161.
[657] Case C-391/95 [1998] ECR I-7091.   [658] Ibid, para 40.
[659] Lord Donaldson MR in *Rosseel NV v Oriental Commercial Shipping (UK) Ltd* [1990] 1 WLR 1387 at 1389.
[660] *Crédit Suisse Fides Trust SA v Cuoghi* [1998] QB 818.
[661] *Belletti v Morici* [2009] ILPr 57; *Mobil Cerro Negro Ltd v Petroleos de Venezuela SA* [2008] 1 Lloyd's Rep 684.
[662] [1990] 1 QB 202.

to the Republic. The Republic applied to the English court for a worldwide Mareva injunction and a disclosure order requiring the defendants to reveal the whereabouts of their assets, wherever located. The Court of Appeal decided that it was an appropriate case for the grant of a worldwide Mareva injunction, notwithstanding the fact that the substantive proceedings were being conducted in France, where the defendants were domiciled. Opinion is divided as to whether the requirement to show a real connecting link with England could have been satisfied in these circumstances. For example, in *Banco Nacional de Commercio Exterior Snc v Empresa de Telecommunicaciones de Cuba SA*,[663] a case involving an application for protective measures in the context of the enforcement in England of an Italian judgment under the 2002 Regulation, the Court of Appeal granted a domestic freezing injunction, but refused to make a worldwide order on the basis that there is no connecting link at all between the subject-matter of a measure directed at assets abroad and the territorial jurisdiction of the court.[664] By contrast, it has been suggested that the ruling in *Van Uden* does not necessitate a reconsideration of the *Republic of Haiti* case (because a real connecting link was provided by the fact that the defendants had solicitors in England who held assets for them abroad)[665] and Lawrence Collins LJ reiterated this view in *Masri v Consolidated Contractors International (UK) Ltd (No 2)*.[666] Nevertheless, it has to be conceded that, in the *Republic of Haiti* case, the link with England was, in objective terms, very weak and it is at least possible that the effect of the ruling in the *Van Uden* case is to deprive the English courts of the power to grant extraterritorial measures in circumstances such as those which arose in *Republic of Haiti v Duvalier*.[667]

2.296 In *Motorola Credit Corpn v Uzan (No 2)*[668] a worldwide freezing injunction in support of substantive proceedings in New York was granted against a defendant who, although domiciled in Turkey, had substantial assets in England (including a house in London).[669] Even more controversially, in *Royal Bank of Scotland plc v Fal Oil Co Ltd*[670] a worldwide freezing injunction in support of proceedings in Sharjah was granted against UAE companies even though the defendant companies had no assets in England. It is very doubtful whether the fact that directors of the defendant companies made regular visits to England can legitimately be regarded as a real connecting link between the subject-matter of the injunction (that is, the defendants' assets) and England.

2.297 Where the court exercises its discretion in favour of granting extraterritorial relief, it is important that steps should be taken to ensure that oppression of the defendants by way of exposure to a multiplicity of proceedings and the misuse of information is

---

[663] [2007] 2 Lloyd's Rep 484. [664] See Tuckey LJ at [49].
[665] Although earlier editions strongly supported the decision in *Republic of Haiti v Duvalier*, the current edition is more equivocal, suggesting that the decision 'may perhaps be justified': Dicey, Morris and Collins, *The Conflict of Laws* (15th edn, 2012) p 275.
[666] [2009] QB 450 at [106]. [667] Peel (1998) 18 YBEL 689, 698. [668] [2004] 1 WLR 113.
[669] In its judgment the Court of Appeal referred to the *Van Uden* case and it seems that the court would have reached the same decision if the substantive proceedings had been in a Member State.
[670] [2013] 1 Lloyd's Rep 327.

avoided and that the position of third parties is protected. Where the court grants extraterritorial relief the claimant is normally required to give an undertaking not to take any action abroad in respect of the defendant's assets without the court's permission.[671] Furthermore, a worldwide freezing injunction normally contains appropriate provisions for the protection of third parties.[672] As a general rule, a third party will not be in contempt, even if he is subject to English jurisdiction, if he was not able to prevent the wrongful acts or omissions outside the jurisdiction or if the reason for his failure to comply with the freezing injunction is that he acted in accordance with his obligations under the law of the country in which the acts were committed: 'it would be an exorbitant exercise of jurisdiction to put a third party abroad in the position of having to choose between being in contempt of an English court and having to dishonour its obligations under a law which does not regard the English order as a valid excuse.'[673] This protection of third parties is of particular importance to banks which might otherwise find themselves in contempt of court for dealing with the defendant's assets in accordance with the defendant's instructions.

V Restraining foreign proceedings: anti-suit injunctions

A Introduction

2.298 The English court cannot stay proceedings in a foreign court. However, on the basis of section 37 of the Senior Courts Act 1981, it can grant an injunction restraining a party from instituting or pursuing such proceedings.[674] An anti-suit injunction is most likely to be sought where D has started foreign proceedings against C, who claims that the matter should be (or has been[675]) decided by the English court (or by arbitration in England) rather than abroad. Normally in such cases, unless the application is to restrain proceedings brought in breach of an arbitration agreement, C will already have started proceedings in England at the time of the application for the anti-suit

---

[671] See *Dadourian Group International Inc v Simms* [2006] 1 WLR 2499; *Dadourian Group International Inc v Simms (No 2)* [2007] 1 WLR 2967.

[672] For consideration of the 'Babanaft proviso', the mechanism whereby the courts have sought to provide protection for third parties, see Lord Donaldson MR in *Derby & Co Ltd v Weldon (Nos 3 and 4)* [1990] Ch 65 at 84; *Baltic Shipping v Translink Shipping Ltd* [1995] 1 Lloyd's Rep 673; *Bank of China v NBM LLC* [2002] 1 WLR 844. A reformulated Babanaft proviso is included in the CPR's model freezing injunction order: CPR PD25.

[673] Lawrence Collins LJ in *Masri v Consolidated Contractors International (UK) Ltd (No 2)* [2009] QB 450 at [47].

[674] In an appropriate case, the court may grant an injunction preventing a defendant from relying abroad on a foreign judgment (see *Bank of St Petersburg OJSC v Arkhangelsky* [2014] 1 WLR 4360) or restraining a defendant from bringing or pursuing arbitration proceedings (*Albon v Naza Motor Trading Sdn Bhd (No 4)* [2008] 1 All ER (Comm) 351; *Republic of Kazakhstan v Istil (No 2)* [2008] 1 Lloyd's Rep 382; *Claxton Engineering Services Ltd v TXM Olaj-és Gázkutató Kft (No 2)* [2011] 2 All ER (Comm) 128; *Excalibur Ventures LLC v Keystone Inc* [2011] 2 CLC 338; but, see *Weissfisch v Julius* [2006] 2 All ER (Comm) 504; *Elektrim SA v Vivendi Universal SA (No 2)* [2007] 2 Lloyd's Rep 8).

[675] See, eg, *Masri v Consolidated Contractors International (UK) Ltd (No 3)* [2009] QB 669.

injunction. In such cases, if the English court has jurisdiction over the substantive claim against D, it also has jurisdiction to grant the anti-suit injunction sought by C: 'once the court has jurisdiction over the substance of the case, it has jurisdiction to make ancillary orders, including anti-suit injunctions to protect the integrity of its process.'[676]

2.299 As an anti-suit injunction is a measure which is designed to have an extraterritorial effect, a major area of controversy is the exercise of the court's discretion. It is recognised that, because an injunction which orders a litigant to discontinue proceedings abroad involves an indirect interference with the process of justice in the foreign court, the court's approach should be cautious.[677]

2.300 At one time the courts took the view that the principles to be applied to an application for an anti-suit injunction were the same as those which governed the staying of English proceedings.[678] This approach has since been rejected. There are two broad categories of case in which the courts may consider granting injunctive relief: (i) where a person has behaved, or threatens to behave, in a manner which is unconscionable; (ii) where a litigant has invaded, or threatens to invade, a legal or equitable right of another.[679] The fundamental test for the grant of an anti-suit injunction is whether it is in the interests of justice.

B Unconscionable behaviour

2.301 Where a remedy for a particular wrong is available both in England and in a foreign forum, the court will, as a general rule, only restrain the claimant from pursuing proceedings in the foreign court if two conditions are satisfied: first, England is

---

[676] Lawrence Collins LJ in *Masri v Consolidated Contractors International (UK) Ltd (No 3)* [2009] QB 669 at [59]; see also *The Golden Endurance* [2015] 1 Lloyd's Rep 266. If the English court is not already seised of the substantive claim against D, the English court may consider the grant of an anti-suit injunction only if D is otherwise amenable to the court's jurisdiction. In a case governed by the traditional rules, if the defendant does not submit to the court's jurisdiction and cannot be served with process in England, the claimant may apply for permission to serve process abroad, for example, under CPR PD 6B para 3.1(6)(c), on the basis that the claim is in respect of a contract governed by English law: *Schiffahrtsgesellschaft Detlev von Appen GmbH v Voest Alpine Intertrading GmbH* [1997] 2 Lloyd's Rep 279; *Steamship Mutual Underwriting Association (Bermuda) Ltd v Sulpicio Lines Inc* [2008] 2 Lloyd's Rep 269; *Elektrim SA v Vivendi Holdings 1 Corporation* [2009] 1 Lloyd's Rep 59. For the position where an anti-suit injunction is sought to restrain proceedings brought in breach of an arbitration clause, see *AES Ust-Kamenogorsk Hydropower Plant LLP v Ust-Kamenogorsk Hydropower Plant JSC* [2013] 1 WLR 1889. Although it is generally thought that an anti-suit injunction is not one of the types of provisional measure which fall within the scope of art 35 of the Brussels I Recast, in *Masri v Consolidated Contractors International (UK) Ltd (No 3)* [2009] QB 669 at [66] Lawrence Collins LJ suggested (obiter) that an interim anti-suit injunction qualifies as a provisional measure.

[677] See Lord Diplock in *British Airways Board v Laker Airways Ltd* [1985] AC 58 at 95. For the English courts' reaction to a foreign anti-suit injunction restraining the commencement of proceedings in England, see *General Star International Indemnity Ltd v Stirling Cooke Brown Reinsurance Brokers Ltd* [2003] ILPr 19.

[678] *Castanho v Brown & Root (UK) Ltd* [1981] AC 557.

[679] Lord Brandon in *South Carolina Insurance Co v Assurantie Maatschappij De Zeven Provincien NV* [1987] AC 24 at 40. For a summary of the key principles, see *Deutsche Bank AG v Highland Crusader Offshore Partners LP* [2010] 1 WLR 1023 at [50].

the appropriate forum[680] and, second, the pursuit of the foreign proceedings would be vexatious or oppressive.[681] It is, of course, notoriously difficult to define concepts such as 'vexatious or oppressive'. The fact that the foreign proceedings are not being conducted in the appropriate forum does not necessarily mean that such proceedings are vexatious or oppressive; the court should not grant an injunction if, by doing so, it would deprive the claimant of advantages in the foreign forum of which it would be unjust to deprive him.[682] A party cannot be said to be acting unconscionably when it seeks a legitimate juridical advantage in a foreign court, especially where that is the court of its domicile.[683] However, the court may conclude that foreign proceedings are vexatious if they are not brought in good faith.[684] So, an anti-suit injunction may be granted where the purpose of the foreign litigation is to disrupt proceedings between the parties in England,[685] to make a collateral attack on an English arbitration[686] or to undermine an English judgment.[687] It should be stressed, however, that the purpose of an anti-suit injunction 'is not to ensure that an English judgment is recognised by a friendly foreign state, but to prevent unconscionable conduct'.[688]

2.302 There is a difficult dividing-line to be drawn between, on the one hand, situations where foreign proceedings are brought with the purpose of obtaining an unfair advantage (which is vexatious or oppressive) and, on the other, cases where a claimant brings proceedings abroad to obtain an advantage of which it would be unjust to deprive him (which is not). There is a tendency for the court to decide that it is vexatious or oppressive for a litigant to pursue a claim abroad if England is overwhelmingly the most appropriate forum and either the foreign proceedings are obviously doomed to failure or the advantages to the claimant in the foreign proceedings are relatively minor or not legitimate.[689] Such cases are, however, fairly uncommon. The mere fact that a foreign court will not apply the law which would be the applicable law according to English choice of law principles does necessarily render proceedings brought in that forum vexatious or oppressive.[690]

2.303 In *Société Nationale Industrielle Aérospatiale v Lee Kui Jak*[691] the Privy Council, sitting on appeal from the Court of Appeal of Brunei, held that an injunction should be granted to restrain the plaintiff from continuing proceedings in Texas. The Brunei court

---

[680] *Airbus Industrie GIE v Patel* [1999] 1 AC 119. If England is not the natural forum, an application for an anti-suit injunction should fail: *Oceanconnect UK Ltd v Angara Maritime Ltd* [2010] 2 CLC 448.
[681] *Société Nationale Industrielle Aérospatiale v Lee Kui Jak* [1987] AC 871.
[682] Lord Goff at 896.
[683] *Star Reefers Pool Inc v JFC Group Co Ltd* [2012] 2 All ER (Comm) 225.
[684] *Turner v Grovit* [2002] 1 WLR 107; *Cadre SA v Astra Asigurari SA* [2006] 1 Lloyd's Rep 560.
[685] *Albon v Naza Motor Trading Sdn Bhd (No 4)* [2008] 1 All ER (Comm) 351; *Tonicstar Ltd v American Home Assurance Co* [2005] Lloyd's Rep IR 32.
[686] *Noble Assurance Co v Gerling-Konzern General Insurance Co* [2007] 1 CLC 87.
[687] *Trafigura Beheer BV v Kookmin Bank Co (No 2)* [2007] 1 Lloyd's Rep 669; *Masri v Consolidated Contractors International (UK) Ltd (No 3)* [2009] QB 669.
[688] Clarke LJ in *The Western Regent* [2005] 2 Lloyd's Rep 359 at [48].
[689] See, eg, *Simon Engineering plc v Butte Mining plc (No 2)* [1996] 1 Lloyd's Rep 91.
[690] *The Golden Endurance* [2015] 1 Lloyd's Rep 266.
[691] [1987] AC 871.

was the most appropriate forum and the continuation of the Texas proceedings would be oppressive or vexatious. The defendants would suffer serious injustice on account of the fact that they were unable, in the Texas proceedings, to claim an indemnity from a third party (because the third party was unwilling to submit to Texas jurisdiction); the claim for indemnity could, however, be brought in the Brunei proceedings because the third party was prepared to submit to Brunei jurisdiction. As a result of undertakings given by the defendants in relation to the litigation in Brunei, there would be no injustice to the plaintiff in not being able to continue with the proceedings in Texas.

2.304 In the context of an application for an anti-suit injunction, the court should not take too forum-centric a view and should have regard to the requirements of comity, a notoriously difficult concept to pin down.[692] Because the effect of an anti-suit injunction (if complied with) is to interfere, albeit indirectly, with foreign proceedings and there is 'something of a touch of egoistic paternalism' in restraining the continuation of proceedings in a foreign forum, comity should cause the court to pause long and hard before granting an injunction in other than exceptional cases.[693]

2.305 In the *Société Nationale Industrielle Aérospatiale* case the Privy Council indicated that an anti-suit injunction should not normally be granted unless England is the most appropriate forum. This limitation was taken further in *Turner v Grovit*.[694] According to Lord Hobhouse, the English court will not grant an anti-suit injunction unless the applicant is a party to litigation in England and establishes that there is a clear need to protect existing English proceedings.[695] On the basis of Lord Hobhouse's speech, some of the earlier cases are of doubtful authority. For example, the decision in *Midland Bank plc v Laker Airways Ltd*[696] is inconsistent with the approach in *Turner v Grovit*: an injunction was granted to restrain an English plaintiff from pursuing proceedings against an English defendant in the United States claiming damages under the United States anti-trust legislation, even though there were no proceedings in England. Similarly, Lord Hobhouse's speech contradicts Lord Goff's suggestion (obiter) in *Airbus Industrie GIE v Patel* that, notwithstanding the fact that England is not the appropriate forum (as a result of which there are no English proceedings), the grant of an anti-suit injunction might be justified in an exceptional case where 'the conduct of the foreign state is such as to deprive it of the respect normally required by comity'.[697]

C Infringement of a legal or equitable right

2.306 A defendant in foreign proceedings may apply for an anti-suit injunction in a case where the bringing of those proceedings involves a breach of the legal or equitable rights of the defendant. A right not to be sued abroad may be contractual (for example, where there is an arbitration clause or a clause conferring exclusive jurisdiction on the

---

[692] See Sim, 'Choice of Law and Anti-Suit Injunctions: Relocating Comity' (2013) 62 ICLQ 703.
[693] See Rix LJ in *Star Reefers Pool Inc v JFC Group Co Ltd* [2012] 2 All ER (Comm) 225 at [39]–[40].
[694] [2002] 1 WLR 107.   [695] [2002] 1 WLR 107 at [28].   [696] [1986] QB 689.
[697] [1999] 1 AC 119 at 140.

English courts) or may arise by virtue of an equitable defence to the claim (such as estoppel). Most of the recent cases have involved foreign proceedings brought in breach of the terms of a contractual dispute-resolution clause.

2.307 Traditionally, the courts at least paid lip-service to the principle that an anti-suit injunction should be regarded as an exceptional remedy.[698] More recently, in *The Angelic Grace*[699] (a case 'followed on many occasions since'[700]), it was held that where proceedings abroad involve the breach of a jurisdiction or arbitration agreement the court should not feel reticent about granting an anti-suit injunction; in such a case damages are not an adequate remedy for the breach of contract. In the situation where foreign proceedings involve the breach of an exclusive jurisdiction clause or an arbitration clause, an anti-suit injunction is granted almost as a matter of course, with judges referring to the remedy in such cases as something to which the claimant is prima facie entitled.[701] Accordingly, if there is a binding dispute-resolution agreement between the parties and the subject-matter of the foreign proceedings falls within the scope of that agreement, an injunction should ordinarily be granted unless there are 'special countervailing factors',[702] or unless good reason is shown why the court's discretion should not be exercised in the applicant's favour.[703]

2.308 Notwithstanding the fact that the foreign proceedings were brought in breach of a dispute-resolution clause, relief may be refused if the applicant is guilty of misconduct which amounts to having 'unclean hands'[704] or if there has been delay on the part of the claimant in applying for the order; a party who is sued abroad in breach of the terms of a dispute-resolution clause should apply promptly for an anti-suit injunction from the English court.[705] If the application is made at the last minute in an attempt to frustrate foreign proceedings which have been ongoing for an appreciable period of time, an anti-suit injunction will be refused.[706] The general principle that equity will not act in vain applies to anti-suit injunctions as much as to any other type of injunction; if it is

---

[698] *Tracomin v Sudan Oil Seeds Co Ltd (No 2)* [1983] 1 WLR 1026; *Sohio Supply Co v Gatoil (USA) Inc* [1989] 1 Lloyd's Rep 588.
[699] [1995] 1 Lloyd's Rep 87. On the question of damages for breach of a dispute-resolution agreement, see *Donohue v Armco Inc* [2002] 1 All ER 749; *Union Discount Co Ltd v Union Discount Cal Ltd* [2002] 1 WLR 1517; *Starlight Shipping Co v Allianz Marine & Aviation Versicherungs AG* [2014] 1 All ER 590; *Starlight Shipping Co v Allianz Marine & Aviation Versicherungs AG (No 2)* [2014] 2 Lloyd's Rep 544; *SwissMarine Services SA v Gupta Coal India Private Ltd* [2015] 1 Lloyd's Rep 456. See also the discussion by Briggs (2001) 72 BYIL 446; Yeo and Tan, 'Damages for Breach of Exclusive Jurisdiction Clauses' in Worthington (ed), *Commercial Law and Commercial Practice* (2003) pp 403–31.
[700] Cooke J in *Compania Sud Americana de Vapores SA v Hin-Pro International Logistics Ltd* [2015] 1 Lloyd's Rep 301 at [35].
[701] See, eg, Longmore LJ in *OT Africa Line Ltd v Magic Sportswear Corp* [2006] 1 All ER (Comm) 32 at [39].
[702] Steyn LJ in *Continental Bank NA v Aeakos Compania Naviera SA* [1994] 1 WLR 588 at 598.
[703] *The Angelic Grace* [1995] 1 Lloyd's Rep 87. See also *Louis Dreyfus Commodities Kenya Ltd v Bolster Shipping Co Ltd* [2010] 2 CLC 71; *Vitol SA v Capri Marine Ltd* [2011] 1 All ER (Comm) 366; *Ecom Agroindustrial Corp Ltd v Mosharaf Composite Textile Mill Ltd* [2013] 2 All ER (Comm) 983.
[704] *Royal Bank of Scotland plc v Highland Financial Partners LP* [2012] 2 CLC 19.
[705] See *The Skier Star* [2008] 1 Lloyd's Rep 652 (delay of more than two years; injunction refused); *The MD Gemini* [2012] 2 Lloyd's Rep 672.
[706] *Toepfer International GmbH v Molino Boschi SRL* [1996] 1 Lloyd's Rep 510.

clear that an anti-suit injunction would be disregarded or would be a *brutum fulmen*, the court should refrain from granting the relief sought by the applicant.[707]

2.309 The fact that the claimant in the English proceedings, instead of seeking to rely on the jurisdiction clause or arbitration agreement to contest the foreign court's jurisdiction, submitted in the foreign proceedings normally provides a good reason for the court to refuse to grant an anti-suit injunction.[708] The court may also refuse an injunction if, in a case involving a multiplicity of parties, foreign proceedings provide the best means of submitting the whole dispute to a single tribunal which is able to make a comprehensive judgment on all issues between the parties.[709]

2.310 Where the parties' contract includes a non-exclusive jurisdiction agreement in favour of the English courts, there is no presumption that the grant of an injunction to restrain foreign proceedings is appropriate. The grant of an anti-suit injunction in such cases depends upon the foreign proceedings being shown to be vexatious or oppressive.[710] If the parties agreed to the non-exclusive jurisdiction of the English courts, the commencement of proceedings abroad will be considered vexatious or oppressive if their purpose is to prevent or hamper proceedings in England.[711]

2.311 The approach adopted in cases involving dispute-resolution clauses was inexplicably extended in *Samengo-Turner v Marsh & McLennan (Services) Ltd*[712] to a case involving an employment contract in which the English court had exclusive jurisdiction under Brussels I. When the employer brought proceedings in New York against three of its English employees, the employees applied to the English court for an anti-suit injunction to restrain the New York action. Although the contract of employment included a New York jurisdiction clause, the employees argued that, under what is now article 23 of the Recast, the jurisdiction clause was not enforceable against them and that, accordingly, they had a legal right not to be sued other than in the Member State of their domicile. The Court of Appeal granted an anti-suit injunction to protect the employees' right to be sued only in the English courts.

2.312 This decision is plainly wrong, the Court of Appeal's error being to accept the idea that Brussels I was the source of a 'right' for the employees not to be sued other than in England. Properly understood, Brussels I does no more than direct the courts of Member States either to assume or to decline jurisdiction in certain specified circumstances; it does not purport to confer rights (or impose obligations) on natural and

---

[707] *Stichting Shell Pensioenfonds v Krys* [2015] AC 616.
[708] *A/S D/S Svendborg v Wansa* [1997] 2 Lloyd's Rep 183.
[709] *Donohue v Armco Inc* [2002] 1 All ER 749. See also *Bouygues Offshore SA v Caspian Shipping Co (Nos 1, 3, 4 and 5)* [1998] 2 Lloyd's Rep 461. However, an injunction will normally be granted to restrain proceedings brought in breach of a jurisdiction clause if the goal of having all related disputes determined by a single forum cannot be achieved: *Skype Technologies SA v Joltid Ltd* [2011] ILPr 8.
[710] *Royal Bank of Canada v Coöperative Centrale Raiffeisen-Boerenleenbank BA* [2004] 1 Lloyd's Rep 471; *Deutsche Bank AG v Highland Crusader Offshore Partners LP* [2010] 1 WLR 1023; *The MD Gemini* [2012] 2 Lloyd's Rep 672.
[711] *Sabah Shipyard (Pakistan) Ltd v Islamic Republic of Pakistan* [2003] 2 Lloyd's Rep 571.
[712] [2007] 2 All ER (Comm) 813.

legal persons.⁷¹³ Although the grant of an anti-suit injunction in the *Samengo-Turner* case cannot be supported, the decision was followed unquestioningly in *Petter v EMC Europe Ltd*.⁷¹⁴

D Anti-suit injunctions and the Brussels I Recast

2.313 In principle, the court's general jurisdiction to grant equitable remedies exists regardless of whether proceedings are brought in a Member State in accordance with the terms of Brussels I or in a non-Member State. Nevertheless, the grant of an injunction which interferes (albeit indirectly) with the process of justice in another Member State hardly seems compatible with the Brussels I Recast. Given that articles 29 and 30 of the Recast establish rules for dealing with conflicts of jurisdiction between Member States, any measure taken by the courts of one Member State which has the effect of pre-empting the decision of the courts of another Member State on questions of jurisdiction disrupts the scheme of the Recast. Where, for example, a claimant brings proceedings in France against a defendant who is domiciled in England for breach of contract (on the basis that France is the place of performance of the obligation in question) there should be no question of the English court granting an anti-suit injunction restraining the claimant from pursuing the French proceedings, even if the defendant will be deprived of advantages which he would have enjoyed had the proceedings been brought in England.

2.314 Despite the formidable arguments against anti-suit injunctions being granted in cases where jurisdiction is conferred by Brussels I, the English courts took the view that a claimant is entitled to an injunction restraining the defendant from pursuing proceedings in another Member State either where the foreign proceedings are (in the eyes of the English court) brought in breach of an English jurisdiction clause⁷¹⁵ or where the claimant is already a litigant in England and the foreign proceedings are brought with the purpose of harassing and oppressing him.⁷¹⁶ This approach was, however, subject to widespread criticism⁷¹⁷ and, when questions concerning the compatibility of anti-suit injunctions with the Brussels Convention were referred to the Court of Justice, the doctrine of the English courts was conclusively shown to be wrong.

2.315 In *Turner v Grovit*⁷¹⁸ the English plaintiff, who had temporarily worked in Spain, resigned from his job and started proceedings in England against the defendant, his former employer, claiming constructive dismissal. When the defendant then began proceedings for breach of contract against the plaintiff in Spain, the plaintiff applied

---

⁷¹³ See Briggs, 'Who Is Bound by the Brussels Regulation?' [2007] LMCLQ 433.   ⁷¹⁴ [2016] ILPr 3.
⁷¹⁵ *Continental Bank NA v Aeakos Compania Naviera SA* [1994] 1 WLR 588.
⁷¹⁶ *Turner v Grovit* [2002] 1 WLR 107.
⁷¹⁷ See, eg, Asariotis, 'Antisuit Injunctions for Breach of a Forum Agreement: A Critical Review of the English Approach' (1999/2000) 19 YBEL 447.
⁷¹⁸ Case C–159/02 [2004] ECR I–3565. For criticism of the decision, see Briggs (2004) 120 LQR 529; Dickinson, 'A Charter for Tactical Litigation in Europe?' [2004] LMCLQ 273.

for an anti-suit injunction to restrain the Spanish proceedings. Notwithstanding the argument that, as the Spanish court should be allowed to decide for itself whether or not to assume jurisdiction, the grant of an anti-suit injunction was inappropriate,[719] neither the Court of Appeal[720] nor the House of Lords[721] thought that it was incompatible with the Brussels Convention for the English court to grant an anti-suit injunction restraining Spanish proceedings if those proceedings had been brought only to harass and oppress the English plaintiff. Nevertheless, the House of Lords recognised that the issue was controversial and referred the matter to the Court of Justice.

2.316 Although the House of Lords was at pains to emphasise that an anti-suit injunction is directed at the litigant rather than the foreign court,[722] the Court of Justice considered that an injunction prohibiting the bringing of proceedings in a particular court constitutes an interference with the jurisdiction of that court.[723] For the English court to grant an anti-suit injunction which prohibits a litigant from commencing or continuing legal proceedings in another Member State is incompatible with Brussels I even where that person is acting in bad faith with a view to frustrating existing English proceedings.[724]

2.317 The logic of the Court of Justice's ruling is that, in cases which fall within the scope of article 1 of the Recast, the English court is prevented from granting an anti-suit injunction in relation to proceedings in another Member State not only where the foreign court's jurisdiction is based on the direct jurisdiction provisions of Chapter II of the Brussels I Recast, but also in cases where the foreign court has assumed jurisdiction under its traditional rules against a defendant not domiciled in a Member State (as authorised by article 6). However, the Court of Justice's ruling extends neither to cases where the application is for an injunction restraining proceedings in a non-Member State[725] nor to proceedings which are outside the material scope of the Recast.

2.318 For several years, the English courts took the view that, in a case where the parties had agreed to refer their dispute to arbitration, the subject-matter of an application for an anti-suit injunction to restrain a litigant from pursuing proceedings in breach of the arbitration agreement was 'arbitration' and that, by virtue of article 1(2)(d), such an application fell outside the scope of Brussels I.[726] However, in *West Tankers Inc v Allianz SpA*,[727] a case in which the claimant applied for an anti-suit injunction to restrain the defendant from pursuing Italian proceedings which allegedly had been brought in breach of an arbitration clause, the House of Lords, while supporting the

---

[719] See the decision of the first instance judge: [1999] 1 All ER (Comm) 445. [720] [2000] 1 QB 345.
[721] [2002] 1 WLR 107.   [722] [2002] 1 WLR 107 at [23].
[723] Case C-159/02 [2004] ECR I-3565, para 27.   [724] Ibid, para 31.
[725] *OT Africa Line Ltd v Magic Sportswear Corp* [2006] 1 All ER (Comm) 32; *Midgulf International Ltd v Groupe Chimique Tunisien* [2010] 1 CLC 113.
[726] See, eg, *Through Transport Mutual Insurance Association (Eurasia) Ltd v New India Assurance Co Ltd* [2005] 1 Lloyd's Rep 67.
[727] [2007] 1 Lloyd's Rep 39.

practice endorsed by *The Angelic Grace*,⁷²⁸ decided to refer the following question to the Court of Justice: 'Is it consistent with [Brussels I] for a court of a Member State to make an order to restrain a person from commencing or continuing proceedings in another Member State on the ground that such proceedings are in breach of an arbitration agreement?'⁷²⁹

2.319 The Court of Justice answered this question in the negative.⁷³⁰ In the Court's view, a crucial issue ignored by the English practice was the nature of the proceedings towards which the anti-suit injunction was directed: the decisive question was not whether the application for an anti-suit injunction fell within the scope of Brussels I, but whether the proceedings against which the anti-suit injunction was directed did so.⁷³¹ Even where the purpose of an injunction is to promote respect for an arbitration agreement, the courts of one Member State are not entitled to prevent the court of another Member State from determining for itself whether it has jurisdiction to resolve the dispute before it. So, if Italian proceedings are within the scope of the Brussels I Recast, an English anti-suit injunction would be incompatible with the Recast and would run counter to 'the trust which the Member States accord to one another's legal systems and judicial institutions and on which the system of jurisdiction under [Brussels I] is based'.⁷³² The Court of Justice had no hesitation in concluding that the Italian proceedings were civil or commercial in nature and did not concern arbitration: whether or not proceedings fall within the scope of Brussels I has to be determined from the substantive subject-matter of the dispute; the subject-matter of the Italian proceedings was a claim in tort (possibly also in contract) which fell within the scope of article 1 and the fact that, as a preliminary issue, the Italian court had to examine the validity and scope of an arbitration agreement did not lead to the conclusion that the subject-matter of the Italian proceedings was 'arbitration'. Accordingly, an anti-suit injunction which restrains the defendant from continuing civil or commercial proceedings in Italy interferes with proceedings which are within the scope of the Brussels I Recast and is incompatible with it. The effect of the ruling in the *West Tankers* case is that the practice so robustly promoted in *The Angelic Grace*⁷³³ (and enthusiastically followed in numerous cases for more than a decade) is limited to situations where the offending proceedings are brought in a non-Member State.⁷³⁴

2.320 In policy terms, the problems with the *West Tankers* case echo some of those generated by the decision in *Erich Gasser GmbH v MISAT Srl*,⁷³⁵ since reversed by the

---

⁷²⁸ [1995] 1 Lloyd's Rep 87.   ⁷²⁹ [2007] 1 Lloyd's Rep 391 at [25].
⁷³⁰ Case C-185/07 [2009] 1 AC 1138. Perhaps not surprisingly, the Court of Justice's decision was not warmly received in England; see, eg, Briggs [2009] LMCLQ 161; Fentiman [2009] CLJ 278; Peel (2009) 125 LQR 365. See also Carducci, 'Arbitration, Anti-suit Injunctions and *Lis Pendens* under the European Jurisdiction Regulation and the New York Convention' (2011) 27 Arb Int 171.
⁷³¹ Case C-185/07 [2009] 1 AC 1138 at [24]-[25].   ⁷³² Ibid at [30].
⁷³³ [1995] 1 Lloyd's Rep 87.
⁷³⁴ For consideration of further implications of the *West Tankers* decision (particularly, in the context of the enforcement of arbitral awards), see *African Fertilizers and Chemicals Nig Ltd v BD Shipsnavo GmbH & Co Reederei KG* [2011] 2 Lloyd's Rep 531.
⁷³⁵ Case C-116/02 [2003] ECR I-14693. See paras 2.195-2.198.

amendments implemented by the Recast. A party who is intent on undermining the effect of an arbitration clause can initiate proceedings in any Member State which, but for the clause, would have jurisdiction over the substantive dispute; by contesting the validity or effectiveness of the arbitration clause, a party can drag out these proceedings in the non-contractual forum. Even if such a tactic does not ultimately prevent the dispute being referred to arbitration, it will be a source of aggravation and costs.

2.321 One way of attempting to address these concerns would have been to amend Brussels I with a view to strengthening the enforcement of arbitration agreements. Although various options were considered during the process which led to the enactment of the Recast,[736] none of the proposals relating to the potential amendment of the arbitration exception was adopted. Accordingly, the problems generated by the ruling in *West Tankers* remain largely unresolved under the Recast.

---

[736] See European Commission, *Brussels I Recast Proposal*, COM (2010) 748 final.

3

Foreign judgments

I Introduction

A General considerations

3.1 Although the conflicts process can be broken down into three elements (jurisdiction; choice of law; and the recognition and enforcement of judgments), the English court will rarely have to address all three elements in the same case. Where, for example, the court assumes jurisdiction and grants a judgment in the claimant's favour, there are no special conflicts aspects to the enforcement of the judgment against the defendant's assets in England. Where, however, the court does not have jurisdiction in relation to a particular dispute—which is then determined by a foreign court—a question may arise concerning the effect of the foreign judgment in England. When considering this question it is important to draw a number of distinctions.

1. Recognition and enforcement

3.2 The enforcement of a judgment, which necessarily involves its recognition, will be sought by a judgment-creditor—that is, a litigant who has obtained a judgment in a foreign court which awards him some relief, and who now wishes to obtain that relief in England. Where, for example, a claimant is awarded damages by a French court in an action for breach of contract and the defendant has no assets in France, if the claimant wishes to have the judgment satisfied out of the defendant's assets in England, the question arises whether the English court will enforce the French judgment.

3.3 Although there can be no enforcement without recognition, situations arise in which a litigant in English proceedings wishes to have a foreign judgment recognised only. Where, for example, a foreign court dismisses a claim for breach of contract on the basis that no breach was committed and gives judgment in the defendant's favour, if the claimant starts proceedings in England on the same cause of action, the defendant will want the English court to recognise the foreign judgment, but no question of enforcement arises. In this type of case, the defendant raises the foreign judgment as a defence to the claim. Whereas enforcement of a foreign judgment is essentially a positive process whereby the English court authorises the judgment-creditor to take the necessary steps so that the judgment is satisfied, recognition of a foreign judgment merely provides a barrier which prevents proceedings being pursued in England.

2. Judgments in personam and judgments in rem

3.4 A judgment in personam is a court order which determines the rights and obligations of the particular parties to the litigation. In a typical case—based on an allegation of a breach of contract or on the commission of a tort by the defendant—the judgment either will order the defendant to pay damages to the claimant (or may order the defendant to do, or refrain from doing, something) or will decide that the defendant is not liable.

3.5 A judgment in rem may affect the position of third parties as well as the parties to the litigation. Many judgments in rem involve questions of status and arise in the context of family proceedings; the court may, for example, declare that an alleged marriage is valid or that a foreign divorce is (or is not) entitled to recognition in England.[1] In the commercial sphere judgments in rem are most frequently found in the context of Admiralty proceedings, typically in cases involving the ownership or possession of a ship. In this type of case a judgment in rem determines not only the rights of the parties, but also ownership or possession of the ship, and is effective against the whole world. The fact that a foreign judgment has property as its underlying subject-matter does not necessarily mean that it is a judgment in rem; a distinction has to be drawn between a judgment purporting to transfer, dispose of, or determine the ownership of property (a judgment in rem) and a judgment establishing the parties' contractual rights in relation to property (a judgment in personam).[2] At common law a foreign judgment in rem may not be recognised or enforced in England unless the ship or other property was situated in the country of origin at the time of the commencement of proceedings.[3] Recognition or enforcement may be refused, however, on the same grounds which apply to foreign judgments in personam.[4]

3. Various legal regimes

3.6 Foreign judgments may be entitled to recognition and enforcement under one of a number of different legal regimes. Which set of rules is applicable depends primarily on the country of origin. The common law rules are still applicable to judgments given by the courts of many countries around the world, including most countries in the Middle East, some countries in Eastern Europe, and most non-Commonwealth countries in the Americas (including the United States), Africa, and Asia. The Administration of Justice Act 1920 applies to the enforcement of some Commonwealth judgments. The Foreign Judgments (Reciprocal Enforcement) Act 1933, which is a virtual codification of the common law, governs the recognition and enforcement of the judgments of some Commonwealth countries and judgments given by some non-Commonwealth countries (including countries in Western Europe and Israel). As regards judgments given by the courts of most European countries, however, the

---

[1] The recognition of foreign divorces and nullity decrees is considered in Chapter 8.
[2] See Lord Mance in *Pattni v Ali* [2007] 2 AC 85 at [25].
[3] *Castrique v Imrie* (1870) LR 4 HL 414. Judgments in rem granted by the courts of Member States may also be entitled to recognition and enforcement under the Brussels I Recast. See para 3.89.
[4] See paras 3.60–3.79.

1933 Act has been superseded, in civil and commercial matters, by the Brussels I Recast (and by the Lugano Convention). As regards matters within the scope of article 1 of the Brussels I Recast,[5] Chapter III of the Recast applies to judgments given by the courts of EU Member States.[6] There is also provision for the recognition and enforcement in England of judgments granted by the courts of Scotland and Northern Ireland.[7]

3.7 Whereas, at common law, foreign judgments are enforced by bringing ordinary proceedings on the judgment, under the various statutory regimes there are special procedures prescribed leading to registration of the judgment. Once registered, a foreign judgment may be enforced in the same way as a judgment of the English court. There is, however, no special procedure for the recognition of foreign judgments.

B The basis of recognition and enforcement

3.8 In theory, the English court could recognise and enforce all foreign judgments; alternatively, it would be possible for the English court not to recognise or enforce any foreign judgment. Such extreme positions are not very attractive from a practical point of view.[8] As Slade LJ noted in *Adams v Cape Industries plc*, the law is based on 'an acknowledgement that the society of nations will work better if some foreign judgments are taken to create rights which supersede the underlying cause of action, and which may be directly enforced in countries where the defendant or his assets are to be found'.[9] The crucial question, therefore, is not *whether* foreign judgments should be recognised and enforced in England but *which* judgments should be recognised and enforced.

3.9 There are, broadly speaking, two theories. The first is the theory of obligation, which is premised on the notion that if the original court assumed jurisdiction on a proper basis the court's judgment should prima facie be regarded as creating an obligation between the parties to the foreign proceedings which the English court ought to recognise and, where appropriate, enforce. In effect, a foreign judgment which orders a defendant to pay damages is to be regarded as creating a debt which the claimant can enforce in England. The alternative theory is based on the idea of reciprocity: the courts of country X should recognise and enforce the judgments of country Y if, mutatis mutandis, the courts of country Y recognise and enforce the judgments of country X. The theory of obligation was adopted by the English courts in the nineteenth century[10] and still

---

[5] See paras 2.14–2.15.
[6] Although Denmark did not participate in the adoption of the Recast, Denmark entered an agreement with the EU so that, under international law, the provisions of the Recast apply to relations between Denmark and the other EU Member States: see OJ 2013 L79/4. Title III of the Lugano Convention applies to judgments granted by the courts of Iceland, Norway, and Switzerland. Most provisions of the Lugano Convention 2007 are identical to the equivalent provisions of the 2002 Regulation.
[7] Civil Jurisdiction and Judgments Act 1982, schs 6 and 7.
[8] See paras 1.173–1.175.   [9] [1990] Ch 433 at 552.
[10] *Schibsby v Westenholz* (1870) LR 6 QB 155. For a modern defence of the theoretical foundations of the common law, see Briggs, 'Recognition of Foreign Judgments: A Matter of Obligation' (2013) 129 LQR 87.

forms the basis of recognition and enforcement at common law (and the statutory regimes which are based on the common law). English law is, however, radically affected by the Brussels I Recast, which—as regards civil and commercial matters—provides for the reciprocal recognition and enforcement of judgments granted by the courts of EU Member States.

3.10 Whichever theory is adopted, the recognition and enforcement of foreign judgments is limited by a range of defences which may be invoked by the party wishing to resist the judgment in question. It would be unrealistic to expect the English court to give effect to a foreign judgment which conflicts with fundamental notions of justice and fairness. So, the recognition and enforcement of foreign judgments is a two-stage process: (i) are the basic conditions for recognition or enforcement satisfied, and (ii) if so, is there a defence by reason of which the foreign judgment should nevertheless not be recognised or enforced?

II Recognition and enforcement at common law

A Conditions for enforcement

3.11 For a judgment to be entitled to enforcement at common law a number of conditions must be satisfied: (i) the original court must have been a court of competent jurisdiction; (ii) the judgment must be final and conclusive; (iii) the judgment must be for a fixed sum of money, not being a tax or penalty. If the judgment-creditor can satisfy the court that these criteria are satisfied, the foreign judgment is prima facie entitled to enforcement. The burden then shifts to the judgment-debtor; the foreign judgment will be enforced unless the judgment-debtor establishes a defence which negatives the effect of the judgment in England.

1. A court of competent jurisdiction

(A) Introduction

3.12 The important question when considering whether the original court was a court of competent jurisdiction is not whether the foreign court was entitled to assume jurisdiction according to the foreign law, but whether the foreign court had jurisdiction according to the English rules of private international law.[11] The decided cases indicate that there are, broadly speaking, two situations in which the original court will be regarded as a court of competent jurisdiction: first, where the judgment-debtor submitted to the jurisdiction of the foreign court; secondly, where there is a sufficient territorial connection between the judgment-debtor and the country of origin.

3.13 Other types of connection between the parties or the cause of action and the original court are not sufficient. For example, it is irrelevant that the cause of action arose in the

---

[11] *Buchanan v Rucker* (1808) 9 East 192.

country of origin[12] or that the defendant has assets in the country of origin.[13] Similarly, even though the English court may assume jurisdiction over absent defendants under CPR rule 6.36 on the ground that England is the forum conveniens, a foreign judgment founded on a similar basis of jurisdiction is not entitled to enforcement in England. As Lord Collins noted in *Rubin v Eurofinance SA*, '[t]here is no necessary connection between the exercise of jurisdiction by the English court and its recognition of the jurisdiction of foreign courts. . . . The English court does not concede jurisdiction in personam to a foreign court merely because the English court would, in corresponding circumstances, have power to order service out of the jurisdiction.'[14]

(B) Submission

3.14 A foreign judgment is prima facie enforceable in England if the judgment-debtor submitted to the jurisdiction of the foreign court. Submission can take one of three forms.[15]

(i) Consent

3.15 The foreign court is regarded as a court of competent jurisdiction if the judgment-debtor consented to the jurisdiction of the forum in which the judgment was obtained.[16] Such consent usually takes the form of a contractual clause providing for the exclusive or non-exclusive jurisdiction of the foreign court.[17] A doubtful question is whether the original court should be regarded as a court of competent jurisdiction in a case where an agreement to submit, although not expressly stated in the contract, can be implied into it. In *Blohn v Desser*[18] Diplock J decided, albeit obiter, that a defendant, an English resident, who had been a sleeping partner in a firm which carried on business in Austria, could be regarded as having impliedly agreed with all people who made contracts with the firm in the course of its business in Austria to submit to the jurisdiction of the Austrian courts in any dispute arising from such contracts. Later decisions, however, have diverged on the question of whether it is possible for an agreement to submit to the jurisdiction of a foreign court to be implied.[19] *Adams v Cape Industries plc*,[20] in which there was a review of the earlier cases, casts further doubt on the correctness of Diplock J's observations in *Blohn v Desser*. Scott J thought that the minimum requirement is 'a clear indication of consent to the exercise by the foreign court of jurisdiction'.[21]

---

[12] *Sirdar Gurdyal Singh v Rajah of Faridkote* [1894] AC 670.   [13] *Emanuel v Symon* [1908] 1 KB 302.
[14] [2013] 1 AC 236 at [127].   [15] *Emanuel v Symon* [1908] 1 KB 302 at 309.
[16] *Feyerick v Hubbard* (1902) 71 LJKB 509.
[17] The Hague Choice of Court Convention 2005 (see paras 2.244–2.248) provides that a judgment given by the court of a Contracting State which is chosen by an exclusive choice of court agreement must be recognised and enforced in other Contracting States: art 8. This is subject to art 9 which lists grounds on which recognition or enforcement may be refused; these grounds are largely equivalent to defences to recognition or enforcement under English common law.
[18] [1962] 2 QB 116.
[19] *Vogel v R & A Kohnstamm Ltd* [1973] QB 133 (agreement must be express); *Sfeir & Co v National Insurance Co of New Zealand* [1964] 1 Lloyd's Rep 330 (agreement may be implied).
[20] [1990] Ch 433.   [21] Ibid, 466.

3.16 A further issue which was considered by Scott J in *Adams v Cape Industries plc* is the extent to which consent to the jurisdiction of the original court might amount to submission notwithstanding that such consent does not form part of a contractually binding agreement. As a matter of principle, there is no reason why, in appropriate circumstances, a defendant should not be estopped from denying that the original court was a court of competent jurisdiction. Where the defendant consents to the jurisdiction of the foreign court otherwise than by contractual agreement and, before the consent is withdrawn, the claimant relies upon it to his detriment, the defendant should be regarded as having submitted to the foreign court's jurisdiction. For example, if D, an English resident, orally assures C that he will submit to the jurisdiction of the Russian courts and, in reliance on this assurance, C fails to commence proceedings against D in England within the relevant limitation period, and then C, having obtained a judgment in Russia, seeks enforcement in England D should be estopped from denying that the Russian court was a court of competent jurisdiction. However, no such estoppel can arise if the defendant's consent is not acted upon by the claimant or if it is withdrawn before it is acted upon.

(ii) Voluntary appearance

3.17 A defendant who voluntarily participates in the foreign proceedings submits to the jurisdiction of the foreign court. A foreign judgment can be enforced against a defendant in England if he entered an appearance to defend the case (even if he took no further steps) or if he took any step designed to contest the claim on the merits or even if he filed an appeal against the judgment to a higher court in the country of origin, not previously having taken any steps in the action.[22] It is not sufficient that the judgment-debtor submitted in the eyes of the foreign court; it must be shown that the judgment-debtor took part in the foreign proceedings in a way accepted by English law as amounting to a voluntary appearance.[23] However, acts which would be regarded as submission in English law are not sufficient to found jurisdiction in the international sense if those acts would not constitute submission under the law of the original court.[24]

3.18 If D submits to proceedings brought by C1 in a foreign country this is not an implied submission to related proceedings commenced by C2 in the same court, even if the proceedings commenced by C1 and C2 involve almost identical issues. In *Adams v Cape Industries plc*[25] an English company, which had been involved—through subsidiary and associated companies—in the mining and sale of asbestos, was the defendant in two sets of proceedings (the *Tyler 1* actions and the *Tyler 2* actions) brought by more than 600 asbestos workers in Texas. The defendant took part in the *Tyler 1* actions, which were settled, but contested the jurisdiction of the original court in relation to the *Tyler 2* actions and took no further part in those proceedings. Scott J rejected the argument that, by taking part in the *Tyler 1* actions, the defendant had submitted to

---

[22] *SA Consortium General Textiles v Sun and Sand Agencies Ltd* [1978] QB 279; *Pattni v Ali* [2007] 2 AC 85.
[23] Roch LJ in *Desert Sun Loan Corpn v Hill* [1996] 2 All ER 847 at 862. See also *Akande v Balfour Beatty Construction Ltd* [1998] ILPr 110.
[24] *Starlight International Inc v Bruce* [2002] ILPr 35.   [25] [1990] Ch 433.

the jurisdiction of the original court as regards the *Tyler 2* actions. As the two sets of proceedings were not to be regarded as 'one unit of litigation', the steps taken by the defendant in the *Tyler 1* actions could not be regarded as constituting submission for the purposes of the *Tyler 2* actions.[26] However, where D submits in foreign proceedings brought by C, D's submission to the foreign court's jurisdiction extends not only to further claims concerning the same subject-matter, but also to claims which are connected or related to the original claim; whether a claim is connected or related is a question of degree to be decided by the English court.[27]

3.19 A defendant is not to be regarded as having submitted to the jurisdiction of a foreign court only by reason of the fact that he appeared to contest the court's jurisdiction or to ask the court to dismiss or stay the proceedings on the ground that the dispute should be submitted to arbitration or to the determination of the courts of another country.[28] As long as it is clear from the defendant's first defence, rather than in some subsequent defence, that he is contesting the foreign court's jurisdiction, his conduct does not amount to submission even if the first defence contains some additional material which constitutes a plea to the merits of the case.[29] If, however, the defendant's jurisdictional challenge is rejected and the defendant subsequently defends the claim on the merits, the defendant has submitted to the court's jurisdiction.[30]

3.20 The defendant does not submit to the jurisdiction of the foreign court if his appearance in the original proceedings was not voluntary. Whether the defendant appeared voluntarily is to be determined by English law, rather than by the law of the country of origin.[31] An appearance is not voluntary if it is due to duress or undue influence brought to bear by the other party.[32] It is also provided by legislation that a defendant shall not be regarded as having submitted to the jurisdiction of the foreign court by reason only of the fact that he appeared 'to protect, or obtain the release of, property seized or threatened with seizure in the proceedings'.[33] This rule safeguards a defendant who is sued in a foreign country whose courts assume jurisdiction on the ground of the presence of the defendant's property in that country. In the absence of a sufficient territorial connection between the defendant and the country of origin, if the defendant does not appear in the proceedings the judgment is not enforceable in England. This might well be of little comfort to the defendant if his property in the country of origin is seized in order to found the court's jurisdiction and he loses this property as a result of an adverse judgment. The effect of the law is that the defendant may enter an appearance to protect his property but that, since this is not regarded as voluntary submission, the final judgment of the foreign court is not enforceable in England by virtue of the defendant's participation.

---

[26] See Scott J at 462–3. [27] *Murthy v Sivajothi* [1999] 1 WLR 467.
[28] Civil Jurisdiction and Judgments Act 1982, s 33(1)(a) and (b).
[29] Neill LJ in *Marc Rich & Co AG v Società Italiana Impianti PA (No 2)* [1992] 1 Lloyd's Rep 624 at 633.
[30] *Spliethoff's Bevrachtingskantoor BV v Bank of China Ltd* [2015] 2 Lloyd's Rep 123.
[31] *Desert Sun Loan Corpn v Hill* [1996] 2 All ER 847.
[32] *Israel Discount Bank of New York v Hadjipateras* [1984] 1 WLR 137.
[33] Civil Jurisdiction and Judgments Act 1982, s 33(1)(c).

(iii) Invoking the jurisdiction of the original court

3.21 The judgment-debtor will be held to have submitted to the jurisdiction of a foreign court if he took part in the proceedings as claimant.[34] If, for example, C brings an action for breach of contract against D in New York and the New York court gives a judgment in D's favour and orders C to pay D's costs, the order for costs is enforceable in England on the ground that C had submitted to the jurisdiction of the original court. Similarly, if D counterclaims in proceedings commenced by C and obtains a judgment in his favour, that judgment is, in principle, entitled to recognition and enforcement in England.

(C) A sufficient territorial connection

(i) Individuals

3.22 It is well established that a foreign judgment is enforceable in England if there was a sufficient territorial connection between the defendant and the country of origin. As regards individuals there is some uncertainty whether the appropriate connecting factor is residence or presence.[35] There are three types of case to consider.

3.23 The first situation is where the defendant is not only resident in the country of origin but also is present there when the proceedings are commenced. There is no doubt that in this case the foreign court is a court of competent jurisdiction.[36]

3.24 The second case is where the defendant is present in the country of origin at the commencement of proceedings, but is not resident in that country. There is some ambiguity in the cases as to the correct solution in this situation. For many years the textbooks relied on Buckley LJ's judgment in *Emanuel v Symon*[37] in which it was stated that a foreign court is to be regarded as a court of competent jurisdiction if the defendant was resident in the country of origin at the time of the commencement of the foreign proceedings.[38] The law was, however, subjected to extensive review in *Adams v Cape Industries plc*.[39] The Court of Appeal expressed the view[40] that the jurisdiction of the foreign court—in the private international law sense—depends on the defendant's voluntary presence in the country of origin, rather than his residence.[41] In reaching this conclusion the Court of Appeal placed particular emphasis on *Carrick v Hancock* in which Lord Russell of Killowen CJ stated that the jurisdiction of a court is based upon the principle of territorial dominion, and that 'all persons within any territorial dominion owe their allegiance to its sovereign power and obedience to all its laws and to the lawful jurisdiction of its courts'.[42] The Court of Appeal also sought to derive support

---

[34] *Emanuel v Symon* [1908] 1 KB 302.
[35] Although there are dicta which suggest that the English court will prima facie enforce a foreign judgment if the judgment-debtor is a national of the country of origin (see, in particular, *Emanuel v Symon* [1908] 1 KB 302), as nationality is not a connecting factor which has traditionally been adopted by the common law, the correctness of such dicta is doubtful.
[36] *Adams v Cape Industries plc* [1990] Ch 433.   [37] [1908] 1 KB 302 at 309.
[38] See, eg, Jaffey, *Introduction to the Conflict of Laws* (1988) p 224.   [39] [1990] Ch 433.
[40] Ibid, 518.   [41] See also the decision of the Supreme Court in *Rubin v Eurofinance SA* [2013] 1 AC 236.
[42] (1895) 12 TLR 59 at 60.

from the principles governing the English court's jurisdiction, according to which service of process on the defendant during a temporary visit to England is sufficient to found the court's jurisdiction.[43]

3.25 The third situation is where the defendant is resident in the country of origin at the commencement of proceedings, but is not present there at that time. The Court of Appeal expressly left open this third situation.[44] If presence is properly regarded as a sufficient connection, residence—even if not accompanied by presence—should also be adequate since residence is a more substantial connection than mere presence.

(ii) Companies

3.26 Since a company is a legal person without a physical existence, any test which is based on presence or residence has to be applied analogistically rather than literally. One approach would be to look at the activities of the company and ask whether the company was economically present in the country of origin—by doing business there.[45] The common law has not adopted this approach. Rather than looking for economic presence, the court applies a more physical test based on the notion of a place of business. There are two possibilities to consider with regard to companies: direct presence and indirect presence (through a representative).

(a) Direct presence

3.27 A company has direct presence in the country of origin if 'it has established and maintained at its own expense (whether as owner or lessee) a fixed place of business of its own in the other country and for more than a minimal period of time has carried on its own business at or from such premises by its servants or agents'.[46] The mere fact that a company carries on business in a foreign country is not enough to make its court a court of competent jurisdiction. In *Littauer Glove Corpn v FW Millington*[47] proceedings in New York were commenced against an English company, which carried on business in the United States. The originating process was served on one of the company's directors in New York while he was there on business. The company took no part in the proceedings and resisted enforcement of the New York judgment in England. The court held that the judgment was not enforceable in England: the company had not submitted to the jurisdiction of the original court and did not have a place of business in New York. It is equally clear that the mere selling of goods in country B by a seller, established in country A, does not amount to the presence of the seller in country B; by the same token, the fact that the defendant runs a website which is accessible in country B does not mean that the defendant is present in country B.[48]

---

[43] *Maharanee of Baroda v Wildenstein* [1972] 2 QB 283.   [44] [1990] Ch 433 at 518.
[45] See Fawcett, 'A New Approach to Jurisdiction over Companies in Private International Law' (1988) 37 ICLQ 645.
[46] Slade LJ in *Adams v Cape Industries plc* [1990] Ch 433 at 530.   [47] (1928) 44 TLR 746.
[48] *Lucasfilm Ltd v Ainsworth* [2010] Ch 503.

(b) Indirect presence

3.28 As regards indirect presence the position is more complex. The leading authority is *Adams v Cape Industries plc*[49] in which the Court of Appeal had to consider a case involving the defendant (an English company) which, it was alleged, transacted business in the United States (and elsewhere) through subsidiaries or associated companies, including a US marketing company. When the defendant was sued in the United States, the question arose whether the defendant was indirectly present there—through the marketing company. The Court of Appeal held that it was not. A company is indirectly present in a foreign country only if a representative of the company has for more than a minimal period of time been carrying on the company's business in the other country at or from some fixed place of business.[50] For the purposes of this rule it is of crucial importance that the *company's* business has been transacted at or from the fixed place of business. On the facts of the case the Court of Appeal held that the US marketing company was carrying on its own business—rather than the defendant's business.

3.29 Whether a representative in the country of origin is carrying on the company's business depends on a range of factors including: the extent to which the company contributes to the financing of the business carried on by the representative; the way in which the representative is remunerated (for example, by commission or by fixed regular payments); the degree of control the company exercises over the running of the business conducted by the representative; whether the representative displays the company's name at his premises or on his stationery; what business, if any, the representative transacts as principal exclusively on his own behalf; whether the representative makes contracts with customers or other third parties in the name of the company and, if so, whether the representative requires specific authority in advance before binding the company to contractual obligations.[51] Although no single factor is decisive, whether the representative is able to contract on behalf of the company is of particular significance. In *Vogel v R & A Kohnstamm Ltd*[52] D, an English company, sold goods to C in Israel. D was assisted by an agent in Israel who acted as a channel of communication between D and its Israeli customers. C obtained a judgment against D from the Israeli courts and sought to enforce it in England. D had taken no part in the foreign proceedings and contended that the agency in Israel could not be regarded as its place of business. The court held that the Israeli judgment was not enforceable; it could not be said that D was indirectly present in Israel through the agent who sought customers and transmitted correspondence but who 'had no authority whatever to bind the defendant in any shape or form.'[53]

(iii) *A problem with federal states*

3.30 Particular problems may arise in the context of cases involving foreign judgments granted by the courts of federal states which comprise a number of separate law districts. The problem results from the fact that there may be two different types of

---

[49] [1990] Ch 433. [50] At 530. [51] At 530–1.
[52] [1973] QB 133. [53] Ashworth J at 143.

judgment: the judgments of local courts and the judgments of federal courts. Whether a case is assigned to a local court or a federal court is determined by the constitutional law of the state in question.

3.31 Where the claimant seeks enforcement in England on the basis of the defendant's presence at the commencement of the proceedings, does the claimant have to show that the defendant was present in the particular law district in which the judgment was granted or is it enough that the defendant was present in the larger political unit? In *Adams v Cape Industries plc*[54] the US marketing company was incorporated in Illinois, but the proceedings against the defendant were conducted in Texas. Was the Texas court to be regarded as a court of competent jurisdiction only if the defendant had been present in Texas (the law district in which the original proceedings took place) or was it sufficient for the defendant to have been present somewhere in the United States of America (the political unit)? The Court of Appeal disposed of the appeal by deciding that the defendant was not present—either directly or indirectly—anywhere in the United States. Accordingly, consideration of what the position would have been if the defendant had been present in the United States was unnecessary. However, since the question had been argued, the Court of Appeal decided to express its view on the matter.

3.32 The defendant contended that, for the purposes of the English conflict of laws, the relevant territorial unit should be the law district rather than the larger political unit. On the basis of this analysis the original court could not have been regarded as a court of competent jurisdiction, since, if present anywhere, the defendant was present in Illinois, rather than in Texas. The plaintiffs, however, sought to place emphasis on the fact that the proceedings in Texas had been conducted in a federal court, rather than in a local court. It was accepted that, if proceedings are conducted in a local court, the defendant's presence in the relevant law district must be established; it was argued, however, that if the original proceedings are conducted in a federal court, it has to be established only that the defendant was present somewhere in the political unit.

3.33 Although the Court of Appeal did not purport to reach a definitive conclusion, it favoured the plaintiffs' analysis. As regards proceedings conducted in local courts, the defendant must have the appropriate territorial connection with the law district in which the court sits. In the words of Slade LJ: 'The fact that Chicago is in the United States does not make Texas any the less a foreign court for a resident in Illinois than if Chicago were in France.'[55] In federal matters, however, the political unit should be treated as a single country, so that any federal court should be regarded as a court of competent jurisdiction as long as the defendant was present somewhere within the political unit. So, if the plaintiffs had been able to establish the defendant's presence in Illinois through the marketing company, the Court of Appeal would have been inclined to regard the Texas court as a court of competent jurisdiction.

---

[54] [1990] Ch 433. [55] Ibid, 555.

3.34 The basic approach adopted by the Court of Appeal has much to recommend it; the distinction between local and federal matters seems to be a logical one. The analysis is, however, premised on the notion that, as regards federal matters, there is a single, national system of jurisdiction. All three members of the Court of Appeal thought, 'albeit with varying degrees of doubt',[56] that there is a national system of jurisdiction in federal matters in the United States of America. It has been questioned whether this is really the case: US legislation provides for the registration of judgments of federal courts in other states of the Union; and, for the purposes of enforcement, US law treats the judgment of a federal court in the same way as the judgment of a local court.[57] The Court of Appeal's approach might lead to a situation in which a judgment of a federal court sitting in Texas would be enforceable in England but not be enforceable in other parts of the United States. Since the Court of Appeal's view was both tentative and obiter, a court in a subsequent case may feel free not to follow it.

(D) Immovable property

3.35 Just as the English court will not adjudicate on questions relating to title to, or the right to the possession of, immovable property outside England,[58] it will not regard a foreign court as a court of competent jurisdiction on such a question in respect of immovable property outside its country, even if the defendant was present in the country of origin at the commencement of the proceedings or submitted to the jurisdiction of its courts.[59]

(E) Forum conveniens?

3.36 The foundations of the common law rules relating to foreign judgments were laid in the second half of the nineteenth century when the primary bases of the English court's jurisdiction were presence and submission. At this time there was only a very limited form of 'long-arm' jurisdiction, introduced by the Common Law Procedure Act 1854, and the doctrine of forum non conveniens was not even a glimmer in the eye of the House of Lords. It is hardly surprising that, when deciding whether or not to enforce a foreign judgment, the courts in the nineteenth century looked to see whether the defendant had been present in the country of origin or had submitted to the jurisdiction of its courts.

3.37 The traditional rules on jurisdiction have undergone a profound transformation in the intervening years; extraterritorial jurisdiction—now under CPR rule 6.36—has been significantly extended and the test of appropriateness has come to dominate the jurisdictional inquiry. It is no longer true to say that the English court assumes jurisdiction on the grounds of presence and submission; the English court may assume jurisdiction over an absent defendant if England is the forum conveniens and may decline jurisdiction against a defendant who is present in England if another forum is more

---

[56] Slade LJ at 557.
[57] See Carter (1990) 61 BYIL 402; Collier [1990] CLJ 416.
[58] See para 2.257.
[59] Dicey, Morris and Collins, *The Conflict of Laws* (15th edn, 2012) pp 716–19.

appropriate.[60] There has not, however, been a similar shift in attitude to jurisdictional questions in cases concerning foreign judgments.[61]

3.38 The decision of the Court of Appeal in *Adams v Cape Industries plc*[62] only served to widen the gulf between the common law principles which determine the English court's jurisdiction and those which, at the enforcement stage, determine whether a foreign court is to be regarded as a court of competent jurisdiction. To a very significant extent the traditional rules fall into a pattern which has been described as a 'sort of law of the jungle' in that they display 'the twin vices of . . . exorbitant national jurisdictional rules, and extremely narrow judgment recognition practices'.[63] If, for example, an English defendant, while visiting a foreign country, causes injury to a local inhabitant in a driving accident, the English court will not enforce a judgment against the defendant granted by the foreign court, unless the defendant submitted to the jurisdiction of the original court or was served with the originating process while abroad. To reach the defendant's assets the claimant must sue in the English court. This hardly seems just to the claimant who has been injured in his own country. Moreover, the foreign court is prima facie the more appropriate forum. (If the facts were reversed—a foreigner injures an English resident in a road accident in England—the English court would be prepared to assume jurisdiction.[64]) There is something fundamentally suspect about a system of rules which refuses to enforce a judgment given by a foreign court which is obviously the most appropriate forum for the trial of the action. The current rules may also work an injustice on a person with assets in England who finds himself the defendant in foreign proceedings. If, for example, an English defendant is served with process in New York while on holiday there, the ensuing judgment of the New York court is prima facie entitled to enforcement in England even if the defendant's presence in New York was fleeting and the claim has no connection at all with the country of origin. Since this is a situation in which the English court would, mutatis mutandis, stay the proceedings, it seems somewhat irrational to say that the New York judgment creates an obligation which the English court should enforce.

3.39 It might be concluded that, if the English court assumes jurisdiction when it is the appropriate forum, it ought to be prepared to enforce a foreign judgment when the original court was the appropriate forum (and should refuse to enforce a foreign judgment if the original court was not an appropriate forum).[65] There are, however, certain problems with this approach. The test of appropriateness is fundamentally open-textured and turns on the exercise of the court's discretion. There would be considerable

---

[60] See paras 2.150–2.176 and 2.212–2.238.
[61] See, however, the approach of the Canadian Supreme Court in *Saldhana v Beals* (2003) 234 DLR (4th) 1.
[62] [1990] Ch 433.
[63] Borchers, 'Comparing Personal Jurisdiction in the United States and the European Community: Lessons for American Reform' (1992) 40 Am J Comp L 121, 128.
[64] CPR r 6.36, PD 6B para 3.1(9). The court will almost invariably conclude in such a case that England is the appropriate forum: *The Albaforth* [1984] 2 Lloyd's Rep 91; *Berezovsky v Michaels* [2000] 1 WLR 1004. See, however, *VTB Capital plc v Nutritek International Corpn* [2013] 2 AC 337.
[65] See Briggs, 'Which Foreign Judgments Should We Recognise Today?' (1987) 36 ICLQ 240; cf Harris, 'Recognition of Foreign Judgments—the Anti-suit Injunction Link' (1997) 17 OJLS 477.

uncertainty if the enforceability of foreign judgments at common law depended on the English court having to determine whether it would have assumed jurisdiction in similar circumstances. There is no easy answer to the question whether such uncertainty would be a price worth paying for a more coherent system of rules.

2. Final and conclusive

3.40 Even if the foreign court was a court of competent jurisdiction, the judgment cannot be enforced in England unless it is final and conclusive in the country of origin. This means that the judgment must conclusively and permanently decide the matter between the parties; whether the foreign judgment has these characteristics is to be determined by reference to the law of the country of origin.[66] If, according to the foreign law, the judgment can be challenged by the losing party in the same court with the possibility of its being varied or set aside, the judgment will not normally be regarded as final and conclusive and will not be enforced in England.[67] Nevertheless, a default judgment (which is valid unless and until it is set aside) may be final and conclusive for the purposes of this rule.[68] As long as the decision of the foreign court is not provisional or subject to revision it will be regarded as final and conclusive even if the decision is made on a procedural matter at a stage of the proceedings prior to the final determination of the claim.[69] Furthermore, the fact that a judgment is subject to appeal in the country of origin does not mean that it is not final and conclusive, although in such a case the English court might stay enforcement proceedings pending the outcome of the appeal.[70]

3. For a fixed sum of money, not being a tax or penalty

3.41 At common law a foreign order for the delivery of goods (or other specific performance) or for an injunction is not entitled to enforcement. The only judgments which can be enforced at common law are judgments for a fixed sum of money. Nevertheless, a foreign judgment for a tax or for the payment of a fine or other penalty will not be enforced. This is an aspect of the general principle that the English court will not enforce the revenue or penal laws of foreign countries.[71]

3.42 As a general rule, if the defendant is ordered to pay a sum of money to a private person—rather than to the state—the judgment is enforceable. A judgment which orders the defendant to pay exemplary or punitive damages is in principle enforceable.[72] Similarly, an order by a criminal court that the defendant must compensate his victim may be enforced in England.[73] The mere fact that a judgment orders the defendant to pay a sum to the state does not, in itself, mean that the judgment cannot be enforced in England; the

---

[66] *Joint Stock Co 'Aeroflot-Russian Airlines' v Berezovsky* [2014] 1 CLC 53.
[67] *Nouvion v Freeman* (1889) 15 App Cas 1; *Buehler v Chronos Richardson Ltd* [1998] 2 All ER 960; *The Irini A (No 2)* [1999] 1 Lloyd's Rep 189.
[68] *Vanquelin v Bouard* (1863) 15 CBNS 341.
[69] Stuart-Smith LJ in *Desert Sun Loan Corpn v Hill* [1996] 2 All ER 847 at 863.
[70] *Colt Industries Inc v Sarlie (No 2)* [1966] 1 WLR 1287.   [71] See paras 1.145–1.151.
[72] *SA Consortium General Textiles v Sun and Sand Agencies Ltd* [1978] QB 279.
[73] *Raulin v Fischer* [1911] 2 KB 93.

question is whether the sum is a tax or is payable by way of punishment. In *United States of America v Inkley*[74] the US government sought to enforce a judgment for the amount of an appearance bond given by the defendant. Although the judgment resulted from civil proceedings in Florida, the appearance bond had been required to encourage the defendant to answer various criminal charges. The Court of Appeal concluded that the judgment was not enforceable because the payment was in the nature of a penalty.[75]

B **Conditions for recognition**

3.43 The recognition of a foreign judgment is dependent on various conditions being fulfilled: (i) the court must be a court of competent jurisdiction; (ii) the judgment must be final and conclusive; (iii) the judgment must be on the merits; (iv) the foreign proceedings must have been between the same parties and have involved the same cause of action or the same issue. The first and second of these four requirements apply equally in enforcement cases and have already been discussed.[76] The final condition determines not only the extent to which matters determined by the foreign court are regarded as conclusive but also the person or persons who are bound by the foreign court's decision. Where the relevant conditions are established a foreign judgment is prima facie entitled to recognition; the foreign judgment establishes either a cause of action estoppel (if the English and foreign proceedings involve the same cause of action) or an issue estoppel (if an issue raised before the English court is the same as an issue decided by the original court). The party wishing to deny the effect of a foreign judgment may, however, resist recognition of the judgment if he can establish one of the available defences.

3.44 Broadly speaking, there are three types of situation in which the recognition of a foreign judgment may arise. First, a defendant who is successful in foreign proceedings may wish to rely on a foreign judgment as a defence to English proceedings involving the same issue or cause of action. In such cases there is little difficulty in establishing that the foreign court was a court of competent jurisdiction. Where, for example, C sues D abroad and the foreign court gives judgment in D's favour, if C starts proceedings in England on the same cause of action the judgment is prima facie entitled to recognition as a judgment of a court of competent jurisdiction since C submitted to the original court by participating in the proceedings as claimant.

3.45 Secondly, the defendant may seek to rely on a foreign judgment, not only where the judgment has been given in his favour, but also where the judgment has been given in the claimant's favour. Section 34 of the Civil Jurisdiction and Judgments Act 1982 provides that no proceedings may be brought by a person in England on a cause of action in respect of which a judgment has been given in his favour in proceedings between the same parties[77] in a foreign court unless that judgment is not enforceable or entitled

---

[74] [1989] QB 255.
[75] See also *Pocket Kings Ltd v Safenames Ltd* [2010] Ch 438.   [76] See paras 3.12–3.40.
[77] For the purposes of s 34 of the 1982 Act, English proceedings in rem brought by C in relation to a ship owned by D involve the same parties as foreign proceedings in which C sued D in personam: *Republic of India v India Steamship Co Ltd (No 2)* [1998] AC 878. For further consideration of this case, see para 3.54.

to recognition in England.[78] As long as the conditions laid down in section 34 are satisfied a claimant who has been awarded a sum of money by a foreign judgment cannot sue in England on the original cause of action.

3.46 In *Black v Yates*[79] the plaintiff's husband had been killed in Spain in a road accident caused by the defendant's negligence. The defendant was prosecuted and, in the context of the criminal proceedings to which the plaintiff joined a civil claim for damages, the Spanish court awarded the plaintiff compensation. The plaintiff subsequently commenced proceedings against the defendant in England, in the hope of obtaining higher damages under the Fatal Accidents Acts. It was held that the plaintiff's action was barred by section 34, notwithstanding the fact that the Spanish proceedings started out as a criminal prosecution to which the plaintiff was not an original party. However, section 34 is not a mandatory provision. In *Republic of India v India Steamship Co Ltd*[80] the House of Lords decided that section 34 merely provides the defendant with a defence, which may be defeated by estoppel, waiver, or contrary agreement. If a claimant, having obtained a judgment in his favour abroad, starts proceedings in England on the same cause of action and the defendant consents to the jurisdiction of the English court, section 34 does not bar the English proceedings.

3.47 Thirdly, a judgment-creditor may wish to raise issue estoppel as a means of limiting the grounds on which the judgment-debtor may challenge enforcement of a foreign judgment in England. Consider the situation where C seeks to enforce in England the judgment of a foreign court which assumed jurisdiction on the basis of D's submission. If in the course of its decision the original court determined that D authorised a local lawyer to accept service of process on his behalf, the foreign judgment prima facie creates an issue estoppel in relation to that factual question. If the factual issues definitively determined by the original court establish that D submitted to the jurisdiction of the foreign court *according to English conflict of laws rules* D is effectively estopped from arguing that the foreign court was not a court of competent jurisdiction.[81]

1. On the merits

3.48 For a foreign judgment to be a good defence to proceedings in England it must have been a judgment on the merits.[82] It is provided by statute that where a foreign court dismisses an action on the ground that it is time-barred the action is deemed to have been determined on its merits.[83]

3.49 As a general rule, if the foreign court dismisses an action on the basis that it lacks jurisdiction under its own law, that does not preclude the claimant from suing on the same cause of action in the English court. This general principle is qualified, however,

---

[78] See *Karafarin Bank v Mansoury-dara* [2009] 2 Lloyd's Rep 289.
[79] [1992] QB 526.   [80] [1993] AC 410.
[81] See *Desert Sun Loan Corpn v Hill* [1996] 2 All ER 847.
[82] *Harris v Quine* (1869) LR 4 QB 653; *Black-Clawson International Ltd v Papierwerke Waldhof-Aschaffenburg AG* [1975] AC 591.
[83] Foreign Limitation Periods Act 1984, s 3.

by the decision of the House of Lords in *The Sennar (No 2)*.[84] This case concerned a Dutch judgment which had been given in the context of litigation involving two foreign companies. Although there was a contract between the parties conferring exclusive jurisdiction on the courts of Sudan, C had sought to avoid the impact of the jurisdiction clause by framing the claim in tort. The Dutch courts dismissed the claim on the ground that C was entitled to found the claim only in contract and was bound by the jurisdiction clause. When C started proceedings against D in England with a view to obtaining damages in tort, D sought to rely on the Dutch judgment. C argued, however, that, since the Dutch court had dismissed the claim on jurisdictional grounds, the judgment was not on the merits and, therefore, was not entitled to recognition in England. The House of Lords was not persuaded by C's argument. Lord Brandon went some way towards clarifying what is meant by a decision 'on the merits': although a decision on procedure alone, if looked at negatively, is not a decision on the merits, if looked at positively 'a decision on the merits is a decision which establishes certain facts proved or not in dispute, states what are the relevant principles of law applicable to such facts, and expresses a conclusion with regard to the effect of applying those principles to the factual situation concerned'.[85]

3.50 On the basis of this analysis, the Dutch judgment was 'on the merits' in a positive sense as regards two questions: first, C's only claim against D was for breach of contract; secondly, C was bound by the jurisdiction clause in favour of the Sudanese courts. Accordingly, D was entitled to rely on the Dutch judgment in support of its application for a stay.

3.51 It follows from *The Sennar (No 2)* that a foreign judgment which, in general terms, decides a procedural or jurisdictional question may be regarded as determining an issue (or a number of issues) 'on the merits'. In order for the decision of a foreign court on such an issue to be regarded as a decision 'on the merits' not only must there have been an express submission of the procedural or jurisdictional issue in question to the foreign court but also the specific issue of fact must have been raised before, and decided by, that court.[86]

2. Cause of action and issue estoppel

3.52 Where a foreign judgment operates as a defence, this is by way of estoppel per rem judicatam, just as where the prior judgment is given by the English court. There are two forms of such estoppel: cause of action estoppel (where the claimant is prevented from suing on the same claim) and issue estoppel (where, although the cause of action is different, the claimant is estopped from contending that a particular issue should be decided differently from the way the identical issue was decided in an earlier case). Whichever form the estoppel takes, there are two fundamental conditions which must be satisfied, in addition to those already considered: first, the parties to the foreign proceedings and the English proceedings must be the same; secondly, the cause of action (or issue) in the English proceedings must be the same cause of action (or issue) as was determined by the foreign court.

---

[84] [1985] 1 WLR 490.   [85] At 499.   [86] *Desert Sun Loan Corpn v Hill* [1996] 2 All ER 847.

(A) Identity of the parties

3.53 In the straightforward case, where a foreign court gives judgment in proceedings involving C and D and C then starts proceedings against D on the same cause of action in England, the foreign judgment gives rise to a cause of action estoppel. The position is more complicated, however, in cases involving multi-party litigation and in cases involving a foreign judgment in personam and English proceedings in rem (or a foreign judgment in rem and English proceedings in personam).

3.54 A cause of action estoppel is not only effective as between the parties to the foreign proceedings but is also binding on the parties' 'privies'. Although there is a dearth of authority as to who are privies for the purposes of the doctrine of res judicata,[87] it seems that two parties are in a relationship of privity if there is privity of blood, title, or interest.[88] Privies include, for example, a person who succeeds to the rights and liabilities of another on the latter's death. In *Republic of India v India Steamship Co Ltd (No 2)*[89] the court had to consider the impact of a foreign judgment in personam on later proceedings in rem commenced in England. C sued D in India and obtained damages for breach of contract. Subsequently, C started proceedings in rem in England in respect of one of D's vessels. D applied for the claim to be dismissed under section 34 of the Civil Jurisdiction and Judgments Act 1982[90] on the ground that the English proceedings involved the same cause of action and the same parties as the Indian proceedings. C argued, however, that the parties to the two sets of proceedings were different because, in proceedings in rem, the defendant is the vessel, rather than its owner. The House of Lords rejected C's argument. The purpose of section 34 is to prevent the same cause of action being tried twice over between those who are, in reality, the same parties. Where C obtains a judgment in personam against D in foreign proceedings and then starts proceedings in rem in England, section 34 bars the English action if D is the owner of the vessel on which process is served in the Admiralty claim in rem.

(B) Identity of the cause of action or the issue

(i) Identity of the cause of action

3.55 The fundamental principle underlying cause of action estoppel is that a litigant should be prevented from asserting or denying, as against the other party, the existence of a particular cause of action, the non-existence or existence of which has been determined by a court of competent jurisdiction in previous litigation between the same parties.[91] For the purposes of this principle a cause of action consists of the minimum facts which a claimant has to plead and (if necessary) prove in order to obtain the relief claimed.[92] Where a set of facts gives rise to two types of loss the question facing the court is whether there are two causes of action or one cause of action involving two types of damage.

---

[87] See Spencer Bower and Turner, *The Doctrine of Res Judicata* (2nd edn, 1969) pp 209–11.
[88] *Carl Zeiss Stiftung v Rayner & Keeler Ltd (No 2)* [1967] 1 AC 853. [89] [1998] AC 878.
[90] See para 3.45.   [91] *Thoday v Thoday* [1964] P 181.   [92] *Letang v Cooper* [1965] 1 QB 232.

3.56 This question was considered by the House of Lords in *Republic of India v India Steamship Co*,[93] a case which involved litigation arising out of bills of lading under which C's cargo was carried from Sweden to India in a ship owned by D. During the course of the voyage there was a fire on board the ship; some of the cargo was jettisoned and the rest was damaged. C sued D in India and the Indian court awarded damages for short delivery. C then started English proceedings claiming compensation for delivery of the cargo in a damaged condition. D argued that the Indian judgment created a cause of action estoppel which barred C's claim.[94] The House of Lords accepted that the same cause of action was involved in both the Indian and the English proceedings; for each claim C sought to rely on the same breach of contract.[95] The general principle is that a cause of action estoppel extends to matters which might have been raised (but were not raised) in the original proceedings; it was, therefore, irrelevant that C pleaded in the English proceedings particulars of damage which were not pleaded in the Indian proceedings.

3.57 There is every reason to think that the court would take the same approach to different types of loss and different heads of damage in a tort claim. Where, for example, the victim of a road accident suffers property damage and loses both an arm and a leg, if the victim sues abroad and pleads only the loss of the leg, the foreign judgment creates a cause of action estoppel as regards not only the other physical injuries (the loss of the arm) but also the other head of damage (property damage).[96]

(ii) Identity of the issue

3.58 Even if a foreign judgment does not create a cause of action estoppel, it may give rise to an issue estoppel. As a general rule, once an issue has been determined between the parties neither party is allowed to fight that issue all over again.[97] But, the issue determined by the foreign court must be *identical* to the issue raised in the English proceedings.[98] The nature of an issue estoppel can be illustrated by the following simple example: a dispute having arisen out of a contract between C and D, the parties enter a settlement agreement according to the terms of which C undertakes to pay specified sums to D; subsequently, C obtains a declaration from a foreign court that the original contract was illegal and void and refuses to honour the settlement agreement; when D seeks to enforce the settlement agreement in England, C challenges its validity. No cause of action estoppel arises in this situation because the central question in the English proceedings (the validity of the settlement agreement) is different from the central question in the foreign proceedings (the validity of the underlying contract).

---

[93] [1993] AC 410.   [94] Under Civil Jurisdiction and Judgments Act 1982, s 34.
[95] It was also held that if the defendant consents to the jurisdiction of the English court the defence provided by s 34 of the 1982 Act is waived.
[96] *Talbot v Berkshire County Council* [1994] QB 290. Compare, however, *Brunsden v Humphrey* (1884) 14 QBD 141.
[97] See Lord Denning MR in *Fidelitas Shipping Co Ltd v V/O Exportchleb* [1966] 1 QB 630 at 640.
[98] *Yukos Capital Sarl v OJSC Rosneft Oil Co (No 2)* [2014] 1 WLR 458 (whether recognition of a foreign judgment is contrary to Dutch public policy is not the same issue as whether recognition of that judgment would be contrary to English public policy); Mills [2012] CLJ 465.

However, the issue decided by the foreign court is relevant to the English proceedings. On the assumption that the conditions necessary for the creation of an issue estoppel are satisfied, the effect of the foreign judgment is that, in the context of the English proceedings, D is estopped from denying that the underlying contract was void for illegality. However, issue estoppel may be relied upon only if the determination of the issue by the foreign court was necessary for its decision.[99]

3.59 There may be considerable difficulty in deciding whether a foreign judgment has already determined a particular issue which is raised in proceedings in England and, if so, whether that determination was necessary for its decision. Accordingly, the courts have tended to be rather cautious when questions of issue estoppel are raised. If in doubt, the court will refuse to recognise the foreign judgment as having conclusive effect.[100] Indeed, it is accepted that the court has a discretion not to recognise a foreign judgment if it would be unjust to do so, even if the technical criteria for the creation of an issue estoppel are satisfied.[101] Moreover, the principle of issue estoppel may be held not to operate in a case where, subsequent to the foreign judgment, further material, which could not by reasonable diligence have been adduced in the foreign proceedings, becomes available.[102]

C Defences to recognition and enforcement

3.60 The positive conditions which must be satisfied by the party wishing to enforce or rely on a foreign judgment are only one half of the equation. Even if the foreign court was a court of competent jurisdiction and the other relevant conditions are satisfied, recognition or enforcement will be refused if the party seeking to deny the impact of the foreign judgment establishes one of a number of defences.

3.61 There are two general points which should be mentioned before the specific defences are considered. First, as a general rule, it is not possible to raise at the recognition or enforcement stage defences which were raised, or could have been raised, in the foreign proceedings. Secondly, it is not a defence to recognition or enforcement that the judgment was wrong on the merits, whether on the facts or the law. It is even immaterial that the foreign court misapplied English law in reaching its decision.[103]

3.62 The court has to strike a difficult balance: on the one hand, defences should be kept within limits, otherwise the English court will assume the unacceptable role of a Court of Appeal in relation to the foreign proceedings; on the other hand, it is not reasonable to expect the English court to recognise or enforce a foreign judgment which conflicts

---

[99] *Carl Zeiss Stiftung v Rayner & Keeler Ltd (No 2)* [1967] 1 AC 853; *The Good Challenger* [2004] 1 Lloyd's Rep 67.
[100] *Desert Sun Loan Corpn v Hill* [1996] 2 All ER 847. See also *Baker v Ian McCall International Ltd* [2000] CLC 189.
[101] *Carl Zeiss Stiftung v Rayner & Keeler Ltd (No 2)* [1967] 1 AC 853.
[102] See *C (a minor) v Hackney London Borough Council* [1996] 1 WLR 789 (a case involving a domestic judgment).
[103] *Godard v Gray* (1870) LR 6 QB 139.

with fundamental notions of justice and fairness. Whether English law manages to deal adequately with these competing tensions may be questioned.

1. Natural justice

3.63 The English court will not recognise or enforce a foreign judgment which was obtained in a manner contrary to natural justice. The traditional understanding of natural justice is that it requires two conditions to be satisfied: first, the litigant must have been given notice of the foreign proceedings; secondly, the litigant must have been given a proper opportunity of presenting his case before the court.[104] Whether either of these elements is lacking is a question which should be determined by English law, rather than by the law of the country of origin. It would seem that if a method of serving notice on the defendant was used which was in accordance with a contract between the parties (for instance, service at a stated address) that will be sufficient for the English court, even if the defendant did not in fact receive the notice with the consequence that the judgment was obtained against him by default.[105] Indeed, although there are many cases in which it has been confirmed that breach of the principles of natural justice is a defence to the recognition or enforcement of a foreign judgment, the English court is not easily persuaded that natural justice has not been complied with. The fact that under the law of the country of origin the parties were not competent to give evidence themselves has been held not to preclude enforcement.[106]

3.64 There is also a strand in the cases which indicates that a foreign judgment will not be recognised or enforced if the original proceedings 'offend against English views of substantial justice'.[107] The question of 'substantial justice' was one of the many issues considered (obiter) by the Court of Appeal in *Adams v Cape Industries plc*.[108] Following the defendant's decision not to take part in the *Tyler 2* actions, the proceedings took—to English eyes—a slightly unusual turn. The proceedings in Texas did not involve a judicial investigation of the injuries of any of the individual plaintiffs; the judge simply directed that the average award for each of the plaintiffs should be $75,000 and counsel placed the plaintiffs in four bands according to the seriousness of their injuries. The defendant argued that, even if the plaintiffs could establish that the original court was a court of competent jurisdiction, the way in which the proceedings were conducted meant that the judgment was unacceptable.

3.65 The Court of Appeal asked itself the following question: did the proceedings in the foreign court offend against English views of substantial justice?[109] This question was answered in the affirmative; in cases involving a claim for unliquidated damages for a tortious wrong, the notion of substantial justice requires the amount of compensation to be assessed objectively by an independent judge, rather than subjectively by or on behalf of the claimant.[110]

---

[104] *Jacobson v Frachon* (1927) 138 LT 386. [105] *Feyerick v Hubbard* (1902) 71 LJKB 509.
[106] *Scarpetta v Lowenfeld* (1911) 27 TLR 509.
[107] Lindley MR in *Pemberton v Hughes* [1899] 1 Ch 781 at 790.   [108] [1990] Ch 433.
[109] Slade LJ at 564.   [110] At 567. See also *Masters v Leaver* [2000] ILPr 387.

3.66 The relationship between natural justice and substantial justice is far from clear. Although parts of the judgment in the Court of Appeal in *Adams v Cape Industries plc* seem to be couched in the language of public policy, the judgment does not suggest what the relationship between substantial justice and public policy might be. Furthermore, the content of substantial justice is inherently vague and there is no indication in the judgment in *Adams v Cape Industries plc* as to what are the principles of substantial justice. The approach adopted by the Court of Appeal invests the English court with a broad discretion and makes it difficult to predict how similar questions will be dealt with in subsequent cases.

2. Fraud

3.67 The English court will not recognise or enforce a judgment which was obtained by fraud. Fraud may take one of a number of forms. Most cases involve allegations by one party that the judgment was obtained by the presentation of evidence which the other party knew to be false. The defence of fraud also covers cases where a litigant has been deprived of the opportunity to take part in the foreign proceedings either by a trick of the other party[111] or as a result of threats of violence,[112] and cases in which the defendant's objection relates to fraud by the foreign court (where, for example, the court has accepted a bribe). The court is prepared to investigate allegations of fraud in this third category even if the allegations raise potentially sensitive political or diplomatic issues. In *Korea National Insurance Corporation v Allianz Global Corporate & Specialty AG*[113] it was argued that a North Korean judgment in favour of a North Korean insurance company against foreign reinsurers should not be enforced on the basis that (i) it had been procured by fraud instigated or approved by senior officials of the North Korean state and (ii) the North Korean judiciary was not independent of the state. The Court of Appeal decided that, notwithstanding the fact that the allegations might embarrass both the North Korean state and diplomatic relations between the United Kingdom and North Korea, the English court should normally look into such allegations.

3.68 The defendant is entitled in the English proceedings to establish the fraud in the original proceedings even if the allegations of fraud were considered and rejected by the foreign court. Although this rule, which was formulated by the courts in the nineteenth century[114] (when the prevailing attitude was judicial chauvinism, rather than judicial comity), was challenged in the second half of the twentieth century, it was confirmed by decisions of the Court of Appeal[115] and the House of Lords.[116] The defence of fraud is, therefore, an exception to the general rule that the English court will not question the merits of the foreign judgment or re-open questions determined by the original court.[117] It has also been held that the defence of fraud may be invoked in

---

[111] *Ochsenbein v Papelier* (1873) 7 Ch App 695. [112] *Jet Holdings Inc v Patel* [1990] 1 QB 335.
[113] [2009] Lloyd's Rep IR 480.
[114] *Abouloff v Oppenheimer & Co* (1882) 10 QBD 295; *Vadala v Lawes* (1890) 25 QBD 310.
[115] *Jet Holdings Inc v Patel* [1990] 1 QB 335. [116] *Owens Bank Ltd v Bracco* [1992] 2 AC 443.
[117] *Abouloff v Oppenheimer & Co* (1882) 10 QBD 295.

English proceedings even if the defendant failed to raise the issue in the foreign proceedings when he could have done so.[118]

3.69 There are, however, circumstances in which fraud cannot be raised as a defence to recognition or enforcement—namely, where there have been separate proceedings abroad leading to a judgment which creates an issue estoppel on the question of fraud; in such cases it is an abuse of the process of the English court for the defence of fraud to be raised again.[119] In *House of Spring Gardens Ltd v Waite*[120] the plaintiff obtained a judgment in Ireland (the first judgment).[121] The defendant subsequently started separate proceedings in Ireland with a view to having the first judgment set aside on the basis of fraud. The Irish court dismissed the defendant's allegation of fraud (the second judgment). When the plaintiff brought proceedings in England to enforce the first judgment, the defendant sought to raise the defence of fraud. The Court of Appeal held that the defendant was estopped: the second judgment, in which it had been decided that the first judgment had not been obtained by fraud, created an issue estoppel, thereby preventing the defendant from raising the question of fraud again.

3. Public policy

3.70 The court will not recognise or enforce a foreign judgment if to do so would be contrary to public policy. As elsewhere in the conflict of laws, there is no closed list of cases where public policy can be invoked. One instance is where, if the original proceedings had been brought in England, the cause of action under the foreign law would have been rejected on the ground of public policy even though the foreign law would otherwise have been applicable. There are very few cases involving commercial judgments in which public policy has been successfully invoked. It is not, for example, contrary to public policy to enforce a foreign judgment which orders the defendant to pay exemplary damages[122] or to enforce a foreign judgment ordering payment of a gambling debt.[123] It is, however, contrary to public policy to recognise or enforce a foreign judgment if recognition or enforcement of the judgment would lead to a breach of the defendant's rights under the European Convention on Human Rights (ECHR),[124] such as where the foreign proceedings did not respect the defendant's right to a fair trial under article 6, whether or not the country of origin is a signatory to the ECHR.[125]

---

[118] *Syal v Heyward* [1948] 2 KB 443.   [119] *Owens Bank Ltd v Etoile Commerciale SA* [1995] 1 WLR 44.
[120] [1991] 1 QB 241.
[121] The judgment pre-dated the entry into force of the Brussels Convention between the United Kingdom and Ireland.
[122] *SA Consortium General Textiles v Sun and Sand Agencies Ltd* [1978] QB 279.
[123] See, eg, *Liao Eng Kiat v Burswood Nominees Ltd* [2005] 4 LRC 8 (Court of Appeal, Singapore).
[124] *Merchant International Co Ltd v Natsionalna Aktsionerna Kompaniia Naftogaz Ukrainy* [2012] 1 WLR 3036.
[125] See, however, the controversial decision in *Government of the United States v Montgomery (No 2)* [2004] 1 WLR 2241 in which the House of Lords held, in the context of an application to register a US confiscation order under the Criminal Justice Act 1988, that art 6 of the ECHR was engaged only if the procedure of the original court involved a flagrant denial of justice. For criticism of the decision, see Fawcett, 'The Impact of Article 6(1) of the ECHR on Private International Law' (2007) 56 ICLQ 1, 23. For a more general discussion of the impact of art 6 of the ECHR on recognition and enforcement at common law, see Fawcett, Ní Shúilleabháin and Shah, *Human Rights and Private International Law* (2016) ch 7.

3.71 In *Re Macartney*,[126] a Maltese judgment under which personal representatives were ordered to pay maintenance to an illegitimate child of the deceased was refused enforcement on grounds of public policy, because the judgment entitled the child to receive maintenance even after her minority. The decision has been criticised,[127] for the only objection to the Maltese law on which the judgment was based was that it was different from English law, which should not be sufficient reason to reject the foreign law. In *Israel Discount Bank of New York v Hadjipateras*[128] the defendant sought to resist enforcement of a New York judgment on the basis that it was only as a result of his father's undue influence that he had entered the contract of guarantee on which the judgment was based. The defendant argued that it would be contrary to public policy to enforce the judgment. The Court of Appeal rejected the defence on the ground that the defendant, having failed to raise the issue of undue influence in the New York proceedings, was unable to raise the matter in the English enforcement proceedings. However, the Court of Appeal seems to have accepted the notion that a foreign judgment based on an agreement which contravenes public policy may be unenforceable on the ground of public policy.[129]

4. Conflicting judgments

3.72 A prior English judgment is a defence not only to subsequent English proceedings, but also to the recognition or enforcement of a subsequent foreign judgment.[130] It could hardly be otherwise; it is not reasonable to suppose that the English court would give effect to a foreign judgment which conflicts with an English judgment. If there are two conflicting foreign judgments—both of which satisfy the conditions for recognition or enforcement—the earlier judgment prevails unless the circumstances are such that the party wishing to rely on the earlier judgment is estopped from doing so.[131]

5. Judgment invalid under the foreign law

3.73 Will the English court recognise or enforce a judgment which otherwise qualifies for recognition or enforcement if it is invalid by the law of the country where it was granted—for example, because the court which granted it lacked jurisdiction under that law? Under the Family Law Act 1986 a foreign divorce decree cannot be recognised in England unless it is 'effective under the law of the country in which it was obtained';[132] similarly, under the Brussels I Recast cross-border enforcement of a judgment depends on the judgment being enforceable in the country of origin.[133] It follows that, as a general rule, a judgment that has been set aside in the country of origin will not be recognised or enforced in England.[134]

---

[126] [1921] 1 Ch 522.
[127] Patchett, *Recognition of Commercial Judgments and Awards in the Commonwealth* (1984) p 159.
[128] [1984] 1 WLR 137.
[129] Nevertheless, as a matter of English law, an agreement entered into under duress, while unenforceable, does not contravene public policy.
[130] *Vervaeke v Smith* [1983] 1 AC 145; *ED & F Man (Sugar) Ltd v Haryanto (No 2)* [1991] 1 Lloyd's Rep 429.
[131] *Showlag v Mansour* [1995] 1 AC 431.
[132] S 46(1)(a) and s 46(2)(a). See paras 8.91–8.93.   [133] Art 39.
[134] But, see Harder, 'Recognition of a Foreign Judgment Overturned by a Non-Recognisable Judgment' (2012/13) 14 Yb PIL 103.

3.74 So far as judgments in personam are concerned, the requirement that the judgment must be final and conclusive should mean that if the judgment is void under the foreign law, in the sense of being a nullity even without its having been set aside by the court, it cannot be recognised or enforced in England.[135] It has been held, however, that if the judgment is merely voidable under the foreign law, being valid unless and until it is set aside, it will be recognised or enforced. So, the omission in a French default judgment to recite the steps taken to bring the summons to the defendant's knowledge, as required by French law, was held not to prevent enforcement of the judgment in England, as it was, at most, only voidable under French law.[136] This is perhaps the best explanation also of *Vanquelin v Bouard*,[137] where the English court enforced a judgment of a French commercial court, even though by French law such a court had jurisdiction only over defendants who were traders, and the defendant was not a trader.

6. Foreign judgment in breach of arbitration or jurisdiction clause

3.75 By virtue of section 32 of the Civil Jurisdiction and Judgments Act 1982, if the claimant sues in a foreign country on a contract which contains a provision that the courts of some other country shall have exclusive jurisdiction, or that the dispute shall be submitted to arbitration (whether in England or abroad), the ensuing judgment shall normally be refused recognition or enforcement. A jurisdiction or arbitration agreement cannot provide a defence to recognition or enforcement, however, if it was illegal, void, unenforceable, or incapable of being performed.[138] Similarly, a defendant cannot rely on such a clause if the proceedings in the original court were brought with the defendant's agreement or if he counterclaimed in those proceedings or otherwise submitted to the jurisdiction.[139]

3.76 Where a foreign court assumes jurisdiction over a dispute on the basis that an alleged jurisdiction or arbitration clause is void (or that the defendant submitted to the court's jurisdiction), the original court's decision on this point does not establish an issue estoppel. In the context of proceedings in England for the recognition or enforcement of the foreign judgment on the merits, the English court is entitled to decide, according to its own conflicts rules, whether or not the alleged clause is void (or the defendant submitted).[140]

3.77 In *Tracomin SA v Sudan Oil Seeds*[141] the parties concluded a contract which contained a clause referring any dispute which might arise to arbitration in England. The plaintiff sued the defendant for breach of contract in Switzerland. Although the defendant contested the court's jurisdiction, the Swiss court concluded that the arbitration

---

[135] See, however, *Merker v Merker* [1963] P 283 where the court recognised a German divorce decree even though it was a complete nullity in Germany.
[136] *SA Consortium General Textiles v Sun and Sand Agencies Ltd* [1978] QB 279.
[137] (1863) 15 CBNS 341.   [138] S 32(2).
[139] S 32(1)(b) and (c). *Marc Rich & Co AG v Società Italiana Impianti (No 2)* [1992] 1 Lloyd's Rep 624; *Spliethoff's Bevrachtingskantoor BV v Bank of China Ltd* [2015] 2 Lloyd's Rep 123.
[140] S 32(3).   [141] [1983] 1 WLR 662.

clause was of no effect and handed down a judgment ordering the defendant to pay damages. When the plaintiff started enforcement proceedings in England, the defendant sought to rely on section 32 of the 1982 Act. The Court of Appeal refused to enforce the judgment, notwithstanding the fact that the Swiss court had decided that the arbitration clause was of no effect. According to English law, which was the law governing the contract, the arbitration clause was a valid clause which provided for the dispute to be settled otherwise than by proceedings in the Swiss courts. The defendant was, therefore, able to rely on the arbitration clause as a defence to the Swiss judgment.

7. Multiple damages

3.78 The Protection of Trading Interests Act 1980 was passed to counteract, in particular, the extraterritorial effect of US anti-trust laws. One of the features of the US legislation is that, where the law requires the claimant to be compensated for losses caused by anti-competitive behaviour, the defendant is required to pay 'triple damages'. Other American legislation, such as the Racketeer Influenced and Corrupt Organisations (RICO) statute, also makes provision for the trebling of damages.

3.79 Section 5 of the 1980 Act provides that a judgment for multiple damages shall not be enforced by any court in the United Kingdom.[142] In a situation where a foreign court makes a composite award of damages which includes an element of multiple damages, only the multiple element is rendered unenforceable by the 1980 Act; the judgment as a whole is not tainted by the part of the judgment which awards multiple damages. If, for example, a US court awards the claimant $8 million and that award includes multiple damages of $1.2 million under the RICO statute (ie, $400,000 multiplied by three), the claimant is unable to enforce the RICO element (ie, $1.2 million); however, section 5 of the 1980 Act does not bar enforcement of the non-RICO elements of the judgment (ie, $6.8 million) in England.[143]

III Statutory regimes based on the common law

A Administration of Justice Act 1920

3.80 The Administration of Justice Act 1920 provides for the reciprocal enforcement of money judgments as between the United Kingdom and Commonwealth countries. It applies only to the judgments of Commonwealth countries to which the Act has been extended by Order in Council, on the basis that such countries have made reciprocal

---

[142] Provision is also made in s 6 for the recovery in a UK court by certain defendants of the excess paid under a judgment for multiple damages.

[143] *Lewis v Eliades* [2004] 1 WLR 692. The 1980 Act also provides that a judgment is not to be enforced if it is based on particular competition law rules specified by the Secretary of State. The effect of the Protection of Trading Interests (Australian Trade Practices) Order 1988 (SI 1988/569), for example, is that a judgment based on s 81(1A) of the Australian Trade Practices Act 1974 is not enforceable in the United Kingdom.

provision for the enforcement of UK judgments.[144] It cannot be extended to any further country since the enactment of the Foreign Judgments (Reciprocal Enforcement) Act 1933, which was intended to take its place for the future.

3.81 Enforcement is by means of registration of the foreign judgment by the English court, but there are few differences from the substantive requirements at common law. The foreign court must have been a court of competent jurisdiction,[145] the only difference in this regard being that presence in the country of origin is not a sufficient territorial connection: the defendant must either have been resident (rather than merely present) in the country of origin or must have carried on business there.[146]

3.82 A foreign judgment shall not be enforced in England under the 1920 Act in the following circumstances: if the defendant 'was not duly served with the process of the original court and did not appear';[147] if the judgment was obtained by fraud; if an appeal is pending in the country of origin; or if the judgment was in respect of a cause of action which for reasons of public policy or for some other similar reason could not have been entertained by the English court.[148] Defences are also provided by section 32 of the Civil Jurisdiction and Judgments Act 1982 and section 5 of the Protection of Trading Interests Act 1980. Presumably, a judgment would also be refused enforcement if it were to conflict with an English judgment.

3.83 The 1920 Act does not abrogate the common law. It does not deal with recognition, as opposed to enforcement, and, as regards a judgment which falls within the scope of the Act, a claimant may choose to bring an action at common law instead of applying to register the judgment under the Act. However, a claimant who does not proceed under the Act when he could have done so will normally be deprived of his costs.[149]

B Foreign Judgments (Reciprocal Enforcement) Act 1933

3.84 The Foreign Judgments (Reciprocal Enforcement) Act 1933 provides for the recognition and enforcement of money judgments given by foreign courts (including those of Commonwealth countries). Like the Administration of Justice Act 1920, it applies only to judgments of countries to which it has been extended by Order in Council, on the basis of their having made reciprocal provision for the recognition and enforcement of UK judgments. The Act has in fact been extended to very few countries.[150]

---

[144] Although the 1920 Act applies to many Commonwealth countries it does not apply to Australia, Bangladesh, Canada, Gibraltar, Hong Kong (which is no longer part of the Commonwealth), India, Pakistan, and South Africa.
[145] S 9(2)(a).   [146] S 9(2)(b) and (c).
[147] It was said in *Sfeir & Co v National Insurance Co of New Zealand* [1964] 1 Lloyd's Rep 330 that 'duly served' means duly served under the foreign rules of procedure, rather than by reference to the standards of the English court.
[148] S 9(2)(d)–(f).   [149] S 9(5).
[150] The Act applies to judgments granted by the courts of Guernsey, Jersey, the Isle of Man, Australia (including the states and territories), Canada (including the provinces, other than Quebec), India, Pakistan, Tonga, Israel, and Suriname. Although the Act was extended to a number of western European countries (Austria, Belgium, France, Germany, Italy, the Netherlands, and Norway) it has since been largely superseded as regards these countries by Brussels I and the Lugano Convention.

3.85 The foreign court must have been a court of competent jurisdiction, the grounds being broadly similar to those recognised at common law.[151] It is worth noting, however, that the 1933 Act is in one respect more restrictive than the common law. The legislation refers to a defendant who was resident in or had its principal place of business in the country of origin;[152] the defendant's presence in the country of origin does not suffice. In addition, the Act provides that the original court will be regarded as a court of competent jurisdiction if the defendant had an office or place of business in the country of origin and the proceedings were in respect of a transaction effected through or at that office or place.[153] The other common law requirements apply: the judgment must be final and conclusive; only money judgments, not being for a tax or penalty, may be enforced;[154] a judgment which is not on the merits is not entitled to recognition.[155] Once the Act has been extended to a country, proceedings for the enforcement of a judgment from that country must be by way of registration under the Act and not by an action at common law.[156]

3.86 As regards defences, the 1933 Act largely follows the common law. A foreign judgment may be refused recognition or enforcement if it was obtained by fraud,[157] if its recognition or enforcement would be contrary to public policy,[158] or if the judgment is irreconcilable with an earlier judgment of the English court or another court of competent jurisdiction.[159] As regards natural justice, the legislation provides that a judgment shall be refused recognition or enforcement if the defendant 'did not (notwithstanding that process may have been duly served on him in accordance with the law of the country of the original court) receive notice of those proceedings in sufficient time to enable him to defend the proceedings and did not appear'.[160] Defences are also provided by section 32 of the Civil Jurisdiction and Judgments Act 1982 and section 5 of the Protection of Trading Interests Act 1980.

IV Recognition and enforcement under the Brussels I Recast

3.87 The Brussels I Recast, which is directly effective in England, is divided into three chapters: the first defines its scope; the second regulates jurisdiction; the third covers the recognition and enforcement of judgments. Although considerable energy is devoted to questions of jurisdiction,[161] it must not be forgotten that the fundamental purpose of the Brussels I Recast is to facilitate the free movement of judgments between the EU Member States. The harmonisation of jurisdiction rules is not an end in itself; it

---

[151] S 4(1)(a)(ii) and (2)(a).   [152] S 4(2)(a)(iv).
[153] S 4(2)(a)(v). This jurisdictional basis is phrased differently from the common law test of indirect presence laid down in *Adams v Cape Industries plc* [1990] Ch 433 (see paras 3.28–3.29) and its scope is somewhat different.
[154] S 1(2)(a) and (b).
[155] *Black-Clawson International Ltd v Papierwerke Waldhof-Aschaffenburg AG* [1975] AC 591.
[156] S 6.   [157] S 4(1)(a)(iv).   [158] S 4(1)(a)(v).   [159] S 4(1)(b).
[160] S 4(1)(a)(iii).   [161] See Chapter 2.

is considered necessary in order to achieve the primary objective of Brussels I. As has been seen in the context of the common law rules, one of the main obstacles to the recognition and enforcement of foreign judgments in England is the fact that a foreign court may decide a question in relation to which, for the purposes of English conflicts rules, it was not a court of competent jurisdiction. The theory underlying Brussels I is that, if international consensus is achieved in relation to bases of jurisdiction, the recognition and enforcement of judgments can be significantly simplified.

3.88 Chapter III is built on the principle of mutual trust between the courts of the Member States.[162] As a consequence, a judgment which is recognised under the Recast should, in principle, have the same effects in the state in which recognition is sought as it does in the state of origin.[163] As regards enforcement, however, if a judgment contains a measure which is not known in the law of the Member State addressed, that measure must be adapted, as far as possible, to an equivalent measure which is known in the law of that Member State; any such adaptation must not produce effects which go further than those provided for in the law of the Member State of origin.[164]

A Judgments falling within the scope of the Brussels I Recast

1. A judgment of a Member State

3.89 Article 2(a) defines 'judgment' as 'any judgment given by a court or tribunal of a Member State, whatever the judgment may be called, including a decree, order, decision or writ of execution'.[165] This definition covers any judicial decision which was (or was capable of being) the subject of an enquiry in contested proceedings in the court of origin,[166] including judgments by consent.[167] In principle, no distinction is made between judgments in personam and judgments in rem. A judicial decision may be a 'judgment' for the purposes of the Recast even though it does not determine the substantive merits of the parties' dispute (such as a judgment by which a court declines jurisdiction on the basis of a foreign jurisdiction clause[168]). It must be remembered

---

[162] Brussels I Recast, recital (26); Case C-302/13 *FlyLAL-Lithuanian Airlines SAS v Starptautiska Lidosta Riga VAS* [2015] ILPr 2. This principle does not operate between arbitral tribunals and Member State courts: the Recast is not engaged in a case involving recognition of an arbitral award in the form of an anti-suit order (restraining a litigant from pursuing proceedings in a Member State); whether the award is entitled to recognition in a Member State is to be decided solely by reference to the New York Convention (as implemented into the law of the Member State in question): Case C-536/13 *Proceedings concerning Gazprom OAO* [2015] 1 WLR 4937. For discussion of the decision, see Briggs, [2015] LMCLQ 284; Hartley, (2015) 64 ICLQ 965.

[163] Case 145/86 *Hoffmann v Krieg* [1988] ECR 645; Case C-456/11 *Gothaer Allgemeine Versicherung AG v Samskip GmbH* [2013] QB 548.

[164] Art 54.

[165] A judgment of a Cypriot court concerning ownership of land situated in Northern Cyprus falls within the scope of Brussels I even though the operation of the *acquis communautaire* is suspended in relation to Northern Cyprus: Case C-420/07 *Apostolides v Orams* [2009] ECR I-3571; see De Baere (2010) 47 CML Rev 1123.

[166] Case 125/79 *Denilauler v SNC Couchet Frères* [1980] ECR 1553; Case C-39/02 *Maersk Olie & Gas A/S v Firma M de Haan en W de Boer* [2004] ECR I-9657.

[167] *Landhurst Leasing plc v Marcq* [1998] ILPr 822.

[168] Case C-456/11 *Gothaer Allgemeine Versicherung AG v Samskip GmbH* [2013] QB 548.

that article 1(2)(d) excludes 'arbitration' from the Recast and that an arbitral award is not a judgment for the purposes of article 2(a).[169]

3.90 As regards provisional measures, article 2(a) of the Recast confirms much of the case law of the Court of Justice under Brussels I: the Recast covers 'provisional, including protective, measures ordered by a court or tribunal which by virtue of this Regulation has jurisdiction as to the substance of the matter',[170] but excludes provisional measures rendered 'without the defendant being summoned to appear, unless the judgment containing the measure is served on the defendant prior to enforcement'.[171] Chapter III does not apply to: (i) interlocutory decisions which regulate procedural matters only;[172] (ii) court orders falling outside the range of provisional measures which may be granted under article 35 (because their provisional character is not guaranteed);[173] or (iii) court settlements.[174] It also seems likely that provisional measures granted by courts other than those with jurisdiction over the substantive dispute in question are outside Chapter III.[175]

3.91 Although Chapter III applies to judgments given by the courts of Member States, it applies only to international recognition. Accordingly, the Brussels I Recast does not apply to the recognition and enforcement in England of judgments given by the courts of Scotland and Northern Ireland.[176]

2. Within the material scope of the Recast

3.92 To be entitled to recognition or enforcement under Chapter III the judgment must fall within the material scope of the Brussels I Recast ('civil and commercial matters') as defined by article 1. The issue whether a particular matter falls within the ambit of article 1 may arise both at the jurisdiction stage and at the stage of recognition or enforcement. For example, when a claimant applies to the English court to enforce a judgment given by a French court, the English court must determine for itself whether the judgment is within the scope of the Recast; the fact that the French court, prior to assuming jurisdiction under Chapter II, has already decided that the case is covered by article 1 does not preclude the English court from reconsidering the material scope of the Recast. It is theoretically possible for the original court to assume jurisdiction under Chapter II (on the basis that the case falls within the scope of article 1) and

---

[169] Case C-536/13 *Proceedings concerning Gazprom OAO* [2015] 1 WLR 4937.
[170] Case C-80/90 *Italian Leather SpA v WECO Polstermöbel GmbH & Co* [2002] ECR I-4995; Case C-394/07 *Gambazzi v Daimler Chrysler Canada Inc* [2009] ECR I-2563; Case 406/09 *Realchemie Nederland BV v Bayer Cropscience AG* [2012] ILPr 1.
[171] Art 2(a).
[172] Schlosser Report, OJ 1979 C59/127, para 187; *CFEM Façades SA v Bovis Construction Ltd* [1992] ILPr 561.
[173] See para 2.284. See also *Comet Group plc v Unika Computer SA* [2004] ILPr 10.
[174] Case C-414/92 *Solo Kleinmotoren GmbH v Boch* [1994] ECR I-2237. Special rules on the enforcement of court settlements are laid down in Chapter IV on authentic instruments and court settlements. See Case C-260/97 *Unibank A/S v Christensen* [1999] ECR I-3715.
[175] This follows *a contrario* from the definition in art 2(a).
[176] See paras 3.127-3.128.

for the English court to refuse enforcement under Chapter III (on the basis that it does not). This type of case is likely to generate a reference to the Court of Justice.[177] Although the scope of the Brussels I Recast is considered in Chapter 2,[178] there is one further question which should be addressed at this point.

3.93 What is the correct solution in a case where, notwithstanding the defendant's argument that the dispute should be referred to arbitration, the foreign court assumes jurisdiction, decides that the arbitration clause is invalid and gives a judgment on the merits in the claimant's favour? If the claimant seeks to enforce the judgment in England, the question is whether this judgment concerns 'arbitration' for the purposes of article 1. If the judgment does not concern 'arbitration' it falls within the scope of article 1 of the Brussels I Recast and, in principle, is enforceable under Chapter III; if the judgment does concern 'arbitration' it falls outside the scope of article 1 and, if the arbitration clause is valid according to English conflicts rules and the defendant did not submit to the jurisdiction of the foreign court, the judgment is unenforceable.[179]

3.94 The uncertainty caused by apparently inconsistent case law of the Court of Justice,[180] and the vigorous debate which it provoked,[181] was not put to rest until the Court of Justice's ruling in the *West Tankers* case.[182] Although *West Tankers* was concerned with the question whether or not an anti-suit injunction to restrain proceedings brought in breach of an arbitration clause was within the scope of Brussels I, the way in which the Court of Justice addressed that question[183] necessarily means that where a Member State court grants a judgment on the merits, notwithstanding the defendant's allegation that there is a binding arbitration agreement between the parties, the judgment does not concern 'arbitration'. On the basis of the ruling in *West Tankers*, in *The Wadi Sudr*[184] the Court of Appeal accepted that, in a case where the subject-matter of the underlying dispute between the parties is civil and commercial in nature, Brussels I covers a Spanish judgment which, before proceeding to address the substantive dispute between the parties, decides as a preliminary issue that an alleged arbitration clause is not incorporated into the contract; for the purposes of article 1 of the Recast, the Spanish judgment does not concern 'arbitration'.

3.95 In the wake of *West Tankers*, the process that resulted in the adoption of the Recast involved consideration of the question whether the arbitration exception should be reformed or deleted. Ultimately, the Recast retained the arbitration exception without

---

[177] Under art 267 TFEU.   [178] See paras 2.14–2.15.
[179] Civil Jurisdiction and Judgments Act 1982, s 32. This provision applies only to judgments falling outside the scope of the Brussels I Recast: s 32(4).
[180] Compare Case C–190/89 *Marc Rich & Co AG v Società Italiana Impianti, The Atlantic Emperor* [1991] ECR I–3855 and Case C–391/95 *Van Uden Maritime BV v Firma Deco-Line* [1998] ECR I–7091.
[181] A judgment given in breach of an arbitration clause concerns 'arbitration': *The Ivan Zagubanski* [2002] 1 Lloyd's Rep 106; Briggs, (1991) 11 YBEL 527 at 529; a judgment given in breach of an arbitration clause does not concern 'arbitration': *The Heidberg* [1994] 2 Lloyd's Rep 287.
[182] Case C–185/07 *West Tankers Inc v Allianz SpA* [2009] 1 AC 1138.   [183] See paras 2.318–2.319.
[184] [2010] 1 Lloyd's Rep 193. See also *DHL GBS (UK) Ltd v Fallimento Finmatica SPA* [2009] 1 Lloyd's Rep 430.

amendment. However, a new recital (12) of the Recast[185] states that a judgment on the validity of an arbitration clause does not fall within the scope of the Recast. In addition, article 73(2) explicitly notes that the Recast shall not affect the application of the New York Convention of 1958 (on the enforcement of arbitration agreements and arbitral awards).

3.96 It would appear that the combined effect of recital (12) and article 73(2) is as follows. First, if a Member State court hands down a judgment declaring an arbitration clause to be null and void, inoperative or incapable of being performed, this judgment concerns arbitration and falls outside the scope of the Recast, regardless of whether the court decided the matter as a principal issue or as an incidental question. Secondly, however, where a Member State court decides a dispute on the merits, having first determined that an alleged arbitration agreement is null and void, inoperative or incapable of being performed, this judgment on the merits falls within the scope of the Recast and is, in principle, entitled to recognition or enforcement, as the case may be, under Chapter III. Thirdly, enforcement of an arbitral award under the New York Convention cannot be impeded or blocked by an inconsistent judgment of a Member State court, even though the judgment is, in principle, entitled to recognition under the Recast. In such a case, the court faced with a Member State judgment (under the Recast) which is inconsistent with an arbitral award (which is entitled to enforcement under the New York Convention) can give priority to the award and decline to give effect to the inconsistent judgment.

3. Regardless of the basis of jurisdiction in the original proceedings

3.97 Although the purpose of Chapter II (jurisdiction) is to simplify Chapter III (judgments), recognition and enforcement under Chapter III does not depend on the original court having assumed jurisdiction on the basis of the heads of direct jurisdiction laid down in Chapter II. The basic requirements of Chapter III are that the original court is the court of a Member State and that the judgment falls within the material scope of the Brussels I Recast. The English court is required to recognise and enforce judgments granted by the courts of other Member States where the court of origin assumed jurisdiction on an exorbitant basis over a defendant who is not domiciled in a Member State (as authorised by article 6). Where, for example, the French court gives judgment against a New Yorker—having assumed jurisdiction on the basis of article 14 of the Civil Code, which confers jurisdiction on the French court if the claimant is a French citizen—the ensuing judgment is enforceable even though the French court would not have had jurisdiction under Chapter II if the defendant had been domiciled in a Member State.[186] As this example shows, the structure of the Brussels I Recast

---

[185] See Camilleri, 'Recital 12 of the Recast Regulation; a new hope?' (2013) 62 ICLQ 899; Carducci, 'The New EU Regulation 1215/2012 of 12 December 2012 on Jurisdiction and International Arbitration: With Notes on Parallel Arbitration, Court Proceedings and the EU Commission's Proposal' (2013) 29 Arb Int 467; Wilhelmsen, 'The Recast Brussels I Regulation and Arbitration: Revisited or Revised?' (2014) 30 Arb Int 169; Wilhelmsen, 'European Perspectives on International Commercial Arbitration' (2014) 10 Journal of Private International Law 113.
[186] Art 5(2).

discriminates against defendants who are not domiciled in a Member State.[187] Not only does the Recast authorise the courts of Member States to assume jurisdiction on exorbitant bases against defendants not domiciled in a Member State, it also enhances the effect of the ensuing judgments by requiring their automatic recognition throughout the Member States.[188]

B Recognition

3.98 If a judgment falls within the scope of Chapter III, article 36(1) provides simply that it 'shall be recognised in the other Member States without any special procedure being required'. It is not necessary that the person seeking to rely on the foreign judgment should establish that the original court was a court of competent jurisdiction. To obtain recognition the party relying on the foreign judgment need do no more than produce a copy of the judgment and a formal certificate issued by the court of origin.[189] Recognition is, however, subject to a limited range of defences.[190]

3.99 Although article 36 states that judgments given by courts of the Member States shall be recognised, questions of cause of action estoppel and issue estoppel are not addressed. It is clear, however, that a judgment falling within Chapter III may create an estoppel of either type. In *Gothaer Allgemeine Versicherung AG v Samskip GmbH*,[191] C brought proceedings relating to a contractual dispute against D in Belgium. The Belgian court declined jurisdiction on the basis that the parties' contract included a jurisdiction clause in favour of the courts of Iceland. When C started similar proceedings in Germany, D contested jurisdiction by seeking to rely on the Belgian judgment as establishing the existence and validity of the Icelandic jurisdiction clause. C argued that, as the Belgian judgment was procedural, it was not entitled to recognition. On a reference by the German courts, the Court of Justice ruled that, if the court of one Member State has ruled that the jurisdiction clause was valid, it would be contrary to the principle of mutual trust to allow the courts of another Member State to review the same question. Although the Court of Justice did not use the language of issue estoppel, the substance of the decision is that the effect of the Belgian judgment was to estop C from reopening the issue of the jurisdiction clause's validity in the subsequent German proceedings. In the words of the Court of Justice: 'the court before which recognition is sought of a judgment by which a court of another member state has declined jurisdiction on the basis of a jurisdiction clause is bound by the finding ... regarding the validity of that clause'.[192]

---

[187] For the United States' reaction, see Nadelmann, 'The Outer World and the Common Market Experts' Draft of a Convention on Recognition of Judgments' (1967–68) 5 CML Rev 409; Von Mehren, 'Recognition and Enforcement of Sister-state Judgments: Reflections on General Theory and Current Practice in the European Economic Community and the United States' (1981) 81 Col LR 1044.
[188] Borchers, 'Comparing Personal Jurisdiction in the United States and the European Community: Lessons for American Reform' (1992) 40 Am J Comp L 121, 132–3.
[189] Art 37(1). See also art 53 and Annex 1. [190] Art 45.
[191] Case C–456/11 [2013] QB 548. [192] Ibid, para 43.

3.100 For the purposes of Brussels I, the Court of Justice adopted a broad concept of res judicata, which attaches to not only the operative part of the judgment, but also the reasons for the judgment in question (ratio decidendi). In this regard, the Court of Justice's analysis mirrors the English courts' approach to the question whether a judgment is 'on the merits' at common law. Indeed, the Court of Justice's ruling in the *Gothaer* case has much in common with the House of Lords' decision in *The Sennar (No 2)*.[193]

C Enforcement

3.101 There is no requirement under the Brussels I Recast that the foreign judgment should be final and conclusive or for a fixed sum of money; it must, however, be enforceable in the country of origin.[194] As long as the foreign order is a 'judgment' for the purposes of article 2(a),[195] a decree of specific performance or an injunction is as entitled to enforcement under Chapter III as a money judgment.[196] It is also provided that a judgment which orders a payment 'by way of a penalty' is enforceable, though only if the amount of the payment has been finally determined by the court of origin.[197] Where the payment accrues to the state, rather than to an individual or company, the likelihood is that the judgment concerns public law questions rather than 'civil and commercial matters' and, therefore, falls outside the scope of the Brussels I Recast altogether. However, in *Realchemie Nederland BV v Bayer Cropscience AG*[198] the Court of Justice ruled that Chapter III covered the recognition and enforcement of a judicial decision which included a fine (to be paid to the German state) in order to ensure compliance with a judgment given in a civil and commercial matter.

3.102 The procedure for enforcement under the Recast is simpler than that under the instruments which the Recast replaces. Although the judgment-creditor is not required to obtain a declaration of enforceability (exequatur) in order for a judgment to be enforced under the Recast,[199] Chapter III contains a detailed series of provisions regulating the procedure whereby enforcement is to be obtained.[200] In very general terms, the procedure can be broken down into a number of elements. First, the claimant makes an application for enforcement, providing a copy of the judgment and the certificate issued pursuant to article 53, certifying that the judgment is enforceable in the country

---

[193] [1985] 1 WLR 490 (discussed at para 3.49).
[194] Art 39. Whether a judgment is 'enforceable' for the purposes of art 39 is a legal question, rather than a practical one: Case C-267/97 *Coursier v Fortis Bank* [1999] ECR I-2543; Case C-420/07 *Apostolides v Orams* [2009] ECR I-3571.
[195] See paras 3.89–3.91.
[196] Case 143/78 *De Cavel v De Cavel* [1979] ECR 1055. See also Viet and Sprange, 'Enforcing English Worldwide Freezing Injunctions in Switzerland' (2004) 5 Bus Law Int 400.
[197] Art 55. See Case C-4/14 *Bohez v Wiertz* [2015] ILPr 43.
[198] Case C-406/09 [2012] ILPr 1. See also Case C-4/14 *Bohez v Wiertz* [2015] ILPr 43.
[199] Art 39. See Timmer, 'Abolition of *Exequatur* under the Brussels I Regulation: Ill Conceived and Premature?' (2013) 9 Journal of Private International Law 129.
[200] Arts 39–51.

of origin.²⁰¹ This certificate must be served on the judgment-debtor.²⁰² Secondly, the judgment-debtor may apply to the court for a decision refusing enforcement on the basis of one or more of the defences listed in article 45.²⁰³ Thirdly, the court's decision to enforce or refuse enforcement is subject to appeal.²⁰⁴ Fourthly, provision is made for a further appeal (against the third-stage appeal).²⁰⁵ In England, the second and third stages are conducted in the High Court; the final appeal at the fourth stage is heard by the Court of Appeal. A claimant who obtains a judgment in another Member State may enforce it in England only through the procedure laid down in Chapter III; the claimant cannot choose to bring an action on the judgment at common law.²⁰⁶

D Defences to recognition and enforcement

3.103 Chapter III starts from the premise that a judgment falling within its scope is entitled to recognition and, where appropriate, enforcement. The conditions which must be satisfied by the person seeking to rely on a foreign judgment are minimal. Under no circumstances may a foreign judgment falling within Chapter III be reviewed as to its substance.²⁰⁷ It is important, however, that the scales are not tilted too much in favour of the claimant. It is, therefore, not surprising that Chapter III includes a number of defences to recognition and enforcement; these defences are exhaustively set out in article 45.²⁰⁸ If the judgment is being challenged in legal proceedings in the Member State of origin, recognition or proceedings for the enforcement of the judgment in another Member State may be stayed.²⁰⁹ As a general rule, the defences are mandatory: if the defendant establishes the conditions of the defence relied upon, recognition or enforcement must be refused.²¹⁰

1. Limited review of jurisdiction

3.104 It is normally for the original court alone to ensure that it had jurisdiction, whether according to the bases of jurisdiction laid down in Chapter II or according to its traditional rules if the case fell within article 6. The general policy of the Recast is to draw the defendant into the original proceedings so that any jurisdictional problems can

---

²⁰¹ Art 42.   ²⁰² Art 43.   ²⁰³ Art 46.   ²⁰⁴ Art 49.   ²⁰⁵ Art 50.
²⁰⁶ Case 42/76 *de Wolf v Harry Cox BV* [1976] ECR 1759.   ²⁰⁷ Art 52.
²⁰⁸ Where the original proceedings fall within the scope of one of a number of Regulations in the field of civil procedure, the enforcement process is simplified even further and the only basis on which a judgment of the court of origin may be refused recognition or enforcement in another Member State is that the judgment conflicts with an earlier judgment involving the same cause of action and the same parties; even this ground is available only if the irreconcilability was not, and could not have been, raised as an objection in the original proceedings. See the European Enforcement Order Regulation, Reg (EC) No 805/2004, OJ 2004 L143/15 (considered in Case C–292/10 *G v de Visser* [2013] QB 168); the European Small Claims Procedure Regulation, Reg (EU) No 861/2007, OJ 2007 L199/1 (amended by Reg (EU) No 2015/2421, OJ 2015 L341/1); the European Order for Payment Procedure Regulation, Reg (EC) No 1896/2006, OJ 2006 L399/1 (considered in Case C–215/11 *Szyrocka v SiGer Technologie GmbH*, unreported; Case C–144/12 *Goldbet Sportwetten GmbH v Sperindeo* [2014] ILPr 1; Joined Cases C–119/13 & C–120/13 *eco cosmetics GmbH & Co KG v Dupuy* [2015] 1 WLR 678; Case C–245/14 *Thomas Cook Belgium NV v Thurner Hotel GmbH* [2016] 1 WLR 878).
²⁰⁹ Arts 38, 51.
²¹⁰ Case C–80/90 *Italian Leather SpA v WECO Polstermöbel GmbH & Co* [2002] ECR I–4995.

be resolved as early as possible. If the original court declines jurisdiction, the claimant will have to try his luck elsewhere. If, however, the court assumes jurisdiction, the court's judgment on the merits is generally effective throughout the Member States. Accordingly, the court addressed is not normally entitled to question whether the original court was justified in assuming jurisdiction. Article 45(3) expressly provides that the test of public policy (which is one of the available defences to recognition and enforcement) may not be applied to the rules relating to jurisdiction.[211]

3.105 The fact that the original court was not a court of competent jurisdiction according to English common law notions is irrelevant. Where, for example, an English defendant visiting France injures someone in a motor accident, a French judgment ordering the defendant to pay damages is enforceable in England, even if the defendant chose not to defend the claim. Had the accident taken place in Texas, a judgment of the Texas court would not be enforceable at common law unless the defendant either was present in Texas when the originating process was served on him or submitted to Texas jurisdiction.

3.106 There are, however, two exceptions to the general rule that the jurisdiction of the original court may not be reviewed.[212] First, a judgment shall not be recognised or enforced if the judgment conflicts with articles 10–16 (matters relating to insurance), articles 17–19 (consumer contracts), or articles 20–23 (employment contracts) and the defendant was the policyholder, the insured, a beneficiary of the insurance contract, the injured party, the consumer, or the employee. Secondly, a judgment shall be refused recognition or enforcement if the assumption of jurisdiction by the original court was contrary to the provisions relating to exclusive jurisdiction (article 24). When examining the grounds of the original court's jurisdiction in such a case, the English court is bound by the findings of fact on which the original court based its jurisdiction.[213]

3.107 The fact that the original court assumed jurisdiction, notwithstanding an agreement between the parties to refer the dispute to the courts of another Member State, is not a defence. Accordingly, if a defendant wishes to rely on such an agreement he must commence proceedings in the contractual forum (thereby requiring the non-contractual forum to stay its proceedings under article 31(2) and giving the contractual forum the opportunity to determine whether or not the jurisdiction agreement is valid): he cannot afford to ignore the foreign proceedings and hope to rely on the jurisdiction clause to resist enforcement of the ensuing default judgment in another Member State.

2. Public policy

3.108 A judgment will not be recognised or enforced in England if such recognition or enforcement is manifestly contrary to English public policy.[214] Some of the problems relating to the notion of public policy have already been considered.[215] Within the context of the Brussels I Recast, although it is not for the Court of Justice to define

---

[211] See Case C–7/98 *Krombach v Bamberski* [2000] ECR I–1935.   [212] Art 45(1)(e).
[213] Art 45(2).   [214] Art 45(1)(a).   [215] See paras 3.70–3.71.

public policy (as this is a question for the law of each of the Member States), the Court of Justice does have a role in reviewing the limits within which the courts of a Member State might have recourse to public policy for the purpose of refusing recognition or enforcement of a judgment.[216] Unsurprisingly, the Court of Justice has stressed that public policy is a concept which should be given a restricted interpretation[217] and should be invoked only in exceptional cases.[218] Public policy cannot be relied upon simply because the law applied by the court of origin is different from the law which the court addressed would have applied to the claim in question or because the court addressed considers that the court of origin failed to determine the facts of the case accurately.[219] Unless recognition of the foreign judgment would constitute a breach of a fundamental principle or of a rule of law regarded as essential in the legal order of the state addressed recognition cannot be refused on the basis of public policy.[220]

3.109 On the one hand, the fact that the court of origin made a mistake in the application of EU law is not enough to justify non-recognition of the judgment.[221] Similarly, it is not contrary to public policy for an English court to recognise or enforce a Spanish judgment in a situation where the Spanish court failed to refer the parties to arbitration on the basis of an arbitration agreement which the English court would have regarded as binding on the parties.[222] The position may well be different, however, if the parties' dispute has been determined by an arbitral tribunal (which regarded the arbitration agreement as valid) and the arbitral award is entitled to recognition and enforcement under the New York Convention of 1958.[223] It has also been held that, in a case where there can be no suggestion that the foreign judgment is inconsistent with principles of public international law, the mere fact that the judgment in question is rendered against the background of an unresolved international dispute does not justify recognition and enforcement being refused on the basis of public policy.[224]

3.110 On the other hand, as the right to a fair trial requires all judgments to be reasoned so that a defendant can understand why judgment was pronounced against him and can bring an appropriate and effective appeal, public policy is engaged if the court of origin failed to give adequate reasons for its decision.[225] The defence of public policy may also be applied in a situation where the law of the state of origin has failed to

---

[216] Case C-302/13 *FlyLAL-Lithuanian Airlines SAS v Starptautiska Lidosta Riga VAS* [2015] ILPr 2, para 47.
[217] Case C-414/92 *Solo Kleinmotoren GmbH v Boch* [1994] ECR I-2237.
[218] Case C-145/86 *Hoffmann v Krieg* [1988] ECR 645; Case C-78/95 *Hendrikman v Magenta Druck & Verlag GmbH* [1996] ECR I-4943.
[219] Case C-302/13 *FlyLAL-Lithuanian Airlines SAS v Starptautiska Lidosta Riga VAS* [2015] ILPr 2, para 48.
[220] Case C-7/98 *Krombach v Bamberski* [2000] ECR I-1935; Case C-38/98 *Régie Nationale des Usines Renault SA v Maxicar SpA* [2000] ECR I-2973; Case C-420/07 *Apostolides v Orams* [2009] ECR I-3571; Case C-681/13 *Diageo Brands BV v Simiramida-04 EOOD* [2015] 3 WLR 1632.
[221] Case C-38/98 *Régie Nationale des Usines Renault SA v Maxicar SpA* [2000] ECR I-2973.
[222] *The Wadi Sudr* [2010] 1 Lloyd's Rep 193.
[223] This conclusion would appear to follow from Brussels I Recast, art 73(2), which expressly gives priority to the New York Convention.
[224] *Apostolides v Orams* [2010] ILPr 20.
[225] Case C-619/10 *Trade Agency Ltd v Seramico Investments Ltd*, para 53; Case C-302/13 *FlyLAL-Lithuanian Airlines SAS v Starptautiska Lidosta Riga VAS* [2015] ILPr 2, para 51.

prevent a manifest breach of the defendant's rights under the European Convention on Human Rights (such as where the defendant's right to a fair trial under article 6 of the Convention has been infringed).[226] However, in *Gambazzi v Daimler Chrysler Canada Inc*[227] the Court of Justice accepted that recognition or enforcement of a judgment granted against a defendant who had been excluded from the proceedings (because of a failure, at an earlier stage, to comply with obligations imposed by orders of the court) is not necessarily contrary to public policy, notwithstanding the fact that the defendant's procedural rights have been restricted. The *Gambazzi* case involved an attempt by the claimant to enforce an English judgment in Italy. Because the defendant had failed to comply with freezing and disclosure orders, the High Court had barred him from taking any further part in the substantive proceedings and given judgment for the claimant. According to the Court of Justice, the right of a litigant to defend himself is not an unfettered prerogative and it may be subject to restrictions. Whether enforcement of the English judgment would be contrary to public policy depended on whether the sanction imposed by the English court was disproportionate, having regard to the aim being pursued. It was for the Italian court, as the court addressed, to assess whether or not the sanction was disproportionate (and, therefore, whether enforcement of the English judgment was contrary to public policy).[228]

3.111 Although there is no separate defence of fraud under article 45 it is generally accepted that, in certain circumstances, a foreign judgment which has been obtained by fraud may be refused recognition or enforcement on the ground of public policy. However, the common law approach to fraud is not compatible with the Brussels I Recast, under which a judgment cannot be reviewed as to its merits.[229] To the extent that fraud is a defence under the Recast, it is significantly narrower than the defence at common law.

3.112 In *Interdesco SA v Nullifire Ltd*[230] the High Court considered whether fraud could be raised as a defence under the heading of public policy. A number of points emerge from the judgment of Phillips J.[231] First, where the foreign court has ruled on precisely the matters which the defendant seeks to raise when challenging the judgment, the court is not entitled to review the conclusion of the foreign court. Secondly, a defendant who believes that a foreign judgment has been obtained by fraud should pursue any available remedy in the country of origin. Thirdly, the English court should not

---

[226] Case C-7/98 *Krombach v Bamberski* [2000] ECR I-1935; van Hoe (2001) 38 CML Rev 1011. See also *Maronier v Larmer* [2003] QB 620; *Citibank NA v Rafidian Bank* [2003] 2 All ER (Comm) 1054; Fawcett, Ní Shúilleabháin and Shah, *Human Rights and Private International Law* (2016) ch 5.

[227] Case C-394/07 [2009] ECR I-2563.

[228] See also Case C-619/10 *Trade Agency Ltd v Seramico Investments Ltd*, unreported (a case involving enforcement of an English default judgment in Latvia).

[229] Art 52.

[230] [1992] 1 Lloyd's Rep 180.

[231] The approach of Phillips J was approved by the Court of Appeal in *Société d'Informatique Service Réalisation Organisation v Ampersand Software BV* [1994] ILPr 55. Although a number of issues were subsequently referred to the Court of Justice, the fraud question was not: Case C-432/93 [1995] ECR I-2269.

normally entertain a challenge to a judgment in circumstances where it would not permit a challenge to an English judgment.[232]

3.113 On the basis of these principles it will be extremely rare for a judgment falling within the scope of Chapter III to be denied recognition or enforcement on the basis of fraud. The defendant would have to establish not only that further evidence of the fraud has come to light since the judgment was handed down by the original court but also that there is no means of recourse in the state of origin.

3. Natural justice

3.114 Article 45(1)(b) provides that a judgment shall not be recognised 'where it was given in default of appearance, if the defendant was not served with the document which instituted the proceedings or with an equivalent document in sufficient time and in such a way as to enable him to arrange for his defence, unless the defendant failed to commence proceedings to challenge the judgment when it was possible for him to do so'. It should be stressed that the defence provided by article 45(1)(b) is available only if the judgment was given 'in default of appearance'. If the defendant took part in the proceedings on the merits, reliance cannot be placed on article 45(1)(b).[233] Indeed, it seems that a defendant will be regarded as having appeared if he plays any part in the proceedings—even if only to contest the court's jurisdiction or to ask for a postponement of the proceedings.[234] However, the Court of Justice has ruled that where proceedings are initiated against a defendant without his knowledge and a lawyer appears on his behalf, but without his authority, the ensuing judgment is to be regarded as given in default of appearance even if, under the law of the state of origin, the original proceedings are regarded as having been inter partes.[235]

3.115 Article 45(1)(b) is potentially available only if the defendant was not 'served' with the originating process; the omission of the word 'duly' (which appeared in the equivalent provision of the Brussels Convention) is significant.[236] Whether a defendant can resist recognition or enforcement under article 45(1)(b) appears to be primarily a question of fact, rather than a question of law; in other words, whether there has been appropriate service is a question of substance, not form.[237]

3.116 On the one hand, even if service was effected in a manner which constituted 'due service' in the country of origin, the court addressed nevertheless has to determine, in light of all the relevant circumstances, whether the manner of service had enabled the defendant to arrange for his defence. A defendant should be able to resist recognition or enforcement if, even though he was served with the document initiating the proceedings,

---

[232] Under English law, a domestic judgment cannot normally be challenged on the basis of fraud unless new evidence, which was not considered at the trial, is forthcoming: *Henderson v Henderson* (1843) 3 Hare 100.
[233] Case C-172/91 *Sonntag v Waidmann* [1993] ECR I-1963.
[234] Case C-39/02 *Maersk Olie & Gas A/S v Firma M de Haan en W de Boer* [2004] ECR I-9657.
[235] Case C-78/95 *Hendrikman v Magenta Druck & Verlag GmbH* [1996] ECR I-4943.
[236] Case C-283/05 *ASML Netherlands BV v Semiconductor Industry Services GmbH (SEMIS)* [2006] ECR I-12041.
[237] *Reeve v Plummer* [2015] ILPr 19.

there was not enough time in which to arrange for his defence (between when process was served and when, in the event of the defendant's failure to take part in the proceedings, a default judgment could have been issued against him).[238] Similarly, a judgment should not be entitled to recognition or enforcement if the method whereby process was served fails to give the defendant a reasonable opportunity to prepare his defence. For example, the defendant should be able to rely on article 45(1)(b) if the claimant, not knowing the defendant's address, employed a form of fictitious or substituted service as a result of which the defendant was wholly unaware of the proceedings which led to the judgment against him.[239]

3.117 It is for the court addressed to decide whether service was in sufficient time and effected in an appropriate manner. In a straightforward case, where the originating process is served on the defendant in a standard way (for example, where process is sent by post to the defendant's business address), time should start to run from the moment of service, even if the defendant only has actual knowledge that proceedings have been commenced at some subsequent point. In this type of case, the claimant should not have to prove that the originating process was actually brought to the defendant's knowledge.[240] For the purposes of article 45(1)(b) 'the document which instituted the proceedings' is the document which, when served on the defendant, enables him to assert his rights before an enforceable judgment is given in the country of origin.[241] In assessing whether the time available is sufficient, any period after the grant of a default judgment—during which the judgment might be set aside—should be ignored.

3.118 An illustration of the problems which the courts have to confront is provided by *Debaecker v Bouwman*.[242] Shortly after taking a lease of premises in Belgium, the defendant, who was domiciled in the Netherlands, left without giving notice and without leaving a forwarding address. The plaintiff issued Belgian proceedings and, not knowing the defendant's address, served the originating process on the local Police Commissariat—in accordance with Belgian law. A few days later the defendant sent the plaintiff details of a post office box through which he could be contacted. The plaintiff made no attempt to inform the defendant of the proceedings and, in due course, the Belgian court gave a default judgment in the plaintiff's favour. When the plaintiff applied to enforce the judgment in the Netherlands, the defendant resisted enforcement on the ground that he had been given insufficient time to arrange for his defence. The Court of Justice ruled that, in examining whether service had been effected in sufficient time, the Dutch court was entitled to take account of exceptional circumstances which arose after service of the originating process. The exceptional circumstances

---

[238] Case 166/80 *Klomps v Michel* [1981] ECR 1593. See also *TSN Kunststoffrecycling GmbH v Jurgens* [2002] 1 WLR 2459.
[239] *Reeve v Plummer* [2015] ILPr 19.
[240] Case 166/80 *Klomps v Michel* [1981] ECR 1593.
[241] Case C-123/91 *Minalmet GmbH v Brandeis Ltd* [1992] ECR I-5661; Case C-474/93 *Firma Hengst Import BV v Campese* [1995] ECR I-2113.
[242] Case 49/84 [1985] ECR 1779 (a case decided under art 27(2) of the Brussels Convention which is replaced, with modifications, by art 45(1)(b) of the Recast).

included the conduct of the defendant (who had returned to the Netherlands without leaving a forwarding address) and the conduct of the plaintiff (who had failed to inform the defendant of the proceedings even after receiving details of the defendant's new postal address). The Court of Justice gave no indication, however, as to the relative importance of the competing factors. Ultimately, whether a defendant has been given enough time is a question of fact to be determined in the light of all the circumstances by the court of the Member State in which recognition or enforcement is sought.

3.119 On the other hand, a mere formal irregularity in the service procedure will not debar recognition or enforcement if it has not prevented the defendant from arranging his defence.[243] If service of the relevant document has taken place in sufficient time, even if service was defective in some technical way, the defendant cannot rely on article 45(1)(b). However, the defendant must have been 'served';[244] if the proceedings were not served at all, the defendant should be able to rely on article 45(1)(b) even if, through some other means, he became aware that the proceedings against him were taking place.

3.120 Although the text of article 45(1)(b) attempts to prevent defendants being able to mount purely technical defences to recognition or enforcement, the rights of defence must be effectively respected. A defendant may rely on article 45(1)(b) notwithstanding the fact that the issues which are relevant—service and sufficiency of time—have already been considered by the original court under article 28. Even if the original court concludes that the defendant was served in sufficient time, this conclusion is not binding on the court of the country in which recognition or enforcement is sought.[245]

3.121 A defendant who was not served in sufficient time to enable him to arrange his defence prior to a judgment being made against him in the court of origin will lose the defence provided by article 45(1)(b) if, after the judgment has been made, he fails to take an opportunity to challenge the judgment in the country of origin. The idea behind this proviso is that, if the defendant can appeal in the state of origin on grounds of a procedural irregularity, he should not be able to invoke that procedural irregularity as a ground for resisting recognition or enforcement.[246] However, a defendant cannot lose the right to rely on article 45(1)(b) unless, having been informed of the contents of the default judgment (as opposed to the mere fact of its existence), he neglects to mount a challenge in the country of origin; this pre-supposes that the default judgment must be served on the defendant.[247] Failure by the claimant to take steps to serve the default judgment on the defendant leaves open the possibility of the defendant successfully invoking article 45(1)(b) at the stage of recognition or enforcement.

---

[243] See European Commission, *Brussels I Proposal*, COM (1999) 348 final, p 23.
[244] *Tavoulareas v Tsavliris (No 2)* [2007] 1 WLR 1573.
[245] Case C-619/10 *Trade Agency Ltd v Seramico Investments Ltd*, unreported. See also Case 228/81 *Pendy Plastic Products BV v Pluspunkt Handelsgesellschaft mbH* [1982] ECR 2723.
[246] European Commission, *Brussels I Proposal*, COM (1999) 348 final, p 23.
[247] Case C-283/05 *ASML Netherlands BV v Semiconductor Industry Services GmbH (SEMIS)* [2006] ECR I-12041, para 40.

3.122 If there is no possibility of a default judgment being challenged in the country of origin, the proviso to article 45(1)(b) can have no application. However, in cases where a challenge is possible, a defendant who makes an unsuccessful challenge against a default judgment in the country of origin is not able to invoke article 45(1)(b) in recognition or enforcement proceedings; there is no reason why a defendant who makes an unsuccessful challenge should be treated any more favourably than a defendant who could have made a challenge, but failed to do so. In *Apostolides v Orams*, the Court of Justice accepted that, if a defendant seeks to challenge a default judgment in the country of origin (and that challenge fails), the defendant cannot rely on article 45(1)(b) at the enforcement stage as long as the proceedings challenging the judgment 'enabled him to argue that he had not been served with the document which instituted the proceedings . . . in sufficient time and in such a way as to enable him to arrange for his defence'.[248] The effect of the Court of Justice's approach to the proviso is that the circumstances in which the recognition or enforcement of a default judgment will be refused on the basis of article 45(1)(b) are fairly narrow.[249]

4. Irreconcilable judgments

3.123 The jurisdiction provisions of Chapter II go a long way towards reducing the incidence of conflicting judgments. There are, however, limits to what can be achieved by article 8 and articles 29–34—even if they are applied consistently and correctly by the courts of all the Member States. Although articles 33 and 34 allow a Member State court to stay its proceedings on the basis of parallel or related proceedings in a non-Member State, the Recast cannot prevent litigation involving the same issues being conducted in the courts of a non-Member State. In addition, because the material scope of the Recast is limited by article 1, it is possible for there to be a conflict between a judgment of one Member State in a matter falling within the scope of article 1 and a judgment of another Member State in a matter falling outside its ambit. Points (c) and (d) of article 45(1) are designed to deal with the problems posed by irreconcilable judgments.

3.124 Article 45(1)(c) provides that a judgment shall not be recognised if the judgment is irreconcilable with a judgment given in a dispute between the same parties in the state in which recognition is sought. Two judgments are irreconcilable for the purposes of this provision if they entail legal consequences that are mutually exclusive.[250] So, a German judgment ordering an estranged husband to pay maintenance to his

---

[248] Case C-420/07 *Apostolides v Orams* [2009] ECR I-3571, para 80. The defence in art 45(1)(b) is not lost, however, if the court of origin has not yet determined the defendant's challenge to the default judgment when the judgment-creditor applies for enforcement: *Reeve v Plummer* [2015] ILPr 19.

[249] On the question of whether the operation of art 45(1)(b) is compatible with the right to a fair trial under art 6 ECHR, see *Avotins v Latvia* (2016) App No 17502/07 (Grand Chamber, ECtHR.)

[250] Case 145/86 *Hoffmann v Krieg* [1988] ECR 645, para 22.

wife—which is premised on the existence of a matrimonial relationship between the parties—is irreconcilable with a Dutch decree dissolving the marriage.[251] Similarly, an Italian decision on interim measures ordering the defendant not to carry out certain acts is irreconcilable with a German decision on interim measures refusing to grant such an order in a dispute between the same parties.[252]

3.125 Article 45(1)(d) is a simple provision for dealing with two foreign judgments (whether granted by the courts of Member States or third states).[253] Its effect is that the English courts shall not recognise a judgment if it is irreconcilable with an earlier judgment given in a Member State or a third state involving the same cause of action and between the same parties, provided that the earlier judgment fulfils the conditions necessary for its recognition under English law.

3.126 Suppose, for example, that the English court is faced with conflicting foreign judgments in civil and commercial matters, one granted by the courts of New York, the other by the Italian courts. In order to determine whether the Italian judgment is entitled to recognition or enforcement under Chapter III, the court must consider the effect of the New York judgment under the common law. If both judgments satisfy the conditions for recognition or enforcement (the New York judgment under the common law and the Italian judgment under the Recast) the English court must give priority to the earlier judgment. If the New York judgment was granted first, article 45(1)(d) provides that the Italian judgment shall be refused recognition. Similarly, if the English court is faced with two Member State judgments, article 45(1)(d) gives priority to the earlier judgment—as long as it satisfies the conditions for recognition under the Recast.

V United Kingdom judgments

3.127 Provision is made by the Civil Jurisdiction and Judgments Act 1982 for the recognition and enforcement in one part of the United Kingdom of judgments obtained in another part.[254] Under this legislation, a judgment obtained in Scotland or Northern Ireland can be registered and enforced in England. No jurisdictional requirements need to be satisfied in respect of the proceedings in the original court; it is sufficient that the judgment was granted[255] and that the time for an appeal has expired or any appeal has been disposed of. Enforcement is not confined to money judgments; decrees of specific performance and injunctions are equally enforceable.

---

[251] Case 145/86 *Hoffmann v Krieg* [1988] ECR 645. See also *African Fertilizers and Chemicals NIG Ltd (Nigeria) v BD Shipsnavo GmbH & Co Reederei KG* [2011] 2 CLC 761.
[252] Case C-80/90 *Italian Leather SpA v WECO Polstermöbel GmbH & Co* [2002] ECR I-4995.
[253] It has no application, however, in a case where there are two inconsistent judgments emanating from the courts of one Member State: Case C-157/12 *Salzgitter Mannesmann Handel GmbH v SC Laminorul SA* [2014] 1 WLR 904.
[254] Ss 18 and 19; schs 6 and 7.   [255] S 19.

3.128 It would seem that the common law defences of fraud, natural justice, and public policy do not apply to judgments given by the courts of other parts of the United Kingdom;[256] the aggrieved party must seek relief in the original court. It is also expressly provided that section 32 of the 1982 Act does not apply to such judgments.[257] However, a judgment of the courts of Scotland or Northern Ireland cannot be enforced in England if it conflicts with an English judgment.[258]

---

[256] See *Clarke v Fennoscandia Ltd* 1998 SC 464 (a case concerning the enforcement of an English judgment in Scotland).
[257] S 32(4).
[258] Sch 6, para 10(b) and sch 7, para 9(b).

4

Contractual obligations

I Introduction

4.1 A dispute about a contract which comes before the English court may have foreign elements of various types: one or both of the parties may be foreign; the making or performance of the contract may be connected with a number of foreign countries. For example, according to the terms of a contract of sale concluded by telephone, an English seller may undertake to deliver goods to a French buyer in Italy. In a claim for breach of contract brought by the French buyer in England, a question may arise on which the rules of English, French, and Italian law are different. In this type of case which law is the court to apply? It would be possible, in theory, for the court to apply English law as the lex fori. This solution has the attraction of simplicity and certainty. It would not, however, be consistent with the objectives which the conflict of laws seeks to achieve. If each country were simply to apply the lex fori to cases with a foreign element, there would be a significant likelihood that the outcome of many international disputes would depend solely on the location of the litigation. Even though one of the purposes of jurisdiction rules is to ensure that international litigation is conducted in an appropriate forum, the law of the country which assumes jurisdiction in relation to a contractual dispute is not necessarily the most appropriate law to govern the contract. Certain factors which are relevant for the allocation of jurisdiction—in particular, questions of practical litigational convenience (such as the location of evidence and witnesses)—have no significance for the determination of the governing law.

4.2 The general principle is that every international contract has a governing law—known at common law as the 'proper law' and under EU law as the 'applicable law'—by reference to which most of the significant issues arising out of the contract are to be determined. Subject to certain limitations, parties to a contract are free to choose the applicable law; if the parties fail to make a choice, the governing law is, as a general rule, the law of the country with which the contract is most closely connected.

A The proper law doctrine

4.3 During the nineteenth and twentieth centuries the English courts developed the doctrine of the 'proper law of the contract', which comprises a hierarchy of three rules. First, the parties might make an express choice of law. At common law, the court gives effect to an express choice of law, as long as it is bona fide, legal, and not contrary to public policy.[1] Secondly, in the absence of express choice, the proper law of the contract may be 'the system of law by reference to which the contract was made'.[2] This formula allows for the possibility of an implied choice. At common law, the court may imply a choice of law from the form of the contract (such as use of a particular standard form[3]) or from an arbitration clause[4] or from a jurisdiction agreement.[5] Thirdly, if the parties fail to make a choice, a contract should be governed by the 'objective' proper law—that is, the law 'with which the transaction has its closest and most real connection'.[6]

4.4 These rules can be explained by reference to a number of objectives which the law seeks to achieve. First, the law promotes certainty by allowing the parties to choose the governing law. Secondly, the rule that effect will be given to an express or implied choice of law is consistent with the principle of party autonomy which underpins the whole of the law of contract. Thirdly, in cases where the parties have not made a choice, the application of the law of the country with which the contract is most closely connected gives effect both to the reasonable expectations of the parties and to the interests of the country which is likely to have the greatest interest in the outcome of the parties' dispute.

B Harmonisation

4.5 Although one of the aims of the choice of law process is to promote uniformity of result regardless of where the claim is litigated, the conflict of laws cannot achieve such uniformity if different countries have different choice of law rules. Generally speaking, it is the claimant who benefits from the flexibility which results from the fact that the outcome of a contractual dispute may differ depending on the country in which the proceedings are brought. If the courts of more than one country have jurisdiction, the claimant is able to choose the most advantageous forum in which to sue the defendant. There are various ways in which the balance may be tilted back in favour of the defendant. First, as a result of the operation of a sophisticated framework of jurisdiction rules, the claimant may be deprived of choice at the jurisdiction stage. Secondly, attempts may be made to harmonise law at the substantive level. If, for example, the law of contract were the same throughout Europe, the choice of law process would be circumvented entirely as regards contractual disputes connected only with European countries because the domestic contract law of each country would be identical. However, harmonisation at a substantive level is fraught with difficulty. It is dependent not only

---

[1] *Vita Food Products Inc v Unus Shipping Co Ltd* [1939] AC 277. There is no reported English case in which an express choice was disapplied on the basis of the proviso. See, however, *Golden Acres Ltd v Queensland Estates Pty Ltd* [1969] Qd R 378 (a decision of the Queensland courts) and the discussion of the Singapore Court of Appeal in *Peh Teck Quee v Bayerische Landesbank Girozentrale* [2001] 2 LRC 23.
[2] *Bonython v Commonwealth of Australia* [1951] AC 201 at 219.
[3] *Amin Rasheed Shipping Corpn v Kuwait Insurance Co* [1984] AC 50.
[4] *James Miller & Partners Ltd v Whitworth Street Estates (Manchester) Ltd* [1970] AC 583; *Compagnie Tunisienne de Navigation SA v Compagnie d'Armement Maritime SA* [1971] AC 572.
[5] *The Komninos S* [1991] 1 Lloyd's Rep 370.
[6] *Bonython v Commonwealth of Australia* [1951] AC 201 at 219.

on international agreement being reached on the substance of the law itself, but also on the implementation into domestic law of the internationally agreed rules. Thirdly, an attempt may be made to harmonise choice of law rules. This third option has been pursued by the Member States of the European Union. As a consequence of developments at the European level, for most practical purposes, the proper law doctrine has been superseded in England—although it still forms the foundation of the law in most other parts of the English-speaking world.

C **Europeanisation**

4.6 The harmonisation achieved by the Brussels I Recast in relation to jurisdiction and judgments is not sufficient to achieve uniformity in the commercial sphere if there is lack of uniformity at the conflict of laws level (for example, because different countries have different choice of law regimes). In the 1970s the first steps were taken, at the European level, to harmonise choice of law rules relating to contractual and non-contractual obligations. This led to the Rome Convention on the Law Applicable to Contractual Obligations of 1980, which was implemented in the United Kingdom by the Contracts (Applicable Law) Act 1990 and came into force on 1 April 1991.[7] Just as the Brussels Convention was translated into a Regulation (now the Brussels I Recast), in 2008 the regime established by the Rome Convention was replaced (and amended) by the Rome I Regulation.[8] The Regulation applies to contracts concluded on or after 17 December 2009.[9] Although there are significant differences between the Rome I Regulation and the traditional common law choice of law rules, the Regulation's basic approach to the choice of law process is similar to that of the proper law doctrine.

II Rome I Regulation: general considerations

A **The scope of the Regulation**

4.7 The Regulation applies, subject to exceptions, 'in situations involving a conflict of laws, to contractual obligations in civil and commercial matters'; it does not apply to revenue, customs, or administrative matters.[10] The Regulation does not define 'contractual obligations'. Although, at common law, classification is to be determined by reference to the conceptual categories of the lex fori, for the purposes of the Regulation a broader, European approach should be adopted; the term 'contractual obligations' must have

---

[7] The goal of European harmonisation of choice of law rules relating to non-contractual obligations was not attained until the enactment of Regulation (EC) No 864/2007 (known as the Rome II Regulation), OJ 2007 L199/40. See Chapter 5.

[8] Regulation (EC) No 593/2008, OJ 2008 L177/6. For discussion of the Regulation, see McParland, *The Rome I Regulation on the Law Applicable to Contractual Obligations* (2015); Lando and Nielsen, 'The Rome I Regulation' (2008) 45 CML Rev 1687.

[9] Art 28. The common law rules continue to apply only to contracts concluded before 1 April 1991 and to contractual questions which are not regulated by the Regulation or other statutory provisions.

[10] Art 1(1). This phraseology follows the text of the Brussels I Recast, art 1.

an autonomous meaning and the simple fact that a particular situation would not be regarded as contractual according to English law is not sufficient to exclude that situation from the Regulation's scope.[11] In line with the Court of Justice's interpretation of article 7(1) of Brussels I, a 'contractual obligation' for the purpose of Rome I, is 'a legal obligation freely consented to by one person towards another'.[12]

1. Exclusions

4.8 Various matters are excluded from the Regulation's scope even though they involve contractual obligations.[13] The excluded matters are a mixed collection with no internal consistency. First, the rules in the Regulation do not apply to questions involving the status or legal capacity of natural persons. This is subject, however, to article 13, which lays down a limited, uniform rule with regard to contractual capacity.[14] Secondly, the Regulation does not apply to contractual obligations relating to matrimonial relationships, matrimonial property regimes, wills, and succession. Thirdly, obligations arising under bills of exchange, cheques, and promissory notes are excluded from the Regulation's scope.[15] Fourthly, the Regulation does not apply to arbitration agreements and agreements on the choice of court.[16] This exclusion is said to be justified by the fact that such agreements lie within the sphere of procedure and are, to some extent, regulated by other provisions of an international nature—namely, the New York Convention of 1958 and the Brussels I Recast.[17] Fifthly, matters excluded from the Regulation include questions governed by the law of companies and other bodies corporate or unincorporated, such as whether a company is bound by a contract which is not executed in accordance with the company's constitution.[18] Sixthly, although contracts of agency are not excluded entirely, the Regulation does not apply to the question whether an agent is able to bind a principal (or whether an organ is able to bind a company or body corporate or unincorporated) to a third party. Seventhly, excluded matters cover the constitution of trusts and the relationship between settlors, trustees, and beneficiaries. Eighthly, obligations arising out of dealings prior to the conclusion of a contract are excluded.[19] Ninthly, although article 7 lays down choice of law rules for contracts of insurance,[20] there is an exclusion

---

[11] For example, within the framework of the Regulation, gifts and promises to give are to be regarded as involving contractual obligations: Giuliano-Lagarde Report, OJ 1980 C282/10. Even at common law, for conflict of laws purposes, the conceptual category 'contract' includes a claim to enforce a promise which is not supported by consideration: *Re Bonacina* [1912] 2 Ch 394.

[12] Joined Cases C-359/14 & C-475/14 *'ERGO Insurance' SE v 'If P&C Insurance' AS*, para 44.

[13] Art 1(2)-(3).   [14] See paras 4.161–4.164.

[15] These matters are governed by the Bills of Exchange Act 1882.

[16] On the law governing an arbitration agreement, see *Sul América Cia Nacional de Seguros SA v Enesa Engenharia SA* [2013] 1 WLR 102.

[17] Giuliano-Lagarde Report, OJ 1980 C282/11–12.

[18] See *Integral Petroleum SA v SCU-Finanz AG* [2015] ILPr 50 (which involved a contract signed on behalf of the defendant company by one 'prokurist' when the company's constitution required the signature of two 'prokurists').

[19] Such obligations are non-contractual and are covered by the Rome II Regulation, art 12: recital (10). See paras 5.83–5.85.

[20] See paras 4.126–4.132.

relating to a narrow category of life insurance contracts concerning the provision of benefits for employed or self-employed persons affected by sickness related to work or accidents at work. Finally, questions of evidence and procedure are excluded. This is consistent with the general principle that procedural questions are governed by the lex fori.

2. Universal application

4.9 Article 2 provides that the law specified by the Regulation shall be applied whether or not it is the law of a Member State.[21] Indeed, the Regulation applies regardless of the territorial connections of the parties and whether or not the contract or the dispute has any connection with a Member State. So, in the context of a contractual dispute between a US corporation and an Iranian company, the English court applies the Rome I Regulation to determine the law governing the contract.[22] However, in practice, most cases in which the Regulation is applicable have a significant connection with a Member State, since, for the Regulation to apply, the court of a Member State must have jurisdiction in relation to the dispute.

4.10 The United Kingdom is made up of three legal systems: England, Scotland, and Northern Ireland. Although the United Kingdom is not required to apply the Regulation to disputes which are internal to it,[23] secondary legislation provides that the Regulation rules are applicable in the case of conflicts between the laws of different parts of the United Kingdom.[24]

B Interpretation

4.11 The Court of Justice has jurisdiction under article 267 TFEU to interpret the provisions of the Rome I Regulation. Under article 267 TFEU, a court against which there is no judicial remedy under national law 'shall' make a reference if a ruling on a point of European law is necessary to enable the court to make its decision;[25] any other court or tribunal 'may' make such a reference.

4.12 Some of the concepts which determine the scope of the Rome I Regulation are borrowed from Brussels I and are also employed in the Rome II Regulation (on choice of law relating to non-contractual obligations). It is intended that the various instruments should be interpreted consistently and harmoniously.[26] It also needs to be

---

[21] Denmark is not a Member State for the purposes of the Rome I Regulation: recital (46). Ireland opted into the Regulation and the United Kingdom, having originally decided not to do so (see recital (45)), changed its mind and is bound by the Regulation: see Commission Decision, OJ 2009 L10/22.

[22] See *Iran Continental Shelf Oil Co v IRI International Corp* [2004] 2 CLC 696 (a case decided under the Convention).

[23] Art 22(2).

[24] Law Applicable to Contractual Obligations (England and Wales and Northern Ireland) Regulations 2009, SI 2009/3064; Law Applicable to Contractual Obligations (Scotland) Regulations 2009, SSI 2009/410.

[25] In the context of English civil proceedings, the Supreme Court is, for nearly all practical purposes, the only court against whose decisions there is no judicial remedy.

[26] Recital (7).

emphasised that many of the provisions of the Rome I Regulation follow the text of the Convention which it replaced. Interpretation of the Convention was assisted by the Giuliano-Lagarde Report[27] and it is reasonable to suppose that, along with the travaux préparatoires of the Regulation itself,[28] the report remains relevant for the courts' interpretation of the Regulation.

C Exclusion of renvoi

4.13 The doctrine of renvoi has no role to play in relation to choice of law in contract. The Rome I Regulation provides that where its choice of law rules require the application of the law of a country, that means 'the application of the rules of law in force in that country other than its rules of private international law'.[29] So, if Russian law is the law applicable to a contract, the rights and obligations of the parties are to be determined by Russian domestic law, not by reference to the law which would be regarded as the governing law according to Russian choice of law principles.

III Determining the applicable law

4.14 Central to the operation of the Regulation is the identification of the applicable law. The Regulation draws a distinction between cases in which the parties have made a choice (which fall within article 3) and cases where the parties have not made a choice (which are governed by article 4). However, three important qualifications should be made at this stage. First, the determination of the applicable law is only the first stage of the choice of law process. Certain elements of the applicable law may be displaced by the mandatory rules of other countries—or may be disapplied on grounds of public policy. Secondly, the general rules in articles 3 and 4 do not apply to contracts of carriage, consumer contracts, insurance contracts and individual contracts of employment, which are regulated by articles 5 to 8. Thirdly, some contractual questions are not governed by the applicable law or are not governed exclusively by the applicable law. These three further aspects of the choice of law rules are considered in later sections.

A Applicable law chosen by the parties

4.15 Subject to limits which are considered later, article 3 of the Regulation gives effect to the principle of party autonomy: 'The parties' freedom to choose the applicable law should be one of the cornerstones of the system of conflict-of-law rules in matters of

---

[27] OJ 1980 C282/1.
[28] See European Commission, *Proposal for a Regulation of the European Parliament and the Council on the Law Applicable to Contractual Obligations ('Rome I')*, COM (2005) 650 final (hereafter '*Rome I Proposal*').
[29] Art 20. This replicates the common law position: Lord Diplock in *Amin Rasheed Shipping Corpn v Kuwait Insurance Co* [1984] AC 50 at 61–2.

contractual obligations.'[30] Under article 3(1), the parties are free to choose the law to govern their contractual relationship; the only condition is that the choice of the parties must be 'made expressly or clearly demonstrated by the terms of the contract or the circumstances of the case'.[31]

1. Choice: expressly made

4.16 A choice of law is made expressly when the contract contains a provision which specifies the law by which it is to be governed. For example, a contract may include a clause which provides that the contract 'shall be governed by the law of Brazil' or which states that 'any dispute arising out of this contract shall be decided according to Israeli law'. Parties to an international contract are wise to include such a clause in their agreement to avoid the uncertainty which may otherwise arise in ascertaining the applicable law. Where, however, the parties choose a non-national system of law (such as Sharia law or Jewish law) this choice does not constitute a choice of law for the purposes of article 3.[32] In its original proposal, the Commission suggested that the principle of party autonomy should extend to allowing parties to choose as the applicable law a non-state body of rules, such as the UNIDROIT *Principles of International Commercial Contracts*.[33] This suggestion, however, did not survive into the final version of the Regulation, though the recitals make it clear both that parties may incorporate by reference non-national rules or an international convention into their contract[34] and that, in the event of the adoption at the European level of an instrument containing substantive rules of contract law (such as the proposed, but subsequently withdrawn, Regulation on a Common European Sales Law), the parties may choose that instrument as the governing law.[35]

4.17 Article 3 is satisfied if a contract has been concluded by reference to one of the parties' general conditions (which include a choice of law clause), as long as there is consensus that the contract is concluded on those contractual terms.[36] A choice of law in a printed contract does not satisfy article 3 if one of the parties deletes the clause before signing the contract and the other party signs the contract without noticing the deletion.[37]

4.18 Where the parties have directly identified the applicable law—such as English law or French law—the court will normally have no difficulty in giving effect to the parties' choice. More problematical, however, is the case where the parties attempt to select the applicable law indirectly. For example, a bill of lading may provide that it is governed

---

[30] Recital (11).
[31] The Rome Convention, art 3(1), used the phrase 'demonstrated with reasonable certainty', rather than 'clearly demonstrated'.
[32] *Shamil Bank of Bahrain EC v Beximco Pharmaceuticals Ltd* [2004] 1 WLR 1784; *Halpern v Halpern (Nos 1 and 2)* [2008] QB 195; *Musawi v RE International (UK) Ltd* [2008] 1 Lloyd's Rep 326. See Colon, 'Choice of Law and Islamic Finance' (2011) 46 Texas Int LJ 411 and, more generally, Dickinson, 'Territory in the Rome I and Rome II Regulations' [2013] LMCLQ 86.
[33] European Commission, *Rome I Proposal*, COM (2005) 650 final, p 5.
[34] Recital (13). For the distinction between choice and incorporation, see paras 4.36–4.38.
[35] Recital (14). [36] *Iran Continental Shelf Oil Co v IRI International Corp* [2002] CLC 372.
[37] *Samcrete Egypt Engineers and Contractors SAE v Land Rover Exports Ltd* [2002] CLC 533.

by the law of the country in which the carrier's principal place of business is situated; a charterparty may be governed by the law of the flag of the vessel in question. As long as the carrier's principal place of business or the flag of the vessel can be identified, the parties' choice of law is effective. In any particular case where the parties purport to select the applicable law indirectly, whether the alleged choice is effective depends on interpretation of the clause in question. If the applicable law cannot be identified with certainty, the alleged choice of law is unenforceable.[38]

4.19 In *Companie Tunisienne de Navigation SA v Companie d'Armement Maritime SA*[39]—a case decided by the House of Lords under the common law—a contract was made in Paris between D (a French company) and P (a Tunisian company), for the carriage of a number of consignments of oil between Tunisian ports over a period of some months. Although performance of the contract would require at least 12 voyages, the parties adapted a single-voyage charterparty form, clause 13 of which provided that the charterparty was governed by the law of the flag of the vessel carrying the goods. At the time of the conclusion of the contract the parties seemed to have assumed that D would be using its own ships, which flew the French flag. Before performance of the contract was completed, war broke out in the Middle East and D, relying on French law as the governing law, alleged that the contract had been frustrated. One of the questions facing the court was whether, in view of the fact that for the first six voyages the defendant had employed ships flying five different flags, clause 13 was an effective choice of French law.

4.20 A minority of the House of Lords thought that clause 13 was meaningless and approached the case on the basis that the parties had not made an express choice. The majority, however, decided that clause 13 was an effective choice of French law. The parties had envisaged that D would use French vessels in performing the contract and it was reasonable to conclude that the parties had chosen French law as the governing law, even though the parties' assumptions at the time of contracting were erroneous.

2. Choice: clearly demonstrated

4.21 Although a well-drafted international contract will include an express choice of law, it is not uncommon for the parties to fail to select the applicable law—whether because they do not apply their minds to the question at all or because they are unable to agree on which law is to be the applicable law.

4.22 Article 3(1) of the Regulation does not require a choice of law to be expressly made in order to be effective; it is sufficient if a choice is 'clearly demonstrated by the terms of the contract or the circumstances of the case'.[40] The burden of proof is on the party who asserts that a choice has been made. If the court is not satisfied that the parties have

---

[38] See *Sonatrach Petroleum Corp v Ferrell International Ltd* [2002] 1 All ER (Comm) 627.
[39] [1971] AC 572.
[40] Notwithstanding the use of the word 'or' in art 3(1), an implied choice can be based on the combined effect of 'the terms of the contract' and 'the circumstances of the case': Aikens J in *Marubeni Hong Kong and South China Ltd v Mongolian Government* [2002] 2 All ER (Comm) 873 at [42].

chosen the applicable law, the case must be determined in accordance with article 4. Within the structure of the Regulation it is not legitimate for the court to determine the applicable law under article 3 on the basis that, had the parties thought about it, they would have chosen the law of a particular country.[41] While the court must give effect to a choice of law, whether or not express, the court is not entitled to impute a choice to the parties.

4.23 In what circumstances is it possible to say that the parties have made a choice, albeit not an express one? In answering this question some guidance is provided by the Giuliano-Lagarde Report, which gives a number of examples where a choice of law may be clearly demonstrated, notwithstanding the fact that it is not express.[42]

(A) Dispute-resolution clauses

4.24 A choice of jurisdiction is not, in itself, a choice of law. Similarly, the fact that parties agree to refer their disputes to arbitration in England does not necessarily entail a choice of English law. It is important to keep distinct—at least for analytical purposes—the question of forum (where is the dispute to be resolved?) from the question of the applicable law (which law governs the contract?).

4.25 The Giuliano-Lagarde Report states that although 'the choice of a particular forum may show in no uncertain manner that the parties intend the contract to be governed by the law of that forum . . . this must always be subject to the other terms of the contract and all the circumstances of the case'.[43] The Commission wanted the Regulation to go further and provide that, if the parties agreed to the jurisdiction of the courts of a particular country, they should be presumed to have chosen the law of that country as the applicable law.[44] The final version of the Regulation, however, merely echoes the Giuliano-Lagarde Report: a jurisdiction clause is 'one of the factors to be taken into account in determining whether a choice of law has been clearly demonstrated'.[45]

4.26 In practice, where parties have agreed to litigation or arbitration in a particular country, the court is likely to conclude that the contract is governed by the law of that country. Even if the contract has no connections with England (apart from the dispute-resolution clause), the governing law will normally be English law in spite of substantial connections with another country. The mere fact that there are countries with which the contract has a closer connection does not mean that the parties have not chosen English law. The approach of the English courts to situations involving dispute-resolution clauses can be illustrated by some of the cases decided at common law. Underlying the common law doctrine[46] is the idea that, where a contract includes a choice of jurisdiction in favour of the English courts or an agreement to

---

[41] *Lawlor v Sandvik Mining and Construction Mobile Crushers and Screens Ltd* [2013] 2 Lloyd's Rep 98.
[42] OJ 1980 C282/17.   [43] Ibid.
[44] See European Commission, *Rome I Proposal*, COM (2005) 650 final, p 14.   [45] Recital (12).
[46] See *Hamlyn & Co v Talisker Distillery* [1894] AC 202; *Compagnie Tunisienne de Navigation SA v Compagnie d'Armement Maritime SA* [1971] AC 572.

refer disputes to arbitrators in England, the parties intend English law to govern the contract as they are most likely to have in mind that the court or the arbitral tribunal will apply its own law.

4.27 In *The Komninos S*,[47] for example, a cargo belonging to P was shipped on a vessel owned by D. P started proceedings in England for damages alleging that, as a result of the unseaworthiness of the vessel and D's negligence, the cargo had been damaged during the voyage. Although neither the contract nor the parties had any connection with England, the bill of lading, which was drawn up in the English language, provided that any dispute should be referred to 'British courts'.

4.28 On the one hand, D argued that the bill of lading was governed by Greek law according to which P's claim was time-barred. This argument succeeded at first instance.[48] Leggatt J held that the parties had not made a choice of law and that, given that the contract was made in Greece between Greek shippers and Greek managers to carry goods from Greece to Italy for freight payable in Greece in Greek currency, Greece was the country with which the contract was most closely connected.

4.29 On the other hand, P argued that the jurisdiction clause in favour of 'British courts' was an implied choice of English law, under which the limitation period had not expired. The Court of Appeal adopted P's view. First, the choice of 'British courts' was to be interpreted as a choice in favour of English courts.[49] Bingham LJ rejected D's suggestion that the jurisdiction clause was ambiguous; the idea that the parties might have intended to confer jurisdiction on the courts of Scotland or Northern Ireland was 'far-fetched'.[50] Secondly, the Court of Appeal decided that it should be inferred that parties intend their contracts to be governed by the law of the forum where disputes are to be tried unless there are strong indications that they did not intend or may not have intended that result.[51] In the absence of such strong indications, the Court of Appeal concluded that English law was the proper law of the bill of lading.

4.30 The same approach is evident in cases involving arbitration clauses. In *The Parouth*,[52] for example, the contract had connections with, inter alia, Panama, Greece, and Florida, but none at all with England. The Court of Appeal held that English law was the proper law on the basis of an agreement for arbitration in England.

4.31 Nevertheless, a dispute-resolution clause is not conclusive. In *Compagnie Tunisienne de Navigation SA v Compagnie d'Armement Maritime SA*[53] the House of Lords considered what the position would have been if clause 13 of the charterparty had not effected an express choice of French law. The charterparty included a clause which provided that any dispute should be settled by arbitrators in London. The House of Lords decided that, although a choice of English law would normally be implied from an

---

[47] [1991] 1 Lloyd's Rep 370. [48] [1990] 1 Lloyd's Rep 541.
[49] See also *Catlin Syndicate Ltd v Adams Land & Cattle Co* [2006] 2 CLC 425 ('UK courts' means 'English courts').
[50] [1991] 1 Lloyd's Rep 370 at 374. [51] At 376.
[52] [1982] 2 Lloyd's Rep 351. [53] [1971] AC 572.

agreement to refer disputes to arbitration in England, on the facts of the case, French law—as the law of the country with which the contract was most closely connected—was the proper law. The parties and the contract were connected entirely with France and Tunisia (a former French protectorate whose legal system is based on the French system). The contract was negotiated in France in the French language; it was made in France through French brokers; it provided for payment in France in French currency; one party was a French company; the other was Tunisian and Tunisia was the place of performance of that party's obligations.

4.32 The common law approach illustrated by these cases is also adopted in situations governed by the European choice of law rules. In *Egon Oldendorff v Libera Corpn*[54] P, a German company, sought leave to serve a writ on D, a Japanese corporation, out of the jurisdiction on the basis that the contract between the parties was 'by implication' governed by English law.[55] The contract had no connections with England apart from a clause providing for arbitration in England. Leave was given to serve D out of the jurisdiction on the basis that there was a good arguable case that the contract was governed by English law; Mance J found the suggestion that it was contemplated that the arbitral tribunal should apply a foreign law 'unconvincing'.[56] In subsequent proceedings Clarke J held that the contract was indeed governed by English law.[57] In considering the effect of the arbitration clause, Clarke J concluded that, although the test under article 3 is not the same as at common law, it is very similar and that the considerations set out by the House of Lords in the *Compagnie Tunisienne* case are equally relevant to the correct interpretation of article 3.[58] Clarke J considered that 'if [article 3] involves a change in emphasis from the approach by the common law it is a small one'.[59]

(B) Standard forms

4.33 A common indication of an implied choice is the use of standard forms, notably certain types of standard form which are drafted against the background of a particular system of law. For example, in *Amin Rasheed Shipping Corpn v Kuwait Insurance Co*[60] a marine insurance policy was issued in Kuwait by the defendant, a Kuwaiti insurance company, in respect of a ship owned by the plaintiff, a Liberian company which carried on business in Dubai. The policy was based on a Lloyd's form set out in a schedule to the Marine Insurance Act 1906. The House of Lords held that English law was the law governing the contract. In view of the English form of the policy, which could only be interpreted in the light of English law, the parties must have intended English law to govern. Moreover, since at the time the contract was made, Kuwait did not have any

---

[54] [1995] 2 Lloyd's Rep 64.
[55] This jurisdictional basis is now to be found in CPR PD 6B para 3.1(6)(c).
[56] At 69.
[57] [1996] 1 Lloyd's Rep 380.
[58] At 389.
[59] At 390. See also *Marubeni Hong Kong and South China Ltd v Mongolian Government* [2002] 2 All ER (Comm) 873.
[60] [1984] AC 50. See also *James Miller & Partners Ltd v Whitworth Street Estates (Manchester) Ltd* [1970] AC 583.

law of marine insurance (as opposed to a general law of insurance), it was legitimate to conclude that the parties must have had English law in mind. Although this case was decided under the common law, the application of article 3 to the particular facts yields the same result.[61] Where a reinsurance contract is placed in London on the London market and the contract is of a standard type, the implication is that the parties chose English law as the applicable law—unless the contract includes clear indications that a different law was intended.[62]

(C) Previous course of dealing

4.34 According to the Giuliano-Lagarde Report, 'a previous course of dealing between the parties under contracts containing an express choice of law may leave the court in no doubt that the contract in question is to be governed by the law previously chosen where the choice of law clause has been omitted in circumstances which do not indicate a deliberate change of policy by the parties'.[63] Each case will turn on its own facts; it would be wrong for the court to conclude that the parties had impliedly chosen the law of a particular country simply because they had done so in an earlier transaction.

(D) Express choice of law in related transactions

4.35 Where contracts are related to each other, it is not unreasonable to suppose that the parties intended that they should be governed by the same law. According to the Giuliano-Lagarde Report, a choice may be implied into a contract from 'an express choice of law in related transactions between the same parties'.[64] The common law has taken this idea further and may imply a choice of law into a contract between B and C on the basis of an express choice of law in a related contract between A and B. At common law, where a charterparty is expressly governed by English law, a choice of English law may be implied into the related bills of lading;[65] similarly, where Y's obligations to X under a contract which is expressly governed by English law are guaranteed by Z it may be appropriate to imply a choice of English law into the contract of guarantee between X and Z.[66] By contrast, a letter of credit issued in connection with a commercial transaction is not necessarily to be regarded as governed by the law which governs the underlying transaction; a letter of credit is an autonomous contract which does not depend in any way on the performance or non-performance of the underlying transaction.[67]

---

[61] Giuliano-Lagarde Report, OJ 1980 C282/17.
[62] *Gan Insurance Co Ltd v Tai Ping Insurance Co Ltd* [1999] ILPr 729; *Stonebridge Underwriting Ltd v Ontario Municipal Insurance Exchange* [2010] 2 CLC 349; *Gard Marine and Energy Ltd v Glacier Reinsurance* [2011] 2 All ER (Comm) 208; *Wasa International Insurance Co v Lexington Insurance Co* [2010] 1 AC 180.
[63] OJ 1980 C282/17.
[64] Ibid. See *FR Lürssen Werft GmbH & Co KG v Halle* [2011] 1 Lloyd's Rep 265: *Golden Ocean Group Ltd v Salgaocar Mining Industries Pvt Ltd* [2012] 1 WLR 3674.
[65] *The Njegos* [1936] P 90; *The Freights Queen* [1977] 2 Lloyd's Rep 140.
[66] *Broken Hill Proprietary Co Ltd v Xenakis* [1982] 2 Lloyd's Rep 304; *Wahda Bank v Arab Bank* [1996] 1 Lloyd's Rep 470.
[67] See *Attock Cement Co Ltd v Romanian Bank for Foreign Trade* [1989] 1 WLR 1147.

(E) Reference to particular rules

4.36 Just as the use of a standard form which is drafted against the background of the law of a particular country may imply a choice of the law of that country, references to the law of a particular country in a contract may imply a choice of that law. The Giuliano-Lagarde Report suggests that 'references in a contract to specific articles of the French Civil Code may leave the court in no doubt that the parties have deliberately chosen French law, although there is no expressly stated choice of law'.[68]

4.37 However, choice of law should not be confused with incorporation. Where the parties choose the law of a particular country they run the risk that the chosen law might change in a way which is advantageous to one party or the other. If the parties litigate a dispute the court will apply the chosen law as it is at the time of the trial, not as it was when the contract was concluded.[69] Rather than choosing a particular law, the parties may incorporate specific rules—usually statutory provisions—of the law of country X into a contract which is governed by the law of country Y. The English court will apply these provisions of the law of country X just as if they had been written out in extenso as clauses of the contract. For example, a contract for the carriage of goods by sea, whose applicable law is English law, may contain a clause that 'with respect to shipments from a port in the United States, all the terms and provisions of the Carriage of Goods by Sea Act 1936 of the United States are to apply to this contract'.[70]

4.38 Where foreign legal rules are incorporated into a contract by reference, the incorporated provisions are, in principle, to be interpreted in the same way as other contractual terms.[71] The parties are taken to have intended the incorporated provisions to apply as they existed at the date of the contract, unaffected by any subsequent amendments.

(F) Other considerations

4.39 The various examples given by the Giuliano-Lagarde Report of circumstances or contractual terms from which a court may conclude that the parties have impliedly made a choice of law are not exhaustive. In *American Motorists Insurance Co v Cellstar Corporation*[72] there was a question whether a contract of insurance between C, an Illinois company which conducted insurance business in Texas, and D, a Delaware company whose principal place of business was in Texas, was governed by the law of England or Texas. The contract had been negotiated by D on behalf of itself and its subsidiaries and the contract had been issued by C in Texas. It was held that the parties had selected Texas law, even though the contract did not include an express choice. The terms of the contract, which included a clause providing a time limit for suit of 12 months 'by the laws of the state in which such policy is issued', were a strong indication of an understanding that the policy would be governed by Texas law (as Texas was the place where the policy was issued). This conclusion was supported by the fact that the

---

[68] OJ 1980 C282/17.   [69] *R v International Trustee for Protection of Bondholders Akt* [1937] AC 500.
[70] *Stafford Allen & Sons Ltd v Pacific Steam Navigation Co* [1956] 1 WLR 629.
[71] See *The Stolt Sydness* [1997] 1 Lloyd's Rep 273.   [72] [2003] ILPr 22.

circumstances surrounding the conclusion of the contract were overwhelmingly centred on Texas.

4.40 At common law, where a contract—or a particular provision in a contract—is valid under the law of one country with which the contract is connected but invalid under another, the court may imply a choice of the validating law, on the basis that the parties must have intended their contract to be valid, not void. For example, in *Re Missouri Steamship Co*[73] the US plaintiff made a contract in Massachusetts with English shipowners for the carriage of cattle from Boston to England. During the voyage, the cattle were injured through the negligence of the crew. When sued in England, the defendants relied on a clause in the contract exempting them from liability in such circumstances. By the law of Massachusetts this exemption clause was void, but it was valid by English law. It was held that English law was the proper law, for the parties must have intended the provisions of their contract, including the exemption clause, to be valid. However, according to the common law doctrine, such an implication is not conclusive and it may be outweighed by the fact that there are factors pointing more strongly to an implied choice of an invalidating law.[74]

4.41 There are certain problems with the implication of a choice in favour of the validating law. Most fundamentally, such an implication is normally a fiction, for the parties will often have no idea that the contract is valid under one law and invalid under another. In such cases, it is difficult to see how a choice in favour of the validating law can be said to have been clearly demonstrated. Nevertheless, where the parties are aware that a contract (or a clause) is valid under one law but invalid under another, it may be legitimate to imply a choice of the law under which the contract (or clause) is valid under article 3(1).

3. The distinction between implied choice and no choice

4.42 One of the most uncertain aspects of article 3 is the requirement that a choice of law, if not express, must be clearly demonstrated. This uncertainty is not unique to the Regulation; it is also part of the proper law doctrine which was superseded by the European choice of law rules. Although the conceptual distinction between implied choice and an absence of choice is not difficult to understand, the dividing-line is much harder to draw in practice. The truth is that, unless the parties have made an express choice, it is impossible to say whether or not the parties actually made a choice. The cases decided by the English courts and the illustrations given by the Giuliano-Lagarde Report show that, although certain factors *may* be regarded as justifying the implication of a choice of law, no single factor is decisive.

4.43 An alternative and, it is submitted, preferable approach would be to do away entirely with the notion of implied choice.[75] In cases where the contract does not include an

---

[73] (1889) 42 Ch D 321.
[74] *Royal Exchange Assurance Corpn v Sjoforsakrings Aktiebolaget Vega* [1902] 2 KB 384.
[75] See Okoli and Arishe, 'The Operation of the Escape Clauses in the Rome Convention, the Rome I Regulation and the Rome II Regulation' (2012) 8 Journal of Private International Law 513.

express choice, very often the parties will have given no thought at all to the applicable law. The real significance of factors such as jurisdiction clauses and the language and form of the contract is not that they reveal the parties' subjective intentions, but that they point to a law with which the contract is connected. For example, a contract is more likely to give effect to the parties' reasonable expectations if it is governed by the law in whose terminology and concepts it is couched.

4.44 In the absence of an express choice of law, a contract should be governed by the law of the country with which it is most closely connected. In determining the country with which a contract is most closely connected, the court would necessarily have regard to factors such as any dispute-resolution clause and the form and language of the contract; the court would not, however, be tempted to glean the supposed intentions of the parties from flimsy evidence.

4. Splitting the applicable law

4.45 The logic of the principle of party autonomy leads to the idea that different parts of the same contract may be subjected to different laws. The Regulation provides that the parties can, by their choice, 'select the law applicable to the whole or to part only of the contract'.[76] There are problems associated with splitting the applicable law. A legal system is intended to be a coherent whole, the rules of which are interrelated with, and influenced by, each other. To apply the rules of one legal system to one issue in a contractual dispute, but the rules of a different legal system to another issue might distort the true effect of the rules in question, producing a decision which would not be reached under either law alone, and which is not consistent with the objectives of either law.

4.46 Although the Regulation permits splitting the applicable law the Giuliano-Lagarde Report states that the parties' choice 'must be logically consistent, ie it must relate to elements in the contract which can be governed by different laws without giving rise to contradictions'.[77] Accordingly, the parties may decide to subject a particular contractual term (such as an index-linking clause) to a different law from that which governs the rest of the contract.[78] However, if a contract provided that one party's obligations were governed by the law of country X and the other's by the law of country Y, the choice should be regarded as ineffective on the basis that 'the harmony between the obligations of the parties to a bilateral contract'[79] is disturbed if different laws are applied to each party's obligations. In such a case the applicable law should be determined by reference to article 4.

5. Changing the applicable law

4.47 Can the parties, after they have made their contract, by agreement change the applicable law? The principle of party autonomy suggests that this question should be

---

[76] Art 3(1).   [77] OJ 1980 C282/17.   [78] Ibid.
[79] Lando, 'The EEC Convention on the Law Applicable to Contractual Obligations' (1987) 24 CML Rev 159, 169.

answered in the affirmative.[80] Article 3(2) of the Regulation provides that the parties 'may at any time agree to subject the contract to a law other than that which previously governed it'. The freedom to change the applicable law applies both to cases in which the parties made a choice at the time of contracting and to cases where no initial choice was made. However, an agreement changing the applicable law will normally need to be express and the court will be slow to imply any such agreement.[81] A change in the applicable law cannot render a contract formally invalid; nor can such a change adversely affect the rights of third parties.[82] Whether a change in the governing law takes effect retrospectively or only prospectively should, in principle, be determined by the parties' intentions as revealed by their agreement.

4.48 A related question is whether a contract can have a 'floating' applicable law to be determined by an event occurring after the making of the contract. At common law, a clause which provides that a contract should, at the option of one of the parties, be governed either by the law of country X or the law of country Y is void.[83] However, where the factor on which the selection of the proper law depends is not the unilateral choice of one party, but an objectively ascertainable event, the clause is valid. In *The Mariannina*,[84] for example, the Court of Appeal held valid a clause which provided that, if a provision for arbitration in London should be ruled unenforceable, the contract should be governed by Greek law.

4.49 The position under the Regulation would appear to be different. The logic of article 3 is to allow the parties to choose the applicable law at any time. There is no obvious reason why a contractual term which gives one party the power to select the applicable law at some point after the conclusion of the contract should not be regarded as a valid clause. The argument that, until the choice has been made, the alleged contract cannot exist—because it inhabits a legal vacuum—is unsound. Until the party who has been given the power to select the applicable law has exercised that power, the contract is governed by the law which applies in the absence of choice (as determined by article 4); a subsequent exercise of the power should simply be regarded as a variation for the purposes of article 3(2).

B Applicable law in the absence of choice

1. Introduction

4.50 One of the significant ways in which the Rome I Regulation differs from the Rome Convention which preceded it is in relation to the choice of law rules which apply in cases where the parties have failed to choose the applicable law (whether expressly or impliedly). Article 4 was one of the most frequently criticised elements of the Convention and the Regulation seeks to address the problems to which the Convention

---

[80] *Mauritius Commercial Bank Ltd v Hestia Holdings Ltd* [2013] 2 All ER (Comm) 898.
[81] *The Aeolian* [2001] 2 Lloyd's Rep 641.   [82] Art 3(2).
[83] *Armar Shipping Co Ltd v Caisse Algérienne d'Assurance et de Réassurance* [1981] 1 WLR 207; *Sonatrach Petroleum Corp v Ferrell International Ltd* [2002] 1 All ER (Comm) 627.
[84] [1983] 1 Lloyd's Rep 12. See also *Bhatia Shipping and Agencies PVT Ltd v Aclobex Metals Ltd* [2005] 2 Lloyd's Rep 336.

gave rise while retaining the basic principle that, in the absence of choice by the parties, a contract should be governed by the law of the country with which it is most closely connected. Unlike article 4 of the Convention (which was structured around various presumptions, which could be disregarded in certain circumstances),[85] article 4 of the Regulation starts with a series of rules—to which there are a number of qualifications.[86] The intention of the drafters of article 4 of the Regulation is that 'the rules applicable in the absence of a choice should be as precise and foreseeable as possible'.[87]

2. General choice of law rules: article 4(1)

4.51 Subject to the provisions which apply to certain specific types of contracts,[88] article 4(1) lays down a series of general choice of law rules which determine the applicable law in cases involving a variety of typical contracts. Article 4(1) provides that, to the extent that the law applicable to the contract has not been chosen in accordance with article 3, the governing law is determined as follows:

(a) a contract for the sale of goods shall be governed by the law of the country where the seller has his habitual residence;

(b) a contract for the provision of services shall be governed by the law of the country where the service provider has his habitual residence;

(c) a contract relating to a right in rem in immovable property or to a tenancy of immovable property shall be governed by the law of the country where the property is situated;

(d) notwithstanding point (c), a tenancy of immovable property concluded for temporary private use for a period of no more than six consecutive months shall be governed by the law of the country where the landlord has his habitual residence, provided that the tenant is a natural person and has his habitual residence in the same country;

(e) a franchise contract shall be governed by the law of the country where the franchisee has his habitual residence;

(f) a distribution contract shall be governed by the law of the country where the distributor has his habitual residence;

(g) a contract for the sale of goods by auction shall be governed by the law of the country where the auction takes place, if such a place can be determined.[89]

---

[85] See Hill, 'Choice of Law in Contract under the Rome Convention: The Approach of the UK Courts' (2004) 53 ICLQ 325; Atrill, 'Choice of Law in Contract: The Missing Pieces of the Article 4 Jigsaw?' (2004) 53 ICLQ 549; Fons, 'Commercial Choice of Law in Context: Looking Beyond Rome' (2015) 78 MLR 241.

[86] See Tang, 'Law Applicable in the Absence of Choice—The New Article 4 of the Rome I Regulation' (2008) 71 MLR 785; Arzandeh, 'The Law Governing International Contractual Disputes in the Absence of Express Choice by the Parties' [2015] LMCLQ 525.

[87] European Commission, *Rome I Proposal*, COM (2005) 650 final, p 5.

[88] Contracts of carriage (art 5), consumer contracts (art 6), contracts of insurance (art 7), individual contracts of employment (art 8).

[89] Para (h) lays down a rule for contracts concluded in the context of certain types of multilateral trading system; individual contracts concluded within the particular trading system are governed by the law applicable to the trading system.

4.52 For the purposes of these rules, a party's habitual residence is determined by article 19 of the Regulation.[90] The concepts used in the first two paragraphs of article 4(1) ('provision of services' and 'sale of goods') should be interpreted in the same way as in the context of article 7(1)(b) of the Brussels I Recast.[91] Although franchise and distribution contracts are contracts for services, they are the subject of specific rules in paragraphs (e) and (f).

4.53 The different approaches adopted in the various rules in article 4(1) are motivated by different considerations. First, as regards contracts for the sale of goods and for the provision of services, points (a) and (b) select the law of one of the parties (rather than, say, the law of the country of performance); the purpose behind this approach is to give priority to the convenience of the parties. The choice of the law of the characteristic performer—that is, the party who is to provide the goods (article 4(1)(a)) or the services (article 4(1)(b)), rather than the one who is to pay the price—may be justified by the likelihood that, as that party's performance is the more active, that party is more likely to have to consult the law during the course of performance. There is also an argument based on economic efficiency. Many contracts are concluded on standard forms. Although a contract of sale may be concluded on the seller's standard conditions of sale or on the buyer's standard conditions of purchase, it is more common for the seller to frame the contract. Where a seller sells goods to buyers in different countries the application of the seller's law may be supported on the ground that 'mass bargaining, like mass production, brings down the cost and the price'.[92]

4.54 Secondly, some paragraphs of article 4(1) seek to identify the law with which the contract is typically most closely connected and which the parties would legitimately expect to govern the contract in question. This rationale explains the rule in point (c) which requires the application of the lex situs to contracts concerning rights in rem in immovable property; for example, it is obvious that, regardless of the territorial connections of the parties, a contract for the sale of land in England is most closely connected with England. Point (g) also reflects party expectations; parties to a contract concluded at an auction would reasonably anticipate that the contract would be governed by the law of the country in which the auction took place.[93]

4.55 Thirdly, points (e) and (f), by favouring the law of the franchisee (over the franchisor) and the distributor (over the manufacturer), are consistent with a desire to protect the position of the weaker party in the contractual relationship.[94] Similar considerations

---

[90] See paras 4.82–4.86.
[91] Recital (17). For discussion of Brussels I Recast, art 7(1)(b), see paras 2.81–2.89.
[92] Lando, 'The EEC Convention on the Law Applicable to Contractual Obligations' (1987) 24 CML Rev 159, 202.
[93] This rule does not normally apply to internet auctions as, in such cases, the place where the auction takes place cannot be determined.
[94] European Commission, *Rome I Proposal*, COM (2005) 650 final, p 6.

apply in point (d) which deals with short lettings where the tenant is an individual (rather than a company) and both the landlord and tenant are habitually resident in the same country; the application of the law of the parties' habitual residence (rather than the lex situs) protects the tenant's legitimate expectations. These provisions reflect the policy adopted by the Regulation in relation to other types of contract which display an imbalance of bargaining power between the parties, notably consumer contracts and employment contracts.[95]

3. Other contracts: article 4(2)

4.56 In a case which is not covered by any of the sub-paragraphs of article 4(1) (or is covered by more than one of them), article 4(2) lays down a choice of law rule according to which the contract is governed by the law of the country in which the party required to effect the characteristic performance of the contract is habitually resident. This rule is structured around two ideas: (i) the party who is to effect the performance which is characteristic of the contract (the 'characteristic performer'); and (ii) the characteristic performer's habitual residence (as defined by article 19, which gives 'habitual residence' a special meaning[96]).

4.57 The notion of characteristic performance is one which was adopted from Swiss law.[97] In a unilateral contract, it follows from the fact that only one party is under a legal obligation that it is the performance of that obligation which is characteristic of the contract. Where, for example, A promises to pay B a £25,000 termination fee in the event of deciding not to go ahead with a joint venture with B, A is the characteristic performer.[98] The Regulation indicates that 'the characteristic performance of the contract should be determined having regard to its centre of gravity'.[99] In an ordinary bilateral contract under which one party pays money in return for the other party's performance, the characteristic performance is the other party's performance, rather than the payment of the price.[100]

4.58 So, in a contract for the licensing of an intellectual property right (such as a patent or trademark), the licensor is the characteristic performer; similarly, in a contract of guarantee, the guarantor is the characteristic performer. Where there are two performances involving the payment of money, the characteristic performer is the party carrying the greater risk.[101] For example, in a contract of reinsurance, the reinsurer, rather than the reinsured, is the characteristic performer; in a gambling contract, the party who offers the facility for the placing of bets, rather than the gambler, is the characteristic

---

[95] See paras 4.122–4.125 and 4.133–4.139.   [96] See paras 4.82–4.86.
[97] D'Oliveira, '"Characteristic Obligation" in the Draft EEC Obligation Convention' (1977) 25 Am J Comp L 303.
[98] *Ark Therapeutics plc v True North Capital Ltd* [2006] 1 All ER (Comm) 138. See also *Ophthalmic Innovations International (United Kingdom) Ltd v Ophthalmic Innovations International Inc* [2005] ILPr 10.
[99] Recital (19).
[100] Giuliano-Lagarde Report, OJ 1980 C282/20.
[101] D'Oliveira, '"Characteristic Obligation" in the Draft EEC Obligation Convention' (1977) 25 Am J Comp L 303, 314.

performer.[102] In *Bank of Baroda v Vysya Bank*,[103] D (an Indian bank) issued a letter of credit in favour of an Irish company which had sold a quantity of iron to an Indian buyer. The credit was confirmed by C, another Indian bank, through its branch in London. Mance J held that the performance which characterised the contract was C's confirmation of the letter of credit and its honouring of the obligations in relation to the seller, rather than D's obligation to reimburse C.

4.59 The limits of the doctrine of characteristic performance should be noted. First, it is impossible to determine the characteristic performance in relation to a contract where both parties undertake to perform obligations of the same type.[104] In a contract of exchange—as opposed to sale—the characteristic performance cannot be identified. Secondly, it is not easy to see how the notion of characteristic performance can be applied in a complex contract, such as a joint venture agreement. If the case falls outside the scope of article 4(1) and the characteristic obligation of the contract cannot be determined for the purposes of article 4(2), the applicable law is determined by article 4(4).[105]

4. Escape clause: article 4(3)

4.60 The fundamental principle underlying article 4 is that, in the absence of choice by the parties, a contract should be governed by the law of the country with which it is most closely connected. The application of the law of closest connection will not only normally accord with the parties' reasonable expectations but also give effect to the policies of the law of the country which has the greatest interest in the contractual situation. It is for this reason that the rules in article 4(1) and (2) are subject to an important qualification; article 4(3) provides that, where it is clear from all the circumstances of the case that the contract is manifestly more closely connected with a country other than that indicated in paragraph (1) or (2), the law of that other country applies. So, in a case involving a contract for the sale of goods between a French seller and an English buyer, although the governing law under article 4(1)(a) would be French law, the applicable law will be English law if the contract is manifestly more closely connected with England. There is no obvious limit to the range of factors which are relevant to the question whether a contract is more closely connected with one country than another. When comparing connections between a contract and different countries, the court is entitled to have regard to the circumstances as a whole, including the existence of other contracts connected with the contract in question (such as other contracts in the same chain of contracts).[106] Whether a contract is more closely connected with country X than with country Y does not turn simply on the number of connections with each country, but depends on an assessment of the significance of those connections.

---

[102] *Hillside (New Media) Ltd v Baasland* [2010] 2 CLC 986 (a decision under the Rome Convention; under the Regulation such a contract could well be treated as a contract for services within art 4(1)(b), according to which the result would be the same).
[103] [1994] 2 Lloyd's Rep 87.
[104] See *Apple Corps Ltd v Apple Computer Inc* [2004] ILPr 34.   [105] See paras 4.77–4.81.
[106] Case C-305/13 *Haeger & Schmidt GmbH v Mutuelles du Mans assurances IARD* [2015] QB 319.

4.61 Article 4(3) is designed to address one of the most controversial features of the Convention. Article 4 of the Convention sought to determine the applicable law in the absence of choice by reference to a number of presumptions (article 4(2)–(4)); however, these presumptions could be disregarded if the contract was more closely connected with a country other than the country identified by the relevant presumption (article 4(5)). Article 4 of the Regulation seeks to resolve the difficulties, under the Convention, surrounding the relationship between the presumptions and the possibility of the presumptions being disregarded if the contract was more closely connected with another country. Nevertheless, many of the same difficulties have been perpetuated under article 4 of the Regulation through the relationship between the rules in paragraphs (1) and (2) and the 'escape clause'[107] in paragraph (3).[108] On the face of it, the Regulation's addition of the word 'manifestly' in the escape clause does not radically transform the situation, although arguably article 4(3) of the Regulation 'sets the bar higher'[109] than article 4(5) of the Convention. The question remains whether the case law decided under article 4 of the Convention continues to be relevant in the context of the Regulation.

(A) Two theories

4.62 In broad outline, there are two possible approaches to article 4. The first is to treat the application of the rules in article 4(1) and (2) as usual, with the escape clause being applicable only in exceptional cases. This approach is supported by the fact that article 4(3) can be applied only if the contract is manifestly more closely connected with another country. Further support may be drawn from the travaux préparatoires of the Rome II Regulation (which contains a similar escape clause); according to the Commission, the application of the escape clause 'really must be exceptional'.[110] The alternative is to take a more liberal approach to the escape clause and not to make the condition for its application too difficult to satisfy. The stipulation that, for the application of article 4(3), a contract must be manifestly more closely connected with another country requires only that it is clear that the contract is more closely connected with one country than with another; according to this approach, a contract may be manifestly more closely connected with a particular country without it necessarily being overwhelmingly more closely connected with it.

4.63 Until article 4 of the Regulation has spawned a body of case law, there will remain some uncertainty over the operation of the escape clause. However, there is no particular reason to think that, notwithstanding the addition of the word 'manifestly' in article 4(3) of the Regulation, the general approach to article 4 of the Convention adopted by both the English courts and the Court of Justice is inappropriate in the context of article 4 of the Regulation.

---

[107] This is the expression used in recital (20) to describe art 4(3).
[108] Okoli and Arishe, 'The Operation of the Escape Clauses in the Rome Convention, the Rome I Regulation and the Rome II Regulation' (2012) 8 Journal of Private International Law 513.
[109] Dickinson, 'Rebuttable Assumptions' [2010] LMCLQ 27, 35.
[110] European Commission, *Proposal for a Regulation of the European Parliament and the Council on the Law Applicable to Non-Contractual Obligations ('Rome II')*, COM (2003) 427 final, p 12 (hereafter '*Rome II Proposal*').

(B) When should the escape clause be applied?

4.64 Under the Convention, there was a strand in the cases which took a very narrow view of the exception in article 4(5). The most extreme example of this strand is the decision of the Dutch Supreme Court in *Société Nouvelle des Papeteries de l'Aa SA v BV Machinefabrike BOA*.[111] The Dutch claimant sold a paper press to the French defendant. The contract, which was drawn up in French, was negotiated in France. The machine was delivered to the defendant in France, where it was assembled by the claimant. The price was expressed in French currency. When the defendant failed to pay the purchase price, the claimant started proceedings in the Netherlands. One of the questions facing the Dutch court was whether the contract was governed by Dutch law (on the basis that the seller was a Dutch company) or French law (on the basis that the contract was more closely connected with France).

4.65 The Dutch court thought that Dutch law was the applicable law. It decided that the exception in favour of the law of closest connection should be applied restrictively and only if, in the special circumstances of the case, the seller's place of business has no real significance as a connecting factor.[112] The court, however, considered that the seller's place of business was not without significance and that, therefore, the contract's closer connection with France did not lead to French law being the applicable law.

4.66 This decision is impossible to square with the actual text of the Convention and it would be equally indefensible under the Regulation. Apart from the fact that the seller was a Dutch company, all the elements of the contract were connected with France; on any plausible reading of the Convention, the contract should have been regarded as governed by French law. The fact that the Dutch court's extremely narrow view of the role played by the principle of closest connection was not the correct interpretation of the Convention is demonstrated by the ruling of the Court of Justice in *Intercontainer Interfrigo SC (ICF) v Balkenende Oosthuizen BV*,[113] the only reference under the Rome Convention prior to the entry into force of the Regulation.

4.67 In the *ICF* case, the question was whether a contract for the provision by a Belgian company of railway wagons to a Dutch company (for the purpose of the carriage of goods from the Netherlands to Germany) was governed by Belgian law (on the basis that the characteristic performer was a Belgian company) or Dutch law (on the basis that the contract was more closely connected with the Netherlands). The Court of Justice accepted that, where it is clear from the circumstances as a whole that a contract is more closely connected with a country other than the characteristic performer's country, the applicable law under article 4 is the law of the country with which the contract is most closely connected.[114] As the Court of Justice pointed out, the objective of article 4 of

---

[111] 1992 Nederlands Jurisprudentie 750; noted and discussed by Struycken, 'Some Dutch Judicial Reflections on the Rome Convention, Art 4(5)' [1996] LMCLQ 18.
[112] Translated and quoted by Struycken [1996] LMCLQ 18, 20.
[113] Case C–133/08 [2009] ECR I–9687.   [114] At para 64.

the Convention is to balance 'the requirements of legal certainty ... with the necessity of providing for a certain flexibility in determining the law which is actually most closely connected with the contract in question'.[115] Of course, the objective of article 4 of the Regulation is no different and a good argument can be made for applying the approach adopted by the Court of Justice in the *ICF* case to situations falling under the Regulation; if it is *clear* that a contract is more closely connected with country X than with country Y, it is only a very small step to the conclusion that the contract is *manifestly* more closely connected with country X.

4.68 Nevertheless, the English authorities decided under the Convention (in which the courts repeatedly favoured the application of the law with which the contract was most closely connected, rather than the characteristic performer's law) 'must be used with caution'[116] in the context of cases governed by the Regulation. On the one hand, the ruling of the Court of Justice in the *ICF* case can be read as an endorsement of the English courts' approach to article 4 (that is, that the court should apply the characteristic performer's law 'unless there is a valid reason, looking at the circumstances as a whole, not to do so',[117] or 'except where the evidence clearly shows that the contract is more closely connected with another country'[118]). On the other hand, the re-drafting of article 4 in the form of a series of rules (article 4(1) and (2)) followed by an escape clause (article 4(3)) suggests that the escape clause should not be applied too readily. In *Molton Street Capital LLP v Shooters Hill Capital Partners LLP*, Popplewell J indicated that 'the new language and structure [of the Rome I Regulation] suggests a higher threshold, which requires that the cumulative weight of the factors connecting the contract to another country must clearly and decisively outweigh the desideratum of certainty in applying the relevant test in Article 4.1 or 4.2'.[119]

4.69 In the English cases decided under the Convention, there was a tendency for the characteristic performer's law to be displaced in favour of the law of the place of performance—at least where the characteristic performance took place in a single country.[120] For example, in *Definitely Maybe (Touring) Ltd v Marek Lieberberg Konzertagentur GmbH*,[121] the claimant was an English company which provided the services of the pop group 'Oasis' to concert organisers; the defendant was a German-based company which organised pop festivals in Germany. The defendant contracted with the claimant for live performances by 'Oasis', but, because of a rift between the Gallagher brothers, Noel Gallagher did not play in Germany. As a result, the defendant refused to pay the

---

[115] At para 59.
[116] Popplewell J in *Molton Street Capital LLP v Shooters Hill Capital Partners LLP* [2015] EWHC 3419 (Comm) at [105].
[117] Mance J in *Bank of Baroda v Vysya Bank* [1994] 2 Lloyd's Rep 87 at 93.
[118] Keane LJ in *Ennstone Building Products Ltd v Stanger Ltd* [2002] 1 WLR 3059 at [41]. See also Potter LJ in *Samcrete Egypt Engineers and Contractors SAE v Land Rover Exports Ltd* [2002] CLC 533 at [45].
[119] [2015] EWHC 3419 (Comm) at [94].
[120] The characteristic performer's law is less likely to be displaced if the characteristic performer's obligations are to be performed in more than one country: *Ennstone Building Products Ltd v Stanger Ltd* [2002] 1 WLR 3059; *Iran Continental Shelf Oil Co v IRI International Corp* [2004] 1 CLC 696.
[121] [2001] 1 WLR 1745.

full price due under the contract and the question arose whether the contract was governed by English law or German law.

4.70 Morison J recognised that, if English law is the characteristic performer's law, the mere fact that Germany is the place of performance of the contract is not sufficient to justify the conclusion that the contract is more closely connected with Germany. This is a very important point. It is not legitimate to treat the place of performance as a more significant connecting factor than the territorial connections of the characteristic performer. If the drafters had wanted the place of performance to play a special role in the determination of the applicable law, they could have drafted article 4 to reflect that (instead of focusing on the territorial connections of the characteristic performer). It is not reasonable for the court to consider applying the escape clause in preference to the rule unless a combination of connecting factors justifies the conclusion that the contract is manifestly more closely connected with a country other than that identified by the rule.

4.71 Nevertheless, in the *Definitely Maybe* case, Morison J held that, on the facts, the contract was more closely connected with Germany: the contract, which provided for payment in German currency, required the performance of contractual obligations in Germany by both parties and, apart from the territorial connections of one of the parties, there was no other connection between England and the contract. Is there any reason to think that, were the same facts to arise under the Regulation, it would be illegitimate for the court to conclude that the contract was manifestly more closely connected with Germany than with England?

4.72 Although several cases decided under the Convention would be decided in exactly the same way under the Regulation,[122] there are some pre-Regulation authorities which are no longer of much value. In *Kenburn Waste Management Ltd v Bergman*,[123] for example, a contractual agreement under which the German characteristic performer undertook not to do certain acts in England was held to be governed by English law on the basis that the contract, which was designed to achieve negative results in England, was more closely connected with England than with Germany. Similarly, in *Marconi Communications International Ltd v PT Pan Indonesia Bank Ltd*[124] the Court of Appeal held that, as regards a letter of credit involving Indonesian banks, English law applied on the basis that the territorial connections of the banks were less significant than the fact that England was the place of performance (that is, where the documents necessary to procure payment were to be presented and checked and the place where payment to the beneficiary was to be made against those documents).[125] These cases fall into the trap of according special weight to the place of performance and, arguably, were the same facts to arise under the Regulation, the court would not be justified in concluding that the contracts in question were manifestly more closely connected with England.

---

[122] See, eg, *Lawlor v Sandvik Mining and Construction Mobile Crushers and Screens Ltd* [2012] 2 Lloyd's Rep 25.
[123] [2002] CLC 644.   [124] [2007] 2 Lloyd's Rep 72.
[125] For criticism of this aspect of the decision, see Hare, 'The Rome Convention and Letters of Credit' [2005] LMCLQ 417.

4.73 The only guidance offered by the Regulation itself is the indication that, when deciding whether or not to apply the escape clause, the court should take account, inter alia, of whether the contract in question has a very close relationship with another contract or contracts.[126] Consider the case where, within the framework of a distributorship between A, a French company, and B, an English company, A sells goods to B. If the distributorship is expressly governed by English law, it would be reasonable to conclude that, even though French law would be the law governing the sale under article 4(1)(a), English law should be the applicable law under article 4(3) on the basis that, by virtue of its very close connection with the distributorship, the contract of sale is, manifestly more closely connected with England. Nevertheless, the position cannot be regarded as settled.

4.74 In *Bank of Baroda v Vysya Bank*[127] it was held that the contract between the parties was governed by English law (which was the characteristic performer's law).[128] Although not strictly necessary for the decision, Mance J also considered the law applicable to other contractual relationships which arose out of the same letter of credit. As regards the relationship between the Indian defendant and the Irish seller, Indian law was the characteristic performer's law. Nevertheless, Mance J thought that the applicable law was English law on the basis that, as a general principle, closely related contracts should be governed by the same law.[129] A similar approach was taken, albeit in less clear-cut circumstances, in *Samcrete Egypt Engineers and Contractors SAE v Land Rover Exports Ltd*.[130] D (an Egyptian company) and C (an English company) had entered into a contract under the terms of which D undertook to act as guarantor in relation to obligations owed to C by X (another Egyptian company). Although Egyptian law was the characteristic performer's law, it was held that England was the country with which the contract was most closely connected. The Court of Appeal relied not only on the fact that England was the place of payment under the contract of guarantee between D and C but also on the fact that England was the place of performance of C's obligations under the contract between C and X. Although this decision might be regarded as very close to the dividing-line, it was followed in *Commercial Marine & Piling Ltd v Pierse Contracting Ltd*,[131] another case decided under the Convention. This case concerned a contract of guarantee under which the guarantor was an Irish company. However, it was held that English law, rather than Irish law, was the applicable law; the contract was more closely connected with England than with Ireland because the contract guaranteed the performance of obligations by an English company and England was the place of payment under the guarantee. It is not certain that, were the facts of either of these cases to arise under the Regulation, it would be legitimate to conclude that the contract of guarantee was manifestly more closely connected with England than with the guarantor's country.

---

[126] Recital (20). [127] [1994] 2 Lloyd's Rep 87. [128] See para 4.58.
[129] See also *Marconi Communications International Ltd v PT Pan Indonesia Bank Ltd* [2005] 2 All ER (Comm) 325; *Gard Marine and Energy Ltd v Glacier Reinsurance AG* [2011] 2 All ER (Comm) 208; *British Arab Commercial Bank v Bank of Communications* [2011] 1 Lloyd's Rep 664.
[130] [2002] CLC 533. [131] [2009] 2 Lloyd's Rep 659.

(C) Conclusions

4.75 If an appropriate balance is struck between the rules in article 4(1) and (2) and the escape clause in article 4(3), article 4 can promote certainty and predictability in most cases. Where the connecting factors are equally balanced between two or more countries the rules in article 4(1) and (2) avoid the need for the court to engage in the difficult task of weighing the various factors against each other and enable the applicable law to be easily identified. This certainty and predictability depends, however, on the courts not being too liberal in their use of the escape clause. The re-drafting of article 4 will not achieve its objective if courts turn article 4 on its head by making the escape clause the rule, rather than the exception.

4.76 The key to finding the appropriate balance between the rules and the escape clause is provided by article 4(3) itself: the rules in article 4(1) and (2) should be displaced only if the contract is *manifestly* more closely connected (or, to put it another way, only if it is *clearly* the case that the contract is more closely connected) with another country. Several of the English cases decided under the Convention in which the court applied the law of closest connection in preference to the characteristic performer's law do not reach this threshold. To justify the application of the escape clause, there must be a combination of connecting factors which causes the balance to be clearly tilted in favour of a law other than the characteristic performer's law.

5. Non-applicability of article 4(1) and (2): article 4(4)

4.77 It is to be expected that the majority of contracts will fall within the rules already considered; either the contract will be of one of the types listed in article 4(1) or, if not one of those types of contracts, it will be possible to identify the characteristic performer. However, not every contract has a characteristic performance—for example, a contract of exchange or a joint venture agreement. If the parties have failed to make a choice of law, how is the applicable law to be determined in such cases? Article 4(4) provides that, if the applicable law cannot be determined pursuant to article 4(1) or (2), the contract shall be governed by the law of the country with which it is most closely connected.

4.78 How is the court to decide with which country a contract is most closely connected? The terms of the Regulation do not provide much guidance—other than to note that 'account should be taken, inter alia, of whether the contract in question has a very close relationship with another contract or contracts'[132]—and the Giuliano-Lagarde Report is of limited help. In the absence of case law from the Court of Justice, the courts in England are likely to be tempted to turn to cases decided under the proper law doctrine prior to the Rome Convention's entry into force. In determining which law is the applicable law the court looks for the 'centre of gravity' of the contract. The theory advocated by Cheshire is that, in cases where the parties fail to make a choice, the court should have regard to 'localising elements'[133]—that is to say, the elements which connect the contract with the various countries involved; the governing law should be the law of the country in which the localising elements are most densely grouped.

---

[132] Recital (21). [133] *International Contracts* (1948) pp 27–8.

4.79 This 'localisation' or 'centre of gravity' approach can be justified on the basis that it is the country in which the elements of the contract are most densely grouped whose interests and policy are most likely to be affected by the contract. To some extent this approach involves a mere enumeration of the links with the different countries; in many cases, the applicable law is the law of the country with the greatest number of localising elements. Where, however, there is no clear preponderance of connections with one country, the weight or quality of the different elements must be assessed.

4.80 Particular significance may be given to the place of performance of the contract—especially when the whole performance of both parties takes place in the same country. Such emphasis on the place of performance may be explained on the basis that a contract is most likely to impinge on the interests of a country if it is to be performed in that country, rather than elsewhere. If both parties have strong links with one country, this is a significant factor in determining the country with which the contract is most closely connected.

4.81 The cases decided at common law show that, except in those cases where the connections with one country are clearly predominant, it is often far from clear why the court finally concludes that one country is more closely connected than another. In such cases there may be great uncertainty for the parties, as it is difficult for them to predict in advance which law will be held to be the governing law.

6. Habitual residence: article 19

4.82 Within the context of article 4(1) and (2) the factor which localises a contract is normally a territorial link between the active or characteristic performer and a country. Although the Regulation uses the term 'habitual residence', this concept is fleshed out by article 19 to mean different connecting factors in different contexts depending on whether the relevant party to the contract is a legal person or an individual. Whatever 'habitual residence' means in the particular circumstances, the appropriate point in time for assessing the relevant connecting factor is when the contract was concluded.[134]

4.83 As a general rule, the habitual residence of a company or other similar body is the place of central administration.[135] If, for example, an English shoe manufacturer contracts to sell a thousand pairs of shoes to a French buyer, the applicable law under article 4(1)(a) is English law, as England is the country in which the seller's central administration is located. In a situation where a company's decision-making centre is in country X, but its main business operations take place in country Y, it would appear that the company's habitual residence under the Rome I Regulation is country X.

4.84 Article 19(2) deals with the case where the contract is concluded in the course of the operations of a branch, agency, or any other establishment, or where, under the contract, performance is the responsibility of such a branch, agency, or establishment. In this type of situation, the active performer's habitual residence is the place where the branch, agency, or any other establishment is situated. So, in the context of a bank loan which

[134] Art 19(3).   [135] Art 19(1).

is made by a French bank through its London branch, the bank's habitual residence is England (because the London branch is responsible for performance of the bank's obligations), rather than France (where the bank's central administration is located).

4.85 For the purposes of article 19(2), it is not enough that the parties anticipate that performance will be effected through a branch, agency, or other establishment; either the contract must have been concluded in the course of the branch's operations or performance of the contract must be the responsibility of the branch. Consider *Bank of Baroda v Vysya Bank*[136] in which the characteristic performance was held to be confirmation of a letter of credit by an Indian bank. In the normal course of events, this would lead to Indian law being the governing law on the basis that the characteristic performer's central administration was situated in India. However, in the *Bank of Baroda* case, the credit was confirmed by the Indian bank through its branch in London. In this type of situation, the combined effect of articles 4(2) and 19(2) is that, in the absence of choice by the parties, English law is the applicable law. It should be noted, however, that it may be difficult, in any given situation, to determine whether a contract is concluded by a branch in the conduct of its operations or whether the branch is acting only as a channel of communication on behalf of the headquarters.[137]

4.86 With regard to individuals, article 19(1) provides that the habitual residence of a natural person acting in the course of his business activity shall be his principal place of business. Where, for example, X, who resides in the Netherlands, runs a business whose activities take place in Belgium, X is habitually resident in Belgium (as regards contracts entered into in the course of X's business activities). In situations where an individual is not acting in the course of business activity, article 19 provides no guidance as to how that person's habitual residence should be ascertained. Fortunately, in the commercial context, there will be few such cases. Consider the case where A, a multimillionaire who divides his time between his homes in Monte Carlo, New York, and London, sells a luxury yacht to B, an Italian playboy. If the parties fail to make a choice of law in accordance with article 3, article 4(1)(a) provides that the contract is governed by the law of the country in which A is habitually resident. If B sues A in England under the contract, article 19 is silent on how A's habitual residence is to be determined. Although there is a significant body of English case law on the meaning to be ascribed to habitual residence,[138] for the purposes of the Regulation habitual residence must be regarded as an autonomous concept which has to be understood by reference to EU law. It remains to be seen the extent to which the Court of Justice finds it necessary to develop different meanings for habitual residence in different contexts. In a series of cases decided in contexts other than choice of law in contract,[139] the Court

---

[136] [1994] 2 Lloyd's Rep 87.
[137] In the context of a similar question under the Rome Convention, compare the first instance decision in *Iran Continental Shelf Oil Co v IRI International Corp* ([2002] CLC 372) with the decision of the Court of Appeal ([2004] 1 CLC 696).
[138] See paras 6.69–6.100.
[139] See, eg, Case C-90/97 *Swaddling v Adjudication Officer* [1999] ECR I-1075; Case C-523/07 Re *Proceedings Brought by A* [2009] ECR I-2805; Case C-497/10 *Mercredi v Chaffe* [2011] 3 WLR 1229.

of Justice has indicated that, for the purposes of EU law, an individual can have only one place of habitual residence, which is the place where the person has established, on a fixed basis, his permanent or habitual centre of interests.[140]

IV The limits of the applicable law

A Introduction

1. Mandatory provisions and public policy

4.87 One justification for giving the parties complete freedom to select the applicable law is that it gives them the certainty of knowing what the governing law is. Another is that, in domestic systems of contract law, the parties are largely free to choose the terms of their contract for themselves; the power to choose the governing law follows as an obvious and reasonable extension. Most domestic contract rules are optional, in the sense that their function is to fill gaps in the contract, but giving way to the parties' agreement to the contrary. Why should not the parties to an international contract, instead of making express provision for various matters, simply agree on which law should be applied to fill the gaps? The answer, of course, is that not all rules of contract law are optional; some are mandatory.

4.88 In cases where the parties fail to make a choice, should the law of the country with which the contract is most closely connected be the only source of rules governing the rights and obligations of the parties? Although it is reasonable to assume that the country with which a contract is most closely connected has, from a policy point of view, the greatest interest in the way in which the contractual relationship is regulated, this does not mean that other countries do not also have an interest when a particular contractual relationship impinges on their policies. Accordingly, a choice of law regime may well provide that in certain types of case the applicable law should yield to policies embodied in the law of another country.

4.89 Although the Regulation allows the parties freedom to choose the applicable law and provides that the applicable law should play the predominant role in determining the rights and obligations of the parties, the drafters recognised that a balance has to be struck between the applicable law (whether chosen by the parties or determined in accordance with article 4) and the legitimate interests of those countries whose law is not the applicable law. This balance is implemented in two ways: first, a number of provisions allow for the application of the mandatory rules of countries whose law is not the applicable law; secondly, the applicable law may be limited by the public policy of the forum.

2. Two types of mandatory provision

4.90 The articles of the Regulation which allow for the application of mandatory provisions which do not form part of the applicable law refer to two different types of rule: (i)

---

[140] See para 6.91.

'provisions ... which cannot be derogated from by agreement'[141] (which, for convenience, might be called 'mandatory provisions') and (ii) 'overriding mandatory provisions', which are defined as 'provisions the respect for which is regarded as crucial by a country for safeguarding its public interests, such as its political, social or economic organisation, to such an extent that they are applicable to any situation falling within their scope, irrespective of the law otherwise applicable to the contract'.[142]

B Limits on freedom of choice

4.91 The main practical objection to giving the parties complete freedom to choose the applicable law is that it allows evasion of the mandatory provisions of the law of a country with which the contract is closely connected, whose purpose may be to protect the public interest, or to protect the interests of a particular class (such as employees or consumers). Moreover, the choice may be, in effect, the choice of the stronger party—where, for example, a standard form contract includes a non-negotiable choice of law clause.

4.92 There is no requirement under article 3 of the Regulation that there should be any objective connection between the country whose law is chosen as the applicable law and the parties to, or the substance of, the contract. So, a choice of English law in a contract between a Greek seller and an Italian buyer is prima facie valid. Article 3(3), however, provides that, where the parties choose the law of one country and 'all other elements relevant to the situation at the time of the choice are located in a country other than the country whose law has been chosen', the mandatory provisions of that other country must be applied.[143] So, if a contract entirely connected with France contains a provision for disputes to be litigated in England under Brazilian law the English court, while applying Brazilian law generally, must nevertheless apply any relevant mandatory provisions of French law.

4.93 Article 3(3) defines mandatory provisions as provisions 'which cannot be derogated from by agreement'. The distinction between mandatory and non-mandatory provisions can be illustrated by a couple of simple examples. Section 39(1) of the Marine Insurance Act 1906 provides that in a 'voyage policy' there should be an implied warranty that at the commencement of the voyage the ship shall be seaworthy. This rule is not, however, mandatory; the implied warranty can be excluded by an appropriately drafted term of the contract[144] or may be waived by the insurer.[145] The implied warranty of seaworthiness may be contrasted with certain implied terms under the Landlord and Tenant Act 1985. In a lease of residential premises for a term of less than seven years, there is an implied statutory covenant by the landlord to keep the

---

[141] See arts 3(3), 3(4), 6(2), 8(1).   [142] See art 9(1).
[143] A similar rule in art 3(4) makes provision for the application of mandatory provisions of EU law in cases where the parties have chosen the law of a third state and all other elements relevant to the situation at the time of the choice are located in one or more Member States.
[144] *Parfitt v Thompson* (1844) 13 M & W 392.   [145] S 34(3).

structure and exterior in repair.¹⁴⁶ This implied statutory covenant is a mandatory rule, as the 1985 Act also provides that an agreement which purports to exclude or limit the landlord's statutory obligations is void (unless authorised by the county court).¹⁴⁷ So, with regard to a short lease of residential premises in England which includes a choice of Italian law, as long as all the elements relevant to the situation are connected with England, the effect of article 3(3) is to enable the tenant to rely on the covenants implied by the 1985 Act, even though Italian law governs other aspects of the contract.

4.94 The application of article 3(3) does not depend on the parties' motives. What triggers the operation of article 3(3) is a choice of the law of country X and the fact that all the other elements relevant to the situation are connected with country Y. Although the purpose of article 3(3) is to nullify an evasive choice, whether or not article 3(3) applies depends on a consideration of objective factors, rather than subjective ones.

4.95 Article 3(3) gives the courts considerable room to manoeuvre, since neither the text of the Regulation nor the Giuliano-Lagarde Report gives much guidance on which elements are 'relevant to the situation'. Although article 3(3) has no application where the parties are based in different countries (because the territorial connections of the parties are 'relevant to the situation'),¹⁴⁸ there are situations in which it is unclear whether article 3(3) is potentially applicable. For example, if an English manufacturer contracts to sell goods to an English buyer is it relevant for the purposes of article 3(3) where the goods are manufactured?

4.96 The effect of article 3(3) is not to invalidate the choice of law in relation to non-mandatory provisions. Where article 3(3) applies, the chosen law is superseded only to the extent that it is in conflict with the mandatory provisions of the law of the country with which the situation is connected.

C Overriding mandatory provisions

4.97 Whereas article 3(3) is concerned entirely with cases where the parties have made a choice of law, article 9 is potentially applicable in cases where the applicable law is determined in accordance with article 4 as well as cases falling within the scope of article 3. Article 9 is premised on the idea that the country whose law is the applicable law is not the only country which, from the point of view of policy, has an interest in how a contractual relationship is to be regulated. Article 9(1) defines a category of mandatory provisions which are 'regarded as crucial by a country for safeguarding its public interests' and must be applied even in the case of an international contract which is governed by a foreign law; an overriding mandatory provision is one which must be applied 'irrespective of the law otherwise applicable to the contract'. Whether or not a provision is overriding is a question of interpretation.¹⁴⁹

---

[146] S 11(1)(a).   [147] S 12.
[148] See *Caterpillar Financial Services Corpn v SNC Passion* [2004] 2 Lloyd's Rep 99.
[149] This issue is considered further at paras 4.102–4.108.

1. Overriding rules of a third country

4.98 The effect of article 9(3) is that where the applicable law is the law of country X but the obligations arising out of the contract have to be, or have been, performed in country Y, effect may be given to the overriding mandatory provisions of the law of country Y in so far as those overriding mandatory provisions render performance of the contract unlawful. Article 9(3) goes on to say that the court, in considering whether to give effect to these overriding mandatory provisions, should have regard to their nature and purpose and to the consequences of their application or non-application.

4.99 Article 9(3) replaces article 7(1) of the Convention which, because it was drafted in a more open-textured way and was potentially much broader in scope, caused considerable controversy.[150] Article 9(3) avoids many of the problems posed by its predecessor by limiting its operation to situations where contractual performance is unlawful under the law of the place of performance (lex loci solutionis). In this revised form, article 9(3) is consistent with the line of English cases at common law in which the court denied enforcement of a contract which, although valid by its proper law, was illegal according to the law of the place of performance.

4.100 Article 9(3) confers a discretion but gives no guidance on how that discretion is to be exercised; the requirement that the court, when considering whether to apply overriding mandatory provisions under article 9(3), should have regard to 'their nature and purpose and to the consequences of their application or non-application' does not take the matter much further. Nevertheless, given the traditional English approach to the types of case which are covered by article 9(3), it would be reasonable to expect that the English court will normally exercise its discretion in favour of giving effect to overriding mandatory provisions of the lex loci solutionis if performance of the contract is rendered illegal by those provisions.

2. Overriding mandatory provisions of the forum

4.101 Article 9(2) provides that nothing in the Regulation shall restrict the application of the overriding mandatory provisions of the law of the forum. This provision is potentially relevant in cases in which the applicable law is determined in accordance with article 4 as well as in cases in which the parties have made a choice of law.[151] In a situation in which the parties choose the applicable law, it is theoretically possible for both article 3(3) and article 9(2) to be relevant. Where, for example, a contract entirely connected with California contains a provision for disputes to be litigated in England under Mexican

---

[150] Such was the opposition to art 7(1) of the Convention that several Contracting States (including the United Kingdom, Germany, Ireland, and Luxembourg) took advantage of the opportunity of entering a reservation on this provision; it was provided that art 7(1) did not form part of English law: Contracts (Applicable Law) Act 1990, s 2(2).

[151] In Case C-184/12 *United Antwerp Maritime Agencies NV v Navigation Maritime Bulgare* [2014] 1 Lloyd's Rep 161 the Court of Justice accepted that the rules of the chosen law implementing the Commercial Agents Directive (Directive No 86/653/EEC, OJ 1986 L382/17) could be displaced by the forum's implementing legislation if the forum's legislation, providing commercial agents with a higher level of protection than the chosen law, was overriding in nature.

law, the English court must have regard to a number of different laws: (i) according to article 3(1) Mexican law is the law which generally governs the contract; (ii) article 3(3) indicates that Mexican law yields to any provisions of Californian law which cannot be derogated from by agreement; (iii) article 9(2) provides for the application of any overriding mandatory provisions of English law. In the event of conflict between the mandatory provisions of Californian law and the overriding mandatory provisions of English law, the overriding mandatory provisions of the forum should prevail. It should be emphasised that the fact that aspects of Mexican law (the law chosen by the parties) may be overridden by specific mandatory rules of English law does not mean that the contract is governed by English law.[152]

4.102 As a general rule, if an English statute makes no provision, express or implied, for the circumstances in which it is to apply, it will apply to a contract which has foreign elements only if English law is the applicable law. Where, for example, a contract of sale is, by virtue of article 4 of the Regulation, governed by Italian law, the implied terms contained in the Sale of Goods Act 1979 do not apply. Although the non-excludable implied terms in the 1979 Act are provisions which cannot be derogated from by contract under article 3(3), they are not overriding mandatory provisions for the purposes of article 9 as they are not applicable to an international contract whose governing law is not English law.

4.103 Some statutes which apply to contractual situations make complete or partial provision for their sphere of application. A statute may provide that it is to apply only if specified connections exist; if the territorial connections are not present the statute does not apply to the contract. What is the position if those territorial connections do exist, but English law is not the applicable law?

4.104 One possibility is that the statute expressly determines its scope of operation. One example of a statute of this type is the Unfair Contract Terms Act 1977. First, the Act defines the circumstances in which its provisions are not applicable even though English law is the law governing the contract.[153] Secondly, and, in the context of the current discussion, more importantly, the Act determines the circumstances in which it is applicable notwithstanding a choice of a foreign law. The 1977 Act contains provisions which invalidate exemption and similar clauses in certain contracts, in some cases automatically and in others unless they satisfy a test of reasonableness. Although much of the Act is directed at consumer contracts,[154] its ambit is wider than that. The Act

---

[152] *Fern Computer Consultancy Ltd v Intergraph Cadworx & Analysis Solutions Inc* [2014] 2 CLC 326.

[153] Under s 27(1) the Act's controls do not apply if English law is the applicable law only by the choice of the parties and, in the absence of such choice, a foreign law would have been the applicable law; s 26 excludes 'international supply contracts' from the Act's scope. See *Trident Turboprop (Dublin) Ltd v First Flight Couriers Ltd* [2010] QB 86. It is provided by s 12 of the Late Payment of Commercial Debts (Interest) Act 1998 that, in a case where the parties choose English law to govern their contract, the Act does not apply if, but for the parties' choice, the applicable law would not have been English law and there is no 'significant connection' between the contract and the United Kingdom: see *Martrade Shipping & Transport GmbH v United Enterprises Corpn* [2015] 1 WLR 1.

[154] For consideration of consumer contracts, see paras 4.122–4.125.

contains provisions designed to ensure that its protective rules apply in appropriate cases even if a foreign law is the applicable law.

4.105 The extent to which the controls in the 1977 Act are to be regarded as overriding for the purposes of article 9 is fixed by section 27(2). The effect of this provision is that the Act applies to a contract, notwithstanding the choice of a foreign law, if (a) such a choice was 'imposed wholly or mainly for the purpose of enabling the party imposing it to evade the operation of the Act' or (b) 'in the making of the contract one of the parties dealt as a consumer, and he was then habitually resident in the United Kingdom, and the essential steps necessary for the making of the contract were taken there, whether by him or by others on his behalf'. The operation of section 27(2) can be illustrated by the following example: the claimant, an English resident, purchases a train ticket from the defendant, a foreign railway operator, for a journey between two foreign cities;[155] the claimant takes all the essential steps necessary for the making of the contract in England; the contract contains a clause which excludes the railway operator's liability for death or personal injury; the contract includes an express choice of the law of the country where the place of departure is situated,[156] according to which the contractual exclusion is valid. If the claimant is injured as a result of the defendant's negligence and brings proceedings in England for breach of contract, the defendant cannot rely on the exclusion clause in the contract. The effect of section 27(2) is that, for the purposes of article 9(2), the provisions of the Act (which render void any contract term which seeks to exclude or restrict liability for death or personal injury resulting from negligence[157]) are overriding in these circumstances.

4.106 If the statute does not expressly identify the circumstances in which it applies, the court has to decide whether or not its provisions are overriding. It seems that the courts are quite likely to hold that, on its true construction, the statute was impliedly intended by the legislator to be applicable if a particular territorial connection exists, whether or not English law is the applicable law.

4.107 An example is *Boissevain v Weil*,[158] a case decided at common law, where statutory provisions laid down that no person should borrow foreign currency, the prohibition being expressed to apply to British subjects in various countries including Monaco. It was held that these statutory provisions, on their true construction, rendered void a contract under which a British subject borrowed foreign currency in Monaco, even if the law of Monaco was the law governing the contract. The statutory rules considered in *Boissevain v Weil* would be overriding mandatory provisions for the purposes of article 9(2) of the Regulation. A similar approach is illustrated by *English v Donnelly*,[159] a Scottish case decided prior to the Rome Convention. An English company entered into a hire-purchase agreement (which included an express choice of English law) in Scotland with a Scottish hirer. The company sued in Scotland for breach of the

---

[155] This contract is not a consumer contract for the purposes of the Regulation: art 6(4).
[156] Such a choice is valid under art 5(2).   [157] Unfair Contract Terms Act 1977, s 2(1).
[158] [1950] AC 327.   [159] 1958 SC 494.

agreement, but the hirer successfully relied on the provisions of the Hire-Purchase and Small Debt (Scotland) Act 1932, a statute which was part of Scots law but not English law, under which the contract was void because the company had not delivered a copy of the agreement to the hirer within a specified period. It was held that, on its true construction, the statute applied to all hire-purchase contracts made in Scotland, irrespective of whether Scots law was the governing law. In effect, the court decided that the statutory rule relied upon by the hirer was an overriding mandatory provision.

4.108 In *Ingmar GB Ltd v Eaton Leonard Technologies Inc*[160] C, a UK company, was engaged by D, a Californian company, as D's exclusive agent in the United Kingdom and Ireland. The contract contained an express choice of Californian law. When the agency contract was terminated, C started proceedings in England to recover payment of commission and, more significantly, compensation as stipulated by the Commercial Agents (Council Directive) Regulations.[161] The High Court rejected the claim on the basis that, as the contract was governed by Californian law, the regulations were not relevant. However, on a reference from the Court of Appeal under what is now article 267 TFEU, the Court of Justice ruled that the regulations, the purpose of which is to guarantee certain rights to commercial agents after the termination of agency contracts, apply regardless of the law applicable to the contract; accordingly, a commercial agent who carries on his activity in a Member State can rely on the regulations, even though the principal is established in a non-Member State.[162]

D Public policy

4.109 In addition to the application of overriding mandatory provisions of the law of the forum under article 9(2), the Regulation also gives a role to the public policy of the forum. According to article 21: 'The application of a provision of the law of any country specified by this Regulation may be refused only if such application is manifestly incompatible with the public policy (*ordre public*) of the forum.' Public policy in the conflicts sphere has a more restricted role than in the domestic sphere. The fact that a contract is void on grounds of public policy by English domestic law does not necessarily mean that public policy can be invoked to invalidate it if it has foreign elements and a foreign applicable law. It is intended that, under the Regulation, public policy should have a very narrow scope.

4.110 According to traditional English notions, there are two categories of case where the court may on grounds of public policy refuse to enforce a contract which is valid by

---

[160] Case C-381/98 [2000] ECR I-9305. See Verhagen, 'The Tension between Party Autonomy and European Union Law' (2002) 51 ICLQ 135.
[161] SI 1993/3053, implementing Directive No 86/653/EEC, OJ 1986 L382/17.
[162] According to the approach endorsed by the *Ingmar* case, a dispute resolution clause may be overridden if the contractual forum would fail to give effect to the relevant overriding rules: see *Accentuate Ltd v Asigra Inc* [2010] 2 All ER (Comm) 738; *Fern Computer Consultancy Ltd v Intergraph Cadworx & Analysis Solutions Inc* [2014] 2 CLC 326 and a similar decision of the German courts: BGH, 5 September 2012, VII ZR 25/12.

its governing law. The first is where to enforce the contract would infringe fundamental English ideas of justice or morality. The best-known case of this sort is *Kaufman v Gerson*.[162] The French defendant had promised to pay the French plaintiff a sum of money in return for the plaintiff refraining from instituting criminal proceedings against the defendant's husband in France. Though the agreement was valid by French law, the plaintiff failed in English proceedings to recover the money on the ground that, under English law, the agreement was illegal and had been made under duress. Romer LJ said that the English court will not enforce a contract which contravenes 'what by the law of this country is deemed an essential moral interest'.[164] Similarly, it would be contrary to public policy for the English court to enforce a contract of slavery or a contract involving bribery, even if the contract were valid under its applicable law. Under this exceptional category, there is no requirement that the contract should have any connection with England.

4.111 In the second category of public policy case, it is the public interest that is at stake. Enforcement of a contract may be refused if it would tend to injure the public interest in a way which an English invalidating rule is designed to prevent. In this type of case public policy is invoked only if the contract has relevant connections with England. It has been held that public policy may be relied upon to refuse enforcement of a restraint of trade clause in a contract of employment, restraining competition in England, even though the clause is valid by its proper law.[165] In this example the English public interest in free competition, which English law is designed to protect, is liable to be injured; if the restraint of trade provision were to operate only abroad, public policy would have no role to play. It should not be thought, however, that doing an act abroad can never be injurious to the public interest. For example, public policy will preclude the enforcement of a contract under which a British subject trades abroad with an enemy.[166] Similarly, as public policy may be invoked to protect the public or national image of the United Kingdom, the court may refuse to enforce a contract where the parties intend to circumvent or breach the laws of another country. In *Regazzoni v KC Sethia (1944) Ltd*[167] a contract provided for the sale of jute bags by Indian sellers to Swiss buyers. Although the contract provided for the goods to be shipped to Genoa, the sellers were aware that the buyers intended to reship the goods from Genoa to South Africa. Under Indian law the shipment from India of jute destined for or intended to be taken to South Africa was prohibited, as both parties well knew. When the sellers repudiated the contract it was held by the House of Lords that the contract should not be enforced by the English court.[168]

4.112 In the commercial sphere, it is very unusual for the law governing a contract to be disapplied on the ground of public policy. If there is no express choice of a foreign law,

---

[163] [1904] 1 KB 591. See also *Royal Boskalis Westminster NV v Mountain* [1999] QB 674.
[164] At 599–600.
[165] *Rousillon v Rousillon* (1880) 14 Ch D 351 (a case decided at common law); *Duarte v Black & Decker Corporation* [2008] 1 All ER (Comm) 401 (a case decided under the Rome Convention).
[166] *Dynamit Act v Rio Tinto Co Ltd* [1918] AC 260.   [167] [1958] AC 301.
[168] It is unclear whether the same principle applies in a situation where breach of the foreign law is inadvertent, rather than intended: see, eg, *Emeraldian Limited Partnership v Wellmix Shipping Ltd* [2010] 1 CLC 993.

public policy will not often need to be relied upon, for if the contract is sufficiently closely connected with England to affect the public interest, English law, as the law of the country with which the contract is most closely connected, is likely to be the applicable law.

4.113 Within the context of the Regulation, it is possible that some of the cases which were traditionally considered as raising questions of public policy should be dealt with by reference to the provisions relating to overriding mandatory provisions. It may be difficult to maintain a clear dividing-line between article 9(2) and article 21. Whereas the effect of article 9(2) is positive (by providing that the applicable law should be displaced by the overriding mandatory provisions of the forum), article 21 operates negatively (by excluding the applicable law). In practical terms, however, it is irrelevant whether an agreement is legally ineffective because it conflicts with the public policy of the forum or because an overriding mandatory provision of the law of the forum renders it unenforceable; whichever analysis is employed the result is the same.[169]

V Specific contracts: articles 5 to 8

4.114 Notwithstanding the possible application of overriding mandatory provisions which do not form part of the applicable law, the starting-point for the Regulation's choice of law regime is the principle of party autonomy. However, it has come to be recognised that freedom of contract should not be unrestricted in areas where there is a structural inequality in socio-economic terms between the parties. Accordingly, the Regulation contains specific provisions dealing with consumer contracts, insurance contracts, and individual contracts of employment. The Regulation also includes specific choice of law rules for contracts of carriage.

A Contracts of carriage: article 5

4.115 Article 5 contains separate choice of law rules for the carriage of goods and the carriage of passengers: whereas the former are generally commercial contracts in relation to which it is reasonable to allow the principle of party autonomy to operate, the latter are typically a type of consumer contract in which the passenger is in a weaker position than the carrier and some modification of the parties' freedom to choose the applicable law is justifiable.

1. Carriage of goods

4.116 In terms of its scope, article 5(1) of the Regulation follows its predecessor, article 4(4) of the Convention: contracts for the carriage of goods cover 'single-voyage charter parties

---

[169] Lando, 'The EEC Convention on the Law Applicable to Contractual Obligations' (1987) 24 CML Rev 159, 208.

and other contracts the main purpose of which is the carriage of goods'.[170] For the purposes of article 5, the important distinction is between an obligation to carry goods, on the one hand, and an obligation to make available a means of transport by which goods may be carried, on the other; a contract involving the former obligation is a contract for the carriage of goods, whereas a contract involving only the latter obligation is not.[171] It follows that a time charter is not a contract for the carriage of goods.[172] Generally, a commission contract for the carriage of goods does not constitute a contract for the carriage of goods; however, a commission contract for the carriage of goods can fall within article 5(1) if its principal purpose is the actual carriage of the goods, as opposed to only organising the carriage of goods.[173] For the purposes of the Regulation, the term 'consignor' refers to any person who enters into a contract of carriage with the carrier and the term 'carrier' refers to the party who undertakes to carry the goods, whether or not he performs the carriage himself.[174]

4.117 To the extent that the parties to a contract for the carriage of goods have not chosen the applicable law, article 5(1) provides that, as long as certain conditions are satisfied, the applicable law should be the law of the country of the carrier's habitual residence.[175] In essence, article 5(1) follows the same basic approach as article 4 by providing for the application of the law of the characteristic performer.[176]

4.118 The qualification is that, in order for the carrier's law to apply under article 5(1), the carrier's place of habitual residence must coincide with at least one of the following connecting factors: the place of receipt of the goods; the place of delivery of the goods; or the habitual residence of the consignor. If these requirements are not met, the applicable law is the law of the country where the place of delivery as agreed by the parties is situated.[177] So, if a Spanish carrier undertakes to carry goods from Mexico to Spain (or vice versa), in the absence of choice by the parties, Spanish law governs. However, where an English carrier undertakes to carry goods from Singapore to Shanghai for a New York consignor, the applicable law is not determined by the carrier's habitual residence. In this situation, in the absence of choice, the contract of carriage is governed by the law of the country where the parties agreed the goods were to be delivered (that is, Chinese law).

4.119 It has to be added that article 5(1) is subject to an escape clause. Article 5(3) is drafted in basically the same terms as article 4(3) and gives rise to the same questions and potential difficulties.[178] In a case where the parties to a contract for the carriage of goods have failed to choose the applicable law, where it is clear from all the circumstances of

---

[170] Recital (22).
[171] Case C-133/08 *Intercontainer Interfrigo SC v Balkenende Oosthuizen BV* [2009] ECR I-9687.
[172] *Martrade Shipping &Transport GmbH v United Enterprises Corpn* [2015] 1 WLR 1.
[173] Case C-305/13 *Haeger & Schmidt GmbH v Mutuelles du Mans assurances IARD* [2015] QB 319.
[174] Ibid.
[175] For the purpose of this rule, 'habitual residence' is determined by art 19. See paras 4.82–4.86.
[176] See Okoli, 'Choice of Law for Contracts of Carriage of Goods in the European Union' [2015] LMCLQ 512.
[177] Art 5(1).   [178] See paras 4.60–4.76.

the case that the contract is manifestly more closely connected with a country other than the country of the carrier's habitual residence or the country of the agreed place of delivery (as the case may be), the law of that other country applies.

2. Carriage of passengers

4.120 As regards contracts for the carriage of passengers, party autonomy is limited; article 5(2) provides that the parties' freedom of choice is restricted to the law of one of the following: (a) the country where the passenger has his habitual residence; (b) the country where the carrier has his habitual residence; (c) the country where the carrier has his place of central administration; (d) the country where the place of departure is situated; (e) the country where the place of destination is situated. In essence, article 5(2) enables the parties to choose a law which has an objective connection with the parties or the contract's performance.

4.121 If the contract for the carriage of passengers includes a choice which is not permitted by article 5(2) or fails to make a choice, the applicable law is the law of the country where the passenger has his habitual residence, provided that either the place of departure or the place of destination is situated in that country. So, if an English airline passenger buys an airline ticket for a journey from New York to London (or vice versa), the contract of carriage, in the absence of a choice of law, is governed by English law. If, however, the journey was from New York to Paris, the contract is not sufficiently closely connected to the country in which the passenger is habitually resident to justify the application of the law of that country. In this type of case, article 5(2) provides that the contract is governed by the law of the country where the carrier has his habitual residence. So, in the absence of a choice of law, if an English airline passenger buys an airline ticket for a journey from St Petersburg to Istanbul from a Finnish airline, the contract is governed by the law of Finland.

B Consumer contracts: article 6

1. Protecting the consumer

4.122 The purpose of article 6 is to ensure that, as regards contracts falling within its scope, a consumer is not deprived of the protection provided by the consumer legislation of the country in which he is habitually resident.[179] This purpose is achieved by two basic rules. First, where the contract does not include a choice of law, it is provided that the law of the consumer's habitual residence is the applicable law.[180] This is an inflexible rule, which applies irrespective of whether the contract is more closely connected with the country in which the consumer is habitually resident or with another country. Secondly, in cases where a consumer contract includes a choice of law, this choice cannot have the effect of depriving the consumer of the protection afforded to him by provisions that cannot be derogated from by agreement under the law which, in the absence of choice, would have been applicable (that is, the law of the country in which the

---

[179] See Hill, *Cross-Border Consumer Contracts* (2008) ch 12.   [180] Art 6(1).

consumer is habitually resident).[181] However, if the law chosen by the parties is more advantageous to the consumer than the law of the country in which the consumer is habitually resident, the chosen law should govern.[182]

2. The scope of article 6

4.123 The significance of the consumer contract provisions is relatively limited. The ambit of article 6 is circumscribed by a number of factors. First, one of the parties to the contract must be a 'consumer' (that is, a natural person who enters the contract for a purpose which can be regarded as being outside his trade or profession) and the other must be a 'professional' (that is, a person acting in the exercise of his trade or profession).[183] Secondly, the professional must either pursue his commercial or professional activities in the country where the consumer has his habitual residence, or direct, by any means, such activities to that country or to several countries including that country, and the contract must fall within the scope of such activities.[184] In this regard, article 6 is drafted in the same way as article 17 of the Brussels I Recast and the two instruments must obviously be interpreted in the same way.[185] If the professional does not pursue activities in the country of the consumer's habitual residence or direct activities to that country, the contract is governed by the rules in articles 3 and 4.[186] Thirdly, article 6 does not apply to: (a) a contract for the supply of services where the services are to be supplied to the consumer exclusively in a country other than that in which he has his habitual residence; (b) a contract of carriage other than a contract relating to a package holiday or tour; (c) a contract relating to a right in rem in immovable property or a tenancy of immovable property, other than a timeshare contract; (d) contracts relating to certain financial instruments.[187] Fourthly, even where a contract of insurance or a contract of carriage is in the nature of a consumer contract for the purposes of article 6, the applicable law is determined by article 7 (insurance) or article 5 (contracts of carriage), rather than article 6.[188]

3. Overriding mandatory provisions of the forum

4.124 Consumer contracts are subject to the general provisions of the Regulation concerning overriding mandatory provisions and public policy. In principle, where litigation takes place in England, a consumer contract is, by virtue of article 9, subject to the overriding mandatory provisions of English law and EU law. The Consumer Rights Act 2015[189] implements rules which are common to all the EU Member States.[190] Part 2 of the 2015 Act provides that certain types of contractual term ('unfair terms') are not binding on consumers.[191] If the contract has a close connection with the United Kingdom, the provisions of Part 2 apply notwithstanding the fact that the law of a country other than an

---

[181] Art 6(2).
[182] See Morse, 'Consumer Contracts, Employment Contracts and the Rome Convention' (1992) 41 ICLQ 1, 8–9.
[183] Art 6(1).   [184] Ibid.   [185] Recital (24).   [186] Art 6(3).   [187] Art 6(4).
[188] Recital (32).
[189] Which revokes the Unfair Terms in Consumer Contracts Regulations, SI 1999/2083.
[190] Directive No 93/13/EEC, OJ 1993 L95/29.   [191] S 62(1).

EEA member state[192] is chosen by the parties to be the applicable law.[193] Accordingly, for the purposes of the Rome I Regulation, the provisions relating to unfair terms are overriding mandatory provisions under article 9(2) in cases where the contract has a close connection with the United Kingdom.

4.125 Nevertheless, in many cases article 9 is redundant. If a contract falls within the scope of article 6, the consumer receives the protection of the mandatory rules which form part of the law of the country where he is habitually resident. A consumer who is resident in England will, therefore, often receive the protection of English consumer legislation by virtue of article 6.[194]

C Insurance contracts: article 7

4.126 Prior to entry into force of the Regulation, choice of law rules relating to contracts of insurance were largely to be found in rules derived from various European directives which had been enacted as part of the drive towards the harmonisation of insurance law in the European Union. Whereas most of the provisions of the Regulation are reasonably simple and focus on the important principles, article 7, which deals with the law applicable to insurance contracts, is complex and addresses many points of detail.

4.127 The scope of the choice of law rules relating to insurance contracts is determined by article 7(1) and (2). There are three fundamental points. First, article 7 does not apply to contracts of reinsurance (which fall within the scope of articles 3 and 4). Secondly, article 7 applies to some types of insurance contract regardless of whether the risk is situated in a Member State or a non-Member State.[195] These are contracts relating to so-called 'large risks',[196] which include contracts covering not only the insurance of property such as railway rolling stock, aircraft, and ships but also liability insurance relating to aircraft and ships. Thirdly, as regards insurance contracts not covered by the preceding point, article 7 applies only if the risks covered are situated in a Member State.

4.128 As regards insurance contracts governing large risks, the pattern follows articles 3 and 4. The principle of party autonomy is given free rein and the parties can choose the applicable law—whether or not there is any objective connection between the substance of the contract and the chosen law. If the parties have failed to choose the governing law, the contract is governed by the law of the country in which the insurer is habitually

---

[192] The EEA (European Economic Area) comprises the Member States of the European Union, Iceland, Liechtenstein, Norway, and Switzerland.

[193] S 74(1).

[194] There are circumstances in which, although art 6 does not apply, the Unfair Contracts Terms Act 1977 and/or Part 2 of the Consumer Rights Act 2015 are overriding. For example, if a contract includes a choice of the law of a foreign country, the court may, relying on art 9(2), apply the Unfair Contract Terms Act 1977 if it appears that the purpose of the choice of law was to evade the operation of the Act. See also the example at para 4.105.

[195] Art 7(6) provides that the country in which the risk is situated is determined in accordance with Directive No 88/357/EEC, art 2(d); in the case of life assurance, the country in which the risk is situated is the country of the commitment within the meaning of Directive No 2002/83/EC, art 1(1)(g).

[196] As defined by Directive No 73/239/EEC, art 5(d).

resident; however, this is subject to an escape clause in favour of the law of another country if the contract is manifestly more closely connected with that country.

4.129 As regards contracts of insurance not relating to large risks—which are covered by article 7 of the Regulation only if the risk is situated in a Member State—the parties' freedom to select the governing law is limited to the choice of one of the following:

  (a) the law of any Member State where the risk is situated at the time of conclusion of the contract;
  (b) the law of the country where the policy holder has his habitual residence;
  (c) in the case of life assurance, the law of the Member State of which the policy holder is a national;[197]
  (d) for insurance contracts covering risks limited to events occurring in one Member State other than the Member State where the risk is situated, the law of that Member State;
  (e) where the policy holder . . . pursues a commercial or industrial activity or a liberal profession and the insurance contract covers two or more risks which relate to those activities and are situated in different Member States, the law of any of the Member States concerned or the law of the country of habitual residence of the policy holder.

4.130 Where, in the cases set out in points (a), (b), or (e), the Member States referred to grant greater freedom of choice of the law applicable to the insurance contract, the parties may take advantage of that freedom.[198]

4.131 This provision is similar in inspiration to article 5(2) (which applies to contracts for the carriage of passengers) in the sense that the parties are free to select only a law which has an objective connection with the parties to the contract or the contract's substance.

4.132 If a contract of insurance not relating to large risks does not contain a choice of law, it is provided that the applicable law is the law of the Member State in which the risk is situated at the time the contract is concluded.[199] In contrast to the position pertaining to insurance contracts covering large risks, this rule is not qualified by an escape clause in favour of the law of another country with which the contract is most closely connected.

D Individual contracts of employment: article 8

4.133 Whereas article 6 defines what is meant by a consumer contract for the purposes of the Regulation, article 8, which covers individual contracts of employment, contains no equivalent definition. Although the question has not yet been settled,

---

[197] Where the contract covers risks situated in more than one Member State, the contract is considered as constituting several contracts each relating to only one Member State: art 7(5).
[198] Art 7(3).
[199] Ibid. Art 7(4) sets out additional rules that apply to insurance contracts covering risks for which a Member State imposes an obligation to take out insurance (such as motor insurance).

there are strong arguments in favour of applying the governing law to determine whether or not a contract is an individual employment contract for the purposes of article 8: this approach is most likely to achieve uniformity and it has the added advantage of avoiding a situation where the court applies the employment law of a particular country to a contract which is not a contract of employment according to that law.[200]

4.134 If the parties do not make a choice, the law applicable to an individual contract of employment is determined by article 8, which adopts the same basic approach as article 4. Article 8 adopts a hierarchy of choice of law rules which contain three elements: (i) the country in which the employee works; (ii) the place of business through which the employee was engaged; (iii) the country with which the contract is most closely connected. The first of these three elements should be given priority.[201]

4.135 First, the contract is governed by the law of the country in which or, failing that, from which the employee habitually carries out his work in performance of the contract.[202] The country in which the employee habitually carries out his work is a concept which should be given a broad interpretation.[203] As a general rule, an employee is to be regarded as habitually carrying out his work at the place where he establishes the effective centre of his working activities.[204] Where an employee works in more than one country, the place where the employee habitually works is the place in which or from which, in the light of all the factors which characterise his employment activity, the employee performs the main part of his obligations towards his employer.[205] The place where work is habitually carried out does not change simply because the employee is temporarily employed in another country.[206] Work carried out in another country should be regarded as temporary if the employee is expected to resume working in the country of origin after carrying out his tasks abroad; similarly, the conclusion of a new contract of employment with the original employer or an employer belonging to the same group of companies as the original employer should not preclude the employee from being regarded as carrying out his work in another country temporarily.[207]

4.136 Secondly, if the country in which or from which the employee works cannot be determined, typically because it is not possible to identify a country with which the employment has a significant connection, the applicable law is the law of the country where the place of business through which the employee was engaged is situated.[208] The relevant connecting factor for this rule is the place of business which concluded

---

[200] See Morse, 'Consumer Contracts, Employment Contracts and the Rome Convention' (1992) 41 ICLQ 1, 13.
[201] Case C-384/10 *Voogsgeerd v Navimer SA* [2012] ILPr 16, para 32.   [202] Art 8(2).
[203] Case C-29/10 *Koelzsch v Grand Duchy of Luxembourg* [2012] QB 210; Case C-384/10 *Voogsgeerd v Navimer SA* [2012] ILPr 16.
[204] Case C-383/95 *Rutten v Cross Medical Ltd* [1997] ECR I-57 (case decided in the context of the Brussels Convention, art 5(1)).
[205] Case C-29/10 *Koelzsch v Grand Duchy of Luxembourg* [2012] QB 210, para 50.   [206] Art 8(2).
[207] Recital (36).   [208] Art 8(3).

the contract of employment, rather than the place of business of the undertaking to which the employee is connected through his actual employment.[209]

4.137 Thirdly, these two choice of law rules are subject to the usual escape clause; the contract is governed by the law of another country if it appears from the circumstances as a whole that the contract is more closely connected with that other country.[210] Although a contract of employment will normally be most closely connected with the country where the employee habitually works, the relevant connecting factors may indicate that another country is clearly more closely connected—even if the employee has worked habitually in one country for a lengthy period of time; relevant factors may include the country in which the employee pays taxes on the income from his employment and the country in which the employee is covered by schemes relating to social security, pension, sickness insurance, and invalidity.[211]

4.138 If the parties make a choice of law, the chosen law prima facie governs the contract.[212] This rule is subject to an important limitation: a choice of law shall not have the result of depriving the employee of the protection afforded to him by the provisions that cannot be derogated from by agreement under the law which would have been applicable in the absence of choice. So, if a French resident is employed to work in France under a contract which is expressly governed by German law, the provisions of French law that cannot be derogated from by agreement prevail over German law. If the applicable law gives the employee more protection than the law which would be applicable in the absence of choice, the employee should be given the benefit of the law which is more favourable. For the purposes of article 8, provisions that cannot be derogated from by agreement are provisions in employment statutes whose purpose is to protect employees; the English rules relating to restrictive covenants in employment contracts are part of the general law of contract and are not mandatory rules as that term is to be understood in the context of article 8.[213]

4.139 Whether or not the parties have made a choice of law, the applicable law has to give way to any relevant overriding mandatory provisions of the law of the forum. Similarly, the rules on individual employment contracts should not prejudice the application of the overriding mandatory provisions of the country to which a worker is posted in accordance with Directive 96/71/EC.[214]

VI Particular aspects of the contract

4.140 Although the applicable law, as identified by articles 3–8 (and modified by any relevant mandatory rules), is central to the determination of the rights and obligations of the parties, it cannot be assumed that all aspects which arise under a contract are governed

---

[209] Case C–384/10 *Voogsgeerd v Navimer SA* [2012] ILPr 16.
[210] Art 8(4). Unlike art 4(3), art 8(4) does not include the word 'manifestly'; whether this omission is meant to be significant is unclear.
[211] Case C–64/12 *Schlecker v Boedeker* [2014] QB 320. [212] Art 8(1).
[213] *Duarte v Black & Decker Corporation* [2008] 1 All ER (Comm) 401. [214] Recital (34).

exclusively by the applicable law. In the sections which follow, the choice of law aspects of various contractual issues are considered.

A Consent and material validity

4.141 Article 10 of the Regulation identifies the law which determines whether a contract or a term of a contract is materially valid. One of the most important aspects of material validity is the formation of the contract. Have the parties reached an agreement by offer and acceptance? Is consideration required for the agreement to be enforceable? Did the parties have the necessary intention to create legal relations? Have the parties freely given their consent? What is the effect of mistake or duress?[215] Is the alleged contract void for illegality? These are all questions of material validity which fall within the scope of article 10. Article 10 comprises two paragraphs: the first lays down a general rule; the second contains an exception.

1. The general rule

4.142 The general rule is that the existence and validity of a contract, or of any term of a contract, are determined by the law which would govern it if the contract or term were valid.[216] This rule is difficult to defend from the point of view of logic. As a matter of logic, questions of formation cannot be governed by the applicable law, for until such questions have been decided it is not clear that there is a contract at all. The Regulation ignores these logical problems and lays down the rule that the putative applicable law governs these issues.

4.143 The application of the general rule may be illustrated by a couple of simple examples. Suppose a Swiss seller sends by post an offer to sell goods to an English buyer, who posts back an acceptance which is lost in the post. By English law there is a contract, because acceptance is effective on posting; by Swiss law there is no contract because acceptance is effective only on receipt. Which law is to decide whether a contract was made? The putative applicable law approach adopted by the Regulation requires the court to determine which law would be the applicable law on the assumption that a contract was made. In the absence of choice by the parties, this would normally be the law of the country in which the seller was habitually resident.[217] So, unless the alleged contract is manifestly more closely connected with England, Swiss law would be applied to decide whether there was a contract, with the result that there would not be.

4.144 A similar analysis can be applied in the situation in which an Italian donor promises to make a gift to an English donee. According to Italian law the promise is legally binding; under English law it is unenforceable because the donee gave no consideration for the promise. In the absence of choice, the putative applicable law would be Italian law, the law of the country in which the donor was habitually resident. Accordingly, the promise would be enforceable.

---

[215] See *Lupofresh Ltd v Sapporo Breweries Ltd* [2014] 1 All ER (Comm) 484 (a case of alleged duress).
[216] Art 10(1). See *Toyota Tsucho Sugar Trading Ltd v Prolat Srl* [2015] 1 Lloyd's Rep 344.
[217] Art 4(1)(a).

4.145 The position is slightly more complicated if it is alleged that the supposed contract contains a choice of law clause. Article 3(5) provides that the existence and validity of the consent of the parties as to the choice of the applicable law is to be determined according to the general principles which apply to other questions relating to the existence and validity of contractual terms. So, the existence and validity of a choice of English law is to be determined by English law.

4.146 What is the position, as regards the substance of the contract, if according to its putative applicable law the alleged choice of law does not exist? Suppose that an English buyer offers to buy goods from a German seller on terms which include a choice of English law. Although the buyer purports to withdraw the offer before the seller replies, the seller accepts the offer. Under English law the revocation is effective; under German law it is not. Is there a valid contract?

4.147 There are two possible ways of looking at the problem. First, if the contract—including the alleged choice of law—is looked at as a single entity, the answer is that no contract comes into being: if the contract exists it is governed by English law; but according to English law there is no contract. The logic of this approach, however, may be questioned. Furthermore, both article 3(5) and article 10 can be interpreted as suggesting that the existence of the alleged choice of law clause should be considered independently, before the contract as a whole is examined.

4.148 According to the second approach, the first step is to consider the existence of the alleged choice of English law by reference to its putative applicable law. Under English law there is no effective choice because of the revocation of the offer prior to the seller's acceptance. Following the disposal of the choice of law clause, the putative applicable law—as regards the remainder of the disputed contract—has to be determined by article 4, the rule being that German law, being the seller's law, governs. According to German law the purported revocation is ineffective and, subject to the exception in article 10(2), the contract is validly created with German law as its applicable law.

2. **The exception**

4.149 One of the problems posed by the putative applicable law approach is that it could be unjust to hold a party bound under a foreign law in circumstances in which he is not bound by his own law. For example, an offeree might find himself bound under a contract even though he did not accept the offer on the basis that according to the putative applicable law (but not the offeree's law) silence can amount to consent. To deal with this problem, the Regulation contains an exception to the general rule: a party may rely upon the law of the country in which he is habitually resident to establish that he did not consent if it appears from the circumstances that it would not be reasonable to determine the effect of his conduct in accordance with the law specified by the general rule.[218]

---

[218] Art 10(2).

4.150 There are a number of points to make about this provision. First, its effect is entirely negative. The exception cannot be invoked to validate a contract which would be materially invalid under the general rule. Secondly, the exception allows a contracting party to invoke the law of the country in which he is habitually resident. Habitual residence has to be understood by reference to article 19.[219] Thirdly, the exception—which is based on a reasonableness test—is rather open-textured and the text of the Regulation does not give any guidance on how the test should be applied. The reported cases suggest that the English courts will not readily allow a litigant to rely on the exception—at least in cases where the transaction is an 'entirely conventional one'.[220] In *Egon Oldendorff v Libera Corpn*,[221] a case concerning an alleged charter agreement which, if it existed, was governed by English law, the Japanese defendant sought to rely on Japanese law, according to which, it was argued, consent was not established. Mance J, adopting 'a dispassionate, internationally minded approach',[222] held that, as the alleged contract included an English arbitration clause from which a choice of English law could be implied, it was reasonable to determine the effect of the defendant's conduct in accordance with English law. In Mance J's view, to ignore the arbitration clause would have been contrary to ordinary commercial expectations, given that the arbitration clause was precisely the sort of clause which would be expected in an international charter agreement and the circumstances suggested that the defendant must actually have considered and accepted the clause.

B Formal validity

4.151 Article 11 of the Regulation lays down the choice of law rules which apply to questions of formal validity. Although the Regulation does not attempt to define the scope of formal (as opposed to material) validity, the Giuliano-Lagarde Report states that formal validity covers 'every external manifestation required on the part of a person expressing the will to be legally bound, and in the absence of which such expression of will would not be regarded as fully effective'.[223] So, for example, a requirement that certain types of contract—such as contracts for the sale of land[224]—must be made in writing is an aspect of formal validity.[225] The regime set out in article 11 is very liberal with the consequence that an international contract will rarely be invalid as a result of the parties' failure to comply with formal requirements.

4.152 A contract which is concluded by parties (or agents of the parties) in the same country is formally valid if it satisfies the formal requirements of either the applicable law (as determined by article 3 or 4) or the law of the country in which the contract is concluded (lex loci contractus).[226] Where the parties to the contract (or

---

[219] See paras 4.82–4.86.　　[220] David Steel J in *The Epsilon Rosa* [2002] 2 Lloyd's Rep 701 at [12].
[221] [1995] 2 Lloyd's Rep 64.　　[222] At 70.　　[223] OJ 1980 C282/29.
[224] Law of Property (Miscellaneous Provisions) Act 1989, s 2.
[225] For consideration of the classification questions raised by the Statute of Frauds and its interpretation in *Leroux v Brown* (1852) 12 CB 801, see para 1.95.
[226] Art 11(1).

their agents) are in different countries when the contract is concluded, the contract is formally valid if it satisfies the requirements of (i) the applicable law or (ii) the law of the country in which either party (or agent) was located when the contract was concluded or (iii) the law of the country in which either party is habitually resident.[227] If, for example, an English resident and a French resident conclude by telephone a contract which contains a choice of German law, the contract will be formally valid if it satisfies the formal requirements of the laws of England, France, or Germany.

4.153 Article 11 lays down rules for acts intended to have legal effect relating to an existing or contemplated contract as well as to concluded contracts. Such an act—for example, an offer or an invitation to treat—is formally valid if it is formally valid according to the putative applicable law or the law of the country where the act was done or the law of the country where the person by whom it was done had his habitual residence at that time.[228] Article 11 also includes a special rule for consumer contracts. The formal validity of a consumer contract—within the scope of article 6—is governed by the law of the country in which the consumer has his habitual residence.[229] Finally, special provision is made for contracts concerning rights in rem in immovable property and tenancies of immovable property. Such contracts are subject to the formal requirements of the lex situs if by that law (a) those requirements are imposed irrespective of the country where the contract is concluded and irrespective of the law governing the contract, and (b) those requirements are mandatory—in the sense that they cannot be derogated from by agreement.[230]

C Capacity

4.154 Rules relating to capacity define classes of person who lack the power which people in general have to make or to be bound by a contract. (If it is contended that no person can validly make the contract in question, the issue is one of material validity, not capacity.) In the context of the conflict of laws, 'capacity' should be given a broad, internationalist interpretation. The commonest kind of incapacity to contract is that of minors. Others who may lack capacity under a particular legal system are married women, mentally disordered people, and corporations.[231] Whether a corporation is legally able to exercise specific rights, such as enter a valid contract with a third party, is a question of capacity; a lack of substantive power to conclude a contract of a particular type is equivalent to a lack of capacity for conflict of laws purposes.[232] Similarly, in a case where a company's constitution requires contracts to be signed by two officers of the company, the question whether the signature of one officer can bind the company is a question of capacity, rather than one of formal validity.[233]

---

[227] Art 11(2).   [228] Art 11(3).   [229] Art 11(4).   [230] Art 11(5).
[231] See *Merrill Lynch Capital Services Inc v Municipality of Piraeus* [1997] 6 Bank LR 241.
[232] *Haugesund Kommune v Depfa ACS Bank* [2012] QB 549.
[233] *Integral Petroleum SA v SCU-Finanz AG* [2015] ILPr 50.

4.155 In general, questions of capacity are excluded from the scope of the Regulation on the ground that such issues are part of the law of persons, rather than the law of obligations. Accordingly, the relevant rules have to be located in the common law. There is, however, a specific rule in article 13 providing that, in certain circumstances, an incapacity under the law governing that question should be disregarded.

1. Capacity rules at common law

4.156 It is well established that the capacity of a company is governed by the law of its place of incorporation.[234] As regards natural persons, the position at common law is not definitively settled, there being very few modern authorities. There are dicta in some older cases[235] that capacity to contract is governed by the law of domicile. By contrast, in the old case of *Male v Roberts*[236] it was held that Scots law, as the lex loci contractus, governed the capacity of a party to make a contract, even though that party was domiciled in England. At that time, however, it was generally assumed that contracts were governed by the law of the country where they were made and few commentators favour the general application of the lex loci contractus to questions of capacity.

4.157 In *Bodley Head Ltd v Flegon*[237] it was held obiter that capacity is governed by the proper law.[238] The author, Solzhenitsyn, had executed in Russia a power of attorney in favour of a Swiss lawyer, empowering him to deal with Solzhenitsyn's books outside Russia. It was contended that this contract of agency was void, as Solzhenitsyn lacked capacity under Russian law to make it. Russian law governed capacity, it was argued, either as the domiciliary law or the lex loci contractus. It was held, however, that the issue was not one of capacity, for the relevant rule of Russian law—that Russian citizens were not permitted to trade abroad—was a rule of material validity, rather than a capacity rule. The question was, therefore, governed by the proper law, which was Swiss law. However, Brightman J went on to say that, even if it had been the case that Solzhenitsyn lacked capacity by Russian law, the contract would still have been valid, for capacity is also governed by the proper law.

4.158 In view of the confusion surrounding the authorities it is difficult to state the current law with confidence. One suggestion is that a party to an international contract should be regarded as having capacity if he has capacity either by his personal law or by the objective proper law.[239] This suggestion not only draws on the decided cases but also is defensible from the point of view of principle.

4.159 If a party lacks capacity by the law of the country with which the contract is most closely connected, he should still be bound if he has capacity by the law of his domicile.[240] To the extent that an incapacity is protective of the party concerned, the law of

---

[234] See, eg, *Integral Petroleum SA v SCU-Finanz AG* [2015] ILPr 50.
[235] *Cooper v Cooper* (1888) 13 App Cas 88 at 99.   [236] (1790) 3 Esp 163.   [237] [1972] 1 WLR 680.
[238] See also *Charron v Montreal Trust Co* (1958) 15 DLR (2d) 240 (Court of Appeal, Ontario); *Homestake Gold of Australia Ltd v Peninsula Gold Pty Ltd* (1996) 131 FLR 447 (Supreme Court, New South Wales).
[239] Dicey, Morris and Collins, *The Conflict of Laws* (15th edn, 2012) p 1865.
[240] For the meaning of 'domicile' in this context, see Chapter 6.

the country to which a person belongs is best able to decide whether he needs such protection. There is no reason why a party who has capacity by his own law should be able to rely on any other law to avoid being bound.

4.160 However, to allow a party to rely on an incapacity under the law of his domicile could be unjust to the other party, who may have no reason to suppose that his contracting partner is domiciled in a foreign country, let alone to know what the capacity rules in that country are.[241] Where both parties have capacity by the proper law, it would be unfair to allow one party to avoid being bound by invoking an incapacity under his personal law. In this context the proper law should be objectively ascertained; the relevant law is the law of the country with which the contract is most closely connected. If the proper law were determined subjectively a person would be able to confer capacity on himself by his mere agreement to a contractual clause which selected a law according to which he had capacity.

2. The significance of article 13

4.161 Although capacity questions are, in general, excluded from the Regulation's scope,[242] article 13 provides as follows:

> In a contract concluded between persons who are in the same country, a natural person who would have capacity under the law of that country may invoke his incapacity resulting from the law of another country, only if the other party to the contract was aware of that incapacity at the time of the conclusion of the contract or was not aware thereof as a result of negligence.

4.162 The Giuliano-Lagarde Report explains that the purpose of this provision is to protect a party who in good faith believed himself to be contracting with a person of full capacity and who, after the conclusion of the contract, is confronted by the incapacity of the other contracting party.[243] Nevertheless, article 13 is not without its difficulties.

4.163 It is not at all clear how the negligence test is to be applied. In what circumstances, if any, would it be negligent for a foreign trader not to know that a 17-year-old English youth does not have capacity to conclude a commercial contract? The Giuliano-Lagarde Report indicates only that the burden of proof is on the incapacitated party to prove that the other party knew or should have known of the incapacity.[244]

4.164 Care is needed when considering the possible application of article 13. Take, for example, the situation where D, an English youth of 17, agrees—while on holiday in France—to buy a motorbike from C, a French seller; the youth has capacity under French law by virtue of the fact that, even though he is under the age of majority, he is married.[245] When C seeks to enforce the contract in England, can D rely on the fact that he does not have capacity under English domestic law? At first glance, this might

---

[241] *McFeetridge v Stewarts and Lloyds Ltd* 1913 SC 773 at 784. [242] Art 1(2)(1).
[243] OJ 1980 C282/34. [244] Ibid. [245] See French Civil Code, arts 476, 481, 1123, and 1124.

appear to be the type of situation in which, on the assumption that the seller knew of the incapacity or was negligent in not knowing about it, article 13 allows an incapacitated person to invoke his incapacity. This would, however, be too superficial a view. According to the Giuliano-Lagarde Report, article 13 applies only if there is a conflict of laws: 'The law which, according to the private international law of the court hearing the case, governs the capacity of the person claiming to be under a disability must be different from the law of the country where the contract was concluded'.[246] So, if D has capacity not only under French law, but also according to English *conflicts rules* (because French law is the objective proper law of the contract), D cannot invoke his incapacity under English domestic law.

D The effect and construction of a contract

4.165 Questions may arise concerning the nature or extent of the parties' rights and obligations under a valid contract. As questions of substance are governed by the applicable law, it follows that this law governs the interpretation of contractual provisions.[247] Primarily, the court will seek to ascertain the intention of the parties, but to the extent that any rules of law or canons of construction are needed to determine what the terms are, the court will use those of the applicable law.

4.166 The applicable law also governs performance.[248] The Regulation provides, however, that '[i]n relation to the manner of performance and the steps to be taken in the event of defective performance regard shall be had to the law of the country in which performance takes place'.[249] The precise significance of this provision is somewhat opaque; the Giuliano-Lagarde Report states that matters falling within the scope of the phrase 'manner of performance' include 'rules governing public holidays, the manner in which goods are to be examined, and the steps to be taken if they are refused'.[250] The Regulation does not state that, as regards questions relating to the manner of performance, the law of the place of performance (lex loci solutionis) governs but simply provides that 'regard shall be had' to it. Questions of substance are governed by the applicable law and the lex loci solutionis should not, as a general rule, be allowed to impinge upon such questions so as to alter the rights and obligations of the parties.

4.167 The consequences of breach are within the province of the applicable law.[251] So, the applicable law determines whether a party is entitled to recover a particular type of loss (such as non-pecuniary losses) and whether or not such losses are too remote. The right to claim interest should be regarded as a substantive matter for the applicable law under article 12(1)(c). The applicable law also governs questions of causation and the question whether the defendant can rely on a defence (such as set-off or contributory negligence) as a means of limiting his liability.[252]

---

[246] OJ 1980 C282/34.   [247] Art 12(1)(a).   [248] Art 12(1)(b).
[249] Art 12(2). See *East West Corpn v DKBS 1912* [2002] 2 Lloyd's Rep 182.   [250] OJ 1980 C282/33.
[251] Art 12(1)(c).   [252] *Meridien BIAO Bank GmbH v Bank of New York* [1997] 1 Lloyd's Rep 437.

E Discharge

4.168 The circumstances in which a contract, or obligation under it, comes to an end is for the applicable law to determine.[253] The applicable law, therefore, governs such matters as frustration, termination for breach or by agreement or as a result of any other factor (such as insolvency). The applicable law also determines whether a claim is barred by lapse of time.

F Illegality

4.169 There are no provisions of the Regulation which deal with illegality as such. Problems of illegality have to be dealt with by applying those articles of the Regulation which deal with material validity, the performance and discharge of contractual obligations and overriding mandatory provisions. Two issues can be dealt with simply. First, if a contract or contractual provision is invalid because it is illegal under the putative applicable law, the English court will not enforce it.[254] Secondly, the fact that a contract is illegal under a foreign law which is neither the applicable law nor the law of the place of performance (lex loci solutionis) will be ignored if the contract is valid according to the applicable law.[255]

4.170 Problems are most likely to arise in cases where the contract is prima facie valid by the applicable law, but is illegal under the lex loci solutionis. Although the position under the Convention was uncertain, article 9(3) of the Regulation provides a clear solution to this scenario. In considering problems of illegality under the lex loci solutionis it is useful to draw a number of distinctions: first, cases of initial illegality (where the contract is illegal at the outset) should be distinguished from cases of subsequent illegality (where the contract is valid at the outset, but is rendered illegal by a change in the law); secondly, a distinction should be made between cases in which English law is the applicable law and cases in which a foreign law is the applicable law.

1. Contracts governed by English law

4.171 A contract which is governed by English law will not be enforced if performance is illegal under the lex loci solutionis. This general principle applies equally to cases of initial and subsequent illegality.

4.172 So, a contract of sale involving the export of goods from country X will not be enforced if, by the law of country X, such export is permitted only under licence and an appropriate licence has not been obtained.[256] The courts' refusal to enforce contracts which are illegal under the lex loci solutionis was extended to cases in which the parties'

---

[253] Art 12(1)(d).
[254] Art 12(1). See *Zivnostenska Banka National Corpn v Frankman* [1950] AC 57 (a case decided at common law).
[255] This principle is illustrated by *Kleinwort Sons & Co v Ungarische Baumwolle Industrie Akt* [1939] 2 KB 678 (a case decided at common law).
[256] *AV Pound & Co Ltd v MW Hardy & Co Inc* [1956] AC 588.

common intention was the commission in country X of acts which are illegal by the law of that country even if performance in country X was not necessarily required by the terms of the contract.[257] For example, in *Foster v Driscoll*[258] the Court of Appeal refused to enforce an agreement to ship a cargo of whisky across the Atlantic during Prohibition; although the contract did not require performance in the United States, the parties' intention was to smuggle the cargo into the United States. This case, which involved a contract whose proper law was English law, would be decided the same way under the Regulation.[259] The leading case relating to subsequent illegality is *Ralli Bros v Compania Naviera Sota y Aznar*,[260] in which English defendants chartered a Spanish ship to carry a cargo of jute from Calcutta to Barcelona at an agreed freight, part of which was to be paid in Barcelona when the ship arrived there. Spanish legislation passed after the making of the contract, but before the arrival of the ship, laid down that the freight payable on jute imported into Spain should not exceed a certain rate, and made it an offence to pay or receive freight above that amount. As the freight agreed in the charterparty to be payable in Spain exceeded the statutory rate, the issue for the English court was whether the ship-owners were entitled to recover the excess. The Court of Appeal held that the excess was not recoverable; the contract, which was governed by English law, was not enforceable to the extent that it required performance in Spain which was illegal under Spanish law.

2. Contracts not governed by English law

4.173 What is the position with regard to contracts governed by a foreign law if performance of the contract is illegal under the law of the place of performance? If the contract is valid by its applicable law (notwithstanding the illegality under the lex loci solutionis), the question is whether the applicable law should prevail over the lex loci solutionis or vice versa. The answer to this question is provided by article 9(3) of the Regulation, which stipulates that effect may be given to the overriding mandatory provisions of the law of the place of performance to the extent that those overriding mandatory provisions render performance of the contract unlawful. Although article 9(3) does not require the application of the overriding mandatory provisions of the lex loci solutionis, a court which is faced with a conflict between the applicable law and the overriding mandatory provisions of the law of the place of performance is entitled to decide, having regard to the nature and purpose of the overriding mandatory provisions involved, that the applicable law should yield to the overriding mandatory provisions.

4.174 Suppose that A and B enter a contract to smuggle carpets out of Iran and that, under Iranian law, performance of the contract is illegal. However, the contract is expressly governed by Ruritanian law, according to which the contract is valid and enforceable, notwithstanding the illegality under Iranian law. If B fails to perform his side of the bargain and A sues B in England, the English court may, relying on article 9(3), give

---

[257] *Beijing Jianlong Heavy Industry Group v Golden Ocean Group Ltd* [2013] 2 Lloyd's Rep 61.
[258] [1929] 1 KB 470.
[259] See also *S v A Bank* [1997] 6 Bank LR 163; *Ispahani v Bank Melli Iran* [1998] Lloyd's Rep Bank 133.
[260] [1920] 2 KB 287.

effect to the provisions of Iranian law which render performance of the contract illegal and dismiss A's claim. Given that there is a long line of common law authorities in which the English courts have decided (or stated obiter) that they will not enforce a contract which is illegal under the lex loci solutionis,[261] it can be anticipated that an English court will typically exercise the discretion conferred by article 9(3) in favour of giving priority to overriding mandatory provisions of the lex loci solutionis which render contractual performance illegal—at least in a case involving initial illegality.

4.175 The arguments are more finely balanced in cases of subsequent illegality. Under the Regulation, whether or not a contract is frustrated is a question of substance which is determined by the applicable law.[262] There is a case for saying that subsequent illegality by the lex loci solutionis should discharge the defendant's obligations only to the extent that those obligations are discharged under the applicable law. Having said that, as article 9(3) is drafted in wide enough terms to cover any case of illegality, an English court would be entitled, in cases of subsequent illegality, to give priority to the overriding mandatory provisions of the lex loci solutionis that render contractual performance illegal.

G Nullity

4.176 Article 12(1)(e) provides that the applicable law governs the consequences of nullity of the contract. This repeats the equivalent provision of the Convention on which the United Kingdom entered a reservation[263] on the basis that the consequences of nullity should be classified as restitutionary, rather than contractual.

4.177 The reservation was hardly necessary as the common law choice of law rules would normally lead to the same result as the Convention and the fact that the Regulation, being uniform EU legislation, does not permit reservations poses no problems. Article 12(1)(e) simply repeats the choice of law rule adopted by the Rome II Regulation for restitutionary obligations: article 10(1) of Rome II provides that, if a non-contractual obligation arising out of unjust enrichment concerns a contractual relationship between the parties that is closely connected with that unjust enrichment, the law governing the contract also governs the non-contractual obligation.

H Remedies and damages

4.178 The traditional view is that questions relating to the nature of the remedy to be granted for a breach of contract are procedural matters determined by English law, as the lex fori, even if the contract is governed by a foreign law. According to this approach, in

---

[261] See, eg, *Euro-Diam Ltd v Bathurst* [1987] 2 All ER 113; *Libyan Arab Foreign Bank v Bankers Trust Co* [1989] QB 728; *Royal Boskalis Westminster NV v Mountain* [1999] QB 674; *Mahonia Ltd v JP Morgan Chase Bank* [2003] 2 Lloyd's Rep 911. See also Carter, 'Rejection of Foreign Law: Some Private International Law Inhibitions' (1984) 55 BYIL 111.
[262] Art 12(1)(d).   [263] See Contracts (Applicable Law) Act 1990, s 2(2).

deciding whether or not to grant specific performance or an injunction the court refers exclusively to the principles of English law. Similarly, it used to be thought that the quantification of damages is a question of procedure governed solely by the lex fori, rather than a substantive matter for the applicable law.

4.179 It is provided that 'evidence and procedure' are excluded from the material scope of the Regulation.[264] It could be argued, on the basis of this provision, that the traditional distinction between, on the one hand, questions of liability (substance) and, on the other, questions relating to remedies and damages (procedure) is unaffected by the Regulation. If this argument were accepted, where a particular type of loss is recoverable according to the applicable law, it would be for English law, as the law of the forum, to determine how damages for that loss are to be quantified.

4.180 However, article 12(1)(c) provides that 'within the limits of the powers conferred on the court by its procedural law' the applicable law governs 'the consequences of a total or partial breach of obligations, including the assessment of damages in so far as it is governed by rules of law'. The significance of this provision is uncertain. Developments in relation to other areas of private international law suggest that the court should classify as procedural only matters which relate to the mode and conduct of the proceedings. Since the question whether or not a remedy of specific performance or an injunction is available is not inextricably linked to the mode of trial, there is a good argument for saying that the applicable law should, subject to the limitations of the procedural law of the forum, determine the type of remedy to which the claimant is entitled.[265]

4.181 As regards damages, article 12(1)(c) seeks to locate a half-way house between the idea that quantification of damages is a procedural matter (for the lex fori) and the view that quantification is substantive and within the province of the applicable law. Even under the Regulation, to the extent that the assessment of damages is not governed by rules of law, the measure of damages is procedural and is, therefore, subject to the law of the forum. Nevertheless, there is every reason to think that, to a large extent, quantification of damage should be governed by the applicable law. This is because quantification of damage is mainly determined by the operation of legal rules (such as rules relating to: whether tax that would have been payable on lost earnings is to be deducted; the time at which the loss is to be assessed; whether the claimant is entitled to the loss value of damaged property or the cost of repairing it; whether loss of value is to be assessed in relation to market value). There is no reason why rules of this type which impact upon the assessment of damages—and which are concerned with the extent of the rights of the party in the event of the contract being breached—should not be seen as 'rules of law' under article 12(1)(c).

4.182 A further question relates to the currency in which a judgment should be expressed. Suppose that, in an international contract of sale which is the subject of litigation in

---

[264] Art 1(3).
[265] See Panagopoulos, 'Substance and Procedure in Private International Law' (2005) 1 Journal of Private International Law 69, 87.

England, the price of the goods sold is expressed in US dollars. Can the court give judgment for that amount in US dollars, rather than sterling? Can the court award a sum expressed in a foreign currency as damages for breach of contract? Until the 1970s the rule was that the court could give judgment only in sterling.[266] The law in this respect was changed by the House of Lords in *Miliangos v George Frank (Textiles) Ltd*;[267] where a party is entitled to an amount under a contract which is expressed in a foreign currency the court will give judgment in that currency. Similarly, the court may give judgment for damages for breach of contract in a foreign currency in which the loss was sustained by the claimant.[268] When judgment is given in a foreign currency the defendant may pay either the sum awarded in that currency or the sterling equivalent at the date of actual payment. If the claimant has to enforce the judgment, the date of conversion into sterling is the date when the court authorises enforcement of the judgment.[269]

---

[266] *Tomkinson v First Pennsylvania Banking and Trust Co* [1961] AC 1007.   [267] [1976] AC 443.
[268] *Services Europe Atlantique Sud (SEAS) v Stockholms Rederiaktiebolag Svea* [1979] AC 685; *The Texaco Melbourne* [1994] 1 Lloyd's Rep 473.
[269] *Miliangos v George Frank (Textiles) Ltd* [1976] AC 443.

5

Non-contractual obligations

Non-contractual obligations cover both tortious obligations and obligations which arise from unjust enrichment and analogous doctrines. Choice of law in tort has been one of the most fertile areas for theoretical writing about choice of law questions (especially in the United States). As regards unjust enrichment, the volume of material—both in terms of decided cases and literature discussing them—is less extensive. Indeed, choice of law rules for unjust enrichment have been somewhat peripheral when compared to choice of law rules for contracts and torts. Until relatively recently, choice of law rules formulated by the courts held sway in relation to both torts and restitution. However, the expanding role of the European Union in the field of private international law has led to Europe-wide legislation—in the form of the Rome II Regulation.[1]

I Choice of law in tort: introduction

A General considerations

5.1 As regards choice of law in tort, the obvious starting-point is the law of the country in which the tort occurs (lex loci delicti). In the simple case where an English motorist injures an Italian pedestrian in a road accident in Italy, it seems reasonable that the driver's liability should be determined by Italian law: when in Rome do as the Romans do. It is widely accepted that, as a general rule, a person's criminal liability should be determined by the law of the country in which the alleged crime occurs. Although the analogy between tort and crime is by no means exact, it seems obvious that the law of the place where the tort was committed should normally be the applicable law. In most cases both parties might, if they applied their minds to the question, reasonably anticipate that liability in tort would be governed by the lex loci delicti.

5.2 The basic appeal of the lex loci delicti does not mean, however, that the law of the country in which the tort occurs should invariably govern or that it should govern all aspects of a tortious situation. In most cases, the application of the lex loci delicti will produce a just solution. It would perhaps always be right to apply the lex loci delicti in the usual case where one or both of the parties belong to the country

---

[1] Regulation (EC) No 864/2007, OJ 2007 L199/40.

where the tort is committed. Then a party who acts, or is injured, in his own country will not be deprived of the protection of his own law, while if he loses he can have no complaint of injustice if his own law is applied against him. Equally, a foreign party can have no cause for complaint if he is subjected to the lex loci delicti in such a case. Where, however, both parties belong to the same country, which is not that in which the tort was committed, justice may often be served better by applying the law of that country.

5.3 The idea that the lex loci delicti should normally be the applicable law, but that some other law might be more appropriate in particular cases, leads to the suggestion that issues in tort should be governed by the 'proper law of the tort'—that is, the law of the country with which the tort is most closely connected—just as issues in contract, in the absence of choice by the parties, are governed by the law of the country with which the contract is most closely connected.[2]

B The development of English law

5.4 Until the 1990s, choice of law in tort was one of the areas of the English conflict of laws which was regulated by the common law. In the nineteenth century, the English courts adopted the rule that liability for a foreign tort could not be imposed unless the defendant's conduct was not only wrongful under the law of the country where the defendant had acted but also gave rise to tortious liability under English law.[3] Although, in the second half of the twentieth century, this so-called 'double actionability' rule was refined (and qualified by an exception),[4] choice of law in tort retained the traditional common law approach which, in most situations, involved having regard to the laws of two countries—the locus delicti and the forum.

5.5 However, dissatisfaction with the common law led to proposals for legislative reform. Part III of the Private International Law (Miscellaneous Provisions) Act 1995 largely replaced the common law choice of law rules with a new statutory scheme.[5] Having said that, Part III of the 1995 Act was clearly derived, in structural terms, from the common law. The statutory choice of law rules were built around a general choice of law rule (which, normally, identified the lex loci delicti as the applicable law), qualified by an exception (which was applicable in cases where the tort was significantly more closely connected with a country other than that whose law would have governed under the general rule). It is worth noting, however, that defamation claims, which were excluded from Part III of the 1995 Act, continued to be governed by the common law. Furthermore, in historical terms, Part III of the 1995 Act should be seen as, to a very large extent, a short interlude between, on the one hand, the common law and, on the other, the European choice of law rules which came into effect in 2009.

---

[2] Morris, 'The Proper Law of the Tort' (1951) 64 Harv LR 881.   [3] See paras 5.108–5.111.
[4] See, in particular, *Boys v Chaplin* [1971] AC 356.   [5] See paras 5.122–5.127.

II The Rome II Regulation: introduction

A Background

5.6 The harmonisation of choice of law rules for non-contractual obligations has been on the European agenda ever since the start of the negotiations which led to the Rome Convention on the Law Applicable to Contractual Obligations in 1980. Although the issue was dropped in the 1970s (when it became clear that differences between the laws of various Member States were such that finding a consensus was impossible), the idea was revived in the late 1990s, when the European Community acquired legislative competence in the field of private international law under the Treaty of Amsterdam. In July 2003 the European Commission published a proposal for a Regulation in the field of choice of law relating to non-contractual obligations (the so-called 'Rome II Regulation')[6] and a revised proposal was presented in February 2006.[7] The Rome II Regulation, which was enacted in 2007,[8] applies to events giving rise to damage which take place after 11 January 2009.[9]

5.7 The Rome II Regulation lays down choice of law rules not only for tortious obligations, but also for other non-contractual obligations (arising from unjust enrichment, negotiorum gestio, and culpa in contrahendo). Because the material scope of the Regulation is limited in certain ways, the choice of law rules which preceded the entry into force of the European choice of law regime continue to apply to some common torts (in particular, defamation).[10]

B Scope

5.8 The material scope of the Rome II Regulation is broadly the same as that of the Brussels I and Rome I Regulations. Where the various instruments use the same terminology, the relevant concepts should be given a uniform interpretation.[11] The Rome II Regulation applies, in situations involving a conflict of laws, to non-contractual obligations in civil and commercial matters; it does not apply to revenue, customs, or administrative matters.[12] The Regulation also explicitly states that its scope does not

---

[6] European Commission, *Proposal for a Regulation of the European Parliament and the Council on the Law Applicable to Non-Contractual Obligations ('Rome II')*, COM (2003) 427 final (hereafter 'Rome II Proposal').

[7] European Commission, *Amended proposal for a European Parliament and Council Regulation on the Law Applicable to Non-Contractual Obligations ('Rome II')*, COM (2006) 83 final (hereafter 'Amended Rome II Proposal').

[8] Regulation (EC) No 864/2007, OJ 2007 L 199/40. For an exhaustive analysis of the Regulation, see Dickinson, *The Rome II Regulation: The Law Applicable to Non-contractual Obligations* (2008). For the purposes of the Regulation, both Ireland and the United Kingdom, having decided to participate in the adoption of the Regulation, are 'Member States': recital (39). Demark is not: recital (40).

[9] Arts 31 and 32 as interpreted in Case C-412/10 *Homawoo v GMF Assurances SA* [2011] ECR I-11603. In a product liability case, the date of the events giving rise to the damage is the date of manufacture or distribution of the defective product, rather than the date of damage: *Allen v Depuy International Ltd* [2015] 2 WLR 442.

[10] See paras 5.108–5.121.   [11] Recital (7).   [12] Art 1(1).

extend to the liability of the state for acts and omissions in the exercise of state authority.[13] This exclusion covers, inter alia, claims against officials who act on behalf of the state and liability for acts of public authorities, including liability of publicly appointed office-holders.[14] In view of the Court of Justice's interpretation of 'civil and commercial matters' in the context of Brussels I,[15] it is doubtful whether, in substantive terms, the additional wording of the Rome II Regulation was necessary.[16]

5.9 Article 1(2) and (3) lists a series of exclusions, some of which mirror the exclusions in related EU instruments. As one would expect, the Regulation does not apply to evidence and procedure;[17] these matters are determined by the law of the forum, though whether a rule is to be classified as procedural or substantive is a matter of EU law.[18] For example, in the context of English proceedings relating to a road traffic accident in France, the question of what expert evidence the court should order and whether there should be one single joint expert (the normal practice in French proceedings) or more than one expert (the usual practice in England) concerns 'evidence and procedure' and is, therefore, regulated by English law.[19] Similarly, as regards a dispute concerning patent infringement, the rules determining the admissibility of a declaration of non-infringement are procedural in nature.[20]

5.10 The Regulation does not apply to non-contractual obligations arising out of family (and equivalent) relationships or to non-contractual obligations arising out of matrimonial property regimes, wills, and succession.[21] Similarly, Rome II does not cover non-contractual obligations arising under bills of exchange, cheques, and promissory notes and other negotiable instruments to the extent that the obligations under such other negotiable instruments arise out of their negotiable character.[22] Nor does it apply to non-contractual obligations arising out of the law of companies and other similar bodies regarding matters such as the creation, legal capacity, internal organisation, or winding-up of such bodies, the personal liability of officers and members as such for the obligations of the body in question, and the personal liability of auditors to a company or to its members in the statutory audits of accounting documents.[23] Although Rome II excludes non-contractual obligations arising out of the relations between settlors, trustees, and beneficiaries of a trust created voluntarily,[24] the EU choice of law rules apply to non-contractual obligations concerning involuntary trusts. So, whether a constructive trustee is liable for wrongful interference is a question falling within the scope of the Regulation.

---

[13] Ibid. [14] Recital (9). [15] See para 2.14.
[16] See, eg, Case C-292/05 *Lechouritou v Dimosio tis Omospondiakis Dimokratias tis Germanias* [2007] ECR I-1519.
[17] Art 1(3).
[18] Floyd LJ in *Activis UK Ltd v Eli Lily and Co* [2015] Bus LR 1068 at [133].
[19] *Wall v Mutuelle de Poitiers Assurances* [2014] 1 WLR 4363.
[20] *Activis UK Ltd v Eli Lily and Co* [2015] Bus LR 1068.
[21] Art 1(2)(a) and (b). [22] Art 1(2)(c). [23] Art 1(2)(d).
[24] Art 1(2)(e). Questions involving the administration of a trust and the personal liability of the trustees for breach of trust are governed by the law applicable to the trust: Art 8 of the Convention on the Law Applicable to Trusts and on their Recognition, as implemented by the Recognition of Trusts Act 1987, s 1(1).

5.11 The final two exclusions are unique to the Rome II Regulation. First, the Regulation does not cover non-contractual obligations arising out of nuclear damage.[25] Such questions are governed by other international instruments which pre-date the European Union.[26] Secondly, and in practical terms more significantly, non-contractual obligations arising out of violations of privacy and rights relating to personality (including defamation) are outside the scope of the Regulation.[27] The law applicable to these matters is determined by national choice of law rules.[28]

5.12 The Regulation is effectively limited to cases falling into one of the following four categories: tort/delict, unjust enrichment, negotiorum gestio, and culpa in contrahendo.[29] Although the Regulation indicates that these concepts should be given an autonomous interpretation,[30] limited guidance is given by the Regulation itself. Accordingly, it is not unlikely that national courts and, in due course, the Court of Justice will have to take some difficult decisions when working out the parameters of the various provisions of the Regulation in the light of the particular circumstances that arise.

5.13 Although it has been asserted that the enactment of the Regulation (laying down uniform choice of law rules for non-contractual obligations) is justified by the need to promote the proper functioning of the internal market within the European Union,[31] application of the Regulation does not depend on the factual situation giving rise to the parties' dispute having any connection with the Member States. Article 3 provides that any law specified by the Regulation is to be applied whether or not it is the law of a Member State. It would be unnecessarily complex for each Member State to operate two sets of choice of law rules, one for cases connected with one or more of the Member States, the other for cases with no internal market dimension. It is more straightforward for all concerned if there is a single choice of law regime.

5.14 Of course, situations coming before the courts of a Member State will normally have some connection with that state, otherwise the court would not have jurisdiction. Nevertheless, because article 4 of the Brussels I Recast provides for general jurisdiction, proceedings may be brought against a person domiciled in a Member State in relation to a matter which has little or no factual connection with any of the Member States. Accordingly, it is perfectly possible for the Regulation to require the application of the law of a non-Member State to govern a non-contractual obligation.

---

[25] Art 1(2)(f).
[26] See the Paris Convention of 29 July 1960 on Third Party Liability in the Field of Nuclear Energy and the Vienna Convention of 21 May 1963 on Civil Liability for Nuclear Damage.
[27] Art 1(2)(g). It is intended that, in due course, EU-wide choice of law rules for defamation will be established: see art 30(2).
[28] See paras 5.104–5.127.
[29] Art 2. See Joined Cases C–359/14 & C–475/14 'ERGO Insurance' SE v 'If P&C Insurance' AS, paras 45–6.
[30] Recital (11).   [31] See Recital (1).

C Anticipated wrongs

5.15 The Rome II Regulation covers anticipated wrongs, just as much as it applies to harmful events which have already taken place. Although key provisions of the Regulation are drafted in terms such as 'the country in which the damage occurs'[32] or 'the person sustaining damage'[33] or 'damage caused by a product',[34] this does not mean that the Regulation has no application in cases where the claimant is seeking to prevent the commission of a wrong by the defendant. Article 2(2) provides that the Regulation applies to 'non-contractual obligations that are likely to arise'; for the purposes of the Regulation, damage includes 'damage that is likely to occur'.[35] So, in relation to a matter which is within the material scope of the Regulation, an application for a prohibitory injunction to restrain the commission of a threatened tort by the defendant is covered by the Regulation and the law applicable to such a claim is determined by the Regulation's choice of law rules.

D Exclusion of renvoi

5.16 The doctrine of renvoi is generally excluded from the European choice of law regime. Article 24 of the Regulation (which mirrors article 20 of Rome I) provides that the application of the law of any country specified by the Regulation means the application of that country's rules of law other than its rules of private international law. So, if a claimant is injured in a road accident in Mexico in circumstances in which Mexican law is the applicable law under the Rome II Regulation, the rights of the claimant against the defendant are to be determined by Mexican tort law, even if Mexican choice of law rules would stipulate that the law of another country should be the applicable law.

E Intra-UK disputes

5.17 In a case where a Scot is injured in a road accident in England through the negligence of a driver who is habitually resident in Northern Ireland, the United Kingdom is not required to apply the choice of law rules contained in the Rome II Regulation.[36] It would, however, be more complicated than necessary for English law to run two sets of choice of law rules in tandem: one for cases with connections with foreign countries and the other for cases connected only with the constituent legal systems of the United Kingdom. Just as the Rome I Regulation applies to intra-UK cases involving contractual obligations, the Rome II Regulation determines the law applicable to non-contractual obligations in cases which have connections with more than one of the legal systems of the United Kingdom, but no connections with any foreign country.[37]

---

[32] Art 4(1).   [33] Art 4(2).   [34] Art 5(1).   [35] Art 2(3).   [36] Art 25(2).
[37] Law Applicable to Non-Contractual Obligations (England and Wales and Northern Ireland) Regulations 2008, SI 2008/2986; Law Applicable to Non-Contractual Obligations (Scotland) Regulations 2008, SSI 2008/404.

III The Rome II Regulation: tortious obligations

A What is a tortious obligation?

5.18 The fundamental characteristics of a tort are (i) a wrongful act committed by the defendant, (ii) causing damage to the claimant. Such a broad definition runs the risk of covering the whole of the law of obligations. To distinguish torts from contracts, a tort is a wrongful act which takes the form of a breach of the general law as opposed to the breach of an obligation owed to the claimant individually by virtue of an agreement between the parties. This raises the question whether the Rome I and Rome II Regulations are mutually exclusive—by analogy with the Court of Justice's interpretation of what are now article 7(1) and article 7(2) of the Brussels I Recast.[38] It would be perfectly possible to interpret 'contractual obligations' for the purposes of the Rome I Regulation as obligations freely assumed by one party to another and to regard 'non-contractual obligations' under the Rome II Regulation as a residual category of obligations which are not freely assumed in this way.[39]

5.19 While it seems reasonable to think that, in general terms, the distinction between 'freely assumed' obligations (contractual) and 'not freely assumed' obligations (non-contractual) determines the scope of the two Regulations, there is an important distinction between the Brussels I Recast, on the one hand, and the choice of law regime, on the other, and it is clear that the approach to article 7 of the Brussels I Recast cannot simply be transposed to the Rome I and II Regulations. Whereas the Brussels I Recast treats 'matters relating to a contract' and 'matters relating to tort' as mutually exclusive categories—to the extent that claims arising out of a single set of facts can fall within either article 7(1) or article 7(2), but not both—a single set of facts which include the existence of a contract between the parties can give rise to 'contractual' and 'non-contractual' obligations for the purposes of the two Rome Regulations. Various provisions of the Rome II Regulation refer to situations where a non-contractual obligation either has a close connection with 'a pre-existing relationship between the parties, such as a contract'[40] or 'concerns a relationship existing between the parties, such as one arising out of a contract... that is closely connected with that non-contractual obligation'.[41] It follows that the existence of a contract between the parties does not preclude the possibility of conduct by one of the parties which is wrongful under the general law being characterised as non-contractual under the Rome II Regulation. This interpretation is also supported by the Regulation's travaux préparatoires: in its original proposal, the European Commission drew attention to 'Member States whose legal system allows

---

[38] See para 2.67.
[39] In Case C-26/91 *Jakob Handte & Co GmbH v Traitements Mécano-chimiques des Surfaces SA* [1992] ECR I-3967, para 15, the Court of Justice decided that art 5(1) of the Brussels Convention 'is not to be understood as covering a situation in which there is no obligation freely assumed by one party towards another'. See also Case C-147/12 *ÖFAB v Koot* [2015] QB 20, para 33; Case C-519/12 *OTP Bank Nyilvánosan Müködö Részvénytársaság v Hochtief Solution AG* [2015] ILPr 30.
[40] See arts 4(3) and 5(2).
[41] See art 11(1); see also the similar wording of art 10(1).

both contractual and non-contractual obligations between the same parties'.[42] This implies that where particular conduct constitutes not only the breach of a contractual obligation (whether express or implied) but also a tort under the general law, the claimant may, if the procedural law of the forum permits it, formulate his claim as a breach of contract (with the applicable law being determined by the Rome I Regulation) and/or a tort (whose applicable law is determined by the Rome II Regulation).[43] Whether the Court of Justice will be prepared to endorse this interpretation of the Regulations remains to be seen.

5.20 Given that, for the purposes of article 4 of the Rome II Regulation, the phrase 'non-contractual obligation arising out of a tort' must be given an autonomous definition, the scope of this provision will not necessarily be co-terminous with matters that are regarded as tortious under English domestic law. It is well recognised that the categories employed for choice of law purposes do not necessarily mirror precisely the categories of domestic law;[44] in an international instrument such as the Regulation, it is almost inevitable that the scope of article 4 may cover a relationship which is covered by the law of tort in one Member State and the law of contract in another.[45]

5.21 Although the idea of a 'not freely assumed' obligation lacks precision, the vast majority of day-to-day situations are not too difficult to classify. For example, where C is injured in a road accident as a result of D's negligence, there is no doubt that a tortious obligation is involved; the same would be true if the driver's liability were strict.[46] Similarly, cases involving wrongful interference with goods, trespass to land, nuisance, and the infringement of intellectual property rights are unmistakably tortious.[47]

5.22 There are other cases which are less clear. English law has not traditionally assimilated equitable wrongs with torts for choice of law purposes.[48] However, in the context of the European choice of law regime, the courts have little room for manoeuvre. It must be the case that, with the exception of obligations which are excluded from their material scope, the Rome I and II Regulations are intended, together, to cover the whole field of civil and commercial obligations. Where an equitable obligation arises otherwise than within the framework of a contractual relationship, there is no option but to treat an equitable wrong—such as breach of a fiduciary obligation, breach of confidence, or dishonest assistance in a breach of trust[49]—as a non-contractual obligation for the purposes of the Rome II Regulation. The fact that, in English law, certain types of wrongful

---

[42] *Rome II Proposal*, COM (2003) 427 final, pp 12–13. See also art 14 (considered at paras 5.86–5.90), which is premised on the idea that parties involved in a tortious claim may have selected the applicable law (which, in practice, must be by virtue of a contractual choice of law) before the commission of the tort.
[43] See Dickinson, *The Rome II Regulation* (2008) paras 3.124–3.139.
[44] *Re Bonacina* [1912] 2 Ch 394.
[45] *Rome II Proposal*, COM (2003) 427 final, p 13.   [46] See recital (11).
[47] Some of these torts are governed by art 4, others by special rules in arts 5–9. See paras 5.45–5.66.
[48] See, eg, *Grupo Torras SA v Al-Sabah (No 5)* [2001] Lloyd's Rep Bank 36.
[49] It is uncertain whether liability for knowing receipt should be classified as tortious (within art 4) or as based on unjust enrichment (within art 10).

conduct under the general law are equitable wrongs, rather than common law torts, is little more than an accident of history.

B The general rules: article 4

5.23 The basic aim of the Regulation is to combine certainty and flexibility. There is a school of thought according to which the proper functioning of the internal market creates a need for choice of law rules to be certain, so that, when coupled with rules in the field of jurisdiction and judgments, they create a high degree of predictability in the outcome of litigation.[50] It is recognised, however, that, notwithstanding the fact that choice of law rules should be highly foreseeable, what is needed is a flexible framework of choice of law rules which enables the court seised to treat individual cases in an appropriate manner.[51]

5.24 Opinion is divided on whether the Regulation strikes an appropriate balance between certainty and flexibility. In terms of its rhetoric, English law has traditionally favoured a more flexible approach than that apparently promoted by the Regulation. Whether the Regulation really gives too little room for flexibility—and less flexibility than the traditional English choice of law rules that the Regulation replaced—is, however, open to question. In practical terms, there are relatively few common situations in which the applicable law under the Regulation is different from the law which would have resulted from the operation of the English choice of law rules that the Regulation replaced.

1. The lex loci damni under article 4(1)

5.25 As a general rule, the law applicable to a tortious obligation is 'the law of the country in which the damage occurs'.[52] This approach is fundamentally an approach based on the lex loci delicti, with a preference for the law of the place of damage (lex loci damni) in multiple locality cases—where D commits the wrongful act in country A but harm is inflicted on C in country B. It is important, for the purposes of article 4(1), that the place where 'the damage occurs' is narrowly circumscribed; the applicable law is determined by where direct damage happened, irrespective of where the event giving rise to the damage occurred and irrespective of the country or countries in which the indirect consequences of that event occur.[53] This rule based on the lex loci damni is said to strike a fair balance between the interests of the person claimed to be liable and the person sustaining the damage, and also to reflect the modern approach to civil liability and the development of systems of strict liability.[54]

5.26 In a case involving personal injury or property damage, the damage occurs at the place where the injury is sustained or the property is damaged.[55] So, if a French driver (D)

---

[50] Recital (6)   [51] Recital (14).   [52] Art 4(1).
[53] Art 4(1); recital (17).   [54] Recital (16).
[55] Recital (17). See *Bianco v Bennett* [2015] ILPr 24.

negligently runs down an English resident (C) in Scotland, the applicable law under the general rule is Scots law; the fact that C has to deal with his injuries and their economic consequences in England is irrelevant under article 4(1). The same law also applies to claims by indirect victims of the tort—such as C's dependants and relatives in the event of the accident causing C's death.[56]

5.27 If the defendant's act produces harmful effects in more than one country, the operation of article 4(1) means that 'the laws of all the countries concerned will have to be applied on a distributive basis'.[57] If, for example, an aircraft belonging to a German airline explodes while flying near to the Franco-Belgian border and, as a consequence, X suffers personal injury in Belgium and Y suffers personal injury in France, the general rule provides that X's claim is governed by Belgian law, whereas Y's claim is governed by French law.[58]

5.28 Although the lex loci damni rule in article 4(1) is less straightforward to apply in cases not involving personal injury or property damage, it is legitimate to be guided in such situations by the Court of Justice's analysis of the place where the damage occurred in the context of article 7(2) of the Brussels I Recast (and the provisions it replaced).[59] It seems clear that the place where the damage occurred for the purposes of article 7(2) of the Recast[60] equates to 'the country in which the damage occurs' for the purposes of article 4(1) of Rome II.[61] Accordingly, in a case like *Marinari v Lloyds Bank plc*[62] (in which an Italian claimant suffered financial loss in Italy consequential upon initial damage arising from the defendant's refusal to return promissory notes which the claimant had deposited in England), article 4(1) designates English law as the applicable law.[63] Where the harm suffered by the claimant takes the form of failing to receive a payment to which he was entitled, the applicable law is the law of the country where the payment should have been made.[64]

5.29 In the context of online activity, there had been a debate about the relationship between the Rome II Regulation and the E-Commerce Directive.[65] Some had argued that, in the field of activity covered by the Directive, the general rule in article 4(1) of Rome II was

---

[56] Case C–350/14 *Lazar v Allianz SpA* [2016] 1 WLR 835. See also *Brownlie v Four Seasons Holdings Inc* [2016] 1 WLR 1814.

[57] European Commission, *Rome II Proposal*, COM (2003) 427 final, p 11.

[58] The question may then arise whether the tort is manifestly more closely connected with another country for the purposes of art 4(3). See paras 5.34–5.42.

[59] See recital (7). In Case 21/76 *Handelskwekerij GJ Bier BV v Mines de Potasse d'Alsace SA* [1976] ECR 1735 the Court of Justice ruled that 'the place where the harmful event occurred' can mean either the place where the damage occurred or the place of the event giving rise to it. As regards art 4(1) of the Rome II Regulation, it is only the Court's interpretation of the first of these alternatives that is relevant.

[60] See paras 2.99–2.101.

[61] See European Commission, *Rome II Proposal*, COM (2003) 427 final, p 11.

[62] Case C–364/93 [1995] ECR I–2719.

[63] *Hillside (New Media) Ltd v Baasland* [2010] 2 CLC 986 (Norway was not the locus damni in a case where a Norwegian gambler lost funds betting via an English gambling website).

[64] Following the analysis in *Dolphin Maritime & Aviation Services Ltd v Sveriges Angfartygs Assurans Forening* [2009] 2 Lloyd's Rep 123 (a case decided under art 5(3) of Brussels I).

[65] Directive 2000/31/EC on certain aspects of information society services, OJ 2001 L 12/1.

displaced by a 'country of origin rule' in article 3 of the Directive, justifying the application of the law of the Member State in which the defendant is established, rather than the law of the Member State in which the damage occurred. The debate was put to rest by *eDate Advertising GmbH v X*,[66] in which the Court of Justice ruled that the E-Commerce Directive does not include choice of law rules that require transposition into national law.

2. The exception: common habitual residence under article 4(2)

5.30 The general rule in article 4(1) is subject to an exception in article 4(2): if both the person claimed to be liable and the person sustaining damage have their habitual residence[67] in the same country at the time when the damage occurs, the law of that country applies.[68] If, in a road accident case, C sues D1, the driver of the car, and D2, D1's insurer, it is the habitual residence of C and D1 which is relevant for the purposes of article 4(2); the habitual residence of D2 is immaterial.[69] The operation of article 4(2) is mechanical—in the sense that it does not depend on the weighing of factors in favour of one country or another—unlike the analogous provision of the Private International Law (Miscellaneous Provisions) Act 1995.

5.31 The rule in article 4(2) is premised on the idea that where C and D are based in country X and the tort is committed in country Y, country X is the country with which the tort is more closely connected and the application of the law of country X reflects the parties' legitimate expectations.[70] In policy terms, there is a strong argument for saying that a law other than the lex loci damni should be the applicable law if neither party is connected with the country in which the tort is committed. In *Edmunds v Simmonds*,[71] for example, the claimant and the defendant, both of whom were resident in England, hired a car while on holiday in Spain. The claimant was injured when, as a result of the defendant's negligence, the car hit a Spanish lorry. It was held that, in these circumstances, the general rule in favour of Spanish law was displaced; English law was the applicable law. Given that both parties were English and the accident was caused by the defendant's negligence, there is no reason why the involvement of the Spanish lorry should have any bearing on the determination of the applicable law.

5.32 In practice, in the majority of cases involving the exception, the parties will be habitually resident in the forum and the effect of article 4(2) will be the displacement of the lex loci damni by the law of the forum. The situations falling within the exception are illustrated by some of the cases which were at the forefront of the development of tort

---

[66] Joined Cases C-509/09 & C-161/10 *eDate Advertising GmbH v X; Martinez v MGN Ltd* [2012] QB 654.
[67] For the purposes of the Regulation, 'habitual residence' is (partially) defined by art 23. See paras 5.95–5.96.
[68] Notwithstanding the fact that art 4(2) refers to a 'person' (in the singular), it is potentially applicable in a case involving more than two parties: *Marshall v Motor Insurers' Bureau* [2015] EWHC 3421 (QB).
[69] *Winrow v Hemphill* [2015] ILPr 12.
[70] European Commission, *Rome II Proposal*, COM (2003) 427 final, p 12.
[71] [2001] 1 WLR 1003. This case was decided under Part III of the Private International Law (Miscellaneous Provisions) Act 1995 (see paras 5.122–5.127); the result would be the same under the Rome II Regulation.

choice of law at common law—cases such as *Babcock v Jackson*[72] (where two New York residents were involved in a road accident in Ontario) and *Boys v Chaplin*[73] (where two English servicemen were involved in a road accident in Malta). It was recognised that, in this type of case, the application of the law of the country with which the parties were closely connected is more appropriate than the application of the law of the country where the tort was committed.

5.33 Of course, the operation of the common habitual residence rule in article 4(2) is not limited to cases in which the law specified by article 4(1) is displaced by the law of the forum; it is theoretically possible for the law applicable under article 4(2) to be the law of a country which is neither the forum nor the locus damni. For example, if, following a road accident in Malta involving two Scottish residents, the dispute between the parties is litigated in England, Scots law is the applicable law under article 4(2). Such cases will, however, be rare because it is extremely unusual, in the context of tort claims, for a court to be able to assume jurisdiction in a case which has such strong connections with other countries and so little connection with the forum.

3. The escape clause under article 4(3)

5.34 The general rule in article 4(1) and the exception in article 4(2) are subject to an 'escape clause',[74] the purpose of which is to enable the court 'to adapt the rigid rule to an individual case so as to apply the law that reflects the centre of gravity of the situation'.[75] According to article 4(3), if a tortious obligation is manifestly more closely connected with another country, the law of that other country applies.[76] Article 4(3) goes on to say that a manifestly closer connection with another country might be based on a preexisting relationship between the parties, such as a contract, that is closely connected with the tort in question.[77]

5.35 Article 4(3) gives rise to a number of potentially difficult issues. First, there is a question of interpretation. Consider the case where a tort is committed in New South Wales, but both parties are habitually resident in England. In this situation, article 4(1) would identify the law of New South Wales as the applicable law under the general rule, but this law would be displaced under the exception in article 4(2) by English law on the basis that both parties were habitually resident in England. The question then arises whether it would be possible to apply the escape clause in favour of the law of New South Wales on the basis that the tort was manifestly more closely connected with New South Wales. The underlying rationale of article 4—to designate the law of the country with which the tort is most closely connected—suggests that the escape clause should be applied;[78] also, in the Regulation's travaux préparatoires, article 4(3) is described as

---

[72] [1963] 2 Lloyd's Rep 286. See paras 1.47–1.48.
[73] [1971] AC 356. See paras 5.108–5.114. [74] Recital (18).
[75] European Commission, *Rome II Proposal*, COM (2003) 427 final, p 12.
[76] Art 4(3).
[77] See Okoli, 'The Significance of the Doctrine of Accessory Allocation as a Connecting Factor under Article 4 of the Rome II Regulation' (2013) 9 Journal of Private International Law 449.
[78] Dickinson, *The Rome II Regulation* (2008) para 4.89.

a 'general exception clause'.⁷⁹ However, the wording of article 4(3) can be read as pointing to the opposite conclusion.⁸⁰ The application of article 4(3) depends on it being clear from all the circumstances of the case that the tort is manifestly more closely connected with a country other than that indicated in article 4(1) (the locus damni) or article 4(2) (the parties' common habitual residence). Although a literal reading of article 4(3) might suggest that the escape clause can operate only in favour of a third country, the better view is that 'a governing law mandated by article 4(1), but excluded by article 4(2), might be required by article 4(3)'.⁸¹ *Marshall v Motor Insurers' Bureau*⁸² was a case in which A, an English resident, was killed, and D, another English resident, was injured on the hard shoulder of a French motorway as a result of a collision with a car driven by X, a French driver. It was accepted that the claim by C, A's widow, against D was governed by French law, rather than English law, notwithstanding the fact that C and D were both habitually resident in England.

5.36 Secondly, there is the question of how liberally the courts may resort to the escape clause. One view is that, since article 4(3) generates a degree of unforeseeability as to the law that will be applicable, it must remain exceptional; this explains why the escape clause requires the tort to be *manifestly* more closely connected with another country.⁸³ It seems clear that article 4(3) places a 'high hurdle in the path of a party seeking to displace the law indicated by article 4(1) or article 4(2)'.⁸⁴ Nevertheless, that hurdle is not insurmountable.⁸⁵

5.37 Apart from the case where the country where the damage occurs is manifestly more closely connected with the tort than the country in which the parties are habitually resident, the situation in which the escape clause is most likely to come into the picture is where a tort, committed in country A, is closely connected with a contract between the parties which is governed by the law of country B. It is hard to think of many other circumstances in which it could be said that the tort is manifestly more closely connected with a country which is neither the locus damni nor the common habitual residence of the parties.

5.38 The range of connecting factors in a standard tort case is not very extensive. In essence, there are only four significant elements: the territorial connections of the claimant and of the defendant, the place where the claimant was injured and the place where the defendant committed the wrongful act. In typical cases, some of these connections will overlap; for example, in many cases, the claimant will be injured in the country in which he is habitually resident or the defendant will commit the wrongful act in the country in which he is habitually resident, or the claimant and the defendant will be

---

[79] European Commission, *Rome II Proposal*, COM (2003) 427 final, p 16.
[80] See Rushworth and Scott, 'Rome II: Choice of Law for Non-contractual Obligations' [2008] LMCLQ 274.
[81] Dingemans J in *Marshall v Motor Insurers' Bureau* [2015] EWHC 3421 (QB) at [19].
[82] [2015] EWHC 3421 (QB).
[83] European Commission, *Rome II Proposal*, COM (2003) 427 final, p 12.
[84] Slade J in *Winrow v Hemphill* [2015] ILPr 12 at [63].
[85] See *Marshall v Motor Insurers' Bureau* [2015] EWHC 3421 (QB).

habitually resident in the same country or the claimant will be injured in the country in which the defendant commits the wrongful act. As a result, the number of countries potentially involved is quite limited. In a case where either of the parties is habitually resident in the country in which the tort is committed, the case for arguing that there is another country which is manifestly more closely connected with the tort than the locus damni is very weak; similarly, if both parties are habitually resident in the same country, it is highly unlikely that another country (other than possibly the locus damni) can be significantly more closely connected with the tort.

5.39 In *Winrow v Hemphill*[86] the court considered the possibility of applying the escape clause in a situation where both C and D1 were British nationals who had been habitually resident in Germany at the time of C's injury. The judge thought that, for the purposes of article 4(3), there is no temporal limitation on the factors which should be taken into account and that relevant factors included: the habitual residence of C at the time when consequential loss was suffered; the links of the consequences of the tort to a particular country; the fact that, at the time of the court hearing, both C and D1 had become habitually resident in England. Despite the post-tort connections with England, C failed to persuade the court that the tort was manifestly more closely connected with England than with Germany (which was not only the locus damni but also the common habitual residence of the parties at the time of the accident).

5.40 Thirdly, as regards the operation of article 4(3), what significance should be attached to the fact that there is a pre-existing relationship between the parties?[87] A tort which would normally be governed by the law of country A (lex loci damni) is not governed by the law of country B simply because there is, between the victim and the tortfeasor, a pre-existing contractual relationship governed by the law of country B: 'the law applicable to the pre-existing relationship does not apply automatically, and the court enjoys a degree of discretion to decide whether there is a significant connection between the non-contractual obligations and the law applicable to the pre-existing relationship.'[88] Nevertheless, in policy terms, there is much to be said in favour of applying one law as far as possible to all aspects of a case.[89]

5.41 Much depends on the degree of connection between the contract and the tort. Consider, for example, the situation where C, who is habitually resident in country Z, purchases a rail ticket from a rail operator (D) for a journey from country X to country Z (via country Y). D is habitually resident in country X and the contract of carriage is governed by the law of country X. During the journey, C is injured in country Y as a result of D's negligence. If C sues D in tort for his personal injuries, it seems reasonable to assume that the law of country Y (which is the lex loci damni under article 4(1))

---

[86] [2015] ILPr 12.
[87] Such relationship will typically be contractual, but there is no reason, in principle, why it should not be any other relationship (such as a family relationship).
[88] European Commission, *Rome II Proposal*, COM (2003) 427 final, p 12.
[89] See Czepelak, 'Concurrent Causes of Action in the Rome I and II Regulations' (2011) 7 Journal of Private International Law 393.

should yield to the law of country X, which governs the contract between the parties. The tort has a close connection with the contract and it should be regarded as manifestly more closely connected with country X than with country Y; it makes sense for the legal relations between the parties (both contractual and tortious) to be governed by the same law. The other factor which increases the likelihood that the law governing the contract will also govern any tort that has a connection with the contract is the fact that, subject to certain qualifications, the Regulation permits parties to select the law governing a tort. Depending on its drafting, a contractual choice of law clause may be broad enough to cover the situation where the tortfeasor is one contracting party and the victim of the tort is the other party to the contract.[90]

5.42 It must be remembered, however, that not every tortious situation which involves parties to a contract will necessarily be governed by the contractual law. Where, for example, it is purely coincidental that the tortfeasor and the victim are in a contractual relationship (for example, where the parties involved in a road accident are, by chance, also parties to a contract which is wholly unconnected with road transport), there is no reason to give preference to the contractual law over the law of the country which would otherwise govern the tort (either the lex loci damni or the law of the country in which the parties are habitually resident).

4. The significance of article 17

5.43 Article 17 provides that '[i]n assessing the conduct of the person claimed to be liable, account shall be taken, as a matter of fact and in so far as is appropriate, of the rules of safety and conduct which were in force at the place and time of the event giving rise to the liability'. This is not a choice of law rule and does not authorise the application of the law of the place where the tortfeasor committed the harmful act in preference to the applicable law as determined by article 4.[91] Nevertheless, the court should 'take account' of rules of safety—which should be understood as 'all regulations having any relation to safety and conduct, including, for example, road safety rules in the case of an accident'[92]—and rules of conduct in general as laid down by the law of the country where the harmful act took place. For example, the court should take account of rules of safety and conduct of the law of the country where the harmful conduct occurred 'when assessing the seriousness of the fault or the author's good or bad faith for the purposes of the measure of damages'.[93]

5.44 The significance of such rules of safety and conduct, and the extent to which they should be taken into account, will vary from case to case. In a situation in which the tortfeasor's liability is strict, there is no obvious role for the rules of safety of the law of the country where the tortfeasor acted; in this type of case an evaluation of the

---

[90] Art 14. See paras 5.86–5.90.
[91] Although, for convenience, art 17 is discussed here in relation to art 4, it should be noted that art 17 is of general application and is potentially relevant in the context of any of the Regulation's choice of law provisions.
[92] Recital (34).
[93] European Commission, *Rome II Proposal*, COM (2003) 427 final, p 25.

defendant's conduct is not a component of civil liability. Conversely, where the defendant's liability depends on fault, the court should have regard to the standards required by the law of the country where the tortfeasor committed the harmful act. At the relatively trivial level, rules of the highway code in the country where an accident occurred (such as the applicable speed limit or the priority of vehicles at junctions and roundabouts) are relevant facts to be taken into account when assessing whether a driver was or was not at fault. Similarly, if liability depends upon a finding that the defendant acted dishonestly, the court may need to take account of the standards of probity imposed by the law (or even customs) of the country where the defendant acted,[94] even though that law is not the applicable law under the Regulation.

C Specific rules: articles 5–9

5.45   Many common tortious situations (such as road accident cases) are covered by the rules contained in article 4. Indeed, it would have been possible for article 4 to have been adopted as the choice of law regime for all tortious situations. This would have had the benefit of simplicity. The Regulation, however, includes a series of separate choice of law rules for different types of tort. These specific provisions, rather than laying down completely different choice of law rules, involve a modification or refinement of (or addition to) the general rules in cases where it is thought that 'the general rule does not allow a reasonable balance to be struck between the interests at stake'.[95]

1. Product liability: article 5

5.46   Article 5 is one of the more complex (some would say too complex) provisions of the Regulation; it sets out a series of choice of law rules for cases involving non-contractual obligations arising out of 'damage caused by a product'. The Regulation does not define the boundary between article 4 (torts in general) and article 5 (product liability). Presumably, not every case in which a 'product' is involved in the tort (in some way) falls within article 5, otherwise article 4 would be deprived of most of its content. A straightforward road accident case falls within the scope of article 4, even if a motor car is the instrument through which damage is inflicted. It is reasonable to suppose that article 5 is limited to cases where some physical attribute of the product itself (such as a defect[96]), as opposed to operation of the product by human activity, is the direct cause of the damage. The classic types of case covered by article 5 include situations in which the claimant suffers injury as a result of taking harmful pharmaceuticals, or is injured by malfunctioning electrical equipment. By departing from the rules that apply to torts generally, article 5 is designed 'to meet the objectives of fairly spreading the risks inherent in a modern high-technology society, protecting consumers' health, stimulating innovation, securing undistorted competition and facilitating trade'.[97]

---

[94] See Dickinson, *The Rome II Regulation* (2008) para 15.32.   [95] Recital (19).
[96] The European Commission's original proposal referred to 'damage caused by a defective product': COM (2003) 427 final, p 13.
[97] Recital (20).

5.47 The approach taken by article 5 seeks not only to give effect to the parties' legitimate expectations, but also to reflect 'the wide scatter of possible connecting factors (producer's headquarters, place of manufacture, place of first marketing, place of acquisition by the victim, victim's habitual residence)'.[98] With a view to balancing the competing factors, article 5 gives effect to 'a cascade system of connecting factors, together with a foreseeability clause'.[99]

5.48 First, the basic rule in article 5(1)(a) is that the applicable law in product liability cases is the law of the country in which the person sustaining the damage had his or her habitual residence when the damage occurred; this is, however, conditional on the product being marketed in that country. Secondly, if the product was not marketed in the country of the victim's habitual residence, the applicable law is the law of the country in which the product was acquired; again, this rule depends on the product having been marketed in that country.[100] Thirdly, if the product was not marketed in either the country in which the victim is habitually resident or the country in which the product was acquired, the applicable law is the law of the country in which the damage occurred, as long as the product was marketed in that country.[101] Fourthly, even if the product was marketed in the country whose law would be the applicable law under one of the three foregoing rules, the law of the defendant's habitual residence applies instead if the defendant could not have reasonably foreseen the marketing of the product (or of a product of the same type) in the country in question.[102]

5.49 The operation of these rules can best be illustrated by a simple example. Consider the following situation involving C, who is habitually resident in country X, and D, who is habitually resident in country A: while in country Y, C purchases some headache pills manufactured by D;[103] C takes the pills, which are defective, in country Z, and C suffers personal injury there. If D's pills are marketed in countries X, Y, and Z, the law of country X applies (under article 5(1)(a)). If D's pills are marketed in countries Y and Z, the law of country Y applies (under article 5(1)(b)). If D's pills are marketed only in country Z, the law of country Z applies. If D could not reasonably foresee his pills being marketed in any of those countries, the law of country A applies.

5.50 A central component of the scheme established by article 5 is that the product which caused the damage (or products of the same type) are *marketed* in a particular country. The Regulation provides no guidance on the meaning of marketing for the product liability choice of law rules. Marketing obviously covers cases where the product is sold through a network of retail outlets in the country in question; there is also a good argument for saying that where a product is advertised and sold through a website that is

---

[98] European Commission, *Rome II Proposal*, COM (2003) 427 final, p 13.
[99] Recital (20). [100] Art 5(1)(b). [101] Art 5(1)(c). [102] Art 5(1), proviso.
[103] Note that art 5 refers to 'the person claimed to be liable' and covers not only product liability cases where the defendant is the manufacturer of a finished product, but also situations where the defendant is the producer of a component which forms part of the finished product, an intermediary or a retailer: European Commission, *Rome II Proposal*, COM (2003) 427 final, p 16.

accessible in a particular country, the product is marketed in that country. Conversely, if the product is sold only on the black market in country X (for example, where medicine is licensed in some countries, but is not licensed in country X and cannot lawfully be sold there), the product should not be regarded as being marketed in country X for the purposes of article 5.

5.51 As noted above, even if a product is marketed in country X, where the claimant is habitually resident, the applicable law is not the law of country X if the defendant could not reasonably foresee the marketing of the product (or a product of the same type) in that country. The precise operation of this proviso is uncertain; in particular, there is a question over whether the reference to 'a product of the same type' covers only products for whose production the defendant is responsible or whether similar products of different manufacturers are contemplated. The more reasonable interpretation of the proviso is that the question is whether the defendant could reasonably foresee the marketing of the product which caused the damage or of the defendant's similar products in the country in question.[104] It is arguable that the foreseeability proviso is unduly generous to potential defendants in product liability cases.[105]

5.52 There are two further points which need to be made about article 5. First, the special choice of law rules for product liability are subject to article 4(2). Accordingly, if the tortfeasor and the victim are habitually resident in the same country, the law of that country applies. Secondly, the choice of law rules in article 5 are subject to the same escape clause as article 4: article 5(2) provides that, where it is clear from all the circumstances of the case that a tort is manifestly more closely connected with a country other than that indicated in article 5(1), the law of that other country applies. If there is a contractual relationship between the claimant and the tortfeasor, it may be appropriate for the court to conclude that the tort should also be governed by the law applicable to the contract on the basis that the tort is manifestly more closely connected with the country whose law governs the contract. Consider the case where C (habitually resident in country X) and D (habitually resident in country Y) enter a contract for the sale of a toaster; the contract is concluded in, and governed by, the law of country Y. C takes the toaster to a holiday cottage in country Z where it explodes, causing personal injury to C. If C sues D in tort, the applicable law under article 5(1)(a) is the law of country X (assuming that D's toasters are marketed in country X). This is obviously a situation where there is a very close connection between the tort and the contract and all the arguments point towards the law of country Y being the law which governs not only the contract, but also the parallel tort. Accordingly, this is a suitable case for the application of the escape clause in article 5(2).

2. Unfair competition and acts restricting free competition: article 6

5.53 Whereas the legal system of several of the Member States includes a civil wrong known as 'unfair competition', there is no such nominate tort in English law.[106] This does not

---

[104] See Dickinson, *The Rome II Regulation* (2008) para 5.35.
[105] See, eg, Symonides, 'Rome II and Tort Conflicts: a Missed Opportunity' (2008) 56 Am J Comp Law 173.
[106] See *L'Oreal SA v Bellure NV* [2008] ETMR 1 at [161].

mean, of course, that English law does not impose tortious liability for acts of unfair competition; English law includes a number of torts which have a similar purpose and content to the wrong of unfair competition in other legal systems; some of the most significant of the common law torts in this area are passing off and malicious falsehood (in the area of misleading advertising). Other matters that are covered by article 6 include forced sales, disruption of deliveries by competitors, enticing away a competitor's staff and boycotts.[107]

5.54 Under article 6(1), the law applicable to a non-contractual obligation arising out of an act of unfair competition is the law of the country where competitive relations (or the collective interests of consumers) are, or are likely to be, affected. Article 6(2) goes on to deal with the situation where an act of unfair competition affects exclusively the interests of a specific competitor; in this situation, article 4 applies. It seems that the dividing-line between article 6(1) and article 6(2) is based on the scope of impact of an act of unfair competition rather than on the nature of the remedy sought by the claimant. Although, in English law, an action in passing off is brought by a claimant in order to protect his own interests, it appears that article 6(1) is engaged as the deception of consumers is a significant element of the alleged tort. So, in a case where a German company (C), the market leader for product X in England, alleges that another German company (D) is committing acts of unfair competition by selling a competing product in a confusingly similar package in the English marketplace, the English law of passing off applies under article 6(1). While the common habitual residence of C and D would result in the application of German law if article 6(2) were applicable, the fact that the collective interests of English consumers are affected brings the case within article 6(1).

5.55 Article 6(3) deals with restrictions on competition under both national and EU competition law; the concept of a restriction on competition covers matters which fall foul of articles 101 and 102 TFEU—that is, not only agreements between undertakings, decisions by associations of undertakings, and concerted practices which have as their object or effect the prevention, restriction, or distortion of competition within a Member State or within the internal market, but also the abuse of a dominant position within a Member State or within the internal market.[108] Under article 6(3), the law which governs non-contractual obligations involving damage resulting from restrictions on competition is the law of the country where the market is, or is likely to be, affected. In cases where the market is (or is likely to be) affected in more than one country, the claimant can, in certain circumstances, choose to base his claim on the law of the country in which the claim is brought. This option to choose the law of the forum is available only if the market in the forum country is one of the markets which are directly and substantially affected by the restriction of competition which gives rise to the claim.

---

[107] European Commission, *Rome II Proposal*, COM (2003) 427 final, p 16.
[108] Recital (23).

5.56 Article 6 lays down hard-and-fast rules: (i) there is no exception in cases where the parties are habitually resident in the same country; (ii) there is no escape clause in favour of the law of another country with which the tort is manifestly more closely connected; (iii) the applicable law under article 6 cannot be derogated from by an agreement pursuant to article 14.[109]

3. Environmental damage: article 7

5.57 Article 7 lays down a special rule for civil liability in relation to violations of the environment; the rule, which reflects developments in the substantive law, covers not only damage to property and persons but also damage to the ecology itself, provided such damage is the result of human activity.[110] The dividing-line between article 4 and article 7 may be difficult to draw in certain cases. For example, on one possible reading, article 7 might be thought to cover cases which English law treats as private nuisance or a tort under the rule in *Rylands v Fletcher*. However, this reading would be too broad: 'environmental damage' should be understood as meaning adverse change in a natural resource, such as water, land, or air, impairment of a function performed by that resource for the benefit of another natural resource or the public, or impairment of the variability among living organisms.[111] A case like *Bier v Mines de Potasse d'Alsace*[112] (in which a French defendant discharged pollution into the Rhine, causing damage to the plants of a market gardener in the Netherlands) would fall within article 7, rather than article 4. Conversely, the law governing a claim by an English landowner against a Scottish pig farmer based on private nuisance should be determined by article 4.

5.58 With a view to encouraging the highest possible level of environmental protection, in accordance with the 'polluter pays' principle,[113] article 7 supplements the rule in article 4 by giving the claimant the possibility of choosing a law which is more favourable to his interests. Of course, the claimant can choose only between laws which have a relevant connection with the situation. According to article 7, the law applicable to a non-contractual obligation arising out of environmental damage or damage sustained by persons or property as a result of such damage is either the law determined pursuant to article 4(1) or, if the claimant so chooses, the law of the country in which the event giving rise to the damage occurred. So, in a situation like the *Bier* case,[114] the claimant can opt for the law of France (where the defendant acted), rather than the law of the Netherlands (where the damage occurred). The question of when the person seeking compensation can make the choice of the applicable law is determined in accordance with the law of the Member State in which the claim is brought.[115]

---

[109] For discussion of art 14, see paras 5.86–5.90.
[110] European Commission, *Rome II Proposal*, COM (2003) 427 final, p 19.
[111] Recital (24).
[112] Case C-21/76 *Handelskwekerij GJ Bier BV v Mines de Potasse d'Alsace SA* [1976] ECR 1735.
[113] See recital (25).
[114] Case C-21/76 *Handelskwekerij GJ Bier BV v Mines de Potasse d'Alsace SA* [1976] ECR 1735.
[115] Recital (25).

5.59 One of the advantages of this either/or rule is that, if a defendant established in a country with a high level of environmental protection causes environmental damage in a low-protection country, the defendant will be subject to the standards of the high-protection country as the claimant will rationally choose the law of the country where the defendant acted. By the same token, the defendant cannot escape liability by setting up in a country with a low level of environmental protection because, if the defendant causes environmental damage in a high-protection country, the claimant will rely on the law of the country where the damage occurs.

5.60 However, as the Commission noted in its original proposal for the Rome II Regulation, one of the difficulties relating to civil liability for violations of the environment is the relationship between the law of the country where the damage occurs and the public law rules with which industrial operators are required to comply in their home country.[116] A defendant who is sued for environmental damage incurred in a foreign country may feel that it can legitimately exculpate itself by pointing to the fact that its activities are authorised in its home country.

5.61 This issue is addressed, up to a point, in article 17, the purpose of which is to allow the court 'to have regard to the fact that the perpetrator has complied with the rules in force in the country in which he is in business'.[117] As already noted in the context of article 4, article 17 states that, in assessing the conduct of the person claimed to be liable, account shall be taken, as a matter of fact and in so far as is appropriate, of the rules of safety and conduct which were in force at the place and time of the event giving rise to the liability.

5.62 The intended significance of article 17 (which, in certain respects, is not unlike article 12(2) of the Rome I Regulation) is not completely clear. What does the phrase 'account shall be taken ... of' actually mean? As a general rule, legal rules are either applied to a particular situation or they are not; it is also accepted that article 17 is not a choice of law rule. In principle, issues of substance should be governed by the applicable law; if, for example, liability for environmental damage is strict under the lex loci damni (country A), but is based on fault under the law of the place where the defendant acted (country B), article 17 cannot enable the defendant to escape liability under the lex loci damni by showing that he was not negligent (and, therefore, not liable) under the law of country B. To allow the defendant to escape strict liability in these circumstances would go much further than 'taking account of' the law of country B; it would involve applying it in preference to the law of country A. This is not what article 17 envisages.

5.63 Perhaps a more plausible example for the operation of article 17 would be where the defendant's liability under the law of country A is based on fault. In assessing whether the defendant was or was not negligent, it would make sense for the court to consider whether or not the defendant had acted appropriately, having regard to the safety requirements imposed by the law of country B, the place where the defendant acted.

---

[116] See European Commission, *Rome II Proposal*, COM (2003) 427 final, p 20.   [117] Ibid.

Nevertheless, uncertainty over the precise relationship between the applicable law and the law of the country in which the alleged tortfeasor acted—which gives national courts a certain amount of room for manoeuvre—may have the effect of undermining the intended uniformity of the regime introduced by the Regulation.

4. Infringement of intellectual property rights: article 8

5.64 Intellectual property rights are strictly territorial in nature. In most legal systems, the 'territorial principle' enables each country to apply its own law to an infringement of an intellectual property right which is in force in its territory.[118] To maintain the status quo, it was important that the general rules in article 4 were not applied to the infringement of intellectual property rights and that 'the universally acknowledged principle of the *lex loci protectionis* should be preserved'.[119] Article 8 provides that the law applicable to a non-contractual obligation arising from an infringement of an intellectual property right is the law of the country for which protection is claimed.[120] This is a hard-and-fast rule which is not subject to exceptions, provisos, or an escape clause. It is expressly provided that the lex loci protectionis may not be derogated from by an agreement pursuant to article 14.[121]

5. Industrial action: article 9

5.65 The rationale for a specific choice of law rule dealing with industrial action is the fact that the exact concept of industrial action, such as strike action or lock-out, varies from one Member State to another and is invariably governed by the rules of the national law of the place where the action is brought.[122] Although article 9 resembles article 4, it is less complex as it does not include an escape clause; it provides that the law applicable to a non-contractual obligation in respect of liability for damages caused by an industrial action, whether pending or already carried out, is the law of the country where the action is to be, or has been, taken. This rule applies to industrial action on the part of a worker or an employer or an organisation which represents the interests of workers or employers. The rule in article 9 is, however, without prejudice to article 4(2); so if the parties to the dispute are habitually resident in the same country, the law of that country applies.

5.66 It is worth emphasising that article 9 is concerned only with questions of civil liability. It does not purport to have any bearing on either the conditions relating to the exercise of industrial action in accordance with national law or the legal status of trade unions or of the representative organisations of workers as provided for in the law of the Member States.[123]

---

[118] Ibid.   [119] Recital (26).
[120] As regards infringement of a unitary EU intellectual property right, the applicable law for any question that is not governed by the relevant EU instrument is the law of the country in which the act of infringement was committed: art 8(2). See also art 13, which applies the lex loci protectionis to non-contractual obligations other than torts.
[121] Art 8(3). For consideration of art 14, see paras 5.86–5.90.
[122] Recital (27).   [123] Recital (28).

IV The Rome II Regulation: other non-contractual obligations

5.67 The scheme for non-contractual obligations which do not arise from torts has certain features in common with the rules which apply to tortious obligations. However, because other non-contractual obligations frequently can arise in the context of pre-existing legal relationships, there are some significant differences between the tort choice of law rules and the choice of law rules for other non-contractual obligations.

5.68 When the Rome II Regulation was being negotiated, the common law choice of law rules relating to unjust enrichment were regarded as being still in their infancy—which is not altogether surprising as it was only towards the end of the twentieth century that the law of unjust enrichment was recognised in English law as being based on a coherent principle.[124] As it is almost inevitable that the development of choice of law rules in relation to claims based on unjust enrichment would lag some way behind the development of the rules which identify the circumstances in which such causes of action arise, there was a body of opinion which was opposed to the United Kingdom's participation in the adoption of the Rome II Regulation on the ground that it was premature to attempt to codify choice of law rules in the field of unjust enrichment. However, this viewpoint did not prevail and the United Kingdom decided to opt in to the Regulation. Whatever the strengths and weaknesses of the rules contained in the Rome II Regulation, it is hard to see how they could not be an improvement on the pre-existing common law rules which were, at best, somewhat opaque.

A Unjust enrichment: article 10

1. Classification: what is covered by article 10?

5.69 The Regulation contains little indication of the types of issues which should be classified as 'unjust enrichment' for the purposes of article 10. The text of that article simply refers to 'a non-contractual obligation arising out of unjust enrichment, including payment of amounts wrongly received'. Within the framework of English law, there is a vigorous debate about what exactly falls within the general category 'restitution' and, within that general category, what should be classified as relating to 'unjust enrichment'. The extent to which the boundaries of the English law of restitution are the same as the parameters of article 10 is uncertain. It must always be remembered that, for the purposes of the Regulation, 'unjust enrichment' must be given an autonomous meaning, rather than a national one. The fact that a particular situation is regarded as part of the English law of restitution is far from conclusive; the conceptual categories for choice of law purposes may differ from those categories as applied in entirely domestic cases.

5.70 Within the English law of restitution, there are two fundamental distinctions. The first is between, on the one hand, the most significant part of the law of restitution, often

---

[124] *Lipkin Gorman v Karpnale Ltd* [1991] 2 AC 548.

referred to as 'autonomous unjust enrichment', which is concerned with the identification of the circumstances in which the claimant has a claim against the defendant on the basis of unjust enrichment (as opposed to contract or tort) and, on the other, that part of the law known as 'restitution for wrongs', which is concerned with whether the claimant is entitled to restitution (rather than compensation or some other remedy) for a wrong—whether a breach of contract, tort, or equitable wrong—committed by the defendant.[125] The second distinction is between circumstances in which the defendant owes a restitutionary obligation to the claimant and cases involving proprietary restitution, in which the claimant asserts a legal or equitable proprietary right in property in the hands of the defendant. To what extent do autonomous unjust enrichment, restitution for wrongs, and proprietary restitution come within the scope of article 10?

5.71 On the one hand, there seems little doubt that, as a general rule, matters which English law would treat as autonomous unjust enrichment are subject to the choice of law rules in article 10. So, if C, having paid D a sum of money under a mistake of law, brings a claim for unjust enrichment against D, article 10 determines the law governing C's claim. Whether article 10 covers a claim for restitution of benefits paid under a void contract is less straightforward. Although domestic law may classify such a claim as restitutionary in nature, for the purposes of the European choice of law regime, such claims should be classified as contractual and within the scope of the Rome I Regulation.[126] Having said that, in practical terms, it does not much matter whether the claim is classified as contractual or based on unjust enrichment; whatever the analysis, the law governing the contract is the applicable law.[127]

5.72 On the other hand, restitution for wrongs is focused on whether restitution is available as a remedy—which is not an unjust enrichment question as such. This question should be approached by classifying the underlying cause of action; whether the claimant is entitled to restitution for the wrong should be answered by reference to the law which governs the cause of action.[128] So, in a so-called 'waiver of tort' case, whether the claimant can claim restitution, rather than damages, should depend on the law governing the tort. However, the significance of whether restitution for wrongs is classified by reference to the underlying wrong or as an issue of unjust enrichment is limited, as either classification will normally lead to application of the law governing the wrong.[129]

5.73 It is far from clear that questions of proprietary restitution should properly be regarded as part of the law of restitution under English domestic law and there is a strong argument for saying that such questions are outside the scope of the Rome II Regulation altogether. As its title indicates, the Regulation is concerned with non-contractual *obligations*; it does not purport to address questions of property ownership. Accordingly, questions relating to an obligation to make restitution for unjust enrichment should be

---

[125] See Birks, *An Introduction to the Law of Restitution* (1989) ch 1; and Birks, *Restitution—The Future* (1992) ch 1.
[126] See paras 4.176–4.177.
[127] Rome I Regulation, art 12(1)(e); Rome II Regulation, art 10(1).
[128] Art 15(c). See, further, para 5.91.   [129] See art 10(1).

decided by the law governing unjust enrichment, whereas any question of legal and/or equitable title in relation to specific property in the hands of the defendant should be classified as part of the law of property for conflict of laws purposes.[130]

5.74 Potential difficulties may be posed by the traditional division between substance and procedure. One of the problems is that, in cases of autonomous unjust enrichment, the question whether the claimant has a cause of action and the question whether the claimant is entitled to restitution collapse into each other. The danger is that the law of unjust enrichment may be seen as an aspect of procedure and, as a result, governed by the law of the forum. Although some of the common law cases seem to fall into this trap,[131] there can be no doubt that unjust enrichment is a substantive category for the purposes of article 10.

2. Choice of law rules

5.75 Many unjust enrichment claims are for the restitution of benefits bestowed on the defendant under a contract which, for one reason or another, turns out to be ineffective. The contract may be void, frustrated, or unenforceable. The obvious starting-point in these cases is the law which governed (or would have governed) the contract. Under the Rome II Regulation, as a general rule, if a non-contractual obligation arising out of unjust enrichment is connected with a relationship previously existing between the parties (such as contract or tort), the law governing the relationship also governs the non-contractual obligation.[132] So, where the claimant seeks to enforce a restitutionary obligation arising on the termination of a contractual relationship, the law governing the contract also governs the claim to restitution; similarly, a claim for unjust enrichment which arises out of a void contract should be governed by the law which would have governed the contract had it been valid.

5.76 There are two good reasons for this rule. First, where there is a connection between an unjust enrichment claim and a contract, if the parties to the unjust enrichment claim had applied their minds to the question, they might reasonably have expected that the law which governed (or would have governed) the contract would also govern the restitutionary consequences of the situation. Secondly, one of the advantages of the general rule under article 10(1) is that the significance of questions of classification is much reduced; where, for example, a claim to restitution is closely connected with a contract, the law governing the contract will generally apply whether a particular issue is classified as contractual or relating to unjust enrichment.[133]

---

[130] *Macmillan Inc v Bishopsgate Investment Trust (No 3)* [1996] 1 WLR 387. For choice of law in relation to property, see Chapter 9.

[131] See, eg, *Arab Monetary Fund v Hashim (No 9)* (1994) *The Times*, 11 October; noted by Briggs, 'The International Dimension to Claims for Contribution' [1995] LMCLQ 437.

[132] Art 10(1). This rule is consistent with the (rather opaque) common law rules which applied before the entry into force of the Regulation: see, eg, *Fibrosa Spolka Akcyjna v Fairbairn Lawson Combe Barbour Ltd* [1943] AC 32; *Arab Bank Ltd v Barclays Bank* [1953] 2 QB 527; *Dimskal Shipping Co SA v International Transport Workers' Federation* [1992] 2 AC 152.

[133] See also Rome I Regulation, art 12(1)(e), which provides that the law applicable to a contract also governs the consequences of nullity of the contract.

5.77 As regards situations involving claims to restitution for the breach of fiduciary obligations (such as the obligations owed by company directors to the company or by an agent to his principal), the law governing the relationship between the parties also governs the claim to restitution. This principle can be illustrated by the facts of *Kuwait Oil Tanker SAK v Al Bader*,[134] in which the claimants, a number of Kuwaiti oil companies, argued that the defendants, who were members of the senior management of the first claimant, were liable as constructive trustees for breach of fiduciary duties. In this situation, the claim for restitution must be governed by the law applicable to the fiduciary relationship—which, in the *Kuwait Oil Tanker* case, was Kuwaiti law (on the basis that the law of the place of the company's incorporation governs the relationship between a company director and the company[135]).

5.78 If the applicable law cannot be determined by the general rule in article 10(1)—typically because there is no legal relationship between the parties—but the parties had their habitual residence in the same country when the event giving rise to unjust enrichment occurred, the law of that country applies.[136] If, however, the parties do not have the same habitual residence, article 10(3) provides that the law applicable to non-contractual obligations arising out of unjust enrichment is 'the law of the country in which the unjust enrichment took place'.[137] This rule follows the common law position: for example, in *Chase Manhattan Bank NA v Israel-British Bank (London) Ltd*,[138] a case involving payment of money under a mistake of fact, the law of New York, being the place where the money was received, was applied to the plaintiff's claim.[139] It has been convincingly argued that, in the case of enrichment through receipt of tangible assets, the applicable law under article 10(3) is the law of the country where the defendant assumed control over the asset; where the enrichment is in the form of a transfer into a bank account, the place of enrichment is the location of the branch in which the account is operated.[140]

5.79 Article 10, like article 4 in the context of tortious obligations, includes an escape clause. The three choice of law rules set out in article 10(1) to (3) may be displaced: if a non-contractual obligation arising out of unjust enrichment is manifestly more closely connected with another country, the law of that other country applies.[141] Although the escape clause in article 10(4) is potentially applicable in cases covered by any of the rules contained in the other three paragraphs, it is most likely to come into the picture where there was no pre-existing relationship between the parties and the parties do not share a common habitual residence—that is, in cases where the applicable law is prima facie the law of the place of enrichment under article 10(3). In such cases, the application of the law of the country where the enrichment took place may, in the circumstances of the case, be inappropriate; the place of enrichment is a potentially arbitrary

---

[134] [2000] 2 All ER (Comm) 271.
[135] See *Base Metal Trading Ltd v Shamurin* [2005] 1 WLR 1157.   [136] Art 10(2).
[137] Art 10(3). See *Banque Cantonale de Genève v Polevent Ltd* [2016] QB 394.
[138] [1981] Ch 105.
[139] See also *El Ajou v Dollar Land Holdings plc* [1993] 3 All ER 717; *Re Jogia (a bankrupt)* [1988] 1 WLR 484. But, compare *Barros Mattos Junior v MacDaniels Ltd* [2005] ILPr 45.
[140] See Dickinson, *The Rome II Regulation* (2008) para 10.34.   [141] Art 10(4).

connecting factor which may have very little connection with the substance of the parties' dispute. If the court is satisfied that the situation is manifestly more closely connected with, for example, the country where the defendant committed the acts which led to the enrichment, the law of that country should be the applicable law by virtue of article 10(4). It must be emphasised that it is intended that the escape clause should be applied only rarely and in exceptional circumstances.

B Negotiorum gestio: article 11

5.80 Although there is no specific institution in English law which corresponds to negotiorum gestio (which is sometimes translated as 'agency without authority'), the fact that the institution exists under the laws of several other EU legal systems provides a good reason for including appropriate choice of law rules in the Regulation. Negotiorum gestio covers the legal relationship between a person (A) who intervenes in the affairs of another person (B); in its most typical manifestation, A's intervention is for B's benefit, but without B's authority. The rules and principles relating to negotiorum gestio determine whether, and in what circumstances, B is under an obligation to A (for example, to compensate A for expenditure undertaken for B's benefit). Article 11(1) provides that, if a non-contractual obligation arising out of an act performed without due authority in connection with the affairs of another person concerns a relationship existing between the parties, such as one arising out of a contract or a tort/delict, that is closely connected with that non-contractual obligation, the non-contractual obligation is governed by the law that applies to that relationship.

5.81 Article 11, like article 10, is drafted on the assumption that non-contractual obligations arising from agency without authority may well arise in situations where there is a pre-existing relationship between the parties. It makes sense in such cases for the liability of the defendant in cases of agency without authority to be governed by the law which governs the pre-existing relationship. If, for example, an agent properly constituted by contract interferes in the principal's affairs, the law applicable to the contract of agency also applies to any non-contractual obligations which arise as a consequence of the agent's interference which goes beyond the scope of his mandate. However, article 11(1) is subject to an escape clause in favour of the law of a country with which a non-contractual obligation arising from agency without authority is manifestly more closely connected.[142]

5.82 If the applicable law cannot be determined by reference to article 11(1), the following choice of law rules apply: if the parties are habitually resident in the same country, the law of the parties' common habitual residence applies;[143] if, however, the parties do not share a habitual residence, the governing law is the law of the country in which the claimant's act of intervention was done.[144] These two rules are subject to the escape clause: where it is clear from all the circumstances that the non-contractual obligation arising out of an act performed without due authority is manifestly more closely connected with another country, the law of that other country governs.[145]

---

[142] Art 11(4).   [143] Art 11(2).   [144] Art 11(3).   [145] Art 11(4).

C Culpa in contrahendo: article 12

5.83 Article 12 was added into the Regulation at a late stage of the legislative process—after the publication of the amended proposal in 2006. For the purposes of the Regulation, culpa in contrahendo is an autonomous concept and should not necessarily be interpreted in accordance with national law.[146] The Regulation indicates that article 12 covers cases involving 'violation of the duty of disclosure and the breakdown of contractual negotiations'; it also covers 'non-contractual obligations presenting a direct link with the dealings prior to the conclusion of a contract'.[147] However, article 12 does not apply to a non-contractual obligation which is only tangentially connected with an anticipated contract. Whereas, under German law, a potential purchaser who is injured when he slips on the floor of a car-showroom can base a claim on culpa in contrahendo,[148] the Regulation classifies this situation as one involving tortious obligations; it does not come within the scope of article 12.

5.84 The choice of law rules in article 12 follow a similar pattern to articles 10 and 11. First, the general rule is that the law applicable to a non-contractual obligation arising out of dealings prior to the conclusion of a contract, whether or not the contract was actually concluded, is the law that applies to the contract or that would have governed it if it had been entered into.[149] This general rule, which is a hard-and-fast rule and is not subject to the escape clause, has the effect of largely side-stepping the question whether a particular obligation should be classified as contractual or non-contractual; either classification leads to the application of the law which governs (or would have governed) the contract. So, in a scenario like the *Tacconi*[150] case, in which the Court of Justice ruled that, for the purposes of Brussels I, a claim based on breach of a pre-contractual obligation to conduct contractual negotiations in good faith was not a matter relating to a contract, the relevant choice of law rule would be article 12 of the Rome II Regulation.

5.85 Secondly, where the applicable law cannot be determined on the basis of the general rule, the governing law is the law of the country in which the damage occurs (lex loci damni), irrespective of the country in which the event giving rise to the damage occurred and irrespective of the country or countries in which the indirect consequences of that event occurred.[151] Thirdly, however, if the parties have their habitual residence in the same country at the time when the event giving rise to the damage occurs, the law of that country applies.[152] Finally, the lex loci damni or the law of the parties' common habitual residence (as the case may be) is subject to the escape clause: where it is clear from all the circumstances of the case that the non-contractual obligation arising out of dealings prior to the conclusion of a contract is manifestly more closely

---

[146] See Hage-Chahine, '*Culpa in Contrahendo* in European Private International Law: Another Look at Article 12 of the Rome II Regulation' (2012) 32 Northwestern Journal of International Law and Business 451.
[147] Recital (30).
[148] See Zweigert and Kötz, *Introduction to Comparative Law* (2nd edn, 1992) pp 674–5.
[149] Art 12(1).
[150] Case C–334/00 *Fonderie Officine Mecchaniche Tacconi SpA v Heinrich Wagner Sinto Maschinenfabrik GmbH* [2002] ECR I–7357.
[151] Art 12(2)(a). [152] Art 12(2)(b).

connected with another country, the law of that other country applies.¹⁵³ It must be remembered, however, that the escape clause does not apply to cases where the applicable law can be determined under the general rule, which operates as a hard-and-fast rule in favour of the contractual law.

V The Rome II Regulation: general provisions

A Freedom of choice: article 14

5.86 In contrast to the common law which was, at best, equivocal on the question whether it was open to parties to select the law to govern a tort or other non-contractual obligation,¹⁵⁴ the Regulation aims to give effect to the principle of party autonomy. According to the Regulation, to respect the principle of party autonomy and to enhance legal certainty, the parties should be allowed to make a choice as to the law applicable to a non-contractual obligation.¹⁵⁵ Whatever the benefits of allowing party autonomy in the context of non-contractual obligations, it is less obvious that parties should be allowed complete freedom in cases where, in socio-economic terms, the parties are not on an equal footing. Article 14 attempts to find a reasonable compromise between the extremes of ignoring any purported choice by the parties, on the one hand, and giving the principle of party autonomy free rein, on the other.

5.87 Article 14(1) provides that parties may choose the law to govern a non-contractual obligation in two situations: first, by means of an agreement entered into after the event giving rise to the damage occurred; secondly, in cases where all the parties concerned are pursuing a commercial activity, by means of an agreement freely negotiated before the event giving rise to the damage occurred. Article 14 requires any choice to be 'expressed or demonstrated with reasonable certainty by the circumstances of the case'.¹⁵⁶

5.88 It is not easy to predict the circumstances in which the first alternative is likely to come into the picture. Once the event giving rise to the damage has occurred, it should be relatively straightforward, in most cases, to predict which law is designated by the Regulation to govern the non-contractual obligation which has arisen. In these circumstances, the effect of a choice of law would be either to confirm the law which the parties anticipate to be the governing law under the Regulation, the value of which would be relatively limited, or to select a different law. If the parties choose a law which is substantively different from the law which would apply in the absence of such choice, the choice is bound to be detrimental to the interests of one or other of the parties. Why would the party who is going to be disadvantaged by the chosen law

---

[153] Art 12(2)(c).
[154] See, eg, *Morin v Bonhams & Brooks Ltd* [2004] 1 Lloyd's Rep 702.   [155] Recital (31).
[156] See the discussion of the slightly differently worded art 3(1), the equivalent provision of the Rome I Regulation, at paras 4.15–4.20.

agree to that law? It remains to be seen whether the freedom to choose the law applicable to a non-contractual obligation after the event comes to have much of a role to play in practice.

5.89 As regards the second alternative, it seems likely that it will arise in commercial cases where the parties to the dispute relating to a non-contractual obligation are already parties to a contract and that contract contains a choice of law clause which is drafted broadly enough to cover non-contractual obligations as well as contractual obligations. Indeed, it might be thought that article 14(1)(b) provides a positive incentive to contracting parties to draft choice of law clauses in a way which extends to non-contractual obligations, thereby avoiding any uncertainty over the applicable law which might otherwise arise in the context of a dispute concerning a non-contractual obligation. However, the significance of such agreements on choice of law may be doubted. This is because several of the provisions laying down choice of law rules for non-contractual obligations provide for an escape clause in favour of the law of a country with which the non-contractual obligation is manifestly more closely connected; the most obvious situations in which the escape clause is relevant are where there is a contractual relationship between the parties and there is such a close connection between the non-contractual obligation and the contract that the law governing the contract should also govern the non-contractual obligation—on the basis that the non-contractual obligation is manifestly more closely connected with the country whose law governs the contract.[157] Consider the situation where parties (C and D) enter a contract which includes a choice of English law as the governing law; C alleges that D's fraudulent activity amounts to both a breach of the contract and commission of the tort of deceit. In this type of case involving parallel claims in contract and tort, it is more than likely that English law, the law governing the contract, will also govern the tort claim, whether or not the choice of law clause in the contract is drafted with a view to including within its scope any potential tort claim by one contracting party against the other. Obviously, if the choice of law clause is broadly drafted, English law governs the claim for deceit by virtue of article 14; if, however, the choice of law clause does not extend to tortious claims, English law will nevertheless, in all probability, govern the tort claim on the basis of article 4(3).

5.90 There are a couple of other points to note about the operation of article 14. First, parties are not free to select the applicable law in relation to cases involving either unfair competition and acts restricting free competition (article 6) or the infringement of intellectual property rights (article 8). Secondly, a choice of law by the parties may be limited by the effect of mandatory provisions.[158] It is provided that, where all the elements relevant to the situation at the time when the event giving rise to the damage occurs are located in a country other than the country whose law has been chosen, the choice of the parties shall not prejudice the application of provisions

---

[157] See arts 4(3), 5(2), 10(4), 11(4), 12(2)(c).
[158] For consideration of the distinction between mandatory provisions and overriding mandatory provisions, see para 4.90.

of the law of that other country which cannot be derogated from by agreement.[159] So, in a case involving a tort committed in country A involving two parties who are habitually resident in country A, if the parties select the law of country B to govern the tort, that choice cannot prevent the application of mandatory provisions of the law of country A. As there has been little or no experience to date on the operation of choice of law clauses in the field of non-contractual obligations, it is hard to know what practical significance (if any) article 14(2) will have. If experience with equivalent provisions of the Rome I Regulation is anything to go by, it seems unlikely that the courts will frequently be faced by the potential problems posed by mandatory rules under article 14(2).

B Scope of the applicable law

5.91 In principle, all substantive elements of a non-contractual obligation are governed by the same law: in a tort case, one system of law governs the entire tortious claim.[160] Article 15 lists a number of issues which are governed by the law applicable to a non-contractual obligation. The list, which is non-exhaustive, illustrates the basic point that questions of substance are governed by the applicable law:

(a) *The basis and extent of liability, including the determination of persons who may be held liable for acts performed by them:* This paragraph is particularly concerned with the following questions: the nature of liability (strict or fault-based); the definition of fault, including the question whether an omission can constitute a fault; the causal link between the event giving rise to the damage and the damage; the persons potentially liable. The phrase 'extent of liability' refers to the limitations laid down by law on liability, including the maximum extent of that liability and the contribution to be made by each of the persons liable for the damage which is to be compensated for.[161]

(b) *The grounds for exemption from liability, any limitation of liability, and any division of liability:* The law governing a non-contractual obligation determines the effect of the grounds for release from liability, such as force majeure, necessity, third-party fault, and fault by the victim. If, for example, contributory negligence is a complete defence under the applicable law, the claim will be rejected, even if the lex fori provides for apportionment.[162] Whether the defendant's liability is limited as a result of a failure by the claimant to mitigate his loss is a substantive question governed by the law governing the non-contractual obligation.[163] In a case where a victim is injured in Germany by a tractor pulling a trailer, the law of the country where the victim was injured (that is,

---

[159] Art 14(2). A similar rule in art 14(3) makes provision for the application of mandatory provisions of EU law in cases where the parties have chosen the law of a non-Member State and all other elements relevant to the situation at the time of the choice are located in one or more Member States. Art 14(2) and (3) are the equivalent of art 3(3) and (4) of the Rome I Regulation.
[160] *Winrow v Hemphill* [2015] ILPr 12 at [45].
[161] European Commission, *Rome II Proposal*, COM (2003) 427 final, p 23.   [162] Ibid.
[163] See *Cox v Ergo Versicherung AG* [2014] AC 1379 (a case decided under the Private International Law (Miscellaneous Provisions) Act 1995).

German law) determines how (if at all) the obligation to compensate the victim is to be apportioned between the owner of the tractor and the owner of the trailer.[164]

(c) *The existence, the nature, and the assessment of damage or the remedy claimed:* At common law, the English courts consider that, while the availability of heads of damage in tort is a substantive issue which is governed by the law governing the tort,[165] quantification of damages is procedural and governed by the law of the forum.[166] Although the Regulation does not apply to evidence and procedure,[167] it would be difficult to maintain—in the face of the clear wording of article 15(c)—that the Regulation has left the common law position untouched.[168] In *Maher v Groupama Grand Est*[169] Blair J accepted (obiter) that the position under article 15(c) was different from the pre-existing English law and that, under the Regulation, the applicable law governs not only whether damages may be awarded for certain heads of damage, but also the quantification of damage. This view was confirmed by the Court of Appeal in *Wall v Mutuelle de Poitiers Assurances*.[170] In this context, the applicable law includes 'judicial conventions and practices, for example particular tariffs, guidelines or formulae used by judges in the calculation of damages under the applicable law'.[171]

5.92 One of the recitals states that, in road accident cases, the court 'should take into account all the relevant actual circumstances of the specific victim, including in particular the actual losses and costs of after-care and medical attention'.[172] However, this recital, far from being a rule of law, does not even correspond with any of the substantive provisions of the Regulation; accordingly, it has no legal effect.[173] What significance, if any, should be attached to it is uncertain; its effect cannot be to displace or otherwise modify the applicable law.

5.93 It is sometimes suggested that the choice of law rule for unjust enrichment should also apply to the issue of restitution for wrongs.[174] This, however, is unsound in principle. The law of restitution for wrongs is built on the foundation of the general law of civil liability; it determines the circumstances in which the claimant is entitled to restitution as a remedy in cases where the basis of the defendant's liability is a breach of contract, a tort or an equitable wrong. When, for example, can the defendant be required to give up a gain made at the claimant's expense rather than simply to compensate the claimant for the loss he has suffered?

5.94 Article 15(c) of the Regulation provides that the law applicable to a non-contractual obligation extends to questions surrounding 'the remedy claimed'. It follows that

---

[164] Joined Cases C-359/14 & C-475/14 *'ERGO Insurance' SE v 'If P&C Insurance' AS*, paras 51–2.
[165] *Boys v Chaplin* [1971] AC 356.   [166] *Harding v Wealands* [2007] 2 AC 1.   [167] Art 1(3).
[168] See also recital (32) which only makes sense on the basis that questions of quantification are governed by the applicable law.
[169] [2009] 1 WLR 1752.
[170] [2014] 1 WLR 4263. See also *Jacobs v Motor Insurers' Bureau* [2010] 1 All ER (Comm) 1128; reversed on other grounds: [2011] 1 All ER 844.
[171] Longmore LJ in *Wall v Mutuelle de Poitiers Assurances* [2014] 1 WLR 4263 at [21].
[172] Recital (33).
[173] Dickinson, *The Rome II Regulation* (2008) para 3.17.
[174] See *Arab Monetary Fund v Hashim* [1996] 1 Lloyd's Rep 589 (although the analysis is somewhat confused). Compare Bird, 'Choice of Law' in Rose (ed), *Restitution and the Conflict of Laws* (1995) p 92.

if C sues D in tort and claims to be entitled to restitution for the wrong (rather than, or as well as, damages), the law governing the cause of action in tort should also determine whether restitution is available. It is well established that whether a claimant may recover in tort for a particular head of damage falls to be determined by the law governing the tort; by analogy, whether restitution may be awarded for a particular wrong should be determined by the law governing the wrong.

(d) *Within the limits of powers conferred on the court by its procedural law, the measures which a court may take to prevent or terminate injury or damage or to ensure the provision of compensation:* This paragraph refers to forms of compensation, such as the question whether the damage can be repaired by payment of damages, and ways of preventing or halting the damage, such as interlocutory injunctions; however, article 15(d) does not oblige a court to order measures that are unknown in the procedural law of the forum.[175]

(e) *The question whether a right to claim damages or a remedy may be transferred, including by inheritance.*

(f) *Persons entitled to compensation for damage sustained personally:* The applicable law answers the question whether a person other than the direct victim can obtain compensation for damage sustained on a 'knock-on' basis following damage sustained by the immediate victim.[176] So, where the direct victim of a tort dies, the law applicable to that tort, as designated by the Regulation, also determines whether members of the deceased's family (such as a widow or other dependant) have a claim and, if so, the extent of that claim.

(g) *Liability for the acts of another person:* Where C is injured by the negligence of X, an employee of D, the law governing the tort determines whether D is vicariously liable for the wrong committed by X. The law applicable to a tort also governs the liability of parents for their children and of principals for their agents.

(h) *The manner in which an obligation may be extinguished and rules of prescription and limitation, including rules relating to the commencement, interruption, and suspension of a period of prescription or limitation:* Whether C's claim in tort against D is barred by lapse of time is a substantive question for the law governing the tort, rather than a procedural question for the law of the forum.[177]

C Habitual residence

5.95 There are various provisions of the Regulation which depend on the habitual residence of the parties. For example, article 4(2) provides that, if a tort is committed by the defendant in country X, but both the defendant and the claimant are habitually resident in country Y, the law governing the tort is the law of country Y, rather than the law

---

[175] European Commission, *Rome II Proposal*, COM (2003) 427 final, p 24.   [176] Ibid.
[177] But, see the possible relevance of public policy, paras 5.97–5.102.

of country X.¹⁷⁸ Article 23, which is similar to article 19 of the Rome I Regulation,¹⁷⁹ defines what is meant by habitual residence for the purposes of the Regulation.

5.96 First, the habitual residence of companies and other similar bodies is the place of central administration.¹⁸⁰ Secondly, where the event giving rise to the damage occurs, or the damage arises, in the course of the operations of a branch, agency, or other establishment, the place where the branch, agency, or other establishment is located is to be treated as the place of habitual residence.¹⁸¹ Where, for example, C suffers financial loss as a result of a negligent misstatement by a Swiss bank, the bank's habitual residence will normally be Switzerland; if, however, the misstatement was made by the bank's Paris branch, the bank would be regarded as habitually resident in France for the purposes of the tort claim in question. Thirdly, a natural person acting in the course of his business is habitually resident at his principal place of business.¹⁸² Fourthly, the Regulation does not attempt to define the habitual residence of a natural person who is not acting in the course of business. For the purposes of EU law, it has been assumed that an individual can have only one place of habitual residence, which is where the person has established, on a fixed basis, his permanent or habitual centre of interests.¹⁸³

D Overriding mandatory provisions and public policy

5.97 The applicable law has to be balanced against the overriding mandatory rules of the laws of other countries: article 16, a provision which mirrors article 9(2) of the Rome I Regulation, states that the applicable law yields to the overriding mandatory rules which form part of the law of the forum. The original proposal included a rule-making provision for the discretionary application of the overriding mandatory rules of a closely connected law which was neither the applicable law nor the law of the forum,¹⁸⁴ but this proposal was dropped during the legislative process. It is also provided that the application of a provision of the law of any country specified by the Regulation may be refused if such application is manifestly incompatible with the public policy (ordre public) of the forum.¹⁸⁵ The use of the word 'manifestly' is intended to signify that 'the use of the public policy exception must be exceptional'.¹⁸⁶

5.98 According to the Regulation, if the governing law has the effect of causing non-compensatory, exemplary, or punitive damages of an excessive nature to be awarded, it is legitimate for the forum to decide that the application of the governing law is contrary to public policy; this depends, however, on the circumstances of the case and the legal order of the forum.¹⁸⁷ In England, there is authority that it is not contrary to English public policy to enforce a foreign judgment which awards exemplary or

---

¹⁷⁸ See also arts 5(1), 10(2), 11(2), 12(2)(b).   ¹⁷⁹ See paras 4.82–4.86.   ¹⁸⁰ Art 23(1).
¹⁸¹ Art 23(1).   ¹⁸² Art 23(2).
¹⁸³ See paras 6.90–6.95. A person, born in England, who lives in Germany for more than eight years prior to being injured in a road accident in Germany and who remains in Germany for 18 months following the accident, is habitually resident in Germany at the time of the accident: *Winrow v Hemphill* [2015] ILPr 12.
¹⁸⁴ See European Commission, *Rome II Proposal*, COM (2003) 427 final, p 25.   ¹⁸⁵ Art 26.
¹⁸⁶ European Commission, *Rome II Proposal*, COM (2003) 427 final, p 28.   ¹⁸⁷ Recital (32).

punitive damages.¹⁸⁸ Accordingly, it is reasonable to suppose that the English court would not normally have any qualms about applying the governing law of a foreign country which allows the award of punitive damages.¹⁸⁹

5.99 To date, questions involving overriding mandatory provisions of the forum and public policy have not generally loomed large in tort cases in English law. There is a simple explanation for this: at common law, liability can be imposed for a tort committed abroad only if the conduct in question would have given rise to tortious liability under English law had the tort been committed in England—as well as giving rise to civil liability under the law of the place where the tort was committed; this is the double actionability rule.¹⁹⁰ From a functional point of view, the double actionability rule operates as a rule of public policy which excludes the application of any foreign rule which imposes tort liability unless there is a corresponding rule of English law.

5.100 To a large extent, whether the imposition of liability for a tort under a foreign law would be contrary to English public policy is a matter for speculation. Public policy should be invoked rarely and only in cases where the content of the foreign law is repugnant in English eyes. It would, for example, be wrong for the court to refuse to give effect to the applicable law on grounds of public policy simply because liability under the applicable law is strict whereas English law would impose liability only in the event of the defendant's fault. The potential application of public policy is not limited to the rejection of a foreign rule which imposes liability (in circumstances where no liability arises under English law); public policy may also have the effect of excluding the operation of a foreign rule which denies liability.

5.101 Notwithstanding the narrowness of the public policy exception, there is no reason to think that the small number of English cases in which public policy has been successfully invoked in the tort context would be decided differently under the Regulation. For example, in *Jones v Trollope Colls Cementation Overseas Ltd*¹⁹¹ C, who had been injured in a road accident in Pakistan, started proceedings in England against D, the negligent driver's employer. Not long after the accident C had been flown to Germany, where she spent seven months in hospital. Although the proceedings in England were commenced within the three-year limitation period under English law, the claim was time-barred under the law of Pakistan, which imposed a limitation period of one year. It was held, in this case, that it would be contrary to public policy to allow the claim to be defeated by the rule of Pakistani law laying down a one-year limitation period. Of particular significance was the fact that, before starting proceedings in England, C had been in correspondence with a representative of D, who had made statements suggesting that her claim would be settled by D's insurers. It does not follow, however, that public policy can be invoked simply on the ground that the limitation period under the

---

¹⁸⁸ *SA Consortium General Textiles v Sun and Sand Agencies Ltd* [1978] QB 279.
¹⁸⁹ There may be a question whether the result would be the same if the level of damages were so excessive that it 'shocks the conscience' of the court and is not consistent with the English court's notions of substantive justice.
¹⁹⁰ See paras 5.108–5.111.   ¹⁹¹ *The Times*, 26 January 1990.

applicable law is shorter than the period provided by English law; it all depends on the circumstances.[192]

5.102 In *Kuwait Airways Corpn v Iraqi Airways Co (Nos 4 and 5)*[193] some of the claimant's aircraft were seized by the Iraqi military on its invasion of Kuwait in 1990. The aircraft were then taken to Iraq and transferred to the defendant under Iraqi law. When the claimant brought proceedings in England for the return of the aircraft, the defendant denied its liability under the law of the place where the alleged wrong was committed by relying on an Iraqi decree which had purported to expropriate the aircraft and vest them in the defendant. The House of Lords held that the Iraqi decree was a gross breach of established rules of public international law and, as such, should be denied recognition on grounds of public policy. Accordingly, the defendant was liable; but for the decree, under Iraqi law the defendant's conduct amounted to usurpation, a civil wrong which broadly corresponds to the tort of conversion.

D Direct actions against insurers

5.103 Article 18 states that the victim of a tort may sue the tortfeasor's insurer directly to recover compensation if such possibility is available under either the law applicable to the non-contractual obligation or the law applicable to the insurance contract in question. In *Pruller-Frey v Brodnig*[194] C, an Austrian resident, was a passenger in an aircraft operated by X in Spain. The aircraft, which was insured under a policy issued by D and governed by German law, was involved in an accident in which C was injured. C brought a direct action in Austria for compensation against D. D argued that C was not entitled to bring the action as German law makes no provision for an injured party to sue the tortfeasor's insurer directly. The Court of Justice ruled that, if the law governing the tort allows for a direct action against the insurer, such direct action cannot be barred by the law governing the insurance policy.

VI Non-contractual obligations excluded from the Rome II Regulation

5.104 It has already been seen that certain matters are excluded from the material scope of the Regulation. The most important exclusion is in article 1(1)(g) which concerns 'non-contractual obligations arising out of violations of privacy and rights relating to personality, including defamation'. This means that cases falling within this exception are governed by English choice of law rules, rather than by the European regime. In fact, for historical reasons, there are two sets of choice of law rules which cover matters excluded from the Regulation. In the mid-1990s, the English choice of law rules for international torts were put on a statutory footing by Part III of the Private International

---

[192] *Harley v Smith* [2010] CP Rep 33 (in which the application of the 12-month limitation period under Saudi law was not regarded as contrary to public policy).
[193] [2002] 2 AC 883.   [194] Case C-240/124, [2015] 1 WLR 5031.

Law (Miscellaneous Provisions) Act 1995. However, before the enactment of that legislation, there had been a vigorous debate on the question whether the 1995 Act should apply to defamation claims. When the bill first appeared it caused a furore in the newspapers, even provoking a hostile editorial in *The Times*.[195] As a result of concerted lobbying by the press, it was decided that defamation claims should be excluded from the legislation.[196] Accordingly, as regards matters excluded from the scope of the Rome II Regulation, the law governing defamation claims is determined by the traditional common law choice of law rules; the law applicable to other tortious matters excluded from the Regulation (such as a claim for breach of privacy) depends on the choice of law rules set out in the 1995 Act.[197]

A Defamation claims: common law choice of law rules

5.105 At common law, if a tort occurs in England, English law applies, even if the case has strong connections with a foreign country.[198] If, however, the tort occurs abroad, the applicable law is determined in accordance with the rule in *Phillips v Eyre*[199] (as adapted by subsequent cases). For the purposes of these rules, the first issue to consider is the place where the tort occurs (locus delicti).

5.106 In many situations the locus delicti is simple to determine: it is the country in which the defendant commits the wrongful act and in which the harm is suffered by the claimant. The position is slightly more complicated in a case where the defendant acts in one country and the victim suffers harm in another. In this type of case the locus delicti is to be determined by answering the following question: where in substance did the cause of action arise?[200] Such an open-textured question gives the courts considerable room for manoeuvre and, as a consequence, it is impossible to lay down hard-and-fast rules. However, it has been held that, where a libel is contained in a letter written by the defendant abroad, but received by the addressee in London, the place of the tort is England, where the defamatory material is published.[201]

5.107 The common law choice of law rules comprise a general rule and an exception. The leading authority is the decision of the House of Lords in *Boys v Chaplin*,[202] a case which both built on the foundation of two important nineteenth-century cases—*The Halley*[203]

---

[195] 19 January 1995.
[196] See Private International Law (Miscellaneous Provisions) Act 1995, ss 9(3) and 13.
[197] There is no equivalent English legislation setting out choice of law rules for non-contractual obligations which are not tortious obligations (such as restitutionary obligations). Accordingly, if a choice of law question concerning unjust enrichment arises in relation to a matter excluded from the Regulation, the common law choice of law rules apply. For consideration of unjust enrichment choice of law rules at common law, see the 3rd edition of this work.
[198] *Szalatnay-Stacho v Fink* [1947] KB 1; *Metall und Rohstoff AG v Donaldson Lufkin & Jenrette Inc* [1990] 1 QB 391.
[199] (1870) LR 6 QB 1.
[200] The question was formulated, in the context of a jurisdiction case, by Lord Pearson in *Distillers Co (Biochemicals) Ltd v Thompson* [1971] AC 458 at 468. It was subsequently applied both to jurisdiction and choice of law issues. See, in particular, *Metall und Rohstoff AG v Donaldson Lufkin & Jenrette Inc* [1990] 1 QB 391.
[201] *Bata v Bata* [1948] WN 366.   [202] [1971] AC 356.   [203] (1868) LR 2 PC 193.

and *Phillips v Eyre*²⁰⁴—and brought about a significant change in the law through its reinterpretation of the rule in *Phillips v Eyre*.

1. The general rule: double actionability

5.108 In *Boys v Chaplin*²⁰⁵ P and D were both members of the British armed forces, resident in England. While both were temporarily stationed in Malta, they were involved in a road accident in which P was injured as a result of D's negligence. P sued D in England. Under the laws of England and Malta D was liable to P. Under Maltese law, however, P was entitled to recover only pecuniary loss, which amounted in this case to £53, whereas by English law P was also entitled to recover damages for pain and suffering and loss of amenity, which the trial judge assessed at £2,250. P succeeded in recovering for his pecuniary and non-pecuniary losses. Notwithstanding the varied reasons given by the five members of the House of Lords (which make it difficult to determine the ratio decidendi of the case), it has been accepted that Lord Wilberforce's approach is the one to be followed.²⁰⁶

5.109 A majority of the House of Lords decided that, as a general rule, a claimant can recover damages for a tort committed abroad only if two requirements are satisfied: (i) the defendant's conduct must be actionable as a tort under English law (a requirement ultimately derived from the decision of the Privy Council in *The Halley*²⁰⁷) and (ii) the defendant must be civilly liable under the lex loci delicti.²⁰⁸ According to Lord Wilberforce, the general rule requires 'actionability as a tort according to English law, subject to the condition that civil liability in respect of the relevant claim exists as between the actual parties under the law of the country where the act was done'.²⁰⁹ Under this revised version of the rule in *Phillips v Eyre*, the defendant is liable only to the extent that he is liable under both the law of the forum and the lex loci delicti; moreover, not only must the defendant be civilly liable to the claimant under both laws, he must also be liable in respect of the particular loss claimed by the claimant. In adopting this approach the House of Lords followed the interpretation of the rule in *Phillips v Eyre* favoured by the Scottish courts.²¹⁰

5.110 For the purposes of the double actionability rule, it is the position as between the actual parties in the particular circumstances of the case which determines whether or not the defendant's conduct is actionable. If the defendant has a defence under either the lex loci delicti or the lex fori this has the effect of barring the claim.²¹¹

---

²⁰⁴ (1870) LR 6 QB 1.   ²⁰⁵ [1971] AC 356.
²⁰⁶ See, eg, *Church of Scientology of California v Metropolitan Police Commissioner* (1976) 120 Sol Jo 690; *Coupland v Arabian Gulf Petroleum Co* [1983] 1 WLR 1136.
²⁰⁷ (1868) LR 2 PC 193.
²⁰⁸ This decision involved overruling *Machado v Fontes* [1897] 2 QB 231, which had held that the rule in *Phillips v Eyre* was satisfied if the defendant's conduct gave rise either to civil or criminal liability under the law of the place of the wrong.
²⁰⁹ [1971] AC 356 at 389.
²¹⁰ *M'Elroy v M'Allister* 1949 SC 110; *Mackinnon v Iberia Shipping Co* [1954] 2 Lloyd's Rep 372.
²¹¹ *Anderson v Eric Anderson Radio and TV Pty Ltd* (1966) 114 CLR 20 (an Australian case in which the lex fori denied recovery but the lex loci delicti provided for apportionment).

5.111 The double actionability rule is unusual—in the sense that, instead of identifying one law to govern the relationship between the parties, it requires the claimant to overcome a double hurdle in order to establish the defendant's liability. Accordingly, the double actionability rule gives the claimant the worst of both worlds.[212] If, for example, the limitation period has expired under either the lex loci delicti or the lex fori, the effect of the double actionability rule is to bar the claim for lapse of time.

2. The exception

5.112 The application of the double actionability rule to the facts of *Boys v Chaplin* would have led to P's claim for non-pecuniary losses failing because they were not recoverable by Maltese law, the lex loci delicti. To avoid this unfortunate solution, Lord Wilberforce propounded an exception to the double actionability rule.

5.113 In formulating the exception to the general rule, the House of Lords in *Boys v Chaplin* was influenced, up to a point, by developments which had occurred in the United States. The envisaged exception was along the lines of the American Second Restatement: 'The rights and liabilities of the parties with respect to an issue in tort are determined by the local law of the state which, as to that issue, has the most significant relationship to the occurrence and the parties.'[213] There is no suggestion in the House of Lords that the proper law approach should become the general rule; rather, the view was that, where the application of the double actionability rule would lead to an unjust decision, a particular issue may, by way of exception, be governed by a single law. Lord Wilberforce indicated that 'the general rule must apply unless clear and satisfying grounds are shown why it should be departed from'.[214] *Boys v Chaplin*, however, was a suitable case in which to apply the exception. The issue was whether a particular kind of loss was recoverable; it was appropriate to apply English law to that issue, given that England was the country to which both parties belonged. Accordingly, the plaintiff was entitled to recover damages for non-pecuniary losses, even though such recovery was denied by Maltese law.

5.114 According to Lord Wilberforce, the exception seeks to identify the law appropriate to a particular issue and it is envisaged that different laws may be applicable to different issues in the same case.[215] Also, Lord Wilberforce seems to favour US interest analysis rather than the 'centre of gravity' approach which has traditionally been applied in contract cases.[216] It can perhaps be gleaned from his speech that the general rule should not be departed from unless it is found that only one country's law has an interest to be applied. So, if in *Boys v Chaplin* the defendant, or both of the parties, had been

---

[212] The classic illustration of the injustice to which the double actionability rule can give rise is the Scottish case of *M'Elroy v M'Allister* 1949 SC 110, in which the pursuer brought proceedings in Scotland in respect of an accident in England, caused by the defender's negligence, in which her husband had been killed. Although the pursuer had a substantial claim under Scots law (damages for bereavement and loss of support) and English law (damages for loss of expectation of life), the operation of the double actionability rule meant that she was able to recover only for funeral expenses as this was the only head of damage which was common to both English and Scots law.
[213] S 145.   [214] [1971] AC 356 at 391.   [215] Ibid.   [216] See paras 1.44–1.60.

Maltese, the claim for non-pecuniary losses would have been rejected on the application of Maltese law.[217]

5.115 Some of the uncertainties surrounding the exception were considered by the Privy Council in *Red Sea Insurance Co Ltd v Bouygues SA*.[218] In *Boys v Chaplin* the application of the exception led to a segregated issue being governed by English law.[219] In the *Red Sea Insurance* case the central question was whether a defendant can rely solely on the lex loci delicti to establish liability in tort when the lex fori does not recognise such liability. The Privy Council decided that, although the application of the lex loci delicti to the exclusion of the lex fori is a departure from the strict rule in *The Halley*,[220] in principle the exception can be applied in an appropriate case to enable a claimant to rely exclusively on the lex loci delicti.[221] Although the *Red Sea Insurance* case does not directly address the question whether the general rule can be displaced in favour of the law of a country which is neither the forum nor the locus delicti, the logic of the decision is that, in an appropriate case, it can.

5.116 The other question raised by *Red Sea Insurance Co Ltd v Bouygues SA* was whether the whole case, as opposed to an isolated issue, can be governed by the law of the country which has the most significant relationship to the tort, rather than by the general rule. The Privy Council decided that, although the application of the exception to the whole case is not likely to happen very frequently, the exception is not limited to specific isolated issues but may apply to the whole claim (for example, where all or virtually all of the significant factors point towards the locus delicti).[222]

5.117 Although the exception to the double actionability rule is theoretically important, there is no case involving a defamation claim in which the exception has been applied—and it would only be in exceptional circumstances that the court would consider applying it in favour of a law other than English law. One of the rationales for the retention of the common law choice of law rules for defamation claims is English law's interest in protecting free speech (as understood in England) and to protect English publishers against foreign claims which the English legal system does not consider to be legitimate.

5.118 Suppose an English newspaper, which is circulated in countries throughout the world, runs a story alleging that the president of Ruritania has rigged the local parliamentary elections. The president brings proceedings in England alleging libel. Whereas under English law the newspaper may plead justification and fair comment, no such defences are available under Ruritanian law. Under the double actionability rule the newspaper has nothing to fear. Liability cannot be imposed for a tort committed abroad unless the defendant would be liable according to English law; as long as the newspaper has a good defence under English law the libel claim is bound to fail. In view of the policy underlying the retention of the double actionability rule for this kind of case, scope for the application of the common law exception would appear to be very limited indeed.

---

[217] [1971] AC 356 at 379, 382.   [218] [1995] 1 AC 190.
[219] See also *Johnson v Coventry Churchill International Ltd* [1992] 3 All ER 14.
[220] (1868) LR 2 PC 193.   [221] [1995] 1 AC 190 at 206.   [222] At 207.

3. Substance and procedure

5.119 It is a general principle of the conflict of laws that questions of procedure are governed by the law of the forum, regardless of the law governing the substantive dispute between the parties. Historically, the common law has been open to the criticism that it has tended to classify certain matters as procedural, rather than substantive, thereby expanding the sphere of application of the lex fori at the expense of the lex causae.[223] This tendency is most obvious with regard to the classification of rules relating to the quantification of damages.

5.120 The leading common law authority is *Boys v Chaplin*,[224] in which the issue facing the court was whether damages for non-pecuniary losses could be recovered notwithstanding the fact that Maltese law did not award damages for such losses. A minority decided that this central question was a procedural one and was, therefore, governed by English law; the fact that Maltese law did not give damages for pain and suffering and loss of amenity was irrelevant. A majority decided, however, that whether there is recovery for a particular head of damage is a substantive question which has to be decided by reference to the law (or laws) governing the tort. The classification adopted by the majority is clearly correct and has not been seriously questioned.

5.121 This still leaves the question of where exactly the line between substance and procedure is to be drawn. The traditional view reiterated in *Boys v Chaplin* is that questions of pure quantification are to be regarded as procedural and this view, which is contrary to that adopted in the Rome I and II Regulations,[225] was confirmed by the House of Lords in *Harding v Wealands*.[226] Nevertheless, a rule which requires the victim of a tort to mitigate loss is substantive because it determines 'the extent of the loss for which the defendant ought fairly, reasonably or justly to be held liable'.[227]

B Other tortious obligations excluded from the Rome II Regulation: Part III of the Private International Law (Miscellaneous Provisions) Act 1995

1. Background of the statutory rules

5.122 Dissatisfaction with the common law rules prompted a review of choice of law in tort by the Law Commission in the 1980s[228] and led ultimately to the enactment of Part III

---

[223] For example, at common law, rules on the limitation of actions were regarded as procedural. This common law classification was not reversed until the Foreign Limitation Periods Act 1984 (considered in *Re Iraqi Civilian Litigation* [2016] 1 WLR 1290). See also Rome I Regulation, art 12(1)(d); Rome II Regulation, art 15(h).

[224] [1971] AC 356.   [225] See Rome I Regulation, art 12(1)(c); Rome II Regulation, art 15(c).

[226] [2007] 2 AC 1. See also *Maher v Groupama Grand Est* [2010] 1 WLR 1564; *Cox v Ergo Versicherung AG* [2014] AC 1379. Compare the conflicting view of the Court of Appeal in *Harding v Wealands* [2005] 1 WLR 1539. See also the inconsistent decisions of the High Court of Australia: *Stevens v Head* (1993) 176 CLR 433 (procedural); *John Pfeiffer Pty Ltd v Rogerson* (2000) 203 CLR 503 (substantive); *Régie Nationale des Usines Renault SA v Zhang* (2002) 210 CLR 491 (question left open).

[227] Lord Sumption JSC in *Cox v Ergo Versicherung AG* [2014] AC 1379 at [17].

[228] Law Com Working Paper No 87, *Private International Law: Choice of Law in Tort and Delict* (1984); Law Com No 193, *Private International Law: Choice of Law in Tort and Delict* (1990).

of the Private International Law (Miscellaneous Provisions) Act 1995.[229] The essence of the Law Commission's proposals was to replace the double actionability rule with a general rule that the lex loci delicti alone should govern, but to retain an exception to the general rule along the lines of the 'proper law' exception. Following the entry into force of the Rome II Regulation, Part III of the 1995 Act applies only to issues which not only are excluded from the Regulation's scope, but also do not concern defamation (which, as has been seen, is still governed by the common law rules). As the scope of the 1995 Act is very limited, the paragraphs which follow provide only a brief overview of the legislation.

2. The statutory rules

5.123 The choice of law rules set out in the 1995 Act determine the applicable law in relation to 'issues relating to tort'.[230] As regards matters excluded from the Regulation, the 1995 Act applies not only to those areas which are regarded as tortious for the purposes of English domestic law, but also to wrongs which, although they do not give rise to tortious liability under English domestic law, are to be classified as torts for the purposes of the English conflict of laws. The statutory rules ought to apply, for example, to a claim for damages for invasion of privacy,[231] notwithstanding the fact that there is no such tort in English law; the claim is 'tort-like' and it is obviously neither contractual nor founded on unjust enrichment. In addition, Part III of the 1995 Act applies both to torts committed abroad and to torts committed in England.[232]

5.124 Under the 1995 Act the general rule is to be found in section 11. This provision draws a distinction between cases in which the events constituting the tort occur in a single country and cases in which those events occur in two or more countries. In effect, though not in form, the general rule in section 11 is that, under the 1995 Act, a tort is governed by the lex loci delicti.[233]

5.125 The simplest situation is where the events constituting a tort occur in a single country. In this case the applicable law under the general rule is the law of that country.[234] In situations where elements of the events constituting the tort occur in different countries, the 1995 Act adopts different approaches to different types of claim. With regard to cases involving personal injury or property damage, the general rule takes the same

---

[229] See Briggs, 'Choice of Law in Tort and Delict' [1995] LMCLQ 519; Morse, 'Torts in Private International Law: A New Statutory Framework' (1996) 45 ICLQ 888.
[230] S 9(1).
[231] Such a claim is excluded from the Rome II Regulation by art 1(2)(g) and, as it does not concern defamation, it is not governed by the common law.
[232] See *Roerig v Valiant Trawlers Ltd* [2002] 1 WLR 2304.
[233] Like the Rome II Regulation, the 1995 Act excludes the operation of the doctrine of renvoi: s 9(5). Compare *Neilson v Overseas Projects Corporation of Victoria Ltd* (2005) 221 ALR 213, in which the High Court of Australia accepted the availability of renvoi in the case of an international tort.
[234] S 11(1). See *Glencore International AG v Metro Trading International Inc* [2001] 1 Lloyd's Rep 284 (an interference with goods case); *Hulse v Chambers* [2001] 1 WLR 386; *Roerig v Valiant Trawlers Ltd* [2002] 1 WLR 2304; *Bristow Helicopters Ltd v Sikorsky Aircraft Corporation* [2004] 2 Lloyd's Rep 150.

approach as that adopted by article 4(1) of the Rome II Regulation: the applicable law is the law of the country where the victim was when he sustained the injury[235] or the law of the country where the property was located when it was damaged.[236] By contrast, in other cases, the applicable law under the general rule is 'the law of the country in which the most significant element or elements of [the events constituting the tort] occurred'.[237]

5.126 The general rules in section 11 are subject to an exception in section 12 which, although drafted in a rather complex way, has the effect that the applicable law under the general rule may be displaced by the law of another country if it would be substantially more appropriate to apply the law of that other country; in effect, section 12 applies if the tort is substantially more closely connected with a country other than that identified by section 11. Although this exception is flexible and potentially far-reaching—in the sense that it can apply to an issue or a number of issues arising out of a tortious situation or to the whole claim—in practice, if the exception is invoked, the decision facing the court is normally whether the lex loci delicti or the lex fori is the most appropriate law.

5.127 The inherent flexibility of section 12 makes it impossible to lay down hard-and-fast rules about its application. Nevertheless, the law applicable under the general rule is most likely to be displaced either where both parties are foreigners to the country where the tort is committed and come from the same country[238] or where both parties are foreigners to the country where the tort is committed and, although they belong to different countries, the relevant rules of their countries are the same on the issue in question. If one of the parties is closely connected with the country in which the tort is committed it is difficult to envisage circumstances in which it is substantially more appropriate to apply the law of another country.[239] If the circumstances surrounding the tort have connections with several countries, there is no plausible argument for the exception displacing the general rule.[240]

VII The interaction of non-contractual obligations and contractual obligations

5.128 There are cases in which questions of both non-contractual and other obligations may arise. For example, the claimant may argue that the defendant's conduct amounts to more than one type of wrong—such as both a breach of contract and a tort or a breach of fiduciary duty as well as a breach of contract. Another type of case is where a defendant seeks to rely on a foreign contract as a defence to a tort alleged to have

---

[235] S 11(2)(a). [236] S 11(2)(b). [237] S 11(2)(c).
[238] *Edmunds v Simmonds* [2001] 1 WLR 1003.
[239] *Harding v Wealands* [2007] 2 AC 1; *Donkers v Storm Aviation Ltd* [2015] 1 All ER (Comm) 282.
[240] *Anton Durbeck GmbH v Den Norske Bank* [2006] 1 Lloyd's Rep 93.

been committed either in England or abroad. In *Galaxias Steamship Co Ltd v Panagos Christofis*[241] the defendants were employed under a contract of employment governed by Greek law to work on a ship belonging to the plaintiff. While the ship was in England, the plaintiff purported to terminate their contract of employment. When the defendants refused to leave the ship, the plaintiff sued them for trespass. The defendants argued that, as a consequence of the fact that the contract of employment had not been validly terminated, they were entitled to remain on the ship. To succeed in the action for trespass, the plaintiff had to establish that the defendants' continued occupation of the ship was unlawful. The plaintiff's claim in tort, which was governed by English law, was bound to fail if the plaintiff's purported termination of the contract was not effective under Greek law, the law governing the contract. The court held that, since according to Greek law the contract had been validly brought to an end, the defendants were trespassers. This type of case is relatively straightforward since the tort question and the contract question can be segregated and the relevant choice of law rules applied to each question.

5.129 More problematical are cases in which questions of tort and contract interact. The defendant to a tort claim may, for example, set up as a defence a clause in a contract which exempts him from the liability in question. In *Sayers v International Drilling Co NV*,[242] one of the few English cases in which the interaction of contract and tort choice of law rules has arisen, the plaintiff, an English resident, and the defendant, a Dutch company, entered into a contract of employment under which the plaintiff was to work on an oil rig in Nigerian territorial waters. The contract contained a clause exempting the company from liability for any injury which the plaintiff might suffer in the course of his employment. This exemption clause was valid by Dutch law, but was rendered void in English law by section 1(3) of the Law Reform (Personal Injuries) Act 1948. There was no evidence of Nigerian law on the point. The plaintiff was injured in the course of his employment and sued the defendant in tort in England. The defendant sought to rely on the exemption clause in the contract.

5.130 The first question in this type of case is whether the claimant is able to advance his claim in contract and/or tort. As regards jurisdiction under the Brussels I Recast, article 7(1) and article 7(2) are mutually exclusive. A claim involves either matters relating to a contract or matters relating to tort (or neither); claims cannot fall within both categories and the claimant is not able to formulate his claim (as either contractual or tortious) so as to take advantage of whichever of the jurisdiction rules seems most advantageous to him.[243] There is an argument in favour of taking the same approach to choice of law questions. It would, in theory, have been possible for the Rome I and Rome II Regulations to have been mutually exclusive and for their respective spheres of operation (namely, contractual obligations and non-contractual

---

[241] (1948) 81 Ll L Rep 499. See North, 'Contract as a Tort Defence in the Conflict of Laws' (1977) 26 ICLQ 914, 915–16.
[242] [1971] 1 WLR 1176.   [243] See para 2.67.

obligations) to have been determined by the pan-European criteria which draw the demarcation between article 7(1) and article 7(2) of the Brussels I Recast. Under this approach, the nature of the claim would be classified by reference to the European criteria and the claim would succeed or fail under the applicable law as determined by Rome I or Rome II, as the case may be.

5.131 However attractive this solution might appear in theory, it is not the one adopted by the Regulations. It is clear that the Rome II Regulation envisages situations arising in which, although there is a contractual relationship between the parties, the claimant is able to advance a claim for breach of a tortious (or other non-contractual) obligation and the law applicable to the claim will be determined by reference to the choice of law rules which govern non-contractual obligations.[244] It follows that, assuming that the law of the forum allows the claimant to advance claims with alternative legal bases, even though they rely on the same set of facts, a claimant may, in appropriate circumstances, advance parallel claims in contract and tort. It was always assumed in England that this was the position at common law,[245] and the traditional understanding was endorsed by the Court of Appeal in *Base Metal Trading Ltd v Shamurin*,[246] a case decided before the enactment of the Rome II Regulation. The Court of Appeal held that English conflict of laws (as well as English domestic law) allows concurrent actions in contract, tort, and breach of equitable duty. There is no reason to think that the basic analysis adopted in this case has ceased to be applicable following the entry into force of the Rome I and II Regulations. It follows that, as far as the English court is concerned, a claimant who has concurrent claims in contract and tort has an unrestricted choice to rely on any way of presenting his case with a view to maximising his chances of success through the application of the most advantageous choice of law rules.

5.132 How, therefore, should a case like *Sayers* be dealt with under the Rome Regulations? There are two issues to be considered: one is the validity of the exclusion clause; the other is the effect of the clause as a defence to a claim in tort. If the contractual exclusion clause is invalid under the law applicable to the contract, there is no reason why it should be given any effect, regardless of the clause's effect according to the law governing the tort. If, however, the clause is valid according to its applicable law, it should be for the law applicable to the tort to determine whether the exclusion clause is an effective defence to the claim in tort. Assuming the exclusion clause to be valid according to the law governing the contract, if the exemption clause affords a good defence under the law applicable to the tort the claim should fail; if, however, the exemption clause does not provide a defence under the law governing the tort the claim should succeed.

---

[244] See, in particular, art 4(3).
[245] See, eg, *Coupland v Arabian Gulf Oil Co* [1983] 1 WLR 1136.
[246] [2005] 1 WLR 1157 (in which the court rejected the argument of Briggs, 'Choice of Choice of Law?' [2003] LMCLQ 12).

5.133 In *Sayers v International Drilling Co NV* the majority of the Court of Appeal seemed to assume that, if the exclusion clause were valid under the law governing the contract, that was the end of the matter; the claim failed. The majority simply decided that Dutch law (under which the exemption clause was valid) was the law governing the contract and that, therefore, the defendant was not liable;[247] no reference at all was made by the majority to the choice of law rules for tort, even though the action was brought in tort. In a minority judgment which is not always easy to follow, Lord Denning MR decided that the contract was governed by English law, that Dutch law was the law applicable to the tort and that Dutch law should determine the issue whether the exemption clause was a defence to the action in tort.

5.134 At common law, there are a few cases which proceed on the basis that the law governing the tort may be different from the law governing the contract, especially when the law governing the contract is chosen by the parties and, in objective terms, has little connection with the tort. In *Brodin v A/R Seljan*,[248] a Scottish case, the pursuer's husband (X) was employed to work on a ship belonging to the defender, a Norwegian company, under a contract of employment which was governed by Norwegian law. X was killed in an accident which took place on the ship while it was in Scottish waters. When the pursuer brought proceedings in Scotland, alleging that the accident was caused by the defender's negligence, the defender sought to rely on an exclusion clause in the contract of employment. Although the clause was valid under Norwegian law, the court held that the clause was not effective to exclude the defender's liability in tort; under Scots law the exclusion of liability was void by virtue of section 1(3) of the Law Reform (Personal Injuries) Act 1948 and Scots law, as the law governing the tort, prevailed over the law governing the contract.[249]

5.135 Under the Rome Regulations it seems unlikely that this case would be decided in the same way; at any rate, the analysis would be different. On the facts of *Brodin v Seljan*, the law applicable to the tort under the Rome II Regulation would be determined by article 4. According to article 4(1), Scots law would prima facie be the governing law. However, article 4(3) provides that where a tort is manifestly more closely connected with another country, the law of that other country applies; for the purpose of this rule, a manifestly closer connection with another country might be based on a pre-existing relationship between the parties, such as a contract that is closely connected with the tort in question. In *Brodin*'s case, there can be little doubt that the pre-existing contractual relationship between X and the defender was closely connected with the tort; without the contract of employment, the tort would not have taken place. So, under

---

[247] See also *Coupland v Arabian Gulf Oil Co* [1983] 1 WLR 1136. Although in this case Robert Goff LJ might be thought to lend some support to the majority view in the *Sayers* case (at 1153), the case is weak authority; any discussion of the relationship between contract and tort was obiter as, on the facts of the case, there was no contractual defence available to the defendant.

[248] 1973 SLT 198.

[249] See also the similar analysis (albeit leading on the facts to the opposite conclusion) in *Canadian Pacific Rly Co v Parent* [1917] AC 195.

the Rome II Regulation, the arguments in favour of the tort being governed by the law applicable to the contract are very strong. As a result, prima facie the defendant would not be liable, regardless of whether the claim was advanced in contract or tort.

5.136 However, both of the Rome Regulations balance the applicable law against the mandatory provisions of other legal systems which have a close connection with the situation. It is important not to forget that, in cases involving consumers and employees, the Rome I Regulation seeks to limit the effect of a choice of law so as not to deprive the weaker party of the legal protection to which he might reasonably expect to be entitled. As regards contracts of employment, a choice of law cannot have the effect of depriving the employee of the protection of the provisions which cannot be derogated from by agreement under the law which would have been applicable in the absence of choice.[250] Suppose that the place where X habitually worked could not be determined, but that the place of business through which X had been engaged was in Scotland. In such circumstances, in the absence of a choice of law in the contract, Scots law would have been the applicable law;[251] as a result, section 1(3) of the Law Reform (Personal Injuries) Act 1948 would have applied as a provision which could not be derogated from by contract. If, however, X did not habitually work in Scotland and had not been recruited through a place of business in Scotland, section 1(3) of the 1948 Act would apply to defeat the defence based on the contractual exclusion clause only if that section were an overriding mandatory provision for the purposes of article 9(2) of the Rome I Regulation (if the claim were brought for breach of contract) or for the purposes of article 16 of the Rome II Regulation (if the claim were in tort). The analysis in the *Sayers* case indicates that section 1(3) of the 1948 Act is not an overriding mandatory provision (otherwise the majority could not have decided that the validity of the exclusion clause under Dutch law was a complete answer to the plaintiff's claim). As a consequence, in *Brodin*'s case unless Scots law were the law which would have governed the contract of employment in the absence of choice, any claim in contract would fail. The position would be the same if the claim were based on tort; if article 4(3) leads to the conclusion that the law governing the contract (Norwegian law) is also the law applicable to the tort, success of the tort claim would depend on the defence under the exclusion clause being defeated (by virtue of section 1(3) of the 1948 Act being an overriding mandatory provision of the law of the forum for the purposes of article 16 of the Rome II Regulation).

5.137 As this analysis of *Brodin v Seljan* shows, the significant change brought about by the Rome Regulations is not to prevent a claimant from bringing parallel claims in contract and tort (if that is permitted according to the procedural law of the forum), but to bring the law governing the contract and the law governing the tort into alignment in such cases. In a case like *Brodin*, it is only possible for a claim in tort to succeed—when a parallel claim in contract fails—if the choice of law rules lead to the law governing the tort being different from the law applicable to the contract. Article 4(3) of the Rome II

---

[250] Rome I Regulation, art 8(1). [251] Rome I Regulation, art 8(2).

Regulation reduces the chance of the law governing a tort and the law applicable to a contract between the parties diverging; it does not, however, eliminate the possibility: 'the law applicable to the pre-existing relationship does not apply automatically, and the court enjoys a degree of discretion to decide whether there is a significant connection between the non-contractual obligations and the law applicable to the pre-existing relationship.'[252] So, even though, where there is a contractual relationship between the parties, there is a natural tendency for the court to want also to apply the law which governs the contract to any parallel tortious claim,[253] it is possible for a court to follow the analysis in *Brodin v Seljan* in a case where, under the Rome II Regulation, the law governing the tort is not the same as the law applicable to the parties' contractual relationship.

---

[252] European Commission, *Rome II Proposal*, COM (2003) 427 final, p 12.

[253] *Middle Eastern Oil LLC v National Bank of Abu Dhabi* [2009] 1 Lloyd's Rep 251; *Trafigura Beheer BV v Kookmin Bank Co* [2006] 2 Lloyd's Rep 455 (both cases decided under the Private International Law (Miscellaneous Provisions) Act 1995). Compare *Morin v Bonhams & Brooks Ltd* [2004] 1 Lloyd's Rep 702 (in which the issue was left open).

6

Domicile, nationality, and habitual residence

I Introduction

6.1 In previous chapters it has been seen that the object of jurisdictional rules is to determine an appropriate forum and that choice of law rules are designed to lead to the application of the most appropriate law, the law that generally the parties might reasonably expect to apply. The test for recognition of foreign judgments is not dissimilar. A judgment granted by an appropriate forum should normally be recognised. The problem is one of ascertaining the connecting factor (or factors) which would best satisfy the criterion of appropriateness.

6.2 The test of appropriateness, and therefore the required link with a country, varies in different areas of law. For example, in the fields of status, marriage, and succession the traditional view is that a much closer connection between a person and a country is required than in the commercial sphere. Laws on marriage and the family are intimately connected with the culture and the moral standards of the community. However, even in these personal areas of law, the test of appropriateness will vary depending on the purpose for which the connecting factor is being employed. The policy considerations underlying jurisdictional, choice of law, and recognition rules are somewhat different and, accordingly, different, or a different range of, connecting factors might be appropriate for each purpose. With regard to jurisdiction, the rules are designed to ensure that England is an appropriate forum. For example, England has a legitimate interest in facilitating divorce for those who reside in England (even if only for the medium term) because financial and custody arrangements can have an impact upon British society. However, this does not mean that only current residents should be afforded access to the English courts for this purpose. Where English spouses are residing elsewhere but intend ultimately to return to England, English law has an interest in their marriage and its dissolution and the consequences that flow from a divorce decree. Accordingly, the connecting factor or factors utilised for jurisdiction in divorce cases need to be flexible enough to encompass all such persons. Similar considerations apply to connecting factors employed for recognition of foreign personal judgments, such as divorce decrees. If English law deems certain connecting factors to be appropriate for founding English jurisdiction, arguably it should be prepared to recognise foreign decrees in similar circumstances. Indeed, one could adopt an even broader range of connecting factors for purposes of recognition than for jurisdiction so that recognition would be given in any case where the parties had some legitimate connection with the country in which the judgment was obtained. Such flexibility is desirable in so far as questions of recognition, by their nature, arise after the event, often many years after the grant of the foreign divorce.

6.3 In contrast, with regard to choice of law in the fields of marriage and succession, the prevailing view has been that the applicable law should be the law of the country with which the parties have a substantial connection, on the basis that people should be subject to the law of the country to which they primarily belong. This law is known as the personal law. Wherever a person goes in the world this personal law accompanies him and governs his status and personal relationships. Thus, if a man's personal law is English, he cannot go to Saudi Arabia and contract a polygamous marriage there which is valid in the eyes of English law. English law, which does not permit polygamous marriages, will continue to be applicable. However, even with regard to choice of law, different degrees of connection might be appropriate for different areas affected by the personal law. For example, in relation to the formal validity of wills, policy considerations in favour of upholding the validity of wills militate against insisting on compliance with the law of the country to which a person most closely belongs. In respect of such matters, a more flexible approach is appropriate and a wider range of connecting factors can be employed.

6.4 Bearing in mind these different purposes for which personal connecting factors are used, it is hardly surprising that there is little international agreement as to the appropriate test of 'belonging'. In England and most common law countries, the traditional personal connecting factor is *domicile*, which loosely translates as a person's permanent home. One of the problems here is that domicile is a connecting factor which is interpreted differently in various parts of the world. In the United States, for instance, domicile is given a significantly different meaning from that ascribed by English law. In contrast, most of continental Europe and other civil law countries have traditionally used *nationality* as the basic connecting factor, especially for choice of law purposes; the personal law is the law of the country of which the person is a citizen. An alternative approach for choice of law is adopted in yet other countries where the personal law is based on *adherence to a particular religion*. In these countries what matters is whether one is a Muslim, Hindu, or Christian. In Pakistan, for example, the marriage laws of these various religions apply in determining validity of marriage. Finally, in some countries, including England, another connecting factor, *habitual residence*, has emerged. This is increasingly being used for the purposes of jurisdiction rules and in the law relating to recognition of foreign judgments. As has been seen, habitual residence also plays a prominent role in choice of law for tort and contract. It is also used for other choice of law rules, for example, in relation to the formal validity of wills.

6.5 Each of these personal connecting factors will be examined. Primary emphasis is laid on domicile and habitual residence as the two main connecting factors employed by English law.

II Domicile: introduction

A A variable meaning

6.6 While it has been stated by the House of Lords that domicile has 'the same meaning in whatever context it arises',[1] in reality the term 'domicile' has a variable meaning in English law and, indeed, within the conflict of laws. The traditional concept that is discussed in this chapter has a relatively long history, but it was during the Victorian era that it developed most of its essential characteristics. However, the use of domicile is not restricted to the conflict of laws; it is also employed in tax law where it generally bears the same meaning.[2] Indeed, several of the leading authorities on the meaning of 'domicile' are, in fact, tax cases. This is somewhat regrettable and has perhaps impeded the rational development of the concept for conflict of laws purposes. When significant reforms to the law of domicile were proposed in the Domicile Bills of 1958 and 1959, it was concern over the tax implications that led to abandonment of the proposed reforms.

6.7 Further problems resulted from developments at the European level in the field of jurisdiction and the recognition of judgments in civil and commercial matters. The Brussels I Recast,[3] dealing with civil and commercial matters, utilises the continental concept of 'domicile', which is markedly different from the traditional English one. It might have been preferable, and less confusing, if the connecting factor used by the Brussels I Recast had been given a different name. Domicile for the purposes of the Brussels I Recast is discussed in Chapter 2. This chapter is concerned only with the traditional concept as employed mainly in the fields of family law and succession. The reader must always be alert as to which conception of domicile is being used.

B General principles

6.8 In broad terms, domicile means 'permanent home'. The general rationale for the use of this connecting factor is that people are deemed to 'belong' to the community in which they have made their home. This is their 'centre of gravity'.[4] As permanent members of a community it is only right that its laws be applied to them. Further, domicile is supported as a connecting factor on the ground that it allows respect to be shown to the freedom of individuals, who can choose where they wish to live and, thus, indirectly, the law to which they are to be subject.

6.9 There are three kinds of domicile: domicile of origin, domicile of dependence, and domicile of choice. At any given time, a person's domicile will be one of these. The *domicile of origin* is the domicile which a person obtains at birth. A *domicile of dependence* is the domicile which a dependent person, such as a child, has by virtue of being

---

[1] *Mark v Mark* [2006] 1 AC 98 at [37].
[2] There are some statutory modifications which are limited to the field of tax. See, eg, Inheritance Tax Act 1984, s 267.
[3] Regulation (EU) No 1215/2012. See Chapter 2.   [4] *Re Flynn* [1968] 1 All ER 49.

dependent on another person. A *domicile of choice* is a domicile which an independent person acquires by residing in a country with the intention of settling there permanently or indefinitely.

6.10 Several general introductory points in relation to the law of domicile need to be made.

1. Only one domicile

6.11 Because so many important areas of law are governed by the law of domicile, every person must have a domicile, and only one domicile. A person could not have two competing laws governing the same status or relationship. However, in reality, there are some people who might not actually have a home anywhere or who might have more than one home. In order to ensure that a domicile, and only one domicile, is attributed to all such people, detailed rules have been developed. As shall be seen, these rules are structured in such a way that a domicile can always be assigned to every person.

6.12 The rule that a person cannot have two domiciles is perhaps an oversimplification. It would be more accurate to say that one cannot have more than one domicile for the same purpose. It has already been seen that a country for the purposes of the conflict of laws is a law district, a territorial unit having a separate legal system, which may for political purposes be part of a larger political state.[5] It is normally the law district, not the composite state, in which a person is domiciled. For the purposes of the conflict of laws, a person is domiciled in England, Scotland, or Northern Ireland, not in the United Kingdom as a whole. However, there are some statutory exceptions to this orthodoxy. For example, under section 54(4)(b) of the Human Fertilisation and Embryology Act 2008 either one or both of the applicants for a parental order (in respect of a child born through surrogacy) must be 'domiciled in the United Kingdom'.[6] Also some federal states, such as Australia,[7] have introduced statutory rules according to which, for the purpose of matrimonial proceedings, a person can be domiciled in the federal state. Thus, for the purposes of divorce a person can be domiciled in Australia while being domiciled in, say, Queensland for other purposes.

6.13 While, apart from the above exception, a person can have only one operative domicile and while it has been stressed that domicile should bear the same meaning in all contexts,[8] the way in which the court applies the rules—and the conclusion which it reaches—may be coloured by the context in which the question of a person's domicile arises.[9] For example, in *Ramsay v Liverpool Royal Infirmary*[10] George Bowie left Scotland, where he was domiciled, and moved to Liverpool where he lived for the last 36 years of his life, sponging off his brother and sister. During that whole period he

---

[5] See para 1.10.
[6] Also for tax purposes one can be domiciled in the United Kingdom. See, eg, Inheritance Tax Act 1984, s 267.
[7] Australian Family Law Act 1975, s 39(3); *Lloyd v Lloyd* [1962] VR 70.
[8] *Mark v Mark* [2006] 1 AC 98.
[9] Cook, *The Logical and Legal Bases of the Conflict of Laws* (1942); Fawcett, 'Result Selection in Domicile Cases' (1985) 5 OJLS 378.
[10] [1930] AC 588.

never set foot in Scotland. The House of Lords concluded that Bowie was still domiciled in Scotland at the date of his death. However, it is relevant to note that the issue before the court was the formal validity of Bowie's will and that, by holding him domiciled in Scotland, the court was able to uphold the validity of his will. Had the court concluded that he was domiciled in England, the will would have been invalid. It seems likely that the nature of the issue before the court strongly influenced the court's interpretation of the rules on domicile. If the issue had been the capacity of Bowie to marry or a question of domicile for the purpose of taxation, it is quite possible that the court would have concluded that he was domiciled in England. 'Result selection' would also appear to be in evidence in the English courts' handling of applications for parental orders in respect of children born through surrogacy overseas. As indicated above, it is formally necessary for one of the applicants to prove a domicile in the United Kingdom; however, in their concern to regularise the status of such children, it appears that the courts will readily accept that foreign applicants living in the United Kingdom have acquired a British domicile of choice,[11] and that British applicants have retained their domicile of origin even if they have been living abroad for many years.[12] The forensic scrutiny of life patterns, so typical of other litigation concerned with domicile, is notably absent in these cases.

2. 'Domicile' according to the lex fori

6.14 English courts will normally apply their own rules of domicile to determine where a person is domiciled.[13] The connecting factor, domicile, must be construed according to English law, the lex fori. There is one statutory exception to this rule. Under section 46(1) of the Family Law Act 1986 a foreign divorce (or other matrimonial decree) is entitled to recognition on the basis that one of the parties is domiciled in the country where the judgment is obtained. For the purpose of this rule, according to section 46(5), domicile may mean either domicile according to English law or domicile according to the law of the country in which the divorce was obtained.

6.15 While domicile must normally be determined according to English law, if this results in a reference to a country where the law is not territorially based it is necessary to adopt that country's criterion of the personal law to lead to the applicable law. For instance, in determining the essential validity of a marriage, English choice of law rules will normally lead to the parties' domiciliary law. If one is dealing with a country such as Pakistan where the personal law is based on adherence to a religion, there is no such thing as a general Pakistani law of marriage. The solution to this problem is that having used the English concept of domicile and having been referred to the law of Pakistan, one then has to adopt the Pakistani test of the personal law which will refer to the appropriate religious law. This is not really an exception to the proposition that domicile

---

[11] See, eg, *Re A and B (Parental Order: Domicile)* [2014] 1 FLR 169; *Re W* [2013] EWHC 3570 (Fam); *Re G and M* [2014] EWHC 1561 (Fam).
[12] See, eg, *CC v DD* [2014] EWHC 1307 (Fam); *Re A (Foreign Surrogacy: South Africa)* [2015] EWHC 1756 (Fam).
[13] *Re Annesley* [1926] Ch 692; *Chandler v Chandler* [2011] EWCA Civ 143 at [4].

must be construed according to English law. One is utilising the English concept of domicile and then applying 'Pakistani law'. It just so happens that Pakistani law in this case will mean one of a number of religious laws and Pakistani law indicates which religious law is, in the circumstances, the relevant law.

3. Presumption in favour of existing domicile

6.16 There is a presumption in favour of the continuance of an existing domicile. The burden of proving a change of domicile lies on the person alleging the change.[14] While the standard adopted is the normal civil one of proof on a balance of probabilities, it is often stated that a higher standard is required when alleging that a domicile of origin has been lost.[15] This point is elaborated in the next section.

III Species of domicile

A Domicile of origin

1. Bases of attribution

6.17 The domicile which a person acquires at birth is called the domicile of origin. Apart from the exceptional case of the foundling whose domicile of origin is assumed to be the place where he was found,[16] the domicile of origin is conferred on the basis of parentage. Accordingly, in most cases it does not matter where a child is born. The domicile of origin reflects the domicile of the parents at the date of the child's birth. The common law view is that if the child is legitimate and born during the lifetime of the father, the child's domicile of origin is the father's domicile at the time of the child's birth;[17] if the child is illegitimate, the child's domicile of origin is the mother's domicile at the time of the child's birth.[18] The domicile of origin acquired at birth does not change unless the child is the subject of an adoption or parental order. Where a child is adopted, or a parental order is made in respect of a child born through surrogacy, statute provides that the child is treated in law as if the child of the adopting or commissioning parents[19] and the child's domicile of origin is assumed to be adjusted accordingly.[20]

6.18 The common law rules on domicile of origin are archaic and unsatisfactory. First, the rule that domicile depends on legitimacy overlooks the fact that, in many cases, legitimacy depends upon domicile. One cannot ascertain whether a child is legitimate until one has established the child's domicile, but the domicile cannot be established until

---

[14] *Winans v A-G* [1904] AC 287; *Re Fuld's Estate (No 3)* [1968] P 675.
[15] *Henderson v Henderson* [1967] P 77.
[16] *Re McKenzie* (1951) 51 SRNSW 293 (illegitimate child whose mother's domicile was unknown was treated as found in the child's country of birth and therefore having a domicile of origin there).
[17] *Udny v Udny* (1869) LR 1 Sc & Div 441 at 457; *Henderson v Henderson* [1967] P 77.
[18] *Udny v Udny* (1869) LR 1 Sc & Div 441 at 457; *Henderson v Henderson* [1967] P 77.
[19] Adoption and Children Act 2002, s 67(1); Human Fertilisation and Embryology Act 2008, s 54(1).
[20] Dicey, Morris and Collins, *The Conflict of Laws* (15th edn, 2012) p 141.

the question of legitimacy has been resolved. As there is no logical way out of this impasse, perhaps the best solution would be to regard the child as legitimate if he or she is so regarded by the law of either parent's domicile. However, authority favours the application of the father's domiciliary law at the date of the child's birth.[21] Secondly, there is no longer any rational basis for the rule that a legitimate child takes the domicile of the father. The historical explanation for this rule was that, on marriage, a woman took her husband's domicile as a domicile of dependence. This rule was abolished in the 1970s largely because of its discriminatory character. To abolish the basic rule but allow its consequences to continue makes little sense. Thirdly, as shall be seen, when parents are living apart, children take the domicile of the parent with whom they have a home.[22] If a married mother and father are living apart when their child is born and the child lives with the mother, it makes little sense to assert that the child takes the domicile of origin of the father which could then instantly be replaced by a domicile of dependence on the mother. Finally, the existing common law rules provide no clear guidance as to the basis for attributing domicile of origin where a child is adopted by a same-sex couple, or where a parental order is made in favour of a same-sex couple,[23] or where a child is born to a woman in a same-sex marriage or civil partnership.[24] The common law rules assume that the parents of a legitimate child are not of the same gender and provide no answer to the question of how the domicile of origin should be determined in these situations.

6.19 In view of all of these objections there is a strong case for a substantial overhaul of these rules. In the 1980s the Law Commission proposed that dependent children should be regarded as domiciled in the country with which they are most closely connected.[25] If the concept of domicile of origin is to be retained[26] there should be a coincidence of domicile of origin and dependence at birth and the Law Commission's proposals should be followed.

2. **Tenacity**

6.20 A distinctive feature of the domicile of origin is that it has traditionally been regarded as more difficult to lose than any other form of domicile because a domicile of origin is generally 'associated with a person's native character'.[27] The burden of proof in such cases was until recently said to go 'beyond a mere balance of probabilities'.[28] For

---

[21] *Re Bischoffsheim* [1948] Ch 79; *Hashmi v Hashmi* [1972] Fam 36.
[22] Domicile and Matrimonial Proceedings Act 1973, s 4(2).
[23] The child who is the subject of an adoption order or a parental order is considered the legitimate child of the adoptive or commissioning parents: Adoption and Children Act 2002, s 67(2); Human Fertilisation and Embryology (Parental Orders) Regulations 2010, SI 2010/985, sch 1.
[24] Under s 42 of the Human Fertilisation and Embryology Act 2008 the civil partner or female spouse of a woman giving birth to a child is deemed to be the child's parent. Under s 48(6), such child 'is the legitimate child of the child's parents'. See further para 6.30.
[25] Law Com No 168, paras 4.13–4.20. Several rebuttable presumptions for determining this country of closest connection are suggested. See para 6.32.
[26] See para 6.25.
[27] *Henwood v Barlow Clowes International Ltd* [2008] EWCA Civ 577.
[28] *Henderson v Henderson* [1967] P 77 at 80; *R v R (Divorce: Jurisdiction: Domicile)* [2006] 1 FLR 389.

example, in *Ramsay v Liverpool Royal Infirmary*[29] it was held that a Scottish domicile of origin had not been lost despite the fact that the propositus (as the person whose domicile is in question is referred to) had lived in England for the last 36 years of his life without expressing any intention of returning to Scotland and despite even having made arrangements to be buried in England. In *Winans v A-G*[30] it was similarly held that a man who resided primarily in England for the last 37 years of his life had not lost his domicile of origin despite not having visited that place for the last 47 years of his life. In *IRC v Bullock*[31] a man who had lived in England for the previous 44 years was also held not to have abandoned his domicile of origin. Later cases have endorsed this approach. In *R v R (Divorce: Jurisdiction: Domicile)* it was emphasised that the standard of proof required to establish loss of a domicile of origin was a heavy one.[32] In *Cyganik v Agulian*[33] it was held that the burden of proof on losing a domicile of origin is heavier than the burden on losing a domicile of choice. This led the Court of Appeal to conclude that a man who had lived and worked in England for the last 43 years of his life had not lost his domicile of origin in Cyprus.

6.21 When one recalls that domicile is meant to indicate a person's permanent home, this excessive importance attached to a domicile of origin can only be regarded as out of touch with today's realities, when people are far more mobile and establish permanent homes in new countries with greater ease and readiness than in the mid-Victorian era when the common law rules were developed.[34] Unsurprisingly, the Law Commission recommended that there should be no 'special tenacity' given to the domicile of origin, and some modern cases have been more willing to allow a domicile of origin to be replaced by a domicile of choice.[35] In *Brown v Brown*, for example, it was emphasised that there is 'no warrant for ... using the words "heavy burden"'.[36] In *Henwood v Barlow Clowes International Ltd*,[37] the *Cyganik* case was expressly disapproved; the normal civil burden of balance of probabilities applies. The acquisition of a new domicile should 'in general always be treated as a serious allegation'[38] and 'the more serious an allegation the more substantial will need to be the evidence to prove it on a balance of probabilities'.[39] However, where the domicile of origin is only operative under the 'default rule' (that the domicile of origin revives when a domicile of choice is abandoned) there was no need for 'evidence to meet a more serious case'.[40] In short, it is easier to satisfy the balance of probabilities test when displacing a revived domicile of origin than when the person's domicile of origin has not previously been replaced by a domicile of choice.

3. Revival

6.22 A further distinctive feature of the domicile of origin is that, while it can be replaced by a different domicile of dependence or choice, it is never totally lost, but rather held in

---

[29] [1930] AC 588. [30] [1904] AC 287. [31] [1976] 3 All ER 353.
[32] [2006] 1 FLR 389 at 398. [33] [2006] 1 FCR 406. [34] Law Com No 168, para 4.24.
[35] For example, *Sekhri v Ray* [2014] 1 FLR 612 (affirmed on appeal: [2014] 2 FLR 1168); *Perdoni v Curati* [2012] WTLR 505.
[36] [1981] 3 FLR 212 at 218. [37] [2008] EWCA Civ 577. [38] At [94].
[39] At [88]. [40] At [95].

abeyance. If a domicile of choice is abandoned without being replaced by a new domicile of choice, then the domicile of origin revives. In fact, this revival rule (described in *Henwood v Barlow Clowes International Ltd* as a 'default rule'[41]) is the only reason why the concept of domicile of origin is needed; apart from that, the domicile of a child at birth could be a domicile of dependence, just as it is thereafter until the age of 16.[42]

6.23 The rule that a domicile of choice can be abandoned without a new one being acquired, the domicile of origin reviving to fill the gap, was settled by the House of Lords in 1869 in *Udny v Udny*.[43] A more recent example is *Henwood v Barlow Clowes International Ltd*. In this case a man had a domicile of origin in England. He disliked England intensely and in 1975 moved to the Isle of Man where he acquired a domicile. In 1992, because of the collapse of his business, he was ostracised and felt forced to leave. Thereafter he spent most of his time in a house he bought in France and in a rented villa in Mauritius. It was held that he lost his domicile of choice in the Isle of Man when he left. There was insufficient evidence that he had acquired a domicile of choice in either France or Mauritius. Accordingly, his English domicile of origin revived and he was held to be domiciled in the one country where it was clear he was never going to live, having 'formed an aversion to living in the United Kingdom as the result of his tragic early life history'.[44]

6.24 This revival of the domicile of origin rule, conceived and developed in Victorian England, assumes that, if ever a person ceases to have a permanent home, the most appropriate personal law to allocate to him is the law of the original native home. Rather like elephants who allegedly return to their birthplace to die, British colonists, for whom these rules were primarily designed, would naturally return to Britain to see out their final days. These rules were designed for the class of person who might have an ancestral home to which they would long feel a commitment.[45] However, in the more migratory modern world it would normally be more sensible to attribute to a person the law of the country which was most recently the home, rather than that of a country which has been abandoned, perhaps very many years previously. A person may have few or no connections with the domicile of origin, and even may never have been there. Suppose the propositus is born in Ontario when his father, domiciled in England, is working temporarily in Canada. After his birth his father decides to settle in Ontario permanently. Although the propositus has a domicile of dependence in Ontario, his domicile of origin is still English. If in later life he leaves Ontario for good, but dies before settling in another country, the succession to his movable estate will be governed by English law—rather than the law of Ontario—even though he may never have set foot in England, and until shortly before his death had lived his whole life in Ontario.

---

[41] [2008] EWCA Civ 577 at [21].   [42] See paras 6.27–6.30.
[43] (1869) LR 1 Sc & Div 441.   [44] [2008] EWCA Civ 577 at [46].
[45] It has been suggested that the rules on revival of the domicile of origin were developed as a response to the growing rise and popularity of nationality in the middle of the nineteenth century; it was a mechanism for endowing domicile with enduring qualities similar to those attached to nationality. See Carter, 'Domicil: The Case for Radical Reform in the United Kingdom' (1987) 36 ICLQ 713, 716.

6.25 In some countries, such as the United States, the doctrine of the revival of the domicile of origin has been abolished. Instead, a domicile of choice continues until a new one is obtained. While it might previously have been argued that this divergence of approach was explicable on the basis that the population in the United States was more migratory and less influenced by birth, locality, and the local history of families, such an explanation can no longer be accepted. Accordingly, the Law Commission proposed in the 1980s that the doctrine of revival of the domicile of origin be abolished and that an existing domicile should continue until a new one is established. If enacted, this recommendation, along with the proposal that it should be no harder to lose a domicile acquired at birth than any other domicile, would mean that no special significance would be attached to such a form of domicile and, accordingly, it should be abolished as a separate species of domicile.[46]

B Domicile of dependence

6.26 A domicile of dependence is the domicile conferred on legally dependent persons by operation of law. The domicile of a dependent person is the same as the domicile of the person upon whom he is dependent and will change with any change in the latter's domicile. The underlying rationale of this rule (apart from being another mechanism for ensuring that every person always has an operative domicile) is twofold. First, certain classes of person are regarded as being incapable of forming the necessary intention to acquire a domicile of choice. A young child, for instance, cannot intend to reside permanently anywhere; his home will generally be with his parents and, accordingly, the law directs that he follows their domicile as one of dependence. Similarly, a mentally incapable person is regarded as unable to form the necessary intention for acquisition of a domicile of choice and is, therefore, assigned a domicile of dependence. Secondly, there are advantages in preserving a unity of domicile for all members of a family. The potential for further conflict between laws is exacerbated when different members of the same family have separate domiciles. A child's domicile is dependent on that of his parents and, before the Domicile and Matrimonial Proceedings Act 1973, a wife was regarded as having a domicile of dependence on her husband.

1. Children

6.27 It has already been seen that at birth all children are assigned a domicile of origin, normally on the basis of parentage. This domicile of origin can never be completely lost as it may revive at some later stage in life, but it is not determinative of domicile during childhood. Until the child reaches the age of 16 or marries under that age,[47] his domicile is one of dependence. The child's domicile of dependence may be the same as his domicile of origin but this is not necessarily so. Even if the child's initial domicile of dependence coincides with his domicile of origin (as will be the case for most children),

---

[46] Law Com No 168, para 4.24.   [47] Domicile and Matrimonial Proceedings Act 1973, s 3(1).

the domicile of dependence will change if the relevant parent's domicile changes. The law on the child's domicile of dependence is a combination of common law principles and rules contained in the Domicile and Matrimonial Proceedings Act 1973.

(A) Bases of attribution of the child's domicile of dependence

6.28 First, if the child is illegitimate he takes the domicile of his mother.[48] Secondly, if the child is legitimate and his parents are alive and living together, the child takes the domicile of his father. (In such a case the mother may have a different domicile from the father and the child, even though they are all living together.) Thirdly, if, in this latter situation, the father then dies, the child thereafter normally takes the domicile of the mother.[49] However, in these circumstances, the child's domicile does not always automatically follow a change in the mother's domicile. Where the child lives with the mother when she acquires a new domicile, the child's domicile will follow the mother's. It has been decided, however, that if she changes her domicile, but leaves the child permanently resident in the former country (for example, in the care of a relative), the child's domicile does not change with the mother's. In *Re Beaumont*[50] a widow, domiciled in Scotland, remarried an English domiciliary, thereby acquiring an English domicile (of dependence). She moved to England with her new husband leaving one daughter in Scotland. It was held that the daughter's domicile remained Scottish because the change of a child's domicile is the 'result of the exercise by [the mother] of a power vested in her for the welfare of the infants, which in their interest she may abstain from exercising, even when she changes her own domicile'.[51] It has even been suggested that a mother in such cases can confer a domicile on her child in a third country by placing the child there under the care of a competent person.[52] Such an interpretation seems implausible. Why should a widow have such extensive powers not possessed by anyone else? A father who sends a child to another country has no such power. The underlying rationale behind the decision in *Re Beaumont* was the desire to prevent a child effectively obtaining a domicile of dependence on a stepfather. As a married woman no longer acquires a domicile of dependence on her husband, there seems little point any longer in singling out widows for special treatment.

6.29 Fourthly, if a legitimate child's parents are 'alive but living apart', then as long as the child has a 'home' only with the mother he takes her domicile, but if he has a home with the father alone, or a home with each parent, then he takes the father's domicile.[53] If the child ceases to have a home with the parent whose domicile he shares, that domicile continues unless and until he has a home with the other parent.[54] These statutory provisions, designed to introduce a correlation between the legal rules on domicile of

---

[48] *Udny v Udny* (1869) LR 1 Sc & Div 441 at 457; Domicile and Matrimonial Proceedings Act 1973, s 4(4).
[49] *Potinger v Wightman* (1817) 3 Mer 67 at 79.   [50] [1893] 3 Ch 490.   [51] At 497.
[52] Blaikie, 'The Domicile of Dependent Children: A Necessary Unity' [1984] Jur Rev 1, 7; Cheshire, North and Fawcett, *Private International Law* (14th edn, 2008) p 177.
[53] Domicile and Matrimonial Proceedings Act 1973, s 4(2)(a).
[54] S 4(2)(b). In a similar vein, under s 4(3), if the mother dies at a time when the child has her domicile by virtue of s 4(2), the child retains that domicile unless and until he has a home with his father.

dependence and the factual realities of a child's dependence on a parent, present certain problems of interpretation. What is the meaning of 'home'? A 'home' clearly combines notions of both physical presence and an emotional link. It is appropriate here to consider the duration and regularity of the residence and whether the child regards the parent's house as his 'home . . . or . . . proper abode'.[55] Also, do these rules apply to amicable arrangements where the parents have two separate homes, or do they apply only to situations where the marriage has broken down? There is a strong argument for saying that the Domicile and Matrimonial Proceedings Act 1973 should be applicable to all cases of parents living apart. The rules are designed to mirror reality. If a happily married couple choose to maintain separate homes in different countries—for, say, employment reasons—the child's domicile should be the same as that of the parent with whom he has his home. In such situations, however, it is likely that it would be held that the child has a home with each parent and would, therefore, follow the father's domicile.

6.30 There remain some further grey areas. The question arises as to whether, after the death of both parents of a legitimate child, or of the mother of an illegitimate child, the child's domicile must remain unchanged until he is old enough to have an independent domicile.[56] Questions also arise in respect of a child's domicile of dependence following the making of an adoption or parental order. The law is tolerably clear where such an order is made in favour of a heterosexual married couple (it mirrors the position of the legitimate child as outlined above[57]); however, there is uncertainty as to which parent's domicile ought to be determinative where such an order is made in respect of same-sex spouses. Leading commentators suggest that where a parental order is made, the child ought to take the domicile of the parent with the genetic connection to the child.[58] There are similar questions concerning the determination of the dependent domicile of a child born to a woman in a same-sex marriage where the spouse is treated as a parent.

(B) Loss of domicile of dependence

6.31 How is a child's domicile of dependence lost? Section 3(1) of the Domicile and Matrimonial Proceedings Act 1973 provides that a child becomes capable of acquiring an independent domicile upon reaching the age of 16 or by marrying under that age. Prior to the 1973 Act an independent domicile could be acquired only at the age of majority. However, as one can leave school, marry, and live an independent life at the age of 16, this is the appropriate age for an emancipated child to acquire an independent domicile.[59] As a domicile of dependence 'cannot survive the destruction of the factors essential to its creation and continued existence'[60] it is lost immediately when the minor turns 16, and is replaced by a domicile of choice (if the person is already in that country with the requisite intention of remaining there indefinitely) or, alternatively, by the

---

[55] Law Com No 168, para 4.20; *Re Y* [1985] Fam 136 at 140.
[56] Dicey, Morris and Collins, *The Conflict of Laws* (15th edn, 2012) p 169.
[57] Adoption and Children Act, s 67(1); Human Fertilisation and Embryology Act 2008, s 54(1). See para 6.18.
[58] Dicey, Morris and Collins, *The Conflict of Laws* (15th edn, 2012) p 170.
[59] Law Com No 48, *Report on Jurisdiction and Matrimonial Causes* (1972) para 33.
[60] Wade, 'Domicile: A Re-Examination of Certain Rules' (1983) 32 ICLQ 1, 17.

domicile of origin. This can be illustrated by the case of *Harrison v Harrison*.[61] Harrison was born with an English domicile of origin. When he was 18 (the age of majority at which an independent domicile could be acquired was then 21) his parents emigrated to South Australia and acquired a domicile there, leaving him in England. Under the rules described above he acquired a South Australian domicile of dependence. When he was 20 he emigrated to New Zealand, intending to remain there permanently, and married a New Zealander. Shortly thereafter he returned to England, where he turned 21. His wife petitioned the English court for a divorce and at that time the English court could have exercised jurisdiction only if Harrison were domiciled in England. It was held that the court did have jurisdiction. When Harrison turned 21 he lost his South Australian domicile of dependence. As he had not yet acquired a New Zealand domicile of choice (because he had not resided there since turning 21) his English domicile of origin revived.

(C) Reform

6.32 Despite the reforms effected by the Domicile and Matrimonial Proceedings Act 1973, these rules are highly artificial. If the facts of *Harrison* were to recur today (with Harrison being under 16) he would still acquire a South Australian domicile of dependence in a country in which he had never set foot. More than 40 years ago, judges in other jurisdictions were questioning this approach. For example, Wilson J in the New Zealand case of *Re G* stated that 'the true position may now be that a dependent person's domicile changes when his parent intends it to change and the change is for his benefit, irrespective of whether the domicile of the parent also changes'.[62] The Law Commission, conscious of the artificiality of the present law, proposed that a child under the age of 16 should have a domicile 'in the country with which he is for the time being most closely connected'.[63] In order to introduce a degree of certainty, this test would be combined with rebuttable presumptions that the child would have the same domicile as his parents where they are both domiciled in the same country and he has his home with either of them, or, where the parents are domiciled in different countries, that the child would share the domicile of the parent with whom he has his home.[64] In other cases, for example where the child has a home with both parents in different countries, or has no home with either parent, the basic test of closest connection would be applied without the aid of any presumption.[65]

2. Married women

6.33 Until 1 January 1974 the domicile of a married woman was necessarily the same as that of her husband.[66] On the death of the husband or on divorce, the woman's former domicile of dependence continued as her domicile of choice[67] (if it was not her

---

[61] [1953] 1 WLR 865. [62] [1966] NZLR 1028 at 1031.
[63] Law Com No 168, para 4.13. [64] Ibid, paras 4.15, 4.16.
[65] Ibid, para 4.17. In Scotland the Family Law (Scotland) Act 2006, s 22, introduced rules (not presumptions) along these lines. See Harder, 'Domicile of Children: the New Law in Scotland' (2006) 10 Edinburgh Law Review 386.
[66] *Lord Advocate v Jaffrey* [1921] 1 AC 146; *A-G for Alberta v Cook* [1926] AC 444.
[67] *Re Wallach* [1950] 1 All ER 199. For a criticism of this approach, see Wade, 'Domicile: A Re-Examination of Certain Rules' (1983) 32 ICLQ 1, 17.

domicile of origin) unless and until she abandoned it (which would happen at the moment of the death or divorce, if she had previously ceased to reside in, and did not intend to return to, the country in question).[68]

6.34 The Domicile and Matrimonial Proceedings Act 1973 provided that from 1 January 1974 a married woman should have her own independent domicile.[69] As the Act is not retrospective,[70] if the domicile of a married woman has to be ascertained as at a date before 1974 the common law applies. A woman who was already married on 1 January 1974 retains her former domicile of dependence as her domicile of choice (or origin), unless and until she changes it by acquisition or revival of another domicile on or after that date.[71] This means that the independent domicile of a married woman when the Act came into effect was not necessarily the domicile she would have had if her domicile had never been dependent on her husband.[72] Her domicile of choice might be a country in which she had never decided to settle permanently if that was her husband's domicile and she was resident there on 1 January 1974. In *IRC v Duchess of Portland*[73] the propositus, who had a domicile of origin in Quebec, married an English domiciliary in 1948, thereby acquiring an English domicile of dependence. Despite the fact that she had always planned to return to Canada with the consequence that an acquisition of an English domicile of choice under the normal rules would have been 'an impossibility in the real world'[74] it was held that on 1 January 1974 her English domicile of dependence became converted into an English domicile of choice which she could lose only by satisfying the strict rules on abandonment of a domicile of choice. She could 'only free herself from the shackles of dependency by choosing to leave her husband for permanent residence in another country'.[75] A more realistic approach that would enable such women to avoid this 'last barbarous relic of a wife's servitude'[76] would be to hold that, in such cases, where the woman, according to the normal rules, does not herself acquire a domicile of choice on 1 January 1974, her domicile of origin should revive on that date.[77]

3. Mentally incapable people

6.35 It seems that a mentally disordered person who is incapable of forming the necessary intention to acquire a domicile of choice retains whatever domicile he had immediately before becoming incapable.[78] The Law Commission proposed that such a person should be domiciled in the country with which he is for the time being most closely connected.[79]

C Domicile of choice

1. Acquisition of domicile of choice

6.36 A domicile of choice in a country is acquired by residing there with the intention of remaining permanently or indefinitely. There are thus two requirements to be satisfied:

---

[68] *Re Scullard* [1957] Ch 107. [69] S 1(1). [70] Ibid. [71] S 1(2).
[72] See, eg, *Breuning v Breuning* [2002] 1 FLR 888. [73] [1982] Ch 314. [74] At 318.
[75] At 320. [76] *Gray v Formosa* [1963] P 259 at 267.
[77] Wade, 'Domicile: A Re-Examination of Certain Rules' (1983) 32 ICLQ 1.
[78] *Urquhart v Butterfield* (1887) 37 Ch D 357. [79] Law Com No 168, para 6.6.

the objective one of residence (or, perhaps, presence[80]) and the subjective one of intention. The two factors must coexist for a domicile of choice to be acquired.

(A) Residence

6.37 Residence is the easier factor to establish. The test of residence for the purpose of acquiring a domicile is a qualitative one rather than a quantitative one.[81] The residence need be of no particular duration, and may indeed be only momentary.[82] So, if the propositus has firmly decided before he arrives in the country to settle there permanently, then the residence factor will be satisfied as soon as he arrives, and the domicile will immediately be acquired. In such cases it seems more apt to say that only presence in a country is required for acquisition of a domicile of choice. Indeed, because of such cases, the Law Commission proposed that 'presence' is a more appropriate term than 'residence'.[83] In the United States it has been suggested that where a person sends his family and belongings ahead of him to establish a home in a new state, a domicile might be vicariously acquired even before the propositus himself arrives there.[84] In view of the somewhat stricter nature of the English rules on domicile, it is unlikely that such a notion would be accepted by an English court.

6.38 In less clear-cut cases, it has been held that 'residence' for these purposes means physical presence 'as an inhabitant'.[85] This excludes presence merely as a visitor. In *IRC v Duchess of Portland*,[86] the propositus with a domicile in England spent between 10 and 12 weeks every year in Quebec and maintained her links with Canada with a view to retiring there. This was not sufficient to make her an inhabitant of Quebec and accordingly she could not acquire a domicile there. (The same result could have been reached—even if it were accepted that mere presence always amounts to residence—on the ground that at the relevant time the propositus had the intention of residing permanently in Quebec only at some future time.)

6.39 In *Plummer v IRC*[87] it was held that, as regards a person with two homes, a person is an inhabitant of the country in which he has his chief residence. The propositus in this case had a home in England where she finished school, did a secretarial course, and went to university, and a home in Guernsey where her family lived and where she spent many weekends and some holidays. It was concluded that Guernsey was not her place of chief residence and that a domicile had not been acquired there. The test for determining a person's chief residence is, again, a qualitative one and is not dependent on the size or amenities of the homes in question or the length of time spent in each.[88]

---

[80] See *Divall v Divall* [2014] 2 FLR 1104 at [28].
[81] *Ramsay v Liverpool Royal Infirmary* [1930] AC 588 at 595, 598.
[82] *Bell v Kennedy* (1868) LR 1 Sc & Div 307.
[83] A similar recommendation has been made by the Law Reform Commission of Hong Kong, in *Rules for Determining Domicile* (2005).
[84] Scoles and Hay, *Conflict of Laws* (2nd edn, 1992) p 178–9.
[85] *IRC v Duchess of Portland* [1982] Ch 314 at 319.   [86] [1982] Ch 314.
[87] [1988] 1 WLR 292.
[88] *Henwood v Barlow Clowes International Ltd* [2008] EWCA Civ 577 at [104].

6.40 Until recently it was accepted that an English domicile could not be acquired if the residence in England was unlawful.[89] However, it has been ruled by the House of Lords that a domicile can be acquired in such circumstances.[90] In matters of civil status, as opposed to political status, it is 'in everyone's interests that the affairs of such long-term residents [are] governed by the laws of the country with which they [are] so closely connected'.[91] It is not a matter of the person benefiting from unlawful action: domicile gives rise to liabilities as well as rights.

(B) Intention

6.41 For a domicile of choice to be acquired, the propositus's residence must be accompanied by the intention to remain permanently or indefinitely. If a person moves to a new country but has not finally made up his mind whether to remain there indefinitely, the pre-existing domicile is retained.[92] It is the intention requirement that is most likely to lead to dispute for, from the legal point of view, it is imprecise, and, on the facts, it may be difficult to prove.

6.42 What is meant by the intention to remain permanently or indefinitely? If the propositus's intention is to remain only temporarily, say for the duration of a job[93] or to receive medical treatment,[94] then, however long that is, a domicile will not be acquired. At the other extreme, if the propositus has decided to make the country his home, having no intention ever of leaving, nor having in mind any circumstances which may cause him to leave, then clearly he has the requisite intention.

6.43 The difficult cases are those where the propositus intends to remain in the country unless and until the occurrence of some event, which may or may not happen; if it does happen, then he will, or may, leave. Older cases suggested that no domicile could be acquired in such circumstances. If the propositus foresaw any event that would cause him to leave, no matter how remote or unlikely that event, the intention required by law was lacking.[95] However, in the latter half of the twentieth century a more flexible and realistic approach was adopted so that today the fact that the propositus has in mind such a contingency does not necessarily mean that he does not have the intention to remain permanently or indefinitely. In *Re Fuld's Estate (No 3)* Scarman J stated that:

> if a man intends to return to the land of his birth upon a clearly foreseen and reasonably anticipated contingency, eg, the end of his job, the intention required by law is lacking; but, if he has in mind only a vague possibility, such as making a fortune (a modern example might be winning a football pool), or some sentiment about dying in the land of his fathers, such a state of mind is consistent with the intention required by law.[96]

---

[89] *Puttick v A-G* [1980] Fam 1.
[90] *Mark v Mark* [2006] 1 AC 98. See Forsyth, 'The Domicile of the Illegal Resident' (2005) 1 Journal of Private International Law 335.
[91] *Mark v Mark* [2006] 1 AC 98 at [45]. [92] *Holliday v Musa* [2010] 2 FLR 702 at [23].
[93] In *Irvin v Irvin* [2001] 1 FLR 178 a man worked in the Netherlands for 25 years but always intended to return to England on retirement. It was held that he had not acquired a Dutch domicile.
[94] *Re Haji-Ioannou (Deceased)* [2009] ILPr 56 at [54].
[95] *Udny v Udny* (1869) LR 1 Sc & Div 441; *Ramsay v Liverpool Royal Infirmary* [1930] AC 588.
[96] [1968] P 675 at 684–5.

6.44 Accordingly, it is necessary to distinguish between two types of contingency that might cause a person to leave the country of residence. If the contingency is vague and uncertain, or not at all likely to happen ('no more than a pipe dream'[97]), then a domicile of choice may be acquired. Where the propositus's intention was to remain in England, but to return to France if he 'made his fortune', this vague contingency did not prevent him from acquiring a domicile of choice in England.[98] Similarly, where the intention was to leave England if the propositus ceased to be capable of leading an active life on his farm, the contingency was sufficiently vague and uncertain (especially as whether or not it occurred would depend on the propositus's own assessment) and so a domicile was acquired in England.[99]

6.45 If, on the other hand, it is a definite event that the propositus has in mind, and this contingency is 'clearly foreseen and reasonably anticipated'[100] and the propositus firmly intends to leave if it does happen, then he will not have the requisite intention. For example, in *IRC v Bullock*[101] the domicile of origin of the propositus was in Nova Scotia. In 1932 he had come to England to join the RAF and England was his home for the next 44 years. At first, his intention had been to return to Canada when he retired from the Air Force. However, in the meantime, he had married an Englishwoman, and when he retired in 1959 he remained in England. His wife disliked Canada and was not willing to live there. Thereafter, his intention was to remain in England unless his wife died before him, in which event he would return to Canada. The Court of Appeal held that he had not acquired a domicile of choice in England, for he had in mind a definite, not a vague, contingency—the death of his wife before him—and there was a 'sufficiently substantial possibility of the contingency happening' and he firmly intended to leave if it happened.

6.46 This approach raises several questions. First, while the *Fuld (No 3)* test asked whether the contingency was 'clearly foreseen and reasonably anticipated', in the *Bullock* case this was rephrased as 'was there a sufficiently substantial possibility of the contingency happening?' These two tests are not the same. Although in *Bullock* there was a substantial possibility of his wife dying before him (there was a fair chance that this would happen), it seems unlikely that the propositus would reasonably anticipate or expect his wife (who was three years younger than him) to die before him. The test in *Fuld (No 3)* is clearly preferable and was more recently approved in *Perdoni v Curati*.[102] Had it been applied in *Bullock*, the propositus would have been held to have acquired a domicile in England, which after 44 years' residence here would have been a more realistic result.

6.47 Secondly, must the contingency be subjectively foreseen as reasonably likely to occur, or is it enough that it is objectively likely to occur or objectively a sufficiently substantial

---

[97] *Sekhri v Ray* [2014] 1 FLR 612 at [29].
[98] *Doucet v Geoghegan* (1878) 9 Ch D 441; see also *Perdoni v Curati* [2012] WTLR 505 at [27].
[99] *Re Furse* [1980] 3 All ER 838.   [100] *Re Fuld's Estate (No 3)* [1968] P 675 at 684.
[101] [1976] 1 WLR 1178.
[102] [2012] WTLR 505 at [25], [27]; also in *Z and B v C (Parental Order: Domicile)* [2012] 2 FLR 797 at [16].

possibility? In *Cramer v Cramer*[103] a French domiciliary came to England with the hope of marrying her lover and establishing a home here. Her intention to remain was, however, conditional upon her being able to marry him (he was already married) and their relationship lasting until then. While she hoped to remain in England, it was decided that an objective assessment of the situation had to be made. A mere desire to remain would not suffice. Her intentions were too speculative and, accordingly, no domicile was acquired in England. While there are also dicta in *Bullock* suggesting that the test was whether the wife was in fact likely to die before the propositus,[104] the better test is that favoured in *Fuld (No 3)* of examining the 'contingencies in the contemplation of the propositus, their importance to him, and the probability, in his assessment, of the contingencies he has in contemplation being transformed into actualities'.[105] This was confirmed in *Bheekhun v Williams* where it was stated that 'the relevant enquiry is what was in his mind; not what a person who was better informed would have appreciated the position to be'.[106]

6.48 As subjective intentions are often impossible to ascertain, objective considerations are important *evidence* from which intentions can be inferred. If a person claims he intends to return to his country of origin upon the happening of an outlandish contingency—for example, the British National Party winning a general election in the United Kingdom—it would be virtually impossible for him to establish that he foresaw this as reasonably likely to occur. Judges can do little other than draw inferences from conduct and the objective likelihood of contingencies occurring. They are forced to apply their own standards: 'If I had been in that situation, what would I have foreseen?' The only realistic circumstances in which it could be concluded that the propositus foresaw a bizarre contingency as reasonably likely to occur would be where there was clear evidence that the propositus's state of mind was in some material way different from that of the reasonable person—say, because he was mentally disturbed. In such a situation, however, it is unlikely that the propositus would be regarded as sufficiently mentally capable to change his domicile.[107] While it will make little practical difference in most cases whether an objective or subjective test is applied, the test ought ultimately to be a subjective one. As already seen,[108] one of the underlying rationales of the concept of domicile of choice is that it allows full autonomy to persons to choose where they wish to make their home and thus, indirectly, to choose the law to which they are to be subject. Such a principle can only find expression in rules that take full account of a person's subjective hopes, wishes, and expectations. If a person genuinely expects a contingency to occur which will cause him to leave (and the court can be persuaded that this is his genuine belief), then, as the rules are presently structured, he cannot be said to have made a permanent home in the new country.

6.49 Thirdly, what is the position of a person who wants to remain in a country, but realistically will have little prospect of being able to do so—say, for immigration reasons? In *Szechter v Szechter* it was stated that, if a person wished to remain permanently in a country, a domicile would be acquired and it was 'immaterial that their intentions were

---

[103] [1987] 1 FLR 116.   [104] [1976] 3 All ER 353 at 359, 360.   [105] [1968] P 675 at 685.
[106] [1999] 2 FLR 229 at 239.   [107] See para 6.35.   [108] See para 6.8.

liable to be frustrated by the decision of the Secretary of State for the Home Department as to permission for their continued residence here'.[109] This seems to suggest that intention here is to be equated with an aim or desire to remain. The more realistic approach, however, adopted in *Cramer* and *Fuld (No 3)*, is that simply desiring to remain is not sufficient. If the propositus realises that there is a clear contingency, such as a refusal to extend residence rights in a country, that could cause him to leave (whether he wants it to occur or not), the issue becomes whether he anticipates that contingency as reasonably likely to occur. Such an intention, especially if it involved an intention to remain illegally in a country 'would need to be carefully scrutinised'.[110] Under this approach the expectations of the propositus are crucial. In *Henwood v Barlow Clowes International Ltd* it was stated that the need for permission to remain in a country did 'not make it impossible' to acquire a domicile of choice but made it 'less likely'.[111] The issue is whether the propositus foresees himself remaining permanently in a country, rather than whether he wishes to remain there. To adapt terminology employed in other areas of law, the type of intention required here should not be direct intention (what one wants or hopes will happen), but rather oblique intention (what one foresees as reasonably likely to happen). Any other approach could result in the totally unrealistic situation of a person acquiring a domicile in a country in which he would have no prospect of being able to reside permanently. Equally where the propositus *desires* a return to his native land but accepts that in reality he will live permanently and indefinitely in England, he will acquire an English domicile of choice.[112]

(i) Evidence of change of domicile

6.50 How does a court decide where a person was domiciled at a given time? There is a presumption against a change of domicile, so that once it has been shown, or is admitted, that the propositus was domiciled in a particular country, the onus of proving any subsequent change of domicile lies on the party alleging it. This onus may be difficult to discharge because the evidence that must be adduced relates to the intention rather than to the residence factor. The most direct evidence of the propositus's intention is his own statements. Even if such evidence is available, however, it may well not be conclusive or even reliable.[113] For the most part, the intention of the propositus must be judged from his conduct. As the state of mind in question is whether at the relevant time he regarded a given country as his permanent home, there is a very wide range of facts which may be relevant. As Kindersley VC said in *Drevon v Drevon*:

> there is no act, no circumstance in a man's life, however trivial it may be in itself, which ought to be left out of consideration in trying the question whether there was an intention to change the domicile. A trivial act might possibly be of more weight with regard to determining this question than an act which was of more importance to a man in his lifetime.[114]

---

[109] [1971] P 286 at 294.   [110] *Mark v Mark* [2006] 1 AC 98 at [13].
[111] [2008] EWCA Civ 577 at [119].
[112] *Perdoni v Curati* [2012] WTLR 505; *Sekhri v Ray* [2014] 1 FLR 612.
[113] *Wahl v A-G* (1932) 147 LT 382; *Buswell v IRC* [1974] 1 WLR 1631; *M v M (Divorce: Domicile)* [2011] 1 FLR 919: such evidence may be of a 'self-serving nature'.
[114] (1864) 34 LJ Ch 129 at 133.

6.51 It is not surprising then that contested domicile cases may be lengthy and expensive, involving a minute analysis of the significance to be attached to the activities of a person over many years.

6.52 The fact that a person has resided in a country for a substantial time is in itself some evidence that he has made it his permanent home; but, however long such residence lasts, it does not raise any presumption that he is domiciled there. The quality of the residence, and all other indications of the propositus's intention, must still be considered in deciding whether a change of domicile has been proved. The courts have taken into account a wide variety of factors in assessing whether a person possesses the requisite intention. One of the more important factors is naturalisation. Becoming a naturalised citizen of the new country is strong evidence that a person intends to remain there permanently, but it is never decisive and is simply 'one of the totality of facts'.[115] In *Fuld (No 3)* the propositus changed his nationality, but was held not to have changed his domicile. In *Perdoni v Curati*[116] the deceased had retained his Italian citizenship throughout but was found to have acquired an English domicile of choice. In *Bullock*, on the other hand, the fact that the propositus had not changed his nationality was regarded as relevant in deciding he had not changed his domicile. Another factor is the purchase of real property. The fact that a person has purchased a house or a flat in a country rather than renting accommodation is often viewed as evidence of acquisition of a domicile of choice.[117] Where a person (or a couple) own multiple properties in different countries, the location of the main family home will carry weight.[118]

6.53 Also significant are a person's family ties in the new community. The fact that the propositus has married a person from the new country may be significant.[119] The spouse's own attitude is also material. In the context of a longstanding marriage, a husband, residing in England, is likely to be considered domiciled here if the wife is determined to live permanently in England, and the husband is committed to remaining with his wife and family (even if, were he a free agent, he would reside elsewhere).[120] Also relevant (although not decisive[121]) is the degree of social integration into the new community. Details of the daily life of the propositus in the new country are commonly regarded as indicators of whether or not he had the requisite intention to remain. Factors that have been considered include membership of churches and clubs,[122] exercising rights

---

[115] *Wahl v A-G* (1932) 147 LT 382; 'not in itself conclusive, but it is a persuasive factor': *Munro v Munro* [2008] 1 FLR 1613 at [39].
[116] [2011] EWHC 3442.
[117] See, eg, *Sekhri v Ray* [2014] 1 FLR 612 at [29]. Correspondingly, a decision to live in rented accommodation may negate the acquisition of a new domicile: *Gate Gourmet Luxembourg IV Sarl v Morby* [2015] EWHC 1203 (Ch) at [24].
[118] *Perdoni v Curati* [2012] WTLR 505 at [27].
[119] Ibid.
[120] Ibid; *Sekhri v Ray* [2014] 1 FLR 612 at [27]–[29].
[121] *Perdoni v Curati* [2012] WTLR 505 at [11].
[122] *Re Craignish* [1892] 3 Ch 180.

to vote,[123] from which country a pension is received,[124] newspapers read,[125] whether the language of the country has been learned,[126] and general lifestyle in the local community.[127] Also relevant here is the congeniality of the local customs. In older cases it was asserted that stronger evidence was required to establish that a Westerner had acquired a domicile in an Oriental country.[128] Even in more modern times a similar approach has been applied in relation to people from Pakistan coming to England.[129] However, given the multi-cultural nature of British society today, it is doubtful whether too much weight would be attached to this factor. In *F v F (Divorce: Jurisdiction)*[130] a Muslim woman was held to be domiciled in England with account being taken of the fact that she was 'well integrated into a substantial Islamic community' in London. Where a question arises as to the domicile of same-sex partners, evidence of hostility towards such relationships in the person's country of origin may be probative of the acquisition of a domicile of choice.[131] Other relevant factors that have been taken into account include a person's career prospects, business interests, location of pets,[132] answers to income tax questionnaires,[133] age,[134] the motive for moving to the new country,[135] and where the person wishes to be buried.[136]

(ii) Intention freely formed

6.54 It is often said that in forming the intention necessary for the acquisition or loss of a domicile of choice, the propositus must make a free choice, formed independently of external pressures.[137] This proposition, however, seems to have little practical significance. One unlikely case in which it could arise is that of the prisoner under a sentence likely to last his lifetime who is moved to a prison in a different country (say, from England to Scotland). He might then believe that he will spend the rest of his days in Scotland; even if that were regarded as an intention to remain permanently, the prisoner would not acquire a domicile of choice in Scotland, for the intention was not freely formed.[138]

---

[123] *IRC v Bullock* [1976] 3 All ER 353; *Dellar v Zivy* [2007] ILPr 60. For the purposes of tax law, the fact that one registers as an overseas elector to vote in UK elections will not be taken into account in determining the domicile of that individual: Finance Act 1996, s 200.
[124] *Dellar v Zivy* [2007] ILPr 60.
[125] *IRC v Bullock* [1976] 3 All ER 353; *Irvin v Irvin* [2001] 1 FLR 178.
[126] *Irvin v Irvin* [2001] 1 FLR 178; *Re J (Jurisdiction)* [2007] 2 FLR 1196 at [9]; *Morris v Davies* [2011] WTLR 1643 at [71].
[127] *Re Furse* [1980] 3 All ER 838.
[128] *Casdagli v Casdagli* [1919] AC 145. See also *Steel v Steel* (1888) 15 R 896 at 909: 'Nobody in his senses ever goes to Burma sine animo revertendi'.
[129] *Qureshi v Qureshi* [1972] Fam 173.   [130] [2009] EWHC 1448 (Fam).
[131] *Z and B v C (Parental Order: Domicile)* [2012] 2 FLR 797 at [23]; *Re JV* [2014] EWHC 4756 (Fam) at [8]; *Re A and B (Parental Order: Domicile)* [2014] 1 FLR 169 at [25]–[26].
[132] *Z and B v C (Parental Order: Domicile)* [2012] 2 FLR 797 at [23]–[24].
[133] *Buswell v IRC* [1974] 1 WLR 1631. In *Holliday v Musa* [2010] 2 FLR 702 it was stated that while declarations to the Inland Revenue 'cannot be ignored', they 'must be treated with some caution' (at [66]).
[134] Graveson, *Conflict of Laws: Private International Law* (7th edn, 1974) p 202: 'permanence is necessarily relative to the individual's expectation of life'.
[135] *Wood v Wood* [1957] P 254; *Divall v Divall* [2014] 2 FLR 1104 at [43]–[44].
[136] *Holliday v Musa* [2010] 2 FLR 702 at [74].
[137] *Udny v Udny* (1869) LR 1 Sc & Div 441 at 458; *Re Fuld's Estate (No 3)* [1968] P 675 at 684.
[138] *Re late Emperor Napoleon Bonaparte* (1853) 2 Rob Eccl 606.

6.55 Lesser pressures, such as those motivating fugitives from justice, refugees, and people migrating for the sake of their health, do not normally negate intention.[139] For example, in *Donaldson v Donaldson*[140] it was held that an officer with the RAF who was stationed in Florida and liable to be posted elsewhere (and indeed was posted back to England) acquired a domicile in Florida. Any inference that he lacked the necessary intention because of the 'involuntary' nature of his presence there was rebutted by the fact that he married a local woman and clearly intended to return to Florida to make a permanent home there as soon as he was free to do so.

6.56 Whether a person changes his domicile depends on the answers to the usual questions: does the propositus intend to return to his former country? Does he intend to remain permanently in the new country? The fact that he is, for instance, a refugee will, depending on the circumstances of his plight, help to show that he does, or does not, have in mind a sufficiently definite and likely contingency on which he will return home. In *Cyganik v Agulian*[141] a Greek Cypriot was displaced from his home as a result of the Turkish invasion of Cyprus. It was held that although his 'truly free choice' would not have been to live in England, his intention 'adapted over time to his circumstances' and he had acquired a domicile in England. In *Re Martin*[142] it was stated that what mattered was whether the person (in this case a fugitive from justice) was free to return home after a specified number of years. If the fugitive remains perpetually liable to prosecution or punishment, this is a factor which suggests that he does not intend to return and so thereby acquires a domicile in the new country.

2. Abandonment of domicile of choice

6.57 A domicile of choice will be lost if the propositus not only ceases to reside in the country in question but also ceases to intend to reside there permanently or indefinitely. So while a domicile of choice can be acquired only by the concurrence of residence and intention, it continues as long as either one of them remains.

(A) Cessation of residence

6.58 Even when the propositus has ceased to intend to reside permanently, he will not lose his domicile merely through absence from the country. He must cease to reside there as an *inhabitant*. In *IRC v Duchess of Portland*[143] the question was whether the propositus abandoned her English domicile of choice in 1974. At the relevant time, the intention factor for the loss of the domicile was already satisfied, for, though she lived in England, she did not intend to remain there permanently. She had a house in Quebec, where she spent 10 or 12 weeks each year. It was argued that, when she made her annual visit there in 1974, she lost her English domicile on the basis that her absence

---

[139] See *Puttick v A-G* [1980] Fam 1; *Moynihan v Moynihan (Nos 1 and 2)* [1997] 1 FLR 59 (fugitives); *May v May and Lehmann* [1943] 2 All ER 146 (refugees); *Hoskins v Matthews* (1856) 8 De GM & G 13; *Re James* (1908) 98 LT 438 (invalids).
[140] [1949] P 363.
[141] [2005] WTLR 1049; reversed on appeal on other grounds: [2006] 1 FCR 406.
[142] [1900] P 211.   [143] [1982] Ch 314.

from England meant that she ceased to reside in England and that she did not have the intention of residing permanently in England. It was held, however, that she retained her English domicile, for, despite her temporary absence, her residence as an inhabitant in England continued. Where a person has two homes, residence in the old country will be abandoned only when a chief residence is established in the new country.[144]

(B) Cessation of intention

6.59 If the propositus has ceased to reside in the country in question, what precisely is the intention requirement for loss of the domicile of choice? The law on this point is not settled. Certainly, if the propositus positively intends not to return to live in his former country, the domicile will be abandoned. Equally, if he positively intends at some time in the future to resume his residence in the former country, he will retain his domicile there. It is the case in between that causes difficulty: where the propositus is undecided whether or not he will return.

6.60 In some cases it has been held that a domicile of choice will not be lost unless there is a positive intention not to return (except temporarily). In *Re Lloyd Evans*[145] the domicile of choice of the propositus had been Belgium. During the German occupation in the Second World War, he had escaped to England (which was his domicile of origin). While in England he was undecided whether, after the war, he would return to Belgium or go to Australia. He died before he could make up his mind. It was held that he had not lost his Belgian domicile, for he had not definitely decided not to return there as his home. Similarly, in *Re S (Hospital Patient: Foreign Curator)* it was held that a person living in England had not lost his Norwegian domicile because 'he wanted to keep his eventual options [of returning] open although for the time being the die was cast [and he did not anticipate leaving England]'.[146]

6.61 The alternative approach is that, as the intention needed to acquire a domicile of choice is to remain in the country permanently, all that is required for its abandonment is that the propositus should cease to intend to reside there permanently. On this basis, the domicile of choice will be lost if the propositus is undecided whether or not to return because, in such a case, he no longer has the intention of residing permanently (even though, of course, he does not have the intention of not doing so). There is support for this view. In *Re Flynn*[147] it was indicated that there need not be a departure with the intention of not returning permanently, but rather a domicile of choice could be lost where there was a departure without a specific intention of returning. This view was endorsed in *Qureshi v Qureshi* where it was stated that a domicile of choice could be lost if the propositus went to a new country without an intention of returning to the old country of domicile: 'the animus that must be shown is not necessarily non revertendi; it is sufficient that the residence in the new country is sine animo revertendi'.[148] In this respect it was added that an intention to return could 'wither away'.[149]

---

[144] *Plummer v IRC* [1988] 1 WLR 292.   [145] [1947] Ch 695.   [146] [1996] 1 FLR 167 at 179.
[147] [1968] 1 WLR 103. This was followed in *Morgan v Cilento* [2004] WTLR 457.
[148] [1972] Fam 173 at 191.   [149] Ibid. See also *Maples v Melamud* [1988] Fam 14.

6.62 This latter approach, which seems more in touch with modern-day reality, making it easier to lose a domicile of choice and acquire a new one, was accepted by the Court of Appeal in *Henwood v Barlow Clowes International Ltd*.[150] The propositus left the Isle of Man, where he had a domicile of choice, and established homes in France and Mauritius. It was held that he had lost his Manx domicile, even though he had not decided firmly to reside permanently or indefinitely in either France or Mauritius. Such 'indecision'[151] meant he no longer had an intention to reside permanently or indefinitely in the Isle of Man.

3. Reform of domicile of choice

6.63 The central problem with the law here relates to the nature, and difficulty of proof, of the requisite intention requirement. Despite developments in cases such as *Fuld (No 3)*, the law remains rooted in its Victorian origins when the establishment of a home was an affair of a lifetime. It is unrealistic in the modern world to assert that people such as the propositus in *Bullock*, who have lived in England for over 40 years, are not domiciled here. The function of domicile is to connect people to the legal system to which they belong and whose laws are most appropriate to apply to them. For all practical purposes (other than purely emotional and sentimental considerations) the propositus in *Bullock* had made his home in England and should have been held to be domiciled here. Further, because of the infinite range of factors that can prevent a person from acquiring a domicile in a country, and the difficulty of proving a person's state of mind, trials involving domicile of choice tend to be lengthy and expensive with the outcome difficult to predict.

6.64 In an attempt to address these problems, there have been several proposals to reform the law on domicile of choice. As long ago as 1954, reforms were recommended by the Private International Law Committee,[152] the main one being the introduction of a rebuttable presumption that a person should be presumed to intend to live permanently in the country in which he has his home. This proposal was carried forward into the Domicile Bill 1958, which foundered after its second reading in the House of Lords because of intense opposition from US and Commonwealth businesspeople who feared they would become liable to UK income tax and estate duty.[153] A revised Domicile Bill in 1959 was similarly abandoned because of opposition in the House of Commons.[154] In 1963 the Private International Law Committee again proposed similar reforms which were never implemented.[155] In 1985 the Law Commission published a consultation document suggesting that, subject to evidence to the contrary, a person should be presumed to intend to make his home indefinitely in a country in

---

[150] [2008] EWCA Civ 577. See also *Ray v Sekhri* [2014] 2 FLR 1168 at [46]; *Divall v Divall* [2014] 2 FLR 1104 at [35], [41] expressing support for this approach.
[151] [2008] EWCA Civ 577 at [115].
[152] *First Report of the Private International Law Committee*, 1954 (Cmd 9068).
[153] Graveson, *Conflict of Laws: Private International Law* (7th edn, 1974) p 189; Carter, 'Domicil: The Case for Radical Reform in the United Kingdom' (1987) 36 ICLQ 713, 724.
[154] Graveson, *Conflict of Laws: Private International Law* (7th edn, 1974) p 189.
[155] *Seventh Report of the Private International Law Committee*, 1963 (Cmnd 1955).

which he has been habitually resident for seven years.[156] In its final Report in 1987 the Law Commission, responding to criticisms that such a presumption could be difficult (and expensive) to rebut, abandoned the use of presumptions and simply proposed that a domicile of choice should be acquired if a person was present in a country and intended to settle there for an indefinite period.[157] This proposal is little more than a restatement of the present law on domicile of choice and would mean that persons such as the propositus in *Bullock* will continue to be domiciled in a country in which they had not lived for more than 40 years.[158] While several of the Law Commission's proposals are to be welcomed,[159] it is regrettable that the opportunity was not taken to try to modernise the somewhat antiquated rules on domicile of choice.[160]

IV Nationality

6.65 In most civil law systems, such as those operating in continental Europe and the former colonies of those countries, the longstanding test of 'belonging' to a country for conflict of laws purposes is not domicile, but nationality. For example, such countries would traditionally regard French law as the most appropriate law to govern the personal transactions and relationships of a French citizen. In English domestic law, the use of nationality as a connecting factor has been relatively limited. With regard to choice of law, it is used as one of a range of alternative connecting factors compliance with the law of which can render a will formally valid.[161] It is also employed as a basis for the recognition of a foreign divorce or other matrimonial decree; if one of the parties to the marriage was a national of the country in which the divorce or other decree was obtained the decree is prima facie entitled to recognition in England.[162] At common law, British nationality provides a basis for the exercise of wardship jurisdiction by the English courts.[163] Nationality is also used as a secondary connecting factor in EU measures on family aspects of the conflict of laws—for example, as a relevant factor in determining the desirability of a transfer of parental responsibility jurisdiction[164] and as a subsidiary basis for maintenance jurisdiction.[165]

6.66 The advantages of nationality over domicile are that it can easily be ascertained and is, therefore, more certain: whereas most people know what their nationality is, fewer can

---

[156] Law Commission Working Paper No 88 (1985) para 5.15. See Carter, 'Domicil: The Case for Radical Reform in the United Kingdom' (1987) 36 ICLQ 713.
[157] Law Com No 168, cl 2(2) of the Draft Bill.
[158] See also Trakman, 'Domicile of Choice in English Law: an Achilles Heel?' (2015) 11 Journal of Private International Law 317 arguing for emphasis to be placed on a person's habitual or permanent residence.
[159] See paras 6.25 and 6.32.
[160] In 1996 the government announced that it had abandoned any intention of implementing the Law Commission's reform proposals: *Hansard* (HC) vol 269, cols 488–489w, 16 January 1996 (see (1996) 146 NLJ 371).
[161] Wills Act 1963, s 1.   [162] Family Law Act 1986, s 46(1)(b)(iii).
[163] See *Re A (Children)* [2014] AC 1 at [60]–[63].
[164] Brussels II bis Regulation (Regulation (EC) No 2201/2003, OJ 2003 L338/1), art 15(3)(c).
[165] Maintenance Regulation (Regulation (EC) No 4/2009, OJ 2009 L7/1), art 6.

be certain as to where they are domiciled; it is difficult to change one's nationality, making evasion of the law more difficult; in times of crisis a person may turn to his state of nationality for protection and so it is only appropriate that he should be subject to its laws for conflict of laws purposes.[166]

6.67 On the other hand, there are distinct disadvantages to utilising nationality instead of domicile as a connecting factor. First, there is the problem posed by stateless persons or those with dual nationality.[167] Secondly, the concept does not work efficiently when dealing with composite states, such as the United Kingdom or the United States, comprising more than one legal system. Finally, as with domicile, it can lead to highly unrealistic results in that persons who have long since left a country, but failed to become naturalised elsewhere, continue to be subject to the law of their former country. The propositus in *Bullock* would still be subject to Canadian law as, despite 44 years' residence in England, he had retained his Canadian nationality. Accordingly, the Law Commission has recommended against replacing domicile with nationality because, while it 'is a proper test of political status and allegiance, domicile being based on the idea of the country where a person has his home is a more appropriate concept for determining what system of law should govern his civil status and certain aspects of the administration of his property'.[168]

6.68 One possible compromise, not explored by the Law Commission, that would bring English law more into line with the laws of other EU Member States, is the solution adopted in Singapore whereby a person who is a citizen of Singapore is presumed, until the contrary is proved, to be domiciled in Singapore.[169] This approach, assuming it were elevated into a general presumption that a person is domiciled in the country of his nationality, would introduce a great measure of certainty and simplicity into the law and, as the presumption would be rebuttable, would allow nationality to be displaced in cases where its application would be inappropriate. The disadvantage of this approach is that it would solve little, as in all the difficult cases there would need to be the same full inquiry as at present in order to ascertain whether the presumption has been rebutted.

V Habitual residence

A Introduction

6.69 The operation of the conflict of laws depends upon choice of law rules containing connecting factors that lead to realistic and appropriate laws. With regard to the personal law, connecting factors should lead to the law that is most appropriate for governing and controlling the personal transactions of an individual. Also, with regard to

---

[166] See, generally, Nadelman, 'Mancini's Nationality Rule and Non-Unified Legal Systems: Nationality versus Domicile' (1969) 17 Am J Comp Law 418.
[167] See Kruger and Verhellen, 'Dual Nationality = Double Trouble?' (2011) 7 Journal of Private International Law 601.
[168] Law Com No 168, para 3.11. [169] Women's Charter (Ch 353) (revd edn, 1985), s 3(4).

jurisdiction and the recognition of foreign judgments, the system depends on the employment of connecting factors that ensure that appropriate courts have jurisdiction and that the judgments of appropriate foreign courts are recognised.

6.70 As has been explored, the major problem with the concepts of domicile and nationality is that they can lead to unrealistic, unpredictable, and inappropriate laws or jurisdictions. If domicile or nationality were the sole connecting factor employed by English law for choice of law and jurisdictional purposes, the propositus in *Bullock* would not have been able to obtain a divorce in England and, in any choice of law dispute, the law of Nova Scotia would have been applicable to him, despite 44 years' residence in England.

6.71 Accordingly, over the last 40 years habitual residence has emerged to become the predominant connecting factor in English and EU conflict of laws. Initially, this was a concept developed by the Hague Conference on Private International Law and it was employed in UK statutes giving effect to Hague conventions (for example, as a basis for divorce recognition[170] and in handling international child abduction[171]). However, it was also used as a connecting factor in purely domestic initiatives, for example as a jurisdictional basis for divorce[172] and declarations of status.[173]

6.72 When the European Union introduced uniform jurisdictional rules for divorce, separation, and annulment and jurisdictional rules on parental responsibility and provisions on child abductions within the European Union (in the Brussels II *bis* Regulation), habitual residence was adopted as the main connecting factor.[174] It is also the principal connecting factor under the EU Maintenance Regulation.[175] 'Habitual residence' has also taken centre stage in other EU conflict of laws measures in which the United Kingdom is not participating (for example, the Succession Regulation[176] and the Rome III Regulation on choice of law in divorce[177]). Even in commercial areas of private international law the concept is utilised—most importantly, as has been seen, as regards choice of law rules relating to contractual obligations[178] and non-contractual obligations.[179] The concept of habitual residence has also been employed in other areas of EU law beyond the conflict of laws, for example in social security law[180] and in determining the entitlements of EU officials.[181]

---

[170] Recognition of Divorces and Legal Separations Act 1971, s 3(1)(a) (subsequently Family Law Act 1986, s 46(1)(b)(i)).
[171] Child Abduction and Custody Act 1985, sch 1, art 4.
[172] Domicile and Matrimonial Proceedings Act 1973, s 5(2)(b) (since amended to give effect to Brussels II *bis*).
[173] Family Law Act 1986, ss 55–57.
[174] Regulation (EC) No 2201/2003, OJ [2003] L338/1, replacing Regulation (EC) No 1347/2000, OJ 2000 L160/19.
[175] Regulation (EC) No 4/2009, OJ 2009 L7/1, art 3.
[176] Regulation (EU) No 650/2012, OJ 2012 L201/107.
[177] Regulation (EU) No 1259/2010, OJ 2010 L343/10.
[178] Rome I Regulation (Regulation (EC) No 593/2008), OJ 2008 L177/6.
[179] Rome II Regulation (Regulation (EC) No 864/2007), OJ 2007 L199/40.
[180] See Case C–90/97 *Swaddling v Adjudication Officer* [1999] ECR I–1075.
[181] See Case T–90/92 *Magdalena Fernández v Commission* [1993] ECR II–971.

6.73 In English law, a closely related, and also extensively utilised, concept is that of 'ordinary residence', which has been held to bear largely the same meaning as habitual residence.[182]

B A variable meaning

6.74 Originally it was thought that 'habitual' or 'ordinary' residence had the same meaning in all areas of law.[183] However, even under this view, it is likely that the courts paid 'mere lip-service to this rule'[184] and that the meaning of 'habitual residence' varied according to the context in which the issue arose. This approach was endorsed by the House of Lords in *Mark v Mark*,[185] where it was held that the concept could have a 'different meaning in different statutes according to [the] context and purpose' of the statute.[186]

6.75 Further, and even more importantly, it has become established that for purposes of EU law the concept must be given an autonomous, EU meaning,[187] which is somewhat different from the meaning under English law. To complicate matters even further, it has also been established that this autonomous EU meaning of habitual residence itself varies depending on the context. Thus, the 'core' autonomous meaning of habitual residence which applies to, for example, divorce jurisdiction is not applicable for determining the habitual residence of children for the purpose of parental responsibility disputes—despite both matters being dealt with in the same Brussels II *bis* Regulation.[188]

6.76 Accordingly, the following sections will first examine the general meaning of habitual residence as established by English law and will then look at the EU meaning of the concept as employed in the Brussels II *bis* Regulation.

C Meaning of habitual residence in English law

6.77 Over the past 25 years an extensive jurisprudence on the meaning of 'habitual residence' has emerged. Most of the decisions have concerned the habitual residence of children under the Child Abduction and Custody Act 1985, implementing the Hague Convention on Civil Aspects of International Child Abduction of 1980. Under this statute the English court has a prima facie duty to order the return of a child who has been wrongfully removed from a Contracting State in which he is habitually resident.

---

[182] *Shah v Barnet London Borough Council* [1983] 2 AC 309; *Ikimi v Ikimi* [2002] Fam 72.
[183] *Re J (Abduction: Custody Rights)* [1990] 2 AC 562 at 578; *Shah v Barnet London Borough Council* [1983] 2 AC 309; *Nessa v Chief Adjudication Officer* [1999] 1 WLR 1937.
[184] Rogerson, 'Habitual Residence: The New Domicile?' (2000) 49 ICLQ 86, 87.
[185] [2006] 1 AC 98.
[186] At [15], [37]. See also (to the same effect) *R (Cornwall Council) v Secretary of State for Health* [2016] AC 137 at [43].
[187] *L-K v K (No 2)* [2007] 2 FLR 729; *Marinos v Marinos* [2007] 2 FLR 1018; *Munro v Munro* [2008] 1 FLR 1613; *Z v Z (Divorce: Jurisdiction)* [2010] 1 FLR 694.
[188] Case C-523/07 *Re Proceedings Brought by A* [2009] ECR I-2805, para 36.

In determining such a child's habitual residence the courts have laid down principles capable of general application.

6.78 With the adoption of Brussels II *bis* and its supplementary regulation of child abduction, it has recently been decided that the child's 'habitual residence' for Hague Convention purposes should be determined in accordance with the EU conception of 'habitual residence'.[189] It follows that the voluminous case-law on the *English* understanding of 'habitual residence' for Hague Convention purposes is now of limited significance in Hague Convention child abduction cases. This jurisprudence is, however, directly relevant where an English court is required to interpret 'habitual residence' in determining whether a third-country divorce is entitled to recognition under the Family Law Act 1986;[190] or in assessing its jurisdiction to grant a declaration of recognition of a foreign adoption;[191] or in determining the formal validity of a will[192]—in other words, in those areas where English law uses 'habitual residence' as a connecting factor and remains untouched by EU developments.

1. General principles

6.79 The House of Lords in *Re J (Abduction: Custody Rights)*[193] stressed that the ascertainment of habitual residence is a question of fact to be decided by reference to all the circumstances of the case. It is accepted that a 'person may cease to be habitually resident in country A in a single day if he or she leaves it with a settled intention not to return to it but to take up long-term residence in country B instead'.[194] Such person might not, however, become habitually resident in country B on arrival. *Re J* suggested that an 'appreciable period of time' must pass before habitual residence can be established in country B[195]—although other cases have indicated that where the person in question has prior residential connections to country B, he may become habitually resident immediately on returning there with a 'settled purpose' of remaining for the medium term.[196]

6.80 It is implicit in the above analysis that a person may have no habitual residence at a given point in time—where there is a 'gap' between the loss of a former habitual residence and the acquisition of a new one.[197] In certain contexts, this is unproblematic. For example, if habitual residence is used as a basis for divorce jurisdiction alongside other connecting factors, a determination that a newly arrived person is at present not habitually resident in England will not necessarily prevent the immediate assumption of jurisdiction in England or elsewhere. Even if there is no other available basis for jurisdiction in England at the time of the initial petition, English jurisdiction based on 'habitual residence' in England may be established at a later date. A 'gap' can therefore

---

[189] *Re A (Children)* [2014] AC 1 at [35], [54]; *Re KL (a Child)* [2014] 1 AC 1017 at [18]–[19]; *Re LC (Children)* [2014] 1 AC 1038 at [30].
[190] S 46(1)(b)(i).   [191] Family Law Act 1986, s 57(3)(b). See, eg, *Re Z and Z* [2013] EWHC 747 (Fam).
[192] Wills Act 1963, s 1.   [193] [1990] 2 AC 562 at 578.   [194] Ibid.   [195] Ibid.
[196] See, eg, *Nessa v Chief Adjudication Officer* [1999] 1 WLR 1937 at 1942–3; *Re A (Children)* [2014] AC 1 at [44].
[197] See *Nessa v Chief Adjudication Officer* [1999] 1 WLR 1937 at 1942–3.

be tolerated where habitual residence is used as a jurisdictional connecting factor in divorce cases. However, in other contexts (for example in the application of the Hague Child Abduction Convention or in determining the applicable law) a 'gap' in habitual residence may be more problematic. In such contexts, there will be a greater pressure to adopt an interpretation which avoids any such 'gap'—in order to identify the applicable law or to secure the protection of the Hague Convention, as the case may be.[198] It has also been accepted that, for the purposes of English law, a person can have more than one ordinary or habitual residence at the same time.[199] In *Ikimi v Ikimi*[200] it was held that a couple who had consistently maintained matrimonial homes in both England and Nigeria could be habitually resident in both countries at the same time. *Ikimi* was, however, a case concerned with divorce jurisdiction (where dual habitual residence poses no difficulty). In other contexts (for example where habitual residence is used to determine the applicable law), it may be necessary to identify a single habitual residence.[201]

2. 'Residence' and 'settled intention'

6.81 In order to prove habitual (or ordinary) residence it is necessary to establish a concurrence of both the physical element of residence and a mental state of having a 'settled purpose' of remaining there.[202] However, the nature of these two requirements differs markedly from the superficially similar requirements of domicile.

(A) Residence

6.82 An examination of reported cases suggests that, where there has been residence for a year or more, habitual residence is almost always held to be established.[203] In such cases the objective fact of the residence is decisive and the intentions of the person are of little importance—even if it is clear that the person has no desire to live in the country and has no intention of remaining there in the longer term.[204]

6.83 More problematic are cases where the residence has endured for less than a year and where there is no question of resumption of a prior residence. How quickly can habitual residence be established in such circumstances? In *Nessa v Chief Adjudication Officer*[205] a woman from Bangladesh, who had a right of abode in the United Kingdom, arrived in England for the first time and applied for income support four days later. She was entitled to income support only if she was habitually resident in England. It was held

---

[198] Rogerson, 'Habitual Residence: The New Domicile?' (2000) 49 ICLQ 86, 92 and 104.
[199] *Shah v Barnet London Borough Council* [1983] 2 AC 309 at 342. In *Re V* [1996] 3 FCR 173 it was held that for the purposes of the Hague Convention a child who lived in two countries for different parts of the year had consecutive habitual residences rather than being concurrently habitually resident in both.
[200] [2002] Fam 72.
[201] Rogerson, 'Habitual Residence: The New Domicile?' (2000) 49 ICLQ 86, 104.
[202] *Shah v Barnet London Borough Council* [1983] 2 AC 309 at 344.
[203] Clive, 'The Concept of Habitual Residence' [1997] Jur Rev 137, 141.
[204] *M v M (Abduction: England and Scotland)* [1997] 2 FLR 263. See Rogerson, 'Habitual Residence: The New Domicile?' (2000) 49 ICLQ 86, 94.
[205] [1999] 1 WLR 1937.

that, even though she had come to England for the settled purpose of remaining (and so could even be domiciled here), she had not acquired habitual residence within four days.

6.84 However, the period of residence may be short[206] and the amount of time needed to be spent in the new country depends on the degree of settled purpose. In *Re S (A Minor) (Custody: Habitual Residence)*[207] the House of Lords held that if there was an established intention of settling in the country permanently a new habitual residence may be acquired 'very quickly'. On this basis, in *Re F (Child Abduction)*[208] habitual residence was acquired within one month of a family moving to Australia with the intention of remaining there. In *Re S (Habitual Residence)*[209] habitual residence was established after 7 to 8 weeks' residence in England. In *Re A (Abduction: Habitual Residence)*[210] it was held that, in the particular factual context, eight days was not a sufficiently appreciable period of time to acquire a new habitual residence. In *V v B (Abduction)*[211] habitual residence was acquired after a little over two months' residence in Australia. On the other hand, in *A v A (Child Abduction)*[212] it was stated that, if there were doubts over the requisite 'settled intention', eight months' residence in Australia would be insufficient for the acquisition of habitual residence there. As indicated above, where a person is returning 'home', habitual residence may be established very quickly.

6.85 Difficulties also arise in determining the habitual residence of the intermittent resident who regularly spends periods of time in different countries. In *Armstrong v Armstrong*[213] it was decided that spending 71 days in a year in England was not enough for habitual residence to be acquired, whereas in *Ikimi v Ikimi*[214] spending 161 days in a year was enough. Ultimately, each case turns on its facts.

6.86 As is implicit in *Ikimi*, residence need not be continuous in order to qualify as 'habitual'. It is well-established that occasional absences, such as for holidays, will not affect a person's habitual residence. In *Re H (Abduction: Habitual Residence: Consent)*[215] it was held that a student studying abroad for a finite one-year course would not lose her habitual residence.[216] Habitual residence is particularly likely to subsist, even in the face of an extended period of absence, if that absence was involuntary.[217]

6.87 Finally, for conflict of laws purposes, the residence need not be lawful. In *Mark v Mark*[218] it was ruled that an over-stayer who was in this country illegally could nevertheless be held to be habitually resident here for the purposes of divorce jurisdiction.[219]

---

[206] Lord Slynn in *Nessa v Chief Adjudication Officer* [1999] 1 WLR 1937 at 1943 approved *Re F (Child Abduction)* [1992] 1 FLR 548 where it was stated (at 555) that 'a month can be . . . an appreciable period of time'.
[207] [1998] AC 750.   [208] [1992] 1 FLR 548.   [209] [2010] 1 FLR 1146.
[210] [2007] 2 FLR 129.   [211] [1991] 1 FLR 266.   [212] [1993] 2 FLR 225 at 235.
[213] [2003] 2 FLR 375.   [214] [2002] Fam 72.   [215] [2000] 2 FLR 294.
[216] Following *Kapur v Kapur* [1984] FLR 920 it is possible that such a person could also acquire a habitual residence in the country of study.
[217] *Re Z and Z* [2013] EWHC 747 (Fam) at [30], [32].   [218] [2006] 1 AC 98.
[219] This remains the position in defining 'habitual residence' under Brussels II bis: *Chai v Peng* [2015] 2 FLR 424 at [27]. The position is, however, different in other areas of law where the establishment of ordinary or habitual residence results in the entitlement to state benefits: see, eg, *R (Arogundade) v Secretary of State for Business, Innovation and Skills* [2013] ELR 466.

(B) Settled intention

6.88 Residence must be accompanied by a 'settled purpose'[220] or 'settled intention'[221] of remaining 'as part of the settled order of [a person's] life for the time being'.[222] The test is not whether the person has 'settled' in the country 'in the sense of putting down substantial roots'[223] but rather whether the residence was for a 'settled purpose'—and the party must be able to define what that purpose is.[224] The intention need only be to remain for a relatively short or limited period of time.[225] Thus, a person who goes to a country for the purpose of study or of taking up employment under a fixed-term contract can become habitually resident there. In *Re C (Abduction: Habitual Residence)*[226] a person who was transferred to work in Germany for about six months was held to be habitually resident there. In *Kapur v Kapur*[227] a man who came to England to study for the English Bar exams was held to be habitually resident here for the purposes of divorce jurisdiction. In *Re B (No 2)*[228] a couple living in Scotland went to Germany (the wife's place of origin) in order to resolve their matrimonial difficulties and plan their future lives. Despite being there for only six months it was held that they had a sufficient settled purpose to become habitually resident in Germany. As stated in *Shah v Barnet London Borough Council*: 'All that is necessary is that the purpose of living where one does has a sufficient degree of continuity to be properly described as settled.'[229] On the other hand, in *Re B (Child Abduction: Habitual Residence)*[230] two months' residence in Canada trying to effect a marital reconciliation did not indicate a sufficient settled purpose for habitual residence to be acquired.

6.89 It is necessary that the residence be voluntarily adopted. However, as with domicile, it seems that this is less a rule of law than an evidential proposition that, if residence is involuntary, it is unlikely that the propositus would have the requisite settled intention to remain. For example, in *Breuning v Breuning*[231] it was held that a man's presence in England purely for the purpose of receiving medical treatment did not establish habitual residence. In *Re Z (Abduction)*[232] it was held that the operation of fraud or mistake could prevent the acquisition of habitual residence, particularly if a parent had been tricked into removal abroad by the other parent who intended to kidnap the children. In *Shah* Lord Scarman instanced kidnapping, imprisonment, and being stranded on a desert island with no opportunity of escape as factors that may be so overwhelming 'as to negative the will to be where one is'.[233] In *Re A*

---

[220] *Shah v Barnet London Borough Council* [1983] 2 AC 309 at 344.
[221] *Re J (Abduction: Custody Rights)* [1990] 2 AC 562 at 579.
[222] *Re B (Abduction) (No 2)* [1993] 1 FLR 993 at 995.
[223] *Al Habtoor v Fotheringham* [2001] 1 FLR 951 at 966.   [224] *E v E* [2007] 1 FLR 1977.
[225] *Al Habtoor v Fotheringham* [2001] 1 FLR 951 at 966; *Re Z (Abduction)* [2009] 2 FLR 298.
[226] [2004] 1 FLR 217.   [227] [1984] FLR 920.   [228] [1993] 1 FLR 993.
[229] [1983] 2 AC 309 at 344.   [230] [1994] 2 FLR 915 at 918.   [231] [2002] 1 FLR 888.
[232] [2009] 2 FLR 298 at [13].
[233] [1983] 2 AC 309 at 344. In *Re Z (Abduction)* [2009] 2 FLR 298 it was stated that a 'virtual prisoner' was unlikely to acquire habitual residence in that country. In the Scottish case of *Cameron v Cameron* 1996 SC 17 the opposite view was adopted: it was stated (at 20) that Nelson Mandela would have been habitually resident on Robben Island where he was imprisoned.

*(Abduction: Habitual Residence)*²³⁴ it was argued that a member of the US forces stationed in Iceland could not become habitually resident there because of the compulsory nature of the posting. This argument was swept aside on the basis that joining the army involved a 'voluntary election' that was no different from joining a business firm knowing one could be required to work in another country. It was, however, added that a new habitual residence would not be acquired by a member of the armed forces who is posted to a foreign country on active service.

D Habitual residence under EU law

6.90 As seen above, it is clear that habitual residence must bear an autonomous meaning for the purposes of EU instruments. This meaning can vary from instrument to instrument depending on the context and the policies of the law involved. The remainder of this section focuses in particular on the meaning of habitual residence for the purposes of the Brussels II *bis* Regulation.[235] As seen earlier, even within this Regulation, habitual residence is to be interpreted somewhat differently for adults (for example, for divorce jurisdiction) and children (for example, for issues of parental responsibility). Also, as previously mentioned, the Supreme Court has determined that the Court of Justice's interpretation of the child's habitual residence for the purposes of Brussels II *bis* should be utilised in all Hague Child Abduction Convention cases.[236]

1. Adults

6.91 The Explanatory Report on the Brussels II Convention (the Borrás Report),[237] drawing on existing jurisprudence of the Court of Justice in other areas of EU law, encapsulated the meaning of habitual residence as being:

> the place where the person had established, on a fixed basis, his permanent or habitual centre of interests, with all the relevant facts being taken into account for the purpose of determining such residence.

6.92 This has become known as the 'centre of interests' test and it has been applied by the English and French courts in determining an adult's habitual residence under Brussels II *bis*.[238] In *Swaddling v Adjudication Officer* (a case on EU social security law) the Court of Justice gave an indication of the factors which are likely to be influential in the assessment of 'habitual residence':

---

[234] [1996] 1 All ER 24 at 31.
[235] See, generally, Ní Shúilleabháin, *Cross-Border Divorce Law: Brussels II bis* (2010) p 36–66.
[236] *Re A (Children)* [2014] AC 1 at [35], [54]
[237] OJ 1998 C221/27. The Brussels II Convention was recast as a Regulation, the Brussels II Regulation (Regulation (EC) No 1347/2000, OJ 2000 L160/19) before it ever came into force. The Brussels II Regulation was subsequently replaced by the Brussels II *bis* Regulation (Regulation (EC) No 2201/2003, OJ 2003 L338/1).
[238] *Marinos v Marinos* [2007] 2 FLR 1018; *Saward v Saward* [2013] EWCA Civ 1060 at [7]; *Tan v Choy* [2015] 1 FLR 492 at [11], [29]; *Moore v Moore* [2006] ILPr 29.

account should be taken in particular of the employed person's family situation; the reasons which have led him to move; the length and continuity of his residence; the fact (where this is the case) that he is in stable employment; and his intention as it appears from all the circumstances . . . [T]he length of residence in the Member State in which payment of the benefit at issue is sought cannot be regarded as an intrinsic element of the concept of [habitual] residence . . . [i]n particular, when, as in the present case, an employed person [is] returning to his State of origin . . . [and] intends to remain in his State of origin[239]

6.93 The Court of Justice has not yet had the opportunity to offer guidance on the interpretation of an adult's habitual residence in establishing divorce jurisdiction under Brussels II *bis*; however, a number of English cases have sought to shed light on the operation of the connecting factor in this context. The English courts have taken the view that the 'centre of interests' test involves a more qualitative assessment of where a person's interests are centred, rather than the more quantitative evaluation traditionally undertaken in English law.[240] In the English case of *L-K v K (No 2)*[241] it was stated that the EU concept places 'far less, if any, emphasis on the ingredients which English law has developed that there needs to pass an appreciable time' before a person can acquire an habitual residence in a country. In *Marinos v Marinos*[242] and in a number of subsequent English cases,[243] it was also accepted that the autonomous EU concept of habitual residence requires a *single* habitual residence. While a person can be *resident* in two or more states at a given point in time, he can only be *habitually resident* in one state.[244] This is in contrast to the traditional English approach laid down in *Ikimi v Ikimi*.[245]

6.94 In English case-law, the upshot of the application of this 'autonomous' 'centre of interests' test is that 'habitual residence' as a connecting factor for divorce jurisdiction has lost much of its fact-based objectivity and has drifted closer to traditional conceptions of domicile. That is not to say that the English courts have begun to equate the two. On the contrary—it is, for example, still clear that an expatriate working abroad for the medium term will become habitually resident in his new country of residence, even in circumstances where there can be no question of a domicile of choice being acquired.[246] Nonetheless, it is apparent that there is increased reliance on long-standing connections and subjective intention in determining 'habitual residence' for the

---

[239] Case C-90/97 [1999] ECR I-1075, paras 29–30.
[240] *Marinos v Marinos* [2007] 2 FLR 1018 at [56]; *Z v Z (Divorce: Jurisdiction)* [2010] 1 FLR 694 at [37].
[241] [2007] 2 FLR 729 at [31].   [242] *Marinos v Marinos* [2007] 2 FLR 1018 at [40]–[43].
[243] *Z v Z (Divorce: Jurisdiction)* [2010] 1 FLR 694 at [41]; *V v V (Divorce: Jurisdiction)* [2011] 2 FLR 778 at [36]; *Tan v Choy* [2015] 1 FLR 492 at [10]–[11], [29].
[244] *Marinos v Marinos* [2007] 2 FLR 1018 at [48], [78]; *V v V (Divorce: Jurisdiction)* [2011] 2 FLR 778 at [50]–[52].
[245] [2002] Fam 72.
[246] *L-K v K (No 2)* [2007] 2 FLR 729; *Z v Z (Divorce: Jurisdiction)* [2010] 1 FLR 694. See also *Munro v Munro* [2008] 1 FLR 1613 where it was accepted that British nationals were habitually resident in Spain in circumstances where they retained their English domicile of origin. Similarly, in the context of art 4(2) of Rome II in *Winrow v Hemphill* [2015] ILPr 12, the wife of a British serviceman, who had been living in Germany for eight years, was held to be habitually resident there.

purposes of Brussels II *bis*, with a number of cases concluding that a person was not in fact habitually resident in the country in which the day-to-day life of that person was, for the most part, conducted. For example, in *Olafisoye v Olafisoye*[247] a wife was found to be habitually resident in England (and not in Nigeria) in the 12 months prior to the issue of a divorce petition, even though she had spent only 28 days in England in the eight months preceding the petition (having spent most of that time in Nigeria). In *C v S* the wife was found to be habitually resident in England (and not in Italy) between 2003 and 2008 when in fact she spent most of her time in Italy (where her children were at school): she had 'never lost her habitual residence in England'.[248] Similarly, in *Marinos v Marinos* a wife was found to be habitually resident in England at a time when she worked as a flight attendant out of Heathrow and spent most of her time, when she was not working, living with her husband and children in Greece.[249] She was held not to have been habitually resident in Greece at the relevant time. In these cases there is often an emphasis on the kinds of preferences and loyalties that have traditionally weighed heavily in domicile cases. For example, in *Marinos* the court noted that the wife 'had never settled very happily in Greece'.[250] In *Olafisoye* the substantial time spent in Nigeria could be disregarded because it was necessitated by the daughter's schooling.[251] In *C v S* the court emphasised the wife's preference for life in England and accepted that she had moved to Italy out of necessity (not only because, having lost her job in England due to ill-health, she could obtain more advantageous medical treatment in Italy, but also because of her role as primary carer of her children).[252]

6.95 This tendency to focus on long-term connections and preferences as opposed to the factual realities of a person's life is not evident in all English cases[253] and it is not necessarily warranted by the Court of Justice's wider case-law on habitual residence. This tendency appears to be influenced in particular by the assumption that a person can have only one habitual residence: it follows (according to the logic of *Marinos*, *C v S* and *Olafisoye*) that a woman with two homes is habitually resident in the country with which she has more permanent connections. While the Court of Justice case-law has tended to take the view that a person can have only one habitual residence, in *Wencel* the Court linked this to the legislative context in which the concept was used—and in that case, the Court ruled that for the relevant social security purpose a person could have only one habitual residence because this was necessary for the realisation of the aims of the EU legislation at issue.[254] In *C v S* it was suggested that the same considerations applied to the divorce jurisdiction provisions of Brussels II *bis*. Referring to 'the concept of unitary habitual residence', Hedley J opined that this was necessary 'to ensure that at any one time only one court has jurisdiction within the Community'.[255] This view is, however, at odds

---

[247] *Olafisoye v Olafisoye (Jurisdiction)* [2011] 2 FLR 553.
[248] *C v S (Divorce: Jurisdiction)* [2011] 2 FLR 19 at [33].
[249] *Marinos v Marinos* [2007] 2 FLR 1018.   [250] *Marinos v Marinos* [2007] 2 FLR 1018 at [77].
[251] *Olafisoye v Olafisoye (Jurisdiction)* [2011] 2 FLR 553 at [55], [63].
[252] *C v S (Divorce: Jurisdiction)* [2011] 2 FLR 19.   [253] See, eg, *CC v NC* [2015] 1 FLR 404.
[254] Case C–589/10 *Wencel v Zakład Ubezpieczeń Społecznych w Białymstoku* [2013], paras 43–51.
[255] *C v S* [2011] 2 FLR 19 at [27].

with the flat, non-hierarchical structure of article 3 of Brussels II *bis* which by its very nature contemplates and tolerates the possibility of parallel competence. Furthermore, in *Hadadi v Hadadi*, in interpreting nationality as a basis for divorce jurisdiction, the Court of Justice emphasised the virtue of a 'choice' of jurisdictional options under article 3 and refused to interpret nationality in a manner which would reduce that jurisdictional choice and confine a petitioner with dual nationality to one of those nationalities for jurisdictional purposes.[256] The Court noted that the 'system of jurisdiction' established by Brussels II *bis* 'is not intended to preclude the courts of several States from having jurisdiction'.[257] Thus, the logic of the *Hadadi* judgment is inconsistent with some of the assumptions underpinning the English view that 'habitual residence' under article 3 of Brussels II *bis* must be exclusive. In interpreting 'nationality' in *Hadadi*, the Court of Justice also emphasised the need for legal certainty and the desirability of a 'simple and unambiguous connecting factor'.[258] These interests tend to militate against the more subjective approach which has emerged in the English jurisprudence, and may (when the Court of Justice eventually deals with the question) lead to a greater emphasis on factual presence and the day-to-day reality of the individual's life.

2. Children

6.96 The Brussels II *bis* Regulation provides that jurisdiction in matters of parental responsibility is based on the habitual residence of the child.[259] The Regulation also supplements the Hague Convention of 1980 and deals with cases of child abductions between Member States. For these purposes the habitual residence of the child is the critical connecting factor. Whilst previously it was thought that 'habitual residence' was to be understood in the traditional English sense for Hague Convention purposes,[260] in *Re A (Children)*[261] the Supreme Court determined that the same test should be used under the Hague Convention and Brussels II *bis* and that this should be the Court of Justice's test.

6.97 Although there is no Court of Justice guidance, as yet, on the test for determining an adult's habitual residence under Brussels II *bis*, the Court of Justice has pronounced on the nature of a child's habitual residence on a number of occasions. The traditional English approach was to link the child's habitual residence to that of the person exercising parental responsibility (the 'parental intention approach'). An alternative approach focuses on the child as an autonomous individual and determines habitual residence by reference to the child's own connections leaving parental intent out of account (the 'child-centred approach'). The Court of Justice is said to have adopted a third approach which combines elements of both:[262] focusing on the child's connections whilst also viewing parental intent as a relevant factor. This 'combined approach' was laid down in

---

[256] Case C-168/08 [2009] ECR I-6871, paras 53, 58.   [257] Ibid, para 49.
[258] Ibid, paras 48, 55.   [259] Art 8(1).   [260] *Re P-J (Children)* [2010] 1 WLR 1237.
[261] *Re A (Children)* [2014] AC 1 at [35], [54].
[262] See generally Schuz, *The Hague Child Abduction Convention* (2013) pp 186–95; also Beaumont and Holliday, 'Recent Developments on the Meaning of "Habitual Residence" in Alleged Child Abduction Cases' (University of Aberdeen Centre for Private International Law, Working Paper No 2015/3) available at: <http://www.abdn.ac.uk/law/research>.

Re Proceedings Brought by A[263] where the Court of Justice defined 'habitual residence' for the purposes of article 8(1) of Brussels II *bis* as follows:

> it corresponds to the place which reflects some degree of integration by the child in a social and family environment. To that end, in particular the duration, regularity, conditions and reasons for the stay on the territory of a Member State and the family's move to that State, the child's nationality, the place and conditions of attendance at school, linguistic knowledge and the family and social relationships of the child in that State must be taken into consideration.[264]

6.98 The Court also noted that 'the parents' intention to settle permanently with the child in another Member State, manifested by certain tangible steps such as the purchase or lease of a residence in the host Member State, may constitute an indicator of the transfer of the habitual residence'.[265] In the subsequent Court of Justice case of *Mercredi v Chaffe*[266] it was stated that the 'social and family environment' of a child comprises various factors which vary according to the age of the child and that '[a]n infant necessarily shares the social and family environment of the circle of people on whom he or she is dependent'.[267] Therefore, for very young children, parental intent and the primary care-giver's connections will assume a much greater significance in determining the child's habitual residence.

6.99 As indicated above, in *Re A (Children)* the Supreme Court ruled that these Court of Justice principles should henceforth replace the traditional English approach in determining the habitual residence of a child (even outside of the domain of Brussels II *bis*). The Supreme Court also emphasised the 'essentially factual and individual nature of the inquiry' and cautioned against 'legal concepts which would produce a different result from that which the factual inquiry would produce'.[268] Consistent with the increased emphasis on the child as an autonomous individual, the Supreme Court in the later case of *Re LC (Children)* determined that an adolescent child's own state of mind respecting a new country of residence should be material in deciding whether the child had become habitually resident there.[269]

E Conclusion

6.100 The concept of habitual residence is one suited to modern conditions where people move around the world with greater ease than in the past and is ideally suited for purposes such as divorce jurisdiction or child abduction, where the aim is not to establish

---

[263] Case C–523/07 [2009] ECR I–2805.   [264] Ibid, para 44.   [265] Ibid, para 40.
[266] Case C–497/10 PPU [2011] ILPr 23.   [267] Ibid, paras 53, 55.
[268] *Re A (Children)* [2014] AC 1 at [54]. This was further emphasised in *Re KL (a Child)* [2014] 1 AC 1017 at [20] where it was determined that a successful appeal against a decision allowing the removal of a child could not prevent the acquisition of a habitual residence in the country to which the child had been taken. However, the subsequent Court of Justice decision in Case C–376/14 *C v M* raises doubt as to the correctness of this decision (and suggests that the Court of Justice might not fully share the Supreme Court's commitment to a purely factual enquiry).
[269] *Re LC (Children)* [2014] 1 AC 1038. See generally Williams, 'The Supreme Court Trilogy: A New Habitual Residence Rises!' [2014] IFL 84.

a 'real home' but rather to identify a jurisdiction with which a person has a legitimate connection (although he may be more closely connected with some other country). The concept is, however, unsuitable for certain choice of law purposes as it generates a link with a country that may be tenuous. An English domiciliary working in Saudi Arabia on a one- or two-year contract can become habitually resident in that country. If habitual residence were to replace domicile as a general connecting factor for choice of law purposes this would mean that questions such as his capacity to marry more than one wife would be governed by Saudi Arabian law. Such an approach would be inappropriate and could encourage people to engage in deliberate evasion of the law that would normally be applicable to them.[270] Further, one could not countenance habitual residence as a general connecting factor when it is possible for a person to have no, or more than one, habitual residence. Accordingly, the Law Commission has rejected the idea of employing habitual residence as a general substitute for domicile.[271] The road forward seems clear. Habitual residence can, and should, be utilised in many areas of law, particularly in the context of jurisdiction and the recognition of foreign judgments. For many family choice of law purposes, however, the concept of domicile is more appropriate. That concept, however, as has been seen, is somewhat outdated and, accordingly, efforts should be redoubled to reform it. With a more modern and realistic concept of domicile, one could then engage in a functional analysis to determine which connecting factor, domicile or habitual residence (or even, perhaps sometimes, nationality), is most suitable for each conflicts rule.

---

[270] Law Com No 168, para 3.6.   [271] Ibid, paras 3.5–3.8.

7

Marriage

I Introduction

7.1 When the English court has to decide whether a marriage is valid, foreign elements may be involved: one or both of the spouses may be of overseas origin, or the marriage may have been celebrated in a foreign country. This chapter considers which law applies to determine the validity of such marriages.

7.2 There are various defects which may make a marriage invalid. These and the rules that precisely define them differ between various legal systems. For example, the question may be whether the proper formalities for the celebration of the marriage were complied with, or whether one of the spouses was below the minimum permitted age, or whether the spouses are too closely related. On such matters, different countries have different rules.

7.3 For choice of law purposes, rules about the validity of marriage are divided into two classes: those concerned with *formal* validity, on the one hand, and those concerned with *essential* validity, or capacity to marry, on the other. Rules of formal validity lay down the way in which a marriage must be celebrated (for example, to ensure publicity and proof of marriage). Rules of essential validity or capacity are concerned with the permissibility of the marriage relationship itself—whether the parties ought to be allowed to marry each other (or at all). Formal validity is governed by the law of the country where the marriage is celebrated (lex loci celebrationis), while essential validity (or capacity) is governed by the domiciliary laws of the parties at the time of the marriage. These propositions are considered in detail below.

A Marriage

7.4 Under the applicable rules a marriage may be valid or invalid. As will be seen, if the marriage is invalid, it may be void or voidable. However, in order for the applicable rules to be relevant, there must be a 'marriage' as opposed to, say, an engagement.[1] English law has started regarding some ceremonies as 'non-marriages' or 'non-existent marriages'.[2]

---

[1] See, eg, *Alfonso-Brown v Milwood* [2006] 2 FLR 265, where the 'husband' thought he was participating in an engagement ceremony, as opposed to a marriage ceremony, in Ghana.

[2] See Probert, 'The Evolving Concept of "Non-Marriage"' (2013) 25 CFLQ 314; Gaffney-Rhys, 'Am I Married? Three Recent Case Studies on the Effect of Non-compliant Marriage Ceremonies' [2013] IFL 53.

For example, in *A-M v A-M*³ an Islamic ceremony conducted in a flat in London was compared to a staged dramatic marriage ceremony in a soap opera: it did not constitute a 'marriage'. Other examples of non-marriages would be an exchange of promises between small children[4] or a full dress rehearsal of a wedding ceremony.[5] It is important to distinguish non-marriages from void marriages as ancillary relief can be claimed in respect of the latter, but not for the former. In *Hudson v Leigh*[6] the parties went through a religious ceremony on 'a fabulous roof-top setting overlooking a sunlit sea' in South Africa. Both parties and the minister conducting the ceremony knew that this would not constitute a valid marriage under South African law. (The atheist 'husband' was simply humouring his religious 'wife'; they planned to go through a later civil marriage ceremony in England.) It was held that this was a non-marriage because the ceremony was 'but a rehearsal and was neither arranged to, nor intended to, nor was itself purporting to achieve any legal outcome at all'.[7]

7.5 While the lex loci celebrationis determines the basic question as to whether the marriage is formally valid or invalid, the question as to whether an invalid marriage is a 'non-marriage' or a 'void marriage' is normally a matter for the lex fori (English law).[8] In *Hudson v Leigh* it was stated that this question must be determined by considering, not exhaustively, the following matters:

> (a) whether the ceremony or event set out or purported to be a lawful marriage; (b) whether it bore all or enough of the hallmarks of marriage; (c) whether the three key participants (most especially the officiating official) believed, intended and understood the ceremony as giving rise to the status of lawful marriage; and (d) the reasonable perceptions, understandings and beliefs of those in attendance.[9]

7.6 In *Burns v Burns*[10] a couple went through a ceremony of marriage in a hot-air balloon in California but, because of weather conditions, they only obtained a marriage licence after the ceremony rather than before it as required by Californian law. This formal defect rendered the marriage invalid as a matter of Californian law. The defective ceremony was, however, in the eyes of English law (the lex fori), 'nowhere near to the category of cases where the marriage can be described as a non-marriage'.[11] Accordingly, it was a marriage—but was void for non-compliance with the formalities of the lex loci celebrationis. The wife was thus able to seek financial relief.

7.7 It would further seem that, in order to qualify as a marriage, the relationship must be intended at the outset to be permanent. In an Asylum and Immigration Tribunal appeal[12] it was held that a temporary 'marriage', known as mut'a or sighé and celebrated

---

[3] [2001] 2 FLR 6.   [4] Ibid.
[5] *Hudson v Leigh (Status of Non-Marriage)* [2009] 2 FLR 1129 at [71]. In *Galloway v Goldstein* [2012] 1 FLR 1254 an English marriage ceremony (for the benefit of friends and family) between persons who had already contracted a valid marriage abroad, was characterised as a 'non-marriage'.
[6] [2009] 2 FLR 1129.   [7] At [72].   [8] *Assad v Kurter* [2014] 2 FLR 833 at [86]–[87].
[9] [2009] 2 FLR 1129 at [79]. See also *MA v JA* [2013] 2 FLR 68 at [85].
[10] [2008] 1 FLR 813.   [11] At [48].
[12] *LS (Mut'a or sighé) Iran* [2007] UKAIT 00072. See Shah, 'Inconvenient Marriages, or What Happens When Ethnic Minorities Marry Trans-jurisdictionally' (2010) 6 Utrecht Law Review 17.

by some Shia Muslims in Iran, was not a marriage for purposes of the immigration rules, as 'permanence and exclusivity'[13] are essential features of the institution of marriage.

7.8 In 2009 a French woman went through a ceremony of marriage with her dead fiancé.[14] Under article 171 of the French civil code, a bride or groom can marry a dead fiancé if there is clear evidence (which there was in this case) that they planned to marry.[15] It is not clear whether an English court would classify this as a marriage. Several of the key criteria set out in *Hudson v Leigh* would be satisfied—for example, the ceremony purported to be a lawful marriage and those in attendance certainly believed it was a marriage. However, it could well be (but this is speculation) that an English court would, for public policy reasons, insist that, in order to qualify as a marriage, both spouses must be alive.

B Degrees of invalidity

7.9 Assuming one is dealing with a 'marriage', different degrees of invalidity can result from a defect according to different laws. In English law, a marriage which is invalid may be either void ab initio or merely voidable. For example, in the cases of a marriage within the prohibited degrees, or below the permitted age, the marriage is void. Lack of consent of a party makes the marriage voidable. When a marriage is void in English law either party may apply to the court for a nullity decree and will usually do so if they are claiming financial relief, but a decree is not necessary to make the marriage void. Even without a decree, the parties are single and free to marry another person. On the other hand, a marriage which is voidable is valid unless and until it is annulled by the court on the petition of one of the parties. As regards a voidable marriage, if a nullity decree is made, it does not have retrospective effect; the marriage merely ceases to exist for the future.

7.10 Foreign laws also have different kinds of invalidity, but these do not necessarily correspond to the English distinction between void and voidable marriages. Under Scots law, for example, the annulment of a voidable marriage has retrospective effect. Under a particular law there may be more than two categories of invalidity. Older authorities suggest that the law which determines whether the marriage is invalid should also determine the kind of invalidity and its consequences.[16] However, in *Burns v Burns*[17] it was held that once the foreign law has established that the marriage is invalid 'the role of the foreign law is largely exhausted and the lex fori, i.e. England, produces the necessary remedies'.[18] Of course, the English court can grant a decree only of a kind and form known to English law. Nonetheless, 'if the applicable foreign law determines the effect of the defect by reference to concepts which clearly (or sufficiently) equate to the same concepts in English law then the English court is likely to apply those concepts'.[19]

---

[13] [2007] UKAIT 00072 at [19]. [14] *The Independent*, 18 November 2009.
[15] Apparently, some 20 posthumous marriages take place in France each year (ibid).
[16] *De Reneville v De Reneville* [1948] P 100; *Lepre v Lepre* [1965] P 52.
[17] [2008] 1 FLR 813. [18] At [44]. [19] *Assad v Kurter* [2014] 2 FLR 833 at [97].

C Civil partnerships/Same-sex marriages

7.11 The Civil Partnership Act 2004, which came into force in December 2005, allowed persons of the same sex to register a civil partnership. While civil partnership conferred a status which was distinct to that of 'marriage', there was little in terms of legal consequences to distinguish the two. The 2004 Act mirrors the various rules covering marriage and divorce; it specifies the formalities that must be complied with; it lists rules of capacity (described as 'eligibility'); it specifies the proprietary and financial consequences; it contains provisions relating to children; and it provides rules for the dissolution or annulment of such partnerships. While the 2004 Act remains in force, it has, to a large extent, been overtaken by the Marriage (Same Sex Couples) Act 2013, which allows same sex couples to marry. Both the 2004 Act and the 2013 Act include provisions governing the recognition of same-sex relationships formalised abroad. For the sake of convenience, same-sex marriages and civil partnerships will be dealt with separately in this chapter.

D Classification of defects

7.12 Because there are different choice of law rules for questions of formal validity and questions of essential validity, it is necessary that any alleged defect to a marriage be classified as relating to either formalities or essentials. Until this is done, the appropriate choice of law rule cannot be applied. With most alleged defects this classification process is simple and automatic. For example, whether the requisite number of witnesses is present at the marriage ceremony relates to the formalities, whereas the age at which a person can marry is a matter relating to capacity or essential validity. However, in respect of certain other alleged impediments, the appropriate classification may not be self-evident. The general rule is that classification must be effected according to the lex fori. The critical issue is whether English law regards the defect as relating to formalities or essentials. The application of this rule can be seen in the following areas dealing with proxy marriages and parental consent.

1. Proxy marriages

7.13 Under English law, both spouses are required to be present at the marriage ceremony.[20] In some other countries, however, proxy marriages are permitted. In *Apt v Apt*[21] an English domiciliary executed a power of attorney authorising a friend to go through a marriage ceremony on her behalf in Argentina with an Argentinian domiciliary. If the requirement of the parties' presence at the marriage ceremony were classified as relating to the essentials of marriage, the marriage would have been held void as the English woman would have lacked capacity. It was held, however, classifying the issue according to the lex fori,[22] that the requirement of presence related to the method of

---

[20] This is implicit in the Marriage Act 1949, s 44(3), which requires both parties to make various declarations at the marriage ceremony.
[21] [1948] P 83.   [22] See paras 1.70–1.75.

giving consent, as opposed to the fact of consent (which would have been an essential requirement). Accordingly, it related to the method by which the ceremony was performed, which is a matter of formal validity to be governed by Argentinian law, the lex loci celebrationis, according to which the marriage was valid.

2. Parental consent

7.14 Legal systems often provide that persons below a certain age must have the consent of their parents to marry. However, the age below which such consent is necessary, and the consequences of failure to obtain it, differ from one law to another. Does this requirement relate to formalities or essentials? At first sight, it might seem that a requirement of parental consent relates to capacity, at any rate if the marriage is invalid without such consent, presumably because it is thought that the judgment of the person concerned is insufficiently mature. The English requirement of parental consent, however, is regarded by the English courts as a formality, not an incapacity. The main reason for this is that the absence of parental consent in English law does not normally invalidate the marriage. If the parties manage to have the marriage celebrated without it, the marriage is normally valid. So, it is hardly possible to say that there is any incapacity involved.

7.15 It should not necessarily follow that a foreign rule about parental consent should also be classified as one of formalities if by the foreign law the absence of parental consent does affect the validity of the marriage. Nevertheless, following the general rule that classification is to be effected by the lex fori, it has been held that such a foreign rule concerns formalities and, therefore, is only to be applied if the marriage is celebrated in the foreign country concerned. *Ogden v Ogden*[23] involved a marriage which was celebrated in England between a woman domiciled in England and a man aged 19 domiciled in France. According to French law, a man of that age required the consent of his parents to marry and, if such consent was not obtained, the marriage was voidable. The Court of Appeal held that the French requirement of parental consent was a formality and, accordingly, that French law, not being the lex loci celebrationis, was inapplicable. The formal validity of the marriage was tested by English law as the parties had married in England. As the marriage had been celebrated according to the forms required by English law, it was held to be valid.[24]

7.16 This decision has been widely criticised, but in *Lodge v Lodge*[25] it was again accepted that the French requirement was a formality. In this case, the marriage was celebrated in Scotland between a husband domiciled in England and a wife aged 18 domiciled in France who did not have parental consent. The English court, following *Ogden v Ogden*, held the marriage valid under Scots law as the lex loci celebrationis.[26]

---

[23] [1908] P 46.
[24] Another reason for the decision was that since the marriage was celebrated in England and the wife was domiciled here, then according to the rule in *Sottomayor v De Barros (No 2)* (1879) 5 PD 94 the validity of the marriage was to be tested exclusively by English law. See para 7.57.
[25] (1963) 107 Sol Jo 437.
[26] This decision could not have been reached on the basis of the rule in *Sottomayor v De Barros (No 2)*. See para 7.57.

7.17 Critics of this approach would not necessarily claim that all rules relating to parental consent should be treated as rules of capacity. In *Simonin v Mallac*,[27] a couple domiciled in France celebrated their marriage in England without parental consent. The husband was aged 29 and the wife 22. By French law, parties of those ages had to request the consent of their parents 'by a respectful and formal act'. If, however, this was refused, and continued to be refused when the request was repeated twice more at monthly intervals, the parties were free to marry without it. The marriage was held valid. The French rule here can reasonably be regarded as one of formality, in substance analogous to a requirement of notice, unlike the rule considered in *Ogden v Ogden*, under which the parental consent could not be dispensed with. Similar questions of classification may arise with respect to a requirement for the consent of state authorities where a marriage to a foreign national is contemplated. Such a requirement (arising under Syrian law) was assumed to be a formality in *Asaad v Kurter*;[28] however, one might argue that it ought to have been classified as an incapacity in so far as it was a mandatory requirement which arguably had a protective function. On the other hand, in so far as arbitrary state interference in a person's choice of marital partner is considered to violate the right to marry under article 12 of the European Convention on Human Rights,[29] public policy might require an English court to disregard such a requirement under foreign law.[30]

II Formal validity

A The general rule

7.18 Under formal validity one is concerned with the law which governs the ceremony and other procedures required for the valid celebration of a marriage. The following matters relate to the formalities of a marriage: whether a civil ceremony or a religious ceremony is necessary, or whether either suffices; what ancillary formalities as to notices and witnesses are necessary; where, when, and by whom the ceremony must be conducted. Also, as already seen, issues relating to proxy marriages and parental consent are regarded as matters relating to formal validity.

7.19 Under English domestic law, a failure to comply with the English formal requirements relating to a marriage ceremony does not necessarily render the marriage void. Broadly speaking, there are two types of formal requirements. Non-compliance with the first category (for example, parental consent) does not render the marriage void.[31]

---

[27] (1860) 2 Sw & Tr 67.   [28] [2014] 2 FLR 833 at [72].
[29] *R (Baiai) v Secretary of State for the Home Dept* [2008] 3 WLR 549; *O'Donoghue v United Kingdom* (2011) 53 EHRR 1.
[30] See paras 7.100–7.103. Questions of classification—and public policy—might also arise where the lex loci celebrationis imposes a requirement of 'iddah'—a requirement that a (divorced or widowed) woman waits three months before remarrying in order to ensure that she is not pregnant by her former spouse: see *Ismail v Choudhry* [2016] EWCA Civ 17.
[31] Marriage Act 1949, ss 24, 48. The position is different with civil partnerships. If the civil partnership has been 'forbidden' (in writing by the person whose parental consent is required) the civil partnership is void: Civil Partnership Act 2004, s 49(c).

Thus, while a marriage official may refuse to marry persons without the necessary consents, if they go through a marriage ceremony, the marriage is valid. Non-compliance with the second category (for example, that the marriage must be solemnised by a person who is a recognised marriage official) will render the marriage void—but only if both parties were aware of the irregularity at the time of the marriage ceremony.[32] The main sanction for non-compliance with the formalities of marriage is afforded by the criminal law.[33] Many other legal systems, however, are not so indulgent and a failure to comply with formal requirements renders a marriage invalid.

7.20 The basic rule is that questions of formal validity are governed by the lex loci celebrationis, the law of the country where the marriage is celebrated. If the ceremony suffices to create the status of marriage under that law, the marriage will be considered formally valid as a matter of English law. Even if there is some doubt as to the legal basis for recognition of the ceremony under the lex loci celebrationis, the fact that the resulting marriage is in practice recognised for all official purposes under that country's laws will ensure its formal validity under English law.[34] The parties' own expectations are generally irrelevant if the marriage is formally valid under the applicable foreign law: their assumption that the relevant marriage form would not suffice for the purposes of English law will not prevent its recognition.[35] Where there is subsequent legislative validation of formally defective marriages in the place of celebration, English law will normally recognise the retrospective validation and consider the affected marriages to be formally valid.[36]

7.21 While in most cases it is clear where a marriage has been celebrated, this issue can, on occasion, be problematic. For example, in *Westminster City Council v C*[37] a man in England went through an Islamic marriage ceremony over the telephone with a woman in Bangladesh. In such cases it is for English law, as the lex fori, to determine where the marriage was celebrated. The law remains unsettled as to the correct approach but there is some support for the view that such 'telephone marriages' are celebrated in the *principal* place of solemnisation where any additional religious or ceremonial acts are carried out.[38] A question may also arise as to whether a marriage ceremony conducted in consular premises is required to comply with the law of the sending state, or that of the receiving state on whose territory the consulate is located. English law provides a clear answer to this question: the law of the receiving state must be complied with

---

[32] Marriage Act 1949, ss 25, 49. See, eg, *Chief Adjudication Officer v Bath* [2000] 1 FLR 8. The position is the same with civil partnerships: Civil Partnership Act 2004, s 49(b).
[33] Marriage Act 1949, s 75; Marriage (Registrar General's Licence) Act 1970, s 16; Perjury Act 1911, s 3; Civil Partnership Act 2004, ss 32, 33.
[34] *R v M* [2011] EWHC 2132 (Fam).
[35] *N v D (Customary Marriage)* [2015] EWFC 28 at [68].
[36] *Starkowski v A-G* [1954] AC 155. [37] [2009] Fam 11.
[38] See, eg, *MRA v NRK* [2011] CSOH 101 (Court of Session, Scotland). This 'principal place of solemnisation' approach was also supported by the High Court in *City of Westminster v C*, but in the Court of Appeal, Thorpe LJ was not prepared to commit himself on this issue: [2009] Fam 11 at [36]–[42].

as the lex loci celebrationis.[39] Therefore, in *Dukali v Lamrani*,[40] a marriage ceremony taking place at the Moroccan Consulate in London—and valid by Moroccan law—was held to be a non-marriage as a matter of English law, because there had been no attempt to comply with the English formality rules.

7.22 A clear application of the basic rule can be seen in *Berthiaume v Dastous*,[41] where the spouses, who were domiciled in Quebec, married in a Roman Catholic church in France. The marriage was void by French law because, owing to a mistake by the priest, it had not been preceded by a civil ceremony. Even though by the law of Quebec a religious ceremony alone was sufficient, the Privy Council (on appeal from Quebec) held the marriage void.

7.23 Where there is a difficulty in proving a marriage in accordance with the lex loci celebrationis, presumptions of validity of marriage may apply. Even if there is no such presumption under the law of the place of celebration, the English presumption may assist in circumstances where the parties cohabited for many years and had the reputation of being married and where there is insufficient positive evidence that the relevant overseas ceremony could not have constituted a valid marriage.[42] While questions of proof are generally a matter for the lex fori, a copy of a marriage certificate apparently authenticated by the authorities of the place of celebration must be presumed to be valid unless and until evidence to the contrary is adduced.[43]

7.24 The lex loci celebrationis rule is an application of a general principle of the conflict of laws, locus regit actum (the place governs the deed). The principle is partly one of convenience. Parties to a transaction must be free to use a form which is required of or available to them. It would not be reasonable to require a couple who are residing abroad to use a ceremony required by the law of their domicile if that ceremony is not available or has no legal foundation in the jurisdiction in which they are marrying. In most cases, local formalities are easily ascertainable; the parties can rely on local legal advice and the application of such a law would accord with their reasonable expectations.[44] In giving effect to the formalities of the lex loci celebrationis, English law adheres to an internationally accepted standard,[45] thereby promoting the consistent recognition of marriage and the avoidance of 'limping marriages' (that is, marriages which are considered valid in one country and invalid in another).

7.25 Questions have arisen, however, as to the desirability of a mechanical application of the lex loci celebrationis rule where overseas marriage forms pursue a very different policy

---

[39] Although, as will be seen at para 7.32 below, statute makes special provision for the recognition of British consular marriages taking place abroad in compliance with British law (and without regard to the law of the place of celebration).
[40] [2012] 2 FLR 1099.   [41] [1930] AC 79.
[42] See, eg, *Pazpena de Vire v Pazpena de Vire* [2001] 1 FLR 460; also *Al-Saedy v Musawi (Presumption of Marriage)* [2011] 2 FLR 287; *Asaad v Kurter* [2014] 2 FLR 833 at [50]; *K v A* [2015] 2 FLR 461.
[43] *Lukandwa v Birungi* [2012] 1 FLR 898.
[44] Law Com Working Paper No 89, *Private International Law: Choice of Law Rules in Marriage* (1985) para 2.36.
[45] Pålsson, 'Marriage and Divorce', in Lipstein (ed), *International Encyclopaedia of Comparative Law*, vol III, Private International Law (1986) p 27.

agenda from the English domestic rules which are principally concerned with publicity and proof of marriage.[46] Proxy and customary marriage forms may facilitate clandestine marriages and bring about circumstances where neither spouse can give direct testimony as to a marriage ceremony.[47] Customary marriages are often unregistered.[48] Many other countries are much more restrictive in their recognition of such marriage forms—which fail to comply with the UN Convention on Consent to Marriage[49]—and it is arguable that the English courts should reconsider the automatic application of the lex loci celebrationis rule in such cases (in particular where English residents, who might easily marry in accordance with English law, choose to marry abroad in a form which is far less amenable to objective verification[50]).

B Exceptions to the lex loci celebrationis rule

7.26 In certain exceptional situations the parties are exempted from compliance with the lex loci celebrationis. There are both common law and statutory exceptions.

1. Common law exceptions

7.27 In certain circumstances the parties are permitted to ignore the formalities of the lex loci celebrationis and can instead contract a 'common law marriage'. A common law marriage is one that complies with the English common law as it stood before Lord Hardwicke's Clandestine Marriages Act of 1753. All that is required is that the parties take each other as husband and wife in the presence of each other. Originally, when such marriages could still take place in England, it was held that the ceremony had to be performed by an episcopally ordained clergyman,[51] but later decisions have indicated that this requirement is not applicable to marriages celebrated abroad (which is the only place where one can celebrate a common law marriage).[52] Further, such a requirement would discriminate against parties who were not Christians.[53] Whether such marriages can take place only in circumstances of some urgency or where the parties are likely to remain in the foreign country for some appreciable time is an

---

[46] See Fawcett, Ní Shúilleabháin and Shah, *Human Rights and Private International Law* (2016) para 11.99 ff; Crawford and Carruthers, 'Dual Locality Events: Marriage by Telephone' 2011 Scots Law Times 227; Murphy, 'The Recognition of Overseas Marriages and Divorces in the United Kingdom' (1996) 47 NILQ 35, 39–40.

[47] See, eg, *McCabe v McCabe* [1994] 1 FLR 410; *Pazpena de Vire v Pazpena de Vire* [2001] 1 FLR 460.

[48] See *MO v RO* [2013] EWHC 392 (Fam) at [46].

[49] UN Convention on Consent to Marriage, Minimum Age for Marriage and Registration of Marriages 1962 521 UNTS 231. This UN Convention (ratified by the United Kingdom) requires marriages to be celebrated in person and to be registered. Proxy marriages are permitted only in 'exceptional circumstances' and only in the absence of one party (not both).

[50] See, eg, *McCabe v McCabe* [1994] 1 FLR 410; *N v D (Customary Marriage)* [2015] EWFC 28.

[51] *R v Millis* (1844) 10 Cl & Fin 534. See Probert, 'R v Millis Reconsidered: Binding Contracts and Bigamous Marriages' (2008) 28 LS 337.

[52] *Wolfenden v Wolfenden* [1946] P 61; *Isaac Penhas v Tan Soo Eng* [1953] AC 304; *Preston v Preston* [1963] P 411. It has been suggested that the requirement of an episcopally ordained clergyman can be dispensed with only if such a person is not available: Cheshire, North and Fawcett, *Private International Law* (14th edn, 2008) p 889.

[53] *Hooshmand v Ghasmezadegan* (2000) FLC 93-044 (Family Court of Western Australia).

unresolved issue. In such circumstances one can understand the law adopting a flexible approach with a view to trying to uphold the validity of such marriages. However, it would be patently absurd to extend this indulgence to persons who are merely on holiday or present for a short time in the foreign country.[54] Common law marriages may be regarded as formally valid in the following three situations.

(A) Where English common law applies

7.28 In the days of the British Empire there was a rule of constitutional law that settlers took with them as much of the English common law as was applicable to local conditions.[55] This was often achieved by a capitulatory agreement providing that the Crown exercised extraterritorial jurisdiction over British subjects in a foreign country to which an Order in Council had been extended. In *Wolfenden v Wolfenden*[56] an Order in Council of 1925 applied to the province of Hupeh in China. A common law marriage entered into there by an English and a Canadian domiciliary was recognised as valid. This is, of course, not a true exception to the lex loci celebrationis rule because in this type of case the English common law is deemed to be the local law for British subjects. This category of case is now only of historical interest.

(B) Insuperable difficulty in complying with the local law

7.29 If it is impossible (having regard, inter alia, to their religious beliefs) for the parties to comply with the form required by the law of the foreign country in which they marry, or if no form is available, then they may validly contract a common law marriage. In *Ruding v Smith*[57] a common law marriage entered into at the Cape of Good Hope was recognised. The 'insuperable difficulty' in this case was that the local law required the guardian of each party to consent to the marriage; the husband's guardian was in England and the wife had not had a guardian appointed after the death of her father. Another example of an 'insuperable difficulty' would be where the parties were domiciled in England and only a polygamous local form of marriage was available.[58] In the Australian case of *Hooshmand v Ghasmezadegan*[59] the spouses went through a marriage ceremony in Iran in accordance with the Baha'i religion. This marriage was held to be valid despite non-compliance with the lex loci celebrationis as only Christian, Jewish, and Muslim marriages could be contracted in Iran and civil marriage was not available there. Because of their religion, the parties were unable to comply with Iranian law.

(C) Marriages in countries under belligerent occupation

7.30 The exception to the lex loci celebrationis rule was extended at the end of the Second World War to marriages celebrated by members of occupying forces in Germany and Italy. In *Taczanowska v Taczanowski*[60] two Polish domiciliaries married in Italy without complying with the local Italian formalities but in a manner that satisfied the requirements of

---

[54] See however *Nygh & Kasey* [2010] FamCA 145 (Family Court of Australia).
[55] *Maclean v Cristall* (1849) 7 Notes of Cases, Supp xvii.   [56] [1946] P 61.
[57] (1821) 2 Hag Con 371.   [58] Law Com Working Paper No 89, para 2.23.
[59] (2000) FLC 93–044 (Family Court of Western Australia).   [60] [1957] P 301.

English common law. The husband was a member of the Polish occupying forces. It was held that the rationale of the general lex loci celebrationis rule is that parties marrying in a country are presumed to submit themselves to the law of that country. Such a presumption was inapplicable in the case of members of occupying forces as the conqueror could not be presumed to submit to the law of the conquered. As Italian law was inapplicable, it was held that the English common law applied and the marriage was valid. While one can have some sympathy with the court's desire to uphold the validity of such marriages, the result is nevertheless extraordinary in that the validity of a marriage contracted in Italy by two Poles who had never set foot in England was tested by reference to English law as it stood before 1753. A better approach would be that such marriages will only be valid if there had been an insuperable difficulty in complying with the local formalities which was not the case in *Taczanowska*—unless 'insuperable difficulty' is defined so broadly as to include 'merely distasteful'. Alternatively, if the presumption of submission is the basis of the lex loci celebrationis rule, if it is rebutted it should arguably be rebutted in favour of the parties' personal law. It makes no sense to assert that if the parties have not submitted to the lex loci celebrationis they must be deemed to have submitted to the law of a country with which they have never had any connection.

7.31 Despite such criticisms, *Taczanowska* was followed in numerous other cases involving marriages contracted in Europe in the mid-1940s.[61] Doubt still remains, however, over the precise ambit of the rule and whether it covers other persons in war zones, such as Red Cross members in Syria or armed forces in Afghanistan. Perhaps the most authoritative approach is that adopted in *Merker v Merker* which limited the *Taczanowska* rule to 'marriages within the lines of a foreign army of occupation . . . or of persons in a strictly analogous situation to the members of such an army, such as members of an organised body of escaped prisoners of war'.[62] In *Preston v Preston*[63] this category was expanded to military personnel who were in a camp which was serving the overall Allied purpose of hostile occupation of Germany. In *Merker* the court also challenged the underlying rationale of submission put forward in *Taczanowska* on the basis that, if generally applied, it would 'introduce anarchy in a field where order and comity are particularly required'.[64] Instead, the exception was explained on the basis that such an army of occupation or organised body of escaped prisoners of war formed an 'enclave' within which it was unreasonable to apply the local law. However, even accepting this better rationale, one is still left with the question of what law applies within this enclave and, again, it is far from clear why this should be English common law if none of the people within the enclave is, in fact, English.

2. Statutory exceptions

(A) Consular marriages

7.32 Statute makes special provision for the recognition of British consular marriage. The original scheme laid down in the Foreign Marriage Act 1892 was replaced by a new scheme

---

[61] For example, *Kochanski v Kochanska* [1958] P 147; *Preston v Preston* [1963] P 411.
[62] [1963] P 283 at 295. [63] [1963] P 411. [64] [1963] P 283 at 295.

pursuant to Schedule 6 to the Marriage (Same Sex Couples) Act 2013. Various requirements are specified in the Act. One of the parties proposing to marry must be a UK national,[65] and both must be eligible to marry in either England or Scotland.[66] The registration officer must also be satisfied that insufficient facilities exist under the lex loci celebrationis and that the local authorities will not object to the solemnisation of the marriage.[67]

(B) Military marriages

7.33 Special provision is also made under the Marriage (Same Sex Couples) Act 2013, for the solemnisation of military marriages (whether opposite sex or same sex) in foreign countries when one of the parties is either a member of HM Forces serving there or a member of the civilian personnel accompanying such forces, or a child of a forces or civilian personnel member.[68] Such marriages are celebrated by military chaplains or other persons authorised by the commanding officer.[69]

III Essential validity

A Terminology

7.34 'Essential validity' covers all questions of validity other than formal validity. 'Capacity to marry' is a category within essential validity.[70] 'Capacity to marry' ought strictly to be confined to rules which lay down that a particular class of person lacks a power to marry which other people possess (for instance, a rule that a person below a certain age may not marry). In practice, however, capacity to marry also includes cases where the reason for the invalidity is that such a marriage relationship is objectionable in the eyes of the law (for instance, rules prohibiting marriages between relatives of certain degrees). Capacity to marry does not, however, cover the whole field of essential validity; it does not include some instances relating to the consent of the parties (for example, mistake) or the non-consummation of the marriage.

B The choice of law rule

1. Introduction

7.35 Although formal validity is governed by the law of the country where the marriage is celebrated, that law is not generally thought appropriate in the English conflict of laws

---

[65] Marriage (Same Sex Couples) Act 2013, sch 6, para 1(2)(a).
[66] Marriage (Same Sex Couples) Act 2013, sch 6, para 1(2)(b). The notice of intention to marry must specify the part of the United Kingdom elected by the parties: The Consular Marriages and Marriages under Foreign Law (No 2) Order 2014, SI 2014/3265, art 4(4)(a).
[67] Marriage (Same Sex Couples) Act 2013, sch 6, para 1(2)(c) and (d). Similar provisions exist for civil partnerships: Civil Partnership Act 2004, s 210.
[68] Marriage (Same Sex Couples) Act 2013, sch 6, para 8(2). See also the Overseas Marriage (Armed Forces) Order 2014, SI 2014/1108.
[69] Similar provisions exist for civil partnerships: Civil Partnership Act 2004, s 211.
[70] The Civil Partnership Act 2004 uses the term 'eligibility' (s 3).

to govern essential validity.[71] While there is an argument, to be canvassed later,[72] that the lex loci celebrationis may have *some* interest in the essential validity of marriages contracted within its borders, this interest is insufficient to justify utilising the lex loci celebrationis as the primary choice of law rule here. This is because the marriage may be celebrated in a country which in other respects has no connection with the marriage or the parties. Neither of the parties may be domiciled there before the ceremony and they may not establish their home there after it.

7.36 For essential validity, therefore, it is the personal law which is important. The personal law governs certain matters relating to status and personal relationships that are regarded as vital to the maintenance of the institution of marriage in a society and, therefore, all persons 'belonging' to that society have to comply with its rules. Any other approach would open the door to unacceptable evasion of the law with the parties simply making temporary visits to foreign countries in order to marry and thereby evade the provisions of their personal law. It was seen in Chapter 6 that a person is often regarded as 'belonging' to the country of his domicile. With marriage, however, one is dealing with a relationship between two people (at least) who before the marriage might be domiciled in different countries and who after the marriage might set up a home together in another country. What is the appropriate test of belonging in this context? Is it where the parties each belonged before the marriage or is it where the marriage subsequently belongs? The answer to this question is not self-evident and consequently there has been some uncertainty as to the precise nature of the English choice of law rule for essential validity of marriage. Various solutions have been suggested. Each of these is considered in turn.

2. Dual domicile doctrine

7.37 According to the dual domicile doctrine, the law of each party's domicile at the date of the marriage has to be considered. For the marriage to be valid, each party must have capacity by the law of his or her domicile to contract the marriage. Suppose the English court has to determine the validity of a marriage between first cousins, one of whom at the date of the marriage is domiciled in Sweden and the other in Portugal. By Swedish law, let it be assumed, such a marriage is valid, but by Portuguese law it is within the prohibited degrees of relationship. Under the dual domicile doctrine, the marriage would be invalid.

7.38 This rule, which, as will be seen, commands most support in English law, has several advantages. In terms of principle, it is appropriate that people be governed by the law of their existing domicile. This law will usually have governed their status for a long time, if not for their whole life. The reasonable expectations of the parties are often best fulfilled by an application of their existing personal law. The application of any other law (say, the law of the intended matrimonial home) would enable the parties

---

[71] *X City Council v MB* [2006] 2 FLR 968.   [72] See para 7.58.

to evade any restrictions imposed by their ante-nuptial domiciliary laws. As the Law Commission put it:

> The main rationale of the dual domicile rule is that a person's status is a matter of public concern to the country to which he belongs at the time of marriage; and therefore the domiciliary law of each party has an equal right to be heard. The issue of whether a valid marriage has been or may be contracted should, in principle and in logic, depend on the conditions existing at the time of marriage rather than subsequently.[73]

7.39 Another advantage claimed for the dual domicile doctrine is that it is easy to apply in prospective situations. Recourse to some of the other suggested tests, such as the intended matrimonial home doctrine, would involve the validity of the marriage remaining in suspense until the new home is established. Under the dual domicile doctrine, the validity of the marriage can be established from the moment of marriage. It is therefore amenable to application by marriage officials who have to decide in advance of the ceremony whether the parties are entitled to marry one another.

7.40 There are, however, certain disadvantages and criticisms associated with the dual domicile doctrine. It is arguable that in assessing the essential validity of a marriage, the focus should be on the law to which the *marriage* belongs. This is arguably the community which is most affected by the marriage. The country where the parties came from is arguably less interested in the validity of the marriage than the country where the marriage is based. A further objection to the dual domicile doctrine is that, because both parties' ante-nuptial domiciliary laws have to be applied cumulatively, there is a greater chance of the marriage being declared invalid than if any single law were applied. Such an approach runs counter to the well-established policy in favour of upholding the validity of a marriage.

3. Intended matrimonial home doctrine

7.41 An alternative approach is that the law of the intended matrimonial home (sometimes called the matrimonial domicile) governs the essential validity of a marriage. This test, as originally advocated in earlier editions of Cheshire's *Private International Law*,[74] provided a basic presumption in favour of the law of the country in which the husband was domiciled at the date of the marriage. This presumption could be rebutted if at the time of the marriage the parties intended to establish a matrimonial home in a different country and if they implemented that intention within a reasonable time. For example, in *Frankel's Estate v The Master*[75] a man, domiciled in Germany, married a woman, domiciled in Czechoslovakia. The marriage took place in Czechoslovakia. At the time of the marriage the parties had planned to emigrate from Europe to settle permanently in South Africa, which they did four months later. They lived in South Africa for the next 15 years until the husband died. Under the intended matrimonial home doctrine the validity of this marriage would be tested by South African law. At the date of the marriage they intended to settle there and implemented this intention within a reasonable period of time.

---

[73] Law Com Working Paper No 89, para 3.36. [74] Eg, 7th edn, 1965, p 276.
[75] 1950 (1) SA 220 (South Africa). (This case was in fact concerned with matrimonial property and not with the validity of the marriage.)

7.42 Cheshire's original formulation, drawing on the writings of Cook[76] and Savigny,[77] pointed presumptively to the law of the husband's domicile on the basis that, in most cases where the parties have different domiciles, they are likely to make their home in his country. This might have been empirically true 50 years ago, but can only be regarded as questionable today and, given its sexist assumption, cannot be accepted. A further explanation for the original presumption was that at the moment of marriage, the wife acquired a domicile of dependence on the husband. Since the abolition of the married woman's domicile of dependence, this rationale is no longer applicable. Accordingly, Cheshire's basic presumption is no longer tenable and the only issue is whether the dual domicile doctrine should be displaced in clear cases in favour of the intended matrimonial home.

7.43 The perceived advantage of applying the intended matrimonial home doctrine is that it allows the validity of a marriage to be tested by the law of the country most affected by and interested in the marriage. For proponents of this doctrine, that country forms the 'true seat' of the marriage;[78] its law is the 'proper law' of the marriage. If, for example, the issue is the validity of a marriage between cousins, it is arguably the country where the married cousins will live that has the most interest in the marriage. The country from which the parties came might be said to have little interest in the matter. The other advantage of the doctrine is that it tends to favour the validity of marriages, in that it is necessary to have recourse only to one law.

7.44 The disadvantages attached to the doctrine are, however, formidable. First, the doctrine can be applied only retrospectively. If the parties in *Frankel's Estate* had sought advice before their marriage as to whether it would be valid, no definitive answer could have been provided as the validity of the marriage would have depended on whether they implemented their intention within a reasonable time. As noted above, this places marriage officials in a predicament. Such officials cannot operate according to the laws of a place where the parties might establish a home.

7.45 Secondly, what if the parties leave the country of their intended matrimonial home after a limited period and establish a permanent home in another country? In such a case it is the law of the new country that is arguably most interested in the marriage. One could not, however, continually reassess the validity of a marriage every time the parties change their home. Thirdly, and most significantly, there is a fallacy in the assumption that it is the law of the intended matrimonial home that is most interested in the marriage. Most rules on capacity to marry are designed to protect a person. For instance, the rule in English law that no marriage may be contracted until the age of 16 is designed to protect the immature. English law has a legitimate interest in ensuring its domiciliaries do not evade this prohibition. When a 13-year-old English domiciliary went through a marriage ceremony in 1996 with a Turkish domiciliary and set up a home with him in Turkey, the resultant furore indicated very

---

[76] *The Logical and Legal Bases of the Conflict of Laws* (1942) p 448.
[77] *A Treatise on the Conflict of Laws* (Guthrie's translation, 1869) p 240.   [78] Ibid.

clearly that English law maintained a strong interest in her welfare and the validity of her marriage.[79] Fourthly, it is highly questionable whether the application of the law of the intended matrimonial home does accord with the reasonable expectations of the parties. Suppose two cousins domiciled in England decide to marry and set up a matrimonial home in Portugal. In such a case the parties would probably have relied on English legal advice that marriages between cousins are lawful; indeed, they might have been brought up their whole lives with such a belief. An application of Portuguese law which could declare their marriage void would clearly frustrate their reasonable expectations.[80] Fifthly, there are the inevitable practical problems: how can one establish what the parties intended at the time of their marriage[81] and how long is a reasonable period of time? In practice, such questions would not be unanswerable[82]—but they are certainly vaguer questions than those posed in the ascertainment of a person's domicile. Finally, over the last half-century, immigration patterns have shown a greater movement of people from developing countries to developed countries and from countries permitting polygamy to countries practising monogamy than vice versa.[83] Particularly with regard to age restrictions, developing countries tend to have lower age limits than developed countries.[84] Application of the intended matrimonial home test would, therefore, result in the invalidation of marriages which are valid according to the parties' domiciliary law. Similarly, where a couple from a country practising polygamy planned to emigrate to the United Kingdom, there would be a greater chance of their marriage being declared invalid if the intended matrimonial home doctrine were utilised.[85]

4. Real and substantial connection

7.46 Another possibility is that the essential validity of a marriage should be governed by the law of the country with which the marriage has its most real and substantial connection. As with the intended matrimonial home doctrine this rule is trying to connect the marriage (as opposed to either of the parties) with the country to which it 'belongs'. Normally, the country with which a marriage is most closely connected will be the country where the matrimonial home is situated.[86] It is, however, a test that provides extra flexibility in that other factors such as domicile and nationality can be taken into consideration.[87] In *Vervaeke v Smith*[88] this test was considered (obiter) by Lord Simon in a case involving the validity of a marriage of convenience where no matrimonial home had been intended. In this case the marriage had been contracted in England. The man was an English domiciliary and the woman, while a Belgian domiciliary, was

---

[79] *The Times*, 25 January 1996, 1.   [80] Law Com Working Paper No 89, para 3.35.
[81] Jaffey, *Topics in Choice of Law* (1996) p 130, argues that this should not be a requirement in most cases.
[82] Ibid, pp 127–8.   [83] *UN Demographic Yearbook 1996* (48th issue, 1998) pp 1076–93.
[84] As in *Mohamed v Knott* [1969] 1 QB 1. See also Gaffney-Rhys, 'The Law Relating to Marriageable Age from a National and International Perspective' [2009] IFL 228.
[85] Karsten, 'Capacity to Contract a Polygamous Marriage' (1973) 36 MLR 291, 296; Davie, 'The Breaking Up of Essential Validity of Marriage Choice of Law Rules in English Conflict of Laws' (1994) 23 Anglo-Am L Rev 32, 35.
[86] *Lawrence v Lawrence* [1985] 1 All ER 506 at 511.   [87] *Indyka v Indyka* [1969] 1 AC 33.
[88] [1983] 1 AC 145 at 166.

planning to become permanently resident in England and assume British nationality. The marriage was clearly most closely connected with England.

7.47 In *Vervaeke v Smith*, Lord Simon indicated that the real and substantial connection test should be applied 'if not [to] all questions of essential validity, at least [to] the question of the sort of quintessential validity in issue in this appeal, the question of which law's public policy should determine the validity of the marriage'.[89] In *Lawrence v Lawrence*, at first instance, Lincoln J regarded this dictum as referring to 'circumstances in which the public policy of two legal systems pulled in opposite directions'; the judge regarded the issue of capacity to remarry after a foreign divorce as one that 'directly... involve[d] "the quintessential validity" of the marriage contract'.[90] Such an approach is unacceptable. While the issue of a marriage of convenience can perhaps be interpreted as one of quintessential validity, because the question is whether the parties intended a 'marriage', it is difficult to fathom the basis upon which any other impediment can be so classified. All prohibitions on marriage, such as lack of age or marriages within the prohibited degrees of relationship, are little more than crystallisations of public policy. Indeed, it has been suggested that marriages within the prohibited degrees and capacity to contract a polygamous marriage raise questions of quintessential validity of marriage.[91] If this is true, it would seem that all questions of capacity and consent can be so regarded, with the result that only matters such as impotence and wilful refusal would be regarded as essential rather than quintessential. Such a classification hardly seems helpful.

7.48 Further, while the real and substantial connection test has its supporters,[92] it is, in reality, a question-begging test. The question is which choice of law rule will best lead to the application of the law to which the parties and the marriage 'belong'. This test does not answer the question, but rather 'simply restates the problem'.[93] And, as the Law Commission put it:

> It is an inherently vague and unpredictable test which would introduce an unacceptable degree of uncertainty into the law. It is a test which is difficult to apply other than through the courtroom process and it is therefore unsuitable in an area where the law's function is essentially prospective, i.e., a yardstick for future planning.[94]

5. Validity by either party's domiciliary law

7.49 Under this test a marriage would be regarded as essentially valid if it were valid under either party's ante-nuptial domiciliary law.[95] This proposal has the advantage that it

---

[89] Ibid. This dictum was cited with approval in *Westminster City Council v C* [2009] Fam 11 at [84].
[90] [1985] 1 All ER 506 at 511.
[91] Jaffey, *Introduction to the Conflict of Laws* (1988) p 37.
[92] Fentiman, 'The Validity of Marriage and the Proper Law' [1985] CLJ 256; Fentiman, 'Activity in the Law of Status: Domicile, Marriage and the Law Commission' (1986) 6 OJLS 353.
[93] Davie, 'The Breaking Up of Essential Validity of Marriage Choice of Law Rules in English Conflict of Laws' (1994) 23 Anglo-Am L Rev 32, 37.
[94] Law Com Working Paper No 89, para 3.20.
[95] Hartley, 'The Policy Basis of the English Conflict of Laws of Marriage' (1972) 35 MLR 571.

would promote the policy in favour of validity of marriages, but has little else to commend it. As the Law Commission put it:

> If it is accepted that a person's status is a matter of public concern to the country in which he or she is domiciled at the time of marriage, then the rules of that country which are designed to protect its public interest (such as rules laying down prohibited degrees of relationship or requiring monogamy) should be given effect. The proposed rule would enable a party to evade the requirements of his domiciliary law and would also lead to limping marriages.[96]

6. Alternative reference test

7.50 It has been suggested that (at least for some incapacities) a marriage should be regarded as essentially valid if it is so regarded by either the dual domicile doctrine or the intended matrimonial home test.[97] This view was supported in *Lawrence v Lawrence*.[98] This would mean that the marriage would only be invalid if it is so *both* by the law of the intended matrimonial home *and* by the law of the domicile of one or both of the parties. This approach can be justified on the basis that there is no reason to hold a marriage invalid on a ground based on the public interest (such as polygamy or prohibited degrees) if it is valid by the law of the country where the marriage relationship is to exist. However, even if it is invalid by the law of that country, the spouses' expectation that their marriage, which is unobjectionable by the standards of their own countries at the time of the marriage, will be valid should be met.

7.51 This solution was considered and rejected by the Law Commission[99] on the ground that it would be wrong to elevate the general policy in favour of upholding the validity of marriages into a general choice of law rule. The Law Commission's approach has much to commend it. Choice of law rules should be based on sound policy grounds. While there might be some scope for disagreement as to whether those policy considerations point to the ante-nuptial domiciliary laws of the parties or the law of the intended matrimonial home, they cannot point to both. The alternative reference test amounts to little more than an abdication of the quest for a rational choice of law rule. Further, it could necessitate proof of three different laws, which could greatly complicate and lengthen the process.

7.52 Despite these objections, in *Westminster City Council v C*,[100] the Court of Appeal approved a similar approach but with a clearer emphasis. There is a presumption that the dual domicile doctrine applies: 'the rule is of general application'.[101] However, if the marriage would *not* be recognised as valid under the dual domicile doctrine, then the law of the intended matrimonial home *or* the law of the country of most real and substantial connection can be applied in order to ensure recognition of the marriage. As Wall LJ put it:

---

[96] Law Com Working Paper No 89, para 3.38.
[97] Jaffey, 'The Essential Validity of Marriage in the English Conflict of Laws' (1978) 41 MLR 38.
[98] [1985] 1 All ER 506 at 512 (at first instance by Lincoln J); [1985] 2 All ER 733 at 746 (in the Court of Appeal by Sir David Cairns).
[99] Law Com Working Paper No 89, para 3.37.   [100] [2009] Fam 11.   [101] Thorpe LJ at [29].

I fully accept, as a matter of public policy, that, where it is appropriate to do so, the courts will seek to uphold the concept of marriage. It also seems from the authorities that in cases where the dual domicile rule would result in non-recognition, and where non-recognition would contradict or conflict with the principle of upholding the concept of marriage, the courts have looked for alternative ways of recognising particular marriages. This has led, as I read the authorities, to the concept that a marriage will be recognised if the parties have capacity under the law of the country of their intended matrimonial home or under the law of the country with which the marriage has its most real and substantial connection.[102]

7.53 While the clarity of this dictum is to be welcomed, the earlier criticisms of this approach are still applicable. It is highly questionable whether the general policy of upholding the validity of marriages should prevail over the policy considerations inherent in the choice of law rules. Further, this approach only applies 'where it is appropriate to do so'.[103] This is simply opening the door to a broad discretion for the judiciary to achieve whatever result they deem to be just.

7. A variable rule

7.54 Most of the above theories are premised on the notion that there should be one rule applying to all questions of essential validity. However, it can be argued that different choice of law rules should be adopted for different incapacities and impediments. It has already been seen that in *Vervaeke v Smith*[104] it was suggested that some issues, namely those involving quintessential validity, could be dealt with differently from the remaining essentials to a valid marriage. This approach was adopted in *Radwan v Radwan (No 2)*, where Cumming-Bruce J stated:

> It is arguable that it is an over-simplification of the common law to assume that the same test for purposes of choice of law applies to every kind of incapacity—non-age, affinity, prohibition of monogamous contract by virtue of an existing spouse, and capacity for polygamy. Different public and social factors are relevant to each of these types of incapacity.[105]

7.55 It has been argued that the law of the ante-nuptial domicile has a legitimate interest in imposing its own protective rules (for example, those concerned with non-age and consent) while the law of the intended matrimonial home has a greater interest in imposing those restrictions which are concerned to support the wider social fabric and the public interest (for example, restrictions on polygamy and marriage between close relatives).[106] However, upon closer examination, this 'interest analysis'[107] risks an over-simplification of the often very complex policy considerations underpinning

---

[102] At [74], drawing on dicta in *Lawrence v Lawrence* [1985] Fam 106. See also Thorpe LJ at [29].
[103] In the earlier case of *Wilkinson v Kitzinger (No 2)* [2007] 1 FLR 295 it was accepted that the dual domicile rule could 'occasionally' be displaced by the intended matrimonial home or most substantial connection test (at [15]).
[104] [1983] 1 AC 145.   [105] [1973] Fam 35 at 51.
[106] See, eg, Jaffey, 'The Essential Validity of Marriage in the English Conflict of Laws' (1978) 41 MLR 38.
[107] See paras 1.43–1.60.

such capacity restrictions.[108] While restrictions on polygamy are intended to preserve the institution of monogamy, they are also intended to protect women from subjugation, an interest which points towards the domiciliary law. Equally, while non-age rules seek to protect individual children, they also seek to reduce the incidence of unstable marriages (a factor which points towards the intended matrimonial home). Given the complexity and elusiveness of such interest analysis, and the many difficulties associated with the intended matrimonial home doctrine,[109] it is submitted that the variable approach is, on balance, unsatisfactory.

C The role of the lex fori

7.56   As indicated above, the weight of authority supports the dual domicile doctrine as the general choice of law rule for determining essential validity of marriage. However, the lex fori also plays a significant role. As will be seen,[110] statute allows foreign restrictions on remarriage and on same-sex marriage to be overridden, effectively substituting the forum's own views on capacity for those of the domiciliary law in these contexts. It is also accepted that foreign domiciliaries marrying in England must comply with English rules on capacity.[111] In principle they are also required to comply with their own domiciliary requirements but in practice these are unlikely to be investigated by the English registrar at the time of the ceremony.[112] The marriage will, however, be vulnerable to an *ex post facto* challenge if the capacity requirements of the domiciliary law were not complied with.

7.57   The role of the lex domicilii is also restricted where an English domiciliary marries a foreign domiciliary in England. The essential validity of such marriages is governed by English law alone and any invalidity under the law of the foreign domicile of the other party is ignored. This rule was laid down in *Sottomayor v De Barros (No 2)*,[113] in which a marriage was celebrated in England between first cousins, the husband being domiciled at the time of the marriage in England and the wife in Portugal. Even though a marriage between first cousins was prohibited by Portuguese law, the marriage was held valid under English law. The basis of the decision was that it would be unjust to an English party who celebrates in England a marriage which is valid by English law to hold the marriage void under foreign law.[114] This, rule in *Sottomayor v De Barros (No 2)*, as it has become known, has been applied in cases dealing with other impediments and must now be regarded as an accepted part of the law.[115] As will be seen, however, its

---

[108] See Fawcett, Ní Shúilleabháin and Shah, *Human Rights and Private International Law* (2016) para 11.176.
[109] See paras 7.41–7.45.   [110] See paras 7.87 and 7.122.
[111] Cheshire, North and Fawcett, *Private International Law* (14th edn, 2008) p 907.
[112] Law Com Working Paper No 89, para 3.46 (fn 318) but see also *R v Brentwood Superintendent Registrar of Marriages, ex p Arias* [1968] 2 QB 956.
[113] (1879) 5 PD 94.
[114] Ibid at 104, based on a dictum in the judgment of the Court of Appeal in *Sottomayor v De Barros* (1877) 3 PD 1 at 6–7.
[115] *Ogden v Ogden* [1908] P 46; *Vervaeke v Smith* [1981] 1 All ER 55 at 87 (though the point was not considered by the House of Lords on appeal: [1983] 1 AC 145); Wall LJ in *Westminster City Council v C* [2009] Fam 11 at [69] (obiter).

ambit has been somewhat limited by statute in respect of certain marriages within the prohibited degrees of affinity.[116]

7.58 The rule in *Sottomayor v De Barros (No 2)* has been condemned as 'xenophobic'[117] and 'unworthy of a place in a respectable system of conflict of laws'[118] because it only operates in favour of an English person marrying in England, not a foreign person marrying in his own country.[119] In the same vein, English law might also be criticised for imposing English *and* foreign capacity requirements where foreign domiciliaries marry in England—even though there is no equivalent expectation of compliance with the capacity rules of the lex loci celebrationis if a marriage takes place abroad. It is, however, possible to support these rules and practices or, at least, to defend them on the basis that this type of forum preference is not uncommon in the conflict of laws.[120] Inevitably, the lex fori will adopt a role of protecting English interests, values, and institutions. For instance, in relation to contracts, there are special provisions ensuring that English interests in protecting its consumers are not bypassed by the application of foreign laws.[121] Similarly, the doctrine of public policy is particularly likely to be invoked when enforcement of a foreign law will have an impact in England.[122] Marriages contracted in England have a greater potential impact in England than marriages contracted abroad and, accordingly, there is a greater interest in ensuring conformity to the standards of English law. Where parties, one of whom is domiciled in England, marry in England and there is a conflict between the spouses' domiciliary laws, it is inevitable that the English court will lean in favour of the English domiciliary. In view of the fact that the English domiciliary has not stepped into the international arena by marrying abroad, such a person does not deserve to forfeit the right to rely on the law of the country to which he belongs and with which the marriage is more closely connected. The court is justified in ignoring the foreign incapacity on the ground that the English domiciliary has married in England and would reasonably expect the validity of the marriage to be judged by English law.

D The impediments

1. Prohibited degrees of relationship

7.59 While all systems of law impose restrictions on marriage between persons who are related, the precise rules vary between different countries. The prohibitions may extend not only to blood relationships (consanguinity), but also to relationships by marriage (affinity). One reason for the prohibition of marriage between blood relations is the biomedical one of reducing the incidence of children born with genetic disorders. Other reasons for the prohibition on marriages between close relatives are sociological,

---

[116] Marriage (Enabling) Act 1960, s 1(3). See para 7.63.
[117] Cheshire, North and Fawcett, *Private International Law* (14th edn, 2008) p 905.
[118] Falconbridge, *Essays on the Conflict of Laws* (1954) p 711.   [119] *Re Paine* [1940] Ch 46.
[120] Clarkson, 'Marriage in England: Favouring the Lex Fori' (1990) 10 LS 80.
[121] See paras 4.122–4.125.   [122] See paras 1.171–1.172.

moral, and religious.¹²³ It has been argued that it is the public interest, rather than the protection of the spouses themselves, that is the main object of these incapacities and that the intended matrimonial home test might therefore be appropriate.¹²⁴ However, such restrictions are also concerned to protect the wider family circle (in the country of the ante-nuptial domicile) and to protect against sexual exploitation within family networks.

7.60 An examination of the authorities reveals that it is the dual domicile rule that applies to all the prohibited degrees. Admittedly, the only House of Lords decision on the matter leaves the question open. In *Brook v Brook*¹²⁵ the husband wished to marry the sister of his deceased wife. The intending spouses were both domiciled in England. By English law, at that time, a marriage between a man and his former wife's sister, aunt, or niece (or between a woman and her former husband's brother, uncle, or nephew) was prohibited, so the parties celebrated their marriage in Denmark, by whose law it was valid. They returned to live in England after the marriage. The House of Lords held the marriage void, establishing that questions of essential, as opposed to formal, validity are not to be decided by the lex loci celebrationis. Lord Campbell said:

> The essentials of the marriage depend on the lex domicilii, the law of the country in which the parties are domiciled at the time of the marriage and in which the matrimonial residence is contemplated.¹²⁶

7.61 This leaves open the position when one or both of the parties have a different ante-nuptial domicile from the intended matrimonial residence.

7.62 Later cases,¹²⁷ however, with increasing explicitness, have inclined to the dual domicile test, although, at least in most cases, the result under either test would have been the same. In *Re Paine*,¹²⁸ for example, the marriage was celebrated in Germany between a man domiciled in Germany and his deceased wife's sister, who was domiciled in England. By German law such a marriage was valid, but the marriage was held invalid under English law, the judge holding that each spouse must have capacity to marry the other by the law of his or her ante-nuptial domicile. The parties did establish a matrimonial home in England, but this was not the basis of the decision. Statutory support for the dual domicile doctrine in respect of some of these incapacities is to be found in section 1(3) of the Marriage (Enabling) Act 1960. Originally, as has been seen, English domestic law had strict rules prohibiting marriages between relatives by marriage. These were progressively relaxed, and the 1960 Act abolished the remaining restrictions against a man marrying his divorced or deceased wife's sister, niece, or aunt

---

¹²³ Lowe and Douglas, *Bromley's Family Law* (11th edn, 2015) p 45–6.
¹²⁴ See, eg, Jaffey, 'The Essential Validity of Marriage in the English Conflict of Laws' (1978) 41 MLR 38, 44.
¹²⁵ (1861) 9 HL Cas 193.   ¹²⁶ At 207.
¹²⁷ *Mette v Mette* (1859) 1 Sw & Tr 416; *Sottomayor v De Barros* (1877) 3 PD 1; *Cheni v Cheni* [1965] P 85.
¹²⁸ [1940] Ch 46.

and a woman marrying her former husband's brother, nephew, or uncle.[129] Section 1(3) contains a choice of law provision that:

> ... this section does not validate a marriage if either party to it is at the time of the marriage domiciled in a country outside Great Britain, and under the law of that country there cannot be a valid marriage between the parties.

7.63 The provision confirms that, as regards marriages within these degrees of affinity, the dual domicile doctrine is applicable. Accordingly, if a man marries, for example, his former wife's sister who is domiciled in a country forbidding such marriages, the marriage is void even if the intended matrimonial home was England. Section 1(3) also has the effect of excluding the rule in *Sottomayor v De Barros (No 2)*. So, if a man domiciled in England marries, in England, his first cousin, who is domiciled in a country by whose law the marriage is void, the marriage is valid under the *Sottomayor* exception. But if a man domiciled in England marries in England his former wife's sister, who is domiciled in a country by whose law such marriage is void, the marriage is invalid under section 1(3). There is no sense in this distinction; the point must have been overlooked in the drafting of the statute.

7.64 Public policy may come into play where a relationship considered acceptable under the domiciliary law is criminalised as incestuous in England. This was implicit in *Cheni v Cheni*,[130] where the marriage of an uncle and niece domiciled in Egypt at the time of the marriage, and valid under Egyptian law, was subsequently challenged in England on public policy grounds. The English High Court upheld the validity of the marriage emphasising that the relationship was not incestuous under English criminal law.[131]

2. Lack of age

7.65 Countries have varying rules on the minimum age for marriage. The English rule is contained in section 2 of the Marriage Act 1949, which provides that a marriage solemnised between persons either of whom is under the age of 16 shall be void.[132]

7.66 The English courts have applied the dual domicile rule in determining whether a foreign marriage is void for non-age.[133] As has been stated:

> Since children may develop socially and emotionally, and even physically, at different rates in different environments, it seems sensible for English law to rely on the judgment of the law of the country to which a person belongs for the decision whether he or she is mature enough to marry.[134]

---

[129] S 1. See also the Marriage Act 1949 (Remedial) Order 2007 repealing the Marriage Act 1949, s 1(4)–(8) (in response to the judgment of the European Court of Human Rights in *B v UK* [2006] 1 FLR 35) and the Marriage (Prohibited Degrees of Relationships) Act 1986, s 1(7).
[130] [1965] P 85.
[131] [1965] P 85 at 97. Sexual relations between an uncle and adult niece are now subject to criminal sanction: Sexual Offences Act 2003, s 64.
[132] The Civil Partnership Act 2004, s 3(1)(c) specifies the same age for eligibility to register a civil partnership.
[133] For confirmation that this is the correct test, see *A Local Authority v X* [2014] 2 FLR 123 at [9].
[134] Jaffey, 'The Essential Validity of Marriage in the English Conflict of Laws' (1978) 41 MLR 38, 46.

7.67 In *Mohamed v Knott*[135] a man of 26 and a girl of 13, both domiciled in Nigeria, had married each other there, and come to England four months later, where they were to live while the husband was a student. The court accepted that the marriage was valid, because the wife was old enough by Nigerian law, even though she was much too young by English law. *Mohamed v Knott* was referred to with apparent approval in the more recent case of *Re K*;[136] however, one might question the likelihood of the same approach being taken if these facts came before an English court today. In modern times, there is a much greater emphasis on the rights of the child and on the undesirability of child marriage.[137] In contrast to the approach taken in *Cheni*,[138] the court in *Mohamed* did not appear to accept that the criminalisation of the sexual relationship should trigger a public policy objection to the recognition of the marriage,[139] but another court might follow *Cheni* in this regard.[140]

7.68 The extreme pluralism of *Mohamed v Knott* stands in contrast to the more paternalistic approach adopted in *Pugh v Pugh*.[141] In this case, a British army officer, domiciled in England, married in Austria a girl aged 15 who was domiciled in Hungary. The wife had capacity to marry under Hungarian law. On a construction of the English statutory provision—'a marriage solemnised between persons either of whom is under the age of 16 shall be void'—the marriage was held void as the wife was under the age of 16. This decision has attracted adverse comment.[142] The argument is that English law had no reason to invalidate the marriage as the English domiciliary was old enough to marry; Hungarian law also had no reason to invalidate the marriage as the Hungarian domiciliary was, by Hungarian law, old enough to marry. The marriage should, accordingly, have been held valid.

7.69 Such reasoning, however, fails to understand the policy rationale underlying the English prohibition. In reality, there are two policies enshrined in section 2 of the Marriage Act 1949. First, and most obviously, the object of the provision is to protect English domiciliaries from the responsibilities of marriage until they are considered sufficiently mature. However, there is a second, equally important, policy underlying the English provision, namely, that an English domiciliary of whatever age should not be permitted to contract a marriage with a child. English law has an interest in preventing its domiciliaries from sexually exploiting children. Such reasoning was instrumental in the introduction of laws prohibiting, inter alia, British tour operators from organising 'sex package holidays' involving children in foreign countries.[143] Viewed in the context of this second policy, the decision in *Pugh v Pugh* is justifiable.

---

[135] [1969] 1 QB 1. [136] *Re K: A Local Authority v N and Others* [2007] 1 FLR 399 at[31].
[137] Gaffney-Rhys, 'The Law Relating to Marriageable Age from a National and International Perspective' [2009] IFL 228; Fawcett, Ní Shúilleabháin and Shah, *Human Rights and Private International Law* (2016) paras 11.157–11.159.
[138] See para 7.64. [139] [1969] 1 QB 1 at 16–17.
[140] Sixteen is the age at which a person may consent to a sexual relationship under English criminal law: Sexual Offences Act 2003, s 9.
[141] [1951] P 482.
[142] See, eg, Smart, 'Interest Analysis, False Conflicts, and the Essential Validity of Marriage' (1986) 14 Anglo-Am L Rev 225, 230 and 233–4.
[143] Sexual Offences (Conspiracy and Incitement) Act 1996.

7.70 As the rule in *Sottomayor v De Barros (No 2)*[144] has been held to apply to essential validity generally, and not merely to prohibited degrees, it would presumably apply to a case of non-age.[145] So, if one party is domiciled in England, where the marriage is celebrated, a provision of the law of the other party's domicile setting a minimum age higher than the English one would not affect the validity of the marriage.

3. Consent of the parties

7.71 Another question of essential validity is lack of consent. In English domestic law the effect of this defect is to make the marriage voidable rather than void.[146] However, in certain cases, a complete absence of consent can lead to the marriage being denied all recognition. For example, in *Westminster City Council v C*[147] a 26-year-old English domiciliary with a mental capacity of a three-year-old went through a marriage ceremony over the telephone with a Bangladeshi domiciliary. This marriage was denied recognition.[148]

7.72 Lack of consent relates to cases where it is maintained that a party did not consent to the marriage at all, or that the apparent consent was vitiated by some defect such as fraud, duress, mistake (including that the consent related to something other than a marriage), or unsoundness of mind. The only types of mistake affecting the validity of a marriage under English law are mistake as to the identity of the other party and mistake as to the nature of the ceremony.[149] For example, in *Alfonso-Brown v Milwood*[150] the husband thought he was participating in an engagement ceremony in Ghana. It was held that he had not consented to a marriage. Marriages of convenience (where the parties have no intention of cohabiting), however, do not involve a mistake and so are valid under English law.[151] Conflicts of laws will arise because the rules differ from one legal system to another. For example, marriages of convenience are not valid by Belgian law.

7.73 In *Vervaeke v Smith*[152] Lord Simon in the House of Lords suggested, obiter, that whether a marriage of convenience was valid was a matter of 'quintessential validity' to be governed by the law of the country with which the marriage had its most real and substantial connection. Despite this suggestion, however, the authorities are overwhelmingly in favour of the dual domicile doctrine for all matters of consent.[153] In *Szechter v Szechter*[154] the parties were domiciled in Poland, where the marriage was

---

[144] See para 7.57.
[145] This point was accepted in the Singapore case of *Re Maria Hertogh* (1951) 17 MLJ 12, but, as the husband was found not to be domiciled in the forum, the rule could not be applied.
[146] Matrimonial Causes Act 1973, s 12(1)(c). The Civil Partnership Act 2004, s 50(1)(a) contains an identical provision.
[147] [2009] Fam 11. [148] See also *SH v NB (Marriage: Consent)* [2010] 1 FLR 1927.
[149] Lowe and Douglas, *Bromley's Family Law* (11th edn, 2015) p 79.   [150] [2006] 2 FLR 265.
[151] *Vervaeke v Smith* [1983] 1 AC 145. Such (heterosexual) marriages could be voidable on grounds of non-consummation. See para 7.77.
[152] [1983] 1 AC 145.
[153] *Westminster City Council v C* [2009] Fam 11; *SH v NB (Marriage: Consent)* [2010] 1 FLR 1927.
[154] [1971] P 286.

celebrated. The parties entered into the marriage only in order to obtain the wife's release from prison, where her personal safety was threatened. On her release, the parties made their way to England. The wife brought nullity proceedings in the English court on the ground that she had entered the marriage under duress. Simon P, holding that the matter was governed by Polish law as the law of the parties' ante-nuptial domicile, granted a nullity decree, accepting that the marriage was invalid for lack of consent by Polish law. The husband was thus able to remarry his first wife, whom he had divorced as part of the scheme to secure the release of the second wife.

7.74 In *Szechter* both parties were domiciled in Poland. What is the position if, at the time of the marriage, the parties are domiciled in different countries, whose laws give different answers to the question whether or not there was consent? No doubt, if the marriage is invalid by the law of the ante-nuptial domicile of the party whose consent is questioned, then the marriage will be annulled, even if there was consent by the law of the other party's domicile. Suppose, however, that the wife has validly consented by the law of her domicile, but not by the law of the husband's domicile. Will the court grant a nullity decree? It can be argued that, if by the standards of her own law she has validly consented, there is no reason why the marriage should be annulled. By the same token, however, it could be said that the husband would have no cause to complain of injustice if the marriage were annulled, seeing that, by the standards of his own law, the wife has not consented. The answer to this difficult question is unsettled.

7.75 In *Szechter*[155] Simon P agreed obiter with the suggestion in the then current edition of *Dicey & Morris* that 'no marriage is valid if by the law of either party's domicile one party does not consent to marry the other'.[156] According to this, a party *can* rely on lack of consent under the law of the other party's domicile. Earlier, in *Way v Way*[157] a marriage had been celebrated in Russia between a wife domiciled there and a husband domiciled in England. The husband sought a nullity decree in the English court, one of the grounds being lack of consent: he had entered the marriage under the mistaken belief that the wife would be permitted to come to live with him in England. The judge's view seems to have been that whether the husband had consented was to be decided according to English law as the law of his own domicile. By that law the mistake was immaterial, so the marriage was not invalid for lack of consent. There is no suggestion that Russian law, the law of the wife's domicile, could be relevant to test whether the husband had consented. It is thus implicit in the judgment that each party's consent was tested by reference solely to the law of that person's ante-nuptial domicile. This approach is preferable in terms of policy. The rationale of applying the law of ante-nuptial domicile here is that a person is entitled to the protection of his own law; he does not need the protection of his spouse's law.[158] As the Law Commission has pointed out, it

---

[155] Ibid at 294.
[156] *The Conflict of Laws* (8th edn, 1967) p 271. In the present edition of Dicey, Morris and Collins the contrary view is preferred: (15th edn, 2012) p 961.
[157] [1950] P 71 at 78–9. On appeal the judge's statement on this point was assumed to be correct: *Kenward v Kenward* [1951] P 124 at 133.
[158] But see the discussion of public policy at paras 7.100–7.103 below.

is 'difficult to see why, if a party's own law considers that he has validly consented to the marriage, he should nevertheless be entitled to avoid the marriage on the basis of his lack of consent under the other party's domiciliary law'.[159]

4. Physical impediments

7.76 Several disparate impediments (under English law) can be grouped under this heading. First, under section 12(1)(e) of the Matrimonial Causes Act 1973, a marriage is voidable if at the time of the marriage the respondent was suffering from venereal disease in a communicable form, and under section 12(1)(f) if at the time of the marriage the respondent was pregnant by some person other than the petitioner.[160] As it is provided by section 13(3) that a decree shall not be granted in these situations unless the petitioner was at the time of the marriage ignorant of the facts alleged, it has been pointed out[161] that these cases are similar to ones involving lack of consent. However, even if they are not so regarded, the choice of law rule for them should be the same.

7.77 Secondly, there is the problem of non-consummation of a marriage, whether through impotence or wilful refusal to consummate the marriage. Such marriages are voidable according to English law.[162] Other countries may have different rules on the subject. For example, neither impotence nor wilful refusal may affect the validity of the marriage; or the latter may not do so, but may, or may not, be a ground for divorce.[163] Which law governs?

7.78 It was held by the Court of Appeal in *De Reneville v De Reneville* that these issues are to be decided by 'the law of the husband's domicile at the time of the marriage or (preferably . . .) . . . the law of the matrimonial domicile in reference to which the parties may have been supposed to enter into the bonds of marriage'.[164] This approach has been followed in subsequent cases.[165] In *Ponticelli v Ponticelli*,[166] for example, a marriage was celebrated in Italy between a wife domiciled there and a husband domiciled in England, where the parties set up their matrimonial home. The husband petitioned the English court for a nullity decree on the ground of the wife's wilful refusal to consummate the marriage. By Italian law wilful refusal was not a ground of nullity. Sachs J held that English law governed, either as the lex fori or (the view he preferred) as the lex domicilii, by which he meant 'the law of the country in which the parties are domiciled at the time of the marriage, and in which the matrimonial residence

---

[159] Law Com Working Paper No 89, para 5.23. See also *SH v NB (Marriage: Consent)* [2010] 1 FLR 1927 at [3].
[160] The Civil Partnership Act 2004, s 50(1)(c) is to similar effect. This Act contains no provision relating to venereal disease.
[161] McClean and Ruiz Abou-Nigm, *Morris: The Conflict of Laws* (8th edn, 2012) p 223.
[162] Matrimonial Causes Act 1973, s 12(1)(a) and (b). The Civil Partnership Act 2004 contains no comparable provision and s 12(2) provides that s 12(1)(a) and (b) do not apply to the marriage of a same-sex couple.
[163] See Dicey, Morris and Collins, *The Conflict of Laws* (15th edn, 2012) p 1011.
[164] [1948] P 100 at 114.
[165] *Casey v Casey* [1949] P 420; *Way v Way* [1950] P 71. *Robert v Robert* [1947] P 164, in which the lex loci celebrationis was held applicable, cannot stand with *De Reneville v De Reneville*. [166] [1958] P 204.

is contemplated'.[167] This, he said, 'normally coincides with the law pertaining to the country of the husband's domicile at the time of the marriage'.[168] So, a nullity decree was granted.

7.79 While historically, therefore, the courts have favoured the law of the husband's domicile at the time of the marriage, and the law of the intended matrimonial home if that is different, these are dubious authorities. Clearly, any preference for the husband's domicile per se is untenable in the contemporary law given its inherent sexism. Here, as with consent, the concern is with the protection of a party from contracting a marriage that is different in nature from the one anticipated and it is submitted that the petitioner ought to be entitled to rely on the non-consummation grounds of his or her own domiciliary law.[169]

5. Capacity to marry after a foreign decree of divorce or annulment

(A) Introduction

7.80 Here the concern is with cases where none of the potentially applicable laws permit polygamy. A monogamously married person lacks capacity to contract a second monogamous marriage until the first marriage has been dissolved or annulled. Conflicts can arise when the first marriage is dissolved or annulled and one potentially applicable law recognises the divorce or annulment but another does not. The result is that one of the parties is already married according to one of the laws but not according to another. The issue is whether that spouse has capacity to marry again or whether the second marriage would be bigamous. For example, in *Lawrence v Lawrence*[170] the wife, then domiciled in Brazil, obtained a divorce from her first husband in Nevada. The next day, in Nevada, she married the second husband, who was domiciled in England. England was also the intended matrimonial home and the parties set up home in England very soon after the marriage. The wife's Nevada divorce was recognised by English law but not by Brazilian law, under which she remained married to her first husband. The wife petitioned in the English court for a nullity decree on the ground that the second marriage was bigamous. English and Brazilian law agreed that the wife did not have capacity to contract the second marriage unless she was single. The conflict arose because the two laws, taking different views as to the validity of the Nevada divorce, also took different views as to whether the wife was single when she remarried. The wife contended that her capacity to marry her second husband was governed by Brazilian law as the law of her ante-nuptial domicile. Since the Nevada divorce was invalid by Brazilian law she lacked capacity by that law, so the marriage was void. The trial judge, however, held that the validity of the remarriage was governed by English law, because, being the law of the intended matrimonial domicile, it was the law of the country with which the marriage had its most real and substantial connection.[171] Since the divorce was recognised by English law, the remarriage was valid. The Court of Appeal adopted

---

[167] Citing *Brook v Brook* (1861) 9 HL Cas 193 at 207.   [168] At 214.
[169] Jaffey, 'The Essential Validity of Marriage in the English Conflict of Laws' (1978) 41 MLR 38, 48.
[170] [1985] Fam 106.
[171] Following Lord Simon in *Vervaeke v Smith* [1983] 1 AC 145 at 166. See paras 7.46–7.48.

a third approach. English law has its own conflicts rules on recognition of foreign divorces and under these rules the Nevada divorce was entitled to recognition. The wife was, therefore, a single woman at the time of her second marriage. That marriage could not be declared void on the ground of her bigamy. The English conflicts rules (as the law of the forum) should not have to give way to the Brazilian conflicts rules on recognition of foreign divorces.

(B) The incidental question

7.81   As discussed in Chapter 1,[172] an incidental question arises when one country's conflicts rules lead to a foreign law, but under that law an incidental or subsidiary question arises which can only be resolved by the application of a further conflicts rule governing that incidental question. The issue is whether that incidental question should be governed by the conflicts rule of the foreign law (the lex causae approach) or the conflicts rule of the forum (the lex fori approach).

7.82   In *Lawrence v Lawrence*[173] the question before the English court was the wife's capacity to marry the second husband. According to the general rule, this is (contrary to what the trial judge held) governed by the law of her ante-nuptial domicile, Brazilian law. The relevant rule of capacity of Brazilian domestic law was that only a single person can marry. In applying that rule, the English court would immediately be confronted with another question: was the wife single when she married her second husband or was she still married to her first husband? This question—of the validity of the Nevada divorce—could be described as an incidental question because it arises for decision, not independently, but in the course of determining the wife's capacity to remarry, the main question. To this incidental question the conflicts rules of England and Brazil (in this case, their rules for the recognition of foreign divorces[174]) gave different answers, the divorce being recognised by English law but not by Brazilian law.

7.83   In deciding the incidental question, should the English court simply use its own rules for the recognition of foreign divorces (the lex fori approach) or should it use the Brazilian ones, since it is Brazilian law which governs the main question of the wife's capacity to remarry (the lex causae approach)? On the one hand, one could argue that it is pointless referring to Brazilian law as the ante-nuptial domiciliary law and then ignoring the only relevant Brazilian rules, that is, whether the wife was validly divorced. On the other hand, simply to say that the wife lacked capacity under Brazilian law is to conceal the fact that there are two separate questions. First, what is the relevant Brazilian domestic rule of capacity to marry? Answer: only a single person can marry. Secondly, arising from that answer, was the wife single when she remarried? This second question is a question of her status, not her capacity. There would be no logical contradiction in applying the Brazilian domestic rule of capacity that only a single person can marry and English conflicts rules to test whether she is single.

[172] See para 1.131.   [173] [1985] Fam 106.
[174] The recognition of foreign matrimonial decrees is dealt with in Chapter 8.

7.84 It is this latter view that is consistent with the modern English law. It is helpful, however, to distinguish two situations.

(i) Divorce or annulment recognised by English law but not by the domiciliary law

7.85 In earlier cases,[175] the courts took it for granted that the lex causae should decide the incidental question of whether the divorce or annulment should be recognised. In *R v Brentwood Superintendent Registrar of Marriages, ex p Arias*[176] the first marriage of the husband, who was domiciled in Switzerland but a national of Italy, was dissolved by a Swiss court. This divorce was recognised in England but not in Italy. The husband wanted to remarry in England, and the question came before the Divisional Court whether he was entitled to do so. The court held that his capacity was governed by Swiss law, as the law of his ante-nuptial domicile. By Swiss law, since he was an Italian national, his capacity to marry was governed by Italian law.[177] As the divorce was not recognised in Italy, it followed, in the court's view, that the husband lacked capacity to marry again. In other words, the incidental question of the validity of the Swiss divorce was decided by the lex causae,[178] Swiss law. The consequence was that a single person (for that is what he was in the eyes of the English court) was not permitted to marry.

7.86 In *Perrini v Perrini*,[179] however, such reasoning was departed from and a second marriage held valid because a preceding nullity decree obtained from a New Jersey court was entitled to recognition by English law. This result was reached despite the fact that the decree was not recognised by Italian law, the law of the husband's domicile at the date of the second marriage. Similarly, as has been seen, the Court of Appeal in *Lawrence v Lawrence*[180] held that, if a divorce is recognised in England, a remarriage cannot be held void on the ground that the divorce is not recognised in some other country. In other words, the incidental question is to be decided under the conflicts rules of the lex fori.

7.87 The decision in *Lawrence v Lawrence* was confirmed by section 50 of the Family Law Act 1986. Its effect is that where a divorce or annulment has been granted by an English court, or is recognised in England, the fact that the divorce or annulment would not be recognised elsewhere shall not preclude either party to the marriage from remarrying in England or cause the remarriage of either party (wherever the remarriage takes place) to be treated as invalid in England.[181]

(ii) Divorce or annulment recognised by domiciliary law but not by English law

7.88 The converse situation to that in *Lawrence v Lawrence*[182] can also occur, where the divorce is not recognised by the lex fori, but is recognised by the lex causae. In the

---

[175] Eg, *Padolecchia v Padolecchia* [1968] P 314. [176] [1968] 2 QB 956.
[177] The English court's application of the Swiss conflicts rule (renvoi) is discussed at para 7.91.
[178] The court did not in fact analyse the issue in this way, but simply assumed that this was the proper approach.
[179] [1979] Fam 84. [180] [1985] 1 All ER 506.
[181] A similar provision applies with regard to registered partnership dissolutions or annulment: Civil Partnership Act 2004, s 238.
[182] [1985] 1 All ER 506.

Canadian case of *Schwebel v Ungar*[183] the wife and her first husband were originally domiciled in Hungary. On their way to settle in Israel, while in Italy but still domiciled in Hungary, the husband divorced the wife under Jewish law. They then made their way to Israel, where both became domiciled, and where the divorce was recognised as valid. Some years later, the wife, still domiciled in Israel, married in Ontario a second husband who was domiciled there. The divorce obtained in Italy was not recognised in Ontario. The second husband petitioned in the Ontario court for a nullity decree on the ground that, when the wife's second marriage was celebrated, she was still married to her first husband. The Canadian courts held the remarriage valid, because, using the dual domicile rule, the wife's capacity to remarry was governed by the law of Israel, and by that law the divorce was valid, even though it was not valid by the lex fori, Ontario law. In other words, the lex causae approach was used for the incidental question.

7.89 How would such a case as *Schwebel v Ungar* be decided by an English court today? There is no statutory provision dealing with this situation, as there is for the converse case under section 50 of the Family Law Act 1986; nor does the case strictly fall within the ratio of *Lawrence*. Nevertheless, the lex fori approach seems preferable in a case such as *Schwebel v Ungar* as much as in *Lawrence*.[184] In the latter case, the lex fori must decide the validity of the divorce to avoid the consequence that a single person is not free to marry. In a case such as *Schwebel*, the lex fori should be used to avoid the even more startling result that a person is validly and monogamously married to two spouses at the same time. This is because under the forum's own rules of recognition (to be applied when there is no main question governed by a foreign law), the first marriage still subsists, even though the second marriage has been held valid. Intractable problems in relation to succession, matrimonial relief, and other matters could arise.[185] Suppose in a case such as *Schwebel*, the wife, after her second marriage had been held valid in England, became domiciled in England and died intestate. The first husband would be entitled to succeed as the surviving spouse, for the divorce would not be recognised in England. What about the second husband, whose marriage had been held valid?

IV Renvoi

7.90 Generally, when English choice of law rules on both formal and essential validity of marriages lead to the application of a foreign law, this is taken to mean the *domestic* law of the foreign country. However, this is one of the areas of law where the doctrine

---

[183] (1963) 42 DLR (2d) 622 (affd 48 DLR (2d) 644).
[184] For a view that there is no logical answer to the problem of the incidental question and so choices should be made on policy grounds, see Harris, 'Does Choice of Law Make Any Sense?' (2004) 57 CLP 305, 332–44.
[185] It is arguable that *Schwebel v Ungar* (1963) 42 DLR (2d) 622 (affd 48 DLR (2d) 644) decided that in view of the position under Israeli law the divorce had to be recognised in Ontario: Lysyk (1965) 43 Can Bar Rev 363. But if such a case arose in England, the divorce could not be recognised under the English statutory grounds, and the problem of two coexisting monogamous marriages could arise.

of renvoi has at times been applied. According to this, a reference to a foreign law involves applying that country's conflicts rules as opposed to its domestic laws.[186] For example, in relation to formal validity, in *Taczanowska v Taczanowski*,[187] the marriage was celebrated in Italy but the court considered, obiter, whether the marriage was valid under Italian conflict of laws rules which referred the matter to the law of the parties' nationality.

7.91 Similarly, the doctrine of renvoi was employed in *R v Brentwood Superintendent Registrar of Marriages, ex p Arias*[188] in relation to the essential validity of a marriage. In this case the question was the capacity of the husband, domiciled in Switzerland but a national of Italy, to remarry. The English choice of law rule indicated Swiss law as the ante-nuptial domiciliary law but, as under Swiss conflicts rules capacity to marry was governed by the law of nationality, the English court applied Italian law.

7.92 These two cases appear to be the only reported cases where renvoi has been used in the context of formal and essential validity of marriage. However, the doctrine of renvoi has been explicitly adopted by the Civil Partnership Act 2004 when dealing with registered partnerships contracted abroad. As shall be seen,[189] the parties must have capacity to enter into the relationship by the relevant law and must comply with the formalities of the relevant law.[190] The 'relevant law' is defined as the law of the country where the relationship is registered 'including its rules of private international law'.[191]

7.93 Is it desirable to use renvoi for formal and essential validity of marriage? There are two different reasons why an English court might choose to have recourse to the doctrine. First, it could lead to uniformity of result between various countries with an interest in the case. Because different countries have not only different domestic laws but also different conflicts rules, a marriage may be valid in one country and invalid in another. This results in what is called a 'limping marriage'. The hardship and inconvenience which can arise from parties having the status of married persons in one country but not in another is obvious. How can this be avoided? The only sure way would be by the harmonisation, by international agreement, of the conflicts rules of the different countries. Apart from this, where a particular foreign country's choice of law rule is different from the English one, the English court might be able to secure uniformity with that country by using the doctrine of renvoi and employing the foreign country's choice of law rule instead of the English one. For example, in *Taczanowska* the English and Italian conflicts rules were different. By applying the Italian conflicts rule, as opposed to the domestic Italian rule, the English court could (had it not ended up resorting to the common law marriage fiction) have ensured that a limping relationship was avoided. Similarly, in the *Brentwood Marriage Registrar* case, the doctrine enabled uniformity of decision to be achieved. The effect of the decision was that any remarriage by the husband would be void by English law, as well as by Swiss and Italian law, thus

---

[186] See paras 1.106–1.130. [187] [1957] P 301. [188] [1968] 2 QB 956.
[189] See paras 7.113–7.114. [190] S 215(1). [191] S 212(3).

achieving uniformity of status in England and the countries of the husband's domicile and nationality.

7.94 However, this uniformity was achieved at a price. In the *Brentwood Marriage Registrar* case the Swiss divorce was entitled to recognition under English conflicts rules on the recognition of foreign divorces. The husband was, therefore, a single man in English eyes. Utilising renvoi resulted in the English court holding that a single man was not free to remarry. The decisive law was Italian law, the law of the husband's nationality. For reasons explored in Chapter 6, English law has largely rejected nationality as a connecting factor. Renvoi, all too often, simply allows nationality in through the back door.

7.95 Further, renvoi may well produce uniformity with the wrong countries. What is wanted is uniformity with the countries to which the parties belong now, when the question arises. Renvoi can only produce uniformity with the country where the marriage took place or in which the party was domiciled at the time of the marriage (or soon after the marriage, when the intended matrimonial home rule is applicable). That is of no value if he has changed his domicile since the marriage. Renvoi in such a case might even destroy a uniformity which exists with the law of the current domicile. Moreover, uniformity with the country of one spouse may be achieved at the expense of lack of uniformity with the country of the other.

7.96 The second main justification for utilising the doctrine of renvoi is that it provides extra flexibility. Normally, one should try to uphold the validity of a marriage where possible and if one's primary conflicts rules fail in that regard, recourse to the foreign country's conflicts rules may achieve the desired result. This was clearly the reason why the doctrine was flirted with in *Taczanowska*.[192] Such an approach, however, is objectionable and contrary to principle.

7.97 Choice of law rules are designed to lead to the application of appropriate laws. There are strong policy reasons why formal validity of marriage is governed by the lex loci celebrationis and essential validity is governed by the personal law of the parties. If these policy considerations are sound, the whole point of applying the English choice of law rule is defeated if it does no more than lead to another country's choice of law rule. If, on the other hand, the policy considerations underlying the English choice of law rule are questionable and renvoi is being resorted to as a corrective for an unduly strict conflicts rule, then one should re-examine the English rule.

7.98 The Law Commission has favoured application of the doctrine of renvoi in this area of law.[193] However, it is very doubtful whether renvoi is worth the price, which is the sacrifice of the English choice of law rule in favour of the foreign one. As explored earlier,[194] the *Brentwood Marriage Registrar* case has since been reversed by section 50

---

[192] The same cannot be said of the *Brentwood Marriage Registrar* case where, if the second marriage had taken place, it would have been void.
[193] Law Com Working Paper No 89 (1985); Law Com No 165, *Private International Law: Choice of Law Rules in Marriage* (1987).
[194] See para 7.87.

of the Family Law Act 1986, which provides that if a foreign divorce or nullity decree is entitled to recognition under the Act the parties to that divorce are entitled validly to remarry irrespective of whether their law of domicile recognises the divorce or annulment. Apart from its resurrection in relation to civil partnerships, the doctrine of renvoi has thus been ousted from this particular area of law. Courts should hesitate before utilising it in relation to any of the other incapacities.

7.99 Further arguments concerning the doctrine of renvoi are explored in Chapter 1.

V Public policy

7.100 It is a general principle of the conflict of laws that a rule of foreign law which would be applicable under the ordinary choice of law rules may be disregarded if its application would be contrary to English public policy. As regards the validity of marriage, public policy may be invoked if the foreign rule is thought by the court to be grossly offensive or repugnant to English standards of justice, decency, or morality or where the foreign law upholds a relationship which is subject to criminal sanction in England.[195] However, public policy does not insist that English standards must always prevail. Priority is often given to the interests and expectations of the spouses under a foreign law. So, polygamous marriages, even if the spouses come to live in England, may be valid and effective,[196] as may marriages between persons more closely related than English law permits. Because of the danger of public policy being used as a mask for 'judicial cultural imperialism'[197] it is only when the foreign rule is so repugnant to English notions that the conscience of the court simply will not permit it to apply the foreign law, that public policy will be invoked.

7.101 If the doctrine is applied, the effect is either that a marriage is valid despite a foreign incapacity which would otherwise prevail or, conversely, a marriage which is valid under the governing foreign law is held invalid.

7.102 With respect to invalidity under the foreign law, the doctrine of public policy should be invoked only in rare cases where application of the foreign law would be regarded as offensive (for example, restrictions based on race or creed),[198] or where a foreign rule can be construed as penal—such as a prohibition against remarriage before the innocent party to a preceding divorce[199]. With regard to using public policy to deny

---

[195] See the discussion of *Cheni v Cheni* [1965] P 85 at para 7.64. See also *Westminster City Council v C* [2009] Fam 11 at [32], where Thorpe LJ observed that the 'wife' would be guilty of rape if she had sexual intercourse with her severely incapacitated 'husband'.
[196] See paras 7.124–7.160.
[197] Murphy, 'Rationality and Cultural Pluralism in the Non-Recognition of Foreign Marriages' (2000) 49 ICLQ 643, 644.
[198] See *Lepre v Lepre* [1965] P 52 at 64–65, discussing *Chetti v Chetti* [1909] P 67; *Gray v Formosa* [1963] P 259.
[199] *Scott v A-G* (1886) 11 PD 128.

validity to a marriage which is valid under the governing foreign law, the doctrine must be used with great circumspection. As Simon J said in *Cheni v Cheni*, the test is:

> whether the marriage is so offensive to the conscience of the English court that it should refuse to give effect to the proper foreign law . . . [I]n deciding the question the court will seek to exercise common sense, good manners and a reasonable tolerance.[200]

7.103 A sphere in which public policy is likely to operate (with invalidating effect) is that of consent. Indeed, it has been suggested[201] that any foreign rule under which a party had consented when consent was absent according to English law would be rejected on grounds of public policy. For example, a foreign rule allowing a parent to consent to a marriage when the person contracting the marriage did not consent would almost certainly be regarded as contrary to public policy. Such an approach was approved in *Westminster City Council v C*[202] where it was held that it would be contrary to public policy to recognise the validity of a foreign marriage contracted by a severely intellectually impaired 24-year-old person who only had the skills of a three-year-old. Statute has since made provision for the issuance of forced marriage protection orders in such circumstances.[203] The Forced Marriage (Civil Protection) Act 2007 treats force as a question of fact,[204] lending further credence to the idea that English law prioritises its own conceptions of adequate consent and will be intolerant of alternative foreign views.

VI Same-sex marriages and civil partnerships

A Introduction

7.104 In the recent past, same-sex couples were unable to formalise their relationships in any country. This began to change with the introduction of registered partnership in Denmark in 1989. Many other countries followed suit, with the United Kingdom adopting the Civil Partnership Act 2004. Meanwhile the institution of marriage was opened up to same-sex couples in the Netherlands in 2001. Since then, many other Western European countries (including the United Kingdom) have abolished the requirement that spouses be respectively male and female. Same-sex marriage is also permitted in a number of non-European countries including Canada, South Africa, and Argentina. While the past 20 years have therefore witnessed a sea change in attitudes towards formalisation of same-sex relationships, different countries have different views on the scope of that formalisation, and indeed in many countries there has been no change at all. The potential for conflict of laws issues is self-evident in these circumstances. If an English man marries a Ruritanian man in Canada, should the

---

[200] [1965] P 85 at 99.
[201] Hartley, 'The Policy Basis of the English Conflict of Laws of Marriage' (1972) 35 MLR 571, 580.
[202] [2009] Fam 11. See also *XCC v AA* [2013] 2 All ER 988 at [94].
[203] See Chaudhry, 'An Introduction to the Forced Marriage (Civil Protection) Act 2007' (2010) 24 Journal of Immigration, Asylum and Nationality Law 173; *Re RS (Forced Marriage Protection Order)* [2015] EWHC 3534 (Fam).
[204] See Dicey, Morris and Collins, *The Conflict of Laws* (15th edn, 2012) p 963.

marriage be denied recognition on the basis that the Ruritanian man lacked capacity to marry someone of the same gender under his own domiciliary law? Is the outcome any different if Ruritanian law made provision for the registration of same-sex partnerships? The situation is further complicated by the availability, in some countries, of registered partnerships for opposite-sex as well as same-sex couples.

B Same-sex registered partnerships

7.105 In the United Kingdom, the Civil Partnership Act 2004, which came into force in December 2005, allows persons of the same sex to register a civil partnership. This Act contains detailed rules relating to formalities, capacity, proprietary and financial consequences, and dissolution and annulment of such civil partnerships—as well as conflict of laws rules relating to the recognition of foreign 'overseas relationships'. For the most part, the legal regulation of civil partnerships mirrors marriage law; however, as will be seen, there are some notable departures from the corresponding marriage norms in the sphere of the conflict of laws.

7.106 For the purposes of the discussion which follows, it is helpful to distinguish registered partnerships entered into abroad from civil partnerships registered in England.

1. Registered partnerships contracted abroad

7.107 There are two situations in which same-sex partnerships formed abroad are recognised under the Civil Partnership Act 2004.

(A) Registration outside the United Kingdom under an Order in Council

7.108 As with marriages, Orders in Council permit same-sex couples to register a civil partnership at British Consulates, etc, in prescribed countries outside the United Kingdom.[205] Similarly, members of HM Forces serving abroad are permitted to enter a civil partnership in the presence of an appointed officer.[206]

7.109 The rules governing such registrations are broadly the same as those for marriages.[207] For example, with respect to registrations at British Consulates, etc, one of the parties must be a UK national and there must be insufficient facilities in that country for a registered partnership to be formed there and the officer must be satisfied that the authorities of that country would not object to the registration.[208]

(B) Overseas relationships

(i) Introduction

7.110 The 2004 Act provides that if an 'overseas relationship' is recognised, the parties will 'be treated as having formed a civil partnership'.[209] Recognising a variety of 'overseas

---

[205] S 210; Civil Partnership (Registration Abroad and Certificates) Order 2005, SI 2005/2761.
[206] S 211; Civil Partnership (Armed Forces) Order 2005, SI 2005/3188.
[207] See paras 7.32–7.33. [208] S 210(2). [209] S 215(1).

relationships' as civil partnerships can give rise to possible unfairness. Some legal systems allowing registered partnerships do not afford the same rights to, and impose the same responsibilities on, the registered partners as English law. For example, a 'civil pact of solidarity' (PACS) in France gives only limited rights on the breakdown of the relationship; it mainly gives tax and inheritance benefits after registration.[210] Such PACSs will be recognised in England but, by virtue of their being equated to English civil partnerships, many more rights and responsibilities than would have been anticipated by the parties will arise.

7.111 An 'overseas relationship', registered with a responsible authority abroad, can be recognised in England and treated as a civil partnership provided that both parties are of the same sex[211] and neither of them already has a civil partner or is lawfully married.[212] It would appear that whether a person is already a civil partner or is lawfully married is to be determined by English law. Section 212(1)(b)(i) requires the parties to be of the same sex *under the relevant law*.[213] Section 212(1)(b)(ii), specifying that neither be a civil partner nor lawfully married, contains no such indication of the law to determine the issue and, therefore, the assumption is that English law applies.

(ii) Two types of overseas relationships

7.112 There are two types of 'overseas relationship'. First, there are 'specified relationships', which are those that have been registered in one of the specified countries or territories listed in schedule 20.[214] Secondly, there are relationships that meet the 'general conditions',[215] namely that, under the relevant law, the relationship may not be entered into if either of the parties is already a party to a relationship of that kind or lawfully married, the relationship is of indeterminate duration and has the effect of treating the parties as a couple.[216]

(iii) Formalities

7.113 In order for both categories of overseas relationship to be recognised as valid (and not *void*) further conditions are specified. The parties must have complied with all the formalities of the 'relevant law',[217] which is defined as meaning the law of the country where the relationship is registered (including its rules of private international law).[218] This requirement that the parties must have complied with the rules laid down by the lex loci celebrationis is identical to the rule traditionally laid down for marriage. However, what is surprising is the endorsement, by the express reference to the rules of private international law, of the doctrine of renvoi, a doctrine which was thought to be of diminishing importance in the conflict of laws.[219]

---

[210] Harper and Landells, 'The Civil Partnership Act 2004 in Force' [2005] Fam Law 963.
[211] S 212(1)(b)(i).   [212] S 212(1)(b)(ii).
[213] But see also s 216(1), which requires the parties, in addition, to be of the same sex under UK law.
[214] S 213.   [215] S 212(1)(a).
[216] S 214. If the point made in para 7.111 is correct, this means that for this category of overseas relationship neither party must be a civil partner or lawfully married both by English law and by the relevant law (law of the country or territory where the relationship is registered).
[217] S 215(1)(b).   [218] S 212(2).   [219] See paras 1.106–1.130.

(iv) Capacity

7.114 The parties must have capacity to enter into the relationship 'under the relevant law',[220] which is similarly defined as meaning the law of the country where the relationship is registered (including its rules of private international law).[221] Again, the doctrine of renvoi is applicable. A further capacity rule is added for English domiciliaries: where one of the parties is domiciled in England, both parties must be aged 16 or over and not be within the prohibited degrees of relationship.[222]

7.115 This requirement that the parties must have capacity by the lex loci celebrationis is different from the comparable rule laid down for marriage under which such capacity is generally unnecessary.[223] Further, this rule that the applicable law is the lex loci celebrationis is starkly at odds with the common law rules on capacity to marry under which the parties must have capacity by their personal law. However, the personal law is still relevant if the lex loci celebrationis insists on the parties having capacity by their personal law. So, if a 17-year-old Ruritanian domiciliary enters into a same-sex partnership in Arcadia but, under Ruritanian law, either same-sex unions can be entered into only by persons aged 18 or over or same-sex partnerships are prohibited altogether, the registered partnership will not be recognised in England, if Arcadian law refers such matters to the law of domicile. Experience to date suggests, however, that overseas registered partnership regimes tend to insist only on compliance with the capacity requirements of the forum.[224] It follows that the use of renvoi, in the English capacity requirements for overseas relationships, is unlikely to have much impact in practice. The formulation of the English choice of law rule suggests a prioritisation of uniformity with the views of the country of registration and a relative lack of concern for issues of limping status as between English law and the personal law. This implies a legislative willingness to uphold the partnership status of those who wished to formalise a same-sex relationship in another country in the face of hostility towards such relationships under their personal law.

(v) Voidable civil partnerships

7.116 A civil partnership registered outside England is *voidable* (i) if it is voidable under the relevant law[225] or (ii) if one party has obtained an interim gender recognition certificate under the Gender Recognition Act 2004 after entering into a civil partnership[226] or (iii) where either party is domiciled in England or Northern Ireland, and the partnership would have been voidable if registered in England.[227]

---

[220] S 215(1)(a). [221] S 212(2).
[222] S 217; the prohibited degrees of relationship are specified in Pt 1 of sch 1 to the Act.
[223] See paras 7.35–7.36.
[224] See Wautelet, 'Private International Law Aspects of Same-Sex Marriages and Partnerships in Europe—Divided We Stand?', in Boele-Woelki and Fuchs (eds), *Legal Recognition of Same-Sex Relationships in Europe* (2012) pp 151–3.
[225] S 54(8)(a). Again, this means the law of the country where the overseas relationship is registered (including its rules of private international law): s 54(10).
[226] S 54(8)(b).
[227] S 54(8)(c). The grounds on which a civil partnership entered into in England is voidable are: lack of valid consent, mental disorder, pregnancy to another person, and changed gender: s 50. S 216 contains detailed provisions relating to gender change.

(vi) Public policy

7.117 In section 218, provision is made for a public policy exception: overseas registered partnerships will not be recognised if it would be manifestly contrary to public policy to recognise the capacity, under the 'relevant law' (the lex loci celebrationis), of one or both of the parties to enter into the relationship. This is narrower than the common law public policy exception for marriages.[228] At common law, the public policy doctrine has both positive and negative implications: both capacities and incapacities under the relevant foreign law can be disapplied. Furthermore, while questions of public policy have tended to focus on essential validity, the common law doctrine is general in scope and may be invoked with respect to any objectionable foreign law,[229] including foreign rules relating to formalities. By contrast, within the detailed statutory scheme laid down for civil partnerships, it appears that public policy has a more limited role: section 218 suggests that it has only a negative *invalidating* application and may only affect capacity (as opposed to formality) rules. However, given the 'western liberal' value systems that tend to go hand in hand with registered partnership, these statutory limitations on the public policy doctrine may well be of little consequence in practice.[230]

2. Civil partnerships registered in England

7.118 Many other countries permitting registered partnerships restrict the circumstances in which foreigners may contract such unions within the jurisdiction. For example, under Belgian law both parties must be habitually resident in Belgium. In the Netherlands, the Dutch nationality of one of the parties will suffice if the parties reside outside the Netherlands.[231]

7.119 Under English law, however, persons of foreign domicile or nationality are at liberty to enter into a civil partnership in England. The only territorial requirement is that each person must have resided in England for at least seven days before giving notice of a proposed civil partnership.[232] This must normally be followed by a waiting period of 28 days.[233] All persons whether domiciled in England or abroad must comply with the 'eligibility' (capacity) rules specified in section 3[234] and the various formalities (including the parental consent rules for persons under 18[235]). The Act makes no reference to any additional capacity requirements for foreign domiciliaries and it is generally accepted that compliance with the internal English formality and capacity requirements

---

[228] See paras 7.100–7.103.   [229] See para 1.155.
[230] See Norrie, 'Recognition of Foreign Relationships under the Civil Partnership Act 2004' (2006) 2 Journal of Private International Law 137, 149; Fawcett, Ní Shúilleabháin and Shah, *Human Rights and Private International Law* (2016) para 11.181.
[231] Wautelet, 'Private International Law Aspects of Same-Sex Marriages and Partnerships in Europe—Divided We Stand?' in Boele-Woelki and Fuchs (eds), *Legal Recognition of Same-Sex Relationships in Europe* (2012) pp 155–6.
[232] S 8.   [233] S 11(b) as amended by Immigration Act 2014, sch 4(2), para 22.
[234] This is the same as the position for marriage where parties marrying in England must have capacity by English law: see para 7.56.
[235] S 4.

is sufficient.[236] Although this is at variance with the position respecting marriage,[237] it is consistent with the policy objective of facilitating registered partnership for those who are denied such possibility under their personal law.

C Same-sex marriages

1. Marriage in England

7.120   The Marriage (Same Sex Couples) Act 2013 abolished the opposite-sex requirement for marriage in English law. Marriage of same-sex couples became lawful[238] and, in English law, marriage was given the same effect in relation to same-sex couples as it has in relation to opposite-sex couples.[239] While this brings about an extension of the general marriage laws (including the choice of law rules), it is implicit in the 2013 Act that, where either party to a proposed same-sex marriage in England is domiciled in a country which does not permit same-sex marriage, this will not affect the validity of the marriage. In other words, an incapacity to contract same-sex marriage under the personal law will not affect the validity of a marriage celebrated in England. This can be inferred from the provision under the 2013 Act of a 'forum of necessity' jurisdiction to dissolve same-sex marriages celebrated in England in circumstances where the parties have remained domiciled and resident in a jurisdiction which does not recognise their same-sex marriage.[240] There would be no need to make provision for an exceptional divorce jurisdiction for such cases, if incapacity under the domiciliary law invalidated the marriage in the first place. While the irrelevance of an opposite-sex requirement under the personal law is therefore implied, it would be preferable if this point were made more explicitly.[241] In so far as the Act provides for the extension of existing marriage laws to same-sex couples, one must infer that any other incapacity under the domiciliary law (apart from an opposite-sex requirement) will affect the validity of the marriage.

---

[236] Dicey, Morris and Collins, *The Conflict of Laws: Second Cumulative Supplement to the Fifteenth Edition* (2015) p 167.

[237] See para 7.56.   [238] S 1.   [239] S 11(1).

[240] Pt 4 of sch 4, amending the Domicile and Matrimonial Proceedings Act 1973 to include a new sch A1, and providing at para 2(1)(c) for a special forum of necessity jurisdiction to dissolve same-sex marriages. See the Explanatory Notes to the Act at [116]: 'Same sex couples who marry in England and Wales but *remain* or become habitually resident or domiciled in another country may not be able to end their marriage in that country if it does not recognise the existence of the relationship. Part 4 [of sch 4] therefore amends the Domicile and Matrimonial Proceedings Act 1973 to provide a "jurisdiction of last resort" so that those same sex couples who are unable to divorce or obtain other matrimonial orders in the country which would normally have jurisdiction are able to have their case heard in the courts in England and Wales' (emphasis added). This explanatory note clearly envisages that same-sex couples who have *remained domiciled* (ie prior to and since the marriage) in a jurisdiction not permitting same-sex marriage may seek a divorce in England.

[241] See Walker, 'Same-sex Divorce Tourism in Canada' (2012) 128 LQR 344: in Canada (one of the first countries to permit same-sex marriage) emergency legislation was required to confirm (with retrospective effect) the validity of marriages contracted in Canada in violation of opposite-sex requirements under the law of the domicile.

7.121 The 2013 Act also makes provision for the conversion of existing civil partnerships into marriages.[242] In this context, it appears that the validity of the resulting marriage will not be affected by *any* pre-existing incapacity to marry under the domiciliary law:[243] the satisfaction of the English eligibility and formality requirements at the time of registering the civil partnership appears to be sufficient.

2. Recognition of overseas same-sex marriages

7.122 Overseas same-sex marriages were previously recognised in England as civil partnerships;[244] however, they are no longer treated as 'overseas relationships' under the 2004 Act.[245] Section 10(1) of the 2013 Act provides that a marriage under 'the law of any country or territory outside the United Kingdom is not prevented from being recognised under the law of England and Wales only because it is the marriage of a same sex couple'. This provision is capable of either a narrow or a broad interpretation. On a narrow construction, it simply allows for the recognition of overseas same-sex marriages, provided they are formally valid under the law of the place of celebration and essentially valid under the law of the domicile of each party. This (narrow) interpretation would allow opposite-sex requirements under the domiciliary law to preclude recognition in England. On a broader construction, section 10 rules out any denial of recognition of a marriage celebrated abroad 'only because it is the marriage of a same sex couple'. In other words, the same-sex nature of the marriage shall not be a ground for non-recognition (even if that objection arises under the domiciliary law). It is submitted that the second (broader) interpretation is preferable. If domiciliary opposite-sex requirements do not affect the validity of marriages celebrated in England (as outlined above), it is difficult to see why the same understanding should not be brought to bear in interpreting section 10. Furthermore, a policy of facilitating same-sex marriage for those who are denied such a status under their personal law would chime with the policy objectives inherent in the choice of law scheme of the Civil Partnership Act 2004. Even if the narrower interpretation of section 10 were to prevail, it would still be arguable that opposite-sex requirements under the domiciliary law should be disapplied as a matter of public policy. However, given the exceptionality of the public policy doctrine, an English judge might be reluctant to take the view that a foreign rule could offend public policy in circumstances where English law took the very same approach up until 2013.[246]

---

[242] S 9. See also the Marriage of Same Sex Couples (Conversion of Civil Partnership) Regulations 2014, SI 2014/3181. This conversion mechanism applies only to civil partnerships contracted in England and Wales and to those formed overseas under an Order in Council. 'Overseas relationships' recognised as civil partnerships are not eligible for conversion.

[243] Dicey, Morris and Collins, *The Conflict of Laws: Second Cumulative Supplement to the Fifteenth Edition* (2015) p 167.

[244] The denial of the status of 'marriage' under the 2004 Act was challenged (unsuccessfully) on human rights grounds in *Wilkinson v Kitzinger (No 2)* [2007] 1 FLR 295.

[245] So far as English law is concerned: Civil Partnership Act 2004, s 212(1A).

[246] See Briggs, *Private International Law in English Courts* (2014) p 909.

D Opposite-sex registered partnerships

7.123 As indicated earlier, some countries permit registered partnerships between persons of the opposite sex.[247] Such partnerships are not capable of recognition under the Civil Partnership Act 2004: the recognition scheme laid down under the 2004 Act is explicitly confined to same-sex partnerships.[248] It is possible that such partnerships might be recognised as marriage (arguably the closest analogue in English law).[249] This might be considered unsatisfactory in so far as the parties are likely to have opted for registered partnership *in preference* to traditional marriage in the country of origin but recent case-law suggests that any human rights objections to a marriage characterisation are unlikely to succeed.[250] In the alternative, it has been suggested that it might be possible to use the common law to fashion a sui generis solution to the recognition of such partnerships.[251]

VII Polygamous marriages

A Introduction

7.124 The laws of many countries permit polygamous marriages, under which a man may have more than one wife. Islamic countries allow polygamy and in a number of African countries polygamous marriages may be celebrated under Islamic or customary law. Some laws permit a woman to have more than one husband at the same time.[252] Correctly speaking, where a man is allowed more than one wife the marriage is described as *polygynous* and where a woman may have more than one husband it is *polyandrous*. All such marriages are generically termed *polygamous* marriages.

7.125 What is the attitude of English law to polygamous marriages? In *Hyde v Hyde* marriage was defined as 'the voluntary union for life of one man and one woman to the exclusion of all others'.[253] However, part of the function of the conflict of laws is to ensure that a status or relationship created by foreign cultures and religions and valid under foreign legal systems is respected and recognised. In view of immigration over the past half-century from countries permitting polygamy, there would be grave hardship if polygamous marriages were denied all recognition. Accordingly, it has long been clear

---

[247] Examples include France and the Netherlands.   [248] S 212(b)(i); s 216(1).

[249] In *Hincks v Gallardo* [2013] ONSC 129 an English (same-sex) civil partnership was recognised as marriage under Canadian law. See Wiggerich, 'Civil Partnership as Marriage: The Recognition of Foreign Same-Sex Unions Under Canadian Law' [2014] IFL (March).

[250] See *Steinfeld and Keidan v Secretary of State for Education* [2016] 4 WLR 41, where the State's refusal to extend civil partnership to opposite-sex couples was found to be compatible with its obligations under the European Convention on Human Rights.

[251] See Norrie, 'Recognition of Foreign Relationships under the Civil Partnership Act 2004' (2006) 2 Journal of Private International Law 137, 154.

[252] See, generally, Majumdar, *Himalayan Polyandry: Structure, Functioning and Cultural Change: A Field Study of Jaunsar-Bawar* (1962) pp 75–7; *The Guardian*, 4 March 1993, 12.

[253] (1866) LR 1 P & D 130 at 133.

that a polygamous marriage may be entitled to recognition as a valid marriage. The approach of the courts, as stated in *Mohamed v Knott*, is that 'a polygamous marriage will be recognised in England as a valid marriage unless there is some strong reason to the contrary'.[254] Formerly, however, under the rule laid down in *Hyde v Hyde*, while such marriages were entitled to recognition for most purposes, the parties were not permitted to obtain matrimonial relief in England. Although they were regarded as validly married to each other, the courts had no power to grant either spouse a divorce, a decree of judicial separation, a nullity decree or financial relief. This hardship[255] was removed by the Matrimonial Proceedings (Polygamous Marriages) Act 1972.[256] Since then, parties to polygamous marriages have been entitled to the same matrimonial relief as monogamous couples.

7.126 Despite the increased recognition of polygamous marriages, the question whether a marriage is monogamous or polygamous may still need to be answered. For example, the parties may lack capacity to enter into a marriage if it is polygamous.

B Classification

7.127 In order to determine whether the conflicts rules on monogamy or polygamy are applicable, the marriage in question needs to be classified as monogamous or polygamous. For example, under traditional Chinese law a man was permitted only one primary wife (a tsai) but was allowed concubines (tsips) who had legal rights (for example, succession rights) and were often referred to as secondary wives. In *Lee v Lau*,[257] the Privy Council, on appeal from Hong Kong, declared that the marriage to the primary wife was polygamous, despite the fact that Hong Kong law described it as monogamous. Consistent with the normal approach, this classification was effected by the lex fori. The court looked beyond the nomenclature employed by the applicable law and examined the nature and incidents of the foreign marriages or relationships and characterised them according to their nearest analogue in English law. Although the concubines or secondary wives did not have the same full legal status as the primary wife, they nevertheless had sufficient legal rights of a wife for the relationships to be regarded as polygamous marriages. Accordingly, the marriage to the primary wife was also polygamous.

7.128 How is a marriage to be classified where the husband has only one wife in fact but is permitted under his personal law to take more wives? Such marriages, known as *potentially polygamous marriages*, used to be regarded as polygamous even if the husband never took another wife. Accordingly, the conflicts rules on polygamy were applicable both to actually and potentially polygamous marriages. However, the Private International Law (Miscellaneous Provisions) Act 1995 abolished the concept of a potentially polygamous marriage if either party to the marriage is domiciled in England at the time of the marriage.[258] So, if an English domiciled woman marries in Pakistan

---

[254] [1969] 1 QB 1 at 13–14. [255] See, eg, *Sowa v Sowa* [1961] P 70.
[256] Now s 47 of the Matrimonial Causes Act 1973. [257] [1967] P 14.
[258] Para 2(2) of the sch to the Act amending Matrimonial Causes Act 1973, s 11(d).

a man domiciled there who has no other wife, the marriage, which previously would have been regarded as potentially polygamous, will be treated as monogamous.[259] However, if neither party is domiciled in England at the time of the marriage, such marriages are still regarded as potentially polygamous and governed by the conflicts rules on polygamy.

C Law determining nature of marriage

7.129 Where a married man contracts a second marriage, the nature of this marriage is determined by the lex loci celebrationis. For example, if a Muslim domiciled in Pakistan, who already has a wife, marries another woman by Islamic rites in Pakistan the marriage is polygamous. If the second marriage is celebrated in a country only permitting monogamous marriages, then, while the second marriage is monogamous in nature, it will be void, because a monogamous marriage cannot be validly contracted by a person who is already married.

7.130 However, if a single man marries a single woman and neither party is domiciled in England, which law decides whether the marriage is monogamous or potentially polygamous? Suppose the husband, a Muslim domiciled in New York, marries in Pakistan a woman domiciled in Pakistan. The marriage is celebrated by Islamic rites; by Pakistani law the husband would be free to take further wives; by New York law (let it be assumed[260]) he would not. Is the marriage potentially polygamous or monogamous? Is its nature to be decided by Pakistani law as the lex loci celebrationis or by New York law as the law of the husband's domicile?

7.131 The argument in favour of applying the law of the husband's domicile at the time of the marriage is that the question whether the nature of the marriage is such that the husband is permitted to marry another wife is a question of his capacity to be governed by the law of his domicile.[261] If this were the rule, it would mean that, if at the time of the marriage the husband was domiciled in New York, or any other monogamous country, the marriage would be monogamous.[262] If, however, he was domiciled in Pakistan, or any other country whose law permitted him to marry further wives, the marriage would be potentially polygamous. It would not matter where the marriage was celebrated.

7.132 The alternative solution is that the nature of the marriage should be governed by the law of the country where it was celebrated. On this approach, the question whether the marriage is such that the husband is free to marry again is not a question of capacity. The nature of the marriage is determined by the lex loci celebrationis. The role of the law of domicile is limited to the (important) issue of whether the marriage contracted

---

[259] See paras 7.138–7.141.   [260] See n 262.
[261] This assumes the dual domicile doctrine is applicable.
[262] It is a moot point whether reference should be made to the conflict of laws rules, rather than the internal law, of the country concerned (see, by analogy, Dicey, Morris and Collins, *The Conflict of Laws* (15th edn, 2012) p 977). In view of the general trend against extending the use of renvoi, such a suggestion is unlikely to be accepted.

in such a form is valid. The justification for referring to the lex loci celebrationis is that the nature of the marriage should depend on the intentions and expectations of the parties. If they go through a ceremony under which, according to the law of the country where it is celebrated, the husband is entitled to marry again, then presumably they intended the marriage to be of that nature. In *Isaac Penhas v Tan Soo Eng*,[263] a Privy Council decision on appeal from Singapore, it was held that whether a marriage was monogamous or polygamous depended on the intention of the parties. If the lex loci celebrationis permits both religious polygamous marriages and civil monogamous marriages, the parties are free to choose whichever form of marriage to which they wish to subject themselves. A fortiori, if there is only one form of marriage available, the parties must be deemed to have chosen to contract a marriage of that form and nature. On this basis, if a husband domiciled in New York marries in Pakistan by Islamic rites, the marriage is potentially polygamous.

7.133 In order to assess the law's response to this issue, it is necessary to distinguish between marriages contracted in England and those contracted abroad.

1. Marriage in England

7.134 No valid polygamous marriage can take place in England. When England is the locus celebrationis the parties have to comply with the provisions of the Marriage Act 1949 under which only monogamous marriages can be contracted. In *R v Bham*[264] a Muslim man and woman went through a form of 'marriage' in accordance with Islamic rites under which the 'marriage' would have been polygamous. The 'marriage officer' was prosecuted for knowingly solemnising a marriage in an unregistered building contrary to section 75(2)(a) of the Marriage Act 1949. On appeal the defendant's conviction was quashed on the ground that the Islamic ceremony did not constitute a 'marriage'. It was a religious ceremony of no legal significance. In *Qureshi v Qureshi*[265] the husband, domiciled in Pakistan, and the wife, domiciled in India, went through an English register office marriage ceremony which was followed by a further ceremony in accordance with Islamic rites. It was common ground that the register office ceremony gave rise to a valid monogamous marriage and the subsequent religious ceremony was of no legal significance, even though it would have given rise to a potentially polygamous marriage under the law of the husband's domicile. In *A-M v A-M*[266] an Islamic ceremony conducted in a flat in London was compared to a staged dramatic marriage ceremony in a soap opera: it did not constitute a 'marriage'. This rule is not hard to understand. While polygamous marriages celebrated abroad can be recognised, if the parties marry in England the link with England is stronger and the law is entitled to insist on conformity with English standards under which only monogamous marriages can be contracted.

2. Marriage abroad

7.135 Where the parties marry abroad, the courts for many years adopted the view that the nature of the marriage was governed by the law of the country where it was celebrated.

---

[263] [1953] AC 304.   [264] [1966] 1 QB 159.   [265] [1972] Fam 173.   [266] [2001] 2 FLR 6.

In *Re Bethell*[267] the husband, an English domiciliary, married in Bechuanaland (as it then was) a local woman from the Baralong tribe. It was held that this was a Baralong (and hence polygamous) marriage. As the husband was an English domiciliary lacking capacity to contract a polygamous marriage, the marriage was void.

7.136 This approach caused severe hardship in many cases. By the latter half of the twentieth century there were many people domiciled in England whose families had originally come from the Indian subcontinent.[268] It was not uncommon for arranged marriages to persist within such families and often it would be the English domiciled husband who would return to the Indian subcontinent and there contract the arranged marriage.[269] Under the traditional approach, whereby the lex loci celebrationis determines the nature of the marriage, such marriages would be regarded as potentially polygamous in nature and, therefore, void on the ground that one party was domiciled in England.[270] Such an approach amounted to a 'serious interference with the customs of ethnic minority communities'[271] in this country and had many adverse practical consequences affecting the immigration status of the wife, acquisition of British nationality, social security benefits and rights of succession.[272] In an attempt to alleviate these hardships the Court of Appeal in 1982 in *Hussain v Hussain*[273] introduced a new approach. In this case the marriage was celebrated in Pakistan according to Islamic rites, the husband (a single man) being domiciled in England and the wife in Pakistan. The parties set up their matrimonial home in England. In answer to the wife's petition in the English court for a judicial separation, the husband contended that the marriage was void under section 11(d) of the Matrimonial Causes Act 1973. Section 11(d) provides that a polygamous marriage (which then included a potentially polygamous one even if one of the spouses was domiciled in England) shall be void if either party was at the time of the marriage domiciled in England. The husband argued that the marriage was void because he was domiciled in England at the time of the marriage, which was potentially polygamous under the lex loci celebrationis. The Court of Appeal, however, held that the marriage was monogamous. The court's view was that a marriage can be potentially polygamous for the purpose of section 11(d) only if one of the spouses has the capacity to marry a second spouse. Whether the husband had such capacity depended on the law of his domicile, English law, and by that law he had not. Accordingly, the marriage was monogamous and valid.

7.137 How far did *Hussain* go towards overruling the common law rule that the nature of the marriage was to be determined by the lex loci celebrationis? One view is that the

---

[267] (1888) 38 Ch D 220. See also *Risk v Risk* [1951] P 50.
[268] Law Com No 42, paras 23–4; Figures show that from 1985 to 1995 a total of 175,630 people from the Indian subcontinent, Iran, Iraq, and Saudi Arabia were given rights to settle in the United Kingdom. Note, however, that not all these people were Muslims.
[269] Poulter, 'Hyde v Hyde—A Reappraisal' (1976) 25 ICLQ 475, 504.
[270] Matrimonial Causes Act 1973, s 11(d). See para 7.144.
[271] Poulter, 'Polygamy—New Law Commission Proposals' [1983] Fam Law 72.
[272] Ibid.   [273] [1983] Fam 26.

decision is to be limited to cases involving an interpretation of section 11(d), that is, where one of the parties was domiciled in England at the date of the marriage.[274] However, the more widely accepted interpretation is that the *Hussain* principle applies irrespective of the husband's domicile. According to this view, a marriage is monogamous if by the law of the husband's domicile at the date of the marriage he is not permitted to take a further wife. It is immaterial that the marriage is potentially polygamous by the lex loci celebrationis. The converse, however, would not apply. A marriage celebrated in a country by whose law it is monogamous is always monogamous, even if by the law of the husband's domicile at the time of the marriage he is free to take a further wife.[275] In other words, a marriage is potentially polygamous only if it is so under both the lex loci celebrationis and the law of the husband's domicile.[276] The advantage of this interpretation is that more marriages will be held to be monogamous and valid.

D One party domiciled in England with no existing spouse

7.138 Where one of the parties is domiciled in England the decision in *Hussain*[277] has been superseded by the Private International Law (Miscellaneous Provisions) Act 1995. The schedule to this Act amended section 11(d) of the Matrimonial Causes Act 1973 so that where 'either party was at the time of the marriage domiciled in England and Wales . . . a marriage is not polygamous if at its inception neither party has any spouse additional to the other'. A marriage which is 'not polygamous' must, logically, be monogamous. Section 5(1) of the 1995 Act spells out that such marriages are 'not void'. For English domiciliaries, this provision is wider than the principle established in *Hussain* in that it applies even if it is the wife who is domiciled in England. Under *Hussain* if an English domiciled woman married a Pakistani domiciliary (with no existing wife) in Pakistan the marriage would have been polygamous in nature and void under the old section 11(d). Under the 1995 Act, however, assuming the husband did not already have a spouse, this marriage is regarded as 'not polygamous' (that is, monogamous) and, assuming there were no other impediments, valid. The implications of *Hussain* were rightly described as 'sexist' in that 'the daughters of immigrant families [could not] return to marry local men whose domiciliary law permits polygamy'.[278] Under the 1995 Act such a marriage would be monogamous and valid.

7.139 Section 5(2) of the 1995 Act adds:

> This section does not affect the determination of the validity of a marriage by reference to the law of another country to the extent that it falls to be so determined in accordance with the rules of private international law.

---

[274] Carter (1982) 53 BYIL 298, 302.
[275] Compare Briggs, 'Polygamous Marriages and English Domiciliaries' (1983) 32 ICLQ 737, 740 who suggests that the husband's domicile should be determinative in all cases.
[276] Dicey, Morris and Collins, *The Conflict of Laws* (15th edn, 2012) p 968.   [277] [1983] Fam 26.
[278] Schuz, 'When is a Polygamous Marriage Not a Polygamous Marriage?' (1983) 46 MLR 653, 657.

7.140 This provision is best interpreted[279] as a reminder that the other conflicts rules relating to validity of marriage, apart from those relating to polygamy, are applicable. The marriage is only 'not void' if the alleged defect relates to lack of capacity to contract a polygamous marriage. If, however, continuing the example of the English woman marrying the Pakistani man, the parties failed to comply with the formal requirements of the locus celebrationis or if one of them lacked capacity on other grounds, for example, lack of age, the marriage is not to be declared valid on the basis of section 5(1). The normal conflicts rules governing the formalities and essentials of a marriage are still applicable.

7.141 It should be noted that these provisions of the 1995 Act are for most purposes retrospective. Accordingly, if a wife domiciled in England married an Egyptian domiciliary (without an existing wife) by Islamic rites in Egypt before the commencement of the Act, this marriage, which would have been void under the common law rules,[280] is to be regarded as valid.[281] However, such a marriage is not retrospectively validated if one of the parties had, before the commencement of the Act, already entered into another marriage that would be valid either under the common law or under the Act[282] or if the marriage has already been annulled before commencement of the Act.[283] Further, such a marriage is not retrospectively validated for the purposes of succession, benefits, allowances, or pension rights payable before commencement and tax in respect of the period before commencement.[284]

E Capacity to contract a polygamous marriage

7.142 It has been seen above that polygamous marriages are recognised as marriages for most purposes. But it is, of course, only *valid* polygamous marriages that can be recognised. In addition to the general issues of formal and essential validity which arise in relation to all marriages, there is the additional question whether the parties have capacity to enter into a polygamous (as opposed to a monogamous) marriage. In this regard, there has been some debate as to whether the dual domicile doctrine or the intended matrimonial home doctrine is applicable.

7.143 It was decided in *Radwan v Radwan (No 2)*[285] that the intended matrimonial home rule applies to this aspect of capacity. In this case, the marriage was celebrated in France

---

[279] The Law Commission in its Explanatory Notes to the Draft Bill—which eventually became the 1995 Act—states that (what became) s 5(2) 'corresponds to section 14(1) of the Matrimonial Causes Act 1973' (see para 7.145): Law Com No 146, Explanatory Notes to cl 1(3). It would, however, be perverse to argue that s 5(2) similarly excludes the operation of s 5(1) and that, under the intended matrimonial home test, an English domiciliary can contract a potentially polygamous marriage. S 11(d), which is not affected by s 5(2), is clear that if one of the parties is domiciled in England, the marriage is not polygamous. Dicey, Morris and Collins, *The Conflict of Laws* (15th edn, 2012) p 977 suggests that s 5(2) means that one must refer to the conflict rules on polygamy of the law of domicile of the relevant spouse, ie, s 5(2) endorses the doctrine of renvoi. The better interpretation, however, is that the reference in s 5(2) to 'the rules of private international law' means the English rules of private international law.
[280] Assuming Egyptian law is not applied as the law of the intended matrimonial home.
[281] Private International Law (Miscellaneous Provisions) Act 1995, s 6(1).
[282] S 6(2).   [283] S 6(3)–(5).   [284] S 6(6).   [285] [1973] Fam 35.

in Islamic form. The husband was a Muslim domiciled in Egypt who already had a wife married to him in Egypt, also by Islamic rites. The second wife was domiciled in England at the time of the ceremony, but the parties set up their matrimonial home in Egypt after the marriage, as they had intended at the time of the marriage. Five years later they moved to England. When the wife petitioned in the English court for a divorce, the question arose whether the marriage was valid. It was argued that it was void because under English law, the law of her ante-nuptial domicile, the wife lacked capacity to marry a man who was not single. However, applying Egyptian law as the law of the intended matrimonial home, it was held that this was a valid polygamous marriage. The decision was strongly criticised,[286] mainly on the ground that it is well established that other aspects of capacity to marry are subject to the dual domicile rule.

7.144 Since *Radwan* was decided, section 11(d) of the Matrimonial Causes Act 1973 has come into force. This provision reads:

> A marriage celebrated after 31 July 1971 shall be void on the following grounds...
>
> (d) in the case of a polygamous marriage entered into outside England and Wales that either party was at the time of the marriage domiciled in England and Wales.

7.145 This provision must be read with section 14(1) of the Act, the effect of which is that section 11 does not apply if the validity of the marriage is to be determined by a foreign law. In other words, despite the reference to the domicile of a party, it is arguable that section 11(d) is not a conflicts rule, but a rule of English domestic law, to be applied only if, according to the common law rules of the conflict of laws, English law is the governing law. Accordingly, if *Radwan* is not followed and the dual domicile doctrine applied, any polygamous marriage contracted by a party domiciled in England will be void. However, if *Radwan* is applied, the result seems to be as follows. If the intended matrimonial home is any country other than England, section 11(d) does not come into the picture at all. The validity of the polygamous marriage is determined by the law of the foreign country in question.[287] So, *Radwan* would have been decided in the same way even if the marriage had been celebrated after 31 July 1971. This means that it is possible for an English domiciliary to contract a valid polygamous marriage.

7.146 On the other hand, following *Radwan*, if the intended matrimonial home is England, then English law governs and section 11(d) applies. If either of the parties is domiciled in England at the time of the marriage, it is void. If neither of the parties is domiciled in England at the time of the marriage, section 11(d) is not applicable but the same result will be reached and the marriage held void. This is because polygamous

---

[286] Wade, 'Capacity to Marry: Choice of Law Rules and Polygamous Marriages' (1973) 22 ICLQ 571; Karsten, 'Capacity to Contract a Polygamous Marriage' (1973) 36 MLR 291; Pearl, 'Capacity for Polygamy' [1973] CLJ 43. The decision is defended by Jaffey, 'The Essential Validity of Marriage in the English Conflict of Laws' (1978) 41 MLR 38 and Stone, 'Capacity for Polygamy—Judicial Rectification of Legislative Error' [1983] Fam Law 76.
[287] This is, of course, somewhat perverse. Cumming-Bruce J in *Radwan* accepted that s 14 was enacted on the assumption that the dual domicile rule governed the question of capacity to contract a polygamous marriage (at 52).

marriages are not permitted under English domestic law. This was the reason why the marriage in *Radwan*, decided before section 11(d) came into effect, would have been void under the dual domicile doctrine. Further, even if this were not the position at common law in cases where neither party was domiciled in England,[288] section 11(b) of the Matrimonial Causes Act 1973 provides that a marriage is void if 'at the time of the marriage either party was already lawfully married'. Unlike section 11(d), this is not limited to cases where either of the spouses is domiciled in England. So, if England is the intended matrimonial home, the marriage will be void even if both parties are domiciled in an Islamic country when they marry.

F Change in the nature of a marriage

1. Polygamy to monogamy

7.147 A marriage which at its inception is potentially polygamous may subsequently become monogamous as the result of some event or a change in the law.[289] In *Parkasho v Singh*[290] a marriage celebrated in India was at the time of its celebration potentially polygamous according to Indian law. Subsequently, the effect of the Indian Hindu Marriage Act was to debar the husband from marrying further wives. It was held that the marriage had become monogamous in the eyes of English law. Similarly, in *Ali v Ali*,[291] it was held that if the husband in a potentially polygamous marriage becomes domiciled in England (or any other monogamous country), the marriage thereby becomes monogamous. The reasoning was similar to that later used in *Hussain v Hussain*[292] in relation to the nature of the marriage at its inception. Once the husband is domiciled in England, he no longer has capacity to marry again; hence the marriage becomes by definition monogamous. It follows, as was held in *Onobrauche v Onobrauche*,[293] that if the wife, but not the husband, becomes domiciled in England, a potentially polygamous marriage will not become monogamous. An actually polygamous marriage cannot, of course, become monogamous, but there is no reason why, if there is only one wife remaining from a hitherto polygamous marriage, it should not become monogamous.

7.148 The reason why the courts were anxious in the above cases to hold that the potentially polygamous marriages had become monogamous was that, unless they were monogamous, the court could not have granted matrimonial relief. The question is less important following the entry into force of the Matrimonial Proceedings (Polygamous

---

[288] This was the view adopted by Jaffey, *Introduction to the Conflict of Laws* (1988) p 32. The more orthodox position was that stated in Dicey and Morris, *The Conflict of Laws* (12th edn, 1993) p 700: 'All monogamous countries have a rule prohibiting bigamy and, though this was originally intended to apply where both marriages are in monogamous form, it could be applied without undue distortion to an actually polygamous marriage.'

[289] *Sinha Peerage Claim* [1946] 1 All ER 348n; *Cheni v Cheni* [1965] P 85.

[290] [1968] P 233.   [291] [1968] P 564.

[292] [1983] Fam 26. This reasoning casts some doubt on the correctness of the use of the intended matrimonial home test in *Radwan v Radwan (No 2)* [1973] Fam 35.

[293] [1978] Fam Law 107.

Marriages) Act 1972, which gave the courts power to grant matrimonial relief in respect of polygamous marriages. Nevertheless, the question can still arise (for example, in deciding whether the husband is guilty of the crime of bigamy if he marries again). Moreover, as the following discussion shows, if the husband subsequently enters a valid polygamous marriage, the first wife's legal position may be stronger if her marriage has become monogamous.

2. Monogamy to polygamy

7.149 In *A-G of Ceylon v Reid*,[294] an appeal to the Privy Council from Ceylon (as it then was), a couple had contracted a valid Roman Catholic marriage. Twenty-six years later the husband wished to marry a Muslim woman. Accordingly, he converted to Islam and three days later they were married. His conviction for bigamy was quashed with the Privy Council holding, in effect, that his second marriage was a valid polygamous marriage. Similar situations can arise in cases where there has been no change of religion or domicile. In *Nabi v Heaton*[295] the husband, domiciled in Pakistan, married the first wife in England. This marriage was monogamous. He then returned to Pakistan and there married a second wife under Islamic law. It was accepted without argument on appeal that the second marriage was a valid polygamous marriage. In both these cases the result was that the husband had contracted a valid monogamous marriage followed by a valid polygamous marriage. He was validly married to both wives. What is the effect in these cases of the second marriage on the first monogamous marriage? Does the first marriage retain its legal character as monogamous or have the husband's unilateral acts converted it into a polygamous one?

7.150 At first sight it seems that the nature of the initial marriage must have changed. It is a logical, legal, and linguistic nonsense to assert that the husband is monogamously married to the first wife, but polygamously married to the second wife. However, while this is true from his perspective, from the first wife's perspective the nature of her monogamous marriage does not change. As she had the reasonable expectation at the time of the marriage that she would be the only wife, her rights as a monogamous wife should be protected. In *A-G of Ceylon v Reid* it was accepted that while, from the husband's perspective, he might be validly married to his second wife, nevertheless from his first wife's perspective he was committing adultery. The same conclusion was reached in *Drammeh v Drammeh*,[296] where it was held that a husband might well be validly married to his second wife, but from his first monogamous wife's point of view he was committing adultery.

7.151 The nature of the first marriage is important for several reasons. If it remains a monogamous marriage, in matrimonial proceedings the wife can rely on her husband's intercourse with his second wife as adultery, because it falls outside the monogamous relationship.[297] Such intercourse is not adultery if the first marriage is polygamous.[298] Further, the first wife's rights of succession are more likely to be protected if

---

[294] [1965] AC 720.   [295] [1981] 1 WLR 1052.   [296] (1970) 78 Ceylon Law Weekly 55.
[297] Matrimonial Causes Act 1973, s 1(2)(a).   [298] *Onobrauche v Onobrauche* [1978] Fam Law 107.

her marriage remains monogamous, despite the husband's second valid marriage.[299] Finally, the wife under a monogamous marriage is entitled to social security benefits as such, even if there is a subsequent valid marriage.[300] Her status as a monogamous wife remains protected and is not affected by a subsequent marriage by the husband. The first marriage does not become a polygamous marriage.

G Recognition of polygamous marriages

7.152 The approach today is that a valid polygamous marriage is to be recognised unless there is some strong reason to the contrary. It will seldom be that such a reason is found. The old rule that a polygamous marriage was not recognised for the purposes of matrimonial relief was abolished by the Matrimonial Proceedings (Polygamous Marriages) Act 1972. The initial fears that English court procedures would be difficult to adapt to polygamous marriages have proved to be largely unfounded. As shall be seen in the next chapter, English courts always apply the lex fori when granting divorces and separation orders. However, the fact that a man is polygamously married to more than one wife can be relevant to the interpretation of this lex fori. For example, a divorce can only be obtained on the ground that the marriage has irretrievably broken down and this has to be proved by establishing one of a number of stated facts such as adultery, unreasonable behaviour, or desertion.[301] In *Onobrauche v Onobrauche*[302] the husband had two polygamous wives. The second wife claimed that the husband had committed adultery with the first wife. This claim was rejected on the basis that sexual intercourse with a lawful wife could not amount to adultery. In *Poon v Tan*[303] it was held that marrying a second wife was unreasonable behaviour towards the first wife. This, of course, need not always be the case; much should depend on the cultural acceptability of polygamous marriages under the relevant law and the first wife's reasonable expectations. For instance, while polygamous marriages are still tolerated in India, both Indian law and culture are moving firmly against such marriages.[304] The first wife under such an Indian polygamous marriage would certainly have a plausible claim that her husband's second marriage amounted to unreasonable behaviour. Whether such a plea should be accepted from a Muslim first wife who is domiciled in Pakistan is more questionable. Polygamy is more widely practised and accepted by Muslims in Pakistan and, in marrying under Pakistani law, the wife might be deemed to have accepted the possibility of the husband taking further wives. Much, of course, will depend on all the factual circumstances. For example, in *Quoraishi v Quoraishi*[305] it was held that, while it was appropriate to take foreign law into account as part of the background to the marriage, where the husband and wife were professional people who had been resident in England for 10 years, the husband's taking of a second wife could be sufficient to give

---

[299] See paras 7.156–7.157.   [300] See para 7.159.   [301] Matrimonial Causes Act 1973, s 1.
[302] [1978] Fam Law 107.   [303] [1973] Fam Law 161.
[304] Law Com No 42, para 37, n 91. See, generally, Shah, 'Attitudes to Polygamy in English Law' (2003) 52 ICLQ 369, 370–3.
[305] [1985] FLR 780.

the first wife a 'just cause' for deserting him.[306] In matrimonial proceedings, provision is made for notice to be given to other spouses and for conferring on them the right to be heard in the proceedings.[307]

7.153 It has long been established that a polygamous marriage is recognised so as to render void a subsequent monogamous marriage. For example, in *Baindail v Baindail*[308] an Indian domiciliary who had contracted a valid polygamous marriage in India came to England and married an English woman in an English register office. The second 'marriage' was annulled as being bigamous. The validity of his first polygamous marriage was thus recognised. Such second marriages are, however, only civilly bigamous. In *R v Sagoo*[309] it was held that the celebration of the subsequent marriage in such a case does not render the husband liable to conviction for the crime of bigamy, unless the first polygamous marriage has in the meantime become monogamous. This rule is explicable on the basis that the criminal law is normally concerned with the punishment of blameworthy conduct. Where a person from a different cultural background, where polygamy is accepted, goes through another marriage ceremony (possibly thinking it is a polygamous marriage), criminal liability and punishment seem inappropriate. With no excuse of ignorance of the law, English law is perhaps wise to achieve the same result by these circuitous means.

7.154 The children of a polygamous marriage are legitimate[310] and entitled to succeed to all property in England with the possible exception of entailed interests and titles of honour that devolve with property.[311] For example, in *Bamgbose v Daniel*[312] it was held that the children of nine polygamous marriages celebrated in Nigeria between Nigerian domiciliaries were entitled to succeed to their father's property on his intestate death.

7.155 Spouses under polygamous marriages qualify as spouses for succession purposes.[313] In *Cheang Thye Phin v Tan Ah Loy*[314] the Privy Council endorsed the Straits Settlements' practice of dividing the widow's share equally between the surviving widows. A polygamous wife qualifies as the wife of the deceased under the Inheritance (Provision for Family and Dependants) Act 1975, enabling her to apply for a court order for reasonable provision to be made out of her husband's estate. In *Re Sehota*[315] the husband had left the whole of his estate to the second of his two polygamous wives. The court made an order for provision to be made in favour of the first wife.

---

[306] Under the Matrimonial Causes Act 1973, s 1(2)(c), desertion is only a 'ground' for divorce if the deserting spouse has no 'just cause' for the desertion.
[307] Matrimonial Causes Act 1973, s 47(4), as amended by para 2(3)(b) of the schedule to the Private International Law (Miscellaneous Provisions) Act 1995.
[308] [1946] P 122.   [309] [1975] QB 885. See also *R v Sarwan Singh* [1962] 3 All ER 612.
[310] *Sinha Peerage Claim* [1946] 1 All ER 348n; *Baindail v Baindail* [1946] P 122 at 127–8.
[311] *Sinha Peerage Claim* [1946] 1 All ER 348n.   [312] [1955] AC 107.
[313] *Coleman v Shang* [1961] AC 481; *Official Solicitor v Yemoh* [2011] 1 WLR 1450.
[314] [1920] AC 369. See also *Choo Eng Choon v Neo Chan Neo (Six Widows' Case)* (1908) 12 Straits Settlements LR 120.
[315] [1978] 3 All ER 385.

7.156 More problematic in these succession situations is the case where there is a monogamous wife and the husband marries a second wife polygamously. There are two views that can be adopted here. On the one hand, if the polygamous spouse were to be given, say, intestate succession rights this would in reality erode the first wife's status as a monogamous spouse. The monogamous wife should take the whole of the surviving spouse's share, to the exclusion of polygamous wives, in view of her expectation under the monogamous marriage of being the only wife. On the other hand, this result might seem unfair to the second wife who has contracted a valid polygamous marriage and presumably has reasonable expectations that she would receive a polygamous wife's share of her husband's estate on his intestacy. The counter-argument that she could have no such reasonable expectations because she has married a man who has a monogamous wife seems implausible as it involves imputing to her a sophisticated legal knowledge about the nature of the first marriage and its consequences.

7.157 What is the position with respect to family provision where there is a first monogamous wife and a second polygamous wife? The polygamous spouse is entitled to apply for family provision because any person who has lived with the deceased in the same household 'as the husband or wife of the deceased' for two years immediately before the death of the deceased may apply for family provision.[316] But, in doing this she would be in no better position than a woman who had lived with the man outside marriage and would be entitled only to provision for maintenance as opposed to the (more generous) reasonable financial provision available to wives.[317] Such an approach would amount to a negation of the polygamous spouse's status as a wife. The innocent 'wife' of a void bigamous marriage is permitted to apply for family provision as a wife.[318] It would seem odd that such a person should be favoured above a validly married polygamous spouse. Further, if the polygamous spouse divorced her husband, she would be entitled to full financial relief which would ultimately be to the detriment of the first wife. There seems no reason why she should be prejudiced by his dying rather than their being divorced.

7.158 It has been held[319] that a wife under a polygamous marriage can apply to court under the Married Women's Property Act 1882 for a declaration that she is entitled to a share of certain property; an actually polygamous marriage has been recognised under the income tax legislation;[320] and polygamously married spouses are entitled to statutory protection under Part IV of the Family Law Act 1996 which deals with the family home and domestic violence.[321]

7.159 Special statutory provision is made for polygamous marriages in relation to social security benefits.[322] The effect is that a polygamous marriage is treated as having the same consequences as a monogamous marriage but only as regards those periods

---

[316] Inheritance (Provision for Family and Dependants) Act 1975, s 1(1A), as introduced by the Law Reform (Succession) Act 1995, s 2(3).
[317] Inheritance (Provision for Family and Dependants) Act 1975, s 1(2).   [318] S 25(4).
[319] *Chaudhry v Chaudhry* [1976] Fam 148.   [320] *Nabi v Heaton* [1983] 1 WLR 626.
[321] S 63(5).   [322] Social Security Contributions and Benefits Act 1992, ss 121(1)(b), 147(5).

when there was in fact only one wife. So, none of the wives under an actually polygamous marriage is entitled to benefits in respect of contributions paid by the husband. However, a wife under a monogamous marriage is entitled to benefits, even if the husband has subsequently contracted a valid polygamous marriage. Polygamous spouses are denied rights to a widow's pension under the state pension scheme.[323] With regard to income support, the critical issue is no longer whether the parties are married, but rather whether they are partners who are members of the same household; a 'partner' is defined as including a polygamous wife.[324]

7.160 Polygamous marriages are largely denied recognition for immigration purposes if there is another wife who is, or since the marriage has been, in the United Kingdom,[325] but, ironically, such marriages are recognised for purposes of deportation.[326]

---

[323] See *R v Department of Health, ex p Misra* [1996] 1 FLR 129.
[324] Income Support (General) Regulations 1987, SI 1987/1967, reg 2(1).
[325] Immigration Act 1988, s 2(2). See Shah, 'Attitudes to Polygamy in English Law' (2003) 52 ICLQ 369.
[326] Immigration Act 1971, s 5(4), as amended.

8

Matrimonial causes

This chapter examines the jurisdiction of the English court and the choice of law process in proceedings for divorce, judicial separation, and annulment of marriage and the extent to which the decrees of foreign courts in such matrimonial cases are recognised in England.[1] Similar rules which have been introduced in relation to same-sex marriage and civil partnership will also be discussed. Finally, there is a consideration of the powers of the English court to grant financial relief and to recognise foreign maintenance orders.

I Jurisdiction of the English court

A Introduction

8.1 At common law different jurisdictional rules applied to divorce, judicial separation, and annulment of marriage. Originally, English courts would only consider granting a divorce if, at the commencement of the proceedings, the parties were domiciled in England.[2] Such an approach was unduly rigid and caused grave hardship to those who had lived in England for many years but not acquired a domicile here and to wives who, before the entry into force of the Domicile and Matrimonial Proceedings Act 1973, had a domicile of dependence on the husband who might have left England and acquired a domicile in another country. Accordingly, statutory extensions to the court's divorce jurisdiction were made for the protection of married women, enabling a wife to petition for divorce in England in specified circumstances even if neither party was domiciled in England.[3]

8.2 The English common law jurisdictional rules in nullity cases were more complex, with much depending on whether the marriage was void or voidable. Essentially, English courts exercised jurisdiction on the basis of domicile, common residence, or, when the marriage was void, the fact that the marriage had been contracted in England. With

---

[1] Proceedings for presumption of death and declarations of status are not dealt with. See Dicey, Morris and Collins, *The Conflict of Laws* (15th edn, 2012) pp 1057–62.

[2] *Le Mesurier v Le Mesurier* [1895] AC 517.

[3] For example, if the wife had been ordinarily resident in England for the three years immediately preceding her petition: Matrimonial Causes Act 1973, s 46(1)(a), (b) (originally Matrimonial Causes Act 1937, s 13 and Law Reform (Miscellaneous Provisions) Act 1949, s 1).

decrees of judicial separation, because no change of status is involved, domicile was displaced by residence as the basic connecting factor founding jurisdiction.[4]

B Jurisdictional rules

8.3 The exclusive role of domicile having been breached, and married women having independent domiciles, new uniform grounds of jurisdiction were introduced for all three types of matrimonial proceedings by the Domicile and Matrimonial Proceedings Act 1973. These grounds were based on the policy that at least one of the parties, whether husband or wife, applicant or respondent, should have a sufficient connection with England to make it reasonable for the English court to deal with the case and likely that the divorce would be recognised in other countries. Section 5(2) provided that the English court would only have jurisdiction if at least one of the parties had been domiciled in England on the date when the proceedings were begun or had been habitually resident in England throughout the period of one year ending with that date. Section 5(3) laid down broadly similar jurisdictional rules for nullity decrees.[5]

8.4 In 1998 the Brussels II Convention[6] was signed by the Member States of the European Union and (with amendments) was brought into force as a Regulation[7] on 1 March 2001 (hereafter the 'Brussels II Regulation'). The Regulation was revised in 2003[8] and the new Regulation (which is referred to hereafter as the 'Brussels II *bis* Regulation' or 'Brussels II *bis*') came into force on 1 March 2005.[9] Like the Brussels I Recast, the Brussels II *bis* Regulation imposes uniform jurisdictional rules throughout the European Union (except Denmark, which did not participate in the adoption of the Regulation) and provides for almost automatic recognition of divorces, annulments, and separations granted by the courts of the Member States. The Regulation is an important step in avoiding limping marriages in Europe.[10] In particular, there was a problem between France and Germany in that German divorces involving a French national would not be recognised in France unless stringent conditions had been met.[11] However, the real driving force behind the process which led to the Regulation

---

[4] See, further, Graveson, *The Conflict of Laws* (6th edn, 1969) pp 336–46, 363–6.

[5] Additionally, the court had (and still has: see n 14) jurisdiction where either of the parties has died, and at death was domiciled in England or had been habitually resident here for the preceding year.

[6] Convention on Jurisdiction and the Recognition and Enforcement of Judgments in Matrimonial Matters, OJ 1998 C221/1.

[7] Regulation (EC) No 1347/2000, OJ 2000 L160/19.

[8] The revisions were concerned with matters of parental responsibility: the divorce, annulment, and separation provisions of the Brussels II Regulation were carried over into the Brussels II *bis* Regulation without any substantive changes being made.

[9] Regulation (EC) No 2201/2003, OJ 2003 L338/1. See, generally, Ní Shúilleabháin, *Cross-Border Divorce Law: Brussels II bis* (2010); Boele-Woelki and González Beilfuss (eds), *Brussels II bis: Its Impact and Application in the Member States* (2007); Magnus and Mankowski (eds), *Brussels II bis Regulation* (2012).

[10] Remien, 'European Private International Law, the European Community and its Emerging Area of Freedom, Security and Justice' (2001) 38 CML Rev 55, 56.

[11] Karsten, 'Brussels II—An English Perspective' [1998] IFL 75; McEleavy, 'The Brussels II Regulation: How the European Community has Moved into Family Law' (2002) 51 ICLQ 883.

was not so much the eradication of perceived problems regarding jurisdiction or the recognition of foreign judgments, but the promotion of European goals: 'European integration, the creation of a common judicial area, the operation of the single market and the development of European citizenship'.[12]

8.5 As the Brussels II *bis* Regulation largely, but not completely, replaces the 'traditional' jurisdictional rules, section 5(2) of the Domicile and Matrimonial Proceedings Act 1973 was amended[13] and provides that an English court shall have jurisdiction to entertain proceedings for divorce or judicial separation[14] if: (a) the court has jurisdiction under the Brussels II *bis* Regulation; or (b) no court of a Member State has jurisdiction under the Brussels II *bis* Regulation and either of the parties to the marriage is domiciled in England on the date when the proceedings are begun.[15]

1. The grounds of jurisdiction under the Regulation: article 3

8.6 The basic jurisdictional rules are contained in Chapter II of the Regulation. Article 3(1) lists several alternative bases of jurisdiction without any hierarchy being established between them.[16] Thus, the courts of several Member States could potentially assume jurisdiction in a given case. Pursuing the EU goal of freedom of movement, individuals should have the freedom to choose, between the potentially competent courts, the forum for the dissolution of their marriage.[17] Where more than one court is seised, the conflict of jurisdiction can be resolved by applying the rule for staying actions laid down in article 19(1) which is discussed later. These jurisdictional criteria are more complex than were the English traditional rules[18] and give rise to some problems of interpretation. *Jurisdiction lies with the courts of the Member States in whose territory:*

8.7 *(i) The spouses are habitually resident.* As seen in Chapter 6, it is now accepted that habitual residence must, for the purposes of Brussels II *bis*, bear an autonomous, EU meaning to be derived from the jurisprudence of the Court of Justice. In the absence of any guidance (to date) from the Court of Justice, the English courts have expressed the view that 'habitual residence' under article 3 of Brussels II *bis* is an exclusive concept (meaning that a spouse can have only one habitual residence) and is to be determined by

---

[12] McGlynn, 'A Family Law for the European Union?' in Shaw (ed), *Social Law and Policy in an Evolving European Union* (2000) p 235; see also Borrás Report, OJ 1998 C221/27.

[13] European Communities (Matrimonial Jurisdiction and Judgments) Regulations 2001, SI 2001/310, reg 3; European Communities (Jurisdiction and Judgments in Matrimonial and Parental Responsibility Matters) Regulations 2005, SI 2005/265, reg 3.

[14] S 5(3) contains similar provisions for jurisdiction in nullity proceedings but additionally affords jurisdiction in cases where one of the parties has died. See n 5 above.

[15] As will be seen at para 8.15 below, art 6 Brussels II *bis* may in certain circumstances preclude the exercise of jurisdiction by English courts even in the event that no Member State has jurisdiction under the Regulation and one of the parties is domiciled in England.

[16] Case C-168/08 *Hadadi v Hadadi* [2009] ECR I-6871, paras 48–49. These bases have been numbered in the ensuing text. In the Regulation they are simply indents.

[17] Ibid, para 53. This approach is criticised in Meeusen, 'System-Shopping in European Private International Law in Family Matters' in Meeusen et al, *International Family Law for the European Union* (2007).

[18] They have been described as a 'near impenetrable mesh of jurisdictional rules': McEleavy, 'The Communitarization of Divorce Rules: What Impact for English and Scottish Law?' (2004) 53 ICLQ 605, 610.

reference to a qualitative rather than a quantitative assessment of a person's 'centre of interests'.[19] As indicated in Chapter 6, however, there are good grounds for suspecting that the Court of Justice may take a different view—potentially placing a greater emphasis on factual presence and perhaps also accepting the possibility of concurrent habitual residence in two different states.[20] Whatever the test adopted (whether quantitative or qualitative, exclusive or non-exclusive), jurisdiction based on this first ground—and entailing the current habitual residence of both spouses—is unlikely to be contentious. This Member State is likely to be convenient for both parties to the litigation and to be an appropriate forum for any ancillary matters concerning children or financial relief.

8.8 *(ii) The spouses were last habitually resident, in so far as one of them still resides there.* In *Sundelind Lopez v Lopez Lizazo*[21] a Swedish wife and her Cuban husband were habitually resident in France. When the marriage broke down, the husband returned to Cuba but the wife continued to reside in France. It was held that the French court would have jurisdiction under this provision. Where the spouses no longer reside in the same country, the country of their former shared habitual residence (where they are likely to have spent their married life) is arguably a reasonable divorce forum.

8.9 *(iii) The respondent is habitually resident.* This basis of jurisdiction is consistent with the general jurisdictional approach throughout the conflict of laws that an appropriate connection between a defendant (in civil or commercial matters) or a respondent (in family matters) and a country should suffice to found jurisdiction. Where the applicant is willing to petition where the respondent is habitually resident, one might expect that the respondent will be glad of the convenience of that forum. This third ground was therefore also relatively uncontroversial when the text of the Brussels II Convention was agreed.[22] Of course there will be cases where respondents will vigorously contest the jurisdiction of the courts of their own habitual residence[23]—for strategic and financial reasons—but it does not follow that the conferral of jurisdiction on the state of the respondent's habitual residence is per se objectionable.

8.10 *(iv) In the event of a joint application, either of the spouses is habitually resident.* It had been suggested that this provision enables a court to assume jurisdiction in any case where both parties consent to jurisdiction and one of them is habitually resident in the agreed forum.[24] However, given the express reference to a 'joint application' the better view is that this provision applies only in those Member States making explicit provision for joint applications for divorce. Joint applications for divorce cannot be made under English law and so this provision is of no relevance to the jurisdiction of the English court.[25]

---

[19] See para 6.93. [20] See para 6.95. [21] Case C-68/07 [2007] ECR I-10403.
[22] See Ní Shúilleabháin, *Cross-Border Divorce Law: Brussels II bis* (2010) pp 135–6.
[23] See, eg, *Z v Z (Divorce: Jurisdiction)* [2010] 1 FLR 694.
[24] See, eg, Hausmann, 'New International Procedure Law in Matrimonial Matters in the European Union' [2000–01] European Legal Forum 271, 276.
[25] Borrás Report, OJ 1998 C221/27, para 31; Hodson, *A Practical Guide to International Family Law* (2008) p 76.

8.11 *(v) The applicant is habitually resident if he or she resided there for at least a year immediately before the application was made.* As indicated above, the basic rule in civil and commercial matter is that the claimant must sue the defendant in the courts of the country with which that defendant is appropriately connected. The fifth ground under article 3 of Brussels II *bis* was, therefore, a matter of some controversy in so far as it enables a petitioner to proceed in a Member State with which the respondent and the marriage were entirely unconnected. In order to alleviate concerns of forum shopping, the fifth ground requires the petitioner to show something more than habitual residence at the date of institution of proceedings[26]—he or she is also required to show that he or she has resided in that Member State for at least one year immediately prior to the application. The precise nature of this additional requirement has, however, been a matter of debate in the English courts. There is considerable support for the view that petitioners are simply required to prove habitual residence as of the date of institution of proceedings—and a lesser requirement of mere residence for the previous year.[27] An alternative view is that petitioners are required to prove habitual residence for a full year prior to the institution of proceedings[28] (and that the subsequent reference to 'resided' takes colour from the immediately preceding reference to 'habitually resident'[29]). A third view is that the fifth ground deems a petitioner to be habitually resident in a Member State 'if' he or she has resided there for the preceding year—thus, on this interpretation, the petitioner is only required to prove residence for one year.[30] The second of these interpretations is clearly the most onerous and the one which is most likely to be effective in preventing forum shopping. However, the first of the three interpretations is the one which has commanded most support[31] and the English courts, whilst insisting that 'habitual residence' is an exclusive concept, have taken the view that 'residence' is non-exclusive and that a person may be resident in two different countries at the same time.[32] Thus a woman who is splitting her time between Greece and England in the year preceding her divorce petition may be considered resident in both countries—and eligible to petition on this fifth ground if she moves permanently to England prior to the issue of the divorce petition and can be considered habitually resident here as of that date.[33]

8.12 *(vi) The applicant is habitually resident if he or she resided there for at least six months immediately before the application was made and is either a national of the Member*

---

[26] Borrás Report, OJ 1998 C221/27, para 32.
[27] See *Marinos v Marinos* [2007] 2 FLR 1018 at [46]; *V v V (Divorce: Jurisdiction)* [2011] 2 FLR 778 at [47]; *Tan v Choy* [2015] 1 FLR 492 at [9].
[28] See *Tan v Choy* [2015] 1 FLR 492 at [30].
[29] See *V v V (Divorce: Jurisdiction)* [2011] 2 FLR 778 at [44].
[30] See *Tan v Choy* [2015] 1 FLR 492 at [30].
[31] For an account of the views adopted in other Member States (and the text of art 3 in other EU languages), see Hodson, 'What is Jurisdiction for Divorce in the EU? The Contradictory Law and Practice Around Europe' [2014] IFL 170.
[32] See *Marinos v Marinos* [2007] 2 FLR 1018 at [78]; *V v V (Divorce: Jurisdiction)* [2011] 2 FLR 778 at [50].
[33] See *Marinos v Marinos* [2007] 2 FLR 1018—although on the facts of that case, the petitioning wife had an English domicile and was therefore eligible to proceed after only six months of residence—see the sixth ground discussed below. The judge in *Marinos* also accepted that the wife may in fact have been habitually resident in England prior to her permanent return to England: [2007] 2 FLR 1018 at [80].

State in question or, in the case of the United Kingdom and Ireland, has his or her 'domicile' there. As with the fifth ground, this sixth ground allows the habitual residence of the applicant to justify the court's assumption of jurisdiction as long as that habitual residence is buttressed by other connections with the forum, in this instance, six months residence coupled with nationality or, for the United Kingdom and Ireland, domicile. It is not uncommon for English domiciliaries who marry foreigners and live abroad to return home on the breakdown of their marriage. Such persons need only be resident in England for six months before issuing a divorce petition provided they are 'habitually resident' there at the date of instituting proceedings.[34] The meanings of 'nationality' and 'domicile' are discussed in relation to the seventh ground.

8.13 *(vii) Article 3(1)(b) confers jurisdiction on the Member State of the nationality of both spouses or, in the case of the United Kingdom and Ireland, of the 'domicile' of both spouses.* The premise underlying all the jurisdictional bases listed in article 3 is that they provide a 'real link between the party concerned and the Member State exercising jurisdiction'.[35] Habitual residence is regarded as the most appropriate connecting factor to indicate this 'real link'. Nationality and domicile are regarded as providing weaker links with a territory in that *both* spouses must have the relevant connection with the territory, a requirement not necessarily imposed when jurisdiction is based on habitual residence. Article 2(2) of the Brussels II Convention provided that each Member State had to stipulate in a declaration whether it would be applying the criterion of nationality or domicile. The Regulation, however, omitted article 2(2) of the Convention and made it clear that only the United Kingdom and Ireland could apply the criterion of domicile, with the other Member States having to utilise nationality as the alternative connecting factor. In *Re N (Jurisdiction)* it was held that the words 'nationals' and 'domiciled' are to be 'read disjunctively'.[36] This was confirmed by the Court of Justice in *Hadadi v Hadadi*.[37] Accordingly, a court in the United Kingdom cannot assume jurisdiction on the basis that both parties are UK citizens and only UK and Irish courts can use the joint domicile of the parties to found jurisdiction. For the other Member States, the court of the country of which both spouses are nationals has jurisdiction. It is irrelevant that the parties are both also nationals of another Member State and have much closer links with that other country.[38] Article 3(2) provides that '"domicile" shall have the same meaning as it has under the legal systems of the United Kingdom and Ireland'. Accordingly, the concept is not to be given an autonomous meaning. Nevertheless, situations may arise where the courts of Member States other than the United Kingdom and Ireland are called upon to interpret the concept. For instance, if a German court is seised of a case where the jurisdictional bases in articles 3, 4, and 5 are not satisfied, before applying German traditional rules, the court would need to ensure under article 6 (discussed in the next section) that, inter alia,

---

[34] This assumes the correctness of the 'first' of the three interpretations of the fifth ground: the same debate arises here as to whether mere residence in the preceding time is sufficient—or whether six months residence taken with domicile is 'constitutive' of habitual residence: see *Munro v Munro* [2008] 1 FLR 1613 at [48]–[54].
[35] Recital (12) to Regulation (EC) No 1347/2000 (the original Brussels II Regulation).
[36] [2007] 2 FLR 1196 at [7]. [37] Case C-168/08 [2009] ECR I-6871. [38] Ibid.

the respondent was not domiciled in the United Kingdom; 'domicile' would bear the meaning it has in the United Kingdom. This means that not only continental European courts, but also the Court of Justice, might have to explore the intricacies of, for example, the revival of a domicile of origin.

2. The grounds of jurisdiction under the Regulation: articles 4 and 5

8.14 Two further jurisdictional bases are provided. Under article 4 the court in which proceedings are pending on the basis of article 3 shall also have jurisdiction to examine a counterclaim. Under article 5 a court of a Member State which has given judgment on a legal separation shall also have jurisdiction to convert that judgment into a divorce, if the law of that Member State so provides.

3. Exclusive jurisdiction

8.15 The traditional rules (of any of the Member States) may not be utilised if there is exclusive jurisdiction under the Brussels II *bis* Regulation. Article 6 provides that in certain situations the Regulation *must* be used. This is so when the respondent is habitually resident in or a national of or, in the case of the United Kingdom and Ireland, 'domiciled' in, a Member State; such a respondent may be sued in another Member State only in accordance with the Regulation. This means that if the respondent is, say, a Spanish national and the English court does not have jurisdiction under the Regulation, an English court is not permitted to exercise jurisdiction under the traditional rules—on the basis that the applicant is domiciled in England—and so the English court will not have jurisdiction at all. Further, article 7(1) provides that courts of Member States may assume jurisdiction under their traditional rules only if no other court of a Member State has jurisdiction pursuant to articles 3, 4, or 5. So, if a court of another Member State has jurisdiction under the Brussels II *bis* Regulation, an English court cannot exercise jurisdiction under its traditional rules (discussed in the next section).

8.16 These rules on exclusive jurisdiction are illustrated by the Court of Justice's decision in *Sundelind Lopez v Lopez Lizazo*.[39] A Swedish wife sought to divorce her Cuban husband in Sweden by invoking the Swedish domestic (traditional) rule under which jurisdiction could be founded on her Swedish nationality and former residence in Sweden. She argued that as her husband was not habitually resident in, nor a national of, a Member State, article 6 permitted a Swedish court to assume jurisdiction under its domestic law. This argument was rejected by the Court of Justice on the basis that article 7(1) clearly precluded this. In this case the French court had jurisdiction under article 3 as France was the country where the spouses had last been habitually resident and the wife still resided there (second ground)—or, alternatively, because the wife was habitually resident there and had been resident there for at least one year (fifth ground). The Swedish court would have been permitted to assume jurisdiction only if no court of any Member State had jurisdiction under articles 3, 4, or 5.

---

[39] Case C–68/07 [2007] ECR I–10403.

4. Residual jurisdiction

8.17 If the above exclusive jurisdiction rules are not applicable, article 7(1) (the equivalent of articles 5 and 6 of the Brussels I Recast) provides that courts of Member States may avail themselves of their traditional jurisdictional rules. The Borrás Report[40] provides an indicative list of such residual jurisdiction rules. For example, if exercising its traditional jurisdictional criteria, a German court could assume jurisdiction on the basis that one spouse was a German national when the marriage took place.

8.18 Article 7(2) provides that these residual rules may (in cases where there is no exclusive jurisdiction) be utilised by any national of a Member State who is habitually resident within the territory of another Member State. So, a German national who is habitually resident in France is free to utilise the French traditional jurisdictional grounds.

8.19 Although article 7(2) is highly ambiguous, the most plausible interpretation is that it is aimed at those Member States which (unlike England) previously linked divorce jurisdiction to nationality. Accordingly, it is suggested that article 7(2) has no application in England as the English residual grounds are not based on nationality.[41]

8.20 In England the amended section 5(2)(b) of the Domicile and Matrimonial Proceedings Act 1973 specifies the only remaining residual jurisdiction under the traditional rules: if either of the parties to the marriage is domiciled in England on the date when the marriage proceedings are begun. In practical terms the scope of the traditional rules is rather narrow. They will be applicable only when one of the spouses is domiciled in England and the respondent spouse is neither habitually resident in a Member State nor a national of a Member State (other than the United Kingdom or Ireland) nor domiciled in Ireland and no court of a Member State has jurisdiction under article 3 Brussels II *bis*.[42]

5. Overview

8.21 The overall impact of the Brussels II *bis* Regulation has been a narrowing of English divorce jurisdiction. While previously the English domicile of either spouse provided a sufficient basis for jurisdiction, domicile can now be invoked only in circumstances where *both* spouses have an English domicile, or where one of the spouses is domiciled in England in circumstances where the parties' connections are otherwise to a non-EU state.[43] On the face of it, the Regulation is less stringent as respects jurisdiction based on habitual residence: while the 1973 Act originally required a spouse's habitual residence for one year in all petitions based on habitual residence, the Regulation allows reliance on habitual residence per se in certain circumstances. However, in so

---

[40] OJ 1998 C221/27.
[41] McEleavy, 'The Communitarization of Divorce Rules: What Impact for English and Scottish Law?' (2004) 53 ICLQ 605, 615.
[42] An example of jurisdiction being assumed on this statistically rare basis is *F v F (Divorce: Jurisdiction)* [2009] 2 FLR 1496.
[43] For a detailed exposition of when single-party domicile can provide jurisdiction, see Ní Shúilleabháin, *Cross-Border Divorce Law: Brussels II bis* (2010) pp 156–65, 182–3.

far as 'habitual residence' is now assumed to be an exclusive concept under Brussels II *bis*, and was a looser non-exclusive concept under the 1973 Act as it stood previously,[44] in practice it may often be more difficult to establish habitual residence under the Regulation than under the original version of section 5 of the 1973 Act.

C Staying proceedings

8.22 The non-hierarchical structure of article 3 of Brussels II *bis* specifically envisages that multiple Member States may have jurisdiction in parallel. Thus, it is quite possible that there could be matrimonial proceedings between the same parties already pending in the court of another country when proceedings are commenced in England (lis pendens) or, even if there are no proceedings abroad, the parties to English proceedings could be more closely connected with another country (forum non conveniens). The extent to which the English court has power to stay its proceedings (and the legal basis for doing so) depends on whether the rules set out in the Brussels II *bis* Regulation or the traditional rules apply.

1. Brussels II *bis* Regulation: Proceedings pending in another EU Member State

8.23 Under the Regulation the English court may not stay its proceedings on the ground that the courts of another Member State are clearly more appropriate to resolve the issue. Similarly, there is no power to issue an anti-suit injunction restraining a party from pursuing proceedings in any such court.

8.24 Proceedings may be stayed only in two situations.[45] First, if the respondent in the English proceedings is habitually resident elsewhere and does not enter an appearance, the English court shall stay proceedings so long as it is not shown that the respondent has been able to receive the document instituting the proceedings in sufficient time to arrange for his defence (unless all necessary steps have been taken to inform the respondent of the proceedings).[46]

8.25 Secondly, in situations of lis pendens, article 19(1) provides that where proceedings relating to divorce, legal separation, or marriage annulment between the same parties are brought before courts of different Member States, the court second seised shall of its own motion stay its proceedings until such time as the jurisdiction of the court first seised is established. This is the counterpart of article 29 of the Brussels I Recast. So, if divorce proceedings have been commenced in France, the English court *must* stay any divorce proceeding commenced here provided the French court is the court 'first seised'. The cause of action need not be identical in both sets of proceedings as long as they both relate to divorce, legal separation, or marriage annulment. So, for example, if a French

---

[44] See *Ikimi v Ikimi* [2002] Fam 72 discussed at para 6.80.
[45] In *Jefferson v O'Connor* [2014] 2 FLR 759 at [34] the Court of Appeal declined to determine whether a stay might also be granted on the basis of abuse of process or on temporary case management grounds. The Court of Appeal confirmed in *Jefferson* that a stay could not be granted on estoppel grounds (ie, on the basis of the petitioner's promise to discontinue the earlier English action).
[46] Art 18(1).

court is first seised of proceedings for legal separation, an English court must decline jurisdiction if divorce proceedings are commenced in England shortly afterwards.[47]

8.26 Although under the 1968 Brussels Convention there was no definition of when a court was 'seised', the Brussels I Regulation and the Brussels I Recast do provide such a definition[48] and this definition is replicated in article 16 of the Brussels II *bis* Regulation. According to article 16 a court is deemed to be seised when the document instituting the proceedings is lodged with the court or, if the document has to be served before being lodged with the court, at the time when it is received by the authority responsible for service.[49] Despite the provision of an autonomous definition of 'seisin' under article 16, there has developed a substantial body of case-law on this concept. Questions have arisen, for example, as to whether another Member State should be considered first seised where the earlier foreign action has not been progressed[50] or is dormant[51] or requires reactivation,[52] or where an earlier judicial separation action has been followed by a later divorce action in the other Member State,[53] or where there is an appeal pending in the other Member State on the question of seisin.[54] Questions have also arisen as to the precise meaning of 'lodgment' under article 16: is a document 'lodged' upon receipt in the court office or only when it is formally issued?[55] The Court of Justice has begun to provide some guidance on these issues: it has confirmed that the first court potentially remains seised even if those proceedings have been stayed at the initiative of the applicant who brought them[56]—and that the second court seised becomes the first court seised following the expiry of the first action.[57] However, much confusion remains in particular in so far as the procedural rules of other Member States may require the completion of additional procedural steps (or the obtaining of a judicial separation) prior to the formal presentation of an application for divorce.[58]

8.27 Leaving aside the difficulties surrounding the question of seisin, there has also been much criticism of the use of a lis pendens doctrine in regulating divorce jurisdiction.

---

[47] This is tighter than the procedure under art 30 of the Brussels I Recast pursuant to which the court has a discretion to stay proceedings or decline jurisdiction where there are related proceedings pending in another Member State (see paras 2.199–2.204).

[48] See para 2.184.

[49] Provided the applicant has not subsequently failed to take the steps he was required to take to have service effected on the respondent or to have the document lodged with the court: art 16(1)(a) and (b).

[50] *S v S (Brussels II Revised: Art 19(1) and (3): Reference to CJEU)* [2015] 2 FLR 364 at [20]–[23].

[51] *Trussler v Trussler* [2003] EWCA Civ 1830.

[52] See *C v S (Divorce: Jurisdiction)* [2011] 2 FLR 19, where an earlier Italian petition had been declared void but could be revived.

[53] *S v S (Brussels II Revised: Art 19(1) and (3): Reference to CJEU)* [2015] 2 FLR 364; *Ville de Bauge v China* [2015] 2 FLR 873.

[54] See *LK v K (No 3)* [2007] 2 FLR 741; *Leman-Klammers v Klammers* [2008] 1 FLR 692.

[55] *MH v MH* [2015] IEHC 771.

[56] See Case C-507/14 *P v M*, unreported (referring to the lis pendens rule for parental responsibility proceedings under art 19(2)).

[57] Case C-489/14 *A v B* [2016] 1 FLR 31. This judgment dealt with the reference in *S v S (Brussels II Revised: Art 19(1) and (3): Reference to CJEU)* [2015] 2 FLR 364.

[58] See, eg, *C v C (Divorce: Jurisdiction)* [2005] 1 WLR 1469; *Ville de Bauge v China* [2015] 2 FLR 873; *E v E* [2015] EWHC 3742 (Fam).

The 'inflexibility' of the article 19 rule has been described as 'shocking'.[59] The scenario painted is of a couple, one a Swedish national, the other an English domiciliary, who have established a matrimonial home in England, where they have lived for many years. The Swedish spouse could return to Sweden and, having been resident there for six months, then commence Swedish divorce proceedings. The spouse in England cannot institute proceedings in England even though England is the forum conveniens. A further scare-scenario involves a variation of the above example but this time an Irish spouse returns to Ireland, where the only ground for divorce is a four-year period of separation, and commences legal separation proceedings. The English spouse would be barred from commencing divorce proceedings in England and would potentially have to wait for four years before an Irish divorce could be obtained.[60]

8.28 On the other hand, the new provisions could be welcomed as avoiding the sometimes unseemly 'race to the finish' that can occur under the traditional rules as well as eliminating the uncertainty surrounding the operation of the discretionary doctrine of forum non conveniens. While it can be asserted that the new rules simply substitute a 'race to the start'—and are, therefore, likely to operate as a disincentive to mediation and conciliation[61]—the reality is that both the Swedish and Irish spouses in the above examples must have done more than simply return to their respective countries; they must have been resident there for at least six months, signifying a genuine connection with that country. Where an English domiciliary returns to England and has become habitually resident here after six months of residence, it is unlikely that many would describe it as 'shocking' for an English court to exercise jurisdiction. Further, the practical advice to the spouse left behind in England in the above scenarios is that they have a choice: they can institute proceedings in England within the six-month period (on the basis that they were both last habitually resident in England and one of them still resides here) or they can defend the foreign proceedings.

2. Brussels II *bis* Regulation: Proceedings pending in a non-Member State

8.29 If the English court has assumed jurisdiction under the Brussels II *bis* Regulation and there are matrimonial proceedings pending in a non-Member State, can the English proceedings be stayed on grounds of forum non conveniens? After the Brussels II Regulation came into force, English courts assumed the continuing existence of a discretion to stay proceedings[62] when there were proceedings pending in non-Member States. But these cases were all decided before the Court of Justice's decision in *Owusu v Jackson*.[63] This case established the principle that, where the court has jurisdiction under article 2 of the Brussels Convention, such proceedings cannot be stayed even though the court of a non-Member State is a more appropriate forum. In

---

[59] Truex, 'Brussels II—Beware!' [2001] Fam Law 233.
[60] See Mostyn, 'Brussels II—The Impact on Forum Disputes' [2001] Fam Law 359.
[61] Karsten, 'Brussels II—An English Perspective' [1998] IFL 75.
[62] See, eg, *Breuning v Breuning* [2002] 1 FLR 888; *R v R (Divorce: Hemain Injunction)* [2005] 1 FLR 386.
[63] Case C-281/02 [2005] ECR I-1383.

Ella v Ella[64] (a post-*Owusu* case) a stay was granted in favour of Israeli proceedings in a situation where the English court had assumed jurisdiction under article 3 of Brussels II *bis*. However, *Owusu* was not cited and the issue not raised.

8.30 As shall be seen, the English courts have long had discretionary powers to stay proceedings when there are proceedings abroad. These powers are contained in paragraph 9 of Schedule 1 to the Domicile and Matrimonial Proceedings Act 1973. In order to give effect to the Brussels II and Brussels II *bis* Regulations, paragraph 9 was amended[65] to provide that these discretionary powers now exist only in relation to matrimonial proceedings 'other than proceedings governed by the Council Regulation'. The view adopted in a previous edition of this book and by other commentators[66] is that, if jurisdiction has been assumed on the basis of article 3 of the Brussels II *bis* Regulation, the proceedings are 'governed by the Council Regulation' and so there is no scope for the application of the discretionary powers afforded by paragraph 9. This interpretation is consistent with the approach adopted by the Court of Justice in *Owusu v Jackson*.

8.31 However, in *Cook v Plummer* Thorpe LJ stated (obiter) that the application of the *Owusu* principle 'in the context of family proceedings is perhaps not... clear' as there are 'contrary arguments' and the 'decision in *Owusu* is deeply unpopular' and so the point will 'ultimately have to be referred to the ECJ'.[67]

8.32 This point arose directly in *JKN v JCN*[68] where, in a lengthy and detailed judgment considering *Owusu* and subsequent commercial cases, it was concluded that the English court does retain a discretion to stay its proceedings where there are proceedings pending in a non-Member State (in this case, New York). It was held that the *Owusu* principle does not apply to the Brussels II *bis* Regulation because:

(i) There is no 'express connectivity' between the Brussels I and Brussels II *bis* Regulations. While it is permissible to refer to Brussels I in interpreting Brussels II *bis* where the language is identical, the provisions of the Regulations are different in several material respects.[69]

(ii) Article 2 of Brussels I[70] provides a mandatory basis of jurisdiction whereas article 3 of the Brussels II *bis* Regulation merely 'facilitates jurisdiction with no corresponding obligation on a court to exercise that jurisdiction'.[71]

(iii) The principle of legal certainty is 'not so central to [Brussels II *bis*] as the petitioner/claimant could potentially choose between three Member States as to where proceedings are issued, whereas in Brussels I (central to the ratio in *Owusu*) it is the right of the defendant to know in which court he is liable to be sued'.

---

[64] [2007] 2 FLR 35.
[65] European Communities (Matrimonial Jurisdiction and Judgments) Regulations 2001, SI 2001/310.
[66] Cheshire, North and Fawcett, *Private International Law* (14th edn, 2008) pp 962–3; Karsten, 'The State of International Family Law Issues: A View from London' [2009] IFL 35.
[67] [2008] 2 FLR 989.
[68] [2011] 1 FLR 826. See Scott, '*JKN v JCN*: *Owusu v Jackson* Meets BIIR At Last' [2010] Fam Law 740.
[69] At [147]. [70] Now art 4 of the Brussels I Recast. [71] At [147].

(iv) If there are proceedings pending in another Member State, article 19 of the Brussels II *bis* Regulation provides a mechanism to prevent the risk of irreconcilable judgments. If *Owusu* applied where proceedings were pending in a non-Member State, the result would be a lacuna as there would be no mechanism to prevent two sets of proceedings with increased costs[72] and the risk of irreconcilable judgments.

(v) In amending section 5(2)(b) and paragraph 9 of Schedule 1 to the Domicile and Matrimonial Proceedings Act 1973 Parliament did not intend to abolish the power to grant stays in the vast majority of divorce proceedings where the competing forum is a non-Member State. The phrase 'proceedings governed by the Council Regulation' in paragraph 9 refers to the position where there are competing proceedings in another Member State, in which case article 19 applies.

8.33 The Court of Appeal expressed its agreement with the reasoning in *JKN v JCN* in the subsequent case of *Mittal v Mittal*[73] (and confirmed that the High Court in the instant case had been entitled to grant a stay on the basis that India was forum conveniens for divorce proceedings). The Court of Appeal in *Mittal* also emphasised[74] the introduction of express discretionary powers to stay proceedings under articles 33 and 34 of the Brussels I Recast[75] and noted that an English court would clearly have been empowered to grant a stay in the case at hand (where there were prior competing proceedings in India) had such provisions been applicable under Brussels II *bis*.

8.34 As will be discussed below, the reform of Brussels II *bis* is currently under consideration and it seems likely that the eventual reform agenda will include provisions akin to those laid down under articles 33 and 34 of the Brussels I Recast.[76] In those circumstances, the significance of questions as to the impact of *Owusu* and the correctness of the judgments in *JKN v JCN* and *Mittal* may recede into the background somewhat—and a referral to the Court of Justice may become less likely.[77] However, as was noted in Chapter 2, articles 33 and 34 Brussels I Recast only allow an English court to grant a stay where the English court is second seised, and the question of the entitlement to use forum non conveniens may therefore still arise (even after such reform of Brussels II *bis*) in cases where the third country proceedings are commenced after the English action[78] or in cases where the third country action has not yet been commenced. Even if the Court of Justice endorsed the 'reflexive effect' theory discussed in Chapter 2,[79] this would not support the availability of a forum non conveniens doctrine in such circumstances.

---

[72] At this preliminary stage of these High Court proceedings the parties had already incurred legal costs of £900,000.
[73] [2014] 1 FLR 1514 at [37]–[41]. See Frankle, 'It is OK to be Inappropriate: *Mittal v Mittal*' [2014] IFL 17; Bantekas, 'The Pitfalls of Lis Pendens in Transnational Matrimonial Jurisdiction Disputes Before English Courts' [2014] IFL 30.
[74] [2014] 1 FLR 1514 at [37]–[40].   [75] See paras 2.205–2.211.
[76] See the Commission Report on the application of Brussels II *bis* COM (2014) 225 final, p 9 where the Commission refers to arts 33 and 34 of Brussels I Recast as potential templates for reform.
[77] See *JKN v JCN* [2011] 1 FLR 826 at [5], where such a referral was envisaged as a possibility.
[78] As was the case in *JKN v JCN*.   [79] See paras 2.276–2.279.

3. Traditional rules

8.35 The Domicile and Matrimonial Proceedings Act 1973 makes provision for English matrimonial proceedings to be stayed in certain circumstances when proceedings are pending elsewhere in the British Isles or in a non-Member State. Such a stay of proceedings may be obligatory or discretionary.

(A) Staying English proceedings

(i) Obligatory stays

8.36 The English court is bound to order a stay of *divorce* proceedings in the English court if, before the beginning of the trial in England, divorce or nullity proceedings in respect of the same marriage are continuing in another jurisdiction in the British Isles and the parties resided together in that jurisdiction when the English proceedings were begun, or, if they were not then residing together, the place where they last resided together was in that jurisdiction and either of the parties was habitually resident in that jurisdiction throughout the year ending with the date on which they last resided together before the commencement of the English proceedings.[80] It is immaterial in which court the proceedings are instituted first.

8.37 If any of these criteria is not satisfied, for example if the English proceedings are for annulment of marriage, the English proceedings could still be stayed under the following discretionary rules.

(ii) Discretionary stays

8.38 In cases where the English court is not bound to grant a stay, it may have a discretion to do so. Paragraph 9(1) of Schedule 1 to the Domicile and Matrimonial Proceedings Act 1973 provides that such discretionary powers exist in relation to any matrimonial proceedings 'other than proceedings governed by the Council Regulation'. The meaning of this phrase and whether it applies in cases where jurisdiction has been assumed under article 3 of Brussels II *bis* but there are proceedings pending in a non-Member State was discussed in the preceding section.

8.39 Where jurisdiction has been assumed under the traditional rules, section 5(6A) of the Domicile and Matrimonial Proceedings Act 1973 provides that the power to stay the English proceedings is 'subject to Article 19 of the Council Regulation'.[81] This means that where proceedings are pending in another Member State, the English court must stay the action in accordance with the rules contained in Brussels II *bis*, discussed above.

8.40 Where, however, jurisdiction has been assumed[82] under the traditional rules (or under article 3 of Brussels II *bis*, if *JKN v JCN*[83] and *Mittal v Mittal*[84] are followed) and there

---

[80] Domicile and Matrimonial Proceedings Act 1973, s 5(6); sch 1, paras 3(2) and 8.
[81] As amended by reg 3(5) of European Communities (Jurisdiction and Judgments in Matrimonial and Parental Responsibility Matters) Regulations 2005, SI 2005/265.
[82] In any matrimonial proceedings (not merely divorce proceedings).
[83] [2011] 1 FLR 826.   [84] [2014] 1 FLR 1514.

are proceedings in respect of the same marriage continuing[85] in a non-Member State, the court may order the English proceedings to be stayed if it appears to the court that the balance of fairness (including convenience) as between the parties to the marriage is such that it is appropriate for the proceedings in the other jurisdiction to be disposed of before further steps are taken in England.[86]

8.41 In considering the balance of fairness and convenience, the court must have regard to all the factors appearing to be relevant, including the convenience of the witnesses and any delay or expense which may result from the proceedings being stayed, or not being stayed.[87] A determination by the relevant foreign court that it is not an inappropriate forum does not give rise to an issue estoppel:[88] where the test to be applied, and the issue to be determined, in England is distinct, the English discretionary stay proceedings are not precluded.[89]

8.42 It has already been seen[90] that at common law the English courts may stay civil proceedings under the doctrine of forum non conveniens on the ground that a foreign court is a more appropriate forum. In *de Dampierre v de Dampierre*[91] the House of Lords held that, in applying the balance of fairness test for the staying of matrimonial proceedings under the Domicile and Matrimonial Proceedings Act 1973, the courts should have regard to the civil cases on forum non conveniens. The effect of these is that, if by reason of the factors connecting the case to the foreign court, that court is clearly the more appropriate forum for the trial of the action, a stay will ordinarily be granted unless there are circumstances by reason of which justice requires that the stay should not be granted.

8.43 In *de Dampierre v de Dampierre* the parties were both French. In 1979 they moved to England, where the husband was involved in marketing cognac produced on his family estate in France. A few years later the wife set up a business in New York, where she subsequently took their child, informing her husband that she did not intend to return. The husband instituted divorce proceedings in France, and a few months later the wife instituted similar proceedings in England. The husband then applied to the English court for a stay of the English proceedings. He subsequently returned to live in France. Reversing the decision of the lower courts, the House of Lords held that a stay should be granted. The very strong factors connecting the case with France meant that, prima facie, the French court was the appropriate forum. The Court of Appeal had refused a stay on the ground that, if in the French proceedings it was found that

---

[85] In *R v R (Divorce: Stay of Proceedings)* [1994] 2 FLR 1036 it was implied that these statutory powers were available in cases where the foreign proceedings had been stayed. This ignores para 4(2) of the Domicile and Matrimonial Proceedings Act 1973, sch 1, which provides that 'proceedings in a court are continuing if they are pending and not stayed'.

[86] Domicile and Matrimonial Proceedings Act 1973, sch 1, para 9(1). [87] Para 9(2).

[88] On issue estoppel more generally, see paras 3.43–3.59.

[89] *Chai v Peng (Estoppel: Foreign Judgment) (No 1)* [2015] 2 FLR 412; *Peng v Chai* [2015] EWCA Civ 1312 at [19]–[20].

[90] See Chapter 2.

[91] [1988] AC 92. This and most of the cases discussed in this section of the chapter pre-date the Brussels II Regulation.

the wife was exclusively responsible for the breakdown of the marriage, she might be refused any financial relief, except for maintenance of the child, whereas such a finding in the English court would not have that effect. However, the House of Lords held that for the wife to be deprived of that advantage by the application of French law could not be held a substantial injustice to her, in view of the parties' connections with France.

8.44 In *Butler v Butler*[92] Hobhouse LJ stated obiter that the wording of the 1973 Act was different from the test of forum non conveniens laid down in the *Spiliada* case[93] and, therefore, a different test was applicable; while the *Spiliada* test demands that there be another jurisdiction which is clearly or distinctly more appropriate, the 1973 Act merely lays down a criterion of 'an assessment of the balance of fairness'. This was approved in *Otobo v Otobo*, where it was stated that the judge's discretion was 'bounded by the statutory considerations which rest upon an evaluation of fairness to the parties rather than upon a comparison of the competing jurisdictions, save in so far as the comparison relates to convenience of witnesses, delay and expense'.[94] In *Peng v Chai*,[95] however, the Court of Appeal opined that there was no difference of substance between the tests articulated in *de Dampierre* and *Butler*.

8.45 In considering the balance of fairness and convenience the courts have held several factors to be relevant: the locus of the marriage[96] and location of matrimonial assets;[97] whether the English divorce decree will be recognised in the other country;[98] the fact that the parties have concluded a prenuptial contract governed by the law of the other forum[99]—especially if the contract contains a jurisdiction clause in favour of the alternative forum[100]—and whether a party would be at a disadvantage in litigating abroad for, say, reasons of language difficulties and costs.[101] In *Otobo v Otobo* it was stated that in order to minimise the difference between the traditional rules and the Brussels II Regulation, 'greater weight'[102] should be given to a consideration of where proceedings were first issued.

8.46 In exercising its discretion the English court ought not to be too influenced by the fact that a party will receive no, or less, financial relief in the foreign divorce proceedings. Following the *Spiliada* case, the fact that the applicant may be deprived of a significant advantage abroad ought not to be given too much weight.[103] Further, the English court is empowered, when recognising a foreign matrimonial decree, to grant financial relief itself.[104] Despite this, it is clear that financial questions will continue to influence

---

[92] [1997] 2 All ER 822.   [93] [1987] AC 460.   [94] [2003] 1 FLR 192 at 207.
[95] [2015] EWCA Civ 1312 at [32].
[96] *Krenge v Krenge* [1999] 1 FLR 969 at 981: 'the relationship between the parties "budded, blossomed and withered" in Germany'.
[97] *Chai v Peng (Jurisdiction: Forum Conveniens) (No 2)* [2015] 2 FLR 424 at [77].
[98] *C v C* [2001] 1 FLR 624.
[99] Ibid. See also *Ella v Ella* [2007] 2 FLR 35 at [26], [37].
[100] *S v S (Divorce: Staying Proceedings)* [1997] 1 WLR 1200.
[101] *M v M (Divorce: Domicile)* [2011] 1 FLR 919.
[102] [2003] 1 FLR 192 at 207.   [103] See para 2.228.
[104] Matrimonial and Family Proceedings Act 1984. See paras 8.183–8.186.

English courts in the exercise of their discretionary powers. For example, in *R v R (Divorce: Stay of Proceedings)*[105] it was not clear whether England or Sweden was the more appropriate forum, but because the wife was able to apply for property adjustment, a lump sum, and periodic payments in England, whereas a Swedish court could only enforce a marriage contract providing for separation of property, it was held that justice demanded that a stay of the English proceedings be refused. In *S v S*[106] it was stated that it was relevant to take a 'general look' at the financial arrangements that would be made in the foreign court, but these would only tilt the balance of fairness in favour of the English forum if they amounted to a substantial injustice. The absence of legal aid in the other country and the costs involved for an English spouse having to travel to that country can be taken into account, but the weight to be attached to them will be entirely dependent on the circumstances. For example, in *Krenge v Krenge*[107] a stay of English proceedings was granted on condition that the husband deposited a sum of money to meet his wife's reasonable legal and travel expenses in Germany. The relative costs of litigation may also influence an English court in exercising its discretion: where the costs of the litigation are being met from 'fast-diminishing savings' and legal costs are significantly lower in the alternative forum, this will favour the grant of a stay.[108]

8.47 The statutory provisions are additional to the inherent jurisdiction of the English court to stay proceedings on the basis of forum non conveniens.[109] As the statutory scheme largely reproduces the common law as explained in the *Spiliada* case, there seems little scope for the common law powers to be invoked when there are proceedings pending abroad. However, the inherent common law power could usefully be invoked in cases where there were no proceedings abroad. Of course, in view of the more rigorous matrimonial jurisdictional rules there will be far less need to invoke the power than in civil and commercial cases. However, there can be cases where the concept of domicile gives the English court jurisdiction, despite there being only the most tenuous of links with England.[110]

(B) Anti-suit injunctions

8.48 In exceptional cases the common law powers can also be invoked to restrain a party from pursuing matrimonial proceedings in a non-Member State. Following the reasoning in *Turner v Grovit*[111] there can be no question of the English court granting an anti-suit injunction to restrain proceedings, within the scope of the Brussels II *bis* Regulation, in another Member State. Where, however, the English court assumes jurisdiction—whether under article 3 of the Brussels II *bis* Regulation or the traditional rules—and the petitioner seeks to restrain the other party from pursuing matrimonial proceedings in a non-Member State, whether or not relief should be granted depends wholly on English law. Such an injunction would in fact be seeking to uphold

---

[105] [1994] 2 FLR 1036.   [106] [1997] 1 WLR 1200.   [107] [1999] 1 FLR 969.
[108] *T v P (Jurisdiction: Lugano Convention and Forum Conveniens)* [2013] 1 FLR 478 at [52].
[109] Domicile and Matrimonial Proceedings Act 1973, s 5(6)(b). See *W v W* [1997] 1 FLR 257.
[110] See, eg, *T v T* [1995] 2 FLR 660.   [111] Case C-159/02 [2004] ECR I-3565.

the jurisdiction allocated under Brussels II *bis* and so cannot be incompatible with the Regulation.

8.49 In cases where an anti-suit injunction can be issued, there are two mechanisms that can be employed. First, the court can issue a permanent anti-suit injunction to restrain a spouse from pursuing foreign proceedings. The same test applies here as in civil and commercial matters: England must be the natural forum and the pursuit of the foreign proceedings would be vexatious or oppressive—meaning that it would be unconscionable to allow the foreign proceedings to continue.[112] Secondly, the court can issue a *Hemain* injunction.[113] This is a particular type of anti-suit injunction. It is not a perpetual injunction permanently restraining the pursuit by a spouse of foreign proceedings, but is an interim injunction 'to maintain the status quo, to preserve a level playing field, pending the determination, typically, of that spouse's application for a stay of the English proceedings'.[114] It will generally be used, where there are parallel proceedings in two different countries, to restrain a party from litigating substantive issues in the foreign court until the preliminary issues of jurisdiction have been resolved. As a *Hemain* injunction is simply an interim measure, there is no need to establish that England is the natural forum[115] but it must still be shown that the bringing of the proceedings in the foreign court would be vexatious or oppressive.[116] It will be much harder to demonstrate that the litigant abroad is acting unconscionably when the English proceedings are started significantly later than the foreign proceedings.[117]

D Reform of jurisdictional rules

8.50 The Brussels II *bis* Regulation came into force on 1 March 2005. With the ink hardly dry, the European Commission published a Green Paper on 14 March 2005 containing various proposals to reform the European rules on jurisdiction and on applicable law.[118] This was followed in 2006 by a proposed Regulation.[119] Under this proposal the parties would be permitted to choose a court of any Member State to have jurisdiction provided there was a 'substantial connection' with that Member State by virtue of the fact that (a) any of the grounds of jurisdiction listed in article 3 of Brussels II *bis* applies; or (b) it is the place of the spouses' last common habitual residence for a minimum period of three years; or (c) one of the spouses is a national of that Member State or, in the case of the United Kingdom or Ireland, has his or her 'domicile' there.[120]

---

[112] *Ahmed v Mustafa* [2015] 1 FLR 139. See paras 2.298–2.312.
[113] *Hemain v Hemain* [1988] 2 FLR 388.
[114] *R v R (Divorce: Hemain Injunction)* [2005] 1 FLR 386 at 397. See also *Bloch v Bloch* [2003] 1 FLR 1.
[115] *R v R (Divorce: Hemain Injunction)* [2005] 1 FLR 386; *S v S (Hemain Injunction)* [2010] 2 FLR 502 at [19], [27].
[116] *R v R (Divorce: Hemain Injunction)* [2005] 1 FLR 386; *T v T (Hemain Injunction)* [2014] 1 FLR 96.
[117] *S v S (Hemain Injunction)* [2010] 2 FLR 502 at [28].
[118] European Commission, *Green Paper on Applicable Law and Jurisdiction in Divorce Matters*, COM (2005) 82 final.
[119] *Proposal for a Council Regulation amending Regulation (EC) No 2201/2003 as regards jurisdiction and introducing rules concerning applicable law in matrimonial matters*, COM (2006) 399 final.
[120] Art 1(2) (proposing to insert a new art 3(a) into the Brussels II *bis* Regulation).

There were also proposals to repeal article 6 and substantially amend article 7 by introducing a new set of harmonised subsidiary grounds of jurisdiction to replace the various national (traditional) rules on residual jurisdiction. This proposed Regulation also sought to introduce harmonised choice of law rules indicating the applicable law in divorce cases. Because of hostility to these choice of law proposals in some Member States, the entire proposed Regulation was abandoned in 2008 and the choice of law reforms were brought forward as an 'enhanced cooperation' measure ('the Rome III Regulation') binding only on those Member States who desired to be bound. The United Kingdom did not participate in the Rome III Regulation.

8.51 Article 65 of Brussels II *bis* obliged the Commission to present a report on the application of the Regulation by January 2012. This 'Review' process began (somewhat belatedly) in April 2014. The Commission Report[121] suggests that the jurisdictional reforms proposed in 2006 (and abandoned in 2008) are likely to be revived and put back on the table.[122] This suggestion is not unwelcome. The enforcement of spousal jurisdiction agreements could help tackle forum shopping (particularly in 'big money' cases). Any such provision for party autonomy would, however, need to be accompanied by appropriate safeguards to protect against unequal bargaining and to cater for changed circumstances. The lis pendens doctrine would also require amendment in order to ensure the exclusive jurisdiction of the chosen court. The need for a 'substantial connection' to the agreed forum (as laid down in the 2006 proposal) should address the concerns of Member States with restrictive divorce laws (who might otherwise be concerned that the reforms would provide a general opt-out).

8.52 The existing rules on residual jurisdiction are extremely complex and opaque and their replacement with a simple set of subsidiary jurisdiction rules (allowing a European expatriate to divorce in the jurisdiction of nationality[123] or former habitual residence—in the absence of article 3 jurisdiction[124]) has considerable merit. Such 'subsidiary jurisdiction' rules, based on relatively tenuous connections to a Member State, would, however, be susceptible to abuse if they operated without any kind of a forum non conveniens discretion. Of course, as discussed earlier,[125] the Commission has also suggested the introduction of provisions akin to articles 33 and 34 of the Brussels I Recast[126]—but, as has been seen, such provisions provide no protection for a third-country spouse in the event that the EU Member State court is first seised and the third-country divorce proceedings are commenced later. The Commission Report also mentions the possibility of introducing a 'forum necessitatis' clause to allow for the exercise of jurisdiction, on an exceptional basis, where otherwise there would be no access to a divorce court.[127] The introduction of such a clause might allow for the

---

[121] *Report from the Commission to the European Parliament, the Council and the European Economic and Social Committee on the application of Council Regulation (EC) No 2201/2003 concerning jurisdiction and the recognition and enforcement of judgements in matrimonial matters and the matters of parental responsibility, repealing Regulation (EC) No 1347/2000*, COM (2014) 225 final.

[122] COM (2014) 225 final, pp 4–6.   [123] 'Domicile' in the case of the United Kingdom and Ireland.
[124] See COM (2006) 399 final, p 14.   [125] See para 8.34.   [126] COM (2014) 225 final, p 9.
[127] COM (2014) 225 final, p 8.

abolition of the existing residual jurisdiction rules (articles 6 and 7) without the need for any substitute 'subsidiary jurisdiction' rules as was suggested in the 2006 proposal. It is certainly arguable that the availability of a forum necessitatis ground alongside the existing article 3 grounds would provide sufficient jurisdictional access.

8.53 The Commission Report also acknowledges that the non-hierarchical structure of article 3 Brussels II *bis* can induce a 'rush to court'.[128] However, it seems that there is no appetite for any radical restructuring of that provision: instead the Commission appears to take the view that the solution resides in the Rome III Regulation. It observes that 'the ultimate goal' is that 'the Rome III Regulation is taken up by all Member States'.[129] This ambition appears somewhat unrealistic when one considers the entrenched positions adopted by certain Member States in the face of the 2006 choice of law proposals.[130] Furthermore, even if full participation in Rome III were achievable, this would not address financially motivated forum shopping: Rome III only deals with choice of law respecting the grounds for divorce and does not preclude the application of the lex fori in financial and ancillary relief matters. In so far as forum shopping in England tends to be financially motivated,[131] the adoption of Rome III (and the potential application of foreign grounds for divorce) would have little impact on the 'rush to court'.

E Same-sex marriages and civil partnerships

8.54 It is generally assumed that the Brussels II *bis* Regulation does not apply to either same-sex marriages[132] or civil partnerships;[133] therefore, articles 3 and 19 of Brussels II *bis* are not applicable to the dissolution of such relationships. However, English law has made provision for jurisdictional grounds which emulate those laid down in article 3 and for 'residual' jurisdiction based on the domicile of either spouse or civil partner.[134] Schedule 1 to the 1973 Act has been extended to same-sex spouses[135] and similar provision has been made for the grant of obligatory and discretionary stays of civil partnership dissolution proceedings.[136]

---

[128] COM (2014) 225 final p 5. On the risk of forum shopping under Brussels II *bis*, see Ní Shúilleabháin, 'Ten Years of European Family Law: Retrospective Reflections from a Common Law Perspective' (2010) 59 ICLQ 1021, 1030–8.

[129] COM (2014) 225 final p 3. On p 5 the Commission observes that Rome III does not 'yet' apply in all Member States.

[130] See paras 8.50 and 8.60.

[131] See paras 8.172 and 8.180: primary jurisdiction under art 3 of Brussels II *bis* confers ancillary jurisdiction to grant maintenance and other financial relief.

[132] See Dicey, Morris and Collins, *The Conflict of Laws* (15th edn, 2012), Second Cumulative Supplement, p 172.

[133] Ní Shúilleabháin, *Cross-Border Divorce Law: Brussels II bis* (2010) pp 105–19.

[134] See Domicile and Matrimonial Proceedings Act 1973, sch A1 (inserted by Marriage (Same Sex Couples) Act 2013, sch 4(4), para 8); Marriage (Same Sex Couples) (Jurisdiction and Recognition of Judgments) Regulations 2014, SI 2014/543; Civil Partnership Act 2004, ss 219–221; Civil Partnership (Jurisdiction and Recognition of Judgments) Regulations 2005, SI 2005/3334. These legislative provisions also allow for jurisdiction in legal separation and annulment matters.

[135] Domicile and Matrimonial Proceedings Act 1973, s 5(6) as amended by Marriage (Same Sex Couples) Act 2013, sch 4(4), para 6(4).

[136] Family Procedure (Civil Partnership: Staying of Proceedings) Rules 2010, SI 2010/2986.

8.55 In addition to the extension of the pre-existing jurisdictional grounds for divorce, English law makes a special 'forum necessitatis' provision for same-sex spouses and civil partners who married or registered their partnership in England but are unable to obtain a divorce or dissolution in the country in which they reside.[137] In such circumstances the English court may assume jurisdiction if 'it appears to the court to be in the interests of justice' to do so. While almost all countries in the world allow opposite-sex spouses to divorce, many countries make no provision for the dissolution of same-sex relationships; therefore the risk of same-sex couples being deprived of jurisdictional access to a divorce court is much higher. This kind of legal limbo was well-illustrated by the American case of *Rosengarten v Downes*.[138] The plaintiff in this case had entered into a same-sex civil union with the defendant in Vermont but lived in Connecticut. He was unable to seek a dissolution in either state because Vermont based its jurisdiction to dissolve civil unions on residence within the state and Connecticut did not make any provision for the dissolution of same-sex relationships.

II Choice of law

A Divorce and separation

1. Background

8.56 It might be thought that just as the question whether a marriage was valid at its inception may be governed by a foreign law, so also in appropriate cases the question whether there are sufficient grounds for its dissolution should be referred to a foreign law (for instance, the law of the parties' domicile at the date of the proceedings). In fact, however, when the English court has jurisdiction in divorce or legal separation proceedings, it applies English law exclusively to determine whether a divorce or legal separation should be granted.[139]

8.57 There are two main reasons for this approach. The first is historical. Originally, English courts had jurisdiction only if the parties were domiciled in England. English law, both as the lex fori and the lex domicilii, was the only conceivable law that could be applied. While the extended jurisdictional grounds today mean that the English court can grant a divorce to persons domiciled elsewhere, the rules are designed to ensure that at least one of the parties has a genuine connection with England. Accordingly, it is arguably appropriate that English law be applied. Secondly, it is often asserted that the circumstances in which a marriage should be dissolved by the English

---

[137] Domicile and Matrimonial Proceedings Act 1973, sch A1, para 2(1)(c); Civil Partnership Act 2004, s 221(1)(c).

[138] 802 A 2d 170 (Conn App, 2002). See Silberman, 'Same-Sex Marriage: Refining the Conflict of Laws Analysis' (2004–5) 153 University of Pennsylvania Law Review 2195, 2213–14; Hill Kay, 'Same-Sex Divorces in the Conflict of Laws' (2004) 15 King's College Law Journal 63, 85–8.

[139] *Zanelli v Zanelli* (1948) 64 TLR 556.

courts are very much a matter of English public policy, as reflected by English domestic law. It may be distasteful and time-consuming for English courts to have to apply sometimes 'exotic'[140] and often antiquated foreign grounds for divorce. Some 99 per cent of divorces are uncontested, with courts performing little more than a rubber-stamp function that does not involve any inquiry as to whether the grounds for divorce have been established.[141] It would be invidious to treat foreign domiciliaries differently by embarking on a full trial to ascertain whether the foreign grounds for divorce have been satisfied.

8.58 On the other hand, it has been suggested that 'if the courts take jurisdiction over "exotic foreigners" then the pass has been sold and it is arguably no more bizarre to apply their personal law to the dissolution than to apply it to the creation of their marriage'.[142] Divorce involves changing the status of the parties and so there is a strong argument of principle that the law of domicile should be applicable.[143] This would minimise the risk of limping relationships and take account of the reasonable expectations of the parties.[144] The courts of many EU countries have a long tradition of applying foreign laws, including the law of nationality or long-term residence, to determine whether divorces should be granted.[145] There appears to be no reason, in principle, why English law could not follow these approaches. One consequence of the present approach of the English courts is that a divorce granted in England may not be recognised by the law of the parties' domicile outside Europe.[146] One possibility would be a requirement that the divorce be recognised by the law of the parties' domicile before a divorce order can be made by the English court. However, in reality, lack of recognition of English decrees is more likely to be based on the foreign courts' rejection of the relatively wide English jurisdictional grounds than on the English courts' failure to apply foreign law.

2. European developments: Rome III

8.59 As previously discussed,[147] the European Commission in 2006 published a proposal for the amendment of the Brussels II *bis* jurisdictional grounds and for the harmonisation of divorce choice of law rules in the Member States.[148] This proposed allowing

---

[140] McClean and Ruiz Abou-Nigm, *Morris: The Conflict of Laws* (8th edn, 2012) p 252.
[141] Law Com No 170, *Facing the Future: a Discussion Paper on the Grounds for Divorce* (1988) paras 2.8, 5.17.
[142] North, 'Development of Rules of Private International Law in the Field of Family Law' (1980) 166 Hag Rec 9, 83.
[143] Under such an approach, there would need to be a resolution of the problem posed in cases where the spouses have separate domiciles.
[144] Fiorini, 'Rome III—Choice of Law in Divorce: Is the Europeanization of Family Law Going too Far? (2008) 22 Int JLPF 178, 188.
[145] For a list of the choice of law rules applicable in EU countries prior to the coming into force of Rome III, see European Commission, *Commission Staff Working Paper, Annex to the Green Paper on applicable law and jurisdiction in divorce matters* SEC (2005) 331.
[146] In *Kapur v Kapur* [1984] FLR 920 at 926 such lack of recognition was dismissed as 'irrelevant'.
[147] See para 8.50.
[148] *Proposal for a Council Regulation amending Regulation (EC) No 2201/2003 as regards jurisdiction and introducing rules concerning applicable law in matrimonial matters*, COM (2006) 399 final.

the parties to choose the applicable law provided they had a close connection with that law. In the absence of a choice, a hierarchy of connecting factors was suggested (see below).

8.60 There was intense hostility to this proposed Regulation in the United Kingdom, particularly from the legal profession, which feared it would lead to increased costs, delays, and greater difficulties in settling cases.[149] This resulted in the UK government (in 2006) deciding not to opt in to the proposed Regulation. Several other EU countries (particularly the Scandinavian ones) began voicing similar concerns. For example, Sweden objected on the ground that its simple and quick divorce procedures would become more complicated and lengthy and also, given the number of immigrants from the Middle East resident in Sweden, Swedish courts might be forced to apply Sharia law with its restrictive rules.[150] As indicated earlier, in the end the choice of law proposals were adopted by way of an 'enhanced cooperation' measure and the 'Rome III Regulation'[151] is now binding on those 16 Member States who wished to be bound by such a measure. Under the Regulation the spouses are permitted to choose the law applicable to divorce and legal separation provided they have a 'close connection'[152] with that law. This close connection must be evidenced by the chosen law being either the lex fori or the law of the state: (a) where they are habitually resident at the time the agreement is concluded; or (b) where they were last habitually resident and one of them still resides there at the time the agreement is concluded; or (c) of the nationality of one of the spouses.[153] In the absence of a choice by the parties, the applicable law will be the law of the following countries, in hierarchical order: (a) where both are habitually resident; (b) where they were last habitually resident provided that residence did not end more than one year before the court was seised and provided one of the spouses still resides there; (c) of which both spouses are nationals; (d) the lex fori.[154]

B Nullity

8.61 Unlike the position in divorce cases, the governing law in nullity proceedings in the English court may well be a foreign law. The governing law is determined by the choice of law rules examined in Chapter 7—for example, the lex loci celebrationis if the marriage is alleged to be formally invalid, or the laws of the parties' ante-nuptial domiciles if the issue concerns prohibited degrees of relationship. Whether such an invalid marriage will be regarded as void or voidable is discussed in Chapter 7.[155]

---

[149] Hodson, 'Rome III: Subsidiarity, Proportionality and the House of Lords' [2007] IFL 32.
[150] Bateman, 'Brussels Bulletin' [2007] IFL 98.
[151] Regulation (EU) No 1259/2010, implementing enhanced cooperation in the area of the law applicable to divorce and legal separation, OJ 2010 L 343/10. Initially there were 14 participating Member States (see Recital (6)) and subsequently Greece and Lithuania opted in. For a detailed critical analysis of Rome III, see Franzina, 'The Law Applicable to Divorce and Legal Separation under Regulation (EU) No 1259/2010 of 20 December 2010' (2011) 3 Cuadernos de Derecho Transnacional 85.
[152] Recital (14).   [153] Art 5(1).   [154] Art 8.   [155] See paras 7.9–7.10.

III Recognition of foreign judgments

8.62 The Brussels II *bis* Regulation and the Family Law Act 1986 make provision for the recognition of decrees of divorce, legal separation,[156] and annulment. In so far as it is assumed that Brussels II *bis* does not apply to same-sex marriages, separate provision is made for the recognition of Member State decrees in respect of such marriages under the Marriage (Same Sex Couples) (Jurisdiction and Recognition of Judgments) Regulations 2014.[157] Recognition of civil partnership dissolutions, annulments, and legal separations is governed by the Civil Partnership Act 2004.

A Decrees of divorce and legal separation

1. Introduction

8.63 The question often arises whether a divorce granted by a foreign court is recognised as valid in England.[158] If it is not recognised, the parties, although regarded as single persons in the country where the divorce was granted and in any other country which recognises the divorce, remain married to each other in the eyes of English law (and of any other law which does not recognise the divorce). Such a marriage, which still subsists according to one or more laws, but is regarded as having been dissolved according to others, is called a 'limping marriage'. The hardship and inconvenience which can result from people having a marital status which differs from one country to another is obvious. However, for a legal system to try to avoid this simply by recognising all foreign divorces will enable a spouse to evade the requirements of the law of the country or countries with which the parties are connected by obtaining a divorce in a country with which neither has any genuine connection, but whose courts exercise divorce jurisdiction on flimsy grounds.

8.64 It might be argued, therefore, that the rules governing the recognition of foreign divorces should aim to strike the right balance between being too restrictive, thereby unnecessarily creating limping marriages, and being too generous, thereby sanctioning divorces of convenience. It should be noted, however, that one of the hardships that could previously result from the recognition of a foreign divorce has been removed. The rule used to be that once a marriage had been validly dissolved abroad, the English court lacked power to make, for the first time, an order for financial provision in favour of a former spouse (although an existing order could be continued or varied after a divorce). This meant that an English wife, whose husband had obtained

---

[156] The Family Law Act 1986 refers to 'judicial separation' for the purpose of recognising British decrees (s 44), but refers to 'legal separation' for the purpose of recognising overseas decrees (ss 46–52). The Brussels II *bis* Regulation also refers to 'legal separation'.
[157] SI 2014/543.
[158] For reasons of convenience, discussion in the ensuing text is limited to recognition of foreign divorces. The same rules apply to recognition of foreign legal separations. For the implications of recognising foreign nullity decrees, see paras 8.149–8.164; for the separate rules on recognition of same-sex divorces and civil partnership dissolutions, see para 8.148.

a foreign divorce which was recognised in England, could not obtain an order for financial relief in the English court, even if the foreign court had not made adequate provision for her. However, since the 1980s the courts have been able to make orders for financial provision in favour of former spouses who have an appropriate connection with England.[159]

2. Historical development

8.65 Originally the principle was that it was for the courts of the domicile alone to change the status of the parties; just as the English courts would exercise divorce jurisdiction only if the spouses were domiciled in England, so also they would recognise only divorces granted by,[160] or recognised by,[161] the courts of the domicile.[162] When the jurisdiction of the English courts was extended by statute, the recognition rules were expanded so that divorces granted in circumstances in which the English court would have assumed jurisdiction were entitled to recognition.[163] The final common law extension was that a foreign divorce could be recognised if, at the commencement of the foreign proceedings, there was a real and substantial connection between either of the parties and the country in which the divorce was obtained.[164] While this was certainly a generous approach, this basis of recognition was extremely vague, making the status of the parties in England uncertain, and the decision of the court difficult to predict.[165]

8.66 The Recognition of Divorces and Legal Separations Act 1971 replaced these common law rules with statutory provisions that were both reasonably generous and precise. This Act was repealed and replaced by the Family Law Act 1986 which both amended the provisions of the 1971 Act and extended the recognition rules to nullity decrees.

8.67 As seen above, the Brussels II Convention was signed in 1998 and brought into force as an EC Regulation in 2001; a revised version (referred to here as the 'Brussels II *bis* Regulation') came into force in 2005; it applies to all Member States except Denmark. Under this Regulation divorces, legal separations, and annulments from courts of Member States are entitled to almost automatic recognition throughout the European Union. Accordingly, there are two separate regimes for the recognition of divorces: the EU system governs judgments handed down by the courts of Member States since

---

[159] Matrimonial and Family Proceedings Act 1984, s 12. See paras 8.183–8.186.
[160] *Harvie v Farnie* (1881) 8 App Cas 43.   [161] *Armitage v A-G* [1906] P 135.
[162] This remains the position in Ireland: a third country divorce can be recognised only if it was granted in a country where either spouse was domiciled, or if neither was domiciled in the granting country, it was entitled to recognition in the country or countries where they were domiciled: see *H v H* [2015] IESC 7. See further Ní Shúilleabháin, 'Marriage, Divorce and Stagnation in the Irish Conflict of Laws' (2014) 52 Irish Jurist 68.
[163] *Travers v Holley* [1953] P 246.   [164] *Indyka v Indyka* [1969] 1 AC 33.
[165] It was then estimated that, in around 2,500 cases per year, the Registrar-General of Births, Marriages and Deaths had to decide whether, following a foreign divorce, one of the parties was legally able to re-marry in England. After *Indyka v Indyka* this task became extremely difficult and led to a plethora of appeals to the courts. See Law Com No 34, *Hague Convention on Recognition of Divorces and Legal Separations* (1970) para 25, n 42.

March 2001 and the 'traditional rules' contained in the Family Law Act 1986 apply in all other cases.

3. Brussels II *bis* Regulation

(A) Recognition

8.68 The Brussels II *bis* Regulation applies to 'civil matters' 'whatever the nature of the court or tribunal'.[166] Although purely religious procedures are excluded, divorces obtained by administrative proceedings in a tribunal in a Member State fall within the scope of the Regulation.[167]

8.69 The rules here are broadly similar to those contained in the Brussels I Recast. With commercial judgments, however, it is enforcement of the judgment that is usually critical. The Brussels II *bis* Regulation does not cover financial matters that could be the subject of enforcement. Accordingly, with divorces, legal separations, and annulments, the rules relate purely to the recognition of such judgments.[168]

8.70 Chapter III starts from the premise that a judgment falling within its scope is entitled to recognition. The Regulation is based 'on the principle of mutual trust'[169] and so under no circumstances may a foreign judgment from a Member State be reviewed as to its substance.[170] Equally, the jurisdiction of the original court may not be reviewed,[171] irrespective of whether that court assumed jurisdiction under the Regulation or according to its traditional rules (in cases falling within article 7). Further, recognition may not be refused on the ground that the Member State addressed would not allow the divorce on the same facts.[172]

8.71 Article 21 provides that a judgment of divorce, legal separation, or annulment given in a Member State shall be recognised in other Member States without any special procedure being required. Unlike the Brussels I Recast, this only covers positive decisions that grant the decree. Negative decisions denying a decree are not entitled to recognition and so do not give rise to an issue estoppel.[173]

8.72 The recognition of a divorce, legal separation, or annulment is of particular importance for the updating of civil status records (rather than recognition by a court of law). No special procedure is required for this purpose; the mere existence of the decree from a Member State is sufficient.[174] This simple provision 'will be much appreciated by European citizens ... [and] will save time and money'.[175] Another important difference from the Brussels I Recast is that the judgment must be a final one from which no further appeal lies.[176]

---

[166] Art 1(1).
[167] Divorces can be obtained by administrative proceedings in Estonia and Portugal: European Commission, *Green Paper on Applicable Law and Jurisdiction in Divorce Matters*, COM (2005) 82 final.
[168] Borrás Report, OJ 1998 C221/27, para 80. The rules on enforcement apply only to judgments on the exercise of parental responsibility.
[169] Recital (21).   [170] Art 26.   [171] Art 24.   [172] Art 25.
[173] Kennett, 'Current Developments: Private International Law: The Brussels II Convention' (1999) 48 ICLQ 465, 470.
[174] Art 21(2).   [175] Borrás Report, OJ 1998 C221/27, para 63.   [176] Art 21(2).

8.73 A party might wish to obtain a ruling that the decree is entitled to recognition or might wish to contest the recognition of the decree. The Regulation entitles 'any interested party' to apply for a decision whether the judgment should be recognised or not.[177] The meaning of 'any interested party' is to be construed broadly under the national law of the state addressed.[178] The Borrás Report gives the example of a public prosecutor.[179] In England an 'interested party' could be the Registrar-General of Births, Marriages and Deaths who might seek a ruling prior to granting a licence permitting a party to remarry in England.

8.74 A question whether a decree should be recognised can arise incidentally in judicial proceedings: for example, where the validity of a subsequent marriage has to be determined. In such cases, the court may decide whether the foreign decree should be recognised under the Regulation.[180]

(B) Refusal of recognition

8.75 While judgments from Member States (other than Denmark) are normally entitled to automatic recognition, article 22 of the Regulation provides some limited grounds for non-recognition. As the fundamental principle underlying the Brussels II *bis* Regulation is that of mutual trust between Member States, the grounds for non-recognition are 'kept to the minimum required'.[181]

(i) Public policy

8.76 A judgment will not be recognised if such recognition would be manifestly contrary to public policy.[182] Inclusion of this ground in the Regulation is felt to be important because states are 'extremely sensitive' about family cases and there are major discrepancies between the laws of the Member States on divorce.[183] However, this public policy ground for non-recognition has only a limited reach. As already seen, the substance of a judgment[184] may not be reviewed and recognition may not be refused on the ground that the Member State addressed would not allow the divorce on the same facts.[185] Accordingly, a judgment from a state with flexible divorce laws cannot be refused recognition in a state with strict divorce laws on grounds of public policy. In addition to prohibiting the review of the jurisdiction of the court of origin, article 24 specifies that the test of public policy may not be applied to the rules relating to jurisdiction. This might suggest that even where there is a 'conspiracy to pervert the course of justice on an almost industrial scale'[186] (with multiple petitioners falsely asserting habitual residence in England[187]) that the resulting decrees could not be denied recognition in other Member States on grounds of public policy.[188]

---

[177] Art 21(3). [178] Borrás Report, OJ 1998 C221/27, para 65.
[179] Ibid. [180] Art 21(4). [181] Recital (21). [182] Art 22(a).
[183] Borrás Report, OJ 1998 C221/27, para 69. [184] Art 26. [185] Art 25.
[186] *Rapisarda v Colladon* [2015] 1 FLR 597 at [1]. [187] Ibid.
[188] In *Rapisarda* the 'fraudulent conspiracy' was discovered in England and all decrees nisi and absolute were set aside by the English Family Court.

8.77 Despite sensitivities in this area of law, it is likely that the public policy defence will be limited to situations where the corresponding provision under Brussels I[189] has been considered potentially applicable, for example, where the foreign decree has been obtained by fraud or where the respondent's human rights (as protected by the European Convention on Human Rights) have been infringed. This was generally confirmed in *Yordanova v Iordanov*[190] where a Bulgarian divorce was refused recognition under article 22(a) in circumstances where it had been obtained in violation of 'due process' and where the Bulgarian judge had proceeded in reliance on a power of attorney which had been signed by the wife without realising its true nature. It seems likely that the courts will draw on the jurisprudence interpreting the comparable provisions of Brussels I and tightly control the circumstances in which public policy can be used as a basis for non-recognition.[191]

(ii) Natural justice

8.78 A divorce shall be refused recognition where it was given in default of appearance, if the respondent was not notified in sufficient time and in such a way as to enable a defence to be arranged.[192] This ground of non-recognition mirrors article 45(1)(b) of the Brussels I Recast and, presumably, will be interpreted in a similar manner.[193] Like article 45(1)(b) of the Brussels I Recast, article 22(b) contains a qualification that limits the scope of the defence. Even if the respondent was not able to arrange for his defence, the decree must be recognised if the respondent 'has accepted the judgment unequivocally'. An example of such unequivocal acceptance would be a remarriage by the respondent.[194]

(iii) Irreconcilability

8.79 Again, mirroring the Brussels I Recast,[195] recognition must be refused to a judgment which is irreconcilable with a judgment given in proceedings between the same parties in the Member State addressed.[196] This provision applies regardless of which judgment was given first.[197] There is no requirement that the two judgments relate to the same cause of action. For example, if the parties had obtained a decree of legal separation in France and a divorce in England, the French judgment would be refused recognition in England as being irreconcilable with the English divorce.[198]

8.80 Further, the courts of a Member State shall not recognise a judgment if it is irreconcilable with an earlier judgment given in another Member State or in a non-Member State between the same parties, provided the earlier judgment fulfils the

---

[189] Now art 45(1)(a) of the Brussels I Recast.
[190] [2013] EWCA Civ 464. See also *Liaw v Lee (Non-Recognition of Divorce)* [2016] 1 FLR 533 at [9].
[191] See paras 3.108–3.113.   [192] Art 22(b).   [193] See paras 3.114–3.122.
[194] Borrás Report, OJ 1998 C221/27, para 70.   [195] Art 45(1)(c).   [196] Art 22(c).
[197] Borrás Report, OJ 1998 C221/27, para 71.
[198] The result would be different if a decree of judicial separation had first been obtained in England and a later divorce in France. As separation 'may be considered a preliminary to divorce' (Borrás Report, OJ 1998 C221/27, para 71), the French divorce could be recognised: it would not be irreconcilable with the earlier English judicial separation decree.

conditions necessary for its recognition in the Member State in which recognition is sought.[199]

8.81 Suppose, for example, that the English court is faced with a separation decree granted by a New York court which meets the conditions for recognition under the Family Law Act 1986 and a later divorce decree from a French court which meets the conditions for recognition under the Regulation. The French divorce decree is not irreconcilable with the New York separation judgment and so can be recognised.[200] In the converse case, where there is a divorce decree from New York and a later legal separation judgment from France, the French judgment will not be recognised because it is irreconcilable with the New York divorce decree.

8.82 The Regulation specifically covers irreconcilable judgments from the courts of two Member States.[201] The ground for non-recognition applies equally to the situation where, for example, there has been a Spanish divorce decree followed by a French separation judgment.

4. The traditional rules: Family Law Act 1986

8.83 In examining these rules it is necessary to distinguish between recognition of judicial divorces and recognition of extra-judicial divorces.

(A) Judicial divorces

8.84 The recognition of judicial divorces from non-Member States is governed by the Family Law Act 1986. This Act draws a distinction between 'British Isles divorces'[202] and 'overseas divorces'. With regard to the former, section 44(2) of the Family Law Act 1986 provides that a divorce granted by a court[203] in any part of the British Isles is automatically entitled to recognition throughout the United Kingdom, subject to one qualification which is mentioned below.[204] For the purpose of the recognition of divorces obtained outside the British Isles ('overseas divorces'), a distinction is drawn between divorces obtained by means of proceedings and those not 'obtained by proceedings'. The meaning of 'obtained by proceedings' is discussed later. It can safely be assumed that all overseas judicial divorces have been 'obtained by proceedings'.

8.85 The broad policy underlying the recognition rules is that the divorce should have been obtained in a country having an adequate connection with either of the parties. Section 46(1) of the Act provides that an overseas divorce obtained by proceedings qualifies for recognition if it is effective under the law of the country in which it was obtained, and at the date of the commencement of the proceedings either party was: (i) habitually resident in the country in which the divorce was obtained; or (ii) domiciled in that

---

[199] Art 22(d). [200] See n 198. [201] See Brussels I Recast, art 45(1)(d).
[202] The United Kingdom (consisting of England and Wales, Scotland, and Northern Ireland), the Channel Islands, and the Isle of Man.
[203] An administrative divorce obtained at the Russian Consulate in London is not entitled to recognition under s 44 (or s 46): *Solovyev v Solovyeva* [2015] 1 FLR 734.
[204] S 51(1), (2). See para 8.123.

country either according to English law or according to the law of that country in family matters;[205] or (iii) a national of that country.

(i) Habitual residence

8.86 If either spouse was habitually resident in the foreign country at the date of the commencement of the foreign proceedings, a divorce decree obtained in that country is, in principle, entitled to recognition in England. Habitual residence must be interpreted according to English law.[206] Unlike the former English traditional jurisdictional rule, the habitual residence need not have endured for any set period of time. It is not unusual for English divorce recognition rules to be more flexible than the English jurisdictional rules.[207]

(ii) Domicile

8.87 A divorce obtained in a country in which either party is domiciled, according to English law, is entitled to recognition. The common law rule, preserved in the Recognition of Divorces and Legal Separations Act 1971, that a divorce recognised by the law of the parties' domicile, though not obtained in the country in which either was domiciled, was entitled to recognition, was abolished by the Family Law Act 1986. One of the parties must be domiciled in the country where the divorce was obtained if domicile is being used as the basis for recognition.

8.88 Further, however, contrary to the general rule that domicile is defined by the lex fori, a divorce can also be recognised if either party was domiciled in the country of origin according to that country's law in family matters. In *Messina v Smith*[208] the wife obtained a divorce in Nevada where she had resided for six weeks, which was sufficient for her to acquire a domicile according to Nevada law. Such a divorce would qualify for recognition.[209] In this way, provision is made for a connecting factor likely to facilitate the recognition of divorces even when granted by the courts of a country with which the parties have only a fleeting or tenuous connection.

(iii) Nationality

8.89 A divorce obtained in the country of nationality of either party is entitled to recognition. Despite nationality not being a favoured connecting factor in English law, this provision was added as part of the price of reaching international agreement with civil law countries in the 1970 Hague Convention on the Recognition of Divorces and Legal Separations. In *Torok v Torok*[210] the spouses were Hungarian nationals who came to Britain where they became naturalised subjects while retaining their Hungarian nationality. Later, the husband returned to Hungary and there obtained a divorce. It was

---

[205] S 46(5).
[206] As to the relevance of foreign findings of fact, see paras 8.94–8.96.
[207] At common law the recognition rules under *Indyka v Indyka* [1969] 1 AC 33 were more generous than the then current English jurisdictional rules. [208] [1971] P 322.
[209] See Ormrod J (obiter) at 339. The comparable provision of the 1971 Act was not yet in force.
[210] [1973] 1 WLR 1066.

held that the divorce would, on this basis, be prima facie entitled to recognition.[211] It was irrelevant that the husband was also a national of another country.

(iv) Country

8.90 In the case of a state comprising law districts in which separate systems of law are in force in matters of divorce (for example, the United States), if a divorce is sought to be recognised on the basis of habitual residence or domicile in either sense, then it is the law district, not the political state, which counts as the country.[212] So, for the recognition of a divorce obtained in Colorado, the question would be whether either party was habitually resident or domiciled in Colorado, not anywhere else in the United States. If, however, recognition of the divorce is sought on the ground of either party being a national of the country of origin, then 'country' means the political state, not a constituent law district[213] (for normally nationality will relate to the whole political unit). Thus a divorce obtained in Colorado will qualify for recognition if either party is a citizen of the United States.

(v) Effective under foreign law

8.91 At common law, the fact that a divorce was invalid under the law of the country in which it was obtained was not necessarily an obstacle to its recognition. Under the Family Law Act 1986, however, a foreign divorce cannot be recognised on any ground unless it is effective under the law of the country in which it was obtained.[214] This means that if the divorce is not effective under that law, because, for example, the foreign court lacked jurisdiction under its own law to grant divorce decrees, or because of some procedural irregularity, the divorce cannot be recognised in England. For example, in *D v D*[215] the husband, a Ghanaian national, returned to Ghana and there obtained a divorce without the wife being present or notified. After hearing expert evidence of Ghanaian law, the English court concluded that, if the matter were to be appealed to the High Court of Ghana, the divorce would be set aside on the ground that there had been no voluntary submission by both parties. Accordingly, the divorce was not effective under Ghanaian law and so not entitled to recognition in England. In *Abbassi v Abbassi*[216] it was held that English proceedings could be stayed until a Pakistani court had determined whether or not a talak divorce was effective.

8.92 In *Kellman v Kellman*[217] it was held that 'effective' does not necessarily mean 'valid'; 'effective' connotes a less rigorous standard. In this case the parties obtained a 'mail order divorce' from Guam. Both parties regarded this as a valid divorce and the husband remarried. Ten years later, it transpired that the divorce might not have been valid under Guam law and so the wife attempted to have the divorce decree

---

[211] Recognition was, in fact, denied for other reasons.
[212] Family Law Act 1986, s 49(1), (2). [213] S 49(1), (3).
[214] Ss 46(1)(a) and (2)(a). This rule was first introduced, in respect of the statutory bases of recognition, by s 2(b) of the Recognition of Divorces and Legal Separations Act 1971.
[215] [1994] 1 FLR 38. [216] [2006] 2 FLR 415. [217] [2000] 1 FLR 785.

set aside in Guam. The Supreme Court of Guam denied her motion on grounds of equitable estoppel. Accordingly, the divorce, although not 'valid', could be regarded as 'effective'.

8.93 What is the position in relation to states comprising law districts in which different systems of law are in force? If recognition is based on habitual residence or domicile in a particular law district, the divorce must be effective under the law of that law district. For example, if a divorce were obtained in Colorado, it would need to be effective under the law of Colorado. Where recognition is sought on the ground that either party was a national of the political state, then the requirement is that the divorce must be effective throughout the political state.[218] In *Kellman v Kellman*,[219] where the divorce was obtained in Guam, an unincorporated territory of the United States, recognition was sought on the basis that the parties were US nationals. It was held that the divorce had to be effective under the law of the United States. The reason is that, if the connection which justifies the recognition is with the political state, then the effectiveness in the country in which it was obtained should be assessed by the same yardstick.

(vi) Proof of facts relevant to recognition

8.94 For the recognition of a foreign divorce, the English court has to decide whether a party had the required connection (habitual residence, domicile, or nationality) with the foreign country. It is not essential that the foreign court should have assumed jurisdiction on one of these bases. For example, a foreign court could assume jurisdiction on the basis of one party's presence in the country; such a divorce decree could still be recognised provided either party was in fact habitually resident or domiciled there or a national of that country. Very often, however, the foreign court will have itself assumed jurisdiction on the basis of habitual residence, domicile, or nationality and, in such cases, to avoid the unnecessary reopening in the English court of issues already decided in the foreign court, provision is made that:

> any finding of fact made (whether expressly or by implication) in the [foreign] proceedings and on the basis of which jurisdiction was assumed in the proceedings shall—
>
> (a) if both parties to the marriage took part in the proceedings, be conclusive evidence of the fact found; and
> (b) in any other case, be sufficient proof of that fact unless the contrary is shown.[220]

8.95 So, the foreign finding of fact relevant to jurisdiction is conclusive if the respondent as well as the petitioner took part in the proceedings (which includes even a formal appearance without any further participation), because the respondent would have had the opportunity, if so inclined, to contest the fact in the foreign court. If, however, the respondent did not appear, the foreign finding is presumed to be correct, but it is open to a party in the English proceedings to prove otherwise.

---

[218] S 49(1), (3).   [219] [2000] 1 FLR 785.
[220] S 48(1). S 48(3) provides that a party who has 'appeared in judicial proceedings shall be treated as having taken part in them'. See *A v L* [2010] 2 FLR 1418 at [70].

8.96 The foreign finding of fact which is conclusive, or prima facie sufficient, will often be a finding that a party was habitually resident in the foreign country, or was domiciled in that country under its law, or was a national of that country (when the foreign court's jurisdiction under its own law is based on such ground). However, it could merely be a finding of a fact which is a step towards deciding whether a ground of jurisdiction existed. For example, a finding by the foreign court that a party was present in its country at a certain time or for a certain period would be conclusive, or prima facie sufficient, proof of that fact for the purposes of the English court's decision whether the party was habitually resident in that country or domiciled there in the English sense. There is little possibility of an actual finding by the foreign court that a party was domiciled there in the English sense, for that could hardly ever be a relevant question in the foreign proceedings.

(B) Extra-judicial divorces

(i) Introduction

8.97 Although, in England, a marriage can be dissolved only by judicial proceedings in a court of law, this is not so in all countries.[221] Under some foreign legal systems, the proceedings for divorce may be administrative rather than judicial, or the divorce may be obtained merely by the agreement of the parties or by the act of only one of them, either with or without attendant formalities. The kind of extra-judicial divorce which has most often come before the English courts is the Islamic talak. Under some traditions of classical Islamic law, the husband can divorce his wife merely by declaring three times, in writing or orally, 'I divorce you'. In some Islamic countries such a talak divorce is effective. In Pakistan, however, statute has added further requirements to the procedure. Under Jewish religious law, as applied in Israel, a consensual form of divorce may be obtained: the husband appears before the Beth Din (Rabbinical court) and executes a letter of divorce, a get, which is then delivered to the wife, either in person or by proxy, at the Beth Din. The divorce is final when the wife receives the document. Although the procedure takes place at the Beth Din, it is not the court which grants the divorce.

8.98 English conflict of laws rules have long accepted in principle the validity of foreign extra-judicial divorces, as long as the ordinary grounds of recognition are satisfied. At common law, the original grounds for recognition of a foreign divorce were that it should have been obtained in the country of the parties' domicile or be recognised as valid by the law of that country. On this basis, not only were talak divorces obtained in a foreign country recognised in England,[222] but even a talak divorce pronounced in England while the parties were living here was recognised on the ground that it was valid by the law of Pakistan, the country in which the parties

---

[221] There have been no cases on extra-judicial legal separations for well over a century: North, *The Private International Law of Matrimonial Causes in the British Isles and the Republic of Ireland* (1977) p 280. This section is, accordingly, limited to extra-judicial divorces.

[222] *Russ v Russ* [1964] P 315.

were domiciled.[223] It was not thought contrary to public policy to recognise such divorces,[224] even if the foreign law required no formalities of any kind. However, when further grounds of recognition (habitual residence and nationality) were added by the Recognition of Divorces and Legal Separations Act 1971, they extended only to divorces obtained by 'proceedings'. Then in 1973 it was laid down by statute[225] that in future no extra-judicial divorce obtained anywhere in the British Isles should be recognised in England; this principle was re-enacted in the Family Law Act 1986.[226]

8.99 Accordingly, the rules for recognition of extra-judicial divorces are governed by the Family Law Act 1986[227] under which the rules applicable depend on whether the extra-judicial divorce was obtained by means of 'proceedings' or not.

(ii) 'Proceedings'

8.100 What is the reason for having different rules of recognition for divorces obtained by proceedings and for those obtained without proceedings? Historically, the reason is that, before the Recognition of Divorces and Legal Separations Act 1971, the original and primary basis for the recognition of a divorce was that it was obtained in the country of the parties' domicile, or recognised by its law, which was the appropriate law to determine status. This principle was held to require the recognition of divorces however obtained, and the question whether there had been any proceedings was not thought material. Under the 1971 Act, the existing grounds of recognition on the basis of domicile were continued,[228] even in relation to an entirely informal non-judicial divorce, such as a bare talak.[229] The Act, however, introduced new grounds of recognition (habitual residence, nationality, domicile in the foreign sense), but only (following the Hague Convention which was being implemented) for divorces obtained by 'judicial or other proceedings'. Although the courts might conceivably have held that any act by which a divorce is obtained, including a bare talak, constituted proceedings—thus obliterating any distinction between divorces obtained by proceedings and those not so obtained—they ultimately did not do so.

8.101 The Law Commission, in its report which led to the enactment of the relevant part of the 1986 Act, recommended that 'other proceedings' should 'include acts which constitute the means by which a divorce ... may be obtained in [the] country and are done in compliance with the procedure required by the law of that country'.[230] This

---

[223] *Qureshi v Qureshi* [1972] Fam 173. In *Har-Shefi v Har-Shefi (No 2)* [1953] P 220, a case involving the dissolution of a marriage between Israeli domiciliaries, a Jewish religious divorce obtained by the husband's delivering a letter of divorce to the wife at a Rabbinical court in London was recognised on the ground that it was effective by the law of Israel.
[224] *Qureshi v Qureshi* [1972] Fam 173.
[225] Domicile and Matrimonial Proceedings Act 1973, s 16(1).
[226] In somewhat different wording: s 44(1).
[227] The Brussels II *bis* Regulation applies to divorces obtained by administrative proceedings where the divorce is issued by a tribunal in a Member State (such as Portugal or Estonia).
[228] S 6.   [229] *Chaudhary v Chaudhary* [1985] Fam 19.
[230] Law Com No 137, *Recognition of Foreign Nullity Decrees and Related Matters* (1984) para 6.11.

would include bare talaks. However, this recommendation was not implemented in the statute.

8.102 The Family Law Act 1986 merely states that proceedings are 'judicial or other proceedings'.[231] Accordingly, the meaning of 'other proceedings' has been a matter of judicial interpretation.

8.103 In *Quazi v Quazi*[232] the husband, a Pakistani national, had obtained a divorce by talak under the law of Pakistan. Under the 1971 Act, as under the 1986 Act, an overseas divorce was to be recognised if either spouse was a national of the country in which it was obtained, but only if the divorce had been obtained by means of judicial or other proceedings.[233] In this case, the divorce had been obtained in Pakistan under the Muslim Family Laws Ordinance 1961. This provided that the husband, after pronouncing the talak, had to send a written notice of the divorce to the chairman of an administrative body called the union council, and a copy to the wife. The chairman of the union council then had to set up an arbitration council, whose function was to try to bring about a reconciliation. The effect of the talak was suspended until 90 days after notice of the talak had been given to the official, but if within that period the husband did not revoke the talak, it then became effective. The issue was whether a divorce obtained in this way had been obtained by 'proceedings'. The Court of Appeal[234] held that it had not, for it thought that the requirement of 'proceedings' meant that the efficacy of the divorce must depend in some way on the authority of the state expressed in a formal manner. A divorce obtained under the Ordinance did not satisfy this requirement, because the state could not prevent the husband from divorcing his wife if he chose not to be reconciled. This decision was reversed by the House of Lords, for it was plain to them that the pronouncement by the husband of the talak, and the giving of notice to the council and the wife, constituted 'proceedings' by means of which the divorce had been obtained.

8.104 What remained undecided was whether a 'bare' talak, that is, the mere pronouncement, orally or in writing, of a talak without any other formality—which is legally effective in some Islamic countries[235]—would amount to 'proceedings'. One view expressed in *Quazi v Quazi* was that 'any act or acts officially recognised as leading to a divorce in the country where the divorce was obtained'[236] amounted to proceedings; this would seem to include a bare talak. However, after conflicting decisions in the High Court,[237] it was held by the Court of Appeal in *Chaudhary v Chaudhary*[238] that a bare talak did not amount to proceedings. In this case, the husband had gone from England to Kashmir to pronounce the talak three times orally. He did this before two witnesses in a mosque and reinforced the oral declaration with a written document. These latter elements were not required under the law of Kashmir under which bare talaks were permitted. Although the talak was pronounced in that part of Kashmir

---

[231] Family Law Act 1986, s 54(1).   [232] [1980] AC 744.
[233] Recognition of Divorces and Legal Separations Act 1971, s 2.   [234] [1980] AC 744 at 784.
[235] See, eg, *Zaal v Zaal* [1982] 4 FLR 284 (Dubai); *Sharif v Sharif* [1980] Fam Law 216 (Iraq); *Re Fatima* [1986] AC 527 (Kashmir).
[236] [1980] AC 744 at 824.   [237] See cases cited in n 235.   [238] [1985] Fam 19.

which is within the borders of Pakistan, the 1961 Ordinance does not extend to it and by Pakistani law the divorce was effective. As the husband was a national of Pakistan, the divorce would have qualified for recognition under the 1971 Act if it had been obtained by means of 'proceedings'. The Court of Appeal held that the divorce could not be recognised. 'Proceedings', it was held, does not include 'a private act conducted entirely by parties inter se or by one party alone' even if there are witnesses.[239] There must be 'a degree of formality and at least the involvement of some agency, whether lay or religious, of or recognised by the state as having a function that is more than simply probative'.[240] Accordingly, if the only requirement under the law of the country where the talak is pronounced is that there must be a set number of witnesses, this will not be enough to render the divorce one obtained by proceedings. It was added that what is critical are the elements required by the foreign law and whether they amount to proceedings. It is irrelevant if the parties, as in this case, go through extra solemnities not insisted upon by that law.

8.105 In *El Fadl v El Fadl*[241] the husband divorced his wife by talak in Lebanon. Under Lebanese law, the husband is required to pronounce the words of the talak before two witnesses and then register the divorce before the Sharia court. Under Lebanese law some talaks are revocable while others are irrevocable. The Sharia court identified this divorce as irrevocable and recorded this fact. Even though the Sharia court has no power to grant or refuse a divorce, the fact that the process of identifying the type of talak had to be gone through and that formal declarations are taken and registered was enough to render the process 'proceedings'. In *H v S*[242] it was accepted that, even if there was no formal requirement for a talak to be made or registered in court in Saudi Arabia, if it was, as a matter of practice, necessary to do so, this would render a 'proceedings' characterisation appropriate. In *H v H (Validity of Japanese Divorce)*[243] a Japanese divorce, known as a 'kyogi rikon', was held to be a 'proceeding'. Such divorces require the consent of both parties, the signing of a form and its registration. There are specific rules and procedures laid down by the state governing its making. It was held that the registration process, involving the state of Japan, was not 'simply probative'; the registration of the divorce by the state was fundamental to its effect.[244] In *A v L*[245] it was held that a judgment of a foreign court which is necessary, under the applicable law, to validate and confirm a previous bare talak does amount to 'proceedings'.

8.106 It follows from these cases that a wide range of talaks and other informal divorces can be regarded as obtained by proceedings as long as there is 'the intervention of some other body or person with a specific function to fulfil'.[246] However, bare

---

[239] Ibid at 41. [240] Ibid. [241] [2000] 1 FLR 175.
[242] *H v S (Recognition of Overseas Divorce)* [2012] 2 FLR 157. [243] [2007] 1 FLR 1318.
[244] It was stated that 'the consent of itself creates nothing ... no registration, no divorce' (at [96]).
[245] [2010] 2 FLR 1418 at [71].
[246] Balcombe J in *Chaudhary v Chaudhary* [1985] Fam 19 at 46. In *NP v KRP (Recognition of Foreign Divorce)* [2014] 2 FLR 1 an Indian 'panchayat' divorce was considered a 'proceedings' divorce in circumstances where registration was optional and there appeared to be no obligatory role for any external state-sanctioned body. This case is out of line with the generally accepted principles.

talaks in which, for instance, the only legal requirement is that there be witnesses, do not qualify as 'proceedings'. The fact that not all talaks can be regarded as involving 'proceedings' is further underlined by the Family Law Act 1986's express recognition of a category of divorce that does not involve 'proceedings'. This would almost certainly include another kind of Islamic divorce, known as a khula,[247] which is a divorce by mutual consent: the wife makes a written statement that she wishes to end the marriage, and the husband accepts this in writing, in the presence of witnesses. According to the approach in *Chaudhary v Chaudhary*, such a divorce is not obtained by proceedings.[248]

(iii) Extra-judicial divorces obtained by proceedings

8.107 If the divorce was obtained by means of 'proceedings' then the grounds of recognition are those which have already been considered in the context of judicial divorces: a divorce obtained by proceedings will be recognised if either party was habitually resident or domiciled (in either the English or the foreign sense) in, or a national of, the country in which it was obtained, provided that it is effective under the law of that country. As with judicial divorces, it is not sufficient that it is recognised as valid by the laws of the parties' domiciles, if obtained elsewhere.

8.108 These rules indicate that it is possible for English domiciliaries to obtain extra-judicial divorces in their country of nationality or habitual residence (or, indeed, in a country in which they are domiciled in that country's sense). In *Chaudhary v Chaudhary*[249] it was indicated that it would be contrary to public policy for a party to go abroad and obtain a talak divorce when both parties were domiciled in England. However, the real concern in this case appeared to be the desire to prevent husbands domiciled in England evading English law by travelling abroad to obtain a divorce, leaving the wife destitute. However, this has not been a problem since the entry into force of Part III of the Matrimonial and Family Proceedings Act 1984 under which the English court can itself make financial relief orders when recognising foreign divorces. In a number of reported cases since 2000, extra-judicial divorces have been held to be entitled to recognition despite the fact that one of the parties was domiciled in England.[250] The approach illustrated by these cases must be correct, even when both parties are domiciled in England. Denying recognition to divorces involving English domiciliaries would amount to little more than reintroducing the old common law rules based on domicile via the back door and ignoring the clear provisions of the 1986 Act to the effect that divorces should be recognised if obtained in the country of nationality or habitual residence—irrespective of the parties' domiciles.

---

[247] See *Quazi v Quazi* [1980] AC 744 at 820, 824.
[248] Lord Scarman in *Quazi v Quazi* [1980] AC 744 at 824 had, however, thought to the contrary.
[249] [1985] Fam 19 at 39–40, 43–5, 48.
[250] *H v H (Talaq Divorce)* [2008] 2 FLR 857 (recognised); *H v H (Validity of Japanese Divorce)* [2007] 1 FLR 1318 (recognised); *A v L* [2010] 2 FLR 1418 (not recognised on other grounds).

(iv) Divorces obtained otherwise than by means of proceedings

8.109 If the extra-judicial divorce was not obtained by 'proceedings', section 46(2) of the Family Law Act 1986 provides that it can be recognised only if it is effective under the law of the country in which it was obtained and, at the date on which it was obtained:

    (b) (i) each party to the marriage was domiciled in that country; or

        (ii) either party to the marriage was domiciled in that country and the other party was domiciled in a country under whose law the divorce . . . or legal separation is recognised as valid; and

    (c) neither party to the marriage was habitually resident in the United Kingdom throughout the period of one year immediately preceding that date.

8.110 For the purposes of section 46(2), 'domicile' means domicile according to either English law or the foreign law.[251]

8.111 The grounds for recognition of an extra-judicial divorce not obtained by proceedings are much narrower than for a divorce, whether judicial or not, which is obtained by proceedings. It cannot be recognised on the ground that either party was habitually resident in, or a national of, the country, nor even on the ground that one of the parties was domiciled there (whether in the English or foreign sense) unless the divorce is recognised by the law of the domicile of the other party. In *H v H (Validity of Japanese Divorce)*[252] an extra-judicial divorce was obtained in Japan. The husband was domiciled there, but the wife was domiciled in England. It was held (obiter) that, if the divorce had not involved proceedings, it could not have been recognised under section 46(2) because the wife was not domiciled in a country under whose law the divorce is recognised as valid.[253] It is not clear why, if such informal divorces are not thought fit for recognition if obtained in the country of habitual residence or nationality, they are thought fit for recognition if obtained in the country of domicile. The reason can hardly be the peculiar importance in English eyes of a person's status according to his or her domiciliary law, because the primacy of domicile is no longer accepted in the Act's main provisions for recognition.

8.112 A literal interpretation of section 46(2) would suggest that an English domiciliary (in the English sense) can obtain such an extra-judicial divorce provided both parties are domiciled (in the foreign sense) in the country where the divorce was obtained.[254] For example, an English domiciliary (in the English sense) could obtain an extra-judicial divorce in Iran which would be entitled to recognition if both parties were domiciled there according to Iranian law. More problematic is the case where one party is domiciled (in the foreign sense) in the country of divorce and the other is an English domiciliary (in the English sense) but is domiciled in a third country (in that country's

---

[251] S 46(5).   [252] [2007] 1 FLR 1318.
[253] 'To have argued otherwise would have involved circularity' (at [16]). The divorce was actually found to have been obtained by 'proceedings' and so fell to be recognised under s 46(1).
[254] Provided the argument above concerning the interpretation of *Chaudhary v Chaudhary* [1985] Fam 19 is accepted. See para 8.108.

sense) which recognises the divorce. For example, one party could be domiciled in Iran according to Iranian law and there pronounce talak while the other party could be an English domiciliary (in the English sense) but domiciled in Sudan according to Sudanese law, which recognises the divorce. Again, a literal interpretation would dictate that, as the divorce is recognised as valid by the law of domicile (in either sense) of the other party (Sudanese law), it should be entitled to recognition in England. To assert that domicile in the English sense 'trumps' domicile in the foreign sense would involve a bold interpretation—but, given the dicta in *Chaudhary v Chaudhary*,[255] such a possibility cannot be discounted.

8.113 The reason for the additional requirement that neither party should have been habitually resident in the United Kingdom for a year immediately preceding the divorce is that if either had been so resident, then a UK court would have had jurisdiction to grant a divorce before the coming into force of the Brussels II *bis* Regulation. This was thought to be the proper avenue for the applicant in such a case to follow, even if it was not the applicant who was habitually resident in the United Kingdom.[256]

8.114 One might reasonably question the logic of English law in drawing such a sharp distinction between divorces obtained 'otherwise than by means of proceedings' and other extra-judicial divorces.[257] The formalities in extra-judicial divorces obtained by 'proceedings' may have no substantive protective effect and it is difficult to see why these divorces should be subject to a recognition regime which is radically more liberal than that applicable to divorces obtained 'otherwise than by means of proceedings'.

(v) Transnational divorces

8.115 A transnational divorce is one where some steps towards the divorce occur in one country and other steps are performed in another country. Suppose, for example, a husband, being a national of Pakistan, pronounces the talak in England, and then, in terms of the Pakistan Ordinance, sends notice of it to the chairman of the union council in Pakistan, with a copy to his wife there; the arbitration council is set up in Pakistan and the talak is not revoked, and so the divorce becomes effective by Pakistani law. In such cases it is important to determine where the divorce is obtained as section 44 of the Family Law Act 1986 provides that no extra-judicial divorce obtained in the British Islands shall be regarded as effective. Only 'overseas'[258] extra-judicial divorces are entitled to recognition. Or, alternatively, suppose the same husband pronounces the talak in Saudi Arabia, under whose law it would be an effective divorce and sends the appropriate notices to Pakistan. Can such transnational divorces be recognised?

---

[255] [1985] Fam 19.
[256] Young, 'The Recognition of Extra-Judicial Divorces in the United Kingdom' (1987) 7 LS 78, 85–6.
[257] See Young, 'The Recognition of Extra-Judicial Divorces in the United Kingdom' (1987) 7 LS 78; Pearl, 'Family Law Act 1986, Part II' [1987] CLJ 35.
[258] Family Law Act 1986, s 46.

8.116 To decide the effect in England of a transnational divorce it is necessary again to distinguish divorces obtained by proceedings from those obtained otherwise than by means of proceedings.

(a) Divorces obtained by proceedings

8.117 In *Re Fatima*[259] the husband pronounced talak in England and sent the appropriate notices to Pakistan, the country of his nationality. On an interpretation of section 3 of the Recognition of Divorces and Judicial Separations Act 1971 which required him to have been a national of Pakistan 'at the date of the institution of the proceedings in the country in which it was obtained' it was held that the 'institution of the proceedings' was inextricably linked to the 'obtaining' of the overseas divorce and, accordingly, both had to take place in the same country. The proceedings had been instituted in England; the divorce could not be recognised.[260] The wording of the Family Law Act 1986, however, is different in that it simply requires one of the parties to be habitually resident or domiciled in or a national of the overseas country at the 'date of the commencement of the proceedings'[261] and, additionally, specifies that the divorce must be 'effective under the law of the country in which it was obtained'.[262] Arguably, this could mean that if, as in *Fatima*, the husband was a national of Pakistan when he pronounced the talak (albeit in England) and the divorce was 'obtained' in Pakistan, it should be entitled to recognition. However, in *Berkovits v Grinberg*[263] it was held that transnational divorces could still not be recognised. In this case the Jewish get of divorce was written in England and then delivered to the wife in Israel, the country of both parties' nationality. Wall J accepted the expert evidence that the divorce was only final when the wife received the letter of get. However, he concluded that the word 'obtained' connoted a process rather than a single act: 'To obtain a divorce a party must go through a process, in the same way that a person obtains a university degree.'[264] The writing of the get in England was an integral part of the process. This process (the 'proceedings') had to be instituted in the same country in which the divorce was obtained. From this it follows that no transnational divorces obtained by proceedings, whether get or talak, whether initiated in England or another country, are entitled to recognition.

8.118 This conclusion, which has 'far-reaching implications for the Jewish community in the United Kingdom, and also for the Muslims and other communities'[265] living here, has little to commend it. Nothing in the statute dictates that the proceedings must have been commenced in the country where the divorce was obtained. To pursue Wall J's metaphor: under a modularised system, a degree may be commenced at one university and obtained at another. More significantly, in policy terms, the result is that the rich who can afford to fly to Pakistan or Israel to pronounce talak or write a get can

---

[259] [1986] AC 527.
[260] See also *Maples v Melamud* [1988] Fam 14, where a get was executed and received by the wife in England. This divorce was clearly obtained in England. It was not a transnational divorce as the confirmation of the get by a court in Israel was not part of the process by which the divorce was obtained.
[261] S 46(3)(a).   [262] S 46(1)(a).   [263] [1995] Fam 142.   [264] At 157.
[265] Reed, 'Extra-Judicial Divorces since *Berkovits*' [1996] Fam Law 100, 102.

'buy' recognition of their divorce. The ordinary person, such as Mr Grinberg, who complies with the laws of his religion and the country of his nationality (an accepted basis for recognition under the 1986 Act), finds himself in a limping marriage and Mrs Grinberg is placed 'in an extremely vulnerable position, and one she could hardly have anticipated or desired'.[266]

(b) Divorces obtained otherwise than by means of proceedings

8.119 Such divorces can be recognised if each party is domiciled in the country where the divorce is obtained at the date on which it is obtained (or one party is domiciled there and the divorce is recognised by the law of the other party's domicile).[267] As there are no proceedings to be commenced, the issue here is simpler: where is the divorce 'obtained'?

8.120 There is little direct authority on the point but it would appear that most bare talaks are obtained where they are pronounced;[268] any further steps, such as sending notice to the wife, are not an integral part of the divorce. Accordingly, such divorces can be obtained only in the country where the talak is pronounced and cannot be 'transnational'. However, it is arguable that the necessary steps for obtaining a khula could straddle more than one country. A khula would appear to be obtained where the husband accepts the wife's divorce proposal and utters the word 'khul'.[269] So, if a wife in Iraq e-mails her husband in Iran asking for a divorce and he accepts the proposal and utters the words there, the divorce would appear to have been obtained in Iran and if both parties are domiciled in Iran or one of them is domiciled there and the divorce is recognised by the other party's domiciliary law, the divorce is entitled to recognition in England.

8.121 Given the present denial of recognition to extra-judicial transnational divorces obtained by proceedings, it is odd—and little more than a quirk of statutory interpretation—that such 'bare' transnational divorces should be entitled to recognition.

(C) Refusal of recognition

8.122 The grounds on which judgments from non-Member States and Denmark, and pre-2001 judgments, may be refused recognition are discretionary rather than mandatory and are contained in the Family Law Act 1986.

(i) Marriage void or previously annulled or dissolved

8.123 Under section 51(1) and (2) of the Family Law Act 1986, the court may refuse to recognise a British Isles or overseas divorce or legal separation if, at the time it was obtained, the marriage had already been annulled or dissolved by the English court, or by another court whose decree is recognised, or entitled to recognition, in England, or if

---

[266] *Berkovits v Grinberg* [1995] Fam 142 at 159, citing evidence from the expert witness.
[267] Family Law Act 1986, s 46(2) and s 46(3)(b).
[268] *R v Registrar General of Births, Deaths and Marriages, ex p Minhas* [1977] QB 1 at 5–6; *Sulaiman v Juffali* [2002] 1 FLR 479.
[269] Abdur Rahman I Doi, *Shariah: The Islamic Law* (1984) p 192.

the marriage was a nullity in the eyes of English conflict of laws rules even without any such decree. Obviously, a divorce cannot effectively dissolve a marriage which is void or has already been annulled or dissolved.

(ii) Divorce obtained contrary to natural justice

8.124 This ground for refusal of recognition applies only to overseas divorces and legal separations obtained by means of proceedings.

(a) Reasonable steps for giving notice

8.125 Section 51(3)(a)(i) of the Family Law Act 1986 deals with the failure to afford a party to the marriage a proper opportunity to contest the proceedings. In the case of a divorce or legal separation obtained by proceedings, recognition may be refused if it was obtained:

> without such steps having been taken for giving notice of the proceedings to a party to the marriage as, having regard to the nature of the proceedings and all the circumstances, should reasonably have been taken.

8.126 There is no requirement that a party should actually have received notice. Sometimes the whereabouts of the respondent will be unknown to the petitioner and some form of non-personal service, such as publication in a newspaper, may then be allowed. Inevitably, there are cases where a spouse is divorced without knowing of the proceedings. However, the court may refuse recognition if, in its view, such steps for giving notice have not been taken as reasonably should have been taken in the circumstances. This ground for refusing recognition has been narrowly confined: there must be a 'fundamental' breach of natural justice.[270] Further, the mere fact that this provision has not been complied with is not determinative of the issue; it simply generates a discretion on the part of the English court as to whether or not to recognise the foreign divorce.

8.127 In *Sabbagh v Sabbagh*[271] a wife in England who received notice of her husband's initial unsuccessful application for a decree of separation in Brazil received no notice of his (successful) appeal, which, in accordance with Brazilian law, was only published in the official gazette in Brazil—a publication 'not normally circulated in Hendon',[272] where she lived. It was held that, despite the Brazilian procedures having been properly complied with, reasonable steps to give notice had not been taken. However, the court refused to exercise its discretion to refuse recognition to the decree because, in all the circumstances, she had not been prejudiced as she had already made a decision not to take part in the proceedings. In *D v D*[273] the husband, a Ghanaian national, left his wife in England and went to Ghana where he obtained a divorce from the Customary Arbitration Tribunal without informing his wife. The wife's mother was the defendant in the proceedings, which can be permissible under Ghanaian law as the proper parties to the proceedings are the families themselves and not the married couple. However, it was held that the court had to apply the English concept of

---

[270] *B v B (Divorce: Northern Cyprus)* [2000] 2 FLR 707.
[271] [1985] FLR 29. [272] At 32. [273] [1994] 1 FLR 38.

reasonableness, having regard to the nature of the Ghanaian proceedings.[274] On this basis,[275] especially as the mother had objected to the lack of notice to her daughter, the court decided that reasonable steps for notifying the wife had not been taken.

(b) Opportunity to take part

8.128 Section 51(3)(a)(ii) of the Family Law Act 1986 provides that a divorce or legal separation obtained by proceedings may be denied recognition if it was obtained:

> without a party to the marriage having been given (for any reason other than lack of notice) such opportunity to take part in the proceedings as, having regard to those matters, he should reasonably have been given.

8.129 An example of a case falling within this provision is *Joyce v Joyce*.[276] A wife in England had been given notice of proceedings in Quebec, but despite letters by her English solicitors to the registrar of the court, the husband's lawyers, the Quebec Law Society, and the legal aid authorities there, all stating that she wished to contest the proceedings, the case continued without her being represented, and a decree was granted to the husband in default. It was held that the wife had not been given such opportunity to take part in the proceedings as she should reasonably have been given.[277] In *A v L*[278] the wife, who had notice of proceedings in Egypt, obtained a *Hemain* injunction restraining the husband from continuing those proceedings. When he resumed the proceedings (without informing her) it was held that it was incumbent upon him to give her notice but the point was left open as to whether section 51(3)(a)(i) was satisfied. However, in the circumstances, it was clear that she had been deprived of an opportunity to take part in the proceedings.[279]

8.130 What is the position of a spouse in England who receives adequate notice of foreign divorce proceedings but cannot afford to travel to the foreign country to defend the action? In *Mamdani v Mamdani*[280] it was held that an inability to afford to go to the foreign country to defend proceedings and a lack of legal aid available there were relevant considerations in determining whether a spouse had been given a reasonable opportunity of taking part in the proceedings. Even more weight is attached to this point if the lack of finances is attributable to the other spouse's failure to make maintenance payments.[281] However, in *Sabbagh v Sabbagh*[282] it was concluded that an impecunious wife had not been denied an opportunity to take part in the proceedings because her physical presence was not required and she had made no attempt to apply for legal aid or seek financial assistance from her family.

8.131 In *Liaw v Lee* it was suggested that section 51(3)(a) should be informed by the judicial interpretation of article 22(b) of Brussels II *bis*: '[i]t would be bizarre if totally different

---

[274] See also *Duhur-Johnson v Duhur-Johnson (Attorney General Intervening)* [2005] 2 FLR 1042.
[275] It was also held that the divorce was not effective under Ghanaian law. See para 8.91.
[276] [1979] Fam 93.
[277] See also, to similar effect, *Newmarch v Newmarch* [1978] Fam 79.
[278] [2010] 2 FLR 1418.   [279] At [78].   [280] [1984] FLR 699.
[281] *Joyce v Joyce* [1979] Fam 93.   [282] [1985] FLR 29.

rules applied to an application seeking non-recognition of a divorce granted in, say, Cyprus to one granted in Malaysia'.[283]

(iii) Public policy

8.132   Under section 51(3)(c) of the Family Law Act 1986, recognition of a divorce or legal separation, whether or not obtained by means of proceedings, may be refused if recognition 'would be manifestly contrary to public policy'. Public policy is always to be used sparingly in the conflict of laws and the word 'manifestly' emphasises that this is 'a very high hurdle to clear'.[284]

8.133   There is no closed or definitive list of the kinds of cases which can offend public policy.[285] At common law it was settled that fraud in the foreign court as to the merits would not bar recognition,[286] but fraud as to the jurisdiction of the foreign court would result in recognition being refused.[287] Under the Act it would seem that fraud can be a ground for a refusal of recognition only if one party deceived the other and the foreign court.[288] In *Kendall v Kendall*[289] the husband fraudulently procured the commencement of proceedings in Bolivia purportedly by the wife, but without her knowledge, by obtaining her signature on a document which he told her was to enable her to take the children out of Bolivia, but in fact was a power of attorney in favour of Bolivian lawyers to start divorce proceedings on her behalf. A divorce was then granted, purportedly to the wife, by the Bolivian court on the basis of false evidence by witnesses that they had seen the husband assault the wife. Not surprisingly, the English court held that it would be manifestly contrary to public policy to recognise the divorce. Here the fraud was more fundamental than fraud as to the merits or as to the court's jurisdiction. The very proceedings themselves were a fraud on the wife and the Bolivian court. In *A v L*[290] it was stated (obiter) that if a husband obtained a judgment (confirming a bare talak) by dishonestly asserting that he had earlier pronounced the talak, recognition would be refused on public policy grounds.

8.134   In *Eroglu v Eroglu*[291] the husband and wife, acting together, deceived a Turkish court into granting them a divorce on grounds of extreme incompatibility. The parties continued to live together for the next 12 years during which time children were born. The reason for this 'divorce of convenience' was that, under the then Turkish law, university graduates were entitled to privileged and abbreviated national service provided they were not married to a foreign national; the wife was British. It was held that recognition

---

[283] *Liaw v Lee (Non-Recognition of Divorce)* [2015] [2016] 1 FLR 533 at [8].
[284] *Kellman v Kellman* [2000] 1 FLR 785 at 798.
[285] In *B v B (Divorce: Northern Cyprus)* [2000] 2 FLR 707 a divorce obtained in the Turkish Republic of Northern Cyprus was refused recognition on this ground because that country had never been recognised by the United Kingdom. However, this approach was not followed in *Emin v Yeldag* [2002] 1 FLR 956, where such a divorce was recognised.
[286] *Bater v Bater* [1906] P 209.   [287] *Middleton v Middleton* [1967] P 62.
[288] *Eroglu v Eroglu* [1994] 2 FLR 287 at 289.   [289] [1977] Fam 208.
[290] [2010] 2 FLR 1418.   [291] [1994] 2 FLR 287.

of this divorce was not manifestly contrary to public policy: while the Turkish court might have been deceived, neither of the parties was deceived; the motive for obtaining a divorce was 'generally irrelevant' and the discretion to refuse recognition was to be 'exercised sparingly'.[292] Thorpe J concluded that:

> [t]hose who play games with divorce decrees expose themselves to a variety of risks and, having enjoyed the desired benefits during cohabitation, cannot reorder their status now that they have fallen out.[293]

8.135 Another situation in which recognition of a divorce may be refused is if the institution of the proceedings was the result of duress. In the common law case of *Re Meyer*[294] the parties were Germans, the husband, but not the wife, being Jewish. In 1938, when Jews were being persecuted in Germany, the husband escaped to England. The wife then divorced him in the German court, as arranged between them before he left. The necessity for the divorce was that if she remained married to a Jew, she herself would be in danger, would lose her job and her flat, and it would be difficult for her and their child to survive. After the war, the wife joined the husband in England, where they regarded themselves as still husband and wife. On the husband's death, the wife's right to a German pension as the widow of a person who had been persecuted by the Nazis depended on whether, in the view of the English court, she was still married to her husband at his death. The court granted a declaration that the German divorce was not recognised in England because it had been obtained under duress. Under the Act the recognition of a divorce obtained in such circumstances would be regarded as manifestly contrary to public policy.

8.136 In *Golubovich v Golubovich*[295] it was again emphasised that it would only be in 'truly exceptional' cases that recognition would be denied on public policy grounds. In this case there had been a *Hemain* injunction restraining the husband from pursuing divorce proceedings in Russia. In defiance of this injunction (and, at one stage, acting fraudulently) the husband obtained a Russian divorce. However, as the Russian court had been informed of the injunction, it was held that denying recognition would be 'shooting the wrong target. The proper target was not the Russian [court] but the husband.'[296] The Russian divorce was recognised. The behaviour of the husband could be taken into account in a subsequent financial provision hearing under Part III of the Matrimonial and Family Proceedings Act 1984. Thorpe LJ gave an example of when it might be appropriate to deny recognition on public policy grounds:

> I would posit a case in which the court held primary jurisdiction established by a fully reasoned judgment delivered on an application for a forum conveniens stay. If the other jurisdiction seized, then, with full knowledge of the London judgment, defiantly dissolved the marriage of a wife who could not establish jurisdiction for a Part III claim that would be manifestly offensive.[297]

---

[292] At 289.   [293] At 290.   [294] [1971] P 298.
[295] [2010] 3 WLR 1607.   [296] At [59].   [297] At [81].

(iv) Discretion

8.137 Even if a foreign divorce has been obtained without reasonable steps having been taken to give a party notice of the proceedings, or without a party having been given a reasonable opportunity to take part, recognition need not necessarily be refused. The court has a discretion, for the Family Law Act 1986 provides that recognition 'may be refused'.[298]

8.138 It used to be thought that, if recognition was contrary to public policy, there would be a similar discretion.[299] However, this approach was disapproved in *Golubovich v Golubovich* where it was stated that if recognition would be manifestly contrary to public policy, refusal of recognition *must* follow. Unlike the denial of natural justice grounds, there is no 'second stage discretionary' power whether or not to refuse recognition.[300] In reality, it makes little difference which approach is adopted; the decision that recognition of a divorce would be manifestly contrary to public policy turns on a range of contextual factors which have to be evaluated by the court.

8.139 In exercising its 'wide judicial discretion',[301] the court has regard to what is just as between the spouses, and to the interests of any children of the marriage.[302] The decree can nevertheless be recognised if the interests of the spouse denied notice are met by other means.[303] The decision has often turned on the question of financial provision, because usually the objective of a party who contests divorce proceedings is to secure a satisfactory financial and property settlement rather than to keep the marriage going. In *Newmarch v Newmarch*[304] the wife's solicitors in England instructed solicitors in New South Wales to file an answer to the husband's case in proceedings which he had instituted there. The Australian solicitors failed to do so, and the divorce was granted in default. Although the English court held that the wife had not been given a reasonable opportunity to take part in the proceedings, it nevertheless exercised its discretion to recognise the divorce. The wife's object in wishing to contest the divorce had been to obtain adequate maintenance from her husband. As the English court would be in a position to order such maintenance[305] even if the Australian divorce was recognised, no one's interests would be served by refusing recognition.

8.140 On the other hand, in *Joyce v Joyce*,[306] where the wife had not been given the opportunity to take part in the Quebec proceedings, the court exercised its discretion to refuse recognition, because, as the law then stood, the wife would otherwise be deprived of

---

[298] S 51(3).
[299] *Newmarch v Newmarch* [1978] Fam 79 at 97; *H v H (Validity of Japanese Divorce)* [2007] 1 FLR 1318; Cheshire, North and Fawcett, *Private International Law* (14th edn, 2008) p 1020.
[300] [2010] 3 WLR 1607 at [69].
[301] *Duhur-Johnson v Duhur-Johnson* [2005] 2 FLR 1042 at 1052.
[302] The English court, in exercising its discretion, may take events subsequent to the obtainment of the overseas divorce into account: see *H v H (Validity of Japanese Divorce)* [2007] 1 FLR 1318; *NP v KRP (Recognition of Foreign Divorce)* [2014] 2 FLR 1.
[303] *Duhur-Johnson v Duhur-Johnson* [2005] 2 FLR 1042 at 1052.   [304] [1978] Fam 79.
[305] An English interim maintenance order which could be converted to a substantive maintenance order had been obtained by the wife prior to the Australian divorce.
[306] [1979] Fam 93.

the possibility of financial and property relief in the English court. Since then, however, Part III of the Matrimonial and Family Proceedings Act 1984 enables the court to make financial orders even after the recognition of a foreign divorce obtained by proceedings. As a result, the discretion to refuse recognition, when it exists, is being less frequently used.[307]

8.141 While pragmatic considerations and the continuing availability of a jurisdiction to grant financial relief may encourage the English courts to exercise their discretion in favour of recognising overseas divorces, recognition is still likely to be refused where there has been a 'gross' injustice in the foreign court, and where the recognition of the divorce would 'reward dishonesty and sharp practice'.[308] The English courts, in exercising their discretion, may be concerned to avoid sending out 'a signal that such conduct . . . is tolerable'.[309] Thus where parallel foreign proceedings are deliberately concealed from the English courts and from the other spouse, and where the English proceedings are concealed from the foreign court, the English court is likely to exercise its discretion in favour of non-recognition.[310]

(v) Extra-judicial divorces

8.142 Most of the above grounds for refusing recognition of foreign divorces apply to extra-judicial divorces that are obtained by proceedings. However, the application of these rules is somewhat different.

(a) Divorces obtained contrary to natural justice

8.143 Section 51(3)(a)(i) (notice) and section 51(3)(a)(ii) (opportunity to take part) of the Family Law Act 1986 apply only to divorces and legal separations obtained by means of proceedings. With regard to extra-judicial divorces obtained by proceedings, such as a talak obtained under the Pakistan Ordinance, it must be recalled that the question is to be judged 'having regard to the nature of the proceedings and all the circumstances'. Accordingly, it seems unlikely that recognition would be refused if the requirements of the Pakistan Ordinance were complied with. Indeed, in *D v D* it was said that it was 'possible . . . to envisage circumstances, albeit they would be highly unusual, in which it would be reasonable to take no steps'.[311] In *El Fadl v El Fadl*[312] it was held that whether advance notice of a talak should reasonably be given depended on the circumstances. In the context of a Lebanese talak,[313] it was held that, despite being a 'wrong' to the wife, the absence of notice ought not to lead to refusal of recognition for several reasons. First, advance notice could avail the wife nothing. Secondly, although not informed at the time of the talak, the wife had known of the divorce for many years. Thirdly, and most interestingly, as the divorce was obtained in the country

---

[307] In *Golubovich v Golubovich* [2010] 3 WLR 1607 at [53] it was stated that Part III has had 'a fundamental impact on the flow of cases' where refusal of recognition has been sought.
[308] *Liaw v Lee (Non-Recognition of Divorce)* [2016] 1 FLR 533 at [32].   [309] Ibid.
[310] *Liaw v Lee (Non-Recognition of Divorce)* [2016] 1 FLR 533; also *Ivleva (formerly Yates) v Yates* [2014] 2 FLR 1126; *Olafisoye v Olafisoye (No 2) (Recognition)* [2011] 2 FLR 564.
[311] [1994] 1 FLR 38 at 52.   [312] [2000] 1 FLR 175.   [313] See para 8.105.

where both spouses were domiciled, it was 'accomplished in the forum which was the natural forum for both parties. There was no forum shopping.'[314] This is a somewhat surprising basis for the decision. The 1986 Act has specified that for divorces obtained by proceedings, the courts of the habitual residence, domicile, or nationality of either party are a sufficiently appropriate forum to justify recognition. There is no warrant for elevating domicile (or the domicile of both parties) to a privileged category in interpreting the provisions of the Act. In *H v H (Talaq Divorce)*[315] a Pakistan divorce in which the wife was not given notice or an opportunity to participate was recognised even though the wife was domiciled in England.

8.144 The statutory provisions relating to natural justice do not apply to divorces obtained otherwise than by means of proceedings. It is suggested that in such cases recognition could not be refused on the grounds that no notice was given to the wife of the husband's intention to divorce her or that she was denied a reasonable opportunity to be involved in the process. The nature of the talak is that it is a purely unilateral act.

(b) Public policy

8.145 It follows from the fact that the law provides for the recognition of extra-judicial divorces that such recognition is not necessarily contrary to public policy. In *El Fadl v El Fadl*[316] the absence of notice to a wife was described as offending English sensibilities, but the doctrine of public policy was to be used sparingly and accordingly 'comity between nations and belief systems requires ... that our courts should accept the conscientiously held but very different standards of another where they are applied to those who are domiciled in it'.[317]

8.146 However, while this might be the approach in relation to people domiciled in the country where the divorce was obtained and where there is 'no evidence of forum shopping',[318] it has been stated that recognition of such a divorce, when both parties are English domiciliaries, is contrary to public policy.[319] Furthermore, since the power of the English court to grant financial relief is limited to cases where the foreign divorce was obtained by proceedings,[320] the doctrine of public policy may play a greater role in cases where the divorce was obtained otherwise than by means of proceedings (for example, where the recognition of a bare talak would seriously prejudice the financial interests of a spouse with relatively close links to England).

(c) No official document for divorces obtained otherwise than by means of proceedings

8.147 With regard to divorces not obtained by means of proceedings, the court may refuse to recognise a divorce if there is no official document certifying that the divorce is

---

[314] [2000] 1 FLR 175 at 189.   [315] [2008] 2 FLR 857.   [316] [2000] 1 FLR 175.
[317] At 190.   [318] At 191.
[319] *Chaudhary v Chaudhary* [1985] Fam 19. See para 8.108.
[320] It seems to be an error that the power is limited to divorces obtained by proceedings. For the probable reason, see Poulter, 'Recognition of Foreign Divorces—The New Law' (1987) 84 Law Soc Gaz 253, 255.

effective under the law of the country in which it was obtained, or, where one of the parties was domiciled in another country when it was obtained, no official document certifying that it is valid under the law of that country.[321] An official document means one issued by a person or body appointed or recognised for the purpose under the foreign law. As the power to refuse recognition if there is no official document is discretionary, the court could still recognise the divorce if satisfied by expert evidence of its efficacy under the foreign law.[322]

B Dissolutions of same-sex marriages and civil partnerships

8.148 The recognition provisions of the Family Law Act 1986 would appear to apply to same-sex marriages.[323] The Civil Partnership Act 2004 makes equivalent provision for the recognition of dissolutions[324] from non-Member States, emulating the conditions laid down in the Family Law Act 1986.[325] While it is generally assumed that the recognition rules laid down in the Brussels II *bis* Regulation do not apply to same-sex spouses and civil partners, secondary legislation has introduced similar recognition schemes for same-sex divorces and civil partnership dissolutions granted in other EU Member States.[326] The policy of replicating the pre-existing law applicable to opposite-sex marriage has, however, some odd results. For example, the Civil Partnership Act 2004 makes provision for recognition of civil partnership dissolutions obtained other than by proceedings (a prospect described as 'fanciful'[327]). In a departure from the opposite-sex marriage rules, however, secondary legislation also made provision for the recognition of registered partnership dissolutions granted in a country in which neither partner was habitually resident or domiciled and of which neither was a national, where the party seeking the decree was either habitually resident in or domiciled in a country whose law does not recognise same-sex relationships and does not provide for their dissolution.[328] Like the supplementary forum necessitatis rule of jurisdiction,[329] this additional recognition rule acknowledges that, while heterosexual marriage is a global institution, many legal systems provide no protection for same-sex relationships.

---

[321] S 51(3)(b) and (4). [322] *Wicken v Wicken* [1999] Fam 224.
[323] The Marriage (Same Sex Couples) Act 2013, sch 3(1), para 1 provides for the interpretation of legislation referring to marriage as including the marriages of same-sex couples. See also Briggs, *Private International Law in English Courts* (2014) p 923.
[324] While the discussion focuses on recognition of foreign dissolutions, the same rules apply to foreign annulments and legal separations.
[325] Ss 233–238 of the Civil Partnership Act 2004.
[326] See Marriage (Same Sex Couples) (Jurisdiction and Recognition of Judgments) Regulations 2014, SI 2014/543; Civil Partnership (Jurisdiction and Recognition of Judgments) Regulations 2005, SI 2005/3334. The defences to recognition mirror those laid down in the Family Law Act 1986 rather than those contained in art 22 of Brussels II *bis*.
[327] Dicey, Morris and Collins, *The Conflict of Laws* (15th edn, 2012) p 1049.
[328] Civil Partnership (Supplementary Provisions Relating to the Recognition of Overseas Dissolutions, Annulments or Legal Separations) (England and Wales and Northern Ireland) Regulations 2005, SI 2005/3104, reg 3.
[329] See para 8.55.

C Nullity decrees

1. Grounds of recognition

8.149 Under the common law the grounds for recognition of foreign nullity decrees were, for the most part, based on the theory of equivalence: a foreign decree should be recognised if the English court in equivalent circumstances would itself have assumed jurisdiction. In addition, there was a further basis of recognition: if either party had a real and substantial connection with the country in question.[330]

8.150 These common law grounds for recognition were unaffected by the Recognition of Divorces and Legal Separations Act 1971. As it was undesirable and unjustifiable to have different rules for recognition of divorces and judicial separations, on the one hand, and recognition of nullity decrees, on the other, the Family Law Act 1986 abolished the common law rules on recognition of nullity decrees and applied the same rules to recognition of all three types of decree. Similarly, the Brussels II *bis* Regulation draws no distinction between the various types of decree.

8.151 Accordingly, the grounds for the recognition of foreign nullity decrees are exactly the same as those for the recognition of divorces, even to the extent of the distinction between those obtained by means of proceedings and those not so obtained. However, recognition of nullity decrees can give rise to issues somewhat different from recognition of divorces.

2. The effect of recognition

8.152 The notion of recognising a foreign nullity decree, though certainly accepted by the law, is not without difficulties. If a foreign court annuls a marriage on the ground that it is void (under whatever is the governing law according to the foreign court's conflicts rules), it may be that the marriage is also void under English conflict of laws rules. Then no difficulty arises from recognising the decree, and duplication of proceedings in England is avoided. However, it may be that the marriage is valid under English conflict of laws rules. It is well established that even in such a case the foreign decree can be recognised. In *Merker v Merker*[331] a marriage was annulled by a decree of the German court on the ground that the requisite formalities under German conflict of laws rules had not been complied with. The decree was recognised, even though the marriage was formally valid under English conflicts rules. Such recognition means that, in effect, the foreign country's choice of law rules have superseded the English ones.

8.153 The reason for recognising the foreign decree in such a case is no doubt to ensure uniformity of status. If the court of a country having a reasonable connection with one of the parties has decreed that the marriage is invalid, the English court should not create a limping marriage by insisting that it is valid. That is no doubt right, so far as the future is concerned. If, however, the foreign court by its nullity decree has pronounced

---

[330] See, generally, Clarkson, 'Recognition of Foreign Nullity Decrees in Singapore' (1987) 8 Sing LR 166.
[331] [1963] P 283.

a marriage void ab initio, then the effect of recognising it is to render the marriage void ab initio in England. In *Salvesen (or von Lorang) v Austrian Property Administrator*[332] the effect of recognising a German decree declaring a marriage void ab initio, made 27 years after the marriage, was that the wife had not after all become an Austrian national by virtue of the marriage. If the marriage which is declared void ab initio by the foreign decree is valid by English conflicts rules, its recognition can retrospectively nullify rights which have hitherto existed in English eyes.[333]

8.154 Suppose that, while still married to one wife, a man marries another woman, and then dies intestate domiciled in England. His widow is entitled to succeed to his estate. If the first marriage is valid under English conflicts rules, it follows that the second marriage is void for bigamy. The first wife is, therefore, entitled to succeed, and it makes no difference that by the conflicts rules of some other country the first marriage is void, and the second valid. Is it right that the first wife should be disinherited by the husband's obtaining, after his second marriage, a decree in a foreign country declaring that, according to its conflicts rules, his first marriage was void ab initio?

8.155 Such a result would be avoided if the rule were adopted that the recognition of foreign nullity decrees does not operate retrospectively, and the question of the validity of the marriage prior to the granting of the decree is to be decided by the English court according to the English conflict of laws.[334] However, given the relatively clear provisions of the Brussels II *bis* Regulation and the Family Law Act 1986, it is extremely doubtful whether such an approach is permissible. One possible solution could be to declare the foreign annulment contrary to public policy.[335] However, this would mean denying recognition to the nullity decree completely, rather than simply denying its retrospective operation.

3. Refusal of recognition

8.156 The grounds for refusing recognition to a nullity decree which is prima facie entitled to recognition are the same as for a divorce decree, though the different nature of the decree may lead to differences in their operation.

(A) Irreconcilable with a previous decision

8.157 A British Isles or overseas annulment may be refused recognition in England if it was granted at a time when it was irreconcilable with a decision on the subsistence or validity of the marriage of the parties previously given by a court in England, or by a court elsewhere and recognised in England.[336] So, if it is contended in English nullity proceedings that a marriage is invalid on a particular ground, but the marriage is held

---

[332] [1927] AC 641.
[333] But in *Salvesen (or von Lorang)* itself the retrospective effect of the German annulment secured for the wife a benefit which she wanted (although it seems that the marriage was in any event void under English conflicts rules).
[334] Though findings of fact in the foreign court should perhaps be conclusive in the English court on the basis of issue estoppel.
[335] See paras 8.76–8.77 and 8.132–8.136.
[336] Brussels II *bis* Regulation, art 22(c),(d); Family Law Act 1986, s 51(1).

valid, then a subsequent foreign annulment may be refused recognition if granted on that ground. The mere fact that the marriage was valid according to English conflict of laws rules does not preclude recognition, but if the English court has actually held it to be valid, recognition may be refused.

8.158 While this ground of refusal is mandatory under the Brussels II *bis* Regulation, it is discretionary under the Family Law Act 1986. It is suggested that the discretion to refuse recognition should be exercised if the foreign decree declares void ab initio a marriage which is valid by English conflicts rules and the consequent retrospective invalidation of the marriage would alter rights or entitlements which would exist on the basis of the marriage being valid. An example is *Vervaeke v Smith*[337] in which the House of Lords held, before the enactment of the 1986 Act, that this ground of refusal of recognition existed at common law as an aspect of estoppel per rem judicatam.

8.159 The petitioner, a Belgian national, had married her first husband in England. It was a marriage of convenience, for it was never the parties' intention to live together as husband and wife. The husband was paid a sum of money and emigrated immediately after the marriage. The object was solely for the petitioner to obtain UK citizenship by virtue of the marriage, so that she could continue her trade as a prostitute in England. Some years later, this first marriage not having been dissolved, the petitioner married a second husband who died intestate on his wedding night. Wishing to succeed to his estate as his widow, she brought proceedings in the English court for an annulment of her first marriage on various grounds, one being lack of consent. The English court, however, dismissed the petition, holding the marriage valid. Then, after she had been habitually resident in Belgium for over a year, she obtained a decree in the Belgian court declaring the marriage void for lack of consent. The ground for the annulment was that under Belgian law, which was applicable under the Belgian conflicts rules, a marriage in which the parties never intend to cohabit is void ab initio for lack of consent. Under English law, which had been applicable according to English conflicts rules in the earlier English proceedings, such a marriage of convenience is valid.[338] When the petitioner sought a declaration in the English courts that the Belgian decree should be recognised (with the consequence that, the second marriage being valid, she could succeed to her second husband's estate), recognition was refused. One of the grounds was that, under the doctrine of res judicata, recognition would be incompatible with the prior English decision. The same result would be reached under the 1986 Act.

(B) Contrary to natural justice

8.160 Under the Brussels II *bis* Regulation the same provision relating to inadequate service applies as for divorce decrees.[339] Under the Family Law Act 1986 the court has the

---

[337] [1983] 1 AC 145.

[338] As the parties had married in England and the first husband was an English domiciliary, the wife's incapacity under Belgian law could be disregarded under *Sottomayor v De Barros (No 2)* (1879) 5 PD 94. See para 7.57.

[339] Art 22(b).

same discretion to refuse recognition if the decree was obtained without reasonable steps having been taken to notify the respondent of the proceedings, or without his being given reasonable opportunity to take part in them, as in the case of a foreign divorce.[340]

(C) Public policy

8.161 Recognition may be refused if it would be manifestly contrary to public policy.[341] No doubt fraud or duress would lead to refusal to the same extent as with a divorce. Under the Brussels II *bis* Regulation recognition may not be refused to an annulment because the law of the state in which recognition is sought would not allow an annulment on the same facts.[342] However, under the Family Law Act 1986 public policy may lead to a refusal to recognise a nullity decree because the foreign rule by which the marriage is invalid is objectionable. Although recognition will not normally be refused to a divorce merely because the ground of divorce is objectionable (for example, the husband's unilateral repudiation of his wife by talak), a different approach to nullity decrees may be justified by the fact that the recognition of a foreign nullity decree may have the effect of retrospectively invalidating a marriage which is valid according to English choice of law rules.

8.162 In *Gray v Formosa*[343] the husband, who was a Roman Catholic domiciled in Malta, married a woman domiciled in England in an English register office. Subsequently, the husband deserted his wife and children, leaving them without support in England, and returned to Malta. There he obtained a nullity decree, granted on the ground that, under Maltese law, a Roman Catholic could not validly marry except by a religious ceremony. By Maltese conflicts rules this incapacity was applicable even to a marriage celebrated in England. The Court of Appeal refused to recognise the Maltese decree on the ground that to do so would be contrary to substantial justice. The marriage was valid by English conflicts rules, under which the question whether a civil as opposed to a religious ceremony is sufficient is regarded as one of form, governed by the lex loci celebrationis. Recognition was not refused merely because the marriage was valid under English conflicts rules, but because it was:

> an intolerable injustice that a system of law should seek to impose extraterritorially, as the condition of the validity of a marriage, that it should take place according to the tenets of a particular faith.[344]

8.163 In *Gray v Formosa* it was the foreign country's conflicts rule, that the Maltese requirement of a church marriage applied to a marriage celebrated in England, which was thought objectionable. In *Vervaeke v Smith*[345] a second reason for refusing recognition to the Belgian decree was that recognition would be contrary to public policy. Here

---

[340] Family Law Act 1986, s 51(3)(a).
[341] Brussels II *bis* Regulation, art 22(a); Family Law Act 1986, s 51(3)(c).
[342] Art 25. [343] [1963] P 259.
[344] Simon P in *Lepre v Lepre* [1965] P 52 at 64, explaining the basis of the decision in *Gray v Formosa* [1963] P 259.
[345] [1983] 1 AC 145.

it was not the Belgian conflicts rule that was the obstacle, but the Belgian domestic rule by which a marriage under which the parties never intend to cohabit is void. By English law, on the contrary, such a marriage is valid. Lord Hailsham held that, as the English rule is one of public policy, it would be contrary to public policy to recognise the Belgian decree declaring void such a marriage which was celebrated in, and had other connections with, England. Bearing in mind the very narrow scope of the doctrine of public policy in the English conflict of laws, this conclusion seems unwarranted. Given that, on the facts of the case, the doctrine of res judicata dictated that the Belgian decree should be denied recognition,[346] there was no need for the doctrine of public policy to have been invoked.

(D) Decree invalid under the foreign law

8.164 At common law, if a foreign nullity decree was invalid under the law of the foreign country in which it was obtained, it would nevertheless be entitled to recognition in England if the reason for the invalidity was a mere procedural defect,[347] but not if the reason was that the court was not competent to grant a nullity decree.[348] Under the Family Law Act 1986, however, the decree can be recognised only if it is effective under the law of the country in which it was obtained.[349] It makes no difference what the basis of the invalidity is under the foreign law.

IV Financial provision

A Jurisdiction of the English court

8.165 English courts are able to make orders for financial provision in three situations. First, such an order can be made ancillary to the granting of a divorce, separation, or annulment. Secondly, financial provision may be ordered quite independently of other matrimonial proceedings in situations where the parties are still married but one spouse is failing to provide reasonable maintenance to the other spouse and/or children of the family. Thirdly, when recognising a foreign divorce, legal separation, or annulment, the English court may itself grant financial provision to either party.

8.166 The Brussels II *bis* Regulation has no direct application here as it does not apply to maintenance obligations[350] or the 'property consequences of the marriage or any other ancillary measures'.[351] 'Matters relating to maintenance' were previously, for respondents domiciled in a Member State, governed by article 5(2) of the Brussels I Regulation.[352] Accordingly, as with civil and commercial claims, the jurisdictional rules of the English court were a blend of the English traditional rules and the Brussels

---

[346] See para 8.159.   [347] *Merker v Merker* [1963] P 283.
[348] *Papadopoulos v Papadopoulos* [1930] P 55.
[349] Family Law Act 1986, s 46(1)(a), (2)(a).   [350] Art 1(3)(e).   [351] Recital (8).
[352] Regulation (EC) No 44/2001, OJ 2001 L12/1. Art 1(2)(e) of the Brussels I Recast provides that it does not apply to maintenance obligations.

I Regulation. These rules were replaced by Regulation (EC) No 4/2009 of 18 December 2008 on jurisdiction, applicable law, recognition and enforcement of decisions and cooperation in matters relating to maintenance obligations[353] (referred to hereafter as the 'Maintenance Regulation') which came into force on 18 June 2011.

1. The Maintenance Regulation

8.167 Under the pre-existing law, article 5(2) of the Brussels I Regulation applied only if the person being sued was domiciled in a Member State. In other cases the jurisdiction of the English court was determined by its traditional rules.[354] The Maintenance Regulation replaced the maintenance provisions of the Brussels I Regulation[355] and applies in all cases in 'matters relating to maintenance obligations'.[356] Article 10 excludes the application of the traditional rules by providing: 'Where a court of a Member State is seised of a case over which it has no jurisdiction under this Regulation it shall declare of its own motion that it has no jurisdiction.' This rule is reinforced by recital (15) which states that the 'circumstance that the defendant is habitually resident in a third State should no longer entail the non-application of Community rules on jurisdiction, and there should no longer be any referral to national law'.

8.168 Accordingly, the jurisdictional rules of the Maintenance Regulation apply to all three situations, mentioned above, when an English court is asked to make an order for financial provision by way of maintenance. The jurisdictional rules in the Maintenance Regulation will be outlined and then their implications in the above three situations are assessed.

8.169 Following the model of Brussels I, the Maintenance Regulation allows the parties to choose a court to settle any disputes or to submit to a court's jurisdiction, failing which there are general provisions allocating jurisdiction. Further, and unlike in Brussels I, there are provisions dealing with subsidiary jurisdiction and forum necessitatis.

(A) Choice of court

8.170 Article 4 provides that, in matters other than child maintenance,[357] the parties may agree that the court of a Member State shall have jurisdiction to settle any disputes between them. Allowing such a choice is designed to 'increase legal certainty, predictability and the autonomy of the parties'.[358] However, unlike under Brussels I, this freedom of choice is not unrestricted. The parties may choose only a court of a Member State with which either of them, or their marriage, has a specified connection. Under article 4(1) parties may choose either the courts of a Member State in which one of them is habitually resident or the courts of a Member State of which one of them is a national (or in which one of them is domiciled, in the case of the United Kingdom);[359] alternatively, spouses or former spouses may choose the court of a Member State which has

---

[353] OJ 2009 L7/1. The United Kingdom has not opted into the provisions on applicable law. See para 8.187.
[354] Art 4.   [355] Art 68(1); recital (44).
[356] Art 3. The meaning of 'maintenance obligations' is discussed at para 8.179.
[357] Art 4(3).   [358] Recital (19).
[359] Art 2(3) provides that the concept of 'domicile' shall replace that of 'nationality' in arts 3, 4 and 6 in those Member States which use domicile as a connecting factor in family matters.

jurisdiction to settle their dispute in matrimonial matters or in which the spouses last had a common habitual residence for a period of at least a year.[360] Such a jurisdiction agreement is exclusive in effect (unless the parties have agreed otherwise).[361] To be effective, the agreement must be in writing.[362]

(B) Appearance

8.171 Article 5 provides that a court of a Member State before which a defendant enters an appearance shall have jurisdiction. This rule does not apply, however, if the appearance was entered to contest jurisdiction. As article 5 follows the wording of article 26(1) of the Brussels I Recast, it is likely to be interpreted in the same way. Accordingly, an appearance in English proceedings is effective to confer jurisdiction on the English court even if the parties had agreed, prior to the dispute, that the courts of another Member State were to have jurisdiction.[363]

(C) General provisions

8.172 In the absence of a choice of court agreement or an appearance, article 3 allocates jurisdiction to the following courts:

(a) the court for the place where the defendant is habitually resident; or

(b) the court for the place where the creditor[364] is habitually resident; or

(c) the court which, according to its own law, has jurisdiction to entertain proceedings concerning the status of a person if the matter relating to maintenance is ancillary to those proceedings, unless that jurisdiction is based solely on the nationality [domicile for the United Kingdom] of one of the parties; or

(d) the court which, according to its own law, has jurisdiction to entertain proceedings concerning parental responsibility if the matter relating to maintenance is ancillary to those proceedings, unless that jurisdiction is based solely on the nationality [domicile for the United Kingdom] of one of the parties.

8.173 If a wife is seeking maintenance from her husband, she can choose to bring proceedings in the courts of either his country of habitual residence or her country of habitual residence. If she has commenced divorce etc proceedings against him, the court seised of that matter will normally[365] have jurisdiction in matters of spousal maintenance. Where, however, parental responsibility proceedings are pending in another Member State, only the court seised of the parental responsibility proceedings will have jurisdiction to determine matters of child maintenance.[366] Child maintenance is

---

[360] Art 4(1).   [361] Ibid.   [362] Art 4(2).
[363] Case 150/80 *Elefanten Schuh GmbH v Jacqmain* [1981] ECR 1671. See para 2.61.
[364] Art 2(1)(10): 'the term "creditor" shall mean any individual to whom maintenance is owed or is alleged to be owed'. As was observed in *M v W (Application After New Zealand Financial Agreement)* [2015] 1 FLR 465 at [39], while the term 'creditor' is generally used where a debt is already in existence, the Regulation would make little sense if the term were to be understood so narrowly. Coleridge J concluded that a 'potential creditor' was a 'maintenance creditor' for the purposes of the Regulation.
[365] The one exception to this rule is discussed at para 8.180.
[366] Case C-184/14 *A v B* [2015] 2 FLR 637.

not—according to the Court of Justice—a matter 'ancillary' to divorce in this context. This approach was justified on the basis that the court seised of parental responsibility proceedings has 'the best knowledge of the key elements for assessing' the claim.[367]

(D) Subsidiary jurisdiction

8.174 Where no court of a Member State[368] has jurisdiction pursuant to any of the above provisions the courts of the Member State of the common nationality (or the common domicile in the United Kingdom) of the parties shall have jurisdiction.[369] So, if a married couple both domiciled in England are working on expatriate contracts in Singapore and have lost their habitual residence in England, one of the spouses is still entitled to commence proceedings for maintenance in England.

(E) Forum necessitatis

8.175 In certain exceptional situations, the parties might be habitually resident in a non-Member State and not be able to obtain maintenance there. In order to prevent a denial of justice[370] in such situations, article 7 provides an exceptional basis of jurisdiction known as forum necessitatis. Where no court of a Member State has jurisdiction under any of the above provisions, the court of a Member State 'may, on an exceptional basis, hear the case if proceedings cannot reasonably be brought or conducted or would be impossible in a third State with which the dispute is closely connected'. Recital (16) gives examples of when this jurisdiction might be exercised: 'because of civil war, or when an applicant cannot reasonably be expected to initiate or conduct proceedings in that State'.

8.176 This jurisdictional basis is, however, restricted to cases where the dispute has 'a sufficient connection with the Member State of the court seised',[371] for example where one of the parties is a national of that Member State.[372] For example, if a British national[373] were living in Ruritania but, because of a civil war there, the Ruritanian courts were not operating, an English court would be able to exercise this exceptional jurisdiction.

(F) Lis pendens and related actions

8.177 The English court must stay ancillary or other maintenance proceedings if prior proceedings involving the same cause of action and between the same parties have been brought in the courts of another Member State (article 12) or may stay such proceedings if prior related proceedings are pending in another Member State (article 13). In *AA v BB*[374] the High Court emphasised that article 12 could come into play only where there were concurrent proceedings in existence in another Member State. Article 12

---

[367] At [44]. See the previous related judgment of the English High Court (taking a different view): *EA v AP* [2014] ILPr 17.
[368] Nor a court of a State Party to the Lugano Convention.
[369] Art 6.   [370] Recital (16).   [371] Art 7.   [372] Recital (16).
[373] Art 2(3) (replacing 'nationality' with 'domicile' in those Member States using domicile as a connecting factor in family matters) does not apply to art 7.
[374] [2015] 2 FLR 1251.

was considered to be inapplicable where earlier proceedings in another Member State had been discontinued or terminated by judgment.[375] Moylan J rejected the contention that article 12 fixed maintenance jurisdiction in the court first seised 'for all time' and to the exclusion of other Member States.[376] In his view, the Regulation 'clearly contemplates jurisdiction existing sequentially in different Member States'.[377] In *AA v BB* it was, however, accepted that where there were ongoing proceedings in Slovenia in relation to marital assets falling within the jurisdiction of the Slovenian court, and maintenance proceedings in England, the earlier Slovenian proceedings could be considered to be a 'related action' under article 13—in so far as both actions involved the wife seeking a share of the marital wealth.[378] In *N v N (Stay of Maintenance Proceedings)*[379] an earlier divorce action in Sweden was considered to be 'related' to a later standalone application for interim maintenance in England.

8.178 What is the position if the parties had entered into a choice of court agreement in favour of England, but proceedings have been commenced in another Member State? Does the article 12 lis pendens rule apply? Following the Court of Justice's decision in *Erich Gasser GmbH v Misat Srl*[380] (a commercial case decided under article 21 of the Brussels Convention), the English court will be required to stay proceedings until the court first seised has decided whether or not it has jurisdiction. Of course, if the court first seised declines jurisdiction (on the basis of the choice of court agreement), the English stay will be lifted. If, however, the court first seised decides that it has jurisdiction (for example, because it considers that the choice of court agreement is invalid), the English court must decline jurisdiction and is not entitled to allow the English proceedings to continue on the basis that it considers, contrary to the conclusion of the court first seised, that the parties are bound by the choice of court agreement.

(G) Meaning of 'maintenance'

8.179 The Court of Justice[381] has provided some guidance on the meaning of 'maintenance'. If periodical payments or payments of a lump sum or transfers of property are intended to ensure the support of a spouse, and the needs and resources of the spouses are taken into consideration, the claim will be classified as one relating to maintenance.[382] However, the Court of Justice has also indicated that orders 'solely concerned with dividing property between the spouses' would not constitute maintenance—and would be excluded from the remit of the Brussels I Recast[383] as concerning 'rights in property arising out of a matrimonial relationship'.[384] Thus, the intended purpose of a lump sum or property adjustment order will determine whether it falls within the scope of the Maintenance Regulation.[385]

---

[375] At [62].   [376] At [70].   [377] Ibid.   [378] At [71].
[379] [2014] 1 FLR 1399.   [380] Case C–116/02 [2003] ECR I–14693.
[381] Case C–220/95 *Van den Boogaard v Laumen* [1997] ECR I–1147.
[382] At [22]–[23], [25].   [383] Ibid.   [384] Brussels I Recast, art 1(2)(a).
[385] See *Moore v Moore* [2007] ILPr 36; *Traversa v Freddi* [2011] 2 FLR 272. If an inter-spousal property dispute does not invoke legal rules which are specific to marital relationships (and does not involve 'maintenance'), the property dispute may fall within the Brussels I Recast: see Case 143/78 *de Cavel v de Cavel (No 1)* [1979] ECR 1055, para 7; *G v G* [2016] 4 WLR 22.

2. Implications of the Maintenance Regulation

(A) Ancillary relief

8.180 When the English court has jurisdiction to grant a primary decree of divorce, separation, or annulment, it has also traditionally had jurisdiction to make ancillary orders for maintenance or other financial provision, or the adjustment of property rights as between the parties and for the benefit of the children of the marriage. As seen earlier in this chapter, in the vast majority of cases, the English court, exercising jurisdiction with regard to a primary decree, will do so under article 3 of the Brussels II *bis* Regulation. Under article 3(c) of the Maintenance Regulation the court has jurisdiction to make a maintenance order in such cases. However, the English court can also exercise jurisdiction under section 5(2)(b) of the Domicile and Matrimonial Proceedings Act 1973 if one party is domiciled in England.[386] In such cases there is no power under the Maintenance Regulation to make a maintenance order as article 3(c) specifically excludes any residual jurisdiction based 'solely on the nationality [domicile in the United Kingdom] of one of the parties'. This is an unfortunate exclusion in terms of its impact on English law. Admittedly, with reasonably broad jurisdictional grounds contained in the Brussels II *bis* Regulation, it is only in relatively rare cases that the English court will exercise jurisdiction under section 5(2)(b) of the Domicile and Matrimonial Proceedings Act 1973. However, as seen earlier, such cases do exist. With the court having no power to award ancillary relief by way of maintenance, it can be anticipated that this basis of jurisdiction will be used infrequently as, in the majority of divorce, etc cases, the only real disputes between the parties concern ancillary financial relief and parental responsibility.

(B) Other maintenance orders

8.181 During the subsistence of a marriage the English court has power to make various orders for financial provision in favour of a spouse or child of the family. It has power to order one spouse, who has failed to provide reasonable maintenance, to make periodic payments or lump sum payments to the other or to make similar payments to or for the benefit of a child. The jurisdiction of the English court to award maintenance in such cases is governed exclusively by the Maintenance Regulation.

8.182 However, there are statutes[387] which make provision, in conjunction with reciprocal laws of other countries, for maintenance orders to be made in the country in which the applicant resides and then, after confirmation of the order in the court of the country in which the respondent resides, to be enforced in the latter country. Provision is also made,[388] in pursuance of a UN Convention, for an applicant resident in one country to make application in the court of another country with the assistance of the authorities

---

[386] See para 8.20.
[387] Maintenance Orders (Facilities for Enforcement) Act 1920; Maintenance Orders (Reciprocal Enforcement) Act 1972. See, further, Cheshire, North and Fawcett, *Private International Law* (14th edn, 2008) pp 1053–5.
[388] Maintenance Orders (Reciprocal Enforcement) Act 1972, Pt II.

of the former country. According to article 69 of the Maintenance Regulation, the Regulation does not affect the application of such bilateral and multilateral conventions and agreements between a Member State and a non-Member State.

(C) Financial relief after a foreign decree

8.183 English courts used not to be able to make an order for financial relief after the dissolution of a marriage by a recognised foreign divorce. This caused great hardship to people living in England if the foreign court made no, or inadequate, provision for a spouse. This was remedied by Part III of the Matrimonial and Family Proceedings Act 1984, which provides that after such a divorce (or annulment or separation) obtained by judicial or other proceedings, the High Court may grant financial relief to either party who has not remarried.[389]

8.184 The jurisdiction of the English court to make such an order is governed by the Maintenance Regulation in most cases.[390] However, article 8(1) of the Maintenance Regulation provides that where the original decision was given by a court of a Member State (or a 2007 Hague Convention Contracting State[391]) in which the creditor is habitually resident, proceedings to modify that decision or to have a new decision given cannot be brought by the debtor in any other Member State as long as the creditor remains habitually resident in the state in which the original decision was given. This provision does not apply if the parties have agreed or submitted to the jurisdiction of the other Member State.[392] So, if a French court orders a husband, to pay maintenance to his wife habitually resident in France, this order cannot be modified in England at his request if the wife is still habitually resident in France at the date when modification is sought—unless the parties agree or submit to the jurisdiction of the English court. If, however, after the French order was made, the wife becomes habitually resident elsewhere, the French order is capable of modification under Part III.

8.185 In cases where article 8(1) does not apply or the judgment is from a court of a non-Member State, proceedings may be brought under Part III of the 1984 Act. However, no application can be made without the permission of the (English) court which must be satisfied that there is a 'substantial ground'[393] for making the application and that, having regard to all the circumstances of the case, it is appropriate for a financial order to be made.[394] The factors to be taken into account include the connections which the

---

[389] S 12. As noted at para 8.146, Part III relief is not available in a case where an overseas divorce is obtained otherwise than by proceedings. Part III relief is also unavailable where an overseas (proceedings) divorce is granted in respect of a marriage which is, in the eyes of English law, a non-marriage: *Dukali v Lamrani (Attorney General Intervening)* [2012] 2 FLR 1099.

[390] See s 15 as amended by the Civil Jurisdiction and Judgments (Maintenance) Regulations 2011, SI 2011/1484.

[391] See n 410.

[392] Art 8(2)(a), (b). This restriction also does not apply in certain cases relating to 2007 Hague Convention Contracting States (art 8(2)(c), (d)).

[393] Matrimonial and Family Proceedings Act 1984, s 13(1). In *Agbaje v Agbaje* [2010] 1 AC 628 it was held that 'substantial' means 'solid'.

[394] S 16(1).

parties have with England and with the country where the decree was obtained or any other country;[395] any financial benefit or relief to which the applicant is entitled and which the applicant is likely to receive under any agreement,[396] foreign law, or order of a foreign court;[397] the availability of property in England in respect of which an order could be made;[398] the extent to which an English order is likely to be enforceable;[399] and the length of time which has elapsed since the divorce.[400]

8.186 In several Court of Appeal decisions an analogy was drawn between exercising jurisdiction under Part III and the grant of stays on grounds of forum non conveniens.[401] This approach was rejected by the Supreme Court in *Agbaje v Agbaje*,[402] where it was stated that the test is whether it is appropriate for an order to be made in England 'notwithstanding that the divorce proceedings were in a foreign country which may well have been the more appropriate forum for the divorce'.[403] Nevertheless, the degree of connection with England is important for the assessment of whether an award should be made.[404] Earlier English decisions had also stressed that these provisions were not designed to permit an applicant to have 'two bites at one cherry'[405] or to empower an English court to exercise jurisdiction to 'second-guess' the foreign court's financial relief orders, and that it would be 'inconsistent with the comity existing between courts of comparable jurisdiction'[406] for the English court to review or supplement the foreign order as though it were sitting on appeal from the judgment of the foreign court.[407] Such reasoning was also rejected in *Agbaje*: the Supreme Court ruled that hardship, injustice (let alone serious injustice) and exceptionality were not pre-conditions of the exercise of jurisdiction.[408] While the object of Part III is not to allow a simple 'top-up' of the foreign award so as to equate with an English award, in cases where the connections with England are very strong the application can be treated as if it were made in purely English proceedings. It has been suggested that since *Agbaje* (with the de-emphasis of hardship), 'the Part III procedure has . . . become the application of choice of the otherwise disappointed forum shopper'.[409]

B Choice of law

8.187 Under article 15 of the Maintenance Regulation the law applicable to maintenance obligations is to be determined in accordance with the 2007 Hague Protocol to the Hague Convention on the International Recovery of Child Support and other forms

---

[395] S 16(2)(a)–(c).   [396] S 16(2)(d).   [397] S 16(2)(e).
[398] S 16(2)(g).   [399] S 16(2)(h).   [400] S 16(2)(i).
[401] *Holmes v Holmes* [1989] Fam 47; *Jordan v Jordan* [2001] 1 WLR 210; *Moore v Moore* [2007] 2 FLR 339.
[402] [2010] 1 AC 628.   [403] At [50].
[404] At [70]. See also *MA v SK; S Investments v MA (Financial Relief After Saudi Divorce)* [2016] 1 FLR 310 at [56].
[405] *Lamagni v Lamagni* [1995] 2 FLR 452 at 454.
[406] *Hewitson v Hewitson* [1995] Fam 100 at 105.
[407] *Agbaje v Agbaje* [2009] 3 WLR 835 (CA).   [408] At [72].
[409] Reeves and Willing, 'The Matrimonial and Family Proceedings Act 1984, Part III: The Apotheosis of Justice, English Judicial Imperialism or Just the Forum Shopper's Friend?' [2014] IFL 220.

of Family Maintenance.[410] While the United Kingdom has opted into the remainder of the Maintenance Regulation,[411] it has not opted into this optional Protocol.[412] Accordingly, as the United Kingdom is not bound by article 15 of the Maintenance Regulation, English courts will continue with the long-standing practice that, in all matters of maintenance, only the lex fori, English domestic law, is applied to determine whether relief is available and, if so, its type and extent.[413] The fact that the parties are domiciled or resident abroad is irrelevant. However, in making its assessment in cases with a 'foreign cultural element', the English court should take into account how the foreign courts would deal with such proceedings.[414]

C Recognition and enforcement of foreign maintenance orders

8.188 A maintenance order made by a foreign court, whether ancillary to a divorce order or not, is a foreign judgment in personam, thus qualifying, in principle, for recognition under the rules discussed in Chapter 3. However, normally such judgments can be varied by the foreign court and, therefore, do not meet the common law requirement of finality necessary for enforcement. Accordingly, several statutory regimes for the recognition and enforcement of foreign maintenance orders have been established.

1. United Kingdom maintenance orders

8.189 Under Part II of the Maintenance Orders Act 1950 a maintenance order made in another part of the United Kingdom may be registered in an English court.

2. Foreign maintenance orders

8.190 Under the Maintenance Orders (Facilities for Enforcement) Act 1920 there is a special regime for the enforcement of Commonwealth maintenance orders applying to countries to which an Order in Council has been extended. Under Part I of the Maintenance Orders (Reciprocal Enforcement) Act 1972[415] there is a similar regime for the reciprocal enforcement of other foreign maintenance orders from countries to which an Order in Council has been extended.

3. The Maintenance Regulation

8.191 The Maintenance Regulation provides for recognition and enforcement without exequatur of decisions given in Member States applying the Hague Protocol[416] and for

---

[410] For a full list of the states which have ratified this 2007 Hague Convention, see <https://www.hcch.net>. Those states ratifying the Convention are referred to as '2007 Hague Convention Contracting States'.
[411] Commission Decision No 2009/451/EC, OJ 2009 L149/73.
[412] Under the Hague Protocol the general rule is that maintenance obligations are governed by the law of the state of the habitual residence of the creditor.
[413] In limited circumstances under the Maintenance Orders (Facilities for Enforcement) Act 1920 and the Maintenance Orders (Reciprocal Enforcement) Act 1972 it may be necessary to have recourse to foreign law. See Dicey, Morris and Collins, *The Conflict of Laws* (15th edn, 2012) p 1088.
[414] *A v T (Ancillary Relief: Cultural Factors)* [2004] 1 FLR 977.
[415] As amended by the Maintenance Orders (Reciprocal Enforcement) Act 1992.
[416] Art 17.

recognition and enforcement with exequatur of the judgments of Member States not bound by the Protocol.[417] It follows that UK judgments require a declaration of enforceability before they can be enforced in other Member States. Provision is made for all Member States to establish Central Authorities to co-operate and discharge the duties imposed by the Regulation.[418] There is, however, at present some uncertainty as to the capacity for direct enforcement without the assistance of a Central Authority.[419]

---

[417] Art 26.   [418] Chapter VII.
[419] See *MS v PS* [2016] EWHC 88 (Fam). See also (on applications for modification) *AB v JJB (EU Maintenance Regulation: Modification Application Procedure)* [2015] 2 FLR 1143.

9

Property

This chapter considers the choice of law rules for the transfer of property. The rules are structured around a number of distinctions. First, a distinction has to be drawn between movables and immovables. As regards movables, a further distinction is drawn between tangibles and intangibles. Secondly, the law distinguishes between cases involving the transfer of property on death and cases where property is transferred inter vivos. Thirdly, transfers which arise as a result of marriage should be distinguished from other types of transfer.

I Movables and immovables

9.1 The English conflict of laws, like other systems, draws a distinction between movable and immovable property. The main reason for making the distinction is that immovable property, which comprises land and things attached to or growing on the land, is subject to the control of the authorities where it is situated to a much greater extent than movable property which can be physically removed from one country to another. As a result, different choice of law rules have been developed for movable and immovable property.

9.2 The traditional English distinction between realty and personalty is not used for choice of law purposes for two reasons. First, the distinction between realty and personalty is known only to those legal systems which are derived from the English common law. Secondly, it is the factual difference between movables and immovables—rather than the more technical and artificial distinction between real property and personal property—which justifies the application of different choice of law rules. So, for conflicts purposes, property in England—as well as elsewhere—must be classified as either movable or immovable. Normally, there will be no dispute whether property is movable or immovable, for the distinction is largely factual. However, in borderline cases different laws may take different views as to whether particular property is movable or immovable. It is well established that the classification of property as either movable or immovable should be made according to the law of the country in which the property is situated (lex situs).[1] This is an exception to the general rule that classification is effected in accordance with the lex fori.

---

[1] *Re Berchtold* [1923] 1 Ch 192 at 199; *Re Cutliffe's Will Trusts* [1940] Ch 565 at 571.

9.3 As regards property situated in England, an interest in land will, generally speaking, be classified as an immovable even if, according to English domestic law, the interest is regarded as personalty. In *Freke v Lord Carbery*,[2] for example, a testator died domiciled in Ireland, leaving a leasehold house in England. A question arose as to whether the validity of the disposition should be governed by English or Irish law. If the property were regarded as immovable, English law, as the lex situs, governed; if the property were classified as movable, Irish law, as the law of the testator's domicile, applied. The court decided that, even though English law traditionally classifies leases as personal property, for choice of law purposes the property in question was to be classified as immovable. So, the validity of the disposition was governed by English law, according to which it was invalid.

9.4 Where the property in question is situated abroad, classification is to be effected by the relevant foreign law. So, even though property situated in country X is by English notions immovable, the English court should classify it as movable if that is the classification according to the law of country X.[3] Similarly, if the situs is abroad, property which according to English law is regarded as movable must be treated as immovable if the lex situs classifies the property as immovable. In *Ex p Rucker*[4] the deeds to a plantation in Antigua were lodged with the petitioner by way of equitable mortgage in 1831 (before slavery was abolished in British colonies). When the petitioner applied for sale of the plantation, including the slaves who worked on it, a question arose as to whether or not the slaves were part of the land. The court held that they were, since that was the position under the law of Antigua at that time.

9.5 The distinction between tangible movables and intangible movables essentially mirrors the traditional English distinction between choses in possession and choses in action. The rules relating to tangible movables apply to things such as motor-cars, paintings, and commodities. It is equally clear that the rules relating to intangible movables apply to interests such as debts, shares, patents,[5] trade marks, and copyright. Property questions become potentially muddied, however, in cases where title to an intangible interest (such as shares in a company) is represented by tangible documents (such as share certificates). It is important to distinguish the question of who is entitled to possession of the share certificates from the question of who is entitled to the shares themselves. In *Williams v Colonial Bank*,[6] share certificates (representing shares in a New York company) were deposited with the defendant bank in England. Bowen LJ formulated the issue facing the court in the following terms:

> The key to this case is whether the defendants have a right to hold these pieces of paper, these certificates. What the effect upon their ulterior rights in America would be if we were to declare that they were entitled to these pieces of paper is another question.[7]

---

[2] (1873) LR 16 Eq 461. See also *Re Berchtold* [1923] 1 Ch 192.
[3] *Re Hoyles* [1911] 1 Ch 179.   [4] (1834) 3 LJ Bcy 104.
[5] Somewhat elliptically, the UK legislation provides that a patent is 'personal property (without being a thing in action)': Patents Act 1977, s 30(1).
[6] (1888) 38 Ch D 388.
[7] At 408. See also *Macmillan Inc v Bishopsgate Investment Trust plc (No 3)* [1996] 1 WLR 387.

II Transfers inter vivos

9.6 Which law determines whether a given act, transaction, or event transfers title to property or other proprietary rights from one person to another? Title to property is often transferred in consequence of a contract, but the law which governs the contract is not necessarily the law which determines whether and when title passes in pursuance of it. It is vital to distinguish contractual questions from proprietary ones. In the case of a contract for the sale of goods, for example, if the contract is valid by its applicable law, the buyer acquires a contractual right to receive delivery of the goods to the extent provided for by the applicable law. However, it is not necessarily the law governing the contract which determines whether title to the goods passes. Whether the buyer has title to the goods is to be determined by the law governing the transfer of movables. Immovables, tangible movables, and intangible movables are dealt with in turn.[8]

A Immovables

9.7 The general rule is that the transfer of proprietary rights in immovables is governed by the lex situs.[9] So, if the property in question is situated in England, English domestic law is applicable. This is no doubt the proper approach as regards the material and formal validity of the transfer (for example, rules requiring the execution of a deed or rules requiring registration of the transfer in a public register). Although it has been questioned whether matters of capacity should also be subjected to the lex situs,[10] the authorities suggest that capacity to transfer immovable property (or to take such a transfer) is also governed by the lex situs.[11]

9.8 There are few cases where the question arises as to the law governing the transfer of a foreign immovable as the English court normally does not have jurisdiction in such a case. One case, where the question of title arose incidentally, is *Adams v Clutterbuck*[12] in which a document executed in England conveyed shooting rights over certain moorland in Scotland. The conveyance was not formally valid under English law, because the document was not under seal, but it was valid by Scots law. It was held that Scots law applied.

9.9 One rationale for the application of the lex situs to questions of title to immovable property is that the property is under the close control of the authorities of the country where the property is situated. Accordingly, there is an argument for saying that the application of the lex situs should involve not simply consideration of the domestic law

---

[8] This chapter deals primarily with the voluntary transfer of property. For problems concerning involuntary assignment (eg, on the appointment of a receiver by secured creditors), see Dicey, Morris and Collins, *The Conflict of Laws* (15th edn, 2012) pp 1372–9, 1595–605.

[9] *Earl Nelson v Lord Bridport* (1846) 8 Beav 547; *Norton v Florence Land and Public Works Co* (1877) 7 Ch D 332.

[10] See Jaffey, *Introduction to the Conflict of Laws* (1988) p 211.

[11] *Bank of Africa Ltd v Cohen* [1909] 2 Ch 129.   [12] (1883) 10 QBD 403.

of the situs, but also its choice of law rules. That is to say, title to immovables is one of the areas in which the doctrine of renvoi might be regarded as playing a useful role. Where, for example, a question of title to land in Russia arises incidentally in English proceedings there is an argument for saying that the English court should seek to decide the question as a Russian court would do.

9.10 There are, however, also arguments against the application of the doctrine of renvoi.[13] Since the purpose of a choice of law rule is to identify the law which, from the perspective of English private international law, is the most appropriate one, it is not obvious that the English court should refuse to apply the lex situs simply on the basis that the courts of the country in which the immovable property is situated would apply the law of another country. Furthermore, it should not be assumed that an English judgment which is based on the application of the lex situs would not be recognised or enforced by the courts of the situs if those courts would have applied the law of another country to the issue in question.

9.11 It is also important to keep the issue of renvoi in proportion. The doctrine of renvoi is potentially relevant only if the foreign choice of law rule is different from the English rule. In a case involving title to immovable property, the doctrine of renvoi cannot have any application if, according to the conflicts rules of the country in which the property is situated, title to immovable property is also governed by the lex situs.

9.12 In all cases involving proprietary questions, the transfer of title must be distinguished from any contract in pursuance of which title has been transferred. A question concerning the contract is to be decided by the law applicable to the contract, which may (or may not) be the lex situs.[14] Moreover, the English court may well assume jurisdiction over a dispute arising out of such a contract.[15] So, in *Re Smith*[16] the deceased, who had been domiciled and resident in England, had made a contract in England with his sisters by which he charged his interest in certain land in Dominica in their favour as security for money which he owed them. He also undertook in the contract to execute a legal mortgage over the land, but never did so. On his death the question arose as to the sisters' rights in relation to the land. By the law of Dominica, the lex situs, the contract was not effective to create a mortgage, because the requisite formalities for the creation of a mortgage had not been complied with. It was held, however, that the validity and effect of the contract was governed by English law, under which, the deceased having become bound to execute a mortgage, the executors were ordered to take the necessary steps to do so.

9.13 If, however, enforcement of a contractual obligation to transfer a proprietary interest in an immovable under a contract which is valid by its applicable law would be impossible under the lex situs, the court could hardly make an order for such enforcement. In *Bank of Africa Ltd v Cohen*[17] a contract was made in England between the plaintiff, an

---

[13] See paras 1.127–1.130. [14] See paras 4.15–4.81. [15] See paras 2.70–2.93 and 2.160–2.166.
[16] [1916] 2 Ch 206. [17] [1909] 2 Ch 129.

English bank, and the defendant, who was domiciled and resident in England. Under the terms of the contract, the defendant undertook to execute a mortgage over land which she owned in South Africa as security for money advanced to her husband. When the defendant failed to execute the mortgage the plaintiff sought a decree of specific performance from the English court. Under South African law a married woman lacked capacity to stand surety for her husband unless she expressly and voluntarily renounced the benefits of certain laws, which the defendant had not done. It was held that the wife's capacity to make the contract was governed by South African law, as the lex situs. As she lacked capacity under that law, a decree of specific performance was refused.

9.14 The reasoning of the decision may be criticised on the ground that there is no obvious reason why the choice of law rules for capacity to make a contract with regard to an immovable should be different from the choice of law rules for capacity to make any other contract. Rather than determining the defendant's capacity by reference to South African law, the lex situs, the law governing this question should have been English law, the law of the country with which the contract was most closely connected and in which the defendant was domiciled and resident.[18] According to English law the defendant had full capacity. This does not mean, however, that the decision not to grant a decree of specific performance cannot be justified. It is a well-accepted maxim of equity that equity does not act in vain; it would have been futile for the court to compel the defendant to renounce the benefits of South African law given that by the lex situs the renouncing of the benefits would not be effective unless it was voluntary.

B **Tangible movables**

1. **Introduction**

9.15 Which law should govern the transfer of tangible movables inter vivos? The various theories that have been suggested include the lex situs, the law of the transferor's domicile and the proper law of the transfer. As between the parties to a contract whose object is to pass title, it might be reasonable for questions of title to be governed by the law applicable to the contract. However, questions of title do not arise only as between the parties to a contract; often they involve third parties.[19] For example, the question whether title passes in pursuance of a sale of stolen goods usually arises between the buyer and the original owner, rather than between the buyer and the seller who stole the goods. Similarly, the extent to which a seller may effectively retain title to goods which he has delivered to a buyer is likely to arise, not between the seller and the buyer, but between the seller and the buyer's creditors or a subsequent buyer.

---

[18] See paras 4.154–4.160.
[19] For the argument that choice of law rules developed in the context of three-party cases should not necessarily apply in two-party cases, see Bridge, 'English Conflicts Rules for Transfers of Movables: A Contract-based Approach?' in Bridge and Stevens (eds), *Cross-Border Security and Insolvency* (2001) p 123.

2. The lex situs rule

9.16 The rule is that the transfer of a movable is governed by the lex situs, the law of the country where the movable is situated at the time of the alleged transfer.[20] Even where the case involves a contractual transfer and the dispute is between the transferor and the transferee, the lex situs rather than the law applicable to the contract governs the proprietary effects of the transfer.[21] The lex situs determines whether a given act or event does or does not transfer proprietary rights and, if so, to what extent.[22] The reason is that a person who acquires goods, or rights in goods, should be able to rely on any title which he obtains according to the law of the country where the goods are located when he acquires them and to rely on that law for the retention of title he obtains. As Staughton LJ said in *Macmillan Inc v Bishopsgate Investment Trust plc (No 3)*:

> A purchaser ought to satisfy himself that he obtains good title by the law prevailing where the chattel is . . . but should not be required to do more than that. And an owner, if he does not wish to be deprived of his property by some eccentric rule of foreign law, can at least do his best to ensure that it does not leave the safety of his own country.[23]

(A) Cases where the situs is constant

9.17 Where the situs of goods remains constant the application of the lex situs is unlikely to present many problems. In *Inglis v Robertson*,[24] for example, an English buyer of whisky which was stored in a warehouse in Scotland received a delivery order from the Scottish seller and endorsed it to the English plaintiff by way of security. Under English law the plaintiff obtained an interest in the goods, but by Scots law he did not. It was held that Scots law applied and, therefore, that the plaintiff acquired no interest.

(B) Cases where the situs changes

9.18 The potential problems increase in cases where the situs of the property in question changes. The leading case is *Cammell v Sewell*.[25] Timber belonging to the plaintiff was shipped from Russia to England. While the timber was in transit the ship carrying it was wrecked and the cargo was sold to the defendant in Norway. Under Norwegian law, but not English law, the defendant acquired title to the goods. The plaintiff claimed the goods when the defendant subsequently brought them to England. It was held that the title acquired by the defendant while the goods were in Norway prevailed.

9.19 In *Winkworth v Christie, Manson and Woods Ltd*,[26] works of art belonging to the plaintiff were stolen from him in England and taken to Italy, where the second defendant bought them in good faith. The second defendant later sent them back to England to

---

[20] *Cammell v Sewell* (1860) 5 H & N 728. See also *Gotha City v Sotheby's (No 2)* (1998) *The Times*, 8 October; *Glencore International AG v Metro Trading International Inc* [2001] 1 Lloyd's Rep 284; *Air Foyle Ltd v Center Capital Ltd* [2003] 2 Lloyd's Rep 753; *Bonhams 1793 Ltd v Lawson* [2015] EWHC 3257 (Comm).
[21] *The WD Fairway (No 3)* [2009] 2 Lloyd's Rep 420.
[22] It may be that, under the lex situs, title will not pass in pursuance of a contract unless the contract is valid, which will have to be tested by the law applicable to the contract.
[23] [1996] 1 WLR 387 at 400. [24] [1898] AC 616.
[25] (1860) 5 H & N 728. [26] [1980] Ch 496.

be sold by auction by the first defendant. The plaintiff brought proceedings against the defendants in England for, inter alia, a declaration that the works of art had at all material times been his property. The success of the claim depended on whether English or Italian law should be applied to determine whether or not title to the goods had passed to the second defendant as a result of the sale to him in Italy. By English law, title would not have passed; by Italian law it would because the buyer acted in good faith at the time of the delivery of the goods to him. Slade J held, following *Cammell v Sewell*, that Italian law, as the law of the country where the goods were situated at the time of the delivery, governed the question. The lex situs rule was held to apply even though this meant that the plaintiff was deprived of his title to goods (under English law) removed from England without his consent and even though the goods were once again situated in England at the time of the proceedings. Any argument based on hardship to the original owner in such circumstances was counterbalanced by the interests of innocent purchasers: 'commercial convenience may be said imperatively to demand that proprietary rights to movables shall generally be determined by the lex situs.'[27]

9.20 Once title has passed as the result of a transaction under the lex situs, it is immaterial that the movable property is removed to another country under whose law title did not pass. So, in *Winkworth v Christie, Manson and Woods Ltd*, the second defendant was held to have retained any title he acquired under Italian law even after the goods were sent back to England. Similarly, if title does not pass as a result of a transaction under the lex situs, it makes no difference that the movable property is then taken to another country under whose law it did pass, until some event occurs when the goods are in that country by virtue of which title passes according to the law of that country. Consider, for example, the following situation: X steals goods from C in England and takes them to New York, where he sells them to Y. Under the laws of England and New York, Y does not acquire title. If Y then takes the goods to France, Y still cannot be regarded as acquiring title to the goods even if Y has title under French law. If, however, while the goods are in France Y sells the goods to Z and under French law Z acquires title, the English court will recognise Z's title even if the goods are subsequently brought to England.

9.21 The proposition that the lex situs governs the transfer of title to movables may be misleading unless it is understood to mean that the relevant rule of the lex situs is applied to decide the question. In *Winkworth v Christie, Manson and Woods Ltd*, the first defendant had sold some of the goods by auction in England before the proceedings were brought. Suppose the question were raised whether title passed to the buyer under that sale. One would obviously reach the wrong result by reasoning that the question whether title passed was governed by English law because the goods were in England at the time of the auction and by concluding that title did not pass, because under English law the plaintiff retained his title to the stolen goods notwithstanding the subsequent sales. The right approach is to say that, because the auction took place in England, the relevant rule of English law as to the passing of title is applicable. That rule is that title

---

[27] Slade J at 512.

will pass in the circumstances in question only if the second defendant had title to the goods. That raises the incidental question whether the second defendant had obtained title under his purchase in Italy.[28] According to the English conflicts rules, that incidental question is governed by Italian law, under which the second defendant did acquire title. Therefore, title passed to the buyer at the auction.

9.22 The same considerations would apply in the converse case, where title does not pass under the foreign law, but it would under English law. Suppose a seller, A, sells and delivers goods to a buyer, B, in Germany. The contract contains a clause which is effective under German law to retain title to the goods in A and to preclude B from reselling them until the price is paid; under English law, however, title would pass on delivery. B brings the goods to England and, before paying the price, sells and delivers them to C who buys in good faith. Does title pass to C? At the time when C acquired the goods they were in England, so the relevant rules of English domestic law must be applied. One such rule is that title will pass if the seller has title. That raises the question whether B had title which, according to the English choice of law rule, must be decided by German law as the lex situs at the time when B purchased the goods. B did not acquire title and his mere bringing of the goods to England does not alter the position. C, therefore, does not obtain title on the basis that his seller had title. Another rule of English domestic law is that where a buyer who obtains possession of the goods with the consent of the seller delivers the goods under a sale to a person receiving them in good faith, the latter obtains good title even though the former did not have title.[29] Title would pass under this rule for at the relevant time the goods were in England and the application of the rule accepts that B did not obtain title under the purchase from A.[30]

3. Exceptions to the lex situs rule

9.23 It would seem that the lex situs rule is not applicable in all circumstances. In *Winkworth v Christie, Manson and Woods Ltd*,[31] it was accepted that there might be some exceptions to the general rule. First, '[i]f the goods are in transit, and their situs is casual or not known, a transfer which is valid and effective by its proper law will be valid and effective in England'.[32] Secondly, the English court may decline to recognise the effect of the lex situs if it is considered to be contrary to English public policy. Where, for example, property is expropriated by a foreign government, in certain circumstances the expropriatory legislation may not be recognised as being effective to confer title on the government.[33] Similarly, where a buyer purchases stolen goods abroad knowing them to be stolen—and, therefore, does not act in good faith—the English court might

---

[28] For further consideration of the incidental question, see paras 1.131–1.137.
[29] Sale of Goods Act 1979, s 25(1).
[30] Based on *Century Credit Corpn v Richard* (1962) 34 DLR (2d) 291. There are many US cases dealing with such problems, which have not arisen in the English courts. See Morris, 'The Transfer of Chattels in the Conflict of Laws' (1945) 22 BYIL 232; Davis, 'Conditional Sales and Chattel Mortgages in the Conflict of Laws' (1964) 13 ICLQ 53.
[31] [1980] Ch 496.
[32] Slade J at 501 (citing Dicey and Morris, *The Conflict of Laws* (9th edn, 1973) p 539).
[33] See para 9.43.

consider that it would be contrary to public policy to recognise a title obtained in such circumstances under the lex situs. Thirdly, the lex situs will yield in the face of any English statute which, according to its proper interpretation, has an overriding effect.[34] The importance of these apparent exceptions should not be exaggerated; there are very few reported cases which illustrate their application.

9.24 Although there have been suggestions that the doctrine of renvoi should be applied to movables,[35] in *Islamic Republic of Iran v Berend*[36] the court expressly held that there was no good reason to introduce the doctrine of renvoi into this area.[37] The main argument which has been used to support the application of renvoi in relation to immovables—namely, that the property is under the control of the authorities in the foreign country—cannot realistically be applied to movables. Movables are not amenable to public control in the same way as immovables, precisely because they are movable. When a case comes before the English court involving the transfer of a movable which took place abroad, the likelihood is that the movable has since been brought to England, so that the control of the foreign authorities does not arise. It will also be the case that, to the extent that the parties relied upon the law of the situs, reliance would have been placed on its domestic law (rather than on its choice of law rules).

C Intangible movables

1. Introduction

9.25 It has been seen that, as a general rule, the transfer of immovables and tangible movables is governed by the lex situs. The rationale for this choice of law rule has already been considered and its application, while not without its complications, is facilitated by the fact that the situs of immovables and tangible movables is in most cases easy to determine. Intangibles give rise to different problems as a consequence of which the merits of applying the lex situs rule may be questioned.[38] Although it is not unreasonable to attribute a situs to certain types of intangibles (for example, France is the situs of a French patent; New York is the situs of shares in a New York corporation), as regards other types of property, such as a debt, the allocation of a situs is rather artificial.[39]

9.26 There are two points which should be borne in mind in cases involving the assignment of intangibles. First, as with all property transactions, it is vital to distinguish contractual issues from proprietary ones. One must not fall into the trap of assuming that where an assignment of an intangible is effected by contract, the only question to consider is the validity of the contract. Secondly, in cases involving the assignment of certain types of intangibles (in particular, debts) there are two transactions to consider:

---

[34] For consideration of overriding mandatory provisions in the contractual context, see paras 4.97–4.108.
[35] *Glencore International AG v Metro Trading International Inc* [2001] 1 Lloyd's Rep 284 at 297.
[36] [2007] 2 All ER (Comm) 132.
[37] See also *Blue Sky One Ltd v Mahan Air* [2010] EWHC 631 (Comm) at [172].
[38] See Moshinsky, 'The Assignment of Debts in the Conflict of Laws' (1992) 108 LQR 591.
[39] Rogerson, 'The Situs of Debts in the Conflict of Laws—Illogical, Artificial and Misleading' [1990] CLJ 441.

the first is the transaction which creates the relationship between the debtor and the creditor; the second is the assignment by the creditor to the assignee.

2. The situs of intangibles

9.27 The law artificially ascribes a situs to intangibles. The basic rule is that an intangible is situated where it is properly recoverable or can be enforced. As regards an intangible which is territorially limited (such as a patent), the situs is obviously the territory in question. Where the intangible arises out of a debtor's obligation to pay a sum of money the general rule is that the situs is where the debtor resides, because that is where the debt is properly recoverable.[40] If the debtor resides in more than one country the situs of the debt is the place where the creditor has stipulated that the debt is to be paid.[41] If it has not been stipulated where the debt is to be paid, the debt is situated in the country where it would be paid in the normal course of business.[42]

3. Choice of law rules

9.28 The question of which law governs the transfer of intangible movables is uncertain. Many of the common law authorities are old and inconsistent. To some extent, the confusion in the case law is generated by the courts' failure to distinguish clearly contractual questions from proprietary ones. A degree of certainty, at least as regards some issues, is injected by article 14 of the Rome I Regulation[43] (on the law applicable to contractual obligations).

9.29 In the discussion which follows, three issues are considered: first, which law governs whether or not a particular intangible is assignable; secondly, which law governs the contractual questions arising out of an assignment between the assignor and the assignee; and thirdly, which law governs 'proprietary' questions (whether between the assignor and the assignee or, if the intangible is assigned more than once, between competing assignees or, in cases involving debts, between the assignee and the debtor)?

(A) Assignability

9.30 Whether a particular intangible is capable of being assigned is to be regarded as an aspect of the law under which the interest in question is created. Where, for example, a right arises under a contract which is governed by English law, it is logical to look to English law to determine whether the right can be assigned. This is the solution adopted by the Rome I Regulation: article 14(2) provides that '[t]he law governing the assigned . . . claim shall determine its assignability'.

---

[40] *New York Life Insurance Co v Public Trustee* [1924] 2 Ch 101.
[41] *Jabbour v Custodian of Israeli Absentee's Property* [1954] 1 WLR 139; *Kwok Chi Leung Karl v Estate Duty Comrs* [1988] 1 WLR 1035.
[42] *Power Curber International Ltd v National Bank of Kuwait SAK* [1981] 1 WLR 1233. See also *Taurus Petroleum v State Oil Marketing Co of the Ministry of Oil, Iraq* [2016] 1 Lloyd's Rep 42.
[43] Regulation (EC) No 593/2008, OJ 2008 L177/6. See Hartley, 'Choice of Law Regarding the Voluntary Assignment of Contractual Obligations under the Rome I Regulation' (2011) 60 ICLQ 29; Verhagen and van Dongen, 'Cross-Border Assignments under Rome I' (2010) 6 Journal of Private International Law 1.

9.31 The Rome I Regulation applies only to contracts falling within its scope. There are two types of cases which are governed by the common law. First, a debt may arise out of a contract or other legal relationship which is not within the Regulation's scope. For example, the Regulation does not apply to maintenance obligations or to wills.[44] It has been suggested by writers that, at common law, the question whether a debt is capable of being assigned is governed by the proper law of the debt—that is, the law governing the contract or other transaction which created the debt[45] (the law with which the right assigned has its most significant connection).[46] There are various reasons in favour of this suggestion: there is some authority to support it;[47] it is sound from the point of view of principle; and it avoids arbitrary distinctions between cases governed by the Rome I Regulation and those governed by the common law. Secondly, some types of intangible, such as intellectual property rights, do not arise out of transactions at all. The assignability of such rights should be determined by the lex situs (which will inevitably be the law under which the right was created). So, whether US copyright is assignable is a question to be answered by reference to US law and German law determines the assignability of a German registered trade mark.

(B) The validity of the assignment: contractual questions

9.32 The voluntary assignment of an intangible will be effected either by contract or by gift. Accordingly, the rights and obligations of the assignor and the assignee fall to be determined by the law applicable to the transaction between the parties. The vast majority of such transactions are within the scope of the Rome I Regulation and the applicable law is determined by the choice of law rules contained in the Regulation. Article 14(1) provides that '[t]he relationship between assignor and assignee under a voluntary assignments . . . of a claim against another person (the debtor) shall be governed by the law that applies to the contract between the assignor and assignee'. If the parties make a choice of law, the chosen law governs;[48] if they have not made a choice, the law of the country with which the contract is deemed to be most closely connected applies.[49] In cases involving a dispute arising out of the transfer of an intangible, one or more of the Regulation's provisions dealing with material validity,[50] formal validity,[51] capacity[52] and the scope of the applicable law[53] may be relevant.[54]

9.33 It must be remembered that the Rome I Regulation's scope is limited. Certain types of contract and certain types of contractual question fall outside the Regulation. For example, some contracts of insurance are not governed by the Regulation[55] and, subject to article 13, questions of contractual capacity are governed by the common law choice of law rules. Contracts of assignment to which the common law applies are governed

---

[44] Art 1(2)(b) and (c).
[45] Cheshire, North and Fawcett, *Private International Law* (14th edn, 2008) p 1231.
[46] Dicey, Morris and Collins, *The Conflict of Laws* (15th edn, 2012) p 1355.
[47] *Campbell Connelly & Co Ltd v Noble* [1963] 1 WLR 252.
[48] Art 3.   [49] Art 4.   [50] Art 10.   [51] Art 11.   [52] Art 13.   [53] Art 12.
[54] For a full discussion of the Regulation, see Chapter 4.   [55] Art 1(2)(j).

(C) The effect of the assignment: 'proprietary' questions

9.34 So far, consideration has been given only to contractual issues as between the assignor and the assignee. Which law should govern 'proprietary' questions? Broadly speaking, there are three issues to consider. First, which law determines whether an assignee has title to the intangible which is the subject-matter of the assignment? Secondly, if an intangible, which is assignable by the law under which it was created, is the subject of successive assignments, each valid by its governing law, which law determines the priority between the assignees? Thirdly, in cases involving debts, which law determines whether or not the assignee is able to enforce the debt against the debtor? Although these questions arise in different factual contexts each raises essentially the same issue and there is an argument for saying that the same choice of law rule should apply to each.[56]

9.35 As a matter of principle the law which governs the contract of assignment is not necessarily the law which should govern 'proprietary' questions—in particular, those which involve third parties. Where, for example, X, by a contract governed by English law, purports to assign US copyright to Y, whether Y becomes the owner of the copyright should not be determined by English law. Indeed, the fact that the law governing the contract of assignment cannot apply as such to proprietary issues is obvious from cases which raise priority questions. If X assigns a debt to Y under a contract governed by Italian law and then assigns the same debt to Z under a contract governed by German law, it makes no sense to try to determine whether Y or Z has priority by reference to the law applicable to the contracts of assignment. Nevertheless, in a case involving the assignment of a debt, it seems that the entire relationship between the assignor and the assignee is governed by the law governing the contract of assignment.[57] Accordingly, the applicable law identified by article 14(1) of the Rome I Regulation determines, for example, whether, and at what point, the subject-matter of the assignment should be regarded as forming part of the assignee's estate.

9.36 From a policy point of view what is required is a choice of law rule which promotes stability in proprietary relations. Accordingly, the choice of law rule should use a single connecting factor which is unlikely to be transient. Essentially, there are two options: the lex situs or the law under which the interest was created. In many cases the law under which the interest was created is also the lex situs. This will normally be the case, for example, where the subject-matter of the dispute is an intellectual property right which is territorially limited (such as a registered patent or trade mark) or where the property in question comprises shares in a company. However, in a case involving the

---

[56] For a contrary view, see Bridge, 'The Proprietary Aspects of Assignment and Choice of Law' (2009) 125 LQR 671.
[57] See Rome I Regulation, recital (38). See also *Raiffeisen Zentralbank Österreich AG v Five Star General Trading LLC* [2001] QB 825.

assignment of a contractual debt, the lex situs may well be different from the law under which the interest was created. Where, for example, an English bank makes a loan to a French company under a contract governed by English law which specifies Paris as the place of repayment, the situs of the debt is France, but the debt arises out of a transaction governed by English law. If the English bank assigns the debt to a German bank, should French law (the lex situs) or English law (the law under which the interest was created) determine whether the German bank can enforce the debt against the French company?

(i) The general principle

9.37 Some commentators have supported the application of the lex situs.[58] Notwithstanding the problems of ascribing a situs to interests which have no physical existence, since the lex situs governs questions of title to immovables and tangible movables, there is an obvious attraction to applying the lex situs to proprietary questions concerning intangibles. *Macmillan Inc v Bishopsgate Investment Trust plc (No 3)*[59] involved competing claims to shares in a company which was incorporated in New York, although the transactions on which the parties' claims were based had been effected in London. The Court of Appeal held that the issue as to who has title to shares in a company should be decided by the lex situs. Auld LJ said:

> [T]here is authority and much to be said for treating issues of priority of ownership of shares in a corporation according to the lex situs of those shares. That will normally be the country where the register is kept, usually but not always the country of incorporation.[60]

9.38 The lex situs, being the law under which the right was created, is equally applicable to proprietary questions in cases involving the assignment of intellectual property rights such as patents, trade marks, and copyright.[61] Indeed, in *Macmillan Inc v Bishopsgate Investment Trust plc (No 3)*, Auld LJ expressed the view that '[i]n general, disputes about the ownership of land and of tangible and intangible movables are governed by the lex situs'.[62]

9.39 The implication of the application of the lex situs to proprietary questions is that an assignee under a contract of assignment which is valid according to its applicable law may, nevertheless, be unable to claim title to the intangible in question. If, for example, the transaction does not comply with the formal requirements of the lex situs, but does comply with the formal requirements of the law governing the contract, the assignee acquires contractual rights against the assignor but will not become the legal owner of the intangible. Similarly, the assignee should not be able to claim title if he lacks capacity under the lex situs. The cases suggest, however, that a person's capacity to make or receive an assignment of an intangible is governed either by the law of that person's domicile or by the law of the place of acting.[63] Such a rule, if it exists, has little

---

[58] See, eg, Collier, *Conflict of Laws* (3rd edn, 2001) pp 256–7.   [59] [1996] 1 WLR 387.   [60] At 411.
[61] *Campbell Connelly & Co Ltd v Noble* [1963] 1 WLR 252; *Peer International Corpn v Termidor Music Publishers Ltd* [2004] 2 WLR 849.
[62] [1996] 1 WLR 387 at 410.
[63] *Lee v Abdy* (1886) 17 QBD 309; *Republica de Guatemala v Nunez* [1927] 1 KB 669.

(ii) Debts

9.40 Although there is English authority for the proposition that, in cases involving the assignment of debts, it is inappropriate to characterise issues involving the relationship between the assignee and the debtor as 'proprietary' as opposed to 'contractual',[64] 'there is no doubt that the terminology of the assignability of debts lends a proprietary flavour to the transaction in question'.[65] Notwithstanding this 'proprietary flavour', it may be questioned whether the lex situs should apply to issues arising out of the assignment of a simple debt. First, it is in relation to debts that the allocation of a situs is most artificial. Secondly, one of the problems with the application of the lex situs to cases involving the assignment of debts is that it may generate uncertainty. Because the debtor's residence may change, the situs is not a connecting factor which promotes stability in legal relations.

9.41 In cases falling within the material scope of the Rome I Regulation, article 14(2) provides that the law governing the right to which the assignment relates shall determine the relationship between the assignee and the debtor and the conditions under which the assignment can be invoked against the debtor. So, where a debt due under a contract governed by English law is assigned by the creditor to an assignee by means of a contract governed by French law, the fact that, under French law, the assignee cannot enforce the debt (because notification of the assignment has not been made to the relevant person) is irrelevant; as long as the contract of assignment is valid according to its applicable law (as determined by article 14(1)), English law—as the law governing the right to which the assignment relates—determines whether or not the assignee can recover from the debtor.[66]

9.42 As regards cases not falling within the scope of the Rome I Regulation, the authorities are inconclusive. Some support for the application of the lex situs may be derived from *Re Maudslay*.[67] However, there is a good argument—both in terms of authority and policy—for the application of the law under which the interest was created (which, in the case of contract debts, is the law applicable to the contract out of which the debt arises). First, *Le Feuvre v Sullivan*[68] and *Kelly v Selwyn*[69] may be read as supporting this argument.[70] Secondly, the law under which the interest was created is a less transient and, therefore, more appropriate connecting factor than the situs of the debt. Finally, the application, at common law, of the law under which the interest was created avoids arbitrary distinctions between cases falling within the scope of the Rome I Regulation and those falling outside its scope.

---

[64] See Mance LJ in *Raiffeisen Zentralbank Österreich AG v Five Star General Trading LLC* [2001] QB 825 at 842.
[65] Dicey, Morris and Collins, *The Conflict of Laws* (14th edn, 2006) p 1187.
[66] *Raiffeisen Zentralbank Österreich AG v Five Star General Trading LLC* [2001] QB 825.
[67] [1900] 1 Ch 602.   [68] (1855) 10 Moo PCC 1.   [69] [1905] 2 Ch 117.
[70] Cheshire, North and Fawcett, *Private International Law* (14th edn, 2008) pp 1234–5.

D Governmental expropriation of property

9.43 The general principle that the transfer of title is governed by the lex situs applies equally when the transfer is the result of expropriation by a state under a decree or other legislation. If the property is in the territory of the state at the time when the transfer is alleged to have occurred, then effect will be given to it,[71] subject to the doctrines of public policy[72] and the non-enforcement of foreign penal laws.[73] However, effect will not be given to an extra-territorial expropriation.[74] Where, for example, the government of state A purports to expropriate by legislation property which is situated in state B the application of the lex situs rule means that the legislative action of state A will not be recognised as effective by the English court.[75]

III Matrimonial property

A Introduction

9.44 Different countries have different rules about the effect of a marriage on the property of the spouses. Some countries have systems of community of property, under which, to varying extents, the spouses jointly own the property which each owned separately before the marriage, and which each acquires after the marriage. For example, until recently under Roman–Dutch law in South Africa, upon marriage all property already owned by the parties fell into a community of property as did all property acquired during the subsistence of the marriage. The more usual civil law model is that only property acquired during the subsistence of the marriage falls into the community, although even here there are variations. For example, under German law the property of the spouses remains their separate property during the marriage but on termination of the marriage, a 'deferred community' comes into existence.[76] Under these community of property regimes, on the death of one of the spouses the surviving spouse already owns his or her share of the property and does not have to inherit it by way of succession. Similarly, on divorce a spouse can assert his or her rights to a share of the community and does not have to apply to the court for a transfer of any of that property as part of a divorce settlement. Of course, in many countries the surviving spouse will

---

[71] *Aksionairnoye Obschestvo AM Luther v James Sagor & Co* [1921] 3 KB 532; *Princess Olga Paley v Weisz* [1929] 1 KB 718; *Williams & Humbert Ltd v W & H Trade Marks (Jersey) Ltd* [1986] AC 368.

[72] *Kuwait Airways Corpn v Iraqi Airways Co (Nos 4 and 5)* [2002] 2 AC 883; *Yukos Capital Sarl v OJSC Rosneft Oil Co (No 2)* [2014] QB 458 at [69], [72].

[73] See *Islamic Republic of Iran v Barakat Galleries Ltd* [2009] QB 22 (in which, on the facts, it was held that the relevant provisions of Iranian law were not penal or otherwise unenforceable); *United States Securities and Exchange Commission v Manterfield* [2010] 1 WLR 172. For further discussion, see paras 1.145–1.172.

[74] *Bank voor Handel en Scheepvaart NV v Slatford* [1953] 1 QB 248.

[75] *Peer International Corpn v Termidor Music Publishers Ltd* [2004] 2 WLR 849.

[76] See, generally, Kiralfy (ed), *Comparative Law of Matrimonial Property* (1972) and Rheinstein and Glendon, *International Encyclopaedia of Comparative Law*, Vol IV, *Persons and Family* (1980) ch 4; Steenhof, 'A Matrimonial Property System for the EU?' [2005] IFL 74.

additionally have succession rights in relation to the deceased's share of the community and a divorcing spouse can request extra financial provision out of the other's portion of the community.

9.45 Other systems, including English law, provide for the separate ownership of property by spouses. Marriage has no effect upon either the ante-nuptial or post-nuptial assets of the spouses. (A spouse may acquire a beneficial interest in the matrimonial home under the rules relating to resulting and constructive trusts; these rules operate, however, quite independently of marriage and apply equally to two friends who purchase a house together.) Under English law, when a spouse dies intestate, the other spouse has fixed rights of inheritance, but has no such rights when the deceased spouse makes a will disinheriting the survivor. In such cases, the disinherited spouse can make an application for family provision under the Inheritance (Provision for Family and Dependants) Act 1975. When a divorce is obtained in England the court order may take the form of a financial provision order or a property adjustment order whereby one spouse is required to pay money or transfer property to the other spouse from his or her separate assets. In making these orders the court exercises a discretion with the safeguarding of the welfare of any children being the first consideration. Very similar rules are applicable to same-sex civil partnerships.[77]

9.46 Under most systems of community of property there is provision for ante-nuptial marriage contracts, by which the parties make express arrangements for their property after the marriage, perhaps altering the system which would otherwise prevail. The basic system of community of property applies only in the absence of such a contract. In South Africa, for example, such ante-nuptial contracts, which had to be notarially executed, were common. In other countries, such as Germany, there are statutory alternatives to the basic property regime which the parties may adopt by agreement. In England, such ante-nuptial contracts are not strictly legally enforceable but they may be taken into account as a factor in the exercise of any judicial discretion. Over the past decade the courts have attached increasing weight to such contracts culminating in the Supreme Court decision in *Radmacher v Granatino*,[78] which ruled that marital contracts should be given effect to unless, in the circumstances, it would not be fair to hold the parties to their agreement.[79]

9.47 There is much scope for conflict of laws problems in this area. If a German domiciliary marries an English domiciliary, is the marriage in community of property or not? If it were in community and the parties subsequently obtained a divorce in England or one of them died domiciled in England, what account would be taken of this fact in the exercise of the court's discretionary powers to grant financial relief and in the rules of succession? If the parties had contracted a German ante-nuptial contract, to what extent would this regulate their proprietary regime and affect the court's discretionary powers on divorce or affect the rights of the survivor on the death of his or her spouse?

---

[77] Civil Partnership Act 2004.   [78] [2011] 1 AC 534.   [79] At [75]. See below, paras 9.63–9.68.

B The applicable law

9.48 It is important to stress that, irrespective of the law governing the matrimonial property regime and irrespective of the domicile of the parties, an English court applies only English law to all matters of maintenance, financial provision, and property distribution on divorce, legal separation, or annulment, to financial relief after a foreign divorce and, finally, to applications for family provision on the death of one of the spouses. In all such proceedings the courts have wide discretionary powers.[80] These matters are of greater practical importance to most married couples than relatively abstract questions of proprietary ownership of matrimonial property. However, such matters can be of importance—for example, in succession cases not involving family provision or in proceedings brought by third parties against a spouse, on bankruptcy or in relation to sales or gifts by one spouse to a third party without the consent of the other spouse. Further, it is argued later that English courts ought, in all cases, to have more regard to the central conflict of laws rules governing matrimonial property.

1. Movable property

9.49 The traditional rule was that the effect of the marriage on movable property was governed by the law of the husband's domicile at the date of the marriage.[81] At the time this rule was established, the wife took the husband's domicile on marriage, so her domicile necessarily became the same as his at the date of the marriage. So, if at the time of the marriage the husband was domiciled in England, where the regime was separation of property, while the wife was domiciled in a country where community of property prevailed, under this rule the English system applied.

9.50 In more recent times, it has been accepted that this traditional rule in favour of the husband's law at the date of the marriage should be reformulated so that the governing law is that of the 'matrimonial domicile'.[82] This reformulation can be justified on a number of grounds. The former rule was established at a time when, on marriage, a woman necessarily acquired a domicile of dependence on her husband. Since the Domicile and Matrimonial Proceedings Act 1973 this is no longer the case and so, when the parties are domiciled in different countries at the date of the marriage, there is no reason to favour the husband's law. One of the reasons for the abolition of the married woman's domicile of dependence was that the rule was sexist. A preference for the husband's domicile in determining the law applicable to matrimonial property rights would also discriminate on grounds of gender and would almost certainly contravene the European Convention on Human Rights.[83]

---

[80] The consequence has been that the importance of the conflict of laws rules on matrimonial property has diminished. This explains why most of the judicial authorities in this area are from the end of the nineteenth century and the beginning of the twentieth century.
[81] *Re Martin* [1900] P 211.
[82] Dicey, Morris and Collins, *The Conflict of Laws* (15th edn, 2012) p 1465; *Slutsker v Haron Investments Ltd* [2014] 1 FLR 1114 at [35].
[83] Art 14 and art 1 of Protocol 1. See Kinsch, 'Choice-of-law Rules and the Prohibition of Discrimination Under the ECHR' [2011] Nederlands Internationaal Privaatrecht 19, 22–3; also *W v W* [1993] 2 IR 476 on the abandonment across Europe of conflict of laws rules favouring the husband's connections.

9.51 Furthermore, even in the older authorities it was accepted that the application of the law of the husband's domicile at the date of the marriage was no more than a presumption which, in clear cases, could be rebutted in favour of another law, the law of the country in which the spouses intended to establish their home. In *Re Egerton's Will Trusts*[84] a man domiciled in England married a woman domiciled in France; the parties intended to settle in France, but they did not in fact move there until two years after the marriage. On the husband's death, the wife contended that the marriage had been in community of property under French law, the law of the intended matrimonial home. It was held that the marriage was governed by English law as the law of the husband's domicile at the time of the marriage. Roxburgh J, however, accepted that, in exceptional cases, some law other than that of the husband's domicile might govern as the result of the parties' agreement, either express or inferred from their conduct. If the spouses set up their domicile in a new country immediately after the marriage, an agreement that their proprietary rights should be governed by the law of that country might be inferred. Whether such an inference could be made would depend on the circumstances. In the present case, although the parties intended to settle in France, there was no evidence that they had intended the effects of the marriage on their property to be governed by French law and, accordingly, the basic presumption in favour of the law of the husband's domicile at the date of the marriage applied.

9.52 In 2013 in *Slutsker v Haron Investments Ltd*,[85] it was accepted by the Court of Appeal that where, at the time of the marriage, both parties are domiciled in the same country, the matrimonial domicile is (in the absence of special circumstances) that country. It is suggested by commentators that in cases where the parties are domiciled in separate countries, the applicable law should be that of 'the country with which the parties and the marriage have the closest connection'.[86] An objective test should be applied to determine the 'centre of gravity of the marriage'.[87] This test allows a potential role for the intended matrimonial home doctrine as envisaged in *Re Egerton's Will Trusts*.

9.53 There are fewer objections to the application of the law of the intended matrimonial home here than to its use as a choice of law rule to determine the essential validity of a marriage.[88] While this test tends to generate more uncertainty than a domicile rule, it follows from *Re Egerton's Will Trusts* that it is only in clear, very exceptional circumstances that a conclusion will be reached not only that, at the date of the marriage, the parties intended to establish a matrimonial home in a new country and that they did so shortly thereafter, but also that an inference can be drawn that they intended to subject themselves to the proprietary regime of that new country. Further, the problems associated with trying to apply the intended matrimonial home test to the essential validity

---

[84] [1956] Ch 593.
[85] *Slutsker v Haron Investments Ltd* [2014] 1 FLR 1114 at [35], referring to Dicey, Morris and Collins, *The Conflict of Laws* (15th edn, 2012) rule 165.
[86] Dicey, Morris and Collins, *The Conflict of Laws* (15th edn, 2012) p 1465.
[87] Hartley, 'Matrimonial (Marital) Property Rights in Conflict of Laws: A Reconsideration' in Fawcett (ed), *Reform and Development of Private International Law* (2002) p 226.
[88] See paras 7.41–7.45.

of a marriage in prospective situations[89] are not likely to arise in cases involving disputes over matrimonial property. Marriage officials do not need to know the proprietary consequences of a marriage. Also, the parties themselves generally do not need to know at the date of the marriage to which proprietary regime the marriage will be subject. In almost all cases, it is only later in the marriage—on death, divorce, or insolvency—that a determination needs to be made.

2. Mutability or immutability

9.54 A controversial question is whether the proprietary regime fixed by the law of the matrimonial domicile at the time of the marriage changes if the parties subsequently change their domicile. Is the original regime mutable or immutable according to English conflict of laws rules? Suppose, for instance, the parties were married under a regime of community of property, but later move to a country where the system is separation of property. Is property thereafter held in community or separately?

9.55 In *De Nicols v Curlier*[90] the spouses were both domiciled in France when they married there. Because they did not make any ante-nuptial contract, they were deemed by French law to have agreed that their marriage should be in community of property. Subsequently, they became domiciled in England, where the husband made a large fortune. On his death, the wife claimed to be entitled to half the estate by virtue of the community of property, so that the husband's will could operate only on the other half. It was held that the community of property continued despite the change of domicile.

9.56 While this case seems to suggest that the doctrine of immutability prevails, it has been argued that this is not necessarily so, because the basis of the decision was that, by French law, the parties were deemed to have agreed that their property should be held in community. As an express marriage contract continues despite a change of domicile, unless and until the parties cancel or alter it by a subsequent valid contract, the position should be the same with an implied contract, as in *De Nicols v Curlier*. Therefore, the original proprietary regime should continue despite a change of domicile. Indeed, the same reasoning should arguably apply in a case where the governing law offers a choice of regimes, whether or not by that law the regime which operates in the absence of an express choice is regarded as having been impliedly agreed.[91]

9.57 Since the parties could have excluded the basic regime, it is not unreasonable to suppose that their joint decision not to do so should be capable of alteration only by their subsequent agreement. There seems no reason why their acquisition of a domicile in a country having a different regime should be treated as such an agreement.

9.58 Does the doctrine of immutability apply even if the original matrimonial regime cannot be regarded as having been agreed between the parties? A case which may seem

---

[89] See para 7.39. [90] [1900] AC 21.
[91] It has been said that there is always a marriage contract, for when there is no actual agreement one is presumed: Goldberg, 'The Assignment of Property on Marriage' (1970) 19 ICLQ 557. But, it seems artificial to say that in English law parties choose separation of property.

to be in favour of mutability is *Lashley v Hog*,[92] where the change of domicile after marriage was from England to Scotland. On the husband's death, the wife having predeceased him, it was claimed that the wife's estate was entitled to a third share of the husband's property under Scots law. The House of Lords held that the wife's estate was so entitled, even though no such right existed under English law, the law of the matrimonial domicile at the time of the marriage. However, the better view[93] is that the basis of the decision was that the wife's claim to a third share under Scots law was a right of succession, governed by Scots law as the law of the deceased's domicile at his death. If so, it does not follow that the proprietary regime of the marriage changed when the parties became domiciled in Scotland.

9.59 A full doctrine of mutability, in the sense that assets already acquired before the change of domicile become subject to the matrimonial regime of the new domicile, is unacceptable. Take the example of a couple married under South African community of property. All assets acquired by either spouse became jointly owned. If they later became domiciled in England, they already each owned their share of the community. It would be 'quite unintelligible'[94] to assert that a change of domicile has the effect of changing the ownership of property. This was particularly true before the Domicile and Matrimonial Proceedings Act 1973 when the change of common domicile could have been effected unilaterally by the husband's act. However, these arguments are limited to vested rights acquired before the parties' change of domicile. The rule has been advocated[95] that, where there is no express or implied ante-nuptial contract, a common change of domicile by the spouses should not affect rights already acquired under the previous regime, but property acquired after the change of domicile should be governed by the regime determined by the new domicile. This change in matrimonial property regime should be permitted only where both spouses move to the new country and it is clear that the law of the new country is the law with which the parties and the marriage have the closest connection. In the case where one spouse leaves the other and alone acquires a new domicile elsewhere, the nature of the proprietary regime should remain unaltered. However, it must be conceded that such an approach is not without difficulties. If a married couple domiciled in England settle in a new country where the regime is community of property, should their property thereafter be held in community regardless of their wishes? While the new country may allow spouses to contract out of community of property, it may not make provision for doing so after the marriage.

3. Immovable property

9.60 The central question in relation to immovables is whether the law of the matrimonial domicile (previously, the law of the husband's domicile at the date of the marriage)

---

[92] (1804) 4 Pat 581.
[93] Goldberg, 'The Assignment of Property on Marriage' (1970) 19 ICLQ 557, 580–4; Cheshire, North and Fawcett, *Private International Law* (14th edn, 2008) p 1298.
[94] *De Nicols v Curlier* [1900] AC 21 at 27.
[95] Cheshire, North and Fawcett, *Private International Law* (14th edn, 2008) p 1299.

is displaced by the lex situs as the governing law. In *Welch v Tennent*[96] the House of Lords, on appeal from Scotland, held that the lex situs governed. In this case the husband and wife were domiciled in Scotland. After the marriage the wife sold land which she owned in England and paid the proceeds to her husband. She later claimed she was entitled under Scots law to reclaim these proceeds. It was held, however, that the rights of the spouses in relation to immovable property were governed by English law as the lex situs. Accordingly, the husband was allowed to keep the proceeds.

9.61 On the other hand, in *Re De Nicols*,[97] which was concerned with the same marriage as *De Nicols v Curlier*, the French couple, having married in France, moved to England and purchased English land. It was held that this property was subject to the community of property regime of French law and was not subject to English law, the lex situs. While this case can be distinguished on the ground that the basis of the decision was that there was an implied contract between the parties, it would be preferable to allow this issue to be determined by the law of the matrimonial domicile rather than the lex situs. Application of the lex situs rule, as in *Welch v Tennent*, can lead to an estate being 'juridically fragmented'.[98] If a couple own immovable property in several countries, each property could be subject to different matrimonial property regimes. If an English couple were to purchase a holiday home in France or Spain, it would hardly be in accordance with their reasonable expectations that such property be held in community of property. Although the precise basis of the decision is unclear, the decision in *Chiwell v Carlyon*[99] provides support for the application of the law of the matrimonial domicile. In this case a husband and wife married under the South African regime of community of property and later acquired land in England. It was concluded that the rights in this property were to be governed by South African law and not by English law as the lex situs.

9.62 In *Slutsker v Haron Investments Ltd*[100] Underhill J in the High Court acknowledged that the position as regards the law governing immovables was 'highly debatable' and that the 'relevant authorities do not speak with one voice'. In *Slutsker*, which was concerned with the ownership of a matrimonial home in London, Underhill J followed *Re De Nicols* and applied the law of the matrimonial domicile (Russian law) and not the lex situs (English law). Underhill J acknowledged the undesirability of confining *Re De Nicols* to cases where there was an implied contract for the application of the law of the matrimonial domicile and accepted that, as a matter of policy, it would be preferable if the lex domicilii matrimonii were of general application (although he also acknowledged that the lex situs might still have a role to play where third parties claimed interests for value).[101] On appeal,[102] Lloyd LJ[103] was 'content' to decide the case on the same basis as Underhill J but left 'open for decision ... the debate as between the law of the matrimonial domicile and the lex situs'.[104]

---

[96] [1891] AC 639.   [97] [1900] 2 Ch 410.
[98] Dicey, Morris and Collins, *The Conflict of Laws* (15th edn, 2012) p 1470.
[99] (1897) 14 SC 61 (Cape of Good Hope). See Cheshire, North and Fawcett, *Private International Law* (14th edn, 2008) p 1303.
[100] [2012] EWHC 2539 (Ch) at [97].   [101] [2012] EWHC 2539 (Ch) at [108]–[111].
[102] [2014] 1 FLR 1114.   [103] Patten and Black LJJ concurring.   [104] [2014] 1 FLR 1114 at [37].

C Nuptial contracts

9.63 There are three types of contract that may be entered into by married couples. First, there are separation agreements, which govern the financial consequences of a separation that has occurred or is impending. Secondly, parties to a marriage may make a post-nuptial agreement,[105] the purpose of which is to regulate the financial consequences in the event of a future separation or divorce. Thirdly, intending spouses may enter into an ante-nuptial contract regulating the proprietary consequences of their marriage. Some legal systems enable the parties to choose between alternative proprietary regimes by an ante-nuptial contract. For example, they may be free by such a contract to exclude community of property, which would be the regime in the absence of any agreement. Alternatively, they may construct their own system of community of property. In most of these jurisdictions, such contracts are legally binding although, in some jurisdictions, courts have power to depart from the terms of the contract to prevent manifest injustice.

9.64 In England, separation agreements have long been regarded as enforceable unless there are overwhelmingly strong considerations for a court to interfere with the terms of the contract.[106] Ante-nuptial and post-nuptial contracts, on the other hand, used to be regarded as contrary to public policy and so void. However, when granting a divorce and making ancillary relief orders under section 25(1) of the Matrimonial Causes Act 1973 the court must have regard to 'all the circumstances of the case' and, in recent years, courts have increasingly been giving considerable effect to nuptial contracts as one of the 'circumstances of the case'. As a result, more couples in England are entering into ante-nuptial agreements. In 2014 the Law Commission published a report on 'Matrimonial Property, Needs and Agreements',[107] recommending the adoption of legislation regulating the conclusion of 'qualifying nuptial agreements' and confirming the enforceability of ante-nuptial and post-nuptial contracts, subject to the courts' powers to provide for financial needs. Thus far, however, there has been no move to adopt legislation to implement these recommendations.

9.65 In *MacLeod v MacLeod*[108] the Privy Council drew a distinction between ante-nuptial agreements and post-nuptial agreements holding that the latter (only) did constitute valid and enforceable contracts—although in a divorce case the arrangements were subject to the court's powers of variation under section 25(1). The distinction between ante- and post-nuptial agreements was swept aside by the Supreme Court in *Radmacher v Granatino*[109] where the court ruled that for both ante- and post-nuptial agreements:

> The court should give effect to a nuptial agreement that is freely entered into by each party with a full appreciation of its implications unless in the circumstances prevailing it would not be fair to hold the parties to their agreement.[110]

---

[105] Such agreements are 'rare' in England: *Radmacher v Granatino* [2011] 1 AC 534 at [47].
[106] Maintenance Agreements Act 1957, s 1, reproduced in Matrimonial Causes Act 1973, ss 34, 35; *Smith v McInerney* [1994] 2 FLR 1077.
[107] Law Com No 343.   [108] [2010] 1 AC 298.
[109] [2011] 1 AC 534 at [57]: there is no 'material distinction' between 'an agreement concluded the day before the wedding, and, one concluded the day after it'.   [110] At [75].

9.66 In *Radmacher v Granatino* an ante-nuptial contract was entered into in Germany by a German wife and a French husband. The contract, which contained a German choice of law clause, was valid and legally enforceable both by German law and French conflict of laws rules.[111] The Supreme Court held that, in exercising its jurisdiction to make an order for financial relief under the Matrimonial Causes Act 1973, the English court 'will normally apply English law, irrespective of the domicile of the parties, or any foreign connection'.[112] The main relevance of the German law and the German choice of law clause is that 'they clearly demonstrate the intention of the parties that the ante-nuptial agreement should, if possible, be binding on them'.[113] Accordingly, the fact that the contract is legally binding under a foreign law is not directly relevant. The same principles apply to all cases whether the ante-nuptial contract is foreign or English.[114] In giving weight to the contract as part of 'all the circumstances' of the case under section 25(1) the existence of the ante-nuptial contract is 'but one factor in the process and, perhaps, in the right case ... the most compelling factor'.[115] The Supreme Court concluded that, in the circumstances of the case, it was fair to hold the husband to the terms of the ante-nuptial contract and that 'it would be unfair to depart from it'.[116]

9.67 Because the terms of an ante-nuptial contract are always capable of being varied by the court in a divorce case under the discretionary powers conferred by section 25(1), it is not necessary to decide whether an ante-nuptial contract is legally binding. Nevertheless, it is implicit in the judgment in *Radmacher v Granatino* that both post- and ante-nuptial agreements are binding contracts (although capable of variation by the courts in a divorce case). This is clearly the interpretation that Lady Hale, the one dissenting judge in the case, placed upon the majority judgment when she stated that she disagreed with that view which was 'mercifully obiter to the decision in this case'.[117]

9.68 While the issue whether an ante-nuptial contract is a legally binding contract is a 'red herring'[118] in divorce cases, the matter could be of crucial importance in different contexts, for example in bankruptcy proceedings brought against a spouse during the subsistence of a marriage, or in a succession case after the death of a spouse.[119] Whether nuptial contracts will be enforceable in these other contexts is, at present, pure speculation although, in principle, they should be—especially foreign marriage contracts that are valid under the foreign law. Under the laws of most other jurisdictions where ante-nuptial contracts are common, such contracts are legally enforceable in all contexts. If such an approach were to be accepted by English law (at least, in the case of foreign marital contracts), it is unclear what conflict of laws rules would determine their validity as there is no modern case law on the subject. There are old

---

[111] At [101].   [112] At [103].   [113] At [108].
[114] See *Luckwell v Limata* [2014] 2 FLR 168.
[115] [2011] 1 AC 534 at [83], endorsing the comments of the first instance judge, Baron J.
[116] At [123].   [117] At [138].   [118] At [63].
[119] This point was recognised by Lord Mance at [128] in a separate judgment.

authorities on the law governing marriage settlements which were entered into before 1882 when married women were unable to own certain property (particularly land) unless it was 'settled' on them for their own use in which case it became separate property free from the husband's control. It is doubtful whether these antiquated conflicts rules would be applicable to modern ante-nuptial contracts and, accordingly, these rules are not discussed here.[120] The only general point that needs to be made is that, should the English courts determine that it is necessary to decide the issue, the validity and effect of an ante-nuptial contract is governed by the law governing the contract. The Rome I Regulation[121] is not applicable because article 1(2)(c) excludes contractual obligations 'arising out of matrimonial property regimes'. Accordingly, the common law rules are applicable. Under the common law, a contract is governed by its proper law. This law may be chosen, expressly or impliedly, by the parties. Failing such choice, the proper law of a contract is the law with which the contract is most closely connected.[122] In the matrimonial context, the factors relevant to establishing the law of closest connection are not the same as in commercial contracts. In particular, the matrimonial domicile is often the most important factor in the determination of the proper law.[123]

D **Matrimonial property rights and succession**

9.69 When spouses are married in community of property, on the death of one of them, the survivor is entitled to half the joint estate by virtue of the community. This is generally taken into account in the provision which the law of the country concerned makes for any share in the deceased's half to which a surviving spouse is entitled on intestacy. Anomalies can occur when parties, married in community, move to a country where separation of property is the rule, and one of them dies intestate domiciled in the new country. That country's rules of intestate succession will not take into account the possibility of the survivor taking half the joint estate before any question arises as to the succession to the deceased's half. The consequence may be that the survivor inherits a large share in the deceased's half of the estate as well as taking his own half, thereby receiving considerably more than he would have done if the spouses had always been domiciled in either the original or the new country, at the expense of the children or other relatives entitled on intestacy.[124] However, with respect to persons dying domiciled in England, dependants of the deceased can apply for family provision under the Inheritance (Provision for Family and Dependants) Act 1975.

9.70 Problems arising from the interaction of matrimonial property regimes and succession rules would be avoided if the doctrine of mutability applied. But, that in turn could deprive the survivor of half the property which would have been held in community

---

[120] For a discussion of these rules, see the second edition of this work, pp 504–6.
[121] Regulation (EC) No 593/2008, OJ 2008 L177/6.   [122] See para 4.3.
[123] *Re Fitzgerald* [1904] 1 Ch 573 at 587; *Duke of Marlborough v A-G* [1945] Ch 78. Cf *Re Bankes* [1902] 2 Ch 333.
[124] *Beaudoin v Trudel* [1937] 1 DLR 216.

under the original law if the deceased made a will leaving all or much of his property away from the survivor. Again, the Inheritance (Provision for Family and Dependants) Act 1975 can provide corrective assistance; however, a truly satisfactory solution can be achieved only if the rules of succession of the new country make special provision for people formerly domiciled in countries having community regimes.

E Matrimonial property rights and divorce

9.71 Under the Matrimonial Causes Act 1973, when granting a divorce, the English court has a broad discretion to make orders for financial relief and property adjustment orders whereby one spouse is ordered to transfer property to another. In exercising this discretion, the courts often appear to pay little or no attention to the fact that the parties might be married under some proprietary regime other than separation of property. Similarly, the fact that the parties have drawn up an ante-nuptial contract regulating the proprietary consequences of their marriage is no more than a matter that the courts can consider in the exercise of their discretion. It is true that in the *Radmacher* case[125] the Supreme Court ruled that such contracts should be given effect unless, in the circumstances, it would not be fair to hold the parties to their agreement—but subsequent cases suggest that the English courts will frequently allow parties to escape obligations under an ante-nuptial contract.[126]

9.72 Such an approach is unfortunate. Where the parties have married under a proprietary regime that provides for, say, community of property, there must be a strong argument that the English courts ought to give effect to it, at least as a starting-point in the exercise of its discretion. For example, the parties might have been domiciled and married in Texas according to whose law their matrimonial property would be subject to a regime of community of property. The parties might have sought legal advice and been content with that regime and could have lived for the next 20 years subject to that law. If they then come to England and, after the requisite period of habitual residence, one of the parties petitions for a divorce, it would be highly anomalous and not in accord with the couple's reasonable expectations for the English court to disregard the fact that the parties were married in community of property.

9.73 Section 25 of the Matrimonial Causes Act 1973 should be amended so that the fact that the parties were married under a particular matrimonial regime should be given more weight. The courts should retain their discretionary powers to make the necessary maintenance awards to a spouse and the children.[127] Indeed, for most marriages a couple's resources on divorce will probably be exhausted after maintenance issues have been resolved. However, for more wealthy couples, once maintenance matters have

---

[125] [2011] 1 AC 534.
[126] See, eg, *Z v Z (No 2) (Financial Remedy: Marriage Contract)* [2012] 1 FLR 1100; *B v S (Financial Remedy: Marital Property Regime)* [2012] 2 FLR 502; *AH v PH (Scandinavian Marriage Settlement)* [2014] 2 FLR 251.
[127] Such matters are governed by the Maintenance Regulation (Council Regulation (EC) No 4/2009, OJ 2009 L7/1).

been determined, the fact that the parties were married under a particular matrimonial property regime should be taken into account as a starting-point for the distribution of their property.

F Proposals for reform within Europe

9.74 In 2011 the European Commission published a Proposal on Matrimonial Property Regimes.[128] Under this Proposal there would have been uniform choice of law rules throughout the European Union, with the aim of ensuring that whichever Member State court had jurisdiction in disputes concerning matrimonial property, movable or immovable, whether on divorce or otherwise, the same law would be applied. One of the aims of the Proposal was to ensure that, regardless of jurisdictional issues, questions of substance would be given uniform answers. The Proposal favoured the principle of party autonomy with the parties being free to conclude a marital property contract choosing the law to govern their matrimonial property. In the absence of such a contract, harmonised choice of law rules would have applied. The Council of the European Union had hoped to secure political agreement on the proposed Regulation in December 2015;[129] however, the necessary consensus was not achieved. Subsequently, 17 Member States addressed a request to the Commission to proceed with the project by way of 'enhanced cooperation' (in other words, by way of a measure which would be binding only on those Member States desiring to be bound).[130] It is extremely unlikely that the United Kingdom would participate in any such 'enhanced cooperation' measure, having already 'opted out' of the original Proposal in 2011 (citing concerns about increased costs—in proving foreign law—and the non-existence in English law of the concept of the matrimonial property regime).[131]

IV Succession

A Introduction

9.75 The only person entitled to deal with the property of a deceased person is a personal representative who has been appointed by a grant of representation as an executor (where appointed by a will) or an administrator (where a testamentary appointment

---

[128] European Commission, *Proposal for a Council Regulation on jurisdiction, applicable law and the recognition and enforcement of decisions in matters of matrimonial property regimes*, COM (2011) 126 final. There was also a separate Proposal, along similar lines, regarding the property consequences of civil or registered partnerships: European Commission, *Proposal for a Council Regulation on jurisdiction, applicable law and the recognition and enforcement of decisions regarding the property consequences of registered partnerships*, COM (2011) 127/2.

[129] See JUSTCIV 276, 14651/15 (Brussels, 26 November 2015).

[130] European Commission, *Proposal for a Council Decision authorising enhanced cooperation in the area of jurisdiction, applicable law and the recognition and enforcement of decisions on the property regimes of international couples, covering both matters of matrimonial property regimes and the property consequences of registered partnerships*, COM (2016) 108 final.

[131] Ministry for Justice, *European Commission Proposed Regulations on Matrimonial Property Regimes and the Property Consequences of Registered Partnerships: Response to Public Consultation* (2011).

fails or the deceased dies intestate). In theory, there are no limits to the English court's power to make a grant of representation. However, the court has a discretion to grant representation and will not normally do so unless the deceased has left property in England or there are other good reasons for the making of such a grant—for example, because the testator died domiciled in England and a foreign court, where the assets are situated, requires such a grant before it will allow the personal representative to deal with the estate in that foreign country.[132] Where the deceased has left property in England, the court may also deal with entitlement to immovable property abroad, as an exception to the normal rule about lack of jurisdiction over foreign immovables.

9.76 The personal representative must first collect all the assets and clear the estate by paying all debts and taxes and must then distribute the remaining estate among the beneficiaries under the will or according to the rules of intestacy. This chapter does not deal with the administration of the estate (for example, payment of debts). This is regarded as a matter of procedure and, consistent with the general rule, is governed by English law, the lex fori. The concern in this section is with the distribution of the estate of a deceased person among the beneficiaries, either under a will or on intestacy.

9.77 The following discussion of the choice of law rules for succession deals separately with testate and intestate succession. Within each of these categories, it is necessary to distinguish between the rules relating to movable and immovable property. An EU Regulation on succession—in which the United Kingdom is not a participant—is discussed at the end of this chapter.

B Wills

1. Movables

(A) Introduction

9.78 Like contracts, wills express the intentions of the people who make them, and many of the different issues which may arise are similar to those considered in Chapter 4. One difference, however, is that a will is made at one time but takes effect at another, so connecting factors at two different times may be relevant. As has been seen, the governing law for a contract is (broadly speaking) the law of the country with which it is most closely connected, unless the parties expressly or impliedly choose a different law. The country with which a will is most closely connected is the place where the testator is domiciled, for that is the country to which the beneficiaries are likely to, and the testator is deemed to, belong, and in which all or some of the estate is likely to be situated. For some issues it is the domicile of the testator at death that matters, while for others it is the testator's domicile at the date of making the will. As for the testator intending a different law, this is effective only in respect of non-mandatory rules of succession, such as those governing the construction of wills. With respect to mandatory rules, such as those governing essential validity, the testator is unable to evade the provisions of the law to which he is deemed to belong by choosing another law to govern the will.

---

[132] Dicey, Morris and Collins, *The Conflict of Laws* (15th edn, 2012) p 1394.

(B) Capacity

9.79 The concern here is with issues such as whether the testator was old enough to make a will and whether his mental state was such as to preclude him from doing so. While it is appropriate that the law of the country to which the testator belongs should determine his capacity,[133] it has not yet been decided whether domicile should be assessed when the will was made or when the testator died. The former view seems preferable,[134] not only because it refers to the law of the testator's country at the time of the legal act in question, but also because it avoids the possibility of a hitherto valid will being invalidated by a change in the testator's domicile.

9.80 Another issue that can arise is whether a legatee has capacity to take under a will. While it seems that, in principle, this question should be governed by the law of the legatee's domicile at the date when he claims the legacy,[135] it has been held that it is sufficient if the legatee has capacity either under that law or under the law of the testator's domicile at the date of the latter's death.[136] However, in exceptional cases, the interests of the testator's domiciliary law in the issue may be so great that it alone should determine whether the legatee has capacity to take under a will. For example, if a foreign domiciled legatee murdered an English domiciled testator, the English rule disqualifying the beneficiary from taking under the will would almost certainly be applied irrespective of the law of the beneficiary's domicile.[137]

(C) Formal validity

9.81 The choice of law rules for the formal validity of a will are contained in the Wills Act 1963, which gives effect to the Hague Convention on the Conflict of Laws Relating to the Form of Testamentary Dispositions of 1961.[138] The policy of the Convention and the 1963 Act is to ensure uniformity of decision in different countries and to uphold the formal validity of a will wherever possible. There is little point in invalidating a will on purely formal grounds if the testator has complied with a law with which he (or the will) has a connection. Accordingly, section 1 of the 1963 Act provides that a will is formally valid if the testator complies with any of seven possible laws: the laws of the territory of his domicile, habitual residence, or nationality at the time of executing the will or at the time of his death, and the law of the place where the will was executed. Moreover, further alternative possibilities are added, for if the will was executed on board a vessel or aircraft, it is sufficient if the execution of the will conformed to the internal law in force in the territory with which, having regard to its registration and other relevant circumstances, the vessel or aircraft may be taken to have been most

---

[133] *Re Lewal's Settlement Trusts* [1918] 2 Ch 391; *Re Fuld's Estate (No 3)* [1968] P 675.
[134] Cheshire, North and Fawcett, *Private International Law* (14th edn, 2008) pp 1265–6; Dicey, Morris and Collins, *The Conflict of Laws* (15th edn, 2012) p 1418.
[135] *Re Schnapper* [1928] Ch 420.
[136] *Re Hellmann's Will* (1866) LR 2 Eq 363.
[137] Miller, *International Aspects of Succession* (2000) p 164.
[138] Cmnd 1729. See also the *Fourth Report of the Private International Law Committee*, 1958 (Cmnd 491).

closely connected.¹³⁹ Also, it is sufficient if the will complied with the formalities of any of the possible laws at the time of execution or at a subsequent time if that law is altered with retrospective effect.¹⁴⁰

(D) Essential validity

9.82 Rules of essential validity are those concerned with matters such as whether the testator is obliged to leave a certain proportion of his estate to particular relatives and whether certain kinds of gifts are invalid—for example, as infringing a rule against perpetuities. Where the issue is the protection of relatives against disinheritance, the appropriate law to govern essential validity is the law of the country to which the testator belongs (and to which the relatives will also often belong). Where the issue is whether the will should be rendered invalid by a rule designed to protect the public interest, the law of the country whose interests are most likely to be affected by the disposition should apply. In either case, this law is normally the law of the testator's domicile at the date of his death. Accordingly, matters of essential validity of a will disposing of movables are governed by the law of the testator's domicile at his death.¹⁴¹

9.83 For example, if a testator dies domiciled in France leaving his estate to friends and failing to leave to his wife and children the share to which they are entitled under French law, this will is essentially valid only with respect to that portion of the estate which remains after the wife and children have received their statutory portions. If the testator had died domiciled in England, under whose law relatives are not entitled to any fixed share of the estate, the whole will would be essentially valid and the entire estate would pass to the friends. However, in such cases, certain dependants of the deceased can apply for family provision under the Inheritance (Provision for Family and Dependants) Act 1975. This power to grant family provision is limited to cases where the testator died domiciled in England.¹⁴² It follows that, if the testator had died domiciled in a country under whose law complete freedom of testation is permitted, members of the family living in England could be disinherited and left destitute.

9.84 It would appear, however, that not all questions of essential validity are exclusively subject to the law of the testator's domicile at death. Where that law invalidates a disposition because it infringes a rule against perpetuities or accumulations, it ought not to be applied if the subject-matter of the disposition is situated, and is to be administered, in another country. If, for example, an English testator leaves foreign property for a purpose which is not charitable under English law but is charitable under the law of the country where the property is located, there is no reason why English law should be applied to render the disposition invalid. The issue in such a case should be governed by the lex situs. To apply the testator's domiciliary law would be to invalidate dispositions which are not capable of infringing the public interest which the invalidating rule was

---

¹³⁹ Wills Act 1963, s 2(1)(a).   ¹⁴⁰ S 6(3).
¹⁴¹ *Re Annesley* [1926] Ch 692; *Re Ross* [1930] 1 Ch 377; *Al-Bassam v Al-Bassam* [2004] WTLR 757; *Dellar v Zivy* [2007] ILPr 60.
¹⁴² S 1(1).

designed to protect or advance (such as ensuring the marketability of property in the country concerned). This approach is supported by the old case of *Fordyce v Bridges*.[143] The will of the testator, who died domiciled in England, contained a bequest of movable property on trust to sell and use the money to buy land in Scotland according to certain limitations which infringed the English rule against perpetuities, but were valid by Scots law. The gift was held valid.

(E) Construction

9.85 Which law should govern questions of interpretation such as what the testator meant by phrases such as 'next-of-kin'[144] and what the testator would have intended when an event occurs, such as the death of a legatee before the death of the testator, for which no provision is made in the will? In such cases, the domestic rules of construction of the potentially applicable laws are non-mandatory rules; they are not rules which override the testator's intention, but rather they help to ascertain his intention when it is obscure, or they fill gaps in his expressed intention. So, the governing law should be the law intended by the testator. This is normally presumed to be the law of the testator's domicile at the time he made the will (as opposed to the law of domicile at the date of death), for, unless there is strong indication to the contrary, it is only reasonable to suppose that he was making his will by reference to the law of his own country at the date of making the will.[145]

9.86 In *Re Cunnington*[146] the testator, domiciled in France, made a will in England, in English form and language, bequeathing his residuary estate to ten legatees, all of whom were English. Two of the legatees died before the testator. By English law their shares would go as on intestacy, while by French law they would be divided among the surviving legatees. It was held that French law governed, a decision which shows that the presumption that the testator intended the law of his domicile to govern is a strong one, for there were weighty indications pointing to English law. *Curati v Perdoni*[147] adopts the same approach. Although the testator wrote the will in the Italian language in Italy, the presumption that the testator intended the law of his domicile (in this case English law) to govern was not displaced. Nevertheless, the presumption is rebuttable. In *Dellar v Zivy*[148] a testator who was (probably) domiciled in France made a will in England where he was living. On the facts, the presumption that a person intends his will to be interpreted according to the law of his domicile at the date of making the will was rebutted. It was clear that the testator intended his will to be interpreted according to English law because the will had been made in England by English solicitors and was written in English; the will stated that the testator regarded himself as domiciled in England (even though he was probably domiciled in France); it appointed an English solicitor as executor and directed that English solicitors were to be consulted in all matters concerning the administration of the estate; and it created a trust for sale (which is

---

[143] (1848) 2 Ph 497.   [144] *Re Fergusson's Will* [1902] 1 Ch 483.
[145] Wills Act 1963, s 4 provides that the 'construction of a will shall not be altered by reason of any change in the testator's domicile after the execution of the will'.
[146] [1924] 1 Ch 68.   [147] [2013] WTLR 63.   [148] [2007] ILPr 60.

not known in French law). All these factors made it 'absolutely clear'[149] that the testator intended the will to be interpreted according to English law.

(F) Revocation

9.87 There are various ways in which it may be claimed that a will, or a provision in a will, has been revoked. If it is alleged that the will has been revoked (whether expressly or impliedly) by a subsequent will, the relevant issues concern the validity or construction of the later will; these matters are discussed above. If the question concerns the formal validity of the subsequent will, section 2(1)(c) of the Wills Act 1963 provides that it is sufficient if the subsequent will complies with any law which the revoked will might have complied with, in addition to any law with which the subsequent will may comply.

9.88 There is no English authority on which law determines whether a will is revoked by destroying it. Should this question be governed by the law of the testator's domicile at the date of the purported revocation or at the date of death? The better view is that this should be governed by the law of the testator's domicile at the time of the purported revocation. If the revocation is effective under that law, the will ceases to exist and, therefore, there is no will upon which the later domiciliary law can operate.[150] If the revocation is ineffective under the testator's then domiciliary law, the will should not be retrospectively revoked by a change of domicile because no revoking act has taken place at the time the testator was subject to the new domiciliary law.[151]

9.89 Under English law, but not under the laws of many other countries, a will is revoked by the subsequent marriage of the testator. What is the position if a man domiciled in France makes a will, then acquires an English domicile and marries, and finally dies domiciled in Scotland? (Under French and Scots law, marriage does not revoke a will.) In *Re Martin*,[152] it was held that this issue was to be classified as a matter of matrimonial property (and not succession) to be governed by the law of the husband's domicile at the date of the marriage.[153] Accordingly, in the above example, the will would be revoked. What are the implications of *Re Martin* where a woman marries having made a will? *Re Martin* was decided at a time when a wife automatically acquired her husband's domicile on marriage. Since the Domicile and Matrimonial Proceedings Act 1973 came into force this is no longer the case. Previously, where a French domiciled woman made a will and then, while still domiciled in France, married an English domiciliary, the authority of *Re Martin* would suggest that her will was revoked. With the abolition of the wife's dependent domicile, the position is unclear. It has been suggested that the question whether a will is revoked by subsequent marriage should be reclassified as a separate conflicts category being governed in all cases by the law of the testator's domicile at the date of the marriage.[154] Alternatively, if it

---

[149] At [33].
[150] Dicey, Morris and Collins, *The Conflict of Laws* (15th edn, 2012) p 1442.
[151] Mann (1954) 31 BYIL 231. Cf Miller, *International Aspects of Succession* (2000) pp 191–2.
[152] [1900] P 211.
[153] See para 9.49.
[154] Dicey, Morris and Collins, *The Conflict of Laws* (15th edn, 2012) p 1444.

is still to be classified as a matter of matrimonial property, it should be subject to the proposed new choice of law rule for this category—namely, in the absence of a shared domicile, the law of the country with which the parties and the marriage have their closest connection.[155]

2. Immovable property

9.90 To what extent are the choice of law rules for wills different in relation to the disposition of immovable property? Is the lex situs exclusively relevant? There are two reasons why questions relating to immovable property may be subjected to the lex situs. One is that the property is under the control of the authorities of the country where it is situated, and a decision different from that which would be given by the court of that country may not have any effect. This reason only applies to foreign land. The other reason, which applies to immovable property in England, is that the interests of the country where the land is situated may be affected by the disposition of the land. Whether this is so, however, depends on the nature of the domestic rules in question.

9.91 Because the rationale underlying the application of the lex situs rule depends on whether the property is situated in England or not, it is convenient to explore the two situations separately.

(A) English immovables

9.92 Many questions relating to the disposition by will of immovables situated in England are governed by English domestic law, as the lex situs. However, as the land is situated in England and under the control of English authorities which will clearly follow any English court decision, the main rationale for the application of the lex situs does not apply and a more flexible approach can be adopted.

(i) Capacity

9.93 There is no authority as to the law governing capacity to make a will disposing of immovables in England. As English interests can scarcely be affected by whether or not a testator domiciled abroad has power to dispose of property by will (assuming that the disposition would be essentially valid by English law), there seems no reason why the law of the testator's domicile should not govern, as with movables.[156]

(ii) Formal validity

9.94 Under the Wills Act 1963, the provisions relating to the formal validity of wills disposing of immovable property are the same as for movables, except that, in addition, compliance with the lex situs is sufficient.[157]

---

[155] See paras 9.50–9.53.
[156] This view is not supported by either Dicey, Morris and Collins, *The Conflict of Laws* (15th edn, 2012) p 1419 or Cheshire, North and Fawcett, *Private International Law* (14th edn, 2008) p 1279; both envisage that this issue would be governed by the lex situs.
[157] S 2(1)(b).

(iii) Essential validity

9.95 The essential validity of a will disposing of immovable property has been held to be governed by the lex situs, English law. For example, in *Freke v Lord Carbery*[158] a disposition by a testator domiciled in Ireland of a leasehold house in England was held invalid on the basis that it infringed English legislation, although the disposition was valid by Irish law. Similarly, as regards English land, the questions of what estates can be created, and with what incidents, are governed by English law.[159]

(iv) Construction

9.96 The construction of a gift by will of immovables in England is not necessarily governed by English law; if no mandatory rules of English law are in issue, the interests of England are not involved, so, as with movables, the intention of the testator is to be ascertained, or gaps in his provisions are to be filled, by the law intended by him. It is normally presumed that the law of the testator's domicile at the date of making the will is the law which he would reasonably expect to apply.[160] This is illustrated (in relation to the Scottish conflict of laws) by the Scottish case of *Studd v Cook*,[161] in which a testator, domiciled in England, by his will devised land in Scotland. The effect of the disposition by English law was to give the beneficiary a life interest, but by Scots law a fee simple. The House of Lords (on appeal from the Scottish court) held that the English construction was to be applied. Of course, when the English court is dealing with English land, the essential validity of the disposition is governed by English law, which may mean that the disposition as construed by the law of the domicile has to be accommodated to what is legally possible under English law.[162]

(v) Revocation

9.97 There seems no reason why the rules determining which law governs revocation of a will of English immovables should not be the same as for movables; English interests are not especially involved in relation to that question, merely because the property is English land. This is certainly true where it is claimed that a will is revoked by a later will. However, with regard to revocation by destruction, it was held in the US case of *Re Barrie's Estate*[163] that whether a will had been revoked by writing 'void' across it was to be determined by the lex situs. As regards revocation by subsequent marriage, it has been held in England[164] that the will of a testator domiciled in Scotland at the date of the marriage and disposing of land in England was revoked by his subsequent marriage under English law even though the marriage did not have that effect by Scots law. The decision was, however, not followed by the New South Wales court in *Re Micallef's Estate*[165] in relation to land in New South Wales (whose law has the same rule as English law). The reasons were that the law of New South Wales could have no interest in imposing its rule on a testator domiciled in another country, and that in any

---

[158] (1873) LR 16 Eq 461. [159] *Re Miller* [1914] 1 Ch 511.
[160] *Philipson-Stow v IRC* [1961] AC 727. [161] (1883) 8 App Cas 577.
[162] *Re Miller* [1914] 1 Ch 511. [163] 240 Iowa 431, 35 NW 2d 658 (1949).
[164] *Re Earl Caithness* (1891) 7 TLR 354. [165] [1977] 2 NSWLR 929.

event the rule is not one of succession but of matrimonial property, which is governed by the law of the domicile at the date of the marriage.

(B) *Foreign immovables*

9.98 The reason why the lex situs should govern wills of foreign land is not merely that the foreign country's interests may be affected, but that the land is under the control of the authorities there. If the English court is to make any decision about the entitlement to such land it should, arguably, be in line with the decision which would be made by the foreign court, thereby reducing the likelihood that the matter would be disposed of differently by the foreign court. So, the lex situs should apply.

9.99 Although this reasoning should logically extend to all issues which might arise in relation to foreign immovables, the lex situs does not in fact govern all such issues.

(i) Capacity

9.100 Even if in the case of English land the law of the domicile should govern, for foreign land there is a strong case that the governing law should be whatever domestic law would be applied by the court of the situs. There is little point applying the law of domicile if the result would not be accepted by the authorities of the situs.

(ii) Formal validity

9.101 The position in relation to formal validity is regulated by the Wills Act 1963 and the relevant provisions are the same as those applicable to land situated in England.

(iii) Essential validity

9.102 It is well settled that the essential validity of the will is governed by the lex situs.[166]

(iv) Construction

9.103 So far as the construction of the will is concerned, the authority that the governing law is the law intended by the testator, normally presumed to be the law of the testator's domicile at the time of making the will, rather than the lex situs, is not confined to English immovables.[167] However, the fundamental question here is simply one of ascertaining the intention of the testator, and it may be that the presumption may be more easily rebutted in favour of the lex situs, especially if the testator uses technical language only known to the lex situs. Similarly, if a construction of a will according to the law of domicile would be illegal or impossible to give effect to under the lex situs, then the canons of construction of the lex situs must apply.[168]

(v) Revocation

9.104 As regards revocation of wills of foreign immovables, there seems no reason in principle why the rules should not be the same as for revocation of wills of English immovables, and this is almost certainly the position as regards revocation by subsequent will

---

[166] *Re Ross* [1930] 1 Ch 377.   [167] *Philipson-Stow v IRC* [1961] AC 727.   [168] Ibid.

and revocation by marriage. However, with regard to revocation by destruction, the arguments for application of the lex situs are, as with all issues relating to land abroad, more compelling, and accordingly it is more likely that the US decision of *Re Barrie's Estate*[169] would be followed and the lex situs applied to determine the effect of the destruction of a will.[170]

C Intestate succession

1. Movables

9.105 The law which governs the disposition of a person's movable property on his death, to the extent not validly disposed of by will, is the law of the deceased's domicile at his death.[171] It is appropriate that the matter be determined by the law of the country to which the deceased belongs. A person may reasonably expect that the law of that country will apply and, in not making a will, he may be presumed to be content that his property should devolve in accordance with its intestacy rules.

2. Immovables

9.106 Intestate succession to immovable property, whether situated in England or a foreign country, is governed by the lex situs.[172] This no doubt is the right approach in those exceptional cases when the English court is willing to determine entitlements to land situated abroad. However, there seems little reason why English domestic law should govern the intestate succession of land in England left by a person who died domiciled elsewhere. English interests are not affected by the way the property is divided amongst the deceased's relatives and, if the law of domicile is the appropriate law for movables, it is equally so for immovables. It is unsatisfactory that the different kinds of property of a deceased should be distributed according to different regimes, which can lead to results not contemplated by either law.[173]

D Renvoi in succession cases

9.107 When succession to immovable property in a foreign country is governed by the lex situs, this is traditionally regarded as meaning the whole law of the situs, including its conflicts rules, so that the domestic law to be applied by the English court is that which would be applied by the foreign court,[174] which, in a case of intestate succession for example, might be the law of the deceased's nationality.

9.108 The doctrine of renvoi has also been used in relation to succession to movables.[175] The justification for this is not that the property is in the control of the foreign authority (indeed, it will probably be in England), but that it may produce uniformity of

---

[169] 240 Iowa 431, 35 NW 2d 658 (1949). See para 9.97.
[170] Dicey, Morris and Collins, *The Conflict of Laws* (15th edn, 2012) p 1442, n 193.
[171] *Re Collens* [1986] Ch 505.   [172] Ibid.   [173] Ibid.   [174] *Re Ross* [1930] 1 Ch 377.
[175] *Re Annesley* [1926] Ch 692; *Re Ross* [1930] 1 Ch 377; *Re O'Keefe* [1940] Ch 124; *Re Haji-Ioannou (Deceased)* [2009] ILPr 56.

distribution of the deceased's property, whether determined by the English court or the foreign court, in respect of property in either country. In Chapter 1 it is argued that the doctrine of renvoi is inappropriate in such cases. Effectively, it involves the English court sacrificing its own notions of the appropriate governing law for the sake of uniformity. However, whatever view one adopts in relation to renvoi, one thing seems certain: it is not desirable to use renvoi when the governing law is the law of the domicile at the date of making the will (as opposed to the date of death), as is the case with the construction of a will, at any rate if the deceased changed his domicile after making the will. For then uniformity would be achieved with the wrong country, perhaps at the expense of uniformity with the domicile at death.

9.109 The Wills Act 1963 expressly refers to the 'internal law' of the relevant countries, which is defined in relation to any country as 'the law which would apply in a case where no question of the law in force in any other territory or state arose'.[176] Thus, renvoi is excluded for formal validity[177] (even in respect of immovable property). Uniformity can be hoped for here to the extent that other countries adopt the international convention which was implemented by the 1963 Act.

E The incidental question

9.110 When English conflicts rules lead to the application of the domestic law of a foreign country, an incidental question may arise which itself requires the application of a conflicts rule for its solution. The problem is whether the incidental question is to be decided by the English conflicts rules (lex fori) or by those of the foreign country whose domestic law governs the main question (lex causae).[178] Suppose, for example, a succession is governed by Mexican law and, under Mexican law, the wife and legitimate children of the deceased are entitled to succeed. The question may arise whether a particular claimant is the surviving wife of the deceased, which depends on whether her marriage to the deceased was valid; or the question may arise whether a particular child is legitimate. Are the English or Mexican conflicts rules as to the validity of the marriage or the legitimacy of the child to be applied by the English court?

9.111 The tendency of the courts has been to apply the conflicts rules of the lex causae to decide the incidental question, often, however, without any express discussion of the problem. It is possible to support the use of the lex causae as a general rule in the field

---

[176] S 6(1).
[177] At common law the doctrine of renvoi was applied to formal validity: *Re Fuld's Estate (No 3)* [1968] P 675. As there is nothing in the Act which abolishes the common law rule that formal validity is governed by the law of the testator's domicile at death or the application of renvoi in that connection, it has been argued that renvoi may be applied in such cases: Dicey, Morris and Collins, *The Conflict of Laws* (15th edn, 2012) p 1424; Cheshire, North and Fawcett, *Private International Law* (14th edn, 2008) p 1269. Such a view seems implausible as the Act specifically provides that the testator's law of domicile at the date of death is one of the bases governing formal validity.
[178] There has been a great deal of academic debate of this topic. See, eg, Gotlieb, 'The Incidental Question Revisited—Theory and Practice in the Conflict of Laws' (1977) 26 ICLQ 734.

of succession, for otherwise the application of the foreign domestic rule may be an empty gesture. If the English court applies the foreign rule of succession, say that the surviving spouse or legitimate child of the deceased is entitled to succeed, it might seem only reasonable for it to accept the foreign country's view as to who the spouse or legitimate child is. Why allow the foreign law to determine the class of persons entitled to succeed, but not the members of the class?

9.112 Such little authority as there is supports the view that in the field of succession an incidental question is to be decided by the conflicts rules of the lex causae.[179] In *Re Johnson*[180] an intestate succession was governed under English conflicts rules by the law of Malta. By Maltese law, the next-of-kin were entitled to succeed, but who the next-of-kin were depended on whether or not the deceased was legitimate. He had not been born in lawful wedlock and, although he had been legitimated by subsequent marriage according to Maltese conflicts rules, he had not been legitimated under the English conflicts rules.[181] It was held that the next-of-kin were to be determined under Maltese law on the basis that he had been legitimated. Similarly, in *Haque v Haque*[182] an Australian court was concerned with a succession governed by Indian law, under which the legitimate children of the deceased were entitled to succeed. It was held that a child could succeed who, although illegitimate under the Australian rules, was legitimate under Indian conflicts rules (being the child of a marriage which was void for bigamy under Australian conflicts rules, but which was a valid polygamous marriage under Indian choice of law rules).

9.113 However, despite these authorities, it was suggested in Chapter 1 that the better view is that the lex fori approach should normally be applied, but that in clear cases this could be displaced by the lex causae approach. For example, suppose, as in the illustration above, that in a succession governed by Mexican law the issue arises as to whether a woman was the wife of the deceased. The parties could be validly married under English law and have lived for years in England. It would be extremely unfortunate if the Mexican rules on the validity of this marriage were allowed to prevail with the result that the 'wife' (by English law) would be excluded from the succession. The same argument applies where the incidental question involves a person's legitimacy. If a person is regarded as legitimate by English conflicts rules, there seems no justification for excluding him from a succession simply because Mexican law has different rules on legitimacy. Such a person might even, in separate proceedings, have obtained a declaration of legitimacy,[183] the effect of which would be practically meaningless were the lex causae approach to be adopted.

9.114 However, there can be situations where the lex fori approach should give way to the lex causae approach. For example, if there is no spouse or legitimate child under English

---

[179] *Baindail v Baindail* [1946] P 122 at 127–8.   [180] [1903] 1 Ch 821.
[181] Because, although his father had been domiciled in Malta (which provided for legitimation by subsequent marriage) at the time of the marriage, he had been domiciled in England at the time of the birth.
[182] (1962) 108 CLR 230.
[183] Family Law Act 1986, s 56 (as substituted by the Family Law Reform Act 1987, s 22).

conflicts rules, but there is such a person under Mexican law, policy dictates that they be allowed to succeed.

9.115 Of course, problems arise if X is a spouse or legitimate child under Mexican law and Y is a spouse or legitimate child under English conflicts rules. In such cases, the English rules should not be expected to give way to the Mexican rules and Y should be entitled to succeed. If Y were a wife under English law, she would be entitled to maintenance, family provision, a divorce, and so on from the English courts. The lex fori approach, while perhaps sacrificing uniformity of result, does nevertheless achieve 'internal harmony'[184] within English law.

F EU Succession Regulation

9.116 In 2009 the European Commission published a Proposal for a Regulation on matters of succession.[185] Under this proposal there would be uniform jurisdiction and choice of law rules throughout the European Union and automatic recognition and enforcement of judgments from courts of Member States.

9.117 After extensive consultation[186] the UK government decided in December 2009 not to opt into the proposed Regulation because:

> [t]here were several provisions that were likely to cause significant problems in practice. Of key concern were the problems in relation to clawback, the lack of certainty surrounding the connecting factor of habitual residence and . . . the fact that notaries, not acting in a judicial capacity, will remain unregulated by the Regulation when they issue authentic instruments . . . [T]he benefits that were likely to be achieved were far outweighed by the potential and significant risks that were likely to be imposed, particularly on charities, trusts and land registration matters.[187]

9.118 The Succession Regulation[188] came into force in August 2015 and applies to the succession of persons who died on or after 17 August 2015.[189] It is binding on all of the EU Member States apart from the United Kingdom, Ireland, and Denmark. It seeks to confer jurisdiction on one single Member State with respect to all questions of testate and intestate succession and with respect to movable and immovable property—and general jurisdiction is conferred on the Member State where the deceased had his habitual residence at the time of death.[190] It also lays down a unitary choice of law rule:

---

[184] Dicey, Morris and Collins, *The Conflict of Laws* (15th edn, 2012) p 56.

[185] *Proposal for a Regulation of the European Parliament and of the Council on jurisdiction, applicable law, recognition and enforcement of decisions and authentic instruments in matters of succession and the creation of a European Certificate of Succession*, COM (2009) 154 final.

[186] Ministry of Justice, *European Commission proposal on Succession and Wills: response to public consultation* (2010); House of Lords European Union Committee, *The EU's Regulation on Succession: Report with Evidence* HL Paper 75 (2010).

[187] Ministry of Justice, *European Commission proposal on Succession and Wills: response to public consultation* (2010) paras 4–5. 'Clawback' potentially arises where the applicable law provides for forced inheritance rights and allows protected family members to claim assets which the testator had given away during his lifetime. English succession law makes no provision for forced inheritance or clawback.

[188] Regulation (EU) No 650/2012, OJ 2012 L201/107.   [189] Art 83(1).   [190] Art 4.

'the law applicable to the succession as a whole shall be the law of the State in which the deceased had his habitual residence at the time of death'.[191] Where 'by way of exception, it is clear from all the circumstances of the case that, at the time of death, the deceased was manifestly more closely connected with a State other than the State [of habitual residence at the time of death], the law applicable to the succession shall be the law of that other State'.[192] The Regulation also allows the deceased limited freedom to choose the applicable law: he 'may choose as the law to govern his succession as a whole the law of the State whose nationality he possesses at the time of making the choice or at the time of death'.[193] This freedom of choice is arguably a 'sensible counterbalance to . . . a weakly constructed general rule'.[194] The narrowness of the choice is attributed to the interest of some Member States in preventing evasion of their forced inheritance rules.[195] The Regulation also makes limited provision for renvoi where the law of a third country is applicable.[196]

9.119 Even though the United Kingdom has opted out of this scheme, the operation and ultimately the effectiveness of the Regulation will be a matter of great interest to English law. There remains the possibility that the United Kingdom might still decide to participate. Even if that is unlikely, the workability of a unitary choice of law rule (which does not draw sharp distinctions between movable and immovable property as English law does) and the success of a connecting factor based on habitual residence (as opposed to domicile) may challenge some of the assumptions underpinning the English conflict of laws rules. Alternatively, difficulties may be encountered in the operation of these rules, thus lending support to the status quo in England. Some commentators expressed doubt as to the practicality of the unitary rule: 'the lex situs rule is based on the incontrovertible fact that the situs must be satisfied, and so any unified rule rests on the presumption that the lex situs will acquiesce in recognising title conferred by some other law, and will permit the registration etc processes necessary in accordance with the formalities of the lex situs'.[197] The appropriateness of the habitual residence criterion has also been questioned—although the recitals suggest that the connecting factor will be interpreted in a manner which ensures a 'close and stable connection' and with reference to 'an overall assessment of the circumstances of the life of the deceased during the years preceding his death'.[198]

---

[191] Art 21(1).
[192] Art 21(2). Art 20 acknowledges that the applicable law may be the law of a Member State or the law of a third country.
[193] Art 22(1).
[194] Carruthers, 'Party Autonomy in the Legal Regulation of Adult Relationships: What Place for Party Choice in Private International Law?' (2012) 61 ICLQ 881, 904.
[195] House of Lords European Union Committee, *The EU's Regulation on Succession: Report with Evidence* HL Paper 75 (2010), 14.
[196] Art 34(1).
[197] Written evidence of Janeen Carruthers and Elizabeth Crawford, House of Lords European Union Committee, *The EU's Regulation on Succession: Report with Evidence* HL Paper 75 (2010), 64. The Regulation does defer to the lex situs to some extent: see, eg, art 1(2)(k)–(l); Art 30.
[198] Recital (23). See also Briggs, *Private International Law in the English Courts* (2014) pp 791–4.

9.120 At the time of the consultation on the Commission's proposal, the idea of allowing the testator to choose the applicable law met with general approval;[199] it was observed that this approach would align well with the English emphasis on testamentary freedom[200] and that there was no sound reason for the very limited acceptance of the testator's freedom to choose the applicable law under the existing English rules.[201] It was argued that English law could accommodate even greater freedom of choice; there would be no need to confine the choice of applicable law, as the Regulation does, since forced inheritance is not a feature of English succession law.

9.121 Whether or not the United Kingdom ever opts in, the Regulation and its operation in practice provides valuable insights for those interested in the development and reform of the English conflict of laws rules.

---

[199] House of Lords European Union Committee, *The EU's Regulation on Succession: Report with Evidence* HL Paper 75 (2010), 21.

[200] Carruthers, 'Party Autonomy in the Legal Regulation of Adult Relationships: What Place for Party Choice in Private International Law?' (2012) 61 ICLQ 881, 904.

[201] At present, the testator's freedom of choice is confined to matters of construction. See paras 9.85 and 9.96.

Index

abduction of children 6.71–6.72, 6.77–6.80, 6.84–6.90, 6.96–6.100
abuse of process 2.125, 2.142, 8.24
Administration of Justice Act 1920 3.6, 3.80–3.83
Admiralty claims in rem 2.5–2.6, 2.31–2.35, 3.5, 3.54
adoption 1.75, 6.17–6.18, 6.30, 6.78
adultery 7.150–7.152
age
    domicile 6.30–6.31, 7.70
    essential validity 7.34, 7.45, 7.47, 7.55, 7.65–7.70
    intended matrimonial home rule 7.45
    marriage 7.14–7.15, 7.34, 7.45, 7.47, 7.55, 7.65–7.70
    wills 9.79
agency 2.162, 4.8, 4.108, 5.80
    see also **branches, agencies or other establishments**
air transport 2.89
ancillary relief 8.53, 8.165–8.191, 9.64
annulment of marriage *see* divorce, separation, and annulment
ante-nuptial agreements 9.45–9.47, 9.55, 9.59, 9.63–9.68, 9.71
anticipated wrongs 5.15
anti-suit injunctions 2.298–2.321
    arbitration clauses 2.306–2.309
    Brussels I Recast 2.313–2.321
    Brussels I Regulation 2.16
    Brussels II bis 8.48
    collateral attacks 2.301
    comity 2.304
    costs 2.320
    declining jurisdiction 2.312
    discretion 2.299, 2.307
    domicile 2.311, 2.313
    extraterritoriality 2.299
    Hemain injunctions 8.49
    jurisdiction 2.313–2.321
    legal or equitable rights, infringement of 2.306–2.312
    matrimonial causes 8.23, 8.48–8.49
    multiplicity of parties 2.309
    recognition and enforcement of foreign judgments 3.94
    refusal 2.309
    stay of proceedings 2.298
    traditional rules 2.317
    unconscionability 2.300, 2.301–2.305
    vexatious or oppressive litigation 2.301–2.303, 2.310
applicable law *see also* choice of law
    choice of law 1.28–1.172
    contract 4.1–4.182
    divorce 8.56–8.61
    forum non conveniens, stay on grounds of 2.225
    immovables 9.7–9.14, 9.60–9.62, 9.90–9.104, 9.106
    inter vivos transfers 9.6–9.43
    maintenance 8.187
    marriage 7.1–7.160
    movables 9.15–9.42, 9.49–9.53, 9.78–9.89, 9.105
    non-contractual obligations 5.1–5.137
    nuptial contracts 9.63–9.68
    substance and procedure 1.92–1.101
    Succession Regulation 9.118–9.121
    wills 9.78–9.104
appropriate forum 1.20–1.27, 1.63, 2.217–2.243, 6.1–6.5
arbitration clauses
    anti-suit injunctions 2.306–2.309
    breach 3.75–3.77
    Brussels I Recast 2.16, 2.318–2.321
    capable of being settled by arbitration, subject-matter must be 2.252
    Civil Jurisdiction and Judgments Act 1982 3.75
    defences 3.75–3.77
    exclusive jurisdiction 3.75
    forum non conveniens, stay on grounds of 2.249–2.255
    injunctions 2.16, 2.306–2.309, 2.318–2.321
    issue estoppel 3.76
    New York Convention 1958 2.249
    proper law 4.3
    recognition and enforcement of foreign judgments 3.75–3.77, 3.89, 3.93–3.96
    Rome I Regulation 4.8, 4.24–4.32, 4.44
    writing or evidenced in writing 2.250
armed forces marriages 7.33
arrest of ships 2.5–2.6, 2.34
articles of association 2.49
assignment 9.30–9.42
auction, sale by 4.51, 4.54
audits 5.10
autonomy *see* party autonomy

bargaining power, inequality of 2.130, 2.132–2.133, 4.55, 4.114–4.139, 8.51
bigamy 7.80–7.89, 7.148–7.149, 7.153, 7.157
bills of exchange 4.8, 5.10
Borrás Report 6.91, 8.17, 8.73
branches, agencies or other establishments 2.64, 2.109–2.113, 2.131, 4.84–4.85, 5.96
Brussels Convention 1968 1.13–1.15, 2.8–2.11

INDEX

Brussels I Recast
Admiralty claims in
 rem 2.31–2.35
aims of Regulation 3.87
anti-suit injunctions 2.313–
 2.321
appearance 8.171
arbitration clauses 2.16,
 2.318–2.321
bases of jurisdiction 2.37–
 2.176
branches, agencies or other
 establishments 2.64,
 2.109–2.113, 2.131
Brussels I Regulation,
 replacement of 1.15, 2.9
civil and commercial
 matters 2.14–2.16, 3.9,
 3.92
Civil Jurisdiction and
 Judgments Act
 1982 2.21–2.23, 2.62,
 2.285
claim forms, issue and service
 of 2.62
close connection 2.64,
 2.90–2.93
companies and other legal
 persons 2.29, 2.39,
 2.143–2.145
connecting factors 2.30, 5.14
consumer contracts 2.129–
 2.130, 2.134–2.137,
 4.123
contract 1.91, 2.66–2.89,
 2.129–2.139, 4.6, 4.8,
 4.52, 4.123
Court of Justice 2.10–2.13
declining jurisdiction 2.19,
 2.40, 2.177–2.280
development 2.8–2.9
domicile 1.18, 1.105,
 2.17–2.20, 2.27–2.30,
 2.37, 2.39, 2.62, 6.7
employment contracts 2.119,
 2.129–2.130, 2.138–2.139
exclusions 1.18, 2.15–2.16, 3.92
exclusive jurisdiction 2.39–
 2.45, 2.197, 3.106–3.107
first seised rule 2.20,
 2.184–2.185, 2.193
flexibility 2.18
foreign judgments, invalidity
 of 3.73
forum non conveniens,
 stay on grounds
 of 2.212–2.280

fraud 1.161, 3.111–3.113
free flow of judgments 2.181,
 3.87
Hague Choice of Court
 Convention 2.244–
 2.248
harmonisation 4.6
holiday accommodation 2.44
immovables 2.39, 2.42–2.45,
 2.256–2.264
in personam claims 2.5–2.30,
 2.33, 2.35–2.36
in rem claims 2.33–2.35,
 2.42–2.43
inequality of bargaining
 power 2.130, 2.132–
 2.133
injunctions 2.313–2.321
intellectual property
 rights 2.39, 2.81
interpretation 2.10–2.13
irreconcilable
 judgments 2.20, 2.177,
 3.123–3.126
Jenard and Schlosser
 Reports 2.11
jurisdiction 2.9, 2.14, 2.19,
 2.36–2.139, 2.177–2.211
 agreements 2.46–2.57,
  2.136, 2.197–2.198,
  2.239–2.243, 2.311,
  3.107
 declining 2.19, 2.40,
  2.177–2.211, 2.265–2.280
 prorogation 2.46–2.57
 submission 2.56,
  2.59–2.61
legal certainty 2.18
lis pendens 2.20, 2.35,
 2.180–2.198
matrimonial property 8.179
multiple parties and
 claims 2.64, 2.114–
 2.128
natural justice 3.114–3.122
non-Member States 2.265–
 2.280
nuisance 2.43
online, torts
 committed 2.103
parallel proceedings 2.20,
 2.35, 2.180–2.199,
 2.205–2.211
place of performance 2.76–
 2.89
preliminary rulings 2.10–
 2.13

prorogation of
 jurisdiction 2.46–2.57
provisional measures 2.281–
 2.297
public authorities 2.14
public policy 3.108–3.113
public registers, entries
 in 2.39
recognition and
 enforcement of foreign
 judgments 2.9, 2.39,
 2.182, 3.6, 3.73,
 3.87–3.126, 8.69, 8.78
related proceedings 2.64,
 2.199–2.211
Rome II Regulation 5.18–
 5.19, 5.28, 5.130
scope 2.9, 2.14–2.21, 2.37
special jurisdiction 2.63–
 2.139
squatters 2.42
stay of proceedings 2.20,
 2.177–2.280
submission to
 jurisdiction 2.57,
 2.59–2.61
tenancies of immovable
 property 2.44–2.45
timeshares 2.44
tort and other non-
 contractual
 obligations 1.91, 2.17,
 2.66–2.69, 2.94–2.108,
 5.18–5.19
traditional rules 2.18–2.26,
 2.38, 2.58–2.59, 2.140–
 2.176, 2.212–2.264
travaux préparatoires 2.11
trust, declarations that land
 held on 2.43
uniformity 2.13
unjust enrichment 2.69
Brussels I Regulation
amendment 2.9
anti-suit injunctions 2.16
Brussels Convention
 1968 2.9, 2.11
Brussels I Recast, replacement
 by 1.15, 2.9
comprehensiveness of
 regulations, lack of 1.18
development 2.9
exequatur 3.102
maintenance 8.167, 8.179
revised Regulation, proposal
 for 2.9
travaux préparatoires 2.11

Brussels II bis Regulation
abduction 6.78, 6.96–6.99
anti-suit injunctions 8.48–8.49
entry into force 8.4, 8.50, 8.67
exclusive jurisdiction 8.15–8.16
forum shopping 8.27–8.28, 8.51–8.53
habitual residence 6.72, 6.75–6.76, 6.78, 6.90–6.99, 8.7, 8.11
jurisdiction 8.3–8.54
lis pendens 8.23–8.28
Maintenance Regulation 8.180
matrimonial causes 1.15
  anti-suit injunctions 8.48–8.49
  habitual residence 6.72, 6.91–6.95, 8.7–8.11
  jurisdiction 8.3–8.54
  recognition of foreign judgments 8.62, 8.68–8.82
  Rome III Regulation 8.50, 8.59–8.60
  stay of proceedings 8.22–8.39
matrimonial property 8.166, 8.179
parental responsibility 1.15, 6.72, 6.75, 6.96–6.99
recognition of judgments 8.62, 8.67–8.82
reform 8.34, 8.50–8.53, 8.59–8.60
Rome III Regulation 8.50, 8.59–8.60
same-sex marriage 8.54, 8.62, 8.148
stay of proceedings 8.22–8.34, 8.38–8.39
traditional rules 8.5, 8.17–8.20, 8.50
Brussels II Convention 6.91, 8.4, 8.9, 8.13, 8.67 *see also* **Borrás Report**
Brussels II Regulation 8.4, 8.29, 8.45

capacity
civil partnerships and same-sex marriages 7.104–7.105, 7.114–7.122
contract 4.154–4.164
divorce or annulment, capacity to marry after foreign 7.80–7.89
immovables 9.7, 9.13–9.14, 9.93, 9.100
inter vivos transfers of property 9.7, 9.13–9.14
marriage
  consent 7.14, 7.17
  essential validity 7.34–7.99, 7.104, 7.120–7.122
  formal validity 1.71–1.75
  polygamy 7.126, 7.131–7.132, 7.135–7.136, 7.140–7.147
  same-sex marriage 7.120–7.122
mental capacity 6.26, 6.35, 6.48, 7.71, 7.100, 9.80, 9.93
polygamy 7.126, 7.131–7.132, 7.135–7.136, 7.140–7.147
Rome I Regulation 4.8, 4.154–4.164
same-sex marriage 7.120
wills 9.79–9.80, 9.93, 9.100
carriage contracts 4.115–4.121
cause of action estoppel 3.43, 3.52–3.59, 3.99
centre of gravity approach 4.78–4.79, 5.114, 6.8, 9.52
centre of interests test 6.91–6.94, 8.7
champerty 1.171
characterisation *see* **classification or characterisation and choice of law**
characteristic performance 4.53, 4.56–4.59, 4.117
cheques 4.8, 5.10
children *see also* **parents**
abduction 6.71–6.72, 6.77–6.80, 6.84–6.90, 6.96–6.100
adoption 6.17–6.18, 6.30, 6.78
age of majority 6.30–6.31
attribution of domicile, bases of 6.17–6.19, 6.28–6.30
change in domicile 6.27, 6.30
closest connection 6.32
custody 6.2
death of parents 6.30

dependence, domicile of 6.26–6.32
domicile
  dependence, of 6.26–6.32
  independent domicile 6.30–6.31
  loss of domicile of dependence 6.31
  origin, of 6.9, 6.17–6.25
habitual residence 6.71–6.72, 6.75, 6.77–6.80, 6.84–6.90, 6.96–6.100
Hague Protocol to the Hague Convention on the International Recovery of Child Support and other forms of Family Maintenance 8.187, 8.191
home, definition of 6.29
independent domicile 6.30–6.31
legitimacy 1.131, 6.17–6.18, 6.28–6.30, 7.154, 9.110, 9.113
living apart, parents who are 6.29
Maintenance Regulation 8.170, 8.173, 8.180–8.181
origin, domicile of 6.9, 6.17–6.25
polygamy 7.154
reform of domicile 6.32
choice, domicile of *see* **domicile of choice**
choice of law
applicable law 1.28–1.175
application of foreign law 1.64
burden of proof under Rome I Regulation 4.22
classification 1.66–1.101
clearly demonstrated choice 4.21–4.32
connecting factors 1.102–1.105
contract 4.1–4.182, 5.128–5.137
consumer contracts 4.122–4.125
culpa in contrahendo 5.83–5.85
defamation 5.104–5.121
definition 1.4–1.5
divorce, separation, and annulment 1.15, 6.72, 8.50, 8.53, 8.59–8.60

choice of law (*Contd.*)
  employment
    contracts 4.133–4.139
  environmental damage 5.57–5.63
  exclusion of foreign
    law 1.145–1.172
  express choice 4.3–4.4, 4.15–4.23, 4.112
  foreign law
    exclusion 1.145–1.172
    proof 1.138–1.144
  habitual residence 6.69–6.72, 6.100
  immovables 1.109, 9.1–9.5, 9.7–9.14, 9.60–9.62, 9.90–9.104, 9.106
  implied choice 1.119, 4.3–4.4, 4.21–4.44, 4.47
  incidental questions 1.131–1.137, 7.81–7.89, 9.110–9.115
  industrial action 5.65–5.66
  insurance 4.126–4.132
  intangible movables 9.25–9.42
  intention 1.32–1.35
  interest analysis 1.44–1.60, 7.55
  inter vivos transfers of property 9.3, 9.6–9.43
  justice between parties, achieving 1.31–1.40
  legitimate expectations 1.35–1.40
  lex situs 9.2–9.43, 9.60–9.62, 9.90–9.104, 9.107, 9.119
  Maintenance
    Regulation 8.187
  marriage, validity of 1.37, 6.2–6.4, 7.35–7.55, 7.62, 7.76
  matrimonial causes 8.50, 8.53, 8.56–8.61, 8.152, 8.161
  mechanics of process 1.65–1.175
  movables 9.1–9.3, 9.25, 9.28–9.42, 9.53
  nature of subject 1.4–1.5
  negotiorum gestio 5.80–5.82
  nuptial agreements 9.66
  no choice and implied choice, distinction between 4.42–4.44
  non-contractual obligations and contractual

    obligations, interaction of 5.128–5.137
  party autonomy 1.34–1.40
  penal laws 1.146–1.149
  place of performance 2.79
  previous course of dealing 4.34
  Private International Law (Miscellaneous Provisions) Act 1995 5.122–5.127
  process 1.28–1.175
  product liability 5.46–5.52
  proof of foreign law 1.138–1.144
  proper law 1.39–1.40, 4.3–4.4
  public interest 1.41–1.68
  public laws 1.152–1.154
  public policy 1.155–1.172, 4.109–4.113, 5.97–5.102, 7.100–7.103, 9.43
  rationale 1.29–1.63
  reform of choice of law for matrimonial property 9.74
  religion 6.4
  renvoi 1.106–1.137, 4.13, 5.16, 7.90–7.99, 9.107–9.109
  revenue laws 1.150–1.151
  Rome I Regulation 4.7–4.182
  Rome II Regulation 1.15, 5.6–5.103
  Rome III Regulation 1.15, 6.72, 8.50, 8.53, 8.59–8.60
  standard forms 4.33
  substance and procedure 1.92–1.101
  succession 1.106–1.136, 9.75–9.121
  uniformity 1.61–1.63
  unjust enrichment, restitution for 5.69–5.79
  wills 9.78–9.104
choses in action 9.5
choses in possession 9.5
civil jurisdiction *see* **jurisdiction**
Civil Jurisdiction and Judgments Act 1982
  Administration of Justice Act 1920 3.82
  allocation of jurisdiction 2.22–2.23
  arbitration clauses, breach of 3.75

  Brussels I Recast 2.22–2.23, 2.62, 2.285
  domicile 2.22–2.23, 2.62
  Foreign Judgments (Reciprocal Enforcement) Act 1933 3.86
  forum non conveniens, stay on grounds of 2.269
  immovables 2.260
  jurisdiction agreements, breach of 3.75
  provisional measures 2.285
  recognition and enforcement of foreign judgments 3.45, 3.54, 3.127
  traditional rules of jurisdiction 2.23
civil partnerships 7.104–7.119
  see also **same-sex marriages**
  abroad, formed 7.106–7.117
  annulment 7.11, 7.105
  capacity 7.104–7.105, 7.114–7.119
  conversion to marriage 7.121
  dissolution 7.11, 7.105, 7.110, 7.116–7.117, 8.54–8.55, 8.148
  domicile 7.56, 7.114–7.116, 7.118
  England, in 7.106, 7.110–7.111, 7.114–7.116, 7.118–7.119
  essential validity 7.117
  European Convention on Human Rights 7.123
  formal validity 7.11, 7.32, 7.105, 7.113, 7.115, 7.117, 7.119
  France, civil pacts of solidarity (PACS) in 7.110
  habitual residence 7.118
  gender recognition certificates 7.116
  jurisdiction 7.118, 8.54–8.55
  lex loci celebrationis 7.113, 7.115, 7.117
  limping relationships 7.115
  marriage, comparison with 7.11
  matrimonial causes 7.11, 8.13, 8.22, 8.59–8.60
  nationality 7.109, 7.118–7.119
  opposite-sex registered partnerships abroad, recognition of 7.123

overseas relationships 7.105, 7.110–7.117
public policy 7.117, 7.119
recognition of overseas relationships 7.11, 8.148
renvoi 1.110, 1.130, 7.92, 7.98
stay of proceedings 8.54
traditional rules 7.113, 7.123
two types of overseas relationships 7.112
UK, in 7.104–7.119
validity 7.105, 7.113, 7.115, 7.117, 7.119
voidable civil partnerships 7.116
claim forms
Brussels I Recast 2.62
companies 2.144–2.145
domicile 2.62
fraud 2.142
in personam claims 2.5–2.6
issue 2.62
presence 2.142, 2.144–2.145
service 2.5, 2.62, 2.141
traditional rules 2.141
classification or characterisation and choice of law 1.66–1.101
approaches to classification 1.69–1.88
autonomous interpretation 1.91
burden of proof 1.94
damages 1.98–1.101
evidence 1.94–1.95
immovables 1.66
intestacy 1.66
lex causae 1.77–1.83
lex fori 1.70–1.75, 1.92
limitation periods 1.96–1.97
marriage
  capacity 1.71–1.75
  domicile 1.66
  essential validity 1.70, 1.82, 6.15
  formal validity 1.66, 1.70–1.77, 1.86
  proxy marriage 7.12–7.13
  validity 1.66, 1.70–1.77, 1.86, 7.12–7.13
movables 1.66
polygamy 7.80, 7.124–7.126
procedure 1.91–1.101
property 9.1–9.5

remedies 1.98–1.101
Rome I Regulation 1.91, 1.94, 4.7
Rome II Regulation 1.91, 1.94
specific performance 1.98
substance 1.91–1.101
unjust enrichment, restitution for 5.69–5.79
wills 1.66, 1.90
close connection
branches, agencies or other establishments 2.113
Brussels I Recast 2.64, 2.90–2.93
capacity to marry after foreign divorce or annulment 7.80–7.89
carriage of goods contracts 4.118
characteristic performance 4.56–4.59
children, domicile of 6.32
co-defendants 2.121
competition 5.53–5.56
contract 1.102, 2.90–2.93, 4.124, 4.132, 5.135–5.136
consumer contracts 4.124
culpa in contrahendo 5.83–5.85
dependence, domicile of 6.32
divorce, separation, or annulment 7.80–7.89
domicile 2.64, 6.32
employment contracts 4.134
escape clauses 4.60–4.66, 5.34–5.42
forum non conveniens, stay on grounds of 2.218–2.220, 2.272
insurance 4.128
legitimate expectations 1.35–1.40
Maintenance Regulation 8.175
marriage
  essential validity 7.46–7.48, 7.58
  formal validity 1.37
matrimonial causes 8.13, 8.22, 8.59–8.60
matrimonial property and financial relief 8.175
multiple parties and claims 2.121, 2.123
negotiorum gestio 5.80–5.82

non-contractual obligations and contractual obligations, interaction of 5.135–5.136
place of performance 2.90–2.93
presumptions 4.61
Private International Law (Miscellaneous Provisions) Act 1995 5.126–5.127
product liability 5.46–5.52
public interest 1.44
related proceedings 2.199, 2.202
Rome I Regulation 4.44, 4.54, 4.60–4.66, 4.88, 4.128, 4.159
Rome II Regulation 5.30–5.33, 5.89–5.90, 5.135
sale of goods 2.90–2.93
service out of the jurisdiction 2.157–2.158
services 2.90–2.93
specific obligation theory 2.90
unjust enrichment, restitution for 5.75–5.79
collateral attacks 2.301
colonials, domicile of 6.24
comity 1.164, 2.233, 2.238, 2.304
common law marriage 7.27–7.33
Commonwealth 3.6, 3.80–3.84, 8.190
community of property systems 9.44–9.51, 9.54–9.56, 9.59–9.63, 9.69–9.72
companies and other legal persons
articles of association 2.49
Brussels I Recast 2.29, 2.39, 2.143–2.145
central administration 2.29
Companies Act 2006 2.143–2.145
dissolution 2.39
domicile 2.29
exclusive jurisdiction 2.39
formation 2.39
habitual residence 5.96
overseas companies 2.143–2.145
presence 2.143–2.145, 3.26–3.34

companies and other legal persons (*Contd.*)
principal place of business 2.29
representatives 3.29
Rome I Regulation 4.7
Rome II Regulation 5.96
service of claim forms 2.144–2.145
sufficient territorial connection 3.26–3.34
competent jurisdiction, courts of 3.12–3.39, 3.44, 3.60, 3.81, 3.85–3.87, 3.98
competition 5.53–5.56
composite states 1.10–1.11, 3.30–3.34, 6.67
concurrent claims in contract and tort 5.131
conflicting judgments *see* **irreconcilable judgments**
conflicts process 1.19–1.175
connecting factors *see also* **close connection; domicile; habitual residence; nationality**
appropriate forum 6.1–6.5
Brussels I Recast 2.30, 5.14
carriage of goods contracts 4.118
choice of law 1.22–1.25, 1.102–1.105, 6.4–6.5
contract 1.102–1.105, 4.118
definition 1.102
divorce, separation, and annulment 1.103–1.105, 8.2–8.3, 8.12–8.13
domicile 1.102–1.105, 2.30
environmental damage 5.57–5.63
forum non conveniens, stay on grounds of 2.218–2.220, 2.273–2.280
habitual residence 1.103, 6.4
insurance 4.128
jurisdiction 1.22–1.25, 1.102–1.105, 2.3
Maintenance Regulation 8.175
marriage
essential validity 7.46–7.48, 7.58
formal validity 1.102
matrimonial causes 1.102–1.105, 8.2, 8.13, 8.22, 8.59–8.60, 8.88–8.89

multiple locality cases 2.97–2.98
passengers 4.121
personal law 6.2–6.5
proper law 1.39–1.40
provisional measures 2.289–2.291
real and substantial connection 6.3, 7.46–7.48, 7.52, 7.73, 7.80, 8.50–8.51, 8.65, 8.149
recognition and enforcement of foreign judgments 1.103, 6.2
residence 2.36, 3.22–3.23
Rome I Regulation 4.9, 4.50, 4.54–4.77, 4.128
Rome II Regulation 5.31
sufficient territorial connection 3.22–3.24, 8.3
tort and other non-contractual obligations 2.98
unjust enrichment, restitution for 5.76
wills 9.78, 9.81, 9.89
consent to marriage *see* **marriage, consent to**
constructive trusts 2.95, 5.10
consular marriages 7.32
consumer contracts 2.129–2.130, 2.134–2.137, 4.55, 4.120–4.125, 4.153
consummation of marriage 7.34, 7.77–7.79
contempt of court 2.290, 2.297
contract 4.1–4.182 *see also* **Rome I Regulation on the Law Applicable to Contractual Obligations**
agents 2.162
applicable law 4.2
breach of contract 2.71, 2.166
Brussels I Recast 2.66–2.89, 2.129–2.139, 4.6, 4.8, 4.52, 4.123
choice of law 4.3–4.5, 5.128–5.137
close connection 1.102, 2.90–2.93, 4.21, 4.132, 4.134, 5.135–5.136
concurrent claims in contract and tort 2.66–2.67, 5.19, 5.131

consumer contracts 2.129–2.130, 2.134–2.137, 4.55, 4.122–4.125, 4.153
distribution 4.51–4.55
domicile 2.69
employment contracts 2.119, 2.132–2.133, 2.138–2.139, 4.55, 4.133–4.139
exemption clauses 1.132, 5.129–5.133
existence of contract, denial of 2.72
foreign element 4.1
formation of contract 2.161–2.162
governing law 4.1–4.4
guarantee, contracts of 1.95
harmonisation 4.5
incidental questions 1.131–1.137
insurance contracts 2.129–2.133, 4.8, 4.126–4.132, 5.103
inter vivos transfers of property 9.6–9.7, 9.12–9.16, 9.22, 9.26–9.42
jurisdiction 2.70–2.93
lex fori 4.1, 4.7, 4.8, 4.178, 4.181
matrimonial property 8.174
multiple parties and claims 2.119, 2.123
non-contractual obligations and contractual obligations, interaction of 5.128–5.137
overriding mandatory provisions 5.136
place of performance 2.76–2.89
pre-contractual negotiations 2.73
proper law 4.3–4.4
renvoi 1.119
Rome Convention 1980 1.13–1.15
Rome II Regulation 5.18–5.19, 5.41–5.42
slaves, sale of 1.169
tort, matters relating to 2.66–2.69
traditional rules 2.140
unfair contract terms and exclusion clauses 4.104–4.105
uniformity 4.6

unjust enrichment, restitution for 2.69, 2.74
validity 1.132
contributory negligence 4.167, 5.91
convenience, divorces of 8.64, 8.134
convenience, marriages of 7.46–7.47, 7.72–7.73
conversion 5.102
costs 2.231, 2.320, 3.83, 8.45–8.46
counterclaims 2.127–2.128, 3.21, 8.14
country, definition of 1.10–1.11
criminal law 1.146–1.149, 7.19, 7.27
culpa in contrahendo 5.12, 5.83–5.85
currency of damages 4.182

damages
classification 1.98–1.101
currency 4.182
defamation 1.99, 2.96, 5.104–5.121
exemplary or punitive damages 3.42, 5.98
forum non conveniens, stay on grounds of 2.131–2.132, 2.238
industrial action 5.65–5.66
lex fori 1.99
multiple damages 3.78–3.79
pain and suffering 5.120
procedure 1.98–1.101, 4.178–4.182
provisional measures 2.288
quantification 1.99–1.100, 5.91
recognition and enforcement of foreign judgments 3.78–3.79
Rome I Regulation 1.99, 4.178–4.182
Rome II Regulation 1.99, 5.91–5.94
substance 4.178
transfer 5.94
debts, assignment of 9.35, 9.40–9.42
deceit 5.89
declining jurisdiction
anti-suit injunctions 2.312
Brussels I Recast 2.19, 2.40, 2.58–2.128, 2.177–2.179

Brussels I Regulation 2.177–2.180
Brussels II bis Regulation 8.22–8.34
definition 2.177
exclusive jurisdiction 2.40
first seised rule 2.193–2.198, 8.23–8.28
forum non conveniens, stay on grounds of 2.177, 2.265, 2.268
jurisdiction 2.3, 2.40, 2.58–2.128
matrimonial causes 8.25
parallel proceedings 2.177–2.199, 2.205–2.211
recognition and enforcement of foreign judgments 3.104
defamation 5.104–5.121
choice of law 2.96
common law 5.5
harm, determination of 2.96
lex fori 5.110–5.111, 5.115, 5.119
lex loci delicti 5.105–5.106, 5.109–5.112, 5.115–5.116
Rome II Regulation 1.99
threatened wrongs 2.106
default judgments 3.40, 3.107, 3.114–3.118, 3.121–3.122
defences
Administration of Justice Act 1920 3.82
arbitration clauses, breach of 3.75–3.77
enforcement of foreign judgments 3.10
Foreign Judgments (Reciprocal Enforcement) Act 1933 3.84–3.86
fraud 3.67–3.69, 3.111–3.113
irreconcilable judgments 3.72
jurisdiction agreements, breach of 3.75–3.77
natural justice 3.63–3.66, 3.114–3.121
public policy 3.70–3.71, 3.108–3.113
recognition and enforcement of foreign judgments 3.10,

3.43–3.44, 3.60–3.79, 3.103–3.126
deferred community property regimes 9.44
dependence, domicile of 6.26–6.35
adoption 6.30
age of majority 6.30–6.31
attribution, bases of 6.28–6.30
change in domicile 6.27–6.28, 6.30
children 6.26–6.32
choice, domicile of 6.31, 6.33–6.34
closest connection 6.32
death of parents 6.30
definition 6.9, 6.26
discrimination 9.50
families, unity of 6.26
fathers 6.28
home, definition of 6.29
independent domicile 6.30–6.31
irreconcilable judgments 3.123–3.126
Law Commission 6.32, 6.35
legitimacy 6.28–6.30
living apart, parents living 6.29
loss of domicile of dependence 6.31
married women 6.26, 6.28, 6.33–6.34, 9.50
matrimonial causes 8.1
mental incapacity 6.26, 6.35
mothers 6.28–6.30
origin, domicile of 6.18–6.19, 6.22–6.24, 6.31, 6.33
parents 6.26, 6.28–6.30
reform 6.32–6.35
deportation 7.160
discrimination
Brussels I Recast 3.97
expropriation 1.167
religion 7.27
sexism 6.18, 7.42, 7.79, 7.138, 9.50
dishonest assistance 2.95
dispute resolution clauses *see also* **arbitration clauses**; **jurisdiction agreements**
forum non conveniens, stay on grounds of 2.239–2.243
habitual residence 4.51–4.52
Rome I Regulation 4.51–4.52

divorce, separation, and annulment 8.1–8.16, 8.61 *see also* **matrimonial causes; matrimonial property and financial provision**
administrative proceedings 8.68, 8.97
appropriate forum 6.2, 8.27–8.28, 8.52–8.53
background to choice of law approach 8.56–8.58
balance of fairness and convenience 8.41
bigamy 7.148–7.149, 7.153, 7.157
British Isles divorces 8.84, 8.115
Brussels I Recast 8.4, 8.71–8.72
capacity to marry after foreign divorce or annulment 7.80–7.89
choice of law 1.15, 4.50, 6.72, 8.50, 8.53, 8.56–8.60
civil partnerships and same-sex marriage 8.54–8.55, 8.148
close connection 7.80–7.89
community of property systems 1.75, 9.44–9.51, 9.54–9.55, 9.59–9.63, 9.69, 9.72
composite states 3.30–3.34
connecting factors 1.103–1.105, 8.2–8.3, 8.12–8.13
convenience, divorces of 8.64, 8.134
discretion 1.165, 8.43, 8.46, 8.127, 8.134, 8.137–8.141, 8.158, 9.47–9.48, 9.67
domicile 8.1–8.5, 8.65, 8.85–8.100
  choice of law 8.56–8.60
  counterclaims 8.14
  exclusive jurisdiction 8.15
  extra-judicial divorces 8.107–8.112
  habitual residence 8.12, 8.21, 8.117
  historical development 8.65
  nationality 8.13
  nullity 8.61
  other than by proceedings, obtained 8.119
  proceedings, obtained by 8.117–8.119
  recognition 8.119–8.120, 8.143–8.148, 8.154, 8.162
  residual jurisdiction 8.20
  stay of proceedings 8.47
domiciliary law but not by English law, divorce or annulment recognised by 7.88–7.89
duress 8.135
English law but not by domiciliary law, divorce or annulment recognised by 7.85–7.86
equivalence, theory of 8.149
estoppel 8.71, 8.92
European Convention on Human Rights 8.77
extra-judicial divorces 8.97–8.122
foreign law, effective under 8.91–8.93
forum shopping 8.11, 8.143, 8.146, 8.186
fraud 8.77, 8.133, 8.136, 8.161
habitual residence 6.70–6.72, 6.75, 6.78, 6.80, 6.87–6.90, 6.93–6.95, 6.100, 8.6–8.12, 8.21
historical development 8.65–8.67
harmonisation 8.50, 8.59–8.60
impecuniousness 8.130
irreconcilable judgments 8.32, 8.79–8.82
Islam 1.163–1.164, 8.91, 8.97–8.108, 8.112, 8.115–8.117, 8.120
Japanese divorces 8.105, 8.111
Jewish law 8.97
judicial divorces 8.83–8.96
jurisdiction 8.1–8.55, 8.71–8.72, 8.149
Law Commission 8.101
legal aid 8.130
legitimate expectations 8.58
lex causae 7.81, 7.85, 7.88
lex fori 7.78, 7.81–7.83, 7.86–7.89
lex loci celebrationis 8.61, 8.162–8.163
limping relationships 8.4, 8.58, 8.63–8.64, 8.118
lis pendens 8.25
mutual trust, principle of 8.70, 8.75
nationality 6.65, 6.67, 8.12–8.13, 8.16, 8.19, 8.52, 8.58–8.60, 8.93
natural justice 8.78, 8.124–8.131, 8.160
notice, steps taken to provide reasonable 8.125–8.129, 8.143–8.145
obtained by proceedings 8.84–8.85, 8.100–8.108
official documents for divorced obtained otherwise than by means of proceedings 8.147
opportunity to take part in proceedings 8.95, 8.125, 8.128–8.144, 8.160
overseas divorces 8.97–8.106
party autonomy 1.71
previously annulled or dissolved marriages 8.123
proceedings
  definition of 8.32, 8.107–8.108
  otherwise than by means of proceedings, obtained 8.109–8.114
proof of facts 8.94–8.96
public policy 1.165, 8.57, 8.132–8.136
real and substantial connection 7.80, 8.65, 8.149
recognition 1.6, 8.113, 8.131, 8.150, 8.160–8.161
  automatic recognition 1.173
  Brussels II bis 8.68–8.74
  close connection 1.175
  domicile 1.105
  effect of recognition 8.152–8.155
  limping marriages 8.64
  refusal 8.156–8.164
  renvoi 1.106
refusal of recognition 8.156–8.164

religious procedures 2.235, 4.16, 7.29, 7.88, 8.68, 8.97, 8.104, 8.117, 8.135
res judicata 8.159, 8.163
retrospectivity 8.153, 8.155, 8.158, 8.161
Rome III Regulation 1.15, 4.50, 6.72, 8.50, 8.53, 8.59–8.60
Sharia law 8.60, 8.105
traditional rules 8.35–8.49
transnational divorces 8.115–8.118
uniformity 8.4, 8.153
void marriages 8.2, 8.61, 8.123, 8.152–8.155, 8.158, 8.163
voidable marriages 8.2, 8.61
domestic violence 7.158
domicile 6.6–6.64 *see also* **dependence, domicile of; domicile of choice; domicile of origin; dual domicile rule**
acquisition of domicile 6.13, 6.17
Admiralty claims in rem 2.34
air transport 2.89
anti-suit injunctions 2.311, 2.313
branches, agencies or other establishments 2.109
Brussels I Recast 1.18, 1.105, 2.17–2.20, 2.27–2.30, 2.37, 2.39, 2.58–2.128, 6.7
Brussels I Regulation 1.15
burden of proof 6.16
capacity 4.160, 6.13
centre of gravity 6.8
change of domicile 6.16
choice of law 7.35–7.42
Civil Jurisdiction and Judgments Act 1982 2.22–2.23, 2.62
civil partnerships and same sex marriage 7.56, 7.114–7.116, 7.118, 8.54
claim forms, issue and service of 2.62
classification 6.9
close connection 2.64
companies and other legal persons 2.29, 2.143
connecting factors 1.102–1.105

consumer contracts 2.129–2.130, 2.134–2.137
contract 2.69, 2.129–2.139
declarations 8.13
definition 1.104, 2.27–2.30, 6.6–6.7
divorce, separation, and annulment 7.88–7.89, 8.1–8.5, 8.65, 8.85–8.100
choice of law 8.56–8.60
counterclaims 8.14
exclusive jurisdiction 8.15
extra-judicial divorces 8.107–8.112
habitual residence 8.12, 8.21, 8.117
historical development 8.65
nationality 8.13
nullity 8.61
other than by proceedings, obtained 8.119
proceedings, obtained by 8.117–8.119
recognition 8.119–8.120, 8.143–8.148, 8.154, 8.162
residual jurisdiction 8.20
stay of proceedings 8.47
dual domicile doctrine 7.37–7.42, 7.50–7.52, 7.56, 7.60–7.63, 7.66, 7.73, 7.88
employment contracts 2.138
essential validity of marriage 7.45–7.46, 7.55–7.70, 7.73–7.82, 7.86–7.89
choice of law 7.35–7.42
connecting factors 1.102
domiciliary law, validity by either party's 7.49
dual domicile doctrine 7.37–7.42, 7.50–7.52, 7.56, 7.60–7.63, 7.66, 7.73, 7.88
formal validity 1.66
lex fori 1.70, 6.15
public policy 1.160
forum non conveniens, stay on grounds of 2.256, 2.278
general principles 6.8–6.16
habitual residence 6.70, 6.81, 6.83, 6.89, 6.94, 6.100
husbands, of 7.41–7.42, 7.57, 7.74–7.75, 7.78–7.80, 7.85–7.88

in personam claims 2.27–2.30
insurance 2.131–2.133
intellectual property 2.81
inter vivos transfers 9.12–9.15, 9.39
intestacy 8.154, 9.69, 9.105–9.108
jurisdiction 2.46–2.57, 8.1–8.5, 8.12–8.15, 8.20–8.21, 8.50
lex fori 6.14–6.15
Maintenance Regulation 8.167, 8.172, 8.174, 8.180
matrimonial property 9.69–9.70, 9.72
intestacy 9.105–9.108
inter vivos transfers 9.12–9.15, 9.39
lex situs 9.3, 9.39
nuptial agreements 9.66–9.68
succession 9.69–9.70, 9.75
wills 9.78–9.81, 9.84–9.89, 9.93, 9.96–9.97, 9.100, 9.103
multiple parties and claims 2.115–2.128
nationality 1.129, 6.65–6.68
nuptial agreements 9.66–9.68
only one domicile 6.11–6.13
parallel proceedings 2.180–2.199
place of performance 2.79, 2.88–2.89
polygamy 7.128–7.149, 7.153–7.154
presumption in favour of existing domicile 6.16
prohibited degrees of relationship 7.37, 7.60–7.61, 7.70
provisional measures 2.285
public policy 1.160
recognition and enforcement of foreign judgments 3.97, 3.118, 6.7
related proceedings 2.180
religious law 6.4, 6.15
renvoi 1.106, 1.117, 1.123, 1.126, 1.128–1.129
Rome I Regulation 4.154–4.164
special jurisdiction 2.66–2.128
standard of proof 6.15

domicile (*Contd.*)
  stay of proceedings 8.47
  submission to
      jurisdiction 2.57,
      2.59–2.61
  succession 6.13, 9.69–9.70,
      9.75
  tax 6.6, 6.13
  third parties 2.124–2.126
  tort and other non-
      contractual
      obligations 2.94
  traditional rules 2.59, 2.140
  United States 6.4
  wills 6.13, 9.78–9.89,
      9.93–9.97, 9.100, 9.103
domicile of choice 6.36–6.64
  abandonment 6.56–6.62
  absences 6.58
  acquisition 6.36–6.57,
      6.61–6.64
  burden of proof 6.20
  cessation of intention 6.59–
      6.62
  cessation of residence 6.58
  change of domicile 6.50–6.53
  contingencies causing
      person to change
      domicile 6.43–6.49,
      6.56
  definition 6.9
  dependence, domicile
      of 6.31, 6.33
  duration 6.37
  evidence of change of
      domicile 6.50–6.53
  foreseeability 6.45, 6.48–6.49
  freely formed, intention
      which is 6.54–6.56
  fugitives 6.55–6.56
  immovable property,
      purchase of 6.52
  integration 6.53
  intention 6.37–6.56
  Law Commission 6.37, 6.64
  married women 6.33–6.34
  mental capacity 6.48
  naturalisation 6.52
  origin, domicile of 6.20–
      6.25
  permission to remain 6.49
  presence 6.36–6.38, 6.55,
      6.64
  prisoners 6.54
  reform 6.63–6.64
  residence 6.37–6.40, 6.58
  tax 6.53, 6.64

  temporary, intention that
      residence is 6.42, 6.59
  United States 6.37
  unlawful, where residence
      is 6.40
  visitors 6.38, 6.58
domicile of origin 6.9,
      6.17–6.25
  adoption 6.30
  attribution, bases of 6.17–6.19
  burden and standard of
      proof 6.20
  children 6.9, 6.17–6.25
  choice, domicile of 6.20–6.25
  colonials 6.24
  default rule 6.22
  definition 6.9
  dependence, domicile
      of 6.18–6.19, 6.22–6.24,
      6.31, 6.33
  discrimination 6.18
  fathers 6.17–6.19
  Law Commission 6.19, 6.25
  legitimacy 6.17–6.18
  living apart, parents who
      are 6.19
  loss of domicile 6.20–6.21
  married women 6.19,
      6.33–6.34
  mothers 6.19
  parentage 6.17–6.19
  revival 6.22–6.25
  special tenacity of domicile of
      origin 6.20–6.21
double actionability rule 5.4,
      5.99, 5.108–5.118
dual domicile rule
  civil partnerships and same-
      sex marriage, validity
      of 7.56, 7.104–7.123
  intended matrimonial
      home 7.52
  marriage, essential
      validity 7.37–7.42,
      7.50–7.52, 7.56, 7.60–
      7.63, 7.66, 7.73, 7.88
  polygamy 7.142–7.146
dual nationality 6.67
duress 1.167, 2.48, 2.54, 3.20,
      4.110, 4.141, 7.72–7.73,
      8.135, 8.161

EC law *see* EU law
economic loss 2.101, 2.169
employment contracts 2.119,
      2.129–2.130, 2.138–
      2.139, 4.55, 4.133–4.139

enforcement of foreign
    judgments *see*
    recognition and
    enforcement of foreign
    judgments
environmental damage 5.57–
    5.63
equitable wrongs 5.22
escape clause
  carriage of goods
      contracts 4.119
  close connection 4.60–4.66,
      5.34–5.42
  competition 5.56
  culpa in contrahendo 5.83–
      5.85
  employment contracts 4.137
  intellectual property
      rights 5.64
  product liability 5.32
  Rome I Regulation 4.60–4.66
  Rome II Regulation 4.62,
      5.34–5.42, 5.64, 5.89
  unjust enrichment, restitution
      for 5.79
essential validity of marriage
    see marriage, essential
    validity of
estoppel
  cause of action 3.43,
      3.52–3.59
  competent jurisdiction, court
      of 3.16
  divorce, separation, and
      annulment 8.71, 8.92
  irreconcilable
      judgments 3.72
  issue estoppel 3.52–3.59, 8.71
  recognition, refusal of 8.158
  submission to
      jurisdiction 3.16
EU law *see also* Brussels I
    Recast; Brussels I
    Regulation; Brussels
    II bis Regulation;
    Maintenance
    Regulation; Rome I
    Regulation; Rome II
    Regulation; Rome III
    Regulation
  Brussels Convention
      1968 1.13–1.15,
      2.8–2.11
  Brussels II Convention 6.91,
      8.4, 8.9, 8.13, 8.67
  Brussels II Regulation 8.4,
      8.29, 8.43

INDEX

comprehensiveness of
regulations, lack of 1.18
enforcement of foreign
judgments 1.14
European Judicial
Network 1.144
foreign law, proof of 1.144
habitual residence 6.90–6.99
Insolvency Regulation 1.15
matrimonial property 1.15,
8.166–8.167, 8.169–
8.171, 8.179
Posted Workers
Directive 4.139
preliminary rulings 2.10–
2.13
public policy 1.157
recognition and
enforcement of foreign
judgments 1.14, 1.173
residual English rules,
application of 1.18
Rome Convention
1980 1.13–1.15
Service Regulation 1.15
Succession Regulation 9.116–
9.121
uniformity 1.16
**European Convention on
Human Rights**
dependence, domicile of 9.50
gender discrimination 9.50
fair hearing, right to a 1.167,
2.4, 3.70, 3.110
Human Rights Act 1998 2.4
marry, right to 7.17
matrimonial causes 8.77
**European Judicial Network
(EJN)** 1.144
European Union see **EU law**
evidence
classification 1.94–1.95
domicile, change of 6.50–6.53
experts 1.64, 1.139, 1.141,
2.226
foreign law
application of 1.64
proof 1.138–1.144
forum non conveniens, stay
on grounds of 2.226
fraud 3.67
lex fori 1.94–1.95
procedure 1.94–1.95
Rome I Regulation 1.94–
1.95, 4.8, 4.179
Rome II Regulation 1.94,
1.129, 5.9

Statute of Frauds 1.95
writing or evidenced in
writing 2.51–2.53,
2.250
exclusion of foreign law 1.145–
1.172
penal laws 1.146–1.149, 9.43
proof 1.145–1.172
public laws 1.152–1.154
public policy 1.155–1.172
revenue law 1.150–1.151
exclusive jurisdiction 8.7, 8.51
Brussels I Recast 2.39–2.45,
2.194, 2.272–2.273,
2.280
immovables 2.41–2.45,
2.61, 2.256
jurisdiction
agreements 2.55–2.56,
2.197, 2.241, 2.280,
2.306–2.307, 2.311
multiple parties and
claims 2.114
parallel proceedings 2.211
tenancies 2.44–2.45
traditional rules 2.20
Brussels II bis 8.15–8.16,
8.51
habitual residence 8.7
jurisdiction
agreements 2.55–2.56,
2.197, 2.241, 2.280,
2.306–2.307, 2.311, 3.75
lis pendens 8.51
multiple parties and
claims 2.114
parallel proceedings 2.211,
2.272–2.273
recognition and enforcement
of judgments 3.106
residual jurisdiction 8.17–
8.18
traditional rules 2.20
executors 9.75
exemplary damages 3.42, 5.98
exemption clauses 1.132, 4.104–
4.105, 5.129–5.133
**exorbitant or long-arm
jurisdiction** 2.150, 3.42,
3.97
expatriate contracts 6.94, 8.174
experts 1.64, 1.139, 1.141, 2.225
expropriation 1.149, 1.167, 9.43
extra-judicial divorces 8.97–
8.122
extraterritoriality 2.290–2.297,
3.37, 7.28

facts, application of
foreign 1.64
fair hearing, right to a 1.167,
2.4, 3.70, 3.110
family home 7.136, 7.142–7.146,
7.158 see also **intended
matrimonial home**
fault 5.91
**federal or composite
states** 1.10–1.11,
3.30–3.34, 6.67
fiduciary relationships 5.77
financial provision/relief see
**matrimonial property
and financial provision**
first seised rule 2.20, 2.184–
2.185, 2.193, 8.25–8.26,
8.34, 8.52, 8.177–8.178
force majeure 5.91
foreign element in conflict of
laws 1.1–1.18
foreign currency 4.182
foreign judgments see
**irreconcilable
judgments; recognition
and enforcement of
foreign judgments**
Foreign Judgments (Reciprocal
Enforcement) Act
1933 3.6, 3.84–3.86
foreign law
application 1.64
divorce, separation, and
annulment 8.56–8.60,
8.91–8.93
evidence 1.64
exclusion 1.145–1.172
experts 1.64
foreign facts, application
of 1.64
marriage, validity of 7.15
penal laws 1.146–1.149, 9.43
proof 1.138–1.144
public laws 1.152–1.154
public policy 1.155–1.172
revenue law 1.150–1.151
formal validity of marriage
see **marriage, formal
validity of**
**forum conveniens/forum non
conveniens** see also
**forum non conveniens,
stay on grounds of**
enforcement of foreign
judgments 3.13,
3.36–3.39
presence 2.146–2.147

forum non conveniens, stay on grounds of 2.212–2.280
Admiralty claims in rem 2.32
applicable law 2.225
appropriate forum 2.146–2.147, 2.217–2.243
arbitration clauses 2.249–2.255
balance of convenience test 2.224, 2.234
Brussels I Recast 2.212–2.280
Cambridgeshire factor 2.224
choice of law rules, divergence in 2.233
Civil Jurisdiction and Judgments Act 1982 2.269
Civil Procedure Rules 2.213, 2.217
close connection 2.218–2.220, 2.273–2.280
comity 2.233, 2.238
connecting factors 2.218–2.220, 2.273–2.280
costs 2.131–2.132
damages 2.131–2.132, 2.238
declining jurisdiction 2.177, 2.265, 2.273–2.280
definition 2.177
delay 2.131–2.132
development of doctrine 2.212–2.214
discretion 2.268, 2.277–2.279
dispute resolution clauses 2.239–2.255
documentary evidence 2.226
domicile 2.256, 2.278
expert evidence 2.225
first stage test 2.218–2.226
forum shopping 2.213
fundamental question 2.215–2.216
general principles 2.215–2.238
immovables 2.256–2.264, 2.270, 2.273, 2.279
judicial chauvinism 2.216, 2.238
jurisdiction 2.146–2.147, 2.212–2.280
legal certainty 2.268, 2.278
lis alibi pendens 2.221–2.222
mandatory jurisdiction 2.268
matrimonial causes 8.22, 8.27–8.29, 8.33–8.34, 8.42–8.44, 8.47, 8.52
more appropriate forum 2.141
multiple parties 2.175, 2.223
outstanding questions 2.270–2.279
parallel proceedings 2.269–2.273
procedural advantages 2.131–2.132
procedural fairness 2.234–2.236
public policy 2.225
reflexive effect theory 2.276–2.280
related proceedings 2.269–2.273
second stage test 2.227–2.236
service out of the jurisdiction 2.155–2.158, 2.175, 2.177, 2.213
submission to jurisdiction 2.148
territorial connections 2.220
time bars 2.230
traditional rules 2.177, 2.213, 2.222
uniformity 2.278–2.279
vexatious or oppressive litigants 2.214
weighing factors 2.237–2.238
forum necessitatis 8.169, 8.175–8.176
forum shopping
appropriate forum 1.61
Brussels II bis 8.27–8.28, 8.51–8.53
divorce, separation, and annulment 8.11, 8.143, 8.146, 8.186
forum non conveniens, stay on grounds of 2.213
jurisdiction 1.20
matrimonial causes 8.3, 8.6–8.14, 8.18, 8.50–8.59
recognition and enforcement of foreign judgments 1.175
renvoi 1.125
uniformity 1.61
France, civil pacts of solidarity (PACS) in 7.110
franchises 4.51–4.55
fraud
Administration of Justice Act 1920 3.82
Brussels I Recast 1.161, 3.111–3.113
claim forms, service of 2.142
defences 3.67–3.69, 3.111–3.113
divorce, separation, and annulment 8.77, 8.133, 8.136, 8.161
evidence 3.67
fiduciary relationships and unconscionability 1.168
Foreign Judgments (Reciprocal Enforcement) Act 1933 3.84–3.86
guarantee, contracts of 1.95
habitual residence 6.89
issue estoppel 3.69
merits of foreign judgments, questioning the 3.68
public policy 1.161, 3.111
recognition and enforcement of foreign judgments 3.67–3.69, 3.128
Statute of Fraud 1.95
unjust enrichment, restitution for 2.170–2.171
freezing injunctions 2.281–2.297
fugitives, domicile of 6.55–6.56

gender discrimination 6.18, 7.42, 7.79, 7.138, 9.50
gender recognition certificates 7.116
Giuliano-Lagarde Report 4.12, 4.39, 4.46, 4.78, 4.151, 4.162–4.166
choice of law 4.23, 4.42, 4.95
dispute resolution clauses 4.25
previous course of dealing 4.34
reference to particular rules 4.36
governing law *see* **lex causae**
government expropriation of property 1.149, 9.43
grants of representation 9.75
gratuitous passengers, liability to 1.47–1.54

habitual residence 6.69–6.100
abduction of children 6.71–6.72, 6.77–6.80, 6.84–6.90, 6.96, 6.100
adoption 6.72
adults 6.90–6.95, 6.97

annulment of marriages 6.72
autonomous meaning 6.75, 6.90, 6.93–6.94
branches, agencies or other establishments 5.96
Brussels II bis 6.72, 6.75–6.76, 6.78, 6.90–6.99, 8.7, 8.11
Brussels II Convention 6.91
carriage contracts 4.118, 4.120–4.121
centre of interests test 6.91–6.94
characteristic performance 4.56
children 6.96–6.99
   abduction 6.71–6.72, 6.77–6.80, 6.84–6.90, 6.96, 6.100
   social and family environment 6.97
choice of law 6.69–6.72, 6.100
civil partnerships and same sex marriage 7.118
companies 5.96
competition 5.56
connecting factors 1.103, 6.4–6.5
consumer contracts 4.120–4.121
continuous residence 6.86, 6.88
culpa in contrahendo 5.85
definition 4.86, 6.74–6.89
distribution contracts 4.51
divorce, separation, and annulment 6.70–6.72, 6.75, 6.78, 6.80, 6.87–6.90, 6.93–6.95, 6.100
domicile 6.70, 6.81, 6.83, 6.89, 6.94, 6.100
duration of residence 6.97
EU law 6.90–6.99
expatriate contracts 6.94
franchises 4.51–4.52, 4.55
fraud 6.89
illegally, persons in country 6.87
immovables 4.51
industrial action 5.65–5.66
insurance 4.129
intention 6.79, 6.81–6.89, 6.92–6.94, 6.97–6.98
joint applications 8.10
jurisdiction 6.69–6.72, 6.75, 6.78–6.80, 6.87–6.90, 6.93–6.96, 6.100

Law Commission 6.100
lex loci delicti 5.25
loss of residence 6.80
Maintenance Regulation 6.72, 6.80, 8.167, 8.170, 8.172–8.175, 8.184
matrimonial causes 6.100, 8.143, 8.148, 8.159
   general principles 6.80
   jurisdiction 8.3, 8.7–8.21, 8.50–8.52
   recognition of dissolution of marriages 8.76, 8.85–8.86, 8.90, 8.93–8.96, 8.107–8.113, 8.117
   Rome III Regulation 8.60
   settled intention 6.88
   stay of proceedings 8.24, 8.27–8.28, 8.36
matrimonial property 8.167, 8.170, 8.172–8.175, 8.184
mistake 6.89
more than one country, residence in 6.67, 6.80, 6.100
nationality 6.70, 6.95, 6.97, 6.100,
negotiorum gestio 5.80–5.82
ordinary residence 6.73–6.74, 6.80–6.81
parents 6.72, 6.75, 6.89, 6.90, 6.96–6.98
passengers 4.120–4.121
principal place of business 4.86
product liability 5.48–5.49
recognition of foreign judgments 6.7, 6.69–6.71, 6.78, 6.100
reform 6.100
residence 6.81, 6.82–6.87
Rome I Regulation 4.51, 4.82–4.86, 4.105, 4.117–4.121, 4.129, 4.143, 4.149–4.152
Rome II Regulation 5.30–5.33, 5.90, 5.96
sale of goods 4.51
services 4.51
settled intention/purpose 6.81, 6.88–6.89
social and family environment 6.97–6.98
social security 6.72, 6.92, 6.95

students studying abroad 6.86, 6.88
succession 9.117–9.119
tenancies 4.51, 4.55
unfair contract terms and exclusion clauses 4.104
unjust enrichment, restitution for 5.79
voluntary adoption 6.89
wills 6.4, 6.78, 9.81
Hague Choice of Court Convention 2.244–2.248
Hague Protocol to the Hague Convention on the International Recovery of Child Support and other forms of Family Maintenance 8.187, 8.191
harmonisation 1.62, 3.87, 4.5–4.6, 4.12, 4.126, 5.6, 8.50, 8.59–8.60
holiday accommodation 2.44
human rights *see* **European Convention on Human Rights**

identity, mistake as to 7.72
illegality 1.146–1.149, 4.110, 4.169–4.175, 6.87
immigration 7.125, 7.136, 7.138, 7.160
immovable property
   applicable law 9.7–9.14, 9.60–9.62, 9.90–9.104, 9.106
   Brussels I Recast 2.39, 2.42–2.45, 2.256–2.264
   Brussels I Regulation 2.256–2.264
   capacity 9.7, 9.13–9.14, 9.93, 9.100
   choice of law 9.1–9.3, 9.9–9.11, 9.14, 9.25, 9.90
   Civil Jurisdiction and Judgments Act 1982 2.260
   classification 1.66
   competent jurisdiction, courts of 3.35
   domicile of choice and purchase of property 6.52
   enforcement of foreign judgments 3.35
   exclusive jurisdiction 2.39, 2.42–2.45

immovable property (*Contd.*)
forum non conveniens, stay on grounds of 2.256–2.264, 2.270, 2.273, 2.279
habitual residence 4.51
in rem claims 2.39, 2.42–2.45
intangible movables 9.5, 9.6, 9.25–9.42
intestacy 1.66, 9.106
lex fori 1.91
lex situs 1.168, 9.2–9.14, 9.25, 9.27, 9.31, 9.43, 9.60–9.62, 9.90–9.106
matrimonial property 9.60–9.62
mortgages 9.4, 9.12–9.13
public policy 1.167–1.168
realty and personalty, difference between 9.2
renvoi 9.9–9.11, 9.107–9.109
Rome I Regulation 4.51, 4.153
specific performance 2.262, 9.13
squatters 2.42
succession 9.74–9.77, 9.90–9.104, 9.106, 9.109, 9.118–9.119
tenancies 2.44–2.45
title 2.260–2.261
traditional rules 2.256–2.257
transfers 9.7–9.14, 9.25–9.42
trust, declarations that land held on 2.43
wills 9.31, 9.90–9.104
in personam claims 2.5–2.30, 2.36–2.176
bases of jurisdiction 2.36–2.176
Brussels I Recast 2.5–2.30, 2.33, 2.35–2.36
Brussels I Regulation 2.9, 2.11
Civil Jurisdiction and Judgments Act 1982 2.22–2.23
claim forms, service of 2.5, 2.24–2.25
definition 2.5
discretion of court 2.25
domicile 2.27–2.30
exclusive jurisdiction 2.43
jurisdiction 2.5–2.30, 2.36–2.176
nationality 2.36
outside the jurisdiction 2.24–2.25

recognition and enforcement of foreign judgments 3.4–3.5, 3.89
residence 2.36
service 2.5, 2.24–2.25
stay of proceedings 2.25
traditional rules 2.24, 2.36, 2.140–2.176
in rem claims
Admiralty claims in rem 2.5–2.6, 2.31–2.35, 3.5, 3.54
Brussels I Recast 2.31–2.35, 2.42–2.43
immovables 2.39, 2.42–2.43
nuisance 2.43
parallel proceedings 2.192
recognition and enforcement of foreign judgments 3.5, 3.89
squatters 2.42
third parties 3.5
incidental questions 1.131–1.137, 3.96, 7.81–7.89, 9.110–9.115
income support 7.159
incorporation of particular rules by reference 4.36–4.38
industrial action 5.65–5.66
inequality of bargaining power 2.130, 2.132–2.133, 4.55, 5.86
Inheritance (Provision for Family and Dependants) Act 1975 9.45, 9.69–9.70, 9.83
injunctions *see also* anti-suit injunctions
arbitration clauses 2.16
classification 1.98
freezing injunctions 2.281–2.297
Hemain injunctions 8.49
recognition and enforcement of foreign judgments 3.101
Rome I Regulation 4.178
Rome II Regulation 5.15, 5.94
worldwide freezing injunctions 2.290–2.297
Insolvency Regulation 1.15
insurance
Brussels I Recast 2.129–2.133
contracts 2.129–2.133, 4.8, 4.126–4.132, 5.103

direct actions against insurers 5.103
habitual residence 4.129
intangible movables
assignability 9.30–9.42
choice of law 9.28–9.42
immovables 9.5, 9.6, 9.25–9.42
situs 9.27
intellectual property
rights 2.39, 2.81, 5.64, 5.90, 9.31, 9.36, 9.38
intended matrimonial home 7.38–7.46, 7.50–7.52, 7.55, 7.59–7.63, 7.70, 7.79–7.80, 9.53
intention *see also* intended matrimonial home
choice of law 1.32–1.35
domicile of choice 6.37–6.56, 6.59–6.62
freely formed, as being 6.54–6.56
habitual residence 6.79, 6.81–6.89, 6.92–6.94, 6.97–6.98
justice between parties, achieving 1.31–1.40
legitimate expectations 1.35
Rome I Regulation 4.165
settled intention/ purpose 6.81, 6.88–6.89
wills 9.78, 9.85, 9.96, 9.103
inter vivos transfers of property 9.6–9.43
capacity 9.7, 9.13
choice of law 9.3, 9.9–9.11, 9.14, 9.22, 9.25, 9.28–9.42
contract 9.6–9.7, 9.12–9.16, 9.22, 9.26–9.42
debts, assignment of 9.35, 9.40–9.42
formal validity 9.7
government expropriation of property 9.43
immovables 9.7–9.14, 9.25–9.42
intangible movables 9.25–9.42
intellectual property rights 9.31, 9.36, 9.38
jurisdiction 9.8, 9.12
lex situs 9.16–9.24, 9.27
material validity 9.32
mortgages 9.12–9.13
movables 9.6, 9.15

penal laws, non-enforcement of foreign 9.43
renvoi 9.10, 9.24
Rome I Regulation 9.28, 9.30–9.35, 9.41–9.42
specific performance 9.13–9.14
tangible movables 9.15–9.25
title, passing of 9.6
interest analysis 1.44–1.60, 7.55
interim measures *see* **provisional or interim measures**
intestate succession 9.105–9.106
classification 1.66
domicile 8.154, 9.69, 9.105–9.108
EU law 9.118
immovables 1.66, 9.106
legitimate expectations 1.36
lex causae 1.77–1.81
matrimonial property 9.69, 9.76, 9.86, 9.105
movables 1.66, 1.77–1.81, 9.105
renvoi 1.106, 1.109
irreconcilable judgments
Brussels I Recast 2.20, 2.177, 3.123–3.125
defences 3.72, 3.123–3.125
divorce, separation, and annulment 8.32, 8.79–8.82
estoppel 3.72
matrimonial clauses 8.32, 8.79–8.82, 8.157–8.159
multiple parties and claims 2.121
parallel proceedings 2.181, 3.123
recognition and enforcement of foreign judgments 3.72, 3.82, 8.79–8.82
related proceedings 2.199–2.203
Islam
khula divorces 1.163, 8.106, 8.120
polygamy 7.124, 7.129–7.134, 7.141–7.143, 7.146, 7.149, 7.152
Sharia law 8.60, 8.105
talak divorces 1.163–1.164, 8.91, 8.97–8.108, 8.112, 8.115–8.117

issue estoppel 3.43, 3.52–3.59, 3.99

Jenard and Schlosser Reports 2.11
judgments *see* **irreconcilable judgments; recognition and enforcement of foreign judgments**
judicial chauvinism 2.216, 2.238
jurisdiction 2.1–2.321 *see also* **declining jurisdiction; exclusive jurisdiction; jurisdiction agreements;** *see under* **individual main entries; service out of the jurisdiction; traditional rules**
Admiralty claims in rem 2.5–2.6, 2.31–2.35
appropriate forum 1.20–1.27, 1.63
contest jurisdiction, appearing to 3.19
foreign element 1.3, 1.21
Human Rights Act 1998 2.4
negative considerations 2.2
original court, invoking the jurisdiction of the 3.21
positive considerations 2.3
residual jurisdiction 8.17–8.20, 8.50–8.54
submission to jurisdiction 2.57, 2.59–2.61, 3.14–3.21, 3.37
subsidiary jurisdiction 8.169, 8.174
voluntary appearance 3.17–3.20
jurisdiction agreements
anti-suit injunctions 2.307–2.312
articles of association 2.49
Brussels I Recast 2.46–2.57, 2.136, 2.164, 2.239–2.243
Brussels II *bis* 8.50–8.51
Civil Jurisdiction and Judgments Act 1982 3.75
consumer contracts 2.136
defences to recognition of judgments 3.75–3.77
discretion 2.240

domicile 2.47, 2.50, 2.241
employment contracts 2.139
English courts, in favour of 2.239–2.240
exclusive jurisdiction 2.55–2.56, 2.197, 2.241, 2.280, 2.306–2.307, 2.311, 3.75
first seised rule 2.193–2.198
formal requirements 2.51–2.53
forum non conveniens, stay on grounds of 2.239–2.248
Hague Choice of Court Convention 2.244–2.248
insurance 2.132
interpretation 2.48, 2.64, 2.66
issue estoppel 3.76
limitation periods 2.242
mandatory jurisdiction 2.239
non-exclusive jurisdiction agreements 2.55–2.56
non-Member States, in favour of courts of 2.241–2.243
nuptial contracts 9.63–9.68
oral agreements 2.52
parallel claims 2.48
proper law 4.3
prorogation of jurisdiction 2.46–2.57
Rome I Regulation 4.8, 4.24–4.32, 4.43
separability, doctrine of 2.48
service out of the jurisdiction 2.164, 2.240
standard clauses 2.48
submission to jurisdiction 2.57, 2.59–2.61, 3.14–3.21
trade usage 2.51
traditional rules 2.240
validity 2.48
writing or evidenced in writing 2.51–2.53
justice
between parties, achieving 1.31–1.40
morality, justice, and decency, offensive to standards of 1.167–1.170, 4.110

khula divorces in Islam 1.163, 8.106, 8.120

land *see* **immovable property**
law of the forum *see* **lex fori (law of the forum)**
leases 2.44–2.45, 4.51, 4.55

legal aid 2.232, 8.46, 8.130
legal certainty 2.18, 2.268,
    2.278, 4.67–4.68, 4.81,
    5.23, 5.86, 8.32
legal separation *see* **divorce,
    separation, and
    annulment**
legitimacy 1.131, 6.17–6.18,
    6.28–6.30, 7.154, 9.110,
    9.113
legitimate expectations
  choice of law 1.35–1.40
  close connection 1.35–1.40
  intention 1.35
  intestacy 1.36
  justice between parties,
    achieving 1.31–1.40
  marriage
    essential validity 1.37,
      7.38, 7.45
    formal validity 1.35–1.38,
      7.24
    polygamy 1.37, 7.150,
      7.152, 7.156
  matrimonial property 9.61,
    9.72
  party autonomy 1.35
  polygamy 1.37, 7.150, 7.152,
    7.156
  product liability 5.48–5.49
  proper law 1.39, 4.4
  renvoi 1.119
  Rome I Regulation 4.55
  Rome II Regulation 5.31
lex causae
  capacity to marry after
    foreign divorce or
    annulment 7.81–7.85
  classification 1.76–1.83
  defamation 5.119
  divorce, separation, or
    annulment 7.81, 7.85,
    7.88
  incidental questions 1.132
  intestate succession to
    movables 1.77–1.81
  lex fori 1.76–1.83
  marriage, formal validity
    of 1.5, 1.76, 1.82,
    7.18–7.25
  penal laws, non-enforcement
    of foreign 1.146,
    1.150–1.151
  renvoi 1.106, 1.132
  succession 1.77–1.81,
    9.110–9.114
  title to movables 1.77–1.81

lex fori (law of the forum)
  capacity to marry after
    foreign divorce or
    annulment 7.81–7.83,
    7.88–7.89
  classification 1.70–1.75,
  contract 4.1, 4.7, 4.8, 4.178,
    4.181
  defamation 5.110–5.111,
    5.115, 5.119
  divorce and separation 8.56–
    8.58
  domicile 6.14–6.15
  evidence 1.94–1.95
  immovables 1.91
  incidental questions 1.132
  lex causae 1.76–1.83
  marriage
    essential validity 7.56–
      7.58, 7.78, 7.81–7.83,
      7.86–7.89
    formal validity of 1.70–
      1.75, 7.5, 7.10, 7.23
    non-marriages 7.4–7.8
    polygamy 7.127, 7.152
    proxy marriage 7.12–7.13
    validity 1.1, 1.4–1.5,
      1.70–1.75, 7.15
  movables 1.91
  penal laws, non-enforcement
    of foreign 1.147
  polygamy 7.127, 7.152
  procedure 1.68
  proxy marriage 7.13
  public policy 1.159
  renvoi 1.74, 1.131–1.136
  revenue laws, enforcement of
    foreign 1.151
  succession 9.76
lex loci damni (law of place of
    damage) 2.94–2.102,
    5.25–5.44, 5.79, 5.85
lex loci delicti (law of place
    where tort occurs) 5.1–
    5.3
  defamation 5.105–5.106,
    5.109–5.112, 5.115–
    5.116
  habitual residence 5.25
lex loci celebrationis *see* **place of
    celebration, law of (lex
    loci celebrationis)**
lex situs *see* **place where
    property situated, law
    of (lex situs)**
life assurance 4.8, 4.129
limitation of liability 5.91

limitation periods 1.96–1.97,
    2.230, 2.242, 3.116–
    3.122, 5.94, 5.101
limping marriages and
    partnerships 1.61, 7.24,
    7.49, 7.115, 8.4, 8.58,
    8.63–8.64, 8.118
lis pendens
  Brussels I Recast 2.20, 2.35,
    2.181, 8.25, 8.33
  Maintenance
    Regulation 8.177–8.178
  matrimonial causes 8.22,
    8.25–8.27, 8.51
  related proceedings 2.181
  traditional rules 2.221–2.222
Lugano Convention 1988 2.9,
    3.6
Lugano Convention 2007 2.9,
    3.6

maintenance 8.166–8.191
  see also **Maintenance
    Regulation**
Maintenance Regulation 1.15,
    8.166–8.187
  ancillary relief 8.172–8.173,
    8.177, 8.180
  applicable law 8.166
  appearance 8.171–8.172
  bilateral and multilateral
    conventions 8.182
  Brussels II bis
    Regulation 8.180
  children 8.170, 8.173,
    8.180–8.181
  choice of court 8.170, 8.172,
    8.178
  choice of law 8.170, 8.172,
    8.178, 8.187
  close connection 8.175
  definition of
    maintenance 8.179
  domicile 8.167, 8.172, 8.174,
    8.180
  first seised rule 8.177–8.178
  foreign cultural
    element 8.187
  foreign decree, financial relief
    after a 8.183–8.186
  forum necessitatis 8.169,
    8.175–8.176
  general provisions 8.172–
    8.173
  habitual residence 6.72, 6.80,
    8.167, 8.170, 8.172–
    8.175, 8.184

INDEX

Hague Protocol to the Hague Convention on the International Recovery of Child Support and other forms of Family Maintenance 8.187
hardship 8.183, 8.186
implications 8.180–8.186
jurisdiction 8.167–8.186
lis pendens 8.177–8.178
lump sum payments 8.179, 8.181
matrimonial property 8.166, 8.179
nationality 8.172, 8.174, 8.180
parental responsibility 8.172–8.173, 8.180
periodic payments orders 8.181
recognition and enforcement of foreign maintenance orders 8.191
related actions 8.177–8.178
spouses 8.170, 8.174, 8.179
subsidiary jurisdiction 8.169, 8.174
malicious falsehood 5.53
marriage 7.1–7.160 *see also* **civil partnerships; marriage, consent to; marriage, essential validity of; marriage, formal validity of; marriage, validity of; married women; matrimonial causes; matrimonial property and financial provision; polygamy; same-sex marriages;**
choice of law 1.5
convenience, of 7.46–7.47, 7.72–7.73
definition 7.4–7.8
party autonomy 1.34
proxy marriages 1.70, 1.90, 7.12–7.13, 7.18
public interest 1.41
renvoi 1.109–1.110, 1.126, 7.90–7.99
revocation of will by subsequent 1.66, 9.89, 9.97
Rome I Regulation 4.8
substantial connection 6.3
uniformity 1.61

marriage, consent to
age 7.14–7.15
capacity 7.14, 7.17
domicile 7.73–7.75
essential validity 7.34, 7.47, 7.55, 7.71–7.76, 7.79
formal validity 7.15–7.19, 7.25, 7.29
identity, mistake as to 7.72
lex fori 7.15
lex loci celebrationis 7.14–7.17
marriages of convenience 7.72–7.73
mistake 7.72
nature of ceremony, mistake as to 7.72
parental consent 7.14–7.17
proxy marriages 7.13
void marriages 7.71
voidable marriages 7.15, 7.71
marriage, essential validity of 7.3, 7.34–7.89
age 7.34, 7.45, 7.47, 7.55, 7.65–7.70
alternative reference test 7.50–7.53
annulment, capacity to marry after foreign 7.80–7.89
capacity 7.34, 7.37, 7.45–7.47, 7.54–7.58, 7.62, 7.68, 7.71, 7.80–7.89
change of country 7.36, 7.41–7.42
choice of law 7.35–7.55, 7.62, 7.76
civil partnerships and same sex marriages 7.104–7.123
classification 1.70, 1.82, 6.15
close connection 7.46–7.48, 7.58
consent 7.34, 7.47, 7.55, 7.71–7.76, 7.79
consummation 7.34, 7.77–7.79
definition 1.66, 7.12, 7.34
discrimination 7.58
disease, parties suffering from venereal 7.76
divorce, capacity to marry after foreign 7.73–7.75, 7.80–7.89
domicile 1.102, 1.160, 6.15, 7.35–7.42, 7.45–7.46, 7.55–7.70, 7.73–7.82
domiciliary law, validity by either party's 7.49

dual domicile doctrine 7.37–7.42, 7.50–7.52, 7.56, 7.60–7.63, 7.66, 7.73, 7.88
husbands, of 7.41–7.42, 7.57, 7.74–7.75, 7.78–7.80, 7.85–7.88
lex fori 1.70, 7.86–7.89
dual domicile doctrine 7.37–7.42, 7.50–7.52, 7.56, 7.60–7.63, 7.66, 7.73, 7.88
formal validity 7.34–7.35
husbands, domicile of 7.41–7.42, 7.57, 7.74–7.75, 7.78–7.80, 7.85–7.88
identity, mistake as to 7.72
impediments 7.47, 7.54, 7.57, 7.59–7.89
incidental question 7.81–7.89
intended matrimonial home doctrine 7.38–7.46, 7.50–7.52, 7.55, 7.59–7.63, 7.79–7.80
interest analysis approach 7.55
Law Commission 7.38, 7.48–7.49, 7.51, 7.75
legitimate expectations 1.37, 7.38, 7.45
lex fori 1.70, 7.56–7.58, 7.78, 7.81–7.83, 7.86–7.89
lex loci celebrationis 7.35, 7.58–7.62, 7.70, 7.73
limping marriages 7.49
marriages of convenience 7.46–7.47, 7.72–7.73
married women 7.42–7.43
matrimonial property 9.53, 9.78
mental capacity 7.71
mistake 7.34, 7.72, 7.75
nationality 7.46
nullity 7.73–7.75, 7.78–7.80, 7.86, 7.88
physical impediments 7.76–7.79
polygamy 1.37, 7.45, 7.47, 7.54–7.55, 7.80, 7.140, 7.142
prohibited degrees of relationship 7.37, 7.47, 7.57, 7.59–7.64, 7.70
proper law 7.43
public interest 7.49–7.50, 7.55, 7.59

marriage, essential
    validity (*Contd.*)
  public policy 1.155, 7.47,
    7.52, 7.58, 7.64, 7.67,
    7.100–7.103
  real and substantial
    connection 7.46–7.48,
    7.52, 7.73, 7.80
  religion 7.59, 7.88
  retrospectivity 7.44
  same-sex marriage 7.120–
    7.122
  social factors 7.54–7.55
  temporary visits 7.36
  terminology 7.34
  variable approach 7.54–7.55
  void marriages 7.45, 7.57,
    7.60, 7.63–7.68, 7.71,
    7.75–7.77, 7.80, 7.86,
    7.89
  voidable marriages 7.71,
    7.76–7.77
**marriage, formal validity
    of** 7.18–7.33
  belligerent occupation,
    marriage in countries
    under 7.30–7.31
  capacity 1.71–1.75
  civil partnerships and same
    sex marriage 7.11, 7.32,
    7.105, 7.113, 7.115,
    7.117, 7.119, 7.122
  classification 1.66, 1.70–1.77,
    1.86, 7.12–7.17
  clergy, ceremonies performed
    by 7.27
  common law marriage 7.27–
    7.33
  connecting factors 1.102
  consent 7.18–7.19, 7.25, 7.29
  consular marriages 7.21, 7.32
  criminal law 7.19
  defects, classification
    of 7.12–7.17
  definition 1.66
  difficulty in complying
    with local law,
    insuperable 7.29–7.30
  domicile 1.66
  essential validity 7.34–7.35
  exceptions *to* lex loci
    celebrationis 7.26–7.33
  extraterritoriality 7.28
  general rule 7.18–7.25
  governing law 1.5
  legitimate expectations 1.35–
    1.38, 7.24

lex causae 1.5, 1.76, 1.82
lex fori 1.70–1.75
lex loci celebrationis 1.66,
    1.70–1.71, 1.102,
    7.20–7.33
limping marriages 7.24
local customs and laws 7.24,
    7.28–7.32
military marriages 7.33
nationality 1.126, 1.129
occupation, countries under
    belligerent 7.30–7.32
parental consent 7.14–7.17
polygamy 1.37, 7.121–7.122,
    7.140–7.142
proxy marriages 7.13
religion 7.18, 7.21, 7.29
renvoi 1.126
retrospective validation 7.20
same-sex marriage 7.121–
    7.122
telephonic marriage 7.21
void marriages 7.19, 7.22,
    7.24
marriage, validity of 7.1–7.160
    see also **marriage,
    essential validity of;
    marriage, formal
    validity of**
  age 7.14–7.15
  appropriate forum 6.2–6.4
  choice of law 6.2–6.4
  civil partnerships 7.105,
    7.113, 7.115, 7.117,
    7.119
  classification of defects 7.14–
    7.15
  dead fiancés 7.8
  degrees of invalidity 7.9–7.10
  domicile 1.102, 1.160
  foreign law 7.15
  lex fori 1.4, 7.15
  lex loci celebrationis 1.66,
    1.70–1.71, 1.102
  non-existent or non-
    marriages 7.4–7.8
  permanence 7.7
  polygamy 7.125, 7.132–
    7.145, 7.148–7.153,
    7.156–7.159
  public policy 1.155, 1.160,
    1.167, 7.100–7.103
  same-sex marriage 7.120–
    7.122
  temporary marriages 7.7
  void marriages 7.5–7.6
  voidable marriages 7.4

married women
  choice, domicile of 6.33–6.34
  dependence, domicile
    of 6.33–6.34, 9.50
  discrimination 6.18
  domicile 6.18, 6.33–6.34
  essential validity of
    marriage 7.42–7.43
  Married Women's Property
    Act 1882, declarations
    under 7.158
  origin, domicile of 6.18,
    6.33–6.34
matrimonial causes 8.1–
    8.164 *see also*
    **divorce, separation,
    and annulment;
    matrimonial property
    and financial provision**
  anti-suit injunctions 8.23,
    8.48–8.49
  balance of fairness and
    convenience 8.40–8.46
  Borrás Report 8.17
  Brussels I Recast 8.4, 8.17,
    8.25–8.26, 8.33–8.34,
    8.69–8.72, 8.78–8.79
  Brussels I Regulation 8.26
  Brussels II Convention 8.4,
    8.9, 8.13, 8.67
  Brussels II bis 1.15, 8.148–
    8.150, 8.158–8.160
    anti-suit injunctions 8.48–
      8.49
    habitual residence 6.72,
      8.11–8.12
    jurisdiction 8.4–8.21,
      8.50–8.54
    recognition of foreign
      judgments 8.62,
      8.68–8.82
    Rome III Regulation 8.59
    stay of proceedings 8.22–
      8.39
  Brussels II Regulation 8.4,
    8.29, 8.45
  centre of interests test 6.91–
    6.95, 8.7, 8.11–8.12
  choice of law 8.50, 8.53,
    8.56–8.61, 8.152, 8.161
  civil and commercial
    matters 8.11, 8.47, 8.49
  civil partnerships and same
    sex marriage 7.11,
    8.54–8.55, 8.62, 8.148
  close connection 8.13, 8.22,
    8.59–8.60

connecting factors 8.2, 8.13,
    8.22, 8.59–8.60, 8.88–8.89
consent to jurisdiction 8.10
counterclaims 8.14
declining jurisdiction 8.25
dependence, domicile of 8.1
discretion 8.28–8.47,
    8.52–8.54, 8.122, 8.126,
    8.134, 8.137–8.141,
    8.147, 8.158–8.160
domicile 8.143–8.148, 8.154,
    8.162
  civil partnerships 8.54
  connecting factors 1.102–
    1.105
  divorce and
    separation 8.56–8.58,
    8.65, 8.85–8.90,
    8.94–8.100, 8.107–8.112,
    8.117–8.119
  jurisdiction 8.1–8.5,
    8.12–8.15, 8.20–8.21,
    8.50
  stay of proceedings 8.47
European Convention on
    Human Rights 8.77
exclusive jurisdiction 8.7,
    8.15–8.18, 8.51
first seised rule 8.25–8.26,
    8.52
forum non conveniens, stay
    on grounds of 8.22,
    8.27–8.29, 8.33–8.34,
    8.42–8.44, 8.47, 8.52
forum shopping 8.11, 8.51,
    8.53, 8.143, 8.146
grounds for jurisdiction 8.3,
    8.6–8.14, 8.18, 8.50–8.59
habitual residence 6.100,
    8.143, 8.148, 8.159
  general principles 6.91–
    6.95
  jurisdiction 8.3, 8.7–8.21,
    8.50–8.52
  recognition of dissolution
    of marriages 8.76, 8.85–
    8.86, 8.90, 8.93–8.96,
    8.107–8.113, 8.117
  Rome III Regulation 8.60
  settled intention 6.88
  stay of proceedings 8.24,
    8.27–8.28, 8.36
irreconcilable
    judgments 8.32,
    8.79–8.82, 8.157–8.159
jurisdiction 8.3, 8.6–8.14,
    8.17–8.20, 8.50–8.59

last habitually resident, where
    spouses were 8.8, 8.28,
    8.60
legal certainty 8.32
lis pendens 8.22, 8.25–8.27,
    8.51
nationality 6.65–6.68, 8.12–
    8.13, 8.16, 8.19, 8.85
parallel proceedings 8.22,
    8.49, 8.141
party autonomy 8.51, 8.170
prenuptial contracts 8.45,
    8.61
real link 8.13
reflexive effect theory 8.34
reform 8.34, 8.50–8.53
residual jurisdiction 8.17–
    8.20, 8.50–8.54
Rome III Regulation 8.50,
    8.53, 8.59–8.60
stay of proceedings 8.6,
    8.22–8.49, 8.54, 8.91
substantial connection 8.50–
    8.51, 8.65, 8.149
sufficient connection 8.3
traditional rules 8.5–8.6,
    8.13–8.22, 8.28,
    8.35–8.50, 8.67, 8.70,
    8.83–8.147
unconscionability 8.49
vexatious or oppressive
    proceedings 8.49
void marriage 8.2, 8.61,
    8.123, 8.152–8.154,
    8.158–8.159, 8.163
voidable marriage 8.2, 8.61
**matrimonial property
    and financial
    provision 8.165–
    8.191, 9.1–9.121** see
    also **family home;
    immovable property;
    intended matrimonial
    home; Maintenance
    Regulation; movable
    property;
    place where property situated,
    law of (lex situs)**
ancillary relief 7.4, 8.53,
    8.165–8.166, 8.172–
    8.173, 8.177, 8.180,
    8.188, 9.64
ante-nuptial
    agreements 8.51, 8.170,
    9.45–9.47, 9.55, 9.59,
    9.63–9.68, 9.71
Brussels I Recast 8.171, 8.179

Brussels I Regulation 8.167,
    8.169–8.170
Brussels II bis Regulation 8.53,
    8.166, 8.180
centre of gravity test 9.52
change of domicile 9.18–
    9.22, 9.40, 9.54–9.59,
    9.79, 9.88, 9.108
choice of law 8.57–8.60
  Maintenance
    Regulation 8.187
  nuptial agreements 9.66
  reform 9.74
  succession 9.116–9.118
  wills 9.81, 9.89–9.90
close connection 8.175
Commonwealth maintenance
    orders 8.190
community of property
    systems 9.44–9.51,
    9.54–9.56, 9.59–9.63,
    9.69–9.72
contract 8.174
deferred community 9.44
dependence, married women's
    domicile of 9.50
domicile
  divorce 9.72
  intestacy 9.105–9.108
  inter vivos transfers 9.12–
    9.15, 9.39
  lex situs 9.3, 9.39
  nuptial agreements 9.66–
    9.68
  succession 9.69–9.70, 9.75,
  wills 9.78–9.81, 9.84–9.89,
    9.93, 9.96–9.97, 9.100,
    9.103
English courts, jurisdiction
    of 8.165–8.179
essential validity of
    marriage 9.53, 9.78
EU law 1.15, 8.166–8.167,
    8.169–8.171, 8.179
financial relief after foreign
    divorce 8.183–8.186
foreign cultural element 8.187
habitual residence 8.167,
    8.170, 8.172–8.175,
    8.184
Hague Protocol to the Hague
    Convention on the
    International Recovery
    of Child Support and
    other forms of Family
    Maintenance 8.187,
    8.191

place where property situated, law of (lex situs) (*Contd.*)
Inheritance (Provision for Family and Dependants) Act 1975 9.45, 9.69–9.70, 9.83
intestacy 9.69, 9.76, 9.86, 9.106
jurisdiction 8.165–8.180, 8.184, 8.186, 9.8, 9.12, 9.63, 9.66–9.68, 9.74–9.75, 9.116, 9.118
legitimate expectations 9.61, 9.72
maintenance 8.165–8.191
Maintenance Regulation 8.166–8.191
mutability or immutability 9.54–9.59, 9.70
nuptial agreements 9.45–9.47, 9.55, 9.59, 9.63–9.68, 9.71
party autonomy 1.35, 8.170
post-nuptial agreements 9.45, 9.63–9.67
property adjustment orders 8.46, 8.179–8.180, 9.45, 9.71
public policy 8.132–8.141, 8.146, 9.23, 9.43, 9.64
reciprocal enforcement of maintenance orders 8.182, 8.190
recognition and enforcement of foreign maintenance orders 8.69, 8.166, 8.180, 8.188–8.191
reform 9.74, 9.121
regulation, proposal for a 9.74
separate ownership systems 9.45
separation agreements 9.45–9.47, 9.55, 9.59, 9.63–9.68, 9.71
subsistence of marriage, property acquired during 9.44
succession 9.44, 9.47–9.48, 9.58, 9.68–9.70, 9.75–9.121
wills 9.31, 9.78–9.105, 9.109
mental capacity 6.26, 6.35, 7.71, 9.79

military marriages 7.33
mistake
fact, of 5.78
habitual residence 6.89
law, of 5.71
marriage 7.34, 7.72, 7.75
unjust enrichment, restitution for 5.71, 5.78
morality, justice, and decency, offensive to standards of 1.167–1.170, 4.110
mortgages 9.4, 9.12–9.13
movable property
choice of law 9.1–9.3, 9.15–9.42, 9.49–9.59, 9.78–9.89, 9.105
classification 1.66
immovables 9.1–9.6, 9.24–9.25, 9.37, 9.77, 9.119
intangible movables 9.5–9.6, 9.25–9.42
inter vivos transfers of property 9.6, 9.15
intestacy 1.66, 1.77–1.81, 9.105–9.108
lex causae 1.77–1.81
lex fori 1.91
lex situs 9.16–9.24
mutability or immutability 9.54–9.59
realty and personalty, difference between 9.2
renvoi 1.106–1.109, 1.112–1.117, 1.123–1.125, 1.128–1.129
share certificates 9.5
succession 9.58, 9.74–9.89, 9.93–9.97, 9.105–9.108, 9.118–9.119
tangible property 9.5–9.6, 9.15–9.24, 9.37–9.38
title 1.77–1.81
wills 9.31, 9.78–9.89, 9.105
multiple damages 3.78–3.79
multiple parties and claims
anti-suit injunctions 2.309
Brussels I Recast 2.64, 2.114–2.128, 2.172–2.175
cause of action estoppel 3.53
close connection 2.121, 2.123
co-defendants 2.121
contract 2.119, 2.123
counterclaims 2.127–2.128
domicile 2.114–2.128
employment contracts 2.119
forum non conveniens, stay on grounds of 2.223

irreconcilable judgments 2.121
jurisdiction 1.20
service out of the jurisdiction 2.172–2.175
third party proceedings 2.124–2.126
tort 2.123

national security 1.154
nationality 6.4, 6.65–6.68
civil law countries 6.65
civil partnerships and same-sex marriage 7.109, 7.118–7.119
composite states 6.67
connecting factor, as 3.22, 8.13, 8.85, 8.89, 8.174
declarations 8.13
divorce, separation, and annulment 6.65, 6.67, 8.12–8.13, 8.16, 8.19, 8.52, 8.58–8.60, 8.93
domicile 1.129, 6.65–6.68
dual nationality 6.67
habitual residence 1.129, 6.70, 6.95, 6.97, 6.100
Law Commission 6.68
Maintenance Regulation 8.172, 8.174, 8.180
marriage
essential validity 7.46
formal validity 1.126
matrimonial causes
divorce 8.58–8.60, 8.89–8.90, 8.94, 8.100, 8.108, 8.111, 8.117, 8.143
exclusive jurisdiction 8.16
habitual residence 8.12–8.13
residual jurisdiction 8.19
naturalisation 6.67
renvoi 1.106, 1.126, 1.128
stateless persons 6.67
wills 6.65
natural justice
Brussels I Recast 3.114–3.122
Brussels II bis 8.78
conditions 3.63–3.66
default judgments 3.114–3.118, 3.121–3.122
defences 3.63–3.66, 3.114–3.122
definition 3.63

divorce, separation, and
annulment 8.78,
8.124–8.131, 8.160
Foreign Judgments (Reciprocal
Enforcement) Act
1933 3.86
notice of foreign
proceedings 3.63, 3.118
opportunity to present
case 3.63, 3.114–3.121
procedural
irregularities 3.119
recognition and
enforcement of foreign
judgments 3.64–3.66,
3.128
service 3.63, 3.114–3.121
substantial justice 3.64–3.66
time limits 3.114–3.122
**natural persons, status and legal
capacity of** 4.8
naturalisation 6.52, 6.67
nature of conflict of laws 1.1–1.18
changing nature of
subject 1.12–1.18
choice of law 1.4–1.5
country, meaning of 1.10–1.11
EU law, influence of 1.12–1.18
foreign element 1.12–1.18
jurisdiction 1.3
recognition and
enforcement of foreign
judgments 1.6
terminology 1.7–1.9
necessity 5.91
**negotiorum gestio and Rome
II Regulation** 5.12,
5.80–5.82
non-contractual obligations
see **Rome II Regulation
on the Law Applicable
to Non-Contractual
Obligations; tort and
other non-contractual
obligations**
**non-contractual obligations
and contractual
obligations, interaction
of** 5.128–5.137
nuclear damage 5.11
nuisance 2.43, 5.57
nullity of marriage *see* **divorce,
separation, and
annulment**
nuptial agreements 8.51, 8.170,
9.45–9.47, 9.55, 9.59,
9.63–9.68, 9.71

obligation, theory of 3.9
**occupation, marriage in
countries under
belligerent** 7.30–7.32
**opportunity to take part in
divorce, separation,
or annulment
proceedings** 8.95,
8.125, 8.128–8.144,
8.160
Orders in Council 3.80, 3.84,
7.28, 7.108–7.109, 8.190
origin, domicile of *see* **domicile
of origin**

**pain and suffering, damages
for** 5.120
parallel proceedings
Admiralty claims in rem 2.35
Brussels I Recast 2.20, 2.35,
2.180–2.199, 2.205–
2.211
declining jurisdiction 2.177–
2.199
domicile 2.180, 2.183
first seised rule 2.184–2.185
forum non conveniens, stay
on grounds of 2.269–
2.273
in rem proceedings 2.192
irreconcilable
judgments 2.181
jurisdiction agreements 2.48
lis pendens 2.181
matrimonial causes 8.22,
8.49, 8.141
provisional measures 2.188
recognition and
enforcement of foreign
judgments 2.182
Rome II Regulation 5.137
same cause of action 2.186–
2.189
same parties 2.186,
2.190–2.192
same subject-matter 2.186–
2.189
parents
Brussels II bis 1.15, 6.72,
6.75, 6.96–6.99
death 6.30
dependence, domicile
of 6.26, 6.28–6.30
domicile
dependence, of 6.26,
6.28–6.30
origin, of 6.17–6.19

habitual residence 6.72, 6.75,
6.89, 6.90, 6.96–6.98
living apart, parents who
are 6.18, 6.29
Maintenance
Regulation 1.15, 6.72,
6.75, 6.96–6.99
marriage, consent to 7.14–
7.17
origin, domicile of 6.17–6.19
parental responsibility 1.15,
6.72, 6.75, 6.96–6.99
**partnerships, formation and
dissolution of** 2.39
party autonomy
choice of law 1.32–1.40
divorce 8.50–8.51
insurance 4.126–4.132
matrimonial property 1.35,
8.170
proper law 4.4
renvoi 1.119
Rome I Regulation 4.15–
4.16, 4.45, 4.47, 4.114,
4.120, 4.126–4.132
Rome II Regulation 5.86
Rome III Regulation 8.60
passengers 1.47–1.54,
4.120–4.121
passing off 5.53
**penal laws, non-enforcement of
foreign** 1.145–1.172
pending actions *see* **lis pendens**
pensions 7.141, 7.159
personal law 6.2–6.5
personal representatives 9.75–
9.76
**physical impediments to
marriage** 7.76–7.79
**place of celebration, law of (lex
loci celebrationis)**
civil partnerships and same
sex marriage, validity
of 7.113, 7.115, 7.117
divorce, separation, and
annulment 8.61,
8.162–8.163
essential validity of
marriage 7.35,
7.58–7.62, 7.70, 7.73
exceptions 7.26–7.33
formal validity 1.66, 1.70–
1.74, 1.102, 7.18–7.33
polygamy 7.129–7.137, 7.140
validity of marriage 1.66,
1.70–1.74, 1.102,
7.12–7.33

INDEX

place of damage, law of (lex loci damni) 2.94–2.102, 5.25–5.44, 5.79, 5.85
place of harmful event 2.94–2.102
place of performance 2.76–2.89
place where property situated, law of (lex situs) 9.7–9.27, 9.36–9.43, 9.119
  capacity 9.7
  changes, cases where situs 9.18–9.22
  constant, cases where the situs is 9.17
  exceptions 9.23–9.24
  immovables 1.168, 9.2–9.14, 9.25, 9.27, 9.31, 9.43, 9.60–9.62, 9.90–9.106
  intangible movables, inter vivos transfer of 9.25, 9.27
  inter vivos transfers of property 9.16–9.24, 9.27
  movables 9.16–9.24
  renvoi 1.125
  wills 9.84, 9.90–9.104
place where tort occurs see lex loci delicti (law of place where tort occurs)
policy see public policy
polluter pays 5.58
polygamous marriages 7.124–7.160
  abroad, marriage taking place 7.133–7.137
  adultery 7.150–7.152
  bigamy 7.148–7.149, 7.153, 7.157
  capacity 7.121, 7.126, 7.131–7.132, 7.135–7.136, 7.140–7.147
  change in nature of marriage 7.147–7.151
  children 7.154
  classification 7.127–7.128
  deportation 7.160
  discrimination 7.139
  divorce, annulment, or separation 7.125, 7.143, 7.152, 7.157
  domestic violence 7.158
  domicile 7.128–7.149, 7.153–7.154
  dual domicile doctrine 7.142–7.146
  England, marriage in 7.133–7.134
  essential validity 1.37, 7.45, 7.54–7.55, 7.80, 7.140, 7.142
  family home 7.136, 7.142–7.146, 7.158
  formal validity 1.37, 7.121–7.122, 7.140–7.142
  immigration 7.125, 7.136, 7.138, 7.160
  income support 7.159
  Inheritance (Provision for Family and Dependants) Act 1975 7.155
  intended matrimonial home rule 7.142–7.146
  Islam 7.124, 7.129–7.134, 7.141–7.143, 7.146, 7.149, 7.152
  legitimacy of children 7.154
  legitimate expectations 1.37, 7.150, 7.152, 7.156
  lex fori 7.127, 7.152
  lex loci celebrationis 7.129–7.137, 7.140
  Married Women's Property Act 1882, declarations under 7.158
  matrimonial relief 7.125, 7.136, 7.138, 7.144–7.148, 7.151–7.152
  monogamy, change to and from 7.147–7.151
  morality, justice, and decency, offensive to standards of 7.100
  nature of marriage, law determining 7.129–7.137
  one party domiciled in England with no existing spouse 7.138–7.141
  pensions 7.141, 7.159
  potentially polygamous marriages 7.128, 7.130–7.131, 7.132–7.137, 7.147–7.148
  Private International Law (Miscellaneous Provisions) Act 1995 7.128
  public policy 1.163
  recognition 7.125–7.126, 7.134, 7.142, 7.152–7.153, 7.158–7.160
  retrospective validity 7.141
  social security 7.136, 7.151, 7.159
  state pensions 7.159
  substantial connection 6.3
  succession 7.136, 7.141, 7.151, 7.155–7.156
  validity of marriage 7.125, 7.132–7.145, 7.148–7.153, 7.156–7.159
  void marriages 7.129, 7.135–7.146, 7.153
Posted Workers Directive 4.139
post-nuptial agreements 9.45, 9.63–9.67
precedent 1.140
pre-contractual dealings 2.72, 2.74, 2.95, 4.8, 5.83–5.85
preliminary rulings 2.10–2.13
prenuptial agreements 8.45, 8.61
prescription 5.94
presence 2.141–2.147, 3.22–3.34, 6.36–6.38, 6.55, 6.64
principal place of business 2.29, 4.86
prisoners, domicile of 6.54
privacy 5.11
private international law, definition of 1.7
Private International Law (Miscellaneous Provisions) Act 1995 and tort 5.5, 5.122–5.127, 7.128
procedure
  appropriate forum 1.63
  classification 1.91–1.101
  damages 1.98–1.101, 4.178–4.182
  defamation 5.119–5.121
  definition 1.92
  evidence 1.94–1.95
  fairness 2.234–2.238
  first seised rule 2.184–2.185
  forum non conveniens, stay on grounds of 2.131–2.132
  interlocutory decisions 3.90
  lex fori 1.92, 1.94, 1.99, 1.101
  limitation periods 1.96–1.97
  natural justice 3.119
  provisional measures 2.287
  public policy 1.159
  renvoi 1.118, 1.124
  Rome I Regulation 4.8, 4.178–4.182

Rome II Regulation 5.94
substance 1.91–1.101
unjust enrichment, restitution
   for 5.74
product liability 5.46–5.52
**prohibited degrees of
   relationship** 7.37, 7.47,
   7.57, 7.59–7.64, 7.70
promissory notes 4.8, 5.10
proof of foreign law 1.138–
   1.144
proper law
   arbitration clauses 4.3
   certainty 4.4
   choice of law 1.39
   common law 4.3
   connecting factors 1.39
   contract 4.3–4.4
   express choice of law 4.3–4.4
   implied choice of law 4.3–4.4
   jurisdiction agreements 4.3
   legitimate expectations 1.39–
      1.40, 4.4
   marriage, essential validity
      of 7.43
   party autonomy 4.4
   Private International
      Law (Miscellaneous
      Provisions) Act
      1995 5.124
   public policy 4.3
   standard forms 4.3
   system of law by reference
      to which contract
      made 4.3
   tangible movables, inter vivos
      transfer of 9.15, 9.23
   tort and other non-
      contractual
      obligations 5.3
property 9.1–9.121 *see also*
   **immovable property;
   inter vivos transfers of
   property; matrimonial
   property and financial
   provision; movable
   property; place where
   property situated, law
   of (lex situs)**
   choice of law 9.1–9.2
   choses in action 9.5
   choses in possession 9.5
   classification 9.2–9.5
   expropriation 1.149, 1.167,
      9.34, 9.43
   lex fori 9.2, 9.76, 9.110,
      9.113–9.115

lex situs 9.2–9.4
realty and personalty,
   difference between 9.2
share certificates 9.5
tenancies 2.44–2.45, 4.51,
   4.55
**property adjustment
   orders** 8.46, 8.179–
   8.180, 9.45, 9.71
**prorogation of
   jurisdiction** 2.46–2.57
**Protection of Trading Interests
   Act 1980** 3.78, 3.82,
   3.86
provisional or interim measures
   another Member State,
      proceedings in 2.282,
      2.284–2.285
   Brussels I Recast 2.281–2.285
   Civil Jurisdiction and
      Judgments Act
      1982 2.285–2.286
   Civil Procedure Rules 2.287
   connecting factors 2.289,
      2.294–2.296
   contempt of court 2.290,
      2.297
   damages 2.288
   discretion 2.288–2.289,
      2.292–2.293
   domicile 2.285
   extraterritorial orders 2.290–
      2.297
   freezing injunctions 2.281–
      2.297
   good arguable case 2.288
   jurisdiction 2.281–2.297
   non-Member States,
      proceedings in 2.286
   parallel proceedings 2.188
   procedural issues 2.287
   recognition and
      enforcement of foreign
      judgments 3.90
   search orders 2.290
   third parties 2.297
proxy marriages 1.70, 1.90,
   7.12–7.13, 7.18, 7.25
public interest
   choice of law 1.43–1.54
   close connection 1.44
   comparative impairment
      approach 1.52–1.53
   deducting the applicability
      of a legal rule from its
      policy 1.44–1.54
   disinterested forums 1.52

false conflicts 1.46, 1.50
gratuitous passengers,
   liability to 1.47–1.54
interest analysis 1.44–1.60
marriage 1.41, 7.49–7.50,
   7.55, 7.59
policy 1.44–1.54
polygamy 1.41
public policy 1.44–1.54,
   1.166, 4.111–4.112
Rome I Regulation 1.42, 4.90
true conflicts 1.51
United States 1.47–1.54
**public international law,
   definition of** 1.7
public laws, exclusion of 1.152–
   1.154
public policy
   Administration of Justice Act
      1920 3.82
   ante-nuptial agreements 9.64
   appropriate forum 6.2–6.3
   Brussels I Recast 3.108–3.113
   Brussels II *bis* 8.76–8.77
   champerty 1.171
   choice of law 1.155–1.172
   civil partnerships and same
      sex marriage, validity
      of 7.117, 7.119
   close connection 4.112
   comity 1.164
   consumer contracts 4.124
   contract 4.109–4.113
   crystallisations 1.161
   defences to recognition of
      judgments 3.70–3.71,
      3.108–3.113, 8.76–8.77,
      8.132–8.136
   divorce, separation, and
      annulment 1.165, 8.57,
      8.76–8.77, 8.132–8.136
   domicile 1.160
   English interests, threats
      to 1.171–1.172
   EU law 1.157
   express choice of law 4.112
   expropriation 1.167
   fair hearing, right to a 1.167,
      3.70, 3.110
   Foreign Judgments
      (Reciprocal
      Enforcement) Act
      1933 3.86
   foreign law, exclusion
      of 1.155–1.172
   forum non conveniens, stay
      on grounds of 2.225

public policy (*Contd.*)
  forum-oriented bias 1.159
  fraud 1.161, 3.111
  Hague Choice of Court Convention 2.247
  illegality 4.110
  immovables 1.167–1.168
  international public policy 1.164
  lex fori 1.159
  limitations 1.158–1.165
  marriage 1.155, 1.163, 1.165, 1.167, 7.100–7.103
    domicile 1.160
    essential validity 1.155, 7.47, 7.52, 7.58, 7.64, 7.67
    same-sex marriage 7.122
    validity 1.155, 1.160, 1.167, 7.100–7.103
  matrimonial property 9.23, 9.43, 9.64
  morality, decency, human liberty, or justice, contrary to English concepts of 1.167–1.170, 4.110
  natural justice 1.161, 3.66
  nuptial agreements 9.64
  polygamy 1.163
  procedure 1.159
  property 9.43
  public interest 1.44–1.54, 1.166, 4.111–4.112
  recognition and enforcement of foreign judgments 1.155, 1.167, 3.66, 3.108–3.113, 3.128
  renvoi 1.118, 1.121
  Rome I Regulation 1.17, 4.14, 4.79, 4.111–4.112
  Rome II Regulation 1.17, 5.97–5.102
  same-sex marriage 7.122
  scope of doctrine 1.166–1.172
  sanctions 3.110
  slaves, contracts for sale of 1.169
  statute, regulation by 1.157
  substantial justice doctrine 1.165, 1.170
  tort 1.160, 5.97–5.102
  trading with the enemy 1.172, 4.111
  undue influence 3.71
  wills 6.3
public registers, entries in 2.39
punitive damages 3.42, 5.98

real and substantial connection 6.3, 7.46–7.48, 7.52, 7.73, 7.80
real property *see* **immovable property**
realty and personality, difference between 9.2
reasonable expectations *see* **legitimate expectations**
recognition and enforcement of foreign judgments 1.6, 3.1–3.128
  Administration of Justice Act 1920 3.6, 3.80–3.83
  Admiralty in rem proceedings 3.5
  anti-suit injunctions 3.94
  appeals 3.40, 3.82, 3.102, 3.121, 3.127
  appropriate forum 6.1–6.4
  arbitration clauses 3.75–3.77, 3.93–3.96, 3.109
  automatic recognition 1.173, 3.97
  basis of recognition and enforcement 3.8–3.10
  Borrás Report 8.73
  Brussels I Recast 2.9, 2.39, 2.182, 3.6–3.10, 3.73, 3.87–3.126, 8.69, 8.78
  Brussels II bis 8.62, 8.67–8.82
  cause of action and parties, connection between 3.13
  cause of action estoppel 3.43, 3.52–3.58, 3.99
  choice of law 1.103, 6.2
  civil and commercial matters 3.92–3.94, 6.7
  Civil Jurisdiction and Judgments Act 1982 3.45, 3.54, 3.128
  civil partnerships and same-sex marriages 7.123, 8.148
  common law 3.6–3.7, 3.80–3.86
  Commonwealth 3.6, 3.80–3.84
  competent jurisdiction, courts of 3.12–3.39, 3.44, 3.60, 3.81, 3.85–3.87, 3.98
  conditions 3.10, 3.43–3.59, 3.103
  connecting factors 1.103, 6.2–6.4

  damages 3.42, 3.78–3.79
  declining jurisdiction 3.104
  default judgments 3.40, 3.107
  defences 3.10, 3.43–3.44, 3.60–3.79, 3.103–3.126
  divorce, separation, and annulment 1.6, 8.113, 8.131, 8.150, 8.160–8.161
  automatic recognition 1.173
  Brussels II bis 8.68–8.74
  close connection 1.175
  domicile 1.105
  effect of recognition 8.152–8.155
  limping marriages 8.64
  refusal 8.156–8.164
  renvoi 1.106
  domicile 3.118, 6.7
  EU law 1.173
  exclusions 3.89–3.90
  exclusive jurisdiction 2.39
  exemplary or punitive damages 3.42
  exorbitant jurisdiction 3.97
  extraterritoriality 3.37
  federal states 3.30–3.34
  final and conclusive, judgments must be 3.11, 3.40, 3.85, 3.101
  financial provision 8.69, 8.166, 8.180
  first seised rule 2.194
  fixed sum of money, not being a tax or penalty, judgments must be for a 3.11, 3.41–3.42
  Foreign Judgments (Reciprocal Enforcement) Act 1933 3.6, 3.81, 3.84–3.86
  forum conveniens 3.13, 3.36–3.39
  forum shopping 1.175
  fraud 3.67–3.69, 3.128
  free movement of judgments 2.181, 3.87
  habitual residence 6.4, 6.7, 6.69–6.71, 6.78, 6.100
  Hague Choice of Court Convention 2.244
  harmonisation 3.87

identity of cause of
    action 3.55–3.57
identity of issues 3.58–3.59
identity of parties 3.53–3.54
immovables 3.35
in personam judgments 3.4–
    3.5, 3.89
in rem judgments 3.4–3.5, 3.89
injunctions 3.101
invalidity under foreign
    law 3.73–3.74
irreconcilable
    judgments 3.72, 3.82,
    8.79–8.82
issue estoppel 3.43,
    3.52–3.59, 3.99
jurisdiction 1.18, 1.173, 2.39,
    3.73–3.74
jurisdiction agreements,
    breach of 3.75–3.77
limited review of
    jurisdiction 3.104–3.113
maintenance orders 8.182,
    8.190
Maintenance
    Regulation 8.191
matrimonial causes 8.166,
    8.188–8.191
Member States, judgments
    of 3.89–3.91
merits, judgments on
    the 3.43, 3.51, 3.61,
    3.76, 3.85, 3.93–3.94
multiple damages 3.78–3.79
mutual trust, principle
    of 8.70, 8.75
natural justice 3.63–3.66,
    3.128, 8.78, 8.160
notice, proceedings
    without 3.86
obligation, theory of 3.9
opportunity to take part in
    proceedings 3.86
original proceedings, basis of
    jurisdiction in 3.97
penalties 3.11, 3.41–3.42
polygamy 7.125–7.126,
    7.134, 7.142, 7.152–
    7.153, 7.158–7.160
procedure, interlocutory
    decisions on 3.90
provisional measures 3.90
public policy 1.161, 1.167,
    1.173, 3.70–3.71,
    3.108–3.113, 3.128,
    8.76–8.77, 8.161
reciprocity 3.9, 3.84–3.86

recognition without
    enforcement 3.3
refusal of recognition 8.75–
    8.82, 8.158
registration of judgments 3.7
related proceedings 2.182
Rome II Regulation 5.23
same causes of action 3.43–
    3.44, 3.46, 3.49
same parties 3.43, 3.53–3.54
scope 3.92–3.96
service 3.114
settlements 3.90
specific performance 3.101
submission to
    jurisdiction 3.12,
    3.14–3.21
sufficient territorial
    connection 3.12,
    3.22–3.34
tax 3.11, 3.41–3.42
third parties 3.5
traditional rules 3.104, 8.70
United Kingdom, judgments
    in other parts of 3.127–
    3.128
reflexive effect theory 2.276–
    2.280, 8.34
registration 2.39, 3.7, 3.85
related proceedings 2.180–
    2.184
    Admiralty claims in rem 2.35
    Brussels I Recast 2.64,
        2.180–2.211
    close connection 2.199, 2.202
    declining jurisdiction 2.205–
        2.211
    discretion 2.199, 2.202–2.203
    domicile 2.180, 2.183
    first seised rule 2.181
    forum non conveniens, stay
        on grounds of 2.269–
        2.273
    irreconcilable
        judgments 2.199–2.203
    jurisdiction 2.3
    lis pendens 2.181
    Maintenance
        Regulation 8.177–8.178
    recognition and
        enforcement of foreign
        judgments 2.182
    second seised, court 2.200–
        2.203
    stay of proceedings 2.199–
        2.204, 2.269–2.273
    traditional rules 2.193

religion *see also* Islam
    choice of law 6.3–6.4
    common law exception to lex
        loci celebrationis 7.27
    discrimination 7.27
    divorce, separation, and
        annulment 2.235, 4.16,
        7.29, 7.88, 8.68, 8.97,
        8.104, 8.117, 8.135
    domicile 6.4, 6.15
    Jewish divorce 8.97, 8.117
    marriage
        clergy, ceremonies
            performed by 7.27
        essential validity 7.59
        formal validity 7.18, 7.21,
            7.22, 7.29
    personal law 6.3–6.4
renvoi 1.106–1.137
    advantages 1.117–1.127
    application in English
        law 1.107–1.110
    approaches to renvoi 1.111
    choice of law 1.106–1.137, 5.16
    civil partnerships and same
        sex marriage, validity
        of 1.110, 1.130, 7.92,
        7.98
    contract 1.119
    definition 1.106
    disadvantages 1.127–1.130
    domicile 1.106, 1.117, 1.123,
        1.126, 1.128–1.129
    foreign court theory of
        renvoi 1.111, 1.114–
        1.116
    forum shopping 1.124
    immovables 9.9–9.11,
        9.107–9.109
    implied choice of law 1.119
    incidental questions 1.131–
        1.137
    inter vivos transfers of
        property 9.10, 9.24
    intestate succession 1.106,
        1.109
    jurisdiction 1.119
    Law Commission 1.130
    legitimate expectations 1.119
    lex causae 1.106, 1.136
    lex fori 1.74, 1.131–1.136
    lex situs 1.125
    marriage 1.109–1.110, 1.126,
        7.90–7.99
    movables 1.106–1.109,
        1.112–1.117, 1.123–
        1.125, 1.128–1.129

religion *see also* **Islam** (*Contd.*)
   nationality 1.106, 1.126, 1.128
   partial or single renvoi 1.111, 1.113–1.117, 1.122, 1.129
   party autonomy 1.119
   presumption of non-applicability 1.108
   procedure 1.118, 1.124
   public policy 1.118, 1.121
   rejection 1.112
   remission 1.106, 1.113, 1.116
   Rome I Regulation 1.107, 4.14
   Rome II Regulation 1.107
   substance 1.124
   succession 1.106, 1.125, 1.128–1.130, 9.107–9.109, 9.118
   total or double renvoi 1.111, 1.114–1.118, 1.120, 1.122, 1.125, 1.129
   transmission 1.106, 1.116
   undesirable results, avoidance of 1.126
   uniformity 1.120–1.123
   wills 1.109, 1.115, 1.126, 1.128, 9.109
res judicata 3.52–3.54, 8.159, 8.163
residence 1.1, 2.36, 3.22–3.23, 6.37–6.40, 6.58, 6.81, 6.82–6.87 *see also* **habitual residence**
restitution *see* **unjust enrichment, restitution for**
restrictive covenants 4.138
retention of title 9.16
retrospectivity 7.20, 7.141, 8.153, 8.155, 8.158, 8.161
revenue laws, enforcement of foreign 1.150–1.151
Rome Convention 1980 1.13–1.15, 4.6, 4.50, 4.66, 4.78, 5.6
Rome I Regulation on the Law Applicable to Contractual Obligations 1.15, 4.7–4.182
   absence of choice, applicable law in the 4.50–4.86
   agency 4.8, 4.108
   arbitration clauses 4.8, 4.23–4.32, 4.44
   auction, sale by 4.51, 4.54
   autonomous concept 4.86
   bills of exchange, promissory notes and cheques 4.8
   bodies corporate 4.8
   branches, agencies or other establishments 4.84–4.85
   burden of proof 1.94, 4.22
   capacity 4.8, 4.154–4.164
   carriage contracts 4.115–4.121
   changing the applicable law 4.47–4.49
   characteristic performance 4.53, 4.56–4.59, 4.117
   civil and commercial matters 4.7
   classification 1.91, 1.94, 4.8
   clearly demonstrated choice 4.21–4.32
   close connection 4.44, 4.54, 4.60–4.66, 4.88, 4.117, 4.128, 4.159
   companies 4.8
   connecting factors 4.9, 4.117
   consent and material validity 4.141–4.150
   consumer contracts 4.55, 4.104–4.105, 4.122–4.125, 4.153
   Court of Justice 4.11–4.12
   currency 4.182
   damages
      classification 1.98–1.101
      currency 4.182
      procedure 4.178–4.182
      quantification of 1.100, 4.178–4.182
      substance 4.178
   definition of contractual obligations 4.8
   determination of applicable law 4.14–4.86
   discharge of contract 4.168
   discretion 4.100
   dispute resolution clauses 4.24–4.32
   distribution contracts 4.51–4.55
   domicile 4.164
   effect of contracts 4.165–4.167
   employment contracts 4.55, 4.133–4.139
   English law, contracts governed by 4.171–4.172
   escape clauses 4.60–4.66, 4.119, 4.128
   evidence 1.94–1.95, 4.8, 4.179
   exclusions 4.8, 4.14, 4.155
   express choice of law 4.15–4.23, 4.44
   floating applicable law 4.48
   foreign currency 4.182
   formal validity 4.151–4.153
   formation of contract 4.141–4.144, 4.151–4.153
   franchises 4.51–4.55
   freedom of choice 4.15, 4.89
   habitual residence 4.51, 4.82–4.86, 4.105, 4.117–4.121, 4.129, 4.143, 4.149–4.152
   harmonisation 4.12, 4.126
   illegality 4.168–4.175
   immovables 4.51, 4.153
   implied choice of law 4.29, 4.33–4.35, 4.39–4.44
   incorporation of particular rules by reference 4.36–4.38
   inequality of bargaining power 4.55
   injunctions 4.178
   insurance 4.8, 4.126–4.132
   intention of parties 4.165
   interpretation 4.8, 4.11–4.12, 4.18, 4.32, 4.97, 4.154, 4.165–4.167
   inter vivos transfers 9.28, 9.30–9.35, 9.41–9.42
   jurisdiction agreements 4.8, 4.24–4.32, 4.43
   legal certainty 4.67–4.68, 4.81
   legitimate expectations 4.55
   life insurance for self-employed 4.8
   limitation periods 1.97
   limits of applicable law 4.87–4.113
   localisation or centre of gravity 4.78–4.79
   mandatory provisions 1.42, 4.14, 4.87–4.100, 4.169, 4.173
   manner of performance 4.166
   marriage 4.8
   material validity 4.141–4.150, 4.154
   natural persons, status and legal capacity of 4.8

INDEX

no choice and implied choice, distinction between 4.42–4.44
non-applicability of articles 4.77–4.81
non-contractual obligations and contractual obligations, interaction of 5.128–5.137
nullity 4.176–4.177
overriding mandatory provisions 1.42, 4.90, 4.97–4.108, 4.169, 4.173
particular aspects of contract 4.140–4.182
party autonomy 4.15, 4.45, 4.47, 4.126–4.132
place of performance 4.69, 4.99, 4.173
pre-contractual dealings 4.8
previous course of dealing 4.34
principal place of business 4.86
Private International Law (Miscellaneous Provisions) Act 1995 5.30
procedure 4.8, 4.178–4.182
public interest 1.42, 4.90
public policy 1.17, 4.14, 4.87–4.100, 4.109–4.113
reference to particular rules
related transactions, express choice in 4.35
remedies 4.178–4.182
renvoi 1.107, 4.13
reservations 4.177
restitution for unjust enrichment 4.177
Rome II Regulation 4.62, 4.177
sale of goods 4.51–4.53
scope 1.91, 4.7–4.10
services 4.51
specific contracts 4.114–4.139
specific performance 4.178
splitting the applicable law 4.45–4.46
standard forms 4.17, 4.33, 4.53, 4.91
substance 1.91–1.101, 4.178
tenancies of immovable property 4.51, 4.55
territorial connection 4.54, 4.60–4.76

third countries, overriding rules of 4.98–4.100
travaux préparatoires 4.12
trusts 4.8
unfair contract terms and exclusion clauses 4.104–4.105
unincorporated associations 4.8
United Kingdom, different parts of 4.10
universal application 4.9–4.10
unjust enrichment, restitution for 5.71
validity 4.141–4.153
wills and succession 4.8
Rome II Regulation on the Law Applicable to Non-Contractual Obligations 1.15, 5.67–5.137
anticipated wrongs 5.15
applicable law, determination of 4.62
audits 5.10
background 5.6–5.7
basis of liability 5.91
bills of exchange, cheques, and promissory notes 5.10
branches, agencies or other establishments 5.94
Brussels I Recast 5.18–5.19, 5.28, 5.130
burden of proof 1.94
choice of law 1.15, 5.6–5.14, 5.67–5.68, 5.83–5.85
civil and commercial matters 5.8, 5.22
classification 1.91, 1.94
close connection 5.31–5.33, 5.89, 5.135
companies 5.94
competition 5.53–5.56
comprehensiveness of regulations, lack of 1.18
connecting factors 5.30–5.33
constructive trusts 5.10
contractual obligations 5.18–5.19, 5.41–5.42
contractual obligations and non-contractual obligations, interaction of 5.128–5.137
contributory negligence 5.91
conversion 5.102

culpa in contrahendo 5.12, 5.83–5.85
damages 1.99, 5.91–5.94
deceit 5.89
defamation 5.104–5.121
definition of tortious obligation 5.18
division of liability 5.91
domicile 5.14
double actionability rule 5.99
entry into force 5.6
environmental damage 5.57–5.63
equitable wrongs 5.22
escape clause 4.62, 5.34–5.42, 5.65, 5.89
evidence 1.94, 1.129, 5.9
exclusions 5.9–5.12, 5.104–5.127
exemplary or punitive damages 5.98
exemption of liability 5.91
existence of damage 5.91–5.94
extent of liability 5.91
extinguishment 5.94
fault 5.91
flexibility 5.23
force majeure 5.91
freedom of choice 5.86–5.90
freely assumed and not freely assumed obligations 5.19
general provisions 5.86–5.103
general rules 5.23–5.44
habitual residence 5.30–5.33, 5.90, 5.94
harmonisation 5.6
industrial action 5.65–5.66
inequality of bargaining power 5.86
injunctions 5.15, 5.94
intellectual property rights 5.64, 5.90
internal market 5.13, 5.23
interpretation 1.91, 4.12, 5.8–5.14, 5.35
legal certainty 5.23, 5.86
legitimate expectations 5.31
lex loci damni 5.25–5.44
lex loci delicti 5.25
limitation of liability 5.91
limitation periods 1.97, 5.94, 5.101
mandatory provisions 5.90, 5.97–5.102, 5.136

Rome II Regulation on the Law Applicable to Non-Contractual Obligations (*Contd.*)
material scope 5.8–5.14, 5.15, 5.22
matrimonial property 5.10
matters relating to contract 5.19
matters relating to tort 5.19
Member States, connection with 5.13
nature of damage 5.91–5.94
necessity 5.91
negotiorum gestio 5.12, 5.80–5.82
nuclear damage 5.11
overriding mandatory provisions 5.97–5.102, 5.136
parallel proceedings 5.137
party autonomy 5.86
prescription 5.94
privacy 5.11
procedure 5.94
product liability 5.46–5.52
public policy 1.17, 5.97–5.102
punitive damages 5.98
quantification of damages 5.91–5.94
recognition of foreign judgments 5.102
remedies 5.91–5.94
renvoi 1.107, 5.16
Rome I Regulation 4.62, 5.18
scope 5.8–5.15, 5.19, 5.91–5.94
specific rules 5.45–5.52
strict liability 5.25, 5.44, 5.91
succession, transfer of damages or other remedies by 5.94
temporal scope 5.39
territorial connection 5.64
third parties, liability for acts of 5.94
travaux préparatoires 5.19, 5.35
trusts 5.10
unfair competition 5.90
United Kingdom, disputes within the 5.17
unjust enrichment, restitution for 4.177, 5.12, 5.69–5.79, 5.93–5.94
wills and succession 5.9
Rome III Regulation 1.15, 8.59–8.60

Brussels II bis, amendment for 8.59–8.60
close connection 8.59
Commission report 8.53
enhanced cooperation 4.50, 8.50, 8.60
habitual residence 6.72, 8.60
matrimonial causes 8.50, 8.53, 8.59–8.60
opt-outs by UK and Sweden 8.60
Rylands v Fletcher, **rule in** 5.57

sale of goods 2.76–2.89, 4.51, 4.51–4.54
same-sex marriages 7.120–7.122 *see also* **civil partnerships**
Brussels II bis 8.54–8.55, 8.62, 8.148
capacity 7.120
conversion of civil partnerships 7.121
domicile 7.120
domiciliary law, validity under 7.120, 7.122
England, in 7.120–7.121
formal validity 7.121–7.122
interpretation 7.122
necessity, forum of 7.120
overseas marriages, recognition of 7.122
public policy 7.122
validity 7.120–7.122
search orders 2.290
seised, court first *see* **first seised rule**
separability, doctrine of 2.48
separate ownership systems 9.44–9.45
separation *see* **divorce, separation, and annulment**
service *see also* **service out of the jurisdiction**
claim forms 2.5, 2.24–2.25, 2.62, 2.141
Foreign Judgments (Reciprocal Enforcement) Act 1933 3.86
in personam claims 2.5
natural justice 3.63, 3.114–3.122
presence 2.142–2.145
recognition and enforcement of foreign judgments 3.114

Service Regulation 1.15
submission to jurisdiction 2.60
time limits 3.114–3.122
traditional rules 2.141
service out of the jurisdiction
agents 2.162
bases of jurisdiction 2.150–2.176
breach of contract 2.166
Brussels I Recast 2.150–2.176
Civil Procedure Rules 2.150–2.154
close connection 2.157–2.158
contract 2.160–2.166
defamation 2.168
economic loss 2.169
forum non conveniens, stay on grounds of 2.155–2.158, 2.175, 2.213
good arguable case 2.154
in personam claims 2.24–2.25
interpretation 2.153
jurisdiction agreements 2.164, 2.240
long-arm or exorbitant jurisdiction 2.150
multiple defendants 2.172–2.175
negative declarations 2.165
permission of court 2.150–2.176
restitution 2.170–2.171
serious issue to be tried 2.152
stay of proceedings 2.25
tort 2.167–2.169
traditional rules 2.141
services 2.76, 2.81–2.89, 4.51, 4.123
sexism 6.18, 7.42, 7.79, 7.138, 9.50
share certificates 9.5
ships, arrest of 2.5–2.6, 2.34
slaves, contracts for the sale of 1.169
social and family factors 6.97–6.98, 7.54–7.55
social security 6.72, 6.92, 6.95, 7.136, 7.151, 7.159
specific obligation theory 2.90
specific performance 1.98, 2.262, 3.101, 4.178, 9.13–9.14
squatters 2.42
standard forms 2.48, 4.3, 4.17, 4.33, 4.53, 4.91
state pensions 7.159
stateless persons 6.67

stay of proceedings *see also*
    forum non conveniens,
    stay on grounds of
  anti-suit injunctions 2.298,
    2.300
  Brussels I Recast 2.20
  Brussels II bis 8.22, 8.38–8.39
  jurisdiction 2.3–2.4,
    2.177–2.280
  matrimonial causes 8.6,
    8.22–8.49, 8.54, 8.91
  related proceedings 2.199–
    2.204, 2.269–2.273
  service 2.25
strict liability 5.25, 5.44, 5.62, 5.91
students studying abroad,
    habitual residence
    of 6.86, 6.88
submission to jurisdiction 2.57,
    2.59–2.61, 2.148–2.149,
    3.14–3.21, 3.37
substance
  applicable law 1.92
  classification 1.91–1.101
  damages 4.178
  defamation 5.119–5.121
  definition 1.92
  environmental damage 5.62
  jurisdiction 2.2
  procedure 1.91–1.101
  remedies 1.98
  renvoi 1.124
  Rome I Regulation 4.175
  unjust enrichment, restitution
    for 5.74
succession 9.75–9.121 *see also*
    intestate succession; wills
  administrators 9.75
  bigamy 8.143
  choice of law 1.133,
    9.116–9.118
  damages, transfer by
    inheritance of claim 5.94
  domicile 6.13, 9.69–9.70, 9.75
  EU law 1.15, 9.116–9.121
  executors 9.75
  grants of representation 9.75
  habitual residence 9.117–9.119
  immovables 9.74–9.77,
    9.90–9.104, 9.106, 9.109,
    9.118–9.119
  incidental question 1.131,
    1.133, 1.136–1.137,
    9.110–9.115
  Inheritance (Provision for
    Family and Dependants)
    Act 1975 9.45

legitimacy 1.133
lex causae 1.77–1.81,
    9.110–9.114
lex fori 9.76
matrimonial property 9.44,
    9.47–9.48, 9.58,
    9.68–9.70, 9.75–9.121
movables 9.58, 9.74–9.89,
    9.93–9.97, 9.105–9.108,
    9.118–9.119
polygamy 7.136, 7.141, 7.151,
    7.155–7.156
renvoi 1.106, 1.125, 1.128–
    1.130, 9.107–9.109
Rome II Regulation 5.9, 5.94
substantial connection 6.3–6.4
Succession Regulation 9.116–
    9.121

talak divorces in Islam 1.163–
    1.164, 8.91, 8.97–8.108,
    8.112, 8.115–8.117
tangible property 9.5–9.6,
    9.15–9.24, 9.37–9.38
tax
  domicile 6.6, 6.13, 6.53, 6.64
  enforcement of foreign
    judgments 3.11,
    3.41–3.42
  lex fori 1.151
  revenue laws, enforcement of
    foreign 1.150–1.151
temporary residence 6.53, 6.64,
    7.36
tenancies 2.44–2.45, 4.51, 4.55
terminology 1.7
third parties
  branches, agencies or other
    establishments 2.110
  domicile 2.124–2.126
  in rem claims 3.5
  multiple parties and
    claims 2.124–2.126
  provisional measures 2.297
  recognition and
    enforcement of foreign
    judgments 3.5
  Rome II Regulation 5.94, 5.96
  tangible movables, inter vivos
    transfer of 9.15
time limits 1.96–1.97, 2.230,
    2.242, 3.114–3.122, 5.94,
    5.101
timeshares 2.44
title 1.77–1.81, 2.260–2.261,
    9.6–9.12, 9.15–9.23,
    9.34, 9.37, 9.43

tort and other non-contractual
    obligations *see also* Rome
    II Regulation on the
    Law Applicable to Non-
    Contractual Obligations
  Brussels I Recast 1.91, 2.17,
    2.66–2.69, 2.94–2.123,
    2.168–2.170, 5.18–5.19
  choice of law 5.1–5.5
  concurrent claims in contract
    and tort 5.131
  connecting factors 2.98
  constructive trusts
    and dishonest
    assistance 2.95
  contract 2.66–2.69
  contributory negligence 5.91
  damages 2.106
  defamation 1.18, 1.99,
    2.96, 2.106, 2.108, 5.5,
    5.104–5.121
  domicile 2.94
  double actionability rule 5.4,
    5.117
  economic loss 2.101
  English law development
    of 5.4–5.5
  jurisdiction 2.94–2.108
  lex loci delicti 2.94–2.102,
    5.1–5.3
  matters relating to tort 2.66–
    2.69, 2.94–2.108
  multiple locality cases 2.97–
    2.98
  multiple parties and
    claims 2.123
  negligence 4.105, 5.91
  non-contractual obligations
    and contractual
    obligations, interaction
    of 5.128–5.137
  place where loss occurs 2.99–
    2.105
  pre-contractual
    negotiations 2.95
  Private International
    Law (Miscellaneous
    Provisions) Act
    1995 5.5, 5.122–5.127
  proper law 5.3
  public policy 1.160
  threats 2.108
  unfair contract terms
    and exclusion
    clauses 4.104–4.105
  unjust enrichment, restitution
    for 2.69

INDEX

trade usage 2.51
trading with the enemy 1.172
traditional rules
    anti-suit injunctions 2.317
    arbitration 2.140
    breach of contract 2.140
    Brussels I Recast 2.18–2.20,
        2.38, 2.58–2.59,
        2.140–2.141, 2.172
    Brussels II bis 8.5, 8.17–8.20,
        8.35–8.53
    claim forms, service of 2.141
    divorce, separation, and
        annulment 8.17–8.20,
        8.35–8.49, 8.83–8.164
    domicile 2.140
    forum non conveniens, stay
        on grounds of 2.177,
        2.212, 2.222
    Hague Choice of Court
        Convention 2.246
    immovables 2.256–2.257
    in personam claims 2.24,
        2.36, 2.140–2.176
    jurisdiction
        agreements 2.240
    lis pendens 2.221–2.222
    outside the jurisdiction,
        service 2.141
    practice directions 2.141
    presence 2.141
    recognition and
        enforcement of foreign
        judgments 3.104, 8.70
    related proceedings 2.193
    service 2.141
    submission to jurisdiction 2.56,
        2.59–2.61
transfer *see* inter vivos transfers of property
trusts 2.43, 2.95, 4.8, 5.10

unconscionability 2.300,
    2.301–2.305, 8.49
undue influence 3.20, 3.71
unfair competition 5.53–5.56,
    5.90
unfair contract terms
    and exclusion
    clauses 4.104–4.105
uniformity
    appropriate forum 1.63
    Brussels I Recast 2.13
    choice of law 1.63
    contract 4.5
    divorce, separation, and
        annulment 8.4, 8.153

environmental damage 5.63
EU law 1.16, 2.13
forum non conveniens, stay on
    grounds of 2.278–2.279
forum shopping 1.61
harmonisation 1.62
procedural advantages 1.63
renvoi 1.121–1.123
wills 9.81, 9.108–9.109
unincorporated
    associations 4.8
United Kingdom, within the
    country, definition of 1.10–1.11
    proof of foreign law 1.143
    recognition and
        enforcement of foreign
        judgments 3.127–3.128
    Rome I Regulation 4.9–4.10
    Rome II Regulation 5.17
unjust enrichment, restitution for
    autonomous unjust
        enrichment 5.69–5.74
    Brussels I Recast 2.69
    choice of law 5.69–5.74
    classification 5.69–5.74
    close connection 5.75–5.79
    connecting factor 5.75–5.79
    contract 2.69, 2.74
    escape clause 5.82
    fiduciary relationships 5.77
    fraud 2.171
    habitual residence 5.79
    mistake of fact 5.78
    mistake of law 5.71
    Private International
        Law (Miscellaneous
        Provisions) Act
        1995 5.123
    procedure 5.74
    proprietary restitution 5.70
    Rome I Regulation 4.177
    Rome II Regulation 4.177,
        5.12, 5.69–5.79, 5.93–5.94
    substance 5.74
    waiver of tort cases 5.72

vexatious or oppressive
    litigation 2.214,
    2.301–2.303, 2.310, 8.49
visitors, domicile of 6.38, 6.58

wills 9.78–9.89
    age 9.79
    capacity 9.79–9.80, 9.94,
        9.100
    choice of law 9.81, 9.89–9.90

classification 1.66, 1.90
connecting factors 9.78, 9.81,
    9.89
death, domicile at 9.84, 9.108
dependants 9.83
destruction of wills 9.88,
    9.97, 9.104
disinheritance 9.45, 9.83
domicile 6.13, 9.78–9.89,
    9.93–9.97, 9.100, 9.103
essential validity 1.109,
    1.115, 9.82–9.85, 9.102
formal validity 1.90, 6.3–6.4,
    6.13, 9.81, 9.94, 9.101
freedom of testation 9.83,
    9.120
habitual residence 6.4, 6.78,
    9.81
Hague Convention 1961 9.81
immovables 9.31, 9.90–9.104
    English immovables 9.92
    foreign immovables 9.98–9.104
Inheritance (Provision for
    Family and Dependants)
    Act 1975 9.83
intention 9.78, 9.85, 9.96,
    9.103
interpretation 9.85–9.86,
    9.96, 9.103
later wills, revocation
    by 9.87, 9.97
lex situs 9.84, 9.90–9.104
marriage, revocation by
    subsequent 1.66, 9.89,
    9.97
matrimonial property 9.31,
    9.78–9.105, 9.109
mental capacity 9.80, 9.93
movables 9.31, 9.78–9.89,
    9.105
nationality 6.65, 9.81
presumptions 9.85–9.86,
    9.96, 9.103
public interest 9.82, 9.84
public policy 6.3
relatives 9.82–9.83
renvoi 1.109, 1.115, 1.126,
    1.128
revocation 9.87–9.90, 9.97,
    9.104
Rome I Regulation 4.8
Rome II Regulation 5.10
uniformity 9.81, 9.108–9.109
validity 1.109, 1.115, 6.3–6.4
writing or evidenced in
    writing 2.51–2.53, 2.250